AN EXEGETICAL SUMMARY OF
MATTHEW 1–16

AN EXEGETICAL SUMMARY OF
MATTHEW 1–16

David Abernathy

SIL International®
Dallas, Texas

©2013 by SIL International®

ISBN: 978-1-55671-359-0

Library of Congress Control Number: 2013947124
Printed in the United States of America

All Rights Reserved

No part of this publication may be reproduced, stored in a retrieval system, or transmitted in any form or by any means—electronic, mechanical, photocopy, recording, or otherwise—without the express permission of SIL International®, with the exception of brief excerpts in journal articles or reviews.

Copies of this and other publications
of SIL International® may be obtained from

SIL International Publications
7500 West Camp Wisdom Road
Dallas, TX 75236-5629, USA

Voice: 972-708-7404
Fax: 972-708-7363
publications_intl@sil.org
www.sil.org/resources/publications

PREFACE

Exegesis is concerned with the interpretation of a text. Thus, exegesis of the New Testament involves determining the meaning of the Greek text. Translators must be especially careful and thorough in their exegesis of the New Testament in order to accurately communicate its message in the vocabulary, grammar, and literary restraints of another language. Questions occurring to translators as they study the Greek text are answered by summarizing how scholars have interpreted the text. This is information that should be considered by translators as they make their own exegetical decisions regarding the message they will communicate in their translations.

The Semi-Literal Translation

As a basis for discussion, a semi-literal translation of the Greek text is given so that the reasons for different interpretations can best be seen. When one Greek word is translated into English by several words, these words are joined by hyphens. There are a few times when clarity requires that a string of words joined by hyphens have a separate word, such as "not" (μή), inserted in their midst. In this case, the separate word is surrounded by spaces between the hyphens. When alternate translations of a Greek word are given, these are separated by slashes.

The Text

Variations in the Greek text are noted under the heading TEXT. The base text for the summary is the text of the fourth revised edition of *The Greek New Testament,* published by the United Bible Societies, which has the same text as the twenty-sixth edition of the *Novum Testamentum Graece* (Nestle-Aland). Dr. J. Harold Greenlee researched the variants and has written the notes for this part of the summary. The versions that follow different variations are listed without evaluating their choices.

The Lexicon

The meaning of a key word in context is the first question to be answered. Words marked with a raised letter in the semi-literal translation are treated separately under the heading LEXICON. First, the lexicon form of the Greek word is given. Within the parentheses following the Greek word is the location number where, in the author's judgment, this word is defined in the *Greek-English Lexicon of the New Testament Based on Semantic Domains* (Louw and Nida 1988). When a semantic domain includes a translation of the particular verse being treated, **LN** in bold type indicates that specific translation. If the specific reference for the verse is listed in *A Greek-English Lexicon of the New Testament and Other Early Christian Literature* (Bauer, Arndt, Gingrich, and Danker 1979), the outline location and page number is given. Then English equivalents of the Greek word are given to show how it is translated by those commentaries which have translations of the whole Greek text and, after a semicolon, by twelve major versions. "All versions" refers only to those versions used in the lexicon. "All translations" refers to both the versions and the commentaries used in the lexicon. Sometimes further comments are made about the meaning of the word or the significance of a verb's tense, voice, or mood.

The Questions

Under the heading QUESTION, a question is asked that comes from examining the Greek text under consideration. Typical questions concern the identity of an implied actor or object of an event word, the antecedent of a pronominal reference, the connection indicated by a relational word, the meaning of a genitive construction, the meaning of figurative language, the function of a rhetorical question, the identification of an ambiguity, and the presence of implied information that is needed to understand the passage correctly. Background information is also considered for a proper understanding of a passage. Although not all implied information and background information is made explicit in a translation, it is important to consider it so that the translation will not be stated in such a way that prevents a reader from arriving at the proper interpretation. The question is answered with a summary of what commentators have said. If there are contrasting differences of opinion, the different interpretations are numbered and the commentaries that support each are listed. Differences that are not treated by many of the commentaries often are not numbered, but are introduced with a contrastive 'Or' at the beginning of the sentence. No attempt has been made to select which interpretation is best.

The Use of this Book

This book does not replace the commentaries that it summarizes. Commentaries contain much more information about the meaning of words and passages. They often contain arguments for the interpretations that are taken and they may have important discussions about the discourse features of the text. In addition, they often have information about the historical, geographical, and cultural setting. Translators will want to refer to at least four commentaries as they exegete a passage. However, since no one commentary contains all the answers translators need, this book will be a valuable supplement. It makes more sources of exegetical help available than those to which most translators have access. Even if they had all the books available, few would have the time to search through all of them for the answers.

When many commentaries are studied, it soon becomes apparent that they frequently disagree in their interpretations. That is the reason why so many answers in this book are divided into two or more interpretations. The reader's initial reaction may be that all of these different interpretations complicate exegesis rather than help it. However, before translating a passage, a translator needs to know exactly where there is a problem of interpretation and what the exegetical options are.

ABBREVIATIONS

COMMENTARIES AND REFERENCE BOOKS

BAGD Bauer, Walter. A Greek-English Lexicon of the New Testament and Other Early Christian Literature. Translated and adapted from the fifth edition, 1958 by William F. Arndt and F. Wilbur Gingrich. Second English ed. revised and augmented by F. Wilbur Gingrich and Frederick W. Danker. Chicago: University of Chicago Press, 1979.

BECNT Turner, David L. Matthew. Baker Exegetical Commentary on the New Testament Grand Rapids: Baker Books, 2008.

BNTC Filson, Floyd V. The Gospel According to St. Matthew. 2d ed. Black's New Testament Commentary. London: Adam and Charles Black, 1971.

CC Gibbs, Jeffrey A. Matthew 1:1–11:1. Concordia Commentary. Saint Louis: Concordia Publishing House, 2008.

Gibbs, Jeffrey A. Matthew 11:2–20:34. Concordia Commentary. Saint Louis: Concordia Publishing House, 2010.

EBC Carson, D. A. Matthew. The Expositor's Bible Commentary. 2 vols. Grand Rapids: Zondervan. 1995.

ESVSB English Standard Version Study Bible. Wheaton: Crossway Bibles Div, Good News Publishers, 2008.

ICC Davies, W. D. and Dale C. Allison, Jr. The Gospel According to Saint Matthew. The International Critical Commentary. 3 vols. Edinburgh: T. & T. Clark, 1988, 1997, 2004.

LN Louw, Johannes P., and Eugene A. Nida. Greek-English Lexicon of the New Testament Based on Semantic Domains. New York: United Bible Societies, 1988.

Lns Lenski, R. C. H. The Interpretation of St. Matthew's Gospel. Minneapolis: Augsburg, 1943.

My Meyer, Heinrich August Wilhelm. Critical and Exegetical Handbook to the Gospel of Matthew. New York: Funk and Wagnalls, 1884.

NAC Blomberg, Craig L. Matthew. New American Commentary. Nashville, Tenn.: Broadman, 1992.

NIBC Mounce, Robert H. Matthew. New International Biblical Commentary. Peabody, Mass.: Hendrickson, 1991.

NICNT France, R. T. The Gospel of Matthew. New International Commentary on the New Testament. Grand Rapids: Eerdmans, 2007.

NIGTC Nolland, John. The Gospel of Luke. The New International Greek Testament Commentary. Grand Rapids: Eerdmans, 2005.

NTC Hendriksen, William. Exposition of the Gospel According to Matthew. New Testament Commentary. Grand Rapids: Baker, 1973.

PNTC	Morris, Leon. The Gospel According to Matthew. Pillar New Testament Commentary. Grand Rapids: Eerdmans, 1992.
TH	Newman, Barclay, and Philip C. Stine. A Handbook on The Gospel of Matthew. New York: United Bible Societies, 1988.
WBC	Hagner, Donald A. Matthew, 2 vols. Word Biblical Commentary. Dallas: Word Books, 1993, 1995.

GREEK TEXT AND TRANSLATIONS

GNT	The Greek New Testament. Edited by B. Aland, K. Aland, J. Karavidopoulos, C. Martini, and B. Metzger. Fourth ed. London, New York: United Bible Societies, 1993.
LXX	The Septuagint. The Greek translation of the Jewish Scriptures, translated between 300–200 BC in Alexandria, Egypt.
CEV	The Holy Bible, Contemporary English Version. New York: American Bible Society, 1995.
ESV	The Holy Bible, English Standard Version. Wheaton: Crossway Bibles Div, Good News Publishers, 2001.
GW	God's Word. Grand Rapids: World Publishing, 1995.
KJV	The Holy Bible. Authorized (or King James) Version. 1611.
NASB	New American Standard Bible. La Habra, Calif.: Lockman Foundation, 1995.
NCV	New Century Version. Dallas: Word Publishing, 1991.
NET	The NET Bible. New English Translation, New Testament. Version 9.206. www.bible.com: Biblical Studies Press, 1999.
NIV	The Holy Bible, New International Version. Grand Rapids: Zondervan, 1984.
NLT	The Holy Bible, New Living Translation. Wheaton, Ill.: Tyndale House, 1996.
NRSV	The Holy Bible: New Revised Standard Version. New York: Oxford University Press, 1989.
REB	The Revised English Bible. Oxford: Oxford University Press and Cambridge University Press, 1989.
TEV	Good News Bible, Today's English Version. Second ed. New York: American Bible Society, 1992.

GRAMMATICAL TERMS

act.	active	mid.	middle
fut.	future	opt.	optative
impera.	imperative	pass.	passive
imperf.	imperfect	perf.	perfect
indic.	indicative	pres.	present
infin.	infinitive	subj.	subjunctive

EXEGETICAL SUMMARY OF MATTHEW 1–16

DISCOURSE UNIT—1:1–4:16 [CC; NAC]. The topic is the introduction to Jesus' ministry [NAC], Part 1: the presentation of Jesus [CC].

DISCOURSE UNIT—1:1–4:11 [NICNT]. The topic is the introduction of the Messiah.

DISCOURSE UNIT—1:1–2:23 [BECNT, EBC, NAC, PNTC, WBC; CEV]. The topic is the prologue/introduction: the origin of Jesus the Messiah [BECNT], the origin and birth of Jesus the Christ [EBC], Jesus' origin [NAC], the birth and infancy of Jesus [PNTC], the birth and infancy narratives [WBC], the ancestors and birth of Jesus [CEV].

DISCOURSE UNIT—1:1–17 [BECNT, EBC, NICNT, NIGTC; CEV, ESV, GW, NASB, NCV, NET, NIV, NLT, NRSV, REB, TEV]. The topic is the title and genealogy of Jesus the Messiah [BECNT], the genealogy of Jesus the Messiah [NASB, NRSV], the ancestors of Jesus the Messiah [NLT], the ancestors of Jesus [CEV], the genealogy of Jesus [EBC; NIV], the genealogy of Jesus Christ [ESV, NET], the book of origin of the Messiah [NICNT], the stock from which Jesus comes–and its history [NIGTC], the family line of Jesus Christ [GW], the family history of Jesus [NCV], the ancestors of Jesus Christ [TEV], the ancestry of the Messiah [REB].

DISCOURSE UNIT—1:1 [ICC, NAC]. The topic is the title [ICC], the heading [NAC].

1:1 **(The) record^a of-(the)-genealogy/origin^b of Jesus (the) Christ^c (the) son of David (the) son of Abraham.**

LEXICON—a. βίβλος (LN **33.38**) (BAGD 1. p. 141): 'record' [CC, LN, NTC, WBC; NASB, NET], 'account' [BECNT; NRSV], 'book' [BAGD, CC, NICNT, PNTC; ESV, KJV]. The phrase βίβλος γενέσεως 'record of (the) origin' is translated 'genealogy' [BAGD, BNTC; NIV, REB], 'list of ancestors' [CEV, GW, TEV], 'family history' [NASB], 'birth record' [LN]. This noun denotes relatively short statements in written form [LN].

b. γένεσις (LN **10.24**) (BAGD 3. p. 154): 'origin' [BAGD, BECNT, CC, NICNT, NIGTC, WBC], 'ancestry' [NTC], 'generation' [KJV], 'genealogy' [ESV, NASB, NET, NRSV], 'story' [PNTC]. Used in reference to the OT it means 'origin', but here it means 'genealogy' and describes the contents of 1:1–17 [BAGD]. This noun denotes persons of successive generations who are related by birth [LN].

c. Χριστός (LN 53.82, 93.387) (BAGD 2. p. 887): 'Christ' [BAGD, BNTC, CC, LN (53.82, 93.387), NIGTC, NTC, PNTC, WBC; CEV, ESV, GW, KJV, NCV, NET, NIV, REB, TEV], 'Messiah' [BECNT, NICNT; NASB, NLT, NRSV]. This noun denotes the title for Jesus as being the Messiah, but in many contexts, and especially those without an article, the word becomes a part of the name of Jesus [LN (53.82)].

QUESTION—What is Matthew communicating by the use of the word γένεσις 'genealogy/origin'?

It indicates that this is a genealogy [BNTC, NTC, TRT, WBC; CEV, ESV, GW, NASB, NET, NIV, NRSV, REB]. The use of this phrase intentionally echoes Genesis 2:4 and 5:1 [ICC, NICNT, TH, TRT, WBC]. This genealogy surveys the history of God's people and points to the fulfillment of that history in the coming of the Messiah that God had promised [NICNT]. The phrase βίβλος γενέσεως 'book of the origin' means 'genealogical scroll' [WBC]. In keeping with how this word is used in Genesis, it is used to encompass not only the list of his ancestors, but all the events of his birth and childhood as related in the first two chapter [TH].

QUESTION—What is the relationship between the names 'Jesus' and 'Christ' in this verse?

1. 'Jesus Christ' is treated as a personal name [BNTC, EBC, ICC, Lns, My, NTC, PNTC, TH, TRT, WBC; CEV, ESV, GW, KJV, NET, NLT, NIV, REB, TEV]; that is, Jesus Christ is a descendant of David and of Abraham. Even though he uses 'Christ' as part of a full name, 'Christ' has messianic significance [EBC, ICC, Lns, PNTC, WBC], and in 1:16 Christ is used separately as a title [ICC].
2. Jesus is the Christ (or Messiah), the son of David, and the son of Abraham [BECNT, CC, NAC, NICNT, NIGTC; NASB, NRSV]. 'Son of David' is a designation for the Christ or Messiah [BAGD]. 'Christ' is the first of three titles [CC]. While 'Jesus Christ' is used as a double name, the titular significance of 'Christ' is still present [NIGTC].

QUESTION—What is the function of the first verse?

The lack of definite articles suggests that this is a superscription or heading [NIGTC].

1. It is the title for 1:2–17 [BAGD, Lns, My, NIGTC, NTC, TRT, WBC].
2. It primarily focuses on 1:2–25, though there is reference to themes that will be developed throughout the gospel [BECNT]. It primarily focuses on 1:2–17, but also includes 1:18–25, and possibly even all of chapter 2 [NICNT].
3. It is the title for the first two chapters [EBC, NAC, TH].
4. It is the title for the section from 1:2 to 4:16, which describes the origin of Jesus Christ, affirming that he came from God in fulfillment of the scriptures [CC].
5. It is the title for the entire gospel [ICC, PNTC]. It introduces the gospel as Jesus' story [ICC, PNTC], relating it not only to primeval history, but to the coming new creation [ICC].

QUESTION—What does the title 'son of David' mean?

It is a title for the Messiah [BECNT, BNTC, CC, EBC, ICC, NAC, NIBC, NICNT, NTC, TH, WBC]. It points to the lineage necessary for the Messiah [NAC, NIGTC], as well as his royal role [NAC]. The royal Messiah is the Davidic king [ICC].

QUESTION—Why does Matthew also say that Jesus is the 'son of Abraham'?
1. In view of God's promise in Genesis to bless all the Gentiles through Abraham, it suggests that the Jewish Messiah also came for the salvation of the Gentiles [CC, EBC, ICC]. In Jesus is fulfilled God's promise to Abraham to bless the nations [BECNT, NAC, TH, WBC]. Matthew may have in mind the fact that Abraham was to be the ancestor of a multitude of nations and that through him all families of the earth were to be blessed [NICNT].
2. The Messiah was to be the son of Abraham *par excellence*, the one through whom God would bless anyone who would exercise the faith that Abraham exercised [NTC].
3. It simply shows that Jesus belongs to the people of God, but is not intended to hint at blessings for Gentiles based on promises to Abraham [NIGTC].

DISCOURSE UNIT—1:2–17 [ICC, NAC, PNTC]. The topic is from Abraham to Jesus [ICC], genealogy [NAC], the genealogy of Jesus [PNTC].

1:2 **Abraham begat**[a] **Isaac, and Isaac begat Jacob, and Jacob begat Judah and his brothers,**
LEXICON—a. aorist act. indic. of γεννάω (LN **23.58**) (BAGD 1.a. p. 155): 'to beget' [BAGD, CC, LN; KJV], 'to be/become the father of' [BAGD, BNTC, BECNT, LN, NICNT, NTC, WBC; ESV, GW, NASB, NCV, NET, NIV, NLT, NRSV, REB], 'to father' [PNTC], 'to produce' [NIGTC], not explicit [CEV, TEV]. This verb refers to the male role in causing the conception and birth of a child [LN].
QUESTION—What does γεννάω 'begat' mean in this genealogy?
It can be used in a general sense of being or becoming the ancestor of someone else [BECNT, EBC, NAC, NICNT, NTC, PNTC, TRT]. It can refer to being the father of a line of descendants, or possibly even to being adopted into that royal line [CC].

1:3–10 **and Judah begat Phares ...and Manasseh begat Amos,**
TEXT—In 1:7, instead of Ἀσάφ 'Asaph/', some manuscripts have Ἀσά 'Asa', which is the spelling of the name in the LXX. GNT selects the reading 'Asaph' with a B rating to indicate that the text is almost certain. The reading 'Asaph' is taken by BECNT, CC, NIGTC, NIGTC, PNTC, WBC; ESV, NRSV. The reading 'Asa' is taken by NTC, BNTC; CEV, GW, KJV, NASB, NCV, NET, NLT, NIV, REB, TEV.
TEXT—In 1:10, instead of Ἀμώς 'Amos', some manuscripts have Ἀμών 'Amon', which is the spelling of the name in the LXX. GNT selects the reading 'Amos' with a B rating to indicating that the text is almost certain. The reading 'Amos' is taken by BNTC, BECNT, CC, NIGTC, PNTC, WBC; ESV, NRSV. The reading 'Amon' is taken by NTC; CEV, GW, KJV, NASB, NCV, NET, NLT, NIV, REB, TEV.

1:11 and Josiah begat Jechoniah and his brothers at the time of the deportation[a] to Babylon.

TEXT—In 1:11–12, instead of Ἰεχονίαν 'Jechoniah', some manuscripts have Ἰωακίμ 'Jehoiachim'. GNT selects the reading 'Jechoniah' with an A rating to indicate that the text is certain. This is the reading taken by BNTC, BECNT, CC, NICNT, NIGTC, NTC, PNTC, WBC; ESV, GW, KJV, NASB, NET, NIV, NRSV, REB. (REB spells this name 'Jeconiah', and KJV spells it 'Jechonias'). The reading 'Jehoiachim' is not used by any of the versions, but 'Jehoiachin' is taken by CEV, NCV, NLT, TEV, presumably because the LXX does not distinguish between 'Jehoiachim' and 'Jehoiachin', representing them both as 'Jehoiachim'.

LEXICON—a. μετοικεσία (LN **85.83**) (BAGD p. 514): 'deportation' [BAGD, BNTC, CC, LN, NICNT, NTC; ESV, NASB, NET, NRSV, REB], 'exile' [BECNT, NICNT, WBC; CEV, NLT, TEV], 'removal' [PNTC]. The phrase 'the deportation to Babylon' is translated 'the Babylonian captivity' [BAGD], 'the people were exiled to Babylon' [GW], 'the time they were carried away to Babylon' [KJV], 'the time the people were taken to Babylon' [NCV]. The deportation is mentioned because it is the low point in Israel's history [BECNT, BNTC]. This word occurs only in 1:11-12 and 1:17 in the NT.

1:12–16 And after the exile to Babylon Jechoniah begat Shealtiel,...and Matthan begat Jacob, and Jacob begat Joseph, the husband[a] of Mary, from[b] whom was-born[c] Jesus, the (one) called[d] Christ[e].

LEXICON—a. ἀνήρ (LN 10.53) (BAGD 1. p. 66): 'husband' [BAGD, BECNT, BNTC, CC, LN, NICNT, NIGTC, NTC, PNTC, WBC; all versions except TEV], 'who married' [TEV].

b. ἐκ (LN 89.3): 'from' [BECNT, CC, LN, PNTC], 'of' [BNTC, NTC], 'out of' [NIGTC, WBC; KJV, NRSV], 'by' [NASB, NET], not explicit [NICNT; CEV, GW, NCV, NLT, REB, TEV]. This preposition marks the source from which someone or something is physically or psychologically derived [LN].

c. aorist pass. indic. of γεννάω (LN 23.52): 'to be born' [BNTC, BECNT, CC, LN, NTC; ESV, KJV, NET, NRSV], 'to be produced' [NIGTC], 'to be fathered' [PNTC]. The phrase 'from whom was born' is translated 'who was the mother of' [NICNT], 'was the mother of' [GW, NCV], 'the mother of' [CEV, TEV], 'from whom God brought forth' [WBC], 'gave birth to' [NLT, REB]. After thirty-nine uses of this verb in the active voice, the passive form is used here to communicate that Jesus' birth results from the activity of God, as is made more explicit in 1:18-25 [BECNT, Lns, NICNT, NIGTC, PNTC, WBC]. This verb means to give birth to a child [LN].

d. pres. pass. participle of λέγω (LN 33.129, 33.131) (BAGD II.3 p. 470): 'to be called' [BAGD, BECNT, BNTC, CC, LN (33.129, 33.131), NICNT, NIGTC, NTC, PNTC, WBC; all versions], 'to be named' [LN

e. Χριστός: 'Christ' [BNTC, CC, NIGTC, NTC, PNTC, WBC; ESV, GW, KJV, NCV, NET], 'the Messiah' [BECNT, NICNT; CEV, NASB, NLT, NRSV, TEV], 'Messiah' [REB].

33.129, 33.131]. This verb means to speak of a person by means of a proper name [LN 33.129] or to use an attribution in speaking of a person [LN 33.131].

QUESTION—Why does Matthew's genealogy differ so much from Luke's?

It may be that Matthew is tracing the royal lineage, whereas Luke traces the actual physical descent of Joseph [EBC, NIBC, WBC]. Matthew may be tracing the legal royal lineage, which could include instances of adoption into the royal line, whereas Luke traces the lineage of Mary, who could actually be a descendant of David as well [CC, Lns, NTC]. Attempts to harmonize the two are speculative in nature [NICNT, NIGTC].

1:17 So[a] all[b] the generations[c] from Abraham to David (were/are)[d] fourteen generations, and from David to the deportation to Babylon fourteen generations, and from the deportation to Babylon to the Christ fourteen generations.

LEXICON—a. οὖν (LN 89.50) (BAGD 1.a. p. 593): 'so' [BAGD, BECNT, BNTC, LN, NICNT, NIGTC, NTC; ESV, GW, NASB, NCV, NET, NRSV], 'thus' [REB], 'therefore' [CC, LN, WBC], 'so then' [LN], 'consequently, accordingly' [LN], not explicit [PNTC; CEV].

b. πᾶς (LN 59.23): 'all' [BNTC, CC, LN, NIGTC, NTC, PNTC, WBC; ESV, NASB, NET, NRSV], 'in all' [NICNT; REB], not explicit [BECNT; CEV, GW, NCV, TEV]. This adjective describes the totality of any object, mass, collective, or extension [LN].

c. γενεά (LN 10.28) (BAGD 3.a. p. 154): 'generation' [BAGD, BECNT, BNTC, CC, LN, NICNT, NIGTC, NTC, PNTC, WBC; all versions]. This noun denotes successive following generations of those who are biologically related to a reference person [LN].

d. There is no lexical entry in the Greek text for this verb; it is implied. It is expressed in translation as 'were' [BNTC, CC, NTC, PNTC; ESV], 'there were' [BECNT, NICNT; CEV, GW, NCV, REB, TEV], 'are' [NIGTC; NASB, NET, NRSV], 'are reckoned' [WBC].

QUESTION—What is Matthew's purpose for the genealogy?

He is showing that Jesus is the goal or focal point of the history of Israel, and even his ancestors depend on him for their meaning [CC]. As son of David he is the Messiah, and as a son of Abraham he is part of the people of God [NIBC]. He wants to show that Jesus is the Messiah from the royal line of David [EBC, NICNT], who will bring God's blessing to the nations [EBC]. God's covenantal promises to Abraham and David culminate in Jesus, who will rule over Israel and extend God's blessings to the nations [BECNT]. By showing that Jesus is a descendant of both Abraham and David, Matthew is creating a potential bond between Jewish believers and Gentile believers as heirs of the covenant promises made to David and Abraham [ICC].

QUESTION—Why are there three sections in this genealogy?

Matthew wants to emphasize the importance of Abraham, David, and the captivity in Jesus' genealogy [BNTC]. This shows the line of ancestors rising to a peak with David, sinking to the depths with the deportation, and rising again to Christ [BECNT, Lns, NTC, TRT]. Israel's history is fulfilled through Jesus, son of Abraham and David, who brings relief to Israel from the punishment of the exile as well as renewal of the promises made to its ancestors [BECNT].

QUESTION—How does each of the three sections add up to fourteen generations?

Counting only the names of Jesus' *ancestors* who are listed as begetting a son (or descendant) there are thirteen names in the first section (Abraham to Jesse), fourteen names in the second section (David to Josiah), and thirteen names in the third section (Jechoniah to Joseph) [NAC]. However, in the summary, three equal groups of fourteen can be counted by also including David at the end of the first group ('from *Abraham* to *David*') and by counting from Jechoniah to Christ in the third group ('from the *deportation* to *the Christ*'). That is, from Abraham to David there are fourteen generations, from David to Josiah at the time of the deportation there are fourteen generations, and from Jechoniah at the deportation to Jesus there are fourteen generations [NIBC, probably NAC]. Another explanation is that three equal groups of fourteen can be counted by including Jechoniah at the end of the second list as well as at the beginning of the third list, reflecting the demise of the decadent nation and its subsequent re-creation, as exemplified by Jechoniah's own reversal of fortunes after many years in prison. Then there would be fourteen names in each group: from Abraham to David, from Solomon to Jechoniah, and from Jechoniah to Jesus [CC, NTC]. Although he says 'all the generations', we should understand him to mean 'all the generations listed in this list' [EBC, ESVSB, Lns, NTC, TRT], since the omissions from the genealogy were known to Matthew as well as his readers [EBC]. Matthew is not claiming to give a comprehensive and complete genealogy that includes every name [BECNT].

QUESTION—Why does Matthew mention Tamar, Rahab, Ruth, and the wife of Uriah in the genealogy?

Each of the women evokes an important aspect of the story of Israel's history [NIGTC]. The four women mentioned show how unexpected providential workings led to the birth of the Messiah [BNTC, EBC, My, NIBC]. These four women are a diverse group, and by using them Matthew seems to be saying that God has unforeseen and surprising ways of bringing the Messiah and blessing the nations [CC]. The presence of non-Israelite women and of both men and women of mixed moral character in Jesus' genealogy help emphasize the facts that Jewish boasting of descent from Abraham was foolish and that Jesus is the savior of the world [NTC].

DISCOURSE UNIT—1:18–2:23 [NICNT, NIGTC, NLT; REB]. The topic is a demonstration that Jesus of Nazareth is the Messiah [NICNT], infancy [NIGTC], the birth and infancy of Jesus [REB], the birth of Jesus the Messiah [NLT].

DISCOURSE UNIT—1:18–25 [BECNT, ICC, NAC, PNTC; CEV, GW, NASB, NCV, NET, NIV, NRSV, TEV]. The topic is the birth of Jesus the Messiah [BECNT; NRSV], the virgin birth of Jesus [GW], conceived of the Holy Spirit [ICC], the virginal conception: God becomes human [NAC], the birth of Jesus Christ [NCV; ESV, NET, NIV, TEV], the birth of Jesus [PNTC; CEV], the conception and birth of Jesus [NASB].

1:18 Now[a] the birth[b] of Jesus Christ happened[c] like-this.[d]
  TEXT—Instead of Ἰησοῦ Χριστοῦ 'Jesus Christ', some manuscripts have Χριστοῦ Ἰησοῦ 'Christ Jesus', Χριστοῦ 'Christ', or Ἰησοῦ 'Jesus'. GNT selects the reading 'Jesus Christ' with a B rating to indicate that the text is almost certain. The reading Χριστοῦ 'Messiah' is taken only by NICNT.
  LEXICON—a. δέ (BAGD 2. p. 171): 'now' [BAGD, BECNT, BNTC, CC, NTC, PNTC, WBC; ESV, KJV, NASB, NET, NRSV], not explicit [NICNT, NIGTC; CEV, GW, NCV, NIV, NLT, REB, TEV].
    b. γένεσις (LN **23.46**) (BAGD 1. p. 154): 'birth' [BAGD, BECNT, BNTC, LN, NIGTC, NTC, PNTC, WBC; all versions except CEV, NLT], 'origin' [CC, NICNT], 'was born' [CEV, NLT].
    c. imperf. act. indic. of εἰμί (LN 13.4, 13.104): 'to happen' [BECNT, LN (13.104), NTC, WBC; NET], 'to occur' [BNTC], 'to come about' [NCV, NIV, REB], 'to take place' [NIGTC; ESV, GW, NRSV, TEV], 'to be' [CC, LN (13.4), NICNT, PNTC; KJV, NASB], not explicit [NLT].
    d. οὕτως (LN 61.10) (BAGD 5. p. 598): 'like this' [BAGD, BECNT, NICNT, NIGTC, PNTC, WBC], 'this way' [ESV, NET], 'in this way' [GW, NRSV], 'this is how' [NCV, NIV, NLT, REB, TEV], 'on this wise' [KJV], 'as follows' [BNTC, LN, NTC; NASB], 'of this sort' [CC]. This sentence is translated 'this is what happened when Jesus Christ was born' [LN], 'this is how Jesus Christ was born' [CEV].

Mary the mother of-him, having-been-betrothed[a] to Joseph, before their coming-together[b] was found (to-be) having (a child) in (her) womb[c] by[d] the Holy Spirit.
  LEXICON—a. aorist pass. participle of μνηστεύομαι (LN 34.74) (BAGD p. 525): 'to be betrothed' [BAGD, BNTC, CC, NTC; ESV, NASB, REB], 'to be engaged' [BECNT, LN, NICNT, PNTC, WBC; CEV, NET, NRSV, TEV], 'to be engaged to be married' [NLT], 'to be engaged to marry' [NCV], 'to become engaged' [BAGD, NIGTC], 'to be promised in marriage' [LN; GW], 'to be pledged to be married' [NIV], 'to be espoused' [KJV]. This verb means to promise a person for marriage [LN].
    b. aorist act. infin. of συνέρχομαι (LN **23.61**) (BAGD 1.b. p. 788): 'to come together' [BNTC, CC, NICNT, NIGTC, PNTC; ESV, KJV, NASB, NET,

NIV], 'to begin to live together' [BECNT, NTC], 'to live together' [NRSV], 'to consummate marriage' [WBC], 'to be married' [CEV, GW, TEV], 'to marry' [NCV], 'to have sexual intercourse' [LN]. The phrase 'before their coming together' is translated 'before the marriage took place, while she was still a virgin' [NLT], 'before their marriage' [REB]. This sense of συνέρχομαι is a figurative extension of the more basic sense 'to come together' [LN].

c. γαστήρ (LN 23.50) (BAGD 2. p. 152): 'womb' [BAGD, LN]. The phrase ἐν γαστρὶ ἔχουσα 'having in the womb' is translated 'to be pregnant' [BAGD, BECNT, CC, LN, NICNT, NIGTC, NTC, PNTC; GW, NCV, NET], 'to become pregnant' [NLT], 'to have conceived' [BNTC], 'to be with child' [WBC; ESV, KJV, NASB, NIV, NRSV], 'going to have a baby' [CEV, TEV], 'going to have a child' [REB]. The idiom 'to have in the womb' means to be in a state of pregnancy [LN].

d. ἐκ (LN 90.16) (BAGD 3.a. p. 234): 'by' [BAGD, BNTC, LN, NTC, PNTC; CEV, GW, NASB, TEV], 'by the agency of' [WBC], 'by the power of' [NCV], 'from' [BAGD, CC, LN, NIGTC; ESV, NRSV], 'through' [BECNT, NICNT; NET, NIV, REB], 'through the power of' [NLT], 'of' [KJV]. The phrase ἐκ πνεύματος ἁγίου 'by the Holy Spirit' is Matthew's preliminary explanation of how she conceived, not of what was known or 'found' at the time [BECNT, WBC]. This preposition marks the source of an activity or state, with the implication of something proceeding from or out of the source [LN].

1:19 Now[a] Joseph her husband, being righteous[b] and not wishing to-disgrace- her -publicly,[c] planned[d] to-divorce[e] her quietly.[f]

LEXICON—a. δέ (LN 89.87, 89.124): 'now' [CC, NTC], 'and' [LN (89.87), PNTC; ESV, NASB], 'but' [LN (89.124), WBC], 'then' [KJV], not explicit [BECNT, BNTC, NICNT, NIGTC; CEV, GW, NCV, NIV, NLT, NRSV, TEV].

b. δίκαιος (LN 88.12) (BAGD 1.a. p. 195): 'righteous' [BAGD, BECNT, BNTC, LN, NICNT, NIGTC, WBC; NASB, NET, NIV, NRSV], 'just' [BAGD, LN, PNTC; ESV, KJV], 'upright' [BAGD], 'good' [CEV, NCV, NLT], 'honorable' [GW], '(a man) of principle' [REB], '(a man who) always did what was right' [TEV], 'intent on doing what was right' [NTC]. This adjective describes that which is in accordance with what God requires [LN].

c. aorist act. infin. of δειγματίζω (LN **25.200**) (BAGD p. 172): 'to disgrace publicly' [CC, WBC; GW, NLT, TEV], 'to disgrace in public' [**LN**; NCV], 'to disgrace' [BAGD; NASB, NET], 'to put to shame' [LN; ESV], 'to expose' [BAGD, BNTC, LN], 'to expose publicly' [NIGTC, PNTC], 'to expose to public disgrace' [BECNT, NTC; NIV, NRSV], 'to expose to scandal' [NICNT], 'to embarrass in front of everyone' [CEV], 'to make a public example' [KJV]. The phrase μὴ θέλων αὐτὴν δειγματίσαι 'not wishing to disgrace her publicly' is translated 'wanting to save her from

MATTHEW 1:19 19

exposure' [REB]. This verb means to cause someone to suffer public disgrace or shame [LN].

d. aorist pass. (deponent = act.) indic. of βούλομαι (LN **30.56**) (BAGD 2.a.β. p. 146): 'to plan' [LN, WBC; NASB, NCV, NRSV], 'to make plans' [TEV], 'to decide' [BECNT, BNTC, NICNT, NIGTC, PNTC; CEV, GW, NLT], 'to resolve' [ESV], 'to be minded' [KJV], 'to have in mind' [NIV], 'to make up one's mind' [REB], 'to have in view' [NTC], 'to want' [CC], 'to intend' [**LN;** NET], 'to purpose' [LN]. This verb means to think, with the purpose of planning or deciding on a course of action [LN], to come to a decision of the will after deliberation [BAGD].

e. aorist act. infin. of ἀπολύω (LN 34.78) (BAGD 2.a. p. 96): 'to divorce' [BAGD, BECNT, BNTC, CC, LN, NIGTC, NTC, PNTC, WBC; ESV, NCV, NET, NIV], 'to put away' [KJV], 'to send away' [BAGD; NASB], 'to dismiss' [BAGD; NRSV] 'to break the engagement' [NICNT; NLT, TEV], 'to break the marriage agreement' [GW], 'to call off the wedding' [CEV], 'to have the marriage contract set aside' [REB]. This verb means to dissolve the marriage bond [LN].

f. λάθρᾳ (LN 28.71) (BAGD 1. p. 462): 'quietly' [CC, NIGTC, NTC; CEV, ESV, NIV, NLT, NRSV, REB], 'privately' [BECNT, LN, NICNT, WBC; NET, TEV], 'secretly' [BAGD, BNTC, LN, PNTC; GW, NASB, NCV], 'in secret, in private' [LN], 'privily' [KJV]. This adverb describes an action that is not able to be known by the public but known by some in-group or by those immediately involved [LN].

QUESTION—What relationship is there between the subordinate clause 'being righteous…publicly' and the main clause 'was planning…secretly'?

1. Because he was righteous he was going to divorce her [BECNT, BNTC, CC, EBC, Lns, NIBC, NICNT, NIGTC, NTC, PNTC, WBC; RB, TEV]. Betrothal was legally binding, so breaking the engagement required a legal act of divorce [CC]. Because he was righteous he was going to divorce her, as the law stipulated, *but* because he did not want to disgrace her, he was going to do it privately [BECNT, BNTC, EBC, Lns, NIBC, NICNT, NIGTC, NTC, PNTC, WBC; REB, TEV].

2. Because he was righteous he was not going to disgrace her by a public divorce [TH; CEV, GW, NCV, NIV, NAC; NLT; probably ESV, NASB, NRSV]: Joseph her husband was righteous *and so* he did not wish to disgrace her publicly.

QUESTION—What is meant by 'quietly'?

Joseph was planning to settle things out of court, to avoid public censure for adultery [NAC]. He would seek a private divorce before two witnesses, not a public divorce, which would have brought disgrace [EBC]. All that would have been needed was to give her a bill of divorce before two witnesses [BECNT, PNTC, TH, WBC]. He would break the engagement before two witnesses without pressing charges [NIBC, TH].

1:20 But he having-thought-about[a] this behold[b] an-angel of-(the)-Lord appeared[c] to-him in a-dream[d] saying,

LEXICON—a. aorist pass. (deponent = act.) participle of ἐνθυμέομαι (LN 30.1) (BAGD p. 266): 'to think about' [LN; CEV, NCV, TEV], 'to think on' [KJV], 'to think' [BAGD], 'to consider' [BAGD, BECNT, LN, NIGTC, WBC; ESV, NASB, NIV, NLT], 'to have in mind' [GW], 'to reflect on' [BAGD, CC], 'to mull over' [NTC], 'to contemplate' [NET], 'to decide' [NICNT], 'to reach a decision' [BNTC], 'to make up one's mind' [PNTC], 'to resolve' [NRSV, REB]. This verb means to process information by giving consideration to various aspects [LN].

  b. ἰδού (LN 91.13) (BAGD 1.b.α. p. 371): 'behold' [BAGD, BNTC, WBC; ESV, KJV, NASB], 'look' [BAGD, CC, LN, PNTC], 'listen, pay attention' [LN], 'suddenly' [BECNT, NICNT], 'what happened?' [NTC], not explicit [NIGTC; CEV, GW, NCV, NET, NIV, NLT, NRSV, REB, TEV]. This particle is a prompter of attention, serving to emphasize the following statement [LN].

  c. aorist pass. indic. of φαίνω (LN 24.18) (BAGD 2.c. p. 852): 'to appear' [BAGD, BECNT, BNTC, CC, LN, NICNT, NIGTC, NTC, PNTC, WBC; all versions except CEV, NCV], 'to come' [CEV, NCV]. This verb means to become visible to someone [LN].

  d. ὄναρ (LN **33.486**) (BAGD p. 569): 'dream' [BAGD, BECNT, BNTC, CC, LN, NICNT, NIGTC, NTC, PNTC, WBC; all versions]. This noun denotes a dream that is used as a means of communication [LN].

QUESTION—What is the function of ἰδού 'behold'?

After a genitive absolute (such as 'he having thought about this' in this verse) it introduces something new which calls for special attention [BAGD]. It marks the importance of what follows [NICNT, NIGTC, WBC], particularly with the genitive absolute, though it is often untranslatable in English [NIFGTC]. It indicates an unexpected development in the story [NICNT, TRT] and adds vividness to the narrative [NICNT, NTC, PNTC]. This particle, which occurs sixty-two times in Matthew, usually expresses something surprising or remarkable, or introduces a divine intervention [BECNT]. Matthew uses it for emphasis, to introduce something new or unusual [ESVSB], or to get the reader to pay special attention [ESVSB, TH]. It sets up a contrast between what Joseph was going to do and what God intended for him to do [CC].

"Joseph, son of-David, do- not -be-afraid[a] to-take[b] Mary your wife; for that (which) is-conceived[c] in her is from[d] the Holy Spirit.

LEXICON—a. aorist pass. (deponent = act.) subj. of φοβέομαι (LN 25.252) (BAGD 1.a. p. 863): 'to be afraid' [BAGD, BECNT, BNTC, CC, NICNT, NIGTC, PNTC, WBC; NASB, NCV, NET, NIV, NLT], 'to fear' [LN; ESV, KJV, NRSV, REB, TEV], 'to hesitate' [NTC], 'to shrink from doing' [BAGD], not explicit [CEV]. This verb means to be in a state of fear [LN]. Here it has the connotation of shrinking from doing something [PNTC, TRT].

b. aorist act. infin. of παραλαμβάνω (LN **34.53**) (BAGD 1. p. 619): 'to take, to take into one's home, to take to oneself' [BAGD], 'to receive, to welcome' [LN]. The phrase παραλαβεῖν Μαριὰμ τὴν γυναῖκά σου 'to take Mary your wife' [BNTC, PNTC], is also translated 'to take unto thee Mary thy wife' [KJV], 'to take into your home Mary, your wife' [CC], 'to take (Mary), your wife, into your home' [NTC], 'to take Mary as your wife' [NIGTC, WBC; ESV, NASB, NCV, NET, NLT, NRSV], 'to take Mary home as your wife' [BECNT; NIV], 'to take Mary home with you to be your wife' [REB], 'to take Mary to be your wife' [TEV], 'to accept Mary as your wife' [**LN**, NICNT], 'go ahead and marry her' [CEV]. This verb means to accept the presence of a person with friendliness [LN].

c. aorist. pass. participle of γεννάω (LN 23.58) (BAGD 1.a. p. 155): 'to be conceived' [BAGD, BECNT, NTC, WBC; ESV, KJV, NASB, NET, NIV, NLT, NRSV], 'to be made to conceive' [BNTC], 'to conceive' [NICNT; REB, TEV], 'to be begotten' [CC, LN], 'to be produced' [NIGTC], not explicit [CEV, NCV]. The phrase τὸ γὰρ ἐν αὐτῇ γεννηθέν 'that which is conceived in her' is translated 'the baby that Mary will have' [CEV], 'the baby in her' [NCV].

d. ἐκ (LN 90.16): 'from' [CC, LN, NIGTC, PNTC; CEV, ESV, NCV, NET, NIV, NRSV], 'by' [BNTC, LN; NIV, TEV], 'through' [BECNT; REB], 'of' [NTC, WBC; KJV, NASB]. This preposition marks the source of an activity or state, with the implication of something proceeding from or out of the source [LN].

QUESTION—Why does the angel call Joseph 'son of David'?

By doing so he reminds Joseph of his messianic descent [Lns, NAC]. It alerts Joseph to the importance of his own role in the life of the Messiah [EBC, Lns]. It emphasizes the royal line of Jesus [CC, PNTC]. It marks the importance of Joseph in incorporating Jesus into the line of David [NIGTC]. Joseph's marrying Mary means that the child is legally Joseph's son and therefore also a 'son of David' [CC, NAC]. Legal descent from David passes to Jesus through Joseph [BNTC, NICNT, NIGTC, NTC, WBC]. The angel calls upon Joseph to prove himself a true son of David by having the messianic faith that David did, as well as by protecting the Messiah God was sending [Lns]. The angel addresses him this way because he is bringing news about the Messiah [My]. He does this to strengthen and comfort Joseph, in view of the messianic promises [NTC].

1:21 And she-will-bear a-son, and you(sg)-shall-call his name[a] Jesus, for he-will-save[b] his people from their sins."

LEXICON—a. The idiomatic phrase καλέσεις τὸ ὄνομα αὐτοῦ 'call his name' [CC, NIGTC, NTC, PNTC, WBC; ESV, KJV, NASB], is also translated 'name him' [BECNT, BNTC; CEV, NCV, NET, NIV, NRSV, TEV], 'give him the name' [NICNT; NIV, REB]. The future tense verb καλέσεις

'you shall call' is an implied imperative [BECNT, BNTC, EBC, ICC, Lns, NICNT, NTC, WBC; CEV, ESV, KJV, NASB, NIV, NLT, NRSV, REB]. By giving Mary's son a name, Joseph would be officially accepting Jesus as his child, thus giving Jesus the status of a descendent of David [NICNT, PNTC].
   b. fut. act. indic. of σῴζω (LN 21.27) (BAGD 2.a. α. p. 798): 'to save' [BAGD, BECNT, BNTC, CC, LN, NICNT, NIGTC, NTC, PNTC, WBC; all versions]. This verb means to cause someone to experience divine salvation [LN]. The phrase αὐτὸς γὰρ σώσει 'for he will save' [BECNT, BNTC, NTC] is also translated 'he himself will save' [CC], 'it is he who will save' [NICNT, NIGTC], reflecting the emphasis given by the pronoun αὐτός 'he', that it is he and no one else who saves [Lns, My, PNTC, WBC].

QUESTION—What is the logical connection between the name 'Jesus' and γὰρ σώσει 'for he will save' etc.?

The name 'Jesus' is a Greek transliteration for the Hebrew name 'Joshua' [LN (93.169)]. In the OT this Hebrew name is Yehoshua, (meaning, 'Yahweh is salvation' [EBC, CC, WBC]) and it also has a shortened form Yeshua (meaning 'Yahweh saves' [EBC, NAC]). Giving Jesus this name implies that he is the one who will bring in the eschatological salvation that God had promised [EBC]. The angel then explains the significance of this name by referring to Psalm 130:8 [BECNT, EBC, ICC, TH, WBC], which promises that God will redeem Israel from all their sins [EBC].

QUESTION—Who are the 'people' that he is to save?

They are those people who belong to the Messiah, the identity of which is progressively unfolded throughout Matthew's gospel [EBC]. It refers to the Israelites [NIGTC, TH], the historic people of God [NIGTC]. This implies the biblical concept of the remnant, the genuine Israel within the larger nation of Israel [BECNT]. 'His people' are the Jews, but the salvation offered to them would also extend to all nations [Lns, My]. Initially it refers to Israel [NICNT], but ultimately it will be the church [ICC, NICNT, WBC].

QUESTION—Where does the angel's statement end?

1. It ends at the conclusion of this verse [BECNT, BNTC, CC, ICC, My, NIBC, NICNT, NIGTC, NTC, PNTC, TH, TRT, WBC; all versions]. The perfect tense of γέγονεν is translated as an aoristic perfect: '(this) happened' [BECNT, BNTC, ICC, NIBC, NICNT, NIGTC, NTC, PNTC; all versions].
2. It extends all the way into 1:23 [EBC, Lns]. The angel explains that what has already happened in Mary's virginal conception is the fulfillment of the Isaiah prophecy. The perfect tense of γέγονεν should be translated as a true perfect tense, '(this) has happened' [EBC]. The words of the angel either include all of verse 23 or they end with the word 'Immanuel' [ESV]. The words of the angel do not include the brief explanation of the meaning of 'Immanuel' [Lns].

1:22 Now all this happened so-that it-might-be-fulfilled[a] that (which) was-spoken by the Lord through the prophet saying,

LEXICON—a. aorist pass. subj. of πληρόω (LN **13.106**) (BAGD 4.a. p. 671): 'to be fulfilled' [BAGD, BNTC, CC, LN, NIGTC, NTC, PNTC, WBC; KJV, NET], 'to fulfill' [BECNT, NICNT; ESV, NASB, NIV, NLT, NRSV, REB], 'to bring about' [NCV], 'to make come true' [TEV], 'to come true' [CEV]. This verb means to cause to happen, with the implication of fulfilling some purpose [LN]. 1:22 is translated 'So the Lord's promise came true, just as the prophet had said' [CEV]. Matthew uses this verb ten times, but only to describe fulfillments concerning Jesus [CC].

QUESTION—In what sense do the events narrated in this passage 'fulfill' Isaiah 7:14?

In Matthew it is clear that Mary is the virgin and Jesus is her son, Immanuel, but because this is a quotation from Isaiah 7:14, there are complex issues about Matthew's use of the passage [ESVSB]. There are three senses in which the Isaiah passage could be considered to be fulfilled in Jesus birth: (1) a typological sense, in which there was an immediate fulfillment in the time of Isaiah and Ahaz, but which would be fulfilled in a greater sense in the birth of Jesus, (2) a predictive sense in which Isaiah's words only referred to Christ's birth, (3) a multiple fulfillment sense, in which two fulfillments are intended, one in the immediate situation which the prophet understood, and the other much later, which God intended, but of which the prophet was unaware [BECNT].

1. Isaiah was initially referring to the imminent birth of a child in his own day that would have had a typological significance [BECNT, BNTC, NIBC, NICNT], such as Hezekiah, Ahaz' son [BECNT, NIBC], or Maher-Shalal-Hash-Baz in Is 8:4, 8 [NAC]. This would be supernatural in some way but not a virgin birth [BNTC]. It is best to understand Isaiah's prophecy as something that was partially fulfilled in Isaiah's time through the normal birth of some child, but would be fulfilled in a more complete and glorious way through the birth of Jesus, who truly is Immanuel, 'God with us' [My, NAC]. Events that happened in OT times contain theological motifs that foreshadowed Christ's incarnation and ministry, and they can be understood that way in hindsight by any who investigate those historical events and theological motifs [BECNT].
2. It specifically predicts the birth of Christ in the distant future [CC, EBC, Lns]. OT history and people are paradigms pointing to the Messiah, at least for those who can recognize it [EBC]. Isaiah intended the 'sign' not as an immediate event that will persuade Ahaz about the reliability of a subsequent future event, but of the more distant future event of the virginal conception and birth of the Messiah. This would confirm all that Isaiah had been prophesying about the present decadent and faithless state of the royal dynasty, of which Ahaz is the current representative; this requires seeing the prophecy in Isa. 7:14 in the larger context of Isa. 7–9,

and Immanuel's eating the bread of affliction as fulfilled in the fact that Jesus the Messiah who is born into poverty and as heir to a dynasty that no longer exists as such [EBC]. As a rebuke to Ahaz, who had turned away from relying on God, Isaiah says that the help that God will send won't come through Ahaz' own wicked male descendants [Lns]. While there is a connection between prophecies concerning Immanuel in Isa. 7:14 and the birth of Maher-Shalal-Hash-Baz in Isa. 8:1ff, they are not the same person, and only Jesus fulfills the prophecy of Isa. 7:14 [CC].

1:23 "Behold[a] the virgin[b] will-have in womb[c] and will-bear a-son, and they-will-call his name Immanuel,[d]" which is translated 'God with us.'

LEXICON—a. ἰδού (LN 91.13): 'behold' [BNTC, NTC, WBC; ESV, KJV, NASB], 'look' [BECNT, CC, LN, NICNT, NIGTC, PNTC; NET, NLT, NRSV], 'listen, pay attention' [LN], not explicit [CEV, NCV, NIV, TEV]. This particle is a prompter of attention, serving to emphasize the following statement [LN].
- b. παρθένος (LN 9.39) (BAGD 1. p. 627): 'virgin' [BAGD, LN; all translations]. This noun denotes a female person beyond puberty but not yet married and a virgin [LN].
- c. The idiom ἐν γαστρὶ ἕξει 'will have in womb' is translated 'will/shall conceive' [BNTC, NTC, PNTC, WBC; ESV, NRSV, REB], 'will conceive a child' [NLT], 'will become pregnant' [BECNT, NICNT; TEV], 'will be pregnant' [CC, NIGTC; NCV], 'will be with child' [KJV, NASB, NIV]. The phrase 'will conceive and will bear a son' is translated 'will have a baby boy' [CEV].
- d. Ἐμμανουήλ (LN 93.115) (BAGD p. 255): 'Immanuel' [BECNT, CC, NICNT; CEV, ESV, NASB, NCV, NIV, NLT, TEV], 'Emmanuel' [BAGD, BNTC, LN, NIGTC, NTC, PNTC, WBC; KJV; NET, NRSV, REB]. (Note that 'Immanuel' is the transliteration of the Hebrew spelling of the name, and 'Emmanuel' is the transliteration of the Greek spelling of it.) That God is present in Jesus reappears at the end of the gospel in 28:20 [BECNT, CC, NAC, NIBC, NICNT, WBC]. This creates a 'frame' or 'bookend' effect with that passage [BECNT, ICC, NICNT]. God's presence is a key theme in Matthew [BECNT, NAC]. This word occurs only here in the NT.

QUESTION—What connection does Matthew see between the virginal conception and birth, and Jesus' identity as Immanuel, 'God with us'?

The virginal conception means that Jesus is God's son [EBC, CC, WBC], and because he is the Son of God he is God with his people [BECNT, My]. The virginal conception and the fact that he is 'God with us' means that the Messiah is more than a son of David, and prepares the reader for the idea that will be developed later that he is the very Son of God [NICNT]. Jesus' birth as a result of divine intervention means that he is God's very son, he is the promised Messiah and he is 'God with us' [EBC]. As the son of God he is the Messiah, but at the same time he is more than that, he is 'God with us'

[BNTC]. Matthew obviously sees the Isaiah passage as speaking of a virginal conception and birth, though his focus is more on the fact of the child being Immanuel, God with us, clearly affirming Jesus' full deity, a fact that is re-affirmed at the end of the gospel in Mt 28:18-20 [NAC].

QUESTION—What is the relationship between the Greek word παρθένος 'virgin' and the corresponding word עלמה *almah* in the Hebrew OT text of Isaiah 7:14?

The Greek word παρθένος almost always connotes virginity [BECNT, EBC], and this is certainly how Matthew understands it [BECNT]. The Hebrew word עלמה *almah* refers to a young girl of marriageable age, and in the OT texts where it is used it also usually connotes virginity [CC, ICC, NICNT, NTC]. Likewise, the Hebrew word בתלה *betulah* has approximately the same semantic content, referring to a girl of marriageable age, and also normally implying virginity, though neither *betulah* nor *almah* specifically focus primarily on virginity as such [BECNT]. It would be unusual for the Hebrew word עלמה *almah* to refer to a married woman, so the use of the word suggests something other than normal childbirth within marriage [NICNT, NTC], which accounts for why the LXX translators chose παρθένος as the Greek equivalent [NICNT]. It seems to make more sense to understand the OT text as claiming that a virgin will be pregnant than that a young woman who is a virgin at the time of the prophecy will later become pregnant through the normal means [NIGTC].

1:24 And having-arisen from sleep Joseph did as the angel of-(the)-Lord directed[a] him and took[b] his wife, **1:25** but was- not -knowing[c] her untill[d] she-bore a-son; and he-called his name Jesus.

LEXICON—a. aorist act. indic. of προστάσσω (LN **33.325**) (BAGD p. 718): 'to direct' [NICNT, NTC, PNTC; REB], 'to instruct' [LN], 'to command' [BAGD, BNTC, CC, LN, NIGTC; ESV, NASB, NIV, NLT, NRSV], 'to order' [BAGD, LN, WBC], 'to tell' [**LN**, CEV, NCV, NET, TEV], 'to say' [BECNT], 'to bid' [KJV]. This aorist tense verb is translated as perfect: 'had directed' [BECNT, BNTC, NICNT, NIGTC, NTC, WBC; CEV, KJV, NIV, REB, TEV]; as aorist: 'directed' [CC, PNTC; ESV, NASB, NET, NLT, NRSV]. It means to give detailed instructions as to what must be done [LN].

b. aorist act. indic. of παραλαμβάνω (LN 34.53) (BAGD1. p. 619): 'to take (to oneself)' [BAGD], 'to accept, to welcome, to receive' [LN]. The idiom παρέλαβεν τὴν γυναῖκα αὐτοῦ 'took his wife' [BNTC, PNTC, WBC; ESV, NET], is also translated 'took Mary as his wife' [NASB, NCV, NLT], 'took her as his wife' [NRSV], 'took Mary home as his wife' [BECNT; NIV], 'took Mary home to be his wife' [REB], 'took his wife into his home' [CC, NTC], 'he accepted his wife' [NICNT], 'took his wife to himself' [NIGTC], 'took unto him his wife' [KJV], 'he married Mary' [TEV]. This verb means to accept the presence of a person with friendliness [LN].

c. imperf. act. indic. of γινώσκω (LN 23.61) (BAGD 5. p. 161): 'to know' [CC; ESV, KJV], 'to have sexual intercourse with' [LN], 'to have intercourse with' [NICNT, PNTC, WBC; REB], 'to have sexual relations with' [NIGTC, NTC; NCV, NLT, TEV], 'to be intimate with' [BECNT], 'to have marriage relations with' [BNTC], 'to have marital relations with' [NET, NRSV], 'to have union with' [NIV], 'to sleep together' [CEV]. The phrase 'was not knowing her' is translated 'kept her a virgin' [NASB].

d. ἕως οὗ (LN 67.119) (BAGD II.1.b. α. p. 335): 'until' [BAGD, BECNT, BNTC, CC, LN, NICNT, NTC, PNTC, WBC; all versions except CEV, TEV], 'before' [NIGTC; CEV, TEV]. This prepositional phrase indicates the continuous extent of time up to a point [LN].

QUESTION—What is implied by the statement ἐκάλεσεν τὸ ὄνομα αὐτοῦ 'he called his name'?

His giving the child a name implies that Joseph adopted him legally [PNTC], that he accepted legal paternity [BECNT]. Of course Joseph's recognition of Mary's son as his own was not adoption in the sense of bringing a child in from a different family, but the legal effect was the same [NICNT].

QUESTION—What does the phrase ἕως οὗ 'until' imply about their abstention from sexual relations?

One cannot conclude on the basis of this word alone that they did engage in sexual relations after Jesus was born [BECNT, CC, Lns, My, NIGTC, NTC, TH, TRT], though other evidence argues for that, such as the fact that Jesus had brothers and sisters [BECNT, CC, My, NTC], or the fact that Matthew said nothing to indicate that the abstention continued past the time of Jesus' birth [Lns, My]. It does not prove, but does strongly suggest that they had normal sexual relations after Jesus' birth [NAC, BECNT, BNTC, EBC, NIBC, NICNT, WBC]

DISCOURSE UNIT—2:1–23 [PNTC]. The topic is the infant Jesus.

DISCOURSE UNIT—2:1–12 [BECNT, EBC, ICC, NAC; CEV, ESV, GW, NASB, NCV, NET, NIV, NLT, NRSV, TEV]. The topic is the visit of the Magi [BECNT, EBC; NASB, NIV], the wise men visit [GW], the visit of the wise men [ESV, NET, NRSV], magi from the east [ICC], Bethlehem: Herod versus the magi [NAC], wise men come to visit Jesus [NCV], visitors from the east [NLT, TEV].

2:1 Now Jesus having-been-born[a] in Bethlehem of-Judea in (the) days of-Herod the king, behold,[b] magi[c] from (the) east[d] arrived in Jerusalem

LEXICON—a aorist pass. participle of γεννάω (LN 23.52) (BAGD 2. p. 155): 'to be born' [BAGD, LN, all translations], 'to be given birth' [LN]. This verb means to give birth to a child [LN].

b. ἰδού (LN 91.13) (BAGD 1.b. p. 370): 'behold, see' [BAGD], 'look' [BAGD, LN], 'listen, pay attention' [LN]. See translations of this word at 1:20. This particle is a prompter of attention, and serves to emphasize the following statement [LN].

c. μάγος (LN **32.40**) (BAGD 1. p. 484): 'a magus, a wise man and priest' [LN]. This plural noun is translated 'magi' [BAGD, BNTC, CC, **LN**, NICNT, NIGTC, WBC; NIV], 'wise men' [LN, NTC, PNTC; CEV, ESV, GW, KJV, NCV, NET, NLT, NRSV], 'men who studied the stars' [BECNT; TEV], 'astrologers' [REB]. This noun denotes a person noted for unusual capacity of understanding based upon astrology, and as having both secular and religious aspects of knowledge and understanding [LN].

d. ἀνατολή (LN 82.1) (BAGD 2.b. p. 62): 'east' [BAGD, LN, all translations except NLT], 'eastern lands' [NLT]. This plural form of ἀνατολή denotes east as a direction [LN].

QUESTION—What would have been the approximate date of Jesus' birth?

The calendar in use today that dates things relative to the birth of Christ was based on calculations done by Dionysius Exiguus in 525 AD [BECNT, NAC, PNTC, WBC], but his calculations were approximately four years off [BECNT, PNTC, WBC]. Herod the Great died in 4 BC [CC, EBC, NICNT, NIGTC, NTC], so Jesus could have been born in approximately 6 BC [NAC], or between 6 BC and 5 BC [C0C, NIGTC], or late 5 BC to early 4 BC [EBC, NTC], or sometime in 4 BC [BNTC].

QUESTION—Who was Herod the Great?

Herod, who was born about 74 BC, claimed to be born of wealthy Jewish nobility, but was actually the son of an Edomite (Idumean) father, Antipater, and a Nabatean Arab mother. He was made king of Judea by the Roman senate and granted an army to subdue opposition [NTC]. He pretended to practice Jewish religion, and built the temple in Jerusalem, but he was also devoted to Hellenistic culture and built a pagan temple in Caesarea. Josephus depicts him as crafty and cruel, and as generally hated by his subjects. He murdered his favorite wife, three of his sons, various in-laws, and countless others. He died about 4 BC [NTC]. Herod executed large numbers of prominent citizens, plus some of their families and supporters [NICNT]. He was guilty of numerous atrocities, but was particularly unscrupulous and ruthless when it came to protecting his throne [WBC], especially toward the end of his life [NICNT]. His final years were full of bloodshed [PNTC].

QUESTION—Who were the magi?

They were astrologers [NIBC, NIGTC, TH, WBC]. They were wise men and priests who practiced astrology, dream interpretation, and other secret arts [BAGD, My, NICNT, PNTC]. The term in NT times referred generally to men who were interested in astrology, magic, dreams, and interpreting the future; these men probably had built up their expectations by drawing from various Jewish writings, including the OT, and came to Bethlehem based on astrological calculations [EBC]. They enjoyed a certain amount of religious and political prominence in their own land, and mixed astronomical observations with astrology [NAC]. They were priestly professionals who tried to discern the signs of the times based on the stars [BECNT]. They were respected members of their own communities [NIBC], teachable and wise people, not crafty magicians [BNTC]. The magi were not kings

[BECNT, CC, My, NAC, NIBC, NICNT, NTC, PNTC]. Later Christian tradition, probably dating from the third century, described them as kings based on an interpretation of Isaiah 60:3 [BNTC, EBC, NIBC, NICNT, WBC]. The idea that there were three of them also comes from later Christian tradition, based on the number of gifts [BNTC, EBC, My, NIBC, NTC, PNTC, WBC], but it is not known how many there actually were [NTC, WBC].

QUESTION—How long after Jesus' birth did the magi arrive?
Jesus was at least several weeks old when they arrived [Lns]. Since the time of Jesus' birth, it had been between six and twenty months [EBC], about a year [My], one to two years [NAC], as much as two years [BECNT].

2:2 saying, "Where is the (one) having-been-born^a king of the Jews? For we-saw his star^b in (its) rising/in the east^c and we-came to-worship^d him."

LEXICON—a. a. aorist pass. participle of τίκτω (LN 23.52) (BAGD 1. p. 816): 'to be born' [BAGD, BECNT, CC, LN, NICNT, PNTC, WBC; ESV, KJV, NET, NIV, NRSV], 'to be given birth' [BAGD, LN]. The phrase 'the one having been born king' is translated 'the one who was born king' [BECNT], 'the one born King' [WBC], 'he who has been born King' [PNTC], 'the one who has been born as King' [NICNT], 'the one/baby/child who was born to be the king' [CEV, GW. NCV, TEV], 'the new-born king' [NIGTC, NTC; REB], 'the newly born king' [BNTC], 'the king...who has been born' [CC]. This verb means to give birth to a child [LN].

b. ἀστήρ (LN 1.30): 'star' [LN, all translations]. This noun denotes a star or a planet [LN].

c. ἀνατολή (LN **15.104**) (BAGD 1. p. 62). The phrase ἐν τῇ ἀνατολῇ is translated 'in its rising' [BAGD, CC, NTC], 'at its rising' [NIGTC, PNTC; NRSV], 'as it rose' [NLT], 'when it arose/rose' [BAGD, BECNT, BNTC, LN, NICNT; ESV, NET], 'rising' [GW, REB], 'rising above the eastern horizon' [WBC], 'as it came up in the east' [TEV], 'in the east' [LN; CEV, KJV, NCV, NIV]. This singular form of ἀνατολή denotes the upward movement of the sun, stars, or clouds [BAGD, LN].

d. aorist active infin. of προσκυνέω (LN **53.56**) (BAGD 5. p. 717): 'to worship' [BAGD, BECNT, BNTC, **LN**, NTC, PNTC, WBC; all versions except NRSV, REB], 'to bow down and worship' [LN], 'to show reverence' [CC], 'to pay homage' [NICNT; NRSV, REB], 'to do obeisance' [BAGD, NIGTC]. This verb means to express one's allegiance to and regard for deity by attitude and possibly by posture [LN].

QUESTION—What is the significance of 'born' in the phrase ὁ τεχθεὶς βασιλεύς 'the one having been born king'?
Jesus has the right to the throne by birth, but Herod does not [BECNT, NAC, NICNT]. In this chapter there is a contrast between the false king Herod and the true king Jesus [BNTC, CC]. Herod was a usurper [Lns], and feared the arrival of a bona fide king [NIBC].

1. He was born a king [BECNT, CC, EBC, NICNT, NIGTC, NLT, NRSV, NTC, PNTC, WBC; ESV, KJV, NASB, NET, NIV, REB], He was not born to become a king later on [EBC, PNTC].
2. He was born to become a king [TH; CEV GW, NCV, TEV].

QUESTION—In what sense is it 'his' star?

It is a sign that the expected king has arrived [Lns, WBC], the king of the Jews [PNTC]. They may have connected the star with the king of the Jews through their study of the OT and other Jewish writings [EBC]. The star signaled his birth [TH, TRT], it heralded a royal birth [NICNT, NIGTC]. In the phrase αὐτοῦ τὸν ἀστέρα 'his star' the word αὐτοῦ 'his' comes first, indicating emphasis [Lns, My].

QUESTION—What does ἐν τῇ ἀνατολῇ 'in its rising/in the east' refer to?

1. They saw the star as it rose [BAGD, BECNT, BNTC, CC, EBC, LN, My, NAC, NICNT, NIGTC, NTC, PNTC, WBC; ESV, GW, NET, NLT, NRSV, REB]. In the plural and without the definite article this noun connotes the east, as in 2:1, but here in 2:2 it is in the singular and has the definite article, so it means 'in its rising', a designation of when it was seen, not where [CC, EBC]. (Note that 'as it rose' could mean 'when it first appeared', indicating the time and not the direction of its appearing.)
2. The star came up in the east [TEV]. Several versions translate 'in the east' [CEV, KJV, NCV, NIV], which probably means that the star was in the east, though it could also mean that the magi were in the east when they saw it. (Note that stars always come up in the eastern sky and move all the way across to the western horizon during the night.)

QUESTION—What action or attitude is implied by προσκυνέω 'worship'?

It is speculative to assume too much Christology from the use of this verb, since it can have a wide variety of meanings in secular Greek [EBC].

1. They came to worship him [BECNT, Lns, NAC, TRT]. Matthew's overall use of this verb implies that more than reverence for a human being is meant [BECNT]. Their coming to worship him has significance for what is to come later on [NAC]. They would not have done all that they did just for an earthly king [Lns].
2. They came to offer him the homage due to a king [EBC, NTC, PNTC, TH], or Messiah [NTC]. They were giving him homage, but they did not have the full understanding of who he was such that they would worship him as deity. Nevertheless, Matthew's readers would see the honor given by the magi as a foreshadowing of true worship later given him [CC, NICNT, PNTC, WBC]. Matthew's use of the word here seems intended to blur the distinction between homage and religious worship, but wherever he uses it, his readers will see religious worship in the term, regardless of what the participants in the story actually intended [ICC, NIGTC].

QUESTION—What relationship is indicated by γάρ 'for' when they said 'for we saw his star'?

This conjunction indicates the reason why the magi were asking where this baby was [My, TH]; it could be translated, 'We ask because…' or 'We want to know because…' [TH].

2:3 But having-heard,^a the king Herod was-disturbed^b and all Jerusalem with him,

LEXICON—a. aorist act. participle of ἀκούω (LN 33.212): 'to hear, to receive news' [LN]. This aorist participle is translated as expressing a temporal relationship: 'when King Herod heard this' [BNTC, NICNT, NTC, PNTC, WBC; NCV, NET, NIV, NRSV; similarly ESV, KJV, NASB. NLT, REB], 'when King Herod heard about this' [BECNT, NIGTC; CEV, TEV; similarly GW], 'when King Herod had heard' [CC]. This verb means to receive information about something, normally by word of mouth [LN]. This news also serves to give the reason why Herod was so deeply troubled [PNTC, WBC].

b. aorist pass. indic. of ταράσσω (LN 25.244) (BAGD 2. p. 805): 'to be disturbed' [NIGTC; GW, NIV], 'to be deeply disturbed' [NLT], 'to be greatly perturbed' [REB], 'to be very upset' [TEV], 'to be alarmed' [BECNT; NET], 'to be thoroughly alarmed' [NICNT], 'to be troubled' [BAGD, BNTC, CC, PNTC, WBC; ESV, KJV, NCV], 'to be frightened' [BAGD, NTC; NRSV], 'to be worried' [CEV], 'to be terrified' [BAGD], 'to be caused great mental distress' [LN]. This verb means to cause acute emotional distress or turbulence [LN]. It is a very strong term, possibly meaning to be terrified or in turmoil [NAC].

QUESTION—What is the function of the conjunction δέ 'but'?

It introduces an explanation [BECNT], and possibly a note of mild contrast [BECNT, CC, EBC]. It is not translated by any other commentaries other than CC or by any versions.

QUESTION—Why was 'all Jerusalem' upset along with Herod?

People were probably troubled because of fear of what Herod might do in such as situation [Lns, My, NICNT, NTC, PNTC, TRT]. People knew Herod's cruelty and the paranoia that prompted him to murder his favorite wife and two of his sons, so they were fearful that the Magi's search for 'the one having been born king of the Jews' would provoke more acts of cruelty from him [EBC]. Jerusalem's leaders would have been allies of Herod, and naturally they would be concerned if a potential rival for Herod were to appear [BECNT]. 'All' is used in the sense of a large portion of the people [TH]. Some think that 'all Jerusalem' refers only to the chief priests and teachers of the law who could be quickly consulted about what the magi had said to Herod [EBC, NAC]. Matthew may be foreshadowing the opposition that Jesus would later receive by most of the Jewish leaders in the time leading up to his death [NICNT, NIGTC].

2:4 and having-gathered-together[a] all the chief-priests[b] and scribes[c] of the people he-was-questioning[d] them where the Christ is-born.

LEXICON—a. aorist act. participle of συνάγω (LN **15.125**) (BAGD 2. p. 782): 'to gather together' [CC, **LN**, NIGTC], 'to gather' [BAGD, PNTC, WBC; KJV], 'to call a meeting' [NCV, NLT], 'to call together' [BAGD, BNTC, LN; GW, NIV, NRSV, REB, TEV], 'to bring together' [BAGD; CEV], 'to summon' [BECNT, NICNT], 'to assemble' [NTC; ESV, NET]. This verb means to cause to come together, whether of animate or inanimate objects [LN].

b. ἀρχιερεύς (LN 53.88) (BAGD 1.b. p. 112): 'chief priest' [BECNT, BNTC, CC, LN, NICNT, NIGTC, NTC, WBC; all versions except NCV, NLT], 'leading priest' [NCV, NLT], 'high priest' [PNTC]. This noun denotes someone who became a principal priest because he was a member of one of the high-priestly families [LN].

c. γραμματεύς (LN 53.94) (BAGD 2. p. 165): 'scribe' [BAGD, BNTC, CC, NICNT, NIGTC, NTC, PNTC, WBC; ESV, GW, KJV, NRSV, REB], 'teacher of the law' [CEV, NCV, NIV, TEV], 'teacher of religious law' [NLT], 'expert in the Law' [BAGD, LN; NET], 'legal expert' [BECNT]. This noun denotes a recognized expert in Jewish law (including both canonical and traditional laws and regulations) [LN].

d. imperf. mid. or pass. (deponent = act.) indic. of πυνθάνομαι (LN 33.181) (BAGD 1. p. 729): 'to question' [NICNT], 'to inquire' [BAGD, BECNT, BNTC, CC, LN, NIGTC, PNTC; ESV, NRSV], 'to ask' [BAGD, LN, WBC; CEV, NCV, NET, NIV, NLT, REB, TEV], 'to seek to learn' [BAGD, NTC], 'to try to find out' [GW], 'to make an inquiry' [LN], 'to demand' [KJV]. This verb means to inquire about something [LN].

QUESTION—Who are being described by the noun ἀρχιερεῖς 'chief priests'?
1. It refers to the high priest and all the former high priests, plus a number of other leading priests [BECNT, EBC, ICC, Lns, NIGTC, NTC, PNTC, TRT, WBC], including the heads of the twenty-four main divisions of priests [BECNT, NAC, NIGTC, PNTC], and temple officers [BECNT, NIGTC, PNTC]. The high priest was supposed to remain in office for life [Lns], but, contrary to the law, Herod appointed the high priest himself and made frequent changes, so there were many living former high priests [EBC].
2. It refers to the current and former high priests, but none of the other priests [My].

QUESTION—Who were the scribes and what did they do?
They were experts in OT law [EBC, NIGTC, PNTC, TRT], as well as in the sizeable oral tradition and interpretation related to it, and also in the civil law based upon it [EBC]. They taught the law's application to Jewish life [BECNT], interpreting that law, administering justice, and teaching people [ICC]. Many of them were Pharisees [BECNT, EBC]. They were scholars of Scripture [NTC, TRT, WBC], experts in the Jewish religion [NTC]. They

were the intellectual and spiritual leaders of Judaism, and lived mostly in and around Jerusalem [ICC].
QUESTION—Was Herod convening the Sanhedrin?
1. In calling together a meeting of the chief priests and scribes, he was convening the Sanhedrin [Lns, NTC].
2. He convened a special meeting of all those who composed the Sanhedrin, though it was not a normal meeting of the Sanhedrin [My]. This was not a meeting of the Sanhedrin, though these groups would have composed the Sanhedrin [WBC].
3. He probably met with the priests and scribes separately [EBC].
QUESTION—Why did Herod need to ask this question, since the answer is plainly stated in Micah's prophecy?
Herod was ignorant of the Hebrew scriptures [BECNT]. His knowledge of scripture was superficial [NAC]. He was ill-informed about Jewish traditions [NICNT].

2:5 And they said to-him, "In Bethlehem of-Judea; for thus it-is-written through the prophet: **2:6** 'And you, Bethlehem, land of-Judah, you-are by-no-means[a] least[b] among the rulers[c] of-Judah; for from you will-come one-ruling,[d] who will-shepherd[e] my people Israel.'"

LEXICON—a. οὐδαμῶς (LN **69.6**) (BAGD p. 591): 'by no means' [BAGD, BECNT, BNTC, CC, **LN**, NTC, PNTC, WBC; ESV, GW, NASB, NIV, NRSV, REB, TEV], 'in no way' [NET], 'certainly not' [NICNT], 'most certainly not' [LN], 'not at all' [NIGTC], 'not' [KJV, NLT], not explicit [CEV, NCV]. This adverb marks strongly emphatic negation [LN]. This word occurs only here in the NT.

b. ἐλάχιστος (LN **87.66**) (BAGD 2.a. p. 248): 'least' [BAGD, BECNT, BNTC, CC, NIGTC, NTC, PNTC, WBC; all versions except CEV, NCV], 'least important' [LN, NICNT], 'lowest, last' [LN], 'quite unimportant, insignificant' [BAGD]. The litotes 'by no means least' is translated as a positive statement: '(you are) very important' [CEV], 'you…are important' [NCV]. This adjective describes being of the lowest status [LN].

c. ἡγεμών (LN **37.59**) (BAGD 1. p. 343): 'ruler' [BECNT, CC, **LN**, NICNT; ESV, NET, NIV, NRSV, REB], 'prince' [BAGD, BNTC, NTC, WBC; KJV], 'leader' [NIGTC, PNTC; GW NASB], or, 'important place' [**LN**], 'leading city' [**LN**; TEV], 'ruling city' [NLT]. The clause 'you are by no means least among the rulers of Judah' is translated 'you are very important among the towns of Judea' [CEV], 'you…are important among the tribes of Judah' [NCV]. This noun denotes one who rules, and it implies that he has a preeminent position. In the context of Matthew 2:6 it is possible to understand ἡγεμόσιν 'rulers' as a figurative reference to important places, and therefore one may also translate 'you are by no means the least among the leading cities of Judah' [LN]. The town is

MATTHEW 2:5–6

addressed as though as though it were a person who is a leader in the country of Judah [TH].

d. pres. mid. or pass. (deponent = act.) participle of ἡγέομαι (LN 37.58) (BAGD 1. p. 343): 'to rule, to govern' [LN], 'to lead, to guide' [BAGD]. This participle 'one ruling' is translated 'a ruler' [BECNT, BNTC, CC, NIGTC, NTC, WBC; ESV, NASB, NCV, NET, NIV, NLT, NRSV, REB], 'a leader' [NICNT, PNTC; CEV, GW, TEV], 'a Governor' [KJV]. This verb means to rule over, with the implication of providing direction and leadership [LN].

e. fut. act. indic. of ποιμαίνω (LN 37.57, 44.3) (BAGD 2.a.β. p. 683): 'to shepherd' [BECNT, BNTC, CC, LN (37.57), NICNT, NIGTC, NTC, PNTC, WBC; ESV, GW, NASB, NET, NIV, NRSV], 'to be shepherd for/of' [NLT, REB], 'to be like a shepherd for' [CEV, NCV], 'to lead' [BAGD], 'to guide' [BAGD; TEV], 'to rule' [BAGD, LN (37.57); KJV], 'to govern' [LN (37.57)]. This verb means to rule, with the implication of direct personal involvement [LN (37.57)], or, to herd and tend flocks of sheep or goats [LN (44.3)]. '

QUESTION—Why is the land called both Judea and Judah?

'Judea' is the Greek form, and 'Judah' is the Hebrew form [EBC].

QUESTION—What is the relationship between the names 'Bethlehem' and γῆ Ἰούδα 'land of Judah' in this sentence?

1. Bethlehem is a town in the land of Judah [BECNT, BNTC, EBC, TRT, TH; CEV, ESV, GW, KJV, NCV, NET, NIV, NLT, NRSV, REB, TEV].
2. The terms are in apposition: 'Bethlehem, land of Judah', meaning that Bethlehem is a district of Judah [Lns, NICNT, NIGTC, probably PNTC]

QUESTION—Is there a contradiction between the passage in Matthew that begins, 'And you, Bethlehem, land of Judah, *you are by no means least* among the rulers of Judah' and the passage Jesus is citing in Micah that begins, 'But you, O Bethlehem Ephrathah, *who are too little to be* among the clans of Judah' [EBC]?

There is no substantial contradiction, as both are affirming Bethlehem's insignificance apart from being the birthplace of the Messiah [BECNT, EBC, NIGTC, NTC, PNTC] Jesus just heightens the contrast that is already implicit in the OT text [CC]. Both contrast Bethlehem's geographical significance with its theological significance in redemptive history as birthplace of the Messiah [BECNT]. Matthew has adapted Micah's words to reflect how the prophecy has actually been fulfilled [NIBC, NICNT]. Micah's statement should be understood as a rhetorical question, 'Bethlehem, are you really too small,' while Matthew's form of it states in a positive manner that Bethlehem is undoubtedly an important place' [My]. There may have been a slight textual variant in the Hebrew text, resulting in Matthew's variant reading [WBC].

MATTHEW 2:5–6

QUESTION—Why does Matthew have 'leaders' whereas the Hebrew text has 'clans'?

A slight change in vowel points in the Hebrew text could change 'clans' to 'chiefs' [ICC, Lns, My, NICNT, NIGTC], and Matthew is probably following such a text [NICNT]. The leaders or chiefs represent the 'clans' or 'thousands' [Lns, My].

2:7 Then Herod secretly[a] having-called[b] the magi ascertained[c] from them the time of- the -appearing[d] of- (the) -star,

LEXICON—a. λάθρᾳ (LN 28.71) (BAGD 1. p. 462): 'secretly' [BAGD, BECNT, BNTC, CC, LN, NIGTC, NTC, PNTC, WBC; CEV, ESV, GW, NASB, NIV, NRSV, REB], 'privately' [LN; NET], 'in secret, in private' [LN], 'privily' [KJV]. The phrase 'secretly having called' is translated 'called for a private meeting with' [NLT], 'had a secret meeting with' [NCV], 'called...to a secret meeting' [TEV], 'called...to a private meeting' [NICNT]. This adverb describes what is not known by the public but is known by some in-group or by those immediately involved [LN].

b. aorist. act. participle of καλέω (LN 33.307) (BAGD 1.d. p. 399): 'to call' [CC, LN, NICNT, PNTC; GW, KJV, NASB, NIV, TEV], 'to call for' [NLT, NRSV], 'to call in' [CEV], 'to summon' [BAGD, BECNT, BNTC, LN, NIGTC, NTC, WBC; ESV, NET, REB], 'to have a meeting' [NCV]. This verb means to communicate directly or indirectly to someone who is presumably at a distance, in order to tell such a person to come [LN].

c. aorist act. indic. of ἀκριβόω (LN **27.9**) (BAGD p. 33): 'to ascertain' [BAGD, CC, LN, NIGTC, NTC; ESV, REB], 'to ascertain carefully' [WBC], 'to ascertain exactly' [PNTC], 'to find out' [NIV, TEV], 'to find out exactly' [BECNT, **LN**; GW], 'to find out accurately' [LN], 'to determine' [NCV, NET], 'to learn' [NCV, NLT, NRSV], 'to learn exactly' [BNTC, LN], 'to inquire diligently' [KJV], 'to get (them) to tell' [NICNT], 'to ask' [CEV]. The aspect of exactness implied by this verb is also translated as an adjective describing χρόνος 'time': 'exact time' [NASB, NCV, NIV, NRSV, REB, TEV]. This verb means to acquire information in an exact and accurate manner or to acquire information which is exact and accurate [LN]. This verb occurs only here and in 2:16 in the NT.

d. pres. mid. or pass. (deponent = act.) participle of φαίνω (LN 14.37) (BAGD 2.a. p. 851): 'to appear' [BECNT, BNTC, NICNT, PNTC; all versions except CEV, NCV], 'to begin to appear' [CC], 'to make an appearance' [NIGTC, NTC], 'to become visible' [WBC], 'to shine' [BAGD, LN]. The phrase 'the time of the appearing of the star' is translated 'when they had first seen the star' [CEV], 'they first saw the star' [NCV]. This verb means to shine or to produce light, as in the case of heavenly bodies [LN].

QUESTION—What is the function of τότε 'then' in this passage, and in Matthew's gospel generally?
Matthew normally uses it as a loose connective, though sometimes it has temporal force, which is how he uses it here [EBC]. It is used sixty-one times in Matthew as a connector introducing new narrative [PNTC, WBC]. Matthew probably uses this to show a parallelism between the account of Jesus and Herod (where it occurs in 2:7, 16, and 17), the account of Jesus and John (where it occurs in 3:5, 13, and 15), and the account of Jesus and the devil (where it occurs in 4:1, 5, 10, and 11) [NIGTC].

2:8 **and having-sent[a] them to Bethlehem he-said, "Go, diligently[b] make-careful-inquiry[c] about the child; and when you-find (him), inform[d] me, so-that I-too having-gone may-worship[e] him."**

LEXICON—a. aorist act. participle of πέμπω (LN 15.66) (BAGD 1. p. 641): 'to send' [BAGD, LN; all translations except CEV, NLT], not explicit [CEV, NLT]. This verb means to cause someone to depart for a particular purpose [LN]. Bethlehem was about five or six miles from Jerusalem [BECNT, EBC, ICC, NAC, NIBC, NIGTC, PNTC].
  b. ἀκριβῶς (LN 72.19) (BAGD p. 33): 'carefully' [BAGD], 'well' [BAGD], 'accurately' [BAGD, LN]. This adverb describes strict conformity to a norm or standard, involving both detail and completeness [LN]. Its use here indicates a very high concern on the part of Herod [WBC]. See the next lexicon entry for how ἐξετάσατε ἀκριβῶς 'diligently make careful inquiry' is translated.
  c. aorist act. impera. of ἐξετάζω (LN **27.37**) (BAGD 1. p. 275): 'to make a careful search, inquire' [BAGD], 'to try to find out, to make a diligent effort to learn' [LN]. The phrase ἐξετάσατε ἀκριβῶς 'diligently make careful inquiry' is translated 'make careful inquiry' [BNTC], 'carefully find out' [**LN**], 'make detailed inquiries' [NICNT], 'make careful search' [NTC; NIV, REB, TEV], 'carefully search' [BECNT], 'search carefully' [WBC; CEV, GW, NASB, NLT], 'look carefully' [NCV, NET], 'search diligently' [PNTC; ESV, KJV, NRSV], 'inquire diligently' [NIGTC], 'inquire accurately' [CC]. This verb means to engage in a careful search in order to acquire information, though primarily by inquiry [LN].
  d. aorist act. impera. of ἀπαγγέλλω (LN 33.198) (BAGD 1. p. 79): 'to inform' [LN; NET], 'to tell' [BAGD, LN, NICNT, PNTC, WBC], 'to come/come back (and) tell' [NCV, NLT], 'to report' [BAGD, BECNT, BNTC, CC, NIGTC, NTC; GW, NASB, NIV], 'to let (someone) know' [CEV, TEV], 'to bring word' [ESV, KJV, NRSV, REB], 'to announce' [BAGD]. This verb means to announce or inform, with possible focus upon the source of information [LN].
  e. aorist active subj. of προσκυνέω. See this word at 2:2.

QUESTION—Why did the Jewish leaders not go to Bethlehem also?
They were apathetic about the matter [BECNT, EBC, PNTC]. Of the various religious groups current in that day, only the Essenes were expecting the Messiah to come imminently [EBC].

2:9 **And they having-heard the king went and behold, the star, which they-saw in the east/in the rising, was-going-before[a] them, until having-come it-stood[b] above[c] where the child was.**

LEXICON—a. imperf. act. indic. of προάγω (LN 15.143) (BAGD 2.a. p. 702): 'to go before' [BAGD, BNTC, NIGTC, PNTC, WBC; ESV, KJV, NASB, NCV], 'to be (there) before (them)' [REB], 'to go ahead of' [BECNT, NTC; CEV, NIV, NLT, NRSV, TEV], 'to go in front of' [LN], 'to precede' [BAGD, LN], 'to lead' [GW, NET], 'to lead the way' [BAGD, CC]. This verb means to move in front of or ahead of someone, with the implication that both parties are moving in the same direction [LN].

b. aorist pass. indic. of ἵστημι (LN 85.8) (BAGD II.1.a. p. 382): 'to stand' [BNTC, CC, NIGTC, PNTC, WBC; KJV, NASB], 'to stand still' [BAGD, NTC], 'to stop' [BAGD; CEV, GW, NCV, NET, NIV, NLT, NRSV, REB, TEV], 'to come to rest' [NICNT; ESV], 'to be (in a place)' [LN]. This verb means to be in a location, with the possible implication of standing but with the focus upon the location [LN].

c. ἐπάνω (LN 83.49) (BAGD 2.a. p. 283): 'above' [BAGD, BNTC, CC, LN, NICNT, WBC; NET, REB], 'over' [BAGD, BECNT, LN, NIGTC, NTC, PNTC; all versions except NET, REB]. This preposition describes a position above something else, whether or not in contact [LN].

QUESTION—What did the star do when the magi saw it?
This says that the star moved through the sky in front of them so as to lead them to the very building where the child was [TH]. The star kept going ahead of them until it came to the place where Jesus was located and then it stood still [PNTC, WBC]. It seems impossible that a star could be seen to be standing over a precise house [EBC, ICC, NICNT, PNTC, WBC]. It hovered over Bethlehem, but not over the precise house [EBC]. It may have actually led them to the precise location [BECNT]. The star moved toward Bethlehem, but then stopped when they got to the right house [Lns]. Some have thought that the star did not remain on high, but came down to stand over Jesus' head, while others have reasoned that the 'star' of Bethlehem must have been an angel [ICC]. Perhaps this was not a natural astronomical occurrence but a miraculous provision of some sort that appeared to be a star that moved and then stopped over the child [NICNT]. It had not precisely guided them prior to this time [CC]. At this point it became a guiding star for the first time [NIGTC]. The real point is that God guided the magi to find the child [WBC].

2:10 **And seeing the star they-rejoiced (with) exceedingly[a] great joy.[a]**

LEXICON—a. σφόδρα (LN 78.19) (BAGD p. 796): 'exceedingly' [LN], 'greatly' [BAGD, LN], 'very much, extremely' [BAGD]. The phrase 'they rejoiced with exceedingly/exceeding great joy' [PNTC; KJV] is also translated 'they rejoiced exceedingly with great joy' [**LN**; ESV, NASB], 'they rejoiced with extremely great joy' [BNTC], 'they rejoiced with a very great joy' [WBC], 'they rejoiced with extremely strong joy' [CC], 'they were overwhelmed with joy' [BECNT; GW, NRSV], 'they were overcome with joy' [NIGTC], 'they were filled with joy' [NCV, NLT], 'they were absolutely delighted' [NICNT], 'they were overjoyed' [NTC; NIV, REB], 'they were thrilled and excited' [CEV], 'they shouted joyfully' [NET], 'what joy was theirs' [TEV]. This adjective describes a very high point on a scale of extent [LN]. This is an emphatic way of expressing an extremely heightened joy [WBC]. They were exhilarated [BECNT] with an extravagantly expressed joy [NICNT], happy in the extreme [PNTC], overwhelmed with joy [NIBC].

QUESTION—What caused their great joy?

They rejoiced that the star had reappeared [EBC, Lns, My, NAC, NIBC, NIGTC, NTC, PNTC, WBC]. They rejoiced because they knew they were receiving divine guidance [Lns, NAC, PNTC] and that they would soon find what they sought [My], they would see the newborn king [Lns]. They were overjoyed in seeing the star come to rest over the house, showing them the exact place for which they were searching [NICNT, TH, TRT].

2:11 **And having-come into the house**[a] **they-saw the child with Mary his mother, and having-fallen-down**[b] **they-worshipped**[c] **him**

LEXICON—a. οἰκία (LN 7.3) (BAGD 1.a. p. 557): 'house' [BAGD, LN, all commentaries and versions]. This noun denotes a building or place where one dwells [LN].
b. aorist act. participle of πίπτω (LN **17.22**) (BAGD 1.b.α. p. 659): 'to fall down' [BAGD, BNTC, CC, NIGTC, PNTC; ESV, KJV], 'to fall down before' [LN], 'to fall to the ground' [WBC; NASB], 'to prostrate oneself' [NICNT], 'to prostrate oneself before' [**LN**], 'to kneel down' [BECNT; CEV, NRSV, TEV], 'to bow down' [GW, NCV, NET, NIV, NLT], 'to bow low in homage' [REB], 'to cast oneself to the ground' [NTC]. This verb means to prostrate oneself before someone [LN]. This means to throw oneself to the ground as a sign of devotion to a high-ranking person or divine being [BAGD].
c. aorist act. indic. of προσκυνέω. See this verb at 2:2.

QUESTION—What is implied by the action of πεσόντες 'having fallen'?

It intensifies the verb προσεκύνησαν 'they worshipped' and indicates that it was more than just kneeling to a superior; it was true worship [BECNT]. It indicates submission [WBC]. Their prostrating themselves indicates humble worship [PNTC].

QUESTION—How does Jesus' birth in a stable (Luke 2:7) fit in with Jesus being in a house?

Either there has been sufficient time after Jesus' birth in a manger for the family to relocate to a house, or in a little Palestinian home the manager was not in a separate building from a family's home [Lns, NICNT, PNTC]. A considerable amount of time has passed since the birth of the child, so they have apparently moved to new quarters [NIBC, NTC]. Perhaps as much as two years have passed since his birth [BECNT].

and having-opened their treasure-chests[a] they-presented[b] to-him gifts,[c] gold and frankincense[d] and myrrh.[e]

LEXICON—a. θησαυρός (LN **6.140**) (BAGD 1.a.α. p. 361): 'treasure chest' [BAGD, BNTC, NICNT, NIGTC, NTC, WBC; GW, NLT, NRSV, REB], 'treasure box' [BAGD, **LN**; NET], 'treasure' [CC, PNTC; ESV, KJV, NASB, NIV], 'wealth, riches' [LN (65.10)], 'baggage' [BECNT], 'gifts' [NCV], not explicit [CEV, TEV]. This noun denotes a box containing valuable objects [LN (6.140)].
- b. aorist act. indic. of προσφέρω (LN **57.80**) (BAGD 2.a. p. 719): 'to present to/with' [BAGD, **LN**, NTC; KJV, NASB, NIV, REB, TEV], 'to offer' [BAGD, BECNT, BNTC, CC, NICNT, NIGTC, PNTC, WBC; ESV, GW, NRSV], 'to bring to' [BAGD, LN], 'to give' [CEV, NCV, NET, NLT]. This verb means to present something to someone, often involving actual physical transport of the object in question [LN]. It suggests offerings made to God [Lns].
- c. δῶρον (LN 57.84) (BAGD 1. p. 210): 'gift' [BAGD, LN, all translations except NCV], 'treasure' [NCV], 'present' [LN]. This noun denotes that which is given or granted [LN].
- d. λίβανος (LN **6.212**) (BAGD p. 473): 'frankincense' [BAGD, LN, all translations except NIV], 'incense' [NIV]. This noun denotes the aromatic resin of certain trees [LN].
- e. σμύρνα (LN 6.208) (BAGD p. 758): 'myrrh' [BAGD, LN, all translations]. This noun denotes the aromatic resin of certain bushes [LN].

QUESTION—What is frankincense?
It is a resinous gum derived from certain trees in Arabia that was used in worship and for medicinal purposes [BAGD, NIGTC], as well as on important social occasions [NICNT, NIGTC, NTC]. It is a glittering, odorous gum [EBC]. It is imported from India, Arabia, and Somalia [NIGTC].

QUESTION—What is myrrh?
It is a resinous gum derived from the *balsamodendron myrrha* bush used for incense [BAGD], spice, and perfume [EBC]. It was a luxurious fragrance, used cosmetically [NICNT].

QUESTION—Is Matthew implying anything of deeper significance from the mention of these three particular gifts?
1. No symbolic meaning should be seen in these items [CC, BECNT, My, NIGTC, PNTC, TH, WBC], either in their number or their kind [CC]. There is no basis to see in these gifts anything more than what the magi considered to be gifts fit for a king [CC, EBC, NAC, TH]. They were luxury gifts [BECNT, NICNT, NIGTC, PNTC, WBC]. Matthew is

alluding to Psalm 72:10–11 and Isaiah 60:6 [BECNT, EBC, ICC, WBC]. Matthew may intend an allusion to Isaiah 60:6 in which the nations will bring gold and frankincense [NICNT, NIGTC], or to 1 Kings 10:1-10 where the queen of Sheba brought gold and spices to Solomon [NICNT].
2. Gold was often associated with royalty, especially Solomon, incense was associated with worship, and myrrh was associated with death and burial [NTC, TRT]. Gold would be natural as a gift for a king, frankincense suggests worship of deity, and myrrh is associated with death [Lns].

2:12 And having-been-warned^a in a-dream not to-return to Herod, they-departed^b through a different road^c to their country.^d

LEXICON—a. aorist pass. participle of χρηματίζω (LN 28.39) (BAGD 1.b.α. p. 885): 'to be warned' [BAGD, all translations except BNTC], 'to be given a revelation' [BAGD], 'to be divinely instructed' [BNTC], 'to be made to know God's message, to receive a message revealed from God' [LN]. This verb means to make known a divine revelation [LN].
  b. aorist act. indic. of ἀναχωρέω (LN 15.89) (BAGD 2.a. p. 63): 'to depart' [BNTC, CC, NIGTC, WBC; ESV, KJV], 'to leave' [GW, NASB, NRSV], 'to go away' [NICNT], 'to withdraw' [BECNT], 'to return' [BAGD, LN; NCV, NIV, NLT, REB, TEV], 'to go back' [PNTC; CEV, NET], 'to retire' [NTC]. This verb means to move back to a point or area from which one has previously departed, but with more explicit emphasis upon the return [LN]. It is often used by Matthew to express strategic withdrawal from opposition or danger [BECNT, Lns, NAC].
  c. ὁδός (LN 1.99) (BAGD 1.a. p. 553): 'road' [BAGD, BNTC, LN, WBC; CEV, GW, NRSV, TEV], 'way' [BAGD, LN, PNTC; ESV, KJV, NASB, NCV], 'route' [BECNT, BNTC, NICNT, NIGTC, NTC; NET, NIV, NLT, REB], 'highway' [BAGD, LN]. This noun is a general term for a thoroughfare, either within a population center or between two such centers [LN].
  d. χώρα (LN 1.79) (BAGD 1.b. p. 889): 'country' [BECNT, BNTC, NICNT, NTC, PNTC, WBC; all versions except CEV], 'region' [BAGD, LN, NIGTC], 'place' [BAGD], 'land' [CC, LN], 'home' [CEV]. This noun denotes a region of the earth, normally in relation to some ethnic group or geographical center, but not necessarily constituting a unit of governmental administration [LN].

DISCOURSE UNIT—2:13–23 [ICC; NET]. The topic is the Messiah's flight and return [ICC], the escape to Egypt [NET].

DISCOURSE UNIT—2:13–18 [GW, NIV, NLT]. The topic is the escape to Egypt.

DISCOURSE UNIT—2:13–15 [BECNT, EBC, NAC; CEV, ESV, NASB, NCV, NRSV, TEV]. The topic is the escape to Egypt [BECNT, EBC; CEV, NRSV, TEV], the new exodus from Egypt [NAC], Jesus' parents take him to Egypt [NCV], the flight to Egypt [ESV, NASB].

2:13 And they having-departed, behold, an-angel of-(the)-Lord appears[a] in a-dream to Joseph saying, "Get-up[b] take[c] the child and his mother and flee[d] to Egypt and be[e] there until I-tell you; for Herod is-about to-search-for[f] the child to-destroy[g] him."

LEXICON—a. pres. indic. mid. or pass. of φαίνω (LN 24.18) (BAGD 2.c. p. 852): 'to appear' [BAGD, LN, all commentaries and versions except NCV], 'to come to' [NCV], 'to become visible' [LN]. This verb is translated as aorist tense: 'appeared' [all translations except NIGTC, PNTC]; as present tense: 'appears' [NIGTC, PNTC]. It means to become visible to someone [LN].

b. aorist pass. participle of ἐγείρω (LN 23.74) (BAGD 2.b. p. 215): 'to get up' [BAGD, BECNT, CC, NICNT, NIGTC, NTC, PNTC; all versions except ESV, KJV], 'to rise' [BAGD, BNTC, WBC; ESV], 'to arise' [KJV], 'to wake up' [LN]. This verb means to become awake after sleeping [LN].

c. aorist act. impera. of παραλαμβάνω (LN 15.168) (BAGD 1. p. 619): 'to take' [BAGD, all translations except NLT], 'to take with' [BAGD], 'to take along' [BAGD, LN], 'to bring along' [LN], not explicit [NLT]. This verb means to take or bring someone along with [LN].

d. pres. act. impera. of φεύγω (LN 15.61) (BAGD 1. p. 855): 'to flee' BAGD, BECNT, BNTC, CC, LN, NIGTC, PNTC, WBC; ESV, GW, KJV, NASB, NET, NLT, NRSV], 'to run away' [LN, NICNT], 'to escape' [NTC; NCV, NIV, REB, TEV], not explicit [CEV]. This verb means to move quickly from a point or area in order to avoid presumed danger or difficulty [LN].

e. pres. act. impera. of εἰμί (LN 85.1) (BAGD I. 3. p. 223): 'to be' [CC, LN, PNTC; KJV], 'to stay' [BAGD, BECNT, BNTC, NICNT, WBC; CEV, GW, NCV, NET, NIV, NLT, REB, TEV], 'to remain' [NIGTC, NTC; ESV, NASB, NRSV], 'to reside' [BAGD]. This verb means to be in a place [LN].

f. pres. act. infin. of ζητέω (LN 27.41) (BAGD 1.a.β. p. 338): 'to search for' [BECNT, BNTC, NICNT, NIGTC, NTC; ESV, GW, NASB, NIV, NLT, NRSV, REB], 'to look for' [BAGD, LN, PNTC, WBC; CEV, NCV, NET, TEV], 'to seek' [BAGD, CC; KJV], 'to try to learn where something is, to try to find' [LN]. This verb means to try to learn the location of something, often by movement from place to place in the process of searching [LN].

g. aorist act. infin. of ἀπόλλυμι (LN 20.31) (BAGD 1.a.α. p. 95): 'to destroy' [BAGD, CC, LN, NICNT, NIGTC, NTC, PNTC, WBC; KJV, NASB, NRSV], 'to kill' [BAGD, BECNT, BNTC; CEV, ESV, GW, NCV, NET, NIV, NLT, REB, TEV], 'to put to death' [BAGD]. This verb means to destroy or to cause the destruction of persons, objects, or institutions [LN]. Its recurrence in 27:20 connects the passion narrative to the persecution by Herod [ICC].

QUESTION—Why does Matthew use the present tense of the verb φαίνεται 'appears'?

The use of the historical present tense of this verb adds vividness to the narrative [EBC, PNTC, WBC]. It shows emphasis, and also links 2:13–18 to 2:19–23, since 2:19 has this same verb used in the historical present [CC]. The use of the historical present here marks the beginning of a section, as it also does in 2:19 [NIGTC]. It may indicate that the appearing of the angel coincides with the departure of the magi [BECNT].

QUESTION—What would the angel tell Joseph?

This is incomplete [TH], and it is filled out in some translations: 'until I tell you to return' [CEV, NCV, NLT] 'until I tell you to leave' [NTC; TEV]. Joseph is to wait for further orders [PNTC].

2:14 **And having-risen he-took the child and his mother by-night[a] and departed[b] to Egypt, 2:15 and he-was there until the death[c] of Herod, so-that it-might-be-fulfilled[d] that (which was) spoken by (the) Lord through the prophet saying, 'Out-of Egypt I-have-called[e] my son'.**

LEXICON—a. νύξ (LN 67.192) (BAGD 1.b. p. 546): 'night' BAGD, LN]. 'at night, in the night-time' [BAGD]. This is in the genitive case and it is translated 'by night' [NIGTC, PNTC, WBC; ESV, KJV, NRSV, REB], 'at night' [BAGD, BECNT], 'in the night' [NTC], 'in the night-time' [BAGD], '(he arose) while it was night' [BNTC], 'while it was still night' [NASB], 'during the night' [NCV, NET, NIV, TEV], 'that same night' [NICNT], 'that night' [CEV, GW, NLT]. This noun denotes the period between sunset and sunrise [LN].

b. aorist act. indic. of ἀναχωρέω (LN 15.53) (BAGD 2.b. p. 63): 'to depart' [BECNT, BNTC, CC, NIGTC, WBC; ESV, KJV], 'to go away' [LN, PNTC], 'to go off' [LN], 'to go' [NET, NRSV], 'to leave' [GW, NASB, NIV, NLT, TEV], 'to set off' [NTC], 'to escape' [NICNT], 'to seek refuge' [REB], 'to take refuge' [BAGD], not explicit [CEV]. This verb means to move away from a location, implying a considerable distance [LN]. See this word at 2:12.

c. τελευτή (LN **23.102**) (BAGD p. 810): 'death' [BNTC, CC, LN, NIGTC, NTC, PNTC, WBC; ESV, KJV, NASB, NIV, NLT, NRSV, REB], 'end' [BAGD]. This noun is translated as a verb: '(Herod) died' [BECNT, NICNT; CEV, GW, NET, TEV]. This noun is figurative extension of τελευτή 'end' and means the end of one's life, a euphemistic expression for death [BAGD, LN]. This is the only occurrence of the noun in the New Testament.

d. aorist pass. subj. of πληρόω (LN 13.106) (BAGD 4.a. p. 671): 'to be fulfilled' [BAGD, LN, all commentaries; KJV, NET, NIV]. This passive verb is also translated actively: 'to fulfill' [ESV, NASB, NLT, NRSV, REB], 'to bring about' [NCV]. The phrase 'so that it might be fulfilled' is translated '...came true' [CEV, GW], 'to make come true' [TEV]. This

verb means to cause to happen, with the implication of fulfilling some purpose [LN].
e. aorist act. indic. of καλέω (LN 33.307) (BAGD 1.d. p. 399): 'to call' [LN, all translations], 'to summon' [BAGD, LN]. This verb means to communicate directly or indirectly to someone who is presumably at a distance, in order to tell such a person to come [LN].

QUESTION—When did they leave for Egypt?
They left that same night after Joseph's dream [BECNT, CC, BNTC, ICC, Lns, NAC, NICNT, NIGTC, NTC, TH; CEV, GW, NCV, NET, NIV, NLT, TEV]. The verb μέλλει 'is about to' in 2:13 indicates the imminence of the danger [BECNT, ICC, NAC, WBC].

QUESTION—In what sense does Jesus' return from Egypt 'fulfill' the quotation from Hosea 11:1?
The fulfillment is typological [CC, BECNT, EBC, ICC, Lns, NIBC, NICNT, NIGTC, PNTC, WBC]. Typology involves the use of transferable models from OT stories [NICNT]. 'Fulfill' does not necessarily refer to predictive prophecy, because in the NT the history and laws of the OT are seen to have prophetic significance as well [EBC]. There is a typological identification of Jesus, God's Son, re-enacting what Israel, as God's son, did in coming out of Egypt [CC, BECNT, EBC, ICC, NAC, NICNT, NTC, PNTC]. Just as the nation of Israel came out of Egypt when the first covenant is being initiated, so also Jesus comes out of Egypt when the new covenant is being initiated [NAC].

QUESTION—Why is the quotation from Hosea placed here, when they go to Egypt, rather than later, when they actually leave?
In 2:21 Matthew's geographical orientation is shifting to Nazareth, so he maintains the focus on Egypt here rather than distract from the focus on Nazareth later on [BECNT, EBC, ICC, WBC]. Placing it here instead of after 2:21 allows each section to have a fulfillment formula [NIGTC]. It allows a parallelism with the previous section, 2:13–14, and with the following section, 2:19–21 [ICC]. Its placement here lends symmetry to the structure of the chapter, and also introduces the exodus motif before the exile motif [WBC].

DISCOURSE UNIT—2:16–23 [CEV, NASB]. The topic is the killing of the children [CEV], Herod slaughters babies [NASB].

DISCOURSE UNIT—2:16–18 [BECNT, EBC, ESV, NAC; NCV, NRSV, TEV]. The topic is the massacre at Bethlehem [BECNT], the massacre of Bethlehem's boys [EBC], the massacre of the infants [NRSV], Ramah: weeping for dead children [NAC], Herod kills the baby boys [NCV], Herod kills the children [ESV], the killing of the children [TEV].

2:16 **Then Herod, seeing that he-was-tricked[a] by the magi, was-enraged[b] greatly, and having-sent (soldiers) he-killed[c] all the boys in Bethlehem and**

MATTHEW 2:16 43

in all the region^d of-it from two-years (of age) and below, according to the time which he-ascertained from the magi.

LEXICON—a. aorist pass. indic. of ἐμπαίζω (LN 88.156) (BAGD 2. p. 255): 'to be tricked' [BAGD, **LN**, NICNT, NTC, PNTC; ESV, NASB, NET, NRSV, REB], 'to be deceived' [BAGD, BECNT, BNTC, CC, WBC], 'to be made a fool of' [BAGD, LN, NIGTC], 'to be outwitted' [NIV], 'to be mocked' [KJV]. This passive verb is also translated actively with the magi as the subject: 'to trick' [CEV; GW, NCV, TEV], 'to outwit' [NLT]. This verb means to trick someone into thinking or doing something and thus to make a fool of such a person [LN].

b. aorist pass. indic. of θυμόομαι (LN **88.179**) (BAGD p. 365): 'to be/become enraged' [CC; NASB, NET], 'to fly into a rage' [REB], 'to be/become furious' [NTC; ESV, GW, NCV, NIV, NLT, TEV], 'to be infuriated' [NRSV], 'to be angered' [BNTC], 'to be/become angry' [BAGD, LN, NIGTC, WBC; CEV], 'to be wroth' [KJV]. The phrase 'was enraged greatly' is translated 'was furiously angry' [PNTC], 'was filled with fury' [BECNT], 'was absolutely furious' [NICNT]. This verb means to be extremely angry, even to the point of being in a rage [LN]. This word occurs only here in the NT.

c. aorist act. indic. of ἀναιρέω (LN **20.71**) (BAGD 1.a. p. 55): 'to kill' [BAGD, LN], 'to execute' [LN], 'to destroy' [BAGD]. The phrase 'having sent he killed' is translated 'he sent and killed' [NIGTC, PNTC; ESV, NRSV], 'he sent and murdered' [WBC], 'he sent and slew' [NASB], 'he sent forth, and slew' [KJV], 'he gave orders/an-order to kill' [NCV, NIV, TEV], 'he gave orders for his men to kill' [CEV], 'he sent soldiers/men to kill' [NICNT; GW, NET, NLT], 'he sent men to murder' [BECNT], 'he sent and put to death' [BNTC], 'he sent and did away with' [CC], 'he gave orders for the massacre of' [REB], 'he had…killed' [NTC]. This verb means to get rid of someone by execution, often with legal or quasi-legal procedures [LN].

d. ὅριον (LN **1.79**) (BAGD p. 581): 'region' [BAGD, BECNT, **LN**; ESV], 'region around' [NTC], 'surrounding region' [BNTC, WBC; NET], 'surrounding area' [NCV], 'district' [BAGD, CC, LN, NICNT; REB], 'environs' [NIGTC], 'neighborhood' [PNTC; TEV], 'vicinity' [NASB, NIV], 'coasts' [KJV], 'in or near' [CEV, GW], 'in and around' [NLT, NRSV], 'territory' [LN]. This noun, which is always used in the plural, denotes a region or regions of the earth, normally in relation to some ethnic group or geographical center, but not necessarily constituting a unit of governmental administration [LN].

QUESTION—Why did Herod specify those of two years of age or younger?

Herod had learned from the magi that the star had appeared approximately two years earlier [CC, PNTC WBC]. The two-year limit was to make sure the specific child would not be missed [EBC, NAC], but it was not necessarily the age of Jesus [EBC]. Two years was not necessarily the exact time of the appearance of the star, it may only be Herod's rough guideline to his soldiers to insure that his potential rival would not be missed [NICNT]. Herod probably allowed for a margin of error [BNTC, Lns, NIBC, NTC, WBC], possibly a very wide margin [NTC].

QUESTION—How many boy babies would have been killed?

It would have been about twenty [CC, NAC, NIBC, NICNT, NIGTC, PNTC, WBC], possibly fifteen or twenty [NTC], or thirty [NIBC], or possibly no more than a dozen or so [EBC].

2:17 Then[a] was-fulfilled that (which was) spoken through Jeremiah the prophet saying, **2:18** 'A-voice was-heard in Ramah, weeping[b] and great lamentation;[c] Rachel is-weeping-for her children, and was- not -willing to-be-comforted,[d] because they-are not'.[e]

TEXT—Instead of κλαυθμός καὶ ὀδυρμός 'weeping and lamentation', some manuscripts have θρῆνος καὶ κλαυθμὸς καὶ ὀδυρμός 'wailing and weeping and lamentation'. GNT selects the reading κλαυθμός καὶ ὀδυρμός 'weeping and lamentation' with a B rating to indicate that the text is almost certain. The reading θρῆνος καὶ κλαυθμὸς καὶ ὀδυρμὸς πολύς is taken only by KJV, which translates it as 'lamentation, and weeping, and mourning'.

LEXICON—a. τότε (LN 67.47) (BAGD 1.a. p. 823): 'then' [BAGD, BECNT, BNTC, CC, LN, NICNT, NIGTC, NTC, PNTC, WBC; ESV, GW, KJV, NASB, NET, NIV, NRSV], 'so' [CEV, NCV, REB], 'in this way' [TEV], not explicit [NLT]. This temporal particle denotes a point of time subsequent to another point of time [LN].

b. κλαυθμός (LN 25.138) (BAGD p. 433): 'weeping' [BAGD, BNTC, CC, LN, NICNT, NIGTC, PNTC, WBC; ESV, KJV, NASB, NET, NIV, NLT], 'wailing' [BECNT, NTC; NRSV], 'crying' [BAGD, LN; CEV, GW], 'painful crying' [NCV], 'sobbing' [REB]. The phrase 'wailing and great mourning' is translated 'the sound of bitter weeping' [TEV]. This noun denotes weeping or wailing, with emphasis upon the noise accompanying the weeping [LN].

c. ὀδυρμός (LN **52.3**) (BAGD p. 555): 'lamentation' [BAGD, BNTC, **LN**, NICNT, NIGTC, NTC, PNTC, WBC; ESV, NRSV], 'mourning' [BAGD, CC; KJV, NASB, NIV, NLT], 'weeping' [CEV], 'grief' [BECNT; GW, REB], 'wailing' [LN; NET], 'lamenting' [LN], 'sadness' [NCV], not explicit [TEV]. This noun denotes ritualized wailing and crying as an expression of grief and sorrow at funerals [LN].

d. aorist pass. infin. of παρακαλέω (LN 25.150) (BAGD 4. p. 617): 'to be comforted' [BAGD, BNTC, CC, NICNT, NIGTC, PNTC, WBC; all versions except NRSV], 'to be consoled' [BECNT, LN, NTC; NRSV], 'to be encouraged' [BAGD, LN]. This verb means to cause someone to be encouraged or consoled, either by verbal or non-verbal means [LN].

e. The phrase ὅτι οὐκ εἰσίν 'because they are not' [CC; KJV], is translated 'because they are/were no more' [BECNT, NICNT, NIGTC, NTC, PNTC,

WBC; ESV, NASB, NIV, NRSV, REB], 'because they are/were dead' [BNTC; CEV, GW, NCV, NLT, TEV], 'because they were gone' [NET].

QUESTION—Why does he use τότε 'then' in this fulfillment formula instead of ἵνα 'so that' as in other places?

Matthew uses τότε here and in 27:9 (concerning Judas' death) to avoid the implication that the evil that happened was intended by God [BECNT, CC, Lns, NICNT, WBC], or should be attributed to God [EBC], although God does take and use evil deeds to bring his scriptural plan and promise to pass [CC]. God's providence overrules evil as he works out his gracious purpose [WBC]. He avoids the normal fulfillment formula here and in the passage about Judas because the actions described have a human and sinful origin, and also because neither Herod nor Judas intended to fulfill scripture [NIGTC].

QUESTION—In what sense does the slaughter of the children fulfill the passage from Jeremiah 31:15?

The Jeremiah passage speaks of the sorrow and grief the people of Judah experienced as they were being assembled at Ramah in 596 BC to be deported to Babylon [BECNT, EBC, NICNT, NTC]. Rachel represents the Jewish nation which is poetically represented as weeping over the deportation of the Jews [EBC, Lns, NAC, PNTC, TRT, WBC], and that passage has a typological correspondence to the Jewish mothers of Bethlehem were weeping over the death of their children [TRT, WBC]. Some commentaries note that the Jeremiah passage depicts mourning within the context of a hope of restoration with a new covenant. Now the tears begun in Jeremiah's days are ended with the tears of the mothers of Bethlehem. The heir to David's throne has come and the Exile is over, the true Son of God will introduce the new covenant promised by Jeremiah [BECNT, EBC, NIBC, NICNT, NIGTC, NTC].

QUESTION—What is meant by 'because they are not'?

In the Jeremiah passage it refers to the fact that the Jewish people are not there anymore due to being taken into captivity, but in Matthew it means that they have died [EBC, ICC, Lns, NAC, NIBC, NICNT, NIGTC, NTC, PNTC, TRT, WBC]. In being removed from the land, they were no longer a nation [EBC], and because they were taken into captivity, they were reckoned as being dead [WBC]. The Jeremiah passage speaks of the deportation of the northern kingdom, and it was as though those ten tribes no longer existed [Lns]. It is possible that the weeping of the Jeremiah passage may also be for those who had died in the conquest of the land by the enemy forces [BECNT, NIGTC, NTC].

DISCOURSE UNIT—2:19–23 [BECNT, EBC, NAC; CEV, ESV, GW, NCV, NIV, NLT, NRSV, TEV]. The topic is the return to Nazareth [BECNT, EBC; ESV, NIV, NLT], Nazareth: coming home to obscurity [NAC], from Egypt to Nazareth [GW], Joseph and Mary return [NCV], the return from Egypt [CEV, REB, TEV].

2:19 And Herod having-died[a] behold, an-angel of-(the)-Lord appears in a-dream to-Joseph in Egypt **2:20** saying, "Rise, take the child and his mother and go to (the) land of-Israel, for those seeking the life of-the child have-died."[b] **2:21** And having-risen he-took the child and his mother and went to (the) land of-Israel.

LEXICON—a. aorist act. participle of τελευτάω (LN **23.102**) (BAGD p. 810): 'to die' [BAGD, LN; BECNT, BNTC, CC, NICNT, NIGTC, PNTC, WBC; all versions except GW, KJV, REB]. This verb is translated as an adjective: '(was) dead' [NTC; GW, KJV]; as a noun: '(Herod's) death' [REB]. This verb means to come to the end of one's life, an euphemistic expression for death [LN].

    b. perf. act. indic. of θνῄσκω (LN **23.99**) (BAGD 1. p. 362): 'to be dead' [BECNT, BNTC, PNTC; all versions] 'to die' [BAGD, CC, LN, NICNT, NIGTC]. This verb refers to the process of dying [LN].

QUESTION—Why does he use the plural in the phrase 'those seeking the life of the child'?

The plural is a generalizing or categorical plural, but it refers only to Herod [BECNT, EBC, My]. It forms a link with the story of Moses, using wording drawn from Ex 4:19 LXX [ICC, NICNT, NIGTC]. Matthew draws an analogy between Moses and Christ, particularly in terms of the danger both faced as infants from the king; consequently the wording here is drawn from very similar wording in Ex 4:19 LXX, although here it applies only to Herod [NICNT]. It refers mainly to Herod [BNTC, TRT], but it also includes those whom he had ordered to find and kill Jesus [BNTC]. The plural may be intended to include Herod's servants, who had not died, but were no longer in power [PNTC, WBC], or some of his royal advisors [NAC, TH]. The angel is simply saying that no one remains who is seeking to kill the child [NTC].

2:22 But having-heard that Archelaus was-ruling Judea in-place-of his father Herod he-was-afraid to-go there; and having-been-warned[a] in a-dream he-withdrew[b] to the region[c] of-Galilee,

LEXICON—a. aorist pass. participle of χρηματίζω (LN 28.39) (BAGD 1.b.α. p. 885): 'to be warned' [BECNT, CC, NICNT, NIGTC, NTC, PNTC, WBC; all versions except CEV, REB, TEV], 'to be given a revelation' [BAGD], 'to be divinely instructed' [BNTC], 'to be given instructions' [TEV], 'to be directed' [REB], 'to be told' [CEV], 'to be made to know God's message, to receive a message revealed from God' [LN]. This participle is used to indicate the cause of the next action, as is 'having heard' earlier in the verse [BECNT]. This verb means to make known a divine revelation [LN]. See this word at 2:12.

    b. aorist act. indic. of ἀναχωρέω (LN 15.53) (BAGD 2.b. p. 63): 'to withdraw' [BAGD, LN, NTC; ESV, NIV, REB], 'to retire' [BAGD, LN], 'to take refuge' [BAGD], 'to depart' [BNTC, CC, NIGTC, WBC], 'to leave' [GW, NASB, NLT], 'to go' [CEV, NCV, NCV, NET, TEV], 'to go

MATTHEW 2:22   47

away' [BECNT, LN; NRSV], 'to get safely away' [NICNT], 'to go off'
[LN, PNTC], 'to turn aside' [KJV]. This verb means to move away from a
location, implying a considerable distance [LN]. See this word at 2:12.
  c. μέρος (LN 1.79) (BAGD 1.b.γ. p. 506): 'region' [BAGD, LN, NICNT,
NTC, PNTC, WBC; NASB, NCV, NET, NLT, REB], 'district' [BAGD,
BNTC, LN, NIGTC; ESV, NIV, NRSV], 'territory, land' [LN], 'parts
(of)' [CC; KJV], 'area' [NCV], 'province' [TEV], not explicit [CEV,
GW]. This noun denotes a region or regions of the earth, normally in
relation to some ethnic group or geographical center, but not necessarily
constituting a unit of governmental administration [LN].
QUESTION—Why might Joseph be afraid of Archelaus?
  Archelaus was a cruel tyrant like his father, and Josephus reports an incident
  at the beginning of Archelaus' reign in which he massacred 3,000 people
  [NIBC, NICNT, NTC]. He was notorious for his cruelty [NAC, PNTC], even
  in an age when cruelty was not uncommon [PNTC].
QUESTION—Was the content of the dream only a warning about living in
Judea where Archelaus was, or did it include a divine directive to go to
Nazareth as well?
  1. He was warned not to remain in Judea [BECNT, EBC, PNTC], but it was
     left up to him to decide where to go [BECNT, Lns]. It is unclear whether
     or not he was specifically told to go to Nazareth [EBC, PNTC].
  2. Joseph was warned to avoid Judea and also to go live in Nazareth [BNTC,
     CC, NIBC, NICNT, NTC].

2:23 **And having-come he-settled[a] in a town[b] called Nazareth; thus was-fulfilled that (which was) spoken through the prophets that/because[c] he-will-be-called a Nazarene.**

LEXICON—a. aorist act. indic. of κατοικέω (LN 85.69) (BAGD 1.a. p. 424):
  'to settle' [BAGD, BECNT, BNTC, NIGTC, NTC, PNTC; REB], 'to
  dwell' [CC, WBC; KJV], 'to make one's home' [NICNT; GW, NRSV,
  TEV], 'to live' [LN; CEV, ESV, NASB, NCV, NET, NIV, NLT], 'to
  reside' [BAGD, LN]. This verb means to live or dwell in a place in an
  established or settled manner [LN].
  b. πόλις (LN 1.88) (BAGD 1. p. 685): 'town' [BECNT, LN, NICNT,
  NIGTC, NTC; CEV, NCV, NET, NIV, NLT, NRSV, REB, TEV], 'city'
  [BAGD, BNTC, CC, LN, PNTC, WBC; CEV, GW, KJV, NASB]. This
  noun denotes a population center, in contrast with a rural area or
  countryside and without specific reference to size [LN].
  c. ὅτι (LN 90.21, 89.33) (BAGD 2. p. 589): 'that' [LN (90.21), NICNT,
  PNTC, WBC; NET], 'for' [CC, LN (89.33), NTC], 'because, since, in
  view of the fact that' [LN (89.33)]. The following do not translate
  explicitly, but indicate by quotation marks that ὅτι is understood as
  introducing the content of discourse: BECNT, BNTC, NIGTC; ESV, GW,
  NASB, NCV, NIV, NLT, NRSV, REB, TEV. This particle can mark

discourse content, whether direct or indirect [LN (90.21)], or can mark cause or reason, based on an evident fact [LN (89.33)].

QUESTION—Was Nazareth a city or a town?

The term πόλις could refer to anything from a large city such as Jerusalem, or to a small town of less than 500 people such as Nazareth [NICNT]. Nazareth was an obscure village founded late in the OT period, and would have been smaller than Bethlehem, but with a less lengthy history [NICNT]. It was a small village [BECNT], and unimportant [PNTC]. It was a very unpromising location [WBC]. In the NT, the name 'Nazareth' is spelled three different ways: Ναζαρέτ (here), or Ναζαρά, or Ναζαρέθ [LN 93.536].

QUESTION—What prophetic passage does this fulfill?

The absence of the participle λέγοντος 'saying' that normally occurs in Matthew's OT citations, along with the fact that he does not name a prophet, indicates that he is not citing a specific passage [EBC, BECNT, NICNT, NIGTC, WBC], but is indicating a theme of prophecy rather than a specific prediction-fulfillment quotation [EBC, BECNT, NICNT]. The use of the plural 'prophets' indicates he is referring to a motif common in the prophets [WBC].

1. It fulfills the prophetic predictions that Jesus would be disparaged and rejected, since Nazareth was unimportant, even despised, and to be called a Nazarene was to be scorned [EBC, BECNT, CC, Lns, NAC, NIGTC, NTC, PNTC]. The negative connotations of being a Nazarene in Jesus' day reflects more generally a rejection by the Jewish people, whose expectations Jesus did not meet [CC, NICNT]. Because Nazareth was considered a non-entity, being known as a Nazarene was to invite ridicule, dismissal, or abuse, just as the phrase 'he shall be called' implies a derogatory sense [NICNT].
2. Matthew is engaging in a play on words in Hebrew [ICC, NIBC, NIGTC, WBC]. (This view assumes that the readers or hearers of Matthew's Greek text would know the Hebrew term and would recognize the association with 'Nazarene', or that some among them would be able to explain it to the others.)
2.1. It relates Ναζωραῖος 'Nazarene' with the Hebrew word *netser*, referring either to Isa. 11:1 where it means 'branch' [My, NIGTC, WBC], or to Isa. 42:6 where it means 'to guard, keep' [NIGTC].
2.2. It relates Ναζωραῖος 'Nazarene' with the Hebrew word *nazir* 'Nazirite', alluding to various OT texts [ICC].

QUESTION—What is the function of ὅτι 'that/because'?

1. It indicates direct discourse [BECNT, BNTC, NIGTC; ESV, GW, NASB, NCV, NIV, NLT, NRSV, REB, TEV].
2. It begins indirect discourse [EBC, NICNT, PNTC, WBC; NET].
3. It indicates the reason for the claim of fulfilled prophecy. *Because* he would be called a Nazarene, the OT prophets' prediction that Jesus would be disparaged is fulfilled [CC, Lns, NTC].

DISCOURSE UNIT—3:1–7:29 [BECNT, EBC]. The topic is the early days of kingdom word and deed [BECNT], the gospel of the kingdom [EBC].

DISCOURSE UNIT—3:1–4:25 [BECNT; EBC]. The topic is Narrative 1: John and Jesus and the kingdom of God [BECNT], narrative [EBC].

DISCOURSE UNIT—3:1–4:16 [NAC]. The topic is Jesus' preparation for ministry.

DISCOURSE UNIT—3:1–4:11 [PNTC, WBC]. The topic is the preliminaries to Jesus' ministry [PNTC], the preparation for the ministry [WBC].

DISCOURSE UNIT—3:1–17 [ICC, PNTC; REB]. The topic is John the Baptist and Jesus [ICC; REB], John the Baptist [PNTC].

DISCOURSE UNIT—3:1–12 [NAC, NICNT, NIGTC; CEV, ESV, GW, NASB, NCV, NET, NIV, NLT, NRSV, TEV]. The topic is John the Baptist: the prophetic forerunner to the Messiah [NAC], the Messiah's herald [NICNT], John proclaiming in the wilderness [NIGTC], John the Baptist prepares the way [ESV, NIV, NLT], John prepares the way [GW], the preaching of John the Baptist [CEV, NASB, TEV], the proclamation of John the Baptist [NRSV], the work of John the Baptist [NCV], the ministry of John the Baptist [NET].

3:1 And in those days[a] John the Baptist comes[b] preaching[c] in the wilderness[d] of Judea

LEXICON—a. ἡμέρα (LN 67.142) (BAGD 4.b. p. 347): 'day' [BAGD], 'time' [LN]. The phrase 'in those days' [BNTC, CC, NICNT, NIGTC, NTC, PNTC, WBC; ESV, KJV, NASB, NET, NIV, NLT, NRSV] is also translated 'some years later' [BECNT], 'years later' [CEV], 'later' [GW], 'about that time' [NCV], 'at that time' [TEV], 'in the course of time' [REB]. This noun denotes an indefinite unit of time (whether grammatically singular or plural), but not particularly long [LN].

   b. pres. mid. or pass (deponent = act.) of παραγίνομαι (LN **85.7**) (BAGD 2. p. 613): 'to come' [BNTC, NIGTC, WBC; ESV, KJV, NASB, NET, NIV, NLT, TEV], 'to appear' [BAGD, BECNT, CC, **LN**, NICNT, PNTC; GW, NRSV, REB], 'to make a public appearance' [LN, NTC]. This verb means to come to be in a place [LN].

   c. pres. act. participle of κηρύσσω (LN 33.256) (BAGD 2.b.β. p. 431): 'to preach' [BAGD, BECNT, BNTC, CC, LN, NTC, PNTC, WBC; CEV, ESV, KJV, NASB, NIV, TEV], 'to proclaim' [NICNT, NIGTC; NET, NRSV, REB]. The phrase 'comes preaching' is translated 'started preaching' [CEV], 'came...and started preaching' [TEV], 'began preaching' [NCV], 'came...and began preaching' [NLT], 'appeared...his message was' [GW]. This verb means to publicly announce religious truths and principles while urging acceptance and compliance [LN].

   d. ἔρημος (LN 1.86) (BAGD 2. p. 309): 'wilderness' [BNTC, LN, NICNT, NIGTC, NTC, PNTC, WBC; ESV, KJV, NASB, NET, NLT, NRSV, REB], 'desert' [BECNT, CC, LN; CEV, GW, NCV, NIV, TEV]. This noun denotes a largely uninhabited region, normally with sparse vegetation [LN].

QUESTION—What time period in referred to by the phrase 'in those days'?

It is indefinite [My, TH]. The phrase is intentionally vague [BECNT, EBC], but the events of course occurred years later than what was just narrated [BECNT]. 'Those days' does not refer to the previous narrative, it is imprecise and general, probably referring to the critical time in which the important events occurred [PNTC]. It refers to the time in which Christ lived [NAC, NTC]. The phrase indicates little more than that he intends the account to be understood to be historical [EBC]. It indicates that the ministry of John occurred while Jesus was still in Nazareth [BNTC, My]. It indicates that the time of the gospel events was a critical period in history [NIBC]. It links the fulfillment theme found in Mt 2 with the materials that now follows in Mt 3 [NICNT]. It connects conceptually with the remarkable events that have been narrated before [Lns]. 'Those days' links chapters 1, 2, and 3; that is, 'those days' of Jesus' birth as well as of John's coming were both prophetic fulfillments of God's promises [CC]. The date was sometime between A.D. 27 and 29 [BECNT, EBC, NAC], or between A.D. 26 and 27 [NTC].

QUESTION—Why does the author use the present tense of the verb παραγίνεται 'comes'

It makes the description of the events more vivid [BECNT, Lns, PNTC]. It adds emphasis [CC, NIGTC]. The present tense introduces a change of scene [ICC]. It is used here, as well as in 2:1 and 3:13, to introduce a new character in the story, but in this uninhabited desert area where it signifies the beginning of a dramatic new mission it has the connotation of 'appeared' [NICNT].

QUESTION— What kind of place is the wilderness?

It was a remote semi-arid area [EBC, NICNT], and sparsely populated [BECNT, EBC]. It was mostly uninhabited, except by ascetics and hermits [Lns]. It was dry and barren [BECNT]. It was the wasteland to the west of the Dead Sea [NIBC]. It was a place of light rainfall and little agriculture [PNTC]. In the OT era the desert was associated with the giving of the law and with the prophetic ministry [EBC]. The desert was a place of refuge, of testing, of the giving of the law, of the exodus, and of renewal movements [BECNT]. The area to the west of the Jordan was a barren expanse of chalky, rocky soil, although John's ministry extended even to the east side of the Jordan [NTC].

QUESTION—What may be implied by the use of the present participle κηρύσσων 'preaching'?

The present participle is circumstantial and modal, meaning that the key feature of John's arrival was that he was proclaiming something [BECNT]. The verb implies a message given by someone in authority, and not one that is composed freely by the one making the proclamation [PNTC]. John speaks as a herald, as though representing someone else [Lns, NAC].

3:2 and saying, "Repent;[a] for the kingdom[b] of-the heavens[c] has-drawn-near.[d]"

LEXICON—a. pres. act. impera. of μετανοέω (LN 41.52) (BAGD p. 512): 'to repent' [BAGD, BECNT, BNTC, CC, LN, NICNT, NIGTC, PNTC, WBC; ESV, KJV, NASB, NET, NIV, NRSV, REB], 'to change one's way' [LN], 'to be converted' [BAGD, NTC]. This imperative is translated 'repent of your sins and turn to God' [NLT], 'turn back to God' [CEV], 'change your hearts and lives' [NCV], 'turn to God and change the way you think and act' [GW], 'turn away from your sins' [TEV]. This verb means to change one's way of life as the result of a complete change of thought and attitude with regard to sin and righteousness [LN].

b. βασιλεία (LN 37.64) (BAGD 3.a., 3.g. p. 135): 'kingdom' [BAGD, BECNT, BNTC, NICNT, NIGTC, NTC, PNTC, WBC; all versions], 'reign' [CC, LN], 'royal reign' [BAGD], 'rule' [LN]. This noun denotes the rule of a king, with the implication of having complete authority and the possibility of being able to pass on the right to rule to one's son or near kin [LN].

c. οὐρανός (LN 1.11, 12.16) (BAGD 1.e. p. 594, 3. p. 595): 'heaven' [BAGD, LN (1.11), all translations], 'God' [BAGD, LN (12.16)]. This noun denotes the supernatural dwelling place of God and other heavenly beings, and there seems to be no semantic distinction in NT literature between the singular and plural forms [LN (1.11)], and it is used as a figurative extension of the meaning οὐρανός 'heaven' to refer to God based on the Jewish tendency to avoid using a name or direct term for God [LN (12.16)]. It is plural here, following normal usage, as is the case in 3:16 and 3:17.

d. perf. act. indic. of ἐγγίζω (LN 67.21) (BAGD 5.b. p. 213): 'to draw near' [BNTC, NIGTC, PNTC], 'to come near' [BAGD, BECNT, LN, WBC; NRSV], 'to stand near' [CC], 'to be near' [GW, NCV, NET, NIV, NLT, TEV], 'to be here' [CEV], 'to be upon you' [REB], 'to arrive' [NICNT], 'to be at hand' [NTC; ESV, KJV, NASB]. This perfect tense verb is translated with a present tense meaning: 'stands near' [CC], 'is near' [GW, NCV, NET, NIV, NLT, TEV], 'is at hand' [NTC; ESV, KJV, NASB], 'is upon you' [REB]; with a future tense meaning: 'will soon be here' [CEV]. This verb refers to the occurrence of a point of time close to a subsequent point of time [LN].

QUESTION—What does John mean by 'repent'?

He is speaking of a turnaround of the entire person, involving the thinking as well as behavior, with overtones of grief [EBC]. It is the turning of the entire person to God and away from sin in a radical conversion to a new way of life, done as a response to the message about the kingdom, and involving sorrow about sin, recognizing one's need, and resulting in an obedient lifestyle [BECNT]. It is turning from an evil way of life to a completely new way of living [PNTC]. It is to stop sinning and serve and obey God instead [TRT]. It is a radical change of attitude and actions [NAC], a change of attitudes and conduct [TH], a radical change of mind [BNTC], a complete change of direction and lifestyle [NIBC]. John implies a complete conversion from a state of unbelief to faith [CC]. It is to be converted in a radical turnabout of mind, heart and will that changes the entire life [NTC]. It is a transforming of one's moral disposition [My].

QUESTION—What is the 'kingdom of heaven'?

It is God's rule [My, TH, TRT]. The kingdom is the manifest exercise of God's saving sovereignty on earth, and in human society [EBC]. In Matthew 'kingdom of heaven' is synonymous with 'kingdom of God' [BECNT, CC, EBC, Lns, NAC, NIBC, PNTC, TH], though it leaves more room to conceive of Jesus as the king of that kingdom [EBC], and also that it extends beyond this earth [PNTC]. It is the kingdom of which heaven is its very nature, but also is wherever the king is ruling with his power and grace [Lns]. It is God's rule effectively at work in his people [BNTC]. Jewish people often substituted 'heaven' for 'God' out of reverence [BECNT, CC, NAC, NIBC, PNTC]. 'Kingdom' is dynamic, pointing to a rule as opposed to a place, a 'realm' [PNTC, TH]. God's power to rule history has come in a new and dramatic way with the coming of the Messiah, to whom all power and authority are given [NAC]. God's reign is the exerting of his royal power, his kingly ruling [CC, NICNT]. Among first century Jews the phrase also reflected the hope of God's coming and of his asserting his authority over all who opposed it [NICNT]. The era of fulfillment of the Messianic prophecies had begun, resulting in God ruling the hearts and lives of men and bringing great blessing [NTC].

QUESTION—In what sense has the kingdom 'drawn near'?

With the coming of the Messiah the messianic age has dawned, though there were widely varying ideas of what that might mean [EBC]. It has drawn near in redemptive history, and has also become morally present as a dynamic and life-changing reign [BECNT]. There is a sense in which the kingdom is future, but here the focus is on the present, that the kingdom appears when Jesus appears [PNTC]. There is an overlapping of ages in the sense that the arrival of the kingdom was imminent, but also that they were in the decisive moment of its arrival; the kingdom, then as well as now, is both present and future [NAC]. God's ruling activity, especially his saving work, was about to begin [TH]. God's ruling has begun to operate, but has not fully come [CC]. The time was at hand for people to act decisively in response to God's rule [NICNT]. God is about to establish his effective rule in a way that will bring blessing to those who welcome it, and judgment to those who do not [BNTC]. The kingdom of heaven was drawing near in the form of the king of salvation, who is from heaven [Lns].

3:3 For this is the (one) having-been-spoken-of[a] through Isaiah the prophet saying, "A-voice shouting[b] in the wilderness: 'Prepare[c] the way[d] of-(the) Lord, make straight[e] his paths.[f]"

LEXICON—a. aorist pass. participle of εἶπον (LN 33.69) (BAGD 1. p. 226): 'to be spoken of' [BAGD, BECNT, BNTC, CC, LN, PNTC, WBC; ESV, NIV], 'to be spoken about' [NIGTC; NET], 'to be referred to' [NASB], 'to be announced' [NICNT], 'to speak of' [NTC; NRSV, REB], 'to speak about' [GW, NLT], 'to talk about' [CEV, NCV, TEV]. This verb means to speak or talk, with apparent focus upon the content of what is said [LN].

b. pres. act. participle of βοάω (LN 33.81) (BAGD 2. p. 144): 'to shout' [BAGD, BECNT, BNTC, NICNT; CEV, NET, NLT, TEV], 'to cry out' [BAGD, LN, PNTC; GW, NRSV], 'to cry' [CC, NTC, WBC; ESV, NASB, REB], 'to call' [BAGD; NIV], 'to call out' [NIGTC; NCV]. This verb means to cry or shout with unusually loud volume [LN].

c. aorist act. impera. of ἑτοιμάζω (LN 77.3) (BAGD 1. p. 316): 'to prepare' [BAGD, BECNT, BNTC, CC, LN, NICNT, NIGTC, PNTC, WBC; all versions except CEV, NASB], 'to make ready' [LN, NTC; NASB], 'to get ready' [CEV]. This verb means to cause to be ready [LN].

d. ὁδός (LN 1.99) (BAGD 1.a. p. 554): 'way' [BAGD, LN, all translations except NCV, NLT], 'road' [BAGD; CEV, TEV]. The phrase 'prepare the way of the Lord' is translated 'prepare the way for the Lord's coming' [NLT]. This noun is a general term for a thoroughfare, either within a population center or between two such centers [LN].

e. εὐθύς (LN **79.88**) (BAGD 1. p. 321): 'straight' [BAGD, **LN**; all translations], 'direct' [LN]. The phrase 'make straight his paths' is translated 'clear the road for him' [NLT], 'clear a straight path for him' [REB], 'make a straight path for him to travel' [TEV]. This adjective describes being straight in contrast to what is crooked [LN].

f. τρίβος (LN 1.100) (BAGD p. 826): 'path' [BAGD, LN, all translations except NCV, NLT], 'road' [NCV, NLT], 'beaten path' [BAGD]. This noun denotes a well-worn path or thoroughfare [LN].

QUESTION—What relationship is indicated by γάρ 'for'?

It introduces a traditional *pesher* or explanatory formula [BECNT, EBC], and is used here to identify John as fulfilling the prophecy of Isa. 40:3 [BECNT, EBC, TH]. It indicates an answer to the unstated question, "Why is John preaching this message?", the answer to which is, "Because he is the one prophetically spoken of in Isa. 40:3" [CC]. It indicates an explanation of the coming of John as well as of his message [Lns].

QUESTION—Who is making this explanatory statement?

1. Matthew is explaining John's ministry as fulfillment of prophecy [BECNT, BNTC, CC, My, NICNT, NIGTC, NTC, TRT, WBC; CEV, ESV, GW, NASB, NCV, NET, NIV, NLT, NRSV, REB, TEV].

2. This comment is part of John's message; John quotes from Isa. 40:3 to explain that what is happening in himself and his ministry is the fulfillment of prophecy [PNTC].

QUESTION—What does it mean to prepare his way and make his paths straight?

He is using a road-building metaphor [BECNT, EBC, PNTC]. In the ancient world a visiting king would be honored by the building or repairing of roads before his arrival [BECNT, NAC, NIBC, PNTC], but here John is demanding moral change [BECNT], calling people to repentance [NIBC]. John is calling them to rebuild highways of holiness in the sense of preparing for God's coming in Christ through moral living [NAC]. Whereas Isaiah has 'the way of our God', here he says 'the way of the Lord' [BECNT, CC, NICNT, PNTC, TH], which refers to the coming Messiah [TH]; since Jesus is 'God with us', his way is the way of God [BECNT, CC]. The 'wilderness' is ultimately the human heart, and they must correct what is not straight in the sense of not being in line with God's will, and must remove such things as self-righteousness, complacency, slander, cruelty or greed that would be obstacles between them and God [NTC]. The wilderness and its obstructions are within the human heart [Lns].

QUESTION—Does 'in the wilderness' refer to the paths, or to the voice crying out?

Following the reading of the LXX, it refers to the voice that is crying out in the wilderness [BECNT, CC, ICC, My, NTC, PNTC, TH]. Both Mark and Matthew follow the wording of the LXX, so one should not read too much into the difference between the OT Hebrew form and what Matthew has here [EBC]. There is really little difference here [CC, EBC, Lns, NIBC, NTC], and the command is intended to be spread everywhere anyway, not just the wilderness [EBC]. Both the voice as well as the preparation are in the wilderness [Lns]. In the lonely wilderness there is an openness to God's message [PNTC].

3:4 And this[a] John had his garment[b] of camel hair and a-leather belt[c] around his waist, and his food was locusts[d] and wild honey.[e]

LEXICON—a. αὐτός (LN 92.37) (BAGD 1.h. p. 123): 'this' [BECNT, BNTC, NICNT, NIGTC, NTC], 'this very, this same' [BAGD], 'the same' [KJV], '(John) himself' [CC, WBC; NASB], not explicit [PNTC; all versions except CEV, KJV]. This pronoun marks emphasis by calling attention to the distinctiveness of the lexical item with which it occurs [LN].

    b. ἔνδυμα (LN 6.162) (BAGD 1. p. 263): 'garment' [BAGD, NICNT, NTC; ESV, WBC; ESV, NASB], 'clothes' [BECNT; CEV, GW, NCV, NIV, NLT, TEV], 'clothing' [BAGD, BNTC, CC, LN, NIGTC, PNTC; NET, NRSV, REB], 'apparel' [LN], 'raiment' [KJV]. This noun refers to any kind of clothing [LN]. His clothing was coarse [NLT], being woven from camel hair [My, TRT].

    c. ζώνη (LN 6.178) (BAGD p. 341): 'belt' [BAGD, BECNT, BNTC, CC, LN, NICNT, NTC, PNTC, WBC; all versions except CEV, KJV], 'strap' [CEV], 'girdle' [BAGD, LN; KJV]. The phrase ζώνην δερματίνην 'leather belt' is translated 'a stripe of hide' [NIGTC]. This noun denotes a

band of leather or cloth worn around the waist outside of one's clothing [LN].
d. ἀκρίς (LN 4.47) (BAGD p. 33): 'locust' [BAGD, all translations except CEV], 'grasshopper' [BAGD, LN; CEV]. This noun denotes an insect of the family Acrididae. In Europe the term 'locust' is used for the large varieties of these insects and the term 'grasshopper' is used for smaller varieties, while in North America all these insects are generally called 'grasshoppers', and the term 'locust' refers to cicadas of the family Cicadadae [LN].
e. μέλι (LN 5.20) (BAGD p. 500): 'honey' [BAGD, LN, all commentaries and versions]. The phrase μέλι ἄγριον, literally 'wild honey,' refers to bee honey gathered in the fields and not the result of keeping bees in hives; the equivalent of 'wild honey' in a number of languages is 'forest honey' or 'tree honey' [LN].

QUESTION—What is intended or implied by the use of αὐτός 'this'?

It is emphatic, giving emphasis to John [BECNT, PNTC]. It shifts the focus from the 'voice' in the prophecy to John [My, NICNT], who is mentioned in 3:1, who fulfills the prophecy, and whose introduction to the story is now resumed [NICNT].
1. It is demonstrative [BECNT, BNTC, Lns, NICNT, NIGTC, NTC; KJV]: this John.
2. It is intensive [CC, My, WBC; NASB]: John himself.

QUESTION—What is the relevance of John's dress and diet to this passage and to his message?

John's lifestyle and appearance is as rugged as his message, and symbolized his prophetic ministry [EBC, PNTC]. His clothing associates him with the prophet Elijah [EBC, CC, ICC, Lns, NAC, NIBC, NICNT, NTC, PNTC, TH]. John's food and clothing were that of the poor [EBC, Lns, PNTC], and of those who lived in the desert [NAC]. He ate the food available in the wilderness [BNTC]. Such clothing was appropriate to the desert in that it was durable and not expensive, but it also symbolized the prophetic office, and his modest diet and clothing was a protest against self-indulgence and all that goes with it [NTC].

3:5 Then Jerusalem was-going-out[a] to him and all Judea and all the region[b] of-the Jordan, **3:6** and they-were-being-baptized in the Jordan River by him, confessing[c] their sins.

LEXICON—a. imperf. mid. or pass (deponent = active) indic. of ἐκπορεύομαι (LN 15.40) (BAGD 1.c. p. 244): 'to go out' [BAGD, BNTC, CC, LN, NICNT, NIGTC, NTC, PNTC; ESV, GW, KJV, NASB, NET, NIV, NRSV], 'to go out to see and hear' [NLT], 'to go' [CEV], 'to come out' [BECNT, WBC], 'to come' [NCV, TEV], 'to flock' [REB]. The imperfect tense of this verb is translated as having an inceptive sense: 'started coming' [BECNT], 'began to go out' [CC], 'began coming out' [WBC].

This verb means to move out of an enclosed or well defined area [LN]. The imperfect tense suggests repeated action [TH, WBC].
- b. περίχωρος (LN 1.80) (BAGD p. 653): 'region' [BECNT, BNTC], 'region around' [BAGD, NICNT; NET], 'region about' [ESV], 'region round about' [KJV], 'region along' [NIGTC; NRSV], 'neighboring region' [CC], 'surrounding region' [LN, WBC], 'whole region' [NIV], 'country by' [PNTC], 'district around' [NASB], 'area around' [NCV], 'neighborhood' [BAGD, NTC]. The phrase 'all the region of the Jordan' is translated 'the Jordan Valley' [REB], 'the Jordan River Valley' [CEV], 'the whole Jordan Valley' [GW], 'all over the Jordan Valley' [NLT], 'all over the country near the Jordan River' [TEV]. This noun denotes an area or region around or near some central or focal point [LN].
- c. pres. mid. participle of ἐξομολογέω (LN 33.275) (BAGD 2.a. p. 277): 'to confess' [BAGD, BECNT, CC, LN, NICNT, NIGTC, NTC, PNTC, WBC; all versions except CEV], 'to confess openly' [BNTC], 'to admit' [BAGD, LN], 'to tell how sorry (they were)' [CEV]. This verb means to acknowledge a fact publicly, often in reference to previous bad behavior [LN].

QUESTION—How many were being baptized?

People were streaming out to John from the entire region [CC, Lns]. The personification of the place names 'Jerusalem', 'Judea', and 'all the region of the Jordan' indicate that the response to John was quite sensational [BECNT]. That *all* the people were going out to John is hyperbole to emphasize the great number of people who went to hear John [ICC, WBC], and this means that many of the people from those areas went out [PNTC, TH]. The imperfect tense of the verb suggests that John's ministry extended for some period of time [NAC]. John's preaching brought a very large response [BNTC]. John was a sensation, and his influence was far-flung [ICC]. He may have baptized between 200,000 and 500,000 people [Lns].

QUESTION—What was the relationship between repentance and the time of baptism?

John baptized those who had repented of their sins [BECNT, CC, EBC, Lns, NTC]. He baptized those who had confessed their sins [TH]. He baptized those who had confessed and renounced their sins, as a confirmation of their repentance [EBC]. John's preaching brought about repentance, which prompted people to come for baptism, at which time they confessed their sins, with the result that they experienced ongoing repentance and faith [CC]. Matthew does not specify when the repentance occurred relative to the baptism, only that they confessed their sins when they were being baptized [NICNT]. The confession happened as they were being baptized [My, TRT].

QUESTION—In what way did John's baptism correspond with existing baptismal practices?

The baptisms of the Qumran community were for ritual purification and were repeated [EBC, NIBC], and the baptism done by the rabbis was for non-Jewish proselytes only, but John's baptism was unique in what it signified [EBC]. In the OT, cleansing by water symbolizes forgiveness, spiritual purity, and blessing [BECNT]. Since normally only Gentile proselytes were baptized, John's baptizing Jews was startling and new [NTC], and may have been considered an insult by some [PNTC]. Unlike baptismal practice of his own day, John baptized Jews and not Gentile proselytes, and it was directed toward the entire Jewish nation, not a sect within it [BECNT, CC], and it was a single act rather than a repeated ritual [BECNT, NAC]. The fact that he called Jews to repent and be baptized indicated that Jews could not count on their Jewishness to insure salvation [NAC]. The fact that he baptized Jews means he did not automatically view them as the holy people of God [NICNT]. John's baptism was unusual in that in OT washings people typically baptized themselves, whereas John performed baptisms on those who came [NICNT, PNTC]. As with existing baptismal practice among the Jews, John's baptism was not by immersion [Lns].

3:7 **But seeing many of-the Pharisees and Sadducees coming to/for[a] his baptism he-said to-them, "Offspring[b] of vipers,[c] who warned you to-flee from the wrath[d] about-to-be[e]?**

LEXICON—a. ἐπί (LN **89.60**) (BAGD III.1.b. p. 289): 'to (the/his baptism)' [BNTC, NICNT, NIGTC, PNTC, WBC; ESV, KJV, NET], 'for' [BAGD, BECNT, CC, NTC; NASB, NRSV, REB], 'for the purpose of, for the sake of, in order to' [LN]. The phrase 'to/for his baptism' is translated 'to the place where John was baptizing' [NCV], 'to where he was baptizing' [NIV], 'to watch him baptize' [NLT], 'to be baptized' [**LN**; CEV, GW, TEV]. This preposition is used as a marker of purpose [LN].

b. γέννημα (LN **23.53**, **58.26**) (BAGD p. 156): 'offspring' [BAGD, BECNT, CC, LN (23.53), **LN** (58.26), NIGTC, NTC, PNTC; NET], 'brood' [BAGD, BNTC, **LN** (23.53), NICNT, WBC; ESV, NASB, NIV, NLT, NRSV, REB], 'bunch' [CEV], 'generation' [KJV], not explicit [GW, NCV, TEV]. This noun denotes that which has been produced or born of a living creature [LN (23.53)], or a kind or class of persons, with the implication of possessing certain derived characteristics [LN (58.26)].

c. ἔχιδνα (LN 88.123) (BAGD p. 331): 'viper' [BAGD, BECNT, BNTC, CC, LN, NICNT, NIGTC, NTC, WBC; ESV, KJV, NASB, NET, NIV, NRSV, REB], 'snake' [BAGD, LN, PNTC; CEV, NCV, NLT, TEV], 'poisonous snakes' [GW]. This noun is a figurative extension of meaning of ἔχιδνα 'viper,' denoting a dangerous and despised person [LN].

d. ὀργή (LN 38.10) (BAGD 2. b. p. 579): 'wrath' [BECNT, BNTC, CC, NIGTC, PNTC, WBC; ESV, KJV, NASB, NET, NIV, NRSV, REB], 'God's wrath' [NLT], 'outpouring of wrath' [NTC], 'God's anger' [GW], 'judgment' [BAGD, NICNT; CEV], 'punishment' [LN; TEV], 'God's punishment' [NCV]. This noun denotes divine punishment based on God's angry judgment against someone [LN].

e. pres. act. participle of μέλλω (LN 67.62) (BAGD 2. p. 501): 'to be about to' [LN], 'to come' [BAGD]. This idiom is translated 'coming' [BECNT, CC, NICNT, NIGTC, PNTC; CEV, GW, NCV, NET, NIV, NLT], 'about to come' [WBC; NRSV], 'to come' [ESV, KJV, NASB, REB], 'approaching' [NTC], 'impending' [BNTC], 'God is about to send' [TEV]. This expression stresses the imminence of the eschatological judgment [BECNT, ICC] and its certainty [PNTC]. This verb means to occur at a point of time in the future which is subsequent to another event and closely related to it [LN]. The participle refers to something being future or coming [BAGD].

QUESTION—What relationship is indicated by the conjunction δέ 'but'?

It indicates a contrast between the popular response to John's message and how the religious establishment responded [BECNT].

QUESTION—Who were the Pharisees?

The Pharisees emphasized strict adherence to the law of Moses, but also to the oral tradition that interpreted that law [BECNT, CC, PNTC]. They were very concerned about ritual purity [CC]. They numbered in the thousands [BECNT], perhaps as much as 6,000 [ICC]. Some were fine people [PNTC] and not all were hypocrites [BECNT, NAC], but many had a tendency to pay far too much attention to small details of the law and lose sight of more important aspects [PNTC]. They were laymen, reformers who focused their activities in the synagogues [CC, NIBC]. They were conservative politically, but religiously were liberal [NAC]. They were generally respected by the Jewish people [CC, NAC], and their influence was widespread [CC]. Although together the Pharisees and Sadducees comprised only about five percent of the Jewish people, most members of the Sanhedrin were members of one group or the other [NAC]. The Pharisees worked through the synagogue system, whereas the Sadducees were concentrated around the temple in Jerusalem [BNTC].

QUESTION—Who were the Sadducees?

The Sadducees were priests [BECNT, NIBC, NTC], relatively few in number, but well-to-do, and generally favorable toward Roman rule; they gave attention to the literal interpretation of the law of Moses [BECNT]. The priestly and temple hierarchy was drawn from the Sadducees [NICNT], and the focal point of their influence was the temple [BNTC]. The Sadducees apparently did not believe in the resurrection of the dead or in any form of life after death [CC]. They were liberal politically, but religiously they were conservative, and did not believe any doctrine that could not be drawn from the five books of Moses [NAC]. They did not enjoy favor with the general population, but their cooperation with the Romans afforded them political power [PNTC]. They were influential among people of wealth and power [My].

MATTHEW 3:7 59

QUESTION—Why does he introduce Pharisees and Sadducees with a single definite article?

Though they are diverse factions, in Matthew's gospel they are often viewed from the standpoint of being united against a common opponent [BECNT, CC, NAC, PNTC]. Although Matthew distinguishes them elsewhere, here he lumps them together as being leaders of the Jewish people [EBC]. It suggests that a delegation consisting of members of the two groups came to investigate what John was doing [NICNT]. John sees them as one class of similar people [Lns, My], namely unworthy people [My] and impenitent hypocrites [Lns].

QUESTION—Were the Pharisees and Sadducees coming to be baptized or to watch?

The Greek text may be taken to mean that they came to be baptized, or that they came to where John was baptizing either to examine what he was doing or to be baptized to show that they were for the Messiah even though they had not repented. In either case John recognized that they were not repentant [ESV].

1. They were coming to be baptized [BAGD, BECNT, CC, Lns, LN, My, NIBC, NTC, PNTC, TH, TRT; CEV, GW, NASB, NRSV, REB TEV]. Although they came for baptism they were repulsed by John's message of repentance and punishment and refused to be baptized [My].
2. They were coming to the place where John was baptizing [BNTC, NICNT, NIGTC, NAC, WBC; ESV, KJV, NCV, NET, NIV, NLT]. They came to watch John baptizing the people [NLT]. They came to investigate John's ministry [NICNT].

QUESTION—What is the point of the rhetorical question?

John's question shows that he doubts the genuineness of their motivations in coming for baptism [BECNT, CC, NICNT, PNTC], or their genuineness in appearing to support his ministry [NAC]. John's question is heavy with sarcasm [NAC, NICNT]. They have no reason to expect to escape judgment if they are not repentant [EBC]. He is asking them who deluded them into thinking they could evade God's judgment [Lns], or to evade God and the call to repentance [NTC]. It is an ironic statement, expressing surprise that they should recognize their need to escape from God's coming judgment [TH]. Vipers flee before a sweeping fire [BNTC, ICC, NICNT, WBC]. Jews considered snakes to be deceitful and evil [TRT]. John was accusing them of being cunning and malignant, and saying that they will not escape God's judgment [My].

3:8 Produce[a] **therefore fruit**[b] **worthy**[c] **of-repentance**

LEXICON—a. aorist act. impera. of ποιέω (LN **13.86**) (BAGD I.1.b. p. 681): 'to produce' [BNTC, NICNT, PNTC, WBC; NET, NIV], 'to produce results' [LN], 'to bear' [BECNT, CC, NIGTC, NTC; ESV, NASB, NRSV, REB], 'to do' [CEV, GW, NCV], 'to bring forth' [KJV], 'cause, bring

about, accomplish' [BAGD]. The idiom ποιέω καρπόν 'to make fruit' means to cause results to exist [LN].
   b. καρπός (LN **13.86**) (BAGD 2.a. p. 405): 'fruit' [BAGD, BECNT, BNTC, CC, NICNT, NIGTC, NTC, PNTC, WBC; ESV, KJV, NASB, NET, NIV, NRSV, REB], 'results' [BAGD, **LN**], 'outcome, product' [BAGD]. The phrase ποιήσατε καρπὸν ἄξιον τῆς μετανοίας 'produce fruit worthy of repentance' is translated 'do something to show you have really given up your sins' [CEV], 'do that which shows that you have turned from your sins' [**LN**], 'do things that show you really have changed your hearts and lives' [NCV], 'do those things that will show that you have turned from your sins' [TEV], 'do those things that prove you have turned to God and have changed the way you think and act' [GW], 'prove by the way you live that you have repented of your sins and turned to God' [NLT], 'prove your repentance by the fruit you bear' [REB]. The phrase ποιέω καρπόν 'to make fruit' is an idiom meaning 'to produce results, to cause results' [LN].
   c. ἄξιος (LN 66.6) (BAGD 1.b. p. 78): 'worthy of' [CC, LN, NIGTC, PNTC; NRSV], 'proper, fitting' [LN], '(that) befits' [BNTC], 'which fits' [NICNT], 'showing' [BECNT], 'in keeping with' [NTC, WBC; ESV, NASB, NIV], 'meet for' [KJV]. 'that will show' [TEV]. This adjective describes that which pertains to being fitting or proper in corresponding to what should be expected [LN].
QUESTION—What relationship is indicated by οὖν 'therefore'?
   They are facing imminent judgment; therefore, if they truly want to escape it, their lives must show that their repentance is genuine [EBC, ICC]. If they want to be recognized as truly converted people, *then* they must show it by a repentant lifestyle and not just depend on their Jewish ancestry [BECNT]. It is used to make his statement more emphatic, that they should *really* show repentance [PNTC].
QUESTION—What is the fruit he is demanding?
   He expects genuine repentance to result in a changed lifestyle [BECNT, NAC, NICNT, NTC]. He is calling for a total re-orientation in the entirety of life [PNTC]. He is calling them to show a radical break with their past actions [ICC]. They must show by their actions that their hearts have been changed [Lns]. It means to obey God [TRT].

3:9 **and do- not -think^a to-say to/among^b yourselves, We-have Abraham (as) father. For I-tell you that God is able from these stones to raise-up^c children to-Abraham.**

LEXICON—a. aorist act. subj. of δοκέω (LN 31.29) (BAGD 1.a. p. 201): 'to think' [BAGD, BECNT, CC, NIGTC, PNTC, GW, KJV, NCV, NET, NIV, TEV], 'to think smugly' [NICNT], 'to suppose' [BAGD, BNTC, LN; NASB], 'to presume' [LN, NTC; ESV, NRSV], 'to imagine' [LN; REB], 'to assume' [LN], 'to consider' [WBC], 'to believe' [BAGD, LN], not explicit [CEV, NLT]. This verb means to regard something as

MATTHEW 3:9 61

presumably true, but without particular certainty [LN]. Note that this verb is subjunctive because it is a negated imperative, which typically requires a subjunctive form.
b. ἐν (LN 31.5) (BAGD I.5.b. p. 259): 'to' [BAGD, BECNT, BNTC, LN, NICNT, NIGTC, NTC; ESV, NASB, NCV, NET, NIV, NLT, NRSV], 'among' [CC, WBC], 'in' [BAGD], 'within' [PNTC; KJV], not explicit [GW, REB, TEV]. The phrase μὴ δόξητε λέγειν ἐν ἑαυτοῖ 'do not think to say in/among yourselves' is translated 'don't start telling yourselves' [CEV], 'don't think you can say' [GW]. The idiom λέγειν ἐν ἑαυτοῖς 'to think to oneself, to say to oneself' means to think about something without communicating the content to others, and is often used to introduce a direct quotation of one's thoughts [LN].
c. aorist act. infin. of ἐγείρω (LN 13.83) (BAGD 1.a.ε. p. 214): 'to raise up' [BAGD, BECNT, BNTC, LN, NICNT, NIGTC, NTC, PNTC, WBC; ESV, GW, KJV, NASB, NET, NIV, NRSV], 'to raise' [CC], 'to make' [NCV, REB, TEV], 'to create' [NLT], 'to cause to exist, to provide' [LN], 'to bring into being' [BAGD]. The phrase 'from these stones to raise up children' is translated '(God can) turn these stones into children' [CEV]. This verb means to cause to come into existence [LN].

QUESTION—What is the significance of his comment about Abraham being their father?

Despite the discipline of Israel by God in the OT era, by NT times there had arisen the belief that the merits of the patriarchs were sufficient for the salvation of all their descendents [EBC]. Many believed that their descent from Abraham would insure salvation for themselves [BECNT, ICC, Lns, My, NIBC, NTC, PNTC, TH]. Contrary to expectation John has called them the offspring of snakes, not of Abraham [ICC]. Physical descent is useless without repentance and obedience [BNTC]. Many believed that Abraham had amassed a treasury of merit that was sufficient for all his descendants [NIBC], and that his righteousness would be reckoned to them [My].

QUESTION—What is meant by the phrase ἐγεῖραι τέκνα τῷ Ἀβραάμ 'to raise up children to Abraham'?

The noun 'Abraham' is in the dative case, and a preposition needs to be supplied to show its relationship: God is able to raise up children 'to Abraham' [BNTC, NIGTC, PNTC, WBC; NASB, NRSV; similarly KJV]. But 'to Abraham' is not natural English [TH], so some translate it 'for Abraham' [BECNT, CC, NICNT, NTC; CEV, ESV, GW, NCV, NET, NIV, REB, TEV], 'of Abraham' [NLT]. It means that God could make descendents of Abraham out of those stones [TH]. There is a play on words because the words for 'stones' and 'children' are similar in Aramaic [EBC, ICC, NAC, NIBC, NICNT, PNTC], as well as in Hebrew [BECNT, EBC, ICC, NIBC, NICNT, TH]. Using this play on words, Jesus made the point that even out of those stones on the ground around them God could raise up those who were true sons of Abraham in contrast with those Pharisees who could claim no more than physical descent [PNTC]. Even stones had more chance of being God's true people than they had [NICNT].

3:10 And already^a the axe is-laid^b to the root of-the trees; therefore every^c tree not producing fruit is cut-down^d and is-cast^e into (the) fire.

LEXICON—a. ἤδη (LN 67.20) (BAGD 1.a. p. 344): 'already' [BAGD, BECNT, CC, LN, NICNT, NIGTC, NTC, PNTC, WBC; NASB, NIV], 'even now' [BNTC; ESV, NET, NLT, NRSV], 'now' [KJV], not explicit [CEV, GW, NCV, REB, TEV]. The use of this particle is emphatic [EBC, ICC]. This temporal particle indicates a point of time preceding another point of time and implying completion [LN].
- b. pres. pass. indic. of κεῖμαι (LN 85.3) (BAGD 1.b. p. 426): 'to be laid' [BAGD], 'to lie, to be' [LN]. The phrase 'already the axe is laid to the root of the trees' [CC, NIGTC, NTC], is translated 'even now the axe is laid to the root of the trees' [ESV; similarly WBC; KJV], 'even now the ax is laid at the root of the trees' [NET], 'already/even now the ax is lying at the root of the trees' [PNTC; NRSV], 'the axe is already laid at the root of the trees' [NASB], 'the ax is already at the root of the trees' [NIV], 'the axe lies ready at the roots of the trees' [REB], 'even now the axe lies at the root of the trees' [BNTC], 'the ax has already been placed against the root of the trees' [NICNT], 'the ax is now ready to cut the roots of the trees' [GW], 'an ax is ready to cut the trees down at their roots' [CEV; similarly TEV], 'the ax is now ready to cut down the trees' [NCV], even now the ax of God's judgment is poised, ready to sever the roots of the trees' [NLT], 'the ax is already being swung at the root of the trees' [BECNT]. This verb means to be in a place, frequently in the sense of 'resting on' [LN]. It is laid at the root in order to judge where the first blow should fall [NIGTC].
- c. πᾶς (LN 59.23) (BAGD 1.a.α. p. 631): 'every' [BAGD, BECNT, BNTC, CC, LN, NICNT, NIGTC, NTC, WBC; all versions except CEV, GW], 'any' [BAGD, PNTC; CEV, GW], 'all' [BAGD, LN]. This adjective describes the totality of any object, mass, collective, or extension [LN].
- d. pres. pass. indic. of ἐκκόπτω (LN **19.18**) (BAGD 1. p. 241): 'to be cut down' [BAGD, BECNT, BNTC, CC, **LN**, NIGTC, NTC, PNTC, WBC; all versions except CEV, KJV, NLT], 'to be chopped down' [NICNT; CEV, NLT], 'to be hewn down' [KJV], 'to be cut off' [LN]. This verb means to cut in such a way as to cause separation [LN].
- e. pres. pass. indic. of βάλλω (LN 15.215) (BAGD 1.b. p. 131): 'to be thrown' [BAGD, BECNT, BNTC, CC, LN, NICNT, NIGTC, NTC, PNTC; all versions except KJV], 'to be cast' [WBC; KJV].

QUESTION—Why is the cutting action focused on the roots of the trees instead of the trunk?

The judgment will be so complete that not even the stump will be left [Lns, PNTC]. The action is one of final removal, not of pruning [NICNT]. The axe

MATTHEW 3:10 63

is at the base of the trunk in order to judge correctly the first blow to be given [NIGTC].

QUESTION—Why does John use present tense verbs?

It gives a sense of immediacy and certainty [BECNT, ICC, My], which is heightened by the use of ἤδη 'already' [BECNT, CC, ICC, NTC]. These things were already beginning to happen [PNTC]. It communicates timeless propositions as well as emphasis [Lns].

QUESTION—Who is the agent of the passive verbs 'is laid', 'is cut down', and 'is cast'?

1. God is the agent of the passive verbs [ICC, TH].
2. Jesus is the agent of the passive verbs [BECNT, NIGTC].

3:11 I baptize you with/in[a] water for[b] repentance, but the (one) coming after me is stronger-than[c] me,

LEXICON—a. ἐν (LN 90.10): 'with' [BECNT, BNTC, CC, LN, NIGTC, NTC; all versions], 'in' [NICNT, PNTC, WBC]. This preposition can mark an immediate instrument [LN].

b. εἰς (LN 13.62) (BAGD 6.a. p. 230): 'for' [BNTC, CC, LN, NIGTC, PNTC; ESV, NASB, NET, NIV, NRSV, REB], 'with a view to' [NICNT, NTC], 'to' [LN], 'unto' [KJV], 'at' [BAGD], 'associated with' [WBC], 'in reference to' [BECNT], 'so that you will…' [CEV, GW], 'to show that…' [NCV, TEV], not explicit [NLT]. This preposition marks a change of state [LN].

c. ἰσχυρός (LN 87.44) (BAGD 1.a. p. 383): 'strong' [BAGD], 'mighty, powerful' [BAGD, LN], 'great' [LN]. This comparative form of this word (ἰσχυρότερος) is translated 'stronger' [BNTC, NICNT, WBC], 'mightier' [CC, NIGTC, NTC; ESV, KJV, NASB, REB], 'more powerful' [CEV, GW, NET, NIV, NRSV], 'greater' [BECNT, PNTC; NCV, NLT, TEV]. This adjective describes a high status, probably on the basis of significant personal capacity [LN]. It means that the coming one would be more important than John and would have more authority than John had [TH].

QUESTION—Whom is John addressing now?

He is addressing everyone in the crowd [CC]. He is speaking to those whom he is baptizing [NICNT]. He is speaking to the Pharisees and the Sadducees [NIGTC]. He is addressing the Pharisees and the Sadducees, but through them the entire Jewish nation that they represent [My].

QUESTION—What relationship is indicated by the conjunction δέ 'but'?

This conjunction introduces the second element in the μέν…δέ construction that balances two contrasting propositions [BECNT, CC, NICNT, PNTC], a contrast that is strengthened by the use of the emphatic personal pronouns ἐγώ 'I' and αὐτός 'he' [BECNT, CC, ICC, PNTC].

QUESTION—Does ὁ δὲ ὀπίσω μου ἐρχόμενος 'the one coming after me' indicate that this person will follow John in time, or follow John as a disciple?

1. He was to follow John in time, that is, coming subsequent to John [BECNT, BNTC, CC, ICC, Lns, My, NIGTC, NTC, PNTC, TH, TRT,

WBC]. It refers to a man who would appear later to proclaim his own message [TH].
2. The one coming was to be, in one sense, a disciple of John, though also being superior to John [NAC, NIBC, NICNT]. At first Jesus led a baptizing ministry similar to John's, and this paradoxical language speaks of the follower who becomes the leader [NICNT].

QUESTION—What relationship is indicated by the preposition ἐν 'with/in' in the phrase ἐν ὕδατι 'with/in water'?

John's baptism is 'with' water in that it uses water [BECNT, TH], but it was also done 'in' water [BECNT]. John's baptism is in connection with water, just as the baptism Jesus brings is in connection with the Holy Spirit and fire [Lns]. It indicates the element in which baptism takes place [My].

QUESTION—What relationship is indicated by εἰς 'for' in the phrase εἰς μετάνοιαν 'for repentance'?

It indicates purpose: John baptizes people with a view toward repentance [NICNT]. It indicates purpose as well as result: John's public preaching and baptizing were a call to repentance, and also produced repentance [CC, NTC]. It indicates that baptism presupposes and expresses repentance [BECNT, CC, ICC, NIBC, PNTC; CEV, GW]. They have presumably already repented [EBC]. His baptism also *results* in a true reformation of character in conjunction with God's own work [ICC]. Through God's work, it also results in continued repentance [BECNT]. John baptizes them *with reference to* repentance, as distinguished from other ritual washings that do not symbolize repenting of sin [NAC]. Baptism imposes the obligation to repent [My]. It indicates that their repentance is the reason he baptizes them; that is, he baptizes them *at* their repentance or *in view of* their repentance [BAGD].

QUESTION—Who or what did John think the coming one would be?

He expected that the coming one would be the Messiah [ICC, Lns, My, NAC, TRT]. He would be the agent of God's judgment that had just been mentioned [NIGTC].

of-whom I-am not worthy[a] to-carry[b] the sandals;[c] he will-baptize you with/in[d] (the) Holy Spirit and fire;

LEXICON—a. ἱκανός (LN 75.2) (BAGD 2. p. 374): 'worthy' [BAGD, BNTC, CC, NIGTC, PNTC, WBC; ESV, GW, KJV, NET, NLT, NRSV], 'fit' [BECNT, NICNT, NTC; NASB, NIV, REB], 'good enough' [CEV, NCV, TEV], 'adequate' [LN], 'qualified' [BAGD, LN]. This adjective describes being adequate for something [LN].

b. aorist act. infin. of βαστάζω of (LN 15.188) (BAGD 3.a. p. 137): 'to carry' [BECNT, CC, LN, NIGTC, PNTC; CEV, ESV, NCV, NET, NIV, NRSV, TEV], 'to be his slave and carry' [NLT], 'to carry away' [BAGD], 'to remove' [BAGD, BNTC, NTC; GW, NASB, REB], 'to take off' [NICNT], 'to bear' [LN, WBC; KJV]. This verb means to bear or carry a relatively heavy or burdensome object [LN]. Matthew has not included

the word ἱμάντα 'strap' that is used in Mark 1:7, and here the picture is not of untying the straps of the master's sandal, but of a disciple carrying his master's sandals [ICC].
c. ὑπόδημα (LN 6.182) (BAGD p. 844): 'sandal' [BAGD, LN, all commentaries and all versions except KJV], 'shoe' [LN; KJV]. This noun denotes any type of footwear [LN].
d. ἐν (LN 90.10): 'with' [BECNT, BNTC, CC, NIGTC, NTC, PNTC; all versions], 'in' [NICNT, WBC].

QUESTION—What is the relationship between 'Holy Spirit' and 'fire'?

The words 'Holy Spirit' and 'fire' are governed by the single preposition ἐν 'with' to indicate indicating they are considered together as a single concept [EBC, Lns, NAC], or as one baptism with two aspects [BECNT], or as two closely related baptisms [PNTC]. Both 'spirit' and 'fire' are purifying agents, [BECNT, EBC, Lns, NICNT, NTC].

1. Those who believe and repent will receive the Holy Spirit, but those who don't will experience the fire of judgment [HNTC, My, TH, TRT]. It is one eschatological event; for believers, it is a baptism with the Holy Spirit in eschatological salvation on the last day, and for unbelievers it is a baptism with fire on the last day [CC]. The changed life of anyone who repents and believes will culminate in a final purification done by the Holy Spirit, but those who rejected the call to repentance will be judged [NIGTC]. It will be a final eschatological baptism of fiery breath (*ruah*, spirit) from God, which will overcome the wicked and purify the righteous [ICC].
2. This represents two different events at two different times. The believer is baptized with the Holy Spirit at conversion, and continually purified by the 'fire' of the Holy Spirit; the unbeliever however experiences only the fire, which will be at the time of judgment [NAC, NTC].
3. The word 'Holy Spirit' and 'fire' may be a hendiadys indicating a single concept, meaning that it is one purifying baptism for believers, with two aspects that are so closely related that they might be considered one thing [BECNT].
4. He speaks here of two closely related baptisms at the same time for believers only [PNTC]. The one preposition ἐν 'with' closely connects the two baptisms, so that the coming Messiah will baptize his followers with the Holy Spirit, that is, bring them into vital contact with the Spirit, and at the same time baptize them with the fire of purification [PNTC].

QUESTION—When was that baptism to happen?

1. It is an eschatological event that will happen on the last day [BECNT, CC, ICC, NIGTC]. The Holy Spirit will finally purify the believer, and fire will finally destroy the unbeliever [NIGTC].
2. It occurred at Pentecost, and was for purifying and enabling believers [Lns, PNTC]. It occurred in a special sense at Pentecost, but will have ultimate fulfillment at the last day [NTC].

3. For believers it occurs at conversion, but for unbelievers it occurs at the judgment [NAC, TRT]. It occurs at the time of Christian baptism [NICNT].

3:12 Of-whom the winnowing-fork[a] (is) in his hand and he-will-clean his threshing-floor[b] and he-will-gather his wheat into the granary,[c] and he-will-burn-up the chaff[d] in-fire unquenchable.[e]"

LEXICON—a. πτύον (LN **6.6**) (BAGD p. 727): 'winnowing fork' [BNTC, PNTC, WBC; ESV, NASB, NET, NIV, NLT, NRSV], 'winnowing shovel' [BAGD, CC, LN, NICNT, NIGTC, NTC; GW, REB, TEV], 'threshing fork' [CEV], 'pitchfork' [BECNT], 'fan' [KJV], not explicit [NCV]. The phrase 'the winnowing fork is in his hand' is translated 'he will come ready to clean the grain' [NCV]. This noun denotes a fork-like shovel for throwing threshed grain into the air so that the wind may separate the chaff from the grain [LN].

b. ἅλων (LN **3.43, 7.65**) (BAGD 2. p. 41): 'threshing floor' [**LN** (7.65)], 'threshed grain' [LN 3.43)]. The phrase 'he will clean up his threshing floor' [GW; similarly NET, NLT] is also translated 'he will clear his threshing floor' [ESV, NIV, NRSV, REB; similarly NASB], 'he will thoroughly purge his floor' [KJV], 'he will clean his threshed grain' [**LN** 3:43)], 'he will cleanse (winnow) what he has threshed' [BAGD], 'he will come ready to clean the grain' [NCV], 'he is ready to separate the wheat from the husks' [CEV], 'to thresh out completely all the grain' [LN (7.65); similarly TEV]. This noun denotes the surface of hard ground or stone upon which the grain was threshed out. 'He will clean up his threshing floor' could mean that he gathers up the grain and gets rid of the straw and chaff [LN (7.65)], or the threshing floor may be taken as a metonymy to refer to the threshed grain that is lying on the threshing floor, and it would mean 'he will clean his threshed grain' [LN (3.43)]. This is used figuratively of the threshed grain still lying on the threshing floor [BAGD].

c. ἀποθήκη (LN **7.25**) (BAGD p. 91): 'granary' [BNTC, NICNT, NIGTC, NTC; NRSV, REB], 'barn' [BAGD, BECNT, CC, LN, PNTC, WBC; CEV, ESV, GW, NASB, NCV, NIV, NLT, TEV], 'garner' [KJV], 'storehouse' [BAGD, **LN**; NET]. This noun denotes a building for storage [LN].

d. ἄχυρον (LN **3.57**) (BAGD p. 129): 'chaff' [BAGD, LN, all commentaries, all versions except CEV, GW], 'husks' [CEV, GW]. This noun denotes the husks of grain [LN].

e. ἄσβεστος (LN 14.71) (BAGD 1. p. 114): 'unquenchable' [CC, LN, NTC, WBC; ESV, KJV, NASB, NIV, NRSV], 'inextinguishable' [BAGD, BNTC, NIGTC; NET], 'never-ending' [NLT], 'that cannot be extinguished' [BECNT], 'that cannot be/can never be put out' [NICNT, PNTC; GW, NCV, REB], 'that never goes out' [CEV, TEV]. This adjective describes a fire that cannot be put out [LN].

QUESTION—What is the process of winnowing and threshing that he is describing here?
>Grain was threshed to separate the wheat from the chaff, and then tossed into the air by means of a winnowing fork so the wind would blow the chaff away from the wheat, after which the chaff would be swept up and burned [BECNT, NICNT, NTC, PNTC]. The threshing was by oxen treading on it [PNTC], or by oxen pulling a sled with stones under it [NTC]. Winnowing was done first with a winnowing fork, and then with a winnowing shovel [NICNT, PNTC]. It is noteworthy that the wheat is described as 'his wheat' but the chaff is not described as 'his' [BECNT, ICC].

QUESTION—What is implied by describing the fire as 'unquenchable'?
>It is more than a metaphor, signifying the fearful reality of eschatology*cal judgment [EBC]. It indicates that the judgment cannot be averted [PNTC], that it is irreversible [NIGTC].
>>1. It supports the doctrine of eternal punishment as opposed to annihilation [BECNT, Lns, NAC]. It tells us that the punishment is eternal [My, NAC, NTC].
>>2. It does not necessarily address the issue of annihilation versus eternal suffering [NICNT].

DISCOURSE UNIT—3:13–4:12 [NIGTC]. The topic is preparation.

DISCOURSE UNIT—3:13–17 [NAC, NICNT; CEV, ESV, GW, NASB, NCV, NET, NIV, NLT, TEV]. The topic is John and Jesus: the Messiah's baptism [NAC], the Messiah revealed as the Son of God [NICNT], John baptizes Jesus [GW], the baptism of Jesus [CEV, ESV, NET, NASB, NIV, NLT, TEV], Jesus is baptized by John [NCV].

3:13 **Then Jesus arrives[a] from Galilee to the Jordan to John to be baptized by him.**
LEXICON—a. pres. mid. or pass. (deponent = act.) indic. of παραγίνομαι (LN 15.86) (BAGD 1. p. 613): 'to arrive' [BAGD, BECNT, NICNT, LN; NASB, NCV, NET, NIV, REB, TEV], 'to come' [BAGD, BNTC, NIGTC, LN, PNTC, WBC; ESV, GW, KJV, NRSV], 'to appear' [CC], 'to make a public appearance' [NTC], 'left (Galilee) and went (to the Jordan)' [CEV], 'to go' [NLT]. This verb means to come to be present at a particular place [LN]. The use of the present tense of this verb parallels its use in 3:1 where it is similarly used to describe John arriving on the scene [BECNT, Lns, NICNT, PNTC], moving from private life to public ministry [Lns], and links the account of Jesus' arrival with that of John [CC, NIGTC].

3:14 But John was-preventing[a] him saying, "I have need to-be-baptized by you, and-yet[b] you come to me?" **3:15** But Jesus answering said to him, "Allow[c] (this) now,[d] for thus it-is fitting[e] for-us to-fulfill all righteousness.[f]" Then he-allows him.

LEXICON—a. imperf. act. indic. of διακωλύω (LN **13.146**) (BAGD p. 185): 'to prevent' [BAGD, BECNT, CC, **LN**, NIGTC, NTC; ESV, NASB, NET, NRSV], 'to forbid' [BNTC; KJV], 'to hinder' [LN, WBC], 'to deter' [NIV], 'to stop' [PNTC; GW, NCV], 'to put (him) off' [NICNT], 'to object' [CEV], 'to try to dissuade' [REB], 'to try to make (him) change his mind' [TEV], 'to talk (him) out of it' [NLT]. This verb means to cause something not to happen [LN]. The imperfect tense of the verb is translated as having a conative sense, indicating intent: John *tried to* prevent him or stop him [BAGD, BECNT, BNTC CC, ICC, NICNT, **LN**, NIGTC, NTC, PNTC, WBC; GW, NASB, NCV, NET, NIV, NLT, REB, TEV], or would have done so [ESV, NRSV]. It is translated as having a continuative sense: 'he kept objecting' [CEV]. This word occurs only here in the NT.

b. καί (LN **91.12**) (BAGD I.2.g. p. 392): 'and yet' [BAGD, NICNT, WBC; NET, TEV], 'yet' [BECNT, LN], 'and' [BNTC, CC, NIGTC, NTC, PNTC; ESV, KJV, NASB, NIV, NRSV], 'why' [CEV, GW, NCV, NLT], 'how is it then' [**LN**], not explicit [REB]. As it is used here, this conjunction marks emphasis, involving surprise and unexpectedness [LN]. Contrast is strengthened by the use of the personal pronouns ἐγώ 'I' and σύ 'you' [EBC, CC, NTC, PNTC].

c. aorist act. impera. of ἀφίημι (LN **13.140**) (BAGD 4. p. 126): 'to allow' [CC, LN, NIGTC], 'to let' [LN], 'to let it happen' [NET], 'to let it be done' [BECNT], 'to let it be so/this way' [BAGD, NICNT, PNTC, WBC; ESV, NCV, NIV, NRSV, REB, TEV], 'to permit it' [BNTC; NASB], 'to suffer it to be so' [KJV], 'to yield (to me)' [NTC], not explicit [CEV, GW]. The phrase 'allow this now' is translated 'for now this is how it should be' [CEV], 'this is the way it has to be now' [GW], 'it should be done' [NLT]. This verb means to leave it to someone to do something, with the implication of distancing oneself from the event [LN].

d. ἄρτι (LN **67.38**) (BAGD 2. p. 110): 'now' [BAGD, BNTC, LN, NIGTC, PNTC; ESV, GW, KJV, NET, NIV, NRSV], 'for now' [NICNT, WBC; CEV, NCV, TEV], 'for the present' [REB], 'right now' [BECNT], 'this time' [NTC], 'at this time' [CC; NASB], not explicit [NLT]. This temporal particle describes a point of time simultaneous with the event of the discourse itself [LN].

e. pres. act. participle of πρέπω (LN **66.1**) (BAGD p. 699): 'to be fitting' [BAGD, BNTC, CC, LN, NIGTC, PNTC, WBC; ESV, NASB], 'to be proper' [BECNT, NTC; NIV, NRSV], 'to be right' [LN; NET, REB], 'to be the right way' [NICNT], 'to become (us)' [KJV], not explicit [NCV, TEV]. The phrase 'thus it is fitting' is translated 'this is how it should be' [CEV], 'this is the way it has to be' [GW], 'for we must' [NLT]. This verb means to be fitting or right, with the implication of possible moral judgment involved [LN].

f. δικαιοσύνη (LN 88.13) (BAGD 2.a. p. 196): 'righteousness' [BAGD, LN], 'doing what God requires, doing what is right' [LN]. The phrase 'to fulfill all righteousness' [BECNT, BNTC, CC, NIGTC, PNTC, WBC; ESV, KJV, NASB, NET, NRSV] is also translated 'to fulfill all that is required of us' [NICNT], 'to fulfill every righteous requirement' [NTC], 'to do all that God wants us to do' [CEV], 'carry out all that God requires' [NLT], 'to do all that God requires' [REB, TEV], 'to do everything that God requires of us' [GW], 'to do all things that are God's will' [NCV]. This noun denotes the act of doing what God requires [LN].

QUESTION—What does John's reluctance to baptize Jesus say about the meaning of his baptism?

John's baptism signified repentance and confession, but John recognized that Jesus did not need to repent or to confess sin [BECNT, CC, EBC, Lns, NAC, PNTC]. John was concerned about the difference between his lowly status relative to the superior status of Jesus [NICNT].

QUESTION—What is implied by ἄρτι 'now'?

It focuses on that particular moment in salvation history, when it was time for Jesus to show his willingness to take on his role as Suffering Servant [EBC]. In his preaching John has been focusing on eschatological realities, but Jesus is shifting the focus to what is needed in the present, though things will not remain that way forever [CC]. Jesus acknowledges the truth of what John has just said, but 'now' implies that eventually their roles will be reversed [BNTC, Lns, NICNT, PNTC].

QUESTION—How would Jesus' being baptized fulfill all righteousness?

To fulfill all righteousness is to do what God wants or requires [TH, TRT]. It is a reference to Isa. 53:11–12 in which the righteous Suffering Servant is numbered with the transgressors and justifies many by bearing their sins. Although Jesus did not need repentance, Israel, whom he typologically represents did need it [PNTC]. For Jesus to be baptized showed that he yielded to God's will by carrying out his role as the Suffering Servant [EBC, NICNT]. Jesus did not need to repent, but he shows his solidarity with the people of Israel and identifies himself with this national movement of repentance, of which one ethical expression was baptism [NIBC]. Jesus put himself alongside sinners and shows that he is ready to assume the redemptive work of taking the load of their sins [Lns]. In the OT there is a strong correlation between God's righteousness and his saving acts, and now Jesus is relating righteousness to salvation, which Jesus will effect by standing in the place of sinners, as symbolized by his submitting to the baptism that sinners receive [CC]. Righteousness was fulfilled in the sense that this was the way God wanted Jesus to be set apart and consecrated to his Messianic ministry, to which he was now devoting himself [My].

3:16 And having-been-baptized Jesus immediately[a] went-up[b] from[c] the water; and behold, heaven was-opened[d] [to him], and he-saw the spirit of God descending[e] like[f] a-dove and coming[g] on him;

TEXT—Some manuscripts include αὐτῷ 'to him' after ἠνεῴχθησαν 'were-opened'. It is omitted by GNT with a C rating to indicate that choosing it over a variant text was difficult. It is included by BECNT, CC, NIGTC, WBC; ESV, KJV, NRSV. It is excluded by BNTC, NICNT, NTC, PNTC; GW, NASB, NCV, NET, NIV, NLT, REB; not explicit CEV.

LEXICON—a. εὐθύς (LN 67.53) (BAGD p. 321): 'immediately' [BAGD, LN, NIGTC, NTC, WBC; ESV, GW, NASB], 'at once' [BAGD, BNTC, CC], 'as soon as' [BECNT, NICNT; CEV, NCV, NIV, TEV], 'just as' [NET, NRSV], 'as' [NLT], 'no sooner' [REB], 'right away' [LN], 'straightway' [KJV], 'straightaway' [PNTC]. This adverb describes a point of time immediately subsequent to a previous point of time (the actual interval of time differs appreciably, depending upon the nature of the events and the manner in which the sequence is interpreted by the writer) [LN].

b. aorist. act. indic. of ἀναβαίνω (LN 15.101) (BAGD 1.a.α. p. 50): 'to go up' [BAGD, BNTC, CC, LN; ESV, KJV, NIV], 'to come up' [BECNT, LN, NICNT, NIGTC, PNTC, WBC; GW, NASB, NCV, NET, NLT, NRSV, REB, TEV], 'to come out' [CEV], 'to step up' [NTC]. This verb means to move up [LN].

c ἀπό (LN 84.3): 'from' [BNTC, CC, LN, NIGTC, PNTC; ESV, GW, NASB, NRSV], 'out of' [BECNT, NICNT, NTC, WBC; CEV, KJV, NCV, NET, NIV, NLT, REB, TEV]. This preposition denotes extension from or away from a source [LN].

d. aorist pass. indic. of ἀνοίγω (LN 79.110) (BAGD 1.b. p. 71): 'to be opened' [LN; all translations except CEV, NCV, NET], 'to open' [CEV, NCV, NET]. This verb means to cause something to be open [LN]. Note that this verb form is plural because the subject 'the heavens' is a plural noun.

e. pres. act. participle of καταβαίνω (LN 15.107) (BAGD 1.b. p. 408): 'to descend' [BECNT, BNTC, CC, LN, NTC, PNTC; ESV, KJV, NASB, NET, NIV, NLT, NRSV, REB], 'to come down' [BAGD, LN, NICNT, NIGTC; GW, NCV, TEV]. The phrase 'descending...and coming on him' is translated 'coming down on him' [CEV]. This verb means to move down, irrespective of the gradient [LN].

f. ὡσεί (LN **64.12**) (BAGD 1. p. 899): 'like' [BECNT, CC, LN, NICNT, NTC, PNTC; all versions except GW, NASB], 'in a form like' [NIGTC], 'as' [BNTC, LN; GW, NASB], 'as...might' [WBC]. This particle is a relatively weak marker of a relationship between events or states [LN].

g. pres. mid. or pass. (deponent = act.) participle of ἔρχομαι (LN 15.81) (BAGD I.2.c. p. 311): 'to come' [BAGD, BECNT, BNTC, CC, LN, NICNT, PNTC, WBC; NET], 'to come to rest' [ESV], 'to settle' [NLT], 'to alight' [NIGTC; NRSV, REB], 'to light (on)' [NTC; KJV, NASB,

NIV, TEV], not explicit [GW, NCV]. This verb means to move toward or to the reference point of the viewpoint character or event [LN].

QUESTION—What does it mean that Jesus 'went up from' the water?

1. As soon as he was baptized he left the river [BECNT, EBC, Lns, NIBC, NTC, PNTC, TRT].
2. It suggests that he had been immersed [NICNT].

QUESTION—Does 'like a dove' refer to the visible form, or to the manner of movement?

1. The form was that of a dove [BECNT, EBC, My, NAC, NICNT, NIGTC, NTC, PNTC]. Some visual form is required to make the Spirit's descent visible, so little is gained by saying that he came in a dove-like manner [NICNT].
2. The Spirit of God descended as a dove would descend [BNTC, TH, WBC], which is gently [BNTC]. He saw God's Spirit coming down and landing on him in a manner that a dove would [TH].

QUESTION—Who is referred to by the verb εἶδεν 'he saw' in the phrase 'he saw the spirit descending'?

Jesus saw the Spirit coming down upon himself [BECNT, EBC, Lns, NICNT, NIGTC, PNTC, TRT, WBC]. Matthew says that 'he' (Jesus) saw the Spirit descending, and the other Gospels simply imply that it was Jesus who saw this. But from John 1:32 we learn that John the Baptist also saw it. Since none of the Gospels say anything about the crowd seeing this event, we can assume that no one else saw it [WBC]. Matthew does not make clear whether anyone else saw this; he is emphasizing that Jesus did [PNTC]. This passage is speaking of what John saw, but all who were present with John and Jesus would have also seen this miracle [NAC, NTC].

QUESTION—What symbolic significance is there in the dove?

The Holy Spirit has no body and cannot be seen, and although it is not clear why God chose the form of a dove to represent the Holy Spirit some commentaries think the form of a dove could point to a dove's purity and gentleness [NTC]. A dove symbolizes the graciousness that characterizes the Holy Spirit [Lns]. The dove was a ceremonially clean animal and symbolized innocence [NIBC]. Perhaps a dove was chosen because doves were used as messengers [NIGTC]. The dove flying down from heaven recalls the Spirit of God hovering over the waters in Gen. 1:2, and therefore signals a connection between creation and Jesus as the starter of a new creation, since the Spirit of God is also the Spirit of the Messiah [ICC]. It recalls God's supervision over creation in Gen 1:2, the coming of peace in Gen. 8:10, and generally of gentleness [NAC]. It is not precisely known what symbolic significance doves may have had in that time [ICC, PNTC]. Speculation about any symbolism connected with the appearance of a dove is unimportant since this is describing the coming of the Holy Spirit in terms of the flight of a bird that was common and familiar to all [NICNT].

3:17 and behold, a-voice from heaven saying, "This is my son, the beloved,[a] in whom I-am-well-pleased.[b]"

LEXICON—a. ἀγαπητός (LN **58.53**) (BAGD 1. p. 6): 'beloved, only beloved' [BAGD], 'only dear, only' [LN]. This adjective is translated in apposition to 'Son': 'my Son, the Beloved' [PNTC; NRSV]; as an attribute: 'my beloved Son' [BNTC, CC, EBC, NICNT, NIGTC, WBC; ESV, KJV, NASB, REB], 'my dearly loved Son' [NLT], 'my own dear Son' [CEV, TEV], 'my one dear Son' [**LN**; NET]; as a separate phrase: 'my Son, whom I love' [BECNT; GW, NCV, NIV]. This adjective describes one who is the only one of his or her class, but at the same time is particularly loved and cherished [LN].

  b. aorist act. indic. of εὐδοκέω (LN **25.87**) (BAGD 2.a. p. 319): 'to be well pleased (with/in)' [BAGD, BNTC, CC, NTC, PNTC, WBC; CEV, ESV, GW, KJV, NASB, NIV, NRSV], 'to be very pleased (with)' [BECNT; NCV], 'to be pleased (with)' [**LN**; TEV], 'to be delighted (with)' [NICNT], 'to take delight (in)' [BAGD; REB], 'to take great delight (in)' [NET], 'to come to delight (in)' [NIGTC], 'to take pleasure (in)' [LN]. The phrase 'in whom I am well-pleased' is translated 'who brings me great joy' [NLT]. This verb means to be pleased with something or someone, with the implication of resulting pleasure [LN].

QUESTION—What does it mean that Jesus is God's Son in this passage, and in Matthew's gospel generally?

  Bible scholars and theologians recognize and discuss four senses in the NT in which Jesus is said to be the son of God, all of which are inseparably interrelated. One is the messianic sense; a second is the nativistic sense, meaning that he has no human father. A third is an ethical and religious sense in which he is perfectly obedient to the will of the Father as other 'sons', such as Adam or Israel, were not. The fourth sense is the eternal sense, that he has been the Son of the Father from all eternity, as articulated in the creeds. Many commentaries take God's words, 'My son' to be focusing on Jesus' roles as Messiah and Suffering Servant and as reflected in Isaiah 42 and Psalm 2 [BECNT, BNTC, ICC, NAC, NIBC, PNTC, TH, WBC], and used with 'beloved' it speaks of the strong affection of the Father for the Son [PNTC] and of the relationship Jesus had with his heavenly Father that is both intimate [NIBC] and unique [BNTC, NIBC]. It has associations with his role as Suffering Servant, the Davidic Messiah, and the true Israel, but also hints at his ontological (i.e., eternal) sonship [EBC]. Jesus is 'son' typologically in the sense that Israel was [CC, ICC, NIGTC]. Matthew links Jesus' divine sonship with his obedience [BECNT]. At the Exodus from Egypt God constituted Israel as his 'son', and now Jesus typologically embodies the nation and becomes the summation and representative of God's 'son' Israel as he perfectly carries out the Father's will; Jesus is truly the son of God, both in the sense of this mission or purpose, as well as in his very person [CC]. Like Israel of old, who in becoming 'God's Son', went through the waters of the sea and into a time in the desert, so Jesus as the Son also goes from the waters of the Jordan into the desert for testing [ICC]. The significance of Jesus' sonship is not limited to his being Messiah [BECNT, EBC, Lns, My, NAC, NIBC, NICNT, NIGTC, NTC]. His sonship means that he is in some way on a par with deity [NAC]. Jesus is the Messiah, but he is also the Son of God from all eternity [Lns], the Son by eternal generation [NTC]. Throughout his gospel Matthew presents Jesus as the Son of God, who consequently is often worshipped as God the Son [BECNT]. While there may be allusion to Isa. 43, Psalm 2, or even Gen. 22, this passage is primarily saying that Jesus is God's own Son in whom he delights, and in later passages in Matthew, 'Son' expresses a supernatural dimension that is greater than Jesus' role as Messiah [NIGTC]. Although it includes a messianic element, 'son' is not simply another word for 'messiah'; rather, sonship refers to a special status and relationship with God that the Messiah may experience, and this sonship as status and relationship is what unites the different strands involved in identifying Jesus as Son of God in Matthew's gospel [NICNT]. Other christological titles such as Son of Man, Son of David, Messiah, Servant, and Lord give content to the title 'Son of God' [ICC]. It indicates that he is the Messiah in the sense of Psalm 2, but also describes his metaphysical being as well, that he comes forth from the Father's being [My]. The heavenly voice affirms both that Jesus is the messianic Son of God, as well as the divine love that has eternally existed between the Father and the Son [ESVSB].

QUESTION—Why was the Father 'well pleased' with the Son?

God was pleased with Jesus as the Messiah and Suffering Servant [PNTC]. It suggests his pre-temporal election as Messiah [EBC, Lns]. The Father was pleased by Jesus being baptized [BECNT, BNTC, NICNT]. The Father was pleased that Jesus has accepted the role of Suffering Servant [ICC]. The Father has been delighted in the Son from all eternity, but is also pleased with the Son's acceptance of his mission of atoning for sin [NTC]. The aorist verb is used in a way similar to a perfect tense, and means that God's pleasure continues to remain on Jesus [CC]. It is a timeless aorist [NTC].

QUESTION—Who heard the heavenly voice?

Probably only John and Jesus heard it [ICC]. Jesus and John heard it [EBC, Lns], and possibly others as well [EBC]. It was addressed to the bystanders as an affirmation of who Jesus is [NICNT, PNTC]. The statement 'this is my son' indicates that others witnessed it [NIBC]. The statement is heard in heaven, before the heavenly court, and by Jesus as well [NIGTC].

DISCOURSE UNIT—4:1–22 [ICC]. The topic is the beginning of the ministry.

DISCOURSE UNIT—4:1–11 [NAC, NICNT, PNTC; CEV, GW, NASB, NCV, NET, NIV, NLT, NRSV, REB, TEV]. The topic is Jesus alone: the Messiah's temptation [NAC], the testing of the Son of God: the Messiah as the true Israel [NICNT], the temptation of Jesus [GW, NASB, NCV, NET, NIV, NLT, NRSV, REB, TEV], Jesus' temptation [PNTC], Jesus and the devil [CEV].

4:1 Then Jesus was-led-up[a] into the wilderness by the Spirit to-be-tempted[b] by the devil.[c] **4:2** And having-fasted[d] forty days and forty nights, afterwards[e] he-hungered.[f]

LEXICON—a. aorist pass. indic. of ἀνάγω (LN 15.176) (BAGD 1. p. 53): 'to be led up' [BAGD, BNTC, CC, ESV, LN, NIGTC, NTC, PNTC, WBC; KJV, NASB, NRSV], 'to be led' [GW, NET, NIV, NLT, REB], 'to be led away' [BECNT], 'to be taken up' [NICNT]. The passive voice is translated as active: 'the Spirit led Jesus' [CEV, NCV, TEV]. This verb means 'to bring or lead up' [LN].

b. aorist pass. infin. of πειράζω (LN 88.308) (BAGD 2.d. p. 640): 'to be tempted' [BAGD, BECNT, BNTC, CC, LN, NIGTC, NTC, PNTC; all versions except CEV], 'to be tested' [NICNT, WBC], 'to be led into temptation' [LN]. The phrase 'to be tempted by the devil' is translated 'so that the devil could test him' [CEV]. This verb means to endeavor or attempt to cause someone to sin [LN]. It can have a positive connotation of testing to achieve approval or of tempting to achieve disapproval [BECNT]. In Matthew the intent is always negative, meaning to tempt or to trap, and Jesus is always the object of temptation [CC].

c. διάβολος (LN **12.34**) (BAGD 2. p. 182): 'the devil' [BAGD, BECNT, BNTC, LN, NICNT, NIGTC, NTC, PNTC, WBC; all versions], 'slanderer' [CC]. This noun is a title for the devil, literally 'slanderer' [BAGD, LN]. The terms 'devil' and 'Satan' are used interchangeably in the gospels, and throughout the NT [NICNT].

d. aorist active participle of νηστεύω (LN 53.65) (BAGD p. 538): 'to fast' [BAGD, BECNT, BNTC, CC, LN, NIGTC, PNTC, WBC; ESV, KJV, NASB, NET, NIV, NLT, NRSV, REB], 'to go without food' [NICNT, NTC], 'to go without eating' [CEV], 'to not eat' [GW], 'to eat nothing' [NCV], 'to spend (forty days and nights) without food' [TEV]. This verb means to go without food for a set time as a religious duty [LN].

e. ὕστερον (LN 67.50) (BAGD 2.a. p. 849): 'afterward' [BNTC, LN, NIGTC, WBC; KJV, NRSV], 'after this' [NCV], 'later' [BAGD, LN], 'in the end' [NICNT], 'at the end' [REB], 'at the end of that time' [GW], 'then' [BAGD], not explicit [NLT]. The phrase '(having fasted)... afterward' is translated 'after (he had fasted/gone without food/fasting)' [BECNT, NTC, PNTC; CEV, ESV, NET, NIV, TEV], 'after (he had fasted)...then' [NASB], 'after (he had fasted)...at the end' [CC]. This adverb describes something that pertains to a subsequent event, but not necessarily the second in a series [LN].

f. aorist act. indic. of πεινάω (LN 23.29) (BAGD 1. p. 640): 'to be hungry' [BECNT, CC, LN, NIGTC, PNTC, WBC; ESV, GW, NIV, TEV], 'to become hungry' [NASB], 'to be very hungry' [CEV, NCV], 'to become very hungry' [NLT], 'to grow hungry' [BNTC], 'to be famished' [NICNT, NTC; NET, NRSV, REB], 'was an hungred' [KJV]. This verb means to be in a state of hunger, without any implications of particular contributing circumstances [LN]. Jesus' hunger was caused by the forty-day fast, but it does not mean that his hunger began at the end of the forty days [BECNT].

QUESTION—Why does it say he was led *up*?

The river is the topographical low point, from which movement into the wilderness would be up [Lns, My, NICNT, NIGTC, TH]. He is going into the highlands west of the Jordan [BNTC, WBC]. The Jordan is below sea level at this point [BNTC].

QUESTION—What relationship is indicated by τότε 'then'

It connects 4:1–11 with the account of his baptism in 3:13–17 [Lns, NIGTC]. Matthew frequently uses τότε 'then' to connect one account to another, just as Mark frequently uses εὐθύς 'immediately' as a connective [WBC]. It is a temporal connector, in that the temptation occurs after his baptism, but also a logical connector, in that he is first attested by the Father before being tested by the devil [BECNT].

QUESTION—What relationship is indicated by the use of the infinitive πειρασθῆναι "to be tested"?

It indicates the Holy Spirit's purpose for leading Jesus into the wilderness [BECNT, CC, ICC, Lns, My, TH, WBC]. Jesus is tested to confirm him in his messianic role [BECNT]. God intended to test Jesus just as Israel was tested in the wilderness [EBC, NIGTC]. It was God's good purpose to test his Son [NICNT]. Whereas the devil tried to entice Jesus to sin, God used the same situation as a test to prove Jesus' faithfulness [NAC].

QUESTION—At what point during the forty days did the temptation occur?

It occurred at the end of the forty days [BECNT, BNTC, NIBC, NTC, WBC]. These particular temptations occurred at the end of the forty days, but the Luke account indicates that he was tempted throughout the entire period, but what those temptations were is not recorded [Lns].

4:3 And the (one) tempting[a] having-come[b] he-said to-him, "If you-are (the) son of-God, say[c] that these stones become[d] bread.[e]"

LEXICON—a. pres. act. participle of πειράζω. See above in 4:1. The phrase 'the one tempting' is translated 'the tempter' [BECNT, BNTC, CC, NICNT, NIGTC, NTC, PNTC, WBC; ESV, GW, KJV, NASB, NET, NIV, NRSV, REB], 'the devil' [CEV, NLT, TEV], 'the devil (came) to tempt (him)' [NCV].

b. aorist act. participle of προσέρχομαι (LN 15.77) (BAGD 1. p. 713): 'to come' [BECNT, NIGTC, NTC, WBC; all versions except CEV, REB], 'to come to (him)' [BAGD; CEV], 'to come near to' [LN], 'to approach' [BAGD, BNTC, CC, LN, NICNT, PNTC; REB]. This verb means to move toward a reference point, with a possible implication in certain contexts of a reciprocal relationship between the person approaching and the one who is approached [LN].

c. aorist act. indic. of λέγω (LN 33.69) (BAGD 3.c. p. 226): 'to command' [BNTC, CC; ESV, KJV, NASB, NET, NRSV], 'to tell' [LN, NTC, PNTC; GW, NCV, NIV, NLT, REB], 'to speak' [WBC], 'to say' [LN,

NIGTC], 'to tell' [BAGD, LN; CEV], 'to order' [BAGD, BECNT; TEV], 'to give orders' [NICNT]. This verb means to speak or talk, with apparent focus upon the content of what is said [LN].

d. aorist mid. (deponent = act.) subj. of γίνομαι (LN 13.48) (BAGD I.4.a. p. 159): 'to become' [BAGD, BECNT, CC, LN, NICNT, NIGTC, PNTC, WBC; all versions except CEV, KJV, TEV], 'to be made' [KJV], 'to turn into' [BNTC, NTC; CEV, TEV]. This verb means to come to acquire or experience a state [LN].

e. ἄρτος (LN 5.8) (BAGD 1.a. p. 110): 'bread' [BAGD, CC, NIGTC, NTC, PNTC, WBC; all versions except ESV, NLT, NRSV], 'loaf' [BAGD], 'loaf of bread' [BECNT, BNTC, LN, NICNT; ESV, NLT, NRSV]. This noun denotes a relatively small and generally round loaf of bread (considerably smaller than present-day typical loaves of bread and thus more like rolls or buns) [LN].

QUESTION—What relationship is indicated by the conjunction εἰ 'if'?

This temptation is directly linked to the preceding passage in which Jesus is affirmed as God's son at his baptism [BECNT, CC, EBC, NICNT, WBC].

1. The 'if' does not imply uncertainty, but presupposes that he indeed *is* God's son [EBC, ICC, My, NAC, NIBC, NICNT, NIGTC, NTC, TH, WBC]. It could be translated 'since' [NTC, WBC].
2. The intent was to introduce doubt [BNTC, CC, Lns]. The 'if' assumes the truthfulness of the first clause for the sake of argument, but Satan's intent was to leave the question somewhat open [CC]. Although the 'if' expresses a condition of reality, Satan was introducing a cloud of doubt to induce Jesus to prove his sonship by making bread of stone [Lns].

QUESTION—Why is there no definite article with the word υἱός 'son'?

1. The word υἱός is a predicate nominative preceding the verb, which normally does not take a definite article [CC, WBC]. The position of this noun indicates emphasis [My].
2. Satan's statement implies that Jesus is merely one of a class, '*a* son of God', and even that must be proved by some unusual act on Jesus' part [Lns].

QUESTION—What was the intent of Satan's temptation?

The issue was not whether or not Jesus was the Son of God, but whether Jesus will be obedient to the Father as a son, since fasting at this time was the Father's will [WBC]. The issue is what kind of son he will be [NAC]. He was tempted to be a self-serving son instead of an obedient son [CC], to doubt God's good care and, by acting in his own interests, change the course of salvation history [ICC]. He was tempted to act in his own interest instead of trusting God to provide [NIBC]. He was tempted to doubt and also to act in self interest [BNTC], to doubt God's care and take matters into his own hands [NTC]. He was tempted to exploit the privileges of sonship to meet his own needs [NIGTC]. The object of the temptation was that Jesus should obey Satan's suggestion rather than God's will, which would also represent a failure to trust God to meet his needs [Lns]. Jesus was being tempted to use his sonship selfishly to meet his own needs instead of trusting in the Father's provision and using his sonship to fulfill his mission as God's servant [BECNT]. Satan's intent was not to bring Jesus' sonship into question, but to challenge its meaning, getting Jesus to use his sonship, and the power he had willingly abandoned, for his own interests instead of following God's mission for him as son [EBC]. Satan was trying to drive a wedge into the relationship between the Son of God and the Father by tempting Jesus to use his power to indulge himself rather than obey God's will, which at that time was fasting [NICNT]. There is a typology of a time of testing in the desert after having come out of the water; Jesus is being tested over forty days as Israel was over forty years, but he will stand the test where they failed it [CC, ICC, NICNT]. He was tempted to act in his own behalf to alleviate a condition that was supposedly beneath his dignity as God's son [My].

4:4 But answering^a he-said, "It-is-written, 'Not on bread alone^b man^c shall live, but on every word^d going-forth^e through (the) mouth of God.'"

LEXICON—a. aorist pass. (deponent = act.) participle of ἀποκρίνομαι (LN 33.28) (BAGD 1. p. 93): 'to answer' [BAGD], 'to reply' [BAGD], 'to speak, to declare, to say' [LN]. The phrase 'answering he said' is translated 'he answered and said' [BNTC, CC, NTC, WBC; KJV, NASB], 'he/Jesus answered' [BECNT, CC, NIGTC; all versions except KJV, NASB, NLT], 'Jesus told him' [NLT], 'Jesus/he replied' [NICNT, PNTC]. This verb introduces or continues a somewhat formal discourse [LN].

b. μόνος (LN 58.51) (BAGD 1.a.γ. p. 527): 'alone' [BAGD, BECNT, BNTC, CC, LN, NICNT, NIGTC, NTC, PNTC, WBC; all versions except CEV, NCV], 'only' [BAGD; CEV, NCV]. This adjective describes the only item of a class in a place [LN].

c. ἄνθρωπος (LN 9.1) (BAGD 3.b. p. 69): 'man' [BNTC, NTC, PNTC; KJV, NASB, NET, NIV, REB], 'person' [BAGD, CC, LN, NICNT, NIGTC; ESV, GW, NCV], 'people' [BECNT; NLT], 'human being' [BAGD, LN; TEV], 'one' [WBC; NRSV], '(no) one' [CEV], 'individual' [LN]. This noun denotes a human being (normally an adult) [LN].

d. ῥῆμα (LN **33.98**) (BAGD 1. p. 735): 'word' [BECNT, BNTC, CC, **LN**, NICNT, NIGTC, NTC, PNTC, WBC; all versions except NCV], 'saying, message, statement' [LN], not explicit [NCV]. This noun denotes that which has been stated or said, with primary focus upon the content of the communication [LN].

e. pres. mid. or pass. (deponent = act.) participle of ἐκπορεύομαι (LN 15.40) (BAGD 2. p. 244): 'to come out of' [BECNT, NIGTC; REB], 'to come from' [BNTC, NICNT; ESV, NET, NIV, NLT, NRSV], 'to come out through' [NTC], 'to go out through' [PNTC], 'to come through' [CC], 'to proceed out of' [WBC; KJV, NASB], 'to go out of' [LN]. The phrase 'every word going forth through the mouth of God' is translated '(people need) every word that God has spoken' [CEV], 'every word that God speaks' [GW, TEV], 'everything that God says' [NCV].

QUESTION—What is the significance of bread here?

There is an echo of Israel's wilderness experience with manna [NICNT]. God's 'son' Israel failed when tested concerning bread in the desert, but now Jesus, as God's true Son, will succeed, being obedient to God concerning bread in the desert [Lns, WBC]. Whereas Israel had demanded bread and died in the wilderness, Jesus refused bread and lived in submission to God's word [EBC]. Whereas Israel was supernaturally provided with bread in the desert for forty years, God's Son will hunger in the desert for forty days [NIBC]. Adam and Eve were well-fed in Eden and failed, whereas Jesus was hungry in the wilderness and succeeded [Lns, NTC].

QUESTION—What is the significance of the word ἄνθρωπος 'man' here?

Jesus has been tempted to use supernatural power to act in his own behalf, but he chooses to be obedient *as a man* even though he is Son of God [BECNT, WBC]. Jesus' responded in terms of what is proper to human actions, not to his status as son of God [Lns, NIGTC]. Jesus identifies with humanity here [TH].

QUESTION—Does the future tense ζήσεται 'he shall live' indicate an implied imperative or a statement of fact?

1. It is a statement of fact [BECNT, CC, NIGTC, PNTC, TH; CEV, GW, My, NCV, NET, NIV, NLT, NRSV, TEV; probably BNTC, NIBC, NTC]; man will not live only by bread. The OT text is saying that it is not bread that sustains man, but God who sustains by what he decrees [NTC].
2. It is an implied imperative [Lns, NICNT, WBC; probably ESV, KJV, NASB, REB]; man *shall* not live only by bread. It expresses God's will [Lns].

4:5 Then the devil takes[a] him into the holy city and he-set[b] him on the high-point[c] of (the) temple,

LEXICON—a. pres. act. indic. of παραλαμβάνω (LN 15.168) (BAGD 1. p. 619): 'to take' [BAGD, BECNT, BNTC, CC, NIGTC, NTC, PNTC, WBC; all versions except NCV], 'to transport' [NICNT], 'to take along' [BAGD, LN], 'to bring along' [LN], 'to take with' [BAGD], 'to lead' [NCV]. This verb means to take or bring someone along with [LN]. The historical present in this temptation narrative and in the temptation in Gethsemane in chapter 26 is used to give emphasis [NICNT, NIGTC] and to make it more vivid [CC].

b. aorist act. indic. of ἵστημι (LN 85.40) (BAGD I.1.a. p. 382): 'to set' [BAGD, LN, NTC, PNTC, WBC; ESV, KJV, REB, TEV], 'to place' [BAGD, BNTC, LN, NIGTC; NRSV], 'to put' [LN], 'to make (him) stand' [LN, NICNT], 'to have (him) stand' [BECNT; CEV, GW, NASB, NET, NIV], 'to stand (someone upon)' [CC], 'to put' [NCV], not explicit [NLT]. This verb means to cause to be in a place, with or without the accompanying feature of a standing position [LN].

c. πτερύγιον (LN **7.53**) (BAGD p. 727): 'pinnacle' [BAGD, BNTC, CC, **LN**, NIGTC, NTC, WBC; ESV, KJV, NASB, NRSV], 'the highest point' [BECNT; NET, NIV, NLT, TEV], 'the highest part' [CEV, GW], 'high corner' [NICNT], 'high place' [NCV], 'wing' [PNTC], 'parapet' [REB]. This noun denotes the tip or high point of a building [LN].

QUESTION—Why do Matthew's and Luke's accounts differ in the order of the second and third temptation?

Matthew has probably preserved the chronological order [BECNT, EBC, Lns, NAC, NTC], whereas Luke probably has the temptation at the temple last in order to focus on Jerusalem [BECNT, EBC, NAC, NICNT].

QUESTION—Was Jesus physically transported to Jerusalem, or was this temptation visionary?

1. The second and third temptations are visionary [BECNT, EBC, NAC, NICNT, NTC]. They are nevertheless real [NTC].
2. It was an actual physical experience [Lns].

QUESTION—What was the πτερύγιον 'high point' of the temple?

This word occurs only here in the NT and its meaning is uncertain [ICC]. It is clear from the context that it was a high point of the temple where there was a substantial drop to the ground level [NICNT]. The word 'Temple' probably applies to the entire complex, not the sanctuary itself [ESV]. This may be the southeastern corner of the temple complex, which overlooks the Kidron valley [BECNT; ESVSB].

4:6 and he-says to him, "If you-are (the) son of-God, throw[a] yourself down; for it-is-written, 'He will-command[b] his angels concerning[c] you and on (their) hands they-will-take- you –up,[d] lest[e] you-strike your foot against a-stone.'"

LEXICON—a. aorist at. impera. of βάλλω (LN 15.122) (BAGD 1.b. p. 131): 'to throw' [BAGD, LN]. The phrase 'throw yourself down' [BECNT, BNTC, CC, NICNT, NIGTC, NTC, PNTC; ESV, NASB, NET, NIV, NRSV, REB, TEV] is translated 'cast thyself/yourself down' [KJV], 'jump down' [NCV], 'jump off' [CEV, NLT], 'jump!' [GW].

b. future mid. (deponent = act.) indic. of ἐντέλλομαι (LN 33.329) (BAGD p. 268): 'to command' [BAGD, LN, WBC; ESV, NASB, NET, NIV, NRSV], 'to give command' [PNTC], 'to order' [BAGD; NLT], 'to give orders' [BNTC, CC; CEV, TEV], 'to direct'[NIGTC] 'to give instructions' [NTC], 'to give charge' [KJV], 'to put in charge' [BECNT; GW, NCV, REB], 'to make responsible' [NICNT]. This verb means to give definite orders, implying authority or official sanction [LN].

c. ὑπέρ with genitive (LN 90.36): 'concerning' [BNTC, NIGTC, NTC; ESV, KJV, NASB, NET, NIV, NRSV], 'about' [CC, PNTC; CEV, TEV], 'for' [LN, NICNT], 'on behalf of, for the sake of' [LN], 'around' [WBC]. The phrase 'he will command his angels concerning you' is translated 'he will order his angels to protect you' [NLT], 'he will put his angels in charge of you' [BECNT; GW, NCV, REB]. This preposition marks a

participant who is benefited by an event or on whose behalf an event takes place [LN].
- d. fut. act. indic. of αἴρω (LN 15.203) (BAGD 2. p. 24): 'to carry' [BNTC, CC; GW], 'to lift up' [NICNT; NET, NIV], 'to lift up and carry along [BAGD], 'to carry away, to carry off' [LN], 'to carry along' [BAGD, BECNT], 'to hold' [PNTC], 'to carry (away), to carry off' [LN], 'to hold (you) up' [NLT, TEV], 'to bear' [WBC], 'to bear (you) up' [ESV, KJV, NASB, NRSV], 'to support' [REB], 'to raise up' [NIGTC], 'to catch' [CEV, NCV]. This verb means to lift up and carry (away) [LN].
- e. μήποτε (LN **89.62**) (BAGD 2.b.α. p. 519): 'lest' [BNTC, CC, LN, NTC, PNTC, WBC; ESV], 'lest at any time' [KJV], 'for fear that' [REB], 'that…not' [BAGD], 'so that…not' [BECNT, LN, NIGTC; NASB, NCV, NET, NIV, NRSV], 'so that…not even' [NLT, TEV], 'so that…never' [NICNT; GW], 'in order that…not' [**LN**], 'and (you will) not' [CEV]. This subordinating conjunction marks negative purpose, often with the implication of apprehension [LN].

QUESTION—What relationship is indicated by the conjunction ὅτι, which occurs in the Greek text before 'He will command his angels'?
1. It functions as an untranslated marker of direct discourse [BECNT, BNTC, NICNT, NIGTC, NTC, WBC; all versions]: it is written, 'He will give orders' etc.
2. It introduces indirect discourse [CC, NICNT]: it is written *that* he will give orders, etc.
3. The word ὅτι is cited from the LXX text of Psalm 91 where the meaning is causal. Satan is suggesting that Jesus throw himself down *because* the angels are there to help him [PNTC]: it is written, '*Because* he will give orders' etc.

QUESTION—What was the object of this temptation?
The devil was trying to tempt Jesus to test whether or not God will actually fulfill his promise of protection instead of trusting God to do what he promises [CC, EBC, NAC, NICNT]. Jesus was tempted to force a situation where he is brought to safety instead of staying on the path of continuing danger and hardship [WBC]. Jesus was tempted to demand, based on his status as God' Son, that God release him from danger [NIGTC], Jesus was tempted to demand from God a release from any danger due to his status as Son of God [NIGTC]. He was tempted to compel God to act, thus becoming lord over God himself [NICNT]. He was being tempted to prove his trust in God's promises as well as God's trustworthiness by acting to force the issue [Lns]. It was a choice between forcing God to act and being obedient to him [ICC]. He was tempted to test and prove his sonship [BNTC], to demand proof of God's goodwill [NIBC], to force God to prove his love [TRT]. Whereas the first temptation was not to trust God, the second was to act presumptuously on a false trust [NTC].

4:7 Jesus said to-him, "Again[a] it-is-written, 'You-shall- not -test[b] (the) Lord your God.'"

LEXICON—a. πάλιν (LN 89.129) (BAGD 4. p. 607): 'again' [BNTC, CC, NIGTC, PNTC, WBC; ESV, GW, KJV, NRSV], 'once again' [NET], 'on the other hand' [BAGD, LN; NASB], 'also' [NICNT, NTC; CEV, NCV, NIV, NLT, REB], 'but...also' [BECNT], 'but' [TEV], 'but in turn, however' [LN]. This adverb marks contrast, with the implication of a sequence [LN].

b. fut. act. indic. of ἐκπειράζω (LN 88.308) (BAGD p. 243): 'to test' [CC, WBC; NCV, NLT], 'to put to the test' [BAGD, BECNT, BNTC, NICNT, NIGTC, NTC, PNTC; ESV, NASB, NET, NIV, NRSV, REB, TEV], 'to try to test' [CEV], 'to tempt' [BAGD, LN; GW, KJV]. The future tense functions as an implied imperative here [CC].

QUESTION—What relationship is indicated by πάλιν 'again'?

'Again' introduces a counterpoint to what Satan told him to do [NICNT]. Jesus uses a second scripture passage to point out that such an act would contradict other passages of scripture [WBC]. The idea is 'Don't try to force God to prove himself' [TH]. Satan was trying to tempt Jesus to test God, but Jesus recognized that such testing was expressly forbidden in Scripture [EBC].

4:8 Again the devil takes him to (a) very high mountain and shows[a] him all the kingdoms of-the world and their glory[b] **4:9** and he-said to-him, "These I-will-give to-you, if falling-down[c] you-worship[d] me."

LEXICON—a. pres. act. indic. of δείκνυμι (LN 28.47) (BAGD 1.a. p. 172): 'to show' [BAGD, LN; all translations]. This verb means to make known the character or significance of something by visual, auditory, gestural, or linguistic means [LN].

b. δόξα (LN **87.23**) (BAGD 2. p. 204): 'glory' [BECNT, CC, LN, NICNT, NIGTC, WBC; ESV, GW, KJV, NASB, NLT, REB], 'magnificence' [BAGD], 'splendor' [BAGD, BNTC, NTC, PNTC; NCV, NIV, NRSV], 'grandeur' [NET], 'greatness' [**LN**; TEV], 'power' [CEV]. This noun denotes a state of being great and wonderful [LN].

c. aorist act. participle of πίπτω (LN 17.22) (BAGD 1.b.α. p. 659): 'to fall down' [BNTC, CC, NIGTC, PNTC, WBC; ESV, KJV, NASB, NRSV, REB], 'to fall down before' [LN], 'to bow down' [NICNT; CEV, GW, NCV, NIV], 'to prostrate oneself before' [LN, NTC], 'to kneel down' [BECNT; NLT, TEV], 'to throw oneself to the ground' [NET]. This verb means to prostrate oneself before someone, implying supplication [LN]. The aorist participle πεσών 'falling down' is an attendant circumstance, and thus takes the tense of the verb it accompanies [CC].

d. aorist act. subj. of προσκυνέω (LN 53.56) (BAGD 3. p. 717): 'to worship' [BAGD, LN; all translations except REB], 'to do homage' [REB], 'to do obeisance to, to do reverence to, to prostrate oneself before' [BAGD], 'to prostrate oneself in worship, to bow down and worship'

[LN]. This verb means to express by attitude and possibly by position one's allegiance to and regard for deity [LN].

QUESTION—What is the object of the third temptation?

Satan tempted Jesus to violate the first commandment, to worship someone other than God, just as Israel did in the wilderness. However, Jesus succeeds where Israel failed [BECNT]. He tempted Jesus to grasp messianic power without going to the cross as the suffering servant who takes away sin, which would deprive God of his exclusive claim of worship [EBC]. Jesus clearly faced a choice over whether he would exercise his ministry based on God's authority or the devil's authority [NIGTC]. It was a choice between glory versus self-sacrificial obedience [NICNT]. It was a choice between instant power over the world's kingdoms by violating the first commandment, versus obtaining all authority after the path of suffering [ICC, Lns, NAC, NIBC], to obtain the crown without enduring the cross [NTC]. It was a temptation to be disloyal to God both in goal as well as in method [BNTC].

QUESTION—Was this a real mountain in a geographical place?

1. It was not a real mountain, it was a visionary experience [BECNT, BNTC, EBC, NAC, NTC, WBC], though that does not make the temptation any less real [NTC]. Since no mountain exists where the entire world may be viewed from the top of it, Satan must have brought all the kingdoms of the world before the mind of Jesus [PNTC].
2. It was a real mountain [Lns].

QUESTION—What is the δόξα 'glory' Jesus is shown?

It is wealth [NTC, WBC], and all the world has to offer [WBC]. Satan showed the splendor but not the sin [EBC]. He showed their greatness and beauty [TH]. It is their external splendor [My].

4:10 Then Jesus says to-him, "Go-away,[a] Satan;[b] for it-is-written, '(The) Lord your God you-shall-worship and him only[c] you-shall-serve.[d]'"

LEXICON—a. pres. act. impera. of ὑπάγω (LN 15.35) (BAGD 1. p. 836): 'to go away' [BAGD], 'to go, to go away from, to depart, to leave' [LN]. The imperative is translated 'go away' [PNTC; CEV, GW, NET, TEV], 'go' [NASB], 'go away from me' [NCV], 'get away' [BECNT, NIGTC], 'get away from me' [WBC], 'away from me' [NIV], 'away with you' [NICNT; NRSV], 'depart' [BNTC], 'leave' [CC], 'be gone' [NTC; ESV], 'get thee hence' [KJV], 'get out of here' [NLT], 'out of my sight' [REB]. This verb means to move away from a reference point, perhaps more definitively than in the case of πορεύομαι and ἄγω [LN]. This is a decisive rejection of Satan's proposition [PNTC].

b. Σατανᾶς (LN 93.330) (BAGD p. 744): 'Satan' [BAGD, BECNT, BNTC, LN, NICNT, NIGTC, NTC, PNTC, WBC; all versions], 'Adversary' [BAGD, CC]. This noun denotes the usual proper name of the Devil, and is a borrowing from Greek and Aramaic words which literally mean 'adversary' [LN].

MATTHEW 4:10 83

    c. μόνος (LN 58.50) (BAGD 1.a.β. p. 527): 'only' [BAGD, BECNT, BNTC, NIGTC, NTC, PNTC; all versions except REB] 'alone' [BAGD, CC, LN, WBC; REB], 'only one' [LN]. The clause 'him only you shall serve' is translated 'he is the only one you are to serve' [NICNT]. This adjective describes the only entity in a class [LN].
    d. fut. act. indic. of λατρεύω (LN 53.14) (BAGD p. 467): 'to serve' [BAGD; all translations except REB], 'to worship' [LN; REB], 'to perform religious rites, to venerate' [LN]. This verb means to perform religious rites as a part of worship [LN].

QUESTION—What relationship is indicated by τότε 'then'?
    It marks a climax where Jesus speaks for the last time in this account [NIGTC].

4:11 **Then the devil leaves him, and behold^a angels came and were-ministering^b to-him.**

LEXICON—a. ἰδού (LN 91.13) (BAGD 1.b. p. 370): 'behold' [BAGD] 'see' [BAGD], 'look' [BAGD, LN], 'listen, pay attention' [LN]. See translations of this word at 1:20. This particle is a prompter of attention, and serves to emphasize the following statement [LN].
    b. imperf. act. indic. of διακονέω (LN35.37) (BAGD 2. p. 184): 'to minister to' [BNTC, WBC; ESV, KJV, NASB, NET], 'to serve' [BAGD, CC], 'to help' [BECNT; CEV, TEV], 'to wait on' [BAGD, NIGTC; NRSV], 'to render service' [NTC], 'to take care of' [LN, NICNT, PNTC; GW, NCV, NLT], 'to attend' [NIV], 'to attend to (his) needs' [REB]. The imperfect tense of this verb is translated as having an inceptive sense: 'began to help/minister/serve' [BECNT, CC; NASB, NET]; or as having a durative sense: 'were ministering/rendering service' [NTC, WBC; ESV]. This verb means to take care of someone by rendering humble service to him [LN].

QUESTION—In what way did the angels minister to him?
    They provided for his hunger [BNTC, EBC, Lns, My, NICNT, NIGTC, NTC, WBC], and fed him supernaturally [EBC]. They also acknowledged his victory [Lns, WBC]. They gave spiritual support as well [BNTC]. The imperfect tense of the verb indicates an ongoing help [EBC, NICNT].

DISCOURSE UNIT—4:12–18:35 [CEV]. The topic is Jesus in Galilee.

DISCOURSE UNIT—4:12–16:20 [NICNT]. The topic is Galilee: the Messiah revealed in word and deed.

DISCOURSE UNIT—4:12–13:52 [PNTC]. The topic is Jesus' ministry in Galilee.

DISCOURSE UNIT—4:12–25 [WBC; REB]. The topic is the Galilean ministry [WBC], the first disciples [REB].

DISCOURSE UNIT—4:12–17 [NICNT, PNTC; ESV, GW, NASB, NET, NIV, NLT, NRSV, TEV]. The topic is the introduction [PNTC], the light dawns in Galilee [NICNT], a light has risen [GW], Jesus begins his ministry [ESV,

NASB], Jesus begins his work in Galilee [TEV], Jesus begins his ministry in Galilee [NRSV], the ministry of Jesus begins [NLT], preaching in Galilee [NET], Jesus begins to preach [NIV].

DISCOURSE UNIT—4:12–16 [NAC; NCV]. The topic is Jesus settles in Capernaum [NAC], Jesus begins work in Galilee [NCV].

4:12 And[a] having-heard that John was-arrested[b] he-departed/withdrew[c] into Galilee.

LEXICON—a. δέ (LN 91.3): 'and' [LN, PNTC], 'now' [CC, ESV, NET], not explicit [BECNT, BNTC, NICNT, NIGTC, NTC, WBC; all versions except ESV]. This particle marks linkage in discourse, but is often left untranslated [LN].

  b. aorist pass. indic. of παραδίδωμι (LN 37.111) (BAGD 1.b. p. 614): 'to be arrested' [BECNT, PNTC; ESV, NLT, NRSV, REB], 'to be imprisoned' [BNTC; NET], 'to be handed over' [CC, LN, NIGTC], 'to be taken into custody' [NTC, WBC; NASB], 'to be put/cast into prison [CEV, GW, KJV, NCV, NIV, TEV], 'to be handed over, to be given up' [BAGD], 'to be turned over to' [BAGD, LN], 'to be betrayed' [LN]. This verb means to deliver a person into the control of someone else, involving either the handing over of a presumably guilty person for punishment by authorities or the handing over of an individual to an enemy who will presumably take undue advantage of the victim [LN].

  c. aorist act. indic. of ἀναχωρέω (LN 15.53, 15.89) (BAGD 2.b. p. 63): 'to depart' [BNTC, CC, LN (15.53), NIGTC, WBC; KJV], 'to go' [CEV, NET], 'to go away' [LN (15.53); TEV], 'to withdraw' [BAGD, LN (15.53), NTC, PNTC; ESV, NASB, NRSV, REB], 'to return' [BECNT, LN (15.89); NIV, NLT], 'to go back' [GW, NCV], 'to move back' [LN (15.89)], 'to retire' [BAGD, LN (15.53)], 'to take refuge' [BAGD]. This verb means to move away from a location, implying a considerable distance [LN (15.53)], or to move back to a point or area from which one has previously departed, but with more explicit emphasis upon the return [LN (15.89)]. This verb occurs in 2:12, 13, 14, where it means 'to depart' and in 2:22 where it means 'to withdraw'. It implies a strategic withdrawal done in recognition of possible danger [BECNT, CC, EBC, NICNT].

QUESTION—Why did Jesus depart to Galilee?

Jesus knew that the Jewish leaders in Jerusalem would be less likely to directly oppose his ministry if he moved farther away to Galilee [My, NTC]. Galilee was a place of travel and trade and was open to new ideas [PNTC]. It was a good base for ministry as it had two major highways and a significant population [NIBC]. Matthew presents Jesus' going there as the fulfilling of prophecy, but also in terms of Jesus ministering in a place that was shunned or scorned by the establishment in Jerusalem [BECNT].

QUESTION—How soon after the events related in 4:1–11 did Jesus go into Galilee?

Matthew gives no indication of the time involved [ICC, NICNT, WBC] There was probably an interval of time, but Matthew does not indicate how long it was [Lns, NIGTC]. It may have been as much as a year after his baptism that he went into Galilee [NTC]. He went there fairly soon after John's arrest [BECNT, CC].

DISCOURSE UNIT—4:13–25 [NIGTC]. The topic is the establishment of his ministry.

4:13 And having-left Nazareth (and) having-come he settled[a] in Capernaum beside-the-lake[b] in (the) region of-Zebulon and Naphtali;

LEXICON—a. aorist act. indic. of κατοικέω (LN 85.69) (BAGD 1.a. p. 424): 'to settle' [BAGD, BNTC, NICNT, NTC; NASB, REB], 'to dwell' [BECNT, CC, LN, WBC], 'to live' [BAGD, LN, NIGTC, PNTC; ESV, NCV, NIV, TEV], 'to reside' [BAGD, LN], 'to make one's home' [GW, NET, NRSV], 'to move to' [NLT]. This verb means to live or dwell in a place in an established or settled manner [LN].

b. παραθαλάσσιος (παρα θαλάσσιος) (LN **1.71**) (BAGD p. 616): 'beside the lake' [NICNT], 'by the lake' [BAGD, BECNT, **LN**; NIV], 'by Lake Galilee' [TEV], 'near Lake Galilee' [NCV], 'by the sea' [BAGD, BNTC, CC, NIGTC, NTC, PNTC; ESV, NASB, NET, NRSV], 'beside the sea' [WBC], 'beside the Sea of Galilee' [NLT], 'by the seaside' [LN], 'on the shores of the Sea of Galilee' [GW], 'upon the sea coast' [KJV], 'on the sea of Galilee' [REB]. This adjectival noun denotes a location beside the sea or along the shore [LN]. This word occurs only here in the NT.

QUESTION—What was the size and significance of Capernaum?

Capernaum was a Jewish town with possibly as many as 10,000 people in it [NICNT]. It was located about two miles west of the Jordan River, near the trade route between Damascus and Ptolemais [ICC]. The presence of tax collectors was due to its thriving fishing industry [EBC]. Other places in Galilee and surrounding areas were easily accessible, either from the nearby road going from Damascus to the Mediterranean, or by boat on the lake itself [NTC]. For Matthew, the significance of Capernaum has to do with fulfilling the prophecy from Isa. 9:1 [BECNT, ICC, PNTC] since Capernaum was in the traditional territory of Naphtali, and Nazareth was in Zebulon [NIGTC].

4:14 so-that it-might-be-fulfilled[a] that (which) was-spoken through Isaiah the prophet saying, **4:15** "Land of-Zebulon and land of-Naphtali, (the) way[b] of-(the) sea, beyond[c] the Jordan, Galilee of-the Gentiles,

LEXICON—a. aorist pass. subj. of πληρόω (LN 13.106) (BAGD 4.a. p. 671): 'to be fulfilled' [BAGD, LN], 'to be caused to happen, to made to happen' [LN]. The phrase ἵνα πληρωθῇ 'so that it might be fulfilled' is translated 'that/so that...might be fulfilled' [BNTC, NIGTC, NTC, PNTC; ESV, KJV, NRSV], 'in order that...might be fulfilled' [CC, WBC], 'so

that...would be fulfilled' [NET], 'to fulfill' [BECNT, NICNT; NIV], 'this was to fulfill' [NASB, REB], 'this fulfilled' [NLT], 'to bring about' [NCV], 'so...came true' [CEV, GW], 'this was done to make come true' [TEV]. This verb means to cause to happen, with the implication of fulfilling some purpose [LN].
- b. ὁδός (LN 1.99) (BAGD 1.a. p. 554): 'way, road, highway' [BAGD, LN]. The phrase ὁδὸν θαλάσσης 'the way of the sea' [BECNT, NICNT, WBC; ESV] is also translated 'the way/road to the sea' [NIV, REB], 'way of the sea' [BNTC, NIGTC, PNTC], 'as far as the way of the sea' [CC], 'toward the sea' [NTC], 'on the way/road to the sea' [GW, TEV], 'by the way of the sea' [KJV, NASB], 'on the road by the sea' [NRSV], 'the way by the sea' [NET], 'beside the sea' [NLT], 'along the sea' [NCV], 'lands along the road to the sea' [CEV]. This noun is a general term denoting a thoroughfare, either within a population center or between two such centers [LN].
- c. πέραν (LN 83.43) (BAGD 2.c. p. 644): 'beyond' [BNTC, NICNT, NTC, PNTC; ESV, KJV, NASB, NCV, NET, NLT, REB], 'across' [NIGTC, WBC; GW, NRSV], 'on the other side of' [BAGD, CC, LN; TEV], 'along' [BECNT; NIV], 'east of' [CEV], 'opposite, across from' [LN]. This adverb describes a position opposite another position, with something intervening [LN].

QUESTION—What relationship is indicated by ἵνα 'so that'?
1. The conjunction ἵνα indicates the consequence of Jesus' move, not his purpose for moving [EBC; CEV, GW, NLT].
2. It indicates the purpose for Jesus' move [BECNT, BNTC, CC, NICNT, NIGTC, NTC, PNTC, TRT, WBC; all versions except CEV, GW, NLT]. This fulfilled God's purpose expressed in the prophecy [PNTC, WBC]. Most commentators don't specifically say whether the move was God's purpose or Jesus' purpose, but it is likely that they are assuming that Jesus' move fulfilled God's purpose. However, the translation 'Jesus did this to bring about what the prophet had said' [NCV] could be taken to mean that Jesus moved to Capernaum with the express purpose of fulfilling the OT prophecy.

QUESTION—What is the way of the sea?
There is a highway called the *Via Maris*, 'the way of the sea', going from Damascus through Galilee to the Mediterranean sea [BNTC, NAC, NIBC, NTC]. The area near the Sea of Galilee can be thought of as the way of the Sea of Galilee [EBC, ICC, Lns, My, NICNT, NIGTC, PNTC, TH, TRT], beside which the *Via Maris* passes [WBC].

QUESTION—Why is it called 'Galilee of the Gentiles'?
In using this passage from Isaiah Matthew indicates that the mission that begins here will extend beyond Israel [CC, NICNT]. The message is for all nations [BECNT, EBC], and there is a connection with 28:19–20 [CC, EBC, NICNT], or it is a possible foreshadowing of 28:19–20 [WBC]. Galilee had a

mixed population [BECNT, NICNT], and it was surrounded by Gentiles [My, NIBC, PNTC].

QUESTION—What is meant by 'beyond the Jordan'?
1. From Matthew's perspective, it refers to west side of the Jordan [EBC, NAC, NICNT, NIGTC, TH, TRT]. This text from Isaiah reflects the path that the conquering armies would have taken, moving from northeast to the west side of the Jordan [EBC, NAC].
2. It is the area to the east of the Jordan [Lns, My, NTC, PNTC, WBC]. Matthew intends to include the Decapolis, which is east of the Jordan [WBC]. Jesus may have worked on the east side of the Jordan more than is recorded in the NT [PNTC]. All five of the designations Matthew uses represent different territories, and this one describes Perea [Lns].

4:16 the people[a] living[b] in darkness[c] saw a-great light, and to-those dwelling in (the) territory and shadow[d] of-death a-light dawned[e] on-them."

LEXICON—a. λαός (LN 11.55): 'people' [LN; all translations], 'nation' [LN]. This noun denotes the largest unit into which the people of the world are divided on the basis of their constituting a socio-political community [LN].
b. pres. mid. or pass. (deponent = act.) participle of κάθημαι (LN 85.63): 'to live' [BECNT; CEV, GW, NCV, NIV, REB, TEV], 'to sit' [BNTC, CC, NICNT, NIGTC, NTC, PNTC, WBC; KJV, NASB, NET, NLT, NRSV], 'to dwell' [ESV], 'to remain, to stay, to reside, to inhabit, to be, to settle' [LN]. This verb means to remain for some time in a place, often with the implication of a settled situation [LN].
c. σκότος (LN 88.125) (BAGD p. 758): 'darkness' [BAGD, LN; all translations], 'gloom' [BAGD], 'evil world, realm of evil' [LN]. This noun denotes the realm of sin and evil [LN].
d. σκιά (LN 14.61) BAGD 1.a. p. 755): 'shadow' [BAGD, BECNT, BNTC, CC, LN, NICNT, PNTC, WBC; all versions except GW, TEV]. The phrase 'territory and shadow' is translated 'region/land overshadowed by' [NIGTC; GW], 'dark land of' [TEV]. This noun denotes the shape or shade cast by an object which blocks rays of light [LN].
e. aorist act. indic. of ἀνατέλλω (LN **14.41**) (BAGD 2. p. 62): 'to dawn' [BECNT, BNTC, **LN**, NTC, PNTC, WBC; ESV, NASB, NET, NIV, NRSV, REB], 'to rise' [CC, LN, NICNT; GW], 'to shine' [CEV, NCV, NLT, TEV], 'to spring up' [KJV], 'to become light' [LN]. This verb means to change from darkness to light in the early morning hours [LN].

QUESTION—Who are the λαός 'people', and what is the relationship of λαός 'people' to 4:15?

All the noun phrases in 4:15 stand in apposition to 'land', which is the subject of the sentence [CC, NICNT].
1. Λαός normally refers to the Jewish people [Lns, NAC, TH]. Matthew only uses λαός to refer to the Jewish people, and here he probably is

referring to the Jewish people who were living in frustration among pagan Gentiles [WBC].

2. Matthew is referring to all peoples, whether Jew or Gentile [PNTC].

QUESTION—What is the 'darkness'?

This darkness is the lack of knowledge of God [My, NAC]. Galilee was looked down on by the Jerusalem establishment as being unenlightened [BECNT]. They lacked the religious advantages of Jerusalem and Judea [EBC]. It refers to the danger, fear, hopelessness, and despondency of a people that had suffered under foreign oppression, and had sunk into moral decay because of paganism [NTC]. It speaks of the frustration and despair of Jewish people living among pagans [WBC]. It is a moral and spiritual darkness [ICC, TH]. It is about religious falsehood and delusion [Lns], living in sin and ignorance of God [TRT]. Darkness stands in contrast to salvation, symbolized by light [NIGTC].

DISCOURSE UNIT—4:17–16:20 [CC; NAC]. The topic is the development of Jesus' ministry [NAC], part 2: ministry and opposition in Israel—Who is this Jesus? [CC].

DISCOURSE UNIT—4:17–11:1 [CC]. The topic is Jesus' ministry with authority in Israel.

DISCOURSE UNIT—4:17–9:35 [NAC]. The topic is Jesus' authority in preaching and healing.

DISCOURSE UNIT—4:17–25 [NAC]. The topic is the introduction.

DISCOURSE UNIT—4:17–22 [CC; NCV]. The topic is Jesus chooses some followers [NCV], Jesus' proclamation begins and he calls disciples [CC].

4:17 From then Jesus began to-preach[a] and to-say, "Repent;[b] for the kingdom of-heaven has-drawn-near."

LEXICON—a. pres. act. infin. of κηρύσσω (LN 33.256) (BAGD 2.b.β. p. 431): 'to preach' [BAGD, BNTC, CC, LN, NTC, PNTC, WBC; CEV, ESV, KJV, NASB, NCV, NET, NIV, NLT], 'to preach (his) message' [TEV], 'to proclaim' [BECNT, NIGTC; NRSV], 'to proclaim this/the message' [NICNT; REB], 'to tell people' [GW]. This verb means to publicly announce religious truths and principles while urging acceptance and compliance [LN].

b. pres. act. impera. of μετανοέω (LN 41.52) (BAGD p. 512): 'to repent' [BAGD, BECNT, BNTC, CC, LN, NIGTC, PNTC, WBC; ESV, KJV, NASB, NET, NIV, NRSV, REB], 'to repent of (your) sins' [NLT], 'to turn away from (your) sins' [TEV], 'to be converted' [BAGD, NTC], 'to turn back to God' [CEV], 'to change (your) hearts and lives' [NCV], 'to turn to God and change the way you think and act' [GW], 'to change one's way' [LN]. This verb means to change one's way of life as the result of a complete change of thought and attitude with regard to sin and righteousness [LN].

QUESTION—What does ἀπὸ τότε 'from then' mark?
It marks a new stage in Jesus' ministry [BECNT, EBC, PNTC], and it ties this new stage to what has just been narrated [EBC]. Each occurrence of ἀπὸ τότε, here, at 16:21, and at 26:16, marks a transition [NIGTC] to a change in the pattern of Jesus' activity [BNTC, CC, NICNT]. Here it marks the beginning of the section about Jesus' Galilean ministry, which ends in 16:21 with the same phrase [WBC].

DISCOURSE UNIT—4:18–25 [PNTC; NLT]. The topic is the first disciples and the first teaching [PNTC], the first disciples [NLT].

DISCOURSE UNIT—4:18–22 [NET, NICNT; CEV, ESV, GW, NASB, NIV, NRSV, TEV]. The topic is the founding of the messianic community [NICNT], the first disciples [NASB], the call of the disciples [NET], the calling of the first disciples [GW, NIV], Jesus calls the first disciples [ESV, NRSV], Jesus calls four fishermen [TEV], Jesus chooses four fishermen [CEV].

4:18 Walking beside Lake Galilee he-saw two brothers, Simon the (one)-called Peter and Andrew his brother, casting a-net[a] into the lake, for they-were fishermen.[b] **4:19** And he-says to-them, "Come[c] after[d] me, and I-will-make you fishermen of-men.[e]"

LEXICON—a. ἀμφίβληστρον (LN **6.12**) (BAGD p. 47): 'net' [BECNT, BNTC, NIGTC, PNTC, WBC; all versions], 'casting-net' [BAGD, CC, **LN**, NICNT, NTC]. This noun denotes a round casting-net used in fishing [LN]. This word occurs only here in the NT.

b. ἁλιεύς (LN **44.10**) (BAGD p. 37): 'fisherman' [BAGD, **LN**; all translations except KJV, NLT], 'fisher' [KJV]. The phrase 'they were fishermen' is translated 'they fished for a living' [NLT]. This noun denotes one whose occupation is to catch fish [LN].

c. δεῦτε is an adverb (BAGD, CC, LN (84.24), PNTC) that serves as an aorist act. impera. of δεῦρο 'to come' (BAGD 2. p. 176): 'here, hither, come here' [LN]. The clause Δεῦτε ὀπίσω μου 'Come after me' [CC] is translated 'Come with me' [CEV; REB, TEV], 'Come, follow me' [BNTC, NTC; GW, NCV, NIV, NLT], 'Come and follow me' [NICNT], 'Come after me' [PNTC, WBC], 'Come on! After me!' [NIGTC], 'Follow me' [BAGD, BECNT; ESV, KJV, NASB, NET, NRSV]. This adverb indicates an extension toward a goal at or near the speaker and implies movement [LN]. The idiom δεῦτε ὀπίσω μου 'follow after me', along with ἀκολουθέω 'follow' in the next verse, are used to describe being a disciple of someone [CC, NICNT].

d. ὀπίσω (LN 36.35) (BAGD 2.a.β. p. 575): 'after' [BAGD, LN], 'to follow' [LN]. See translations of the clause 'come after me' in the preceding lexical item. This preposition occurs with a variety of verbs indicating a change of state or movement and it refers to some one who is followed as a leader [LN].

90   MATTHEW 4:18–19

  e. The phrase ποιήσω ὑμᾶς ἁλιεῖς ἀνθρώπων 'I will make you fishermen of men' is translated 'I will make you fishers of men' [NTC, PNTC; ESV, KJV, NASB, NIV, REB], 'I will make you to be fishers of men' [CC], 'I will make you fishers who catch men' [BNTC], 'I will make you fishers of human beings' [WBC], 'I will turn you into fishers of people' [NET], 'I will make you fish for people' [BECNT; NCV, NRSV], 'I will make you those who fish for people' [NIGTC], 'I will send you out to fish for people' [NICNT], 'I will teach you how to bring in people instead of fish' [CEV], 'I will make you fish for people' [NCV], 'I will teach you to catch people' [TEV], 'I will teach you how to catch people instead of fish' [GW], 'I will show you how to fish for people' [NLT].
QUESTION—Which of the two was the older brother?
  It is not known which was older, but Simon Peter was usually mentioned first, meaning either that he was older, or the more prominent one [TH, TRT].
QUESTION—In what sense will they 'fish' for people?
  They are to help Jesus recruit new subjects for God's kingdom [My, NICNT, NTC], laboring to bring others into the kingdom [EBC, Lns, WBC]. They will bring in human lives for Christ [CC], bring people into contact with God [PNTC], cause people to follow Christ [TRT]. They will gather people in [NIGTC]. They may not have understood what he meant very well, but no doubt they realized that it was something worthwhile [PNTC].

4:20 **And immediately[a] leaving[b] the nets[c] they-followed[d] him.**
LEXICON—a. εὐθέως (LN 67.53) (BAGD p. 320): 'immediately' [BAGD, BECNT, CC, LN, NICNT, NIGTC, WBC; ESV, GW, NASB, NCV, NET, NRSV], 'at once' [BAGD, BNTC, NTC; NIV, REB], 'straightway' [PNTC; KJV, TEV], 'right then' [CEV], 'right away, 'then' [LN]. This adverb describes a point of time immediately subsequent to a previous point of time; the actual interval of time differs appreciably, depending upon the nature of the events and the manner in which the sequence is interpreted by the writer [LN]. It indicates an unusual readiness on the part of the disciples to follow a relative stranger [NICNT].
  b. aorist act. participle of ἀφίημι (LN **85.45**) (BAGD 3.a. p. 126): 'to leave' [BAGD, LN; all translations except CEV], 'to drop' [CEV], 'to leave behind' [LN]. This verb means to let something be put behind in a place [LN].
  c. δίκτυον (LN **6.11**) (BAGD p. 198): 'net' [BAGD, LN; all translations], 'fishnet' [LN]. This noun denotes any kind of net, but in the NT it refers only to nets used for catching fish [LN].
  d. aorist act. indic. of ἀκολουθέω (LN 36.31): 'to follow' [LN; all translations except CEV], 'to go with' [CEV], 'to be a disciple of' [LN]. This verb means to be a follower or a disciple of someone, in the sense of adhering to the teachings or instructions of a leader and in promoting the cause of such a leader [LN].

QUESTION—Was this the first time Peter and Andrew had encountered Jesus? Matthew presents the action as unpremeditated, and Jesus as a relative stranger to them [NICNT]. John tells us that some of the disciples had already known of him [CC, EBC, Lns, NAC, NTC], but Matthew's focus seems to be on the great authority with which Jesus called them, and to which they immediately responded [BNTC, CC]. The call was urgent, and the response was immediate [NIBC]. Matthew emphasizes unconditional and unhesitating obedience to the call [WBC], a decisive response [NAC], immediate obedience [PNTC]. From the other gospels we gather that these men probably had followed Jesus at an earlier date, and returned to their homes and trade, but it was at this point that the decisive change occurred to become full-time disciples, for which their earlier associations with Jesus had prepared them [EBC]. Their leaving everything and following Jesus was not as abrupt as it might appear, but it was still decisive [NAC]. Matthew does not mention any previous contact, but that does not mean there wasn't any, only that he is not interested in that aspect [PNTC]. Matthew presents Jesus' call as coming abruptly, disruptively, urgently, and requiring radical response [NIGTC].

4:21 And having-gone-on from-there he-saw two other brothers, James the (son) of-Zebedee and John his brother, in the boat[a] with Zebedee their father mending[b] their nets, and he-called[c] them. **4:22** And immediately leaving the boat and their father they-followed him.

LEXICON—a. πλοῖον (LN 6.41) (BAGD 2. p. 673): 'boat' [BAGD, LN; all translations except KJV], 'ship' [KJV]. This noun denotes any kind of boat, from small fishing boats as on Lake Galilee to large seagoing vessels [LN].
  b. pres. act. participle of καταρτίζω (LN 75.5) (BAGD 1.a. p. 417): 'to mend' [BECNT, NIGTC, NIGTC; CEV, ESV, KJV, NASB, NCV, NET, NRSV, REB], 'to make adequate' [LN], 'to put in order' [BAGD, BNTC, WBC], 'to prepare' [CC, NICNT, PNTC; GW, NIV], 'to repair' [NLT], 'to get ready' [TEV], 'to restore' [BAGD]. This verb means to make completely adequate or sufficient for something [LN].
  c. aorist act. indic. of καλέω (LN 33.312) (BAGD 1.e. p. 399): 'to call' [LN; all translations except CEV, NCV, NLT], 'to call to come' [NLT], 'to call to a task' [LN], 'to summon' [BAGD]. The phrase 'he called them' is translated '(Jesus) asked them to come with him too' [CEV], 'Jesus told them to come with him' [NCV]. This verb means to urgently invite someone to accept responsibilities for a particular task, implying a new relationship to the one who does the calling [LN]. He called them to be disciples [CC, WBC] and believers [CC].
QUESTION—Is there any indication of which brother was older?
James appears to have been the older one [PNTC, TRT].

DISCOURSE UNIT—4:23–5:2 [ICC]. The topic is an introduction to the sermon on the mount.

DISCOURSE UNIT—4:23–25 [NICNT; CEV, ESV, GW, NASB, NCV, NET, NIV, NLT, NRSV, TEV]. The topic is an overview of the Messiah's revelation in Galilee [NICNT], spreading the good news in Galilee [GW], ministry in Galilee [NASB], Jesus teaches and heals people [NCV], Jesus teaches, preaches, and heals [CEV, TEV], Jesus' healing ministry [NET], Jesus ministers to great crowds [ESV], Jesus ministers to crowds of people [NRSV], Jesus heals the sick [NIV], crowds follow Jesus [NLT].

DISCOURSE UNIT—4:23–24 [CC]. The topic is a summary of Jesus' ministry.

4:23 **And he was-going-about[a] in all Galilee teaching[b] in their synagogues[c]**
LEXICON—a. imperf. act. indic. of περιάγω (LN 15.23) BAGD 2. p. 645): 'to go about, to go around' [BAGD], 'to travel through' [LN]. The phrase 'he was going about in all Galilee' is translated 'Jesus was going throughout all Galilee' [BECNT], 'he traveled about in all Galilee' [BNTC], 'he began to go around in the whole of Galilee' [CC], 'he began traveling around throughout the whole of Galilee' [NICNT], 'Jesus traveled around in the whole of Galilee' [NIGTC], 'he/Jesus went throughout all Galilee' [ESV, NIV, NRSV], 'he went through all Galilee' [NTC], 'he went about in all Galilee' [PNTC], 'he was going about the whole of Galilee' [WBC], 'Jesus went all over Galilee' [CEV, GW, TEV], 'Jesus went about all Galilee' [KJV], 'Jesus was going throughout all Galilee' [NASB], 'Jesus went everywhere in Galilee' [NCV], 'Jesus went throughout all of Galilee' [NET], 'Jesus traveled throughout the region of Galilee' [NLT], 'he traveled throughout Galilee' [REB]. This verb means to move about from place to place, with significant changes in direction [LN].

b. pres. act. participle of διδάσκω (LN 33.224) (BAGD 1. p. 192): 'to teach' [BAGD, LN; all translations]. This verb means to provide instruction in a formal or informal setting [LN].

c. συναγωγή (LN 7.20) (BAGD 2.a. p. 782): 'synagogue' [BAGD, LN; all translations except CEV], 'meeting places' [CEV], 'place of assembly' [BAGD]. This noun denotes a building of assembly, associated with religious activity (normally a building in which Jewish worship took place and in which the Law was taught) [LN].

and preaching[a] the good-news[b] of-the kingdom and healing[c] every[d] disease[e] and every sickness[f] among the people.
LEXICON—a. pres. act. participle of κηρύσσω. See 4:17.

b. εὐαγγέλιον (LN 33.217) (BAGD 1.c., 2.b.α. p. 318): 'the good news' [BAGD, BECNT, CC, LN, NICNT; CEV, GW, NCV, NIV, NLT, NRSV, REB, TEV], 'the gospel' [BAGD, BNTC, LN, NIGTC, NTC, PNTC, WBC; ESV, KJV, NASB, NET]. This noun denotes the content of good news [LN].

MATTHEW 4:23

c. pres. act. participle of θεραπεύω (LN 23.139) (BAGD 2. p. 359): 'to heal' [BAGD, LN; all translations except GW, NRSV], 'to cure' [LN; GW, NRSV], 'to restore' [BAGD]. This verb means to cause someone to recover health, often with the implication of having taken care of such a person [LN].

d. πᾶς (LN 59.23) (BAGD 1.a.β. p. 631): 'every' [BNTC, CC, LN, NIGTC, NTC, PNTC, WBC; ESV, GW, NIV, NRSV], 'every kind of' [BAGD, BECNT; CEV, NASB, NLT, REB], 'all' [LN; NCV], 'all kinds of' [NET, TEV], 'all sorts of' [BAGD, NICNT], 'all manner of' [KJV]. This adjective describes the totality of any object, mass, collective, or extension [LN].

e. νόσος (LN 23.155) (BAGD 1. p. 543): 'disease' [BAGD, BECNT, BNTC, CC, LN, NIGTC, PNTC, WBC; all versions except CEV, KJV, REB], 'sickness' [LN; CEV, KJV], 'illness' [LN, NICNT, NTC; REB]. This noun denotes the state of being diseased [LN].

f. μαλακία (LN 23.154) (BAGD 1. p. 488): 'sickness' [BAGD, BECNT, BNTC, LN, NIGTC; CEV, GW, NASB, NCV, NET, NIV, NRSV, TEV], 'illness' [PNTC; NLT], 'affliction' [ESV], 'ailment' [CC], 'infirmity' [NTC; REB], 'malady' [WBC], 'disease' [LN; KJV], 'disability' [NICNT]. This noun denotes a state of weakness resulting from disease [LN].

QUESTION—Is there any significant difference between 'teaching' and 'preaching'?

There is probably no sharp difference [CC, NICNT, NIGTC, TH, WBC], though teaching was a common function of synagogue life [EBC, NIGTC]. Preaching would have been more informal, and suited for crowds, whereas teaching would have been more formal, and would have been by invitation at a weekly synagogue assembly [NAC, NICNT]. Preaching would have been more oriented toward conversion, whereas the content of teaching would depend on the context [CC]. The content of his preaching would have been the foundation for the teaching as well as for healing [WBC]. Teaching is systematic whereas preaching is forthright proclamation of a message people may or may not want to hear [PNTC]. Teaching involves explaining in more detail, whereas preaching is acting as a herald, announcing and proclaiming a message [NTC]. Teaching was in synagogues whereas preaching was in the open [BNTC, TH], expressing an urgent appeal [BNTC].

QUESTION—What was the good news of the kingdom?

It is the good news that God's reign is breaking upon the scene in the person of his Son the Messiah [EBC]. His preaching involved proclaiming that God was beginning to act with sovereign power in human affairs [NIBC]. It is the good news about God's rule [PNTC, TH], as shown in the work that his Son was doing [PNTC]. The reality of God's rule is displayed in Jesus' acts of power by which he shows his kingly power and demonstrates mercy, and also as he defeats the devil [BECNT]. This verse summarizes what is to be described in detail in subsequent chapters [EBC]. It is about God's rule in the lives of people [NTC].

4:24 **And the news**[a] **of-him went into all**[b] **Syria, and they-brought to-him all those having illness,**[c] **various**[d] **diseases and those-suffering**[e] **pain**[f]

LEXICON—a. ἀκοή (LN **33.213**) (BAGD 2.a. p. 31): 'news' [BECNT, **LN**, NTC; CEV, GW, NASB, NCV, NIV, NLT, TEV], 'report' [BAGD, BNTC, CC, LN, NICNT, PNTC; NET], 'fame' [NIGTC, WBC; ESV, KJV, NRSV, REB], 'rumor' [BAGD], 'information' [LN]. This noun denotes the content of the news that is heard [LN].

b. ὅλος (LN **63.1**): 'all' [BECNT, BNTC, LN, PNTC; ESV, KJV, NASB, NCV, NIV, NRSV], 'whole' [CC, LN, NICNT, NIGTC, WBC], 'whole country of' [TEV], 'complete, entire' [LN]. The phrase 'went into all' is translated 'spread throughout' [NTC; GW, NET, REB], 'spread all over' [CEV], 'spread as far as' [NLT]. This adjective describes that which pertains to being whole, complete, or entire, with focus on unity [LN].

c. κακῶς ἔχω (LN **23.148**) (BAGD 1. p. 398). The phrase 'having illness' is translated 'to be ill' [BAGD, BECNT, LN, PNTC, WBC; NASB, NIV], 'to be seriously ill' [BNTC], 'to be sick' [BAGD, CC, LN, NIGTC; GW, NLT, TEV], 'to be afflicted' [NTC], '(people with) sickness' [CEV], '(the) sick' [ESV, NCV, NRSV], 'sick people' [KJV]. The phrase 'having illness, various diseases' is translated 'suffering from all kinds of illnesses' [NICNT], 'sufferers from various diseases' [REB]. The phrase 'all those having illness, various diseases, and those suffering pain' is translated 'all who suffered with various illnesses and afflictions' [NET]. The phrase κακῶς ἔχω 'to have badly' or 'to fare badly' is an idiom meaning to be in a bad state, and here, 'to be ill' [LN].

d. ποικίλος (LN **58.45**) (BAGD 1. p. 683): 'various' [BNTC, CC, LN, PNTC, WBC; ESV, NASB, NET, NIV, NRSV, REB], 'various kinds' [BAGD, LN, NIGTC], 'different kinds' [NCV], 'all kinds of' [NICNT, NTC; TEV], 'every kind' [CEV], 'any kind' [GW], 'divers' [KJV], 'whatever' [NLT]. This adjective describes that which exists in a variety of kinds, diversified [LN].

e. pres. pass. participle of συνέχομαι (LN **90.65**) (BAGD 5. p. 789): 'to suffer' [BECNT; GW, NASB, NCV, NET, NCV, NIV, TEV], 'to be tormented' [BNTC, CC, WBC], 'to be afflicted' [NICNT, NIGTC; ESV, NRSV], 'to be distressed' [NTC], 'to be gripped' [PNTC], 'to be taken with' [KJV], 'to be racked with' [REB], 'to experience, to have' [LN], not explicit [CEV, NLT]. This verb means to experience a state or condition, generally involving duration, and in the passive voice means to be sick, to suffer [LN].

f. βάσανος (LN **24.90**) (BAGD 2. p. 134): 'pain' [BECNT, NICNT, WBC; ESV, GW, NASB, NRSV, REB], 'severe pain' [BAGD, BNTC, CC, **LN** NIGTC; NIV], 'great pain' [NCV], 'torment' [BAGD, **LN**, NTC, PNTC; KJV], 'severe suffering' [LN], 'affliction' [NET], 'disorder' [TEV], not

MATTHEW 4:24

explicit [CEV, NLT]. This noun denotes severe pain associated with torment and torture [LN].

QUESTION—What region is referred to here as 'Syria'?
1. It was the region north of Galilee [Lns, NIBC, NTC, TH, TRT]. It was probably the area north of Palestine [ICC, NIGTC, NTC]. This would of course include Gentiles [NIGTC].
2. It was the entire Roman province of Syria, which included all of Palestine, and indicates an extremely successful program of healings [NICNT].

QUESTION—What is the object of the verb 'suffering'?
1. They suffer pain [BNTC, NICNT, NIGTC, PNTC; NIV, REB]: those having illness and various diseases, and those-suffering from pain.
2. They suffer various diseases *and* pain [BECNT, CC, Lns, My, NTC, WBC; ESV, GW, NASB, NET, NRSV, TEV]: those having illness, and those suffering from various diseases and pain.

and (those who) were-demon-possessed^a and epileptics^b and paralytics,^c and he-healed them.

LEXICON—a. pres. mid. or pass. (deponent = act.) participle of δαιμονίζομαι (LN 12.41) (BAGD 169): 'to be demon possessed' [BECNT, CC, LN; NIV, NLT], 'to be possessed by a demon' [BAGD, NICNT, NIGTC, WBC; GW, NET, REB], 'to be possessed by devils' [KJV], 'to be oppressed by demons' [ESV], 'to have demons' [NCV], 'to have a lot of demons in' [CEV], 'with demons' [TEV], 'demoniac' [BNTC, NTC, PNTC; NASB, NRSV]. This verb means to be possessed by a demon [LN].

b. pres. mid. or pass. (deponent = act.) participle of σεληνιάζομαι (LN 23.169) (BAGD p. 746): 'epileptic' [BECNT, NTC; ESV, GW, NASB, NCV, NLT, NRSV, REB, TEV], 'to be subject to epilepsy' [NIGTC], 'to suffer epileptic seizures, to be an epileptic' [LN], 'to be subject to seizures' [WBC], 'to have seizures' [NET, NIV], 'to be subject to fits' [NICNT], 'lunatic' [BNTC, PNTC; KJV], 'thought to be crazy' [CEV], 'to be moon-struck' [BAGD, CC]. This verb means to suffer epileptic seizures, which was associated in ancient times with the supernatural power of the moon [LN].

c. παραλυτικός (LN 23.171) (BAGD p. 620): 'paralytic' [BAGD, BECNT, BNTC, CC, NTC, PNTC; ESV, NASB, NET, NRSV, TEV], 'paralyzed' [LN, NICNT, NIGTC, WBC; GW, NCV, NIV, NLT, REB], 'lame' [BAGD, LN], 'could not walk' [CEV], '(that had) the palsy' [KJV]. This adjective describes that which pertains to being lame and/or paralyzed [LN].

QUESTION—What does 'epileptic' mean here?
1. This refers to epileptic seizures [BAGD, BECNT, LN, NAC, NIGTC, NTC, TH, TRT, WBC; ESV, GW, NASB, NCV, NLT, NRSV, REB, TEV]; the ancient world actually could and did distinguish between ordinary afflictions and those caused by demons [NAC]. It may refer to

epilepsy and it can also be associated with demon possession [WBC]. The symptoms of epilepsy could also be linked to demon possession, but are not necessarily that [NICNT]. It may refer to more than just epilepsy [NIGTC].
2. It refers to insanity [BNTC, Lns, PNTC; CEV, KJV]. This could refer to insanity or irrational behavior that may or may not be caused by demon possession [EBC]. This appears to be differentiated from demon possession and many think it refers to epilepsy. However, the Greek word is equivalent to 'lunatic' and there is no reason for denying that meaning here [PNTC].

QUESTION—What does 'paralytic' mean here?
It means that they were lame or unable to walk, for whatever reasons [BECNT, TH]. It is not necessarily the same as how we use the word today [BECNT].

DISCOURSE UNIT—4:25–8:1 [CC]. The topic is the sermon on the mount: Jesus blesses and calls with authority.

4:25 **And many crowds[a] from Galilee and Decapolis and Jerusalem and Judea and (the region) across the Jordan (River) followed him.**

LEXICON—a. ὄχλος (LN 11.1) (BAGD 1. p. 601): 'crowd' [BAGD, LN], 'multitude' [BAGD, LN]. The phrase ὄχλοι πολλοί 'many crowds' [CC] is translated 'large crowds' [BECNT, BNTC; CEV, GW, NASB, NET, NIV, NLT, REB, TEV], 'great crowds' [NICNT, NIGTC, PNTC; ESV, NRSV], 'huge crowds' [NTC], 'great multitudes' [KJV], 'many people' [NCV]. This noun denotes a casual non-membership group of people, fairly large in size and assembled for whatever purpose [LN].

QUESTION—What is Decapolis?
Decapolis refers to ten Hellenistic cities southeast of Galilee that were ruled by Rome from Syria [BECNT]. It is a Gentile region east of Galilee that stretched from Damascus in the north to Philadelphia in the south [EBC]. Most of the inhabitants were non-Jewish [My]. It is northeast of Samaria, and to a certain extent northeast of Galilee as well [NTC]. The region to the east of the Jordan had a sizeable Jewish minority [NIGTC]. This league of originally ten Hellenistic cities was, with one exception, east of the Jordan and the Sea of Galilee [BNTC]. It was considered part of Syria for administrative purposes [NIBC].

QUESTION—How much time did these people actually spend with Jesus?
The word 'follow' here does not indicate full discipleship, as their following was sporadic and temporary [NICNT]. They didn't attain the status of the other disciples who follow Jesus continually [CC]. These were not opponents, but neither were they adherents [PNTC]. No doubt there were some among the crowds who were to be true disciples [WBC]. This may include some who at various times followed Jesus around and were disciples in a more loose sense of the term [EBC]. These were not committed followers [NIGTC].

MATTHEW 5:1

DISCOURSE UNIT—5:1–8:1 [NIGTC]. The topic is the sermon on the mount.

DISCOURSE UNIT—5:1–7:29 [BECNT, EBC, NAC, NICNT, PNTC, WBC; CEV, REB]. The topic is the first discourse: the sermon on the mount [BECNT, EBC, WBC], paradigmatic preaching: the sermon on the mount [NAC], the Messiah's authority revealed in his teaching: the discourse on discipleship [NICNT], the sermon on the mount [PNTC; REB].

DISCOURSE UNIT—5:1–12 [GW, NASB, NCV, NET, NIV, NRSV]. The topic is the sermon on a mountain: the beatitudes [GW], the sermon on the mount; the beatitudes [NASB], the beatitudes [NET, NIV, NRSV], Jesus teaches the people [NCV].

DISCOURSE UNIT—5:1–2 [NLT, TEV]. The topic is the sermon on the mount.

DISCOURSE UNIT—5:1 [CEV, ESV]. The topic is the sermon on the mount.

5:1 **And having-seen the crowds[a] he-went-up[b] on[c] the mountain;[d]**
  LEXICON—a. ὄχλος (LN 11.1) (BAGD 1. p. 600): 'crowd' [BAGD, LN; all translations except KJV], 'multitude' [BAGD, LN; KJV]. This noun denotes a casual non-membership group of people, fairly large in size and assembled for whatever purpose [LN].
  b. aorist act. indic. of ἀναβαίνω (LN **15.101**) (BAGD 1.a.α. p. 50): 'to go up' [BAGD, **LN**, all translations], 'to ascend' [BAGD, LN].
  c. εἰς (LN 83.47, 84.16): 'on' [BECNT, CC, LN (83.47)], CEV, ESV, NASB, NCV, NIV, NLT], 'into (the mountain)' [BNTC, NTC, PNTC], 'into (a mountain)' [KJV], 'into (the hills)' [NICNT], 'to' [LN (84.16), WBC], 'toward, in the direction of' [LN (84.16)], not explicit [NIGTC; GW, NET, NRSV, REB, TEV]. This preposition describes a position on the surface of an area [LN (83.47)] or extension toward a special goal [LN (84.16)].
  d. ὄρος (LN 1.46) (BAGD p. 582): 'mountain' [BAGD, BECNT, BNTC, CC, LN, NIGTC, NTC, PNTC, WBC; ESV, GW, KJV, NASB, NCV, NET, NRSV, REB], 'side of a mountain' [CEV], 'mountainside' [NIV, NLT], 'hill' [BAGD, NICNT; TEV]. This noun denotes a relatively high elevation of land, and it contrasts with βουνός 'hill', which is by comparison somewhat lower [LN].
QUESTION—Where did this sermon occur?
  The word ὄρος can mean either a mountain or a hill [TH]. The majority of the translations state that Jesus went up on a 'mountain'. However, since this concerns the hill country on the northwest side of the Lake of Galilee where the hills rise steeply from the lake, the phase τὸ ὄρος need not denote a specific mountain. It is a general term for the hill country and we are to understand that that Jesus went into the hills, that is, he was in the hill country [NICNT]. Jesus went up into the hills, not literally on a mountain,

98   MATTHEW 5:1

where he gave the discourse on a level plateau [EBC, NAC]. It was on a level place somewhere between heights or along a mountainside [Lns].

and he having-sat-down his disciples came-to[a] **him;**
LEXICON—a. aorist act. indic. of προσέρχομαι (LN 15.77) (BAGD 1. p. 713): 'to come to' [BAGD, BECNT, BNTC, NICNT, NIGTC, NTC, PNTC, WBC; ESV, GW, KJV, NASB, NCV, NET, NIV, NRSV], 'to approach' [BAGD, CC, LN], 'to come near to' [LN], 'to gather around/round' [CEV, NLT, REB, TEV]. This verb means to move toward a reference point, with a possible implication in certain contexts of a reciprocal relationship between the person approaching and the one who is approached [LN].
QUESTION—Why did he sit to teach?
   Sitting was the normal posture for teaching [BNTC, EBC, NAC, NIBC, NICNT, NIGTC, NTC, TH, TRT, WBC]. This was the normal way of teaching in the synagogues and schools [EBC].

DISCOURSE UNIT—5:2–12 [CEV, ESV, TEV]. The topic is true happiness [TEV], the beatitudes [ESV], blessings [CEV].

5:2 and/then[a] **opening**[b] **his mouth he-was-teaching them saying,**
LEXICON—a. καί (LN 89.87): 'and' [BNTC, CC, LN, NTC, PNTC, WBC; CEV, ESV, KJV, NCV, NIV, NLT, TEV], 'then' [NIGTC; NET, NRSV], 'and then' [LN], not explicit [BECNT, NICNT; GW, NASB, REB]. This conjunction marks a sequence of closely related events [LN].
   b. aorist act. participle of ἀνοίγω (LN 33.29) (BAGD 1.e.α. p. 71): 'to open' [BAGD, BECNT, BNTC, CC, NICNT, NIGTC, NTC, PNTC, WBC; ESV, KJV, NASB], 'to open (one's mouth to speak)' [BAGD], 'to address, to start speaking, to begin to speak, to utter' [LN], not explicit [CEV, GW, NCV, NET, NIV, NLT, NRSV, REB, TEV]. This verb is translated as implying the beginning of a speech process [BECNT, CC, NIGTC, NTC, WBC; GW, NASB, NCV, NET, NIV, NLT, NRSV, REB, TEV]: he began to teach. The imperfect tense of 'teach' is also inceptive, indicating the beginning of an ongoing action [CC, EBC]. This Semitic idiom means to begin to speak in a somewhat formal and systematic manner [LN].
QUESTION—Who was the audience for this sermon?
   This sermon was primarily intended for his disciples, though the crowds are there in the background as well [BECNT, CC, Lns, My, NICNT, PNTC, TH, WBC]. The disciples were in the inner circle around Jesus, and the crowds were around the periphery, overhearing what he said [ICC]. The crowds were on the periphery of the conversation, and had varying levels of interest and understanding [BECNT]. The crowds heard what Jesus was saying to his disciples [BNTC, CC, NAC, TH], and were impressed with the authority with which he spoke (7:29) [CC, WBC]. The audience was more than just the twelve [EBC, TH, TRT], who have not been mentioned yet, but was less

than the crowds mentioned in the previous verse. However, more and more people did crowd around to listen in [EBC]. The immediate circle was the twelve disciples, behind whom were other disciples [Lns, NIBC, NTC], and then encircled also by the crowds who were listening [Lns, NTC]. It was addressed to the community of disciples who had already repented and were seeking further instruction, and who were committed to him personally [NAC]. The crowds were also part of the intended audience, although the disciples were the closest to Jesus and were the primary intended audience [NIGTC].

QUESTION—Was this the same sermon as the Sermon on the Plain in Luke 6:17–49?

1. It is the same sermon [EBC, ICC, Lns, NAC, NIBC, NTC, WBC]. Jesus gave the discourse on a level plateau in the hill country, not literally on a mountain [EBC, NAC], and since his teaching could have been for quite a long time, even up to several days, repetition of subject matter and condensing of the discourse by the evangelists can account for the differences between the two accounts in Matthew and Luke [EBC]. This is most likely a condensed version of a much larger body of material given at the time [NAC].

2. It is not the same sermon, although Jesus used similar material on many occasions [PNTC].

QUESTION—What is the purpose of this discourse?

It provides ethical guidelines for how to live in God's kingdom, which is the fulfillment of the scriptural prophecies of the coming messianic reign, and it does so in a way that anticipates the love commandments and grace [EBC]. It describes how the true Christian disciple lives [BNTC]. Jesus is giving the definitive interpretation and full meaning of God's commandments, and describes the ethics of the kingdom, which applies to Christians even now, but will only be fully realized in the coming age; it is also based fundamentally on grace, as is shown by the fact that it begins with the blessings before moving on to exhortation [WBC]. It teaches ethical principles of how Jesus' followers are to live in God's reign, and also how they should understand Jesus' teaching relative to the law of Moses and the Hebrew scriptures [BECNT]. It describes the moral conditions of participating in the coming messianic kingdom [My]. It is an ethical ideal that is applicable to Christians in every age, but which will only be fully realized when Christ returns; that the beatitudes are given first shows that God blesses before making demands [NAC, WBC]. Jesus describes the character and blessedness of the citizens of the kingdom of God, their relation to the world, and the righteousness required by God of those who live in his kingdom; he also concludes with an exhortation to enter the kingdom [NTC].

DISCOURSE UNIT—5:3–12 [ICC; NLT]. The topic is the beatitudes.

5:3 Blessed^a (are) the poor^b in-spirit,

LEXICON—a. μακάριος (LN 25.119) (BAGD 1.b. p. 486): 'blessed' [BAGD, BECNT, BNTC, CC, NTC, PNTC; ESV, GW, KJV, NASB, NET, NIV, NRSV, REB], 'happy' [BAGD, LN, NICNT, WBC; NCV, TEV], 'fortunate' [BAGD], 'good fortune now to' [NIGTC]. The phrase 'blessed are…' is translated 'God blesses those/those people who…' [CEV, NLT]. This adjective describes what pertains to being happy, with the implication of enjoying favorable circumstances [LN]. It describes a privileged recipient of divine favor [BAGD]. This word occurs first in the sentence for emphasis [CC, NTC].

b. πτωχός (LN **88.57**) (BAGD 1.c. p. 728): 'poor' [BAGD], 'humble' [LN]. The phrase οἱ πτωχοὶ τῷ πνεύματι 'the poor in spirit' [BECNT, BNTC, CC, NIGTC, NTC, PNTC; ESV, KJV, NASB, NET, NIV, NRSV, REB] is also translated 'those who are poor in spirit' [NICNT], 'those who are humble before God' [**LN**], 'the oppressed' [WBC], 'those people who depend only on him' [CEV], 'those who recognize they are spiritually helpless' [GW], 'those people who know they have great spiritual needs' [NCV], 'those who know they are spiritually poor' [TEV], 'those who are poor and realize their need for him' [NLT]. This phrase is an idiom that describes one who is humble with regard to his own capacities. In this only NT occurrence this humility is in relationship to God [LN].

QUESTION—What does μακάριος 'blessed' mean?

Some section headings use the word 'Beatitudes', a transliteration of the Latin word meaning 'blessings' [BECNT, EBC].

1. It refers objectively to a state of blessedness wherein God graciously grants his favor [BECNT, PNTC, TRT] and his approval [BNTC, EBC]. It has a strong connotation of salvation, both present and future [CC]. It is similar to a congratulation given for a happy or enviable condition or situation [NAC, NICNT, NIGTC], one which others would want to share or experience [NAC, NICNT]. Instead of being wretched, such people are well-off and fortunate [NTC]. They are to be considered fortunate and blessed, a condition that produces joy in them [NTC]. The beatitudes describe and commend the good life [NICNT]. It describes well-being and God's approval [BNTC]. 'Fortunate' and 'happy' bring out the joy that is conveyed by Jesus' word, but there is more to blessedness than happiness. This is the blessing of membership in the kingdom which is available only to those who are poor *in spirit* [PNTC].
2. It is a subjective state of happiness [NIBC, WBC; NCV, TEV]. It describes the deep inner joy of those who are beginning to experience the fulfillment of God's promises of salvation; they are deeply or supremely happy [WBC].
3. It describes those who are especially well off or fortunate, and who are happy as a result [TH].

QUESTION—What does the phrase πτωχός τῷ πνεύματι 'poor in spirit' mean?

It describes people who have become convinced of their spiritual poverty and utter helplessness [Lns, My, NTC], those who have a contrite spirit [NTC]. The poverty is that of the internal disposition as opposed to an external material condition [BECNT]. This poverty of spirit is an acknowledgement of one's entire dependence on God, both physically and spiritually [BECNT, NIBC, TH]. They are spiritually destitute, with no resources of their own [CC, PNTC]. The poor in spirit know they are spiritually powerless and bankrupt; they feel their spiritual need, and have confidence in God alone [NAC]. It is the opposite of arrogant self-confidence and self-seeking; they are repentant and readily accept God's rule over them [NICNT]. It describes the frame of mind of those who are in fact materially poor, whose only hope is in God [TH, WBC]. It describes people who have experienced social distress and material need such that they acknowledge their spiritual bankruptcy and unworthiness, and have placed their confidence completely in God [EBC].

for theirs is the kingdom of-the heavens.

QUESTION—Is this promise of the kingdom primarily for the future, or the present?

It is not entirely about the future; the blessings already begin in this life, though the full consummation will occur in the future [BECNT, BNTC, EBC, NIBC, NICNT, WBC]. The blessing of membership in the kingdom is available now and the riches of the kingdom now *belong* to them in the fullest measure, while the full blessings in all the other beatitudes are for the future [PNTC]. It is theirs in principle even now [NTC]. These are eschatological blessings, but they are already being experienced by Jesus' disciples in the present era [CC]. They have his grace now, but the glory of the kingdom is not yet revealed [NTC]. It is for the future reversal of all things at the last judgment, though the kingdom is already present in some sense [ICC]. The blessings are in the future [My].

QUESTION—Is there any significance in the word order αὐτῶν ἐστιν 'theirs is'?

The fronting of the word αὐτῶν 'theirs' is emphatic [CC, My, NICNT, PNTC, TRT, WBC], meaning 'theirs alone' [Lns, My, NTC, PNTC], that it *belongs* to them [CC], that it belongs to people like this [NIGTC].

5:4 Blessed (are) those mourning,[a]

LEXICON—a. pres. act. participle of πενθέω (LN **25.142**) (BAGD 1. p. 642): 'to mourn' [BECNT, BNTC, CC, NICNT, NIGTC; all versions except CEV, NCV, REB], 'to grieve' [BAGD, **LN**, WBC; CEV], 'to be sad' [BAGD, LN; NCV], 'to be sorrowful' [REB], 'to weep for' [LN]. The phrase 'those mourning' is translated 'the mourners' [NTC, PNTC]. This verb means to experience sadness or grief as the result of depressing circumstances or the condition of persons; the reference here is not to grieving or mourning for the dead but rather sadness and grief because of wickedness and oppression [LN].

QUESTION—What is the nature of their mourning?

They mourn over sin and its consequences, whether their own sin or the sins of others [Lns, NIBC, NTC]. They mourn over sin as well as over afflictions they experience because of their loyalty to the kingdom, but the focus is more on the afflictions [BECNT]. They mourn over sin and evil, whether in themselves, in the world around them, [CC, EBC, PNTC], or in the church [CC]. They grieve over personal sin, over social evil, and over oppression [NAC]. They mourn over the apparent slowness of God's justice [WBC]. Their situation is intolerable and wretched [NICNT]. They mourn because the righteous suffer and the wicked prevail [ICC]. They mourn over all life's difficulties, but turn in faith to God [BNTC]. They mourn over suffering and distress in general [My]. They mourn over all the kinds of things that cause suffering, such as persecution, death, sin, or illness [TRT]. No reason for the mourning is given, so none should be stated [TH].

for they will-be-comforted.[a]

LEXICON—a. fut. pass. indic. of παρακαλέω (LN 25.150) (BAGD 4. p. 617): 'to be comforted' [BAGD, BAGD, BECNT, BNTC, CC, NICNT, NIGTC, NTC, PNTC, WBC; ESV, GW, KJV, NASB, NET, NIV, NLT, NRSV], 'to be encouraged' [BAGD, LN], 'to be consoled' [LN]. The phrase 'they will be comforted is translated 'they will find comfort' [CEV], 'they will find consolation' [REB], 'God will comfort them' [NCV, TEV]. This verb means to cause someone to be encouraged or consoled, either by verbal or non-verbal means [LN].

QUESTION—In what way will they be comforted?

They will no longer be afflicted by sinners [BECNT]. They will be comforted when sin and evil end at the dawn of the new age [CC]. In the end they will experience God's ultimate triumph over evil [PNTC]. They will be comforted by the coming of the eschatological messianic blessings described in Isa. 61:1–3 [EBC]. They are happy because they know the kingdom has already arrived and their salvation is drawing near [WBC]. They have the comfort that comes in this life from knowing the forgiveness of sin and the blessing of God, but also the comfort that will be theirs in eternity [NTC]. They will be delivered from all evil [Lns]. God will restore happiness to them [TH].

QUESTION—Who is the agent of the passive verbs in the beatitudes?

These are 'divine passives,' meaning that God is the agent of the actions [CC, ICC, Lns, NICNT, NTC, PNTC, TH, TRT, WBC]. God will comfort them [NAC, NIGTC; NCV, TEV].

QUESTION—Is there any significance in the shift in tense between the two clauses from present to future?

The mourning over sin and evil is a very real and present experience, whereas the comfort will come on the last day, though believers now live in the light of the comfort they will experience [CC]. Those who mourn now will receive comfort in the future [BECNT, Lns], though the comfort begins even now [Lns]. They will be comforted at the return of Christ [ICC], in the messianic kingdom [My]. The full blessing of all these beatitudes is future, but that does not exclude blessing right now [NAC, NICNT, PNTC].

5:5 **Blessed (are) the meek,**[a]

LEXICON—a. πραΰς (LN 88.60) (BAGD p. 699): 'meek' [BAGD, BNTC, LN, NICNT, NTC, PNTC; KJV, NET, NIV, NRSV], 'gentle' [BAGD, BECNT, LN; GW, NASB, REB], 'lowly' [CC, NIGTC], 'mild' [LN], 'those who have been humbled' [WBC], 'humble' [BAGD; CEV, NCV, NLT, TEV], 'considerate, unassuming' [BAGD]. This adjective describes what is gentle and mild [LN].

QUESTION—What is the nature and quality of this meekness?

This describes people who are humble and oppressed, and have no recourse other than God [WBC]. The meek are characterized by a humility that depends on God and not on one's own efforts to relieve their oppression by others [BECNT]. They are the humble who refuse to assert their own rights and do not domineer over others [PNTC]. They are humble and completely dependent on God, without complaint or bitterness [BNTC]. It describes a gentleness and self-control that is without malice [EBC], a humility and gentleness without aggression [NAC. NIBC]. They are mild and patient when wronged or abused [Lns]. They suffer without becoming bitter or vengeful, relying on God's help [My]. These meek people are the same lowly people who are described as being poor in spirit in 5:3, but now they are viewed from a different perspective [NTC, TH]. Instead of trying to overpower others, they rest their entire hope on God and are gentle, humble, and non-aggressive [TH]. They trust in God and suffer what others do to them without being resentful or vindictive [NTC].

for they will-inherit[a] **the earth.**[b]

LEXICON—a. fut. act. indic. of κληρονομέω (LN 57.138) (BAGD 2. p. 434): 'to inherit' [BECNT, BNTC, CC, LN, NICNT, NIGTC, NTC, PNTC, WBC; GW, KJV, NASB, NET, NIV, NLT, NRSV], 'to have for a possession' [REB], 'to receive' [TEV], 'to acquire, to obtain, to come into possession of something' [BAGD]. The phrase 'they will inherit the earth' is translated 'the earth will belong to them' [CEV, NCV]. This verb means to receive a possession or benefit as a gift from someone who has died, generally a parent [LN].

b. γῆ (LN 1.39) (BAGD 4. p. 157): 'earth' [LN; all translations except NIGTC; NLT, TEV], 'whole earth' [NLT], 'land' [BAGD, NIGTC], 'world' [LN], 'what God has promised' [TEV]. This noun denotes the surface of the earth as the dwelling place of mankind, in contrast with the heavens above and the world below [LN].

QUESTION—In what sense will they inherit the earth?

For the disciples 'inheriting the earth' will have its fulfillment in the coming kingdom of heaven [NICNT]. Those who are powerless now will be blessed when everything is reversed in the new creation order [CC]. Their place in the coming messianic kingdom will be certain [PNTC]. They will inherit God's kingdom and enjoy the blessings of fellowship with him [BNTC]. In the time of messianic fulfillment they will inherit the regenerated earth [WBC]. They will receive the renewed heavens and earth at Christ's return, but even now they are more fully able to enjoy whatever earthly things they possess and use, instead of being owned by their possessions [NTC]. They will experience the consummation of God's kingdom at the renewal of all things [EBC]. They will be exalted in the coming kingdom of God [ICC]. They experience blessings even now in that the little that the poor have is better than the wealth of the wicked [Lns]. They will one day experience the blessings of heaven as well as the happiness of a redeemed earth [TH]. Many of the poor in Israel did not own land, and were subject to oppression by those who did; this promise looks forward to the time when they will rule with Christ in a re-created earth and heavens [NAC]. This reflects Psalm 37:9, 11[BECNT, CC, EBC, ICC, Lns, My, NAC, NICNT, NIGTC, NTC, TH, WBC].

5:6 **Blessed (are) those hungering[a] and thirsting[b] (for) righteousness,[c]**

LEXICON—a. pres. act. participle of πεινάω (LN 25.17) (BAGD 2. p. 640): 'to hunger' [BECNT, BNTC, CC, NIGTC, NTC, PNTC, WBC; ESV, GW, KJV, NASB, NET, NIV, NLT, NRSV, REB], 'to be hungry' [NICNT], 'to hunger for something, to desire something strongly' [BAGD]. The phrase 'hungering and thirsting' is conflated into one expression and translated 'to desire intensely' [**LN**], 'to desire strongly' [LN]. The phrase 'hungering and thirsting for righteousness' is translated 'who want to obey him more than to eat or drink' [CEV], 'who want to do right more than anything else' [NCV], 'whose greatest desire is to do what God requires' [TEV]. This verb is a figurative extension of πεινάω 'to hunger' [LN 23.39], and means to have a strong desire to attain some goal, with the implication of an existing lack [LN]. In Matthew 5:6 the two terms πεινάω and διψάω mutually reinforce the meaning of great desire [LN].

b. pres. act. participle of διψάω (LN **25.17**) (BAGD 3. p. 200): 'to thirst' [BAGD; all translations except LN. NICNT; CEV, NCV, TEV], 'to be thirsty' [NICNT], 'to long for' [BAGD], 'to have a strong desire' [BAGD], not explicit [CEV, NCV, TEV]. The phrase 'hungering and thirsting' is conflated into one expression and translated 'to desire intensely' [**LN**], 'to desire strongly' [LN]. This verb is a figurative extension of διψάω 'to thirst' and means to have a strong desire to attain some goal, with the implication of an existing lack [LN]. In Matthew 5:6 the two terms διψάω and πεινάω mutually reinforce the meaning of great desire [LN].

c. δικαιοσύνη (LN 88.13) (BAGD 4. p. 197): 'righteousness' [BAGD, BECNT, BNTC, CC, LN, NICNT, NIGTC, NTC, PNTC; ESV, KJV, NASB, NET, NIV, NRSV], 'uprightness' [BAGD], 'justice' [WBC; NLT], 'God's approval' [GW], 'doing what is right' [LN]. The phrase 'for righteousness' is translated as a verb phrase: 'to do right' [NCV], 'to obey him' [CEV], 'to see right prevail' [REB], 'to do what God requires' [TEV]. This noun denotes the act of doing what God requires [LN].

QUESTION—What is meant by 'hungering and thirsting for righteousness'?

It describes people who earnestly desire to live a righteous life as God wants them to live [EBC, ICC, NIBC, NICN, TH]. They desire to conform to God's will in actions, thought, speech, and worship [BNTC]. They want to live righteously, free from guilt [My]. They strongly desire to have a right standing with God and do what is right, something which must be desired in order to be possessed, but which ultimately can only come as a gift of God [PNTC]. They desire to see God's justice and standards applied in all aspects of life [NAC]. Their desire for right behavior before God includes social justice as well as personal piety [BECNT]. It is an intense desire to see a just social order, as lived out in the presence of God [NIGTC]. They long for the day when God's justice will prevail. 'Righteousness' is primarily social justice, although personal righteousness would also necessarily be involved [WBC]. They have a deep desire for personal righteousness as well as for justice in society, a desire that will ultimately be fulfilled at the consummation of the kingdom [EBC]. A different view is that their desire is to be declared righteous in God's sight [Lns]. Conformity to God's will in one's life, which can ultimately only come by imputation of the merits of Christ, satisfies the deepest spiritual need [NTC].

for they-will-be-satisfied.[a]

LEXICON—a. fut. pass. indic. of χορτάζομαι (LN 25.82) (BAGD 2.b. p. 884): 'to be satisfied' [BAGD, BECNT, CC, **LN**, NICNT, NIGTC, WBC; ESV, GW, NASB, NET, NLT, REB], 'to be fully satisfied' [NTC], 'to be filled' [BNTC, PNTC; KJV, NIV, NRSV], 'to be given what one wants' [CEV]. The passive verb phrase 'they will be satisfied' is translated as active: 'God will fully satisfy them' [NCV], 'God will satisfy them fully' [TEV]. This verb means to be satisfied or content with some object or state [LN].

5:7 Blessed (are) the merciful,[a]

LEXICON—a. ἐλεήμων (LN **88.77**) (BAGD p. 250): 'merciful' [BAGD, LN], 'sympathetic' [BAGD]. The phrase 'the merciful' [BAGD, BECNT, BNTC, CC, **LN**, NIGTC, NTC, PNTC; ESV, KJV, NASB, NET, NIV, NLT, NRSV] is also translated 'those people who are merciful' [CEV], 'those who show mercy' [NICNT, WBC; GW, REB], 'those who show mercy to others' [NCV], 'those who are merciful to others' [TEV]. This adjective describes showing mercy [LN].

QUESTION—How is this mercy to be characterized?
  It is forgiving the guilty as well as having compassion on those who suffer or are in need [CC, EBC, NAC]. It includes generosity [NAC, NICNT], kindness [TRT], and focuses on action [WBC], combining pity with action [BECNT]. It is intentional kindness [NIBC]. It is to be gentle and forgiving, and quick to meet the needs of those who suffer [BNTC]. The merciful are kind and forgiving [TH]. It is to be generous, forgiving, and kind to those in serious need, identifying with them emotionally and allowing the other to make a fresh start [NIGTC]. It is characterized by forgiveness of sinners and love for those in misery, and it is expressed in action [NTC]. It also involves being willing not to take offense and being able to see things from the perspective of others [NICNT]. The merciful seek to relieve, cure, and help those experiencing pain, misery, and distress [Lns].

for they will-be-shown-mercy.[a]
LEXICON—a. fut. pass. indic. of ἐλεέω (LN 88.76) (BAGD p. 249): 'to be shown mercy' [BAGD, CC, LN, WBC; NET, NIV, NLT], 'to receive mercy' [BECNT, BNTC; ESV, NASB, NRSV], 'to obtain mercy' [KJV], 'to be treated with mercy' [CEV], 'to be treated mercifully' [GW]. The phrase αὐτοὶ ἐλεηθήσονται 'they will be shown mercy' is translated 'to them mercy will be shown' [NICNT, PNTC; similarly REB], 'they shall have mercy shown to them' [NTC], 'God will show mercy to them' [NCV], 'God will be merciful to them' [TEV]. This verb means to show kindness or concern for someone in serious need [LN].

5:8 **Blessed (are) the pure**[a] **in-heart,**[b]
LEXICON—a. καθαρός (LN 53.29) (BAGD 3. p. 388): 'pure' [BAGD, LN; all translations], 'free from sin' [BAGD]. This adjective describes that which pertains to being ritually clean or pure [LN].
  b. καρδία (LN 26.3) (BAGD 1.b.δ. p. 404): 'heart' [BAGD, LN; all translations except GW, NCV], 'thoughts' [GW], 'thinking' [NCV]. This noun is a figurative extension of meaning of καρδία 'heart' and denotes the causative source of a person's psychological life in its various aspects, especially his thoughts [LN].
QUESTION—What is purity of heart?
  It is an internal integrity that is expressed in behavior [BECNT]. It consists of worshipping only God [CC]. It is undivided devotion of heart along with inner moral purity [EBC], a moral uprightness as opposed to an outward ritual purity, a life-style of pleasing God, a single-minded loyalty to God that arises from inner cleansing [NAC]. Those who truly desire to please God will go beyond mere ritual purity [NICNT]. It is integrity of motive as opposed to deviousness [NIGTC], a moral blamelessness [My]. It is to be single-minded, without ulterior motives [NIBC]. It is to have a single-minded loyalty to God and his will [BNTC, TH, TRT]. It is to will God's will with all one's being, with consistency between outward behavior and inward thought [ICC]. It is an openness and honesty with no hidden motives

or self interest [Lns]. There is a reference here to Psalm 24 [BECNT, CC, EBC, ICC, Lns, NAC, NICNT, NIGTC, NTC, PNTC, TH, WBC].

QUESTION—What does the term καρδία 'heart' describe?

It is the inner self as opposed to outward behavior [BECNT]. It is the central, inner state, including volition, emotion, and thinking [PNTC, TRT]. It is the true self at the deepest level, the seat of emotion, thought, and volition [ICC]. It is the inner, moral self [NAC], the core of the inner life [My], the thoughts and motivations [NIGTC, WBC], the inner core from which actions spring [NIGTC], the innermost being that shapes the life [TH]. It also speaks of single-mindedness [EBC, WBC], an internal integrity [BECNT, NTC], an honesty and guilelessness [NTC]. The person of single-minded commitment to God's kingdom will be morally pure [EBC]. He will worship God in spirit and in truth [NTC].

for they will-see[a] God.

LEXICON—a. fut. mid. (deponent = act.) indic. of ὁράω (LN 24.1) (BAGD 1.a.γ. p. 578): 'to see' [BAGD, LN; all translations except NCV]. The phrase 'they will see God' is translated 'they will be with God' [NCV].

QUESTION—In what sense will they see God?

They will see him in the world to come [BECNT, My, NIBC, PNTC, TH], when they have a glorified body [My], although even in this life they have a knowledge of God that the impure can't know [PNTC]. God will reveal himself to them, and on the last day they will actually see him [CC]. They will eventually see him in the beatific vision of the age to come [EBC, ICC, Lns, NICNT, WBC], but even now they see him with the eyes of faith [EBC], and may have a profound experience of his presence and power [NIBC]. Their 'seeing' God in this age is but a foretaste of how they will see him in heaven [NICNT]. They will experience intimate fellowship with God [BNTC, NAC]. They have a perception of and delight in God's being and attributes even here on earth, but will do so much more in heaven [NTC].

5:9 Blessed (are) the peacemakers,[a]

LEXICON—a. εἰρηνοποιός (LN 40.5) (BAGD p. 228): 'peacemaker' [BAGD, BECNT, BNTC, CC, LN, NICNT, NIGTC, NTC, PNTC, WBC; ESV, KJV, NASB, NET, NIV, NRSV, REB], 'one who works for peace' [LN; NLT, TEV], 'those who work to bring peace' [NCV], 'those people who make peace' [CEV, GW]. This noun denotes a person who restores peace between people [LN]. This word occurs only here in the NT.

QUESTION—What does it mean to be a peacemaker?

It is to be active in reconciling people, seeking harmonious relationships among people and the ultimate welfare of the world [BECNT]. These are people who bring an end to quarrels and hostilities [PNTC]. These people seek harmony in place of strife or discord [NAC]. They preserve friendship and understanding, or try to restore it where it has been lost [BNTC]. They live peaceably and even love their enemies [WBC]. It refers to those who try to handle their own conflicts in peace-seeking ways, and focuses primarily on the socio-political realm [NIGTC]. It includes a disposition, but also the desire to make peace with one's own enemies as well as to help others do the same [NICNT]. They promote peace among people [NTC, TH], and strive to impart reconciliation with God to others [NTC]. They work to solve problems and reconcile relationships [NIBC]. They make peace by preaching the gospel as well as by reconciling people to one another [EBC]. It is to proclaim the gospel of the kingdom of God whereby people are reconciled to God [CC].

for they-will-be-called[a] sons[b] of-God.
LEXICON—a. fut. pass. indic. of καλέω (LN 33.131) (BAGD 1.a.δ. p. 399): 'to be called' [BAGD, LN; all translations except NCV, TEV]. This passive verb is expressed as active: 'God will call them' [NCV, TEV]. The passive of this verb closely approaches the meaning 'to be' [BAGD]. This verb means to use an attribution in speaking of a person [LN].
  b. υἱός (LN 9.4) (BAGD 1.c.γ. p. 834): 'son' [BAGD, BNTC, CC, LN, NIGTC, NTC, PNTC; ESV, NASB, NIV], 'child' [BECNT, NICNT, WBC; all versions except ESV, NASB, NIV]. This noun, when followed by the genitive of class or kind, denotes a person of that class or kind, as specified by the following genitive construction [LN].
QUESTION—What does it mean to be called υἱοὶ θεοῦ 'sons of God'?
It refers to those who bear a resemblance to God, who treat enemies well [BECNT]. Peacemaking is part of what it means to have membership in God's family, and is something to which all God's children should aspire [PNTC]. They reflect the character of their heavenly father [EBC]. They act as their heavenly father acts [NIBC]. They share his nature [BNTC]. God's children reflect the character of God, who is the ultimate peacemaker [NICNT]. Others will see that they are becoming conformed to God's image [NAC]. It means that God will acknowledge them as his covenant people [NIGTC]. They enter into the very sphere of the activity of God, their father [NTC]. They prove their relation to God by their peacemaking, and he will own them as his sons [Lns]. It means to have a share in the Messiah's future kingdom [My]. They will be called 'sons of God' at the fulfillment of all things [CC].

5:10 **Blessed (are) those having-been-persecuted[a] because-of[b] righteousness,[c] for theirs is the kingdom of-the heavens.**
LEXICON—a. perf. pass. participle of διώκω (LN **39.45**) (BAGD 2. p. 201): 'to be persecuted' [BAGD, LN; all translations except CEV, GW, 'to suffer persecution' [**LN**], 'to be treated badly' [CEV, GW]. This verb means to systematically organize a program to oppress and harass people [LN].
  b. ἕνεκεν (LN **89.31**) (BAGD p. 264): 'because of' [BAGD, BECNT, CC, **LN**, NICNT; NIV], 'because (they do)' [TEV], 'in the cause of' [REB], 'on account of' [BAGD, BNTC, LN], 'for the sake of' [NIGTC, NTC, PNTC, WBC; ESV, KJV, NASB, NRSV], 'for' [CEV, GW, NCV, NET,

NLT]. This preposition marks cause or reason, often with the implication of purpose in the sense of 'for the sake of' [LN].
c. δικαιοσύνη (LN 88.13) (BAGD 4. p. 197): 'righteousness' [BAGD, BECNT, BNTC, CC, LN, NICNT, NIGTC, NTC, PNTC, WBC; ESV, KJV, NASB, NET, NIV, NRSV], 'doing what God requires' [**LN**; TEV], 'doing what God approves of' [GW], 'doing what is right' [LN], 'doing right' [CEV, NLT], '(the cause of) right' [REB], 'doing good' [NCV]. This noun denotes the act of doing what God requires [LN].

QUESTION—What relationship is indicated by ἕνεκεν 'because of'?
It indicates that they are persecuted because of their affiliation with Jesus [BECNT]. The persecution comes as a result of righteous living [NAC], because they do what God requires [TH]. Their loyalty to God and his will in their lives is the cause of their mistreatment by others [WBC]. They suffer because what they were in their character was a rebuke to the world [Lns].

5:11 **Blessed are you(pl) when[a] they-revile[b] you(pl), and persecute[c] (you)**

LEXICON—a. ὅταν (LN 67.31) (BAGD 1.b. p. 588): 'when' [BAGD, BECNT, BNTC, LN, NICNT, NIGTC, PNTC; all versions except NCV], 'whenever' [BAGD, CC, LN, NTC, WBC], not explicit [NCV]. This conjunction describes an indefinite point or points of time, which may be roughly simultaneous to or overlap with another point of time [LN].
b. aorist act. subj. of ὀνειδίζω (LN 33.389) (BAGD 1. p. 570): 'to revile' [BAGD; ESV, KJV, NRSV], 'to reproach' [BAGD, BNTC, WBC], 'to insult' [BECNT, BNTC, LN, NICNT; CEV, GW, NASB, CEV, NET, NIV, TEV], 'to heap insults upon' [BAGD, NTC], 'to upbraid' [PNTC], 'to mock' [NLT]. The phrase ὅταν ὀνειδίσωσιν ὑμᾶς 'when they revile you' is translated 'when you suffer insults' [REB]. This verb means to speak disparagingly of a person in a manner which is not justified [LN].
c. διώκω (LN 39.45) (BAGD 2. p. 201): 'to persecute' [BAGD, LN; all translations except CEV, NCV, REB], 'to suffer persecution' [REB], 'to hurt (you)' [NCV], 'to harass' [LN], 'to mistreat' [CEV].

and say[a] all-kinds-of evil[b] against[c] you(pl) lying[d] because-of me.

TEXT—The word ψευδόμενοι 'lying' is included in GNT in brackets with a C rating to indicate that choosing it over a variant text was difficult.
BECNT, NICNT, WBC also include it in brackets. BNTC, NIGTC, PNTC, NTC; CEV, ESV, GW, KJV, NASB, NCV, NET, NIV, NLT, NRSV, REB, TEV place it in the text without brackets. It is not included in the text by CC. Whether or not the word is original, the concept is assumed as part of the sense in the sentence by all translations.
LEXICON—a. aorist act. subj. of λέγω (LN 33.69) (εἶπον–BAGD 1. p. 226): 'to say' [BAGD, BECNT, BNTC, LN, NTC, PNTC; GW, KJV, NASB, NCV, NET, NIV, NLT], 'to speak' [BAGD, LN, NIGTC, WBC], 'to tell' [LN; CEV, TEV], 'to utter' [ESV, NRSV], 'to make accusations' [NICNT]. The phrase 'say...evil against you' is translated 'when you

suffer calumnies' [REB]. This verb means to speak or talk, with apparent focus upon the content of what is said [LN].

b. πονηρός (LN **88.110**) (BAGD 1.b.β. or 2.c. p. 691): 'evil, wicked' [BAGD, LN], 'bad, base, vicious' [BAGD], 'immoral' [LN]. The phrase 'all kinds of evil' [**BAGD**; ESV, NASB, NIV, RSV] is translated 'all manner of evil' [KJV], 'all kinds of evil things' [**LN**; GW, NCV, NET], 'all sorts of evil things' [NLT], 'all kinds of evil lies' [CEV, TEV], 'calumnies of every kind' [REB], 'you have done wicked deeds' [**LN**]. This adjective describes that which pertains to being morally corrupt and evil [LN].

c. κατά with the genitive (LN **90.31**) (BAGD I.2.b.β. p. 405): 'against' [BAGD, BECNT, BNTC, CC, **LN**, NICNT, NIGTC, PNTC; ESV, KJV, NASB, NIV, NLT, NRSV, TEV], 'about' [NTC; CEV, GW, NCV, NET], 'concerning' [WBC], 'in opposition to, in conflict with' [LN], not explicit [REB]. This preposition marks opposition, with the possible implication of antagonism [LN].

d. pres. mid. or pass. (deponent = act.) participle of ψεύδομαι (LN 33.253) (BAGD 1. p. 891): 'to lie' [BAGD, LN, WBC; GW, NCV], 'to tell falsehoods' [NTC]. This verb is translated as an adverb: 'falsely' [BECNT, BNTC, NIGTC, PNTC; ESV, KJV, NASB, NET, NRSV]; as a noun: 'lie(s)' [CEV, TEV]. This verb means to communicate what is false, with the evident purpose of misleading [LN].

QUESTION—What does πονηρός 'evil' describe?
1. It describes their speech [PNTC, WBC; CEV, GW. NCV, NET, NLT, REB]: all the things they say against you are evil.
2. It describes what they accuse them of doing [LN, NICNT]: they say that the things you do are evil.

5:12 Rejoice[a] and be-glad[b],

LEXICON—a. pres. act. impera. of χαίρω (LN 25.125) (BAGD 1. p. 873): 'to rejoice' [BAGD, BECNT, BNTC, CC, LN, NIGTC, NTC, PNTC; ESV, GW, KJV, NASB, NCV, NET, NIV, NRSV], 'to be glad' [BAGD, LN, NICNT], 'to be joyful' [WBC], 'to be happy' [CEV, TEV], 'to be happy about it' [NLT], 'exult' [REB]. This verb means to enjoy a state of happiness and well-being [LN].

b. pres. mid. impera. of ἀγαλλιάω (LN 25.133) (BAGD p. 4): 'to be glad' [BECNT, NIGTC, WBC; all versions except CEV, KJV, NLT], 'to be very glad' [PNTC; NLT], 'to be exceeding glad' [KJV], 'to exult' [BAGD, BNTC, CC], 'to celebrate' [NICNT], 'to be filled with unrestrained gladness' [NTC], 'to be exited' [CEV], 'to be extremely joyful, to rejoice greatly' [LN], 'to be overjoyed' [BAGD, LN]. This verb means to experience a state of great joy and gladness, often involving verbal expression and appropriate body movement [LN].

for your(pl) reward[a] **(is) great**[b] **in the heavens;**[c]
- LEXICON—a. μισθός (LN **38.14**) (BAGD 2.a. p. 523): 'reward' [BAGD, LN; all translations], 'recompense' [LN].
- b. πολύς (LN 59.11) (BAGD I.1.b.α. p. 688): 'great' [BAGD, LN; all translations except REB], 'rich' [REB], 'much' [BAGD, LN], 'extensive' [LN]. This adjective describes a relatively large quantity [LN].
- c. οὐρανός (LN 1.11) (BAGD 2.d. p. 595): 'heaven' [BAGD, LN; all translations]. This noun denotes the supernatural dwelling place of God and other heavenly beings; there seems to be no semantic distinction in NT literature between the singular and plural forms [LN].

for in-the-same-way[a] **they-persecuted the prophets**[b] **before**[c] **you(pl).**
- LEXICON—a. οὕτως (LN 61.9): 'in the same way' [BECNT, NTC, WBC; NET, NIV, NLT, NRSV, REB], 'so' [BNTC, LN; ESV, KJV, NASB], 'thus' [LN], 'in this way' [CC, LN, PNTC], 'in these ways' [GW], 'this is how' [NIGTC; TEV], 'that was how' [NICNT], '(did) these same things' [CEV], '(did) the same evil things' [NCV]. This adverb is used with reference to that which precedes [LN].
- b. προφήτης (LN 53.79) (BAGD 1. p. 723): 'prophet' [BAGD, LN; all translations]. This noun denotes one who proclaims inspired utterances on behalf of God [LN].
- c. πρό with genitive (LN 67.17) (BAGD 2. p. 702): 'before' [BAGD, LN]. The prepositional phrase πρὸ ὑμῶν 'before you' [NIGTC; NET, REB], is translated 'who were before you' [BECNT, CC, PNTC; ESV, GW, NASB, NIV, NRSV; similarly KJV], 'who preceded you' [BNTC], 'who came before you' [NICNT, WBC], 'who lived before you' [NCV, TEV], 'who lived before your time' [NTC], 'who lived long ago' [CEV], 'ancient (prophets)' [NLT]. This preposition describes a point of time prior to another point of time [LN].

DISCOURSE UNIT—5:13–20 [NASB]. The topic is the disciples and the world.

DISCOURSE UNIT—5:13–16 [ICC; CEV, ESV, GW, NCV, NET, NIV, NLT, NRSV, TEV]. The topic is a summary statement of the task of God's people [ICC], God's people make a difference in the world [GW], you are like salt and light [NCV], salt and light [CEV, ESV, NET, NIV, NRSV, TEV], teaching about salt and light [NLT].

5:13 You(pl) are the salt[a] **of-the earth;**[b]
- LEXICON—a. ἅλας (LN **5.25**) (BAGD 2. p. 35): 'salt' [BAGD, **LN**, all translations].
- b. γῆ (LN 9.22) (BAGD 5.b. p. 157): 'earth' [BAGD; all translations except CEV, TEV], 'everyone on earth' [CEV], 'the whole human race' [TEV], 'people, all mankind' [LN], 'men, humankind' [BAGD]. This noun denotes all people who dwell on the earth [LN].

QUESTION—Is there any significance in the explicit use of the plural pronoun ὑμεῖς 'you'?
>It adds a note of emphasis, meaning '*you* are the ones who are the salt of the earth' [CC, EBC, ICC, NIBC, NIGTC, PNTC, WBC]. It is emphatic, but also restrictive: you, and you alone [ICC, Lns, NTC, PNTC, WBC].

QUESTION—In what way were Jesus' disciples like the salt of the earth?
>The genitive phrase 'of the earth' is objective, indicating that the salt is applied to the earth in order to affect it in some way. But it isn't referring to what happens when salt is put into the soil. It is a metaphor and 'the earth' refers to people [PNTC]. The disciples are to be 'like salt for the whole human race' [TEV]. Salt can have a variety of uses, and the disciples of Jesus ought to benefit the world in many ways [BECNT, CC, ICC, NIGTC, WBC]. Salt was a valuable necessity [TRT]. It was used to preserve food [TH]. It may be unwise to limit the metaphor to one element only, since salt had a variety of uses, but the important thing here is that salt was vitally important for everyday life [NIGTC, WBC]. Jesus is focusing on how salt preserves meat from decay and improves the flavor of food [EBC, ICC, NICNT, NTC, PNTC]. Believers are like a moral antiseptic or disinfectant for society [EBC, PNTC]. They preserve society from decay by opposing what is corrupt, and they also generally improve the state of things [PNTC]. They prevent or retard corruption and moral decay [Lns, My, NAC, NIBC]. They preserve human life and society and give tone to it [BNTC].

but[a] if the salt becomes-tasteless,[b]

LEXICON—a. δέ (LN 89.124): 'but' [BECNT, BNTC, CC, LN, NIGTC, NTC, PNTC, WBC; all versions except REB], 'and' [REB], not explicit [NICNT]. This conjunction marks contrast [LN].
- b. aorist pass. subj. of μωραίνομαι (LN **79.44**) (BAGD 2. p. 531): 'to become tasteless' [BAGD, BNTC, CC, LN, NICNT, NTC; NASB, REB], 'to lose (its) saltiness' [BECNT; NIV, TEV], 'to lose (its) taste' [**LN**, PNTC, WBC; ESV, GW, NRSV], 'to lose (its) salty taste' [NCV], 'to lose (its) savor' [KJV], 'to lose (its) flavor' [NET, NLT], 'to become insipid' [BAGD, NIGTC], 'to no longer taste like salt' [CEV]. This verb means to become insipid or tasteless [BAGD, LN].

QUESTION—How could salt become tasteless?
>Pure salt cannot actually lose its taste, but the sodium chloride of impure salt can be leached out, and the remaining substance is accordingly tasteless [EBC, LN, NICNT, PNTC]. Salt in the ancient world could have other minerals in it that would cause it to lose its salty flavor [BECNT, NTC]. By mixing with other, impure substances it would be useless [ICC, NAC], especially as a preservative [NAC]. Salt was obtained by evaporation of minerals from the Dead Sea, and gypsum, which looked like salt, might be considered to be salt that had lost its flavor [WBC]. Since salt cannot lose its flavor, Jesus is giving a hypothetical illustration [TRT].

QUESTION—In what way might the disciples lose their 'saltiness'?
This is a metaphor about the loss of purity or spiritual decline [BECNT]. The world needs what only Jesus can do through his disciples, and if they were to turn away from his calling, they would be useless like tasteless salt [CC]. They would lose their saltiness if they were to conform to the world instead of the norms of the kingdom [EBC]. They would lose their saltiness by making peace with the world to avoid persecution, or by failing to be agents of change and redemption by not arresting corruption [NAC]. It refers to losing their distinctiveness as Christians [NIBC, NICNT, WBC], being assimilated by the world [NICNT], losing sight of their mission [NIBC], losing their Christian faith [BNTC, Lns]. Those who once had a knowledge of the truth and then harden their hearts against the Holy Spirit cannot be renewed to repentance [NTC]. Their spiritual knowledge, wisdom, and way of life might become diluted so that they become ineffective as disciples [TH].

in what-(way)[a] will-it-become-salty?[b]

LEXICON—a. τίνι (LN 92.14) (BAGD 1.b.α. p. 819): 'what?' [BAGD, LN]. The phrase ἐν τίνι 'in what way' is translated 'how (can/shall/will/is)' [BECNT, WBC; CEV, ESV, GW, NASB, NET, NIV, REB], 'with what' [BNTC, NIGTC, PNTC], 'by what means' [CC], 'wherewith' [KJV], 'what will (make it salty)' [NTC], 'can...?' [NLT, NRSV], not explicit [NICNT; NCV]. This rhetorical question is translated as a statement: 'there is no way to make it salty again' [TEV]. This pronoun is an interrogative reference to someone or something [LN].
  b. fut. pass. indic. of ἁλίζω (LN 5.28) (BAGD p. 37): 'to be made salty' [BAGD, **LN**], 'to be made salty again' [NTC; GW, NASB, NCV, NET, NIV], 'to become salty again' [WBC], 'to be salted' [CC, PNTC; KJV], 'to be re-salted' [NIGTC], 'to be seasoned' [BNTC], 'to make salty again' [NLT, TEV], 'flavor to be restored' [BECNT, LN], 'saltiness to be restored' [ESV, NRSV, REB]. The phrase ἐν τίνι ἁλισθήσεται; 'in what way will it become salty?' is translated 'what else is there to salt it with?' [NICNT], 'how can it make food salty?' [CEV].

QUESTION—What is it that must be made salty?
  1. He is asking how the salt itself would be made salty again [BECNT, EBC, NICNT, NIGTC, NTC, PNTC, TH, WBC].
  2. He is asking how the earth would be made salty if believers do not 'salt' it [CC].

It-is-good[a] for nothing any-longer except[b] (for) being-thrown[c] out[d]

LEXICON—a. pres. act. indic. of ἰσχύω (LN 74.9) (BAGD 2.a. p. 383): 'to be strong enough, to be able, to have the strength to' [LN]. The phrase εἰς οὐδὲν ἰσχύει 'it is good for nothing' [BAGD, CC, NTC, PNTC; KJV, NCV, REB] is also translated 'it is no longer good for anything' [BECNT, BNTC; ESV, GW, NASB, NET, NIV, NRSV], 'it is no good for anything anymore' [NICNT], 'it is worth nothing anymore' [WBC], 'it is

worthless' [TEV], 'it is of no further use' [NIGTC]. This whole clause is translated 'all it is good for is to be thrown out' [CEV], 'it will be thrown out...as worthless' [NLT]. This verb means to be strong enough for some purpose [LN].
  b. εἰ μή (LN 89.131) (BAGD V.8.a. p. 220): 'except' [BAGD, BECNT, CC, NICNT, WBC; ESV, GW, NASB, NCV, NET, NIV], 'but' [BNTC, LN, NTC, PNTC; KJV, NRSV, REB], 'it can only' [NIGTC], 'except that, however, instead, but only' [LN], 'so (it is thrown out)' [TEV], not explicit [CEV, NLT]. This phrase marks contrast by designating an exception [LN].
  c. aorist pass. participle of βάλλω (LN 15.215) (BAGD 1.b. p. 130): 'to be thrown' [BAGD, LN; all translations except KJV], 'to be cast' [KJV].
  d. ἔξω (LN 84.27) (BAGD 1.b. p. 279): 'out' [BAGD, LN, all translations except NTC, REB], 'away' [LN, NTC; REB]. This preposition marks extension to a goal which is outside a presumed area [LN].

and to-be-trampled-under-foot[a] by people.
LEXICON—a. pres. pass. infin. of καταπατέω (LN 19.52) (BAGD 1.a. p. 415): 'to be trampled underfoot/the feet' [BECNT, CC, NICNT, NIGTC, NTC; ESV, NASB, NLT, NRSV], 'to be trampled on/upon' [BAGD, LN, WBC; GW, NET], 'to be trampled' [NIV], 'to be trodden underfoot' [PNTC; KJV, REB], 'to be walked on' [BNTC; CEV, NCV]. This passive verb is translated as active: 'people trample on it' [TEV]. This verb means to step down forcibly upon, often with the implication of destruction or ruin [LN].

5:14 You(pl) are the light[a] of-the world.[b]
LEXICON—a. φῶς (LN 14.36, 88.1) (BAGD 3.b. p. 872): 'light' [BAGD, LN (14.36), all translations]. The phrase 'you are the light' is translated 'you are light' [REB], 'it is you who are the light' [NIGTC], 'you yourselves are the light' [WBC], 'you are that which gives light' [CC], 'you are the light that gives light' [NCV], 'you are like light' [CEV, TEV]. This noun can also denote positive moral qualities of the most general nature [LN (88.1)].
  b. κόσμος (LN 9.23) (BAGD 5.a. p. 446): 'world' [BAGD,], 'people of the world' [LN], 'mankind' [BAGD]. The phrase τοῦ κόσμου 'of the world' [BECNT, BNTC, NICNT, NIGTC, NTC, PNTC, WBC; ESV, KJV, NASB, NET, NIV, NLT, NRSV], is translated 'to the world' [CC; NCV], 'for the world' [GW], 'for all the world' [REB], 'for the whole world' [CEV, TEV]. This noun denotes people associated with a world system and estranged from God [LN].
QUESTION—What relationship is indicated by the genitive construction τὸ φῶς τοῦ κόσμου 'the light of the world'?
  It is objective, indicating that they are that which gives light to the world [CC, ICC, Lns, My, NICNT, NIGTC, NTC, PNTC, TH, WBC; CEV, GW,

NCV, REB, TEV]. They are to bring the light of Christ to a world that is in darkness [PNTC, WBC].

QUESTION—How is the image of light used here?

The disciples are to illuminate a world darkened by sin [EBC]. In the darkness people stumble and are lost, but with the light they can find their way [NICNT]. Believers primarily illumine the world around them by sharing the gospel [NTC]. They mediate God's truth to the world [My]. Some attempts to show the basis of comparing them with light are 'You show people the way to God as a light does,' 'People can see their way to God because of you who are like a light for them' [TH].

A-city[a] situated[b] on a hill[c] is- not -able to-be-hidden;[d]

LEXICON—a. πόλις (LN 1.89) (BAGD 1. p. 685): 'city' [BAGD, BECNT, BNTC, CC, LN, NIGTC, NTC, PNTC, WBC; all versions except REB], 'town' [NICNT; REB]. This noun denotes a population center of relative importance due to its size, economic significance, or political control over a surrounding area [LN].

b. pres. mid. or pass. (deponent = act.) participle of κεῖμαι (LN **85.3**) (BAGD 1.b. p. 426): 'to be situated' [BNTC, NIGTC, NTC], 'to be set' [CC, PNTC; ESV, KJV, NASB], 'to be positioned' [WBC], 'to be built' [BECNT, NICNT; CEV, NCV, NRSV, TEV], 'to be located' [GW, NET], 'to be' [BAGD, **LN**], 'to lie' [BAGD, LN], 'to stand' [REB], not explicit [NIV, NLT]. This verb means to be in a place, frequently in the sense of 'being contained in' or 'resting on' [LN].

c. ὄρος (LN 1.46) (BAGD p. 582): 'hill' [BAGD, BECNT, BNTC, NICNT, NIGTC, NTC, PNTC, WBC; all versions except NLT], 'hilltop'' [NLT], 'mountain' [BAGD, CC, LN]. This noun denotes a relatively high elevation of land [LN].

d. aorist pass. infin. of κρύπτω (LN 24.29) (BAGD 1.a. p. 454): 'to be hidden' [BAGD, BECNT, BNTC, CC, LN, NICNT, NIGTC, NTC, PNTC, WBC except BNTC, all versions except KJV, TEV], 'to be hid' [BNTC; KJV, TEV]. This verb means to cause something to be invisible with the intent of its not being found [LN].

QUESTION—What is the point of this comment about a city on a hill?

This metaphor is about visibility [BECNT, BNTC, CC, EBC, ICC, My, NICNT, NTC, WBC]. The lights of a city on a hillside are highly visible [EBC]. It is unthinkable that a city on a hill would not be seen [WBC]. It is closely related to the idea of being a light; God's illuminating presence in this world flows through Jesus' disciples to the world [BECNT]. Disciples are the light of the world that people cannot fail to see [TH]. Concealment is impossible for a city located on a hill, and since the disciples are the light of the world, they must not be indistinguishable from the people among whom they live [PNTC]. It is about prominence, drawing a contrast between those who build their town in an inconspicuous place so as to have a quiet and secluded life, and those who will have a wider influence such as a city on a hill would have [NIGTC]. It is about visibility and safety; because it is visible from far away, anyone can flee to it for refuge [Lns].

5:15 neither do-they-light^a a-lamp^b and put^c it under the basket,^d

LEXICON—a. pres. act. indic. of καίω (LN **14.65**) (BAGD 1.a. p. 466): 'to light' [BECNT, BNTC, **LN**, NICNT, NIGTC, NTC, PNTC, WBC; all versions except NCV, REB], 'to kindle' [CC, LN], 'to be lit' [REB], 'to ignite, to set ablaze, to start a fire' [LN], not explicit [NCV]. This verb means to cause the process of burning to begin [LN].
- b. λύχνος (LN 6.104) (BAGD 1. p. 483): 'lamp' [BAGD, LN; all translations except KJV, NCV], 'candle' [KJV], 'light' [NCV]. This noun denotes a light made by burning a wick saturated with oil contained in a relatively small vessel [LN].
- c. pres. act. indic. of τίθημι (LN 85.32) (BAGD I.1.a.β. p. 816): 'to put' [BAGD, BECNT, BNTC, CC, LN, NICNT, NIGTC, PNTC, WBC; all versions except NCV, REB], 'to be put' [REB], 'to place' [BAGD, LN, NTC], 'to hide' [NCV]. This verb means to put or place in a particular location [LN].
- d. μόδιος (LN 6.151) (BAGD p. 525): 'basket' [BECNT, LN; ESV, GW, NASB, NET, NLT], 'two-gallon basket' [CC], 'peck-measure' [BNTC, LN, NIGTC, NTC], 'bushel' [KJV], 'bushel basket' [NRSV], 'bowl' [NICNT; NCV, NIV, TEV], 'measuring bowl' [PNTC], 'measuring vessel' [WBC], 'clay pot' [CEV], 'meal tub' [REB]. This noun denotes a container for dry matter with a capacity of about eight liters (about two gallons) [LN]. In this verse the specific quantity of grain is not in mind [PNTC].

but-(rather)^a on the lampstand,^b and^c it-gives-light^d to-all those in the house.

LEXICON—a. ἀλλά (LN 89.125): 'but' [BNTC, LN, NTC, PNT; ESV, KJV, NASB, NET, NRSV, REB], 'instead' [LN; GW, NIV, NLT, TEV], 'on the contrary' [LN], 'rather' [BECNT, CC, NIGTC], not explicit [NICNT, WBC; CEV, NCV]. This conjunction marks emphatic contrast [LN].
- d. λυχνία (LN **6.105**) (BAGD p. 483): 'lampstand' [BAGD, BNTC, CC, **LN**, NICNT, NIGTC, NTC, PNTC, WBC; CEV, GW, NASB, NCV, NET, NRSV, REB, TEV], 'stand' [BECNT; ESV, NIV, NLT], 'candlestick' [KJV]. This noun denotes a stand designed to hold a single lamp or a series of lamps [LN].
- c. καί (LN 89.87, 89.50) (BAGD I.2.f. p. 392): 'and' [BECNT, BNTC, CC, LN (89.87), NIGTC, NTC, PNTC, WBC; ESV, KJV, NASB, NET, NIV, NRSV], 'and then' [BAGD, LN (89.87)], 'then' [GW, LN], 'so' [LN, NCV], 'and so' [BAGD], 'so that' [NICNT]. The phrase καὶ λάμπει 'and it gives light' is translated 'where it can give light' [CEV], 'where it gives light' [NLT, REB, TEV]. This conjunction may be used to mark closely related events [LN (89.87)], or to mark result, often implying the conclusion of a process of reasoning [LN (89.50)].

MATTHEW 5:15 117

d. pres. act. indic. of λάμπω (LN 14.37) (BAGD 1.a. p. 466): 'to give light' [BECNT, CC, LN, NICNT, NTC, PNTC; all versions except GW, NCV], 'to shine' [BAGD, BNTC, LN, WBC; GW, NCV], 'to shine out' [NIGTC], 'to bring light' [LN]. This verb means to shine or to produce light, as in the case of heavenly bodies, lightning, candles, torches, etc. [LN].

QUESTION—What is the meaning of this metaphor?
Just as the idea of unsalty salt or of unseen light is absurd, so also it is a contradiction in terms that a disciple should not live out his or her calling to have a transforming influence on the world [CC]. Without good works one cannot be considered Jesus' disciple [BECNT]. Just as it is the very nature of light to enlighten a dark room, it is the nature of disciples to bring light to the world, and it cannot be otherwise [PNTC].

5:16 In-the-same-way[a] let-shine[b] your(pl) light before[c] the people,[d]

LEXICON—a. οὕτως (LN 61.9) (BAGD 1.b. p. 597): 'in the same way' [NICNT, NIGTC; ESV, GW, NCV, NET, NIV, NLT, NRSV, TEV], 'in this way' [BECNT, CC, LN], 'just so' [BNTC], 'so' [LN, NTC, PNTC], 'thus' [BAGD, LN, WBC], 'in this manner' [BAGD, LN], 'in such a way' [NASB], not explicit [CEV, KJV]. The adverb οὕτως 'in the same way' is translated 'like the lamp' [REB]. This adverb is used with reference to that which precedes it [BAGD, LN].

b. aorist act. impera. of λάμπω (LN 14.37) (BAGD 2. p. 466): 'to let shine' [BECNT, BNTC, CC, NIGTC, NTC, PNTC, WBC; ESV, GW, KJV, NASB, NET, NIV, NLT, NRSV], 'to shine' [BAGD, LN; TEV], 'to make shine' [CEV], 'to shed light' [REB], 'to give light, to bring light' [LN]. The phrase λαμψάτω τὸ φῶς ὑμῶν 'let shine your light' is translated 'your light must shine' [NICNT], 'you should be a light...live (so that)' [NCV]. This verb means to shine or to produce light, as in the case of heavenly bodies, lightning, candles, torches, etc. [LN].

c. ἔμπροσθεν with genitive (LN 83.33) (BAGD 2.c. p. 257): 'before' [BAGD, BECNT, BNTC, CC, LN, NIGTC, NTC, PNTC, WBC; ESV, KJV, NASB, NET, NIV, NRSV, TEV], 'in the sight of' [BAGD], 'in front of' [LN, NICNT; GW], 'among' [REB], not explicit [CEV, NCV, NLT]. This preposition describes a position in front of an object, whether animate or inanimate, which is regarded as having a spatial orientation of front and back [LN].

d. ἄνθρωπος (in the plural) (LN 9.1) (BAGD 1.a.δ. p. 68): 'people' [BECNT, LN; GW, NET, TEV], 'other people' [NICNT; NCV], 'others' [NIGTC, WBC; CEV, ESV, NRSV], 'men' [BNTC, CC, NTC, PNTC; KJV, NASB, NIV], 'mankind' [LN], 'all' [NLT], 'your fellow' [REB]. This plural noun denotes human beings (normally adults) [LN].

so-that[a] they-might-see your(pl) good[b] deeds[c]

LEXICON—a. ὅπως (LN 89.59) (BAGD 2.a.α. p. 577): 'so that' [BECNT, LN,. NICNT, NIGTC, WBC; CEV, ESV, NCV, NET, NRSV, REB,

TEV], 'that' [BAGD, BNTC, NTC, PNTC; KJV, NASB, NIV], 'in order that' [BAGD, CC], 'then' [GW], 'in order to, for the purpose of' [LN]. The phrase ὅπως ἴδωσιν ὑμῶν τὰ καλὰ ἔργα 'so that they might see your good deeds' is translated 'let your good deeds (shine out) for all to see' [NLT]. This conjunction marks purpose for events and states (sometimes occurring in highly elliptical contexts) [LN].
b. καλός (LN 88.4) (BAGD 2.b. p. 400): 'good' [BAGD, LN; all translations], 'fine' [LN], 'praiseworthy' [BAGD, LN]. This adjective describes that which pertains to a positive moral quality, with the implication of being favorably valued [LN].
c. ἔργον (LN 42.11) (BAGD 1.c.β. p. 308): 'deed' [BAGD, LN, NIGTC, WBC, NET, NIV, NLT], 'work' [BECNT, BNTC, CC, NTC, PNTC; ESV, KJV, NASB, NRSV], 'act' [LN]. The phrase ὑμῶν τὰ καλὰ ἔργα 'your good deeds' is translated 'the good you do' [NICNT; CEV, GW, REB], 'the good things you do' [NCV, TEV]. This noun denotes that which is done, with possible focus on the energy or effort involved [LN].

and they-might-glorify^a your(pl) father the-(one) in the heavens.^b
LEXICON—a. aorist act. subj. of δοξάζω (LN 87.24) (BAGD 1. p. 204): 'to glorify' [CC, LN, NIGTC, NTC, WBC; KJV, NASB], 'to give glory to' [NICNT, PNTC; ESV, NRSV], 'to make gloriously great' [LN], 'to praise' [BAGD, BECNT, BNTC; CEV, GW, NCV, NIV, NLT, REB, TEV], 'to give honor' [NET], 'to honor, to magnify' [BAGD]. This verb means to cause someone to have glorious greatness [LN].
b. οὐρανός (LN 1.11) (BAGD 2.a. p. 594). 'heaven' [BAGD, LN]. See this word at 5:12. The phrase ἐν τοῖς οὐρανοῖς 'in the heavens' is translated 'in heaven' [all translations except NLT], 'heavenly' [NLT].
QUESTION—In what way would God be glorified?
People would praise God [BAGD, BECNT, BNTC, NAC, PNTC, TH; CEV, GW, NCV, NIV, NLT, REB, TEV]. This would occur when others are converted to faith and discipleship and when believers are edified [CC]. Kingdom norms exhibited in the lives of the disciples produces a witness of the kingdom [EBC]. God is glorified for having graciously fulfilled his promises [WBC]. People would be impressed by what God is doing [NIGTC], and would acknowledge that he is the author of their good works [My]. People will come to ascribe to God the reverence due him [NTC].
QUESTION—Who are the people who can call God their 'father'?
Jesus is speaking specifically about the disciples, not humanity in general [CC]. God is the father of those who are in relationship with him as members of his kingdom [WBC]. He is father to those who have become subjects of his kingdom through responding to Jesus' message [NICNT]. He is the father of believers [NTC].

DISCOURSE UNIT—5:17–20 [ICC; CEV, ESV, GW, NCV, NET, NIV, NLT, NRSV, TEV]. The topic is Jesus fulfils the law [ICC], Christ came to fulfill the law [ESV], Jesus fulfills the Old Testament scriptures [GW], the importance of the law [NCV], teaching about the Law [NLT, TEV], fulfillment of the law and prophets [NET], the fulfillment of the law [NIV], the law and the prophets [NRSV], the law of Moses [CEV].

5:17 Do- not -think[a] that I-came[b] to-abolish[c] the law[d] or the prophets;[e]

LEXICON—a. aorist act. subj. of νομίζω (LN 31.29) (BAGD 2. p. 541): 'to think' [BAGD, CC, LN, NTC, PNTC, WBC; all versions except CEV, REB], 'to suppose' [BAGD, BECNT, BNTC, LN, NICNT; CEV, REB], 'to make a judgment' [NIGTC], 'to presume, to assume, to imagine' [LN], 'to believe' [BAGD, LN]. The phrase μὴ νομίσητε ὅτι ἦλθον 'do not think that I have come (to)' is translated 'don't misunderstand why I have come' [NLT]. This verb means to regard something as presumably true, but without particular certainty [LN].

b. aorist act. indic. of ἔρχομαι (LN 15.81) (BAGD I.1.η. p. 311): 'to come' [BAGD, LN; all translations], 'to appear' [BAGD]. This verb means to move toward, or up to the reference point, of the viewpoint character or event [LN].

c. aorist act. infin. of καταλύω (LN 76.23) (BAGD 1.c. p. 414): 'to abolish' [BAGD, BECNT, BNTC, NICNT, PNTC; ESV, NASB, NET, NIV, NLT, NRSV, REB], 'to do away with' [BAGD, CC, LN; CEV, TEV], 'to annul' [NIGTC], 'to set aside' [NTC; GW], 'to destroy' [WBC; KJV, NCV], 'to make invalid' [BAGD, LN], 'to invalidate' [BAGD]. This verb means to completely invalidate something which has been in force [LN].

d. νόμος (LN 33.55) (BAGD 4.a. p. 543): 'the law' [BAGD, BECNT, BNTC, CC, LN, NICNT, NIGTC, NTC, PNTC, WBC; CEV, ESV, KJV, NASB, NET, NIV, NRSV, REB], 'the law of Moses' [NCV, NLT, TEV], 'Moses' teachings' [GW]. This noun denotes the first five books of the OT called the Torah (often better rendered as 'instruction') [LN]. The phrase 'the law *and* the prophets' represents the entire Hebrew Bible [BECNT, EBC, NAC, PNTC], and in the next verse just the phrase 'the law' will also refer to the Hebrew Bible as a whole [BECNT, EBC, NAC]

e. προφῆται (in the plural) (LN 33.60) (BAGD 1. p. 723): 'the Prophets' [BAGD, LN; all translations except NCV, NLT, TEV], 'the teachings of the prophets' [NCV, TEV], 'the writings of the prophets' [NLT]. 'The Prophets' is a collective term to refer to all of the writings of the prophets, including both the earlier and the later prophets [LN].

QUESTION—Did the disciples think that Jesus had come to abolish the Law and the prophets?

Jesus saw it was necessary to remove potential misunderstandings that might arise about his kingdom and mission [EBC]. This anticipates material about to be introduced in the next section of the sermon, which could be seen as contrary to the law of Moses [NIGTC]. It is likely that he wanted to prevent his disciples from even considering such an accusation that already was prevalent among others [BECNT]. Some opponents were beginning to accuse him of abandoning traditions [NTC]. Probably there were already some who believed that he was opposing the law and the prophets [NICNT]. Jesus' authoritative interpretations were quite out of step with those of his contemporaries [WBC]. Because Jesus had healed on the Sabbath and did not observe the rituals and feasts to the degree that others did, he was seen as having a lower view of the law [NIBC]. Perhaps some even expected the Messiah to abrogate the law because of the messianic prophecy of Jeremiah 31:31 [My].

QUESTION—Does the phrase 'I have come' indicate a claim to pre-existence on the part of Jesus?

This same language can be used to describe the mission of prophets, but in light of the prologue to Matthew's gospel it seems to affirm Jesus' divine origins [EBC]. It expresses a sense of mission, and that he had come from God into the world [PNTC, TH]. Jesus was fully conscious of his messianic mission and of his pre-existence [NTC]. The words 'I came' hint at his authority [WBC]. They convey a sense of mission, though not necessarily a claim to pre-existence [NICNT].

QUESTION—What does it mean to 'abolish' the law or the prophets?

It means to cancel, repeal, or do away with them [WBC], to abolish them [EBC], to do away with them entirely [PNTC]. It means to undercut their role [NIGTC], to consider them to be no longer normative or relevant [NAC], or no longer valid [NICNT]. It would be to treat them as useless and no longer worthy of respect [Lns].

I-came not to-abolish but to-fulfill.[a]

LEXICON—a. aorist act. infin. of πληρόω (LN **33.144**) (BAGD 4.b. p. 671): 'to fulfill' [BAGD, BECNT, BNTC, CC, NICNT, NIGTC, NTC, PNTC; ESV, KJV, NASB, NET, NIV, NLT, NRSV], 'to complete' [REB], 'to bring to an intended goal' [WBC], 'to give the full meaning' [CEV], 'to give true meaning to' [**LN**], 'to make (them/their teachings) come true' [GW, TEV], 'to bring about (what they said)' [NCV], 'to provide the real significance of' [LN]. This verb means to give the true or complete meaning to something [LN].

QUESTION—What does it mean to 'fulfill' the law and the prophets?

Jesus fulfilled what the law required and what the prophets predicted [BECNT, EBC, TH]. The prophetic scriptures point forward to Jesus' actions and the laws of Moses point forward to his teachings, and both have been realized in a greater and more profound manner [PNTC]. 'Fulfilling' the prophets does not necessarily always refer to fulfilling predictions, but can assume a typological understanding of the OT scriptures which have a foreshadowing, prophetic significance [EBC]. He fulfills the law in the sense of giving a new depth of insight into what it requires [NIGTC]. Although he brings new demands and understanding that surpass those of the law, he confirms the truth and validity of the law [ICC]. In his own person the kingdom is present and the ethical teachings of Jesus make it possible to realize the righteousness of the law. He brings the true intended meaning of the Torah that only he is able to interpret and expound authoritatively [WBC]. The law and the prophets pointed forward to what Jesus is now bringing into being, and in the light of his teaching and practice, his disciples are able to apply the texts of the OT in the new condition which Jesus' coming brought about [NICNT]. 'To fulfill' means to explain or show the true meaning and purpose of the law and prophets [TRT].

5:18 For truly[a] I-say[b] to-you(pl),

LEXICON—a. ἀμήν (LN **72.6**) (BAGD 2. p. 45): 'truly' [BAGD, BECNT, BNTC, CC, LN, NICNT, PNTC, WBC; ESV, NASB, NRSV, REB], 'verily' [KJV], 'amen' [NIGTC], 'solemnly' [NTC], 'indeed, it is true that' [LN], not explicit [CEV, GW, NCV, NET, NIV, NLT, TEV]. This particle expresses strong affirmation of what is declared [LN].

b. pres. act. indic. of λέγω (LN 33.69): 'to say' [CC, LN, NIGTC; NASB], 'to tell' [BECNT, BNTC, LN, NICNT, PNTC, WBC; ESV, KJV, NRSV, REB], 'to declare' [NTC]. The phrase ἀμὴν γὰρ λέγω ὑμῖν 'for truly I say to you' is translated 'for I tell you the truth' [**LN**; NCV, NET, NIV, NLT], 'I can guarantee this truth' [GW], 'I promise you' [CEV], 'remember' [TEV]. This verb means to speak or talk, with apparent focus upon the content of what is said [LN].

QUESTION—What relationship is indicated by γάρ 'for'?

It indicates that this verse further explains and confirms what has been stated in verse 17 [CC, EBC, Lns], that the object of his mission is to fulfill the OT [Lns]. It indicates *why* he came to fulfill and not abolish the law and prophets [CC, PNTC].

QUESTION—What does ἀμήν 'truly' signify?

1. It relates to what is about to be said [BAGD, BECNT, CC, EBC, NICNT, NIGTC, NTC, PNTC, TH, WBC]. It indicates that what follows is of the highest importance [EBC]. It indicates emphasis and solemnity [BECNT, CC, ICC], giving an authoritative explanation of what was said in 5:17 [BECNT]. It marks solemn affirmation [PNTC] and gravity [WBC]. It signifies truth [Lns, NTC], a solemn assertion of divine truth [TH], authority [NICNT], and solemnity [NICNT, NTC]. It expresses Jesus' confidence in his own authority [NIGTC]. This is the first of thirty-one statements of Jesus in Matthew beginning with ἀμήν 'truly' [CC, NICNT, NIGTC].

2. It relates to and emphasizes what was previously said in 5:17 [TRT].

until[a] the heaven and the earth pass-away,[b]

LEXICON—a. ἕως (LN 67.119) (BAGD I.1.b. p. 334): 'until' [BAGD, BECNT, BNTC, CC, LN, NICNT, NIGTC, NTC, PNTC; ESV, GW, NASB, NCV, NET, NIV, NLT, NRSV], 'till' [BAGD; KJV]. The phrase 'until the heaven and the earth pass away' is translated 'as long as heaven and earth last' [WBC; TEV], 'so long as heaven and earth endure' [REB], 'heaven and earth may disappear, but...' [CEV]. The subordinating conjunction ἕως indicates the continuous extent of time up to a point [LN

(67.119)], and ἄν with the subjunctive marks the possibility of the occurrence of some event [LN (71.8)].
b. aorist act. subj. of παρέρχομαι (LN 13.93) (BAGD 1.b.α. p. 626): 'to pass away' [BAGD, BECNT, BNTC, CC, LN, NICNT, NIGTC, PNTC; ESV, NASB, NET, NRSV], 'to pass' [KJV], 'to disappear' [BAGD, NTC; CEV, GW, NIV, NLT], 'to be gone' [NCV], 'to cease to exist, to cease' [LN], 'to come to an end' [BAGD], not explicit [WBC; CEV, REB, TEV]. This verb means to go out of existence [LN].

QUESTION—What is meant by ὁ οὐρανός 'the heaven'?
It is the higher levels of the created order such as the sky, but not the place where God dwells [ICC, NIGTC, PNTC]. Taken together with 'earth' it indicates the present world order [BECNT, EBC, Lns, PNTC, TRT]. It is the sky [Lns].

one smallest-letter[a] or a-single stroke-of-a-letter[b] will- certainly-not[c] disappear[d] from the law

LEXICON—a. ἰῶτα (LN **33.36**) (BAGD p. 386): 'smallest letter' [BECNT, LN; NASB, NCV, NET, NIV], 'small letter' [**LN**, NICNT], 'tiniest letter' [NTC], 'letter' [CC; NRSV, REB], 'iota' [BAGD, BNTC, LN, NIGTC, PNTC; ESV], 'jot' [KJV], 'the least point' [TEV], 'small mark' [LN]. The phrase ἰῶτα ἓν ἢ μία κεραία 'one smallest letter or a single stroke of a letter' is translated 'the slightest aspect' [WBC], 'a period or comma' [CEV, GW], 'the smallest detail (of God's law)' [NLT]. Iota (ι) is the smallest letter of the Greek alphabet, corresponding to the 'yod' (׳) of the Hebrew alphabet [LN].

b. κεραία (LN **33.37**) (BAGD p. 428): 'stroke of a letter' [NET, NRSV], 'stroke of the pen' [BECNT, NICNT; NIV], 'pen stroke' [NIGTC], 'part of a letter' [BNTC, **LN**], 'the smallest part of a letter' [NCV], 'stroke' [CC, LN; NASB], 'little stroke' [PNTC], 'tiniest hook on a letter' [NTC], 'dot' [ESV, REB], 'tittle' [KJV], 'the smallest detail' [TEV], 'short mark, short line of a letter' [LN], 'projection, hook (as part of a letter), serif' [BAGD]. This noun is a part of a letter of the alphabet. The reference to one smallest letter or a single stroke of a letter' is to the small details of the Law, and therefore it may be appropriate in many languages to translate this as 'not one of the smallest parts of the Law will be done away with' or 'not one of the smallest parts of the Law will become null and void' [LN].

c. οὐ μή (LN 69.5) (BAGD D.1.a. p. 517): 'certainly not' [BAGD, CC, LN], 'not' [BAGD, BNTC, LN, NICNT, NIGTC, PNTC, WBC; ESV, NASB, NET], 'not even' [BECNT; CEV, NLT], 'not even…in any way' [NTC], 'in no wise' [KJV], 'by no means' [LN]. The phrase ἤ…οὐ μή '(not)…or…certainly not' is translated 'not…not' [NIV, NRSV, REB], 'not…nor…not' [TEV], 'neither…nor' [GW], 'nothing…not even' [NCV]. The phrase οὐ μή is a marker of emphatic negation [LN]. The use

MATTHEW 5:18

of the two together (οὐ μή) is the most decisive way of negating a future action [BAGD].
d. aorist act. subj. of παρέρχομαι (LN 13.93) (BAGD 1.b.α. p. 626): 'to disappear' [BAGD, NTC; CEV, GW, NIV, NLT, REB], 'to pass away' [BAGD, BNTC, CC, LN, NICNT, NIGTC, PNTC], 'to pass' [BECNT; ESV, KJV, NASB, NET, NRSV], 'to come to an end' [BAGD], 'to fail' [WBC], 'to be lost' [NCV], 'to be done away with' [TEV], 'to cease to exist, to cease' [LN]. This verb means to go out of existence [LN].

QUESTION—What is the κεραία 'stroke of a letter'?
It is the very small serif or mark that differentiates ר from ד, or כ from ב [BECNT, BNTC, Lns, NAC, NTC, PNTC]. It may be ornamental marks added to certain letters [NIGTC, WBC].

QUESTION—What is being affirmed about the authority of the OT?
Here 'law' is considered with respect to its prophetic function, and he is saying that God's redemptive purposes prophesied in the scriptures will be fulfilled in Jesus and the kingdom he is inaugurating [EBC]. The Torah, which Jesus brings to its intended goal, has an ongoing authority that Jesus' disciples are not free to disobey or ignore [BECNT]. Scripture is permanently valid, and its divine purpose will be worked out [PNTC]. The law remains in force [NIBC]. He is saying that the law is to be observed as Jesus definitively and authoritatively interpreted it, and to follow his teaching is to be faithful to its entire meaning [WBC]. The law has an ongoing value and authority; it will never lose its significance, though all must be seen in a new light, since what it points forward to has become a reality in Jesus [NICNT].

until all[a] takes-place/is-accomplished.[b]
LEXICON—a. πᾶς (LN 59.23): 'all' [LN, NIGTC, PNTC; ESV, KJV, NASB, NRSV], 'all it calls for' [NTC], 'all things' [BECNT, BNTC, CC; TEV], 'all that must happen' [REB], 'everything' [NICNT, WBC; GW, NCV, NET, NIV], 'everything written in it' [CEV], 'every' [LN], not explicit [NLT]. This adjective describes the totality of any object, mass, collective, or extension [LN].
b. γίνομαι (LN 13.107) (BAGD I.3.a. p. 158): 'to take place' [BAGD, BNTC, CC, NICNT, NTC, PNTC; NET], 'to be accomplished' [BECNT, WBC; ESV, NASB, NIV, NRSV], 'to happen' [BAGD, LN, NIGTC; CEV, NCV, REB], 'to come true' [GW], 'to be fulfilled' [KJV], 'to be achieved' [NLT], 'to occur, to come to be' [LN]. The phrase ἕως ἂν πάντα γένηται 'until all takes place' is translated 'until the end of all things' [TEV]. This verb means to happen, with the implication that what happens is different from a previous state [LN].

QUESTION—What is the relationship of the first use of ἕως 'until' in this verse to the second use of it?
It introduces phrases that refer to the end of the present era [BECNT, WBC; TEV]. The two phrases are more or less parallel [BNTC, CC, ICC, Lns,

WBC]. The first indicates the time, and the second describes what will occur during that time [Lns]. Jesus fulfilled all things in his ministry, culminating in his death and resurrection by which all things have indeed taken place, and now the new heavens and earth have begun to show themselves in Christ [CC]. Both introduce clauses that indicate how long the authority of the OT will last, but they are not exactly synonymous; the first clause speaks only of the duration of its authority, but the second speaks of its nature, that is, how it reveals God's purposes in redemption and how those will be fulfilled in Jesus and the kingdom he is inaugurating and will consummate [EBC]. The first clause indicates that the law remains in force, and the second one shows how what it points forward to is brought to fulfillment in the greater righteousness that Jesus brings into being [NICNT]. The first use of ἕως indicates that they are in force for all time, but the second qualifies or limits that [My, NAC], since many aspects of the law (such as sacrifices) are brought to an end with the coming of Christ [NAC]. All prophecies will be fulfilled and the law's demands fully met before the universe in its present form disappears; some parts of the OT had already been fulfilled by Jesus' coming, others were in the process of being fulfilled or would be fulfilled in his crucifixion and resurrection and at Pentecost, and still others will be fulfilled at his return in glory [NTC].

QUESTION—What are the things that must take place?
1. Jesus is speaking about God's redemptive purposes that are foreshadowed in the OT scriptures, and which Jesus and his kingdom fulfill [EBC]. Jesus will fulfill the ethical standards as well as the eschatological promises of the law and the prophets [BECNT]. In Jesus' ministry the law and the prophets were fulfilled, and his death was in a sense the day of divine judgment and his resurrection was in a sense the last day; now the new heavens and earth have begun to manifest themselves in Christ [CC]. God's plans with respect to Christ, the Church, mankind, and the universe will take place in full [NTC]. The law will remain in force until what it describes as God's will for the human race has come about [NIGTC]. The validity of the law endures until all that it requires has been accomplished [My]. It refers to the fulfillment of the promises God gave through the prophets and his redemptive purposes in the world [ICC]. It speaks of all the purposes of the OT, some of which were fulfilled in Christ's coming, ministry, death and resurrection, some of which are being fulfilled in the church, and some of which will come about at the final consummation of all things [Lns]. It refers to all that the law points forward to, the reality of which has arrived in the life and ministry of Jesus, who brings into being a greater righteousness that supersedes the old kind of law-keeping [NICNT]. He is speaking of everything written in the law [CEV], the purposes of the law [TH; NLT].
2. He is speaking of the end of all things [TEV, TH]. It refers to the passing of the present era; that is, Jesus' authoritative interpretation of the law is valid until the coming of the eschatological era [WBC].

5:19 Therefore whoever breaks/annuls[a] one of the least[b] of-these commandments[c] and teaches people (to do)-so,[d]

- LEXICON—a. aorist act. subj. of λύω (LN **36.30**) (BAGD 4. p. 484): 'to break' [BNTC, LN, WBC; KJV, NET, NIV, NRSV], 'to annul' [BAGD, NTC; NASB], 'to do away with' [BECNT], 'to transgress' [**LN**], 'to disobey' [TEV], 'to loosen' [CC], 'to relax' [PNTC; ESV], 'to set aside' [NICNT; GW, REB], 'to dismiss' [NIGTC], 'to reject' [CEV], 'to ignore' [NLT], 'to refuse to obey' [NCV], 'to repeal, to abolish' [BAGD]. This verb means to fail to conform to a law or regulation, with a possible implication of regarding it as invalid [LN].
- b. ἐλάχιστος (LN **65.57**) (BAGD 2.a. p. 248): 'least' [BECNT, BNTC, CC, **LN**, NIGTC, NTC, PNTC, WBC; ESV, KJV, NASB, NET, NIV, NLT, NRSV, REB], 'smallest' [NICNT], 'very small, insignificant' [BAGD], 'least important' [CEV, TEV], 'of least importance' [**LN**], 'of very little importance' [LN], 'unimportant' [BAGD], 'that seems unimportant' [GW], 'any' [NCV]. This adjective describes what is of the least importance [LN].
- c. ἐντολή (LN 33.330) (BAGD 2.a.β. p. 269): 'commandment' [BAGD, BECNT, BNTC, CC, LN, NICNT, NIGTC, NTC, PNTC, WBC; ESV, KJV, NASB, NIV, NLT, NRSV, TEV], 'command' [CEV, GW, NCV, NET], 'the law's demand; [REB]. This noun denotes that which is authoritatively commanded [LN].
- d. οὕτως (LN **61.9**) (BAGD 1.b. p. 597): 'so' [BAGD, BNTC, NTC, PNTC, WBC; CEV, KJV, NET], 'accordingly' [BECNT], 'in this way' [CC], 'the same' [NIGTC; ESV, GW, NASB, NIV, NLT, NRSV, REB, TEV], 'thus' [BAGD, **LN**], 'in this way' [LN]. The phrase 'to do so' is translated, 'to disregard them' [NICNT], 'not to obey that command' [NCV]. This adverb refers to that which precedes [LN]. The phrase 'teaches people so' might be filled out to 'teaches people that it is not valid', 'teaches people not to obey', or 'teaches people not to pay attention to them' [TH].

QUESTION—What relationship is indicated by οὖν 'therefore'?

It is inferential [CC, ICC, My, NIGTC]. It indicates the central importance of 5:19, explaining what may be inferred from what he said in 5:18 about himself as the one who fulfills the OT [CC]. This verse explains why the disciples must not do what he has warned them about in 5:18 [BECNT]. It links 5:19 with 5:18, indicating that the 'least' commandments are the smallest letters and strokes of letters mentioned in 5:18, which may not be set aside [NICNT]. It indicates the consequence of the permanence of scripture [PNTC].

QUESTION—What is the difference between λύω 'break/annul' here and its cognate καταλύω 'abolish' in 5:17?

Whereas καταλύω means to abolish the law completely [CC, NAC, NICNT], λύω means to lessen the force or importance of its commands [CC], or to set it aside as not applicable [NAC], to regard it as null and void [PNTC], to willfully disregard it [NTC], to undermine its authority such that it can be ignored [NICNT]. λύω means to dismiss a command as not binding on oneself [NIGTC]. λύω can mean to set aside a command of God through ignorance, misinterpretation, or base motives [Lns].

QUESTION—What commandments is he speaking of here?

It refers back to the commandments of the Mosaic law, as mentioned in 5:18 [BNTC, BECNT, CC, ICC, NAC, NICNT, NIGTC, NTC, WBC]. It refers to the commandments of scripture [EBC, PNTC], which includes both the law and the prophets [EBC]. It is everything that God requires of us as disciples, which would also include repentance and faith in the Messiah [Lns]. While it refers to the Law of Moses, it is not about keeping the minute details as the scribes and Pharisees often emphasized, but the intent of the law as Jesus expounded it [WBC].

will-be-called[a] least[b] in the kingdom of-the heavens.

LEXICON—a. fut. pass. indic. of καλέω (LN 33.131) (BAGD 1.a.δ. p. 399): 'to be called' [BAGD, BECNT, BNTC, CC, LN, NICNT, NIGTC, NTC, PNTC, WBC; CEV, ESV, KJV, NASB, NET, NIV, NLT, NRSV], 'to be named' [BAGD, LN]. The phrase 'will be called least' is translated 'will be least' [TEV], 'will be the least important' [NCV], 'will be unimportant' [GW], 'will have the lowest place' [REB]. This verb means to use an attribution in speaking of a person [LN].

b. ἐλάχιστος (LN 65.57) (BAGD 2. a. p. 248): 'least' [BECNT, BNTC, CC, LN, NIGTC, NTC, PNTC, WBC; ESV, KJV, NASB, NET, NIV, NLT, NRSV, TEV], 'least important' [NCV], 'the least important person' [CEV], 'of least importance' [LN], 'of very little importance' [LN], 'unimportant' [BAGD; GW], 'insignificant' [BAGD], 'smallest' [NICNT], 'lowest place' [REB]. This adjective describes what is of the least importance [LN].

QUESTION—Who will call them 'least'?

God is the one who will either call them 'least' or 'great' [ICC, Lns, NAC, TRT].

but whoever does[a] and teaches (them) this-one will-be-called great[b] in the kingdom of-the heavens.

LEXICON—a. aorist act. subj. of ποιέω (LN 42.7) (BAGD I.1.c.α. p. 682): 'to do, to carry out' [BAGD, LN]. The phrase 'whoever does and teaches (them)' is translated 'whoever does them and teaches them' [BNTC, NICNT, NIGTC; ESV, NRSV; similarly PNTC, WBC; KJV], 'whoever keeps and teaches them' [NASB], 'whoever practices and teaches these commands' [NIV; similarly BECNT, NTC], 'whoever does and teaches what the commands say' [GW], 'whoever obeys them and teaches others to do so' [NET], 'anyone who obeys God's law and teaches them' [NLT], 'if you obey and teach others its commands' [CEV], 'whoever obeys the Law and teaches others to do the same' [TEV], 'whereas anyone who keeps the law, and teaches others to do so' [REB], 'whoever obeys the

commands and teaches other people to obey them' [NCV]. This verb means to do or perform, and it applies to almost any type of activity [LN].
  c. μέγας (LN **87.22**) (BAGD 2.b.α. p. 498): 'great' [BAGD, BECNT, BNTC, CC, LN, NICNT, NIGTC, NTC, PNTC, WBC and all versions except REB], important' [LN]. The phrase 'will be called great' is translated 'will rank high' [REB]. This adjective describes being great in terms of status [LN].

QUESTION—What is meant by being called least or great?
To be called least or great really means to *be* least or great [BNTC, ICC, NTC, PNTC]. It is to be low or high in God's esteem [NICNT]. Being least in the kingdom is to be least in importance, or to be in the lowest position in the kingdom. Being great means to be important or to have high stature [TH]. The least are not excluded from salvation, but they won't have the same degree of reward [BNTC, CC, EBC, Lns, My, NTC, WBC]. Both groups are within the community of God's people in his kingdom [ESV, NAC, NICNT, PNTC].

QUESTION—Does the ranking of 'least' and 'great' in the kingdom of heaven apply to the present age, the future age, or both?
  1. It refers to the eschatological consummation of all things [CC, ICC].
  2. It refers to how God will honor people in the present age [NAC].
  3. This applies both in Christ's present rule as well as in the day of judgment and afterward [Lns, NTC].

5:20 For I-tell you(pl) that unless^a your righteousness^b surpasses^c beyond (that) of-the scribes^d and Pharisees, you(pl)-will- never -enter^e into the kingdom of-the heavens.

LEXICON—a. ἐὰν μή (LN 89.131) (BAGD II. p. 211): 'unless' [BECNT, BNTC, CC, NIGTC, NTC, PNTC, WBC; ESV, GW, NASB, NET, NIV, NLT, NRSV, REB], 'if...does not' [NICNT], 'except' [KJV], 'except that' [LN], not explicit [CEV, NCV, TEV]. This phrase marks contrast by designating an exception [LN].
  b. δικαιοσύνη (LN 88.13) (BAGD 2.a. p. 196): 'righteousness' [BAGD, BECNT, BNTC, CC, LN, NICNT, NIGTC, NTC, PNTC, WBC; ESV, KJV, NASB, NCV, NET, NIV, NLT, NRSV], 'to do what God requires' [LN; TEV], 'to do what is right' [LN], 'to obey God's commands' [CEV], 'to live a life that has God' approval' [GW], not explicit]REB]. This noun denotes the act of doing what God requires [LN].
  c. aorist act. subj. of περισσεύω (LN 59.52) (BAGD 1.a.β. p. 650): 'to surpass' [BAGD, BECNT, WBC; NASB, NIV], 'to go beyond' [NET], 'to go far beyond' [NICNT], 'to exceed' [PNTC; ESV, KJV, NRSV], 'to greatly surpass' [BNTC], 'to abound' [CC, LN], 'to be abundant' [NIGTC], 'to be present in abundance' [BAGD], 'to excel' [NTC], 'to be better than' [CEV, NLT], 'to do (it) more' [GW], not explicit [NCV]. This entire clause is translated 'you must obey God's commands better than the Pharisees and the teachers of the Law obey them' [CEV], 'unless you live

a life that has God's approval and do it more faithfully than the scribes and Pharisees' [GW], 'if you are no more obedient than the teachers of the law and the Pharisees' [NCV], 'unless you show yourselves far better than the scribes and Pharisees' [REB], 'only if you are more faithful than the teachers of the Law and the Pharisees in doing what God requires' [TEV]. This verb means to be or exist in abundance, with the implication of being considerably more than what would be expected [LN].

d. γραμματεύς (LN 53.94) (BAGD 2. p. 165): 'scribe' [BAGD, BNTC, CC, NICNT, NIGTC, NTC, PNTC, WBC; ESV, GW, KJV, NASB, NRSV, REB], 'teacher of the Law' [CEV, NCV, NIV], 'teacher of religious law' [NLT], 'expert in the Law' [BAGD, LN; NET], 'legal experts' [BECNT], 'one who is learned in the Law of Moses' [LN]. This noun denotes a recognized expert in Jewish law (including both canonical and traditional laws and regulations) [LN].

e. aorist act. subj. of εἰσέρχομαι (LN 90.70) (BAGD 2.a. p. 233): 'to enter' [BAGD, BECNT, BNTC, CC, LN, NIGTC, NTC, PNTC, WBC; all versions], 'to get into' [NICNT], 'to come into something, to share in something' [BAGD], 'to begin to experience, to come into an experience, to attain' [LN]. This verb means to begin to experience an event or state [LN].

QUESTION—What relationship is indicated by γάρ 'for'?

It indicates a further explanation of what he has said in 5:19 on the necessity of obeying and teaching the law [BECNT, CC, Lns, My, NIGTC, PNTC], but there is also a link with 5:17 [NIGTC]. It indicates a clarification of what was said in 5:18 [WBC].

QUESTION—How can someone's righteousness exceed that of the scribes and the Pharisees?

This righteousness is described in 5:21–48 [BECNT, BNTC, CC, EBC, ICC, NAC, NIBC, NICNT, NTC], and is both qualitatively and quantitatively greater [EBC]. The righteousness of the scribes and Pharisees was not true righteousness [TRT]. More is needed than punctilious attention to the details of the law [NIGTC]. It is not just a quantitative difference or a focus on the minute details of the law, it is a difference of kind, in which Jesus' authoritative and definitive exposition of the law is followed [WBC]. They are to move beyond scrupulous attention to details of the law, to a deeper and more radical openness to doing what truly pleases God and fulfills his will [NICNT]. Jesus is looking for a radical obedience to the spirit of the law, which is love and not just the letter; he will outline what that means in the rest of this sermon [PNTC]. Jesus requires a more stringent obedience, one that is internalized, and that is defined by his teachings [NAC]. Jesus' disciples must have a truer understanding of God's will and a more complete obedience to it [BNTC].

QUESTION—What is the difference, if any, between the scribes and the Pharisees?
There was considerable overlap between the aims and practice of the two groups [NICNT]. The scribes were legal experts [BECNT, NIBC, NTC], experts in the scriptures [PNTC], and the Pharisees were a religious sect or group [NTC]. The scribes tried to spell out the great principles expressed in the law through rules and regulations; the Pharisees set themselves to carry out all those regulations elaborated by the scribes in order to avoid anything that would defile them [NIBC]. The scribes had a specialized knowledge about Jewish religious traditions; the Pharisees were concerned to broaden the practices of ritual purity in the wider society. Both groups were respected members of Jewish society [NIGTC]. The single definite article is used to describe the two groups described according to what they held in common, which was their failure to achieve the righteousness necessary to enter the kingdom [Lns]. Many scribes were Pharisees, though some were not [CC], and most of the Pharisees were not scribes [TH]. Some men were both [CC, ICC, NICNT, PNTC].

DISCOURSE UNIT—5:21–48 [ICC; NASB]. The topic is the better righteousness [ICC], personal relationships [NASB].

DISCOURSE UNIT—5:21–26 [CEV, ESV, GW, NCV, NIV, NLT, NRSV, TEV]. The topic is Jesus talks about anger [GW], Jesus teaches about anger [NCV], teaching about anger [NLT, TEV], anger [CEV, ESV], concerning anger [NRSV], murder [NIV].

5:21 **You(pl)-have-heard[a] that it-was-said[b] to/by-the ancients,[c]**
LEXICON—a. aorist act. impera. of ἀκούω (LN 33.212): 'to hear' [LN, all translations except CEV], 'to know' [CEV]. This aorist verb is translated as perfect tense: 'have heard' [BECNT, BNTC, NICNT, NIGTC, NTC, PNTC, WBC; all versions except CEV]; as aorist: 'you heard' [CC]; as present: 'you know' [CEV]. This verb means to receive information about something, normally by word of mouth [LN].
b. aorist pass. indic. of λέγω (LN 33.69) (BAGD II.1.e. p. 469): 'to be said' [BAGD, BECNT, BNTC, CC, LN, NICNT, NIGTC, NTC, PNTC, WBC; ESV, GW, KJV, NCV, NET, NIV, NRSV], 'to be told' [CEV, NASB, NLT, REB, TEV], 'to be proclaimed' [BAGD]. This verb means to speak or talk, with apparent focus upon the content of what is said [LN].
c. ἀρχαῖος (LN 67.98) (BAGD 2. p. 111): 'ancients' [CC, LN; NASB], 'the people/men of old' [BECNT, BAGD, NIGTC, PNTC], 'people (were told) in the past' [TEV], 'people of long ago' [NICNT; NCV; similarly NIV], 'men of long ago' [NTC], 'men of ancient times' [BECNT], 'those of ancient times' [NRSV], 'those of earlier times' [WBC], 'them of old time' [KJV], 'those of old' [ESV], 'ancestors' [CEV, GW, NLT], 'forefathers' [REB], 'an older generation' [NET]. This adjective describes that which has existed for a long time in the past [LN].

QUESTION—What relationship is indicated by the use of the dative phrase τοῖς ἀρχαίοις 'to/by the ancients'?
1. The statement was made *to* the people of earlier times [BECNT, BNTC, CC, EBC, My, NICNT, NIGTC, PNTC, TH, TRT, WBC; CEV, ESV, GW, NASB, NCV, NET, NIV, NLT, NRSV, REB, TEV].
    1.1 The people of old were those who heard the ten commandments spoken by Moses [BNTC, PNTC], the original recipients of the Mosaic law [WBC].
    1.2 The verb ἐρρέθη 'it was said' represents a divine passive; the speaker is God himself [ICC]. God was the speaker, and the people of old were the generation of the exodus [NIGTC]. They were those who heard God speak at Sinai, but subsequent generations are also included [TH].
2. The statement was made *by* the people of earlier times [NTC; KJV].

You(sg)-shall- not -murder;[a] and whoever[b] murders, he-will-be liable[c] to-judgment.[d]

LEXICON—a. fut. act. indic. (used as aorist act. impera.) of φονεύω (LN **20.82**) (BAGD p. 864): 'to murder' [BAGD, BECNT, CC, LN, NICNT, NIGTC, PNTC, WBC; CEV, ESV, GW, NCV, NET, NIV, NLT, NRSV], 'to commit murder' [BAGD, LN; NASB, REB, TEV], 'to kill' [BAGD, BNTC, NTC; KJV]. This verb means to deprive a person of life by illegal, intentional killing [LN]. The future tense functions as an imperative [EBC, PNTC, TH].
   b. ὃς ἄν: 'whoever' [BNTC, BECNT, CC, NIGTC, NTC, PNTC, WBC; ESV, GW, KJV, NASB, NET, NRSV], 'anyone who' [NICNT; NCV, NIV, REB, TEV], 'if you' [NLT]. The phrase 'whoever murders' is translated 'a murderer' [CEV].
   c. ἔνοχος (LN 88.313) (BAGD 2.a. p. 267): 'liable' [BAGD, BECNT, BNTC, CC, NICNT, NIGTC; ESV, NASB, NRSV], 'subject' [PNTC; NET, NIV, NLT], 'answerable' [BAGD], 'guilty' [WBC], 'in danger (of)' [KJV], 'to be brought to (justice/trial)' [REB, TEV], 'guilty and deserving, guilty and punishable by' [LN], not explicit [NTC; CEV, GW, NCV]. This adjective describes that which pertains to being guilty and thus deserving some particular penalty [LN].
   d. κρίσις (LN 56.1) (BAGD 2. p. 453): 'judgment' [BECNT, CC, NICNT, NIGTC, WBC; ESV, KJV, NET, NIV, NLT, NRSV], 'court' [BAGD, BNTC, LN; GW, NASB], 'justice' [REB], 'court of justice' [LN], 'trial' [TEV]. The phrase ἔνοχος ἔσται τῇ κρίσει 'he will be liable to judgment' is translated 'deserves to be punished' [NTC], 'shall be guilty in the judgment' [WBC], 'must be brought to trial' [CEV], 'will answer for it in court' [GW], 'will be judged' [NCV]. This noun denotes a court of justice for determining guilt or innocence [LN]. Here it may well represent the whole process of being brought to court, tried, convicted, and punished [NIGTC].

QUESTION—Is the prohibition directed toward all killing, or more selectively only against murder?

It specifically prohibits murder [EBC, My, NAC, NICNT, TH, TRT], but that does not include every instance of taking life [EBC, My, NICNT, TH, TRT], such as killing in self-defense [NAC] or capital punishment according to law [NAC, TH].

5:22 But I say to-you(pl) that everyone-who[a] is-angry[b] (with) his brother[c] will-be liable to judgment;

TEXT—Some manuscripts include εἰκῇ 'without a cause' after τῷ ἀδελφῷ αὐτοῦ 'his brother'. It is omitted by GNT with a B rating to indicate that choosing it over a variant text was difficult. It is included by KJV only.

LEXICON—a. πᾶς (LN 59.24) (BAGD 1.c.γ. p. 632): 'everyone who' [BAGD, BECNT, BNTC, CC, NICNT, NIGTC, PNTC, WBC; ESV, NASB], 'anyone who' [NET, NIV, REB], 'whosoever' [KJV], 'whoever' [BAGD, BNTC; GW], '(if) you' [CEV, NCV, NLT, NRSV, TEV].

b. pres. mid. or pass. (deponent = act.) participle of ὀργίζομαι (LN **88.174**) (BAGD p. 579): 'to be angry' [BAGD, BECNT, BNTC, CC, **LN**, NICNT, NIGTC, NTC, PNTC; all versions except REB], 'to be filled with wrath' [WBC], 'to nurse anger' [REB], 'to be full of anger, to be furious' [LN]. This verb means to be relatively angry [LN].

c. ἀδελφός (LN 11.25) (BAGD 4. p. 16): 'brother' [BNTC, CC, LN, NTC, PNTC; ESV, KJV, NASB, NET, NIV, REB, TEV], 'brother or sister' [BECNT, NICNT, NIGTC, WBC; NCV, NRSV], 'neighbor' [BAGD], 'someone' [CEV, NLT], 'fellow countryman, fellow Jew, associate' [LN], 'another believer' [GW]. This noun denotes a person belonging to the same socio-religious entity and being of the same age group as the so-called reference person [LN].

QUESTION—What is implied by the statement 'but I say to you'?

Jesus is not contradicting the first statement, but is bringing it into sharper focus [ICC, Lns, NIBC]. Jesus authoritatively interprets the law [BECNT, CC, EBC, ICC, NAC, NICNT, PNTC, WBC]. Jesus moves beyond the traditional legal interpretations of the rabbis [CC, EBC, My, NAC], and the misunderstanding of the law that people had [EBC, My]. On the basis of his own authority as the one who fulfills the law, he shows the intent of the law, and the direction to which it points [CC, EBC, NAC]. Jesus is contrasting his teaching with that of Jewish interpreters from the past, whose teaching did not go far enough [NTC]. Jesus deepens the commandments by internalizing them, dealing with the thoughts and motives of people [WBC]. The 'I' is emphatic [CC, EBC, ICC, NIGTC, NTC, PNTC, TH].

QUESTION—Who are included in the category of 'brother'?

1. It is most likely limited to others within one's own religious community [BECNT, NIBC, NIGTC], or at least primarily focused on that group [CC, NAC, NICNT]. In Jewish usage it referred to those who shared membership in the community of God's people, that is, other Jews

[NIGTC]. It is probably directed primarily at relationships with other disciples of Jesus [NICNT, TH], but that does not mean it would be limited only to them [NICNT].

2. It is not to be limited only to other believers, but encompasses all people [ICC, NICNT, PNTC, WBC], as is evidenced by the mention of the Sanhedrin, the altar, and prison, which are not particularly Christian things [ICC].

QUESTION—Is Jesus saying that any anger at all toward someone is wrong?

He is not saying that anger is never justified [NAC, PNTC], although most anger is in fact self-serving [NAC]. There is a legitimate anger, but it is not hostile or unloving [My].

QUESTION—Is Jesus saying that anger is equal to murder?

His point is that anger is the root of murder [EBC], the spiritual cause or attitude that produces the action of murder [ICC, NIBC, NTC]. They are alike in that they both incur God's wrath, but actual murder is much more damaging in human relationships [CC]. The judgment of God is what he is describing, since a human court could not deal very well with the sin of anger [PNTC]. He is saying that anger is equal to murder as God sees it [Lns]. The statement is intentionally puzzling, and cannot be taken and used as a legal principle. Jesus is interpreting the commandment regarding murder in light of the love commandment [NIGTC].

QUESTION—What is the judgment spoken of here?

Although the statement literally refers to a human court, ultimately it is speaking of the judgment of God against human anger [Lns], hostility, and alienation [NIGTC]. The references to 'judgment' in this clause and to 'the council' in the next clause refer to human courts, but cases such as these point to the final judgment [WBC]. The angry person will be subject to judgment, but this presupposes that it is judgment by God since a human court is not competent to try a case of inward anger [EBC]. All three cases metaphorically refer to the final judgment [NAC]. 'Liable to judgment' in this clause might be translated 'be brought before God for judgment' or 'God will judge him' [TH].

and if anyone says to his brother, 'Raka,'ᵃ he-will-be liable to-the council/ Sanhedrin;ᵇ

LEXICON—a. ῥακά (LN **32.61**) (BAGD p. 733): 'raca' [NICNT, PNTC, WBC; KJV, NIV], 'fool' [BAGD, LN; CEV], 'numbskull' [BAGD, CC, LN], 'empty-head' [BAGD, BECNT, BNTC], 'blockhead' [NTC], 'stupid' [NICNT], 'idiot' [NLT], 'good-for-nothing' [NASB, REB, TEV]. The phrase εἴπῃ τῷ ἀδελφῷ αὐτοῦ, Ῥακά 'says to his brother, 'Raka' is translated 'insults his/a brother' [ESV, NET], 'insult a brother or sister' [NRSV], 'calls another believer an insulting name' [GW], 'say bad things to a brother or sister' [NCV]. This noun is a borrowing from Aramaic, and denotes one who is totally lacking in understanding [LN].

MATTHEW 5:22

b. συνέδριον (LN 11.80, 11.79) (BAGD 2. p. 786): 'Sanhedrin' [BAGD, BNTC, CC, LN (11.80), PNTC, WBC; NIV], 'council' [BECNT; ESV, KJV, NCV, NET, NRSV, TEV], 'city council, council of judges [LN (11.79)], 'judgment of the council' [NIGTC], 'court' [CEV, NLT, REB], 'trial' [NICNT], 'high council' [BAGD], 'supreme court' [NTC; NASB], 'highest court' [GW]. This noun denotes the highest Jewish council, exercising jurisdiction in civil and religious matters, but having no power over life and death or over military actions or taxation [LN (11.80)], or a socio-political group acting as a judicial council [LN (11.79)].

QUESTION—What is the significance of the epithet 'raka'?

It was abusive speech [BECNT], expressing contempt [ICC, My, NIBC, NICNT, NTC, PNTC]. It was an objectionable insult, but would have been taken more seriously than in our own contemporary culture [WBC]. 'Raka' was almost a swear-word in Aramaic [NAC]. It was someone with an empty mind [Lns]. It was a commonly used term of contempt [My].

QUESTION—Was the συνέδριον a local council or the Sanhedrin'?

It could be either a local council or the supreme Jewish court [ICC, NIGTC], but in this case it makes little difference [NIGTC].

1. It was any local council convened for judgment [BECNT, NICNT, PNTC; probably CEV, ESV, KJV, NCV, NET, NLT, NRSV, REB]. This is probably the appropriate local court as in 10:17 [NICNT].
2. It was the Jewish supreme court [BAGD, BNTC, Lns, My, NTC, TH, WBC; GW, NASB].

and[a] whoever says, 'Fool,'[b] he-will-be liable to[c] the hell[d] of-fire.

LEXICON—a. δέ (LN 89.94): 'and' [BECNT, BNTC, CC, LN, NICNT, NTC, PNTC, WBC; CEV, ESV, NASB, NCV, NET, NLT, NRSV, TEV], 'but' [KJV], 'again' [NIV], not explicit [NIGTC; GW, REB]. This conjunction marks an additive relation, but with the possible implication of some contrast [LN].

b. μωρός (LN 32.55) (BAGD 1., 3. p. 531): 'fool' [BECNT, BNTC, CC, LN, NICNT, NIGTC, PNTC, WBC; ESV, GW, NCV, NET, REB], 'thou/you fool' [KJV, NASB, NIV, NRSV], 'worthless fool' [TEV], 'idiot' [NTC], 'foolish' [BAGD, LN], 'worthless' [CEV], 'stupid' [BAGD], 'unwise' [LN]. The phrase ὃς δ' ἂν εἴπῃ 'and whoever says 'Fool' is translated 'and if you curse someone' [NLT]. This adjective describes being extremely unwise and foolish [LN].

c. εἰς (LN 84.22) (BAGD 7. p. 230): 'to' [BNTC, CC, NICNT, NIGTC, PNTC, WBC; ESV, NET, NRSV], 'into' [LN, NTC; NASB], not explicit [BECNT; CEV, KJV, NCV, NIV, NLT, REB]. The phrase ἔνοχος ἔσται εἰς 'will be liable to' is translated 'deserves' [REB], 'shall be deserving of' [BECNT], 'deserves to be cast into' [NTC], 'will be sent to' [NET], 'will be in danger of' [CEV], 'will be in danger of going to' [TEV], 'will answer for it in' [GW], 'will be guilty enough to go into' [NASB]. At the entry for ἔνοχος 'liable' (BAGD 2. c. p. 267), the clause is translated 'guilty enough to go into the hell of fire' [BAGD]. This preposition marks extension toward a goal which is inside an area [LN], or motion into something [BAGD].

d. γέεννα (LN 1.21) (BAGD p. 153): 'Gehenna, hell' [BAGD, LN]. The phrase γέενναν τοῦ πυρός 'hell of fire' [BAGD, NTC; ESV, NRSV], is translated 'hellfire' [BECNT, NICNT; GW, KJV, REB], 'fires of hell' [CEV, NLT], 'fire of hell' [NCV, NIV, TEV], 'fiery hell' [NASB, NET], 'fiery Gehenna' [CC, WBC], 'Gehenna of fire' [BNTC, NIGTC, PNTC]. This noun denotes the place of punishment for the dead [LN].

QUESTION—What is the significance of the epithet 'Fool'?

It implies immorality, godlessness, idiocy [NAC], moral apostasy, rebellion, [EBC], wickedness [EBC, My, TRT], moral deficiency [NIBC], impiety [TH]. It is someone of a slow mind [Lns]. It would have been more insulting in that culture than in our own [WBC].

QUESTION—Are these three clauses intended to be seen as parallel, or as increasing in severity?

The three penalties are given in an ascending order of the severity of punishment [BECNT, BNTC, ICC, NIBC, NICNT, WBC]. This seems to suggest that the corresponding offenses are also listed in an ascending order of severity [ICC]. However, no one seems to take this view of the offenses. The three offenses are parallel [NAC, NIGTC], and do not imply that there is an increase in the severity of their crimes [BECNT, BNTC, ICC, Lns, NAC, NIBC, NICNT, NTC, PNTC, WBC]. One crime is not more heinous than the others [ICC]. The mention of the 'hell of fire' indicates that all three judgments represent God's judgment [EBC, TH], which is an eternal judgment [NAC]

QUESTION—Is γέεννα 'hell, Gehenna' the same place as Hades?

Whereas Hades was viewed as the place where the dead led a shadowy existence, Gehenna was understood as the place of final punishment and destruction [My, NICNT], of fiery judgment [NIGTC], of fiery torment of the wicked [PNTC]. It is not just the place of the dead, it is the place of fiery punishment [TH].

5:23 If[a] therefore you(sg)-are-bringing[b] your(sg) gift[c] to the altar[d]

LEXICON—a. ἐάν (LN 89.67, 67.32): 'if' [LN, all translations except NCV, NRSV], 'when' [LN (67.32); NCV], 'when…if' [NRSV]. This particle marks condition, with the implication of reduced probability [LN (89.67)] or it indicates a point of time which is somewhat conditional and simultaneous with another point of time [LN (67.32)].

b. pres. act. subj. of προσφέρω (LN 57.80) (BAGD 2.a. p. 719): 'to bring' [BAGD, CC, LN, NICNT, NTC; KJV, NET], 'to present' [BAGD, BECNT, LN; NASB, NIV, NLT, REB], 'to offer' [BAGD, BNTC, NIGTC, PNTC; ESV, GW, NCV, NRSV, TEV], 'to bear' [WBC], 'to place (on)' [CEV]. This verb means to present something to someone, often involving actual physical transport of the object in question [LN].

c. δῶρον (LN 57.84) (BAGD 2. p. 211): 'gift' [BAGD, BNTC, CC, LN, NIGTC, PNTC, WBC; CEV, ESV, GW, KJV, NET, NIV, NRSV, REB], 'gift to God' [NCV, TEV], 'offering' [BAGD, BECNT, NICNT, NTC; NASB], 'sacrifice' [NLT], 'present' [LN]. This noun denotes that which is given or granted [LN]. This gift is some sort of sacrifice brought to the temple altar [NICNT, PNTC, TH; NLT], probably a sacrificial animal [NICNT, PNTC].

d. θυσιαστήριον (LN **6.114**) (BAGD 1.a. p. 366): 'altar' [BAGD, LN; all translations except NLT], 'altar in the Temple' [NLT]. This noun denotes any type of altar or object where gifts may be placed and ritual observances carried out in honor of supernatural beings [LN].

QUESTION—What is implied by the switch from the second person plural of the previous statements to the second person singular here?

Jesus is addressing each person in particular, so that everyone will examine his or her own heart [NTC]. He is making the lesson more personal [EBC, PNTC]. He is giving individualized illustrations [NICNT], using illustrative material that is to be applied personally [WBC]. It is as though he is speaking to each individual among the disciples listening to him [TH].

and-there[a] you(sg)-remember[b] that your(sg) brother has something[c] against[d] you(sg),

LEXICON—a. κἀκεῖ (BAGD 1. p. 396): 'and there' [BAGD, BECNT, BNTC, CC, NICNT, NIGTC, NTC, PNTC, WBC; ESV, GW, KJV, NASB, NET, NIV, TEV], 'and' [CEV, NCV], 'and suddenly' [NLT, REB], not explicit [NRSV].

b. aorist pass. (deponent = active) subj. of μιμνῄσκομαι (LN 29.7) (BAGD 1.a.δ. p. 522): 'to remember' [BAGD, LN; all translations], 'to recall' [LN], 'to recall to mind' [BAGD], 'to think about again' [LN]. This verb means to recall information from memory, but without necessarily implying that the persons involved have actually forgotten [LN].

c. τις (LN 92.12) (BAGD 1.b.α. p. 820): 'something' [BAGD, BECNT, BNTC, CC, LN, NIGTC, PNTC, WBC; all versions except CEV, KJV, REB], 'anything' [BAGD, LN], 'ought' [KJV], 'complaint' [NICNT], 'grievance' [NTC; REB]. The phrase ἔχει τι κατὰ σοῦ 'has something against you' is translated 'is angry with you' [CEV]. This preposition refers to someone or something indefinite, spoken or written about [LN].

d. κατά with the genitive (LN 90.31) (BAGD I.2.b.γ. p. 406): 'against' [BAGD, LN; all translations except CEV], not explicit [CEV]. This preposition marks opposition, with the possible implication of antagonism [LN].

QUESTION—Do the phrases 'has something against you' and 'be reconciled' imply that the fault is on the part of the person offering the gift at the altar?

1. Genuine fault appears to be with the person offering the gift [EBC, ICC, Lns, My, NAC, NIGTC, PNTC, TH]. Jesus is assuming that the person being described has in fact done something to prompt the anger of another

[EBC, NIGTC]. He is probably talking about a just claim [NAC], a legitimate complaint [PNTC].
2. Jesus is not saying who is at fault, only that his disciples should take the initiative to effect reconciliation regardless of who is at fault [BECNT, NTC].

5:24 leave^a your(sg) gift there before^b the altar,

LEXICON—a. aorist act. impera. of ἀφίημι (LN 85.62) (BAGD 3.a. p. 126): 'to leave' [BAGD, LN; all translations], 'to let remain' This verb means to permit something to continue in a place [LN].
  b. ἔμπροσθεν (LN **83.33**) (BAGD 2.a. p. 257): 'before' [BAGD, BECNT, BNTC, CC, LN, NIGTC, PNTC, WBC; ESV, KJV, NASB, NRSV, REB], 'in front of' [BAGD, LN, NICNT, NTC; CEV, NET, NIV, TEV], 'at' [GW, NCV, NLT]. This preposition describes a position in front of an object, whether animate or inanimate [LN]. The overriding importance of reconciliation is so important that the worshipper must leave the animal to be sacrificed right there in front of the altar and not come back until he is reconciled [PNTC].

and first^a go-away (and) be-reconciled^b to-your(sg) brother, and then coming (back) offer^c your(sg) gift.

LEXICON—a. πρῶτον (LN 60.46) (BAGD 2.a. p. 726): 'first' [BAGD, BECNT, BNTC, CC, LN, NICNT, NIGTC, NTC, PNTC, WBC; ESV, GW, KJV, NASB, NET, NIV, NRSV, REB], 'at once' [TEV], not explicit [CEV, NCV, NLT]. This adverb describes what is first in a series involving time, space, or set [LN].
  b. aorist pass. impera. of διαλλάσσομαι (LN 40.2) (BAGD p. 186): 'to be reconciled' [BECNT, CC, LN, NIGTC, NTC, PNTC, WBC; ESV, KJV, NASB, NET, NIV, NLT, NRSV], 'to become reconciled' [BAGD], 'to effect a reconciliation' [BNTC], 'to make peace with' [LN; CEV, GW, NCV, REB, TEV], 'to make it up (with)' [NICNT]. This verb means to be reconciled to someone [LN].
  c. pres. act. impera. of προσφέρω (LN 57.80) (BAGD 2.a. p. 719): 'to offer' [BAGD, BNTC, CC, NIGTC, PNTC, WBC; all versions except NET], 'to present' [BAGD, BECNT, LN, NTC; NET]. The phrase πρόσφερε τὸ δῶρόν σου 'offer your gift' is translated 'make your offering' [NICNT]. This verb means to present something to someone, often involving actual physical transport of the object in question [LN].

QUESTION—Was Jesus using hyperbole here, or was he intending his statement to be applied literally?
  For a Galilean to do this may mean making an eighty-mile return journey to Galilee and then travel the same distance back to Jerusalem to offer the gift; Jesus is showing that his ethic requires decisive action [NICNT]. Although a potentially long journey might be involved, Jesus is insisting that restoring human relationships be given priority, since worship acceptable to God cannot ignore relationships with other people [NIGTC]. A broken human

MATTHEW 5:24　　　　　　　　　　　137

relationship can damage one's relationship to God [CC]. Reconciliation is more important than the act of sacrifice [PNTC].

5:25 Make-friends-with[a] your(sg) opponent[b] quickly[c] while you(sg)-are-with him on the way[d] (to court),

LEXICON—a. pres. act. participle of εὐνοέω (used in a periphrastic construction with ἴσθι, the pres. act. impera. of εἰμί 'to be, to become') (LN **31.20**) (BAGD p. 323): 'to make friends with' [BAGD, BNTC, NIGTC, NTC, PNTC; CEV, NASB], 'to become friends with' [NCV], 'to make peace with' [GW], 'to be well-disposed (to/toward)' [BAGD, CC, WBC], 'to agree with' [LN; KJV], 'to reach agreement with' [NET], 'to settle with' [BECNT], 'to settle matters' [NIV], 'to settle (your) differences' [NLT], 'to settle the dispute' [TEV], 'to get on good terms with' [NICNT], 'to come to terms with' [ESV, NRSV, REB]. This verb means to come to an agreement with someone [LN]. It occurs only here in the NT.

b. ἀντίδικος (LN 56.11) (BAGD p. 74): 'opponent' [BAGD, BNTC, CC, NICNT, NTC, PNTC; GW], 'opponent at law' [NASB], 'accuser' [LN, NIGTC; ESV, NET, NRSV], 'adversary' [WBC; KJV, NLT], 'adversary who is taking you to court' [NIV], 'enemy' [BAGD; NCV], 'plaintiff' [LN], 'person who has accused you of doing wrong' [CEV], '(when) someone sues you' [REB], '(if) someone brings a lawsuit against you' [TEV]. This noun denotes one who brings an accusation against someone [LN].

c. ταχύ (LN 67.110) (BAGD 2.b. p. 107): 'quickly' [BAGD, LN; all translations except BECNT; CEV, REB, TEV], 'promptly' [BECNT; REB], 'while there is still time' [TEV], 'at once, without delay' [BAGD], 'hurriedly, swiftly, speedily' [LN], not explicit [CEV]. This adverb describes what pertains to a very short extent of time [LN].

d. ὁδός (LN 15.19, 1.99) (BAGD 1. b. p. 554): 'way' [BAGD, LN (1.99)], 'journey' [BAGD, LN (15.19)]. This noun is used to denote a journey or traveling, presumably for some distance [LN (15.19)], or as a general term for a thoroughfare, either within a population center or between two such centers [LN (1.99)]. The phrase ἐν τῇ ὁδῷ 'on the way' [BECNT, BNTC, NICNT, PNTC; NASB, NIV] is also translated 'on the way to court' [NET; similarly NIGTC], 'in the way' [CC; KJV], 'on the road' [WBC]. The phrase ἕως ὅτου εἶ μετ' αὐτοῦ ἐν τῇ ὁδῷ 'while you are with him on the way (to court)' is translated 'while you are on the way to court with him' [GW, NRSV], 'when you are on your way to court' [NLT], 'while you are going with him to court' [ESV], 'while you are both on your way to court' [REB], 'while you still have opportunity to deal with him' [NTC], 'before you are dragged into court' [CEV], 'before you go to/get to court' [NCV, TEV].

QUESTION—What is an ἀντίδικος 'opponent'?

It is someone who has brought legal proceedings [NTC]. It expresses an adversarial legal situation [EBC], an adversary in a lawsuit [BNTC, ICC,

NIGTC, PNTC], any opponent at law [Lns], or any enemy [ICC]. It is a legal opponent to whom a sum of money is owed [NICNT, WBC], a creditor [My].

lest[a] the opponent hand- you(sg) -over[b] to-the judge, and the judge (deliver you) to-the officer,[c]

LEXICON—a. μήποτε (LN 89.62) (BAGD 2.b.α. p. 519): 'lest' [BNTC, CC, LN, NTC, PNTC, WBC; ESV, KJV], 'in order that...not' [BAGD, LN], 'so that...not' [LN, NIGTC; NASB], 'or (your adversary) will' [BECNT], 'or (he/your accuser) may' [NET, NIV, NRSV], 'otherwise (your opponent/he) will' [NICNT; GW], 'otherwise...(your enemy) might' [NCV], 'otherwise (your accuser/he) may' [NLT, REB], 'if you don't, you will be...' [CEV], 'once you are there, you will be' [TEV]. This conjunction marks negative purpose, often with the implication of apprehension [LN].

b. aorist. act. subj. of παραδίδωμι (LN **37.111**) (BAGD 1.b. p. 614): 'to hand over to' [BAGD, BECNT, CC, **LN**, NICNT, NIGTC, NTC, PNTC, WBC; ESV, GW, NASB, NET, NIV, NLT, NRSV, REB], 'to be handed over to' [CEV], 'to turn over to' [BAGD, LN; NCV], 'to deliver' [BNTC; KJV]. This verb means to deliver a person into the control of someone else, involving either the handing over of a presumably guilty person for punishment by authorities or the handing over of an individual to an enemy who will presumably take undue advantage of the victim [LN].

c. ὑπηρέτης (LN 35.20) (BAGD p. 842): 'officer' [NICNT, NTC, PNTC; CEV, GW, KJV, NASB, NIV, NLT, REB], 'court official' [NIGTC], 'servant' [BAGD, CC, LN, WBC], 'assistant' [BECNT], 'attendant' [BNTC], 'guard' [ESV, NCV, NRSV], 'warden' [NET], 'police' [TEV]. This noun denotes a person who renders service [LN]. The primary meaning is 'servant, assistant', and in this setting refers to a servant of the court [PNTC, TH] who looks after imprisonment [PNTC].

and you(sg) will-be-thrown[a] into prison;[b]

LEXICON—a. fut. pass. indic. of βάλλω (LN 15.215): 'to be thrown' [BECNT, CC, LN, NICNT, NIGTC, NTC, PNTC, WBC; NASB, NET, NIV, NLT, NRSV, REB], 'to be put' [BNTC; ESV, TEV], 'to be cast' [KJV]. This passive verb is also translated as active: 'to put' [CEV, NCV], 'to throw' [GW].

b. φυλακή (LN 7.24) (BAGD 3. p. 867): 'prison' [BAGD, BECNT, BNTC, CC, LN, NICNT, NIGTC, NTC, PNTC, WBC; ESV, GW, KJV, NASB, NET, NIV, NLT, NRSV], 'jail' [LN; CEV, NCV, REB, TEV]. This noun denotes a place of detention [LN].

5:26 truly[a] I-say to-you(sg), you(sg)-will- certainly-not[b] -get-out[c] from-there until you(sg)-pay[d] the last penny.[e]

LEXICON—a. ἀμήν. See this word at 5:18.

b. οὐ μή (LN 69.3) (BAGD D.1.a. p. 517): 'certainly not' [BAGD, CC, NIGTC, PNTC], 'surely (will) not' [NLT], 'not' [BAGD, BNTC, NICNT; CEV, NASB, NCV, NIV, REB], 'never' [BECNT, NTC, WBC; ESV, GW, NET, NRSV], 'by no means' [KJV], not explicit [TEV]. The negating particles οὐ and μή mark negative propositions [LN], and the use of the two together (οὐ μή) is the most decisive way of negating a future action [BAGD].
c. aorist act. subj. of ἐξέρχομαι (LN 15.40) (BAGD 1.a. p. 274): 'to get out' [BECNT, CC, NICNT, NIGTC, NTC, WBC; CEV, ESV, GW, NET, NIV, NRSV], 'to be released' [BNTC], 'to be let out' [REB], 'to go out' [BAGD, LN], 'to come out' [BAGD, PNTC; KJV, NASB], 'to go away' [BAGD], 'to leave' [NCV], 'to be free again' [NLT]. The phrase οὐ μή ἐξέλθῃς ἐκεῖθεν 'you will not get out from there' is translated 'there you will stay' [TEV]. This verb means to move out of an enclosed or well-defined two or three-dimensional area [LN].
d. aorist act. subj. of ἀποδίδωμι (LN 57.153) (BAGD 2. p. 90): 'to pay' [BECNT, BNTC, CC, LN, NTC, PNTC, WBC; all versions except NASB], 'to pay up' [NIGTC; NASB], 'to repay' [NICNT], 'to render' [LN], 'to give back, to return' [BAGD]. This verb means to make a payment, with the implication of such a payment being in response to an incurred obligation [LN].
e. κοδράντης (LN **6.78**) (BAGD p. 437): 'penny' [BAGD, **LN**, NICNT, PNTC; ESV, NET, NIV, NLT, NRSV, TEV], 'quarter penny' [WBC], 'cent' [BECNT, CC, LN, NTC; CEV, NASB], 'quadrans' [BAGD, BNTC, LN, NIGTC], 'farthing' [KJV]. The phrase τὸν ἔσχατον κοδράντην 'the last penny' is translated 'every penny of your fine' [GW], 'the last penny of your fine' [TEV], 'the uttermost farthing' [KJV], 'everything you owe' [NCV]. This noun denotes a Roman copper coin worth 1/4 of an assarion or 1/64 of a denarius [LN]. A denarius is a day's wage for a laborer [NTC].

QUESTION—What is the primary application for this illustration?
1. The point is that reconciliation includes being in friendly relations even with one's opponents [PNTC, WBC], including those who are not fellow Christians [ICC, WBC]. Verses 25–26 have a parallel in Luke 12:58–59 which is in an eschatological context about appearing before the great Judge. In Matthew, this passage follows the illustration about the importance of reconciliation between Christian brothers, but here it demands reconciliation between Christians and those outside the church such as opponents and enemies [ICC]. The primary focus is on reconciliation in human relationships, but there is also some suggestion of the final judgment of God as well [WBC].
2. These verses use the story to direct attention to God's final judgment [BNTC, Lns, My, NAC, NICNT, NIGTC, NTC]. It is not primarily about practical legal issues, but about the final judgment [BNTC, Lns, NICNT, NIGTC]. Although the setting of the illustration is human judgment, it is

intended to describe God's final judgment [NIGTC]. Jesus is primarily referring to averting God's wrath at the time of final judgment, when it will be too late to change the outcome [My, NAC]. The words 'I say to you truly' indicate that the ultimate purpose of this illustration is to point to God's judgment on people whose earthly relationships do not conform to the values of the kingdom of heaven [NICNT].

DISCOURSE UNIT—5:27–32 [GW]. The topic is about sexual sin.

DISCOURSE UNIT—5:27–30 [CEV, ESV, NCV, NIV, NLT, NRSV, TEV]. The topic is Jesus teaches about sexual sin [NCV], teaching about adultery [NLT, TEV], lust [ESV], concerning adultery [NRSV], adultery [NIV], marriage [CEV].

5:27 You(pl)-have-heard that it-was-said, You(sg)-shall- not -commit-adultery.[a]

LEXICON—a. fut. act. indic. μοιχεύω (used as aorist act. impera.) of μοιχεύω (LN 88.276) (BAGD 1. p. 526): 'to commit adultery' [BAGD, LN; all translations except CEV, NCV], 'to be guilty of adultery' [NCV]. The phrase οὐ μοιχεύσεις 'you shall not commit adultery' is translated 'Be faithful in marriage' [CEV]. This verb refers to sexual intercourse of a man with a married woman other than his own spouse [LN].

5:28 But I say to-you(pl) that everyone[a] looking-at[b] a woman[c] in-order-to lust-after[d] her

LEXICON—a. πᾶς (LN 59.24): 'everyone' [BECNT, BNTC, NIGTC, PNTC, WBC; ESV, NASB, NRSV], 'anyone' [LN, NTC; NCV, NIV, NIV, NLT, TEV], 'every man' [CC, NICNT], 'whoever' [GW, NET], 'whosoever' [KJV]. The phrase πᾶς ὁ βλέπων 'everyone looking' is translated 'if you look' [CEV], 'if a man looks' [REB].

b. pres. act. participle of βλέπω (LN 24.7) (BAGD 3. p. 143): 'to look at' [BAGD, all translations except KJV], 'to look on' [KJV], 'to notice, to glance at' [LN]. This verb means to see, frequently in the sense of becoming aware of or taking notice of something [LN].

c. γυνή (LN 9.34) (BAGD 2. p.168): 'woman' [BECNT, BNTC, CC, LN, NTC, PNTC, WBC; all versions except CEV], 'another woman' [CEV], '[married] woman' [NIGTC], 'wife' [BAGD], 'someone else's wife' [NICNT]. This noun denotes an adult female person of marriageable age [LN]. It is also the word for 'wife' [BAGD].

d. ἐπιθυμέω (LN **25.20**) (BAGD p. 293): 'to lust after' [NTC, PNTC; KJV], 'to lust for' [BECNT], 'to lust' [LN], 'to desire' [BAGD, CC; GW, NET], 'to covet' [LN]. The phrase πρὸς τὸ ἐπιθυμῆσαι αὐτήν 'in order to lust after/for her' [BECNT, NTC] is translated 'to lust after her' [PNTC], 'with the purpose of lusting after her' [WBC], 'lustfully'[**LN**; NIV], 'with lust' [NLT, NRSV], 'with lust for her' [NASB], 'with a lustful eye' [REB], 'with lustful intent' [ESV], 'with lustful desire for her' [BNTC], 'so as to desire her' [CC], 'in order to desire her [sexually]' [NIGTC], 'and wants to possess her' [TEV], 'and wants to sin sexually with her' [NCV], 'and wants to have sex with her' [NICNT], 'and (you) want her' [CEV], 'and desires her' [GW]. This verb means to strongly desire to have what belongs to someone else and/or to engage in an activity which is morally wrong [LN].

QUESTION—Does βλέπων γυναῖκα 'looking at a woman' refer generally to looking lustfully at any woman or specifically to looking lustfully at a married woman, that is, someone's wife?

  1. It refers to looking lustfully at any woman [BECNT, EBC, Lns, My, TRT, WBC].

  2. It refers to looking lustfully at a married woman [NIBC, NICNT, NIGTC].

QUESTION—Does πρὸς τὸ ἐπιθυμῆσαι αὐτήν 'in order to lust after her' indicate the result of looking at a woman or the purpose or intent of looking at her?

  1. It indicates purpose or intent [BECNT, EBC, Lns, My, NAC, NIBC, NICNT, NIGTC, NTC, WBC].

  1.1 The purpose is to lust [BECNT, My, NIBC, WBC], to intentionally awaken lust [NIBC, NIGTC]. It could also involve contemplating or possibly even planning to engage in actual adultery [NICNT, NIGTC].

  1.2 The purpose is to cause her to lust, to entice her to sin [EBC].

  2. It indicates result [BAGD, ICC]. The sin is not so much that the thought occurred, but allowing it to incite passion [ICC].

  3. It indicates purpose as well as result [CC].

already[a] has-committed-adultery-with[b] her in his heart.[c]

LEXICON—a. ἤδη (LN 67.20) (BAGD 2. p. 344): 'already' [BAGD, LN; all translations except TEV], not explicit [TEV]. This adverb describes a point of time preceding another point of time and implying completion [LN].

  b. aorist act. indic. of μοιχεύω (LN 88.276) (BAGD 2.b. p. 526):'to commit adultery' [BAGD, LN; all translations except CEV, NCV, TEV], 'to be guilty of committing adultery' [TEV], 'to be unfaithful' [CEV], 'to do that sin' [NCV]. This aorist verb is translated as perfect tense by all translations except CEV, TEV. This verb refers to a man having sexual intercourse with a married woman other than his own spouse [LN].

  c. καρδία (LN 26.3) (BAGD 1.b.ε. p. 404): 'heart' [BAGD, LN; all translations except CEV, NCV], 'mind' [LN; NCV], 'thoughts' [CEV], 'inner self' [LN]. This noun denotes the causative source of a person's psychological life in its various aspects, but with special emphasis upon thoughts [LN].

QUESTION—In what sense does he commit adultery with her in his heart?

What Jesus addresses here is the inner desire and consent to the sin in one's own mind, the thoughts and actions that make giving in to the temptation more likely [NAC]. It is to indulge in illicit sexual relations in the imagination, which is sin, and possibly even the planning of actual adultery [NIGTC]. Since the heart is the center of a person's being, to lust in the heart is to be an adulterer in all that really matters [PNTC]. To desire or to imagine sexual involvement with a woman other than one's wife is to violate the real intent of the commandment against adultery as well as the commandment that prohibits coveting another's wife. What occurs in the heart is the foundation of the external act [WBC]. Jesus is saying that the act of continuing to look lustfully indicates that in his heart the man was already an adulterer to begin with [Lns]. By virtue of his adulterous desire he is already an adulterer with respect to his moral constitution [My]. The sin is committed in the lustful thinking of one person, and does not implicate the other party [CC]. It is his intent to entice her into adultery [EBC]. Lust is a violation of the tenth commandment against coveting [NTC].

5:29 And[a] if[b] your(sg) right eye causes- you(sg) -to-sin,[c] pluck- it -out[d] and throw- (it) -away[e] from you(sg);

LEXICON—a. δέ (LN 89.94): 'and' [BECNT, CC, LN, PNTC], 'but' [NICNT, WBC; KJV], not explicit [BNTC; CEV, ESV, NASB, NCV, NET, NIV, NRSV, REB]. The phrase εἰ δέ 'and if' is translated 'so if' [NTC; GW, NLT, TEV], 'if [even]' [NIGTC], This conjunction marks an additive relation, but with the possible implication of some contrast [LN].

b. εἰ (LN 89.65) (BAGD I.1.a. p. 219): 'if' [BAGD, LN; all translations]. This particle marks a condition, real or hypothetical, actual or contrary to fact [LN]. It may express a condition that is thought of as being real, or to mark assumptions regarding something that has already happened [BAGD].

c. pres. act. indic. of σκανδαλίζω (LN **88.304**) (BAGD 1.a. p. 752): 'to cause to sin' [BAGD, BNTC, LN; CEV, ESV, GW, NCV, NET, NIV, NRSV, TEV], 'to make to sin' [BECNT, PNTC], 'to make to stumble' [NASB], 'to cause to stumble' [CC, NICNT, WBC], 'to cause to stumble [into sin]' [NIGTC], 'to cause to fall' [BAGD], 'to cause to lust' [NLT], 'to lure into sin' [NTC], 'to offend' [KJV], 'to cause (your) downfall' [REB]. This verb means to cause to sin, with the probable implication of providing some special circumstances which contribute to such behavior [LN].

d. aorist act. impera. of ἐξαιρέω (LN **85.43**) (BAGD 1. p. 271): 'to pluck out' [NIGTC, NTC, WBC; KJV], 'to gouge out' [BECNT, PNTC; NIV, NLT], 'to tear out' [BAGD, BNTC, CC, NICNT; ESV, GW, NASB, NET, NRSV, REB], 'to take out' [BAGD, **LN**; NCV, TEV], 'to poke out' [CEV], 'to remove' [LN]. This verb means to take something out of its place [LN].

e. aorist act. impera. of βάλλω (LN **15.215**) (BAGD 1.b. p. 131): 'to throw away' [BAGD, BECNT, CC, NICNT, PNTC; all versions except KJV, NASB, REB], 'to throw' [BNTC, **LN**; NASB], 'to cast' [WBC; KJV], 'to cast away' [NIGTC], 'to fling away' [NTC; REB].

QUESTION—What is the nature and severity of the sin described as σκανδαλίζει σε 'causes you to sin'?

It is a sin that leads inexorably to judgment [NAC] and will result in being condemned to hell [BECNT, CC, EBC, Lns, NTC]. This stumbling results in the final loss of salvation [NICNT]. It seems to be equated with giving up one's faith in God or rejecting God [TRT].

for it-is-better[a] for-you(sg) that one of your(sg) members[b] be-lost[c]
- LEXICON—a. pres. act. indic. of συμφέρω (LN 65.44) (BAGD 2.a. p. 780): 'to be better' [BECNT, BNTC, CC, NIGTC, NTC, WBC; CEV, ESV, GW, NASB, NCV, NET, NIV, NLT, NRSV, REB], 'to be much better' [TEV], 'to be better off' [LN, NICNT], 'to be expedient' [PNTC], 'to be advantageous' [BAGD, LN], 'to be profitable' [BAGD; KJV]. This verb means to be of an advantage to someone [LN].
- b. μέλος (LN 8.9) (BAGD 1. p. 501): 'member' [BAGD, BNTC, CC, LN, NIGTC, NTC, PNTC, WBC; ESV, KJV, NET, NRSV], 'part of (your) body' [NICNT; CEV, GW, NASB, NCV, NIV, NLT, REB, TEV], 'body part' [BECNT, LN]. This noun denotes a part of the body [LN].
- c. aorist mid. subj. of ἀπόλλυμι (LN 57.68) (BAGD 2.a. p. 96): 'to be lost' [LN], 'to be destroyed' [NIGTC], 'to perish' [BNTC, CC, PNTC, WBC; KJV], 'to lose' [BECNT, NICNT; all versions except KJV]. This verb means to lose something which one already possesses [LN].

and not[a] (that) your(sg) whole body be-thrown[b] into hell.[c]

LEXICON—a. καὶ μή: 'and not that' [PNTC; KJV], 'and...not' [NIGTC], 'that...not' [CC], 'than for' [BECNT; CEV, NASB, NET, NIV, NLT, NRSV, REB], 'than that' [BNTC, NTC, WBC; ESV], 'than (having)' [NICNT], 'than (to have)' [GW, NCV, NET, TEV].
- b. aorist. pass. subj. of βάλλω (LN 15.215) (BAGD 1.b. p. 131): 'to be thrown' [BAGD, BECNT, BNTC, CC, LN, NICNT, NTC, PNTC, WBC; all versions except CEV, KJV], 'to be cast' [NIGTC; KJV], 'to end up (in hell)' [CEV].
- c. γέεννα (LN 1.21) (BAGD p. 153). See this word at 5:22.

5:30 And if your(sg) right hand causes- you(sg) -to-sin, cut- it -off[a] and throw- (it) -away from you(sg); for it-is-better for-you(sg), that one of your(sg) members be-lost than your(sg) whole body go[b] into hell.

LEXICON—a. aorist act. impera. of ἐκκόπτω (LN 19.18) (BAGD 1. p. 241): 'to cut off' [BAGD, LN; all translations except BECBT; CEV], 'to amputate' [BECNT], 'to chop off' [CEV]. This verb means to cut in such a way as to cause separation [LN].
- b. aorist act. subj. of ἀπέρχομαι (LN 15.37): 'to go' [BECNT, BNTC, NICNT; ESV, GW, NASB, NCV, NET, NIV, NRSV, REB], 'to go off' [NIGTC, PNTC; TEV], 'to go down' [NTC], 'to go away' [LN], 'to depart' [CC, LN, WBC]. The active phrase 'go into hell' is translated as passive: 'to be cast into hell' [KJV], 'to be thrown into hell' [CEV, NLT].

144   MATTHEW 5:30

This verb describes motion away from a reference point with emphasis upon the departure, but without implications as to any resulting state of separation or rupture [LN].

QUESTION—How literally did Jesus intend his statements to be taken and what does it mean?

This is hyperbole [BECNT, CC, My, NAC, NICNT, PNTC, TH, TRT]. He is speaking figuratively, not literally [BNTC, ICC, NAC, NIBC, NICNT, NTC, WBC]. Jesus is not advocating actual mutilation of the body [BECNT, EBC, PNTC]. It means that a person must deal radically and decisively with sin [BECNT, BNTC, CC, EBC, NTC, WBC], and take drastic measures to prevent winding up in hell [NIGTC]. Unconditional self-denial and self-discipline is required [My]. There must be no compromise with evil [PNTC]. Anything that leads to sin and ruin must be stopped [BNTC]. Even self-mutilation is not radical enough, as it does not change the capacity to sin in one's own imagination [EBC]. Jesus is countering poor excuses for sin that claim that the bodily members are the cause of sin and that don't acknowledge that the real problem is in the heart; he is saying that, if that is what you claim, then remove the bodily member, which he of course knows is not really the problem, since a transformed heart, not bodily mutilation, is really the answer [Lns].

DISCOURSE UNIT—5:31–32 [CEV, ESV, NCV, NIV, NLT, NRSV, TEV]. The topic is Jesus teaches about divorce [NCV], teaching about divorce [NLT, TEV], concerning divorce [NRSV], divorce [CEV, ESV, NIV].

5:31 It-was- also -said, Whoever divorces[a] his wife,[b] let-him-give[c] her a-certificate-of-divorce.[d]

LEXICON—a. aorist act. subj. of ἀπολύω (LN **34.78**) (BAGD 2.a. p. 96): 'to divorce' [BAGD, LN; all translations except KJV, NASB], 'to put away' [KJV], 'to send away' [BAGD; NASB]. This verb means to dissolve the marriage bond [LN].

b. γυνή (LN **10.54**) (BAGD 2. p. 168): 'wife' [BAGD, LN; all translations]. This noun denotes a woman who is married to a man [LN].

c. aorist act. impera. (third person imperative) of δίδωμι (LN 57.71) (BAGD 2. p. 193): 'to give' [BAGD, LN; all translations except CEV], 'to hand over' [BAGD]. The third person imperative 'let him give' [BNTC, CC, NIGTC, NTC, PNTC; ESV, KJV, NASB, NRSV], is also translated '(he) must give' [BECNT, NICNT, WBC; GW, NCV, NET, NIV, REB, TEV], 'by merely giving' [NLT], 'he must write out...for her' [CEV]. This verb means to give an object, usually implying value [LN].

d. ἀποστάσιον (LN **33.41**) (BAGD p. 98): 'certificate of divorce' [BAGD, BECNT, CC, WBC; ESV, NASB, NIV, NRSV], 'divorce certificate' [NICNT, NTC], 'certificate of dismissal' [REB], 'bill of divorce' [PNTC], 'writing of divorcement' [KJV], 'certificate of release' [BNTC], 'document of release' [NIGTC], 'divorce papers' [CEV], 'written divorce paper' [NCV], 'written notice' [GW], 'written notice of divorce' [**LN**;

NLT], 'a legal document' [NET]. This noun denotes a written statement prepared by a husband and given to a wife as evidence of a legal divorce [LN].

QUESTION—Does ἐρρέθη δέ 'it was also said' indicate a citation of scripture or a reference to scribal interpretation?

It is an allusion to Deut 24:1ff [BNTC, EBC, ICC, Lns, NAC, NICNT, WBC]. It is an abbreviated citation form, linking it to the preceding passage beginning in 5:27 where scripture is introduced [EBC]. Although this is an abbreviated form for introducing scripture, here Jesus is summarizing how the passage was understood in scribal interpretation, which he opposes [PNTC]. Jesus is introducing what Jewish interpreters have said about how husbands should deal with their wives [CC]. He refers to Deut 24 as the rationale given by scribes and Pharisees to justify their lax divorce practices [Lns, My].

QUESTION—What was a certificate of divorce?

It was a written legal document [BECNT, WBC]. It expressly stated that the woman was free to marry another man and assumed that she would actually do so [CC, NICNT]. It was to be delivered in the presence of two witnesses [NIBC]. The bill of divorce stated that the man is giving up his claims on his wife [BNTC, NIGTC, PNTC, WBC], and that she was free to marry another man [BNTC, NIGTC, PNTC]. It was intended to protect the woman [BNTC, LN, NIBC, TRT], particularly from arbitrary and hasty action on the part of the husband [BNTC, NIBC].

5:32 But I-say to-you(pl) that everyone divorcing his wife except-for[a] (the) reason[b] of-sexual-immorality[c]

LEXICON—a. παρεκτός (LN 58.38) (BAGD 2. p. 625): 'except for' [BAGD, BECNT, CC, PNTC; NASB, NET, NIV], '(for any reason) except' [NICNT], 'except on (the ground of)' [BNTC, NTC, WBC; ESV, NRSV], 'except (in relation to)' [NIGTC], 'other than' [GW, REB, TEV], 'besides' [LN], 'unless' [CEV, NLT], 'saving for' [KJV], 'apart from' [BAGD], not explicit [NCV]. This preposition describes what pertains to being different and in addition to something else, with the implication of something being external to central concerns [LN].

b. λόγος (LN **89.18**) (BAGD 1.a.ε. p. 477; or 2.d. p. 478): 'reason' [BAGD (2.d.)], LN, NICNT; GW, NASB, NCV], 'grounds (of)' [BNTC, NTC, WBC; NRSV], 'matter' [BAGD (1.a.ε□), CC, NIGTC, PNTC], 'cause' [KJV, REB, TEV], not explicit [BECNT; CEV, NET, NIV, NLT]. This noun denotes a reason, with the implication of some verbal formulation [LN]. In this verse it refers to the subject or matter under discussion (1.a.ε.), although the reason or motive (2.d.) is also possible [BAGD].

c. πορνεία (LN 88.271) (BAGD 1. p. 693): 'sexual immorality' [LN; ESV], 'immorality' [NET], 'sexual infidelity' [BECNT, WBC], 'infidelity' [NTC], 'unfaithfulness' [GW, TEV], 'marital unfaithfulness' [NIV], 'sexual unfaithfulness' [NICNT], 'sexual impurity' [NIGTC], 'adultery'

[CC], 'fornication' [BAGD, LN, PNTC; KJV], 'illicit sex' [LN], 'unchastity' [BAGD, BNTC; NASB, NRSV, REB], 'prostitution' [BAGD, LN], 'some terrible sexual sin' [CEV], 'sexual relations with another man' [NCV], 'she has been unfaithful' [NLT]. This noun denotes the act of engaging in sexual immorality of any kind, often with the implication of prostitution [LN]. It encompasses every kind of unlawful sexual intercourse [BAGD].

QUESTION—What is πορνεία 'sexual immorality' in this context?

In this context it means adultery [BNTC, CC, ICC, Lns, My, NAC, NIBC, NICNT, NTC, PNTC, TH, TRT, WBC], a violating of the marriage bond by sexual infidelity [NTC]. It could also refer to sexual sins that occurred before marriage [NICNT, WBC]. It is any sexual activity not involving one's own spouse [BECNT, ICC]. It is sexual sin generally, which would include, but not be limited to, adultery [BAGD, EBC, NICNT, NIGTC, TH, WBC]. Πορνεία, which refers to sexual sin in general, was used more often to refer to female infidelity, whereas μοιχεία (the noun corresponding to the verb μοιχεύω 'to commit adultery') was more often used of male infidelity [ICC, NAC]. By the time of the first century capital punishment as the penalty for adultery had been abolished and divorce took its place [Lns, PNTC], and at least in the case of a woman having committed adultery, divorce may even have been required [PNTC]. Jesus forbids the breaking of a marriage that is intact, but in the case where adultery has occurred, the marriage is already broken and could not continue [NICNT].

he-makes[a] her to-commit-adultery,[b] and whoever marries a-divorced-woman commits-adultery.

LEXICON—a. pres. act. indic. of ποιέω (LN 13.9) (BAGD I.1.b.θ. p. 681): 'to make (to)' [BAGD, BECNT, CC, LN, PNTC; ESV, GW, NASB, NET], 'to make (her the victim)' [NICNT], 'to cause (to)' [BAGD, BNTC, NIGTC, WBC; CEV, KJV, NIV, NLT, NRSV], 'to force to be' [NCV], 'to expose...to (adultery)' [NTC], 'to involve...in (adultery)' [REB], 'to cause to be, to make to be' [LN]. This verb means to cause a state to be [LN].

b. aorist pass. infin. of μοιχεύω (LN 88.276) (BAGD 2.b. p. 526): 'to commit adultery' [BECNT, BNTC, **LN**, PNTC, WBC; ESV, KJV, NASB, NET, NLT, NRSV, TEV], 'to be unfaithful' [CEV], 'to be guilty of adultery' [NCV], 'to become an adulteress' [NIV]. The passive infinitive μοιχευθῆναι, which is usually translated as active ('to commit adultery') is also translated as passive: 'to have adultery committed against her' [CC, NIGTC], '(to be) the victim of adultery' [NICNT], 'to look as though she has committed adultery' [GW], 'involves her in adultery' [REB]. This verb denotes sexual intercourse of a man with a married woman other than his own spouse. From the standpoint of the NT, adultery was normally defined in terms of the married status of the woman involved in any such act. In other words, sexual intercourse of a married man with an unmarried woman would usually be regarded as πορνεία 'fornication' (88.271), but sexual intercourse of either an unmarried or a married man with someone else's wife was regarded as adultery, both on the part of the man as well as the woman [LN].

QUESTION—How would the divorcing husband cause the divorced wife to commit adultery?

1. He causes her to commit adultery when she marries again [BAGD, BECNT, BNTC, ICC, My, NTC, PNTC, TH, TRT, WBC; TEV]. In first century Jewish society the divorced woman had little choice but to marry again just in order to live, so the husband who divorced her is in effect compelling her to remarry and thus become an adulteress [PNTC, NTC, WBC]. Jesus recognized marriage to be a life-long union of one man and one woman, which was not to be dissolved except where it had already been broken by infidelity [PNTC]. If there has been no sexual infidelity to break the marriage there can be no true divorce, and hence any subsequent marriage or sexual union would be adulterous [BECNT, ICC, My, TH]. It is the divorce itself, at least metaphorically, and not a subsequent remarriage, that was adulterous in that it violated the covenantal and lifelong nature of marriage [NAC]. While divorce implies that remarriage is allowed, Jesus is calling his disciples back to God's original intent that marriage should be a lifelong union, a fact that not even divorce can change [WBC].
2. The passive infinitive shows that the woman herself is not the one guilty of adultery [CC, Lns, NIGTC]. A woman who is wrongly divorced and then subsequently remarries is not herself guilty of adultery; rather, adultery is committed against by her first husband who wrongly divorced her [CC, Lns, NIBC]. She is unjustly stigmatized as an adulteress, despite having done no wrong, and the man who marries her likewise is subject to that unjust stigma [Lns]. A husband who divorces his wife causes adultery to be committed against her when he marries someone else [CC, NIGTC]. Likewise, a man is implicated in adultery if he marries a woman who has provoked her husband into divorcing her so she could go to the other man [NIGTC].

DISCOURSE UNIT—5:33–37 [CEV, ESV, GW, NCV, NLT, TEV]. The topic is about oaths [GW], make promises carefully [NCV], teaching about vows [NLT, TEV], oaths [ESV], promises [CEV].

5:33 Again[a] you(pl)-have-heard that it-was-said to-the ancients,[b] You(sg)-shall- not -swear-falsely/break-an-oath,[c] but you-shall-perform[d] your vows[e] to-the Lord.

LEXICON—a. πάλιν (LN 89.97) (BAGD 3. p. 607): 'again' [BNTC, CC, LN, NICNT, NTC, PNTC, WBC; ESV, KJV, NASB, NET, NIV, NRSV, REB], 'also' [LN; NLT], 'and' [LN], 'furthermore' [BAGD, BECNT], not explicit [NIGTC; CEV, GW, NCV, TEV]. This adverb marks an additive relationship involving repetition [LN].

b. ἀρχαῖος. See this word at 5:21.

c. fut. indic. act. of ἐπιορκέω (LN **33.464, 33.465**) (BAGD 2. p. 296): 'to swear falsely' [BAGD, **LN** (33.465), NICNT, NIGTC, WBC; ESV, NRSV], 'to make false vows' [NASB], 'to perjure oneself' [LN (33.465)], 'to commit perjury' [BNTC]. Another meaning is 'to break an oath' [BAGD, BECNT, CC, **LN** (33.464), NTC, PNTC; GW, NET, NIV, REB], 'to swear and fail to keep (an oath)' [**LN** (33.464)], 'to break a promise' [BAGD; NCV, TEV], 'to break a vow' [NLT], 'to foreswear oneself' [LN (33.464); KJV]. The phrase οὐκ ἐπιορκήσεις 'you shall not swear falsely' is translated 'don't use the Lord's name to make a promise unless you are going to keep it' [CEV]. This verb means to take an oath that something is true, when in reality one knows that it is false [LN (33.465)], or to swear that one will do something and then not fulfill that promise [LN (33.464)]. In this verse either 'swear falsely' or 'break one's promise' is possible [BAGD]. This word occurs only here in the NT.

d. fut. act. indic. of ἀποδίδωμι (LN 90.46) (BAGD 1. p. 90): 'to perform' [BNTC, LN; ESV, KJV], 'to keep (an oath/promise)' [BAGD, BECNT, NTC, PNTC; CEV, NCV, NIV, REB], 'to carry out' [NLT, NRSV], 'to pay' [CC], 'to fulfill' [NICNT, WBC; NASB, NET], 'to do' [LN; TEV], 'to give' [LN; GW], 'to hand over' [NIGTC]. This verb denotes an agent relationship with a numerable event, with the probable implication of some transfer involved [LN].

e. ὅρκος (LN 33.463) (BAGD p. 581): 'oath' [BAGD, BECNT, CC, LN, NICNT, NTC, PNTC, WBC; KJV, NIV, REB], 'vow' [NASB, NET, NLT, NRSV], 'promise' [NCV], not explicit [CEV]. This noun is translated by a phrase: 'the things you swear you will do' [BNTC], 'what you have sworn you will give' [NIGTC], 'what you have sworn' [ESV], 'what you swore in an oath to give him' [GW], 'what you have vowed…to do' [TEV]. This noun denotes the statement that is made when calling on a divine being to execute sanctions against a person if the statement in question is not true [LN].

QUESTION—What is the function of πάλιν 'again'?

This adverb, along with the formula that follows, indicates that this is the introduction to a second section of three contrasts [BECNT, BNTC, CC, ICC, NIGTC], the first set being 5:21–26, 5:27–30, and 5:31–32, and the second set consisting of 5:33–37, 5:38–42, and 5:43–48 [BECNT, ICC, NIGTC]. It indicates the beginning of the second of two sets of three contrasts between the Law of Moses and how Jesus teaches that it must be fulfilled [BECNT, BNTC]. It indicates a different subject concerning another scripture quotation [PNTC]. It indicates more teaching of the scribes and Pharisees about the meaning of the OT law [Lns]. It indicates a reference to the elaborate hierarchy that Jewish teachers taught concerning oaths [CC]. It indicates another subject, which confirms that 5:31–32 was an excursus to the antithesis that preceded it, and not a separate one [EBC].

QUESTION—What is the problem Jesus is addressing?

Many believed that if one swore by something other than God or his name, they would not have to fulfill that oath. So they made oaths freely and excused themselves for not fulfilling them [BNTC, EBC, Lns, My, NTC]. There was an elaborate hierarchy of laws in first century Judaism concerning which oaths had to be fulfilled, and which oaths could be left unfulfilled [BECNT, CC, NAC, WBC]. Equivocation on the part of the rabbis had led to the problem of verbal statements being unreliable unless given with a vow [NIBC]. Jesus means that his followers should be truthful at all times and should not need to swear an oath in order to be believed [BECNT, PNTC]. He was also addressing the inflated view that people of his day tended to have regarding their own importance, as reflected in swearing upon one's own head [CC].

QUESTION—Does Jesus contradict what the OT says about oaths and vows?

Jesus' goal is the same as that of the law, which is integrity in speech, so there is no real contradiction [WBC]. While it can be said that Jesus contradicts what the OT says about oaths and vows, he does so in order to uphold its real intent on a deeper level [BECNT, EBC, WBC], and in so doing he actually upholds the commandment against bearing false witness [BECNT]. While the OT laws in question have legitimacy for dealing with specific problems, they cannot form the basis for ethical thinking; Jesus moves beyond the remedial function of the OT law and calls his disciples to a more radical level of righteousness [NICNT].

QUESTION—What is the intent of the OT commands cited?

This is a summary of teachings from various OT passages [BECNT, BNTC, EBC, ICC, Lns, NIBC, NICNT, TH], which are concerned with swearing falsely [EBC, ICC, NTC], and breaking vows [EBC]. It is about violating the second commandment concerning disrespect for God's name [CC, EBC, Lns, My, NICNT, NIGTC] and also violating the ninth commandment concerning false witness [NICNT, TH]. There are different OT passages about people performing what they promised to do [BECNT, BNTC, NIBC], and about being truthful [BECNT, NTC]. The concern here was that people violated the second commandment by making arbitrary distinctions about which oaths were binding and which were not [My].

QUESTION—What is the relationship of the 'vow' to the 'swearing falsely' mentioned in the previous clause?

A vow had to been taken with an oath, which is the real concern of Jesus' statements [BNTC, Lns, NIGTC, NTC]. Both vows and oaths were made in God's name [EBC]. Oaths, which invoke God to substantiate a statement or promise, and vows, which are solemn promises to God, are related, and here Jesus is primarily dealing with oaths [NICNT]. Others think that vows and oaths are treated as being more or less the same [BECNT, TRT].

5:34 **But I say to-you(pl) not to-swear^a at-all;^b**

LEXICON—a. aorist act. infin. of ὀμνύω (or ὄμνυμι) (LN 33.463) (BAGD p. 566): 'to swear' [BAGD, BNTC, CC, LN, NICNT, PNTC; KJV, NIV, NRSV, REB], 'to swear an oath' [BECNT, NIGTC; GW, NCV], 'to take an oath' [BAGD, NTC, WBC; ESV, NET], 'to make an oath' [LN; NASB], 'to make a vow' [NLT]. The phrase μὴ ὀμόσαι 'not to swear' is translated 'not to swear by anything when you make a promise' [CEV], 'do not use any vow when you make a promise' [TEV]. This verb means to affirm the truth of a statement by calling on a divine being to execute sanctions against a person if the statement in question is not true [LN].

b. ὅλως (LN **78.44**) (BAGD p. 565): 'at all' [BAGD, BECNT, BNTC, CC, LN, NICNT, NIGTC, NTC, PNTC, WBC; ESV, GW, KJV, NASB, NET, NIV, NRSV, REB], 'by anything' [CEV]. The phrase μὴ...ὅλως 'not...at all' is translated 'never' [NCV], 'not...any' [NLT, TEV]. This adverb describes the degree of totality or completeness of that which it modifies [LN].

QUESTION—What is Jesus warning them not to do?

He is warning them about dishonesty [BECNT, NIBC, NICNT, NTC, PNTC] and hypocrisy [NTC]. He is telling them not to make oaths in their everyday conversation, and in particular not to make oaths such as those that were thought to be non-binding based on the complicated rules of some rabbis of the day [ICC]. He is telling them not to make oaths generally [Lns, My], but also to avoid lying and perjury, as well as oath breaking [BECNT, Lns]. He is telling them to avoid the use of solemn sounding oaths instead of simple, truthful speech [BNTC]. He is warning them not to follow the false distinctions made by Jewish teachers regarding which oath formulas were binding and which were not [TH].

QUESTION—Is Jesus forbidding the use of any oaths at all?

He is forbidding the use of oaths in common conversation as being unnecessary for truthful people, but he is not forbidding them from taking appropriate oaths such as those that are required in a court of law [ICC, NIBC, NTC, PNTC]. He is forbidding the use of oaths generally as being unnecessary for people who tell the truth, although it is still provisionally necessary in regard to law courts [My]. He is emphasizing the necessity of truthfulness, but this does not mean that court oaths are forbidden [CC, EBC, NICNT]. He is not forbidding religious vows [TH].

neither by^a heaven,^b for^c it-is (the) throne^d of-God;

LEXICON—a. ἐν (LN **90.30**) (BAGD IV. 5. p. 261): 'by' [BAGD, LN; all translations]. This preposition marks objects which serve as symbolic substitutes for supernatural persons or powers presumed to act as guarantors of compliance with oaths [LN].

b. οὐρανός (LN **1.11**) (BAGD 1.a.β. p. 593): 'heaven' [BAGD, LN; all translations]. This noun denotes the supernatural dwelling place of God and other heavenly beings [LN].

MATTHEW 5:34

c. ὅτι (LN 89.33): 'for' [BNTC, CC, LN, NTC; ESV, KJV, NASB, NIV, NRSV, REB, TEV], 'since' [LN], 'because' [BECNT, LN, NICNT, NIGTC, PNTC, WBC; NCV, NET, NLT], not explicit [CEV, GW]. This conjunction marks cause or reason, based on an evident fact [LN].

d. θρόνος (LN 6.112) (BAGD 1.b. p. 364): 'throne' [BAGD, LN; all translations]. This noun denotes a relatively large and elaborate seat upon which a ruler sits on official occasions [LN]. Here, the word 'heaven' refers to the throne of God were he sits to rule [PNTC, TH]

5:35 nor by the earth,[a] for it-is (the) footstool[b] of-his feet; nor by[c] Jerusalem, for it-is (the) city of-the great king;

LEXICON—a. γῆ (LN 1.39) (BAGD 5.a. p. 157): 'earth' [BAGD, LN; all translations], 'world' [LN]. This noun denotes the surface of the earth as the dwelling place of mankind, in contrast with the heavens above and the world below [LN].

b. ὑποπόδιον (LN **6.117**) (BAGD p. 847): 'footstool' [BAGD, LN; all translations except TEV], 'resting place (for his feet)' [TEV]. This noun denotes a piece of furniture on which one may rest one's feet [LN].

c. εἰς (LN 90.30) (BAGD 6.b. p. 230): 'by' [BAGD, BECNT, BNTC, CC, LN, NICNT, NIGTC, NTC, PNTC; all versions], 'with reference to' [WBC]. This preposition marks objects which serve as symbolic substitutes for supernatural persons or powers presumed to act as guarantors of compliance with oaths [LN].

QUESTION—Who is the great king?

God is the great king [BECNT, BNTC, CC, ICC, Lns, My, NIGTC, NTC, PNTC, TH, WBC; probably all versions except CEV since they capitalize 'King'], as is mentioned in Psalm 48:2 [ICC, My, NTC, PNTC, TH] and other OT passages [ICC].

5:36 nor swear[a] by your(sg) head for you(sg)-are- not -able[b] to-make[c] one hair[d] white or black.

LEXICON—a. aorist act. subj. of ὀμνύω (or ὄμνυμι). See this word at 5:34.

b. pres. mid. or pass. (deponent = act.) indic. of δύναμαι (LN 74.5): 'can' [BECNT, BNTC, LN, NICNT, NIGTC, NTC, PNTC; all versions except NET], 'to be able to' [CC, LN, WBC; NET]. This verb means to be able to do or to experience something [LN].

c. aorist act. infin. of ποιέω (LN 13.9) (BAGD I.1.b.ι. p. 682): 'to make' [BAGD, LN; all translations except NCV, NLT, REB], 'to make to be' [BAGD, LN], 'to make to become' [NCV], 'to turn' [NLT, REB], 'to cause to be, to result in, to bring upon, to bring about' [LN]. This verb means to cause a state to be [LN].

d. θρίξ (LN 8.12) (BAGD 2. p. 364): 'hair' [BAGD, LN; all translations except NCV], 'hair on your head' [NCV]. This noun denotes hair, either of a person or of an animal [LN].

QUESTION—Why does Jesus forbid them to swear by heaven, earth, Jerusalem, or one's own head?

He forbids swearing by these things because of the relationship that they all have toward God [My], who is present in all his creation [PNTC]. Even though God is not mentioned when swearing by these things, he is involved [BNTC, EBC, Lns, NIBC, PNTC]. God is the creator and sustainer of all these things [ICC]. Since each of these belongs to God in an important way, it is wrong to think that swearing by them is less binding than swearing by God himself [CC, NAC, PNTC]. To swear by things that God owns *is* actually invoking God [NTC]. All oaths implicate God, and are therefore binding [WBC]. Heaven and earth are God's created domain and under his control, and Jerusalem is the place where he chose to make his presence known on earth, and all of them were metonymies associated with God [BECNT]. Heaven, earth, and Jerusalem are God's dwelling and possession, and he is also the creator and sustainer of the human head and hair [NICNT].

5:37 But[a] let- your(pl) word[b] -be[c] 'Yes yes' (or) 'No no.'

LEXICON—a. δέ (LN 89.124): 'but' [BNTC, CC, LN, PNTC, WBC; KJV, NASB], 'rather' [BECNT, NICNT], not explicit [NIGTC, NTC; CEV, ESV, GW, NCV, NET, NIV, NLT, NRSV, REB, TEV]. This preposition marks contrast [LN].

b. λόγος (LN 33.98) (BAGD 1.a.β. p. 477): 'word' [BECNT, BNTC, CC, LN, NICNT, NIGTC, WBC; NET, NRSV], 'speech' [NTC], 'what you say' [BAGD; ESV], 'message' [LN], 'statement' [BAGD, LN, PNTC; NASB], 'promise' [CEV], 'communication' [KJV], not explicit [NIV, NLT, REB, TEV]. This noun denotes that which has been stated or said, with primary focus upon the content of the communication [LN].

c pres. act. impera. of εἰμί (LN 13.4): 'to be' [LN]. This verb means to be identical with [LN]. The clause ἔστω ὁ λόγος ὑμῶν ναὶ ναί, οὒ οὔ 'let your word be "Yes, yes" or "No, no."' [NET; similarly BNTC, CC, NIGTC; NRSV] is translated 'let your statement be "Yes, yes; no, no"' [PNTC; similarly NASB], 'let what you say be simply "Yes" or "No"' [ESV], 'simply say yes or no' [GW], 'just say "Yes" or "No"' [TEV]. 'let your affirmative word be "Yes" and your negative word be "No"' [BECNT], 'let your words be simply "Yes" and "No"' [NICNT], 'let your speech be such that "yes" is simply "yes" and "no" is simply "no"' [NTC], 'let your word be such that a yes is a yes and a no is a no' [WBC], 'when you make a promise, say only "Yes" or "No"' [CEV], 'let your communication be, Yea, yea; Nay, nay' [KJV], 'say only yes if you mean yes, and no if you mean no' [NCV], 'simply let your "Yes" be "Yes", and your "No," "No"' [NIV], 'just say a simple, "Yes, I will," or "No, I won't"' [NLT], 'plain "Yes" or "No" is all you need to say' [REB].

QUESTION—Why are 'yes' and 'no' reduplicated here?

It shows that what is being said is earnest and decisive [My]. It indicates the positive nature of what is being asserted [Lns], that it is fully sincere [WBC]. Having said 'yes' or 'no', nothing more can be added, other than to repeat the initial assertion [NIGTC].

But more-than^a these is from^b the-Evil-One/evil.^c

LEXICON—a. περισσός (LN 59.51) (BAGD 3. p. 651): 'more than' [BAGD, LN], 'beyond' [BAGD]. The phrase περισσὸν τούτων 'more than these' is translated 'more than this' [NET], 'anything more than this/that' [ESV, GW, NRSV], 'whatsoever is more than these' [KJV], 'anything beyond these' [NASB], 'anything beyond this/that' [NIV, NLT, REB], 'anything else' [CEV], 'anything else you say' [TEV], 'if you say more than yes or no' [NCV]. This adjective pronoun refers to a quantity so abundant as to be considerably more than what one would expect or anticipate [LN].

b. ἐκ (LN 90.16) (BAGD 3.c. p. 235): 'from' [BAGD, BECNT, BNTC, CC, LN, NICNT, NTC, WBC; CEV, ESV, GW, NCV, NET, NIV, NRSV, REB], 'of' [NIGTC, PNTC; KJV, NASB, NLT, TEV], 'by' [LN]. This preposition marks the source of an activity or state, with the implication of something proceeding from or out of the source [LN].

c. πονηρός (LN 12.35, 88.110) (BAGD 2.b. p. 691): The phrase τοῦ πονηροῦ is translated 'the evil one' [BECNT, CC, NTC, PNTC, WBC; GW, NET, NIV, NLT, NRSV, REB], 'the Evil One' [BNTC, LN (12.35); NCV, TEV], 'the devil' [CEV], 'evil' [LN (88.110), NICNT; ESV, KJV, NASB], 'evil (origin)' [NIGTC]. When used as a noun phrase ὁ πονηρός 'the Evil One' functions as a title for the Devil, the one who is essentially evil or in a sense personifies evil [LN (12.35)]. When used as an adjective, πονηρός 'evil' describes what is morally corrupt and evil [LN (88.110)].

QUESTION—Does ἐκ τοῦ πονηροῦ 'from the Evil One/evil' mean that it comes from the devil or from evil more generally?

The expression τοῦ πονηροῦ can be either masculine ('the evil one') or neuter ('evil') [BECNT, CC].

1. It means that it comes from the devil [BAGD, BECNT, BNTC, CC, ICC, LN (12.35), Lns, My, NIBC, NTC, PNTC, TH, TRT, WBC; GW, NCV, NET, NIV, NLT, NRSV, REB].
2. It means that it comes from an evil source, though not specifically the devil [NICNT, NIGTC; probably ESV, KJV, NASB]. The evil that is referred to is our failure to live up to God's standard of truthfulness [NICNT].

DISCOURSE UNIT—5:38–48 [GW]. The topic is love your enemies.

DISCOURSE UNIT—5:38–42 [CEV, ESV, NCV, NET, NIV, NLT, NRSV, TEV]. The topic is don't fight back [NCV], teaching about revenge [NLT,

TEV], revenge [CEV], concerning retaliation [NRSV], retaliation [ESV, NET], an eye for an eye [NIV].

5:38 **You(pl)-have-heard that it-was-said, "An-eye for[a] an-eye and a-tooth for a-tooth."** **5:39** **But I say to-you(pl) not to-resist[b] the evil-person/evil;[c]**

LEXICON—a. ἀντί (LN 57.145) (BAGD 2. p. 73): 'for' [BAGD, BECNT, BNTC, LN, NICNT, NTC, PNTC, WBC; all versions], 'in exchange for' [CC], 'in retaliation for' [NIGTC], 'in place of' [BAGD, LN]. This preposition marks an exchange relationship [LN].
  b. aorist act. infin. of ἀνθίστημι (LN 39.18) (BAGD 1. p. 67): 'to resist' [BAGD, BECNT, BNTC, CC, LN, NICNT, NTC, PNTC, WBC; ESV, KJV, NASB, NET, NIV, NLT, NRSV, REB], 'to oppose' [BAGD; GW], 'to stand up against' [NCV], 'to set oneself against' [NIGTC], 'to get even with' [CEV], 'to take revenge' [TEV]. This verb means to resist by actively opposing pressure or power [LN].
  c. πονηρός (LN 88.110) (BAGD 2.a. p. 691): 'evil person' [BECNT, CC, PNTC; GW, NASB, NCV, NIV, NLT], 'bad person' [NICNT], 'evil man' [BNTC], 'evil-doer' [BAGD, NTC; NET, NRSV], 'one who does evil' [NIGTC], 'one who is evil' [ESV], 'a person who has done something to you' [CEV], 'those who wrong you' [REB], 'someone who wrongs you' [TEV], 'wicked' [LN], 'wicked person' [BAGD], 'evil' [LN, WBC; KJV]. This adjective describes what is morally corrupt and evil, and when used as a substantive, denotes people who are evil [LN (88.110)].

QUESTION—What was the original intent of this saying, and how was it understood in Jesus' day?
  The original intent of this command was to prevent excessive punishment [BECNT, BNTC, CC, NAC, NIBC, NICNT, PNTC, TH]. The intent of this law was to guide civil courts [Lns, NIBC, NICNT], to take revenge out of the hands of the individual and put it in the civil courts [EBC, ICC, Lns, NTC, PNTC]. In Jesus' day it was understood as endorsing retaliation [CC, Lns, NTC, PNTC, TH], even by Jewish teachers [Lns, NTC]. In the OT context it was intended to deal with the seriousness of the crime and to insure that the whole community was not contaminated by the offense [NICNT].

QUESTION—Is he telling them not to resist evil people, or evil in general?
  1. He is telling them not to oppose evil people [BECNT, CC, BNTC, EBC, ICC, Lns, NIBC, NICNT, NIGTC, NTC, PNTC, TH, TRT; CEV, ESV, GW, NASB, NCV, NET, NIV, NLT, NRSV, REB, TEV].
  2. He is telling them not to resist the evil deed [WBC; probably KJV].

but[a] whoever slaps[b] you(sg) on (the) right cheek, turn[c] to-him the other (cheek) also;[d]

LEXICON—a. ἀλλά (LN 89.125): 'but' [BECNT, LN, NTC, PNTC, WBC; ESV, KJV, NASB, NET, NRSV], 'but instead' [NICNT], 'instead' [LN], 'rather' [BNTC, CC, NIGTC], 'on the contrary' [LN], not explicit [CEV, GW, NCV, NIV, NLT, REB, TEV]. The phrase beginning with ἀλλ'

ὅστις 'but whoever...' is translated as the protasis of a conditional sentence: 'if anyone/someone...' [BECNT, NICNT; ESV, GW, NCV, NIV, NLT, NRSV, REB, TEV], 'whenever anyone...' [WBC], 'when someone...' [CEV]. This conjunction marks emphatic contrast [LN].
  b. pres. act. indic. of ῥαπίζω (LN **19.4**) (BAGD p. 734): 'to slap' [BAGD, BNTC, **LN**, NICNT, NTC, PNTC; CEV, ESV, GW, NASB, NLT, REB, TEV], 'to insult by slapping' [WBC], 'to strike' [BAGD, CC, NIGTC; NET, NIV, NRSV], 'to hit' [BECNT, LN], 'to smite' [KJV], 'to whip, to beat' [LN].
  c. aorist act. impera. of στρέφω (LN **16.14**) (BAGD 1.a.α. p. 771): 'to turn' [BAGD, **LN**; all translations except NLT, REB, TEV], 'to turn and offer' [REB], 'to offer' [NLT]. The phrase στρέψον αὐτῷ καὶ τὴν ἄλλην 'turn to him the other (cheek) also' is translated 'let him slap your left cheek too' [TEV]. This verb means to cause something to turn [LN].
  d. καί (LN **89.93**) (BAGD II. 1. p. 393): 'also' [BAGD, BECNT, BNTC, CC, **LN**, NIGTC, NTC, PNTC, WBC; ESV, KJV, NASB, NCV, NIV, NLT, NRSV, REB], 'as well' [NICNT; GW, NET], 'too' [TEV], 'likewise' [BAGD], 'and' [LN; CEV], 'in addition' [LN]. This conjunction marks an additive relationship which is not coordinate [LN].
QUESTION—Is Jesus addressing private ethics as well as public policy?
  This is directed to his disciples in their personal behavior [BNTC, CC, Lns], not to governments [BNTC]. This is a personal ethic that does not contravene the role the state legitimately has to protect its own citizenry [BECNT]. These statements are directed toward believers, and do not address the public law enforcement force [EBC, ICC]. This does not address the legitimacy or justice of war [NAC], nor public order [PNTC]. Jesus is not addressing law, he is guiding personal ethics and the tendency people have of taking things into their own hands to get revenge [NICNT]. Forgoing one's own rights does not mean refusing to take a firm stand for justice and the rights of others [NICNT]. These moral principles and ideals do not preclude seeking one's own legal rights, nor does it dictate what the state or any officer ought to do [My].
QUESTION—What kind of blow is ῥαπίζω 'slap'?
  It is a sharp slap [EBC]. Since most people are right-handed, to strike someone on the right side of the face would mean hitting someone with the back of the hand [BECNT, CC, EBC, ICC, NAC, NIBC, NIGTC, PNTC, TH, TRT, WBC]. A back-handed slap was a form of insult [BECNT, EBC, ICC, NAC, NIBC, NIGTC, PNTC, TH, TRT, WBC].

5:40 **and to-the (one) wanting to-sue[a] you(sg) and to-take[b] your(sg) shirt,[c]**
LEXICON—a. aorist pass. infin. of κρίνω (LN 56.30) (BAGD 4.a.β. p. 451): 'to sue' [BECNT; CEV, ESV, GW, NASB, NET, NIV, NRSV, REB], 'to sue at law' [KJV], 'to sue in court' [NCV], 'to be sued in court' [NLT], 'to go to law' [BAGD, BNTC, CC, NTC, PNTC], 'to take to court' [NICNT, NIGTC, WBC; TEV], 'to be judged as guilty, to be condemned'

[LN]. In the active voice this verb means to judge a person to be guilty and liable to punishment [LN]. In the middle and passive it means to go to law with someone [BAGD].
  b. aorist act. infin. of λαμβάνω (LN **57.55**) (BAGD 1.c. p. 464): 'to take' [BAGD, BECNT, BNTC, CC, **LN**, NTC, PNTC; ESV, GW, NCV, NET, NIV, NRSV, REB], 'to take away' [KJV, NASB], 'to be taken' [NLT], 'to get' [NICNT, NIGTC, WBC], 'to sue for' [TEV], not explicit [CEV]. This verb means to acquire possession of something [LN].
  c. χιτών (LN **6.176**) (BAGD p. 882): 'shirt' [BAGD, BECNT, CC, **LN**, NICNT, NTC; CEV, GW, NASB, NCV, NLT, REB, TEV], 'tunic' [BAGD, BNTC, LN, NIGTC, PNTC; ESV, NET, NIV], 'coat' [KJV, NRSV], 'garment' [WBC]. The χιτών is a garment worn under the ἱμάτιον 'cloak' [LN].

let- him -have^a the coat^b also;^c
  LEXICON—a. aorist act. impera. of ἀφίημι (LN 13.140) (BAGD 3.a. p. 126): 'to let, to allow, to leave it to' [LN], 'let someone have something [BAGD]. The imperative phrase ἄφες αὐτῷ 'let him/them have' [BECNT, BNTC, NICNT, NIGTC; ESV, GW, KJV, NASB, NCV, NIV, REB, TEV] is also translated 'let him take' [NTC, PNTC], 'give that person' [WBC], 'give him' [NET], 'give up (your coat)' [CEV], 'give (your coat/cloak)' [NLT, NRSV], 'release to him' [CC].
  b. ἱμάτιον (LN **6.172**) (BAGD 2. p. 376): 'coat' [BECNT, CC, LN, NICNT, NIGTC, WBC; CEV, GW, NASB, NCV, NET, NLT, TEV], 'outer garment' [BNTC], 'cloak' [LN, PNTC; ESV, KJV, NIV, NRSV, REB], 'robe' [LN, NTC]. This noun denotes any type of outer garment [LN].
  c. καί (LN 89.93) (BAGD II. 1. p. 393): 'also' [BAGD, BECNT, BNTC, CC, **LN**, NIGTC, NTC; KJV, NASB, NCV, NET], 'as well' [NICNT; CEV, ESV, NIV, NRSV, REB, TEV], 'likewise' [BAGD], 'too' [PNTC; GW, NLT], 'and, in addition' [LN], 'even' [LN, WBC]. This conjunction marks an additive relationship which is not coordinate [LN].
QUESTION—What were these two garments?
  The shirt or tunic was an inner garment worn next to the body, and the cloak or coat was an outer garment [EBC, ICC, My, NIBC, NICNT, NIGTC, NTC, PNTC, TH, TRT, WBC]. The cloak often served as a cover during sleep [My, NIBC, NICNT, NIGTC, NTC, TH]. The outer cloak was a possession that could not be taken away from a person [EBC, NICNT, PNTC]. It was more valuable than the inner garment [TH, TRT].

5:41 and whoever will-force^a you(sg) (to-go) one mile,^b go^c with him two.
  LEXICON—a. fut. act. indic. of ἀγγαρεύω (LN 37.34) (BAGD p. 6): 'to force to go' [BAGD, NTC; ESV, GW, NASB, NCV, NET, NIV, NRSV], 'to force into service' [BECNT], 'to force to carry a pack' [CEV, TEV], 'to press into service' [BAGD, LN, NIGTC; REB], 'to conscript' [CC], 'to requisition, to compel' [BAGD], 'to compel to go' [PNTC; KJV], 'to

compel someone to carry a load' [LN], 'to compel into public service to go' [WBC], 'to impress for transport duty' [BNTC], 'to dragoon as a porter' [NICNT]. The phrase καὶ ὅστις σε ἀγγαρεύσει μίλιον ἕν 'and whoever will force you to go one mile' is translated 'if a soldier demands that you carry his gear for one mile' [NLT]. This verb means to force civilians to carry a load for some distance (in NT times Roman soldiers had the authority to enforce such service) [LN]. The present-stem imperative is normally used for this verb [CC].
- b. μίλιον (LN **81.29**) (BAGD p. 521): 'mile' [BAGD, BECNT, BNTC, CC, LN, NICNT, NIGTC, NTC, PNTC, WBC and versions], 'kilometer' [LN]. This noun denotes a Roman mile, consisting of a thousand paces and equivalent to somewhat less than an English mile but equal to about one kilometer and a half [LN]. This word occurs only here in the NT.
- c. pres. act. impera. of ὑπάγω (LN 15.15) (BAGD 2. p. 836): 'to go' [BAGD; all translations except CEV, NLT, TEV], 'to go along' [LN]. The phrase ὕπαγε μετ' αὐτοῦ δύο 'go with him two' is translated 'carry it two miles' [CEV, NLT, TEV]. This verb means to continue to move along [LN].

QUESTION—In what situation might someone be forced to go a mile?
  A Roman soldier could force Jews to carry their goods for a mile [EBC, Lns, NICNT, NIGTC, PNTC]. The Roman mile was 4, 854 feet or 1,478 meters [TH].

5:42 Give[a] to-the (one) asking[b] you(sg), and (do) not turn-away-from[c] the (one) wanting to-borrow[d] from you(sg).

LEXICON—a. aorist act. impera. of δίδωμι (LN 57.71): 'to give' [LN, all translations]. This verb means to give an object, usually implying value [LN].
- b. pres. act. participle of αἰτέω (LN 33.163) (BAGD p. 25): 'to ask' [BAGD, BECNT, BNTC, CC, NICNT, NIGTC, NTC, PNTC, WBC; GW, KJV, NET, NIV, NLT, REB, TEV], 'to ask for' [BAGD, LN; CEV, NCV], 'to beg' [ESV, NRSV], 'to plead for' [LN]. This verb means to ask for with urgency, even to the point of demanding [LN].
- c. aorist pass. subj. of ἀποστρέφω (LN **35.18**) (BAGD 3.a. p. 100): 'to turn away from' [BAGD, BECNT, BNTC, CC, NIGTC, NTC, PNTC, WBC; GW, KJV, NASB, NIV, NLT], 'to turn your back on' [REB], 'to refuse' [ESV, NRSV], 'to refuse to give' [NCV], 'to refuse to help' [LN], 'to turn a cold shoulder to' [NICNT], 'to reject' [NET]. The phrase μὴ ἀποστραφῇς 'do not turn away' is translated 'lend it to them' [CEV, TEV]. This verb means to refuse to provide help to someone [LN].
- d. aorist mid. infin. of δανείζομαι (LN **57.213**) (BAGD 2. p. 170): 'to borrow' [BAGD, LN; all translations except CEV], 'to borrow money' [BAGD, **LN**; CEV]. This verb means to borrow money, normally with the implication of interest to be paid; it is possible, however, that in Matthew 5:42 interest on the loan is not involved [LN].

QUESTION—How literally did Jesus intend the statements in this section to be taken?
> None of these commands should be taken as absolute [NAC]. It is not always possible to live literally and mechanically by these instructions, but they do carry important principles [BNTC]. Jesus' statements are hyperbole [CC, EBC, ICC], but the demands of love must still be taken seriously [CC, EBC]. We are not to give indiscriminately or mindlessly [ICC]. Jesus was teaching the disciples not to take revenge, and to act more generously than the law required and work for the good of others, but he was not requiring them to subject themselves or others to physical abuse and danger [NAC]. Jesus' commands here are somewhat extreme, but they embody ethical themes that must be applied according to how the circumstances dictate [NAC]. He is dealing with great principles here, not laying down new rules [PNTC]. He is not giving a new set of rules, but describing an alternative set of values by which disciples should live as God's people [NICNT]. Jesus' goal is to overcome evil with good, but boundaries concerning how this all applies must be thought through, and in concrete situations other considerations may also need to be looked at [NIGTC]. These injunctions are not to be applied mechanically, but in wisdom and love [Lns]. Jesus did not intend for these principles to be followed in a woodenly literal fashion [My, NIBC] but they should be followed according to their basic principle, which is love, self-denial, and overcoming evil with good [My].

DISCOURSE UNIT—5:43–48 [CEV, ESV, NCV, NET, NIV, NLT, NRSV, TEV]. The topic is love all people [NCV], love for enemies [NET, NIV, NRSV, TEV], love your enemies [ESV], teaching about love for enemies [NLT], love [CEV].

5:43 You(pl)-have-heard that it-was-said, You(sg)-shall-love[a] your(sg) neighbor[b] and you(sg)-shall-hate[c] your enemy.[d]

LEXICON—a. fut. act. indic. of ἀγαπάω (LN 25.43) (BAGD 1.a.α. p. 4): 'to love' [BAGD, LN; all translations], 'to regard with affection' [LN]. This verb means to have love for someone or something, based on sincere appreciation and high regard [LN].
  b. πλησίον (LN 11.89) (BAGD 1.b. p. 672): 'neighbor' [BAGD, LN; all translations except TEV], 'friend' [TEV]. This noun denotes a person who lives close beside others and who thus by implication is a part of a so-called 'in-group,' that is, the group with which an individual identifies both ethnically and culturally [LN].
  c. fut. act. indic. of μισέω (LN 88.198) (BAGD 1. p. 522): 'to hate' [BAGD, LN, all translations], 'to detest' [BAGD, LN]. This verb means to dislike strongly, with the implication of aversion and hostility [LN].
  d. ἐχθρός (LN 39.11) (BAGD 2.b.β. p. 331): 'enemy' [BAGD, all translations], 'being an enemy' [LN]. This word describes the state of being at enmity with someone [LN].

QUESTION—Who said 'hate your enemy'?
> This was a common saying in the Greco-Roman world, but it also reflects a view that is normal to all people [NIGTC]. This sentiment was one expressed by Israel's religious teachers [CC, Lns, My, PNTC], but it is found among sinners everywhere [CC]. It expresses popular attitudes of Jesus' day [TH]. It was a commonly assumed axiom, and even taught by some of Israel's teachers [NTC]. This was the popular understanding of Lev 19:18 [NICNT]. Some concluded that hatred for one's enemies was the logical corollary for Lev 19:18 [BECNT, EBC]. It was an inference some people drew from certain OT passages [BECNT, BNTC, WBC], such as Psalm 139:22–23, Deut 7:2, or Deut 30:7 [BECNT, ICC, WBC], or Psalm 137:7–9, Deut 23:3–6, or Deut 25:17–19 [BECNT, BNTC, ICC]. There were harsh statements in the OT regarding Israel's national enemies, but they were not intended to be applied on a personal level with one's own enemies [Lns, NIBC].

5:44 But[a] I say to-you(pl), love[b] your(pl) enemies and pray[c] for[d] the (ones) persecuting[e] you(pl),

TEXT—After 'love your enemies' some Greek manuscripts read 'bless them that curse you, do good to them that hate you' and that reading is followed by KJV. GNT leaves out the addition with an A rating to indicate its absence was regarded to be certain.

LEXICON—a. δέ (LN 89.124): 'but' [BNTC, CC, LN, NICNT, NIGTC, NTC, PNTC, WBC; all versions except TEV], 'but now' [TEV], 'yet' [BECNT].
- b. pres. act. impera. of ἀγαπάω: 'to love'. See this word at 5:43.
- c. pres. mid. or pass. (deponent = act.) impera. of προσεύχομαι (LN 33.178) (BAGD p. 714): 'to pray' [BAGD, LN; all versions], 'to speak to God, to ask God for' [LN]. This verb means to speak to or to make requests of God [LN].
- d. ὑπέρ with the genitive (LN 90.36): 'for' [BECNT, BNTC, LN, NICNT NIGTC, NTC, PNTC, WBC; all versions], 'on behalf of' [CC, LN], 'for the sake of' [LN]. This preposition marks a participant who is benefited by an event or on whose behalf an event takes place [LN].
- e. pres. act. participle of διώκω (LN 39.45) (BAGD 2. p. 201): 'to persecute' [BAGD, LN; all translations except CEV, NCV, REB], 'to hurt' [NCV], 'to mistreat' [CEV], 'to harass' [LN]. The phrase τῶν διωκόντων ὑμᾶς 'the ones persecuting you' is translated 'your persecutors' [REB]. This verb means to systematically organize a program to oppress and harass people [LN]. See this word at 5:11.

QUESTION—Why are the imperatives ἀγαπᾶτε 'love' and προσεύχεσθε 'pray' in the present tense?
> This indicates emphasis and urgency [CC]. It shows that they are to love constantly and continue praying [Lns].

160   MATTHEW 5:44

QUESTION—Why is there a shift from the singular 'enemy' in verse 43 to the plural 'enemies' here?
> The plural is all-inclusive [PNTC]. The plural indicates comprehensiveness, in that no class of enemies is to be excluded [NICNT].

QUESTION—What does 'love' mean in this context?
> It means to sacrifice oneself generously for the good of another [NAC], acting for the good of another, though controversy and rebuke may be involved [NICNT]. It is trying to be on the same side as others, regardless of how they may treat us [NIGTC]. It is willingly acting for the benefit and well-being of others [WBC]. It is an impartial, kindly, sympathetic, active, and resourceful goodwill that seeks good for all people, even one's enemy [BNTC]. It is a rich and costly love that includes not only action, but concern and sentiment [EBC]. It is active concern [NIBC]. It means to desire and work for the good of others [Lns].

5:45 so that[a] you-may-be[b] sons[c] of-your(pl) father in (the) heavens,

LEXICON—a. ὅπως (LN 89.59) (BAGD 2.a.α. p. 576): 'so that' [BECNT, LN, NICNT, NIGTC, PNTC; ESV, NASB, NRSV, TEV], 'that' [BNTC, NTC; KJV, NET, NIV], 'in order that' [BAGD, CC, WBC], 'in order to, for the purpose of' [LN]. The phrase ὅπως γένησθε 'so that you may be' is translated 'then you will be' [CEV], 'in this way you show that you are' [GW], 'if you do this you will be' [NCV], 'in that way, you will be acting as' [NLT], 'only so can you be' [REB]. This conjunction marks purpose for events and states (sometimes occurring in highly elliptical contexts) [LN].

b. aorist mid. (deponent = act.) subj. of γίνομαι (LN **13.48**) (BAGD I.4.a. p. 159): 'to be' [LN, all translations except TEV], 'to become' [BAGD, **LN**; TEV], 'to be like' [NET], 'to be acting like/as' [CEV, NLT]. This verb means to come to acquire or experience a state [LN].

c. υἱός (LN 9.4) (BAGD 1.c.γ. p. 834): 'son of...' [BAGD, LN], 'person of..., one who is' [LN]. This plural noun is translated 'sons' [BNTC, CC, NIGTC, NTC, PNTC; ESV, NASB, NIV], 'children' [BECNT, WBC; GW, KJV, NRSV, REB, TEV], 'true children' [NICNT; NCV, NLT]. The phrase γένησθε υἱοὶ τοῦ πατρὸς ὑμῶν 'be sons of your father' is translated 'be acting like your Father' [CEV], 'be like your father' [NET]. When followed by the genitive of class or kind, this noun denotes a person of a class or kind, as specified by the following genitive construction [LN].

QUESTION—In what sense would ethical behavior cause people to be or become children of God?
> By living this way they will be acting in a manner appropriate to the family likeness [NIGTC]. They are already God's children [CC, EBC, Lns, NICNT, NTC, PNTC], but they prove it by their actions [CC, Lns, NIBC, NICNT, NTC, TH; GW]. In so doing, they emulate the character of their heavenly father and demonstrate that they are his children [BECNT, ICC]. Living in

this manner is the true outworking of the relationship they already have with God as their father, and shows its legitimacy [NICNT]. The children of God imitate their heavenly father and reflect his character, doing his will, and as they live out the righteousness of the kingdom, they confirm their identity as God's children [WBC]. They prove themselves to be disciples and God's children by being like him in showing goodwill impartially [BNTC]. They already are God's children, but they become his children in the sense of sonship patterned after God's character [EBC]. It does not mean that they become members of the family because of their behavior, but it does indicate their growth in God's service [PNTC]. There are moral standards connected to being God's children that require them to be like him [NIBC]. It refers to the future coming of the kingdom of God and the future sonship the disciples would experience [My].

for he-makes- his sun[a] -rise[b] on evil-(people)[c] and good-(people)[d]

LEXICON—a. ἥλιος (LN 1.28) (BAGD p. 345): 'the sun' [BAGD, LN; all translations except NLT], 'sunlight' [NLT].

b. pres. act. indic. of ἀνατέλλω (LN 15.104) (BAGD 1. p. 62): 'to make to rise' [BECNT, CC, NICNT, PNTC, WBC; CEV, ESV, GW, KJV, NRSV], 'to make to rise and shine forth' [NIGTC], 'to make to shine' [TEV], 'to cause to rise' [BAGD, BNTC, NTC; NASB, NCV, NET, NIV, REB], 'to give (sunlight)' [NLT]. This verb means to move up, especially of the upward movement of the sun, stars, or clouds [LN].

c. πονηρός (LN 88.110) (BAGD 2.a. p. 691): 'evil'. See this word at 5:39. The adjective is translated as a substantive referring to evil people: 'evil people' [NTC, PNTC; NCV], 'the evil' [BECNT, BNTC, NIGTC; ESV, KJV, NASB, NET, NIV, NLT, NRSV], 'the wicked' [CC], 'the bad' [NICNT], 'bad' [REB], 'bad people' [CEV, TEV], '(whether) they are…evil' [GW].

d. ἀγαθός (LN 88.1) (BAGD 1.b.α. p. 3): 'good' [BAGD, LN]. This adjective is translated as a substantive referring to good people: 'good people' [NCV, TEV], 'the good' [BECNT, BNTC, CC, NICNT, NIGTC; ESV, KJV, NASB, NET, NIV, NLT, NRSV]. The phrase πονηροὺς καὶ ἀγαθούς is translated 'evil people and good ones' [PNTC], 'evil people and good' [NTC], 'evil and good people' [WBC], 'bad and good people' [TEV], 'both good and bad people' [CEV], 'good and bad alike' [REB], 'people, whether they are good or evil' [GW]. This adjective describes positive moral qualities of the most general nature [LN].

QUESTION—Why do certain adjectives used as nouns such as πονηρός 'evil' ἀγαθός and 'good' lack the definite article?

The lack of the definite article emphasizes and focuses on the quality itself [Lns, NTC, PNTC]. Evil and good people are not seen as classes of people, but people characterized by evil or goodness [PNTC].

and he-(sends)-rain[a] **on righteous-(people)**[b] **and unrighteous-(people).**[c]

LEXICON—a. pres. act. indic. of βρέχω (LN **14.11**) (BAGD 2.a. p. 147): 'to send rain' [BAGD, BECNT, **LN**, BNTC, NICNT, NTC, PNTC; all versions except GW], 'to cause it to rain' [BAGD, LN, NIGTC], 'to make it rain' [WBC], 'to make rain to fall' [CC], 'to let rain fall' [GW]. This verb means to cause rain to fall [LN]. This verb is used in a causative sense [NIGTC].

b. δίκαιος (LN 88.12) (BAGD 1.b. p. 195): 'righteous' [BAGD, LN, NTC], 'just' [BAGD, LN, PNTC; GW], 'upright' [BAGD]. This adjective is translated as a substantive referring to righteous people: 'the righteous' [BECNT, BNTC, CC, NIGTC; NASB, NIV, NRSV], 'the just' [NICNT, WBC; ESV, KJV, NET, NLT], 'the innocent' [REB], 'the ones who do right' [CEV], 'those who do right' [NCV]. This adjective describes being in accordance with what God requires [LN].

c. ἄδικος (LN 88.20) (BAGD 1. p. 18): 'unrighteous' [LN, NTC], 'unjust' [BAGD, LN, PNTC; GW]. This adjective is translated as a substantive referring to unrighteous people: 'the unrighteous' [BECNT, BNTC, CC, NIGTC; NASB, NET, NIV, NRSV], 'the unjust' [NICNT, WBC; ESV, KJV, NLT], 'the wicked' [REB], 'the ones who do wrong' [CEV], 'those who do wrong' [NCV]. This adjective describes not being right or just [LN].

5:46 For if[a] you(pl)-love (only) the ones-loving you(pl), what reward[b] do-you(sg)-have[c]?

LEXICON—a. ἐάν (LN **89.67**) (BAGD I.1.b. p. 211): 'if' [BAGD, LN, all translations]. This conjunction marks condition, with the implication of reduced probability [LN].

b. μισθός (LN 38.14) (BAGD 2.a. p. 523): 'reward' [BAGD, LN; all translations except CEV], 'recompense' [LN]. This noun is translated as a verb: 'to reward' [CEV]. This noun denotes a recompense based upon what a person has earned and thus deserves, the nature of the recompense being either positive or negative [LN].

c. pres. act. indic. of ἔχω (LN 57.1): 'to have' [BECNT, CC, LN, PNTC, WBC; ESV, KJV, NASB], 'to get' [NICNT; NIV]. The phrase τίνα μισθὸν ἔχετε; 'what reward do you have?' is translated 'what is your reward?' [NTC], 'what reward is due you?' [BNTC], 'what basis do you have for a reward?' [NIGTC], 'will God reward you for that?' [CEV], 'what reward is there for that?' [NLT], 'what reward can you expect?' [REB], 'do you deserve a reward?' [GW], 'why should God reward you?' [TEV], 'you will get no reward' [NCV]. This verb means to have or possess objects or property [LN].

QUESTION—What relationship is indicated by γάρ 'for'?

It indicates an explanation for the imperatives 'love' and 'pray' in 5:44–45 [CC]. It indicates the conclusion with regard to Christian conduct that is to be drawn from the previous statement about God's goodness [PNTC].

QUESTION—In what sense is μισθός 'reward' used here?
The reward is a blessing granted by grace, not something earned [CC, ICC, NTC, TH]. It is given for behavior that befits the kingdom of God [NIGTC]. Although it is a reward, it is not to be understood as strictly meritorious [EBC, ICC]. It is recognition by God [Lns], fellowship with God in his kingdom [ICC].

(Do) not[a] even[b] the tax-collectors[c] do the-same-(thing)?[d]
LEXICON—a. οὐχί (LN **69.12**) (BAGD 3. p. 598): 'do not...' [BAGD, **LN**]. This particle may mark a somewhat emphatic affirmative response [LN]. In this context it is understood as introducing a rhetorical question that expects a 'yes' answer [BAGD, all translations except CEV]. This rhetorical question is translated as a statement: 'Even tax collectors love their friends' [CEV].
  b. καί (LN 89.93) (BAGD II.2. p. 393): 'even' [BAGD, BECNT, BNTC, LN, NICNT, NIGTC, PNTC, WBC; all versions], not explicit [NTC]. This conjunction marks an additive relationship which is not coordinate [LN].
  c. τελώνης (LN 57.184) (BAGD p. 812): 'tax collector' [BAGD, BECNT, BNTC, LN, NICNT, NIGTC, NTC, PNTC, WBC; all versions except KJV, NLT], 'corrupt tax collector' [NLT], 'tax gatherer' [CC], 'publican' [KJV]. This noun denotes one who collects taxes for the government; since Jews who did this were considered traitors to their own people, the term has strongly negative connotations in the NT [LN].
  d. αὐτός (LN **58.31**) (BAGD 4.b. p. 123): 'same' [BAGD, LN]. The phrase τὸ αὐτό 'the same thing' [CC, NTC, WBC] is also translated 'the same' [BECNT, BNTC, NIGTC, PNTC; ESV, KJV, NASB, NET, NRSV], 'as much' [NICNT], 'as much as that' [REB], 'that much' [NLT], 'that' [GW, NCV, NIV, TEV], not explicit [CEV]. This adjective describes that which is identical to something [LN].

5:47 And if you(pl)-greet[a] only your(pl) brothers,[b] what exceptional[c] (thing) are-you(pl)-doing? (Do) not even the Gentiles[d] do the-same-thing?
TEXT—The Greek manuscripts that read ἐθνικοί 'Gentiles' are followed by GNT with a B rating to indicate it was regarded to be almost certain. Other manuscripts read τελῶναι 'tax collectors' instead of ἐθνικοί, a reading that is followed by KJV only.
LEXICON—a. ἀσπάζομαι (LN 34.55) (BAGD 1.a. p. 116): 'to greet' [BAGD, BECNT, BNTC, CC, NIGTC, PNTC, WBC; CEV, ESV, NASB, NET, NIV, NRSV, REB], 'to welcome' [LN, NICNT; GW], 'to salute' [KJV], 'to approach with cordial greeting' [NTC], 'to be nice' [NCV], 'to be kind' [NLT], 'to accept gladly' [LN], 'to speak' [TEV]. This verb means to welcome something or someone, with focus upon the initial greeting [LN].
  b. ἀδελφός (LN 11.25): 'brother' [BNTC, CC, LN, NTC, PNTC; ESV, KJV, NASB, NET, NIV, REB], 'fellow countryman, fellow Jew,

associate' [LN], 'friend' [CEV, GW, NCV, NLT, TEV]. This plural noun is translated 'brothers and sisters' [BECNT, NIGTC; NRSV], 'those of your own circle' [NICNT], 'the members of your own community' [WBC]. It denotes a person belonging to the same socio-religious entity and being of the same age group as the so-called reference person [LN].

c. περισσός (LN 58.57) (BAGD 1. p. 651): 'exceptional' [LN, NTC], 'greater thing' [CC], 'rewardable' [WBC], 'remarkable' [BAGD, LN; GW], 'outstanding, unusual' [LN]. This adjective describes that which is exceptional in the sense of being more than what is expected [LN]. The rhetorical question τί περισσὸν ποιεῖτε; 'what exception thing are you doing?' is translated 'what are you doing more than others?' [BECNT, BNTC, PNTC; NASB, NIV; similarly ESV, KJV, NRSV], 'what is so special about that?' [NICNT], 'what's so great about that?' [CEV], 'what more do you do' [NET], 'what is abundant in what you're doing?' [NIGTC], 'you are no better than other people' [NCV], 'how are you different from anyone else?' [NLT], 'what is there extraordinary about that?' [REB], 'have you done anything out of the ordinary?' [TEV].

d. ἐθνικός (LN **11.38**) (BAGD p. 218): 'Gentile' [BAGD, BECNT, BNTC, CC, LN, NICNT, NIGTC, NTC, PNTC, WBC; ESV, NASB, NET, NRSV], 'unbeliever' [CEV], 'heathen' [BAGD, LN; REB], 'pagan' [LN; NIV, NLT, TEV]. The rhetorical question οὐχὶ καὶ οἱ ἐθνικοὶ τὸ αὐτὸ ποιοῦσιν; 'Do not even the Gentiles do the same thing?' is translated as a statement: 'Everyone does that' [GW]. This adjective describes one who is not a Jew [LN].

QUESTION—What is the nature of the greeting mentioned here?

It expresses a desire for the welfare of the one greeted [TH], of God's blessing and peace for the other person [ICC, WBC]. It expresses goodwill and welcome [PNTC]. It shows that the one being greeted has personal significance to the one greeting him or her [NIGTC]. It expresses concern for the one greeted [NICNT].

QUESTION—Who would be in the category of 'brothers'?

They are the people belonging to the same group [PNTC]. It probably refers to members of the same religious community [TH], to other fellow-Jews [Lns, My, NIGTC], or to other like-minded disciples [EBC].

QUESTION—What answer does this second question expect?

It expects an affirmative answer: yes, of course they do [PNTC, TH].

5:48 Therefore[a] you(pl) shall-be perfect[b] as[c] your(pl) heavenly[d] Father is perfect.

LEXICON—a. οὖν (LN 89.50) (BAGD 1.b. p. 593): 'therefore' [BAGD, BECNT, BNTC, CC, LN, NTC, PNTC, WBC; ESV, KJV, NASB, NIV], 'so' [BAGD, LN, NICNT; NCV, NRSV, TEV], 'consequently' [BAGD, LN], 'so then' [LN; NET], 'that is why' [GW], not explicit [NIGTC; CEV, NLT, REB]. This conjunction marks result, often implying the conclusion of a process of reasoning [LN].

b. τέλειος (LN **88.36**) (BAGD 2.d. p. 809): 'perfect' [BAGD, BECNT, BNTC, CC, LN, NICNT, NTC, PNTC, WBC; all versions except CEV, REB], 'fully developed' [BAGD], 'complete [in reach of your goodness]' [NIGTC]. This sentence is translated 'But you must always act like your Father in heaven' [CEV], 'There must be no limit to your goodness, as your heavenly Father's goodness knows no bounds' [REB]. This adjective describes being perfect in the sense of not lacking any moral quality [LN].

c. ὡς (LN 64.12) (BAGD II.4.a. p. 897): 'as' [BAGD, BECNT, BNTC, CC, LN, NICNT, NTC, WBC; ESV, GW, KJV, NASB, NET, NIV, NRSV, REB], 'just as' [NIGTC; NCV, TEV], 'even as' [PNTC; NLT], 'like' [LN; CEV]. This conjunction marks a relatively weak relationship between events or states [LN].

d. οὐράνιος (LN **1.12**) (BAGD p. 593): 'heavenly' [BAGD, BECNT, BNTC, CC, LN, NICNT, NIGTC, NTC, PNTC, WBC; ESV, NASB, NET, NIV, NRSV, REB], 'in heaven' [LN; CEV, GW, KJV, NCV, NLT, TEV]. This adjective describes what is related to or located in heaven [LN].

QUESTION—What relationship is indicated by οὖν 'therefore'?

It indicates a conclusion to be drawn from 5:45–47 [Lns]. It indicates the conclusion to be drawn from 5:44–47 [My]. It indicates the conclusion that is to be drawn from 5:47 about the necessity of the disciples doing more than people in general would naturally do [PNTC].

QUESTION—What is implied by the use of the personal pronoun ὑμεῖς 'you'?

The personal pronoun ὑμεῖς 'you' is emphatic [ICC, Lns, PNTC, WBC].

QUESTION—What is the nature of the perfection he is calling for in the statement 'you shall be perfect'?

It reflects the Hebrew/Aramaic *tamim* [BECNT, EBC, NAC, NICNT, NIGTC, WBC], which in the OT represents ethical completeness, wholeness, and perfection [WBC]. In the gospel of Matthew τέλειος means to fulfill the law through unrestricted love, which is the reflection of God's love and embodies ethical perfection [WBC]. God's children are called to be perfect in love for all people everywhere, demonstrating the characteristics of God himself, in whose image they are made [NIBC]. It is the maturity of complete love [CC, ICC, My, NAC, NTC, TRT, WBC], similar to their heavenly father's love [CC, TRT]. There should be no limit to their goodness [REB]. It recalls the LXX of Deut 18:13, which calls for complete loyalty to God, and where τέλειος is used to translate the Hebrew *tamim* 'complete loyalty' [Lns, NICNT, PNTC, WBC]; likewise in Mt 19:21 Jesus challenges the rich man to give away all he has if he wants to be τέλειος 'perfect' [NICNT]. It is to fulfill the law by expressing God's will in all the relationships and tasks of life [BNTC]. It is to be complete or mature in benevolence, as God is, and to be upright and blameless in consistently obeying God's law as Jesus interpreted it [BECNT]. For Jesus' disciples, perfection would be to emulate all the perfection of God, as exemplified by Jesus' authoritative interpretation of the law given in the antitheses beginning in 5:17 [EBC]. Disciples are to be fully mature people, achieving the purpose for which God made them and wholehearted in the service of their heavenly father [PNTC]. They are to be wholly devoted to the will of God and to living according to the law of love, but this does not mean sinlessness [Lns]. Their devotion to God must be complete [TH]. The ethics Jesus advocates are suggestive, but not exhaustive, and cannot be formulated into a set of rules [NAC].

QUESTION—What relationship is indicated by ὡς 'as'?

The inspiration for the lifestyle of the disciple is to be drawn from the character of God himself [NICNT]. Their standard is to be the highest possible [PNTC]. God is to be their model and standard, but that does not demand complete equality with how God loves [Lns]. It expresses similarity in the action of loving, in that they do what God does, though not to the same degree [My]. It indicates the motivation for loving: they love because God loves [ICC].

QUESTION—To what portion of the previous material does this statement form a conclusion?

It is a fitting conclusion and summary for all that has been said beginning at 5:17 [BNTC, EBC]. This is the conclusion to all of the antitheses begun in 5:21 [BECNT, ICC, NAC, NICNT, NIGTC, WBC], but also summarizes the section that began in 5:43 [ICC, NICNT, WBC], which is about being like their heavenly father [NICNT]. It concludes the commands to love one's enemy in 5:44 [CC], and may even summarize 5:21–48 [CC]. It confirms the argument of 5:45 [WBC] and is a conclusion to that section [BECNT]. It concludes the section that began in 5:43 [NTC].

DISCOURSE UNIT—6:1–18 [ICC]. The topic is the Christian believers.

DISCOURSE UNIT—6:1–15 [NASB]. The topic is giving to the poor and prayer.

DISCOURSE UNIT—6:1–4 [CEV, ESV, GW, NCV, NET, NIV, NLT, NRSV, TEV]. The topic is the sermon on a mountain continues: Don't do good works to be praised by people [GW], Jesus teaches about giving [NCV], teaching about charity [TEV], giving to the needy [ESV, NIV], pure-hearted giving [NET], concerning almsgiving [NRSV], teaching about giving to the needy [NLT], giving [CEV].

6:1 Be-careful[a] not to-do[b] your(pl) righteous-acts[c] before[d] people in-order-(to)[e] to-be-seen[f] by-them;

LEXICON—a. pres. act. impera. of προσέχω (LN **27.59**) (BAGD 1.b. p. 714): 'to be careful' [BNTC, NICNT, WBC; GW, NCV, NET, NIV, REB], 'to take care' [BAGD, NIGTC, NTC, PNTC], 'to take heed' [KJV], 'to make sure' [BECNT], 'to make certain' [**LN**; TEV], 'to pay attention' [CC, LN], not explicit [CEV]. The verb phrase προσέχετε…μή 'be careful not (to…)' is translated 'beware of' [ESV, NASB, NRSV], 'watch out!'

MATTHEW 6:1

[NLT]. This verb means to be in a continuous state of readiness to learn of any future danger, need, or error, and to respond appropriately [LN].
b. pres. act. infin. of ποιέω (LN 42.7) (BAGD I.1.c.β. p. 682): 'to do' [BAGD, CC, LN; GW, KJV, NCV, NIV, NLT], 'to practice' [BAGD, BECNT, BNTC, NICNT, NIGTC, NTC, WBC; ESV, NASB, NRSV], 'to parade' [PNTC; REB], 'to display' [NET], 'to perform' [LN; TEV], 'to carry out' [LN]. The phrase μὴ ποιεῖν ἔμπροσθεν τῶν ἀνθρώπων 'not to do...before people' is translated 'don't show off' [CEV]. This verb means to do or perform (highly generic for almost any type of activity) [LN].
c. δικαιοσύνη (LN **53.4, 57.111**) (BAGD 2.a. p. 196): 'righteousness' [BAGD, BECNT, CC, NICNT, NIGTC, NTC, PNTC; ESV, NASB, NET], 'acts of righteousness' [NIV], 'good works' [GW], 'good deeds' [CEV, NLT], 'good things' [NCV], 'religious observances' [**LN (53.4)**], 'religious duties' [TEV], 'religious requirements' [LN], 'religion' [REB], 'piety' [BNTC, WBC; NRSV], 'charitableness' [BAGD], 'alms' [LN; KJV], 'acts of charity' [LN], 'giving to the needy' [**LN**]. This noun denotes observances or practices required by one's religion [LN (53.4)], or gifts given to those in need as an act of mercy [LN (57.111)].
d. ἔμπροσθεν (LN 83.33) (BAGD 2.c. p. 257): 'before' [BAGD, BECNT, BNTC, CC, LN, NIGTC, NTC, PNTC, WBC; ESV, KJV, NASB, NIV, NRSV, REB], 'in the sight of' [BAGD], 'in front of' [LN, NICNT; NCV], not explicit [CEV, GW, NET, TEV]. The phrase ἔμπροσθεν τῶν ἀνθρώπων 'before men' is translated 'in public' [GW, TEV], 'publicly' [NLT]. This adverb describes a position in front of an object, whether animate or inanimate, which is regarded as having a spatial orientation of front and back [LN].
e. πρός (with articular infinitive) (LN 89.60) (BAGD III.3.a. p. 710): 'in order to' [BECNT, LN, NIGTC, PNTC, WBC; ESV, GW, NRSV], 'in order that' [CC], 'so that' [NICNT; TEV], 'for the purpose of' [BAGD, LN], 'for' [BAGD], 'for the sake of' [LN], not explicit [CEV, REB]. This preposition is conflated with the following infinitive and translated simply 'to... (be seen/attract attention/be noticed/be admired)' [BNTC, NTC; KJV, NASB, NCV, NET, NIV, NLT]. This preposition marks purpose, pointing to the goal of an event or state [LN].
f. aorist pass. infin. of θεάομαι (LN 24.14) (BAGD 1.c.β. p. 353): 'to be seen' [BNTC, NIGTC, PNTC, WBC; ESV, KJV, NCV, NET, NIV, NRSV], 'to be observed, to be looked at' [LN], 'to be noticed' [BAGD, BECNT; NASB], 'to be visible' [CC], 'to attract attention' [NTC; GW], 'to be admired' [NLT], not explicit [CEV, REB]. This passive verb is translated as active: '(so that they) will notice' [NICNT], '(so that people) will see' [TEV]. This verb means to observe something with continuity and attention, often with the implication that what is observed is something unusual [LN].

168   MATTHEW 6:1

QUESTION—What are the 'righteous acts' he is referring to here?
> He is speaking of acts of mercy and charity [CC]. They are practical piety and religious observance as opposed to ethics [NICNT]. These are any good deeds done in God's service [PNTC]. They are acts of Jewish piety, which was expressed through giving, prayer, and fasting [BNTC, NTC, TH, WBC]. This refers to the acts of religious piety, namely fasting, prayer, and almsgiving, which should be done in secret [ICC]. It is religious activity in terms of functional godliness and obedience to the laws of God [BECNT]. It is righteous living generally, not just particular acts [EBC, My]. It is the entire range of good works [Lns].

QUESTION—How does this statement compare with what was said in 5:16 about letting one's light shine so that others would see our good deeds and glorify God?
> The difference is in the motive concerning who gets the glory [CC, EBC, ICC, Lns, NAC, NICNT, NIGTC, NTC, PNTC, WBC], and who receives the attention and benefit [NIGTC]. In 5:16 it addresses the whole character and lifestyle of the disciples, whereas here it focuses on specific religious duties [NICNT]. In 5:16 he is dealing with the temptation to avoid allowing one's faith to be seen publicly in order to avoid persecution, but here he is focusing on the problem of attracting attention to oneself for the sake of personal gain [NIBC]. There are legitimate outward expressions of religious duties, but they must not be done to seek honor for oneself [BNTC].

otherwise,[a] you(pl)-do- not -have[b] reward[c] with[d] your(pl) Father in the heavens.[e]

LEXICON—a. εἰ (LN 89.65)) (BAGD 1.3.b): The phrase εἰ δὲ μή γε 'otherwise' [BAGD, BECNT, CC, LN, NICNT, NIGTC, NTC, WBC; KJV, NASB, NET] is also translated 'if you do' [BNTC, PNTC; CEV, GW, NCV, NIV, REB, TEV], 'for then' [ESV, NRSV], not explicit [NLT]. This conjunction marks a condition [LN].
  b. pres. act. indic. of ἔχω (LN 57.1): 'to have' [BECNT, BNTC, CC, LN, NIGTC, NTC, PNTC, WBC; ESV, KJV, NET, NIV, NRSV, TEV], 'to expect' [NICNT], 'to get' [CEV], not explicit [GW]. The phrase οὐκ ἔχετε 'you do not have' is translated 'you will lose' [NLT], 'no (reward) awaits you' [REB]. The present tense of this verb is translated as referring to a reward that would be given in the future [NICNT, NIGTC, NTC; CEV, ESV, GW, NCV, NIV, NLT, REB, TEV]. This verb means to have or possess objects or property (in the technical sense of having control over the use of such objects) [LN].
  c. μισθός (LN 38.14) (BAGD 2.a. p. 523): 'reward' [BAGD, LN; all translations except GW], 'recompense' [LN]. This noun is translated as a verb: 'to reward (you)' [GW]. This noun denotes a recompense based upon what a person has earned and thus deserves, the nature of the recompense being either positive or negative [LN].

d. παρά with dative (LN 89.111) (BAGD II.1.b.γ. p. 610): 'with' [BAGD, BECNT, BNTC, CC, LN, NIGTC, NTC, PNTC, WBC; NASB, NET, NIV, REB, TEV], 'from' [NICNT; CEV, ESV, NCV, NIV, NLT, NRSV], 'of' [KJV], not explicit [GW]. This preposition marks association, with the implication of proximity to the so-called viewpoint character [LN].

e. οὐρανός (LN 1.11) (BAGD 2.a. p. 594): 'heaven' [BAGD, LN]. This plural noun, which seems to have the same meaning in NT literature in either the singular or plural form, denotes the supernatural dwelling place of God and other heavenly beings. This word contains a component denoting that which is 'above' or 'in the sky,' but the element of abode' is evidently more significant than location above the earth [LN].

QUESTION—What is implied by the preposition παρά 'with' in this sentence? It means 'with' as in God's presence, but also can mean 'in the judgment of', because God is the one who determines the reward [NICNT]. It is a reward laid up in heaven at the Father's side [Lns].

6:2 **Therefore whenever^a you(sg)-do^b alms,^c do- not -sound-a-trumpet^d before^e you(sg),**

LEXICON—a. ὅταν (LN 67.31) (BAGD 1.a. p. 588): 'whenever' [BAGD, BECNT, LN, NICNT, NTC, PNTC; ESV, NET, NRSV], 'when' [BNTC, CC, LN, NICNT, WBC; all versions except ESV, NET, NRSV]. This conjunction refers to an indefinite point or points of time, which may be roughly simultaneous to or overlap with another point of time [LN].

b. pres. act. subj. of ποιέω (LN 90.45) (BAGD I.1.c.β. p. 682): 'to do' [BAGD, LN; KJV, NET], 'to perform' [LN], 'to practice' [BAGD, LN, NICNT], 'to give (alms, etc.)' [BECNT, BNTC, CC, NICNT, NTC, PNTC, WBC; all versions except KJV, NET]. This verb marks an agent relationship with a numerable event [LN].

c. ἐλεημοσύνη (LN 57.111) (BAGD p. 249): 'alms' [BAGD, BNTC, CC, LN, NICNT, PNTC, WBC; KJV, NRSV, REB], 'almsgiving' [NIGTC], 'charitable giving' [LN; NET], 'acts of charity, giving to the needy, kind deed' [LN]. The phrase ποιῇς ἐλεημοσύνην 'do alms' is translated 'give to the poor' [BECNT, NTC; CEV, GW, NASB, NCV], 'give to the needy' [ESV, NIV], 'give to someone in need' [NLT], 'give something to a needy person' [TEV]. This noun denotes the practice of giving to those in need as an act of mercy [LN].

d. aorist act. subj. of σαλπίζω (LN **6.90**) (BAGD p. 741): 'to sound a/the trumpet' [BAGD, BECNT, BNTC, CC, **LN**, NIGTC, PNTC; ESV, KJV, NASB, NRSV], 'to blow a trumpet' [NICNT, WBC; NCV, NET, NLT], 'to blow a loud horn' [CEV], 'to play the trumpet' [LN], 'to (publicly) announce with the blast of the trumpet' [NTC], 'to announce it with trumpet fanfare/trumpets/a flourish of trumpets' [GW, NIV, REB], not explicit [TEV]. The phrase μὴ σαλπίσῃς ἔμπροσθέν σου 'do not sound a trumpet before you' is translated 'don't make a big show of it' [TEV].

e. ἔμπροσθεν (LN 83.33) (BAGD 2.e. p. 257): 'before' [BAGD, BECNT, BNTC, CC, LN, NIGTC, PNTC; ESV, KJV, NASB, NET, NRSV], 'ahead of' [BAGD], 'in front of' [LN, NICNT], not explicit [CEV, GW, NCV, NIV, NLT, REB, TEV]. In conjunction with the phrase μὴ σαλπίσῃς 'do not sound a trumpet' the phrase ἔμπροσθέν σου 'before you' is translated 'publicly' [NTC], 'to attract attention' [WBC]. This noun denotes a position in front of an object, whether animate or inanimate, which is regarded as having a spatial orientation of front and back [LN].

QUESTION—What relationship is indicated by οὖν 'therefore'?

It indicates that an application is to be made from what was said in 6:1 [NIGTC]. It indicates an inference to be drawn from the principle outlined in 6:1, which also grounds the argument for all of 6:2–18 [CC].

QUESTION—What is the exegetical significance of shifts between 'you' singular and 'you' plural in this verse, and in the following section?

In 6:1 the plural form of 'you' is used in a statement of general principle, and in 6:2 there is a shift to the singular pronoun to express concrete examples [NIGTC]. The shift from plural forms in 6:1 to singular forms in 6:2 makes the application more personal, but the shift back to plural forms in 6:4 does not have much significance [PNTC]. The plurals in 6:1, 5, and 16 shift to singular forms in the verses immediately following them where the focus is on the behavior of an individual disciple. This may be because the almsgiving discussed in 6:2 was done on the basis of individual initiative, whereas prayer (6:5) and fasting (6:16) were prescribed corporately [NICNT]. There is a rhetorical effect, with plural forms used to include all disciples, and singular forms used to focus on each disciple [CC]. The shift from plurals in 6:5 to singulars in 6:6 makes his command more personal [Lns].

QUESTION—Would the listeners actually blow trumpets when they gave alms?

Jesus was using a metaphor [BECNT, BNTC, ICC, My, NIBC, NICNT, NTC, TH, TRT] about drawing attention to themselves when they gave alms [TH, WBC] in order to establish a reputation for piety [PNTC] and be praised by others [WBC]. Blowing a trumpet is a picturesque way of referring to calling attention to oneself [ICC]. This is a warning against becoming hypocrites [PNTC, WBC]. Some consider this figurative language to be hyperbolic [CC, NIGTC].

as[a] the hypocrites[b] do in the synagogues[c] and in[d] the streets,[e]

LEXICON—a. ὥσπερ (LN 64.13) (BAGD 2. p. 899): 'as' [BAGD, BECNT, BNTC, LN, NICNT, NIGTC, NTC, PNTC, WBC; all versions except CEV, GW, NCV], 'just as' [BAGD, CC, LN]. The phrase ὥσπερ οἱ ὑποκριταὶ ποιοῦσιν 'as the hypocrites do' is translated 'that's what show-offs/hypocrites do' [CEV, GW], 'be like the hypocrites' [NCV]. This conjunction indicates similarity between events and states [LN].

b. ὑποκριτής (LN 88.228) (BAGD p. 845): 'hypocrite' [BAGD, LN; all translations except CEV], 'show-off' [CEV]. This noun denotes one who pretends to be other than he really is [LN].

c. συναγωγή (LN 7.20) (BAGD 2.a. p. 782): 'synagogue' [BAGD, LN; all translations except CEV], 'place of assembly' [BAGD], 'meeting place' [CEV]. This noun denotes a building of assembly used for religious activities. The Jewish synagogues were used for worship services where the Law was taught [LN].

d. ἐν (LN 83.13): 'in' [BECNT, BNTC, LN, NICNT, NIGTC, PNTC, WBC; ESV, KJV, NASB, NRSV, REB; implied in CC; NLT], 'on' [BECNT; CEV, GW, NCV, NET, NET, NIV]. This preposition describes a position defined as being within certain limits [LN].

e. ῥύμη (LN 1.104) (BAGD p. 737): 'street' [BECNT, BNTC, NICNT, PNTC, WBC; all versions except CEV], 'city street' [NIGTC], 'narrow street' [BAGD, LN], 'street corner' [CEV], 'lane' [BAGD, CC, LN], 'alley' [BAGD, LN], 'alleyway' [NTC]. This noun denotes a city thoroughfare which is relatively narrow [LN].

QUESTION—What is meant by 'hypocrite'?

It speaks of behavior that is not authentic [CC]. They are not necessarily trying to deceive others as they operate with a false sense of what really matters, and are unable to see things as God sees them [NICNT]. There is a pretence, in that the real but hidden motive was to glorify themselves [WBC]. Their actions were hypocritical in that they were not religiously motivated, but were motivated to elicit approval from others [NIGTC]. A hypocrite is someone who is concerned for show, an actor [BECNT]. It is not so much a matter of intentionally deceiving others, since here the hypocrite not only deceives onlookers about his piety, he also deceives himself [EBC]. Their hypocrisy consisted in the fact that although they pretended to give, they actually intended to receive something, which was honor from others [NTC]. A hypocrite is someone who pretends to be something other than what he really is [NIBC, TRT]. A hypocrite is an actor and pretender, and is guilty of duplicity [ICC]. Conscious deception is involved [TH].

QUESTION—Were there hypocrites who actually blew horns in the synagogues and streets when they gave alms?

It is not certain whether the reference to blowing trumpets is intended to be literal or metaphorical, but there is no evidence that trumpets were blown in connection with almsgiving [NICNT, WBC]. This burlesques the attitude of publicity seekers who gave money to the needy only in order to be praised by men [PNTC]. Probably it is merely a way of referring to the noisy clanging that came from tossing coins into collection receptacles [NAC]. Maybe some unknown custom is being protested [ICC]. Perhaps the mention of trumpets contains a reference to blowing trumpets in the Temple at the time alms were collected for some special need [TH, WBC] with the goal in mind of stimulating others to give as well [WBC]. Trumpets were blown on fast days and alms were asked on such days [ICC]. During times of drought trumpets were blown to announce public assembly for prayer and fasting and at these assemblies financial contributions were made [EBC].

so-that[a] they-might-be-praised[b] by-people; truly[c] I-say to-you(pl), they-are-receiving-in-full[d] their reward.

LEXICON—a. ὅπως (LN 89.59) (BAGD 2.a.α. p. 576): 'so that' [BECNT, LN, NICNT, NIGTC, WBC; NASB, NCV, NET, NRSV], 'that' [BAGD, BNTC; KJV], in order that' [BAGD, CC, PNTC], 'in order to' [LN, NTC; GW], 'for the purpose of' [LN], 'to' [NIV, NLT, REB], not explicit [CEV]. Purpose is expressed in the phrase 'they do it so that' [TEV], 'they are...looking for' [CEV]. This conjunction indicates purpose for events and states (sometimes occurring in highly elliptical contexts) [LN].

b. aorist pass. subj. of δοξάζω (LN **33.357**): 'to be praised' [BECNT, BNTC, LN, PNTC; ESV, GW, NRSV], 'to be glorified' [CC, LN, NIGTC, WBC], 'to have glory' [KJV], 'to be honored' [NASB, NIV], 'to be applauded' [NICNT], 'to win (the) admiration' [NTC], 'to win the praise' [REB], '(to look) for praise' [CEV]. This passive verb is translated as active: 'to honor (them)' [NCV], 'to praise (them)' [NET, TEV]. The phrase ὅπως δοξασθῶσιν ὑπὸ τῶν ἀνθρώπων 'so that they might be praised by people' is translated 'so that people might praise them' [**LN**], 'to call attention to their acts of charity' [NLT]. This verb means to speak of something as being unusually fine and deserving honor [LN].

c. ἀμήν (LN **72.6**) (BAGD 2. p. 45: 'truly' [BAGD, BECNT, BNTC, CC, NICNT, PNTC, WBC; ESV, NASB, NRSV, REB], 'solemnly' [NTC], 'verily' [KJV], 'amen' [NIGTC]. The phrase ἀμὴν λέγω ὑμῖν 'truly I say to you' is translated 'I can assure you' [CEV], 'I assure you' [TEV], 'I can guarantee this truth' [GW], 'I tell you the truth' [NCV, NET, NIV, NLT].

d. pres. act. indic. of ἀπέχω (LN **57.137**) (BAGD 1. p. 84): 'to receive in full' [BAGD, LN, NTC; NIV], 'to receive all they will ever get' [NLT], 'to receive' [CC, NIGTC; NRSV], 'to have in full' [BNTC; NASB], 'to have' [BECNT, PNTC; KJV, NET], 'to have already' [CEV, REB], 'to have at that moment' [WBC], 'to be paid in full' [LN], 'to be paid already in full' [TEV]. This present tense verb is translated as perfect 'they have received' [CC; ESV, NIV, NRSV], 'they have already received' [NTC]. The phrase ἀπέχουσιν τὸν μισθὸν αὐτῶν 'they are receiving in full their reward' is translated 'that will be their only reward' [GW], '(those hypocrites) already have their full reward' [NCV]. This verb means to receive something in full, with the implication that all that is due has been paid [LN].

QUESTION—What is meant by the verb ἀπέχουσιν 'they are receiving'?

This verb is a technical term for a transaction that has been concluded because payment has been received in full [NIBC, NICNT]. It was used in receipts, where it meant 'paid in full' [BNTC, ICC]. Here it means that they have received all of their reward already and can expect nothing more

[NICNT]. This present tense verb has a perfect tense meaning [CC, NIGTC; ESV, NIV, NRSV]: they have *already* received their reward [CC]. The use of the present tense 'they *are having* their reward' implies that this is the only reward they will receive, and it seems to be a deliberate contrast with the future eschatological rewards promised to the people mentioned in verses 4, 6, and 18 [WBC].

6:3 **But you(sg) (when)-doing alms do-not let-know**[a] **your(sg) left-(hand) what your(sg) right-(hand) is-doing,**

LEXICON—a. aorist act. (third person) impera. of γινώσκω (LN **28.74**): 'to let know' [BECNT, BNTC, CC, NIGTC, NTC, PNTC, WBC; all versions except TEV]. The imperative 'do not let know' is translated 'must not know' [NICNT]. The idiom 'do not let your left hand know what your right hand is doing' is translated 'don't let anyone know what you are doing' [NCV], 'don't let anyone know about it' [CEV], 'do it in such a way that others will not know about it' [**LN**], 'do it in such a way that even your closest friend will not know about it' [TEV]. It means to do something without letting people know about it [LN]. This clause is translated 'but when you help a needy person, do it in such a way that others will not know about it' [**LN**].

QUESTION—What relationship is indicated by δέ 'but'?

It is adversative, contrasting the believer with the hypocrites [My, PNTC]. The presence of the pronoun σοῦ 'you' in the phrase 'but *you*' makes this a strongly adversative statement [My, WBC].

QUESTION—How could one hand 'know' or not 'know' what the other is doing?

This is a figure of speech [NAC, TH] called hyperbole [CC, ICC, NIGTC]. It means to give so secretly that we ourselves hardly know what we have given [EBC, NTC]. The hands do everything together, so for one of them not to know what the other is doing would require complete secrecy, and that is how giving should be done [NTC]. It simply means that people should not think too highly of their own giving, so certainly others should not know about it [ICC].

6:4 **so-that your(sg) alms**[a] **may-be in secret;**[b]

LEXICON—a. ἐλεημοσύνη (LN 57.111) (BAGD p. 249): 'alms' [BAGD, LN], 'charitable giving, acts of charity, giving to the needy, kind deed' [LN]. The phrase σου ἡ ἐλεημοσύνη 'your alms' [KJV, NRSV] is also translated 'your almsgiving' [NICNT, PNTC, WBC], 'your giving' [ESV, NASB, NCV, NIV], 'your gift/gifts' [CEV, NET, NLT], 'your contributions' [GW], 'your good deed' [REB], 'it' [TEV]. This noun denotes the practice of giving to those in need as an act of mercy [LN].

b. κρυπτός (LN 28.69, **28.71**) (BAGD 2.b. p. 454): 'what is secret, hidden, not able to be made known' [LN], 'a hidden thing' [BAGD]. The phrase ᾖ ἐν τῷ κρυπτῷ 'may be in secret' [PNTC, WBC; ESV, KJV, NET, NIV] is also translated 'will be in secret' [NASB, REB], 'is in secret' [NICNT], 'will be done secretly' [**LN** (28.71)], 'may be done in secret' [NRSV], 'should be done in secret' [NCV], 'will be given in secret' [CEV], 'will be a private matter' [TEV], 'give in private' [NLT], 'give…privately' [GW]. This word refers to something that is not able to be known in view of the fact that it has been kept secret [LN (28.69)]. The idiom ἐν τῷ κρυπτῷ 'in the hidden' means not being able to be known by the public, but known by some in-group or by those immediately involved [LN (28.71)].

and your(sg) Father, the (one) seeing[a] in secret[b] will-reward[c] you(sg).
TEXT—Some Greek manuscripts add ἐν τῷ φανερῷ 'openly' after ἀποδώσει σοι 'will reward you'. GNT omits this with a B rating to indicate it was regarded to be almost certain. Only KJV follows this reading.
LEXICON—a. pres. act. participle of βλέπω (LN 24.7) (BAGD 1.c. p. 143): 'to see' [BAGD, LN, NICNT; all translations except CEV], 'to notice' [LN], 'to know' [CEV]. This verb means to see, frequently in the sense of becoming aware of or taking notice of something [LN].
  b. κρυπτός. The phrase ἐν τῷ κρυπτῷ 'in secret' [BNTC, CC, NICNT, NIGTC, NTC, PNTC, WBC; ESV, KJV, NCV, NET, NRSV] is translated 'what is done in secret' [BECNT; CEV, NASB, NCV, NIV, REB], 'what you do in private' [GW, TEV], 'everything' [NLT].
  c. fut. act. indic. of ἀποδίδωμι (LN 38.16) (BAGD 3. p. 90): 'to reward' [BAGD, BECNT, CC, LN, NIGTC, NTC, PNTC, WBC; all versions], 'to recompense' [BAGD, BNTC, LN], 'to repay' [NICNT]. This verb means to recompense someone, whether positively or negatively, depending upon what the individual deserves [LN].
QUESTION—What verb does the phrase ἐν τῷ κρυπτῷ 'in secret' modify?
  1. The phrase 'in secret' is the object of the verb 'seeing' [BECNT, EBC, ICC, Lns, My, NIBC, NICNT, NTC, PNTC, TH, TRT; CEV, GW, NASB, NET, NCV, NIV, NLT, REB, TEV]: the one seeing *what is done in secret*. God sees what they do in secret [BECNT; CEV, GW, NASB, NCV, NIV, REB, TEV]. In the OT, God 'sees in secret' in the sense that nothing is hidden from him and here it is the good deeds they do in secret that he sees and will reward [NICNT].
  2. The phrase 'in secret' is the object of the verb 'will reward' [NIGTC]: will reward *you in secret*.
QUESTION—Does this imply that the disciples should give alms for the purpose of receiving a reward from God?
  If good deeds are done only for the reward, they are not truly good; however, God does reward us when we do good as a response to his love, and even in the present time there is the reward of a clear conscience [PNTC]. The reward for holiness is holiness [NIBC]. People cannot earn salvation, but God truly does bless a life lived in gratitude and loyalty to himself [BNTC]. It refers to the reward they will have with their Father in heaven mentioned in 6:1 [NICNT]. The reward is favor with their Father in heaven [Lns]. This does not state when their Father in heaven will reward them, but it probably

refers to the final judgment [TH]. Probably the reward will be both in time and in eternity [EBC].

DISCOURSE UNIT—6:5–18 [NLT]. The topic is teaching about prayer and fasting.

DISCOURSE UNIT—6:5–15 [CEV, ESV, GW, NCV, NET, NIV, NRSV, TEV]. The topic is the Lord's prayer [ESV, GW], Jesus teaches about prayer [NCV], teaching about prayer [TEV], private prayer [NET], concerning prayer [NRSV], prayer [CEV, NIV].

6:5 And[a] whenever[b] you(pl)-pray,[c] you(pl)-will- not -be[d] like[e] the hypocrites,

LEXICON—a. καί (LN 89.92): 'and' [BECNT, BNTC, CC, LN, NICNT, NIGTC, PNTC, WBC; ESV, KJV, NIV, NRSV], 'also' [NTC], 'again' [REB], not explicit [CEV, GW, NASB, NET, NLT, TEV]. This conjunction indicates coordinate relations [LN].

b. ὅταν (LN 67.31) (BAGD 1.a. p. 588): 'whenever' [BAGD, BECNT, LN, NICNT, NTC, PNTC; NET, NRSV], 'when' [BNTC, CC, LN, NIGTC, WBC; all versions except NET, NRSV]. This conjunction indicates an indefinite point of time [LN].

c. pres. mid. or pass. (deponent = act.) subj. of προσεύχομαι (LN 33.178) (BAGD p. 713): 'to pray' [BAGD, LN; all translations], 'to speak to God, to ask God for' [LN]. The present tense of this verb is translated '(when/whenever) you are praying' [CC, NICNT]. This verb means to speak to or to make requests of God [LN].

d. fut. mid. (deponent = act.) of εἰμί (LN 13.1) (BAGD II. 9.b. p. 225): 'to be' [BAGD, LN]. The future tense is translated: 'you shall not be' [BNTC, CC, PNTC; similarly KJV], 'you are not to be' [NICNT, NIGTC; NASB], 'you must not be' [ESV], 'do not be' [BECNT, NTC, WBC; all versions except KJV, NASB, ESV].

e. ὡς (LN 64.12): 'like' [LN; all translations, except KJV], 'as' [LN; KJV]. This conjunction is a relatively weak marker of a relationship between events or states [LN].

for[a] they-love[b] to-pray[c] standing[d] in the synagogues and on the corners of-the streets,[e]

LEXICON—a. ὅτι (LN 89.33): 'for' [BNTC, CC, LN, NTC, PNTC; ESV, KJV, NASB, NIV, NRSV], 'because' [BECNT, LN, NIGTC, WBC; NET], 'since, in view of the fact that' [LN], not explicit [NICNT; CEV, GW, NCV, NLT, REB, TEV]. This conjunction indicates cause or reason, based on an evident fact [LN].

b. pres. act. indic. of φιλέω (LN **25.103**) (BAGD 1.b. p. 859): 'to love to' [BAGD, **LN;** all translations except GW], 'to like to' [BAGD, LN; GW], 'to do often or customarily' [BAGD]. This verb means to particularly like or enjoy doing something [LN].

c. pres. mid. or pass. (deponent = act.) infin. of προσεύχομαι (LN 33.178) (BAGD p. 713): 'to pray' [BAGD, BECNT, BNTC, CC, LN, NICNT, NIGTC, PNTC, WBC; all versions except REB], 'to say their prayers' [NTC; REB]. See this verb in the previous clause.
d. perf. act. participle of ἵσταμαι (LN 17.1): 'to stand' [BNTC, CC, LN, NICNT, NIGTC, PNTC; ESV, GW, KJV, NASB, NCV, NET, NIV, NRSV], 'to stand up' [BECNT, NTC; CEV, REB, TEV], not explicit [WBC; NLT]. The phrase ἑστῶτες προσεύχεσθαι 'to pray standing' [CC, NICNT, PNTC; KJV, NIV], is translated 'to stand and pray' [NIGTC; ESV, NASB, NCV, NRSV], 'to stand and to pray' [GW], 'to stand up and pray' [BECNT; CEV, TEV], 'to pray while standing' [BNTC; NET], 'to say their prayers standing up' [NTC; REB], 'to pray positioning themselves conspicuously' [WBC], 'to pray publicly (on street corners, etc.)' [NLT]. This verb means to be in a standing position [LN].
e. γωνία (LN **79.107**) (BAGD p. 168): 'street corner' [**LN**], 'corner' [LN]. This noun denotes the corner of an area or construction, either an inside corner or an outside corner [LN]. See next entry for the translation of this term.
f. πλατεῖα (LN 1.103) (BAGD p. 666): 'avenue, wide street' [LN], 'wide road' [BAGD]. This noun denotes a wide street within a city [LN]. The phrase ταῖς γωνίαις τῶν πλατειῶν 'corners of the streets' [CC, NICNT; KJV] is also translated 'street corners' [BAGD, BECNT, BNTC, NTC, PNTC; all versions except KJV], 'corners of the public squares' [NIGTC], 'corners of the main roads' [WBC].

QUESTION—What relationship is indicated by ὅτι 'for'?

It indicates an explanatory note about what it is that the hypocrites do that the disciples should not imitate [Lns, PNTC].

so-that[a] they-might-be-seen[b] by people; truly[c] I-say to-you(pl), they-are-receiving-in-full their reward.

LEXICON—a. ὅπως. See this word at 6:2.
b. aorist pass. subj. of φαίνομαι (LN 24.18) (BAGD 2.c. p. 852): 'to be seen' [BAGD, NIGTC, NTC, PNTC; ESV, KJV, NASB, NIV, NRSV], 'to be observed' [WBC], 'to be visible' [CC], 'to become visible' [LN], 'to appear' [BAGD, LN]. The passive verb phrase ὅπως φανῶσιν τοῖς ἀνθρώποις 'so that they might be seen by people' is translated as active: 'so that people may see them' [BECNT], 'so that everyone can see them' [GW, TEV], 'where everyone can see them' [NLT], 'for everyone to see them' [REB], 'so people will/can see them' [NCV, NET], 'so that people will notice them' [NICNT], 'just to look good' [CEV]. This verb means to become visible to someone [LN].
c. ἀμήν (LN 72.6) (BAGD 2. p. 45): 'truly'. See this word at 6:2.

6:6 But[a] you(sg) whenever you-pray, go-into[b] your(sg) inner-room[c]

LEXICON—a. δέ (LN 89.124) (BAGD 1.a. p. 171): 'but' [BAGD, BECNT, BNTC, LN; all translations except CEV, GW, NCV], not explicit [CEV, GW, NCV]. This conjunction indicates contrast [LN].

b. aorist act. impera. of εἰσέρχομαι (LN 15.93) (BAGD 1.a.β. p. 232): 'to go into' [BAGD, BECNT, BNTC, LN, NICNT, NIGTC, PNTC, WBC; CEV, ESV, NASB, NCV, NET, NIV, NRSV, REB], 'to go to' [GW, TEV], 'to go away' [NLT], 'to enter' [BAGD, CC, LN], 'to enter into' [NTC; KJV], 'to come into' [BAGD, LN]. This verb means to move into a space, either two-dimensional or three-dimensional [LN].

c. ταμεῖον (LN 7.28) (BAGD 2. p. 803): 'inner room' [BAGD, BECNT, BNTC, LN; NASB], 'storeroom' [CC, NIGTC], 'most private room' [NICNT, NTC], 'secret, innermost, or hidden room' [BAGD], 'room' [PNTC; ESV, NCV, NET, NIV, NRSV, TEV], 'closet' [WBC; KJV]. The phrase εἴσελθε εἰς τὸ ταμεῖόν σου 'go into your inner room' is translated 'go into a room alone' [CEV], 'go into a room by yourself' [REB], 'go away by yourself' [NLT]. This noun denotes a room in the interior of a house, normally without windows opening to the outside [LN].

QUESTION—What relationship is indicated by the conjunction δέ 'but'?

The conjunction δέ 'but' is adversative and marks contrast [PNTC], and the addition of σύ 'you' makes this an emphatic contrast [ICC, PNTC, WBC]. The pronoun σύ, which is grammatically unnecessary here, is used to emphasize the contrast between what the disciples are to do and what the hypocrites do [CC, Lns].

QUESTION—What was the ταμεῖον 'inner room'?

It could be any inner room, perhaps a storeroom [EBC, ICC] or a bedroom [EBC]. The storeroom was the only room in the house that would have had a door [NIBC, TH]. The important thing is that personal prayer be practiced away from observation by others [ICC, PNTC].

and having-shut[a] your(sg) door[b] pray to your(sg) Father the (one) in secret;[c]

LEXICON—a. aorist act. participle. of κλείω (LN 79.112) (BAGD 1. p. 434): 'to shut' [BAGD, BNTC, CC, LN, NICNT, NIGTC, NTC, PNTC, WBC; ESV, KJV, NLT, NRSV, REB], 'to close' [BECNT, LN; CEV, GW, NASB, NCV, NET, NIV, TEV], 'to make shut' [LN], 'to lock or bar (a door)' [BAGD]. This verb means to cause something to be shut [LN].

b. θύρα (LN 7.49) (BAGD 1.a. p. 365): 'door' [BAGD, LN; all translations], 'gate' [LN]. This noun denotes the door to a house or building [LN].

c. κρυπτός (LN 28.69, **28.71**) (BAGD 2.b. p. 454): 'what is secret, hidden, not able to be made known' [LN], 'a hidden thing' [BAGD]. The phrase τῷ ἐν τῷ κρυπτῷ 'the one in secret' is translated 'who is in secret' [NICNT, WBC; ESV, KJV, NASB, NRSV, REB], 'who cannot be seen' [NCV], 'who is unseen' [EBC; NIV, TEV], '(pray to your Father) in private' [CEV, NLT], '(pray) privately (to your Father who is with you)'

[GW]. This substantive refers to something that is not able to be known in view of the fact that it has been kept secret [LN (28.69)]. The idiom ἐν τῷ κρυπτῷ 'in the hidden' means not being able to be known by the public, but known by some in-group or by those immediately involved [LN (28.71)].

QUESTION—What is meant by praying to their Father τῷ ἐν τῷ κρυπτῷ 'the one in secret'?

The wording of this phrase is awkward [WBC] and the meaning is unclear [TH]. It is unclear whether the Father is in secret or whether the phrase is elliptical and requires a verb, 'who *sees* in secret', or whether the second article τῷ should be omitted to give the translation 'pray to your Father in secret' [ICC].

1. Some translate the phrase quite literally [NICNT, PNTC, WBC; ESV, KJV, NASB, NRSV, REB]: 'pray to your father who is in secret'.
2. Some take this to refer to God's presence in the inner room where the disciples were told to pray. God is omnipresent and he is there with them in the inner room even though they cannot see him [NICNT]. The Father sees in secret, and also *is present* in the secret place of prayer [NTC]. The phrase 'in secret' suggests that the Father is even in that secret place where the disciples are instructed to pray [Lns, NIBC, NICNT, NIGTC]. They are to pray to their Father 'who cannot be seen' [NCV], 'who is unseen' [NIV, TEV]. The following clause, 'who sees in secret' suggests that the emphasis is on the Father's ability to see what takes place in the inner room [TH]. The disciples are to pray in secret before their Father who sees in secret because he is everywhere [WBC]. At the same time, it suggests that God is invisible in contrast to the pretended worshippers who make themselves visible to everyone as they pray [NICNT].
3. Some take this to be an adverbial phrase modifying the verb 'pray': 'pray to your Father in private' [CEV, NLT], 'pray to your Father in secret' [NET], 'pray privately to your Father who is with you' [GW].

QUESTION—Was Jesus saying that prayer should not be done in public?

Jesus prayed both privately and publicly [NICNT]. The problem is in the motive, not the place [NICNT, NIGTC]. He is addressing hypocrisy, not sincere public prayer [BECNT]. The contrast is not with legitimate public prayer, but prayers made for show [ICC, Lns, My]. The early church did not understand this to be forbidding public prayer, because they often engaged in public prayer [EBC]. He is saying that they should not make themselves conspicuous when they pray, and the important thing here is sincerity, not secrecy [NTC]. Jesus is not forbidding public prayers, but is addressing the practice of personal prayer [BNTC, PNTC]. He is focusing on right motives, not forbidding public prayer [ICC, NAC]. He also is emphasizing the private aspect of piety [NAC]. Jesus does not forbid public prayer, as he not only participated in it, but also promised that he would be present whenever people gathered together to pray in his name [Lns].

and your(sg) Father, the (one) seeing in secret will-reward you(sg).
TEXT—Some Greek manuscripts add ἐν τῷ φανερῷ 'openly' after ἀποδώσει σοι 'will reward you'. GNT omits this with a B rating to indicate it was regarded to be almost certain. Only KJV follows this reading.
LEXICON—See this identical clause at 6:4.

6:7 And^a (when) praying do-not babble^b like^c the Gentiles,^d

LEXICON—a. δέ (LN 89.94, 89.124): 'and' [CC, LN (89.94), PNTC, WBC; ESV, NASB, NCV, NIV], 'moreover' [NTC], 'but' [BNTC, LN (89.124); KJV], not explicit [BECNT, NICNT, NIGTC; CEV, GW, NET, NLT, NRSV, REB, TEV]. This conjunction may mark an additive relation, but with the possible implication of some contrast [LN (89.94)], or may be used simply to mark contrast [LN (89.124)].

b. aorist act. subj. of βατταλογέω (LN **33.88**, **33.89**) (BAGD p. 137): 'to babble' [BAGD, BECNT, **LN** (33.89), PNTC, WBC], 'to babble on' [BNTC, CC, NICNT, NIGTC], 'to go babbling on' [REB], 'to babble on and on' [NTC; NLT], 'to keep babbling on' [NIV], 'to babble repetitiously' [NET], 'to talk on and on' [CEV], 'to use many words' [**LN** (33.88)], 'to speak for a long time' [LN (33.88)], 'to heap up empty phrases' [ESV, NRSV], 'to ramble' [GW], 'to use vain repetition' [KJV], 'to use meaningless repetition' [NASB], 'to use a lot of meaningless words' [TEV], 'to continue saying things that mean nothing' [NCV]. This verb can mean to speak much or extensively, with a possible added implication of meaningless words [LN (33.88)], or it can mean to utter senseless sounds or to speak indistinctly and incoherently [LN (33.89)].

c. ὥσπερ (LN 64.13) (BAGD 2. p. 899): 'like' [CC, NICNT, NTC, PNTC; GW, NCV, NET, NIV, REB], 'as' [BAGD, BECNT, BNTC, LN, NIGTC, WBC; CEV, ESV, KJV, NASB, NLT, NRSV, TEV], 'just as' [BAGD, LN]. This conjunction is a somewhat emphatic marker of similarity between events and states [LN]. See this word at 6:2.

d. ἐθνικός (LN 11.38) (BAGD p. 218): 'Gentile' [BAGD, BECNT, CC, LN, NICNT, NIGTC, PNTC, WBC; ESV, NASB, NET, NRSV], 'heathen' [BAGD, LN; GW; KJV, REB], 'pagan' [LN, NTC; NIV, TEV], 'people who don't know the Lord' [CEV], 'those people who don't know God' [NCV], 'people of other religions' [NLT]. This adjective describes one who is not a Jew [LN].

QUESTION—What is meant by the verb βατταλογέω 'to babble'?
The verb refers to the repetition of meaningless syllables [BECNT, NICNT, WBC]. Most think that actual words were being wrongly used in prayer. It means to pray without sincerity or without thinking [TRT]. It means to pray unnecessarily long prayers [BECNT, BNTC, CC, NAC, NIBC, NTC, PNTC], probably using flowery or showy oration [NAC].

for^a they-think^b that because-of^c their many-words^d they-will-be-heard.^e

LEXICON—a. γάρ (LN 89.23): 'for' [BECNT, BNTC, CC, LN, NICNT, NIGTC, NTC, PNTC, WBC; ESV, KJV, NASB, NIV, NRSV], 'because'

[LN; NET], not explicit [CEV, GW, NCV, NLT, REB, TEV]. This conjunction indicates cause or reason between events, though in some contexts the relationship is often remote or tenuous [LN].
b. pres. act. indic. of δοκέω (LN 31.29) (BAGD 1.d. p. 202): 'to think' [BAGD, BECNT, CC, LN, NICNT, NIGTC, PNTC, WBC; all versions except REB], 'to suppose' [BAGD, BNTC, LN], 'to imagine' [LN, NTC; REB], 'to believe' [BAGD, LN]. This verb means to regard something as presumably true, but without particular certainty [LN].
c. ἐν (LN 89.26) (BAGD III.3.a. p. 261): 'because of' [BAGD, BECNT, CC, LN, NIGTC, NTC; NCV, NIV, NRSV], 'merely because of' [WBC], 'merely by' [NLT], 'just because (they)' [BNTC], 'because' [TEV], 'for' [PNTC; ESV, KJV, NASB], 'by' [NET], 'on account of, by reason of' [LN], not explicit [NICNT; CEV]. The phrase ἐν τῇ πολυλογίᾳ αὐτῶν εἰσακουσθήσονται 'because of their many words they will be heard' is translated 'the more they speak, the more likely they are to be heard' [NICNT; similarly REB]. This preposition marks cause or reason, with focus upon instrumentality, either of objects or events [LN].
d. πολυλογία (LN **33.87**) (BAGD p. 687): 'many words' [BAGD, BECNT, **LN**, NIGTC, PNTC; ESV, NASB, NCV, NET, NIV, NRSV], 'flow of words' [NTC], 'abundance of words' [WBC], 'long speaking' [LN], 'much speaking' [LN; KJV], 'wordiness' [CC, LN], 'long prayers' [CEV; similarly TEV]. The noun phrase τῇ πολυλογίᾳ αὐτῶν 'their many words' is translated as a verb phrase: 'they multiply words' [BNTC], 'the more they speak' [NICNT], 'the more they say' [REB], 'if they talk a lot' [GW], 'repeating their words again and again' [NLT]. This noun refers to speaking for a long time or too much [LN].
e. fut. pass. indic. of εἰσακούω (LN 24.60) (BAGD 2.a. p. 232): 'to be heard' [BAGD, BECNT, BNTC, CC, NICNT, NTC, PNTC, WBC; ESV, GW, KJV, NASB, NET, NIV, NRSV, REB], 'to be listened to' [LN, NICNT], 'to be answered' [NLT], 'to be heeded, to be paid attention' [LN]. This passive verb is translated as active: 'God will hear them' [NCV], 'their gods will hear them' [TEV]. The phrase ἐν τῇ πολυλογίᾳ αὐτῶν εἰσακουσθήσονται 'because of their many words they will be heard' is translated 'God likes to hear long prayers' [CEV]. This verb means to listen to someone, with the implication of heeding and responding to what is heard [LN].

QUESTION—What relationship is indicated by γάρ 'for'?

This conjunction indicates the reason the Gentiles babble in their prayers [BECNT, BNTC, CC, LN, NICNT, NIGTC, NTC, PNTC, WBC; ESV, KJV, NASB, NET, NIV, NRSV]. The meaningless repetition was based on the pagan belief that the gods thrive on incantation and repetition [EBC]. The word originally referred to the pagan practice of repeatedly reciting a long list of names of various gods in the expectation that doing so would enable them to invoke the true God, and that saying the name of the right god correctly would enable the person to manipulate that god [NIBC]. Pagans

6:8 Therefore[a] do-not be-like[b] them,

LEXICON—a. οὖν (LN 89.50) (BAGD 1.b. p. 593): 'therefore' [BAGD, LN, NTC, PNTC; KJV], 'then' [BAGD, BNTC, CC, LN], 'so' [BAGD, BECNT, LN, NICNT; NASB], 'so then' [LN] 'consequently, accordingly' [BAGD], not explicit [NIGTC, WBC; all versions except KJV, NASB]. This conjunction indicates result, often implying the conclusion of a process of reasoning [LN].

b. aorist pass. subj. of ὁμοιόω (LN 64.4) (BAGD 1. p. 567): 'to be like' [BAGD, BECNT, CC, LN, NICNT, NIGTC, NTC, PNTC, WBC; all versions except KJV, REB], 'to be like unto' [KJV], 'to become like' [BAGD, BNTC], 'to imitate' [REB], 'to resemble, to be similar to' [LN]. This verb means to be like or similar to something else [LN].

QUESTION—What relationship is indicated by οὖν 'therefore'?

This conjunction indicates the conclusion to be drawn from the preceding clause in 6:7, which itself serves as the reason for the command not to babble like the Gentiles [BECNT, My, NCNT, NTC, PNTC; KJV, NASB]. Since this 'therefore' reinforces the command given in verse 7, many translations omit the conjunction and translate this as a simple command: 'Do not be like them' [all versions except KJV, NASB, REB], 'Do not imitate them' [REB]. It of course means 'do not pray as they do' [PNTC]. They should shun superfluous praying as a heathen error [My]. The disciples should not babble in long prayers like the Gentiles [PNTC]. They should not think they had to demand God's attention and then inform him about needs he may have overlooked [NICNT].

for[a] your(pl) Father knows[b] of-what you(pl)-have need[c] before[d] you(pl) ask[e] him.

LEXICON—a. γάρ (LN 89.23): 'for' [BECNT, BNTC, CC, LN, NIGTC, NTC, PNTC, WBC; ESV, KJV, NASB, NET, NIV, NLT, NRSV, REB], 'because' [LN; NCV], 'since' [NICNT], not explicit [CEV, GW, TEV]. This conjunction indicates cause or reason between events, though in some contexts the relationship is often remote or tenuous [LN].

b. perf. act. indic. of οἶδα (LN 28.1) (BAGD 1.g. p. 556): 'to know' [BAGD, LN; all translations], 'to know about, to have knowledge of, to be acquainted with' [LN]. This verb means to possess information about something. The perfect tense has a present tense meaning [LN].

c. χρεία (LN 57.40) (BAGD 1. p. 885): 'need' [BAGD, CC, LN; KJV], 'lack, what is needed' [LN]. The phrase ὧν χρείαν ἔχετε 'of what you have need' is translated 'what your needs are' [REB], 'what you need' [BECNT, BNTC, NICNT, NIGTC, NTC, PNTC; CEV, ESV, GW, NASB, NET, NIV, NRSV, TEV], 'exactly what you need' [NLT], 'the things you need' [WBC; NCV]. This noun denotes that which is lacking and particularly needed [LN].

d. πρό (LN **67.17**) (BAGD 2. p. 702): 'before' [BAGD, BNTC, CC, **LN**, NICNT, NIGTC, NTC, PNTC, WBC; all versions except NLT], 'even before' [BECNT; NLT]. This preposition describes a point of time prior to another point of time [LN].

e. aorist act. infin. of αἰτέω (LN 33.163) (BAGD p. 25): 'to ask' [BAGD; all translations], 'to ask for' [BAGD, LN], 'to demand, to plead for' [LN]. This verb means to ask for something with urgency, even to the point of demanding [LN].

QUESTION—What relationship is indicated by γάρ 'for'?

This conjunction indicates the reason why they need not pray in the babbling manner of the Gentiles in order to get God to grant their requests [CC, NICNT, PNTC, WBC]. The reason they should not pray like the Gentiles is that God their Father already knows their needs and will grant them what they need [WBC]. The disciples should pray to worship the Father, not to inform him about their needs which he already knows [PNTC]. God is their Father and is both benevolent and omniscient [NICNT].

6:9 You(pl) then[a] pray[b] like-this;[c]

LEXICON—a. οὖν (LN 89.50) (BAGD 1.b. p. 593): 'then' [BAGD, BNTC, LN, NICNT, NTC, PNTC; ESV, NASB, NIV, NRSV, TEV], 'so then' [LN], 'therefore' [BAGD, BECNT, CC, LN, WBC; KJV], 'so' [BAGD, LN; NCV, NET], 'consequently, accordingly' [BAGD, LN], not explicit [NIGTC; CEV, GW, NLT, REB]. This preposition marks result, often implying the conclusion of a process of reasoning [LN].

b. pres. mid. or pass. (deponent = act.) impera. of προσεύχομαι (LN 33.178): 'to pray' [LN; all translations], 'to speak to God, to ask God for' [LN]. This verb means to speak to or to make requests of God [LN].

c. οὕτως (LN 61.9) (BAGD 2. P. 598): 'like this' [BECNT, CC, NIGTC, PNTC; CEV, ESV, NCV, NLT], 'thus' [LN], 'this way' [NET], 'in this way' [BAGD, LN; NASB, NRSV], 'in this manner' [WBC], 'this is the way' [BNTC], 'this is how' [NICNT, NTC; GW, NIV, REB, TEV], 'after this manner' [KJV].

QUESTION—What is the function of the personal pronoun ὑμεῖς 'you'?

The pronoun ὑμεῖς 'you' is stated explicitly in the Greek text as the subject of the imperative verb, emphasizing the contrast between the disciples ('you') and the hypocrites among the Jews [PNTC]. It adds emphasis [CC, Lns, My, WBC] and shows contrast with others who pray [Lns, My].

QUESTION—What is the significance of the use of the present imperative προσεύχεσθε 'pray'?

It points to a habitual practice [PNTC]. It means 'whenever you pray' [Lns]. In this section the present imperatives seem to be used to introduce new topics [CC].

QUESTION—What is meant by praying οὕτως 'like this'?

Jesus is giving them a guide or model for prayer, but it is not intended to be an exact formula [BECNT, EBC, ICC, NAC, NIBC, NIGTC, NTC, PNTC,

TRT]. It is a guide or general pattern [CC], not a liturgical chant [NIBC]. It includes certain elements and attitudes that should be included in the prayer life of disciples [NAC]. It expresses kingdom values, in which the praise of the first three requests precedes and permeates the requests for personal need that follow [BECNT]. Jesus told them that this is *how* they should pray, not *what* they should pray, meaning that it is only a model [EBC].

QUESTION—What is the structure of the prayer?

The first three requests honor God and the rest seek the meeting of human needs [BECNT, BNTC, EBC, NIBC, NICNT, NTC]. The first three petitions are in effect a doxology [NICNT].

Our Father[a] in the heavens,[b] may- your(sg) name[c] -be-held-holy,[d]

LEXICON—a. πατήρ (LN 2.12) (BAGD 3.c.α. p. 636): 'father' [BAGD, LN; all translations]. As a title for God, this noun denotes one who combines aspects of supernatural authority and care for his people [LN].

b. οὐρανός. See this word at 6:1. This plural noun is translated as singular 'heaven' by all translations.

c. ὄνομα (LN 33.126) (BAGD I.4.b. p. 571): 'name' [BAGD, LN; all translations]. This noun denotes the proper name of a person or object [LN].

d. aorist pass. (third person) impera. of ἁγιάζω (LN **88.27**) (BAGD 3. p. 9): 'to be hallowed, to be regarded as holy, to be honored as holy' [LN], 'to be treated as holy, to be held in reverence' [BAGD]. The clause 'may your name be held holy' is translated 'hallowed be your name' [**LN**; ESV, KJV, NASB, NIV, NRSV; similarly NTC], 'let your name be hallowed' [CC], 'may your name be hallowed' [REB], 'may your name be honored as holy' [**LN**], 'may your name be honored' [BECNT; NET], 'may your name be held in reverence' [BNTC, NICNT], 'may your name be kept holy' [PNTC; NLT], 'may your name always be kept holy' [NCV], 'may your holy name be honored' [TEV], 'let your name be sanctified' [NIGTC], 'let your name be kept holy' [GW], 'set apart your holy name' [WBC], 'help us to honor your name' [CEV], 'may you be reverenced as holy', (or even) 'may you be acknowledged as God' [LN]. This verb means to feel reverence for or to honor as holy [LN].

QUESTION—What is implied in the use of the possessive pronoun ἡμῶν 'our' in the phrase 'our Father'?

'Our' speaks of the closeness of relationship to God enjoyed by the disciples [BECNT, EBC, ICC, NAC, NTC]. The possessive pronoun 'our' shows that the disciples are part of a larger community of believers [BNTC, CC, Lns, NAC, NICNT, NIGTC, TH]. Only Jesus' disciples have the right to call upon God as their Father [CC, EBC, ICC, Lns, NICNT], since he is not the father of all people indiscriminately [EBC, ICC, NTC]. Jesus often spoke of God as 'my Father' in speaking of his unique sonship and authority, but since this prayer asks God to forgive ἡμῖν 'us' ἡμῶν 'our' sins, such a prayer would be made only by the disciples, and not by Jesus himself [EBC].

Jesus referred to God as 'my Father' and as 'your Father' but never uses 'our Father' inclusively [EBC, NICNT, PNTC].

QUESTION—What is implied by addressing God as 'our Father in heaven'?

Both Jews and Gentiles occasionally referred to God as 'Father' in prayer, but references to God as transcendent were much more common than intimate references such as 'Father' [EBC, PNTC]. The use of 'Father' to refer to God was unusual but not unknown [BECNT, CC, EBC, ICC, NAC, NICNT, NIGTC, PNTC]. The phrase 'Father in heaven' differentiates the heavenly Father from earthly fathers and it also preserves the distance between God and people [TH]. While the term 'Father' indicates intimacy, the addition of 'in heaven' speaks of his transcendence [BECNT, EBC, Lns, NAC, NIGTC, NTC, PNTC, WBC]. That the Father, who cares for his children, is enthroned in heaven means that he has power to act in their behalf [CC, WBC], and that their hope of heaven is sure [Lns].

QUESTION—What does it mean for God's name to be held as holy?

In that time the name was considered to represent the person with all the qualities that were associated with the person. God is holy, and for his name to be held holy means it should be held in proper reverence, and all that God is and stands for should be revered [PNTC]. God's name represents himself as he is revealed in his works and in his faithfulness toward his covenant people. To treat God's name as holy means to reverence, glorify, honor, and exalt him [NTC]. God's name represents God as he has made himself known [BNTC, ICC, Lns, TH], and to treat his name as holy means to respond to him with worship, gratitude, faith, humility, and acceptance of his will [BNTC]. God's name represents his character as he has revealed himself in history, and to revere God's name is to treat God himself as high and holy [NIBC, TH]. God's name is already holy because it represents him as he is and has revealed himself, so this is a prayer that God may be treated as holy [EBC]. It means to give conscious obedience to his commands [NIGTC]. Since the connection between name and person was very close in Hebrew thought, the petition for God to vindicate his name is to call upon him to vindicate himself by bringing his kingdom and accomplishing his will on earth [WBC]. It is to give God the reverence due him [NICNT]. It is to honor God by obeying him [TRT].

6:10 may- your(sg) kingdom[a] -come,[b]

LEXICON—a. βασιλεία (LN 37.64) (BAGD 3.g. p. 135): 'kingdom' [BAGD, BECNT, BNTC, NICNT, NIGTC, NTC, PNTC; all versions], 'eschatological kingdom' [WBC], 'reign' [CC, LN], 'royal reign' [BAGD], 'rule' [LN]. This noun denotes the rule of a king, with the implication of complete authority and the possibility of being able to pass on the right to rule to one's son or near kin [LN].

b. aorist act. (third person) impera. of ἔρχομαι (LN 13.117) (BAGD I.2.b. p. 311): 'to let come' [BAGD], 'to let happen' [LN]. The phrase 'may your kingdom come' is translated 'your kingdom come' [ESV, NASB,

NIV, NRSV, REB; similarly NTC; KJV], 'let your reign come' [CC], 'let your kingdom come' [NIGTC; GW], 'may your kingdom come' [BECNT, NICNT, PNTC; NCV, NET, TEV; similarly BNTC], 'may your kingdom come soon' [NLT], 'come and set up your kingdom' [CEV], 'bring your eschatological kingdom' [WBC].

QUESTION—What is meant by the coming of God's kingdom?

Most think that the coming of the kingdom focuses on the final establishment of God's reign on earth [BECNT, BNTC, CC, ICC, My, NIBC, PNTC, TH, WBC]. This petition, like the one before it and the one following, is eschatological in focus, looking for the future consummation of history [ICC]. It is the time of God's final victory over sin and evil when the Son of God comes to judge the living and the dead [CC]. The prayer expresses the desire that God's promised rule on earth, which has already begun in Jesus' ministry, would be brought to complete fullness [WBC]. It looks for the advent of God in judgment and salvation, establishing a kingdom of which the ministry of Jesus represented the beginning [NIGTC]. God's kingdom is already present, though hidden to many and unacknowledged by many, and awaits a more public, future manifestation in which people will submit to his sovereignty [NICNT]. Some think that the prayer for the coming of the kingdom includes the growth of the kingdom from the time of Jesus' ministry until its final eschatological establishment [EBC, Lns, NAC, NTC]. It is an appeal that people would bow in submission to God's rule now [EBC]. In conjunction with the next clause it is a petition that people will acknowledge God's reign and that God's purposes will be accomplished in this world [NAC]. It is a prayer for God's rule to be established in human hearts, for the progress of missionary activity, and for believers to acknowledge God more and more as their ruler [NTC]. It is an appeal for the consummation of the kingdom of glory, but also of the rule of grace even here and now [Lns].

may- your(sg) will[a] -be-done,[b]

LEXICON—a. θέλημα (LN **30.59**) (BAGD 1.a. p. 354): 'will' [BAGD, **LN**; all translations except CEV, NCV], 'what you want' [NCV], 'what is willed' [BAGD], 'intent, purpose, plan' [LN]. See the next entry for CEV. This noun denotes that which is purposed, intended, or willed [LN].

b. aorist pass. (third person) impera. of γίνομαι (LN 13.48) (BAGD I.2.a. p. 158): 'to be done' [BAGD, BECNT, BNTC, CC, NICNT, NTC, PNTC; all versions except CEV], 'to be fulfilled' [BAGD, WBC], 'to come into effect' [NIGTC], 'to be performed' [BAGD]. The clauses, 'may your kingdom come, may your will be done on earth as it is in heaven' are conflated and translated as 'come and set up your kingdom, so that everyone on earth will obey you' [CEV]. This verb means to come to acquire or experience a state [LN].

QUESTION—What is God's will that is to be done?

The first and second options are not necessarily mutually exclusive.

1. It is a prayer that people will obey God [TH]. God's rule on earth comes through people who do his will [BECNT]. It petitions God to work in the earth so that people would obey him immediately, completely, and willingly [NTC]. This petition encompasses the other two and focuses on what they have in common, which is that people should conform their behavior to God's will [NIGTC]. The coming of God's kingship would mean that people would obey him and fulfill his purposes, and honor and serve him as king [NICNT]. This is about a practical, moral righteousness that will determine and shape the life of disciples until the fullness of the kingdom comes, a righteousness without which one cannot be admitted to the kingdom when it does come [My].
2. It is a prayer that God's plans be carried out [PNTC]. It asks for the extension of the messianic kingdom here and now, for the consummation of the coming messianic kingdom, and that people will be obedient to God just as he is obeyed in heaven [EBC]. In conjunction with the previous clause it is a petition that people will acknowledge God's reign and that God's purposes will be accomplished in this world [NAC]. This is closely related to the previous petition, and seeks the accomplishment of God's will on earth in terms of overturning the present evil order and a renewal of the earth [WBC]. It is to pray that God will break the will of Satan and sinful men, and bring his own gracious and perfect will on earth, something that will happen fully at the end of the age [CC].
3. It combines both of the above [EBC, ICC]. This request is that God's demands will be obeyed on earth and that God will bring to pass the events in salvation history he has determined [EBC]. God's determination to bring about his will is both ethical and eschatological. The prayer is that people will take the yoke of the kingdom of God upon themselves and live in accord with it ethically, and also that the eschatological realization of heaven on earth will come about wherein God's saving purposes are fully accomplished through the triumph of grace [ICC].

as[a] in heaven (so) also[b] on[c] earth.[d]

LEXICON—a. ὡς (LN 64.12) (BAGD II.1. p. 897): 'as' [BAGD, LN], 'like' [LN]. The phrase ὡς ἐν οὐρανῷ 'as in heaven' [BNTC, CC, NICNT, NIGTC, NTC, PNTC; REB] is translated 'as it is in heaven' [BECNT, WBC; all versions except CEV, GW, REB], 'as it is done in heaven' [GW], 'as you are obeyed in heaven' [CEV]. This conjunction is a relatively weak marker of a relationship between events or states [LN].
  b. καί (LN 89.93) (BAGD II.3. p. 393): 'so also' [BAGD, BNTC, NICNT, NIGTC, NTC], 'also' [CC, LN, PNTC], 'even' [LN], 'and' [LN], not explicit [BECNT, WBC; all versions]. This conjunction indicates an additive relationship which is not coordinate [LN].
  c. ἐπί with genitive (LN 83.46) (BAGD I.1.a.α. p. 286): 'on' [BAGD, LN; all translations except KJV, NCV], 'here on' [NCV], 'in' [KJV], 'upon'

[BAGD, LN]. This conjunction indicates a position on a surface of an object, whether vertical or horizontal, and in contact with the object [LN].
   d. γῆ (LN 1.39) (BAGD 5.a. p. 157): 'earth' [BAGD, LN; all translations], 'world' [LN]. This noun denotes the surface of the earth as the dwelling place of mankind, in contrast with the heavens above and the world below [LN].

QUESTION—With which petition is this phrase connected?
   1. It is connected with the third petition, stated in the preceding clause [EBC, Lns, My, NIBC, NIGTC, NTC, TH, WBC; CEV, GW, KJV, NASB, NET, NIV, NLT, NRSV, TEV]. While it is connected with the last petition, this last petition encompasses the first two, so there is little difference in meaning whether it is linked with all three or only the last one [NIGTC].
   2. It is connected with the last two petitions [NAC; NCV, REB].
   3. It is connected with all three petitions [BECNT, BNTC, CC, NICNT]. In heaven the angels already honor God's name, acknowledge his kingship, and do his will. So those who pray this prayer on earth are committing themselves to honor God's name, accept his kingship, and do his will [NICNT]. All three petitions appeal to the Father in heaven in behalf of those who face the conditions that still exist on the earth [CC].

6:11 Give^a us today^b our daily/needed^c bread;^d

LEXICON—a. aorist act. impera. of δίδωμι (LN 57.71): 'to give' [LN; all translations]. This verb means to give an object, usually implying it is of value [LN].
   b. σήμερον (LN 67.205) (BAGD p. 749): 'today' [BAGD, LN]. This noun denotes the same day as the day of a discourse [LN]. See the next entry for how this term is translated by commentaries and versions.
   c. ἐπιούσιος (LN **67.183, 67.206**) (BAGD p. 297): 'daily, on each day' [LN (67.183)], 'for today' [LN (67.206)]. BAGD says that probably Origen was right in saying that this extremely rare word was coined by Mark and there are numerous suggestions as to how such a word had been derived [PNTC]. BAGD gives all of these possible meanings for the word: (1) 'necessary for existence' (2) 'for the current day, for today', (3) 'for the following day', (4.a) 'for the future', (4.b) 'that belongs to it', (4.c) 'the coming kingdom'. This clause is translated 'give us this day/today our daily bread' [NTC, PNTC; ESV, GW, KJV, NASB, NET, NIV, NRSV, REB], 'give us each day our daily bread' [**LN** (67.183)], 'give us our food for today' [CEV], 'our bread for today give us today' [NIGTC], 'give us our necessary food for today' [BECNT], 'give us the food we need for each day' [NCV], 'give us today the food we need' [NLT, TEV], 'give us today the food we need for today' [**LN** (67.206)], 'give us today our bread that is coming (from you)' [CC], 'give us today our bread for the coming day' [BNTC; similarly NICNT], 'give us today the eschatological bread that will be ours in the future' [WBC]. This noun denotes what recurs on a

daily basis [LN (67.183)], or what pertains to a day which is the same as the day of a discourse [LN (67.206)].

d. ἄρτος (LN **5.1**) (BAGD 2. p. 111): 'bread' [BNTC, CC, **LN**, NICNT, NIGTC, NTC, PNTC; ESV, GW, KJV, NASB, NET, NIV, NRSV, REB], 'eschatological bread' [WBC], 'food' [BAGD, BECNT; CEV, NCV, NLT, TEV]. This noun denotes any kind of food or nourishment [LN].

QUESTION—What is meant by praying that the Father give us today our ἐπιούσιον 'daily/needed' bread?

The word ἐπιούσιον 'daily/needed' occurs only here and in the parallel passage in Luke 11:3, and is unknown outside of these two occurrences [BAGD, BECNT, CC, LN, NIGTC, PNTC]. Its origin and meaning have never been explained to the satisfaction of all [TH]. This word may reflect the fact that laborers were paid a day at a time [BECNT, CC, EBC, NICNT], and many people lived a precarious, hand to mouth lifestyle [EBC].

1. The prayer asks God to supply their daily food [NICNT, NTC, PNTC; CEV, ESV, GW, KJV, NASB, NET, NIV, NRSV, REB]. The word 'daily' fits the facts, and the translation 'the coming day' [BNTC, EBC, ICC, My, NAC] has essentially the same meaning since, if the 'coming day' is prayed in the morning, it refers to the rest of that very day while if prayed in the evening then it would be for next day [NICNT, PNTC]. It concerns the need for food for the coming day, in the sense of 'today' being used in a morning prayer for the day to come after the pattern of Exodus 16 where the manna is given in the morning for the day to come. Yet the eschatological orientation of the three preceding petitions causes one to think of and desire the spiritual eschatological bread which will bring lasting satisfaction [ICC].

2. The prayer asks God to supply food needed for existence [NIBC, WBC; NCV, NLT, TEV]. This text reflects the daily rhythm of making and consuming bread, which represents all recurring basic human needs [NIGTC]. Following the eschatological requests already referred to in the prayer, this request for bread anticipates the messianic banquet of the future by requesting the eschatological benefit of food for their present needs [WBC].

QUESTION—What is meant by ἄρτος 'bread'?

'Bread' represents all food [BECNT, BNTC, EBC, LN, My, PNTC, TH, WBC; CEV, NCV, NLT, TEV]. It may represent all physical needs [CC, EBC, NIGTC, TRT], whatever is necessary to sustain life [Lns, NTC].

6:12 and forgive[a] us our debts,[b]

LEXICON—a. aorist act. impera. of ἀφίημι (LN 40.8) (BAGD 2. p. 125): 'to forgive' [BAGD, LN; all translations except NIGTC], 'to release from' [NIGTC], 'to pardon' [BAGD, LN], 'to cancel, to remit' [BAGD]. This verb means to remove the guilt resulting from wrongdoing [LN].

b. ὀφείλημα (LN **88.299**) (BAGD 2. p. 598): 'debt' [BAGD, BECNT, BECNT, CC, NICNT, NIGTC, NTC, PNTC; ESV, KJV, NASB, NET,

NIV, NRSV], 'sin' [**LN**; NCV, NLT], 'offense' [LN, WBC], '(for) doing wrong' [CEV], 'the wrong/wrongs we have done' [REB, TEV], 'transgression, guilt' [LN], not explicit [GW]. This noun denotes the moral debt incurred as the result of sin [LN].

QUESTION—What is meant by the noun ὀφείλημα 'debt'?
'Debt' is used as a metaphor for sin or as a synonym for sin [BAGD, BECNT, BNTC, EBC, ICC, NIGTC, NTC, PNTC, TH, TRT, WBC], and the parallel passage in Luke 11:4 uses the word ἁμαρτίας 'sins' instead of the word 'debts' [PNTC]. Sin is a debt owed to God [EBC, BNTC, ICC, NAC, NIBC, NTC, WBC], whether it be a sin of omission or of commission [EBC]. It speaks of unfulfilled moral obligations to God [BECNT]. We have an obligation to obey God, and when we fail to do what we should, we owe God a debt and need to have that debt cancelled since we cannot repay it [PNTC]. 'Debt' is used figuratively for 'sin' and if literal translations are likely to be understood as referring to a debt we owe people because we have borrowed something that has to be paid back, then it is better to directly use 'sins' or 'wrongs' [TH].

as^a also^b we-have-forgiven^c our debtors;^d

LEXICON—a. ὡς (LN 64.12) (BAGD II.4.a. p. 897, III.1.b. p. 898): 'as' [BAGD, LN; all translations except NCV], 'just as' [NCV]. This conjunction is a relatively weak marker of a relationship between events or states [LN]. It can mark the cause of an action [BAGD II.4.a. p. 897, III.1.b. p. 898].

b. καί (LN 89.93): 'also' [BECNT, BNTC, CC, LN, NIGTC, NTC, PNTC, WBC; ESV, NASB, NIV, NRSV], 'too' [NICNT], not explicit [CEV, GW, KJV, NCV, NET, NLT, REB, TEV]. This conjunction indicates an additive relationship which is not coordinate [LN].

c. aorist act. impera. of ἀφίημι. See previous clause. This aorist verb is translated as perfect: 'we have forgiven' [BECNT, BNTC, NICNT, NTC, PNTC, WBC; ESV, NASB, NCV, NIV, NLT, NRSV, REB], 'we have released' [NIGTC]; as aorist: 'we forgave' [CC]; as present: '(as) we forgive' [CEV, GW, KJV, TEV].

d. ὀφειλέτης (LN 88.300) (BAGD 2.c.α. p. 598): 'debtor' [BECNT, BNTC, CC, NICNT, NTC, PNTC; ESV, KJV, NASB, NET, NIV, NRSV], 'those indebted to us' [NIGTC], 'those who offend us' [WBC], 'those who sinned/sin against us' [NCV, NLT], 'those who have wronged us' [REB], 'sinner, offender' [LN], 'one who is guilty of sin' [BAGD]. The phrase τοῖς ὀφειλέταις ἡμῶν 'our debtors' is translated 'others' [CEV, GW, TEV]. This noun denotes one who commits sin and thus incurs a moral debt [LN].

QUESTION—What relationship is indicated by ὡς 'as'?
It indicates a needed condition, but not one that causes or merits the forgiveness [Lns, My]. It indicates the reason forgiveness is sought, though not the extent; that is, it is not saying forgive us to the degree we forgive

others [My]. It represents manner: that is, forgive us in the same way we forgive other people [TH].

QUESTION—What is the relationship between forgiving others and being forgiven?

Forgiving others does not earn or merit being forgiven [CC, BNTC, EBC, Lns, ICC, My, NIBC, NTC], but it is the attitude that makes being forgiven possible [EBC]. There is a correlation between our being forgiven and our willingness to forgive, even if we do so imperfectly [PNTC]. The privilege of being forgiven entails the responsibility of forgiving others [BECNT]. Just as faith does not in itself merit salvation, but must be present for salvation to be received, so also a forgiving disposition does not merit forgiveness, but it must be present if forgiveness is to be received [NTC]. Reconciliation at the human level is necessary for us to experience reconciliation with God, not so much because God is unwilling to forgive such people, but that they lack capacity to receive it [NAC]. An unforgiving person is incapable of receiving forgiveness [BNTC, ICC, NIBC]. God wants to use people in the ministry of reconciliation, but he is unable to do that with people who stubbornly hold to grudges and refuse to be his sons by being peacemakers [BNTC]. Being forgiven depends on the grace of Christ, but to receive forgiveness our own hearts must be cleansed of resentments [Lns]. Forgiveness must be reciprocal; those who seek it are hypocritical if they don't grant it to others [NICNT].

QUESTION—What is implied by the aorist tense of the verb ἀφήκαμεν 'we have forgiven'?

It shows that action to forgive others must already have been taken prior to praying for forgiveness [CC, PNTC]. The disciples' daily experience of clearing their debts with God is based on his mercy as Father as well as on their having forgiven others [NIGTC].

6:13 and do-not bring[a] us into[b] temptation/testing,[c]

LEXICON—a. aorist act. subj. of εἰσφέρω (LN 90.93) (BAGD 2. p. 233): 'to bring' [BAGD, CC, LN, NICNT, PNTC, WBC; TEV], 'to lead' [BAGD, BECNT, BNTC, **LN,** NIGTC, NTC; ESV, KJV, NASB, NET, NIV], 'to cause' [**LN**; NCV], 'to allow' [GW]. The negative phrase μὴ εἰσενέγκῃς 'do not bring us' is translated 'keep us from' [CEV], 'don't let us yield' [NLT], 'do not put us (to the test)' [REB]. This verb means to cause someone to enter into a particular event or state [LN]. The literal meaning 'to bring' is used figuratively of bringing or leading someone into temptation [BAGD].

b. εἰς (LN 13.62) (BAGD 4.a. p. 229): 'into' [BECNT, BNTC, CC, NICNT, NIGTC, NTC, PNTC, WBC; ESV, KJV, NASB, NET, NIV], 'to' [LN; NLT, NRSV, REB, TEV], not explicit [CEV, GW, NCV]. This preposition indicates a change of state [LN].

c. πειρασμός (LN 27.46, 88.308) (BAGD 2.b. p. 640): 'temptation' [BAGD, LN (88.308)], 'enticement (to sin)' [BAGD], 'testing' [LN

(27.46)]. Taking the clause to refer to *temptation*, it is translated: 'do not bring us into temptation' [PNTC], 'do not cause us to be tempted' [NCV], 'lead us not into temptation' [ESV, KJV, NIV], 'do not lead us into temptation' [NASB, NET], 'don't allow us to be tempted' [GW], 'don't let us yield to temptation' [NLT], 'keep us from being tempted' [CEV]. Taking the clause to refer to *testing,* it is translated: 'do not bring us into testing' [NICNT, WBC], 'do not bring us to the time of trial' [NRSV], '(that which will be) a trial' [NIGTC], 'do not bring us to hard testing' [TEV], 'do not put us to the test' [REB], 'do not lead us to trial, do not cause us to be tested' [**LN** (90.93)]. This noun denotes an endeavor or attempt to cause someone to sin [LN (88.308)], or an attempt to learn the nature or character of someone by submitting that one to a thorough and extensive testing [LN (27.46)].

QUESTION—What is meant by πειρασμός 'temptation/testing'?

The basic meaning of this word is 'testing' and its meaning could point to testing in general since God does allow his people to be tested by bringing them into difficult circumstances that try their faithfulness. Even though the word does not have the definite article in this verse, a few take it to refer to the fiery trial that will come in the last days. When used of Satan testing people for the purpose of having them fail the test, the word has the meaning 'temptation' [PNTC]. To be tempted is to be enticed to sin, while to be tested is to be brought into difficult circumstances that test one's faithfulness [WBC].

1. It means temptation to sin [BECNT, BNTC, CC, Lns, My, NAC, NTC, PNTC; CEV, ESV, GW, KJV, NASB, NCV, NET, NIV, NLT]. God tempts no one [BECNT, PNTC]. The believer knows his own weaknesses and asks that God will keep him far from anything that might cause him to sin [PNTC].
2. It means testing [ICC, NIBC, NICNT, NIGTC, WBC; NRSV, REB, TEV]. The context indicates that this means 'testing' since God does not lead anyone into temptation by enticing them to sin [NICNT, WBC]. It is a request to be kept from trial so difficult or severe that the disciple would fail [NIBC]. Testing experiences are the normal lot of disciples who try to live according to the principles of the kingdom of God in a world that does not follow such principles [NICNT]. The ordinary testing in the present age anticipates the great final test at the end of the age [ICC, WBC; REB]. The disciples considered every individual test or trial to belong to the eschatological drama, so this is a plea for help so they would not succumb to the apostasy which would characterize the troubles of the last time [ICC].

QUESTION—When πειρασμός is taken to mean 'temptation' (BECNT, BNTC, CC, LN, NTC, PNTC; CEV, ESV, KJV, NASB, NET, NIV, NLT), why would disciples ask God not to lead them into the temptation?

Recognizing one's own helplessness before the Devil, this petition voices a disciple's trust in the Father for deliverance from the Devil's strength and wiles [EBC]. Because we are weak and prone to sin, we need to ask God to keep us from getting ourselves into situations where we might fall into sin [NTC]. It is a prayer to be kept from succumbing to temptations to sin [NAC]. It asks to be kept out of situations where the temptation is too strong, or to be kept from sinning when experiencing times of tempting [BNTC, Lns]. This is an example of dialectical negation, where the first component is formally negated and linked to a second that is affirmed. However, the first element is not actually being negated, but is viewed in the light of the second so that the request means don't just do this, but more importantly *do that*, which in this passage means 'don't *just* lead us into the time of temptation' (which will certainly occur), 'but deliver us from Satan when we're in it' [CC].

QUESTION—When πειρασμός is taken to mean 'testing' (NICNT, NIGNT. WBC; NRSV, REB. TEV), why would disciples ask God not put them into situations where they are tested?

In light of human frailty, vulnerability, and limitation, this petition asks to be spared from great pressures and difficulties [NIGTC]. Testing is not bad in itself, but disciples who are aware of their weaknesses want to avoid such testing [NICNT]. This is a request to avoid a testing of their faith that is beyond their endurance [NIBC, WBC]. It is a plea that God will not to allow disciples to fall victim of such severe testing that they fall into apostasy [ICC].

but[a] deliver[b] us from the evil/the Evil-One.[c]

TEXT—Some Greek manuscripts end the verse with the doxology ὅτι σοῦ ἐστιν ἡ βασιλεία καὶ ἡ δύναμις καὶ ἡ δόξα εἰς τοὺς αἰῶνας. ἀμήν 'For yours is the kingdom and the power and the glory forever. Amen.' and that text is followed by KJV. GNT omits the doxology with an A rating to indicate that its absence in the original text was regarded to be certain. This popular doxology is included in brackets by BECNT, NTC, and NASB, probably to indicate that its absence in the original text is debatable.

LEXICON—a. ἀλλά (LN 89.125): 'but' [BECNT, BNTC, LN, NICNT, NTC, PNTC, WBC; all versions except CEV, GW], 'rather' [CC], 'instead' [LN, NIGTC; GW], 'on the contrary' [LN], 'and' [CEV]. This conjunction indicates emphatic contrast [LN].

b. aorist mid. (deponent = act.) impera. of ῥύομαι (LN 21.23) (BAGD): 'to deliver' [BAGD, BECNT, BNTC, CC, LN, NTC, PNTC, WBC; ESV, KJV, NASB, NET, NIV], 'to rescue [BAGD, LN, NICNT, NIGTC; GW, NRSV], 'to save' [BAGD; NCV, REB], 'to keep safe' [TEV], 'to protect' [CEV], 'to preserve' [BAGD]. This verb means to rescue from danger, with the implication that the danger in question is severe and acute [LN].

c. πονηρός (LN **12.35**, 88.11) (BAGD 2.b. p. 691): 'immoral, evil, wicked' [LN (88.11)], 'the evil one' [BAGD]. The phrase τοῦ πονηροῦ 'the evil' is translated 'evil' [PNTC; CEV, ESV, KJV, NASB], 'that which is evil' [NIGTC], 'he who is evil' [LN (12.35)], 'the evil one' [BAGD, BECNT,

BNTC, CC, NICNT, NTC, WBC; GW, NET, NIV, NLT, NRSV, REB], 'the Evil One; [**LN** (12.35); NCV, TEV]. This adjective refers to being morally corrupt and evil [LN (88.11)], and the pronominal form 'the evil (one)' is a title for the Devil, the one who is essentially evil and in a sense personifies evil [LN].

QUESTION—What relationship is indicated by ἀλλά 'but'?

'But' is a strong adversative that introduces a course of action in marked contrast to the preceding request [PNTC]. It assumes that some testing is inevitable [WBC]. The first clause states the request negatively, and the second clause states it positively [BECNT, NAC, NTC]. The request in this clause is an expansion or elucidation of the request made in the first clause of this verse: the first request is to be kept free from testing, but if testing must occur, the second request is for rescue from that testing [NICNT].

QUESTION—What is meant by 'deliver us from τοῦ πονηροῦ the evil/Evil One'?

The words τοῦ πονηροῦ 'the evil' could be either neuter ('that which is evil') or masculine ('the evil one', a reference to Satan) [EBC].
1. 'The evil' refers to all moral evil in general [Lns, NIGTC, PNTC; CEV, ESV, KJV, NASB]. Neither the Hebrew nor Aramaic communities used the term 'the evil one' to refer to Satan [PNTC].
2. 'The evil' refers to Satan, the evil one [BECNT, BNTC, CC, EBC, ICC, LN (12.35), My, NIBC, NICNT, NTC, WBC; GW, NCV, NET, NIV, NLT, NRSV, REB, TEV]. Satan desires to use any severe testing to his advantage so if testing should come, this is a request to be delivered from the Evil one and his purposes [WBC].

QUESTION—Do the two clauses in this verse represent one petition or two?
1. They constitute one petition [BECNT, BNTC, CC, My, NICNT, NTC], although it is given in two parts [CC, My, NICNT], in two contrasting ways [BECNT].
   1.1 The first clause states the request negatively, and the second clause states it positively [BECNT, NAC, NTC].
   1.2 The relationship between the clauses is one of dialectical negation, in which the first one serves as a foil or introduction to the second one: don't just do this without also doing that, which in this prayer means 'don't only bring us into temptation (that is, without helping us), rather, even more, deliver us from the evil one' [CC].
2. They constitute two petitions [Lns, NIBC, NIGTC, WBC]. The conjunction 'but' assumes that some testing is inevitable and when it comes this is a request for deliverance [WBC].

6:14 For[a] if[b] you(pl)-forgive[c] people[d] their transgressions,[e]

LEXICON—a. γάρ (LN 89.23): 'for' [BECNT, BNTC, CC, LN, NICNT, NIGTC, NTC, PNTC, WBC; ESV, KJV, NASB, NET, NIV, NRSV, REB], 'because' [LN], not explicit [CEV, GW, NCV, NLT, TEV]. This

conjunction indicates cause or reason between events, though in some contexts the relationship is often remote or tenuous [LN].
- b. ἐάν (LN 89.67) (BAGD I.1.b. p. 211): 'if' [BAGD, LN; all translations]. This conjunction indicates condition, with the implication of reduced probability [LN].
- c. aorist act. subj. of ἀφίημι (LN 40.8) (BAGD 2. p. 126): 'to forgive' [BAGD, LN; all translations], 'to pardon' [BAGD, LN]. This verb means to remove the guilt resulting from wrongdoing [LN].
- d. ἄνθρωπος (LN 9.1) (BAGD 1.a.δ. p. 68): This plural noun is translated 'people' [BAGD, BECNT, LN], 'other people' [NICNT, WBC], 'others' [NIGTC; all versions except KJV, NIV, NLT], 'men' [BNTC, CC, NTC, PNTC; KJV, NIV], 'those (who sin)' [NLT]. This noun denotes a human being (normally an adult) [LN].
- e. παράπτωμα (LN **88.297**) (BAGD 1. p. 621): 'transgression' [BAGD, BECNT, CC, **LN**; NASB], 'sin' [BAGD, LN, WBC; NCV, NET], 'trespass' [NIGTC, NTC; ESV, KJV, NRSV], 'misdeed' [BNTC], 'offense' [NICNT, PNTC], 'failures' [GW]. The phrase τὰ παραπτώματα αὐτῶν 'their transgressions' is translated 'the wrongs they do to you' [CEV], 'the wrongs they have done' [REB], 'the wrongs they have done to you' [TEV], 'when they sin against you' [NIV], 'who sin against you' [NLT]. This noun denotes what a person has done in transgressing the will and law of God by some false step or failure [LN].

QUESTION—What relationship is indicated by γάρ 'for'?

It indicates a reason for praying as Jesus has just taught, which is that those who forgive will find forgiveness [PNTC]. It indicates a clarification of the fifth petition in verse 12, which concerns being forgiven [My, NTC].

your(pl) heavenly[a] Father will- also[b] -forgive you(pl).

LEXICON—a. οὐράνιος (LN 1.12) (BAGD p. 593): 'heavenly' [BAGD, BECNT, BNTC, CC, LN, NICNT, NIGTC, NTC, PNTC, WBC; all versions except CEV, NCV, TEV], 'in heaven' [LN; CEV, NCV, TEV]. This adjective describes that which is related to or located in heaven [LN].
- b. καί (LN 89.93): 'also' [BECNT, BNTC, CC, LN, NTC, WBC; all versions except CEV, NLT, REB], 'as well' [NICNT], not explicit [NIGTC; CEV, NLT, REB]. This conjunction indicates an additive relationship which is not coordinate [LN].

QUESTION—Does this mean that forgiving others is the basis for having one's own sins forgiven?

Forgiving others does not merit reward [BNTC, CC, EBC, My, NIBC, NTC], nor is God's forgiveness caused by our forgiving others [WBC]. Our forgiving others arises from our already having been forgiven [BECNT, NIBC, WBC]. While forgiveness, like salvation, is a gift, it does have conditions in that only those who forgive will be forgiven [NICNT]. Forgiving others their offenses is a necessary condition for receiving forgiveness, though not a sufficient one [NIGTC]. It is not that the act of forgiveness merits an eternal reward. Rather, that act is evidence that the grace of God is at work in the forgiving person, and that same grace will also give him forgiveness in due course [PNTC]. Forgiving others does not earn or merit being forgiven, but it is the attitude that makes being forgiven possible [EBC, NTC]. It is not possible that those who have been forgiven will not also extend forgiveness [WBC].

6:15 But[a] if you(pl)- do-not -forgive people, neither[b] will- your(pl) Father -forgive your(pl) transgressions.

TEXT—Some Greek manuscripts add τὰ παραπτώματα αὐτῶν 'their transgressions' after τοῖς ἀνθρώποις 'people'. GNT omits this with a B rating to indicate it was regarded to be almost certain. KJV, ESV, and NIV follow this variant reading.

LEXICON—a. δέ (LN 89.124) (BAGD 1.a. p. 171): 'but' [BAGD, LN; all translations], 'on the other hand' [LN]. This conjunction indicates contrast [LN].
- b. οὐδέ (LN 69.7) (BAGD 2. p. 591): 'neither' [BAGD, BECNT, BNTC, CC, LN, NICNT, NIGTC, NTC, PNTC, WBC; ESV, KJV, NRSV], 'not' [CEV, GW, NASB, NCV, NET, NIV, NLT, REB, TEV]. This adjective is a combination of the negative particle οὐ 'not,' 69.3, and the postpositive conjunction δέ 'and,' 89:94 [LN].

DISCOURSE UNIT—6:16–18 [CEV, ESV, GW, NCV, NET, NIV, NRSV, TEV]. The topic is fasting [ESV, GW, NIV], proper fasting [NET], concerning fasting [NRSV], teaching about fasting [TEV], Jesus teaches about worship [NCV], worshiping God by going without eating [CEV].

DISCOURSE UNIT—6:16–24 [NASB]. The topic is fasting; the true treasure; wealth (mammon).

6:16 And whenever you(pl) fast,[a] do-not be dismal[b] like[c] the hypocrites,

LEXICON—a. pres. act. subj. of νηστεύω (LN 53.65) (BAGD p. 538): 'to fast' [BAGD, LN; all translations except CEV, NCV], 'to go without eating' [CEV], 'to give up eating' [NCV]. This verb means to go without food for a set time as a religious duty [LN].
- b. σκυθρωπός (LN **25.287**) (BAGD p. 758): 'dismal' [NRSV], 'gloomy' [BAGD, BECNT, LN], 'gloomy-looking' [NIGTC], 'gloomy-faced' [CC], 'looking glum' [NTC], 'sullen' [BAGD; NET], 'of a sad countenance' [KJV], 'sad' [BAGD, LN], 'with a sad, gloomy, or sullen look' [BAGD]. The phrase γίνεσθε...σκυθρωποί 'to be dismal' is translated 'to put on a gloomy look' [BNTC; similarly PNTC; NASB], 'to put on a gloomy face' [**LN**], 'to put on a sad face' [NCV, TEV], 'to look miserable' [NICNT], 'to look sullen' [WBC], 'to look gloomy' [CEV, ESV, REB], 'to look somber' [NIV], 'to make it obvious' [NLT], 'looking sad' [GW]. This adjective describes that which is sad and discouraged [LN].

c. ὡς (LN 64.12): 'like' [BECNT, LN, CC, NIGTC, NTC, PNTC; ESV, GW, NCV, NET, NRSV, REB], 'as' [BNTC, LN, NICNT, WBC; CEV, KJV, NASB, NIV, NLT, TEV]. This conjunction is a relatively weak marker of a relationship between events or states [LN].

QUESTION—How does this statement relate to the previous context?

Religious observances are discussed in 6:2–4, 6:5–6, and again here in 6:16–18 [BECNT, BNTC, CC, ICC, NICNT, NIGTC, PNTC, TRT, WBC]. Each of these three sections contrast how people actually practice their piety with how it should be practiced [NICNT, WBC]. In each case Jesus urges them to seek the Father's blessing instead of attention and approval from people [CC]. Each section emphasizes the same concern for complete sincerity [PNTC].

QUESTION—Were the disciples already practicing fasting?

At that time the three primary expressions of Jewish piety were charity, prayer, and fasting and there was an official Jewish day of fasting on the Day of Atonement [TH]. Jesus assumed that his disciples would fast [CC, EBC, NAC, NICNT, PNTC]; the question was not whether it would be done, but how [NICNT, PNTC], when and how often [PNTC], and with what motives [CC]. He did not forbid it, and assumes that it is legitimate if done properly [BNTC].

for they-disfigure[a] their faces[b] so-that[c] they-might-be-seen[d] fasting by-people;

LEXICON—a. pres. act. indic. of ἀφανίζω (LN **79.17**) (BAGD p. 124): 'to disfigure' [BAGD, BECNT, BNTC, CC, LN, PNTC; ESV, KJV, NIV, NRSV], 'to make unsightly' [LN, NTC; REB], 'to make unattractive' [NET], 'to make unrecognizable' [BAGD], 'to make to look sad' [NCV], 'to distort' [WBC], 'to ruin' [BAGD, NIGTC], 'to neglect' [NASB, TEV], 'to hide' [NICNT]. The phrase 'for they disfigure their faces' is translated 'they put on sad faces' [GW], 'they try to look miserable and disheveled' [NLT]. This verb means to cause something to be unattractive or unsightly [LN].

b. πρόσωπον (LN 8.18): 'face' [BNTC, CC, LN, NICNT, NIGTC, NIGTC, NTC, PNTC, WBC; ESV, GW, KJV, NCV, NET, NIV, NRSV, REB], 'appearance' [BECNT; NASB, TEV], not explicit [CEV, NLT]. This noun denotes the front part of the human head [LN].

c. ὅπως (LN 89.59): 'so that' [BECNT, LN, NICNT, NIGTC, PNTC, WBC; NASB, NET, REB, TEV], 'in order that' [CC, NTC], 'that' [BNTC; ESV, KJV], 'so' [NLT], 'so as to' [NRSV], 'in order to' [LN], 'to' [GW, NCV, NIV], not explicit [CEV]. This conjunction indicates purpose for events and states (sometimes occurring in highly elliptical contexts) [LN].

d. aorist pass. subj. of φαίνομαι (LN 28.55) (BAGD 2.c. p. 852): 'to be seen' [BAGD, BNTC, NIGTC, WBC; ESV], 'to be visible' [CC], 'to appear to' [BAGD, BECNT, LN, PNTC; KJV], 'to be noticed' [NASB], 'to give an impression of' [LN]. This passive verb is translated as active:

'(so that) everyone can see' [NICNT; similarly REB, TEV], 'people may see' [NTC; NET], 'people would admire' [NLT], 'to show people' [NCV], 'to show men' [NIV], 'to show others' [NRSV], 'to make it obvious' [GW]. It is conflated with the word 'hypocrite' and the rest of this clause and translated 'those show-offs' [CEV]. This verb means to make known only the superficial and not the real character of someone [LN].

QUESTION—What action is represented by ἀφανίζω 'disfigure'?
There is a play on words between the verb ἀφανίζω, which can mean to cause to disappear, and the verb φαίνομαι, which means to be seen [Lns, My, NIGTC, NICNT]. They would make their faces unrecognizable or nearly so in order to be recognized by others [ICC, NIBC].
1. They disfigure their faces by looking gloomy [BECNT, CC, NIGTC, WBC]. They make their faces unrecognizable by gloominess [WBC], and possibly by putting on ashes [EBC, Lns, NTC, TRT, WBC], making them unsightly [NTC], or by not engaging in normal hygiene [EBC, TRT]. Their countenance is hidden through being unkempt, although their identity is not hidden since the criticism would then be pointless [ICC].
2. The verb ἀφανίζω means 'to hide', and it may be that they veiled their faces or made them less recognizable by smearing them with ashes [My, NICNT]. There is irony in the fact that they 'hid' their faces so as to be seen fasting [NICNT].

truly I-say to-you(pl), they-are-receiving-in-full their reward.
This clause is a repetition of the clause treated at 6:2.

6:17 But[a] you(sg) (when) you-are-fasting anoint[b] your(sg) head and wash[c] your(sg) face

LEXICON—a. δέ (LN 89.124) (BAGD 1.a. p. 171): 'but' [BAGD, BECNT, BNTC, CC, LN, NICNT, NIGTC, NTC, PNTC; ESV, KJV, NASB, NIV, NLT, NRSV, REB], 'on the other hand' [LN], not explicit [WBC; GW, NCV, NET, TEV]. This conjunction indicates contrast [LN]. The phrase σὺ δέ 'but you' indicates contrast by the presence of the pronoun σύ 'you', which is normally omitted [ICC]. This contrast is indicated in translation by italics: 'but when *you* are fasting' [CC]; by reduplication of 'you': 'but you, while/when you (etc.)' [BECNT, NTC, PNTC; KJV (using 'thou'), NASB], 'but as for you, when you (etc.)' [NICNT]; by explicit indication of contrast: 'instead' [CEV], 'by contrast, whenever you (etc.)' [WBC]; not explicit [BNTC, NIGTC; ESV, GW, NCV, NET, NIV, NLT, NRSV, REB, TEV]. The explicit use of the personal pronoun σύ 'you' in conjunction with δέ 'but' gives emphasis [BNTC, PNTC, WBC], showing the contrast between what Jesus' followers should do and what those who primarily want to be seen often do [PNTC].
b. aorist mid. impera. of ἀλείφω (LN 47.14) (BAGD 1. p. 35): 'to anoint' [BAGD, BECNT, BNTC, CC, LN, NICNT, PNTC, WBC; ESV, KJV, NASB, REB], 'to put oil on' [NIGTC; NET, NIV, NRSV]. The phrase

ἄλειψαί σου τὴν κεφαλὴν 'anoint your head' is translated 'comb your hair' [CEV, GW, NCV, NLT, TEV]. This verb means to anoint with a liquid, normally oil or perfume [LN].
- c. aorist mid. impera. of νίπτω (LN 47.9) (BAGD 2.b. p. 540): 'to wash' [BAGD, LN; all translations]. This verb means to wash a part of a body [LN].

QUESTION—What was the reason for anointing the head?

It was a normal part of grooming and hygiene [BECNT, CC, EBC, ICC, NIGTC, PNTC, TRT]. Oil was used for cleaning as well as lubricating dry skin on the scalp [CC]. Anointing with oil caused a person to look and feel at his or her best [NIGTC]. It was done for grooming, for enjoyment, and as a sign of happiness [WBC].

6:18 **so-that you(sg)-may- not -be-seen fasting by-people but[a] by-your(sg) Father the (one) in the secret[b] (place) and your(sg) Father the (one) seeing in the secret (place) will-reward[c] you(sg).**

TEXT—Some Greek manuscripts add ἐν τῷ φανερῷ 'openly' after ἀποδώσει σοι 'will reward you'. GNT omits this with a B rating to indicate it was regarded to be almost certain. Only KJV follows this reading.

LEXICON—a. ἀλλά (LN 89.125): 'but' [BECNT, BNTC, LN, PNTC; CEV, ESV, KJV, NASB, NCV, NRSV], 'but rather' [CC], 'but only' [NICNT, NIGTC, NTC, WBC; NET, NIV, REB], 'only' [TEV], 'except' [NLT], 'instead' [LN; GW], 'on the contrary' [LN]. This conjunction indicates emphatic contrast [LN].
- b. κρυφαῖος (LN 28.72) (BAGD p. 455): 'secret, hidden' [BAGD], 'in secret, privately' [LN]. The phrase τῷ ἐν τῷ κρυφαίῳ 'the one in the secret (place)' is translated 'who is in secret' [BECNT, BNTC, NICNT, NTC, PNTC, WBC; ESV, KJV, NASB, NET, NRSV, REB], 'who is in the secret place' [NIGTC], 'who is in hiddenness' [CC], 'who is unseen' [NIV, TEV], 'whom you cannot see' [NCV], 'who is with you in private' [GW], 'who knows what you do in private' [NLT], not explicit [CEV]. This adjective describes what is secret as a result of people not knowing about it [LN].
- c. fut. act. indic. of ἀποδίδωμι (LN 38.16) (BAGD 3. p. 90): 'to reward' [BAGD, LN]. See this verb at 6:4.

QUESTION—What is the purpose of this command?

Jesus wanted them to pray without being ostentatious [CC, EBC, NIBC, PNTC, WBC], and be as inconspicuous as possible [NTC], just appearing the same as they usually would appear [ICC]. It was to purify the motivation for fasting [EBC, NIGTC], to avoid hypocrisy [Lns], to maintain sincerity [My].

QUESTION—Does the shift from using the noun κρυπτός 'secret place' to the adjective κρυφαῖος 'secret' have any semantic significance?

There is no recognizable difference in meaning between the noun and the adjective [NICNT, PNTC].

MATTHEW 6:19

DISCOURSE UNIT—6:19–34 [ICC; NLT]. The topic is God and mammon [ICC], teaching about money and possessions [NLT].

DISCOURSE UNIT—6:19–24 [ESV, GW, NCV, NET, NIV]. The topic is true riches [GW], God is more important than money [NCV], lay up treasures in heaven [ESV], lasting treasure [NET], treasures in heaven [NIV].

DISCOURSE UNIT—6:19–21 [CEV, NRSV, TEV]. The topic is riches in heaven [TEV], concerning treasures [NRSV], treasures in heaven [CEV].

6:19 Do-not store-up[a] for-yourselves treasures[b] on[c] earth,[d]

LEXICON—a. pres. act. impera. of θησαυρίζω (LN 65.11) (BAGD 1. p. 361): 'to store up' [BAGD, BECNT, NICNT, NIGTC, WBC; CEV, GW, NASB, NIV, NLT, NRSV, REB, TEV], 'to store' [NCV], 'to lay up' [BNTC, PNTC; ESV, KJV], 'to gather' [NTC], 'to gather up, to save' [BAGD], 'to accumulate' [NET], 'to treasure' [CC], 'to treasure up, to keep safe' [LN]. This verb means to keep safe that which is of great value [LN].

  b. θησαυρός (LN 65.10) (BAGD 2.a. p. 361): 'treasure' [BAGD, LN; all translations except TEV], 'that which is stored up' [BAGD], 'wealth' [LN], 'riches' [LN; TEV]. This noun denotes that which is of exceptional value and kept safe [LN].

  c. ἐπί (LN 83.46) (BAGD I.1.a.α. p. 286): 'on' [BAGD, BECNT, BNTC, CC, LN, NICNT, NIGTC, NTC, PNTC; all versions except KJV], 'upon' [BAGD, LN; KJV], 'in' [WBC]. This preposition describes a position on a surface of an object, whether vertical or horizontal, and in contact with the object [LN].

  d. γῆ (LN 1.39) (BAGD 5.a. p. 157): 'earth' [BAGD, BECNT, BNTC, CC, LN, NICNT, NIGTC, NTC, PNTC; all versions], 'world' [LN], 'this world' [WBC]. This noun denotes the surface of the earth as the dwelling place of mankind, in contrast with the heavens above and the world below [LN].

QUESTION—Is there any significance in the use of the present tense of the imperative μὴ θησαυρίζετε 'do not store up'?

Throughout this section the use of a present imperative verb indicates a shift to a new topic [CC]. It is translated as being the same as an ordinary aorist imperative [BECNT, BNTC, CC, NICNT, NIGTC, NTC, PNTC, WBC; all versions except GW]: *do not store up* treasures on earth. The present imperative form of a verb often implies that the act has already begun [Lns, PNTC] and some take this command to indicate that they had been doing this [EBC, NICNT; GW]: '*stop storing up* treasure on earth'.

where moth[a] and corrosion/vermin[b] destroy,[d]

LEXICON—a. σής (LN **4.49**) (BAGD p. 749): 'moth' [BAGD, **LN**; all translations]. This noun denotes the larvae of moths, which eat clothes [LN].

b. βρῶσις (LN **2.62**) (BAGD 2. p. 148): 'corrosion' [BAGD, CC, **LN**, NIGTC, WBC], 'rust' [BAGD, BECNT, BNTC, NTC, PNTC; all versions], 'rusting' [LN], 'tarnishing' [LN], 'vermin' [NICNT]. The noun βρῶσις generally denotes the process of producing rust or tarnish by oxidation, but since this same Greek word occurs in the Septuagint translation of Malachi 3:11 to refer to a type of insect, it might have that meaning here [LN]. This is a general word for 'consuming' and is usually taken to mean corrosion or rust, but in Malachi 3:11 this Greek word is used for 'grasshopper' and could be used here to refer to some other insect that consumes, perhaps a woodworm [BAGD].

c. pres. act. indic. of ἀφανίζω (LN **20.46**) (BAGD p. 124): 'to destroy' [BAGD, BECNT, BNTC, **LN**, PNTC; all versions except KJV, NLT, NRSV], 'to do damage' [LN], 'to ruin' [BAGD, NICNT, NIGTC], 'to completely ruin' [LN], 'to consume' [NTC; NRSV], 'to corrupt' [KJV]. The phrase σὴς καὶ βρῶσις ἀφανίζει 'moth and corrosion destroy' is translated with a verb that collocates with both nouns: 'they are subject to the ravage of such things as moth and corrosion' [WBC], or it is translated with separate verbs that collocate with the different nouns: 'moths eat them and rust destroys them' [NLT]. This verb is singular, indicating that 'moth and rust' are taken together as constituting one subject (known grammatically as a zeugma) [WBC]. In 6:16 this verb means to disfigure, but here it has the meaning of making something disappear [PNTC]. Generally it means to destroy the value or use of something [LN].

QUESTION—What is the σής 'moth'?

It is the moth larva which eats clothing [ICC, LN, NTC, PNTC].

QUESTION—What is meant by βρῶσις 'corrosion/vermin'?

The basic meaning of the word βρῶσις is 'eating' (LN 23.3) [BECNT, EBC, ICC, Lns, My, NIBC, NICNT, PNTC, TH, WBC], and the sort of 'eating' depends on the nature of the treasure [NICNT]. It could refer to the corrosion of metal [EBC, PNTC, WBC], to any rot, deterioration, or decay [BECNT, WBC], or even to wear and tear on something [NIBC]. But it could also refer to animal pests and vermin that eat crops [EBC, NIBC, PNTC] or fabric [NICNT].

1. The noun βρῶσις refers to the corrosion of metal [BECNT, BNTC, NTC, PNTC; all versions]. Since Greek has a specific word for rust, it is better to translate this more generally as 'rot', 'decay', or 'corrosion' [WBC]. This could be corrosion of any type that would bring natural deterioration, such as rust [EBC, NIGTC], decay, staining, or mold growth [NIGTC], rodents [EBC, NAC, NIBC], mildew [EBC], or even wear and tear [NIBC].

2. In this verse the noun βρῶσις refers to animal pests [Lns, NICNT]. The traditional rendering 'rust' is based on the Vulgate translation and assumes that the treasure includes metal, but against this is the fact that the word ἰός is the normal Greek term for rust, as in James 5:3. In the context of 'moth' the word better suits animal pests, such as rodents

nibbling on rich fabrics or woodworms destroying treasure chests [NICNT]. It refers to the eating of food, the topic mentioned later in 6:25 [Lns].

QUESTION—What is the meaning of 'moth and rust' taken together?

It represents all processes that cause earthly treasures to lose their value and no longer serve a useful purpose [NTC].

and where thieves[a] break-in[b] and steal;[c]

LEXICON—a. κλέπτης (LN 57.233) (BAGD p. 434): 'thief' [BAGD, LN; all translations except TEV], 'robber' [TEV]. This noun denotes a person who steals [LN].

b. διορύσσω (LN 19.41) (BAGD p. 199): 'to break in' [BAGD, BECNT, LN, NICNT, NIGTC, PNTC; all versions except KJV, NCV], 'to be able to break in' [WBC; NCV], 'to break into' [LN], 'to break through' [BAGD; KJV], 'to dig through' [BAGD, BNTC, CC, NTC]. This verb means to break through a wall or barrier, normally by the process of digging through (usually implying a wall made of sun-dried brick) [LN].

c. pres. act. indic. of κλέπτω (LN **57.232**) (BAGD p. 434): 'to steal' [BAGD, **LN**; all translations]. This verb means to take the property of someone else secretly and without permission [LN].

QUESTION—What is the nature of this 'breaking in'?

It refers to digging through the mud walls of a house [CC, BNTC, EBC, ICC, My, NICNT, NIGTC, NTC, PNTC, WBC], but also any unlawful entry generally [NIGTC]. It is forceful entry, usually without the owner knowing it [TH]. In those days wealth was often buried under house floors [WBC].

6:20 but[a] store-up for-yourselves treasures in heaven, where neither moth nor corrosion destroys, and where thieves do-not break-in and steal; 6:21 for where your(sg) treasure is, there[b] also will-be your heart.[c]

LEXICON—a. δέ (LN 89.124): 'but' [BECNT, BNTC, CC, LN, NIGTC, NTC, PNTC, WBC; ESV, KJV, NASB, NCV, NET, NIV, NRSV, REB], 'rather' [NICNT], 'instead' [CEV, GW, TEV], not explicit [NLT]. This conjunction indicates contrast [LN].

b. ἐκεῖ (LN 83.2) (BAGD 1. p. 239): 'there' [BAGD, BECNT, BNTC, CC, LN, NICNT, NIGTC, NTC, PNTC, WBC; ESV, KJV, NASB, NET, NIV, NLT, NRSV, REB], 'in that place' [BAGD], 'at that place' [LN], not explicit [CEV, GW, NCV, TEV]. This adverb describes a position relatively far from the speaker, writer, or viewpoint person [LN].

c. καρδία (LN 26.3) (BAGD 1.b.ε. p 404): 'heart' [BAGD, LN; all translations except NLT], 'the desires of your heart' [NLT], 'inner self, mind' [LN]. This noun denotes the causative source of a person's psychological life in its various aspects, but with special emphasis upon thoughts [LN].

QUESTION—What relationship is indicated by γάρ 'for'?

This conjunction indicates the reason why they should obey the command in 6:19–20 [BECNT, BNTC, CC, LN, Lns, My, NICNT, NIGTC, NTC, PNTC,

WBC; ESV, KJV, NASB, NET, NIV, NRSV, REB, TEV]: store up for yourself treasures in heaven *because* your heart will be where your treasure is located. The place of one's investment shows the commitment of one's heart, whether in heaven or on earth [NIGTC], or it even directs and anchors the commitment of one's heart [Lns, My].

QUESTION—What is meant by καρδία 'heart'?

'Heart' is used to refer to what is most important to a person, and represents that which constitutes their true character [NICNT]. The reference to the heart is a metaphor for the center of one's inner being and thus refers to the center of a person's attention and commitment [WBC]. It is the center of one's life [NTC, PNTC], the center of one's affections and commitments [NAC]. It is the center of the personality, embracing the will, the emotions, and the mind [EBC]. In the NT, the heart represents the mind [ICC, LN (26.3)], the source of one's actions [ICC]. It describes one's concerns, feelings, and interests [TH].

QUESTION—How are the two clauses in this verse related?

The word 'heart' stands for what is of central importance to a person and thus indicates one's true character. So whether one values a treasure in heaven or a treasure on earth follows from the orientation of one's heart and at the same time it reveals that orientation to others [NICNT].

1. The orientation of the heart determines where one's treasure will be located [BECNT, EBC, My, NAC, NTC, TH, WBC]; that is, the heart [NTC] and the affections [NAC], will be drawn after whatever one treasures. We set our hearts on what we consider important [BNTC]. Storing up treasures on earth will cause one's commitment and focus to turn to earthly concerns rather than a concern to do the will of God [WBC]. What the heart cherishes will control the direction and values of the entire person [EBC]. The heart will be devoted to what one values most [BECNT].
2. The orientation of the heart depends on where one's treasure is located [CC, ICC, Lns, My, NIBC, NIGTC, PNTC]. This pattern is also found in the next two verses [CC].

DISCOURSE UNIT—6:22–23 [CEV, NRSV, TEV]. The topic is the light of the body [TEV], the sound eye [NRSV], light [CEV].

6:22 The lamp[a] of-the body[b] is the eye.[c]

LEXICON—a. λύχνος (LN 6.104) (BAGD 2. p. 483): 'lamp' [BAGD, BECNT, BNTC, CC, LN, NICNT, NIGTC, NTC; ESV, GW, NASB, NET, NIV, NRSV, REB], 'light' [PNTC; KJV]. The phrase 'the lamp of the body is the eye' is translated: 'the eye is a light for the body' [NCV], 'the eyes are like a lamp for the body' TEV], 'your eye is a lamp that provides light for your body' [NLT], 'the eye enables a person to see light' [WBC], 'your eyes are like a window for your body' [CEV]. This noun denotes the light made by burning a wick saturated with oil contained in a relatively small vessel [LN].

b. σῶμα (LN 8.1) (BAGD 1.b. p. 799): 'body' [BAGD, LN; all translations except WBC], not explicit [WBC]. This noun denotes the physical body of persons, animals, or plants, either dead or alive [LN].
c. ὀφθαλμός (LN 8.23) (BAGD 1. p. 599): 'eye' [BAGD, LN; all translations]. This singular noun is translated as plural: 'eyes' [CEV, TEV].

QUESTION—What is meant by saying that the eye is ὁ λύχνος τοῦ σώματός 'the lamp of the body?'

1. The picture is of the light entering the body through the eye [BECNT, EBC, My, NIBC, NICNT, NIGTC, NTC, PNTC, TH, WBC; CEV, TEV]: *the eye is like a lamp that illumines the body.* The word 'light' is a metonymy for the eye itself. The eye becomes the source for light coming into the rest of the body [NTC, PNTC]. A healthy focus, meaning having proper values, brings in the 'light' of moral and religious insight, which affects the being and action of the entire person [NIGTC]. The eye symbolizes the mind, which should guide us morally and spiritually, keeping us in contact with God, but which will not function that way if darkened by a yearning for earthly treasure [NTC]. It is not entirely clear what the imagery of the lamp means, but it can at least be said that the proper functioning of the body (as representing the whole person) depends on the condition of the eye, which brings light into it. If the person has a healthy orientation to life with the eye bringing in light, it will be exemplified by personal generosity, as opposed to having a 'bad eye', which is greed or stinginess [NICNT].
2. The picture is of light going out of the body through the eye [CC, ICC]: *the eye is the body's lamp, sending forth its light.*

QUESTION—In what way does the eye function metaphorically like a lamp?

1. The eye represents the outlook of a person, that which he or she focuses on, whether good or bad [BECNT, NIGTC, NICNT, WBC]. A healthy focus, meaning having proper values, brings in the 'light' of moral and religious insight, which affects the being and action of the entire person [NIGTC]. Like a lamp, the eye makes sight possible, bringing light to the body [Lns, WBC], and this represents a focus on proper values, such as generosity or singleness of purpose [WBC]. The proper outlook in life is to focus on God's claims and command, which results in clear direction and orientation. To divide one's focus between God and possessions results in being lost in spiritual darkness [BNTC, PNTC]. The eye symbolizes the heart [EBC, NAC]; a good heart stores up treasure in heaven and the bad heart stores up treasure on earth; the way people handle money affects every other aspect of their lives [NAC]. The symbolism means either that the person with loyalty divided between God and possessions will experience a consequent loss of direction and orientation, or that the stingy, selfish person will be morally and spiritually blind [EBC]. The eye symbolizes the mind, which should guide us morally and spiritually, keeping us in contact with God, but which will not function that way if darkened by a yearning for earthly treasure

[NTC]. Generosity of spirit brings health and wholeness, while selfishness prevents one from seeing what really matters [NIBC]. The disciple needs to have an eye for God, meaning the ability to perceive the presence of God [TH]. It is not entirely clear what the imagery of the lamp means, but it can at least be said that the proper functioning of the body (as representing the whole person) depends on the condition of the eye, which brings light into it; that is, if the person has a healthy orientation to life with the eye bringing in light, it will be exemplified by personal generosity, as opposed to having a 'bad eye', which is greed or stinginess [NICNT].
2. The eye's focus reveals what is valued in the inner person, shining its light out in the sense that it directs the body where to go and what to do on the basis of those inner values [CC].
3. The proper focus or outlook on the part of the disciple will bring light into the world around them, dispelling the shades of darkness [ICC].

If therefore your(sg) eye is sound,[a] your(sg) whole[b] body will-be full-of-light;[c]

LEXICON—a. ἁπλοῦς (LN 23.132) (BAGD p. 86): 'sound' [BAGD, BNTC, LN, NICNT, NTC; REB, TEV], 'healthy' [BECNT, LN, NIGTC, PNTC; ESV, NET, NRSV], 'good' [CEV, NCV, NIV, NLT], 'single' [BAGD; KJV], 'unclouded' [GW], 'clear' [BAGD; NASB], 'generous' [CC, WBC]. This adjective describes being healthy, with the implication of sound, proper functioning, and in the NT it has particular reference to the eyes [LN].

b. ὅλος (LN 63.1) (BAGD 2.a. p. 564): 'whole' [BAGD, LN; all translations except CEV], 'entire' [BAGD, LN], 'complete' [BAGD, LN], not explicit [CEV]. This adjective describes what is whole, complete, or entire, with focus on unity [LN].

c. φωτεινός (LN **14.51**) (BAGD p. 872): 'full of light' [BAGD, BECNT, CC, **LN**, WBC; all versions except CEV, NLT, REB], 'filled with light' [NLT], 'illuminated' [NICNT, NIGTC, NTC, PNTC], 'well lighted' [LN], 'shining, bright, radiant' [BAGD]. The phrase 'your whole body will be full of light' is translated 'your whole body will have light' [BNTC], 'you will have light for your whole body' [REB], 'you have all the light you need' [CEV]. This adjective describes being well lighted' [LN].

QUESTION—What relationship is indicated by οὖν 'therefore'?

It indicates the inference to be drawn from what has just been said [CC], the result of the previous chain of reasoning [PNTC].

QUESTION—What is being communicated by the metaphorical term ἁπλοῦς 'sound'?

It means 'single' or 'sound' in the sense of functioning well [NTC], which would represent the quality of sincerity or integrity; someone with such a disposition would also be generous [NTC]. It generally indicates singleness of purpose or sincerity, but when used of the eye it indicates the inner spiritual condition of the person as being generous [CC, ICC, NIBC, NICNT, PNTC]. It describes a generous disposition [ICC, TRT]. It can mean 'generous', but can also imply singleness of purpose [CC, EBC, WBC] and undivided loyalty [EBC]. Its general sense is of being sound and healthy, but the aspect of 'singleness' is related to the concepts of wholeheartedness and integrity, and of sincerity and generosity [NIGTC]. Having singleness of focus means having a healthy outlook [BECNT, BNTC], one that does not look with envy on transient material possessions [BECNT]. It refers to singleness of purpose, which is described more fully in 6:33 where the disciples were told to focus on God's kingdom and righteousness [Lns]. It speaks of the moral capacity of the mind or conscience that rightly and honestly evaluates error and moral evil [My]. It refers to the focus of one's life being healthy, with the result that there is a perception of the presence of God [TH].

6:23 **but if your(sg) eye is bad,**[a] **your(sg) whole body will-be full-of-darkness.**[b]

LEXICON—a. πονηρός (LN 23.149, 57.108, 88.110) (BAGD 1.a.α. p. 690): 'bad' [BECNT, BNTC, NICNT; CEV, ESV, NASB, NIV, NLT, REB], 'no good' [TEV], 'sick' [BAGD, LN (23.149)], 'in poor condition' [BAGD, NTC], 'diseased' [LN (23.149), NIGTC; NET], 'unhealthy' [NRSV], 'evil' [LN (88.110), PNTC; GW, KJV, NCV], 'immoral, wicked' [LN (88.110)], 'greedy' [CC], 'covetous' [WBC], 'stingy, miserly' [LN (57.108)]. This adjective describes what is morally corrupt and evil [LN (88.110)]. It may also function as a figurative extension of 'evil' describing a state of being sickly or diseased [LN (23.149)], or it may be used idiomatically in conjunction with ὀφθαλμός 'eye' to describe being stingy [LN (57.108)].

b. σκοτεινός (LN 14.54) (BAGD p. 757): 'full of darkness' [BECNT, CC, WBC; ESV, GW, KJV, NASB, NCV, NET, NIV, NRSV], 'filled with darkness' [NLT], 'in darkness' [LN; REB, TEV], 'in the dark' [NICNT], 'dark' [BAGD, BNTC, LN, NTC; CEV], 'darkened' [NIGTC, PNTC]. The phrase 'your whole body will be full of darkness' is translated 'everything is dark' [CEV]. This adjective describes being in a state of darkness [LN].

QUESTION—What is a 'bad eye'?

The eye manifests the spiritual condition of the person; the good eye shows generosity and the bad eye exhibits greed [CC]. The bad eye is a wrong outlook on possessions [BECNT, PNTC], which leads to greed and avarice and to hoarding of possessions [BECNT]. A bad eye is a reflector of greed and envy [ICC, NICNT, NIGTC], of covetousness and avarice [WBC], of evil and selfishness [TRT]. It may imply miserliness or lack of generosity [PNTC]. It is a heart set on earthly goods [NAC]. It is a lack of clear spiritual vision [BNTC], an inner condition of a mind darkened by an evil will that resists divine truth [My]. The bad eye has become captivated by earthly treasures that will then win the affection of the heart and body [Lns].

QUESTION—What does the metaphor of light and dark communicate?

Light represents generosity, and darkness indicates greediness [CC]. Light represents proper values, whereas dark represents greed and envy [BECNT]. For the body to be full of light means to be spiritually healthy [BECNT, CC, NICNT]. Light is inner illumination [NIGTC]. Light is a metonymy for the eye itself, which in turn represents generosity and discipleship, or if it is bad, covetousness [WBC]. Light is the brightness of inner goodness, and darkness is perversion at the core of one's life and a total lack of spiritual vision [PNTC]. Light represents proper moral and spiritual guidance for the mind [NTC]. Darkness represents self-deception concerning what is truly worthwhile [Lns]. Darkness represents a grudging or selfish nature [ICC].

If then^a the light in^b you(sg) is darkness,^c how-great^d (is) the darkness.

LEXICON—a. οὖν (LN 89.50): 'then' [BECNT, BNTC, LN, NIGTC, NTC; ESV, NASB, NET, NIV, NRSV, REB], 'therefore' [CC, LN, PNTC, WBC; KJV], 'so' [LN, NICNT; TEV], 'so then' [LN], 'consequently, accordingly' [LN], 'and' [NCV, NLT], not explicit [CEV, GW]. This conjunction indicates result, often implying the conclusion of a process of reasoning [LN].

b. ἐν (LN 13.8): 'in' [BECNT, BNTC, CC, LN, NICNT, NIGTC, NTC, PNTC, WBC; ESV, GW, KJV, NASB, NET, NRSV, TEV], 'within' [NIV], 'inside' [CEV], not explicit [NCV]. The phrase 'the light in you is darkness' is translated 'if the only light you have is really darkness' [NCV; similarly REB], 'if the light you think you have is actually darkness' [NLT]. This preposition marks a state or condition [LN].

c. σκότος (LN 88.125) (BAGD 2.b. p. 758): 'darkness' [BAGD, LN; all translations except CEV, GW], 'dark' [CEV, GW]. This word functions as a figurative extensions of meaning of σκότος 'darkness' (14.53) to denote the realm of sin and evil [LN].

d. πόσος (LN 78.13) (BAGD 1. p. 694): 'how great' [BAGD, BECNT, BNTC, CC, LN, NICNT, NIGTC, NTC, PNTC, WBC; ESV, KJV, NASB, NET, NIV, NRSV, REB], 'how deep' [NLT], 'how terribly (dark)' [TEV], 'how' [LN; GW], 'very, how much, intense, severe' [LN], not explicit [CEV, NCV]. The phrase τὸ σκότος πόσον 'how great is the darkness' is translated 'you surely are in the dark' [CEV], 'how dark it will be' [GW], 'you have the worst darkness' [NCV]. This adjective describes a relatively high point on a scale involving exclamation [LN].

QUESTION—What relationship is indicated by οὖν 'therefore'?

It indicates an emphatic summary conclusion to what has been said [CC]. It summarizes and focuses what he has been arguing [NIGTC].

QUESTION—In what way could light be darkness?

It is a paradoxical statement [CC, ICC, Lns], meaning that instead of having inner light, one has only the darkness of being spiritually unsound [CC].

There is irony here in that when a person believes he has light but really lives in darkness, the darkness is that much worse for not being recognized for what it is [EBC]. This is a call to self-examination so that a perversely ironic situation will not occur in which one's values, which should guide them toward what is good, actually lead the other way [BECNT]. The mind should guide a person morally and spiritually according to the goal of promoting God's kingdom, but if the focus is on the wrong things, then the person can miss everything [NTC]. True perversity occurs when that which should lead us to good actually leads the other way [NAC]. It is to be unable to see the obvious [Lns]. With a dishonest and darkened conscience there is no openness to divine truth that can sanctify and enlighten one inwardly [My].

DISCOURSE UNIT—6:24–34 [TEV]. The topic is God and possessions.

DISCOURSE UNIT—6:24 [CEV]. The topic is money.

6:24 No-one^a is-able^b to-serve^c two masters;^d

LEXICON—a. οὐδείς (LN **92.23**) (BAGD 2.a. p. 591): 'no one' [BAGD, BECNT, BNTC, CC, **LN**, NICNT, NIGTC, NTC, PNTC; all versions except CEV, KJV, TEV], 'no man' [KJV], 'nobody' [LN]. The phrase οὐδείς δύναται 'no one is able' is translated 'it is impossible for anyone' [WBC], 'you cannot' [CEV, TEV]. This pronoun denotes a negative reference to an entity, event, or state [LN].

b. pres. mid. or pass. (deponent = act.) indic. of δύναμαι (LN **74.5**) (BAGD 1.a. p. 207): 'to be able' [BAGD, CC, LN, NIGTC], 'to be possible' [WBC], 'can' [BAGD, BECNT, BNTC, **LN**, NICNT, NTC, PNTC; all versions].

c. pres. act. infin. of δουλεύω (LN **35.27**, 87.79) (BAGD 2.a., b. p. 205): 'to serve' [BAGD, BECNT, BNTC, CC, **LN** (35.27), NTC; all versions except CEV, TEV], 'to give slave service' [NIGTC], 'to be a slave' [LN (87.79), NICNT, PNTC, WBC; CEV, TEV]. This verb means to serve, normally in a humble manner and in response to the demands or commands of others [LN (35.27)], or to be a slave of someone [LN (87.79)].

d. κύριος (LN 57.12) (BAGD 1.a.β. p. 459): 'master' [BAGD, BECNT, BNTC, CC, LN, NIGTC, WBC; all versions], 'owner' [BAGD, LN, NICNT, PNTC], 'lord' [BAGD, LN, NTC]. This noun denotes one who owns and controls property, including especially servants and slaves [LN].

for either^a he-will-hate^b the one^c and he-will-love^d the other,^e

LEXICON—a. ἤ (LN **89.140**) (BAGD 1.b. p. 342). The repetition of ἤ indicates a double alternative 'either…or' [BAGD, BECNT, BNTC, CC, LN, NICNT, NIGTC, NTC, PNTC, WBC; ESV, KJV, NASB, NET, NIV, REB]. In this sentence this first instance of ἤ is left untranslated by CEV, GW, NCV, NLT, NRSV, TEV.

b. fut. act. indic. of μισέω (LN 88.198) (BAGD 1. p. 522): 'to hate' [BAGD, LN; all translations except WBC; CEV], 'to detest' [BAGD, LN], 'to neglect' [WBC]. The phrase 'he will hate the one and he will love the other' is translated 'you will like one more than the other' [CEV]. The future tense here is gnomic, meaning that it expresses things that are true to the way things are in life generally [CC]. This verb means to dislike strongly, with the implication of aversion and hostility [LN].

c. εἷς (LN 92.22) (BAGD 5.d. p. 232): 'one' [BAGD, BECNT, BNTC, CC, LN, NICNT, NIGTC, NTC, PNTC; all versions except GW, NCV, REB], 'one master' [WBC; NCV], 'the first' [REB], '(the) first master' [GW]. This pronominal adjective refers to a single, indefinite person or thing [LN].

d. fut. act. indic. of ἀγαπάω (LN 25.43) (BAGD 1.a.α. p. 4): 'to love' [BAGD, BECNT, BNTC, CC, LN, NICNT, NIGTC, NTC, PNTC; all versions except CEV], 'to like' [CEV], 'to prefer' [WBC], 'to regard with affection' [LN]. This verb means to have love for someone or something, based on sincere appreciation and high regard [LN].

e. ἕτερος (LN 58.37) (BAGD 1.a. p. 315): 'other' [BAGD, LN; all translations except GW, REB], '(the) second' [GW, REB]. This pronominal adjective describes that which is other than some other item implied or identified in a context [LN].

QUESTION—What is implied by the use of the term μισέω 'hate'?

Jesus is using the difficulty of a slave having divided loyalties to describe the problem of disciples having divided priorities [CC]. This is a Semitic idiom that should not be pressed too far; what he is saying is that just as it is inevitable that a slave would be devoted to one master more than another, so also one's loyalties cannot be divided between God and other things [BECNT]. In Semitic thought, 'love' and 'hate' meant to choose or not choose [NAC]. Here 'hate' does not refer to hatred, but to loving and paying attention to one master less than the other, and having partial commitment as opposed to complete commitment [WBC]. 'Hate' and 'love' are not about feelings, but about loyalty to one master or the other [ICC, NIBC, TH]. 'Hate' is not hate as we may think of it, but was a Jewish way of comparing degrees of love and faithfulness [TRT].

or he-will-be-devoted-to[a] one and he-will-despise[b] the other;

LEXICON—a. fut. mid. indic. of ἀντέχομαι (LN **34.24**) (BAGD 1. p. 73): 'to be devoted to' [BAGD, BNTC, NIGTC, NTC; ESV, GW, NASB, NET, NIV, NLT, NRSV, REB], 'to be loyal to' [BECNT; CEV, TEV], 'to take the side of' [NICNT], 'to hold to' [PNTC; KJV], 'to cling to, to hold fast to' [BAGD], 'to adhere to' [**LN**], 'to cling to' [CC], 'to pay attention to' [WBC], 'to follow' [NCV]. This verb means to join with and to maintain loyalty to someone [LN].

b. fut. act. indic. of καταφρονέω (LN 88.192) (BAGD 1. p. 420): 'to despise' [BAGD, BECNT, BNTC, CC, LN, NIGTC, PNTC; all versions except CEV, NCV], 'to have no regard for' [NICNT], 'to disregard' [WBC], 'to look down on' [BAGD, LN, NTC], 'to refuse to follow' [NCV], 'to scorn' [BAGD, LN]. The phrase 'he will be devoted to one and he will despise the other' is translated 'he will be more loyal to one than the other' [CEV]. This verb means to feel contempt for someone or something because it is thought to be bad or without value [LN].

QUESTION—How are the contrasts 'to be devoted to' and 'to despise' to be taken?

This contrast is to be understood in a way similar to the alternatives of love and hate in the previous clause, and it does not mean that that a slave who is not devoted to someone automatically despises that one. The word 'despise' can have the more mild sense of 'disregard.' The point of this verse is that slavery requires absolute loyalty and commitment to a single master [WBC]. The preceding clause refers to *hating* one master and *loving* the other, but as in a chiasm, this clause reverses the qualities and refers to *being devoted* to one master and *despising* the other. If this chiastic feature is not natural in a language, translators should restructure the verse so as to make the whole verse natural in their language [TH]. One translation has put the positive qualities first in both clauses: 'You will like one more than the other or be more loyal to one than the other' [CEV].

you(pl)-are- not -able to-serve God and^a money.^b

LEXICON—a. καί (LN 89.92): 'and' [CC, LN, NTC, PNTC, WBC; ESV, GW, KJV, NASB, NET, NRSV, REB]. This conjunction indicates coordinate relations [LN]. This conjunction is translated 'both … and' [BECNT, BNTC, NICNT; CEV, NCV, NIV, NLT, TEV].

b. μαμωνᾶς (LN 57.34) (BAGD p. 490): 'money' [WBC; CEV, ESV, NET, NIV, NLT, REB, TEV], 'mammon' [BNTC, NIGTC, NTC, PNTC; KJV], 'wealth' [BAGD, BECNT, CC, NICNT; GW, NASB, NRSV], 'worldly wealth' [LN], 'riches' [LN], 'worldly riches' [NCV], 'property' [BAGD]. This Aramaic word denotes wealth and riches, with a strongly negative connotation [LN].

QUESTION—Why is there a switch from the use of the third person verbs in the previous clauses to the second person here?

The switch from third person statements to the second person 'you' helps emphasize the need for single-minded devotion [BECNT]. This statement is the conclusion derived from the first part of his verse [TH, WBC] and the use of the second person verb makes this a personal application to the audience [ICC].

QUESTION—What is meant by the word μαμωνᾶς 'money'?

The translation 'mammon' by some English translations is a transliteration of the Greek word μαμωνᾶς 'mammon' [TH], which in turn is a transliteration of the Hebrew word used in Jewish literature [BECNT, EBC, NIBC, NICNT, NTC, PNTC, TH, WBC]. The root word in Aramaic and Hebrew indicates something in which a person puts confidence [EBC,

NIBC] and can refer to money and property [BECNT, EBC, ICC, NIBC, NICNT, NTC, PNTC, TH, WBC]. It refers to all material resources [ICC, NAC]. The word had no negative connotations to the Jews [NICNT, TH], or a negative connotation has not been firmly established [ICC]. In the contrast of *serving* either God or money, the word is personified as being a slave owner [EBC, NTC], a rival lord [ICC], or even another God [TRT].

QUESTION—What is the application to be derived from this verse?

Disciples must tear their minds away from worldly enticements and fix their attention on their Father in heaven [ICC]. Serving a master demands total and undivided commitment [WBC]. Anyone trying to serve both God and money has not so much a divided loyalty as a deep-seated commitment to the idolatry of worshipping money [EBC]. Service of God must be wholehearted [PNTC]. For disciples, divided loyalty is impossible [BECNT], nor should they be preoccupied with concerns about material possessions [NIGTC]. Greed or concern for possessions should not compete with the disciple's loyalty for God himself [NICNT]. Believers must continually reexamine their priorities to see if they have fallen short of the Lord's calling on their lives [CC].

DISCOURSE UNIT—6:25–34 [CEV, ESV, GW, NASB, NCV, NET, NIV]. The topic is worry [CEV], don't worry [NCV], do not worry [NET, NIV], stop worrying [TEV], do not be anxious [ESV], the cure for anxiety [NASB].

6:25 Therefore[a] I-say[b] to-you(pl) do-not worry[c] (about) your(pl) life[d]

LEXICON—a. διὰ τοῦτο (BAGD B. II. 2. p. 181): 'therefore' [BAGD, NICNT, NTC; ESV, KJV, NET, NIV, NRSV], 'for this reason' [BAGD, BECNT, BNTC, NIGTC, PNTC; NASB], 'so' [GW, NCV], 'with this in view, then' [WBC], 'that is why' [NLT], 'this is why' [REB, TEV], not explicit [CEV]. In real and supposed answers and inferences the phrase διὰ τοῦτο means 'therefore' [BAGD].

b. pres. act. indic. of λέγω (LN 33.69) (BAGD II.1.c. p. 469): 'to say' [BNTC, LN, NIGTC, NTC, PNTC, WBC; KJV, NASB], 'to tell' [BECNT, LN, NICNT; all versions except KJV, NASB], 'to command' [BAGD]. This verb means to speak or talk, with apparent focus upon the content of what is said [LN].

c. pres. act. impera. of μεριμνάω (LN 25.225) (BAGD 1. p. 505): 'to worry about' [BECNT, BNTC, NICNT; CEV, GW, NCV, NET, NIV, NLT, NRSV], 'to be worried about' [LN, NIGTC; NASB, TEV], 'to be anxious about' [BAGD, LN, NTC, PNTC; ESV, REB], 'to be unduly concerned' [BAGD], 'to have anxiety' [BAGD], 'to be filled with anxiety about' [WBC], 'to take thought about' [KJV]. This verb means to have an anxious concern, based on apprehension about possible danger or misfortune [LN].

d. ψυχή (LN 23.88) (BAGD 1.a.β. p. 893): 'life' [BECNT, BNTC, LN, NICNT, NIGTC, NTC, PNTC; CEV, ESV, KJV, NASB, NET, NIV, NRSV], 'everyday life' [NLT], 'earthly life' [BAGD], not explicit [GW].

The phrase τῇ ψυχῇ ὑμῶν 'your life' is translated '(you need) to live' [NCV], 'to keep you alive' [REB], '(you need) in order to stay alive' [TEV]. Here this word has the connotation of life as prolonged by nourishment [BAGD].

QUESTION—What relationship is indicated by διὰ τοῦτο 'therefore'?

It indicates a conclusion to be drawn from what has already been said [BECNT, CC, EBC, NTC, PNTC, WBC], whether in 6:19–24 [CC, EBC, ICC, NTC, WBC], or more specifically in 6:24 [BECNT, My, NICNT, PNTC, WBC]. It forms a rather loose connection with what has preceded it [TH]. Since it is not possible to serve God and money, disciples should not be absorbed with concern over material things, but should trust God for what they need [PNTC]. The right way of viewing earthly possessions is to recognize that Jesus alone is to be the master, so the command not to worry follows naturally from that [CC].

QUESTION—What is implied by the use of the present imperative μὴ μεριμνᾶτε 'do not worry'?

This present imperative expresses emphasis, and also marks a shift to a new section. The theme of this section is that they should not worry and the section boundaries are marked by this beginning command 'Therefore…do not worry about your life' and the ending command at 6:34, 'therefore don't worry about tomorrow' in 6:34 [CC]. There is little distinction between this present imperative and the two aorist imperatives that follow [BECNT]. Some think that the present tense indicates that they are worrying and should stop doing so [Lns, NTC; GW].

QUESTION—Does the command not to worry rule out planning for the future?

Providing for the future and being anxious for the future are not the same thing [NAC, NICNT, NTC]. Worry is being so anxious and bothered about physical needs that we don't trust God [BNTC]. To be anxious is to have one's attention divided in such a way as to be unable to focus on what is important [NTC]. Responsible work is not incompatible with trust [EBC].

what you(pl)-might-eat,[a] or what you(pl)-might-drink[b]

TEXT—The Greek manuscripts that read ἢ τί πίητε 'or what you might drink' are followed by GNT with an a C rating to indicate that choosing it over a variant text was difficult. This reading is followed by BNTC, CC, NTC, and all versions. It is included in brackets by BECNT, PNTC, and WBC. Other manuscripts omit it and they are followed by NICNT, NIGTC.

LEXICON—a. aorist act. subj. of ἐσθίω (LN 23.1) (BAGD 1.a. p. 312): 'to eat' [BAGD, BECNT, BNTC, LN, NICNT, NIGTC, NTC, PNTC, WBC; CEV, ESV, GW, KJV, NASB, NET, NIV, NRSV], 'to consume food, to use food, to drink' [LN]. The phrase τί φάγητε ἢ τί πίητε 'what you might eat, or what you might drink' is translated 'food and drink' [REB], 'the food or drink you need' [NCV, TEV], 'whether you have enough food and drink' [NLT]. This verb means to consume food, usually solids, but also liquids [LN].

b. aorist act. subj. of πίνω (LN 23.34) (BAGD 1. p. 658): 'to drink' [BAGD, BECNT, BNTC, LN, NTC, PNTC, WBC; CEV, ESV, GW, KJV, NASB, NET, NIV, NRSV]. This verb is translated as a noun: 'drink' [NCV, NLT, REB, TEV]. It means to consume liquids, particularly water and wine [LN].

nor[a] (about) your(sg) body[b], what you(pl)-might-wear.[c]
LEXICON—a. μηδέ (LN 69.7) (BAGD 1.a. p. 517): 'nor' [BAGD, BECNT, BNTC, LN, NICNT, PNTC; ESV, KJV, NASB], 'or' [NIGTC, WBC; CEV, GW, NCV, NET, NIV, NLT, NRSV, TEV], 'and' [REB], 'neither' [LN]. This conjunction is a combination of the negative particles μή 'not' (69.3), and the postpositive conjunction δέ 'and' (89.94) [LN].

b. σῶμα (LN 8.1) (BAGD 1.b. p. 799): 'body' [BAGD, LN; all translations except CEV, GW, NLT], not explicit [CEV, GW, NLT]. This noun denotes the physical body of persons, animals, or plants, either dead or alive [LN].

c. aorist mid. subj. of ἐνδύω (LN 49.1) (BAGD 2.a. p. 264): 'to wear' [BNTC, NICNT, NIGTC, NTC; CEV, ESV, GW, NET, NIV, NRSV], 'to clothe' [LN], 'to clothe oneself' [BAGD], 'to dress' [LN], 'to put on' [BAGD, BECNT, LN, PNTC; KJV, NASB]. The clause 'nor about your body, what you might wear' is translated 'or how you will clothe your body' [WBC], 'clothes to cover your body' [REB], 'clothes for your body' [TEV], 'or about the clothes you need for your body' [NCV], 'or enough clothes to wear' [NLT]. This verb means to put on clothes, without implying any particular article of clothing [LN].

Is not[a] life more-than[b] food[c] and the body (more-than) clothing[d]?
LEXICON—a. οὐχί (LN 69.12) (BAGD 3. p. 598): 'not' [BAGD, BECNT, BNTC, L9N, NICNT, NTC, PNTC, WBC; all versions except NCV, REB. The rhetorical question οὐχὶ ἡ ψυχὴ πλεῖόν ἐστιν 'is not life more than…' is translated 'life is more than…isn't it?' [NIGTC], 'surely life is more than' [REB], 'life is more than' [NCV]. This particle marks a somewhat emphatic affirmative response [CC, LN]. It expects a 'yes' answer [BAGD].

b. πλεῖον (LN 78.28) (BAGD II.2.c. p. 689): 'more than' [BAGD, BECNT, BNTC, LN, NIGTC, PNTC; all versions except NET, NIV, TEV], 'something more than' [CC], 'worth more than' [TEV], 'more important than' [NICNT, NTC; NIV], 'more significant than' [WBC], 'greater than' [BAGD]. This question is translated 'isn't there more to life than food and more to the body than clothing?' [NET]. This noun denotes a degree which surpasses in some manner a point on an explicit or implicit scale of extent [LN].

c. τροφή (LN 5.1) (BAGD 1. P. 827): 'food' [BAGD, BECNT, BNTC, LN, NICNT, NIGTC, NTC, PNTC; all versions except KJV], 'nourishment' [LN, WBC], 'meat' [KJV]. This noun denotes any kind of food or nourishment [LN].

d. ἔνδυμα (LN 6.162) (BAGD 1. p. 263): 'clothing' [BAGD, BNTC, LN, NICNT, NIGTC, NTC, PNTC, WBC; CEV, ESV, NASB, NET, NLT, NRSV], 'clothes' [BECNT; GW, NCV, NIV, REB, TEV], 'apparel' [LN], 'raiment' [KJV]. This noun denotes any kind of clothing [LN].

6:26 Look^a at the birds^b of-the air^c

LEXICON—a. aorist act. impera. of ἐμβλέπω (LN **30.1**) (BAGD 1. p. 254): 'to look at' [BAGD, BECNT, CC, NIGTC, NTC, PNTC; all versions except KJV], 'to take a good look at' [NICNT], 'to behold' [KJV], 'to consider' [BNTC, **LN**], 'to consider well' [WBC], 'to think about' [LN]. This verb means to process information by giving consideration to various aspects of it. It is possible to regard ἐμβλέπω in Matthew 6:26 as involving a combination of directing one's vision and attention to a particular object plus intellectual activity [LN].

b. πετεινόν (LN 4.38) (BAGD p. 654): 'bird' [BAGD, LN (4.38); all translations except KJV], 'fowl' [KJV].

c. οὐρανός (LN 1.5) (BAGD 1.d. p. 594): 'air' [BECNT, NIGTC, NTC, PNTC; ESV, KJV, NASB, NCV, NIV, NRSV], 'sky' [CC, LN, WBC; CEV, NET, REB], 'heaven' [BNTC], not explicit [GW, NLT, TEV]. The phrase τὰ πετεινὰ τοῦ οὐρανοῦ 'the birds of the air' denotes wild birds in contrast with domesticated birds such as chickens [LN]. The phrases 'birds of the sky', 'lilies of the field' in 6:28, and 'grass of the field' in 6:30 are not so much concerned with giving their locations as to indicating that they are in their natural states instead of being domesticated or cultivated [NICNT].

that/for^a they-do- not -sow^b nor^c do-they-reap^d

LEXICON—a. ὅτι (LN 90.21, 89.23): 'that' [BECNT, LN, PNTC; NASB], 'the fact that' [LN (90.21)], 'for' [BNTC, CC, NIGTC; KJV]. This conjunction indicates discourse content, whether direct or indirect [LN (90.21)], but may also mark cause or reason, based on an evident fact [LN (89.23)]. This conjunction is left untranslated but appears to be treated as marking discourse content [NICNT, NTC, WBC; CEV, ESV, GW, NCV, NET, NIV, NLT, NRSV, REB, TEV].

b. pres. act. indic. of σπείρω (LN 43.6) (BAGD 1.a.α. p. 761): 'to sow' [BAGD, BECNT, BNTC, CC, LN, NIGTC, NTC, PNTC, WBC; ESV, KJV, NASB, NET, NRSV, REB], 'to sow seed' [NICNT], 'to plant' [CEV, GW, NCV, NLT], 'to plant seeds' [TEV]. This verb means to scatter seed over tilled ground [LN].

c. οὐδέ (LN **69.7**) (BAGD 1. p. 591): 'nor' [BAGD, BNTC, CC, **LN**, NIGTC, NTC, PNTC, WBC; ESV, NASB, NRSV], 'neither' [LN; KJV], 'or' [BECNT, NICNT; CEV, NCV, NET, NIV, NLT], 'and' [REB], 'and not' [BAGD, LN], not explicit [GW, TEV]. This conjunction is a combination of the negative particles οὐ 'not' and the postpositive conjunction δέ 'and' [LN].

d. pres. act. indic. of θερίζω (LN 43.14) (BAGD 1. p. 359): 'to reap' [BAGD, BECNT, BNTC, LN, NIGTC, NTC, PNTC, WBC; ESV, KJV, NASB, NET, NIV, NRSV, REB], 'to harvest' [BAGD, CC, LN; CEV, GW, NCV, NLT], 'to harvest crops' [NICNT], not explicit [TEV]. This verb means to cut ripe grain and to gather bundles of such grain together [LN].

nor do-they-gather^a into barns,^b and-yet^c your(pl) heavenly Father feeds^d them;

LEXICON—a. pres. act. indic. of συνάγω (LN 15.125) (BAGD 1. p. 782): 'to gather' [BAGD, BECNT, BNTC, CC, NIGTC, NTC, PNTC; ESV, KJV, NASB, NET, NRSV], 'to gather crops' [WBC], 'to gather the harvest' [GW], 'to gather together' [BAGD], 'to store' [NICNT; REB], 'to store away' [NIV], 'to store grain' [CEV], 'to store food' [NCV, NLT]. The clause 'nor do they reap, nor do they gather into barns' is translated '(they do not) gather a harvest and put it into barns' [TEV]. This verb means to cause to come together, whether of animate or inanimate objects [LN].
   b. ἀποθήκη (LN 7.25) (BAGD p. 91): 'barn' [BAGD, BECNT, CC, LN, NICNT, NIGTC, NTC, PNTC; all versions], 'storehouse' [BAGD, BNTC, LN, WBC]. This noun denotes a building for storage [LN].
   c. καί (LN 91.12) (BAGD I.2.g. p. 392): 'and yet' [BAGD, BNTC, CC, NICNT, PNTC; ESV, NASB, NIV, NRSV], 'yet' [BECNT, LN, NICNT, NTC, WBC; CEV, GW, KJV, NET, REB, TEV], 'but' [NCV], 'nevertheless' [BAGD], 'for' [NLT]. This conjunction indicates emphasis, involving surprise and unexpectedness [BAGD, LN, PNTC].
   d. pres. act. indic. of τρέφω (LN 23.6) (BAGD 1. p. 825): 'to feed' [BAGD, BECNT, BNTC, CC, NICNT, NIGTC, NTC, PNTC; all versions except CEV, TEV], 'to provide with food' [BAGD, WBC], 'to provide food for, to give food to someone to eat' [LN], 'to take care of' [CEV, TEV], 'to nourish, to support' [BAGD]. This verb means to provide food for someone, with the implication of a considerable period of time and the food being adequate nourishment [LN].

are- you(pl) not^a -worth^b much-more-than^c they?

LEXICON—a. οὐ (LN 69.11) (BAGD 4.c. p. 590): 'not' [BAGD, LN; all translations except NCV]. This rhetorical question is translated as a statement: 'you know you are worth...' [NCV]. This particle marks questions expecting an affirmative answer [LN].
   b. pres. act. indic. of διαφέρω (LN **65.6**) (BAGD 2.b. p. 190): 'to be worth (more than)' [BAGD, BECNT, BNTC, CC, PNTC, WBC; CEV, GW, NASB, NCV, REB, TEV], 'to be valuable' [**LN**; NET, NIV, NLT], 'to be of value' [NIGTC, NTC; ESV, NRSV], 'to have worth' [LN], 'to be (more) important' [NICNT], 'to be better' [KJV]. This verb means to be of considerable value, in view of having certain distinctive characteristics [LN].

c. μᾶλλον (LN 78.28) (BAGD 1. p. 489): 'more than' [LN, NICNT, NIGTC, NTC, PNTC; CEV, ESV, ESV, GW, NET, NRSV, REB], 'to a greater degree' [BAGD, LN], 'even more' [BAGD, LN], 'far more' [NLT], 'much (better)' [KJV]. Taken in conjunction with διαφέρω 'to be worth more (than)' this adverb is translated 'much more than' [BECNT, BNTC, CC, WBC; NASB, NCV, NIV, TEV]. This adverb describes a degree which in some manner surpasses a point on an explicit or implicit scale of extent [LN].

QUESTION—How is the word ὑμεῖς 'you' used here?

'The inclusion of this pronoun makes it emphatic, expressing contrast between the value to God of the disciples and the value of birds [CC, EBC, PNTC].

6:27 And which of you(pl) (by) worrying[a] is-able to-add[b] to his life-span/height[c] one cubit?[d]

LEXICON—a. pres. act. participle of μεριμνάω (LN 25.225) (BAGD 1. p. 505): 'to worry' [BECNT, CC, NICNT, NIGTC; CEV, GW, NCV, NET, NIV, NRSV, TEV], 'to be worried' [NASB], 'to be worried about' [LN], 'to be anxious about' [BAGD, LN, WBC], 'to be anxious' [BAGD, NTC, PNTC; ESV], 'to take thought' [KJV], 'to be unduly concerned' [BAGD]. The participle form of this verb is translated as a noun: 'anxious thought' [REB], 'worry' [BNTC], 'worries' [NLT]. This verb means to have an anxious concern based on apprehension about possible danger or misfortune [LN]. This participle indicates the means by which one's life may or may not be extended [all translations].

b. aorist act. infin. of προστίθημι (LN 59.72) (BAGD 1.a. p. 719): 'to add' [BAGD, LN; all translations except CEV, TEV], not explicit [CEV, TEV]. This verb means to add something to an existing quantity [LN].

c. ἡλικία (LN **67.151**, 81.4) (BAGD 1.a., or 2. p. 345): This verb refers to a period of time: 'life-span' [NICNT, NTC], 'span of life' [BNTC, LN (67.151); ESV, NRSV], 'life' [BECNT, WBC; GW, NASB, NCV, NET, NIV, NLT, REB], 'time of life' [BAGD (1.a.)], 'lifetime' [**LN** (67.151)], 'age' [NIGTC], 'journey of days' [CC]. The verse is translated 'which one of you by worrying can add a single day to his lifetime?'[**LN** (67.151)], 'Can worry make you live longer?' [CEV], 'Can any of you live a bit longer by worrying about it?' [TEV]. Or this verb refers to the height of a person: 'height' [LN (81.4), PNTC], 'stature' [LN (81.4); KJV],'bodily stature' [BAGD (2.)]. This noun denotes the period of time when a person is alive. When taken as time, some adjustment needs to be made to the meaning of πῆχυς 'cubit' (81.25) and for many languages the most appropriate term is one which means 'day' [LN (67.151)], or the noun denotes height as the dimension of stature of an animate object [LN (81.4)].

d. πῆχυς (LN **81.25**, 67.151) (BAGD p. 657): 'cubit' [BAGD, BNTC, CC, LN (81.25), NICNT, NIGTC, NTC, PNTC; KJV], 'eighteen inches' [LN

(81.25)] 'half meter' [**LN** (81.25)], hour' [BECNT, WBC; ESV, GW, NASB, NET, NIV, NRSV], 'moment' [NLT], 'time' [NCV], 'day' [LN (67.151); REB], not explicit [CEV, TEV]. This noun traditionally denotes the distance from the elbow to the end of the fingers, about eighteen inches or one-half meter. In Matthew 6:27 the interpretation of πῆχυς as a measurement of stature rather than length of life may be justified as an instance of literary hyperbole or exaggeration. Most modern translations, however, interpret πῆχυς in this context as a reference to length of life rather than as a measurement of height [LN (81.25)], or it is used to refer to a unit of time [LN (67.151)].

QUESTION—Do ἡλικία 'life span' and πῆχυς 'cubit' refer to a measure of time (life-span, hour) or of spatial distance (height, cubit)?

1. The term πῆχυς, which normally refers to spatial measurement, is used metaphorically here to refer to time [BECNT, EBC, ICC, Lns, My, NAC, NIBC, NICNT, NIGTC, NTC, TH, WBC], as it would not make sense to speak of adding a cubit to one's height [BECNT, EBC, Lns, My, NAC, NICNT, NTC, WBC]. It is a metaphorical reference to spatial distance, meaning that if one views life as a journey, adding a single cubit to the distance traveled would make only a minimal difference [CC, EBC, NTC]. It is translated as representing time by LN (67.151), ESV, GW, NASB, NCV, NET, NIV, NLT, NRSV, REB.

2. It is translated as representing height [PNTC; KJV]. It may be a hyperbole, using humorous exaggeration about physical height for effect, but it is impossible to be absolutely sure which piece of imagery Jesus is using [PNTC].

6:28 And about[a] clothing,[b] why do-you(pl)-worry?[c]

LEXICON—a. περί with genitive (LN 89.6): 'about' [all translations except KJV], 'for' [KJV], 'concerning, with regard to, in relation to' [LN]. This preposition marks a relation, usually involving content or topic [LN].
    b. ἔνδυμα (LN **6.162**) (BAGD 1. p. 263): 'clothing' [BAGD, BECNT, CC, BNTC, **LN**, NIGTC, PNTC, WBC; ESV, NASB, NCV, NET, NLT, NRSV, REB], 'clothes' [NICNT, NTC; CEV, GW, NIV, TEV], 'raiment' [KJV], 'apparel' [LN]. This noun denotes any kind of clothing [LN].
    c. pres. act. indic. of μεριμνάω (LN 25.225) (BAGD 1. p. 505): 'to worry.' See this word at 6:25 and 6:27.

Consider[a] the lilies[b] of-the field[c] how[d] they-grow;[e]

LEXICON—a. aorist act. impera. of καταμανθάνω (LN **30.30**) (BAGD p. 414): 'to consider' [**LN**, NTC, PNTC; ESV, KJV, NRSV, REB], 'to notice' [BECNT; GW], 'to observe' [BAGD, BNTC, LN; NASB], 'to think about' [LN; NET], 'to study closely' [NIGTC], 'to learn well' [CC], 'to learn (something)' [BAGD], 'to learn a lesson from' [WBC], 'to take a lesson from' [NICNT], 'to look at' [CEV, NCV, NLT, TEV], 'to see' [NIV]. This verb means to think about, with the purpose of ultimate understanding [LN]. This word occurs only here in the NT.

b. κρίνον (LN **3.32**) (BAGD p. 451): 'lily' [BAGD, BNTC, CC, **LN**, NICNT, NTC; ESV, KJV, NASB, NCV, NIV, NLT, NRSV, REB], 'flower' [BECNT, PNTC, WBC, NICNT; CEV, GW, NET, TEV], 'wild flower' [LN]. This noun denotes any one of several types of flowers, usually uncultivated [LN].

c. ἀγρός (LN 1.95) (BAGD 1. p. 13): 'field' [BAGD, BECNT, CC, LN, NICNT, NTC, PNTC, WBC; all versions except CEV, TEV]. The phrase 'lilies of the field' is translated 'wild flowers' [NICNT; CEV, TEV], 'wild lily' [BAGD, BNTC]. This noun denotes land under cultivation or used for pasture [LN].

d. πῶς (BAGD 2.a. p. 732): 'how' [BAGD; all translations].

e. pres. act. indic. of αὐξάνω (LN 23.188) (BAGD 3. p. 121): 'to grow' [BAGD, LN; all translations]. This verb means to grow, to increase in size, whether of animate beings or of plants [LN].

QUESTION—What flower is represented by the noun κρίνον 'lily'?

It is a general word for 'flower', not referring to any specific species [WBC]. It could be any of the flowers common in Galilee [EBC, ICC, NICNT]. Jesus may have been thinking of all the flowers that were blooming at that time [NTC], or of wild flowers in general [TRT]. It could have been the purple anemone, which would resemble Solomon's purple robes [NIBC]. It would have been lilies generally [My]. It could have been the white lily, but probably refers more generally to field flowers that were like lilies [NIGTC].

they- (do) not -work[a] nor[b] do-they-spin[c] (thread).

LEXICON—a. pres. act. indic. of κοπιάω (LN 42.47) (BAGD 2. p. 443): 'to work' [NICNT, PNTC; GW, NCV, NET, NLT, REB, TEV], 'to toil' [BAGD, BECNT, LN, NTC; ESV, GW, NASB, NRSV], 'to work hard' [BAGD, LN, NICNT; CEV], 'to labor' [BAGD, BNTC, CC, LN, WBC; NIV]. This verb means to engage in hard work, implying difficulties and trouble [LN].

b. οὐδέ (LN 69.7) (BAGD 1. p. 591): 'nor' [BAGD, CC, **LN**, NTC, PNTC, WBC; NASB, NRSV], 'or' [BECNT, BNTC, NICNT, NICNT; ESV, GW, NCV, NET, NIV, NLT, TEV], 'neither' [LN; KJV], 'and not' [BAGD, LN], not explicit [CEV, REB]. This conjunction is a combination of the negative particles οὐ 'not', and the postpositive conjunction δέ 'and' [LN].

c pres. act. indic. of νήθω (LN 48.2) (BAGD p. 537): 'to spin' [BAGD, BNTC, CC, LN, NICNT, NICNT, NTC, PNTC; ESV, KJV, NASB, NET, NIV, NRSV, REB], 'to spin yarn' [GW], 'to make clothes' [BECNT; CEV, NCV, TEV], 'to make clothing' [NLT], 'to toil' [WBC]. While the work of sowing and reaping for the food harvest was normally a male task, pinning for making clothing was a female task [NICNT, PNTC, WBC]. This verb means to make yarn by twisting fibers together as one of the steps in making cloth [LN].

6:29 But[a] I-say to-you(pl) that not-even[b] Solomon[c] in all his glory[d] clothed-himself[e] like one of-these.[f]

LEXICON—a. δέ (LN 89.124): 'but' [BNTC, CC, LN, NICNT, NICNT, PNTC, WBC; CEV, GW, NCV, TEV], 'yet' [BECNT, NTC; ESV, NASB, NET, NIV, NLT, NRSV, REB], 'and yet' [KJV], 'on the other hand' [LN]. This conjunction indicates contrast [LN].
- b. οὐδέ (LN **69.8**) (BAGD 3. p. 591): 'not even' [BAGD, BECNT, CC, LN, NICNT, NICNT, PNTC, WBC; GW, NASB, NET, NIV, TEV], 'even...not' [BNTC, NTC; ESV, KJV, NCV, NRSV, REB], 'not' [CEV, NLT]. This word is a combination of the negative particle οὐ and the postpositional particle δέ [LN].
- c. Σολομών (LN 93.344) (BAGD p. 759): 'Solomon' [BAGD, LN; all translations]. This is the name of the son and successor of David [LN].
- d. δόξα (LN 87.23) (BAGD 2. p. 204): 'glory' [BECNT, CC, LN, NICNT, PNTC; ESV, KJV, NASB, NET, NLT, NRSV], 'splendor' [BAGD, BNTC, NICNT, NTC, WBC; NIV, REB], 'magnificence' [BAGD], 'majesty' [GW], 'riches' [NCV], 'wealth' [CEV, TEV], 'greatness' [LN]. This noun denotes a state of being great and wonderful [LN].
- e. περιβάλλω aorist mid. indic. of περιβάλλω (LN **49.3**) (BAGD 1.b.ε. p. 646): 'to clothe oneself' [BECNT, CC, PNTC; NASB], 'to clothe' [BAGD, **LN**], 'to be clothed' [NICNT; CEV, NET, NRSV], 'to robe oneself' [NIGTC], 'to dress oneself' [BAGD], 'to dress' [BNTC], 'to be dressed' [GW, NCV, NIV, NLT], 'to be attired' [NTC; REB], 'to be arrayed' [ESV, KJV]. The phrase περιεβάλετο ὡς ἓν τούτων 'clothed himself like one of these' is translated 'could match such clothing' [WBC], 'had clothes as beautiful as one of these flowers' [TEV]. This verb means to put on clothes [LN].
- f. ὡς (LN 64.12): 'like' [BECNT, CC, LN, NTC, PNTC; ESV, GW, KJV, NASB, NET, NIV, NRSV, REB], 'as' [BNTC, LN], 'as well as' [CEV], 'as magnificently as' [NICNT], 'as beautifully as' [NCV, NLT], 'as beautiful as' [TEV]. This conjunction is a relatively weak marker of a relationship between events or states [LN].

QUESTION—What was the δόξα 'glory' of Solomon?

It refers to the kingly splendor and magnificence of Solomon [PNTC], and especially his clothing [BNTC, Lns, NIGTC, NTC, PNTC]. It was all of Solomon's riches and extravagance [EBC], his wealth [TH, WBC]. It refers to the garments that Solomon's great wealth could provide [NIBC]. It included more than just his royal robes [My].

QUESTION—What is being compared by the clause 'like one of these'?

Many use a verb form that would apply to both Solomon and the lily: 'Solomon *was* not *clothed* like one of the lilies of the field (*was clothed*)' [CEV, ESV, GW, KJV, NCV, NET, NIV, NLT, NRSV, REB, TEV]. Some take the middle voice περιεβάλετο to mean that Solomon clothed himself, and since the next verse indicates that God clothes the lilies, the comparison would be: 'Solomon *did* not *clothe himself* like one of the lilies of the field (*was clothed by God*)' [BECNT, CC, NIGTC, PNTC; NASB].

6:30 Now/but^a if God thus^b clothes^c the grass^d of-the field existing^e today^f

LEXICON—a. δέ (LN 89.124): 'now' [BNTC, CC, NTC, PNTC, WBC], 'but' [BECNT, LN; ESV, NASB, NRSV], 'and' [NET, NLT], 'wherefore' [KJV], not explicit [NICNT, NIGTC; CEV, GW, NCV, NIV, REB, TEV]. This conjunction indicates contrast [LN].

b. οὕτως (LN 61.9) (BAGD 1.b. p. 597): 'thus' [BAGD, CC, LN], 'so' [BAGD, BECNT, BNTC, LN, NTC, PNTC; ESV, KJV, NASB, NRSV], 'in this way' [LN], 'like this' [WBC], 'such (clothing)' [NICNT], 'in this manner' [BAGD], 'this is the way' [NIGTC], 'that's the way' [GW], 'this is how' [NET, REB], 'that is how' [NIV], 'so wonderfully' [NLT], not explicit [CEV, NCV]. This adverb is used with reference to that which precedes [LN].

c. pres. act. indic. of ἀμφιέννυμι (LN **49.3**) (BAGD p. 47): 'to clothe' [BAGD, BECNT, BNTC, CC, LN, NTC, PNTC, WBC; all versions except CEV, NLT], 'to give clothes to' [NICNT], 'to dress' [BAGD], 'to deck out' [NIGTC], 'to give such beauty to' [CEV], 'to care for' [NLT]. This verb means to put on clothes, implying the clothing being completely around [LN].

d. χόρτος (LN 3.15) (BAGD p. 884): 'grass' [BAGD, LN]. The phrase 'the grass of the field' [BECNT, CC, NIGTC, NTC, PNTC, WBC; ESV, KJV, NASB, NIV, NRSV] is also translated 'the grass in the field' [GW, NCV, TEV], 'the grass in the fields' [REB], 'everything that grows in the fields' [CEV], 'the wild grass' [BNTC; NET], 'the wild plants' [NICNT], 'wildflowers' [NLT]. This noun denotes small green plants, and in NT contexts it refers primarily to the green grass in a field or meadow [LN].

e. pres. act. participle of εἰμί (LN 13.69): 'to exist' [CC, LN], 'to be' [LN, PNTC; KJV], 'to be here' [BNTC, NICNT; CEV, NET, NIV, NLT, TEV], 'to be there' [NIGTC; REB], 'to be alive' [BECNT, NTC, WBC; ESV, GW, NASB, NCV, NRSV]. This verb means to exist, in an absolute sense [LN].

f. σήμερον (LN 67.205) (BAGD p. 749): 'today' [BAGD, BECNT, BNTC, CC, LN, NICNT, NIGTC, NTC, PNTC; all versions], 'one day' [WBC]. This adjective denotes the same day as the day of a discourse [LN].

QUESTION—What is the function of εἰ 'if' in this verse?

'If' is used to introduce an idea that is presumed to be true and from which conclusions are to be drawn [ICC, NIGTC, PNTC, TH, WBC]. There is no uncertainty here [NIGTC, PNTC].

QUESTION—What difference is there between κρίνον 'lily' in 6:28 and χόρτος 'grass' here in this verse?

Grass was the common fuel for ovens and such grass is said to be clothed by God with the beauty of the flowers [WBC; probably ICC]. Others take 'the grass of the field' to be the same as, or to include, 'the lilies of the field'

[BECNT, My, NICNT, NTC, TH; CEV, NLT]. The lily represents beauty, but here he refers to it as more generally grass because he is focusing on its short existence [BECNT, NTC, PNTC, WBC]. Here he gives the genus of which the κρίνον 'lily' is one species, to indicate their insignificance [My].

and tomorrow[a] is-being-thrown[b] into an-oven[c]

LEXICON—a. αὔριον (LN 67.207) (BAGD 2. p. 122): 'tomorrow' [BAGD, LN; all translations except WBC], 'the next (day)' [WBC], 'soon' [BAGD]. This adjective describes a day following the day of a discourse [LN].

b. pres. pass. participle of βάλλω (LN 15.215) (BAGD 1.b. p. 131): 'to be thrown' [BAGD, BECNT, BNTC, CC, LN, NICNT, NIGTC, NTC, PNTC; all versions except KJV, NET, TEV], 'to be cast' [KJV], 'to be tossed' [NET]. The phrase εἰς κλίβανον βαλλόμενον 'is being thrown into an oven' is translated 'is used as fuel for the oven' [WBC], 'burned up in the oven' [TEV].

c. κλίβανος (LN **7.74**) (BAGD p. 436): 'oven' [BAGD, BNTC, CC, **LN**, NICNT, NIGTC, WBC; ESV, KJV, NRSV, TEV], 'furnace' [BAGD, BECNT, NTC, PNTC; NASB], 'stove' [REB], 'fire' [CEV, NCV, NIV, NLT], 'incinerator' [GW]. The phrase εἰς κλίβανον 'into an oven' is translated 'into the fire to heat the oven' [NET]. This noun denotes a dome-like structure made of clay, in which wood and dried grass were burned, and then after being heated, was used for baking bread [LN].

QUESTION—What was the κλίβανος 'oven'?

It was an oven used for baking food, in which grass was often used as fuel [EBC, ICC, Lns, My, NAC, NICNT, NIGTC, PNTC, TH]. It was made of clay [EBC, PNTC, TH].

(will he) not much more[a] (do so for) you(pl), (you) of-little-faith?[b]

LEXICON—a. The phrase πολλῷ μᾶλλον 'much more' [BECNT, NICNT, NIGTC, PNTC; ESV, KJV, NASB, NIV, NRSV] is also translated 'how much more' [CC; GW], 'much more surely' [BNTC, NTC], 'surely even more' [CEV], 'even more sure' [NCV], 'even more' [NET], 'all the more' [REB], 'all the more sure' [TEV], 'certainly' [NLT].

b. ὀλιγόπιστος (LN 31.96) (BAGD p. 563): 'of little faith' [BAGD, BECNT, BNTC, LN, NIGTC, NTC, PNTC; ESV, KJV, NASB, NET, NIV, NRSV], 'little-faith' [CC], 'who have so little faith' [WBC], 'of little trust' [BAGD], 'who have so little faith' [GW], 'of insufficient faith' [LN], 'faithless' [NICNT]. This word is translated as a rhetorical question: 'why do you have such/so little faith?' [CEV, NLT]; as an imperative: 'Don't have so little faith' [NCV]; as a statement: 'How/what little faith you have!' [REB, TEV]. This adjective describes a person having relatively little faith [LN].

QUESTION—What is the argument given here?

Since God has given such extravagant care to something destined to such an ignoble end, he can be expected to care much more about meeting the essential needs of the disciples [NICNT, NIGTC, PNTC, WBC]. The point is not that the disciples can expect to be dressed more magnificently than Solomon [NICNT, NIGTC]. The statement that God will *much more do so* for them does not mean that God will give them more or better clothing. It is a strong affirmative statement that it is even more sure that God will clothe them [BECNT, BNTC, NIGTC, NTC, TH; CEV, NCV, NLT, TEV].

QUESTION—What does it mean to be ὀλιγόπιστος 'of little faith'?

Their faith was less than what could reasonably be expected of them [NIBC]. It essentially means to be faithless, lacking faith sufficient to face whatever situation is at hand [NICNT]. They were guilty of unbelief [EBC]. Their lack of faith reflected insufficient commitment to the values of God's kingdom [BECNT]. It describes insufficient faith, though not a complete lack of faith since in the NT it is only used of the disciples [ICC]. The disciples failed to trust God completely [WBC], and failed to believe they would be taken care of [NIGTC].

6:31 Therefore[a] do-not-worry,[b] saying,[c] What will-we-eat?[d] or, What will-we-drink?[e] or, What will-we-wear?[f]

LEXICON—a. οὖν (LN 89.50) (BAGD 1.b. p. 593): 'therefore' [BAGD, BECNT, CC, LN, NTC, WBC; ESV, KJV, NRSV], 'so' [BAGD, BNTC, LN, NICNT; NIV, NLT, TEV], 'so then' [LN; NET], 'then' [BAGD, LN, NIGTC; NASB], 'consequently, accordingly' [BAGD, LN], not explicit [CEV, GW, REB]. The phrase μὴ μεριμνήσητε λέγοντες, 'do not worry, saying' is translated 'do not ask anxiously' [REB]. This conjunction indicates result, often implying the conclusion of a process of reasoning [LN].

b. aorist act. subj. or impera. of μεριμνάω (LN 25.225) (BAGD 1. p. 505): 'to worry.' See this verb at 6:25, 6:27, 6:28.

c. pres. act. participle of λέγω (LN 33.69): 'to say' [BECNT, BNTC, CC, LN, NIGTC, NTC, PNTC, WBC; all versions except CEV, REB, TEV], 'to ask oneself' [CEV], 'to ask' [REB], not explicit [NICNT; TEV]. Instead of using the participle 'saying', quotation marks are used to indicate the content of speech or thought by NICNT, TEV. This verb means to speak or talk, with apparent focus upon the content of what is said [LN].

d. aorist act. subj. of ἐσθίω 'to eat'. See this verb at 6:25.

e. aorist act. subj. of πίνω 'to drink'. See this verb at 6:25.

f. aorist mid. subj. of περιβάλλω 'to wear'. See this verb at 6:29.

QUESTION—What relationship is indicated by οὖν 'therefore'?

It indicates a conclusion to be drawn from what has been said [BECNT, CC, EBC, PNTC], which is that they should not worry [CC] or concern themselves with what they will eat, drink or wear [BECNT]. It indicates a summary of the exhortations that have just been given [NTC]. It indicates a recapitulation of what has been said in 6:25–30 [WBC]. It indicates a restating of the premise of 6:25 [NIGTC].

6:32 For[a] the Gentiles[b] seek[c] all these-things;

LEXICON—a. γάρ (LN 89.23): 'for' [BECNT, BNTC, CC, LN, NIGTC, NTC, PNTC, WBC; ESV, KJV, NASB, NET, NIV, NRSV], 'because' [LN], not explicit [NICNT; CEV, GW, NCV, NLT, REB, TEV]. This conjunction indicates cause or reason between events, though in some contexts the relationship is often remote or tenuous [LN].
  b. ἔθνη (LN 11.37) (BAGD 2. p. 218): 'Gentiles' [BAGD, BECNT, BNTC, CC, NICNT, NIGTC, NTC, PNTC, WBC; ESV, KJV, NASB, NRSV], 'heathen' [BAGD, LN; REB], 'pagans' [BAGD, LN; NIV, TEV], 'people who don't know God' [CEV, NCV], 'unconverted' [NET], 'unbelievers' [NLT], 'everyone' [GW]. This plural noun denotes those who do not belong to the Jewish or Christian faith [LN].
  c. pres. act. indic. of ἐπιζητέω (LN 25.9) (BAGD 2.a. p. 292): 'to seek' [BECNT, CC, NIGTC, PNTC; KJV], 'to seek after' [WBC; ESV], 'to eagerly seek' [NASB], 'to run after' [NIV], 'to strive for' [BAGD; NRSV], 'to strive to get' [BNTC], 'to keep trying to get' [NCV], 'to search for' [NICNT], 'to pursue' [NET], 'to crave' [NTC], 'to desire' [LN], 'to always worry about' [CEV], 'to be concerned about' [GW], 'to always be concerned about' [TEV]. This clause is translated 'these things dominate the thoughts of unbelievers' [NLT], 'these are the things that occupy the minds of the heathen' [REB]. This verb means to desire to have or experience something, with the probable implication of making an attempt to realize one's desire [LN].

QUESTION—What relationship is indicated by the first γάρ 'for'?

It indicates the first of two reasons that they should not become anxious about such things [BECNT, BNTC, CC, Lns, My, NIGTC, NTC]. Because of God's bountiful care described in verses 25–30, the thoughtless questions in verse 31 are an affront to God. Anxiety about the necessities of life are the type of things that people who are outside God's family would have. As the Gentiles see it, they must obtain all these things by their own efforts and out of their own resources [PNTC]. This is what the Gentiles were always worrying about [NTC, TH]. Gentiles worried because their deities were capricious and hard to placate, whereas the disciples have a loving heavenly Father [BECNT].

QUESTION—Who are τὰ ἔθνη 'the Gentiles'?

Gentiles are non-Jewish pagans [BECNT, ICC, Lns]. The word 'Gentiles' refers to all people who are not Jews, but in this verse the term is used in a derogatory sense of any people who have not learned to trust in the God of the Jews [TH]. The term refers to all unbelievers [CC, NIBC, TH]. These unbelievers do not belong to the family which calls God their 'heavenly Father' [PNTC, WBC]. They do not know God [Lns]. They do not trust in God's fatherly care [EBC] and providence [ICC].

for[a] your(pl) heavenly Father knows[b] that you(pl)-need[c] all these-things.
LEXICON—a. γάρ (LN 89.23): 'for' [BECNT, CC, LN, PNTC; KJV], 'because' [LN], 'since' [NICNT], 'and' [BNTC; ESV, NCV, NET, NIV], 'and indeed' [NRSV], 'also' [NIGTC], 'besides' [NTC], 'but' [WBC; NLT, REB], not explicit [CEV, TEV]. This conjunction indicates cause or reason between events, though in some contexts the relationship is often remote or tenuous [LN].
   b. perf. act. indic. of οἶδα (LN 28.1) (BAGD 1.e. p. 556): 'to know' [BAGD, LN; all translations except WBC], 'to know about' [LN], 'to be well aware' [WBC]. The perfect tense of this verb has a present tense meaning [LN]. This verb means to possess information about [LN].
   c. pres. act. indic. of χρῄζω (LN 57.39) (BAGD p. 885): 'to need' [BAGD, LN; all translations except KJV], 'to have need' [BAGD, **LN**; KJV], 'to lack, to be without' [LN]. This verb means to lack something which is necessary and particularly needed [LN].
QUESTION—What relationship is indicated by this second γάρ 'for'?
It indicates the second reason that they should not become anxious about such things. God knows their needs and he will provide [BECNT, BNTC, CC, Lns, My, NIGTC, PNTC, NTC]. Such questions should not be asked by God's children [PNTC].

6:33 But[a] seek[b] first[c] the kingdom of God[d] and his righteousness,[e]
TEXT—Manuscripts reading τοῦ θεοῦ 'of God' are given a C rating by GNT to indicate that choosing it over a variant text was difficult. Those that include it are BECNT, NICNT; CEV, ESV, KJV, NCV, NLT, NRSV, REB, TEV. Those that omit it are BNTC, NIGTC, NTC, PNTC; GW, NASB, NET, NIV. Those that include it in brackets are CC, WBC.
LEXICON—a. δέ (LN 89.124) (BAGD 1.d. p. 171): 'but' [BAGD, BECNT, BNTC, CC, LN, NTC, PNTC; CEV, ESV, GW, KJV, NASB, NET, NIV, NRSV], 'rather' [BAGD, NICNT], 'instead' [NIGTC; TEV], 'so' [WBC], not explicit [NCV, NLT, REB]. This conjunction indicates contrast [LN].
   b. pres. act. impera. of ζητέω (LN 25.9) (BAGD 2.a. p. 339): 'to seek' [BECNT, BNTC, CC, NIGTC, NTC, PNTC; ESV, KJV, NASB, NIV, NLT], 'to keep seeking' [WBC], 'to pursue' [NET], 'to strive for' [NRSV], 'to be concerned for/with' [GW, TEV], 'to set your mind on' [REB], 'to desire, to want to' [LN], 'to try to obtain, to desire to possess' [BAGD]. The phrase ζητεῖτε πρῶτον 'seek first' is translated 'make it your priority to find' [NICNT], 'more than anything else put…first' [CEV], 'the thing you should want (most)' [NCV]. This verb means to desire to have or experience something, with the probable implication of making an attempt to realize one's desire [LN].
   c. πρῶτος (LN 60.46) (BAGD 2.c. p. 726): 'first' [BECNT, BNTC, LN, NIGTC, NTC, PNTC; ESV, GW, KJV, NASB, NIV, NRSV], 'most' [NCV], '(your) priority' [NICNT], 'above all' [NET], 'above all else' [WBC; NLT], 'above everything else' [TEV], 'before everything else'

[REB], 'more than anything else...first' [CEV], 'indeed' [CC]. This adverb describes what is done first in a series [LN].

d. βασιλεία (LN 37.64) (BAGD 3.b., 3.g. p. 135): 'kingdom' [BAGD, BECNT, BNTC, CC, NIGTC, NTC, PNTC, WBC; all versions except CEV], 'kingship' [NICNT], 'royal reign' [BAGD], 'rule, reign' [LN], '(God's) work' [CEV]. This verb means to rule as a king, with the implication of complete authority and the possibility of being able to pass on the right to rule to one's son or near kin [LN].

e. δικαιοσύνη (LN 88.13) (BAGD 2.b. p. 196): 'righteousness' [BAGD, BECNT, BNTC, CC, LN, NICNT, NIGTC, NTC, PNTC; ESV, KJV, NASB, NET, NIV, NRSV], 'justice' [REB], 'uprightness' [BAGD], 'doing what God requires, doing what is right' [LN]. The phrase τὴν δικαιοσύνην αὐτοῦ 'his righteousness' is translated 'the righteousness he demands' [WBC], '(do) what he wants' [CEV], 'doing what God wants' [NCV], 'what he requires of you' [TEV], 'what has his approval' [GW], '(live) righteously' [NLT]. This noun denotes the act of doing what God requires [LN].

QUESTION—What relationship is indicated by the use of the present imperative ζητεῖτε 'seek'?

It indicates that the activity is to be ongoing: 'keep seeking' [BNTC, Lns, NTC, PNTC, WBC]. It is used in contrast with the negated aorist imperative μὴ μεριμνήσητε 'do not worry' to indicate emphasis [CC].

QUESTION—What relationship is indicated by the use of πρῶτον 'first'?

It indicates that it is to be done above all else [CC, ICC, NICNT, WBC; CEV, NET, NLT, REB, TEV]. It is of first importance, the highest priority [NTC, PNTC], the dominant concern [BNTC], the most important thing of all [NIGTC]. God's kingdom should be their primary concern, the thing they should be concerned with before anything else [TH]. It expresses priority, one's deepest desire and resolve [NICNT]. To belong to the kingdom here and now should be a disciple's first concern [ICC]. If seeking God's kingdom is the first thing one strives for, any other striving is excluded and unnecessary, because the other needs will be supplied [My]. Seeking the kingdom ought to be the sole priority of the disciples and that toward which they devote their energy [WBC].

QUESTION—How does a person seek the kingdom of God?

1. To 'seek' God's kingdom is to submit to God's rule [TH]. It means to submit to God as one's king and obey him [PNTC, TRT], constantly seeking to do the things that God wills [PNTC]. It is to make God and his will one's dominant concern [BNTC]. Seeking God's 'kingship' means to resolve to live under God's direction and control [NICNT]. Disciples should seek to fully experience God's rule in their hearts and make his kingdom the center of their existence [WBC]. It does not deal with trying to bring about God's kingdom as an eschatological event [NICNT, WBC].

2. It is to seek to be admitted as a participant in the messianic kingdom [My], to seek to belong to the sphere of the working of God's sovereign

rule in the here and now [ICC]. 'Seeking' the kingdom means to desire an increasing participation in the Father's rule by grace in Christ and to enjoy the blessings as well [Lns]. Seeking the kingdom of God includes the effort to bring others into his kingdom [EBC, NTC]. They must pursue the things prayed for in the first three petitions of the Lord's prayer; they should submit to the saving reign of God, and also spread the news about it [EBC]. It means to be absorbed and persevering in a strenuous effort to acknowledge him as king in their own lives, and to work to see him recognized as king in the lives of others and in every sphere of human society [NTC].

QUESTION—What is meant by the phrase 'his righteousness' and how does a person seek this righteousness?

It is the righteousness that God requires [ICC, NIGTC, TH, WBC; CEV, GW, NCV, TEV]. The righteousness of God is both a demand and a gift [WBC]. This righteousness is a right standing before God, something that can only come as a gift from God, yet it involves right conduct as well [PNTC]. It is imputed and imparted, and it produces active effort on their part [NTC]. It is the lifestyle that should accompany a concern for God's kingdom [BECNT]. It is a life lived in submission to God, as Jesus describes it in this discourse [EBC]. It is doing what God requires [TH], living the way God requires, as the distinctive lifestyle of disciples [NICNT], living according to God's will [TRT]. It is obedience to God's will [NIBC]. It is the moral righteousness that God imparts to believers to help them attain the kingdom [My].

and[a] all these-things[b] will-be-added[c] to-you(pl).

LEXICON—a. καί: 'and' [BECNT, BNTC, CC, NIGTC, NTC, PNTC, WBC; all versions except CEV, GW, NCV], 'then' [NICNT; CEV, GW, NCV].

b. ταῦτα πάντα (BAGD 1.e.β. p. 632): This phrase is translated 'all these things' [BECNT, BNTC, CC, NTC, PNTC, WBC; ESV, GW, KJV, NASB, NET, NIV, NRSV], 'all these' [BAGD], 'all these other things' [NICNT; CEV, TEV], 'all these other things you need' [NCV], 'everything you need' [NLT], 'all the rest' [REB].

c. fut. pass. indic. of προστίθημι (LN 57.78) (BAGD 2. P. 719): 'to be added' [BECNT, CC; ESV, KJV, NASB], 'to be granted' [LN, NIGTC], 'to be granted as an extra gift' [NTC], 'to be given' [LN, NICNT, PNTC; NET, NIV], 'to be given as well' [NRSV], 'to be given in addition' [BNTC], 'to be provided' [LN; GW], 'to be granted' [LN]. The phrase προστεθήσεται ὑμῖν 'will be added to you' is translated 'will also be yours' [WBC], 'will be yours as well' [CEV], 'he will give you' [NLT], 'he will provide you with' [TEV], 'will come to you' [REB]. This verb means to place something at the disposal of someone else [LN].

QUESTION—What relationship is indicated by καί 'and'?

It indicates a logical conclusion, showing a causal relation; if you seek the kingdom and God's righteousness first, the rest will be added [BECNT, ICC, My, NICNT].

QUESTION—What are all the things that will be added?

'All these things' refer to 'all these things' in 6:32 where it refers to food, drink, and clothing [ICC, NTC]. The verb 'will be given you' is the divine passive that means the Father who knows your needs will supply those needs [NICNT]. God is the agent of the future passive verb 'will be added' [BECNT, ICC, TH, WBC]. God will provide all the other material things the disciples need [CC, EBC, NIGTC]. God will provide the clothing they need [WBC].

6:34 Therefore^a do- not -worry^b about tomorrow,

LEXICON—a. οὖν (LN 89.50): 'therefore' [BECNT, CC, LN, NTC, PNTC; ESV, KJV, NASB, NIV], 'so' [BNTC, LN; GW, NCV, NLT, NRSV, REB, TEV], 'so then' [LN, WBC; NET], 'then' [LN, NIGTC], 'consequently, accordingly' [LN], not explicit [CEV]. This conjunction indicates result, often implying the conclusion of a process of reasoning [LN].

b. aorist act. subj. of μεριμνάω (LN 25.225) (BAGD 1. p. 505): 'to worry about' [BECNT, BNTC, CC, NIGTC; all versions except ESV, KJV, REB], 'to be worried about' [LN], 'to be anxious about' [BAGD, LN, NTC, PNTC; ESV, REB], 'to have anxiety' [BAGD], 'to be filled with anxiety' [WBC], 'to take thought for' [KJV]. This verb means to have an anxious concern, based on apprehension about possible danger or misfortune [LN]. See this verb at 6:25, 6:27, 6:28, 6:31.

QUESTION—What relationship is indicated by οὖν 'therefore'?

It indicates a conclusion to the section [BECNT, Lns]. It indicates a conclusion to be drawn based on all that has been said [NTC]. It indicates an inference to be drawn from what was said from 6:25 onwards [My]. It indicates a conclusion to be drawn from what was just said about how the personal needs will be met for those seeking God's kingdom and righteousness [EBC, PNTC].

for^a tomorrow will-worry^b about-itself.^c

LEXICON—a. γάρ (LN 89.23): 'for' [BECNT, BNTC, CC, LN, NIGTC, NTC, PNTC, WBC; ESV, KJV, NASB, NET, NIV, NLT, NRSV], 'because' [LN; NCV], 'after all' [GW], not explicit [NICNT; CEV, REB, TEV]. This conjunction indicates cause or reason between events, though in some contexts the relationship is often remote or tenuous [LN].

b. fut. act. indic. of μεριμνάω. 'to worry about' [BNTC, CC, NICNT, NIGTC; GW, NET, NIV], 'to be anxious for/about' [NTC, PNTC; ESV], 'to have its own share of anxiety' [WBC], 'to have worries' [TEV], 'to care for' [BECNT; NASB], 'to take care of' [CEV], 'to take thought for' [KJV], 'to look after' [REB]. This phrase is translated 'because tomorrow will have its own worries' [NCV], 'for tomorrow will bring its own worries' [NLT; similarly NRSV].

c. ἑαυτοῦ (LN 92.25): 'itself' [BECNT, BNTC, LN, NIGTC, NTC, PNTC; CEV, ESV, GW, KJV, NASB, NET, NIV, REB], 'its own (share of anxiety/worries)' [WBC; NCV, NLT, NRSV, TEV]. This pronoun is a reflexive reference to a person or thing spoken or written about.

QUESTION—What does this statement mean?

It is a way of saying that worry should always be deferred [Lns, NIGTC, PNTC], which of course would mean that one should never get around to doing it [Lns, NIGTC, PNTC, WBC]. Jesus may be using a bit of humor by personifying 'tomorrow' and having it worry [My, NTC]. It means that tomorrow will bring its own anxieties [BNTC, WBC]. Tomorrow will have worries of its own [TH; TEV].

Sufficient[a] to[b] the day[c] (is) its-own trouble.[d]

LEXICON—a. ἀρκετός (LN **59.45**) (BAGD p. 107): 'sufficient' [BAGD, BNTC, CC, **LN**, NIGTC, PNTC; ESV, KJV], 'enough' [BAGD, BECNT, NTC; all versions except ESV, KJV, TEV], 'adequate' [BAGD, LN]. The phrase ἀρκετὸν τῇ ἡμέρᾳ 'sufficient to the day' is translated 'each day has its own quite sufficient supply' [WBC], 'there is no need to add to' [TEV]. The position of this word in the sentence is emphatic [WBC]. This adjective describes what is sufficient for some purpose and accordingly resulting in satisfaction [LN].

b. There is no lexical entry for this word, the relationship being indicated by the use of the dative case of τῇ ἡμέρᾳ 'to the day'. It is represented in translation as 'to' [ESV, KJV], 'for' [BNTC, CC, NICNT, NIGTC, PNTC; NRSV], not explicit [BECNT, NTC, WBC; CEV, GW, NASB, NCV, NET, NIV, NLT, REB, TEV].

c. ἡμέρα (LN 67.178) (BAGD 2. p. 346): 'day' [BAGD, BECNT, BNTC, CC, LN, NIGTC, NTC, PNTC; ESV, GW, KJV, NASB, NCV, NIV, REB, TEV], 'today' [NICNT; CEV, NET, NLT, NRSV]. According to Hebrew reckoning (as reflected in the NT), the day was a period of time beginning at sunset and ending at the following sunset [LN].

d. κακία (LN **22.5**) (BAGD 2. p. 397): 'trouble' [BAGD, BECNT, BNTC, NTC, PNTC; all versions except CEV, KJV], 'hardships' [**LN**], 'difficulties' [LN], 'misfortune' [BAGD], 'evil' [**LN**, NIGTC; KJV], 'wickedness' [CC], '(enough) to worry about' [CEV]. This noun denotes a state involving difficult and distressing circumstances [LN].

QUESTION—What κακία 'trouble' is implied?

It refers to the difficulties common to life [CC], whatever brings trouble to people [TH], the problems that call for strength and resourcefulness [BNTC]. It is trouble, pain, and burdens that occur naturally [Lns]. It is the evil that causes people to feel anxious, including such things as drought or robbery [NIGTC].

QUESTION—What did Jesus mean by this saying?

Each day brings us enough challenge so that we don't need to add to it by borrowing some from the next day [CC, My]. Anxiety can be defeated by restricting our concerns to those of the present day, because each day has enough trouble to keep us occupied [PNTC]. The present has enough troubles such that we don't need to go borrowing more from tomorrow to occupy ourselves with [Lns, TH]. Anxiety about possible problems in the future can paralyze one's ability to deal effectively with real problems in the present [BNTC].

DISCOURSE UNIT—7:1–12 [ICC]. The topic is the treatment of one's neighbor.

DISCOURSE UNIT—7:1–6 [CEV, ESV, NASB, NCV, NET, NIV, NLT, TEV]. The topic is be careful about judging others [NCV], judging others [CEV, ESV, NASB, NIV, TEV], do not judge [NET], do not judge others [NLT].

DISCOURSE UNIT—7:1–5 [GW, NRSV]. The topic is the sermon on a mountain continues: Stop judging [GW], judging others [NRSV].

7:1 Do- not -judge,[a] so-that[b] you(pl)- not -be-judged.[c]

LEXICON—a. pres. act. impera. of κρίνω (LN 56.30) (BAGD 6.a. p. 452): 'to judge' [BAGD, BECNT, BNTC, CC, NICNT, NIGTC, PNTC; ESV, GW, KJV, NASB, NET, NIV, NRSV, REB], 'to judge other people/others' [NCV, NLT, TEV], 'to judge unfairly' [WBC], 'to pass judgment upon' [BAGD], 'to pass judgment on others' [NTC], 'to judge as guilty' [LN], 'to condemn' [LN], 'to condemn others' [CEV]. The present tense of this imperative is translated 'stop judging' [GW], 'do not indeed judge' (to indicate emphasis) [CC]. This verb means to judge a person to be guilty and liable to punishment [LN].

b. ἵνα (LN 89.59) (BAGD I.1.c. p. 377): 'so that' [BECNT, CC, LN, NICNT, NIGTC, NTC; NASB, NET, NRSV, TEV], 'that' [BAGD; ESV, KJV], 'in order that' [BAGD, PNTC], 'in order to, for the purpose of' [LN]. The phrase ἵνα μή 'so that…not' is translated 'lest' [BNTC, WBC], 'and God won't' [CEV], 'and you will not (be)' [NLT, REB], 'or you will (be)' [NCV, NIV]. This conjunction indicates purpose for events and states (sometimes occurring in highly elliptical contexts) [LN].

c. aorist pass. subj. of κρίνω (LN 56.30) (BAGD 4.b.α. p. 452): 'to be judged' [BAGD, BECNT, BNTC, CC, NICNT, NIGTC, PNTC; all versions except CEV, TEV], 'to be judged in a similar way' [WBC], 'to have judgment passed (on yourselves)' [NTC], 'to judge as guilty, to condemn' [LN]. The phrase ἵνα μὴ κριθῆτε 'so that you not be judged' is translated 'and God won't condemn you' [CEV], 'so that God will not judge you' [TEV]. This verb means to judge a person to be guilty and liable to punishment [LN].

QUESTION—What is the relationship between this section and what has preceded it?

Demands for superior righteousness and perfection can foster a judgmental attitude [EBC, Lns], which he addresses in 7:1–5, while demands for love may foster a lack of real discernment, which he addresses in 7:6 [EBC]. This saying takes up a new topic that is not directly related to what precedes it, although it continues the general idea of how a person fits into God's reckoning, which is a theme that runs throughout chapter six [NIGTC]. There does not seem to be much connection with preceding material [NICNT, TH], although there is some logical connection with the call to perfection in 5:48 and the exhortation to forgive in 6:12, 14–15 [TH].

QUESTION—What kind of judging is Jesus prohibiting?

The verb κρίνω can refer to legal decisions made at court, but it is also used more generally for forming judgments and reaching conclusions about things and people [NICNT]. The verb is used generally of passing a verdict [PNTC], and here it is specifically used of passing an adverse verdict of condemnation [ICC, NIGTC, PNTC; CEV]. Jesus' prohibition should not be taken as prohibiting all judging or discerning of right and wrong [BNTC, EBC, ICC, Lns, My, NAC, NIBC, NICNT, NIGTC, WBC], nor the need for spiritual discernment [BECNT]. Even the moral distinctions appearing in this sermon show that decisive judgments must be made [My, WBC]. Here the emphasis is on criticizing other people's failings [NICNT, WBC], and being censorious and judgmental [BECNT, BNTC, EBC]. He is warning against being a fault-finder who judges harshly, self-righteously, or mercilessly [NTC]. He is warning them that to make oneself the judge of another is to usurp the place of God as judge [EBC, ICC].

QUESTION—What are the implications of the use of the present tense (negated) imperative?

1. It means that they should stop judging others [NIBC; GW]. It means that they should not make a practice of judging others [PNTC], or should resist doing that as a course of action [Lns].
2. As in other places in the sermon, the shift to a present tense imperative indicates a shift of topic, and adds emphasis [CC].
3. There is no particular significance to the tense [BECNT].

QUESTION—What relationship is indicated by ἵνα 'so that'?

There may be considerable overlap between the two options shown below.

1. It indicates the purpose of not judging others, which is to avoid being judged [BECNT, EBC, NIGTC, PNTC]. Purpose is implied by the wording of BNTC, WBC, and probably LN, NICNT, NTC; NASB, NET, NRSV, TEV.
2. It indicates what will result from not judging, which is being spared from judgment [CC]. Result is implied by the wording of CEV, NCV, NIV, NLT, REB.

QUESTION—Who would judge the person who judges others?

God will judge such a person [BAGD, BECNT, BNTC, CC, EBC, ICC, Lns, My, NAC, NIBC, NICNT, NIGTC, NTC, TH, WBC; CEV, TEV]. The use of the *divine passive* 'be judged' is a way of referring to God as the agent of the action [BECNT, NICNT, WBC]. This pertains to the final judgment [ICC, Lns, PNTC]. Such a person is usurping the place of God and therefore becomes answerable to God [EBC]. Although it is possible to take this to refer to the judgment other people will pass on us, what really matters is the judgment of God. To be quick to call others to account is to invite God to call us to account [PNTC].

7:2 **For with what judgment[a] you(pl)-judge you(pl)-will-be-judged,**

LEXICON—a. κρίμα (LN 56.30) (BAGD 6. p. 451): 'judgment' [BAGD], 'condemnation' [LN]. The phrase ἐν ᾧ κρίματι κρίνετε κριθήσεσθε 'with what judgment you judge you will be judged' [PNTC; KJV] is also translated 'you will be judged by the judgment with which you judge' [CC], 'on the basis of the act of judgment by which you judge you shall yourself be judged' [NIGTC], 'in the way you judge, you will be judged' [NASB; similarly NIV], 'the way you judge others will be the way you are judged' [BECNT], 'with the judgment you use, you will be judged' [BNTC], 'in accordance with the measure whereby you measure, it will be measured back to you' [NTC], 'as you judge others, so you will yourselves be judged' [REB], 'with the judgment you pronounce, you will be judged' [ESV], 'with the judgment you make, you will be judged' [NRSV], 'you will be judged in the same way you judge others' [NCV], 'by the standard you judge, you will be judged' [NET], 'you will be judged by the same standard you use to judge others' [GW; similarly NICNT, WBC], 'you will be treated as you treat others' [NLT], 'God will judge you in the same way you judge others' [TEV], 'God will be as hard on you as you are on others!' [CEV]. This noun denotes the act of judging another person to be guilty and liable to punishment [LN].

QUESTION—What relationship is indicated by γάρ 'for'?

It indicates the reason or motivation for not judging others [BECNT, ICC, PNTC]. This is a reciprocal principle to 7:1 [NICNT].

QUESTION—By whom would the person judging others be judged?

1. God will judge such a person [BNTC, EBC, ICC, Lns, NIGTC, TH, TRT, WBC; CEV, TEV]. God will judge us with the same severity with which we judge others [TH]. By not being forgiving and loving, the judgmental person testifies to his own arrogance and impenitence, and thus shuts himself out from God's forgiveness [EBC].

2. Other people and also God will judge such a person [NAC, NIBC, NICNT, NTC, PNTC]. Society will not tolerate a critical person who exempts himself from standards to which he expects others to conform. Still more seriously, is the judgment of God who maintains impartial judgment [NICNT]. Such people will find that their peers will pass similar

MATTHEW 7:2 231

judgment on them, but the emphasis is surely on being judged by God at the last day [PNTC].

And with what measure^a you(pl)-measure^b it-will-be-measured to-you(pl).

LEXICON—a. μέτρον (LN 81.1) (BAGD 1.a. p. 515): 'measure' [BAGD, CC, LN, NICNT, NIGTC, NTC, PNTC, WBC; ESV, KJV, NET, NIV, NRSV, REB], 'evaluation' [BECNT], 'standard' [GW, NLT], 'standard of measure' [NASB], 'rules' [TEV], 'amount' [NCV], not explicit [CEV]. In ancient sales what was bought and what was sold was often measured with the same measuring instrument to insure equality [NICNT, NIGTC, TH]. This noun denotes a unit of measurement, either of length or volume [LN].

b. pres. act. indic. of μετρέω (LN 57.92) (BAGD 2. p. 514): 'to measure' [BAGD], 'to give, to apportion' [LN]. The clause ἐν ᾧ μέτρῳ μετρεῖτε μετρηθήσεται ὑμῖν 'with what measure you measure it will be measured to you' is translated 'with whatever measure you measure to others, it will also be measured to you' [WBC; similarly PNTC; KJV], 'with the measure you use things will be measured out to you' [BNTC], 'by means of the measure with which you measure, it shall be measured to you' [NIGTC], 'in accordance with the measure whereby you measure, it will be measure back to you' [NTC], 'the same measure which you measure out will be measured out to you' [NICNT], 'the measure you give will be the measure you get' [NRSV], 'the evaluation you give will be the evaluation you get' [BECNT], 'it will be measured to you by the measure with which you measure' [CC], 'with the measure you use, it will be measured to you' [ESV, NIV], 'the measure you use will be the measure you receive' [NET], 'by your standard of measure, it will be measured to you' [NASB], 'whatever measure you deal out to others will be dealt to you' [REB], 'the standards you use for others will be applied to you' [GW], 'the standard you use in judging is the standard to which you will be judged' [NLT], 'he will treat you exactly as you treat them' [CEV], 'he will apply to you the same rules you apply to others' [TEV], 'the amount you give to others will be given to you' [NCV]. This verb means to give a measured portion to someone [LN].

QUESTION—What is the function of this clause?

The principle about judgment that is stated in the preceding clause is now reinforced by quoting a proverbial saying that can be applied to a variety of situations [EBC, ICC, NICNT]. In Mark 4:24 it is used it in reference to paying attention to Jesus' teaching and responding to it [EBC, NICNT, TH]. In a slightly different form in Luke 6:38 it encouraged financial generosity by saying that God will give to a person as that person has given to others [NICNT, TH, WBC].

1. In this verse 'measure' means much the same as 'judgment' [CC, EBC, ICC, NICNT, PNTC, NTC, TH, TRT, WBC] and the point is that one must expect the same standard of measurement to be applied to both

parties. This reinforces the preceding statement about judgment [PNTC]. The punishment fits the crime [NICNT].
2. The measure in this parable is the same as the saying in Luke 6:38: 'the amount you give to others will be given to you' [NCV].
3. The measure in this parable involves both how we evaluate others as well as how we give to others [NIGTC].

7:3 **And why do-you(sg)-look-at^a the speck^b in your(sg) brother's^c eye,**

LEXICON—a. pres. act. indic. of βλέπω (LN 24.7) (BAGD 1.a. p. 143): 'to look at' [BAGD, BECNT, PNTC; NASB, NIV, NRSV, REB, TEV], 'to see' [BAGD, BNTC, LN, NIGTC; CEV, ESV, GW, NET], 'to see so well' [WBC], 'to try to see' [CC], 'to gaze' [NTC], 'to notice' [LN; NCV], 'to focus on' [NICNT], 'to behold' [KJV], 'to worry about' [NLT], 'to become aware of, to glance at' [LN]. This verb means to see, frequently in the sense of becoming aware of or taking notice of something [LN].
b. κάρφος (LN **3.66**) (BAGD p. 405): 'speck' [BAGD, BECNT, BNTC, CC, LN, NIGTC, NTC, PNTC, WBC; CEV, ESV, NASB, NET, NLT, NRSV, TEV], 'speck of sawdust' [NIV, REB], 'piece of sawdust' [GW], 'little piece of dust' [NCV], 'mote' [KJV], 'chip' [BAGD] 'splinter' [LN, NICNT]. This noun denotes a small piece of wood, chaff, or even straw [LN]. The reference is not specific and refers to any small object that could be in an eye [PNTC], any bit of foreign matter [EBC].
c. ἀδελφός (LN 11.89) (BAGD 4. p. 116): 'brother' [BNTC, CC, LN, NICNT, NTC, PNTC; ESV, KJV, NASB, NET, NIV, REB, TEV], 'brother or sister' [NIGTC, WBC], 'neighbor' [BAGD, LN; NRSV], 'friend' [CEV, NCV, NLT], 'fellow disciple' [BECNT], 'another believer' [GW]. This noun denotes a person who lives close beside others and who thus by implication is a part of a so-called 'in-group,' that is, the group with which an individual identifies both ethnically and culturally [LN].

QUESTION—What kind of questions are asked in 7:3–4?
These are rhetorical questions that are given in order to set the stage for the exhortation addressed to the hypocrite in 7:5 [BECNT, ICC, NIGTC].

QUESTION—Who is included in the category of 'brother'?
It is a fellow disciple [CC, NICNT]. Jesus is addressing the Christian community [EBC, WBC].

QUESTION—Why did Jesus talk about a speck in someone's eye?
An insignificant speck of sawdust is used metaphorically to refer to a person's insignificant or slight shortcoming [BECNT, ICC, PNTC, WBC]. It refers to an insignificant wrong that others to do us [TH].

but^a the log^b in your(sg)-own eye you-do- not -notice?^c
LEXICON—a. δέ (LN 89.124): 'but' [BECNT, BNTC, CC, LN, NIGTC, WBC; CEV, ESV, KJV, NASB, NCV, NET, NRSV], 'and' [NICNT, PNTC;

GW, NIV, TEV], 'while' [NTC], 'when' [NLT], 'on the other hand' [LN], not explicit [REB]. This conjunction indicates contrast [LN].

  b. δοκός (LN **7.78**) (BAGD p. 203): 'log' [WBC; CEV, ESV, NASB, NLT, NRSV, TEV], 'beam' [BECNT, CC, LN, NIGTC, NTC; KJV], 'wooden beam' [BNTC; GW], 'beam of wood' [BAGD; NET], 'plank' [NICNT, PNTC; NIV, REB], 'big piece of wood' [NCV]. This noun denotes a beam of wood [LN]. It is lumber used in building [TH], such as a heavy timber used for supporting a roof [BECNT, NIBC, NIGTC, NTC, PNTC] or a main beam in a floor [PNTC].

  c. pres. act. indic. of κατανοέω (LN **24.51**) (BAGD 1. p. 415): 'to notice' [BAGD, BECNT, BNTC, LN, NICNT, NIGTC, PNTC; CEV, ESV, GW, NASB, NCV, NRSV], 'to consider' [CC; KJV], 'to observe' [NTC], 'to pay attention to' [NIV], 'to discover' [LN]. The phrase οὐ κατανοεῖς 'do not notice' is translated 'fail to notice' [NICNT, WBC], 'fail to see' [NET], 'pay no attention to' [TEV], 'with never a thought for' [REB]. This entire clause is translated 'when you have a log in your own' [NLT]. This verb means to discover something through direct observation, with the implication of also thinking about it [LN].

QUESTION—Why did Jesus talk about a log in one's own eye?

The reference to having a log in one's eye is a ludicrous exaggeration in contrast to a tiny speck of sawdust in another's eye. The huge log is used metaphorically to refer to the person's own outrageously huge failures [WBC], one's sizable moral defects [ICC], the enormous sins committed against God [TH]. This is hyperbole [BECNT, EBC, PNTC].

7:4 Or how[a] will-you-say (to) your(sg) brother, "Let[b] (me) take-out[c] the speck from your(sg) eye," and behold,[d] a-log (is) in your(sg) eye?

  LEXICON—a. πῶς (LN **92.16**) (BAGD 1.c. p. 732): 'how?' [BAGD, LN]. The phrase πῶς ἐρεῖς 'how will you say' [CC, PNTC, WBC; KJV], is translated 'how can you say' [BNTC, NICNT, NIGTC, NTC; all versions except KJV, NLT, TEV], 'how dare you say' [BECNT; TEV], 'how can you think of saying' [NLT]. This conjunction is an interrogative reference to means [LN].

  b. aorist. act. impera. of ἀφίημι (LN **13.140**) (BAGD 4. p. 126): 'to let' [BAGD, BECNT, BNTC, CC, **LN**, NICNT, PNTC, WBC; all versions], 'to allow' [BAGD, LN, NIGTC], 'to permit' [BAGD]. This verb means to leave it to someone to do something, with the implication of distancing oneself from the event [LN].

  c. aorist act. subj. of ἐκβάλλω (BAGD 3. p. 237): 'to take out' [BAGD, BECNT, CC, NTC, PNTC, WBC; all versions except KJV, NET, NLT], 'to remove' [BAGD, BNTC; NET], 'to get out' [NICNT], 'to cast out' [NIGTC], 'to pull out' [KJV], 'to get rid of' [NLT].

  d. ἰδού (LN **91.13**) (BAGD 1.b. p. 370): 'behold' [BAGD, BNTC, WBC; KJV, NASB], 'see' [BAGD], 'look' [BAGD, BECNT, CC, LN, NIGTC, NTC], 'listen, pay attention' [LN], not explicit [PNTC; CEV, ESV, GW,

NIV, NLT, NRSV, TEV]. The phrase 'and behold' is translated 'when all the time' [NICNT; REB], 'when all the while' [NIV], 'look at yourself' [NCV]. This particle is a prompter of attention [LN], and serves to emphasize the following statement [LN, WBC].

QUESTION—What relationship is indicated by the conjunction ἤ 'or'?
   This adds another possibility that is really an impossibility since it is absurd to think anyone with a plank in his eye would pose such a question to someone with only a speck in his eye [PNTC].

7:5 Hypocrite,^a first^b throw-out the log out-of your(sg) eye, and then you(sg)-will-see-clearly^c (enough) to-take-out the speck out-of your(sg) brother's eye.

LEXICON—a. ὑποκριτής (LN 88.228) (BAGD p. 845): 'hypocrite' [BAGD, LN; all translations], 'pretender' [BAGD, LN], 'one who acts hypocritically' [LN]. This vocative form is translated 'you hypocrite' [BECNT, BNTC, NICNT, NTC; all versions except CEV, KJV, NLT], 'thou hypocrite' [KJV], 'you are nothing but show-offs' [CEV]. Emphasis is shown in translation by the use of an exclamation point (!) after this word [CC, NIGTC, PNTC, WBC; CEV, GW, NCV, NET, NLT, REB, TEV]. It is a derivative of ὑποκρίνομαι 'to pretend', and denotes one who pretends to be other than he really is [LN].
   b. πρῶτον (LN 60.46) (BAGD 2.a. p. 726): 'first' [BAGD, LN; all translations], 'in the first place, to begin with' [BAGD]. This adverb describes what is first in a series involving time, space, or set [LN].
   c. fut. act. indic. of διαβλέπω (LN **24.35**) (BAGD 2. p. 181): 'to see clearly' [BAGD, **LN**; all versions except NLT], 'to see how' [CEV], 'to see well' [NLT], 'to be able to distinguish clearly' [LN]. The modifier 'enough' is added for clarity by NTC, WBC; NLT. This verb means to be able to see clearly or plainly [LN].

QUESTION—What is the meaning of ὑποκριτής 'hypocrite'?
   The term hypocrite was used in 6:2 of a person who pretends to be good but is actually evil and knows that he being deceptive. But here it may refer to someone who is carried away by his own acting and deceives himself, or it may mean that this person deceives himself into thinking he is acting for the best interests of God and man and also deceives onlookers [EBC]. It is to have an arrogant presumption of knowledge of others' faults and a profound ignorance of our own [PNTC]. It shows that there is deception, whether of oneself or of others [WBC]. It is someone who fails to examine himself and whose estimation of himself is too high [NTC]. Here it means to be blind to one's own failures [BNTC, My, NICNT, NIGTC], to criticize others while being too complacent about one's own moral life [BNTC].

DISCOURSE UNIT—7:6 [GW, NRSV]. The topic is don't throw pearls to pigs [GW], profaning the holy [NRSV].

7:6 Do- not -give[a] the holy[b] (thing) to-dogs,[c]

LEXICON—a. aorist act. subj. or aorist act. impera. of δίδωμι (LN 57.71) (BAGD 1.a. p. 192): 'to give' [BAGD, LN; all translations except NLT], 'to waste' [NLT]. This verb means to give an object, usually implying value [LN].
- b. ἅγιος (LN 53.46) (BAGD 2.a.α. p. 9): 'the holy thing' [CC], 'holy things' [NCV], 'what is holy' [BAGD, BECNT, NIGTC, NTC, PNTC, WBC; ESV, GW, NASB, NLT, NET, NRSV, REB, TEV], 'that which is holy' [KJV], 'what is sacred' [BNTC; NIV], 'sacred thing' [NICNT], 'what belongs to God' [CEV], 'dedicated' [LN]. This adjective describes what pertains to being dedicated or consecrated to the service of God [LN].
- c. κύων (LN 4.34) (BAGD 1. p. 461): 'dog' [BAGD, LN; all translations except NLT], 'people who are unholy' [NLT]. This noun denotes a dog, either a street dog or a watch dog [LN]. This may well be a proverbial saying that eventually came to be taken in a non-literal sense [BAGD].

QUESTION—Why is this verse about the holy thing and pearls inserted here?

It is an independent saying presented as a metaphor with no indication of how it might be applied [NICNT]. This detached saying may be inserted here only because it is another saying of Jesus [WBC]. Some think this is a proverbial saying [CC, ICC, PNTC, WBC] or an adaptation of a proverbial saying to stress the value of holy things and warn against profaning them [EBC]. It counterbalances the warning in the previous verses [BECNT, EBC, ICC, Lns, My, NICNT, NTC, PNTC] since the command not to judge has its limits [Lns, My]. They should not be too severe, but then they should not be too lax either [ICC]. After warning against being judgmental, he then balances it by warning against the opposite problem of extreme gullibility; that is, they should neither be censorious nor naïve simpletons [BECNT, EBC]. Disciples should not be quick to judge, but also they should recognize that their pearls of wisdom may not be appreciated by some, so they should not keep offering the gospel to those who contemptuously reject it [PNTC].

QUESTION—What is meant by not giving the 'holy thing' to dogs?

In the metaphor, the 'holy thing' means something that is sacred and it might be referring to the consecrated food in the temple which could be eaten only by the priests and their families and was not allowed to be thrown to the dogs [NICNT]. It could mean meat from a sacrificial offering which dogs would want [ICC, PNTC]. Dogs were regarded as being unclean animals that could not be given holy things [PNTC]. The 'holy thing' refers to all the things in general that might be classified as holy [TH]. Or the holy thing is not part of the metaphor and refers directly to the holy gospel of the kingdom of the kingdom [EBC].

QUESTION—What is the point of this metaphor?

This stresses the value of holy things and warns against profaning them. The holy thing stands for the gospel of the kingdom [EBC, NICNT, PNTC, WBC]. The dogs refer to people who are unreceptive to the message [BNTC, WBC], who are vicious and vile tempered [Lns], and reject the gospel [EBC,

TRT]. Although the gospel is to be offered to all, there is a limit to the time that it is to be offered to obstinate rejecters [PNTC]. Disciples must be discriminating in sharing the sacred things of the gospel [NICNT]. It is necessary to limit the time and energy a disciple directs towards the hardhearted [ICC]. He is commending a completely God-centered life, and is saying that compared to God, everything and everyone else is comparable to a dog or a pig, with which our resources should not be expended [NIGTC]. Another view is that the holy things are other disciples, and one must not cast them before dogs or pigs by wanton and unjust criticism [CC].

nor[a] throw[b] your(pl) pearls[c] before[d] pigs,[e]
LEXICON—a. μηδέ (LN 69.7) (BAGD 1.b. p. 517): 'nor' [BNTC, LN], 'or' [NICNT; GW, NET], 'and (do) not/don't' [BAGD, BECNT, CC, LN, NIGTC, NTC, PNTC, WBC; ESV, NASB, NCV, NRSV], '(do) not/don't' [NIV, NLT, REB, TEV], 'neither' [LN; KJV], not explicit [CEV, TEV]. This conjunction is a combination of the negative particles μή 'not,' and the postpositive conjunction δέ 'and' [LN].
  b. aorist act. subj. or aorist act. impera. of βάλλω (LN 15.215) (BAGD 1.b. p. 130): 'to throw' [BAGD, BECNT, CC, LN, NIGTC, PNTC; all versions except CEV, KJV], 'to throw down' [BNTC, NICNT; CEV], 'to fling' [NTC], 'to set' [WBC], 'to cast' [KJV].
  c. μαργαρίτης (LN **2.43**) (BAGD 1. p. 491): 'pearl' [BAGD, LN; all translations]. This noun denotes a smooth, rounded concretion formed within the shells of certain mollusks and valued as a gem because of its lustrous color [LN].
  d. ἔμπροσθεν (LN 83.33) (BAGD 2.a. p. 257): 'before' [BAGD, BNTC, CC, LN, NIGTC, NTC, WBC; ESV, KJV, NASB, NCV, NET, NRSV], 'in front of' [BAGD, LN, NICNT, PNTC; CEV, TEV], 'to' [BECNT; GW, NIV, NLT, REB]. This preposition denotes a position in front of an object, whether animate or inanimate, which is regarded as having a spatial orientation of front and back [LN].
  e. χοῖρος (LN 4.36) (BAGD p. 883): 'pig' [BECNT, LN, NICNT, PNTC, WBC; ESV, GW, NCV, NET, NIV, NLT, REB, TEV], 'swine' [BAGD, BNTC, CC, NIGTC; CEV, KJV, NASB, NRSV], 'hog' [NTC]. References to pigs in the OT frequently involve very strong connotations of uncleanness and disgust, though references in the NT are somewhat more neutral [LN].
QUESTION—What is the point of this metaphor?
The pearls represent something that is of high value that must be kept from misuse [NICNT]. Some think the pearls stand for the gospel of the kingdom [ICC, Lns, NICNT, PNTC, WBC]. The pigs, like the dogs, refer to people who give clear evidence of rejecting the gospel with contempt and scorn [EBC, PNTC]. What is precious is not to be given to people who have no appreciation for it [PNTC]. Or, the pearls represent other disciples, who are not to be mistreated by severe criticism [CC]. Alternatively, the pearls and

whatever is holy represent a person's resources, which should be completely dedicated to God and his service [NIGTC].

lest^a they-trample^b them with their feet^c and having-turned^d tear- you(pl) to-pieces.^e

LEXICON—a. μήποτε (LN **89.62**) (BAGD 2.b.γ. p. 519): 'lest' [BNTC, CC, LN, NTC, PNTC, WBC; ESV, KJV], 'in order that ... not' [BAGD, **LN**], 'so that ... not' [LN]. This word is represented in translation as 'otherwise they will' [GW, NET], 'or they will' [BECNT, NIGTC; NASB, NRSV], 'they will only...they will' [CEV], 'they will only' [REB], 'they will only (turn)...they will only (trample)' [TEV], 'they will' [NLT], '(pigs) will only' [NCV], 'or they may' [NICNT], 'if you do they may' [NIV]. This conjunction indicates negative purpose, often with the implication of apprehension [LN].
   b. fut. act. indic. of καταπατέω (LN **19.52**) (BAGD 1.a. p. 415): 'to trample' [BAGD, BECNT, BNTC, CC, **LN**, NICNT, NIGTC, NTC, PNTC; all versions], 'to trample down' [WBC]. This verb means to step down forcibly upon, often with the implication of destruction or ruin [LN].
   c. πούς (LN 8.49) (BAGD 1.a. p. 696): 'foot' [BAGD, BECNT, BNTC, CC, LN, NICNT, NIGTC, NTC, PNTC; ESV, KJV, NASB, NET, NIV, NRSV, TEV], 'hoof' [WBC], not explicit [CEV, GW, NCV, NLT, REB]. The phrase ἐν τοῖς ποσὶν 'with (their) feet' is translated 'under their feet' [KJV, NET, NIV], 'under foot' [BNTC, NICNT, NIGTC; NRSV], 'underfoot' [BNTC; ESV, TEV], 'all over them' [CEV].
   d. aorist pass. participle of στρέφω (LN 16.14) (BAGD 2.a.α. p. 771): 'to turn' [BAGD, BNTC, CC, LN, NIGTC, NTC, PNTC, WBC; all versions except GW, KJV, NET], 'to turn on you' [BECNT], 'to turn round/around' [NICNT; NET], 'to turn again' [KJV], not explicit [GW]. This verb means to cause something to turn [LN].
   e. aorist act. subj. of ῥήγνυμι (LN 19.31) (BAGD 1. p. 735): 'to tear to pieces' [BECNT, NTC, PNTC; GW, NASB, NET, NIV, REB], 'to tear in pieces' [BAGD, BNTC], 'to tear apart' [NIGTC], 'to rend' [CC; KJV], 'to savage' [NICNT], 'to slash with their teeth' [WBC], 'to attack' [CEV, ESV, NCV, NLT, TEV], 'to maul' [NRSV], 'to tear, to rip' [LN]. This verb means to tear, rip, or burst, either from internal or external forces, with the implication of sudden and forceful action [LN].

QUESTION—What is the relationship of the dogs and the pigs to the actions of trampling the pearls and tearing the people to pieces?
   1. The pigs are the ones that trample and also tear to pieces [Lns, My; GW, NIV, NLT, NRSV, REB; probably BNTC, CC, NTC; ESV, KJV, NASB]: lest the pigs tramples the pearls with their feet and then turn and tear you to pieces.
   2. It is a chiastic structure in which the first and last elements correspond and the two middle elements correspond [BECNT, EBC, ICC, NAC, NIBC,

NICNT, NIGTC, PNTC, TH; CEV, NCV, TEV]: lest the pigs trample the pearls with their feet and the dogs turn and tear you to pieces.

DISCOURSE UNIT—7:7–12 [CEV, NASB, NET, NIV, TEV]. The topic is ask, seek, knock [NET, NIV, TEV], ask, search, knock [CEV], prayer and the golden rule [NASB].

DISCOURSE UNIT—7:7–11 [ESV, GW, NCV, NLT, NRSV]. The topic is the power of prayer [GW], ask God for what you need [NCV], ask and it will be given [ESV], ask, search, knock [NRSV], effective prayer [NLT].

7:7 Ask^a and it-will-be-given^b to-you(pl),

LEXICON—a. pres. act. impera. of αἰτέω (LN 33.163) (BAGD p. 26): 'to ask' [BAGD, all translations], 'to ask for' [BAGD, LN], 'to demand' [BAGD, LN], 'to plead for' [LN]. The present tense imperative form of this verb is translated 'keep on asking' [NLT]. This plural verb means to ask for with urgency [LN]. In this context, 'ask' refers to asking God for what one needs [TH].

b. fut. pass. indic. of δίδωμι (LN 57.71): 'to be given' [BECNT, CC, LN, NICNT, NIGTC, NTC, PNTC, WBC; ESV, KJV, NASB, NET, NIV, NRSV]. The phrase δοθήσεται ὑμῖν 'it will be given to you' is translated 'you will receive' [CEV, GW, REB, TEV], 'you will receive what you ask for' [NLT], 'your request will be granted' [BNTC], 'God will give to you' [NCV]. The agent of this passive verb and the one in the next clause is God [TH]. This verb means to give an object, usually meaning to give something of value [LN].

QUESTION—How is this unit related to its context?

The Sermon on the Mount demands that the disciples have the qualities of sincerity, humility, purity, and love, so now Jesus assures them such qualities are theirs if they seek them through prayer [EBC]. It is by prayer for God's help that they can reach the high standards set forth in the preceding section [NTC, PNTC]. This passage gives encouragement to any disciple who is dismayed at what Jesus has been commanding [ICC]. The unit 7:7–11 does not clearly link with the sense of 7:1–6, rather it picks up from the teaching in 6:25–34 where it speaks about trusting their heavenly Father to supply the things they need [NICNT]. Others consider this section to be self contained with no real connection with either the preceding section or the following one [My, WBC].

QUESTION—What is indicated by the use of the present tense of this imperative verb and the two imperative verbs that follow?

1. The present tense implies a continual asking, seeking, and knocking [BECNT, EBC, ICC, Lns, NAC, NIBC, NICNT, NTC, PNTC, WBC; NLT]. It implies the need for persistence [EBC, TH, WBC].
2. It adds emphasis to the imperative, but does not indicate the need to ask continually, since there is also an emphasis in the sermon on the Father's generosity [CC].

MATTHEW 7:7 239

QUESTION—What relationship is indicated by καί 'and'?
The combination of the imperative verb with a future indicative verb linked by καί 'and' is equivalent to a conditional sentence: *if* you ask, it *will be* given [CC].

seek[a] and you(pl)-will-find,[b] knock[c] and it-will-be-opened[d] to-you(pl).
LEXICON—a. pres. act. impera. of ζητέω (LN 27.41) (BAGD 1.a.β. p. 338): 'to seek' [BAGD, BECNT, BNTC, CC, NICNT, NIGTC, NTC, PNTC, WBC; ESV, KJV, NASB, NET, NIV, NLT, REB, TEV], 'to search' [CEV, GW, NCV, NRSV], 'to search for, to look for' [BAGD], 'to try to learn where something is, to look for, to try to find' [LN]. This verb means to try to learn the location of something, often by movement from place to place in the process of searching [LN].
  b. fut. act. indic. of εὑρίσκω (LN 27.27) (BAGD 1.a. p. 324): 'to find' [BAGD, LN; all translations], 'to discover, to come upon' [BAGD, LN], 'to learn the whereabouts of something, to happen to find' [LN]. The implicit object of the verb is supplied: 'to find what you want' [WBC]. This verb means to learn the location of something, either by intentional searching or by unexpected discovery [LN].
  c. pres. act. impera. of κρούω (LN **19.12**) (BAGD p. 454): 'to knock' [BAGD, **LN**; all translations]. This verb means to knock on a door, as a means of signaling one's presence to those inside [LN].
  d. fut. pass. indic. of ἀνοίγω (LN **79.110**) (BAGD 1.a. p. 71): 'to be opened' [BAGD, **LN**; all translations except NCV]. The implicit subject of the passive verb ἀνοιγήσεται 'it will be opened' is made explicit: 'the door will be opened' [BECNT, BNTC, NICNT, WBC; CEV, GW, NET, NIV, NLT, NRSV, REB, TEV], 'the door will open' [NCV]. This verb means to cause something to be open [LN].
QUESTION—What is the significance of the three verbs used to describe prayer?
The order of the verbs 'ask', 'seek', and 'knock' indicate an increasing intensity in one's prayers [CC, Lns, NTC, PNTC]. 'Ask' is a general expression when no particular kind of prayer is in mind, and that prayer will be effective and will be answered. 'Seek' perhaps means that the praying person does not know exactly what he should be praying for, but he knows that the Father will not lead him astray. 'Knock' uses the imagery of a closed door that cannot be opened for the disciple who is serving God, but with a lot of prayer that door will be opened [PNTC]. Others think the use of three elements was a common rhetorical style [NICNT], and here the three verbs merely function as synonyms [NICNT, TRT] for the act of praying [TRT]. The order of the verbs describes the traits of courtesy, persistence, and diligence in prayer: the disciples are to pray ('ask') with both earnest sincerity ('seek'), and an active, diligent pursuit of God's way ('knock') [EBC].

7:8 For everyone asking receives[a] and the (one) seeking finds and to-the (one) knocking it-will-be-opened.

> LEXICON—a. pres. act. indic. of λαμβάνω (LN 57.125) (BAGD 2. p. 465): 'to receive' [BAGD, LN; all translations], 'to get, to obtain' [BAGD]. This verb means to receive or accept an object or benefit for which the initiative rests with the giver, but the focus of attention in the transfer is upon the receiver [LN].

QUESTION—What relationship is indicated by γάρ 'for'?
> It indicates the grounds or basis for the exhortation just given, which is that those who ask receive, etc. [ICC, PNTC].

7:9 Or[a] what man[b] is-there among you(pl), whom (if) his son will-ask-for bread,[c] he-would- not -give him a-stone (will he)?

> LEXICON—a. ἤ (LN 89.139) (BAGD 1.d.δ. p. 342): 'or' [BAGD, BECNT, BNTC, CC, LN, NIGTC, NTC; ESV, KJV, NASB], not explicit [NICNT, WBC; all versions except ESV, KJV, NASB]. This conjunction indicates an alternative [LN]. This word often occurs in interrogative sentences to introduce or add rhetorical questions [BAGD].
>
> b. ἄνθρωπος (LN 9.24) (BAGD 3.a.ζ. p. 69): 'man' [LN], 'who' [BAGD]. The phrase τίς ἐστιν ἐξ ὑμῶν ἄνθρωπος 'what man is there among you' [BNTC, NTC; NASB] is also translated 'what man is there of you' [KJV], 'which man is there among you' [PNTC], 'is there any man among you' [BECNT], 'is there anyone among you' [NET, NRSV], 'who is the man among you' [CC], 'who is the person among' [NIGTC], 'who is there among you' [NICNT], 'there is no one among you…is there?' [WBC], 'would any of you' [CEV, GW, REB], 'would any of you who are fathers' [TEV], 'which of you' [ESV, NCV, NET, NIV], 'you parents' [NLT]. This noun denotes an adult male person of marriageable age [LN].
>
> c. ἄρτος (LN 5.8) (BAGD 1.a. p. 110): 'bread' [BAGD, BNTC, CC, NIGTC, NTC, WBC; all versions except NASB, NLT], 'loaf' [BAGD; NASB], 'loaf of bread' [BECNT, LN, NICNT; NLT]. This noun denotes a relatively small and generally round loaf of bread which is considerably smaller than present-day typical loaves of bread and thus more like 'rolls' or 'buns' [LN].

QUESTION—What relationship is indicated by ἤ 'or' at the beginning of the verse?
> 'Or' makes the same point as that of verses 7–8 in another way. Instead of saying what God will do in answer to prayer, these two verses ask questions from a situation in human life [EBC, PNTC].

QUESTION—What kind of questions did Jesus ask in verses 9 and 10?
> The questions 'would he give him a stone?' and 'would he give him a snake?' are rhetorical questions beginning with the negative particle μή 'not' that indicates that a negative answer is expected [BNTC]. No one would do such a wicked thing [PNTC]. Such questions amount to affirmations: 'he would not give him a stone' and 'he would not give him a snake'. No parent

would respond in such a way! [WBC]. It would be *unthinkable* [ICC, NICNT]. The negative particle is difficult to include in a translation and most omit it in their translations [NICNT, PNTC; all versions except NASB, NLT]. Some show the expected answer by translating the question as a statement ending with a short question: 'Or if he asks for a fish, he will not give him a snake, will he?' [NASB], 'There is no one…who will give a stone, is there? …there is no one who will give a snake…is there? [WBC]. One translates this as a question and then supplies an answer: 'Do you give them a stone instead…do you give them a snake? Of course not!' [NLT].

7:10 Or[a] also (if) he-asks-for a-fish,[b] he-will- not -give to-him a-snake[c] (will he)?

LEXICON—a. ἤ (LN 89.139) (BAGD 1.d.β. p. 342): 'or' [BAGD, LN]. The phrase ἤ καί 'or also' [CC, NTC] is translated 'or' [BECNT, NICNT, NIGTC, PNTC; all versions except CEV], 'and' [WBC], 'or again' [BNTC], not explicit [CEV]. This conjunction indicates an alternative [LN]. It may also be used to introduce a question that is parallel one preceding it [BAGD].
b. ἰχθύς (LN **4.59**) (BAGD p. 384): 'fish' [BAGD, LN; all translations].
c. ὄφις (LN 4.52) (BAGD 1. p. 600): 'snake' [BAGD, BECNT, CC, LN, NICNT, NIGTC, PNTC, WBC; all versions except ESV, KJV], 'serpent' [BAGD, BNTC, NTC; ESV, KJV], 'reptile' [LN].

7:11 If therefore you(pl) being[a] evil[b] know-how[c] to-give good[d] gifts[e] to-your(pl) -children,

LEXICON—a. pres. act. participle of εἰμί (LN 13.1) (BAGD II. 8. p. 224): 'to be' [BAGD, LN; all translations except NLT], not explicit [NLT]. This participle is translated as indicating a concessive relationship: 'even though you are' [BECNT, CC; GW, NCV], 'though you are' [NTC; NIV], 'although you are' [BNTC; NET]. It is translated as indicating contra expectation: 'even you who are sinful (know, etc)' [WBC], 'as bad as you are, (you…know)' [CEV, REB, TEV]. This verb means to possess certain characteristics, whether inherent or transitory [LN].
b. πονηρός (LN 88.110) (BAGD 1.b.α. p. 691): 'evil' [BAGD, BECNT, BNTC, CC, LN, NIGTC, NTC, PNTC; ESV, GW, KJV, NASB, NET, NIV, NRSV], 'sinful' [WBC; NLT], 'bad' [NICNT; CEV, NCV, REB, TEV], 'wicked' [BAGD, LN]. This adjective describes what is morally corrupt and evil [LN].
c. perf. act. indic. of οἶδα (perf. = pres. with this verb) (LN **28.7**) (BAGD 3. p. 556): 'to know how to' [BAGD, **LN**; all translations except CC], 'to know to' [CC]. This verb means to have the knowledge as to how to perform a particular activity or to accomplish some goal [LN].
d. ἀγαθός (LN 65.20) (BAGD 1.a.β. p. 2): 'good' [BAGD, LN; all translations], 'fit, useful' [BAGD], 'nice' [LN]. This adjective describes that which has the proper characteristics or performing the expected function in a fully satisfactory way [LN].

e. δόμα (LN 57.73) (BAGD p. 203): 'gift' [BAGD, LN; all translations except REB, TEV], 'things' [REB, TEV]. This noun denotes that which is given [LN].

QUESTION—What relationship is indicated by the conjunction οὖν 'therefore'?

It indicates that what follows in the next clause is a logical conclusion to be drawn from the statements in 7:9–10 about God's goodness [CC, ICC, NTC]. It indicates the conclusion to be drawn from 7:7–11 about the love of the heavenly Father for his own children [ICC].

QUESTION—What is indicated by the use of the personal pronoun ὑμεῖς 'you' in the phrase ὑμεῖς πονηροὶ ὄντες 'you being evil'?

It makes 'you' emphatic [CC, PNTC], and indicates a distinction between the hearers, who are members of a sinful human race, and Jesus [ICC, NAC, PNTC]. It indicates the contrast between morally flawed human nature and God's nature [NIGTC, TH]. Here Jesus assumes the inherent sinfulness of humanity [BNTC, EBC, ICC].

QUESTION—What relationship is indicated by the use of the present participle ὄντες 'being'?

It indicates a concessive relationship [BECNT, BNTC, CC, Lns, NTC, PNTC, WBC; GW, NCV, NET, NIV]: that is, *although* you are evil.

how-much[a] more[b] your(pl) Father the (one) in the heavens[c] will-give good (things)[d] to-those asking him.

LEXICON—a. πόσος (LN 59.17) (BAGD 1. p. 694): 'how much' [BAGD, LN; all translations except CEV], 'even (more)' [CEV]. This interrogative adjective describes quantity [LN].

b. μᾶλλον (LN 78.28) (BAGD 2.b. p. 489): 'more' [BAGD, LN; all translations], 'more than, to a greater degree, even more' [LN]. The phrase πόσῳ μᾶλλον 'how much more' is translated 'how much more is it true' [WBC], 'even more ready' [CEV]. This comparative adjective describes the degree something that surpasses in some manner a point on an explicit or implicit scale of extent [LN].

c. οὐρανός (LN 1.11) (BAGD 2.a. p. 594): 'heaven' [BAGD, LN]. The phrase ἐν τοῖς οὐρανοῖς 'in the heavens' is translated 'in heaven' [BECNT, BNTC, CC, NICNT, NIGTC, NTC, PNTC; ESV, GW, KJV, NASB, NET, NIV, NRSV, TEV], 'heavenly' [WBC; CEV, NCV, NLT, REB].

d. ἀγαθός (LN 65.20) (BAGD 1.a.β. p. 2): 'good' [BAGD, LN], 'fit, useful' [BAGD], 'nice' [LN]. This adjective is translated as a substantive: 'good things' [all translations except NASB, NET, NIV, NLT], 'good gifts' [NET, NIV, NLT], 'what is good' [NASB].

QUESTION—What are the 'good things' that God will give?

'Good things' describes God's generosity, which is more than just provision for basic human needs [NIGTC]. The good gifts consist of anything that would be beneficial to his children [Lns], whatever is best for them [NIBC].

The good things are those things that are asked for in the Lord's prayer in 6:9–13 [CC], the blessings of the kingdom [EBC]. They are all that is required to live life as a faithful disciple [ICC]. It is everything necessary for seeking God's kingdom and righteousness as first priority [NAC]. He will give them the Holy Spirit and whatever else they need [NTC]. He will give nothing bad [NTC], only what is beneficial [NICNT, PNTC].

DISCOURSE UNIT—7:12–14 [ESV]. The topic is the golden rule.

DISCOURSE UNIT—7:12 [GW, NCV, NLT, NRSV]. The topic is the golden rule [GW, NLT, NRSV], the most important rule [NCV].

7:12 **Therefore all-things whatsoever[a] you(pl)-might-wish[b] that people would-do[c] (for/to)[d] you(pl), so[e] also[f] do (for/to) them;**

LEXICON—a. ὅσος (LN 59.19) (BAGD 2. p. 586): 'as much as' [BAGD, LN]. The phrase πάντα ὅσα 'all things whatsoever' [KJV] is translated 'all things whatever that' [PNTC], 'all things that' [BNTC, CC], 'whatever' [BECNT, NICNT, NTC; ESV, NLT], 'what' [NCV, TEV], 'all of everything that' [NIGTC], 'everything' [WBC], 'in everything' [NASB, NET, NIV, NRSV], 'always' [REB], not explicit [CEV]. This adjective describes a comparison of quantity [LN].

b. pres. act. subj. of θέλω (LN 25.1) (BAGD 1. p. 355): 'to wish' [BAGD, BNTC, CC, LN, NIGTC, PNTC; ESV], 'to want' [BAGD, BECNT, LN, NTC; CEV, NASB, NET, TEV], 'to like' [NICNT, WBC; NLT, REB], 'to desire' [BAGD, LN]. The phrase 'whatsoever you might wish' is translated 'what you would have (them do)' [NIV, NRSV], 'whatsoever you would (that)' [KJV]. This verb means to desire to have or experience something [LN].

c. pres. act. subj. of ποιέω (LN 41.7) (BAGD I.1.d.β. p. 682): 'to do' [all translations except CEV, NASB, NET, REB], 'to do for' [BAGD], 'to do to' [LN], 'to treat' [CEV, NASB, NET, REB], 'to behave toward, to deal with, to act' [LN]. This verb means to behave or act in a particular way with respect to someone [LN].

d. There is no lexical entry for this preposition indicating the relationship between the verb 'to do' and the object 'you'. It is implied by the dative case of the object pronoun ὑμῖν 'you'. This relationship is translated 'for you' [BECNT, BNTC, CC, NICNT, NIGTC, NTC; GW, TEV], 'to you' [PNTC, WBC; ESV, KJV, NCV, NIV, NLT, NRSV]. The phrase ποιῶσιν ὑμῖν 'to do for/to you' is translated 'treat you' [CEV, NASB, NET, REB].

e. οὕτως (LN 61.9): 'so' [LN, NIGTC, PNTC; KJV], 'thus' [LN], 'in this way' [CC, LN], 'the same' [BECNT], 'the same way' [NASB], 'as (you want/would like)' [CEV, NET, REB], not explicit [BNTC, NICNT, WBC; ESV, GW, NCV, NIV, NLT, NRSV, TEV]. This adverb refers to that which precedes [LN].

f. καί (LN 89.93): 'also' [BNTC, CC, LN, NIGTC, NTC, PNTC; ESV], 'too' [NICNT], 'and, and also, in addition' [LN], 'even' [LN; KJV], not explicit [BECNT, WBC; all versions except ESV, KJV]. This conjunction indicates an additive relationship which is not coordinate [LN].

QUESTION—What relationship is indicated by the conjunction οὖν 'therefore'?

QUESTION—What relationship is indicated by the conjunction οὖν 'for'?

It indicates the conclusion to be drawn from the entire contents of the sermon up to this point [PNTC], or from the central core of the sermon, beginning from 5:17 [BECNT, EBC, ICC, My, NICNT, NIGTC, NTC]. This verse ends an *inclusio* construction bracketed by 5:15 where Jesus said he came to fulfill the Law and the Prophets and by this verse which shows how Jesus' disciples should also fulfill the Law and the Prophets. So the conjunction indicates the conclusion to be drawn from everything that has been said since 5:17 [BECNT, EBC, NTC]. In view of all that Jesus has taught them about the true direction of in which the OT points, they should obey the Golden Rule because it sums up the Law and the Prophets [EBC]. Some think that this conclusion refers especially to 7:7–11 so that in gratitude for all the Father's good gifts, we should be motivated to love others as ourselves [NTC]. Since God is such a good Father that he grants what his children need and ask him for, they should live according to this rule as his grateful children [Lns].

for this is[a] the law and the prophets.[b]

LEXICON—a. εἰμί (LN 13.4): 'to be' [LN]. This verb is translated 'is' [BECNT, BNTC, CC, NICNT, NIGTC, NTC, PNTC; ESV, KJV, NASB, NRSV, REB], 'is the essence of' [WBC], 'is the essence of all that is taught in' [NLT], 'is the meaning of' [GW, NCV, TEV], 'is what…are all about' [CEV], 'fulfills' [NET], 'sums up' [NIV]. This verb means to be identical with something [LN].

b. ὁ νόμος καὶ οἱ προφῆται 'the law and the prophets' (LN 33.58): The phrase 'the law and the prophets' [BECNT, NICNT, PNTC, WBC; KJV, NET, NLT, NRSV, REB] is also translated 'the Law and the Prophets' [BNTC, CC, LN, NIGTC, NTC; CEV, ESV, NASB, NIV], 'Moses' teachings and the Prophets' [GW], 'the law of Moses and the teaching of the prophets' [NCV, TEV], 'the sacred writings' [LN]. The idiom 'the Law and the Prophets' denotes all of the sacred writings of the OT, including the Law, the Prophets, and the Writings [LN].

QUESTION—What relationship is indicated by the conjunction γάρ 'for'?

It indicates that the 'golden rule' Jesus articulates is based on the truth that is revealed in the law and prophets [EBC].

QUESTION—What does it mean for Jesus' statement *to be* 'the law and the prophets'?

It means that it sums up the teaching of the OT [NICNT, NIGTC, NTC, PNTC]. Honest and true love that denies self and reaches out to others is a summary of OT teaching [NTC]. It is such an all-embracing principle that it sums up the spirit of the law and the prophets [NICNT]. It states the essence of the meaning of the law and the prophets, and if the disciples of God's kingdom have been inspired by his goodness, they will be like him [BECNT]. Such conduct as described in the golden rule fulfills the goal or intent of the law and the prophets [EBC]. It states the most basic and important demand and goal of the law [ICC].

DISCOURSE UNIT—7:13–29 [ICC]. The topic is three warnings and the conclusion.

DISCOURSE UNIT—7:13–14 [CEV, GW, NASB, NCV, NET, NIV, NRSV]. The topic is the narrow gate [CEV, GW, NET, NRSV, TEV], the way to heaven is hard [NCV], the narrow and the wide gates [NASB, NIV].

7:13 Enter^a through^b the narrow^c gate;^d

LEXICON—a. aorist act. impera. of εἰσέρχομαι (LN 15.93, 90.70) (BAGD 1.f. p. 233): 'to enter' [BAGD, BECNT, BNTC, CC, LN (15.93), NIGTC, NTC, PNTC; all versions except CEV, NLT, TEV], 'to enter God's kingdom' [NLT], 'to go in' [BAGD, NICNT, WBC; CEV, TEV], 'to go into' [BAGD], 'to begin to experience, to come into an experience, to attain' [LN (90.70)]. This verb means to move into a space [LN [15.93]], or to begin to experience an event or state [LN (90.70)].

b. διά with genitive (LN 84.29) (BAGD A.I.1. p. 179): 'through' [BAGD, BECNT, BNTC, CC, LN, NICNT, NIGTC, PNTC, WBC; all versions except ESV, KJV, REB], 'by' [NTC; ESV, REB], 'at' [KJV]. This preposition marks extension through an area or object [LN].

c. στενός (LN **81.19**) (BAGD p. 766): 'narrow' [BAGD, BECNT, BNTC, CC, **LN**, NICNT, NIGTC, NTC, PNTC, WBC; all versions except KJV], 'straight' [KJV]. This adjective describes being narrow or restricted [LN].

d. πύλη (LN 7.48) (BAGD 2. p. 729): 'gate' [BAGD, LN; all translations], 'door' [BAGD, LN]. This noun denotes a door or gate used to close off an entranceway [LN].

QUESTION—What is being entered?
1. The picture is of a person who must pass through one of two gates in order to travel a road that leads to his destination [BECNT, CC, EBC, My, NICNT, NTC]. We may assume that the gate is at the beginning of the road on the basis of the order by which they are presented, and the two roads lead in opposite directions since their destinations are totally apart from each other [NICNT].
2. The picture is of entering one of two roads, each leading up to a different gate through which a traveler must pass in order to arrive at his destination [CC, NIGTC, PNTC].
3. The gate leads into a passageway, which then leads to the rooms of a building [Lns].

4. The words 'road' and 'gate' are used synonymously [ICC, WBC]. The gate and the road seem to function synonymously as though they were side by side, and not one before the other [ICC]. The sequence of gate and road is not significant since this is not talking about entering a gate to get on a road or entering a gate at the end of a road [WBC].

QUESTION—What is a *narrow* gate?

'Narrow' refers to being restrictive [EBC, NIGTC] and it is implied that it is difficult to get through such a gate [ICC]. An effort must be made to enter a narrow gate, and it isn't until the next verse that we find that it is the way into life [NTC].

for wide[a] (is) the gate and broad[b] (is) the road[c] leading[d] to destruction[e]

LEXICON—a. πλατύς (LN 81.16) (BAGD p. 667): 'wide' [BAGD, BECNT, BNTC, LN, NICNT, NIGTC, NTC, WBC; all versions], 'broad' [BAGD, CC, LN, PNTC]. This adjective describes something as being wide [LN].

b. εὐρύχωρος (LN **81.18**) (BAGD p. 326): 'broad' [BAGD, BECNT, BNTC, **LN**, NIGTC, NTC, WBC; KJV, NASB, NIV, NLT, REB], 'wide' [GW, NCV], 'spacious' [BAGD, CC, **LN**, NICNT, PNTC; NET], 'easy' [ESV, NRSV, TEV], 'easy to follow' [CEV]. This adjective describes what is broad and spacious, with the implication of it being agreeable and pleasant [LN].

c. ὁδός (LN 1.99) (BAGD 2.a. p. 554): 'road' [LN, NICNT, PNTC; CEV, GW, NCV, NIV, NRSV, REB, TEV], 'way' [BAGD, BECNT, BNTC, CC, LN, NIGTC, NTC; ESV, KJV, NASB, NET], 'highway' [NLT], 'path' [WBC]. This noun is a general term for a thoroughfare, either within a population center or between two such centers [LN].

d. pres. act. participle of ἀπάγω (LN 15.177) (BAGD 3. p. 79): 'to lead' [BAGD; all translations except NLT], 'to lead off, to lead away, to take away, to take aside' [LN]. The phrase ἡ ὁδὸς ἡ ἀπάγουσα εἰς τὴν ἀπώλειαν 'the road leading to destruction' is translated 'the highway to hell' [NLT]. This verb means to lead or take away from a particular point [LN].

e. ἀπώλεια (LN 20.31) (BAGD 2. p. 103): 'destruction' [BAGD, BECNT, CC, LN, NICNT, NIGTC, NTC, PNTC; all versions except NCV, NLT, TEV], 'ruin' [BAGD, BNTC], 'final ruin' [WBC], 'hell' [NCV, NLT, TEV]. This noun denotes the destruction of persons, objects, or institutions [LN].

QUESTION—What relationship is indicated by the conjunction ὅτι 'for'?

This conjunction indicates the reason for entering the narrow gate instead of the other gate that broad and spacious [Lns, PNTC].

QUESTION—What is meant by the descriptions 'wide' and 'broad'?

They imply easiness and comfort for those who go this way, with no hard demands to be met [WBC]. It is the easy way [BECNT, NAC, NIBC, NICNT]. The adjective 'broad' is almost synonymous with 'wide' and it means that the road is easy to travel on [TH]. The wide gate is more inviting and the spacious road accommodates the crowd [EBC, NIGTC]. 'Wide' and 'broad' represent the excesses and pleasures of sin [My].

QUESTION—What is meant by ἀπάγω 'destruction'?

It is hell [BECNT, TRT]. In 7:14 'life' refers to eternal life, so by analogy 'destruction' must refer to 'eternal destruction' or 'eternal death', which would be equivalent to 'hell' [TH]. This refers to the final ruin brought by eschatological judgment [WBC]. It is the hopeless destiny of death [EBC], it is eschatological doom [CC], God's condemnation at the day of judgment [NIGTC]. It is not annihilation [Lns, TRT].

and many[a] are those-entering through[b] it;

LEXICON—a. πολύς (LN 59.1) (BAGD I.1.a.α. p. 687): 'many' [BAGD, LN; all translations except CEV, NCV], 'many people' [NCV], 'a lot of people' [CEV], 'a great deal of, a great number of' [LN], 'numerous' [BAGD]. This adjective describes a relatively large quantity of objects or events [LN].

b. διά with genitive (LN 84.29) (BAGD A.I.1. p. 179): 'through' [BAGD, BECNT, CC, LN, NIGTC, PNTC; CEV, NASB, NCV, NET, NIV], 'by' [BNTC, NICNT, NTC; ESV, GW], 'thereat' [KJV], 'that way' [REB]. This entire phrase is translated 'there are many who go that way' [WBC], 'there are many who travel it' [TEV], 'for the many who choose that way' [NLT], 'there are many who take it' [NRSV]. This preposition marks extension through an area or object [LN].

7:14 How[a] narrow (is) the gate and difficult[b] the road leading to life[c]

TEXT—Manuscripts reading τί 'how' are given a B rating by GNT to indicate it was regarded to be almost certain. A variant reading is ὅτι 'for/because' and it is followed by BNTC, NTC; ESV, KJV, NASB, NRSV.

LEXICON—a. τί (LN 78.13) (BAGD 3.b. p. 819): 'how' [BAGD, LN, 'very, how great, how much, intense, severe' [LN]. The phrase τί στενὴ ἡ πύλη 'how narrow the gate' is translated 'narrow is the gate' [REB], 'but the gate is narrow' [NET], 'but the gate is small' [NCV; similarly NIV], 'but the gate to life is narrow' [TEV], 'but the gate to life is very narrow' [CEV; similarly GW], 'but the gateway to life is very narrow' [NLT]. Others follow the variant reading ὅτι στενὴ ἡ πύλη 'for the gate is narrow' [ESV, NRSV], 'for the gate is small' [NASB], 'because strait is the gate' [KJV]. This exclamation indicates a relatively high point on a scale [LN].

b. perf. pass. participle of θλίβω (LN **22.21**) (BAGD 2.b. p. 362): 'difficult' [**LN**; NET, NLT], 'straightened' [BNTC], 'restricted' [CC, NICNT], 'constricted' [NIGTC, NTC, PNTC; REB], 'narrow' [BAGD; KJV, NASB, NCV, NIV, TEV], 'confined' [BAGD, WBC], 'hard' [ESV, NRSV], 'hard to follow' [CEV], 'full of trouble' [GW]. The verb from which this participial form is derived means to cause someone to suffer trouble or hardship [LN].

c. ζωή (LN 23.88) (BAGD 2.b.β. p. 341): 'life' [BAGD, LN; all translations except NCV], 'true life' [NCV]. This noun denotes life [LN].

QUESTION—What is the connotation of τεθλιμμένη 'difficult'?

It implies narrowness or lack of space [NICNT]. Pressure from lack of space may point to a secondary meaning of pressure through persecution [CC, ICC, PNTC, NIGTC, WBC]. The narrow road is difficult [BECNT, NAC, TH, TRT]. The restrictive way is the way of persecution and opposition [EBC]. The way is narrow and confining such that there is insufficient room for the sinful ways of the old life [Lns, NTC].

QUESTION—What is ζωή 'life' in this context?

It is to experience fellowship with God in the future eschatological kingdom [BECNT]. It is eschatological life in fellowship with God in Christ, along with all the blessings that flow from such fellowship [NTC]. It is eternal life in the eschatological kingdom of God [ICC, WBC], living with God forever [TRT]. It is eternal life that only Christ brings, and which is full and satisfying [PNTC]. 'Life' is closely connected to the kingdom of God [NIGTC]. It is eternal joy [NIBC], the blessed existence of heaven [Lns], the eternal life of happiness in the Messiah's kingdom [My].

and few[a] are those-finding[b] it.

LEXICON—a. ὀλίγος (LN 59.3) (BAGD 1.b. p. 563): 'few' [BAGD, BECNT, BNTC, CC, LN, NICNT, NIGTC, NTC, PNTC, WBC; ESV, KJV, NASB, NET, NRSV, REB], 'only a few' [NIV, NLT], 'few people' [TEV], 'a few people' [CEV], 'only a few people' [GW, NCV]. This adjective describes a relatively small quantity on any dimension [LN].

b. pres. act. participle of εὑρίσκω (LN 27.27) (BAGD 1.a. p. 324): 'to find' [BAGD, LN; all translations], 'to discover' [BAGD, LN], 'to learn the whereabouts of something, to come upon, to happen to find' [LN]. This verb means to learn the location of something, either by intentional searching or by unexpected discovery [LN].

QUESTION—What is the antecedent to αὐτήν 'it' that so few find?

1. The antecedent is 'gate' [BECNT, Lns, NIGTC, PNTC; GW].
2. The antecedent is 'road' [PNTC, TH, WBC; CEV, NCV]. While 'it' refers to the road, the two metaphors of the path and the gate are used synonymously [WBC].
3. It refers to both the path and the gate [REB].

DISCOURSE UNIT—7:15–23 [GW, NASB, NCV, NIV]. The topic is false prophets [GW], people know you by your actions [NCV], a tree and its fruit [NASB, NIV].

DISCOURSE UNIT—7:15–20 [CEV, ESV, NET, NLT, TEV]. The topic is a tree and its fruit [CEV, ESV, NET, TEV], the tree and its fruit [NLT].

7:15 Beware-of[a] the false-prophets,[b] who come[c] to you in sheep's clothing,[d]

LEXICON—a. pres. act. impera. of προσέχω (LN 27.59) (BAGD 1.b. p. 714): 'to beware' [BAGD, BECNT, BNTC, CC, NIGTC, NTC, PNTC, WBC;

ESV, GW, KJV, NASB, NLT, NRSV, REB], 'to be careful of' [NCV], 'to watch out for' [CEV, NET, NIV], 'to be concerned about, to be on one's guard' [BAGD], 'to be on (your) guard against' [LN, NICNT; TEV], 'to pay attention to' [BAGD, LN], 'to keep on the lookout for, to be alert for' [LN]. This verb means to be in a continuous state of readiness to learn of any future danger, need, or error, and to respond appropriately [LN].

b. ψευδοπροφήτης (LN 53.81) (BAGD p. 892): 'false prophet' [BAGD, LN; all translations]. The definite article with this noun is translated by BECNT, PNTC, WBC; NASB. It is not translated by BNTC, CC, NICNT, NIGTC, NTC; all versions except NASB. This noun denotes one who claims to be a prophet and is not, and thus proclaims what is false [LN].

c. pres. mid. or pass. (deponent = act.) indic. of ἔρχομαι (LN **88.233**) (BAGD I.1.a.β. p. 310): 'to come' [BAGD, **LN**; all translations except CEV], not explicit [CEV]. The phrase ἔρχονται ἐν ἐνδύμασιν προβάτων 'to come in sheep's clothing' is an idiom meaning to pretend to be harmless when in reality one is dangerous and destructive [LN].

d. ἔνδυμα (LN 6.162) (BAGD 2. p. 263): 'clothing' [BAGD, BECNT, BNTC, CC, LN, NIGTC, NTC; ESV, KJV, NASB, NET, NIV, NRSV], 'apparel' [LN], 'garment' [LN]. The phrase ἐν ἐνδύμασιν προβάτων 'in sheep's clothing' is translated 'they dress up like/as sheep' [CEV, REB], 'dressed up as sheep' [NICNT, PNTC], 'disguised as sheep' [GW], 'disguised as harmless sheep' [NLT], 'looking like sheep' [WBC], 'looking like sheep on the outside' [TEV], 'looking gentle like sheep' [NCV]. This noun denotes any kind of clothing [LN].

QUESTION—Who were the false prophets Jesus was referring to?

They are people who falsely claim to speak for God [Lns, NAC, NTC]. The false prophets' teaching will not conform to what Jesus taught [CC]. They are people who will teach and practice a false understanding of God's will, one not in accord with how Jesus illuminates the Law and the Prophets of the OT [NIGTC]. They bring false teaching and have never submitted to kingdom authority [EBC]. They are lawless people [BECNT], and what they proclaim does not accord with how they live [WBC]. These false prophets teach doctrinal errors [CC]. These false prophets were not outsiders, but were outwardly Christian people who said that they proclaimed God's word, but really didn't [TH]. They are false teachers [BNTC, My]. The warnings of 24:11, 24 show that Jesus was aware of this future hazard. That the false prophets were 'coming to you' indicates that they were people from outside the disciple group who would represent themselves as fellow believers, and would even claim inspiration [NICNT]. False prophets were people who claimed falsely to speak in the name of God and there must have been some who were tempted to claim direct inspiration even if it were not true; however, the emphasis of these false teachers actually leads people away from God [PNTC].

250   MATTHEW 7:15

QUESTION—What does it mean to come in ἐνδύμασιν προβάτων sheep's clothing?

They appear to belong to Jesus with outward appearance of good works [CC]. They are putting on an act, hiding their destructive intentions behind a mild façade [NICNT]. Their words and actions appear to promote real Christianity [NAC]. They have smooth speech [NTC] and pious living [BNTC]. They will use orthodox language and exhibit biblical piety [EBC]. They appear to be Christians [NIBC, NIGTC], and act innocently [TRT]. They appear innocent and gentle, but that is not their real inner nature [Lns, My]. They appear to be members of God's people but are not [WBC].

but[a] inwardly[b] they-are ravenous[c] wolves.[d]

LEXICON—a. δέ (LN 89.124): 'but' [BECNT, BNTC, CC, LN, NIGTC, NTC, PNTC; all versions except REB], 'while' [NICNT, WBC; REB], 'on the other hand' [LN]. This conjunction indicates contrast [LN].
  b. ἔσωθεν (LN **26.2**) (BAGD 2. p. 314): 'inwardly' [BNTC, CC, NIGTC, NTC, PNTC; ESV, KJV, NASB, NET, NIV, NRSV], 'inside' [BAGD, NICNT; CEV], 'on the inside' [BECNT; TEV], 'within' [BAGD, WBC], 'in their hearts' [GW], 'underneath' [REB], 'really' [NLT], '(in) the inner being' [**LN**], 'a person's inner self, within oneself' [LN], not explicit [NCV].
  c. ἅρπαξ (LN **20.4**) (BAGD 1. p. 109): 'ravenous' [BAGD, BECNT, BNTC, CC, NTC, PNTC; ESV, NASB, NRSV], 'ravening' [KJV], 'savage' [NICNT; REB], 'predatory' [NIGTC, WBC], 'rapacious' [BAGD], 'voracious' [NET], 'vicious' [**LN**; GW, NLT], 'ferocious' [NIV], 'wild' [TEV], 'destructive' [LN]. This word is translated as a phrase: 'who have come to attack you' [CEV], 'dangerous (like wolves)' [NCV]. This adjective describes what is destructively vicious [LN].
  d. λύκος (LN 88.121) (BAGD 2. p. 481): 'wolf' [BAGD; all translations], 'vicious person, fierce wolf, fierce person' [LN]. This is a figurative extension of meaning of λύκος 'wolf' and denotes a person who is particularly vicious and dangerous [LN].

QUESTION—In what way were the false prophets inwardly like ravenous wolves?

Their false teaching is destructive [Lns, NICNT, NIGTC, WBC]. They try to further their own interests at the expense of other people [PNTC]. They are self-serving [NAC] and mercenary [NICNT]. They endanger the Christian journey of the disciples [BECNT], deceiving and despoiling those who hear them [BNTC]. Their greed for personal gain prompts them to do things that are destructive to other people [NIBC]. They selfishly and maliciously lead others astray by telling them what they want to hear [NTC].

7:16 By[a] their fruits[b] you(pl)-will-recognize[c] them.

LEXICON—a. ἀπό with the genitive (LN 90.11) (BAGD IV.2.b. p. 87): 'by' [BECNT, BNTC, CC, LN, NICNT, NTC, WBC; all versions], 'from'

[BAGD, LN, NIGTC, PNTC]. This preposition marks instrument which serves as a source of information or reason [LN].
- b. καρπός (LN **42.13**) (BAGD 2.a. p. 405): 'fruit' [BECNT, BNTC, CC, NICNT, NIGTC, NTC, PNTC; ESV, KJV, NASB, NET, NIV, NRSV, REB], 'deed' [BAGD, LN, WBC], 'what they do' [CEV, NCV, TEV], 'what they produce' [GW], 'activity' [LN], 'result of deeds' [**LN**], 'result, outcome, product' [BAGD]. This noun is translated as a phrase: '(their) fruit, that is, by the way they act' [NLT]. This noun is a figurative extension of meaning of καρπός 'fruit' and denotes the natural result of what has been done [LN].
- c. fut. mid. (deponent = active) indic. of ἐπιγινώσκω (LN 27.61) (BAGD 2.a. p. 291): 'to recognize' [BAGD, BECNT, BNTC, LN, NICNT, NTC, WBC; ESV, NET, NIV, REB], 'to know' [BAGD, NIGTC, PNTC; GW, KJV, NASB, NCV, NRSV, TEV], 'to know truly' [CC], 'to identify' [NLT]. The phrase 'you will recognize them' is translated 'you can tell what they are' [CEV]. This verb means to identify newly acquired information with what had been previously learned or known [LN].

QUESTION—What 'fruit' would indicate the true nature of these false prophets?

This 'fruit' refers to what one says and does, and such actions will ultimately reveal a person's nature [EBC]. Their true nature would be revealed by the messages they preached [CC, Lns, NIGTC, NTC]. It is the low ethical quality of how they live [BECNT, My, NIBC, NICNT, NIGTC, NTC], their conduct [WBC], their lack of obedience [NAC]. They are lawless [BECNT, BNTC], and antinomian [BECNT], failing to do God's will [BNTC].

(People) do- not -gather[a] grapes[b] from thorn-bushes[c] or figs[d] from thistles[e] (do they)?

LEXICON—a. pres. act. indic. of συλλέγω (LN 18.10) (BAGD p. 777): 'to gather' [BAGD, BECNT, BNTC, CC, NIGTC, PNTC; KJV, NRSV], 'to pick' [LN, NICNT, WBC; CEV, GW, NIV, NLT], 'to pluck' [LN], 'to collect' [BAGD]. This verb is also expressed as a passive: 'to be gathered' [ESV, NASB, NET], 'to be picked' [NTC; REB]. The phrase 'people do not gather grapes from thorn bushes' is translated 'grapes don't come from thorn bushes' [NCV], 'thorn bushes don't bear grapes' [TEV]. This verb means to pluck or pick by pulling off or out of, with the intent of gathering together [LN].
- b. σταφυλή (LN 3.38) (BAGD p. 765): 'grape' [BAGD, LN; all translations], 'bunch of grapes' [BAGD, LN]. This noun denotes the fruit of grapevines [LN].
- c. ἄκανθα (LN **3.17**) (BAGD p. 29): 'thorn bush' [BECNT, BNTC, **LN**, NICNT, NIGTC, PNTC, WBC; ESV, GW, NASB, NCV, NIV, NLT, TEV], 'thorns' [CC, NTC; KJV, NET, NRSV], 'thorn plant' [BAGD, LN], 'brier' [LN; REB], 'thistle,' [LN]. The phrase 'from thorn

bushes...or from thistles' is conflated to 'thornbushes' [CEV]. This noun denotes any kind of thorny plant [LN].
- d. σῦκον (LN 3.36) (BAGD p. 776): 'fig' [BAGD, LN; all translations], 'ripe fig' [BAGD]. This noun denotes the fruit of the fig tree [LN].
- e. τρίβολος (LN **3.17**) (BAGD p. 826): 'thistle' [BAGD, LN; all translations except CEV, NCV, TEV], 'thorny weeds' [NCV], 'thorn bush' [**LN**; TEV], 'thorn plant, thistle, brier' [LN], not explicit [CEV]. This noun denotes any kind of thorny plant [LN].

QUESTION—What kind of a question is this?

This is a rhetorical question which expects the answer 'No' [BECNT, CC, TH, TRT, WBC].

7:17 So/likewise[a] every[b] good[c] tree produces[d] good[e] fruit,[f]

LEXICON—a. οὕτως (LN 61.9) (BAGD p. 597): 'so' [BAGD, BNTC, LN, NTC; ESV, NASB], 'likewise' [PNTC; NIV], 'thus' [BAGD, LN, WBC], 'similarly' [BECNT, CC], 'in this way' [LN], 'in the same way' [NICNT, NIGTC; GW, NET, NRSV], 'even so' [KJV], 'in this manner' [BAGD], not explicit [CEV, NLT, REB, TEV]. This adverb describes or refers to that which precedes [LN].
- b. πᾶς (LN 59.23): 'every' [BECNT, BNTC, CC, LN, NICNT, NIGTC, NTC, PNTC, WBC; ESV, GW, KJV, NASB, NCV, NET, NIV, NRSV], 'all' [LN], 'a' [CEV, NLT, REB, TEV]. This adjective describes the totality of any object, mass, collective, or extension [LN].
- c. ἀγαθός (LN **65.20**) (BAGD 1.a.β. p. 2): 'good' [BECNT, BNTC, **LN**, NICNT, NIGTC, WBC; all versions except ESV, TEV], 'healthy' [CC, NTC; ESV, TEV], 'sound' [PNTC], 'nice, pleasant' [LN], 'fit, useful' [BAGD]. This adjective describes that which has the proper characteristics or performing the expected function in a fully satisfactory way [LN]. A good tree is one that is a healthy tree [TH].
- d. pres. act. indic. of ποιέω (LN 23.199) (BAGD I.1.b. η. p. 681): 'to produce' [BAGD, LN, NICNT, NIGTC, WBC; GW, NCV, NLT], 'to bear' [BAGD, BECNT, BNTC, CC, LN, NTC, PNTC; ESV, NASB, NET, NIV, NRSV], 'to bring forth' [KJV], 'to yield' [BAGD, LN; REB]. The idiom ποιέω καρπόν 'to bear fruit' means to produce fruit or seed of plants [LN].
- e. καλός (LN **65.22**) (BAGD 2.a. p. 400): 'good' [BAGD, LN; all translations except REB], 'sound' [REB], 'fine' [BAGD, **LN**], 'free from defects' [BAGD]. This adjective describes that which has acceptable characteristics or functioning in an agreeable manner, often with the focus on outward form or appearance [LN].
- f. καρπός (LN **3.33**) (BAGD 1.α. p. 404): 'fruit' [BAGD, **LN**; all translations]. This noun denotes any fruit part of plants, including grain as well as pulpy fruit [LN].

MATTHEW 7:17

QUESTION—What relationship does the adverb οὕτως 'so/likewise' indicate?
1. This adverb indicates a conclusion to be drawn from 7:16 [BNTC, Lns, My, NTC, WBC; ESV, NASB]. This is a general principle to be derived from verse 16 [ICC].
2. This adverb indicates a comparison [BECNT, CC, NICNT, NIGTC, PNTC; GW, NET, NIV, NRSV]. This introduces a further but similar point in that the same argument now is about the quality of the fruit rather than the kind, and it extends to the tree that bears the fruit [PNTC].
3. This adverb is used to introduce the next stage in the teaching. There is a shift from the figure of thorny plants to the figure of good trees, which contrast with decaying trees [TH; perhaps CEV, NLT, REB, TEV which do not translate this word].

but/and[a] the unhealthy[b] tree produces bad[c] fruit.
LEXICON—a. δέ (LN 89.124): 'but' [BECNT, CC, LN, NTC, PNTC, WBC; all versions except CEV, NLT, REB], 'and' [BNTC; CEV, NLT, REB], 'while' [NICNT], 'on the other hand' [LN], not explicit [NIGTC]. This conjunction indicates contrast [LN].
b. σαπρός (LN **65.28**) (BAGD 1. p. 742): 'bad' [**LN**, NIGTC; NASB, NCV, NET, NIV, NLT, NRSV], 'worthless' [BECNT, PNTC], 'decayed' [BNTC, WBC], 'diseased' [CC, LN; ESV], 'sickly' [NTC], 'rotten' [NICNT; GW], 'corrupt' [KJV], 'poor' [REB, TEV]. This adjective describes what is of poor or bad quality and hence of little or no value (particularly in reference to plants, either in the sense of seriously diseased or of seedling stock, that is, not budded or grafted) [LN].
c. πονηρός (LN 65.27) (BAGD 1.a.γ. p. 690): 'bad' [BAGD, BNTC, LN, NICNT, PNTC, WBC; all versions except KJV], 'worthless' [BAGD, BECNT, LN, NTC], 'diseased' [CC], 'evil' [NIGTC; KJV]. This adjective describes something that possesses a serious fault and consequently is worthless [LN].

QUESTION—What is the nature of the problem in the case of the σαπρὸν δένδρον 'unhealthy tree' and the καρπὸς πονηρός 'bad fruit'?
1. The problem is not the age or condition of the tree but the kind or species of the tree, it is the wrong kind of tree to bear useful fruit [BECNT, EBC, Lns, NICNT, TRT].
2. The quality of the fruit shows the health of the tree [CC, My, NTC, PNTC, TH]. Now the argument is about the quality of the fruit rather than the kind of fruit [PNTC]. A tree that has decayed with age will give fruit that is bad, small, and useless [My].
3. The quality of the fruit shows the ability or inability of the tree to produce good fruit, which is the standard by which the tree is judged as bad or good [NIGTC].

7:18 A- good -tree is- not -able[a] to-produce bad fruit nor[b] (is) an-unhealthy tree to-produce good fruit.

LEXICON—a. pres. mid. or pass. (deponent = act.) indic. of δύναμαι (LN 74.5): 'to be able' [CC, LN, WBC; NET], 'can' [LN]. The phrase οὐ δύναται 'is not able' is translated 'cannot' [BECNT, BNTC, NICNT, NIGTC, NTC, PNTC; all versions except NET, NLT], 'can't' [NLT]. This verb means to be able to do or to experience something [LN].

    b. οὐδέ (LN 69.7) (BAGD 1. p. 591): 'nor' [BAGD, BECNT, BNTC, CC, LN, NIGTC, WBC; ESV, NASB, NET, NRSV], 'or' [NICNT; REB], 'neither' [LN, NTC, PNTC; KJV], 'and' [GW, NCV, NIV, NLT, TEV], 'and not' [BAGD, LN]. This conjunction is a combination of the negative particle οὐ 'not,' and the postpositive conjunction δέ 'and' [LN].

7:19 Every[a] tree not producing good fruit is-cut-down[b] and is-thrown[c] into (the) fire.

LEXICON—a. πᾶς (LN 59.23): 'every' [BECNT, BNTC, CC, LN, NICNT, NIGTC, NTC, PNTC, WBC; all versions except GW, REB, TEV], 'any' [GW, TEV], 'all' [LN], 'each, whole' [LN], not explicit [REB]. This adjective describes the totality of any object, mass, collective, or extension [LN]. See this word in 7:17.

    b. pres. pass. indic. of ἐκκόπτω (LN 19.18) (BAGD 1. p. 241): 'to be cut down' [BAGD, BECNT, BNTC, CC, LN, NICNT, NIGTC, NTC, PNTC, WBC; all versions except CEV, KJV, NLT], 'to be hewn down' [KJV], 'to be chopped down' [CEV, NLT], 'to be cut off, to be cut in two' [LN]. This verb means to cut in such a way as to cause separation [LN]. When the passive voice must be translated with an active construction, the subject would be 'the farmer' or 'a man' [TH].

    c. pres. pass. indic. of βάλλω (LN 15.215): 'to be thrown' [LN; all translations except CEV, KJV], 'to be cast' [KJV]. The phrase εἰς πῦρ βάλλεται 'is thrown into the fire' is translated 'is burned' [CEV].

QUESTION—What is the function of this verse in the argument?

This verse adds a note that is parenthetical to the subject of recognizing false prophets by their 'fruits' in order to give a warning about what is in store for those prophets and others who do not produce the 'fruits' they promise [My, NICNT]. This is the common metaphorical language of eschatological judgment to indicate that the lack of righteousness will result in condemnation at the end [WBC]. The words 'tree' and 'fruit' look back to the metaphors in 7:16–18 while the prospect of judgment points forward to 7:21–23 where the setting is the final judgment [ICC].

7:20 So[a] then[b] from their fruits you(pl)-will-know[c] them.[d]

LEXICON—a. ἄρα (LN 89.46) (BAGD 4. p. 104): 'so' [BAGD, LN], 'then' [LN], 'consequently, as a result' [BAGD, LN]. This conjunction indicates result as an inference from what has preceded [LN]. The phrase ἄρα γε 'so then' [CC, NIGTC, PNTC; NASB, NET, TEV], is also translated 'so, then' [BECNT], 'so' [BNTC. GW], 'well then' [NICNT], 'clearly, then'

[WBC], 'therefore' [NTC], 'wherefore' [KJV], 'thus' [ESV, NIV, NRSV], 'in the same way' [NCV], 'yes, just as…so' [NLT], 'that is why I say' [REB], not explicit [CEV].
- b. γε (LN 91.6): 'then, indeed' [LN]. This conjunction indicates a relatively weak emphasis and frequently it is not translated, though possibly it is reflected by the word order [LN]. See entry a. above for its translation.
- c. fut. mid. (deponent = active) indic. of ἐπιγινώσκω (LN 27.61) (BAGD 2.a. p. 291): 'to know' [BAGD], 'to recognize' [BAGD, LN]. See this word at 7:16.
- d. αὐτός (LN 92.11): 'them' [BECNT, BNTC, CC, LN, NICNT, NIGTC, NTC, PNTC; ESV, GW, KJV, NASB, NET, NIV, NRSV, REB], 'the false prophets' [WBC; CEV, TEV], 'these false prophets' [NCV]. This entire sentence is translated 'Yes, just as you can identify a tree by its fruit, so you can identify people by their actions' [NLT]. This pronoun is used to refer to a definite person or persons spoken or written about (with an added feature of emphasis in the nominative forms) [LN].

QUESTION—What relationship is indicated by ἄρα γε 'so then'?

It indicates an inference to be drawn from the previous section beginning at 7:16 [BECNT, Lns, My, NIGTC, WBC], or at 7:15 [TH].

DISCOURSE UNIT—7:21–23 [CEV, ESV, NET, NLT, NRSV, TEV]. The topic is I never knew you [ESV, TEV], judgment of pretenders [NET], concerning self-deception [NRSV], true disciples [NLT], a warning [CEV].

7:21 Not everyone[a] saying[b] to-me, "Lord,[c] Lord," will-enter[d] into the kingdom of heaven,

LEXICON—a. πᾶς (LN 59.23): 'everyone' [all translations except NCV], 'all those' [NCV], 'every, all' [LN]. This pronoun denotes the totality of any object, mass, collective, or extension [LN].
- b. pres. act. participle of λέγω (LN 33.131): 'to say' [BECNT, BNTC, CC, NICNT, NIGTC, NTC, PNTC; all versions except CEV, NLT, TEV], 'to call out' [NLT], 'to call, to name' [LN]. The phrase ὁ λέγων μοι, Κύριε κύριε 'saying to me, "Lord, Lord"' is translated 'who acknowledges me with the words, "Lord, Lord"' [WBC], 'who calls me, "Lord, Lord"' [TEV], 'who calls me their Lord' [CEV], 'who say that I am their Lord' [NCV]. This verb means to use an attribute of a person when speaking about or to him [LN].
- c. κύριος (vocative κύριε) (LN 12.9) (BAGD 2.c.β. p. 459): 'Lord' [BAGD, LN; all translations], 'Ruler, One who commands' [LN]. This noun is used as a title for God and for Christ and it denotes one who exercises supernatural authority over mankind [LN].
- d. fut. mid. (deponent = act.) indic. of εἰσέρχομαι (LN 90.70) (BAGD 2.a. p. 233): 'to begin to experience, to come into an experience, to attain' LN], 'to come into something, to share in' [BAGD]. The phrase εἰσελεύσεται εἰς 'to come into' [NICNT] is translated 'to enter into' [KJV, NET], 'to enter' [BECNT, BNTC, CC, NIGTC, NTC, PNTC,

WBC; all versions except CEV, KJV, NET], 'to get into' [CEV]. This verb means to begin to experience an event or state [LN].

QUESTION—What is meant by the word Κύριε 'Lord' when the people say to Jesus 'Lord, Lord'?

The word κύριε has a range of meanings. It originally denoted the owner of anything, and then it was used to refer to important people generally. It became a title of majesty and was used to address the Emperor of Rome [PNTC]. In the Septuagint Greek translation of the OT, the holy name of God, 'Yahweh' is translated 'Lord'. Yet 'Lord' was also used simply as a polite form of address equivalent to 'Sir' [NICNT]. It wasn't until the post resurrection period that 'Lord' was used in worship as a confession of Jesus' deity. In Jesus' day, probably addressing Jesus as 'Lord' meant no more than 'teacher' or 'sir'. However, Jesus is implicitly claiming more than that, since his 'name' becomes the focus of kingdom activity [EBC]. In this verse, the words 'will enter the kingdom of heaven' and the reference to it in the next verse 'Many will say to me in that day, "Lord, Lord..."' cause many to understand that this is talking about what will happen on Judgment Day [BECNT, BNTC, CC, EBC, ICC, Lns, NIBC, NICNT, NTC, PNTC, TH, TRT, WBC; CEV, NLT, TEV]. Here Jesus is linked with entry to the kingdom of heaven and with the working of miracles, but it is too much to claim that the word 'Lord' here attributes divinity to him. It fits in with Jesus' presentation of himself as the ultimate judge who decides who does and who does not enter the kingdom of heaven [NICNT]. Κύριε 'Lord' likely has overtones of divinity [PNTC]. It refers to the exalted Lord [TH]. Matthew's readers would have thought of the primary Christian confession 'Jesus is Lord' (Rom. 20:9; Phil. 2:22; 1 Cor. 12:30) [WBC].

QUESTION—What is the significance of the double vocative in addressing Jesus as 'Lord, Lord'?

It indicates fervency [EBC], earnestness [ICC, My, TRT], and urgency [Lns]. Instead of merely recognizing a superior social status, the effect of doubling the title draws attention to the importance of the title [NICNT]. It gives emphasis to his lordship [PNTC]. The repetition 'Lord, Lord' is somewhat unnatural when following the verb 'saying', so instead of someone actually addressing Jesus in this manner, it might be an effective way of making the point that 'not everyone who is in the habit of saying that I am his Lord', or 'It won't be everyone who constantly acknowledges me as his Lord' [TH].

but[a] the one doing[b] the will[c] of my Father in the heavens.

LEXICON—a. ἀλλά (LN 89.125) (BAGD 1.a. p. 38): 'but' [BAGD, LN, NTC, PNTC; ESV, KJV, NASB], 'but only' [BNTC, NICNT, NIGTC, PNTC; GW, NIV, NRSV, REB, TEV], 'only' [BECNT; CEV, NET, NLT], 'rather' [BAGD, CC], 'instead, on the contrary' [LN]. This word is translated with a phrase: 'the only people who will enter the kingdom of heaven are...' [NCV]. This conjunction indicates emphatic contrast [LN].

MATTHEW 7:21

b. pres. act. participle of ποιέω (LN 42.7) (BAGD I.1.c.α. p. 682): 'to do' [BAGD, BECNT, BNTC, CC, LN, NICNT, NIGTC, PNTC; all versions except CEV, NLT], 'to actually do' [WBC; NLT], 'to carry out' [BAGD, LN], 'to put into practice' [NTC], 'to practice' [BAGD], 'to accomplish, to perform' [LN]. The phrase ποιῶν τὸ θέλημα 'doing the will' is translated 'obey' [CEV]. This verb means to do or perform (highly generic for almost any type of activity) [LN].

c. θέλημα (LN 25.2) (BAGD 1.c.γ. p. 354): 'will' [BAGD, BECNT, BNTC, CC, NICNT, NIGTC, NTC, PNTC, WBC; ESV, KJV, NASB, NET, NIV, NLT, NRSV, REB], 'wish, desire' [LN]. This noun is translated 'what (my Father in heaven) wants' [GW, NCV, TEV]. The phrase 'doing the will of my Father' is translated 'who obey my Father' [CEV]. It denotes that which is desired or wished for [LN].

QUESTION—What relationship is indicated by ἀλλά 'but'?

It indicates that only such a person that does this will enter the kingdom [BECNT, BNTC, My, NICNT, NIGTC, PNTC; CEV, GW, NET, NIV, NLT, NRSV, REB, TEV].

QUESTION—What is implied by the phrase τοῦ πατρός μου '*my* Father'?

This is the first of fourteen occasions in Matthew's gospel where Jesus uses the term 'my Father'. Jesus' unique sonship is shown as being exercised in his unique role as the eschatological judge appointed by the Father [BECNT]. Use of this phrase supports the notion that Jesus alone has authority to reveal the will of the Father [WBC]. Jesus is the Son of God in four senses: (1) an ethical sense of being a child of God, (2) a messianic sense, (3) a nativistic sense as virgin-born, and (4) an eternal sense in that he is eternally the son of the Father, fully partaking of the divine nature, and enjoying a community of essence with the Father in a natural, essential, divine, Trinitarian sonship. It is this forth sense that is the basis for the first three [NTC]. It implies a close personal relationship to the Father that is unique [NICNT, PNTC]. He is *the* Son of the Father, and anyone who does the will of the Father has a genuine and saving relationship with the Son [Lns]. He is the judge, the authorized representative of the Father [ICC, NICNT]. Calling God 'my Father' was rare and striking, indicating Jesus' authority to make known the will of the heavenly Father, and is linked with his identification as God's Son in 3:17, 4:3, 4:6 [NIGTC].

7:22 Many will-say[a] to-me in that day,[b] "Lord, Lord, did-we- not -prophesy[c] in[d]-your(sg) name,[e]

LEXICON—a. fut. act. indic. of λέγω (LN 33.69): 'to say' [LN; all translations except CEV], 'to talk, to tell, to speak' [LN]. The phrase 'will say to me... "Lord, Lord"' is translated 'call me their Lord' [CEV]. This verb means to speak or talk, with apparent focus upon the content of what is said [LN].

b. ἡμέρα (LN 67.178) (BAGD 3.b.β. p. 347): 'day' [BAGD, LN]. The phrase ἐν ἐκείνῃ τῇ ἡμέρᾳ 'in that day' [PNTC; KJV] is also translated 'on that day' [NICNT; ESV, GW, NASB, NET, NIV, NRSV], 'when the day comes' [REB]. Some identify 'that day': 'on the last day' [NCV], 'on the day of judgment' [WBC; CEV], 'on judgment day' [NLT], 'when the Judgment Day comes' [TEV]. This noun denotes a period of time, according to Hebrew reckoning, beginning at sunset and ending at the following sunset [LN]. In this and other contexts it refers to a day appointed for special purposes [BAGD].

c. aorist act. indic. of προφητεύω (LN 33.459) (BAGD 1. p 723): 'to prophesy' [BAGD, LN; all translations except CEV, NCV, TEV], 'to preach' [CEV], 'to speak for (you)' [NCV], 'to speak God's message' [TEV], 'to make inspired utterances' [LN], 'to proclaim a divine revelation' [BAGD]. This verb means to speak under the influence of divine inspiration, with or without reference to future events [LN].

d. There is no lexical entry in the Greek text for the word 'in', but it is supplied in translation to express the relationship indicated by the dative case of the phrase τῷ σῷ ὀνόματι 'your name'. It is translated 'in' [BECNT, BNTC, NICNT, NIGTC, NTC, PNTC, WBC; all versions except NCV], 'by' [CC]. In this clause this relationship is translated 'in your name' [GW, TEV], 'for you' [NCV], but in the subsequent clause it is translated 'by your name' [TEV], 'by the power and authority of your name' [GW], 'through you' [NCV].

e. ὄνομα (LN 33.126): 'name' [LN; all translations except NCV], not explicit [NCV]. This noun denotes the proper name of a person or object [LN].

QUESTION—What 'day' is being referred to here?

It is the day of judgment [BECNT, BNTC, CC, EBC, ICC, Lns, NIBC, NICNT, NTC, PNTC, TH, TRT, WBC; CEV, NLT, TEV], the last day [NCV]. It is the day when people are allowed to enter into the kingdom of heaven or are denied entry into it, and that day is not necessarily judgment day [NIGTC].

and in-your(sg) name we-cast-out[a] demons,[b]

LEXICON—a. aorist act. indic. of ἐκβάλλω (LN 53.102) (BAGD 1. p. 237): 'to cast out' [BECNT, CC, LN, NIGTC, NTC, PNTC, WBC; ESV, KJV, NASB, NET, NLT, NRSV], 'to drive out' [BNTC, LN; NIV, REB, TEV], 'to throw out' [NICNT], 'to force out' [CEV, GW, NCV], 'to expel' [LN], 'to make go out, to exorcise' [LN]. This verb means to cause a demon to no longer possess or control a person [LN].

b. δαιμόνιον (LN 12.37) (BAGD 2. p. 169): 'demon' [BAGD, LN; all translations except KJV], 'devil' [KJV], 'evil spirit' [BAGD, LN]. This noun denotes an evil supernatural being or spirit [LN].

and in-your(sg) name we-performed[a] many miracles[b]?"

LEXICON—a. aorist act. indic. of ποιέω (LN **90.45**) (BAGD I.1.b.β. p. 681): 'to perform' [BAGD, BECNT, BNTC, LN, NICNT, NTC, PNTC, WBC; NASB, NIV, NLT, REB, TEV], 'to do' [BAGD, CC, **LN**, NIGTC; ESV,

GW, KJV, NCV, NET, NRSV], 'to work' [CEV]. This verb marks an agent relationship with a numerable event [LN].
  b. δύναμις (LN 76.7) (BAGD 4. p. 208): 'miracle' [BAGD, BECNT, BNTC, CC, LN, NICNT, WBC; CEV, GW, NASB, NCV, NIV, NLT, REB, TEV], 'mighty work' [NIGTC, NTC, PNTC; ESV], 'wonderful work' [KJV], 'mighty deed' [LN], 'powerful deed' [NET], 'deed of power' [BAGD; NRSV], 'wonder' [BAGD]. This noun denotes a deed manifesting great power, with the implication of some supernatural force [LN].

QUESTION—What is meant by performing miracles τῷ σῷ ὀνόματι 'in your name'?

It means to use the name of Jesus as a means for doing something miraculous [CC]. The name represents the person, and here this is a claim to have acted in Jesus' authority and in submission to his lordship [PNTC]. It is to claim intimate union with Jesus as the source of their power and preaching, as well as to represent him [NTC]. It implies exercising the full authority of the one named [ICC, NIBC]. The name was pronounced when performing miracles or casting out demons [My]. It means to be in accord with the revelation by which the Lord has made himself known, and as representing his true doctrines [Lns]. It is a claim to have done something by his authority or power [TRT].

QUESTION—How is it possible for someone to do such miracles in Jesus' name and not be acknowledged as one of his own?

Miracles are not necessarily an indication of saving faith [ICC] or of discipleship [NICNT]. Charismatic gifts are not as important as the fruit of righteousness, and they are not a proof of real faith or of God's approval [BECNT]. Sometimes their wonders may have been fraudulent, and other times perhaps performed by supernatural power, whether of God or of Satan, but they had degraded the name by using it almost as a magic formula, and had not practiced what they preached [NTC]. Jesus was not with them or empowering their ministry, rather they performed such works through satanic power [CC]. The name itself has a remarkable effect even when used by those who are unworthy of using it [BNTC]. These are lying wonders [Lns].

7:23 And then I-will-declare[a] to-them, "I never knew[b] you(pl).

LEXICON—a. fut. act. indic. of ὁμολογέω (LN **33.221**) (BAGD 4. p. 568): 'to declare' [BAGD, BECNT, **LN**, NICNT; NASB, NET, NRSV], 'to declare openly' [BNTC], 'to declare plainly' [WBC], 'to make a declaration' [NIGTC], 'to say openly' [NTC], 'to say plainly' [PNTC], 'to assert' [LN], 'to acknowledge' [BAGD, CC], 'to tell' [CEV], 'to tell clearly' [NCV], 'to tell plainly' [NIV, REB], 'to tell publicly' [GW], 'to profess' [KJV], 'to reply' [NLT], 'to say' [TEV]. This verb means to make an emphatic declaration, often public, and at times in response to pressure or an accusation [LN].

b. aorist act. indic. of γινώσκω (LN 28.1, 31.27) (BAGD 7. p. 161): 'to know' [LN (28.1); all translations except BECNT, WBC; CEV], 'to recognize' [BAGD, BECNT], 'to acknowledge' [BAGD, LN (31.27), WBC], 'to know about, to have knowledge of, to be acquainted with' [LN (28.1)]. The phrase οὐδέποτε ἔγνων ὑμᾶς 'I never knew you' is translated 'I will have nothing to do with you' [CEV]. This verb may be used to indicate that one does know something [LN (31.27)], or may mean to possess information about [LN (28.1)].

QUESTION—What did Jesus mean when he told them that he never knew them?

This is not to be taken literally. It is a formula of renunciation and means 'I never recognized you as one of my own' [ICC]. He does not acknowledge a personal relationship with them and he renounces them as followers [BECNT]. They are not of his elect [BECNT, WBC]. There is no acknowledgment, fellowship, friendship, or electing love [NTC]. He does not acknowledge them as his true family [NICNT]. They never really believed, and Jesus had never called them to faith and discipleship [CC]. They never really participated as disciples in the kingdom [WBC]. He did not acknowledge them [Lns, PNTC], or recognize them to be what they claimed to be [PNTC]. Despite appearances, he never commissioned them or regarded them as his own [NIBC], and they never had a saving relationship with Jesus Christ [NAC]. It is a formula of renunciation [ICC, NICNT, TH, TRT]. It is a denial of there ever having been any link or relationship between them, based on their failure to do the will of the Father [NIGTC].

Depart[a] from me (you)[b] doers of lawlessness."[c]

LEXICON—a. pres. act. impera. of ἀποχωρέω (LN **15.51**) (BAGD p. 102): 'to depart' [BAGD, BNTC, CC, **LN**, NIGTC, WBC; ESV, KJV, NASB], 'to go away' [BAGD, LN, NTC, PNTC; NET, NRSV], 'to get away' [BECNT, NICNT; GW, NCV, NLT, TEV], 'to leave' [BAGD, LN], 'to get out of one's sight' [CEV]. The phrase ἀποχωρεῖτε ἀπ' ἐμοῦ 'go away from me' is translated 'away from me' [NIV], 'out of my sight' [REB]. This verb means to move away from, with emphasis upon separation [LN].

b. The nominative plural definite article in the phrase οἱ ἐργαζόμενοι 'the (ones) doing' may function as a vocative [BAGD]. It is translated 'you' [all translations except REB], not explicit [REB].

c. ἀνομία (LN 88.139) (BAGD 2. p. 72): 'lawlessness' [BECNT, BNTC, CC, LN, NIGTC, PNTC; ESV, NASB], 'lawless living' [LN], 'lawless deed' [BAGD], 'iniquity' [WBC; KJV], 'evil' [NCV]. The phrase ἐργαζόμενοι τὴν ἀνομίαν 'doers of lawlessness' is translated 'lawbreakers' [NICNT; NET], 'who break God's laws' [NLT], 'law despisers' [NTC], 'wicked people' [TEV], 'evil people' [CEV, GW], 'evildoers' [NIV, NRSV], 'your deeds are evil' [REB]. This noun denotes behavior with complete disregard for the laws or regulations of a society [LN].

QUESTION—What is implied when Jesus sends them away from himself?
Going away *from him* is the essence of being rejected from the kingdom of heaven [NICNT]. He decides who is barred from the kingdom and is banished from his presence [EBC]. They are doomed to destruction of body and soul away from his presence [NTC]. It indicates total rejection [PNTC]. Their rejection in the judgment leads to eternal separation from Christ [NAC]. Jesus is quoting from the passage in Psalm 6:8 which says, 'Depart from me, all you who do iniquity' (NASB) [BECNT, EBC, ICC, Lns, My, PNTC, NICNT, NIGTC, TH, WBC].

DISCOURSE UNIT—7:24–28 [NASB]. The topic is the two foundations.

DISCOURSE UNIT—7:24–29 [CEV, GW, NCV, NET, NIV, NLT, NRSV]. The topic is two kinds of people [NCV], hearers and doers [NRSV], hearing and doing [NET], the wise and foolish builders [NIV], build on the rock [GW], building on a solid foundation [NLT].

DISCOURSE UNIT—7:24–27 [ESV, TEV]. The topic is the two house builders [TEV], build your house on the rock [ESV].

7:24 Therefore^a everyone^b who hears these words^c of mine and does^d them,

LEXICON—a. οὖν (LN 89.50) (BAGD 1.a. p. 593): 'therefore' [BAGD, BECNT, BNTC, CC, LN, PNTC, WBC; GW, KJV, NASB, NIV], 'consequently, accordingly' [BAGD, LN], 'then' [BAGD, LN, NIGTC, NTC; ESV, NRSV], 'so' [BAGD, LN, NICNT; REB], 'so then' [LN; TEV], not explicit [CEV, NCV, NET, NLT]. This conjunction indicates result, often implying the conclusion of a process of reasoning [LN].

b. πᾶς (LN 59.23) (BAGD 1.c.γ. p. 632): 'everyone who' [BAGD, BECNT, BNTC, CC, NICNT, NIGTC, NTC, PNTC, WBC; ESV, GW, NASB, NCV, NET, NIV], 'anyone who' [CEV, NLT, TEV], 'whoever' [BAGD; REB], 'whosoever' [KJV], 'all, every, each' [LN]. This pronominal adjective describes the totality of any object, mass, collective, or extension [LN].

c. λόγος (LN 33.98) (BAGD 1.a.δ. p. 477): 'word' [BAGD, BECNT, BNTC, CC, LN, NICNT, NIGTC, NTC, PNTC, WBC; ESV, NASB, NCV, NET, NIV, NRSV, REB, TEV], 'teaching' [CEV, NLT], 'saying' [LN; KJV], 'message, statement' [LN]. The phrase μου τοὺς λόγους τούτους 'these words of mine' is translated 'what I say' [GW]. The possessive adjective μου 'my' is placed first for emphasis [EBC, WBC]. This noun denotes that which has been stated or said, with primary focus upon the content of the communication [LN].

d. pres. act. indic. of ποιέω (LN 42.7) (BAGD I.1.c.α. p. 682): 'to do' [BAGD, BECNT, BNTC, CC, LN, NIGTC, PNTC, WBC; ESV, KJV, NET], 'to keep' [BAGD], 'to carry out' [BAGD, LN], 'to practice' [BAGD], 'to act on' [NASB, NRSV, REB], 'to put into practice'

[NICNT, NTC; NIV], 'to obey' [CEV, GW, NCV, TEV], 'to follow (it)' [NLT], 'to accomplish, to perform' [LN]. This verb means to do or perform almost any type of activity [LN].

QUESTION—What relationship is indicated by οὖν 'therefore'?

It indicates that an inference is to be drawn from the preceding section [BECNT, CC, EBC, Lns, My, PNTC]. In this section Jesus is drawing an inference either from 7:21–23 [BECNT, CC, EBC], or from 7:15–23 [ICC], or 7:13–23, or possibly even from the entire main body of the sermon from 5:17 on [BECNT]. It indicates that this section is the conclusion of the entire sermon [BNTC, My], though more specifically focusing on conclusions to be drawn from 7:21–23 [My]. It indicates a conclusion to all that Jesus has said so far, but especially in the previous three verses where he was talking about judgment [Lns].

QUESTION—To what does the phrase μου τοὺς λόγους τούτους 'these words of mine' refer?

It refers to the entire sermon [BECNT, BNTC, CC, Lns, NIGTC, NTC, TH, WBC]. It refers specifically to 7:21–23, which summarizes the entire sermon [My]. Jesus' words are the present standard of ethics as well as the future standard of judgment [BECNT]. It refers to everything that Jesus teaches, his entire message [ICC].

QUESTION—To whom was Jesus primarily addressing these comments?

Unlike the very beginning of the sermon where he was primarily addressing his disciples, he is addressing the crowds in this final section [NICNT]. The crowds were at least a secondary audience [ICC, PNTC, WBC]. He is addressing the disciples as well as the crowds [NIGTC].

he-will-be-like[a] a- wise[b] -man, who built[c] his house on the rock;[d]

TEXT—Manuscripts reading ὁμοιωθήσεται 'he will be like' are given a B rating by GNT to indicate it was regarded to be almost certain. A variant reading is ὁμοιώσω αὐτόν 'I will liken him' and it is followed by KJV.

LEXICON—a. fut. pass. indic. of ὁμοιόω (LN 64.4) (BAGD 1., 2. p. 567): 'to be like' [BECNT, CC, NICNT, NIGTC, NTC, WBC; all versions except KJV, NASB, NLT], 'to become like, to be made like' [BAGD 1], 'to be compared (to)' [BAGD 2, BNTC; NASB], 'to be likened (to)' [LN, PNTC], 'to resemble, to be similar to' [LN]. The phrase ὁμοιωθήσεται ἀνδρὶ φρονίμῳ 'he will be like a wise man, who...' is translated 'is wise, like a person who...' [NLT]. This verb means to be like or similar to something else [LN].

b. φρόνιμος (LN **32.31**) (BAGD p. 866): 'wise' [BAGD, BECNT, CC, LN, NIGTC, PNTC, WBC; all versions except REB], 'sensible' [BAGD, NICNT, NTC], 'thoughtful' [BAGD], 'prudent' [BAGD, BNTC], 'with understanding, with insight' [LN]. The phrase ἀνδρὶ φρονίμῳ 'a wise man' is translated 'a man who had the sense (to build)' [REB], 'one who has understanding' [**LN**]. This adjective describes understanding resulting from insight and wisdom [LN].

c. aorist act. indic. of οἰκοδομέω (LN **45.1**) (BAGD 1.a. p. 558): 'to build' [BAGD, **LN**; all translations], 'to construct' [LN]. This verb means to make or erect any kind of construction [LN].

d. πέτρα (LN **2.21**) (BAGD 1.a. p. 654): 'rock' [BAGD, LN], 'bedrock' [LN]. The phrase ἐπὶ τὴν πέτραν 'on the rock' [NICNT, NIGTC; ESV, NASB, NIV] is also translated 'upon a rock' [KJV], 'upon the rock' [CC], 'on rock' [BECNT, NTC, PNTC; GW, NCV, NET, NRSV, REB, TEV], 'on solid rock' [BNTC; CEV, NLT], 'on a foundation of rock' [WBC]. This noun denotes bedrock in contrast with separate pieces of rock or rocky crags and mountain ledges [LN].

QUESTION—What is the function of the future tense of the verb ὁμοιωθήσεται in the phrase 'he will be like a wise-man'?

1. It refers to the future, on the day of judgment [CC, EBC, ICC, Lns, My, NIGTC], at which time the person will be determined to be in the condition that is described here [CC]. It will be in the future that the wisdom of obedience to Jesus will be shown [Lns].
2. It is used with a present tense meaning since this describes something that is true whenever it may occur [TH].

7:25 and the rain[a] came-down[b] and the rivers/floods[c] came

LEXICON—a. βροχή (LN 14.10) (BAGD p. 147): 'rain' [BAGD, LN; all translations]. This noun denotes rain, whether light or torrential [LN].

b. aorist act. indic. of καταβαίνω (LN **15.107**) (BAGD 1.b. p. 408): 'to come down' [BAGD, CC, LN, NIGTC, PNTC; REB], 'to come in torrents' [NLT], 'to fall' [BAGD, BECNT, BNTC, WBC; ESV, NASB, NET, NIV, NRSV], 'to pour down' [NICNT, NTC; CEV, TEV], 'to pour' [GW], 'to descend' [**LN**; KJV], 'to move down, to go down' [LN]. The phrase κατέβη ἡ βροχή 'the rain came down' is translated 'it rained hard' [NCV]. This verb means to move down, irrespective of the gradient [LN].

c. ποταμός (LN 1.76) (BAGD 1. p. 694): 'river, stream' [BAGD, LN]. The phrase ἦλθον οἱ ποταμοί 'the rivers came' is translated 'the floods came' [BECNT, BNTC, NIGTC; ESV, GW, KJV, NASB, NCV, NRSV], 'there came the floods' [NTC], 'the flood came' [NET], 'the rivers came' [CC], 'the rivers flooded' [CEV], 'the rivers flooded over' [TEV], 'the rivers overflowed' [WBC], 'the rivers rose' [NICNT, PNTC], 'the streams rose' [NIV], 'the floods rose' [REB], 'the floodwaters rise' [NLT]. This noun denotes a river or stream normally flowing throughout the year [LN]. It denotes a river or stream and in this verse the plural form refers to mountain torrents or winter torrents which arise in ravines after a heavy rain and carry everything before them [BAGD].

QUESTION—What is the nature of the ποταμοί 'rivers/floods' in this verse?

These are flash floods or torrents that arise after a heavy rain in ravines or *wadis* or normally dry watercourses [BNTC, EBC, NAC, NIBC, NICNT, NTC, PNTC, WBC].

and the winds[a] blew[b] and beat-against[c] that house,
LEXICON—a. ἄνεμος (LN 14.4) (BAGD 1.a. p. 64): 'wind' [BAGD, BECNT, BNTC, CC, LN, NICNT, NIGTC, NTC, PNTC; all translations], 'gale' [WBC]. This plural noun is translated as singular: 'wind' [TEV]. This noun denotes air in relatively rapid movement, but without specification as to the force of the movement [LN].
  b. aorist act. indic. of πνέω (LN 14.4) (BAGD 1.a. p. 679): 'to blow' [BAGD, BECNT, BNTC, CC, LN, NICNT, NIGTC, NTC, PNTC, WBC; ESV, GW, KJV, NASB, NCV, NIV, NRSV, REB]. The phrase ἔπνευσαν οἱ ἄνεμοι καὶ προσέπεσαν 'the winds blew and beat against' is translated 'the winds beat against' [CEV, NET, NLT], 'the wind blew hard against' [TEV]. This verb refers to air in a relatively rapid movement, but without specification as to the force of the movement [LN].
  c. aorist act. indic. of προσπίπτω (LN **19.11**) (BAGD 2. p. 718): 'to beat against' [PNTC; CEV, GW, NET, NIV, NLT], 'to beat upon/on' [BECNT; ESV, KJV, NRSV, REB], 'to strike' [CC], 'to strike against' [BAGD, **LN**], 'to hit' [NCV], 'to hit against' [LN], 'to dash against' [BNTC], 'to fall against' [NIGTC], 'to fall upon' [NTC], 'to attack' [NICNT], 'to assail' [WBC], 'to slam against' [NASB], not explicit [TEV]. This verb means to strike against some object [LN].
QUESTION—What do the floods and storm represent in this illustration?
  They represent the final judgment [BECNT, BNTC, NAC, NIBC, TH, WBC]. They represent the ultimate ordeal, which is death itself [Lns]. They represent the storms of life as well as the final judgment [CC, EBC, My, TRT]. It primarily refers to the day of judgment, but also to the other storms in life as well [NTC]. They represent the eschatological upheaval of the last days prior to the end of the world [ICC, NIGTC].

yet/and[a] it-did- not -fall,[b] for it-had-been-founded[c] on the rock.
LEXICON—a. καί (LN 89.92, 91.12): 'yet' [BECNT, LN (91.12); NIV], 'but' [BNTC, NICNT, NIGTC, NTC, PNTC; CEV, ESV, GW, NCV, NET, NRSV, REB, TEV], 'and yet' [NASB], 'and' [CC, LN (89.92); KJV], not explicit [WBC; NLT]. This conjunction indicates a coordinate relationship [LN (89.92)], or it indicates emphasis, involving surprise and unexpectedness [LN 91.12].
  b. aorist act. indic. of πίπτω (LN 15.119) (BAGD 1.b.β. p. 659): 'to fall' [BAGD, BECNT, BNTC, CC, LN, NIGTC, NTC, PNTC, WBC; all versions except GW, NET, NLT], 'to collapse' [BAGD, NICNT; GW, NET, NLT], 'to fall down' [LN], 'to fall to pieces' [BAGD]. This verb means to fall from a standing or upright position down to the ground or surface [LN].
  c. pluperfect pass. indic. of θεμελιόω (LN **7.42**) (BAGD 1. p. 356): 'to be founded' [BAGD, BNTC, **LN**, NICNT, NIGTC, NTC, PNTC, WBC; ESV, KJV, NASB, NET, NRSV], 'to stand founded' [CC], 'to be built'

[CEV, NCV, NLT, TEV]. The phrase τεθεμελίωτο γὰρ ἐπί 'it had been founded on' is translated 'its foundation was on' [BECNT; GW], 'it had its foundation on' [NIV], 'its foundations were on' [REB]. This verb means to lay or construct a foundation [LN].

7:26 And[a] everyone hearing these words of-mine and not doing them will-be-like the foolish[b] man, who built his house on the sand;[c]
LEXICON—a. καί (LN 89.92): 'and' [BNTC, CC, LN, NTC, PNTC, WBC; ESV, KJV, NRSV, REB], 'but' [BECNT, NICNT; NIV, NLT, TEV], not explicit [NIGTC; CEV, GW, NASB, NCV, NET]. This conjunction indicates coordinate relations [LN].
  b. μωρός (LN **32.55**) (BAGD 1. p. 531): 'foolish' [BAGD, LN; all translations except REB], 'unwise' [LN], 'stupid' [BAGD]. The phrase ἀνδρὶ μωρῷ, ὅστις ᾠκοδόμησεν 'foolish man, who built' is translated 'a man who was foolish enough to build' [REB]. This adjective describes being extremely unwise and foolish [LN].
  c. ἄμμος (LN **2.28**) (BAGD p. 46): 'sand' [BAGD, BECNT, CC, **LN**, NICNT, NIGTC, NTC, PNTC, WBC; all versions], 'sandy soil' [BNTC]. This noun denotes sand. In some areas of the world there is little or no sand, and therefore it may be necessary to render 'sand' in Matthew 7:26 as 'loose soil' or 'unpacked dirt' [LN].

7:27 and the rain fell and the rivers/floods came and the winds blew and beat-against[a] that house, and it-fell and its crash[b] was great.[c]
LEXICON—a. aorist act. indic. of προσκόπτω (LN 19.5) (BAGD 1.b. p. 716): 'to beat against' [BAGD, BNTC, CC, NTC; CEV, ESV, NET, NIV, NLT, NRSV], 'to beat upon' [BECNT], 'to beat upon' [KJV], 'to hammer against' [NICNT], 'to slam against' [NASB], 'to strike against' [LN, NIGTC], 'to batter against' [REB], 'to strike' [PNTC; GW], 'to assail' [WBC], 'to hit' [NCV]. The phrase προσέκοψαν τῇ οἰκίᾳ ἐκείνῃ 'blew and beat against' is translated 'blew hard against' [TEV]. This verb means to strike against something, with the implication of resistance or damage [LN].
  b. πτῶσις (LN 20.50) (BAGD p. 728): 'crash' [NTC, PNTC; CEV, NCV, NIV, NLT, REB], 'fall' [BAGD, BNTC, CC; ESV, KJV, NASB, NRSV, TEV], 'downfall' [NIGTC], 'falling' [BAGD], 'collapse' [BAGD, BECNT, NICNT], 'damage' [WBC], 'destruction' [LN]. The phrase ἡ πτῶσις αὐτῆς μεγάλη 'its crash was great' is translated 'the result was a total disaster' [GW], 'it was totally destroyed' [NET]. This noun, which is a figurative extension of meaning of πτῶσις 'fall,' not occurring in the NT, denotes destruction or ruin, with the implication of having formerly held a position of eminence [LN].
  c. μέγας (LN 78.2): 'great' [BECNT, BNTC, CC, LN, PNTC, WBC; ESV, KJV, NASB, NCV, NIV, NRSV, REB], 'dramatic' [NICNT], 'mighty' [NLT], 'terrible' [LN; TEV], 'tremendous' [NTC], 'on a grand scale'

[NIGTC], not explicit [CEV]. This adjective describes the upper range of a scale of extent [LN].

DISCOURSE UNIT—7:28–29 [ESV, TEV]. The topic is the authority of Jesus.

7:28 And it-happened^a (that) when Jesus finished^b these words,^c

LEXICON—a. aorist mid. γίνομαι (deponent = act.) of (LN 13.107) (BAGD I.3.f. p. 159): 'to happen' [BAGD, BNTC, LN, NIGTC, WBC], 'to come to pass' [PNTC; KJV], 'to occur, to come to be' [LN], 'to take place' [BAGD], not explicit [BECNT, CC, NTC; all versions except NRSV]. The phrase καὶ ἐγένετο 'and it happened' is translated 'and then' [NICNT], 'now' [BECNT, NTC; NRSV]. This verb means to happen, with the implication that what happens is different from a previous state [LN].

b. aorist act. indic. of τελέω (LN 68.22) (BAGD 1. p. 810): 'to finish' [BAGD, BNTC, LN, NIGTC, NTC; all versions except KJV], 'to complete' [BAGD, CC, LN], 'to end' [BECNT, LN, PNTC; KJV], 'to come to the end' [NICNT], 'to bring to an end' [BAGD]. The phrase ἐτέλεσεν τοὺς λόγους τούτους 'finished these words' is translated 'finished speaking these words' [WBC]. This verb means to bring an activity to a successful finish [LN].

c. λόγος (LN 33.98) (BAGD 1.a.δ. p. 477): 'word' [BAGD, BNTC, CC, LN, NIGTC, WBC; NASB], 'saying' [BECNT, LN, NICNT, NTC, PNTC; ESV, KJV], 'message, statement' [LN]. The phrase τοὺς λόγους τούτους 'these words' is translated 'this speech' [GW], 'this discourse' [REB], 'speaking' [CEV], 'saying these things' [NCV, NET, NIV, NLT, NRSV, TEV]. This noun denotes that which has been stated or said, with primary focus upon the content of the communication [LN].

QUESTION—What is the function of this clause?

It contains the first of five instances of a formula that indicates the conclusion of a main discourse and return to narrative [BNTC, CC, EBC, NIBC, NICNT, NICNT, WBC], the other four being found at 11:1, 13:53, 19:1, and 26:1 [BNTC, CC, EBC, NIBC, NICNT, NIGTC, PNTC, TH]. This conclusion to a discourse is different from the other four that follow in that it does not immediately return the reader to the narrative flow [ICC, TH], but provides something of a pause for reflection on what has been said [ICC]. In the other passages this formula transitions to the following narrative, but here it just brings a discourse to a conclusion [TH]. Καὶ ἐγένετο 'and it happened' establishes a structural turning point [EBC].

the crowds^a were-amazed^b at his teaching;^c

LEXICON—a. ὄχλος (LN 11.1) (BAGD 1. p. 600): 'crowd' [BAGD, BNTC, CC, LN, NICNT, NIGTC, NTC, WBC; all versions except KJV, NCV, REB], 'multitude' [BAGD, LN, PNTC], 'throng' [BAGD], 'people' [BECNT; KJV, NCV, REB]. This noun denotes a casual non-membership

group of people, fairly large in size and assembled for whatever purpose [LN].
  b. imperf. pass. indic. of ἐκπλήσσομαι (LN 25.219) (BAGD 2. p. 244): 'to be amazed' [BAGD; GW, NASB, NCV, NET, NIV, NLT, REB, TEV], 'to be astonished' [BECNT, CC, NICNT, NIGTC, NTC, PNTC, WBC; ESV, KJV], 'to be surprised' [CEV], 'to be astounded' [BNTC; NRSV], 'to be greatly astounded' [LN]. This verb means to be so amazed as to be practically overwhelmed [LN].
  c. διδαχή (LN 33.224, 33.236) (BAGD 3. p. 192): 'teaching' [BAGD, LN (33.224), LN (33.236); all translations except KJV, TEV], 'doctrine' [LN (33.224); KJV], 'instruction' [BAGD], 'what is taught' [BAGD]. The phrase τῇ διδαχῇ αὐτοῦ 'his teaching' is translated 'the way he taught' [TEV]. This noun could represent the activity of teaching in the sense of providing instruction in a formal or informal setting [BAGD, LN (33.224)], or it could refer to the content of what is taught [BAGD, LN (33.236)].

QUESTION—Does their amazement reflect a positive attitude toward what Jesus has been saying?

It does not indicate a positive response on their part, and at best their response could only be seen as neutral [CC]. Although they were astonished, they had not yet embraced the way of Christian discipleship [NIGTC].

QUESTION—Were they amazed at how he taught or at what he taught?
  1. They were amazed at how he taught [TH; TEV].
  2. They were amazed at the content of what he taught [Lns; probably KJV].
  3. Here it probably refers both to the manner as well as the content of what he taught [EBC, PNTC].

QUESTION—What is implied by the use of the imperfect tense of ἐξεπλήσσοντο 'were amazed'?

Their astonishment lasted for a while [NTC]. There was an ongoing effect [ICC, PNTC, WBC]. It indicates that they were spellbound [NIBC]. The people may have returned to their homes, struck not only by the novelty of what he was saying, but also with fear because of the note of judgment at the end [ICC].

7:29 for he-was teaching them as[a] having[b] authority[c] and not[d] as their scribes.[e]

  LEXICON—a. ὡς (LN 64.12): 'as' [BECNT, LN, NICNT, NIGTC, NTC, PNTC, WBC; ESV, KJV, NASB, NIV, NRSV], 'like' [LN; CEV, NCV, NET], not explicit [BNTC, CC; NLT, REB, TEV]. This conjunction is a relatively weak indicator of a relationship between events or states [LN].
  b. pres. act. participle of ἔχω (LN 57.1): 'to have' [BECNT, LN, NICNT, NIGTC, NTC, PNTC, WBC; ESV, KJV, NASB, NCV, NET, NIV, NRSV], 'to possess' [LN]. The phrase 'as having authority' is translated 'with authority' [GW, TEV], 'with real authority' [NLT], 'with the note of authority' [BNTC; REB], 'with the conviction that he had authority'

[CC], 'someone with authority' [CEV]. This verb means to have or possess objects or property [LN].
c. ἐξουσία (LN 37.35) (BAGD 2. p. 278): 'authority' [all translations], 'ability, might, power' [BAGD], 'authority to rule, right to control' [LN]. This noun denotes the right to control or govern over [LN].
d. οὐ (LN 69.3): 'not' [BECNT, BNTC, CC, LN, NICNT, NIGTC, NTC, WBC; CEV, ESV, KJV, NASB, NCV, NET, NIV, NRSV]. The phrase οὐχ ὡς 'not as' is translated 'unlike' [GW, REB], 'quite unlike' [NLT], 'instead' [TEV]. This conjunction indicates negative propositions [LN].
e. γραμματεύς (LN 53.94): 'scribe' [BNTC, CC, NICNT, NIGTC, NTC, PNTC; ESV, GW, KJV, NASB, NRSV, REB], 'legal expert' [BECNT], 'professional Torah scholars' [WBC], 'teacher of religious law' [NLT], 'teachers of the law/Law' [NCV, NIV, TEV], 'teacher of the Law of Moses' [CEV], 'expert in the Law of Moses' [LN], 'expert in the Law' [LN; NET], 'one who is learned in the Law' [LN]. This noun denotes a recognized expert in Jewish law (including both canonical and traditional laws and regulations) [LN].

QUESTION—What is the significance of the use of the imperfect tense of ἦν διδάσκων 'he was teaching'?

The crowds were astonished not only at this discourse, but also at Jesus' ongoing ministry of teaching in Galilee [NIC. They were astonished at certain recurring elements in his teaching, such as his repeated 'but *I* say to you' [WBC]. It emphasizes the ongoing nature of the activity [PNTC, WBC], that Jesus continued to teach this way all along [Lns].

QUESTION—What is implied by ὡς ἐξουσίαν ἔχων 'as having authority'?

It means that Jesus was convinced of his own authority [BECNT, CC, EBC, NAC, NICNT, PNTC]. He considered his own words to be authoritative [ICC, WBC]. Jesus claimed authority for himself by contrasting his own teaching with that of the scribes [NICNT, WBC] and even of the Torah [BECNT]. Instead of appealing to prior authorities Jesus said 'But I say to you' [ICC, NICNT, PNTC]. Jesus promised salvation as well as future comfort, and claims that judgment will be based on following or neglecting his words [CC]. He claims that his teaching fulfils the OT, that he has authority to admit or banish from the messianic kingdom, and that he alone knows the will of the Father [EBC]. His authority was readily recognizable [NIGTC]. Instead of quoting from other sources, he spoke from himself [NTC, TH, TRT], and also revealed the mind of God [NTC]. Jesus believed that he was a spokesman from God, bringing a message from God for a new era of history [NAC]. Jesus was invested with prophetic authority and spoke in a candid, forcible, and convincing way [My].

QUESTION—What may be the significance of the possessive adjective αὐτῶν 'their' scribes?

It distinguishes Jewish scribes in general with those scribes who believe in Jesus [BECNT, ICC, NICNT, TH, WBC]. It describes scribes that the crowd is familiar with in contrast to Jesus, who is a new teacher that they don't know [NICNT]. It highlights the contrast between their Jewish scribes and Jesus, who although Jewish himself comes from a source beyond the Jewish race [EBC].

DISCOURSE UNIT—8:1–11:1 [BECNT, EBC]. The topic is the Galilean ministry continues [BECNT], the kingdom extended under Jesus' authority [EBC].

DISCOURSE UNIT—8:1–10:4 [BECNT, EBC]. The topic is narrative 2: three cycles of miracles and discipleship [BECNT], narrative [EBC].

DISCOURSE UNIT—8:1–9:38 [WBC; REB]. The topic is the authoritative deeds of the Messiah [WBC], miracles and teaching [REB].

DISCOURSE UNIT—8:1–9:35 [CC; NAC]. The topic is paradigmatic healing [NAC], Jesus' mighty deeds of authority for the people in need [CC].

DISCOURSE UNIT—8:1–9:34 [NICNT, PNTC]. The topic is the Messiah's authority revealed in his action: an anthology of works of power [NICNT], Jesus' ministry of healing [PNTC].

DISCOURSE UNIT—8:1–22 [ICC]. The topic is a triad of miracle stories.

DISCOURSE UNIT—8:1–13 [NASB]. The topic is Jesus cleanses a leper; the centurion's faith.

DISCOURSE UNIT—8:1–4 [CEV, ESV, GW, NCV, NET, NIV, NLT, NRSV, TEV]. The topic is Jesus cures a man with a skin disease [GW], Jesus heals a sick man [NCV], Jesus heals a man [CEV, TEV], Jesus cleanses a leper [ESV, NRSV], cleansing a leper [NET], the man with leprosy [NIV], Jesus heals a man with leprosy [NLT].

8:1 **And he having-come-down[a] from the mountain, large[b] crowds followed[c] him.**

LEXICON—a. aorist act. participle of καταβαίνω (LN 15.107) (BAGD 1.a.α. p. 408): 'to come down' [BAGD, LN], 'to go down' [BAGD, LN], 'to move down, to descend' [LN]. This aorist participle in the genitive case is part of the genitive absolute construction, in which the subject of the genitive absolute is different from the subject of the verb in the main clause of the sentence. It is translated as an aorist tense verb: 'when he/Jesus came down' [NIGTC, NTC, PNTC; ESV, GW, NASB, NCV, NIV, REB, TEV], 'after he came down' [NET], 'as Jesus/he came down' [CEV, NLT], 'when he was come down' [KJV]; as a past perfect finite verb: 'when he/Jesus had come down' [CC, NICNT, WBC; NRSV], 'after he had come down' [BECNT], 'when he had descended' [BNTC]. This verb means to move down, irrespective of the gradient [LN].

b. πολύς (LN 78.3) (BAGD I.1.a.β. p. 687): 'large' [BAGD, BECNT, NTC, WBC; CEV, GW, NASB, NET, NIV, NLT, TEV], 'great' [BAGD, BNTC, LN, NICNT, NIGTC, PNTC; ESV, KJV, NCV, NRSV, REB],

270   MATTHEW 8:1

'many' [BAGD, CC], 'greatly, much, a great deal' [LN]. This adjective
describes the upper range of a scale of extent [LN].
   c. aorist act. indic. of ἀκολουθέω (LN 15.144) (BAGD 2. p. 31): 'to follow'
      [BAGD, LN; all translations except NTC], 'to accompany' [BAGD,
      NTC], 'to go along with' [BAGD], 'to come behind, to go behind' [LN].
      This verb means to come/go behind or after someone else [LN].
QUESTION—What is meant by the verb 'followed'?
   There is no implication that 'followed' has the sense of discipleship. They
   were gathered to listen to Jesus, but they were not yet ready to commit
   themselves to becoming his disciples [NICNT]. It just means that they were
   present with him [NTC, PNTC], they were not disciples [CC, PNTC]. The
   crowds often had a superficial comprehension of his identity and message
   [BECNT]. Most of these followed out of curiosity, not commitment
   [NICNT, ICC, WBC]. The word introduces a concern about discipleship in
   the narrative section that follows [NAC]. A leper was considered to be
   'unclean' and contagious, so when he approached Jesus, the people must not
   have been crowded around Jesus at that time [BNTC, NICNT].

DISCOURSE UNIT—8:2–9:34 [NIGTC]. The topic is Jesus on the move in
ministry.

8:2 **And behold[a] a-leper[b] having-come[c] bowed-down[d] (before) him saying,**
LEXICON—a. ἰδού (LN 91.13) (BAGD 1.b.β. p. 370): 'behold, see' [BAGD],
      'look' [BAGD, LN], 'listen, pay attention' [LN]. See translations of this
      word at 1:20. This particle is a prompter of attention, and serves to
      emphasize the following statement [LN].
   b. λεπρός (LN 23.162) (BAGD p. 472): 'leper' [BAGD, BECNT, BNTC,
      CC, LN, NICNT, NIGTC, NTC, PNTC, WBC; ESV, KJV, NASB, NET,
      NRSV, REB], 'a man with leprosy' [CEV, NIV, NLT], 'a man with a skin
      disease' [NCV], 'a man with a serious skin disease' [GW], 'a man
      suffering from a dreaded skin disease' [TEV], 'one having a dread skin
      disease' [LN]. This noun denotes a person suffering from a dread skin
      disease [LN].
   c. aorist act. participle of προσέρχομαι (LN 15.77) (BAGD 1. p. 713): 'to
      come/come to' [BECNT, PNTC, WBC; CEV, ESV, GW, NASB, NCV,
      NIV, NRSV, TEV], 'to come up/up to' [NICNT, NIGTC, NTC], 'to
      approach' [BAGD, BNTC, CC, LN; NET, NLT, REB], 'to move toward,
      to come near to' [LN]. This participle is translated 'there came (a leper)'
      [KJV]. This verb means to move toward a reference point, with a possible
      implication in certain contexts of a reciprocal relationship between the
      person approaching and the one who is approached [LN].
   d. imperf. act. indic. of προσκυνέω (LN 17.21) (BAGD 5. p. 717): 'to bow
      down before/in front of' [BECNT; GW, NASB, NCV], 'to bow low
      to/before' [PNTC; NET], 'to bow before' [REB], 'to approach with a
      bow' [NICNT], 'to kneel before/in front of' [NTC; CEV, ESV, NIV,
      NLT, NRSV], 'to kneel down before' [WBC; TEV], 'to fall down in

reverence before' [BNTC], 'to prostrate oneself before' [BAGD, LN], 'to show reverence to' [CC], 'to do reverence to, 'to do obeisance to' [BAGD, NIGTC], 'to worship' [BAGD; KJV]. This verb means to prostrate oneself before someone as an act of reverence, fear, or supplication [LN].

QUESTION—What is the connection between this account and the material that precedes it?

1. Matthew's arrangement is topical rather than chronological [EBC, NAC, NTC, PNTC]. This event may have preceded the Sermon on the Mount [NTC]. What unites the various accounts in this section is a focus on the authority of Jesus [BECNT, CC, ICC, NICNT, WBC].
2. These events occurred the same day, after the Sermon on the Mount had been given [Lns].

QUESTION—What is signaled by the word ἰδού 'behold'?

It indicates that something about the following action was unexpected or sudden [BECNT, Lns, NAC, NTC, TRT, WBC; CEV, NLT]. It introduces vividness [PNTC], or dramatic effect [NIGTC]. It indicates that a new event is about to be narrated [EBC]. It points out something noteworthy, which in this case is the approach of a leper with an unusual degree of faith [CC].

QUESTION—What disease did this man have?

Many think that the biblical term λέπρα 'leprosy' is a collective noun that designates a wide variety of chronic skin diseases, including the leprosy known as Hanson's disease [CC, EBC, LN, NICNT, PNTC]. Because of the uncertainty of the exact nature of the disease, some translate the noun λεπρός 'leper' as 'a man with a skin disease' [NCV], 'a man with a serious skin disease' [GW], 'a man suffering from a dreaded skin disease' [TEV], 'one having a dread skin disease' [LN]. Most, however, translate the word as 'leper'. Some think this man's condition may well have been the true leprosy of Hanson's disease [Lns, My, NTC]. Others think that it could not have been Hansen's disease [BECNT, ICC, NIBC, TH]. Whatever the exact nature of the disease, there was certainly a stigma connected to it [ICC, NICNT, NTC, WBC]. It was considered to be a defiling disease [NIGTC, PNTC] that caused a person to be ceremonially unclean [EBC, ICC, NIBC, NIGTC, NTC, PNTC, TH, TRT] and it excluded him from normal life and worship [NICNT, NIGTC, TRT]. The social and psychological effects were devastating [WBC]. It was a dreaded disease [NIBC] that was regarded with horror [NICNT].

QUESTION—What is meant by the man's action of bowing down and calling Jesus κύριος 'Lord'?

If this man recognized that Jesus was divine, this would be an act of worship, but if he only knows that Jesus is a healer whom he hoped would cure him, this is a way of showing his respect for such a man [PNTC]. He was bowing down to show his great respect for the man Jesus [BECNT, BNTC, CC, EBC, ICC, My, NAC, NIBC, NICNT, NTC, TH, TRT, WBC]. When he calls Jesus 'Lord' he means no more than 'sir' [NIBC, NTC, TH]. He does not view Jesus as deity, but as a prophet and healer [TRT], or as the Messiah [WBC]. He had genuine faith in Jesus, but at this point the fullness of who Jesus is has not yet been shown, so it is not full Christian worship [CC]. He has faith in the divine power and sovereign authority of Jesus [ICC].

"Lord,[a] if you-are-willing[b] you-are-able[c] to-cleanse[d] me."

LEXICON—a. κύριος (LN 12.9, 87.53) (BAGD 2.c.β. p. 459): 'lord' [BAGD, LN (12.9); all translations except GW, REB, TEV], 'Ruler, One who commands' [LN (12.9)], 'sir' [LN (87.53); GW, REB, TEV], 'mister' [LN (87.53)]. As a title for God and for Christ this noun denotes one who exercises supernatural authority over mankind [LN (12.9)]. This noun can also be used as a title of respect used in addressing or speaking of a man [LN (87.53)].

b. pres. act. subj. of θέλω (LN 25.1) (BAGD 2. p. 355): 'to be willing' [BECNT, CC, NICNT, PNTC; GW, NASB, NET, NIV, NLT], 'to will' [BAGD, BNTC, NTC; ESV, KJV, NCV, REB], 'to choose' [NIGTC; NRSV], 'to want' [BAGD, LN, WBC; CEV, TEV], 'to wish' [BAGD, LN], 'to desire' [LN]. This verb means to desire to have or experience something [LN].

c. pres. mid. or pass. (deponent = act.) indic. of δύναμαι (LN 74.5): 'to be able to' [CC, LN, PNTC, WBC], 'can' [BECNT, BNTC, NICNT, NIGTC; all versions except [CEV], 'to have the power to' [CEV]. This verb means to be able to do or to experience something [LN].

d. aorist act. infin. of καθαρίζω (LN 23.137) (BAGD 1.b.α. p. 387): 'to make (someone) clean' [BAGD, BECNT, NICNT, PNTC; all versions except CEV, NCV, NLT], 'to make (someone) well' [CEV], 'to cleanse' [BAGD, BNTC, CC, NTC], 'to cure' [WBC], 'to heal' [NCV], 'to heal and make (someone) clean' [NLT], 'to heal and make ritually pure, to heal and to make ritually acceptable' [LN]. This verb means to heal a person of a disease which has caused ceremonial uncleanness [LN].

QUESTION—What is the significance of the word 'willing'?

It expresses a polite request [TH], and the man leaves it up to Jesus to decide what to do [CC, Lns, My, WBC]. The man was being more than polite. From Jesus' reputation, he assumed that Jesus could heal his disease, but he wasn't sure of Jesus' will to heal him. A Jewish teacher who had a proper concern to maintain ritual purity might be expected to refuse to have anything to do with a leper [NICNT]. The leper had faith in Jesus' healing power; he only feared that he might be passed by [EBC].

QUESTION—Why is the verb καθαρίζω 'cleanse' used instead of 'heal'?

Leprosy was considered to be defiling [NIGTC, PNTC], and those who had it were considered to be unclean [PNTC]. The cleansing was more significant for ceremonial purity than it was physically [NAC]. Leprosy polluted the body [My]. Whereas other diseases would be considered to be cured, healing of leprosy was thought of as cleansing, and the physical

MATTHEW 8:2 273

suffering was not considered to be the worst aspect of the sufferer's problem [NICNT]. The cure would also solve the problem of ritual impurity [TH].

8:3 And^a having-stretched-out^b his hand he-touched^c him saying,

LEXICON—a. καί (LN 89.87): 'and' [BNTC, CC, LN, PNTC, WBC; ESV, KJV], 'and then' [LN], 'then' [NIGTC], 'so' [NTC], not explicit [BECNT, NICNT; CEV, GW, NASB, NCV, NET, NIV, NLT, NRSV, REB, TEV]. This conjunction indicates a sequence of closely related events [LN].
- b. aorist act. participle of ἐκτείνω (LN 16.19) (BAGD 1. p. 245): 'to stretch out' [BAGD, BNTC, CC, LN, NICNT, NIGTC, NTC, PNTC; ESV, NASB, NET, NRSV, REB], 'to extend' [BAGD, LN, WBC], 'to reach out' [BECNT, LN; GW, NCV, NIV, NLT, TEV], 'to put forth' [KJV], not explicit [CEV]. This verb means to cause an object to extend in space (for example, by becoming straight, unfolded, or uncoiled) [LN].
- c. aorist mid. indic. of ἅπτομαι (LN 24.73) (BAGD 2.b. p. 103): 'to touch' [BAGD, LN; all translations except CEV]. The phrase ἐκτείνας τὴν χεῖρα ἥψατο αὐτοῦ 'having stretched out the hand he touched' is translated 'Jesus put his hand on the man' [CEV]. This verb means to touch, with the implication of relatively firm contact [LN].

QUESTION—What is signified by Jesus touching the leprous man?

It expresses compassion to the man, who probably had not been touched by non-lepers for years [PNTC]. Touching the man would normally have been thought to be defiling [EBC, NIBC, NICNT, TH, TRT, WBC], but the point here is that nothing remains defiled when Jesus touches it [EBC]. The gesture would have been considered shocking [NAC, WBC], a violation of a biblical taboo [NICNT]. Normally contact with a leper would make one unclean, but in this case it goes the other way, and Jesus' touch makes the leper clean [CC].

"I-am-willing, be-cleansed." And immediately^a his leprosy^b was-cleansed.

LEXICON—a. εὐθέως (LN 67.53) (BAGD p. 320): 'immediately' [BAGD, BECNT, LN, NICNT, NIGTC, NTC, PNTC, WBC; all versions except CEV, NLT, TEV], 'at once' [BAGD, BNTC, CC; CEV, TEV], 'instantly' [NLT], 'right away, then' [LN]. In this sentence this adverb is emphatic [TH]. This adverb describes an event occurring at a point of time immediately subsequent to a previous point of time (the actual interval of time differs appreciably, depending upon the nature of the events and the manner in which the sequence is interpreted by the writer) [LN].
- b. λέπρα (LN 23.161) (BAGD p. 471): 'leprosy' [BAGD, LN; all translations except GW, NCV, TEV], 'disease' [NCV, TEV], 'skin disease' [GW], 'dread skin disease' [LN]. This noun denotes a dreaded condition of the skin, including what is now regarded as leprosy, as well as certain other types of infectious skin diseases resulting in a person's being regarded as ceremonially unclean and thus excluded from normal relations with other people [LN].

QUESTION—What is implied by Jesus' words, 'I am willing'?
There is a Christological significance in Jesus saying 'I am willing' instead of 'God is willing' [NICNT]. Jesus' willingness is God's 'Yes!' to this man [WBC]. Jesus' action showed that his will is decisive [EBC]. It expresses Jesus' sovereignty [ICC, NAC].

8:4 **And Jesus says to-him, "See[a] (that) you-tell no-one, but go[b] show[c] yourself to-the-priest[d]**

- LEXICON—a. pres. act. impera. of ὁράω (LN 30.45) (BAGD 2.b. p. 578): 'to see that' [BNTC, CC, NICNT, NIGTC, PNTC; ESV, NASB, NET, NIV, NRSV, REB], 'to see' [KJV], 'to see to it' [BAGD], 'to make sure' [BECNT], 'to be sure' [NTC], 'to be careful' [WBC], 'take care' [BAGD], 'to consider, to pay attention to, to concern oneself with' [LN], not explicit [CEV, GW]. The phrase Ὅρα μηδενὶ εἴπῃς 'see that you tell no one' is translated as an imperative: 'don't tell anyone' [GW, NCV, NLT], 'Listen! Don't tell anyone' [TEV]. This verb means to take special notice of something, with the implication of concerning oneself [LN].
- b. pres. act. impera. of ὑπάγω (LN 15.35) (BAGD 2. p. 836): 'to go' [BAGD, BECNT, BNTC, CC, LN, NTC, PNTC, WBC; all versions except GW, KJV, TEV], 'to go straight to' [TEV], 'to go off' [NIGTC], 'to go your way' [KJV], 'to go away from, to depart, to leave' [LN], not explicit [GW]. The imperative ὕπαγε 'go' is translated 'off you go' [NICNT]. This verb means to move away from a reference point [LN].
- c. aorist act. impera. of δείκνυμι (LN 28.47) (BAGD 1.a. p. 172): 'to show' [BAGD, LN; all translations except CEV, NLT, TEV], 'to make known' [BAGD, LN], 'to demonstrate' [LN]. The phrase σεαυτὸν δεῖξον 'show yourself' is translated 'show that you are well' [CEV], 'let him examine you' [NLT, TEV]. This verb means to make known the character or significance of something by visual, auditory, gestural, or linguistic means [LN].
- d. ἱερεύς (LN 53.87) (BAGD 1.b.α. p. 372): 'priest' [BAGD, LN; all translations]. This noun denotes one who performs religious rites and duties on behalf of others [LN].

QUESTION—Why did Jesus forbid him to tell anyone?
Jesus did not want people to misunderstand his motives and conclude that he was a just a wonder-worker, or that he might possibly be someone who could lead a popular revolt against the Romans [EBC, PNTC]. Jesus did not want to inflame messianic expectations among the crowds of people [BECNT, NICNT, WBC], or to have his message of the kingdom overshadowed by emotional excitement that could stem from the healing [BNTC]. Jesus wanted the man to go without delay to perform the proper procedures necessary for being reinstated in normal social contact [CC, NICNT, NIGTC]. Jesus did not want the priests to hear reports of Jesus healing the leper until the temple priest had examined the man and pronounced him cured [Lns].

MATTHEW 8:4

QUESTION—Where would he go to show himself to the priest and offer the gift?

He would have to go to the temple in Jerusalem [BNTC, CC, EBC, Lns, My, NICNT, NTC, TH, TRT].

and offer[a] the gift[b] that Moses commanded,[c] for a-testimony[d] to-them."

LEXICON—a. aorist act. impera. of προσφέρω (LN 57.80) (BAGD 2.a. p. 719): 'to offer' [BAGD, BNTC, CC, NIGTC; ESV, GW, KJV, NCV, NIV, NRSV, TEV], 'to bring' [BAGD, LN, NTC; NET], 'to bring as an offering' [WBC], 'to present' [BAGD, BECNT, LN; NASB], 'to take along' [NLT]. The phrase προσένεγκον τὸ δῶρον 'offer the gift' is translated 'make the offering' [NICNT, PNTC; REB], 'take a gift to the temple' [CEV]. This verb means to present something to someone, often involving actual physical transport of the object in question [LN].

b. δῶρον (LN 57.84) (BAGD 2. p. 211): 'gift' [BNTC, CC, LN, NIGTC, WBC; CEV, ESV, KJV, NCV, NIV, NRSV], 'offering' [BECNT, NICNT, NTC, PNTC; NASB, NET, NLT, REB], 'sacrifice' [GW, TEV], 'present' [LN]. This noun denotes that which is given or granted [LN].

c. aorist act. indic. of προστάσσω (LN 33.325) (BAGD p. 718): 'to command' [BAGD, BECNT, CC, LN, NIGTC, PNTC, WBC; all versions except NLT, REB, TEV], 'to order' [BAGD, LN; TEV], 'to prescribe' [BNTC, NTC], 'to lay down' [NICNT; REB], 'to instruct, to tell' [LN]. The phrase ὃ προσέταξεν Μωϋσῆς 'that Moses commanded' is translated 'required in the law of Moses' [NLT]. This verb means to give detailed instructions as to what must be done [LN].

d. μαρτύριον (LN 33.264) (BAGD 1.a. p. 493): 'testimony' [BAGD, BECNT, BNTC, CC, NIGTC, NTC, PNTC; KJV, NASB, NET, NIV, NRSV], 'witness' [LN, NICNT, WBC], 'proof' [BAGD; ESV, GW]. The phrase εἰς μαρτύριον αὐτοῖς 'for a testimony to them' is translated 'to certify the cure' [REB], 'to prove to everyone that you are cured' [TEV], 'and everyone will know that you have been healed' [CEV], 'as proof to them that you are clean' [GW], 'This will show the people what I have done' [NCV], 'This will be a public testimony to them that you have been cleansed' [NLT]. This noun denotes the content of what is witnessed or said [LN].

QUESTION—What was the gift Moses had commanded to be offered?

The gift was the sacrifice Moses had commanded for the cleansing of a leper in Lev. 14:10, 21–22 [PNTC]. The offering was to be two birds, some cedar wood, scarlet, hyssop, two male lambs and one ewe lamb (or only one lamb if the person was poor), a grain offering, and some olive oil [ICC]. Offering the ritual sacrifices would require eight days, and must be done at the temple in Jerusalem [NICNT].

QUESTION—What is meant by doing this 'for a testimony to them'?

1. This would be a proof to people in general that the man was cleansed [CC, My, NICNT, NIGTC, TRT, WBC]. The man needed to receive a

testimony *from* the priests *for* the people in order to be restored to his place in society [WBC]. The examination by the priest followed by the cleansing ritual and offering of a sacrifice would testify that the cure was complete and the ostracized man should be accepted back among the people [NICNT].
  2. This would be a proof to the priests that Jesus had the power to heal [NTC], and that he obeyed the Mosaic Law by sending the healed leper to the priest for cleansing [BNTC, NTC].
QUESTION—What is included in this testimony?
  The testimony would certify that the man was healed and could take his place in society again [NICNT, PNTC, TH, TRT, WBC]. It would also be a testimony that Jesus not only had healed the man, but that he also had respect for Jewish law [NTC]. It was a testimony of the power of the kingdom [EBC], of Jesus' authority over sickness [NAC].

DISCOURSE UNIT—8:5–13 [ESV, GW, NCV, NET, NIV, NLT, NRSV, TEV]. The topic is a believing army officer [GW], the faith of a Roman officer [NLT], Jesus heals a soldier's servant [NCV], Jesus heals a centurion's servant [NRSV], Jesus heals an army officer's servant [CEV], Jesus heals a Roman officer's servant [TEV], the faith of a centurion [ESV], the faith of the centurion [NIV], healing a centurion's servant [NET].

8:5 And (Jesus) having-entered into Capernaum a-centurion[a] approached him imploring[b] him **8:6** and saying, "Lord,[c] my servant[d] lies[e] in the house[f] paralyzed,[g] suffering[h] terribly.[i]"

LEXICON—a. ἑκατόνταρχος or ἑκατοντάρχης (LN **55.16**) (BAGD p. 237): 'centurion' [BAGD, BECNT, BNTC, CC, **LN**, NICNT, NIGTC, NTC, PNTC, WBC; ESV, KJV, NASB, NET, NIV, NRSV, REB], 'army officer' [CEV, NCV], 'Roman army officer' [GW], 'Roman officer' [NLT, TEV], 'captain' [BAGD, LN]. This noun denotes a Roman officer in command of about one hundred men [LN].
  b. pres. act. participle of παρακαλέω (LN 33.168) (BAGD 3. p. 617): 'to implore' [BAGD, BECNT; NASB], 'to implore urgently' [PNTC], 'to appeal to' [BAGD, LN, NIGTC; NRSV], 'to request' [BAGD, LN], 'to entreat' [BAGD, BNTC], 'to beseech' [CC, PNTC; KJV], 'to ask for help' [NTC; NET, NIV, REB], 'to beg for help' [TEV], 'to beg for' [GW, NCV], 'to ask for (earnestly), to plead for' [LN], 'to plead with' [NLT]. The phrase παρακαλῶν αὐτὸν καὶ λέγων 'imploring him and saying' is translated 'with an urgent request' [NICNT], 'appealing to (him)' [ESV], 'said' [CEV]. This verb means to ask for something earnestly and with propriety [LN].
  c. κύριος (see above at 8:2). 'Lord' [BECNT, BNTC, CC, NICNT, NIGTC, NTC, WBC; all versions except GW, REB, TEV], 'sir' [PNTC; GW, REB, TEV].
  d. παῖς (LN 9.41, 10.36, 87.77) (BAGD 1.a.γ. p 604): 'servant' [BAGD, BECNT, BNTC, CC, NICNT, PNTC; all versions except NLT], 'young

servant' [NLT], 'servant-boy' [NTC], 'slave' [BAGD, LN (87.77)], 'lad' [NIGTC], 'son' [WBC], 'child' [LN (9.41, 10.36)]. This noun denotes a slave, possibly serving as a personal servant who was kindly regarded by his master [LN (87.77)], or a young person, normally below the age of puberty and without distinction as to sex [LN 9.41)], or one's immediate offspring, without specific reference to sex or age [LN (10.36)].
e. perf. pass. indic. of βάλλω (BAGD 1.b. p. 131): 'to lie' [BAGD, BECNT, BNTC, NICNT, PNTC, WBC; all versions except CEV, NCV, TEV], 'to be cast' [CC], 'to be laid out' [NIGTC], 'to be bed-ridden' [NTC], 'to be in bed' [NCV], 'to be sick in bed' [TEV], not explicit [CEV].
f. οἰκία (LN 7.3) (BAGD 1.a. p. 557): 'house' [BAGD, CC, LN, NICNT], 'home' [LN], 'dwelling, residence' [LN]. The phrase ἐν τῇ οἰκίᾳ 'in the house' is translated 'at home' [BAGD, BECNT, BNTC, NIGTC, PNTC, WBC; all versions except NLT], not explicit [NLT]. This noun denotes a building or place where one dwells [LN].
g. παραλυτικός (LN 23.171) (BAGD p. 620): 'paralyzed' [BECNT, BNTC, LN, NICNT, NIGTC, PNTC; ESV, GW, NASB, NET, NIV, NLT, NRSV, REB], 'lame' [BAGD, LN], 'crippled' [WBC], 'sick of the palsy' [KJV]. This adjective is translated as a noun: 'paralytic' [BAGD, CC]; as a prepositional phrase: 'with paralysis' [NTC]; as a verb phrase: 'unable to move' [TEV], 'he can't even move' [CEV], 'he can't move his body' [NCV]. This adjective describes being lame and/or paralyzed [LN].
h. pres. pass. participle of βασανίζω (LN 38.13) (BAGD 2.a. p. 134): 'to suffer torture' [BNTC], 'to be tortured' [LN], 'to be tormented' [CC, LN; KJV, NASB]. This passive verb is translated as active: 'to suffer' [NIGTC, NTC, PNTC, WBC; ESV, TEV]. This participle is translated as a phrase: 'in pain' [NICNT; GW, NCV, NLT], 'in such pain' [CEV], 'in anguish' [NET], 'in suffering' [NIV], 'in distress' [NRSV], 'racked with pain' [NRSV]. This verb means to punish by physical torture or torment [LN].
i. δεινῶς (LN **78.24**) (BAGD p. 173): 'terribly' [BECNT, CC, **LN**, NIGTC, NTC, WBC; ESV, TEV], 'grievously' [KJV], 'fearfully' [NASB], 'bitterly' [LN], not explicit [REB]. This adverb is translated as an adjective describing the suffering: 'terrible' [BNTC, NICNT; CEV, GW, NET, NIV, NLT, NRSV], 'much (pain)' [NCV]; as a noun phrase: 'great (pain)' PNTC]. It describes an extreme point on a scale involving negative values [LN].

QUESTION—What was a 'centurion'?

A centurion was an officer in the Roman army in charge of approximately 100 soldiers [CC, ICC, NICNT, PNTC]. Centurions were the backbone of the Roman forces, maintaining discipline and carrying out orders [EBC]. This centurion was a Gentile [CC, Lns, My, NAC, PNTC], either a Roman [ICC] or Syrian [TH]. He would have commanded men who were in the direct service of Herod Antipas [CC, Lns, My, NICNT], and they would have been recruited from the region under Herod's rule. They were probably

Syrian [CC, NICNT], Idumean [CC], or Phoenician [NICNT], but not Romans or Jews [EBC, NICNT].

QUESTION—What is implied by the centurion calling Jesus κύριος 'Lord'?

It shows that the man acknowledges Jesus' authority [ICC], that at the least he regarded Jesus as having authority over the physical realm [WBC]. It is more than politeness, as indicated by his assumption of Jesus' authority [NICNT]. It expresses submission [NAC]. In calling him 'Lord' he acknowledges Jesus' power to help [BNTC]. It is polite address, similar to 'sir' [EBC, PNTC, TH; GW, REB, TEV]. It suggests that the man has the essence of genuine faith [CC].

QUESTION—Does the word παῖς refer to the man's servant or his son?
1. It means 'servant' [BECNT, BNTC, CC, ICC, Lns, My, NAC, NICNT, NIGTC, NTC, PNTC, TH, TRT; all versions]. He was a servant, but there was a familial affection [NIGTC]. He was a house slave [ICC], or perhaps an orderly [TH]. The word used in the parallel passage at Luke 7:2 is δοῦλος 'servant' [EBC] or 'slave' [PNTC].
2. Here it means 'son' [WBC].

8:7 And (Jesus) says to-him, "I, coming, will-heal[a] him."

LEXICON—a. fut. act. indic. of θεραπεύω (LN 23.139) (BAGD 2. p. 359): 'to heal' [BAGD, LN], 'to cure' [LN], 'to restore' [BAGD]. The direct quotation Ἐγὼ ἐλθὼν θεραπεύσω αὐτόν 'I, coming will heal him' is translated as a statement: 'I will come and heal him' [BECNT, NTC, WBC; ESV, KJV, NASB, NET, NLT; similarly GW], 'I will go and heal him' [CEV, NCV, NIV], 'I will come and cure him' [NRSV, REB], 'I will go and make him well' [TEV]. It is translated as a question: 'Shall I come and heal him?' [BNTC, PNTC], 'Shall I myself come and heal him?' [CC], 'Am I to come and heal him?' [NICNT, NIGTC]. This verb means to cause someone to recover health [LN].

QUESTION—Is Jesus making a statement or asking a question?
1. He is making a statement [BECNT, Lns, My, NAC, NIBC, NTC, WBC; CEV, ESV, GW, KJV, NASB, NCV, NET, NIV, NLT, NRSV, REB, TEV]. The ἐγώ 'I' is emphatic to dispel any doubt that he would go [NTC]. The emphatic pronoun makes this a forceful statement, possibly emphasizing Jesus' authority and control [NAC].
2. He is asking a rhetorical question [BNTC, CC, EBC, ICC, NICNT, NIGTC, PNTC]. That it is a question is indicated by the emphatic ἐγώ 'I' [CC, EBC, ICC, NICNT, PNTC]. The emphatic pronoun draws attention to the highly irregular suggestion that Jesus, being a good Jew, should visit a Gentile home [NICNT]. He is asking, "Shall I, even though I am a Jew, come heal him?" [BNTC, EBC, NICNT, NIGTC]. Jesus is not expressing reluctance to visit a Gentile in his home, he just wants to find out more about the faith of this Gentile who has called him 'Lord' [CC].

8:8 And the centurion answering said, "Lord, I-am not worthy[a] that you-come under my roof,[b] but only speak by-a-word,[c] and my servant will-be-healed.[d]

LEXICON—a. ἱκανός (LN 75.2) (BAGD 2. p. 374): 'worthy' [BAGD, BECNT, BNTC, CC, NIGTC, NTC, PNTC, WBC; ESV, KJV, NASB, NCV, NET, NLT, NRSV, REB], 'fit' [BAGD, NICNT], 'good enough' [CEV], 'adequate' [LN], 'qualified' [BAGD, LN]. The phrase οὐκ εἰμὶ ἱκανός 'I am not worthy' is translated 'I don't/do not deserve' [GW, NIV, TEV]. This adjective describes being adequate for something [LN].

b. στέγη (LN 7.50) (BAGD p. 765): 'roof' [BAGD, LN]. The phrase ὑπὸ τὴν στέγην 'under my roof' [BECNT, BNTC, CC, NICNT, NIGTC, NTC, PNTC, WBC; ESV, KJV, NASB, NET, NIV, NRSV, REB] is also translated 'into my house' [CEV, GW, NCV, TEV], 'into my home' [NLT]. This noun denotes the roof or top of a house [LN].

c. λόγος (LN 33.98) (BAGD 1.a.α. p. 477): 'word' [BAGD, LN], 'saying, message, statement, question' [LN]. The phrase μόνον εἰπὲ λόγῳ 'only speak by a word' is translated 'only say the word' [PNTC; ESV], 'only speak a word' [WBC], 'only speak the word' [NRSV], 'speak the word only' [KJV], 'you need only say the word' [REB], 'just say the word' [NASB, NET, NIV], 'just give the order' [CEV, TEV], 'just issue a command' NICNT], 'just give a command' [GW], 'you only need to command it' [NCV], 'just say the word from where you are' [NLT]. This noun denotes that which has been stated or said, with primary focus upon the content of the communication [LN].

d. fut. pass. indic. of ἰάομαι (LN 23.136) (BAGD 1. p. 368): 'to be healed' [BECNT, BNTC, CC, LN, NIGTC, PNTC, WBC; ESV, GW, KJV, NASB, NCV, NET, NIV, NLT, NRSV], 'to be cured' [LN, NICNT, NTC; REB], 'to get well' [CEV, TEV], 'to be made well' [LN]. This verb means to cause someone to become well again after having been sick [LN].

QUESTION—In what sense does he consider himself unworthy for Jesus to come to his house?

Although this centurion had been given some authority from the Roman emperor, he knew that God had given Jesus a much more important position of authority in his kingdom so that Jesus spoke for God [EBC]. The centurion does not feel that he was worthy to have one with such great authority enter his house [BECNT, EBC, NIGTC, NTC, TH]. He recognizes Jesus' greatness [My, PNTC]. Jesus was too important to enter his house [TH]. Some think that the centurion's feeling of unworthiness involved his sensitivity to the Jewish mores, which prohibited certain associations with Gentiles such as entering their houses [BECNT, BNTC, CC, Lns, My, NAC, NICNT, NIGTC, NTC, WBC]. Although it would not be proper for Jesus to enter his house, Jesus could just speak a word from a distance and the servant would be healed [NICNT].

QUESTION—Why is μου 'my' near the beginning of its clause?

The forefronted position of the pronoun 'my' in the Greek text makes it emphatic [CC, NAC, NICNT, WBC]: that you come under *my* roof. It indicates the man's subordination to Jesus [NAC]. It implies that he recognized the impropriety of asking Jesus to come to the house of a Gentile [NICNT].

QUESTION—What relationship is indicated by the dative case of λόγῳ 'word'?

The dative indicates that the word is the instrument by which he will be healed [My, PNTC]. 'By a word' is redundant, since one always speaks with words, but this redundancy emphasizes his trust in the authority of what Jesus says [CC].

8:9 For I also am a-man under authority,[a] having soldiers under myself, and I-say to-this-one, 'Go', and he-goes, and to-another, 'Come', and he-comes, and to- my -servant,[b] 'Do this', and he-does-(it)."

LEXICON—a. ἐξουσία (LN 37.75) (BAGD 4.a. p. 278): 'authority' [BAGD], 'authority to rule, right to control' [LN]. The phrase 'I also am a man under authority' [NICNT, PNTC; ESV, KJV, NASB, NET, NIV, NRSV] is also translated 'I am also a man/person under authority' [BECNT, NIGTC], 'I myself am a man under authority' [BNTC, NTC], 'even I myself am a man under authority' [CC], 'I am a man under the authority of others' [NCV], 'I am under orders' [REB], 'I am under the authority of my superior officers' [NLT; similarly TEV], 'I have officers who give orders to me' [CEV], 'I'm in a chain of command' [GW]. To be under authority means to have been granted authority by superiors that will in turn be exercised over others, so it is to be translated 'I am a man with authority' [WBC]. This noun denotes the right to control or govern over others [LN].

b. δοῦλος (LN 87.76) (BAGD 1.a. p. 205): 'servant' [CEV, ESV, GW, KJV, NCV, NIV, REB], 'slave' [BAGD, BECNT, BNTC, CC, LN, NICNT, NIGTC, NTC, PNTC, WBC; NASB, NET, NLT, NRSV, TEV], 'bondservant' [LN]. This noun denotes one who is a slave in the sense of becoming the property of an owner (though in ancient times it was frequently possible for a slave to earn his freedom) [LN].

QUESTION—What relationship is indicated by the conjunction γάρ 'for'?

This conjunction indicates the reason why the centurion knew Jesus had the authority to heal by just saying a word [EBC, WBC]. Some translations make this connection explicit: 'I know, for' [REB], 'I know this because' [NLT], 'as you know' [GW]. In the same way the orders of a centurion are to be obeyed, so must Jesus' order be obeyed by the evil powers responsible for the servant's illness [WBC]. There was no reason why the servant's disability should resist Jesus' authority any more than the centurion's subordinates should resist his authority [NICNT].

QUESTION—What is meant by the phrase καὶ ἐγώ 'I also'?

In the Greek text, the pronoun ἐγώ 'I' is in an emphatic position [TH], 'I myself' [BNTC, CC, EBC, Lns, NTC; NIV, REB]. The centurion is saying '*I also/too* am a man under authority' [BECNT, LN, NICNT, NIGTC, PNTC, WBC; ESV, NASB, NCV, NET, NRSV, TEV]. The centurion is emphasizing a point of similarity between himself and Jesus, yet expressing his humility by saying 'even I can have my orders obeyed, though I am not nearly so great as you' [CC, Lns, NIBC, NTC]. The similarity is that 'even I can cause an action to happen at a distance' [PNTC]. Just as the centurion's orders represent all the authority of imperial Rome, so also when Jesus speaks, God is speaking. Jesus' word is effective because it is God's word [EBC].

QUESTION—Why aren't the tenses the same for the three imperatives, Πορεύθητι 'Go!' (aorist), Ἔρχου 'Come!' (present), and Ποίησον 'Do!' (aorist)?

The tense of the imperative is determined by the meaning of the specific verb itself, not by any consideration of aspect or time relative to the action [EBC, PNTC]. The use of the present imperative for the second verb does not appear to indicate any difference in meaning [CC].

8:10 And having-heard (this) Jesus marveled[a] and said to-those following,[b] "Truly[c] I-say-to-you, with[d] no-one in Israel have-I-found[e] such[f] faith.[g]

TEXT—Manuscripts reading παρ' οὐδενὶ τοσαύτην πίστιν ἐν τῷ Ἰσραὴλ εὗρον 'with no one in Israel have I found such faith' are given a B rating by GNT to indicate it was regarded to be almost certain. Other manuscripts read οὐδὲ ἐν τῷ Ἰσραὴλ τοσαύτην πίστιν εὗρον 'I have not found so great faith even in Israel'. Only KJV follows this reading.

LEXICON—a. aorist act. indic. of θαυμάζω: (LN 25.213) (BAGD 1.a.α. p. 352): 'to marvel' [BAGD, BNTC, CC, LN, WBC; ESV, KJV, NASB], 'to wonder' [BAGD, LN], 'to be amazed' [LN, NICNT, NIGTC, NTC; GW, NCV, NET, NLT, NRSV], 'to be astonished' [BAGD, BECNT, PNTC; NIV], 'to be surprised' [CEV, TEV]. The phrase ἀκούσας δὲ ὁ Ἰησοῦς ἐθαύμασεν 'and having heard this Jesus marveled' is translated 'Jesus heard him with astonishment' [REB]. This verb means to wonder or marvel at some event or object [LN], though whether the reaction is favorable or unfavorable depends on the context [BAGD, LN].

b. pres. act. participle of ἀκολουθέω (LN 15.144): 'to follow' [BECNT, BNTC, CC, LN, NICNT, NIGTC, PNTC, WBC; all versions except CEV, TEV], 'to accompany' [NTC], 'to come behind, to go behind' [LN]. This participle is translated as a noun: 'followers' [NICNT]; as a phrase 'the crowd following him' [CEV], 'the people following him' [TEV]. This verb means to come/go behind or after someone else [LN].

c. ἀμήν (LN 72.6) (BAGD 2. p. 45): 'truly' [BAGD, BECNT, BNTC, CC, LN, NICNT, PNTC, WBC; ESV, NASB, NRSV, REB], 'solemnly' [NTC], 'verily' [KJV], 'amen' [NIGTC], 'indeed, it is true that' [LN], not explicit [CEV, TEV]. The phrase Ἀμὴν λέγω ὑμῖν 'truly I say to you' is translated 'I tell you the truth' [NCV, NET, NIV, NLT], 'I can guarantee this truth' [GW]. This particle expresses strong affirmation of what is declared [LN].

d. παρά with dative (LN 90.14) (BAGD II.2.d. p. 610): 'with' [BAGD, BECNT, CC, NTC, PNTC, WBC; ESV, NASB], 'in' [BAGD, BNTC, NIGTC; CEV, GW, NET, NRSV], not explicit [NIGTC; KJV, NCV, NIV, NLT, REB, TEV]. The clause παρ' οὐδενὶ τοσαύτην πίστιν ἐν τῷ Ἰσραὴλ εὗρον 'with no one in Israel have I found such faith' is translated 'I have not found anyone in Israel with faith like this' [NICNT], 'I have not found anyone in Israel with such great faith' [NIV], 'nowhere in Israel have I found such faith' [REB], 'I haven't seen faith like this in all Israel' [NLT], 'I have never found anyone in Israel with faith like this' [TEV], 'this is the greatest faith I have found, even in Israel' [NCV]. This preposition indicates the agentive source of an activity, though often remote and indirect [LN].

e. aorist act. indic. of εὑρίσκω (LN 27.27) (BAGD 1.b. p. 325): 'to find' [BAGD, LN; all translations except NLT], 'to see' [NLT], 'to discover' [LN], 'to come upon' [BAGD, LN], 'to happen to find' [LN]. This verb means to learn the location of something, either by intentional searching or by unexpected discovery [LN].

f. τοσοῦτος (LN 59.18) (BAGD 1.a.β. p. 823): 'such' [NIGTC, NTC, PNTC, WBC; ESV, NET, NRSV, REB], 'such great' [BECNT, BNTC; NASB, NIV], 'so great' [KJV], 'greatest' [NCV], 'so strong' [CC], 'as strong as this' [BAGD], 'as great as this' [GW], 'like this' [NICNT; NLT, TEV], 'this much' [CEV], 'so much, so great, such a large' [LN]. This adjective describes a quantity considerably beyond normal expectations [LN].

g. πίστις (LN 31.85) (BAGD 2.b.α. p. 663): 'faith' [BAGD, LN; all translations], 'trust' [BAGD, LN], 'confidence' [BAGD]. This noun denotes the act of believing to the extent of complete trust and reliance [LN].

QUESTION—Whom was Jesus addressing?
1. He was speaking to the crowds that had been following him [CC, EBC, ICC, NIGTC, TH]. This probably refers to the 'large crowd' mentioned in verse 1 [TH].
2. He was speaking to his disciples. Jesus and his disciples had left the crowd mentioned in verse 1 when they returned to Capernaum [NICNT].
3. He was speaking to his disciples as well as the crowd [BECNT, WBC], including those followers who were less committed to him [BECNT].
4. He was speaking to those Jewish friends whom the centurion had sent (as mentioned in the account of this story in Luke 9) [Lns].

QUESTION—What is meant by τοσοῦτος 'such' faith?
The man's faith is his trust in Jesus' ability and readiness to give help in unexpected ways. The adjective 'such' may refer either to the quantity of his

faith or the quality of his faith, and perhaps it even includes both in this verse [PNTC]. A faith like his could mean that he trusts God *so much*, or he trusts God *in this way*, although the two overlap in this verse [TH]. His great faith was his conviction that Jesus had the authority to heal [NICNT]. It is the kind of faith that recognizes that it is in Jesus that God's help is offered [NIGTC]. The greatness of his faith was not just his strong belief that Jesus could heal from a distance, but even more it was the degree to which he understood the nature of Jesus' person and authority [EBC].

8:11 And I-tell you that many[a] from east and west[b] will-come and will-recline[c] (at table) with Abraham and Isaac and Jacob in the kingdom of heaven,

    LEXICON—a. πολύς (LN 59.1) (BAGD I.2.a.α. p. 688): 'many' [BAGD, BECNT, CC, LN, NICNT, NIGTC, NTC, PNTC, WBC; all versions except CEV, NCV, NLT], 'many people' [CEV, NCV], 'many Gentiles' [NLT], 'a great deal of, a great number of' [LN]. This noun denotes a relatively large quantity of objects or events [LN].

    b. δυσμή (LN 82.2) (BAGD p. 209): 'west' [BAGD, LN]. The phrase 'from east and west' [BNTC, CC, NTC, PNTC; ESV, NASB, NRSV, REB] is translated 'from the east and west' [NICNT; KJV, NET], 'from the east and the west' [NIGTC, WBC; NIV, TEV], 'from the east and from the west' [BECNT; NCV], 'from everywhere' [CEV], 'from all over the world' [GW], 'from all over the world–from east and west' [NLT]. This noun denotes the west as the direction of the setting sun.

    c. fut. pass. indic. of ἀνακλίνομαι (LN **17.23**) (BAGD 2. p. 56): 'to recline at table' [BNTC, CC, NIGTC, NTC, WBC; ESV], 'to recline at the table' [NASB], 'to recline' [BAGD], 'recline for a meal' [BECNT], 'to sit at table' [PNTC], 'to sit down' [KJV], 'to sit and eat' [NCV], 'to sit at the banquet' [REB], 'to share the banquet' [NET], 'to sit down at the feast' [NLT, TEV], 'to enjoy the feast' [CEV], 'to join (Abraham…) for a feast' [NICNT], 'to take their places at the feast' [NIV], 'to eat' [LN; GW, NRSV], 'to recline to eat, to dine, to be at table, to sit down to eat' [LN]. This verb means to be in a reclining position as one eats (with the focus either upon the position or the act of eating) [LN]. In the active voice this verb means to cause someone to lie down or recline, but in the passive voice it means to lie down or recline at meal [BAGD].

QUESTION—What is the significance of λέγω ὑμῖν 'I tell you' at the beginning of Jesus' statement?

    This phrase serves to add emphasis is to what follows [TH]. It indicates that what is to follow is particularly solemn [EBC] What he is saying so important it should not be missed [PNTC].

QUESTION—Who are the 'many from east and west' that will come to the banquet?

    1. They are Gentile believers [BNTC, CC, EBC, Lns, My, NAC, NICNT, TH, TRT; NLT], or at least many Gentile believers will be among those

who come [BECNT, NIGTC, PNTC]. A time is coming when Gentiles will flock to the faith [NAC].
2. They are Jews who believe in Jesus; the contrast is between dispersed or underprivileged Jews versus privileged Jews [ICC].

QUESTION—What is the banquet he refers to here?

It is the eschatological feast [BECNT, NIGTC], the eschatological banquet of the kingdom in the messianic age [WBC], the messianic banquet [BNTC, EBC, My, NAC, NIBC, NICNT, TH], which depicts intimate fellowship among the people of God in the coming age [NAC]. It indicates close fellowship and solidarity [NIBC]. This banquet symbolizes the consummation of the messianic kingdom [EBC], or the joys to be experienced in the kingdom of heaven [TH]. It describes the blessedness of the kingdom, not just in its future realization, but even here and now [Lns].

8:12 but the sons[a] of-the kingdom will-be-cast-out[b] into the outer[c] darkness;[d] in-that-place there-will-be weeping[e] and gnashing[f] of-teeth."

LEXICON—a. υἱός (LN **11.13**) (BAGD 1.c.δ. p. 834): 'son' [BAGD]. The phrase οἱ υἱοὶ τῆς βασιλεία 'the sons of the kingdom' [BECNT, BNTC, NIGTC, NTC, PNTC; ESV, NASB, NET] is also translated 'the children of the kingdom' [KJV], 'the heirs of the kingdom' [NRSV], 'the subjects of the kingdom' [NIV], 'the sons of the reign' [CC], 'those who should be God's people' [**LN**], 'those who should be in the kingdom' [NCV, TEV], 'the ones who should have been in the kingdom' [CEV], 'those who belong to that kingdom' [NICNT], 'the citizens of that kingdom' [GW], 'the kingdom's own children' [WBC], 'many Israelites–those for whom the Kingdom was prepared' [NLT], 'those who were born to that kingdom' [REB], 'people of God's kingdom, God's people' [LN]. The idiom 'sons of the kingdom' refers to the people who should properly be or were traditionally regarded as a part of the kingdom of God. In this context, as well as in most others, the Greek term traditionally rendered 'kingdom' in speaking of 'the kingdom of God' points essentially to the rule of God rather than to any place or time [LN].

b. fut. pass. indic. of ἐκβάλλω (LN 15.44) (BAGD 1. p. 237): 'to be cast out' [BECNT, BNTC, NTC; KJV, NASB], 'to be thrown out' [BAGD, CC, NICNT, NIGTC, PNTC; CEV, NET, REB, TEV], 'to be thrown outside' [GW, NCV, NIV], 'to be thrown' [WBC; ESV, NLT, NRSV], 'to be sent away' [LN], 'to be driven out, to be expelled' [LN]. This verb means to cause to go out or leave, often, but not always, involving force [LN].

c. ἐξώτερος (LN **1.23**) (BAGD 2. p. 280): 'outer' [BECNT, BNTC, LN, PNTC, WBC; ESV, KJV, NASB, NET, NIV, NRSV], 'outermost' [CC], 'most distant' [NTC], 'farthest out' [BAGD], not explicit [CEV, GW, NCV, NIV, REB, TEV]. The phrase τὸ σκότος τὸ ἐξώτερον 'the outer darkness' [**LN**] is also translated 'the darkness outside' [NICNT, NIGTC]. The comparative form of this adjective is used here for the superlative and

MATTHEW 8:12

it means the outermost place of darkness [CC, Lns]. It denotes a place or region which is both dark and removed presumably from the abode of the righteous, a place that serves as the abode of evil spirits and devils [LN].

d. σκότος (LN 14.53) (BAGD 1. p. 757): 'darkness' [LN; all translations except CEV, REB]. The phrase 'the outer darkness' is translated 'the dark' [CEV, REB]. This noun denotes a condition resulting from the partial or complete absence of light [LN].

e. κλαυθμός (LN 25.138) (BAGD p. 433): 'weeping' [BAGD, BECNT, BNTC, CC, LN, NICNT, NIGTC, NTC, WBC; ESV, KJV, NASB, NET, NIV, NLT, NRSV], 'wailing' [PNTC; REB], 'crying' [BAGD, LN]. This noun is translated as a verb phrase: 'they will cry' [CEV, TEV], 'people will cry' [GW, NCV]. It denotes the act of weeping or wailing, with emphasis upon the noise accompanying the weeping [LN].

f. βρυγμός (LN 23.41) (BAGD p. 148): 'gnashing (of teeth)' [BAGD, BECNT, BNTC, CC, LN, NICNT, NIGTC; ESV, KJV, NASB, NET, NIV, NLT, NRSV], 'grinding (of teeth)' [NTC, PNTC, WBC; REB], 'to grind the teeth, to gnash the teeth' [LN]. This noun is translated as a verb phrase: 'they will gnash their teeth' [TEV], 'they will grit their teeth in pain' [CEV], 'people will grind their teeth with pain' [NCV], 'people will be in extreme pain' [GW]. It denotes the grinding or the gnashing of the teeth, whether involuntary as in the case of certain illnesses, or as an expression of an emotion such as anger or of pain and suffering [LN].

QUESTION—Who are the 'sons of the kingdom' who will be cast out into the darkness?

This refers to the Jewish people who, because of their race, should be members of the kingdom of God but had refused to subject themselves to God [LN; CEV, NCV, TEV]. They are Jews who reject the Messiah [NTC, WBC]. They are physical descendants of Abraham who thought they had the fullest rights to the kingdom, but because of unbelief they failed to inherit it [Lns]. They are Jews who wrongly believe they are part of God's covenant [NAC]. The Jewish nation had a special relationship to God [PNTC], and had the right, according to God's promise, to be in the kingdom as its *potential* subjects [EBC, My]. They are the ones who would have been expected to share in the eschatological kingdom [BNTC], and receive God's eschatological blessings [BECNT], and who should have been ruled by God and inherited heaven [TRT]. In Jewish thought, not every Jew might prove worthy of having a place at the banquet, but it would be a Jewish gathering and all non-Jews would be outside in the darkness [NICNT]. Just as 'righteous' is used in 9:13 to refer to those who think they are righteous but are not, here the phrase 'sons of the kingdom' is used to refer to those who think they are such, but actually are not [CC].

QUESTION—What does gnashing of teeth indicate?

It expresses despair [EBC, My], torment [Lns], distress [PNTC], rage [TH], pain [BNTC, TH, TRT], anger [ICC, PNTC], disappointment [BNTC], and vexation [NIGTC, PNTC]. It is a response to final judgment [WBC]. It describes the anguish that comes from being separated from God [BECNT, NAC].

QUESTION—Why is the definite article ὁ 'the' used in the Greek text with 'weeping' and 'gnashing'?

Although not translated, the definite article indicates that the action is unique [Lns, PNTC], and extreme [PNTC]. This reference to *the* weeping and *the* gnashing of teeth emphasizes the horror of what is happening [EBC]. The articles points to the specific effects that accompany that darkness [Lns].

QUESTION—What is 'outer darkness'?

It means that they are far from the light and joy of the kingdom [PNTC]. It describes a great contrast to the illumination of the banquet hall [Lns, NIBC, NICNT, NIGTC, WBC]. It is the opposite of God's light in Christ [NAC]. They are far from the light of God's presence [BECNT, ICC, TH]. The place of perdition was understood to be dark [ICC]. It refers to hell [TH].

8:13 And Jesus said to-the centurion, "Go;[a] as/because[b] you-believed[c] let-it-be-done[d] for-you." And the servant was-healed[e] in that hour.[f]

LEXICON—a. pres. act. impera. of ὑπάγω (LN 15.35): 'to go, to go away from, to depart, to leave' [LN]. The command Ὕπαγε 'Go' [BECNT, BNTC, CC, PNTC, WBC; ESV, GW, NASB, NET, NIV, NRSV], is also translated 'Go home' [NTC; NCV, REB, TEV], 'Go back home' NLT], 'Go thy way' [KJV], 'You may go home now' [CEV], 'Off you go' [NICNT, NIGTC]. This verb means to move away from a reference point [LN].

b. ὡς (LN 64.12, 89.37) (BAGD I.2.b. p. 897): 'as' [BAGD, BNTC, CC, LN (64.12), NICNT, NTC, PNTC, WBC; ESV, KJV, NASB, REB], 'just as' [BECNT, NIGTC; NCV, NET, NIV], 'like' [LN (64.12)], 'according to' [NRSV], 'because' [LN (89.37); NLT], 'on the grounds that' [LN (89.37)], not explicit [CEV, GW, TEV]. This conjunction is a relatively weak marker of a relationship between events or states [LN (64.12)], or it can indicate cause or reason [LN (89.37)].

c. aorist act. indic. of πιστεύω (LN 31.85) (BAGD 2.c. p. 661): 'to believe' [BAGD; all translations except CEV, NRSV], 'to have confidence in' [BAGD, LN], 'to believe in, to have faith in, to trust' [LN]. This verb is also translated as a noun: 'your faith' [CEV, NRSV]. This verb means to believe to the extent of complete trust and reliance [LN].

d. aorist pass. (deponent = act.) impera. of γίνομαι (LN 13.107) (BAGD I.3.b.β. p. 159): 'to happen' [BAGD, LN], 'to occur, to come to be' [LN]. The phrase ὡς ἐπίστευσας γενηθήτω σοι 'as/because you believed, let it be done for you' is translated 'as you have believed, so let it be' [REB], 'just as you believed, it will be done for you' [NET], 'just as you have believed, let it happen for you' [NIGTC], 'as you have believed, so let it be done for you' [NICNT; KJV], 'as you believed, so let it be done for you' [NTC], 'as you believed, so be it to you' [PNTC], 'as you believed, let it happen for you' [CC], 'let it be done for you as you have believed'

MATTHEW 8:13   287

[ESV], 'let it be done for you as you believed' [BNTC], 'let it be done for you just as you believed' [BECNT], 'it shall be done for you as you have believed' [NASB], 'it will be done to you as you have believed' [WBC], 'let it be done for you according to your faith' [NRSV], 'it will be done just as you believed it would' [NIV], 'your servant will be healed just as you believed he would' [NCV], 'what you have believed will be done for you' [GW, TEV], 'as you have believed, so be it to you' [PNTC], 'because you believed, it has happened' [NLT], 'your faith has made it happen' [CEV]. This verb means to happen, with the implication that what happens is different from a previous state [LN].

e. aorist pass. indic. of ἰάομαι (LN 23.136) (BAGD 1. p. 368): 'to be healed' [BECNT, BNTC, CC, LN, NIGTC, PNTC, WBC; all versions except REB], 'to be cured' [LN, NICNT, NTC], 'to be made well' [LN]. This passive verb is translated as active: 'to recover' [REB]. This verb means to cause someone to become well again after having been sick [LN].

f. ὥρα (LN 67.199) (BAGD 3. p. 896): 'hour' [LN], 'the time' [BAGD]. The phrase 'in that hour' [CC; NRSV] is translated 'in that very hour' [NIGTC, WBC], 'in the selfsame hour' [KJV], 'at that hour' [PNTC; NET], 'at that very hour' [NIV], 'that very hour' [BNTC], 'that same hour' [NCV, NLT], 'at that moment' [NICNT; GW], 'that moment' [BECNT], 'that very moment' [NTC; NASB, TEV], 'at that very moment' [ESV, REB], 'right then' [CEV]. 'Hour' is used idiomatically and means 'moment' [TH]. This noun denotes the twelfth part of a day, measured from sunrise to sunset (in any one day the hours would be of equal length, but would vary somewhat depending on the time of the year) [LN].

QUESTION—What relationship is indicated by ὡς 'as'?

1. It indicates a comparative relationship [BECNT, EBC, Lns, NTC; ESV, GW, NASB, NCV, NET, NIV, NRSV, REB, TEV; probably NIC; KJV]. Jesus performed a miracle according to what was expected by the centurion [EBC]. It refers to the fact that the centurion believed his servant could be healed from a distance by a command from Jesus, an expectation that was granted [Lns].

2. It indicates a causal relationship [BNTC, CC, NIGTC, PNTC, TH; CEV, NLT]. His servant was healed on the basis of the centurion's faith [NIBC]. It means, 'God will heal your servant *because* you believed that he would heal him' [TH].

DISCOURSE UNIT—8:14–18 [GW]. The topic is Jesus cures Peter's mother-in-law and many others.

DISCOURSE UNIT—8:14–17 [CEV, ESV, NASB, NCV, NET, NIV, NLT, NRSV, TEV]. The topic is Jesus heals many people [CEV, NCV, NLT, TEV], Jesus heals many [ESV, NIV], Jesus heals many at Peter's house [NRSV], healings at Peter's house [NET], Peter's mother-in-law healed; many healed [NASB].

8:14 And Jesus having-come into the house of-Peter saw (Peter's) mother-in-law lying[a] and burning-with-fever;[b] **8:15** and he touched[c] her hand, and the fever left[d] her, and she-arose[e] and began-serving[f] him.

TEXT—Some manuscripts read διηκόνει αὐτοῖς 'serving them' instead of διηκόνει αὐτῷ 'serving him'. GNT does not mention this variant, and it is taken only by KJV and NET.

LEXICON—a. perf. pass. participle of βάλλω (LN 85.34) (BAGD 1.b. p. 131): 'to lie' [BAGD], 'to be lying in bed' [BECNT, NIV, NRSV], 'to lie sick' [PNTC; ESV], 'to lie sick in bed' [NASB], 'to lie ill' [WBC], 'to be lying down' [NET], 'to be laid up' [NTC], 'to be laid out' [NIGTC], 'to be laid' [KJV], 'to be put' [LN], 'to be cast on a bed' [CC], 'to be sick in bed' [CEV, NCV, NLT, TEV]. This participle is translated as a phrase: 'in bed' [NICNT; GW, REB], as an adjective: 'bedfast' [BNTC]. This verb means to put or place someone in a location [LN].

b. pres. act. participle of πυρέσσω (LN 23.159) (BAGD p. 730): 'to burn with fever' [BNTC, CC], 'to suffer from fever' [NIGTC], 'to have a fever' [LN], 'to be sick of/with a fever' [KJV, NET]. This verb is translated as a phrase: 'with a fever' [BECNT, NICNT, PNTC, WBC; ESV, GW, NASB, NCV, NIV, NRSV, TEV], 'with fever' [NTC; CEV, REB], 'with a high fever' [NLT]. It means to be sick with a fever [LN].

c. aorist mid. indic. of ἅπτομαι (LN 24.73) (BAGD 2.b. p. 103): 'to touch' [BECNT, BNTC, CC, LN, NIGTC, NTC, PNTC, WBC; all versions except CEV, REB], 'to take hold of' [NICNT], 'to take (by the hand)' [CEV, REB]. This verb means to touch, with the implication of relatively firm contact [LN].

d. aorist act. indic. of ἀφίημι (LN 13.37) (BAGD 3.a. p.126): 'to leave' [BAGD, LN; all translations except GW], 'to go away' [GW], 'to cease, to stop' [LN]. This verb means to cease, describing a state [LN].

e. aorist pass. indic. of ἐγείρω (LN 17.9) (BAGD 2.b. p. 215): 'to get up' [BECNT, CC, LN, NICNT, NIGTC, NTC, PNTC; all versions except ESV, KJV, NCV], 'to rise' [BNTC, WBC; ESV], 'to arise' [KJV], 'to stand up' [LN; NCV]. This verb means to get up, normally from a lying or reclining position but possibly from a seated position (in some contexts with the implication of some degree of previous incapacity) [LN].

f. imperf. act. indic. of διακονέω (LN 46.13) (BAGD 2. p. 184): 'to serve' [CC, LN, NIGTC, WBC; CEV, ESV, NCV, NET, NRSV], 'to wait on/upon' [BECNT, BNTC, LN, NICNT, NTC, PNTC; NASB, NIV, TEV], 'to prepare a meal for' [GW, NLT], 'to minister unto' [KJV], 'to attend to (his) needs' [REB]. The imperfect is translated as inceptive (i.e., beginning an action): 'began serving/began waiting, etc.' [BECNT, CC, NIGTC, NTC, WBC; ESV, NCV, NET, NIV, NRSV, TEV]; as aorist: 'served/waited on, etc.' [BNTC, NICNT; CEV, GW, KJV, NASB, NLT,

REB]. This verb means to serve food and drink to those who are eating [LN].

QUESTION—What does the fact that she immediately began serving them show?

It shows the authority of Jesus in providing a complete and instantaneous healing [BECNT, CC, EBC, NTC, PNTC]. The miracle was immediate [EBC, ICC, NICNT, NIGTC] and effective [EBC]. It confirms the reality of the healing [WBC]. No weakness remained as normally happens following a fever [ICC, Lns].

8:16 Evening having-come, they-brought to-him many demonized[a] (people); and he-cast-out[b] the spirits (by) a-word[c] and all the (ones) having-illness[d] he-healed,

- LEXICON—a. pres. mid. or pass. participle of δαιμονίζομαι (LN 12.41) (BAGD p. 169): 'to be demon possessed' [LN], 'to be possessed by a demon' [BAGD]. The phrase δαιμονιζομένους πολλούς 'many demonized people' is translated 'many who were demon-possessed' [BECNT, BNTC, NTC; NASB, NIV], 'many who were being demon-possessed' [CC], 'many demon-possessed people' [NET, NLT], 'many people who were possessed by demons' [NICNT; similarly NIGTC, PNTC; GW, KJV, REB], 'many possessed by demons' [WBC], 'many who were possessed with demons' [NRSV], 'many who were oppressed by demons' [ESV], 'many who had demons' [NCV], 'many people with demons in them' [CEV; similarly TEV]. This verb means to be possessed by a demon [LN].
- b. aorist act. indic. of ἐκβάλλω (LN 53.102) (BAGD 1. p. 237): 'to cast out' [BECNT, CC, LN, NIGTC, NTC, PNTC, WBC; ESV, NLT, NRSV], 'to expel' [BNTC], 'to force out' [CEV, GW, KJV, NASB], 'to drive out' [NET, NIV, REB, TEV], 'to throw out' [NICNT], 'to make go out, to exorcise' [LN], not explicit [NCV]. This verb means to cause a demon to no longer possess or control a person [LN].
- c. λόγος (LN 33.98) (BAGD 1.a.α. p. 477): 'word' [BAGD, LN]. This noun in the dative case is translated 'with a word' [BECNT, BNTC, CC, NIGTC, NTC, PNTC, WBC; ESV, NASB, NET, NIV, NRSV, REB, TEV], 'with his word' [KJV], 'with only a word' [CEV], 'with a command' [NICNT; GW], 'with a simple command' [NLT]. The phrase ἐξέβαλεν τὰ πνεύματα λόγῳ 'he cast out the spirits by a word' is translated 'Jesus spoke and the demons left them' [NCV]. This noun denotes that which has been stated or said, with primary focus upon the content of the communication [LN].
- d. κακῶς ἔχω (LN 23.148) (BAGD 1. p. 398). The phrase τοὺς κακῶς χοντας 'the ones having illness' is translated 'who were ill' [BECNT, BNTC, NIGTC, PNTC; NASB], 'who were/was sick' [CC, NTC, WBC; CEV, ESV, GW, NET, NRSV, REB, TEV], 'that were sick' [KJV], 'who were suffering' [NICNT], 'the sick' [NCV, NIV, NLT]. The idiom κακῶς

ἔχω (literally 'to have badly' or 'to fare badly') means to be in a bad state [LN] or to be ill [BAGD, LN].

QUESTION—Why did they bring the sick for healing in the evening?

From Mark's gospel we get the detail that it was on a Sabbath, and they waited until sunset when normal activities could resume [BNTC, EBC, Lns, NAC, NIBC, NIGTC, NICNT]. Matthew's gospel does not mention it being the Sabbath [BNTC, EBC, NIGTC, NICNT], so his point is more to show the pace of Jesus' ministry [EBC] and that this culminates a long day full of ministry [NIGTC], or that this was simply a convenient opportunity for people to come [BNTC].

8:17 so-that[a] was-fulfilled[b] the-thing-spoken[c] through Isaiah the prophet saying, "He took[d] our sicknesses[e] and bore-away[f] the diseases.[g]"

LEXICON—a. ὅπως (LN 89.59) (BAGD 2.a.α. p. 577): 'so that' [LN, NIGTC, WBC], 'so' [CEV, GW], 'that' [BNTC; KJV], 'in order that' [BAGD, CC, NTC, PNTC], 'in order to, for the purpose of' [LN]. The phrase ὅπως πληρωθῇ 'so that was fulfilled' is translated 'he did this to bring about' [NCV], 'he did this to make come true' [TEV], 'he did this to fulfill' [BECNT], 'this was to fulfill' [NICNT; ESV, NASB, NIV, NRSV], 'in this way...was fulfilled' [NET], 'this fulfilled' [NLT], 'to fulfill' [REB]. This conjunction indicates purpose for events and states (sometimes occurring in highly elliptical contexts) [LN].

b. aorist pass. subj. of πληρόω (LN 13.106) (BAGD 4.a. p. 671): 'to be fulfilled' [BAGD, BNTC, CC, LN, NIGTC, NTC, PNTC, WBC; KJV, NET], 'to fulfill' [BECNT, LN, NICNT; ESV, NASB, NIV, NLT, NRSV, REB], 'to bring about' [NCV], 'to cause to happen, to make happen' [LN], 'to come true' [CEV, GW], 'to make come true' [TEV]. This verb means to cause to happen, with the implication of fulfilling some purpose [LN].

c. aorist pass. participle of λέγω (LN 33.69): 'to be spoken' [LN], 'to be said, to be told' [LN]. This participle, which is used as a substantive, is translated 'what was spoken' [BECNT, CC, NIGTC, NTC, PNTC; ESV, NASB, NET, NIV], 'what had been spoken' [NRSV], 'which was spoken' [KJV], 'the word spoken' [WBC], 'the word which was spoken' [BNTC], 'what had been declared' [NICNT], 'what (Isaiah the prophet) had said' [NCV; similarly TEV], 'the word of the Lord through Isaiah the prophet, who said' [NLT], 'the prophecy of Isaiah' [REB]. The phrase 'was fulfilled the thing spoken through Isaiah the prophet, saying' is translated 'what the prophet Isaiah had said came true' [GW], 'God's promise came true, just as the prophet Isaiah had said' [CEV]. This verb means to speak or talk, with apparent focus upon the content of what is said [LN].

d. aorist act. indic. of λαμβάνω (LN 57.55) (BAGD 1.b. p. 464): 'to take' [BNTC, CC, LN, NIGTC, NTC, PNTC, WBC; all versions except CEV, GW, NIV], 'to take up' [NICNT; NIV], 'to take away' [BAGD, BECNT;

GW], 'to heal' [CEV], 'to acquire, to obtain' [LN]. This verb means to acquire possession of something [LN].
e. ἀσθένεια (LN **23.143**) (BAGD 1.a. p. 115): 'sickness' [BAGD, BNTC, CC, PNTC; NLT, TEV], 'disease' [BAGD, BECNT; CEV], 'weakness' [BAGD, LN, NICNT, WBC; GW, NET], 'infirmity' [NIGTC, NTC; KJV, NASB, NIV, NRSV], 'illness' [LN; ESV, REB], 'suffering' [NCV], 'disability' [LN]. This noun denotes the state of being ill and thus incapacitated in some manner. It may be extremely difficult in some languages to speak of 'taking illness' or 'carrying away diseases.' It may therefore be necessary in some languages to translate Matthew 8:17 as 'he caused us to no longer have illness and disease.' In this way, one may avoid a specific type of shamanistic practice that would be inappropriate in this context [LN].
f. aorist act. indic. of βαστάζω (LN 15.201) (BAGD 3.a. p. 137): 'to bear' [BNTC, NIGTC, WBC; ESV, KJV, NRSV], 'to carry away' [BAGD, LN; NASB, REB, TEV], 'to carry' [CC, NICNT, NTC, PNTC; NCV, NET, NIV], 'to remove' [BAGD, BECNT, LN; GW, NLT], 'to take away' [LN]. The phrase τὰς νόσους ἐβάστασεν 'he bore away the diseases' is translated 'he made us well' [CEV]. This verb means to carry away from a place, with the probable implication of something that is relatively heavy [LN].
g. νόσος (LN 23.155) (BAGD 1. p. 543): 'disease' [BAGD, BNTC, CC, LN, NIGTC, NTC, PNTC, WBC; all versions except CEV, KJV], 'illness' [BAGD, BECNT, NICNT], 'sickness' [LN; KJV], not explicit [CEV]. The definite article 'the' is translated 'our' [all translations except CEV]. This noun denotes the state of being diseased [LN].

QUESTION—What relationship is indicated by ὅπως 'so that'?
1. It indicates purpose [CC, My, NICNT, PNTC; ESV, KJV, NASB, NCV, NIV, NRSV, REB, TEV]. There was a divine purpose, foretold in the prophets, in what Jesus did [PNTC].
2. It is translated as simply indicating that the fulfillment occurs as a result of what Jesus did [WBC; CEV, GW, NET, NLT].

QUESTION—In what sense does Matthew use ἐβάστασεν 'he bore away'?
Matthew is citing Isaiah 53:4 as linking Jesus' healing of sickness during his ministry with his subsequent substitutionary death for sinners [BECNT, CC, EBC, Lns, NAC, NTC]. However, the primary point of the healing miracles is Jesus' messianic authority [BECNT, EBC], not his healing ability [BECNT]. Later citations from Isaiah 53 in Matthew's gospel affirm the idea of vicarious atonement, so that is also in view here due to the understanding that sickness is related to sin, whether directly or indirectly [EBC]. The note of vicarious suffering will appear later in this gospel [WBC]. He also took them upon himself by means of deep sympathy or compassion [NTC].

DISCOURSE UNIT—8:18–27 [NASB]. The topic is discipleship tested.

DISCOURSE UNIT—8:18-22 [CEV, ESV, NCV, NET, NIV, NLT, NRSV, TEV]. The topic is the would-be followers of Jesus [NRSV, TEV], people who want to follow Jesus [NCV], the cost of following Jesus [ESV, NIV, NLT], challenging professed followers [NET], some who wanted to go with Jesus [CEV].

8:18 And Jesus having-seen (the) crowd around him gave-orders[a] to-depart[b] to the other-side[c] (of the lake).

LEXICON—a. aorist act. indic. of κελεύω (LN 33.323) (BAGD p. 427): 'to give orders' [BECNT, NTC, PNTC; ESV, NASB, NET, NIV, NRSV], 'to give the order' [NIGTC], 'to order' [BAGD, LN, CC; GW, TEV], 'to command' [BAGD, LN, WBC], 'to give the command' [BNTC], 'to give commandment' [KJV], 'to give word' [REB], 'to tell' [NICNT; NCV], 'to instruct' [NLT], not explicit [CEV]. Some translations include an implied indirect object: 'his disciples' [CC, NICNT, WBC; GW, NLT, TEV], 'his followers' [NCV]. This verb means to state with force and/or authority what others must do [LN].

b. pres. act. infin. of ἀπέρχομαι (LN 15.37) (BAGD 2. p. 84): 'to depart' [BAGD, BNTC, LN, CC; KJV, NASB], 'to cross' [BECNT; GW, NIV, NLT, REB], 'to go across' [WBC; CEV], 'to go over' [NIGTC, NTC; ESV, NRSV], 'to go off' [PNTC], 'to go away' [LN], 'to go away with him' [NICNT], 'to go' [NCV, NET, TEV]. This verb means to move away from a reference point with emphasis upon the departure, but without implications as to any resulting state of separation or rupture [LN].

c. πέραν (LN 83.43) (BAGD 1. p. 643): 'the other side' [BECNT, NIGTC, PNTC; ESV, KJV, NRSV], 'the other side of the lake' [NICNT, WBC; NCV, NET, NIV, NLT, REB, TEV], 'the other side of the sea' [CC; NASB], 'the other side of the Sea of Galilee' [GW], 'the opposite side' [NTC], 'on the other side of' [BAGD, LN], 'to the opposite shore' [BNTC], 'opposite, across from' [LN]. The phrase 'he gave orders to depart to the other side of the lake' is translated 'he went across Lake Galilee' [CEV]. This adjective describes a position opposite another position, with something intervening [LN].

QUESTION—To whom did Jesus give this order?
This was not a command to the whole crowd that was around him since the crowd appears to be the reason that Jesus gave this command. Evidently Jesus wanted to take his disciples away from the crowd for private instruction, and this is confirmed in verse 23 where it says that the disciples got into the boat and went with him [TH]. This verse assumes that there was a group of disciples who were expected to be his traveling companions. [NICNT]. He gave this order to his band of disciples [BECNT, NIBC, NIGTC, TRT, WBC], that is, the inner circle of disciples [NTC, PNTC]. That group could be the twelve [NAC], but it may not yet be defined as the twelve [WBC].

DISCOURSE UNIT—8:19-22 [GW]. The topic is what it takes to be a disciple.

8:19 And a-certain scribe having-come said to-him, "Teacher,[a] I-will-follow[b] you wherever you may-go." **8:20** And Jesus says to him, "Foxes[c] have dens,[d] and the birds of-the air (have) nests,[e] but the Son of-Man[f] does-not -have (a place) where he-might-lay[g] the head.

LEXICON—a. διδάσκαλος (LN 33.243) (BAGD p. 191): 'teacher' [BAGD, LN; all translations except KJV], 'master' [KJV]. This noun denotes one who provides instruction [LN].

b. fut. act. indic. of ἀκολουθέω (LN 15.156) (BAGD 3. p. 31): 'to follow' [BAGD, LN; all translations except CEV, TEV], 'to accompany as a follower, to go along with' [LN]. The phrase ἀκολουθήσω σοι ὅπου ἐὰν ἀπέρχῃ 'I will follow you wherever you go' is translated 'I'll go anywhere with you' [CEV], 'I am ready to go with you wherever you go' [TEV]. This verb means to follow or accompany someone who takes the lead in determining the direction and route of movement [LN], or, figuratively, to follow someone as a disciple [BAGD].

c. ἀλώπηξ (LN 4.10) (BAGD 1. p. 41): 'fox' [BAGD, LN; all translations]. Though the Greek term ἀλώπηξ and the corresponding Hebrew terms used in the OT may refer to either a fox or a jackal, ἀλώπηξ in the NT seems to refer primarily to a fox [LN].

d. φωλεός (LN 1.56) (BAGD p. 870): 'den' [BAGD, BECNT, CC, LN, NICNT; CEV, NET, NLT], 'hole' [BAGD, BNTC, LN, NIGTC, NTC, PNTC; ESV, GW, KJV, NASB, NIV, NRSV, REB, TEV], 'hole to live in' [NCV], 'lair' [BAGD, LN, WBC]. This noun denotes a hole, typically occupied by an animal as a den or lair [LN].

e. κατασκήνωσις (LN **6.146**) (BAGD 2. p. 418): 'nest' [BAGD, BECNT, BNTC, CC, **LN**, WBC; all versions except REB], 'roost' [NICNT, NTC, PNTC; REB], 'place to settle' [NIGTC]. This noun denotes a construction built by birds in connection with brooding and raising their young. It is, however, possible to understand κατασκήνωσις in this verse as simply a sheltered place, but the most natural interpretation would appear to be 'nest' [LN].

f. ὁ υἱὸς τοῦ ἀνθρώπου (LN **9.3**). This title is translated 'the Son of Man' [**LN**; all translations]. It is a title with Messianic implications used by Jesus concerning himself, which served not only to affirm but also to hide Christ's Messianic role [LN].

g. aorist act. subj. of κλίνω (LN 16.16, **23.83**) (BAGD 1.b. p. 436): 'to lay (down)' BAGD], 'to bow down (the head), to incline' [LN (16.16)]. The phrase οὐκ ἔχει ποῦ τὴν κεφαλὴν κλίνῃ 'does not have a place where he might lay the head' is translated 'has nowhere to lay his head' [BECNT, NIGTC, PNTC, WBC; ESV, NASB, NET, NRSV, REB; similarly KJV], 'has no place to lay his head' [BNTC, WBC; NIV], 'has no place where he can lay his head' [NICNT], 'has no place even to lay his head' [NLT], 'has no place to rest his head' [NCV], 'does not have anywhere he may lay his head' [CC], 'has nowhere to sleep' [GW], 'has no place to lie down and rest' [**LN** (23.83); TEV], 'doesn't have a place to call his own' [CEV]. This verb means to cause something to incline [LN]. The phrase τὴν κεφαλὴν κλίνω 'to lay down the head' means to experience the rest which comes from sleep, and in Mathew 8:20 it implies that Jesus possessed no permanent home [LN (23.83)].

QUESTION—What did the scribe imply when he called Jesus διδάσκαλος 'Teacher'?

In the five other passages in Matthew those who call him 'teacher' are not disciples [BECNT, CC, NIBC, NICNT]. This scribe has a high estimation of Jesus, and Matthew may intend us to see him as a disciple in some sense [PNTC]. Calling Jesus 'teacher' indicates the man is not yet a disciple [CC, NICNT]. The scribe would have been considered a teacher in Israel, yet he considered Jesus to be *his* teacher [NTC]. It was a title of respect, though not a major Christological title in Matthew's gospel [ICC].

QUESTION—Does ἀκολουθέω 'follow' refer to full discipleship?

It does refer to discipleship, although the scribe had a very shallow understanding of what that entailed [BECNT, NAC, NIGTC, NICNT, NTC, PNTC, TH].

QUESTION—Does ὅπου ἐὰν ἀπέρχῃ 'wherever you may go' refer to Jesus' immediate destination at that moment, or to a lifestyle of discipleship?

It refers to a lifestyle of discipleship [BECNT, NAC, NTC, PNTC], as Jesus' answer about that lifestyle shows [BECNT, NAC]. It means not only to follow him across the lake, but also to obey his teaching in a way of life that is completely new, spiritually and ethically [NIBC]. His request to Jesus was not simply to follow him 'wherever you go', but to follow him 'wherever you may be going away to', which could limit his request to just the purposed trip across the lake rather than to a long-term commitment of traveling with Jesus everywhere he would go; however, Jesus' reply focuses on the itinerant lifestyle that his disciples would have commit to [NICNT].

QUESTION—What is the meaning of the phrase ὁ υἱὸς τοῦ ἀνθρώπου 'the Son of Man'?

This phrase is derived from Dan 7:13–14 which begins, 'I saw in the night visions, and behold, with the clouds of heaven there came one like a son of man…and to him was given dominion and glory and a kingdom' (ESV) [BECNT, CC, EBC, ICC, Lns, My, NAC, NIBC, NICNT, NTC, PNTC, TRT, WBC]. It was not commonly understood in Jesus' time as a messianic title [CC, EBC, Lns, PNTC, NTC, WBC]. Its meaning was ambiguous [EBC, CC, NICNT, NTC, TRT, WBC], which is why Jesus used it [EBC, NTC, TRT]. The phrase 'one like a son of man' means that someone appeared in human form [EBC]. The people who heard Jesus refer to 'the Son of Man' probably knew that he was referring to himself, and after the resurrection Christians reading the phrase in the Gospels may have understood that it was being used in reference to the Daniel passage. Since a literal rendering of 'the Son of Man' can be meaningless in a particular language, some translators have indicated that it is a title by translating it 'The One called the Son of Man'. Other translators have focused on the central meaning in Daniel, 'The man whom God has appointed (or chosen)' or 'the man whom God has installed' [TH]. Although Jesus chose this title from Daniel in reference to his future heavenly glory, he also used it with reference to other aspects of his ministry, and in this verse it is used in the context of earthly deprivation [NICNT]. Many commentators mention that Jesus referred to himself as 'the Son of Man' in different contexts where the focus might be either on his suffering or his glory [BECNT, EBC, ICC, NAC, NIBC, NICNT, PNTC]. Early in his ministry Jesus used the term 'the Son of Man' because it was ambiguous. However, especially towards the end of his ministry it had the full messianic significance of the Daniel reference. There are OT passages in which the term 'son of man' contrasts the chasm between frail, mortal man and God himself. God addressed the prophet Ezekiel as 'son of man' and Psalm 8:4 asks God 'What is man that you are mindful of him, and the son of man that you care for him?' (ESV). This aspect of 'son of man' suits the NT passages about the suffering and passion texts [EBC].

QUESTION—What does it mean that Jesus 'has nowhere to lay his head'?

It means that his mission kept him on the move [EBC, ICC, Lns, TRT], and he had no fixed home [Lns, TRT]. He was homeless and itinerant, and when he stayed in a house, it was as a guest in someone else's home [BECNT]. In his itinerant ministry he often did not know where he would spend the night [NTC]. It means that Jesus did not own a home, and in fact owned very little otherwise [PNTC]. He lived with deprivation and had few creature comforts [NAC]. The phrase describes an unsettled life [My]. Jesus had a wandering and homeless ministry [WBC], one in which there was no predictability or stability [CC], only material insecurity [NICNT]. Jesus appears to have had a home in Capernaum but the crowds allow him no rest [TH]. It means he was unwelcome by others [ICC, NIGTC].

8:21 Another of- the -disciples said to-him, "Lord, let^a me first to-go^b and to-bury^c my father." **8:22** But Jesus says to him, "Follow me and let the dead^d bury their-own dead."

LEXICON—a. aorist act. impera. of ἐπιτρέπω (LN 13.138) (BAGD 1. p. 303): 'to let' [BECNT, LN, NIGTC, WBC; all versions except KJV], 'to permit' [BAGD, BNTC, CC, LN; NASB], 'to give permission' [NICNT], 'to allow' [BAGD, LN, NTC, PNTC], 'to suffer' [KJV]. This verb means to allow someone to do something [LN].

b. aorist act. infin. of ἀπέρχομαι (LN 15.37) (BAGD 1.a. p. 84): 'to go' [BECNT, BNTC, NIGTC, WBC; all versions except CEV, NLT, TEV], 'to go away' [BAGD, LN, NICNT], 'to go off' [PNTC], 'to go back' [TEV], 'to go home' [NTC], 'to return home' [NLT], 'to depart' [BAGD, CC, LN], 'to leave' [LN]. The phrase 'permit me first to go and to bury my father' is translated 'let me wait until I bury my father' [CEV]. This verb means to move away from a reference point, with emphasis upon the departure, but without implications as to any resulting state of separation or rupture [LN].

   c. aorist act. infin. of θάπτω (LN 52.4, 35.46) (BAGD p. 351): 'to bury' [BAGD, LN (52.4); all translations], 'to take care of a father, to provide for one's father until his death' [LN (35.46)]. This verb means to bury a dead person [LN (52.4)]. It may possibly be used idiomatically, in this case meaning to take care of one's father until his death [LN (35.46)].

   d. νεκρός (LN 23.121, 33.137) (BAGD 2.b. p. 535): 'dead' [LN (23.121); all translations except NLT], 'spiritually dead' [NLT]. This noun pertains to being dead [LN (23.121)]. It is also possible that this is an adage that means the matter in question is not the real issue, it is not the point [LN (33.137)]. Some scholars, however, understand this expression as merely a figurative reference to various types of people and thus translate 'let those who are spiritually dead take care of their own dead' [BAGD, LN (33.137)].

QUESTION—Does 'another' used of this man indicate that the first man, the scribe, was considered a disciple?

   1. Both men were disciples in a loose sense of the term, but here it does not refer to fully committed discipleship [EBC, My, NAC, NICNT]. In Matthew the term is used about 75 times, but the meaning of the term can vary from one context to another. Here, both were 'followers' in some sense of the term, though the scribe's commitment was very shallow [BECNT]. It may be that both were beginning disciples, but had not yet come to terms with the radical demands of discipleship [WBC]. The first man was a would-be follower [NIBC]. This is translated as 'another of his disciples' (or similarly) indicating that the first man may have been viewed as a disciple, at least in some sense [BNTC, PNTC; CEV, ESV, GW, KJV, NASB, NET, NIV, NLT, NRSV].

   2. This man was a disciple, but the scribe was not [CC, ICC, NIGTC, NTC]. This passage is translated 'someone else, one of his disciples' (or similarly), probably indicating that a distinction is being made between this man, who was a disciple, and the first man, who presumably was not [NIGTC, NTC; NCV, REB, TEV].

QUESTION—Had the man's father actually died yet?

Regardless of whether the man had died or not, the point Jesus is making is about the importance of the ministry [NICNT, NIGTC, WBC]. Jesus' statement showed that he viewed himself as extremely important and had a sense of urgency about the hour in which he was working [NIGTC]. The message of the kingdom was radical, and even the most basic of family ties was of secondary importance by comparison [NICNT]. Although this is hyperbole, the point is that the disciple should not be distracted by anything, however legitimate [WBC].

1. The man's father had already died [BECNT, EBC, ICC, TH]. Jesus' words here are very hard, and speculation that the man's father had not died yet only undermines and lessens that difficulty [BECNT]. It may be that Jesus was not so much forbidding the man to attend the funeral as he was dealing with what he saw as a reservation in the man's commitment, an insincere or qualified response to Jesus' lordship [EBC].
2. It is likely, or at least possible, that the man's father had not died yet [CC, NAC, PNTC]. If he had already died, the son would have been taken up with funeral arrangements and would not have been discussing discipleship with Jesus. Probably he was asking permission to be excused from further responsibilities until his father had actually passed away [PNTC].

QUESTION—How is the term νεκρός 'dead' used in its first occurrence here?

They are those who are spiritually dead, and it is they who are to bury those who are physically dead [EBC, CC, ICC, My, NAC, NICNT, PNTC, TRT]. They are those who are lost to the kingdom [BAGD]. Those who are 'dead' are unresponsive to the rigorous demands of the kingdom, which even supersede duty to one's parents [BECNT, EBC]. Jesus is simply saying that the ordinary priorities of life are less important than the demands of Christian discipleship [NIBC, NIGTC, TH].

DISCOURSE UNIT—8:23–9:17 [ICC]. The topic is a second triad of miracle stories.

DISCOURSE UNIT—8:23–27 [CEV, ESV, GW, NCV, NET, NIV, NLT, NRSV, TEV]. The topic is Jesus calms the sea [GW], Jesus calms a storm [ESV, NCV, TEV], Jesus calms the storm [NIV, NLT], Jesus stills the storm [NRSV], the stilling of a storm [NET], a storm [CEV].

8:23 And he having-gotten into the boat^a his disciples followed him. **8:24** And behold a-great^b storm^c occurred on the lake, such-that the boat (is)-being-covered^d by the waves, but he was-sleeping.

LEXICON—a. πλοῖον (LN 6.41): 'boat' [LN; all translations except KJV], 'ship' [KJV, LN]. This noun denotes any kind of boat, from small fishing boats as on Lake Galilee to large seagoing vessels [LN]. It may be very important to distinguish clearly between small fishing boats and larger ships or vessels. In a number of languages the distinction is based upon whether or not such vessels have decks. For the fishing boats on Lake Galilee there was probably no deck structure, while vessels going for long distances on the Mediterranean would certainly have had decks [LN].
b. μέγας (LN 78.2) (BAGD 2.a.γ. p. 497): 'great' [BAGD, BNTC, CC, LN, NICNT, NIGTC, PNTC, WBC; ESV, KJV, NASB, NCV, NET, NRSV, REB], 'severe' [BECNT; GW], 'violent' [NTC], 'furious' [NIV], 'fierce' [NLT, TEV], 'intense' [LN], 'terrible' [CEV, LN]. This adjective describes the upper range of a scale of extent [LN].

c. σεισμός (LN 14.22) (BAGD p. 746): 'storm' [BAGD, BECNT, BNTC, CC, NICNT; all versions except KJV, NRSV], 'windstorm' [NRSV], 'disturbance' [NIGTC], 'tempest' [KJV], 'storm on the sea' [LN], 'earthquake (under the sea)' [WBC]. This noun denotes a violent action of the surface of a body of water as the result of high waves caused by a strong wind [LN].

d. pres. pass. infin. of καλύπτω (LN 79.114) (BAGD 1. p. 401): 'to be covered' [BAGD, CC, LN, NTC, WBC; KJV, NASB], 'to be covered over' [LN], 'to be swamped' [BECNT, NICNT, NTC; ESV, NRSV], 'to be engulfed' [NIGTC], 'to be submerged' [BNTC], 'to be splashed' [CEV]. This passive verb is translated as active: 'to cover' [GW, NCV], 'to swamp' [NET], 'to sweep over' [NIV], 'to break over' [REB], 'to break into' [NLT]. The phrase τὸ πλοῖον καλύπτεσθαι ὑπὸ τῶν κυμάτων 'the boat is being covered by the waves' is translated 'the boat was in danger of sinking' [TEV]. This verb means to cause something to be covered over and hence not visible [LN].

QUESTION—What type and size boat was this?

This vessel, which had no sails, could fit twelve men plus a catch of fish [EBC]. It would have been crowded if more than thirteen people were aboard [NICNT]. One such boat from approximately the first century that was unearthed by archaeologists from the bottom of Lake Galilee measures 26.5 feet long by 7.5 feet wide, and 4.5 feet deep, with places for four oars and a mast. It could carry a crew of five, plus ten passengers [PNTC].

QUESTION—Is there any significance in adding the clause 'his disciples followed (ἠκολούθησαν) him' after stating that Jesus had gotten into the boat?

The verb ἀκολουθέω 'to follow' is often used to mean 'to accompany as a follower' (LN 15.156) and since verses 19 and 22 concern 'following' Jesus as disciples, the use of the verb 'followed' continues the same idea [ICC, Lns, NICNT, NIGTC, PNTC, TH, WBC]. Disciples are literally 'followers' [NICNT], and discipleship here is about following Jesus [WBC]. The disciples follow Jesus without regard to the cost, as opposed to the two others who did not [NTC]. The passage is about what discipleship means, so here 'follow' means not only to follow literally, but also includes the sense of discipleship [TH]. Some take a different view. When someone is physically following another person, it is too much to invest the word 'follow' with the added meaning of discipleship [EBC]. There are some translations that do not use the word 'followed': the disciples 'went with him' [GW, TEV], Jesus left in the boat 'with the disciples' [CEV, NLT].

QUESTION—What was the nature and intensity of the storm?

The term σεισμός 'storm' normally refers to an earthquake [EBC, Lns, NAC, PNTC], a great shaking [NIGTC, NTC], a violent natural phenomenon [CC], but here it describes tossing waters [Lns], winds and waves [CC]. In this context it can only refer to a storm [TH]. Because four of the disciples were commercial fisherman and were accustomed to storms on the lake, their

fright at this one is especially noteworthy [BECNT, PNTC]. When these experienced sailors could not control the boat they became terrified [BNTC].
QUESTION—What does it mean that the boat was 'covered' by the waves?
It was in a trough, between high waves [ICC, PNTC]. The waves towered over the boat [NIBC, NTC, PNTC], and crashed onto the deck [NIBC]. The waves were running over the boat [My].

8:25 **And going-to (him) they-woke[a] him saying, "Lord, save[b] (us), we-are-perishing.[c]"**
LEXICON—a. aorist act. indic. of ἐγείρω (LN 23.77) (BAGD 1.a.α. p. 214): 'to wake' [BAGD, BECNT, CC, NICNT, NTC, PNTC, WBC; all versions except KJV], 'to awaken someone' [LN; KJV], 'to rouse' [BAGD, BNTC, NIGTC], 'to cause to wake up, to wake up someone' [LN]. This verb means to cause someone to awaken [LN].
b. aorist act. impera. of σῴζω (LN 21.18) (BAGD 1.a. p. 798): 'to save' [BAGD; all translations], 'to save from death' [BAGD], 'to rescue' [BAGD, LN], 'to keep from harm, to preserve' [BAGD], 'to deliver, to make safe' [LN]. This verb means to rescue from danger and to restore to a former state of safety and well being [LN].
c. pres. mid. indic. of ἀπόλλυμαι (LN 23.106) (BAGD 2.a.α. p. 95): 'to perish' [BAGD, BECNT, BNTC, CC, LN, NIGTC, NTC, PNTC, WBC; ESV, KJV, NASB, NRSV], 'to sink' [NICNT; REB], 'to drown' [CEV, NCV, NIV, NLT], 'to die' [BAGD, LN; GW, NET, TEV]. This present tense verb is translated as referring to a future event: 'we are about to die' [NET, TEV], 'we are going to die' [GW], 'we are going to drown' [CEV, NIV, NLT], 'we will drown' [NCV]. This verb means to die, with the implication of ruin and destruction [LN].

8:26 **And he says to-them, "Why are-you afraid,[a] (you-pl)-of-little-faith[b]?" Then having-arisen he-rebuked/commanded[c] the winds and the lake, and a-great[d] calm[e] occurred.**
LEXICON—a. δειλός (LN 25.268) (BAGD p. 173): 'afraid' [BECNT; CEV, ESV, NASB, NCV, NIV, NLT, NRSV], 'timid' [BAGD], 'cowardly' [BAGD, BNTC, CC, LN, NIGTC; NET], 'scared' [NICNT], 'fearful' [WBC; KJV], 'frightened' [NTC, PNTC, TEV]. This adjective is translated as a noun: '(you) cowards' [GW], 'such cowards' [REB]. It describes being cowardly [LN].
b. ὀλιγόπιστος (LN **31.96**) (BAGD p. 563): 'of little faith, of insufficient faith' [LN], 'littleness of faith' [BAGD]. The vocative ὀλιγόπιστοι 'of little faith' is translated 'you of little faith' [NIV, NRSV], 'O you of little faith' [ESV; similarly KJV], 'O men of little faith' [NTC], 'men of little faith' [BECNT], 'you men of little faith' [BNTC, PNTC; NASB], 'you people of little faith' [NIGTC; NET], 'you who have such little faith' [WBC], 'you little-faiths' [CC], 'you faithless people' [NICNT], 'What little faith you have!' [LN; TEV], 'How little faith you have!' [REB], 'You have so little faith!' [NLT], 'you who have such little faith' [WBC],

'You surely don't have much faith' [CEV], 'You don't have enough faith' [NCV]. The whole question is translated 'Why do you cowards have so little faith?' [GW]. This adjective describes someone as having relatively little faith [LN].
   c. aorist act. indic. of ἐπιτιμάω (LN 33.331, 33.419) (BAGD 1. p. 303): 'to rebuke' [BAGD, BECNT, BNTC, CC, NICNT, NIGTC, NTC, LN (33.419), PNTC, WBC; ESV, KJV, NASB, NET, NIV, NLT, NRSV, REB], 'to reprove' [BAGD], 'to command' [LN (33.331)], 'to give a command' [NCV], 'to order...to calm down' [CEV], 'to order...to stop' [TEV], 'to give an order' [GW]. This verb means to command, with the implication of a threat [LN (33.331)], or to express strong disapproval of someone [LN (33.419)].
   d. μέγας (LN 78.2) (BAGD 2.a.γ. p. 497): 'great' [BAGD, CC, LN, NIGTC, PNTC, WBC; ESV, KJV, NLT, TEV], 'complete' [BNTC, NICNT], 'deep' [NTC], 'dead' [NET, NRSV, REB], not explicit [CEV]. This adjective is translated as an adverb: 'perfectly' [BECNT; NASB], 'very' [GW], 'completely' [NCV, NIV]. It describes the upper range of a scale of extent, with the possible implication of importance in relevant contexts [LN].
   e. γαλήνη (LN 14.23) (BAGD p. 150): 'a calm' [BAGD, BNTC, CC, LN, NICNT, NIGTC, NTC, PNTC, WBC; ESV, KJV, NLT, NRSV, REB, TEV]. The noun is translated as an adjective: 'and it was completely calm' [NIV], 'and it became perfectly calm' [BECNT; NASB], 'and it was dead calm' [NET], 'and it became completely calm' [NCV], 'and the sea became calm' [GW], 'And everything was calm' [CEV]. It denotes a calm or unruffled surface of a body of water [LN].
QUESTION—What is meant by the term ἐπετίμησεν 'he rebuked/commanded'?
   1. It may be seen as acknowledging an evil force in the storm [PNTC, WBC], but it also shows that he is sovereign over that force [PNTC]. Jesus exercises authority over nature's destructive forces over which the devil exercises control [NAC]. This verb suggests that Jesus is dealing with the storm as something demonic [BNTC, NIBC].
   2. There is no personal nature assumed about the forces that are rebuked [NIGTC, NICNT]. The verb used here does not require any connotation of demonic involvement; the rebuke shows his authority, which he expects the storm to 'recognize', and which demonstrates that he wields the creator's power when it is stilled [NICNT].

8:27 And the men marveled[a] saying, "What-sort-of[b] (man) is this that even the winds and the lake obey[c] him?"

LEXICON—a. aorist act. indic. of θαυμάζω (LN 25.213) (BAGD 1.a.α. p. 352): 'to marvel' [BAGD, BNTC, CC, LN, NIGTC, WBC; ESV, KJV], 'to wonder' [BAGD, LN], 'to be amazed' [LN, NICNT, NTC; CEV, GW, NASB, NCV, NET, NIV, NLT, NRSV, TEV], 'to be astonished' [BAGD,

BECNT, PNTC; REB]. This verb means to wonder or marvel at some event or object, and whether the reaction is favorable or unfavorable depends on the context [LN].
  b. ποταπός (LN 58.30) (BAGD p. 695): 'what sort of' [BAGD, BNTC, CC, LN, NICNT, NIGTC, WBC; ESV, GW, NET, NRSV, REB], 'what kind of' [BAGD, BECNT, LN, NTC, PNTC; NASB, NCV, NIV, TEV], 'what manner of' [KJV]. The phrase ποταπός ἐστιν οὗτος 'What sort of man is this?' is translated 'Who is this?' [CEV], 'Who is this man?' [NLT]. This interrogative adjective refers to class or kind [LN].
  c. pres. act. indic. of ὑπακούω (LN 36.15) (BAGD 1. p. 837): 'to obey' [BAGD, LN; all translations], 'to be subject to' [BAGD]. This verb means to obey on the basis of having paid attention to someone [LN].
QUESTION—Who are οἱ ἄνθρωποι 'the men' who were so amazed?
  These were the disciples who were in the boat with Jesus [EBC, NICNT, PNTC, TH]. Matthew's use of the words 'the men' instead of 'the disciples' is so unusual that some have wondered if there were other people in the boat besides his disciples, but nothing in the story suggests that to be the case [NICNT]. Others have suggested that this refers to the reaction of others when the news of the miracle became known, but Matthew is probably referring to the disciples as 'the men' in order to emphasize the contrast between mere men and the divine personhood of Jesus who could make the winds and the sea obey [NICNT, PNTC]. These human beings are contrasted with Jesus who has a unique and non-human authority [NICNT].

DISCOURSE UNIT—8:28–9:1 [NRSV]. The topic is Jesus heals the Gadarene demoniacs.

DISCOURSE UNIT—8:28–34 [CEV, ESV, GW, NASB, NCV, NET, NIV, NLT, TEV]. The topic is Jesus cures two demon-possessed men [GW], Jesus heals two demon-possessed men [NLT], Jesus heals two men with demons [ESV, NCV, TEV], healing the Gadarene demoniacs [NET], the healing of two demon-possessed men [NIV], Jesus casts out demons [NASB], two men with demons in them [CEV].

8:28 And he having-come to the other side into the region[a] of the Gadarenes, two demonized[b] (men) coming from the tombs[c] met him, exceedingly[d] violent,[e] such-that not anyone to-be-able to-pass-through that way.[f]
TEXT—Manuscripts reading Γαδαρηνῶν 'of the Gadarenes' are given a C rating by GNT to indicate that choosing it over a variant text was difficult. One variant reading is Γερασηνῶν 'of the Gerasenes' and it is followed by NIGTC. Another variant is Γεργασηνῶν 'of the Gergasenes' and it is followed by KJV.
LEXICON—a. χώρα (LN 1.79) (BAGD 1.b. p. 889): 'region' [BECNT, CC, LN; NET, NIV, NLT], 'territory' [NICNT, NIGTC, LN; GW], 'district' [LN], 'country' [BAGD, BNTC, NTC, PNTC, WBC; ESV, KJV, NASB,

NRSV, REB]. The phrase τὴν χώραν τῶν Γαδαρηνῶν 'the region of the Gadarenes' is translated 'the area of the Gadarene people' [NCV], 'near the town of Gadara' [CEV], 'the territory of Gadara' [TEV]. This noun denotes a region or regions of the earth, normally in relation to some ethnic group or geographical center, but not necessarily constituting a unit of governmental administration [LN].
- b. pres. mid. or pass. participle of δαιμονίζομαι (LN 12.41) (BAGD p. 169): 'to be demon possessed' [LN], 'to be possessed by a demon' [BAGD]. The participle δαιμονιζόμενοι 'demonized men' is translated 'demon-possessed men' [NICNT, NTC, PNTC; ESV, NET, NIV], 'men who were demon-possessed' [BECNT, CC; NASB], 'men who were possessed by demons' [NLT], 'they were possessed by demons' [GW, REB], '(men) possessed with devils' [KJV], 'men with demons in them' [CEV], 'men who had demons in them' [NCV; similarly TEV], 'demoniacs' [BNTC, NIGTC, WBC; NRSV]. This verb means to be possessed by a demon [BAGD, LN].
- c. μνημεῖον (LN 7.75) (BAGD 2. p. 524): 'tomb' [BAGD, LN; all translations except NCV, NLT, TEV], 'burial cave' [NCV, TEV], 'grave' [BAGD, LN], 'cemetery' [NLT]. This noun denotes a construction for the burial of the dead [LN].
- d. λίαν (LN 78.1) (BAGD 2.a. p. 473): 'exceedingly' [BAGD, PNTC], 'exceeding' [KJV], 'extremely' [BECNT, WBC; NASB, NET], 'very' [BAGD, LN, CC, NIGTC], 'really' [NICNT], 'dangerously' [BNTC]. The phrase λίαν ὥστε 'exceedingly…such that' is translated 'so (violent, etc.) that' [NICNT, NTC; all versions except KJV, NASB, NET].
- e. χαλεπός (LN **20.2**) (BAGD p. 874): 'violent' [BAGD, BECNT, BNTC, CC, NTC, PNTC, WBC; NASB, NET, NIV, NLT, NRSV, REB], 'fierce' [**LN**, NIGTC; CEV, ESV, KJV, TEV], 'dangerous' [BAGD, LN; GW, NCV], 'unmanageable' [NICNT]. This adjective describes one who is inclined to violent and dangerous activity [LN].
- f. ὁδός (LN 1.99) (BAGD 1.a. p. 553): 'way' [BAGD, BECNT, LN, NICNT, NIGTC; CEV, ESV, KJV, NASB, NET, NIV, NRSV, REB], 'road' [BAGD, BNTC, CC, LN, NTC, PNTC, WBC; GW, NCV, TEV]. The phrase παρελθεῖν διὰ τῆς ὁδοῦ ἐκείνης 'to pass through that way' is translated 'go through that area' [NLT]. This noun denotes a general term for a thoroughfare, either within a population center or between two such centers [LN].

QUESTION—Why does the name of this area differ from that given in the accounts of Mark and Luke, which have Gerasa?

Gadara was the name of a town, and also the name of its district, which extended to the lakeside [NAC, NICNT, NIGTC, PNTC, TRT]. The town of Gadara, which controlled the district, and the village of Gerasa were both in this area [EBC]. The city of Gadara was about five to six miles from Lake Galilee [BECNT, BNTC, ICC, NICNT, NTC, PNTC, TH, TRT], and the village of Gergesa (modern Khersa) was on the shore, near cliffs that overlook the water [BECNT, BNTC, ICC, NTC, PNTC]. Gadara was one of the ten Greek cities known as the Decapolis [NIBC].)

QUESTION—What were the tombs like?

These were burial caves [CC, NAC, TH, TRT, WBC], located in the hillside [NICNT]. There were many caves in this area that would have been suitable for tombs [My, NTC]. The demoniacs may have lived in the antechambers in front of the rooms where the bodies were placed [EBC, Lns, PNTC, TH], or it may be that some tombs had been abandoned [Lns, PNTC].

8:29 **And behold[a] they-cried-out[b] saying, "What to-us and to-you,[c] Son of God? Did-you-come here to torment[d] us before (the) time[e]?"**

LEXICON—a. ἰδού (LN 91.13) (BAGD 1.b. p. 371): 'behold' [BAGD, BNTC; ESV, KJV], 'see' [BAGD], 'look' [BAGD, CC, LN, PNTC, WBC], 'listen, pay attention' [LN], 'suddenly' [BECNT; CEV, NRSV], 'all at once' [NTC; TEV], not explicit [NICNT, NIGTC; GW, NASB, NCV, NET, NIV, NLT, REB].

b. aorist act. indic. of κράζω (LN 33.83) (BAGD 2.a. p. 447): 'to cry out' [BECNT, BNTC, CC, NIGTC, PNTC, WBC; ESV, KJV, NASB, NET], 'to shout' [LN; CEV, GW, NCV, NIV, NRSV, REB], 'to shout out' [NICNT], 'to scream' [LN, NTC; NLT, TEV], 'to call, to call out' [BAGD]. This verb means to shout or cry out, with the possible implication of the unpleasant nature of the sound [LN].

c. The clause τί ἡμῖν καὶ σοί 'what to us and to you' is translated 'what do you want with us?' [CEV, NCV, NIV, REB, TEV], 'what do you have to do with us' [BECNT; similarly ESV, NRSV], 'what have we to do with you' [BNTC, PNTC; similarly KJV], 'what do we and you have in common' [CC], 'what have we and you to do with each other' [NIGTC], 'what business do we have with each other' [NASB], 'what have we to do with each other' [WBC], 'why do you bother us' [NTC], 'why are you bothering us' [GW], 'why are you interfering with us' [NLT], 'leave us alone' [NICNT; NET].

d. aorist act. infin. of βασανίζω (LN **38.13**) (BAGD 2.a. p. 134): 'to torment' [BAGD, BECNT, BNTC, CC, **LN**, NICNT, NIGTC, PNTC, WBC; ESV, KJV, NASB, NET, NRSV, REB], 'to torture' [BAGD, LN, NTC; GW, NCV, NIV, NLT], 'to punish' [CEV, TEV]. This verb means to punish by physical torture or torment [LN].

e. καιρός (LN 67.1) (BAGD 3. p. 395): 'time' [BECNT, CC, LN, NIGTC, PNTC; ESV, GW, KJV, NASB, NET, NRSV], 'our time' [CEV, REB], 'right time' [NCV, TEV], 'appointed time' [BNTC, WBC; NIV], 'God's appointed time' [NLT], 'proper time' [NICNT], 'occasion' [LN], 'the time of crisis, the last times' [BAGD]. This noun denotes points of time consisting of occasions for particular events [LN].

QUESTION—What is the function of ἰδού 'behold'?

This particle is used in different ways depending on the context. In general it is used to signal a special emphasis, but in this verse, phrases such as 'at once' or 'as soon as they saw Jesus' would be good too [TH]. It moves the narrative along at a quick pace [PNTC]. It calls attention to something exceptional that happens at this point [WBC]. It marks emphasis [NIGTC]. Although it is not made explicit in many translations, it is translated 'behold' [ESV, KJV], 'look' [PNTC, WBC], 'suddenly' [CEV, GW, NRSV], 'at once' [TEV].

QUESTION—Who is speaking to Jesus in these verses?

The words 'they cried out, saying' indicates that the two demon-possessed men are speaking to Jesus, but in verse 31 it says 'the demons were begging him saying'. In both verses, it is to be presumed that the demons were speaking through the men's lips [PNTC]. The men's voices conveyed the demons' thoughts [NICNT, NIGTC]. It is the demons who are speaking [CC, EBC, ICC NAC, NIBC, TRT]. It was the demons who knew that at the eschatological judgment they will experience God's judgment and the end of their power [NICNT, WBC].

QUESTION—What is meant by the question, 'What to us and to you?'

This is a rhetorical question that doesn't expect an answer [WBC], so two translations make this a statement: 'Son of God, leave us alone!' [NET], 'Leave us alone, you Son of God.' [NICNT]. They are telling Jesus not to bother them [NAC, NTC, TH; NLT], to leave them alone [Lns]. They are telling Jesus that they have nothing in common with him [CC, NIGTC PNTC]. This is their way of rejecting or repudiating him [CC]. They don't belong together, so no contact with him would be in their interest [NIGTC].

QUESTION—How did they recognize him to be the 'Son of God'?

The demons had a supernatural recognition of who he was [ICC, NICNT, NIGTC, TH, WBC]. They had an independent knowledge of his identity that was not based on anything that was said or done at that point in time. They were also answering the question raised in the previous episode by the disciples concerning what kind of person Jesus was. Jesus is the Son of God in the richest sense, not just in terms of his power, but also in terms of his person [EBC]. It is not known what they may have meant by the title, but apparently they did understand that he belonged with God in some way and was able to do more than ordinary people could do [PNTC]. They associated his being the Son of God with the final judgment, including the judgment of demons [BECNT, NTC]. Their calling him 'Son of God' meant that they recognized that he truly is God [CC]. That Jesus is the Son of God is a theme in Matthew [BECNT].

QUESTION—Does 'come here' refer to his coming to the tombs, or his coming to earth?

It refers to the fact that Jesus came to earth [EBC, ICC, NIBC, NICNT, NTC, PNTC, WBC]. The eschatological judge had appeared [ICC]. From the idea of his coming to earth one can easily conclude that he was preexistent [EBC].

QUESTION—What is 'the time' they refer to?

It is the time appointed for judgment [BECNT, CC, ICC, Lns, My, NAC, NIBC, NIGTC, NTC, PNTC, TH, TRT, WBC], for the full destruction of the demons' power [EBC]. It is the eschatological end times [BAGD, NICNT, PNTC], the end of the age [BNTC].

8:30 **And some-distance[a] from them there was a herd[b] of-many pigs[c] feeding.[d]**

LEXICON—a μακράν (LN 83.30) (BAGD 1.a.α. p. 487): 'some distance away' [LN, NICNT, NTC, WBC], 'at a distance' [BECNT, BNTC, LN, NIGTC, PNTC; NASB], 'in the distance' [GW, NLT, REB], 'at some distance' [ESV, NET, NIV, NRSV], 'far away' [BAGD, LN], 'far off' [CC], 'a good way off' [KJV], 'not far from there' [CEV], 'not far away' [TEV], 'near that place' [NCV]. This adjective describes a position at a relatively great distance from another position [LN]. It is clear that the pigs were not close by [PNTC], but they were not so far away that that they were out of sight [TH].

b. ἀγέλη (LN **4.8**) (BAGD p. 8): 'herd' [BAGD, **LN**; all translations]. The phrase 'a herd of many pigs' is also translated 'a large herd' [BNTC, NTC; CEV, GW, NCV, NET, NIV, NLT, NRSV, REB, TEV]. This collective noun denotes a group of animals [LN].

c. χοῖρος (LN **4.36**) (BAGD p. 883): 'pig' [CC, **LN**, NICNT, NIGTC, NTC, PNTC; all versions except KJV, NASB, NRSV], 'swine' [BAGD, BECNT, BNTC, WBC; KJV, NASB, NRSV].

d. pres. pass. participle of βόσκομαι (LN **23.9**) (BAGD 2. p. 145): 'to feed' [BAGD, BECNT, **LN**, NICNT, NTC, PNTC, WBC; all versions], 'to graze' [BAGD, BNTC, CC, LN], 'to be grazed' [NIGTC]. This verb refers to the act of eating by animals [LN].

8:31 **And the demons were-begging[a] him saying, "If you-cast- us -out, send[b] us into the herd of pigs."** **8:32** **And he said to them, "Go.[c]" And going-out (of the men) they-went-away into the pigs; and behold all the pigs rushed[d] down the steep-bank[e] into the lake and died in the waters.**

LEXICON—a. imperf. act. indic. of παρακαλέω (LN 33.168) (BAGD 3. P. 617): 'to beg' [BECNT, NIGTC, NTC; all versions except KJV, NASB], 'to plead' [LN, NICNT], 'to implore' [BAGD, WBC], 'to entreat' [BNTC; NASB], 'to beseech' [CC, PNTC; KJV], 'to ask for earnestly, to request, to appeal to' [LN]. The imperfect tense of this verb is translated as inceptive, indicating the beginning of an ongoing action: 'began to (beg, plead, implore, entreat, etc)' [BECNT, CC, NICNT, WBC; NASB]; as durative, indicating an ongoing action: 'kept (entreating)' [BNTC], 'were begging' [NTC]; as aorist: 'begged' (etc.) [NIGTC, PNTC; all versions except NASB]. This verb means to ask for something earnestly and with propriety [LN].

b. aorist act. impera. of ἀποστέλλω (LN 15.66): 'to send' [BECNT, BNTC, CC, LN, NICNT, NIGTC, PNTC, WBC; all versions except CEV, ESV,

KJV], 'to send away' [ESV], 'to suffer, to go away' [KJV]. The imperative phrase ἀπόστειλον ἡμᾶς 'send us' is translated 'please send' [CEV], 'allow us to enter' [NTC]. This verb means to cause someone to depart for a particular purpose [LN].
- c. pres. act. impera. of ὑπάγω (LN 15.52) (BAGD 2. p. 836): 'to go' [BAGD, BECNT, BNTC, CC, NIGTC, PNTC, WBC; all versions except NLT], 'to go ahead' [NTC], 'to go away, to depart, to leave' [LN]. The imperative Ὑπάγετε 'go' is translated 'off you go' [NICNT], 'all right, go' [NLT]. This verb means to depart from someone's presence, with the implication of a changed relationship [LN].
- d. aorist act. indic. of ὁρμάω (LN 15.222) (BAGD p. 581): 'to rush' [BAGD, BECNT, BNTC, LN, NIGTC, PNTC, WBC; all versions except KJV, NLT], 'to rush headlong' [CC, NTC], 'to stampede' [NICNT], 'to run violently' [KJV], 'to run' [LN], 'to plunge' [NLT]. This verb means to move quickly from one place to another [LN].
- e. κρημνός (LN **1.50**) (BAGD p. 450): 'steep bank' [BECNT, BNTC, NIGTC, WBC; CEV, ESV, NASB, NIV, NRSV], 'steep slope' [BAGD, CC, **LN**, PNTC; NET], 'steep place' [KJV], 'bank' [BAGD], 'cliff' [BAGD, NICNT, NTC; GW], 'side of the cliff' [TEV], 'hill' [NCV], 'steep hillside' [NLT], 'steep side of a hill' [LN]. The phrase κατὰ τοῦ κρημνοῦ 'down the steep bank' is translated 'over the edge' [REB]. This noun denotes the upper portion of a precipitous or steep contour of a hill or mountain [LN].

QUESTION—How is εἰ 'if' used in the phrase, 'If you cast us out'?

It states a condition of reality, something about which there is no doubt that it is going to happen [Lns, NAC, PNTC, TH, TRT, WBC]; that is, 'since you are going to cast us out'.

QUESTION—What is the subject of the phrase ἀπέθανον ἐν τοῖς ὕδασιν 'died in the waters'?
1. It is the pigs that died, not the demons [BECNT, BNTC, CC, EBC, NAC, NICNT, NIGTC, NTC, PNTC, WBC; CEV, ESV, GW, KJV, NASB, NCV, NET, NIV, NLT, NRSV, REB, TEV]. Demons were supernatural beings and could not be destroyed by drowning [NICNT]. The demons were dispersed and rendered powerless [WBC]. Mark and Luke say that the pigs choked [PNTC].
2. It is the demons that died, although the pigs would have drowned also [NIBC]. The demons would have been destroyed at the same time [TH].

8:33 And those-herding[a] (them) fled,[b] and having-gone into the town they-reported[c] everything and/including[d] the (things about) the demonized-men. **8:34** And behold, all the town went-out to-meet[e] Jesus, and having-seen him they-pleaded-with him that he-should-depart[f] from their region.

LEXICON—a. pres. act. participle of βόσκω (LN 44.1) (BAGD 1. p. 145): 'to herd' [LN], 'to feed, to tend' [BAGD], 'to take care of, to look after' [LN]. The phrase οἱ βόσκοντες 'those herding' is translated 'the

MATTHEW 8:33-34   307

herdsmen' [BECNT, BNTC, NTC; ESV, NASB, NCV, NET, NLT], 'the herders' [NIGTC], 'the swineherds' [NICNT, PNTC; NRSV], 'those who were tending' [CC], 'those tending the herd' [WBC], 'those tending the pigs' [NIV], 'the people taking care of the pigs' [CEV; similarly TEV], 'those who took care of the pigs' [GW], 'they that kept them' [KJV], 'the men in charge of them' [REB]. This verb means to herd animals so as to provide them with adequate pasture and to take care of what other needs may be involved [LN].

b. aorist act. indic. of φεύγω (LN 15.61) (BAGD 1. p. 855): 'to flee' [BAGD, BNTC, CC, LN, NIGTC, NTC, PNTC, WBC; ESV, KJV, NLT], 'to run away' [BECNT, LN, NICNT; NASB, NCV, TEV], 'to run off' [NET, NIV, NRSV], 'to take to (their) heels' [REB]. The phrase 'fled, and having gone into the town' is translated 'ran to the town' [CEV], 'ran into the city' [GW]. This verb means to move quickly from a point or area in order to avoid presumed danger or difficulty [LN].

c. ἀπαγγέλλω aorist act. indic. of (LN 33.198) (BAGD 1. p. 79): 'to report' [BAGD, BECNT, BNTC, CC, NIGTC, NTC, WBC; GW, NASB, NIV], 'to tell' [BAGD, LN, NICNT, PNTC; all translations except GW, NASB, NIV], 'to announce' [BAGD], 'to inform' [LN]. This verb means to announce or inform, with possible focus upon the source of information [LN].

d. καί (LN 89.92) (BAGD I.3. p. 393): 'and' [LN, PNTC; KJV, NCV, REB, TEV], 'also' [NIGTC], 'including' [BECNT, BNTC, NICNT, NTC, WBC; NASB, NIV], 'especially' [CEV, ESV, GW] 'namely, that is' [BAGD]. Some translations take καί to be explicative and translate the clause 'told everything that had happened to the demon-possessed men' [NET], 'telling everyone what happened to the demon-possessed men' [NLT], 'they told the whole story about what had happened to the demoniacs' [NRSV]. This conjunction indicates coordinate relations [LN]. This conjunction is often explicative so that a word or clause is connected by means of καί with another word or clause that explains it [BAGD].

e. ὑπάντησις (LN **15.78**) (BAGD p. 837): 'coming to meet' [BAGD]. The prepositional phrase εἰς ὑπάντησιν is translated as a verb infinitive: 'to meet' [**LN**; all translations except NCV], 'to see' [NCV]. This noun denotes the action or event of coming near to and to meet, either in a friendly or hostile sense [LN].

f. aorist act. subj. of μεταβαίνω (LN 15.2) (BAGD 1.a.α. p. 510): 'to depart' [LN; KJV], 'to leave' [BECNT, BNTC, NIGTC, NTC, PNTC, WBC; all versions except KJV, NLT], 'to go away' [NICNT], 'to go' [BAGD], 'to pass over from' [BAGD, CC], 'to move from one place to another, to change one's location' [LN]. The phrase μεταβῇ ἀπὸ τῶν ὁρίων αὐτῶν 'that he should depart from their region' is translated 'to go away and leave them alone' [NLT]. This verb means to effect a change of location in space, with the implication that the two locations are significantly different [LN].

QUESTION—Why did these townspeople want Jesus to leave their area?
Matthew and Mark give no reason for their request, but Luke says that they were very much afraid, perhaps because they feared more economic loss or they feared the presence of such an authoritative person [PNTC]. Most think they were disturbed about their pigs and concerned for their livelihood [BECNT, EBC, Lns, NAC, NIBC, NICNT, NIGTC, NTC, PNTC]. They feared that something even worse might happen if he did not leave [My]. They may have feared the presence of someone with that much power [NAC, NIBC, PNTC], possibly fearing that he was divine and holy, and recoiling from that [NAC]. They might have feared that he was a magician and therefore dangerous [BECNT, WBC].

DISCOURSE UNIT—9:1–8 [CEV, ESV, GW, NASB, NCV, NET, NIV, NLT, TEV]. The topic is Jesus forgives sins [GW], Jesus heals a crippled man [CEV], Jesus heals a paralyzed man [NCV, NLT, TEV], Jesus heals a paralytic [ESV, NIV], healing and forgiving a paralytic [NET], a paralytic healed [NASB].

9:1 **And having-gotten**^{a} **into a boat he-crossed-over**^{b} **and came to his own city.**^{c}

LEXICON—a. aorist act. participle of ἐμβαίνω (LN **15.95**) (BAGD p. 254): 'to get into (a boat)' [BAGD, BECNT, CC, **LN**, NICNT, NIGTC, NTC, PNTC, WBC; all versions except KJV, NIV, NLT], 'to enter into' [KJV], 'to step into' [NIV], 'to climb into' [NLT], 'to embark' [BAGD, LN], 'to go on board (a boat)' [BNTC]. This verb means to go into or onto, as in the case of a boat [LN].

b. aorist act. indic. of διαπεράω (LN 15.31) (BAGD p. 187): 'to cross over' [BAGD, BECNT, BNTC, CC, LN, NIGTC, NTC, PNTC, WBC; ESV, NASB, NIV, REB], 'to cross back over' [CEV], 'to cross' [NICNT; GW, NET, NRSV], 'to pass over' [KJV], 'to go back across' [NCV, NLT, TEV], 'to go over' [LN]. Some translations specify what was being crossed: 'the lake' [NICNT; NCV, NLT], 'the sea' [GW, NASB, NRSV], 'to the other side of the sea' [WBC], 'to the other side' [NET]. This verb means to move from one side to another of some geographical object (for example, body of water, chasm, valley, etc.) [LN].

c. πόλις (LN 1.88) (BAGD 1. p. 685): 'city' [BAGD, BNTC, CC, LN, NTC; ESV, GW, KJV, NASB], 'town' [BECNT, LN, NICNT, NIGTC, PNTC; NCV, NET, NIV, NLT, NRSV, REB, TEV]. The phrase 'his own town' is translated 'the town where he lived' [CEV]. This noun denotes a population center, in contrast with a rural area or countryside and without specific reference to size [LN].

QUESTION—What city did he come to?
He came to Capernaum [BECNT, BNTC, CC, EBC, ICC, Lns, NAC, NIBC, NICNT, NIGTC, PNTC, TH, TRT, WBC]. Capernaum is called his own city because after living so long in Nazareth, he had moved to Capernaum (4:13)

and made it the center for his ministry [PNTC]. The information that 'his own town' is Capernaum rather than Nazareth can be put in a footnote, but not in the text [TH].

DISCOURSE UNIT—9:2–8 [NRSV]. The topic is Jesus heals a paralytic.

9:2 **And behold[a] they-brought to-him a-paralytic[b] having-been-put[c] on a-stretcher,[d] and Jesus having-seen their faith[e] said to-the paralytic,**

LEXICON—a. ἰδού (LN 91.13) (BAGD 1.b.β. p. 371): 'behold' [BAGD, BNTC, NTC; ESV, KJV], 'look' [BAGD, CC, LN, PNTC, WBC], 'right away' [BECNT], 'just then' [NET, NRSV], 'see' [BAGD], 'listen, pay attention' [LN], not explicit [BNTC, NICNT, NIGTC; GW, NASB, NCV, NIV, NLT, TEV]. This word is also translated as a phrase indicating a shift of focus or to prompt attention: 'some men appeared' [REB]. See translations of this word at 1:20. This particle is a prompter of attention, and serves to emphasize the following statement [LN].

b. παραλυτικός (LN **23.171**) (BAGD p. 620): 'paralyzed' [LN], 'lame' [BAGD, LN]. This adjective is translated as a substantive: 'paralytic' [BAGD, BECNT, BNTC, CC, **LN**, NIGTC, PNTC, WBC; ESV, NASB, NET, NIV], 'paralyzed man' [NICNT, NTC; GW, NLT, NRSV, REB, TEV], 'man who was paralyzed' NCV], 'man sick of the palsy' [KJV]. This adjective describes being lame and/or paralyzed, and it is often best to speak of a paralytic as 'one who cannot walk' [LN].

c. perf. pass. participle of βάλλω (LN 85.34) (BAGD 1.b. p. 131): 'to be put' [LN]. This passive participle is translated 'lying' [BAGD, BECNT, NICNT, NTC, PNTC, WBC; all versions except GW, NLT, REB], 'placed' [BNTC], 'cast' [CC], 'laid out' [NIGTC], not explicit [GW, NLT, REB]. This verb means to put or place some object or mass in a location, with the possible implication of force in some contexts [LN].

d. κλίνη (LN **6.106**) (BAGD p. 436): 'stretcher' [BAGD, **LN**; GW, NET], 'bed' [BAGD, BECNT, BNTC, CC, LN, NICNT, NIGTC, NTC, PNTC, WBC; ESV, KJV, NASB, NRSV, REB, TEV], 'mat' [CEV, NCV, NIV, NLT], 'pallet' [BAGD], 'couch' [BAGD, LN]. This noun denotes any piece of furniture employed for reclining or lying on [LN].

e. πίστις (LN 31.85) (BAGD 2.b.α. p. 663): 'faith' [BAGD, LN; all translations except CEV, TEV], 'trust' [BAGD, LN]. The phrase 'having seen their faith' is translated 'saw how much faith they had' [CEV, TEV]. This noun denotes the action of believing to the extent of complete trust and reliance [LN].

QUESTION—What is the relationship of this account with what is recorded in 9:1 and before?

1. The account that follows did not necessarily follow chronologically [EBC, NTC]. The exact time of this event was not known [Lns]. All three synoptic gospels put these events together, but none make a specific claim that they occurred in sequence, as they have arranged material topically [EBC]. The call of Matthew probably occurred prior to some of the events

already related in earlier chapters [NTC]. Matthew has arranged his material topically, not chronologically [BECNT, EBC, NAC, NTC].
2. What occurs in the account following 9:1 occurred just after what has been related in chapter 8 [NIBC, PNTC].

QUESTION—What relationship is indicated by the aorist participle ἰδών 'having seen'?

Note that a temporal relationship does not necessarily exclude a causal relationship; that is, when he saw their faith he forgave because of that faith that he saw.
1. It indicates a temporal relationship [BECNT, BNTC, NICNT, NTC, PNTC, WBC; CEV, ESV, GW, NCV, NET, NIV, NRSV, REB, TEV]: when he saw their faith, he healed him.
2. It indicates a causal relationship [CC]: because he saw their faith, he healed him.

QUESTION—What was the κλίνη 'stretcher'?

It is a kind of mat [NTC, PNTC, TH, WBC], a stretcher [NAC, NIBC, TRT; GW, NET]. It was a semi-rigid but lightweight structure [NICNT].

QUESTION—Who is included in the possessive pronoun αὐτῶν 'their'?

It included the man's friends, as well as the man himself [BECNT, BNTC, CC, EBC, Lns, My, NTC, PNTC, WBC]. It primarily refers to the man's friends, but also includes him [ICC, NICNT, TH]. It refers to the man's friends [NIGTC].

"Have-courage,ᵃ child,ᵇ your sinsᶜ are-forgiven.ᵈ"

LEXICON—a. pres. act. impera. of θαρσέω (LN 25.156) (BAGD p. 352): 'to have courage' [BAGD, LN, WBC; NET], 'to take courage' [BECNT, NTC, PNTC; NASB], 'to be encouraged' [NCV, NLT], 'to be courageous' [BAGD, CC, LN], 'to take heart' [NICNT, NIGTC; ESV, NET, NIV, NRSV, REB], 'to be of good cheer' [KJV], 'to cheer up' [GW], 'to be bold' [LN]. This imperative is translated 'Courage!' [BNTC; TEV], 'Don't worry!' [CEV]. This verb means to have confidence and firmness of purpose in the face of danger or testing [LN].
b. τέκνον (LN **9.46**) (BAGD 2.a. p. 808): 'child' [BAGD, BECNT, CC, LN, NIGTC], 'son' [BAGD, BNTC, LN, NICNT, NTC; KJV, NASB, NET, NIV, NRSV]. This vocative is translated 'my child' [BAGD, LN, PNTC, WBC; NLT], 'my son' [BAGD; ESV, REB, TEV], 'friend' [GW], 'my friend' [CEV], 'young man' [NCV], 'my dear man' [**LN**]. This noun may denote a person of any age for whom there is a special relationship of endearment and association. In this context the focus is on affection and endearment, not age [LN].
c. ἁμαρτία (LN 88.310) (BAGD 1. p. 43): 'sin' [BAGD, LN; all translations], 'guilt' [LN]. This noun denotes the moral consequence of having sinned [LN].

d. pres. pass. indic. of ἀφίημι (LN 40.8) (BAGD 2. p. 126): 'to be forgiven' [BAGD, LN; all translations], 'to be pardoned' [BAGD, LN]. This verb means to remove the guilt resulting from wrongdoing [LN].

QUESTION—Why did Jesus call the man τέκνον 'child'?

This is polite form of address to someone of a younger age or lesser social status [TH], or to a person of lesser authority [TRT]. It expresses tenderness [BECNT, Lns], affection [EBC, LN, My], or endearment [ICC, LN, NTC, TH]. It is a term of intimacy [WBC]. It expresses warmth and friendliness to a man in deep need [PNTC]. The informality of the term strengthens the reassurance [NICNT].

QUESTION—Why did Jesus forgive his sins first, instead of healing the paralysis?

Forgiving sins was at the center of Jesus' mission of salvation, and is the ultimate basis for restoring the entire person [CC]. Sin and sickness are tied together [CC, ICC, NICNT], but this does not imply that the man was sick because of his own sin [CC, NICNT]. There is a tie between sin and sickness, but of the two, sin is the more serious problem [EBC]. There is no stated or implied connection between this man's illness and any sin or sins he had presumably committed [My, NTC, WBC]. All sickness and death stem from the entering of sin into the world, so the forgiveness of sins is the most basic need that people have [WBC]. Any possible connection between sin and illness is only in the background of this account [NIGTC]. The man was very conscious of his sins and concerned about his need for forgiveness [Lns, NTC].

QUESTION—What is implied by the use of the present tense of the verb ἀφίενται 'are forgiven'?

Jesus is forgiving his sins right then and there [CC, EBC, ICC, NICNT, NIGTC, PNTC, TRT, WBC]. The man's sins are forgiven in the very act of Jesus saying it [CC, Lns].

9:3 And behold, some of-the scribes^a said within/among^b themselves, "This-man^c blasphemes.^d"

LEXICON—a. γραμματεύς (LN 53.94): 'scribe' [BNTC, CC, NICNT, NIGTC, NTC, PNTC, WBC; ESV, GW, KJV, NASB, NRSV, REB], 'legal expert' [BECNT], 'expert in the law' [NET], 'teacher of the law' [NCV, NIV, TEV], 'teacher of the Law of Moses' [CEV], 'teacher of religious law' [NLT], 'one who is learned in the Law, expert in the Law of Moses' [LN]. This noun denotes a recognized expert in Jewish law (including both canonical and traditional laws and regulations) [LN].

b. ἐν (LN 83.9, 83.13, **31.5**): 'within' [CC, LN (83.13), NTC; KJV], 'among' [LN (83.9), NICNT]. The phrase ἐν ἑαυτοῖς 'within/among themselves' is translated 'to themselves' [BECNT, **LN** (31.5), NIGTC, PNTC, WBC; all versions except KJV, GW], 'inwardly' [BNTC]. The phrase εἶπαν ἐν ἑαυτοῖς 'said within/among themselves' is translated 'thought' [GW]. The idiom λέγω ἐν ἑαυτῷ 'to speak to oneself' means to

think about something without communicating the content to others [LN (31.5)].
  c. οὗτος (LN 92.29): 'this, this one' [LN]. This demonstrative pronoun is translated 'this man' [BNTC, CC, NICNT, PNTC, WBC; ESV, KJV, NCV, NET, NRSV, REB, TEV], 'this fellow' [BECNT, NIGTC, NTC; NASB, NIV], 'he' [GW], 'Jesus' [CEV], not explicit [NLT]. This pronoun refers to an entity regarded as a part of the discourse setting, with pejorative meaning in certain contexts [LN].
  d. pres. act. indic. of βλασφημέω (LN 33.400) (BAGD 2.b.α. p. 142): 'to blaspheme' [BAGD, BECNT, BNTC, CC, LN, NICNT, NIGTC, NTC, PNTC, WBC; ESV, KJV, NASB, NET, NIV, NRSV, REB], 'to speak blasphemy' [TEV], 'to dishonor God' [GW], 'to revile, to defame' [LN]. The phrase Οὗτος βλασφημεῖ 'this man blasphemes' is translated 'Jesus must think he is God!' [CEV], 'This man speaks as if he were God. That is blasphemy!' [NCV], 'That's blasphemy! Does he think he's God?' [NLT]. This verb means to speak against someone in such a way as to harm or injure his or her reputation, and may occur in relation to persons as well as to divine beings [LN].

QUESTION—Were the scribes speaking to one another or were each of them thinking this individually within themselves?
  1. They were thinking this within themselves [CC, Lns, NIBC, NIGTC, NTC, PNTC; GW, KJV].
  2. They were saying this among themselves [EBC], that is, muttering to each other [EBC, NAC] or whispering to one another [NICNT].

QUESTION—What does βλασφημέω 'blaspheme' mean in this verse?
  It means that Jesus claims to be able to do something that only God is able to do [BECNT, BNTC, CC, EBC, ICC, Lns, My, NAC, NIBC, NICNT, NIGTC, NTC, PNTC, TH, TRT, WBC]. Jesus was in effect claiming to be able to speak from God on this [NIGTC].

9:4 **And Jesus having-known[a] their thoughts[b] said, "Why do- you -think evil[c] in your hearts[d]?**

TEXT—Manuscripts reading ἰδών 'having seen' are given a B rating by GNT to indicate it was regarded to be almost certain. Some manuscripts read εἰδώς 'knowing'. Due to the conceptual similarity between 'seeing' and 'knowing' it is difficult to distinguish which text the various translations followed.

LEXICON—a. aorist act. participle of ὁράω (LN 32.11): 'to know' [BECNT, BNTC, NTC, PNTC; CEV, ESV, GW, KJV, NASB, NCV, NIV, NLT], 'to see' [CC, LN, NICNT, NIGTC; NET], 'to discern' [WBC], 'to perceive' [NRSV, TEV], 'to realize' [REB], 'to understand, to recognize' [LN]. This verb means to come to understand as the result of perception [LN].
  b. ἐνθύμησις (LN **30.15**) (BAGD p. 266): 'thought' [BAGD, BECNT, BNTC, CC, LN, NIGTC, NTC, PNTC, WBC; ESV, KJV, NASB, NCV,

NIV, NRSV], '(their) reaction' [NET], 'what is thought, opinion' [LN]. This noun is translated as a phrase: 'what they were thinking' [NICNT; GW, NLT, REB, TEV], 'what was in their minds' [CEV], 'what they were thinking' [**LN**]. It denotes the content of thinking and reasoning [LN].

c. πονηρός (LN 88.110) (BAGD 2.c. p. 691): 'evil' [BAGD, BECNT, LN, NIGTC, NTC; ESV, KJV, NASB, NET, NRSV], 'wicked' [BAGD, LN]. This plural adjectival noun is translated 'evil thoughts' [BNTC, NICNT; NCV, NIV, NLT, REB], 'evil things' [CC, PNTC, WBC; CEV, GW, TEV]. This adjective describes what is morally corrupt and evil [LN].

d. καρδία (LN 26.3) (BAGD 1.b.β. p. 403): 'heart' [BAGD, BECNT, BNTC, CC, LN, NICNT, NIGTC, NTC, PNTC, WBC; ESV, KJV, NASB, NET, NIV, NLT, NRSV], 'inner self' [LN], 'mind' [BAGD, LN], not explicit [CEV, GW, NCV, REB, TEV]. This noun denotes the causative source of a person's psychological life in its various aspects, but with special emphasis upon thoughts [LN].

QUESTION—Did Jesus read their thoughts?

1. He supernaturally discerned what they were thinking [BECNT, BNTC, ICC, Lns, My, NIBC, NTC, PNTC, WBC]. The Holy Spirit revealed this to him [BECNT].
2. It probably did not require supernatural knowledge on Jesus' part to surmise what they were thinking [EBC, NAC]. Here he may have had no more than an acute intuition [NIGTC]. He read their body language [NICNT].

9:5 For which is easier,[a] to say, 'Your sins are forgiven' or to say, 'Rise[b] and walk[c]?'

LEXICON—a. εὐκοπώτερον 'easier' is a comparative form of εὔκοπος (LN 22.39) (BAGD p. 321): 'easy' [LN], 'without trouble' [LN]. This comparative form is translated 'easier' [BAGD; all translations]. This adjective, which occurs only in the comparative form in the NT, describes that which is easy, in the sense of not requiring great effort or work [LN].

b. pres. act. impera. of ἐγείρω (LN 17.9) (BAGD 1.b. p. 214): 'to rise' [BNTC, CC, WBC; ESV], 'to arise' [KJV], 'to get up' [BAGD, BECNT, LN, NICNT, NIGTC, NTC, PNTC; CEV, GW, NASB, NIV, TEV], 'to stand up' [LN; NCV, NET, NLT, NRSV, REB]. This verb means to get up, normally from a lying or reclining position but possibly from a seated position. In some contexts it implies there is some degree of previous incapacity [LN].

c. pres. act. impera. of περιπατέω (LN 15.227) (BAGD 1.c. p. 649): 'to walk' [BAGD, LN; all translations]. This verb means to walk along or around [LN].

QUESTION—What is the logic of Jesus' argument?

It is a greater-to-lesser argument [CC].

1. It is easier to say that his sins are forgiven because it is not immediately apparent whether Jesus actually has the authority for that, whereas it is immediately apparent whether or not he has authority to heal because they could see if it actually happens [BNTC, CC, ICC, NAC, NICNT, PNTC, WBC]. It is easier to *say* that someone's sins are forgiven, but that does not mean it is easier to actually do it [NAC].
2. It is harder to actually forgive sins, since only God can do that; but here the next statement is ironical, in that the 'easier' task of healing was miraculous [EBC].
3. Neither is harder than the other, because both require omnipotent power [Lns, My, NTC].

9:6 **But so-that[a] you-may-know that the Son of Man has authority[b] on the earth to forgive sins—" then he says to-the paralytic, "Rise, take[c] your stretcher and go to your home.[d]" 9:7 And having-risen he-went to his home.**

LEXICON—a. ἵνα (LN 89.59): 'so that' [BECNT, LN, NICNT, PNTC, WBC; NASB, NET, NIV, NRSV], 'that' [BNTC; ESV, KJV], 'in order to/that' [CC, LN, NTC], 'for the purpose of' [LN]. The phrase ἵνα εἰδῆτε 'so that you may know that' is translated 'I will show you that' [CEV], 'I will prove to you that' [NCV, NLT, TEV], 'I want you to know that' [GW], 'to convince you that' [REB]. This conjunction is also translated as indicating this is a parenthetical remark by the author to the reader, not a comment by Jesus to the audience [NIGTC]. This conjunction marks purpose for events and states and sometimes occurs in highly elliptical contexts [LN].

b. ἐξουσία (LN 37.35, 76.12) (BAGD 3. p. 278): 'authority' [BAGD, BECNT, BNTC, CC, NICNT, NIGTC, PNTC, WBC; all versions except CEV, KJV], 'power' [LN (76.12), NTC; KJV], 'right' [CEV], 'authority to rule, right to control' [LN (37.35)]. This noun denotes the power to do something, with or without an added implication of authority [LN (76.12)], or the right to control or govern over [LN (37.35)].

c. aorist act. impera. of αἴρω (LN 15.203) (BAGD 1.a. p. 24): 'to take' [CC, WBC; NCV, NET, NIV, NRSV, REB], 'to take up' [BAGD, BNTC, NIGTC, NTC, PNTC; KJV], 'to pick up' [BAGD, NICNT; CEV, ESV, GW, NASB, NLT, TEV], 'to lift up' [BAGD], 'to carry (away), to carry off, to remove, to take (away)' [LN]. This verb means to lift up and carry (away) [LN].

d. οἶκος (LN 7.2) (BAGD 1.a.α. p. 560): 'home' [BECNT, NIGTC, NTC, PNTC; all versions except KJV], 'house' [BAGD, BNTC, LN, CC, NICNT, WBC; KJV]. This noun denotes a building consisting of one or more rooms and normally serving as a dwelling place [LN].

QUESTION—How is the first clause in 9:6 to be understood?
1. It is a statement made by Jesus to the scribes [BECNT, BNTC, CC, EBC, Lns, My, NAC, NIBC, NICNT, NTC, PNTC, TH, WBC].

MATTHEW 9:6–7

2. It is an aside made by Matthew, the author of this account, to the reader, explaining what Jesus said and did next [ICC, NIGTC].

QUESTION—Why does Jesus add ἐπὶ τῆς γῆς 'on the earth' to his assertion of authority to forgive sins?

First, it is an assertion that there is more to him than just what can be accounted for by his physical manifestation, and secondly, while he does not deny that only God can forgive sins, he is doing it, and inviting those watching to contemplate on what that might mean in the present situation [PNTC]. There is an implied correlation between what the Son of Man does on earth and what God does in heaven [NIGTC]. 'On earth' focuses on the then current moment, as opposed the end of all things at the eschaton [Lns, NTC, WBC], and how he exercises divine right and power while the opportunities of grace are still open [NTC]. The one who would be the eschatological judge had already come on earth with the authority to forgive sins [EBC]. He came to earth with authority brought from heaven [My]. Here he is contrasting his present life with the heavenly preexistence of the Son of Man described in Daniel 7:13–14 [NAC].

9:8 **And seeing (this) the crowds were-afraid**[a] **and glorified**[b] **God the (one) having-given such authority/power**[c] **to men.**[d]

TEXT—Manuscripts reading οἱ ὄχλοι ἐφοβήθησαν 'the crowds were afraid' are given an A rating by GNT to indicate it was regarded to be certain. Some manuscripts read οἱ ὄχλοι ἐθαύμασαν 'the crowds marveled'. Only KJV follows this reading.

LEXICON—a. aorist pass. indic. of φοβέομαι (LN 87.14, 25.252) (BAGD 1.a. p. 862): 'to be afraid' [BAGD, BNTC, CC, LN (25.252), NICNT, NIGTC; CEV, ESV, NET, TEV], 'to be frightened' [BAGD], 'to fear' [LN (25.252, 87.14)], 'to marvel' [KJV], 'to be filled with awe' [BECNT, NTC; GW, NIV, NRSV, REB], 'to be awestruck' [PNTC, WBC; NASB], 'to be amazed' [NCV], 'to show great reverence for, to show great respect for' [LN (87.14)]. The phrase οἱ ὄχλοι ἐφοβήθησαν 'the crowds were afraid' is translated 'fear swept through the crowd' [NLT]. This verb means to be in a state of fear [LN (25.251)], or to have such awe or respect for a person that there is also a measure of fear [LN (87.14)].

b. aorist act. indic. of δοξάζω (LN 33.357) (BAGD 1. p. 204): to glorify' [BECNT, CC, LN, NIGTC, NTC, PNTC, WBC; ESV, KJV, NASB, NRSV], 'to give glory to' [NICNT], 'to praise' [BAGD, BNTC, LN; CEV, GW, NCV, NIV, NLT, REB, TEV], 'to honor' [BAGD; NET], 'to magnify' [BAGD]. This verb means to speak of something as being unusually fine and deserving honor [LN].

c. ἐξουσία (LN 37.35, 76.12) (BAGD 2. p. 278): 'authority' [BECNT, BNTC, CC, LN, NICNT, NIGTC, PNTC, WBC; all versions except KJV, NCV], 'power' [BAGD, LN, NTC; KJV, NCV]. This noun denotes the right to control or govern over some one [LN (37.35)] or the power to do something with or without an added implication of authority. In a number of instances it is difficult to determine whether the focus is upon the power which an individual has or a granted authority to do something which naturally implies strength or power [LN]. It refers to the ability to do something [BAGD].

d. ἄνθρωπος (LN 9.1): The plural form is 'people, persons, mankind' [LN]. This plural noun is translated 'men' [BNTC, NTC, PNTC; ESV, KJV, NASB, NET, NIV, REB],'people' [CEV, TEV], 'humans' [NIGTC; GW], 'human beings' [BECNT, NICNT, WBC; NCV, NRSV] 'the realm of men' [CC], 'a man' [NLT]. This noun denotes a human being (normally an adult) [LN].

QUESTION—Does Matthew include the scribes among the crowds that were fearful and glorifying God?

The plural noun 'crowds' refers to the bystanders in general, and although those people were probably not well disposed to Jesus, they were not hostile like the scribes were [PNTC]. It does not include the scribes in verse three who considered Jesus to be blasphemous [NIGTC]. Matthew doesn't tell us what the effect of all this had on those scribes [PNTC].

QUESTION—What was the authority or power that the crowd believed God had given to men?

1. In verse 6 Jesus had raised up the paralytic so that the scribes (and the other people who were listening) could know that he, the Son of Man, had authority on earth *to forgive sins* [BECNT, BNTC, EBC, ICC, NAC, NIBC, NICNT, NIGTC, TH]. Jesus' authority to forgive sins was demonstrated when he healed the paralytic [NIBC].
2. This refers to the authority to both forgive sins and heal people [CC, Lns, WBC]. Jesus was a human being who was exercising such authority when he forgive the sins of the paralytic and healed him [WBC].
3. This refers to the authority or power to heal people [My, NTC]. The miracle that the crowd had seen was the raising of the paralytic [My, NTC].

QUESTION—What is meant by the statement that God had given such authority/power τοῖς ἀνθρώποις 'to men'?

In verse 6 Jesus said he wanted his opponents to know that he had authority (the same word used in this verse) to forgive sins and then he went on to prove his claim by performing a miracle of healing. The people recognized the hand of God in the healing of the paralytic and were glorifying God for such a miracle. They were amazed that God had given such power to a member of the human race [NTC]. Jesus had receive this authority to exercise for the benefit of people [BNTC, Lns, My]. They were surprised that God would have given such authority to any human being [NICNT], but now they had jus seen a man exercise the authority of God [EBC]. The use of the plural noun ἀνθρώποις 'men' refers just to Jesus [BNTC, EBC, Lns, My, NAC, NICNT, NTC, PNTC, WBC].

Although Jesus seems to be the only man that the present crowd had in mind when they said this, some commentaries think that the use of the plural noun ἀνθρώποις 'men' could includes others, and point out that later on some authority and power to heal would be extended to other men such as the apostles [CC]. This authority has been given to Jesus and his followers, viewed as human beings [BECNT]. It anticipates a coming time when believers will exercise Jesus' authority and also to continue to benefit from what Jesus does by his authority [NIGTC]. In 16:19 and 18:18 Jesus' followers will be given the authority to forgive sin [ICC, TH].

QUESTION—What was the authority or power that God had given?
1. This refers to the authority to forgive sins [BECNT, BNTC, CC, EBC, ICC, NAC, NICNT, NIGTC, TH].
2. This refers to the authority to both forgive sins and heal people [CC, Lns, WBC]. The use of the plural noun ἀνθρώποις 'men' is rhetorical and refers only to Jesus [Lns]. Jesus was a human being who was exercising such authority through forgiving sins and healing the paralytic [WBC].
3. This was the power to heal people [BAGD, NTC]. The effect of the miracle was that the crowds were awe-struck at seeing the men be healed [PNTC].

DISCOURSE UNIT—9:9–13 [CEV, ESV, GW, NASB, NCV, NET, NLT, NRSV, TEV]. The topic is Jesus chooses Matthew to be a disciple [GW], Jesus chooses Matthew [CEV, NCV], Jesus calls Matthew [ESV, NLT, TEV], the call of Matthew: eating with sinners [NET], the call of Matthew [NRSV], the calling of Matthew [NIV], Matthew called [NASB].

9:9 And going-on[a] from-there Jesus saw a-man called[b] Matthew sitting at/in[c] the tax-office,[d] and he-says to-him, "Follow[e] me." And having-risen he-followed him.

LEXICON—a. pres. act. participle of παράγω (LN **15.15**) (BAGD 2.b. p. 614): 'to go on' [BNTC, NICNT; NASB, NET, NIV, REB], 'to go away' [LN, NIGTC], 'to go along' [CC, LN], 'to walk along' [NLT, NRSV], 'to pass by' [BECNT], 'to pass on' [NTC, PNTC; ESV], 'to pass forth' [KJV], 'to leave' [WBC; CEV, GW, NCV], 'to move along' [**LN**]. This participle is translated '(Jesus) left (that place), and as he walked along' [TEV]. This verb means to continue to move along [LN].

b. pres. pass. participle of λέγω (LN 33.129) (BAGD II.3. p. 470): 'to be called' [BAGD, BECNT, CC, LN, NICNT, NIGTC; ESV, NASB, NRSV], 'to be named' [BAGD, BNTC, LN, NTC, PNTC, WBC; CEV, KJV, NCV, NET, NIV, NLT, REB, TEV]. The phrase ἄνθρωπον Μαθθαῖον λεγόμενον 'a man called Matthew' is translated 'the man's name was Matthew' [GW]. This verb means to speak of a person or object by means of a proper name [LN].

c. ἐπί with accusative (LN **83.23**) (BAGD III.1.a.ζ. p. 288): 'at' [BAGD, BECNT, CC, **LN**, NICNT, NIGTC, NTC, PNTC, WBC; ESV, KJV, NET, NIV, NLT, NRSV], 'by' [BAGD, LN], 'in' [BNTC; GW, NASB, NCV, TEV]. The phrase καθήμενον ἐπί 'sitting at/in' is translated 'at his

seat in' [REB]. This preposition describes a position in proximity to or in the immediate vicinity of an object or other position [LN].
d. τελώνιον (LN 57.183) (BAGD p. 812): 'tax office' [BAGD, BNTC, CC, LN, NTC, PNTC; GW], 'office' [TEV], 'tax collection' [WBC], 'tax collector's booth' [BECNT; NASB, NCV, NIV, NLT], 'tax booth' [NIGTC; ESV, NET, NRSV], 'customs booth' [NICNT], 'customs house' [REB], 'receipt of custom' [KJV], 'revenue office' [BAGD, LN]. The phrase 'a man called Matthew sitting at/in the tax-office' is translated 'a tax collector named Matthew sitting at the place for paying taxes' [CEV], 'a tax collector, named Matthew, sitting at his office' [TEV]. This noun denotes a place where taxes or revenue was collected from those entering a town to sell produce [LN].
e. pres. act. impera. of ἀκολουθέω (LN 15.156) (BAGD 3. p. 31): 'to follow' [BAGD, LN; all translations except CEV, NLT], 'to come with' [CEV], 'to follow as a disciple' [BAGD], 'to accompany as a follower, to go along with' [LN]. The command 'follow me' is translated 'follow me and be my disciple' [NLT]. This verb means to follow or accompany someone who takes the lead in determining direction and route of movement [LN].

QUESTION—What was the function and location of this tax office?

It was a toll booth where tax gatherers collected indirect taxes such as customs and sales taxes on commercial goods that passed by that way [CC]. Matthew may have been a minor official in the taxation process there [CC, NTC]. The taxes collected here were levied by Herod Antipas, not by Rome, and were customs duties on goods passing through this district. The booth would have been near the lake where cargoes were unloaded [NICNT, PNTC]. It may have been located near the sea to collect duty on goods brought in by boat [BECNT, BNTC, NAC], or taxes on fish [BECNT]. It was at the edge of town [NAC], on the border between the territories of Philip and Herod Antipas [EBC]. It was near the shore, where traffic in trade goods moved along the highway between Syria and Egypt [Lns, NIBC, NTC, PNTC].

9:10 And it-happened[a] as he was-reclining[b] (at table) in the house, and behold many tax-collectors[c] and sinners[d] having-come were-reclining (at table) -with Jesus and his disciples. **9:11** And seeing (this) the Pharisees were-saying to his disciples, "Why does- your teacher -eat with the tax-collectors and sinners?"

LEXICON—a. aorist mid. (deponent = active) indic. of γίνομαι (LN 13.107) (BAGD I.3.f. p. 159): 'to happen' [BAGD, BNTC, LN, WBC; NASB], 'to occur, to come to be' [LN], 'to come to pass' [BAGD, PNTC; KJV], not explicit [BECNT, CC, NICNT, NTC; CEV, ESV, NCV, NET, NIV, NRSV, REB, TEV]. The phrase Καὶ ἐγένετο...καὶ ἰδού 'and it happened...and behold' is conflated and translated as 'what happened next was' [NIGTC], 'later' [NLT]. The function of the phrase Καὶ

ἐγένετο 'and it happened' as a discourse marker to indicate the shift to a new event is translated 'later' [GW]. This verb means to happen, with the implication that what happens is different from a previous state [LN].
  b. pres. mid. or pass. (deponent = act.) participle of ἀνάκειμαι (LN 23.21) (BAGD 2. p. 55): 'to recline at table' [BECNT, BNTC, NTC, PNTC, WBC; ESV, NASB], 'to recline' [BAGD], 'to recline for a meal' [CC], 'to recline at dinner' [NIGTC], 'to be at table' [BAGD], 'to eat a meal' [LN], 'to be at a meal' [NICNT], 'to have a meal' [NET, REB, TEV], 'to have dinner' [CEV, GW, NCV, NIV], 'to sit at dinner' [NRSV], 'to sit at meat' [KJV]. The phrase αὐτοῦ ἀνακειμένου ἐν τῇ οἰκίᾳ 'as he was reclining (at table) in the house' is translated 'Matthew invited Jesus and his disciples to his home as dinner guests' [NLT]. This verb means to eat a meal, with possible reference to the fact of the people reclining to eat [LN].
  c. τελώνης (LN 57.184) (BAGD p. 812): 'tax collector' [BAGD, BECNT, BNTC, LN, NICNT, NIGTC, NTC, PNTC, WBC; all versions except KJV], 'tax gatherer' [CC], 'publican' [KJV], 'revenue officer' [BAGD, LN]. This noun denotes one who collects taxes for the government [LN].
  d. ἁμαρτωλός (LN 88.295) (BAGD 2. p. 44): 'sinner' [BAGD, BECNT, BNTC, CC, LN, NICNT, NIGTC, PNTC, WBC; all versions except CEV, NLT, TEV], 'other sinners' [CEV], 'other disreputable sinners' [NLT], 'people of low reputation' [NTC], 'other outcasts' [TEV], 'outcast' [LN]. This noun is shown in quotation marks by NCV, NIV. This noun denotes a person who customarily sins, and may refer to persons who were irreligious in the sense of having no concern for observing the details of the Law and as such were often treated as social outcasts [LN].

QUESTION—What is the chronological relationship between the account of this meal and Jesus' call of Matthew in the immediately preceding section?
  1. There is a lapse of time between the two events [EBC, NAC]; Matthew arranges his material topically, not chronologically [EBC].
  2. This meal occurred not long after Matthew's call to discipleship [BECNT].

QUESTION—What is the discourse function of καὶ ἐγένετο 'and it happened'? This transition formula is normally used to introduce narrative, and here sets the scene for an important new development [NICNT]. It indicates a structural turning point in the narrative [EBC].

QUESTION—In whose house did this meal occur?
  1. It was at Matthew's house [BECNT, CC, Lns, NAC, NICNT, NTC, PNTC, WBC; CEV, GW, NCV, NET, NIV, NLT, TEV], as indicated in Luke 5:29 [CC, Lns, NAC, NTC, WBC]. The term 'reclining' suggests a special meal [ICC, WBC], and that Jesus was the guest of honor [WBC].
  2. It was at Jesus' house [My, NIGTC], and the meal is celebrating Matthew's becoming a disciple [NIGTC].
  3. Although it could have been Jesus' house, it was probably the house of Peter [ICC].

QUESTION—What is meant by the term 'sinners'?

The Pharisees considered 'sinners' to be those Jewish people who publicly or flagrantly violated God's laws [CC], and it would have included prostitutes [CC, EBC, NAC]. They had abandoned the law and violated the covenant [ICC]. They are undesirables [NICNT], the lower end of society [WBC], the egregiously ungodly [BECNT], people of low reputation [EBC, NAC, NTC], the immoral [My], those unsavory types who lived outside the boundaries of what was considered respectable [NIGTC]. These 'sinners' were friends of the tax collectors [WBC]. They were disreputable people who were not concerned with righteousness, and may have abandoned any attempt to keep the law [ICC, WBC]. They were people who did not abide by the stricter standards of ceremonial and ritual purity [BNTC, PNTC], and possibly even the moral law [BNTC]. They were people who lived contrary to God's law [Lns]. Tax collectors were part of the larger category more generally described as 'sinners' [Lns; CC; CEV, NLT] or 'outcasts' [TEV].

QUESTION—What was the significance of table fellowship in that time and place?

Sharing a meal was seen as solidifying important social bonds, and as indicating very close fellowship and mutual approval [CC]. It implied deep unity [BECNT], friendship and fellowship [NAC, NTC], close association [PNTC]. Sharing a meal was a sign of identification [NICNT], indicating closeness and even oneness with one another [WBC].

9:12 But he having-heard said, "The ones-being-healthy[a] do- not -need a-physician[b] but the ones-having illness.[c]

LEXICON—a. pres. act. participle of ἰσχύω (LN 23.130) (BAGD 1. p. 383): 'to be healthy' [LN], 'to be in good health' [BAGD]. The phrase 'the ones being healthy' is translated 'those who are healthy' [BECNT, NTC; NASB, NET], 'the healthy' [WBC; NIV, REB], 'healthy people' [CEV, GW, NCV, NLT], 'those who are well' [NICNT, PNTC; ESV, NRSV], 'people who are well' [TEV], 'those in good health' [BNTC], 'those who are in good health' [NIGTC], 'those who are fit' [CC], 'they that be whole' [KJV]. This statement is probably from a proverb [ICC, My, NAC, NICNT, NTC, WBC]. This verb indicates a state of being healthy, with the implication of robustness and vigor [LN].

b. ἰατρός (LN **23.141**) (BAGD 1. p. 368): 'physician' [BAGD, BECNT, BNTC, CC, LN, WBC; ESV, KJV, NASB, NET, NRSV], 'doctor' [**LN**, NICNT, NIGTC, NTC, PNTC; CEV, GW, NCV, NIV, NLT, REB, TEV], 'healer' [LN]. This noun denotes one who causes someone to be healed [LN].

c. κακῶς ἔχω (LN **23.148**) (BAGD 1. p. 398). 'to be ill' [BAGD, LN], 'to be sick' [BAGD]. The idiom κακῶς ἔχω (literally 'to have badly' or 'to fare badly') means to be in a bad state [LN]. The phrase οἱ κακῶς ἔχοντες 'the ones having illness' is translated 'those who are sick' [BECNT, BNTC, CC, **LN**, NIGTC, PNTC, WBC; ESV, GW, NASB,

NET, NRSV, TEV], 'the sick' [NCV, NIV, REB], 'they that are sick' [KJV], 'sick people' [CEV, NLT], 'those who are ill' [NICNT, NTC].

9:13 But go (and) learn[a] what is (the meaning of),[b] "I-desire[c] mercy[d] and not sacrifice,[e]" for I-did- not -come to call[f] (the) righteous[g] but sinners.

TEXT—Manuscripts reading ἀλλὰ ἁμαρτωλούς 'but sinners' are followed by GNT, which does not mention any variant reading. A variant reading is ἀλλὰ ἁμαρτωλούς εἰς μετάνοιαν 'but sinners to repentance' and it is followed by KJV.

LEXICON—a. aorist act. impera. of μανθάνω (LN **27.15**) (BAGD 1. p. 490): 'to learn' [BAGD, **LN**; all translations except TEV], 'to find out' [TEV], 'to come to realize' [LN]. The phrase 'go and learn' is a rabbinic formula [BECNT, EBC, ICC, My, NAC, NIBC, NICNT, NIGTC, PNTC]. This verb means to learn from experience, often with the implication of reflection [LN].

b. This phrase τί ἐστιν 'what is' is translated 'what this means' [BECNT, BNTC, NICNT, PNTC, WBC; ESV, GW, NASB, NCV, NIV, NRSV], 'what this text means' [REB], 'what this saying means' [NET], 'what that meaneth' [KJV], 'what this is' [CC, NIGTC], 'what is meant by' [NTC], 'what is meant by the Scripture that says' [TEV], 'what the Scriptures mean' [CEV], 'the meaning of this Scripture' [NLT].

c. pres. act. indic. of θέλω (LN 25.1, 25.102) (BAGD 4.b. p. 355): 'to desire' [BECNT, BNTC, CC, LN (25.1), NICNT, NIGTC, NTC, WBC; ESV, NASB, NIV, NRSV], 'to want' [LN (25.1), PNTC; CEV, GW, NCV, NLT, TEV], 'to require' [REB], 'to take pleasure in (something)' [BAGD], 'to like, to enjoy' [LN (25.102)]. This verb is translated 'I will have' [KJV]. This verb means to desire to have or experience something [LN (25.1)] or to take pleasure in something in view of its being desirable [LN (25.102)].

d. ἔλεος (LN 88.76) (BAGD 1. p. 250): 'mercy' [BAGD, CC, LN, NICNT, NIGTC, NTC, WBC; ESV, GW, KJV, NET, NIV, NRSV, REB], 'compassion' [BAGD, BECNT, PNTC; NASB], 'kindness' [NCV, TEV]. The phrase Ἔλεος θέλω 'I desire mercy' is translated 'I want you to be merciful to others' [CEV], 'I want you to show mercy' [NLT]. This noun denotes kindness or concern for someone in serious need [LN].

e. θυσία (LN 53.20) (BAGD 2.a. p. 366): 'sacrifice' [BAGD, LN; all translations except NCV, NLT, TEV], 'animal sacrifice' [NCV, TEV], 'offering' [BAGD]. This noun is translated as an infinitive phrase: '(to) offer sacrifices' [NLT]. This noun denotes that which is offered as a sacrifice [LN].

f. aorist act. infin. of καλέω (LN 33.307) (BAGD 2. p. 399): 'to call' [BAGD, LN; all translations except CEV, NCV], 'to summon' [BAGD, LN], 'to invite to be my followers' [CEV], 'to invite' [NCV]. This verb means to communicate directly or indirectly to someone who is presumably at a distance, in order to tell such a person to come [LN].

g. δίκαιος (LN 88.12) (BAGD 1.b. p. 195): 'righteous' [BAGD, BECNT, LN, NICNT, NIGTC, WBC; ESV, KJV, NASB, NET, NIV, NRSV], 'virtuous' [REB], 'upright' [BAGD], 'just' [BAGD, LN]. This plural adjective is translated as a phrase: 'righteous people' [CC, NTC, PNTC], 'righteous men' [BNTC], 'good people' [CEV, NCV], 'respectable people' [TEV], 'people who think they don't have any flaws' [GW], 'those who think they are righteous' [NLT]. This adjective describes being in accordance with what God requires [LN].

QUESTION—What did Jesus mean by saying he did not come to call the righteous?

1. Here 'the righteous' are those who considered themselves righteous [BNTC, Lns, My, NTC; GW, NLT]. The use of 'righteous' is ironic; they weren't really righteous at all [BNTC, CC, EBC, NIBC, WBC]. Here the term is used to describe those who define righteousness in terms of sacrifice and ritual, which is not the same as the righteousness of the kingdom [NICNT].
2. The 'righteous' are those who are already right with God [PNTC], who are attuned to God's purposes and will (such as Joseph in 1:18–2:2), and who don't need any special call [NIGTC].

QUESTION—What is implied by Jesus' use of the verb 'came'?

1. It implies his preexistence [NAC, NIBC, PNTC].
2. It describes his sense of mission, without necessarily implying preexistence [NICNT].

QUESTION—What is the nature of the 'call'?

It is implied that he came to call sinners to repentance [BECNT, NICNT, NTC, PNTC, WBC], and to find true righteousness [NICNT]. He came to call them to leave their old way of life and follow him in faith and service [CC]. He calls them to discipleship [WBC], to full salvation [NTC]. He calls them to inherit the blessings of the kingdom [My].

QUESTION—What is meant by the statement that God did not want sacrifice?

It is not an absolute statement, but expresses a preference of mercy over sacrifices [PNTC, WBC]. This is an example of a dialectical negation, in which one element in the statement is completely negated, even though it is a valid point, in order to emphasize the other element as being more important [CC]. He is dealing with the preoccupation with ritual purity as opposed to concern for those in need [NICNT]. That is, God wants mercy *more than* sacrifice [BECNT, BNTC, NAC, CC].

DISCOURSE UNIT—9:14–17 [CEV, ESV, GW, NASB, NCV, NET, NIV, NLT, NRSV, TEV]. The topic is Jesus is questioned about fasting [GW, NIV], Jesus' followers are criticized [NCV], a discussion about fasting [NLT], a question about fasting [ESV, TEV], the question about fasting [NASB, NRSV], the superiority of the new [NET], people ask about going without eating [CEV].

9:14 Then the disciples of-John approach[a] him saying, "Why (do) we and the Pharisees fast[b] often,[c] but your disciples do- not -fast?"

TEXT—The words νηστεύομεν πολλά 'we fast often' are included in brackets and this reading is given a C rating by GNT to indicate that choosing it over a variant text was difficult. That reading is also included in brackets by BECNT and WBC. It is included but not bracketed by NICNT, NTC, PNTC; CEV, GW, KJV, NCV, NET, NRSV, TEV. A variant reading is νηστεύομεν 'we fast' and it is followed by BNTC, CC, NIGTC; ESV, NASB, NIV, NLT, REB.

LEXICON—a. pres. mid. or pass. (deponent = act.) indic. of προσέρχομαι (LN 15.77) (BAGD 1. p. 713): 'to approach' [BAGD, CC, LN], 'to come to' [BAGD, BECNT, BNTC, NICNT, NIGTC, NTC, PNTC, WBC; all versions except CEV, NIV], 'to go to' [BAGD], 'to move toward, to come near to' [LN]. The phrase προσέρχονται αὐτῷ...λέγοντες 'approach (him) saying' is translated 'came and asked' [CEV, NIV]. This verb means to move toward a reference point, with a possible implication in certain contexts of a reciprocal relationship between the person approaching and the one who is approached [LN].

b. pres. act. indic. of νηστεύω (LN **53.65**) (BAGD p. 538): 'to fast' [BAGD, **LN**; all translations except CEV, NCV], 'to go without eating' [CEV], 'to give up eating for a certain time' [NCV]. This verb means to go without food for a set time as a religious duty [LN].

c. πολλά (LN **67.11**): 'often' [BECNT, **LN**, NTC, PNTC, WBC; CEV, GW, NCV, NET, NRSV, TEV], 'oft' [KJV], 'a lot' [NICNT], 'many times' [LN]. This adverb describes a number of related points of time [LN]. See the note above about textual variants.

QUESTION—What relationship is indicated by τότε 'then'?

It does not necessarily indicate sequence [PNTC], though it may be that Jesus' disciples were feasting on a day when John's disciples were fasting [PNTC]. It shows a logical connection with what precedes it [NIGTC, NTC, WBC]. It shows the relationship between the celebratory meal in 9:10–13 and what is being asked here [NIGTC, NTC]. It indicates an immediate sequential relationship in which the question is raised while Jesus is still at the feast mentioned in the previous section [NIBC, TH], or when he has just come from that feast [Lns].

QUESTION—What was the nature of this fasting?

This is probably the voluntary fasting done twice a week that the Pharisees also practiced [BECNT, BNTC, CC, EBC, NIBC, NICNT, NIGTC, PNTC]. Fasting was practiced often in the ancient world, and could have been seen by some as a way of gaining merit before God [PNTC]. Fasting was an important act of piety in those days [WBC].

9:15 And Jesus said to-them, "The sons-of the wedding-hall[a] are- not -able to-mourn[b] as-long-as[c] the bridegroom[d] is with them, (are they)? But days[e]

MATTHEW 9:15

are-coming when the bridegroom shall-be-taken from them, and then they-will-fast.

TEXT—Instead of πενθεῖν 'to mourn' some manuscripts read νηστεύειν 'to fast'. This variant is not mentioned in GNT. 'To fast' is followed by BNTC and CEV only.

LEXICON—a. νυμφών (LN 7.34, 11.7) (BAGD 2. p. 545): 'wedding hall' [LN], 'bridal chamber' [BAGD]. This noun denotes a relatively large room, often serving as a place for a wedding [LN]. The idiom υἱοὶ τοῦ νυμφῶνος 'sons of the wedding hall' is translated 'sons of the bridal chamber' [CC], 'children of the bridal chamber' [KJV], 'wedding guests' [LN (11.7), NICNT, PNTC; ESV, GW, NET, NLT, NRSV], 'wedding attendants' [NIGTC], 'attendants of the bridegroom' [BECNT; NASB], 'bridegroom's attendants' [BAGD, NTC], 'bridegroom's friends' [REB], 'friends of the bridegroom' [LN (**11.7**); CEV, NCV], 'guests of the bridegroom' [NIV], 'guests at a wedding party' [TEV], 'those who are at the side of the bridegroom' [WBC].

b. pres. act. infin. of πενθέω (LN 25.142) (BAGD 1. p. 642): 'to mourn' [BAGD, BECNT, CC, NIGTC, PNTC; ESV, KJV, NASB, NET, NIV, NLT, NRSV], 'to be mourning' [NTC], 'to be sad' [BAGD, LN, NICNT; GW, NCV, REB, TEV], 'to grieve' [BAGD, LN, WBC], 'to weep' [LN], 'to fast' [BNTC], 'to go without eating' [CEV]. This verb means to experience sadness or grief as the result of depressing circumstances or the condition of persons [LN].

c. ἐφ' ὅσον (LN 67.139): This phrase is translated 'as long as' [BECNT, CC, NICNT, NIGTC, NTC, **LN**, PNTC, WBC; ESV, KJV, NASB, NRSV, TEV], 'while' [BNTC; NCV, NET, NIV, NLT, REB], 'while... still' [CEV, GW].

d. νυμφίος (LN 10.56) (BAGD p. 545): 'bridegroom' [BAGD, BECNT, LN; all translations except GW, NLT], 'groom' [GW, NLT]. This noun denotes a man who is about to be married or has just been married [LN].

e. ἡμέρα (LN 67.142) (BAGD 4.b. p. 347): 'day' [BECNT, BNTC, CC, NIGTC, NTC, PNTC, WBC; ESV, KJV, NASB, NET, NRSV, TEV], 'time' [BAGD, LN, NICNT; CEV, GW, NCV, NIV, REB], 'someday' [NLT]. This noun denotes an indefinite unit of time (whether grammatically singular or plural), but not particularly long [LN].

QUESTION—What kind of a question did Jesus ask?

In Greek the question begins with the negative particle μή 'not' in order to indicate that this question expects a negative answer [BECNT, CC, Lns, NTC, PNTC, TH, WBC]. Some show the expected answer by translating this as a statement followed by 'can they?' [BECNT, BNTC, NICNT; NASB, NET, NRSV], or 'are they?' [CC, WBC]. Some translate this as a question and then supply the answer 'of course not!' [NLT, TEV]. Some translate this as a statement: 'The friends of the bridegroom don't go without eating while he is still with them' [CEV], 'The friends of the bridegroom are not sad while he is with them' [NCV]. Some translate as a rhetorical question with the negative answer implied [NIGTC, NTC, PNTC; ESV, GW, KJV, NIV, REB].

QUESTION—Who are the 'sons of the wedding hall'?

They are the bridegroom's attendants [BECNT, NIGTC, NTC, PNTC], the friends who attend the groom at the wedding ceremony [BECNT, Lns], and who handle the wedding arrangements [Lns]. They are the friends of the bridegroom who would conduct the bride to the house of her parents-in-law for the ceremony [My].

QUESTION—What is meant by the imagery that Jesus is using?

In the OT the imagery of the wedding banquet was used to describe the blessings of the eschatological era [BECNT, EBC], the days of the Messiah [CC]. In OT imagery God was depicted as the husband of his people [NIBC, NIGTC, NTC]. The bridegroom in the OT wedding banquet imagery was God himself [CC, EBC, NAC, PNTC, TRT, WBC], so Jesus is saying that he is the messianic bridegroom and that the messianic age has begun [EBC].

QUESTION—To what does the bridegroom's being taken away refer?

It anticipates his arrest and crucifixion [BECNT, EBC, Lns, My, NAC, NIBC, NICNT, NIGTC, NTC, PNTC, WBC].

9:16 **But[a] no-one sews[b] a-patch[c] of unshrunk[d] cloth on an- old -garment;[e]**

LEXICON—a. δέ (LN 89.124, 89.94): 'but' [LN (89.124), WBC; NASB], 'and' [LN (89.94), PNTC], 'now' [BECNT, CC], 'besides' [NLT], not explicit [BNTC, NICNT, NIGTC, NTC; all versions except NASB, NLT]. This conjunction indicates contrast [LN (89.124)], or indicates an additive relationship with the possible implication of some contrast [LN (89.94)].

b. pres. act. indic. of ἐπιβάλλω (LN 85.51) (BAGD 1.b. p. 290): 'to sew' [BECNT, BNTC, WBC; NCV, NET, NIV, NRSV], 'to put' [BAGD, **LN**, NIGTC, NTC, PNTC; ESV, KJV, NASB, REB]. The phrase ἐπιβάλλει ἐπίβλημα 'sews a patch' is translated 'patches a patch' [CC], 'patches' [NICNT; GW; similarly NLT], 'patches up' [TEV], 'uses a piece of cloth to patch' [CEV]. This verb means to place something on something [LN].

c. ἐπίβλημα (LN **6.157**) (BAGD p. 290): 'patch' [BAGD, BECNT, BNTC, CC, **LN**, NIGTC, NTC, PNTC, WBC; NASB, NCV, NET, NIV, REB], 'piece (of cloth)' [CEV, ESV, GW, KJV, NRSV, TEV], not explicit [NICNT; NLT]. This noun denotes a piece of cloth sewed on clothing to repair a hole or tear [LN].

d. ἄγναφος (LN **48.8**) (BAGD p. 10): 'unshrunk' [BECNT, BNTC, CC, NICNT, NIGTC, PNTC, WBC; ESV, NASB, NCV, NET, NIV, NRSV, REB], 'unshrunken' [BAGD, **LN**], 'new' [BAGD, NTC; CEV, KJV, NLT, TEV], 'a new (piece of cloth) that will shrink' [GW]. This adjective describes an unshrunken condition of cloth, that is, before it has been washed and dried [LN].

e. ἱμάτιον (LN 6.162) (BAGD 1. p. 376): 'garment' [BAGD, BECNT, BNTC, NTC, PNTC, WBC; ESV, KJV, NASB, NET, NIV, REB], 'coat' [CC, NICNT, NIGTC; GW, NCV, TEV], 'cloak' [NRSV], 'clothes'

[CEV], 'clothing' [LN; NLT], 'apparel' [LN]. This noun denotes any kind of clothing [LN].

for it-pulls-away[a] the patch/overlap[b] of-it from the garment and a- bigger - tear[c] happens.[d]

LEXICON—a. pres. act. indic. of αἴρω (LN 20.43) (BAGD 4. p. 24): to pull away' [BECNT, CC, NTC, PNTC; NASB, NET, NIV, NRSV], 'to rip away' [WBC; GW], 'to tear away' [NICNT; ESV, REB], 'to tear out' [BNTC], 'to shrink and pull away' [NCV], 'to shrink and rip away' [NLT], 'to shrink' [CEV, TEV], 'to take away' [BAGD, NIGTC], 'to take (from)' [KJV], 'to remove' [BAGD], 'to destroy' [LN]. This verb means to destroy, with the implication of removal and doing away with [LN].

b. πλήρωμα (LN 59.36) (BAGD 1.b. p. 672): This noun is translated as the subject of the verb 'pulls away': 'patch' [BAGD, BECNT, NICNT, NTC; all versions except KJV, NLT, TEV], 'new patch' [NLT, TEV], 'patch that covers the hole' [BNTC] 'repair' [WBC], 'that which makes full or complete' [BAGD], 'that which fills' [BAGD, LN], 'that which is put in to fill it up' [KJV], 'fullness' [CC, LN], 'completeness' [LN], 'what is meant to restore it' [NIGTC]. This noun is also translated as the object of the verb 'pulls away': 'overlap' [PNTC]. This noun denotes a quantity which fills a space [LN]. It denotes that which makes something complete, such as a patch on a garment [BAGD].

c. σχίσμα (LN 19.28) (BAGD 1. p. 797): 'tear' [BECNT, BNTC, CC, LN, NICNT, NIGTC, NTC, PNTC, WBC; ESV, GW, NASB, NET, NIV, NRSV], 'hole' [CEV, NCV, NLT, REB, TEV], 'rent' [KJV]. This noun denotes the condition resulting from the splitting or tearing [LN].

d. pres mid. or pass. (deponent = act.) of γίνομαι (LN 13.107, 13.48) (BAGD I.1.b.β. p. 158): 'to happen' [BECNT, CC, LN (13.107)], 'to occur' [BNTC, LN (13.107)], 'to result' [NICNT, NIGTC, NTC; NASB], 'to come about' [BAGD], 'to be made' [ESV, KJV, NRSV], 'to become' [LN (13.48)]. The phrase χεῖρον σχίσμα γίνεται 'a bigger tear happens' is translated 'the tear gets/becomes worse' [PNTC; GW, NET], 'making the hole/tear worse' [NCV, NIV], 'would tear a bigger hole' [CEV], 'leaves a bigger hole' [REB], 'make an even bigger hole' [TEV]. This verb means to happen, with the implication that what happens is different from a previous state [LN (13.107)], or to come to acquire or experience a state [LN (13.48)].

QUESTION—How is the noun ἐπίβλημα 'patch/overlap' connected with the verb αἴρει 'pulls away'?

1. This noun refers to the 'patch' that is sewn onto the garment and it is the subject of the verb [ESV, GW, NASB, NCV, NET, NIV, NLT, NRSV, REB, TEV]: 'the patch will pull away from the garment' [NIV; similarly NASB, NET, NRSV], 'the patch tears away from the garment' [ESV, REB], 'the patch will shrink and pull away from the coat' [NCV], 'the new patch would shrink and rip away from the old cloth' [NLT], 'when

the patch shrinks, it will rip away from the coat' [GW], 'the new patch will shrink and make an even bigger hole in the coat' [TEV].
2. This noun refers to the 'overlapped' part of the old garment that is covered by the patch and it is the object of the verb [EBC, ICC, NAC, PNTC]: 'it (the patch) pulls its overlap away from the garment'. The patch of stronger new material would not be torn, so it would tear away some of the garment material with it [PNTC].

9:17 Nor do- they -put[a] new wine[b] into old wineskins;[c] otherwise[d] the wineskins are-burst[e]

LEXICON—a. pres. act. indic. of βάλλω (LN **47.2**, 85.34) (BAGD 2.b. p. 131): 'to put' [BAGD, BECNT, BNTC, CC, **LN** (85.34), NICNT, NIGTC, PNTC, WBC; KJV, NLT, REB], 'to be put' [ESV, NRSV], 'to pour' [**LN** (47.2); CEV, GW, NCV, NET, NIV, TEV], 'to be poured' [NTC]. This verb means to cause a liquid to pour [LN (47.2)], or to put or place some object or mass in a location, with the possible implication of force in some contexts [LN (85.34)].
b. οἶνος (LN 6.197, 6.198) (BAGD 1. p. 562): 'wine' [BAGD, LN (6.197); all translations]. The phrase οἶνος νέος 'new wine' is a set phrase referring to newly pressed grape juice, unfermented or in the initial stages of fermentation [LN (6.198)]. It is translated 'new wine' [BECNT, NICNT, NIGTC, NTC, PNTC, WBC; all versions], 'fresh wine' [BNTC, CC].
c. ἀσκός (LN **6.132**) (BAGD p. 116): 'wineskin' [BAGD, **LN**; all translations except KJV, NCV], 'bottle' [KJV], 'leather bag' [NCV]. This noun denotes a bag made of skin or leather (in the NT it is used only of wineskins) [LN].
d. εἰ δὲ μή γε. This idiomatic phrase is translated 'otherwise' [BECNT, CC, NICNT, NIGTC, NTC, WBC; NASB, NCV, NET, NRSV], 'if they do' [BNTC, PNTC; GW, NIV, REB], 'if it is' [ESV], 'else' [KJV], 'for' [NLT, TEV], not explicit [CEV].
e. pres. pass. indic. of ῥήγνυμι (LN 19.31) (BAGD 1. p. 735): 'to be burst' [BAGD, LN], 'to burst' [BECNT, BNTC, NICNT, NIGTC, NTC, PNTC; ESV, GW, NASB, NET, NIV, NRSV, REB, TEV], 'to burst from the pressure' [NLT], 'to break' [KJV, NCV], 'to be torn' [BAGD, CC, LN], 'to tear' [WBC]. The phrase 'otherwise the wineskins are burst' is translated 'The wine would swell and burst the old skins' [CEV]. This verb means to tear, rip, or burst, either from internal or external forces, with the implication of sudden and forceful action [LN].

QUESTION—What is new wine?
New wine is grape juice in the beginning stages of the process of fermentation [BECNT, BNTC, NAC, NTC, PNTC, TH, WBC]. The buildup of gases emitted from fermentation would rupture a container that was not flexible [EBC, NIBC, NTC, TH].

and the wine pours-out[a] and the wineskins are-ruined;[b] rather[c] they-put new wine into new wineskins, and both are-preserved.[d]"

LEXICON—a. pres. pass. indic. of ἐκχέομαι (LN **14.18**) (BAGD 1. p. 247): 'to pour out' [BAGD, BECNT, **LN**, PNTC, WBC; NASB, TEV], 'to be poured out' [CC], 'to be spilled' [BNTC, NIGTC, NTC; ESV, NET, NRSV], 'to spill' [NCV, NLT], 'to run out' [GW, KJV, NIV, REB], 'to flow out' [LN], 'to be wasted' [NICNT], 'to be lost' [CEV]. This verb means to flow out of a container [LN].

b. pres. mid. indic. of ἀπόλλυμι (LN 20.31) (BAGD 2.a.β. p. 95): 'to be ruined' [BAGD, BECNT, BNTC, LN, NICNT, NTC, PNTC; CEV, GW, NASB, NCV, NIV, REB, TEV], 'to ruin' [NLT], 'to be destroyed' [BAGD, CC, LN, NIGTC, WBC; ESV, NET, NRSV]. This verb means to destroy or to cause the destruction of persons, objects, or institutions [LN].

c. ἀλλά (LN 89.125): 'rather' [BECNT, CC, NIGTC; GW], 'but' [BNTC, LN, NTC, PNTC; ESV, KJV, NASB, NCV], 'no' [NICNT; NIV, REB], 'instead' [LN, WBC; NET, TEV], 'on the contrary' [LN], not explicit [CEV, NLT]. This conjunction indicates emphatic contrast [LN].

d. pres. pass. indic. of συντηρέω (LN 13.33) (BAGD 1. p. 792): 'to be preserved' [**LN**; all translations except CEV, GW, NCV, TEV], 'to be saved' [GW], 'to be safe' [CEV], 'to continue to be good' [NCV], 'to be kept in good condition' [TEV], 'to be kept together' [LN], 'to be protected' [BAGD]. This verb means to cause something to continue along with something else [LN].

QUESTION—What are the 'both' things that are preserved?

1. 'Both' refers to the new wine and the new wineskin [EBC, ICC, NAC, NICNT, NTC, PNTC, WBC; probably all versions]. Jesus is not calling for the old wineskins to be preserved from perishing; it is the new wineskins into which the new wine is put that are to be preserved [PNTC]. The text clearly means that the new skins are preserved along with the new wine [NICNT]. It is obvious that the words 'both are preserved' refer to the new wine of the reality of the kingdom and the new skins (not the old skins) of faithful obedience to the law as expounded by Jesus [WBC].

2. It refers to the new wine and the old wineskin [BECNT, NIBC, NIGTC]. The old wineskin is preserved for use with old wine, and the new wine is not wasted. This illustration is intended to show that those things of value from the old system can be preserved [NIGTC].

QUESTION—What do the old cloth and the old wineskins represent?

They represent the religious system of Jesus' day that had obscured the theology of the OT [CC], the old, restrictive forms of worship [NIBC], the old forms of piety [EBC, My], the limits of the old religious forms of the Jewish system [PNTC], the purely human institutions such as the fasting that was practiced [NTC]. They represent the Pharisaic ways and traditions [BECNT, Lns], the old traditions [BNTC, NICNT], the established patterns of behavior that were considered the expression of right living as defined by the Torah [WBC].

QUESTION—What is the application for the three illustrations?

Jesus is introducing a new situation that would need new forms, because to try to incorporate Jesus and what he represents into current Jewish religious practices would only ruin Judaism as well as what Jesus was teaching [BNTC, EBC, PNTC]. The new reality of the gospel requires new patterns of living that are based on Jesus' own ethical teaching that represents the true intent of the Torah [WBC]. In the new age that Jesus is introducing, new practices of joy and celebration are needed that are appropriate to the new condition [NAC]. Jesus' new teaching about grace and faith, and the life that comes from them cannot be combined with Pharisaic Judaism [Lns]. There is a new and joyful pattern of religious life that is incompatible with the old fasting regimes of the Pharisees and John's disciples [NICNT]. Jesus did not jettison the law and the prophets, but neither does he simply repeat them; rather he fulfils them in the new righteousness of the inaugurated kingdom, not in the tradition of the Pharisees [BECNT]. Jesus and his message are qualitatively different from the practices of Judaism of his day [CC].

DISCOURSE UNIT—9:18-34 [ICC]. The topic is a third triad of miracle stories.

DISCOURSE UNIT—9:18-38 [NASB]. The topic is miracles of healing.

DISCOURSE UNIT—9:18-26 [CEV, ESV, GW, NCV, NET, NIV, NLT, NRSV, TEV]. The topic is the synagogue leader's daughter and the woman with chronic bleeding [GW], Jesus gives life to a dead girl and heals a sick woman [NCV], a dead girl and a sick woman [NIV], a dying girl and a sick woman [CEV], the official's daughter and the woman who touched Jesus' cloak [TEV], a girl restored to life and a woman healed [ESV, NRSV], restoration and healing [NET], Jesus heals in response to faith [NLT].

9:18 **(While) he was-saying these (things) to-them, behold a-certain[a] ruler[b] having-come was-bowing-down[c] to-him saying, "My daughter[d] just-now[e] died, but having-come put your hand on her, and she-will-live." 9:19 And having-risen Jesus and his disciples followed him.**

LEXICON—a. εἷς (LN 92.22): 'a certain' [BECNT, CC, NICNT, NIGTC; KJV], 'one' [LN]. This word is translated simply as an indefinite pronoun: 'a' [BNTC, LN, NTC, PNTC, WBC; all versions except KJV, NLT]; as a definite pronoun: 'the' [NLT]. This cardinal adjective is used to refer to a single, indefinite person or thing [LN].

b. ἄρχων (LN **37.56**) (BAGD 2.a. p. 113): 'ruler' [BNTC, CC, **LN**, NTC, PNTC, WBC; ESV, KJV, NET, NIV], 'official' [BAGD, BECNT, NICNT; CEV, REB, TEV], 'synagogue official' [NASB], 'leader' [NIGTC], 'synagogue leader' [GW], 'leader of the/a synagogue' [NCV, NLT, NRSV], 'governor' [LN]. This noun denotes one who rules or governs [LN].

c. imperf. act. indic. of προσκυνέω (LN 17.21) (BAGD 5. p. 717): 'to bow down before/in front of' [BECNT, PNTC; GW, NASB, NCV], 'to bow low before' [NICNT, WBC; NET], 'to bow before' [REB], 'to kneel before/in front of' [NTC; CEV, ESV, NIV, NLT, NRSV], 'to kneel down before' [TEV], 'to fall down in reverence' [BNTC], 'to show reverence' [CC], 'to prostrate oneself before' [BAGD], 'to do obeisance to' [BAGD, NIGTC], 'to worship' [BAGD; KJV]. The imperfect tense of this verb is translated as indicating an inceptive sense: 'began (bowing, etc)' [BECNT, CC]. This verb means to prostrate oneself before someone as an act of reverence, fear, or supplication [LN 17.21)]. This refers to the custom of prostrating oneself before a person and kissing his feet, and when that person is Jesus it indicates that he is revered and worshipped as Messianic King and Divine Helper [BAGD].

d. θυγάτηρ (LN 10.46) (BAGD 1. p. 364): 'daughter' [BAGD, LN; all translations]. This noun denotes immediate female offspring [LN].

e. ἄρτι (LN **67.39**) (BAGD 1. p. 110): 'just now' [BAGD, CC, **LN**, WBC; CEV], 'just' [BAGD, BECNT, BNTC, NICNT, NIGTC, NTC, PNTC; all versions except CEV, KJV], 'even now' [KJV]. This adverb refers to a time shortly before or shortly after the time of the discourse [LN].

QUESTION—What is the function of ἰδοὺ 'behold' in this and the following verse 20?

It indicates when a new character comes into the narrative [NIGTC, PNTC, TH]. It introduces the new situation in which people are seeking healing [CC, ICC]. It indicates a new development [EBC, WBC], and can also be used as a loose connective between one event and another [EBC]. It expresses vividness [NTC, PNTC], and immediacy of action [NTC].

QUESTION—What kind of 'ruler' was this man?

The word 'ruler' indicates that he was an important man, and the parallel account in Mark 5:22 says that he was one of the rulers of the synagogue [EBC, PNTC, TH]. He was a synagogue official [EBC, BNTC, ICC, Lns, NAC, NIBC, NICNT, NTC, PNTC, WBC].

QUESTION—What is meant by προσκυνέω 'bowed down'?

It is a worshipful posture that expresses strong faith in Jesus [BECNT]. It expresses great respect for Jesus [NTC, TH, TRT], and faith in him [NTC]. It expresses deep reverence, pleading, and homage, but not worship [EBC]. It expresses humility [Lns].

QUESTION—What is implied by the verb ἐγερθείς 'having risen'?

1. When the request came Jesus was still sitting at the table as mentioned in verse 10, so he arose and followed the ruler [EBC, ICC, NIBC, TH, WBC].
2. It simply indicates the beginning of the action that follows [Lns, NTC].

9:20 And behold a-woman hemorrhaging[a] twelve years having-approached behind touched[b] the fringe[c] of his garment;[d] **9:21** for she-was-saying to herself, "If only I-might-touch his garment I-shall-be-healed.[e]"

LEXICON—a. pres. act. participle of αἱμορροέω (LN **23.181**) (BAGD p. 23): 'to suffer with/from hemorrhage' [BAGD, BECNT, CC, NIGTC, NTC, PNTC, WBC; NASB, NET, NRSV, REB], 'to have a hemorrhage' [NICNT], 'to suffer bleeding' [**LN**], 'to suffer from constant bleeding' [NLT], 'to suffer from severe bleeding' [TEV], 'to be subject to bleeding' [NIV], 'to suffer from chronic bleeding' [GW], 'to suffer from a discharge of blood' [BNTC; ESV], 'to bleed' [LN; CEV], 'to be diseased with an issue of blood' [KJV]. This verb means to experience or suffer a loss of blood [LN].

b. aorist mid. indic. of ἅπτομαι (LN 24.73) (BAGD 2.b. p. 103): 'to touch' [BAGD, LN; all versions], 'to take hold of' [BAGD]. This verb means to touch [LN].

c. κράσπεδον (LN 6.180, 6.194) (BAGD 1. p. 448): 'fringe' [BECNT, LN (6.180), WBC; NLT, NRSV], 'edge' [GW, NET, NIV, REB, TEV], 'border' [BAGD], 'hem' [BAGD, CC; KJV], 'tassel' [BNTC, LN (6.194), NIGTC, NTC, PNTC], not explicit [NICNT; CEV, ESV, NASB, NCV]. This noun denotes the border of a garment [LN (6.180)], or the tassels which Jews were obliged to wear on the four corners of the outer garment [LN (6.194)].

d. ἱμάτιον (LN 6.172) (BAGD 2. p. 376): 'cloak' [BAGD, BECNT, LN, NICNT, PNTC; NET, NIV, NRSV, REB, TEV], 'coat' [CC, LN, NIGTC], 'robe' [BAGD, BNTC, LN; NLT], 'garment' [NTC, WBC; ESV, KJV, NASB], 'clothes' [CEV, GW, NCV]. This noun denotes any type of outer garment [LN].

e. σῴζω fut. pass. indic. of (LN 23.136) (BAGD 1.c. p. 798): 'to be healed' [BECNT, BNTC, CC, LN, PNTC, WBC; CEV, NET, NIV, NLT, REB], 'to be cured' [LN], 'to be made well' [LN, NIGTC; ESV, NRSV], 'to get well' [BAGD, NTC; CEV, GW, NASB, TEV], 'to be whole' [KJV], 'to be saved' [BAGD, NICNT]. This verb means to cause someone to become well again after having been sick [LN].

QUESTION—What was the nature of her problem?

It was probably uterine bleeding [BECNT, BNTC, CC, EBC, NAC, NICNT, TRT, WBC]. She would have experienced some social isolation due to ritual impurity [BECNT, CC, EBC, NAC, NIBC, NICNT, PNTC, TRT, WBC]. She would have experienced restrictions in the domestic and cultic realms, though not necessarily in the social realm [NIGTC].

QUESTION—What is implied by the term σωθήσομαι 'I shall be healed', which in other contexts means 'to be saved'?

This term can refer to healing as well as spiritual salvation [TRT]. It means that she will be healed [BECNT, BNTC, CC, LN, NIGTC, PNTC, WBC; all versions]. She expects to be saved from her ailment [Lns]. It describes the healing in terms of divine deliverance [BECNT, NICNT]. In five other passages in Matthew this term refers to salvation, so there may be that nuance in its use here [WBC]. Since in the overall passage Jesus is forgiving sins as well as healing, this term should be understood in its broader theological sense [CC]. Although it is used when asking Jesus to intervene in a situation of pressing need, it also contains a sense of the saving purposes of God in view of the neediness of the people of Israel and the wider world [NIGTC].

9:22 **But Jesus having-turned and having-seen her said, "Take-courage,[a] daughter;[b] your faith[c] has-healed you." And the woman was-healed from that hour.**

LEXICON—a. pres. act. impera. of θαρσέω (LN 25.156) (BAGD p. 352): 'to take courage' [BECNT, NTC, NASB], 'to have courage' [BAGD, LN, WBC; NET], 'to be encouraged' [NCV, NLT], 'to take heart' [NICNT, NIGTC, PNTC; ESV, NIV, NRSV, REB], 'to be courageous' [BAGD, CC, LN], 'to cheer up' [GW], 'to be of good comfort' [KJV], 'to be bold' [LN]. This imperative is translated simply 'Courage!' [BNTC; TEV], 'Don't worry!' [CEV]. This verb means to have confidence and firmness of purpose in the face of danger or testing [LN].

    b. θυγάτηρ (LN **9.47**) (BAGD 2.a. p. 364): 'daughter' [BAGD, LN; all translations except CEV, NCV], 'lady' [LN], 'woman' [LN], not explicit [CEV]. This noun in its vocative form is translated 'my daughter' [**LN**], 'dear woman' [NCV]. Used in this manner this noun is a figurative extension of meaning of θυγάτηρ 'daughter', as used in 9:18, and denotes a woman for whom there is some affectionate concern [LN].

    c. πίστις (LN 31.85) (BAGD 2.b.α. p. 663): 'faith' [BAGD, LN; all translations except NCV], 'trust' [BAGD, LN]. The phrase ἡ πίστις σου σέσωκέν σε 'your faith has healed you' is translated 'you are made well because you believed' [NCV], 'you are now well because of your faith' [CEV]. This verb means to believe to the extent of complete trust and reliance [LN].

QUESTION—After Jesus healed her, why did he say that her faith had healed her?

    The healing was due to her faith, and not to some magical power or some superstitious element supposedly inherent in his clothing [BECNT, BNTC, EBC, NAC, NTC, PNTC]. It was actually Jesus' divine presence and power that ultimately effected the healing [NIBC]. Healing is the work of God's power, but he heals only when faith is present [BNTC]. The efficient cause was Jesus' will and power, but her faith received the gift [Lns, My, WBC]. It was not her grasping the garment that healed her, but the faith that prompted her to do so [ICC]. Jesus' word to her in response to her faith effects her healing, and rules out the possibility of any magic act [TH].

9:23 And Jesus having-come into the house of-the ruler and having-seen the flute-players[a] and the disturbed[b] crowd, **9:24** said, "Go-away,[c] for the girl did- not -die but is-sleeping.[d]" And they-were-ridiculing[e] him.

LEXICON—a. αὐλητής (LN **6.88**) (BAGD p. 121): 'flute player' [BAGD, BECNT, BNTC, CC, NTC, PNTC, WBC; ESV, GW, NASB, NET, NIV, NRSV, REB], 'flutist' [LN], 'piper' [NICNT], 'reed-pipe player' [NIGTC], 'musician' [CEV], 'funeral musician' [NCV], 'musician for the funeral' [TEV], 'minstrel' [KJV]. The phrase ἰδὼν τοὺς αὐλητὰς 'having seen the flute players' is translated 'having heard the funeral music' [NLT]. This noun denotes one who plays the flute [LN].

b. pres. pass. participle of θορυβέομαι (LN 25.234) (BAGD 2. p. 363): 'to be troubled, to be distressed, to be upset' [LN], 'to be aroused in disorder' [BAGD]. This participle is translated as an adjective: 'disorderly' [BECNT, NET], 'distressed' [CC], 'noisy' [NTC, PNTC; GW, NIV, NLT], 'wailing' [NICNT, WBC]; as a phrase: 'in distress' [BNTC], 'making a commotion' [NIGTC; ESV, NRSV], 'making a noise' [KJV], 'in noisy disorder' [NASB], 'many people crying' [NCV], 'all stirred up' [TEV]. The phrase ὄχλον θορυβούμενον 'disturbed crowd' is translated 'crowd of mourners' [CEV], 'general commotion' [REB]. This verb means to be emotionally upset by a concern or anxiety [LN].

c. pres. act. impera. of ἀναχωρέω (LN 15.53) (BAGD 1. p. 63): 'to go away' [BAGD, BECNT, LN, NICNT, NIGTC, NTC, PNTC, WBC; ESV, NCV, NET, NIV, NRSV, REB], 'to depart' [BNTC, CC], 'to leave' [GW, NASB], 'to give place' [KJV], 'to withdraw, to retire, to go off' [LN]. This imperative is translated 'Get out of here!' [CEV], 'Get out!' [NLT], 'Get out, everybody!' [TEV]. This verb means to move away from a location, implying a considerable distance [LN].

d. pres. act. indic. of καθεύδω (LN 23.66) (BAGD 1. p. 388): 'to sleep' [BAGD, BECNT, BNTC, CC, LN, NIGTC, WBC; CEV, ESV, GW, KJV, NRSV, TEV], 'to be asleep' [LN, NICNT, NTC, PNTC; NASB, NCV, NET, NIV, NLT, REB]. This verb describes the state of being asleep [LN].

e. imperf. act. indic. of καταγελάω (LN 33.410) (BAGD p. 409): 'to ridicule' [BAGD, BNTC, LN], 'to laugh at' [BAGD, BECNT, CC, LN, NICNT, NIGTC, PNTC, WBC; all versions except KJV, NET, TEV], 'to laugh in (his) face' [NTC], 'to laugh to scorn' [KJV], 'to make fun of' [LN; NET, TEV]. The imperfect tense of this verb is translated as inceptive: 'began/started to (laugh, etc)' [BECNT, CC; CEV, NASB, NET, TEV]; as indicating ongoing action: 'were laughing' [NTC]. This verb means to make fun of or ridicule by laughing at, but evidently also involving verbal communication [LN].

QUESTION—Why were there flute players present?

It was customary to employ flute players to provide the music at funerals [BECNT, EBC, ICC, Lns, My, NAC, NIBC, NICNT, NIGTC, NTC, PNTC, TH, TRT].

QUESTION—What was Jesus communicating by the verb καθεύδει 'is sleeping'?

He was not saying that she had not really died, but rather that he did not view the death as permanent [BECNT, BNTC, EBC, My, NAC, NICNT, NTC, WBC]. Death does not have the final word [NTC, WBC]. Viewed from the standpoint of what Jesus knew was going to happen, the state of death would be only a temporary condition, similar to sleep [NIGTC].

9:25 But when the crowd was-put-outside[a] having-gone-in he-took[b] her hand, and the girl was-raised-up.[c] **9:26** And the report[d] (of) this went-out into that whole region.[e]

LEXICON—a. aorist pass. indic. of ἐκβάλλω (LN 15.44) (BAGD 1. p. 237): 'to be put out/outside' [BECNT, PNTC; ESV, GW, NET, NIV, NLT, NRSV, TEV], 'to be put forth' [KJV], 'to be cast out' [CC], 'to be sent away' [LN], 'to be sent out' [NASB], 'to be sent out of the house' [CEV], 'to be thrown out of the house' [NCV], 'to be driven out' [BNTC, LN, WBC], 'to be expelled' [BAGD, LN, NTC]. This passive verb is translated as active: 'to throw out' [NICNT], 'to turn out' [REB], 'to expel' [NIGTC]. It means to cause to go out or leave, often, but not always, involving force [LN]. This verb may include an element of force since the crowd of noisy and busy mourners would have resisted being moved out of the house that was the center of their attention [PNTC].

b. aorist act. indic. of κρατέω (LN 18.6) (BAGD 1.b. p. 448): 'to take' [BNTC, NIGTC, PNTC, WBC; GW], 'to take by (the hand)' [BECNT, NTC; all versions except GW, NCV, TEV], 'to take hold of' [BAGD, BNTC, NICNT; NCV, TEV], 'to hold on to, to retain in the hand' [LN], 'to seize' [BAGD, LN], 'to grasp' [BAGD]. This verb means to hold on to an object [LN].

c. aorist pass. indic. of ἐγείρω (LN 17.9, 23.94) (BAGD 2.b. p. 215): 'to get up' [BAGD, LN (17.9)], 'to rise' [BAGD], 'to stand up' [LN (17.9)], 'to be raised to life, to be made to live again' [LN (23.94)]. The phrase ἠγέρθη τὸ κοράσιον 'the girl was raised up' [BECNT], is translated 'the girl was raised' [NICNT, PNTC], 'the girl/she got up' [NIGTC, NTC; NASB, NET, NIV, NRSV, REB, TEV], 'the girl/little girl rose' [BNTC, CC], 'the girl/maid arose' [WBC; ESV, KJV], 'she stood up' [NCV, NLT], 'and helped her up' [CEV], 'the girl came back to life' [GW]. This verb means to get up from a reclining position [LN (17.9)], or to cause someone to live again after having once died [LN (23.94)]. It refers to those who are raised or who get up after being awakened [BAGD].

d. φήμη (LN **33.211**) (BAGD p. 856): 'report' [BAGD, BNTC, CC, LN, PNTC, WBC; ESV, NLT, NRSV], 'word' [**LN**], 'news' [BAGD, BECNT, LN, NICNT, NIGTC, NTC; CEV, GW, NASB, NCV, NET, NIV, TEV], 'fame' [KJV]. The phrase 'report of this went out' is translated 'the story became the talk of (the whole district)' [REB]. This noun denotes information concerning a person or an event [LN].

e. γῆ (LN 1.79): 'region' [BECNT, LN, NICNT, NTC, PNTC, WBC; GW, NET, NIV], 'territory' [LN], 'land' [BNTC, CC, LN; KJV, NASB], 'district' [NIGTC; ESV, NRSV, REB], 'countryside' [NLT], 'that part of the country' [CEV, TEV], 'area' [NCV]. This noun denotes region or regions of the earth, normally in relationship to some ethnic group or geographical center, but not necessarily constituting a unit of governmental administration [LN].

QUESTION—Which of the previously reported miracles was the subject of the report?

They reported the raising of the dead girl [BECNT, BNTC, CC, ICC, Lns, NAC, NICNT, NTC, PNTC, TRT, WBC]. This miracle manifests Christ's power at its highest point [NTC].

DISCOURSE UNIT—9:27-38 [NCV]. The topic is Jesus heals more people.

DISCOURSE UNIT—9:27-34 [NET, NIV, NLT]. The topic is healing the blind and mute [NET], Jesus heals the blind and mute [NIV], Jesus heals the blind [NLT].

DISCOURSE UNIT—9:27-31 [CEV, ESV, GW, NRSV, TEV]. The topic is Jesus heals two blind men.

9:27 **(As) Jesus (was) going-on from-there two blind-men[a] followed (him) crying-out[b] and saying, "Have-mercy-on[c] us, Son of David."**

LEXICON—a. τυφλός (LN 24.38) (BAGD 1.b. p. 830): 'blind' [BAGD, LN]. This adjective is translated as a substantive: 'blind men' [all translations except NIGTC], 'blind people' [NIGTC]. This adjective refers to being unable to see [LN].

b. pres. act. participle of κράζω (LN **33.83**) (BAGD 2.a. p. 447): 'to cry out' [BECNT, CC, NIGTC, NTC, PNTC, WBC; NASB, NCV], 'to cry aloud' [ESV], 'to cry loudly' [NRSV], 'to cry' [BAGD; KJV], 'to call out' [BAGD, BNTC; NIV], 'to call' [BAGD], 'to shout' [**LN**, NICNT; CEV, GW, NET, NLT, REB, TEV], 'to scream' [LN]. This verb means to shout or cry out, with the possible implication of the unpleasant nature of the sound [LN].

c. aorist act. impera. of ἐλεέω (LN 88.76) (BAGD p. 249): 'to have mercy on' [BAGD, BECNT, CC, LN, NIGTC, WBC; all versions except CEV, REB], 'to have pity on' [BAGD; CEV, REB], 'to take pity on' [NTC, PNTC], 'to show mercy' [BAGD, BNTC, LN, NICNT], 'to be merciful toward' [LN]. This verb means to show kindness or concern for someone in serious need [LN].

QUESTION—What does the title 'Son of David' mean?

It is a messianic title [BECNT, BNTC, CC, EBC, ICC, Lns, NAC, NIBC, NICNT, NIGTC, NTC, PNTC, TH, TRT, WBC]. They were confessing Jesus to be the Messiah [EBC], and their use of the title implies that as the Messiah he has authority to heal [BECNT, EBC, ICC]. It shows they believed that he was a wonder worker [BNTC, NIBC]. In Matthew this is a title for the Messiah used by needy people [EBC], or by people of low social standing or theological importance, and it was always used in connection with healing [NICNT]. These blind men were confessing that Jesus is the Messiah [CC, EBC], and it is ironic that blind men were the first to see that fact while the religious leaders never did [CC, NAC]. These blind men knew that OT prophecies about an age of fulfillment would be realized when David's son the Messiah came [WBC].

9:28 Having-gone into the house the blind-men approached him, and Jesus says to-them, "Do-you-believe[a] that I-am-able[b] to-do this?" They-say to-him, "Yes, Lord." 9:29 Then he-touched their eyes saying, "According-to[c] your faith let-it-be-done[d] for-you."

LEXICON—a. pres. act. indic. of πιστεύω (LN 31.85) (BAGD 2.c. p. 662): 'to believe' [BAGD; all translations], 'to believe in, to trust' [BAGD, LN], 'to have confidence in, to have faith in' [LN]. This verb means to believe to the extent of complete trust and reliance [LN].
  b. pres. mid. or pass. (deponent = active) indic. of δύναμαι (LN 74.5): 'to be able to' [BECNT, CC, LN, NIGTC, NTC, PNTC, WBC; ESV, KJV, NASB, NET, NIV, NRSV], 'can' [BNTC, LN; CEV, GW, NCV, NLT, TEV], 'to have the power' [NICNT; REB]. This verb means to be able to do or to experience something [LN].
  c. κατά with accusative (LN 89.8) (BAGD II.5.a.γ. p. 407): 'according to' [BAGD, BECNT, CC, NICNT, NIGTC, NTC, PNTC, WBC; ESV, KJV, NASB, NET, NIV, NRSV], 'in accordance with' [BAGD, LN], 'in relation to' [LN]. The phrase κατὰ τὴν πίστιν ὑμῶν 'according to your faith' is translated 'because of your faith' [CEV, NLT], 'as you have believed' [BNTC; REB], 'just as you believed' [TEV], 'what you have believed' [GW], 'because you believe I can make you see again' [NCV]. This preposition indicates a relationship involving similarity of process [LN].
  d. aorist pass. (deponent = active) impera. of γίνομαι (LN 13.107) (BAGD I.3.b.β. p. 159): 'to be done' [BAGD, BECNT, BNTC, NICNT, NIGTC, NTC, PNTC, WBC; ESV, GW, NASB, NET, NIV, NRSV], 'to be' [KJV, REB], 'to happen' [BAGD, CC, LN; NCV, NLT, TEV], 'to occur, to come to be' LN]. The phrase γενηθήτω ὑμῖν 'let it be done to you' is translated 'you will be healed' [CEV]. This verb means to happen, with the implication that what happens is different from a previous state [LN].

QUESTION—What relationship is indicated by the preposition κατά 'according to'?
  1. It indicates that the healing comes because they have faith [EBC, NAC, NICNT, PNTC, TH, TRT, WBC; CEV, NCV, NLT], not that it comes in proportion to their faith [EBC, NAC, PNTC]. The healing comes because there is faith, not because of the quantity of it [WBC].

2. It indicates that their faith is the norm by which healing is granted to them; that is, the extent of their faith is matched by the extent of the healing received [Lns].

9:30 **And their eyes were-opened.**[a] **And Jesus sternly-warned**[b] **them saying, "See-that**[c] **no-one learns-about (this).** **9:31** **But having-gone-out they-spread-the-news-about**[d] **him in that whole region.**

LEXICON—a. aorist pass. indic. of ἀνοίγω (LN **24.43**) (BAGD 1.e.β. p. 71): 'to be opened' [BAGD, BECNT, BNTC, CC, LN, NICNT, NIGTC, NTC, PNTC, WBC; ESV, KJV, NASB, NET, NRSV], 'to be caused to see' [LN]. The phrase ἠνεῴχθησαν αὐτῶν οἱ ὀφθαλμοί 'their eyes were opened' is translated 'they/the men were able to see' [CEV, NCV], 'then they could see' [GW], 'their sight was restored' [NIV, REB, TEV], 'their eyes were opened and they could see' [NLT]. This idiom means to cause someone to be able to see [LN].

b. aorist. pass. (deponent = act.) indic. of ἐμβριμάομαι (LN **33.320**) (BAGD p. 254): 'to warn sternly' [BAGD, BECNT, BNTC, CC, NTC, WBC; ESV, NASB, NET, NIV, NLT], 'to warn strictly' [CEV], 'to warn fiercely' [NICNT], 'to warn strongly' [NCV], 'to warn' [GW], 'to say sternly' [PNTC; REB], 'to speak sternly' [TEV], 'to order sternly' [NRSV], 'to charge sternly' [LN], 'to charge straitly' [KJV], 'to insist sternly' [**LN**], 'to speak (to them) severely' [NIGTC]. This verb means to state something with sternness [LN]. It is an especially strong word [CC, NICNT, WBC].

c. pres. act. impera. of ὁράω (LN **30.45**) (BAGD 2.b. p. 578): 'to see that' [BECNT, BNTC, NIGTC, NTC, PNTC; ESV, KJV, NASB, NET, NIV, NRSV, REB], 'to see to it (that)' [BAGD, **LN**, WBC], 'to make sure' [NICNT], 'to take care' [BAGD], 'to be sure that' [**LN**], 'to pay attention to, to concern oneself with' [LN], not explicit [CEV]. The phrase Ὁρᾶτε μηδεὶς γινωσκέτω 'see that no one learns about this' is translated 'Look! Let no one know!' [CC], 'don't let anyone know' [GW], 'don't tell anyone' [NCV, NLT], 'don't tell this to anyone' [TEV]. This verb means to take special notice of something, with the implication of concerning oneself with it [LN].

d. aorist act. indic. of διαφημίζω (LN **33.214**) (BAGD p. 190): 'to spread the news about' [BAGD, BECNT, BNTC, CC, LN, NIGTC, NTC, PNTC; GW, NASB, NCV, NET, NIV, NRSV, TEV], 'to spread (his) fame' [WBC; ESV, NLT], 'to spread abroad (his) fame' [KJV], 'to tell people about (him)' [NICNT], 'to talk about (him)' [REB], 'to make known' [BAGD], 'to spread information about' [LN], 'to talk to everyone about' [CEV]. This verb means to spread information extensively and effectively concerning someone or something [LN].

QUESTION—Why did Jesus forbid them to tell others of the miracle?
Jesus wanted to avoid being acclaimed as the Messiah [CC, EBC, Lns, NICNT, WBC]. Since the blind men had called him the Son of David,

bringing attention to what Jesus had done, could stir up misguided messianic expectations among the people, which Jesus wanted to avoid [CC]. Jesus was not interested in getting publicity for himself [BNTC, NIGTC, NTC]. Publicity would appeal to wrong notions about his purpose and mission [CC, WBC], particularly his work on the cross [WBC]. He wanted to avoid causing a reaction by the crowds that would eclipse his ministry of teaching and preaching, or bring interference by religious and government leaders [BECNT]. Jesus' true messianic work would be hindered if he were to become famous as a healer [NIBC]. He wanted to avoid gaining a following built on a wrong basis [NAC]. It may be that he needed some relief from the constant requests for healing [NICNT].

DISCOURSE UNIT—9:32–34 [CEV, ESV, GW, NRSV, TEV]. The topic is Jesus forces a demon out of a man who couldn't talk [GW], Jesus heals a man who could not speak [TEV], Jesus heals a man who could not talk [CEV], Jesus heals a man unable to speak [ESV], Jesus heals one who was mute [NRSV].

9:32 As-they-were-going-out behold they-brought to-him a-demonized mute[a] man. **9:33** And the demon having-been-cast-out the mute spoke. And the crowds marveled[b] saying, "Never has-been-seen[c] such (a thing) in Israel." **9:34** But the Pharisees were-saying, "By[d] the prince[e] of-the demons he-casts-out the demons.

TEXT—Some manuscripts do not include verse 34. GNT includes it with a B rating to indicate it was regarded to be almost certain. Only REB does not include it.

LEXICON—a. κωφός (LN 33.106) (BAGD 1. p. 462): 'mute' [BAGD, BECNT, CC, LN; ESV, NASB, NRSV], 'dumb' [BAGD, BNTC, LN, NICNT, PNTC, WBC; KJV, REB], 'deaf and mute' [NIGTC], 'unable to speak' [LN, NTC], 'couldn't speak' [NLT], 'unable to talk' [GW], 'could not talk' [NCV, NET, NIV, TEV], 'incapable of talking' [LN]. This adjective describes not being able to speak or talk [LN].

b. aorist act. indic. of θαυμάζω (LN 25.213) (BAGD 1.a.α. p. 352): 'to marvel' [BAGD, BNTC, CC, LN, NIGTC, WBC; ESV, KJV], 'to wonder' [BAGD, LN], 'to be amazed' [BECNT, LN, NICNT; all versions except ESV, KJV, REB], 'to be filled with amazement' [NTC], 'to be astonished' [BAGD, PNTC; REB]. This verb means to wonder or marvel at some event or object, and whether the reaction is favorable or unfavorable depends on the context [LN].

c. aorist pass. indic. of φαίνομαι (LN 24.18) (BAGD 2.b. p. 851): 'to be seen' [BAGD, BECNT, BNTC, NICNT, NTC, PNTC, WBC; ESV, KJV, NASB, NET, NIV, NRSV, REB], 'to appear' [BAGD, CC, LN], 'to become visible' [BAGD, LN], 'to be revealed' [BAGD], 'to happen' [BAGD, NIGTC; CEV, NLT]. The phrase οὐδέποτε ἐφάνη 'never has been seen' is translated 'we have never seen' [GW, NCV, TEV]. This verb means to become visible to someone [LN].

MATTHEW 9:32–34

d. ἐν (LN 90.6) (BAGD III.1.b. p. 260): 'by' [BECNT, BNTC, LN, NICNT, NIGTC, NTC, PNTC; ESV, NASB, NET, NIV, NRSV], 'by the power of' [WBC], 'empowered by' [NLT], 'from' [LN], 'with the help of' [BAGD; GW], 'in connection with' [CC], 'through' KJV], 'gives him the power' [CEV, NCV, TEV]. This preposition indicates agent, often with the implication of an agent being used as an instrument, and in some instances relating to general behavior rather than to some specific event [LN].

e. ἄρχων (LN 37.56) (BAGD 3. p. 114): 'prince' [BAGD, NTC, WBC; ESV, KJV, NCV, NIV, NLT], 'ruler' [BAGD, BNTC, BECNT, CC, LN, NICNT, NIGTC, PNTC; GW, NASB, NET, NRSV], 'leader' [CEV], 'chief' [TEV]. This noun denotes one who rules or governs [LN].

QUESTION—Who was going out of the house?
1. The two blind men were leaving the house [ICC, Lns, My, NICNT, NIGTC, NTC, TH, WBC; NCV, NRSV, TEV].
2. Jesus and his disciples were leaving the house [BNTC, NIBC, PNTC; CEV].

QUESTION—What caused the amazement of the crowds?
Demons had been cast out before, but what the crowds had never seen or heard of before was the power of Jesus giving the man the ability to talk again [WBC]. They were amazed at all the miracles that Jesus had been doing [CC, NICNT], particularly those done that day [Lns, NTC]. The amazement mentioned here is the climax of that excitement referred to in verses 26 and 31 [EBC]. They marveled at Jesus' unique authority [NAC], possibly as a response to all of the miracles described in chapters 8 and 9 [NAC, NICNT].

QUESTION—What relationship is indicated by the use of the imperfect tense of ἔλεγον 'were saying'?
It may imply that the ferment of the Pharisees was always going on in the background [CC, EBC]. It indicates that they kept saying this [Lns].

QUESTION—Who is the prince of demons?
It is Satan [BNTC, CC, Lns, NIGTC, PNTC], that is, the Devil [My, TH], Beelzebub [NIBC].

QUESTION—What is Matthew's primary focus in this healing story?
The main point of this incident is the contrast between how the two different groups perceived the miracle [BECNT, BNTC, NIBC, NICNT, NIGTC]. Matthew provides three responses to Jesus: the mute man spoke, the crowds marveled, and the Pharisees give a shockingly wrong assessment of Jesus that portends an increasingly hostile attitude on their part [CC]. The tide of opposition that is now rising becomes an important part of what will be reported in the next chapter [EBC]. This story of the effect of Jesus' miracles on different people is a summary of the entire account of all that Jesus did in chapters 8 and 9 [Lns]. The reaction of the crowds is the climax of chapters 8 and 9, but the opposition of the Pharisees sets the tone for the next chapter's mission discourse, where opposition is more prominent [ICC]. Matthew's

account here is preparing the reader for the opposition to be described in 10:25 [TH, WBC].

DISCOURSE UNIT—9:35–11:1 [NICNT, NIGTC]. The topic is the Messiah's authority shared with his disciples: the discourse on mission [NICNT], workers for the harvest [NIGTC].

DISCOURSE UNIT—9:35–10:42 [PNTC]. The topic is Jesus' second discourse.

DISCOURSE UNIT—9:35–10:4 [ICC]. The topic is the missionary task and its messengers.

DISCOURSE UNIT—9:35–38 [CEV, ESV, GW, NET, NIV, NLT, NRSV, TEV]. The topic is Jesus' compassion for people [GW], Jesus has pity on people [CEV], Jesus has pity for the people [TEV], the harvest is plentiful, the laborers few [ESV], workers for the harvest [NET], the workers are few [NIV], the harvest is great, the laborers few [NRSV], the need for workers [NLT].

9:35 **And Jesus was-going-throughout**[a] **all the cities**[b] **and towns**[c] **teaching**[d] **in their synagogues**

LEXICON—a. imperf. act. indic. of περιάγω (LN 15.23) (BAGD 2. p. 645): 'to go throughout' [ESV, NET], 'to go through' [BECNT, NTC; NASB, NIV], 'to go around' [BAGD, CC, PNTC], 'to go about' [BAGD, BNTC, WBC; KJV, NRSV], 'to go to' [CEV, GW], 'to travel around' [NICNT, NIGTC], 'to travel through' [NCV, NLT], 'to travel about, to wander about' [LN]. This verb means to move about from place to place, with significant changes in direction [LN].

b. πόλις (LN **1.89**) (BAGD 1. p. 685): 'city' [BAGD, BECNT, BNTC, CC, **LN**, NTC, PNTC, WBC; ESV, KJV, NASB, NRSV], 'town' [NICNT, NIGTC; CEV, GW, NCV, NET, NIV, NLT, REB, TEV]. This noun denotes a population center of relatively greater importance than a κώμη, 'village,' due to its size, economic significance, or political control over a surrounding area [LN].

c. κώμη (LN 1.92) (BAGD 1. p. 461): 'village' [BAGD, LN; all translations], 'small town' [BAGD]. This noun denotes a relatively unimportant population center [LN].

d. pres. act. participle of διδάσκω (LN 33.224): 'to teach' [LN; all translations]. This verb means to provide instruction in a formal or informal setting [LN].

QUESTION—What is the relationship of the content in this verse with the very similarly worded statement in 4:23?

These similar verses bracket a section about Jesus' teaching and healing ministry [BECNT, CC, ICC, NAC, NIGTC, NICNT, WBC]. In this section Matthew reports the authoritative words of Jesus (in chapters 5–7) and the authoritative actions of Jesus (in chapters 8 and 9) [CC, NICNT, WBC]. The missional texts preceding 4:23 and following 9:35 indicate that the text in between them contain an important missional perspective [BECNT, NIGTC]. It shows that chapters 5–7 and 8–9 should be read together [BECNT, NIGTC].

QUESTION—How literally should τὰς πόλεις πάσας καὶ τὰς κώμας 'all the cities and towns' be taken?

It is hyperbole [TH, WBC]. It was a comprehensive activity [PNTC]. His ministry covered all of Galilee [BNTC].

and preaching[a] the good-news[b] of the kingdom and healing every disease[c] and every sickness.[d]

LEXICON—a. pres. act. participle of κηρύσσω (LN 33.256) (BAGD 2.b.β. p. 431): 'to preach' [BAGD, BNTC, CC, LN, NTC; CEV, KJV, NCV, NET, NIV, TEV], 'to proclaim' [BAGD, BECNT, NICNT, NIGTC, PNTC, WBC; ESV, NASB, NRSV, REB], 'to announce' [NLT], 'to spread (the good news)' [GW]. This verb means to publicly announce religious truths and principles while urging acceptance and compliance [LN].

b. εὐαγγέλιον (LN 33.217) (BAGD 1.c., 2.b.β. p. 318): 'the good news' [BAGD, CC, LN, NICNT; all versions except ESV, KJV, NASB], 'the gospel' [BAGD, BECNT, BNTC, LN, NIGTC, NTC, PNTC, WBC; ESV, KJV, NASB]. This noun denotes the content of good news (in the NT a reference to the gospel about Jesus) [LN].

c. νόσος (LN 23.155) (BAGD 1. p. 543): 'disease' [BAGD, BECNT, BNTC, CC, LN, NIGTC, PNTC; all versions except KJV, REB], 'sickness' [LN, WBC; KJV], 'illness' [BAGD, NICNT, NTC; REB]. This noun denotes the state of being diseased [LN].

d. μαλακία (LN 23.154) (BAGD 1. p. 488): 'sickness' [BAGD, BECNT, LN, NIGTC, PNTC; CEV, GW, NASB, NCV, NET, NIV, NRSV, TEV], 'illness' [BNTC; NLT], 'ailment' [CC], 'disability' [NICNT], 'infirmity' [NTC; REB], 'malady' [WBC], 'affliction' [ESV], 'disease' [LN; KJV]. This noun denotes a state of weakness resulting from disease [LN].

DISCOURSE UNIT—9:36–12:50 [NAC]. The topic is rising opposition to Jesus' mission.

DISCOURSE UNIT—9:36–11:1 [CC]. The topic is Jesus extends his ministry on behalf of Israel and all peoples: the missionary discourse.

DISCOURSE UNIT—9:36–10:42 [NAC]. The topic is opposition predicted for the disciples' mission.

9:36 **Having-seen the crowds he-felt-compassion[a] concerning[b] them, because they-were harassed[c] and dejected[d] as sheep not-having a-shepherd.**

LEXICON—a. aorist pass. (deponent = act.) indic. of σπλαγχνίζομαι (LN 25.49) (BAGD p. 762): 'to feel compassion' [BECNT, BNTC, LN; NASB], 'to have compassion' [CC, NIGTC, PNTC; ESV, NET, NIV, NLT, NRSV], 'to be moved with compassion' [NTC, WBC; KJV], 'to

feel sorry' [CEV, GW, NCV], 'to have pity' [BAGD], 'to have great affection for' [LN]. The phrase ἐσπλαγχνίσθη περί 'he felt compassion concerning' is translated 'his heart went out to them' [NICNT], 'his heart was filled with pity' [TEV], '(the sight of the crowds) moved him to pity' [REB]. This verb means to experience great affection and compassion for someone [LN].
   b. περί with the genitive (LN 90.24): 'concerning' [CC, LN], 'for' [BECNT, BNTC, NTC, WBC; CEV, ESV, GW, NASB, NCV, NRSV, TEV], 'about' [LN], 'on' [NIGTC, PNTC; KJV, NET, NIV, NLT], not explicit [NICNT; REB]. This preposition refers to general content, whether of a discourse or mental activity [LN].
   c. perf. pass. participle of σκύλλω (LN 22.23) (BAGD 1. p. 758): 'to be harassed' [BAGD, BNTC, CC, LN, NICNT, NIGTC, PNTC, WBC; ESV, NIV, NRSV, REB], 'to be distressed' [BECNT; NASB], 'to be confused' [CEV, NLT], 'to be fatigued' [NTC], 'to be troubled' [LN; GW], 'to be hurting' [NCV], 'to faint' [KJV], 'to be bewildered' [NET], 'to be wearied' [BAGD], 'to be worried' [TEV], 'to be bothered' [LN]. This passive verb means to be caused trouble or harassment [LN].
   d. perf. pass. participle of ῥίπτω (LN 85.37) (BAGD 2. p. 736): 'to be dejected' [BECNT, BNTC, NICNT], 'to be downcast' [CC], 'to be cast down' [PNTC], 'to be helpless' [NIGTC; CEV, ESV, GW, NCV, NET, NIV, NLT, NRSV, REB, TEV], 'to be forlorn' [NTC], 'to be scattered abroad' [KJV], 'to be confused' [WBC], 'to be dispirited' [NASB], 'to be put down' [BAGD, LN]. This passive verb means to be put down, with the possible implication of rapidity of action [LN].
QUESTION—What is the fundamental condition in the people that caused Jesus to be moved with pity?
   They lacked good leadership [BNTC, ICC, Lns, NAC, NICNT, NIGTC, TRT], and were helpless [EBC, NIBC] and lost [ICC]. They were defenseless against being bullied and oppressed by bad leaders [EBC]. He was concerned not only for their obvious needs, but also for their sense of distress, which was made worse by the lack of real leadership from their religious leaders, who were not faithful shepherds [BECNT]. He was concerned for their unmet spiritual needs [Lns, TRT, WBC]. They were in spiritual misery [My], aimless, and subject to futility [WBC]. They had many needs, but very few of them had found true spiritual peace, and they were burdened by the legalism of their leaders [NTC]. They were vulnerable and lacking in resources [PNTC]. They had unmet physical needs [NIGTC].

9:37 Then he-says to-the disciples, "The harvest[a] (is) great,[b] but the workers[c] few. **9:38** Therefore[d] pray[e] to-the Lord of-the harvest that he-send-out[f] workers into his harvest.
LEXICON—a. θερισμός (LN 43.15) (BAGD 2.a. p. 359): 'harvest' [BAGD, BECNT, CC, LN, NICNT, NIGTC, NTC, PNTC, WBC; all versions except CEV, NCV, REB], 'crop' [LN; REB], 'crop in the fields' [CEV].

This metaphor is made more explicit: 'there are many people to harvest' [NCV]. This noun denotes that which is harvested [LN].
b. πολύς (LN 59.11) (BAGD I.1.b.α. p. 688): 'great' [BAGD, CC, LN. NICNT, PNTC; NLT], 'plentiful' [BECNT, NTC; ESV, NASB, NET, NIV, NRSV], 'plenteous' [KJV], 'abundant' [BNTC], 'large' [BAGD, WBC; CEV, GW, TEV], 'many' [NCV], 'heavy' [REB], 'much, extensive' [LN].
c. ἐργάτης (LN 42.43) (BAGD 1.a. p. 307): 'worker' [BECNT, BNTC, CC, LN, NICNT, NIGTC, PNTC, WBC; CEV, GW, NASB, NCV, NET, NIV, NLT], 'laborer' [BAGD, NTC; ESV, KJV, NRSV, REB], 'workman' [BAGD]. This noun is translated as a phrase: 'workers to gather it in' [TEV]. This noun denotes one who works [LN].
d. οὖν (LN 89.50) (BAGD 1.b. p. 593): 'therefore' [BAGD, BECNT, CC, LN, NIGTC, NTC, PNTC, WBC; ESV, KJV, NASB, NET, NIV, NRSV], 'so' [BAGD, BNTC, LN, NICNT; GW, NLT], 'so then' [LN], 'consequently' [BAGD, LN], not explicit [CEV, NCV, REB, TEV]. This conjunction indicates result, often implying the conclusion of a process of reasoning [LN].
e. aorist pass. (deponent = act.) impera. of δέομαι (LN 33.170) (BAGD 4. p. 175): 'to pray' [BNTC, NTC, PNTC, WBC; KJV, NCV, NLT, TEV], 'to pray earnestly' [ESV], 'to ask' [BAGD, NICNT, NIGTC; CEV, GW, NET, NIV, NRSV, REB], 'to beseech' [BECNT, CC; NASB], 'to plead, to beg' [LN]. This verb means to ask for with urgency, with the implication of presumed need [LN].
f. aorist act. subj. of ἐκβάλλω (LN **15.68**) (BAGD 2. p. 237): 'to send out' [BAGD, BECNT, BNTC, CC, **LN**, NICNT, NIGTC, PNTC, WBC; CEV, ESV, NASB, NET, NIV, NRSV, TEV], 'to send' [LN; GW, NCV, NLT, REB], 'to send forth' [LN; KJV], 'to thrust out' [NTC]. This verb means to send out or away from, presumably for some purpose [LN].

QUESTION—What relationship is indicated by the genitive phrase τοῦ θερισμοῦ '(the Lord) of the harvest'?

The Lord owns the harvest [Lns, NIGTC, NTC, PNTC, TH, TRT, WBC]. He is the one who is harvesting [EBC], or who is in charge of the harvest operation [Lns, NICNT, NIGTC]. God himself, not Jesus, is the Lord of the harvest [CC, ICC, NICNT, PNTC, TH, WBC].

QUESTION—What is the harvest?

The harvest represents people who can be brought into the kingdom [EBC, My, NIBC, NICNT, PNTC]. Here the harvest represents those who are ready to be persuaded to respond to the message of salvation and trust in God [TH]. It is all the throngs and multitudes to whom the message of the gospel must be brought [NTC]. It is all those people who need to be reached with the gospel [NAC, WBC], who are ready to hear God's message [TRT]. Harvesting means gathering in the lost [NIBC]. The harvest represents all those in whom God's grace successfully works [Lns].

DISCOURSE UNIT—10:1–11:1 [WBC; REB]. The topic is the second discourse: the missionary discourse [WBC], the twelve are commissioned [REB].

DISCOURSE UNIT—10:1–42 [NIV, NLT]. The topic is Jesus sends out the twelve [NIV], Jesus sends out the twelve apostles [NLT].

DISCOURSE UNIT—10:1–15 [NASB, NCV, NET]. The topic is Jesus sends out his apostles [NCV], sending out the twelve apostles [NET], the twelve disciples; instruction for service [NASB].

DISCOURSE UNIT—10:1–4 [CEV, ESV, GW, NRSV, TEV]. The topic is Jesus appoints twelve apostles [GW], Jesus chooses his twelve apostles [CEV], the twelve apostles [ESV, NRSV, TEV].

10:1 And having-called-to-him[a] his twelve disciples he-gave them authority[b] (over) unclean[c] spirits so-that[d] to-cast- them -out[e] and to-heal every disease[f] and every sickness.[g]

LEXICON—a. aorist mid. participle of προσκαλέομαι (LN 33.308) (BAGD 1.a. p. 715): 'to call to oneself' [BAGD, NICNT, NIGTC, NTC; ESV, KJV, NIV, REB], 'to call together' [WBC; CEV, NCV, NLT, TEV], 'to call' [LN; GW, NET], 'to summon' [BAGD, BECNT, BNTC, CC, PNTC; NASB, NRSV], 'to call to' [LN]. This verb means to call to, with a possible implication of a reciprocal relationship [LN].

b. ἐξουσία (LN 37.35) (BAGD 3. p. 278): 'authority' [BAGD, BECNT, CC, NICNT, NIGTC, NTC, PNTC, WBC; all versions except CEV, KJV], 'power' [BNTC; CEV, KJV], 'authority to rule, 'right to control' [LN]. This noun denotes the right to control or govern over [LN].

c. ἀκάθαρτον (LN 12.39) (BAGD 2. p. 29): 'unclean' [BAGD, BECNT, BNTC, CC, LN, NICNT, NIGTC, NTC, PNTC, WBC; ESV, KJV, NASB, NET, NRSV, REB], 'evil' [CEV, GW, NCV, NIV, NLT, TEV]. The phrase πνεῦμα ἀκάθαρτον 'unclean spirit' denotes an evil supernatural spirit which is ritually unclean and which causes persons to be ritually unclean [LN].

d. ὥστε (LN **89.61**) (BAGD 2.b. p. 900): 'so that' [LN], 'in order to' [**LN**], 'in order that' [BAGD], 'that is' [CC]. This word followed by the infinitive is translated 'so that they could' [NICNT, WBC]. In most cases however, this word is not explicit and the concept expressed by it is expressed by an infinitive 'to (cast out, expel, etc.)' [BECNT, BNTC, NIGTC, NTC, PNTC; all versions]. This conjunction indicates purpose, with the implication that what has preceded serves as a means [LN].

e. pres. act. infin. of ἐκβάλλω (LN 53.102) (BAGD 1. p. 237): 'to cast out' [CC, LN, NIGTC, NTC, PNTC, WBC; ESV, KJV, NASB, NET, NLT, NRSV], 'to drive out' [BAGD; NCV, NIV, REB, TEV], 'to throw out' [NICNT], 'to force out' [CEV, GW], 'to expel' [BAGD, BNTC], 'to exorcise' [LN]. This verb means to cause a demon to no longer possess or control a person [LN].

MATTHEW 10:1

f. νόσος (LN 23.155) (BAGD 1. p. 543): 'disease' [BAGD, BECNT, BNTC, CC, LN, NIGTC, PNTC; all versions except KJV, REB], 'sickness' [LN, WBC; KJV], 'illness' [BAGD, NICNT, NTC; REB]. This noun denotes the state of being diseased [LN]. This word occurs at 4:23, 24; 8:17; 9:35; 10:1.

g. μαλακία (LN 23.154) (BAGD 1. p. 488): 'sickness' [BAGD, BECNT, LN, NIGTC, PNTC; CEV, GW, NASB, NCV, NET, NIV, TEV], 'illness' [BNTC; NLT], 'infirmity' [NTC; REB], 'disease' [LN; KJV], 'ailment' [BAGD, CC], 'affliction' [ESV], 'malady' [WBC], 'disability' [NICNT]. This noun denotes a state of weakness resulting from disease [LN]. This word occurs at 4:23, 24; 8:17; 9:35; 10:1.

QUESTION—Does the phrase 'his twelve disciples' mean that he had only twelve followers, or that these were twelve out of a larger number?

These twelve were chosen from a larger group of disciples [BECNT, EBC, CC, Lns, NICNT, PNTC, WBC]. The twelve were already a recognized group [EBC, My, NAC, NICNT, NTC], and this is a new stage in their training and preparation [EBC]. This is the first time they go out on their own [NAC].

QUESTION—What is the significance of his choosing twelve men to be apostles?

It intentionally corresponds with the twelve tribes of Israel [BECNT, EBC]. Israel lacks godly leaders, and these twelve men are Israel's new leaders [BECNT, ICC]. They are the nucleus of the new Israel [NIBC, NTC, TH], a new community of followers consciously chosen in opposition to the leaders of Israel at that time [NAC]. The number twelve represents Jesus' claim on all Israel, and the expectation that Israel will be restored [NIGTC].

QUESTION—What are these 'unclean' spirits?

They are evil spirits, demons [EBC, Lns, NICNT, NIGTC, NTC, TH, TRT, WBC; CEV, GW, NCV, NIV, NLT, TEV]. This term is a synonym for 'demons' [NICNT]. They instigate filthy thoughts, actions, and speech in human beings [NTC]. They are defiling [Lns]. They are morally evil, opposed to God's purposes and human welfare [BNTC, EBC, PNTC]. A person who was possessed by an evil spirit was considered to be unclean, and therefore not allowed to participate in the cultural or religious life of the community [TH].

QUESTION—What relationship is indicated by ὥστε 'so that'?

It indicates purpose [BAGD, EBC, ICC, LN, My, NICNT, TH]. It indicates purpose but also contemplates result [Lns]. It primarily focuses on result [PNTC]. It adds an explanatory note to indicate what this authority means [CC, My, NIGTC]. Since even Satan would have authority over these spirits, this authority must be further described [NIGTC].

QUESTION—What is the relationship of 'to heal' with what precedes it?

Healing is the second purpose for the authority Jesus gave, the first being to exorcise demons [BECNT, BNTC, CC, Lns, My, NAC, NIBC, NICNT,

NTC, PNTC TRT; CEV, TEV]. The two functions of exorcising and healing are distinguished [BNTC, NIBC, NTC].

10:2 Now^a these are the names of (the) twelve apostles:^b First,^c Simon the-one called Peter and Andrew his brother, and James the (son) of-Zebedee and John his brother, **10:3** Philip and Bartholomew, Thomas and Matthew the tax-collector, James the (son) of-Alphaeus and Thaddaeus,

TEXT—Manuscripts reading Θαδδαῖος 'Thaddaeus' are given a B rating by GNT to indicate it was regarded to be almost certain. Some manuscripts have Λεββαῖος 'Lebbaeus' or other similar variants. KJV reads 'Lebbaeus, whose surname was Thaddaeus'. All other translations read 'Thaddaeus'.

LEXICON—a. δέ: 'now' [BECNT, BNTC, NTC, PNTC, WBC; KJV, NASB, NET], 'and' [CC], not explicit [NICNT, NIGTC; CEV, ESV, GW, NCV, NIV, NLT, NRSV, REB, TEV].
  b. ἀπόστολος (LN 53.74) (BAGD 3. p. 99): 'apostle' [BAGD, LN; all translations], 'special messenger' [LN]. This noun denotes one who fulfills the role of being a special messenger (generally restricted to the immediate followers of Jesus Christ, but also extended, as in the case of Paul, to other early Christians active in proclaiming the message of the gospel) [LN].
  c. πρῶτος (LN 60.46) (BAGD 1.c.β. p. 726): 'first' [BAGD, LN; all translations except GW, NCV], 'first and foremost' [GW], 'foremost, most important, most prominent' [BAGD], not explicit [NCV]. This adjective describes what is first in a series involving time, space, or set [LN].

QUESTION—What does ἀπόστολος 'apostle' mean?
  The term is derived from a verb that means 'send' [EBC, ICC, NAC, NICNT, PNTC, WBC], and these men are sent on a mission [BNTC, NAC]. They are his authorized representatives [ICC, Lns, NIGTC, NTC, PNTC, WBC], men sent out with his authority [CC, PNTC, TH, WBC]. Their mission is an extension of Jesus' own ministry [CC]. In the NT this term can be used broadly to refer to messengers generally, or with a much more narrow meaning to refer to the twelve [EBC]. 'Apostle' is used here because the focus is on their mission [My, NICNT]. This is the only time this noun is used in the gospel of Matthew [BNTC, NAC, NICNT].

QUESTION—What is meant by the word πρῶτος 'first' in this list?
  1. Peter was the leader of the group [BECNT, BNTC, EBC, NICNT, NTC, PNTC]. He was not leader *over* them, but a leader *among* them [PNTC]. He is first among equals [CC, EBC, ICC, Lns, My]. He was prominent [BAGD, NAC, NICNT, NIGTC, WBC], foremost [BAGD, ICC, NIBC; GW], first in rank and spokesman for the rest [CC, WBC]. Peter was also the first disciple chosen [BECNT, BNTC, NICNT, WBC], or was chosen first along with his brother Andrew [My].
  2. This only means that his is the first name given in the list [TH].

QUESTION—Why are the names given in pairs?
Probably their names are given in pairs because of their going out by twos (see Mark 6:7) [BNTC, EBC, Lns, NAC, NTC, PNTC, WBC]. From the way the group of apostles is listed in the gospels and Acts, it seems that they may have been organizationally divided into groups of fours and of twos, each with a leader [EBC].

QUESTION—Is Bartholomew the same person as Nathaniel in John's gospel?
They are the same person [Lns, My, NTC], or are probably the same person [NAC]. There is some evidence to equate the two, though it is uncertain [EBC].

QUESTION—Is Thaddaeus the same as Judas son of James in Luke 6:16?
They are the same person [Lns, My, NAC, NIBC, NTC], or are probably the same person [EBC].

10:4 **Simon the Cananaean[a] and Judas Iscariot who also betrayed[b] him.**

LEXICON—a. Καναναῖος (LN **11.88**) (BAGD p. 402): 'Cananaean' [NIGTC, NTC, PNTC, WBC; ES, NRSV], 'Zealot' [BECNT, BNTC, CC, **LN**, NICNT; GW, NASB, NCV, NET, NIV, REB], 'zealot' [BAGD, LN, NLT], 'Canaanite' [KJV], 'Patriot' [TEV], 'nationalist' [LN], 'eager one' [CEV], 'enthusiast' [BAGD]. This noun is the Aramaic equivalent of ζηλωτής 'Zealot' and it is not in any way related to the geographical terms Cana or Canaan. It means either 'Simon the Zealot,' a member of a Jewish nationalistic group seeking independence from Rome, or 'Simon the Patriot,' an individual who is zealous for national independence [LN].

b. aorist act. participle of παραδίδωμι (LN 37.111) (BAGD 1.b. p. 614): 'to betray' [BECNT, BNTC, CC, NICNT, LN, NTC, PNTC, WBC; all versions except NCV], 'to hand over' [BAGD, LN, NIGTC], 'to turn against' [NCV], 'to turn over to' [BAGD, LN]. This verb means to deliver a person into the control of someone else, involving either the handing over of a presumably guilty person for punishment by authorities or the handing over of an individual to an enemy who will presumably take undue advantage of the victim [LN].

QUESTION—What does the designation 'Cananaean' mean?
This name comes from the Aramaic term for a zealot or enthusiast [BAGD, BECNT, BNTC, CC, EBC, ICC, LN, Lns, My, NAC, NIBC, NTC, PNTC, TH, TRT, WBC], or zealous one [NIGTC]. This designation is not related to the place names 'Canaan' or 'Cana' [BAGD, BECNT, CC, EBC, ICC, LN, Lns, My, NIBC, PNTC, WBC]. The Zealots were Jewish nationalists [EBC, NTC]. There may not yet have been a Zealot party of nationalists at this point in time [BNTC, ICC, NAC, NICNT, PNTC], so it may only mean that he was religiously zealous [NICNT, NIGTC], or zealous for God's law [PNTC]. He may have actually been engaged in terrorist activity against Rome [NAC].

QUESTION—What does 'Iscariot' represent?

It may indicate that his home town was Kerioth [EBC, BNTC, Lns, My, NICNT, PNTC, WBC], but its meaning is not known for certain [CC, EBC, NICNT].

DISCOURSE UNIT—10:5–11:1 [BECNT, EBC; GW]. The topic is mission and suffering [BECNT], second discourse: mission and martyrdom [EBC], Jesus sends out the twelve [GW].

DISCOURSE UNIT—10:5–25 [ICC]. The topic is instructions and prospects for missionaries.

DISCOURSE UNIT—10:5–15 [CEV, ESV, NRSV, TEV]. The topic is the mission of the twelve [NRSV, TEV], Jesus sends out the twelve apostles [ESV], instructions for the twelve apostles [CEV].

10:5 Jesus sent-out[a] these twelve commanding[b] them saying, "Do- not -go into (the) way[c] of- (the) -Gentiles[d] and do- not -enter a-city of-(the) Samaritans. **10:6** But instead[e] go to the lost[f] sheep of-(the) house[g] of Israel.

LEXICON—a. aorist act. indic. of ἀποστέλλω (LN 15.66) (BAGD 1.c. p. 98): 'to send out' [BAGD, BECNT, NICNT, NIGTC, NTC, PNTC, WBC; all versions except KJV], 'to send forth' [BNTC; KJV], 'to send' [CC, LN], 'to send away' [BAGD]. This verb means to cause someone to depart for a particular purpose [LN].

b. aorist act. participle of παραγγέλλω (LN 33.327) (BAGD p. 613): 'to command' [BAGD, LN; KJV], 'to give orders' [BAGD, BECNT], 'to order' [LN], 'to instruct' [LN, BNTC, PNTC, WBC; ESV, NASB, NET], 'to charge' [CC]. The phrase παραγγείλας αὐτοῖς λέγων 'commanding them saying' is translated 'with the following instructions' [NICNT, NIGTC; GW, NIV, NRSV, REB, TEV], 'with these instructions' [CEV, NLT], 'with the following order' [NCV], 'giving them the following charges' [NTC]. This verb means to announce what must be done [LN].

c. ὁδός (LN 1.99) (BAGD 2.a. p. 554): 'way' [BAGD, CC, LN; KJV, NASB], 'road' [BAGD, BNTC, LN, NTC, PNTC; REB], 'direction' [BECNT, NIGTC], 'highway' [BAGD, LN]. The phrase εἰς ὁδὸν...μὴ ἀπέλθητε 'do not go into the way of' is translated 'do not go off to visit' [NICNT], 'don't go to' [NCV, NLT, TEV], 'do not go among' [GW, NIV], 'go neither to' [WBC], 'stay away from' [CEV], 'go nowhere among' [ESV, NRSV], 'do not go into regions' [NET]. This noun denotes a general term for a thoroughfare, either within a population center or between two such centers [LN].

d. ἔθνη (plural form) (LN 11.37): 'Gentiles' [BECNT, BNTC, CC, NICNT, NIGTC, NTC, PNTC, WBC; CEV, ESV, KJV, NASB, NET, NIV, NLT, NRSV], 'Gentile lands' [REB], 'Gentile territory' [TEV], 'non-Jewish people' [NCV], 'people who are not Jewish' [GW], 'heathen, pagans'

MATTHEW 10:5-6

[LN]. This plural noun denotes those who do not belong to the Jewish or Christian faith [LN].

e. μᾶλλον (LN 89.126) (BAGD 3.a.α. p. 489): 'instead' [BAGD, LN, WBC; GW, NET, TEV], 'rather' [BAGD, BECNT, BNTC, CC, NICNT, NIGTC, NTC, PNTC; ESV, KJV, NASB, NIV, NRSV, REB], 'but rather' [LN], 'on the contrary' [LN], not explicit [NCV]. The phrase πορεύεσθε…μᾶλλον 'instead go' is translated 'go only (to)' [CEV, NLT]. This adverb marks a contrast indicating an alternative [LN].

f. perf. act. participle of ἀπόλλυμι (LN 27.29) (BAGD 2.b. p. 95): 'to be lost' [BAGD, LN]. This participle is translated as an adjective: 'lost' [all translations]. This verb means to become unaware of the location of something [LN]. In this verse it refers to sheep which have gone astray [BAGD].

g. οἶκος (LN 11.58) (BAGD 3. p. 561): 'house' [BECNT, BNTC, CC, NICNT, NIGTC, NTC, PNTC, WBC; ESV, KJV, NASB, NET, NRSV, REB], 'people' [LN; CEV, NCV, NLT, TEV], 'nation' [BAGD, GW, LN], 'descendants' [BAGD], not explicit [NIV]. The phrase οἶκος Ἰσραήλ 'the house of Israel' is an idiom that describes the people of Israel as an ethnic entity or nation [LN].

QUESTION—Why would Jesus not allow them to go to Gentiles or Samaritans?

They were to start their ministry with the Jews, but further missions to the Gentiles were to come later [CC, My, Lns, NAC, NICNT, NTC, PNTC, WBC]. It is a principle in the NT that the gospel should go to the Jews first, but then also to the Gentiles [My, NAC, NIBC]. God's plan for bringing salvation to the world involved taking it first to the Jews [TRT]. God had not abandoned the Jews, as the message of salvation went to them first [TH]. Jesus was first and foremost the savior of Israel [WBC]. He was the Jewish Messiah, sent in fulfillment of the Jewish scriptures, and the gospel naturally was to go to them first [NICNT]. Although Jesus had already anticipated ministry to all nations in 8:11, Israel had a priority in redemptive history such that the gospel had to go to them first [BECNT, NTC]. He was limiting their outreach to the geographical area of Galilee for this initial period of preaching while he was primarily focusing on his mission as Israel's Messiah, but the mission would extend to Gentile and Samaritan areas after his resurrection [NICNT]. The apostles were not mentally prepared to minister to Samaritans, but more importantly, since Jesus was the Messiah of Israel, he felt obligated to go to them first, and also to avoid the unnecessary offense to Jews and the rejection of the message that would no doubt happen if the gospel had gone to Gentiles or Samaritans at this stage [EBC].

QUESTION—Does 'lost sheep of the house of Israel' refer to the whole nation as being lost sheep, or only to certain ones who were lost?

1. It refers to all the people of Israel, all of whom are like lost sheep [BECNT, CC, EBC, ICC, My, NAC, NIBC, NICNT, PNTC, TH, WBC].

In Isaiah, Jeremiah, and Ezekiel this term was applied to the people of Israel [EBC, ICC].

2. It refers to those of Israel who are lost, not to all of Israel as being lost [NIGTC].

QUESTION—In what sense were these people 'lost'?

They were spiritually needy and scattered, and their regathering would signal the coming of the messianic age [NIBC]. The term 'lost' indicates a great spiritual need [BNTC]. They were wandering in error [My], having strayed away from serving God [TRT]. Jesus saw them as sheep in need of a shepherd [BECNT, NICNT], but whose human shepherds had failed to give direction and leadership [NICNT]. They were like lost sheep because their leaders had gone astray [ICC]. They needed to respond to the good news and accept Jesus as their Lord and Savior [NTC].

10:7 And (while) going[a] preach[b] saying that 'The kingdom of-the-heavens has-drawn-near.[c]'

LEXICON—a. pres. mid. or pass. (deponent = act.) participle of πορεύομαι (LN 15.10): 'to go' [LN]. This participle is translated 'as you go' [BECNT, BNTC, NICNT, NIGTC, NTC, PNTC, WBC; all versions except NCV, NLT, TEV], 'as you are going' [CC], 'when you go' [NCV], 'go' [NLT, TEV]. This verb means to move from one place to another, with the possible implication of continuity and distance [LN].

b. pres. act. impera. of κηρύσσω (LN 33.256) (BAGD 2.b.β. p. 431): 'to preach' [BAGD, BECNT, BNTC, CC, LN, NIGTC, NTC, PNTC; KJV, NASB, NCV, NET, NIV, TEV], 'to proclaim' [NICNT; ESV, REB], 'to proclaim the gospel' [WBC], 'to proclaim the good news' [NRSV], 'to proclaim aloud' [BAGD], 'to announce' [CEV, NLT], 'to spread the message' [GW]. This verb means to publicly announce religious truths and principles while urging acceptance and compliance [LN].

c. perf. act. indic. of ἐγγίζω (LN 67.21) (BAGD 5.b. p. 213): 'to draw near' [BNTC, NIGTC, PNTC, WBC], 'to be near' [GW, NCV, NET, NIV, NLT, TEV], 'to come near' [BAGD, LN; NRSV], 'to stand near' [CC], 'to approach' [BAGD, LN], 'to be at hand' [BECNT, NTC; ESV, KJV, NASB], 'to arrive' [NICNT]. This perfect tense verb is translated as future: 'will be here soon' [CEV]. This verb denotes the occurrence of a point of time close to a subsequent point of time [LN].

QUESTION—What is the function of ὅτι 'that'?

It is translated as introducing direct discourse [BECNT, BNTC, CC, NICNT, NIGTC, NTC, PNTC; ESV, GW, KJV, NASB, NCV, NET, NIV, NRSV, REB, TEV]; that is, say the following about the coming of the kingdom. It is also translated as introducing indirect discourse [WBC; CEV, NLT]; that is, announce that the kingdom is drawing near.

QUESTION—In what sense had the kingdom drawn near?

God's rule was present [BECNT]. Jesus the king had come to reign graciously and to push back the kingdom of darkness through healings and

MATTHEW 10:7

exorcisms [CC]. They were proclaiming a present reality, which focused on Jesus himself [PNTC]. God's reign in the hearts and lives of people is now asserting itself more powerfully than ever before [NTC]. The kingdom is the rule of grace and power that was present in Jesus, the king [Lns]. God was already at work to establish his rule [TH].

10:8 Heal[a] those-being-sick,[b] raise (the) dead, cleanse[c] lepers, cast-out demons; freely[d] you-received, freely[e] give.

LEXICON—a. pres. act. impera. of θεραπεύω (LN 23.139) (BAGD 2. p. 359): 'to heal' [BAGD, BECNT, BNTC, CC, LN, NICNT, NIGTC, NTC, PNTC, WBC; all versions except GW, NRSV], 'to cure' [BAGD, LN; GW, NRSV], 'to restore' [BAGD]. This verb means to cause someone to recover health [LN].
- b. pres. act. participle of ἀσθενέω (LN 23.144) (BAGD 1.a. p. 115): 'to be sick' [BAGD, LN], 'to be ill, to be disabled' [LN]. This participle is translated as a substantive: 'the sick' [BECNT, BNTC, CC, NIGTC, NTC, WBC; all versions], 'sick people' [PNTC], 'those who are ill' [NICNT]. This verb means to be sick and, as a result, being in a state of weakness and incapacity [LN].
- c. pres. act. impera. of καθαρίζω (LN 23.137) (BAGD 1.b.α. p. 387): 'to cleanse' [BECNT, BNTC, CC, NIGTC, NTC, PNTC, WBC; ESV, GW, KJV, NASB, NET, NIV, NRSV, REB], 'to make clean' [NICNT], 'to cure' [NLT], 'to heal' [CEV, NCV, TEV], 'to heal and make ritually pure, to heal and to make ritually acceptable' [LN]. This verb means to heal a person of a disease which has caused ceremonial uncleanness [LN].
- d. δωρεάν (LN 57.85) (BAGD 1. p. 210): 'freely' [BECNT, BNTC, CC, NTC, WBC; KJV, NASB, NCV, NET, NIV, NLT], 'without cost' [LN, NICNT, PNTC; REB], 'without payment' [BAGD; NRSV], 'without paying' [LN; CEV, ESV, GW, TEV], 'as a gift' [BAGD, NIGTC], 'as a free gift' [LN]. This adverb describes something being freely given [LN].
- e. δωρεάν: 'freely' [BECNT, BNTC, CC, NTC, WBC; KJV, NASB, NCV, NET, NIV, NLT], 'without cost' [CC, PNTC], 'without payment' [NRSV], 'without being paid' [CEV, TEV], 'without pay' [ESV], 'without charge' [REB], 'without charging' [GW], 'as a gift' [NIGTC].

QUESTION—What is it that the apostles had freely received, and were to give freely?

Without charge they had received the gospel message, the authority Jesus had delegated to them, and this commission to preach and heal [EBC]. They were freely given authority and power, and were to offer their ministry without charge [NIGTC, NTC, TH]. They had received without cost the gracious blessings of the kingdom, and were to extend these blessings without being paid for doing so [BECNT]. The way God had treated them in meeting their needs is how they were to treat others [PNTC]. They had received the power to heal as a gift, and were to minister healing to others without charge [ICC]. They had been given power to perform miracles, and of course were to minister accordingly without receiving anything except the basic necessities of living [My]. They received the message of the kingdom of God free of charge, and were to carry out their ministry of teaching and healing free of charge [NICNT]. They had freely received the blessings associated with discipleship, which in this case would also include material resources [NAC]. They would receive all they need materially during their time of ministry, so they should not charge anything for their ministry [NIBC]. Without charge they received forgiveness as well as the power to heal, so they were to heal and offer the message of forgiveness without charging for them [BNTC].

QUESTION—Why are these imperatives, along with the imperatives in verses 6 and 7, in the present tense, whereas most other imperatives in this chapter are in the aorist?

1. There does not seem to be much clear difference in meaning between the use of aorist and present imperatives here, though it may be that the present imperatives in verses 6–8 emphasize the primary task Jesus is giving them for this mission [CC].
2. The present imperatives seem to indicate that the action is to be ongoing [Lns, PNTC].

10:9 **Do- not -acquire^a gold nor silver nor copper-coins^b into your belts,^c**

LEXICON—a. aorist mid. (deponent = active) subjunctive of κτάομαι (LN **57.58**) (BAGD 1. p. 455): 'to acquire' [BAGD, BECNT, CC, LN, WBC; ESV, NASB], 'to get' [BAGD, BNTC, LN, NICNT, NIGTC, PNTC], 'to take' [GW, NET, NLT, NRSV, REB], 'to take along' [CEV, NIV], 'to carry' [NCV, TEV], 'to supply yourself' [NTC], 'to provide' [KJV], 'to gain' [LN]. This verb means to acquire possession of something [LN].

b. χαλκός (LN **6.72**) (BAGD 2. p. 875): 'copper coin' [BAGD, LN, WBC; CEV, GW, NLT], 'copper' [BECNT, NICNT, NIGTC, PNTC; ESV, NASB, NCV, NET, NIV, NRSV, REB], 'copper money' [BNTC, **LN**, NTC; TEV], 'brass' [CC; KJV], 'bronze money' [LN]. This noun denotes coins of bronze or copper, and hence of little value [LN].

c. ζώνη (LN 6.178) (BAGD p. 341): 'belt' [BAGD, CC, LN, NIGTC, NTC; ESV, NET, NIV, NRSV, REB], 'money belt' [BECNT, BNTC, NICNT, PNTC, WBC; NASB, NLT], 'girdle' [BAGD, LN], 'pocket' [GW, TEV], 'purse' [KJV], not explicit [CEV, NCV]. This noun denotes a band of leather or cloth worn around the waist outside of one's clothing. A belt was normally quite wide and could be readily folded, so it was often used to carry money [LN].

QUESTION—Was Jesus commanding them not to take money with them, or not to accept money for their ministry?

1. They were not to take any money with them at all [BNTC, Lns, NAC, NIBC, NTC, PNTC, TH, WBC; CEV, GW, KJV, NCV, NET, NIV, NLT, NRSV, REB, TEV].

2. They were not to acquire any money as payment for their ministry [BECNT, CC, EBC, ICC, NICNT, NIGTC; ESV, NASB], nor were they to take any extra money with them [BECNT, NICNT, NIGTC].

10:10 nor a-bag^a for (the) journey^b nor two tunics^c nor sandals^d nor a-staff;^e

LEXICON—a. πήρα (LN **6.145**) (BAGD p. 656): 'bag' [BECNT, CC, NIGTC, PNTC; ESV, NASB, NCV, NET, NIV, NRSV], 'traveler's bag' [BAGD, **LN**, NTC; NLT], 'traveling bag' [CEV, GW], 'beggar's bag' [BAGD, LN; TEV], 'knapsack' [BAGD, BNTC, WBC], 'pack' [NICNT; REB], 'scrip' (an archaic term for a wallet or small bag) [KJV]. This noun denotes a bag used by travelers (or beggars) to carry possessions [LN].
   b. ὁδός (LN 15.19) (BAGD 1.b. p. 554): 'journey' [BAGD, BECNT, LN, NICNT, NIGTC, PNTC; ESV, KJV, NASB, NET, NIV, NRSV], 'trip' [BNTC; GW, TEV], 'way' [BAGD, CC], 'road' [WBC; REB], not explicit [NCV]. The phrase πήραν εἰς ὁδόν 'bag for the journey' is translated 'traveler's bag' [NTC; NLT], 'traveling bag' [CEV]. This noun denotes the process of traveling, presumably for some distance [LN].
   c. χιτών (LN 6.176) (BAGD p. 882): 'tunic' [BAGD, BNTC, LN, NIGTC, NTC, PNTC; ESV, NET, NIV, NRSV], 'coat' [BECNT; KJV, NASB, REB], 'shirt' [BAGD, CC, LN, WBC; CEV, TEV]. The phrase 'two tunics' is translated 'extra tunic' [NET, NIV], 'extra clothes' [NCV], 'spare clothes' [NICNT], 'a change of clothes' [GW, NLT]. This noun denotes a garment worn under the ἱμάτιον 'cloak' [LN].
   d. ὑπόδημα (LN 6.182) (BAGD p. 844): 'sandal' [BAGD, BECNT, BNTC, CC, LN, NICNT, NIGTC, NTC, WBC; all versions except KJV, TEV], 'shoe' [LN, PNTC; KJV, TEV]. This noun denotes any type of footwear, though ordinarily the reference would be to a sandal rather than to a shoe [LN].
   e. ῥάβδος (LN 6.218) (BAGD p. 733): 'staff' [BECNT, CC, LN, NIGTC, NTC, PNTC, WBC; ESV, KJV, NASB, NET, NIV, NRSV], 'traveler's staff' [BNTC], 'rod' [BAGD, LN], 'walking stick' [CEV, GW, NCV, NLT, TEV], 'stick' [BAGD, LN; REB]. This noun denotes a stick that could be used for a number of different purposes, such as an aid to walking, herding animals, or beating people [LN].

QUESTION—Does πήρα denote a traveler's bag, or a bag used by a beggar to carry possessions?
   1. It is a traveler's bag [ICC, LN, Lns, My, NIBC, NICNT, NIGTC, NTC, PNTC, TRT, WBC; NLT], which could also have been used as a beggar's bag [NICNT].
   2. It is a beggar's bag [TEV].

QUESTION—What was he prohibiting with regard to sandals?
   1. They were not to take extra sandals [BECNT, EBC, ICC, My, NIBC, NICNT, NTC, PNTC, TRT; CEV]. They were not to provide themselves with new sandals, but were to use the ones they already had [Lns]. This

account assumes the disciples already have one cloak, sandals, and a walking stick, and Jesus is forbidding them to acquire anything more [EBC].
2. They were not to wear sandals at all [NIGTC, TH]. This would be a visible demonstration of their vulnerability [NIGTC].

for the worker^a (is) worthy^b of his food.^c

LEXICON—a. ἐργάτης (LN 42.43) (BAGD 1.a. p. 307): 'worker' [BECNT, BNTC, CC, LN, NICNT, NIGTC, NTC, WBC; CEV, GW, NASB, NCV, NET, NIV, REB, TEV], 'workman' [BAGD, PNTC; KJV], 'those who work' [NLT], 'laborer' [BAGD; ESV, NRSV]. This noun denotes one who works [LN].

b. ἄξιος (LN 65.17) (BAGD 2.a. p. 78): 'worthy' [BAGD, BECNT, CC, LN, NICNT, NIGTC, WBC; KJV, NASB]. The phrase 'is worthy of' is translated as a verb: 'to be worth' [NIV], 'to deserve' [BNTC, PNTC; CEV, ESV, GW, NET, NLT, NRSV, REB], 'to be entitled to' [BAGD, NTC], 'should be given' [NCV, TEV]. This adjective describes a relatively high degree of comparable merit or worth [LN].

c. τροφή (LN 5.1) (BAGD 1. p. 827): 'food' [BAGD, BNTC, CC, **LN**, NIGTC; CEV, ESV, NRSV], 'support' [BECNT, NTC, WBC; NASB], 'keep' [NICNT, PNTC; NIV, REB], 'provisions' [NET], 'meat' [KJV], 'what they need' [NCV, TEV]. The phrase ἄξιος...τῆς τροφῆς αὐτοῦ 'worthy of his food' is translated 'deserves to have his needs met' [GW], 'deserve to be fed' [NLT]. This noun denotes any kind of food or nourishment [LN].

QUESTION—What relationship is indicated by the conjunction γάρ 'for'?

This conjunction indicates the reason why the disciple does not need to take the various precautions about obtaining the things needed throughout their journeys. They are workmen for God and God will supply the food and things they need as they work for him [PNTC]. God will provide what they need through those who receive them on their travels [WBC].

10:11 Into whatever city or town you-enter, find-out^a who in it is worthy;^b and stay there until you-leave.

LEXICON—a. aorist act. impera. of ἐξετάζω (LN 27.37) (BAGD 1. p. 275): 'to find out' [ESV, NET, NRSV], 'to inquire' [BAGD, BECNT, BNTC, CC, NIGTC, PNTC; KJV, NASB], 'to make inquiry' [NICNT], 'to look for' [NTC; GW, REB, TEV], 'to search for' [NIV, NLT], 'to search carefully' [WBC], 'to find' [CEV, NCV], 'to try to find out, to make a diligent effort to learn' [LN]. This verb means to engage in a careful search in order to acquire information, though primarily by inquiry [LN].

b. ἄξιός: 'worthy' [BECNT, BNTC, CC, NICNT, NIGTC, PNTC, WBC; ESV, KJV, NASB, NET, NRSV], 'worthy person' [NCV, NIV, NLT], 'suitable person' [REB], 'deserving' [NTC]. This adjective is translated as a phrase: 'worthy enough to have you as their guest' [CEV], '(people) who will listen to you' [GW], 'who is willing to welcome you' [TEV].

10:12 **And on-coming-into the house^a greet^b it;**

LEXICON—a. οἰκία (LN 7.3, 10.8) (BAGD 3. p. 557): 'house' [BECNT, BNTC, CC, LN (7.3), NICNT, NIGTC, NTC, PNTC; ESV, GW, KJV, NASB, NET, NRSV, REB, TEV], 'dwelling, residence' [LN (7.3)], 'home' [CEV, NCV, NIV, NLT], 'household' [LN (10.8), WBC], 'family' [LN 10.8)]. This noun denotes a building or a place where one dwells [LN (7.3)], or it denotes the family consisting of those related by blood and marriage, as well as slaves and servants, living in the same house or homestead [LN (10.8)]. In this verse, the meaning of this noun has a kind of middle position between 'house' and 'household' [BAGD].
- b. aorist mid. (deponent = act.) impera. of ἀσπάζομαι (LN 33.20) (BAGD 1.a. p. 116): 'to greet' [BAGD, BECNT, BNTC, CC, LN, NIGTC, WBC; ESV, GW, NRSV], 'to pronounce greeting' [NTC], 'to give greeting' [PNTC; NASB, NET, NIV], 'to send greetings' [LN], 'to give blessing' [NLT], 'to give your blessing of peace' [CEV], 'to wish peace' [NICNT; REB], 'to salute' [KJV], 'to say Peace be with you' [NCV, TEV]. This verb means to employ certain set phrases as a part of the process of greeting, whether communicated directly or indirectly [LN].

QUESTION—Who is being addressed when they ἀσπάσασθε αὐτήν 'greet it'? The instruction 'greet it' doesn't mean to talk to the house. It means to give your greetings to the people in the house [TH]. Although many of the translations are not clear about this, one translates it, 'When you go into a house, greet the family' [GW].

10:13 **and if the house^a is worthy, let- your(pl) peace^b -come upon it, but if it-is not worthy, let- your(pl) peace -return^c to you.**

LEXICON—a. οἰκία (LN 7.3, 10.8): 'house' [BECNT, BNTC, CC, LN (7.3), NIGTC, PNTC; ESV, KJV, NASB, NET, NRSV], 'household' [LN (10.8), NICNT, WBC], 'family' [GW, LN (10.8)], 'home' [LN, NTC; CEV, NIV, NLT], 'people in that house' [TEV], 'people there' [NCV], not explicit [REB].
- b. εἰρήνη (LN 22.42) (BAGD 2. p. 227): 'peace' [BAGD, LN]. The clause ἐλθάτω ἡ εἰρήνη ὑμῶν ἐπ' αὐτήν 'let your peace come upon/on it' [CC, NICNT, NIGTC, NTC; ESV, KJV, NET, NRSV] is also translated 'let your greeting of peace come upon it' [BECNT, PNTC], 'let your greeting of peace remain' [TEV], 'let your greeting of peace rest upon it' [BNTC], 'let your peace rest on it' [NIV], 'let your peace descend on it' [REB], 'let your peace remain upon it' [WBC], 'let your blessing remain with them' [CEV], 'allow your greeting to stand' [GW], 'let your blessing stand' [NLT], 'give it your blessing of peace' [NASB], 'let your peace stay there' [NCV]. This noun denotes a set of favorable circumstances involving peace and tranquility. In some languages this is best expressed in a negative form, 'to be without trouble' or 'to have no worries' [LN].
- c. aorist pass. impera. of ἐπιστρέφω (LN 15.90) (BAGD 2.a.β. p. 301): 'to return (to)' [BAGD, LN], 'to go back to' [LN]. The clause 'let your peace

return to you' [CC, NICNT, NIGTC, NTC, PNTC, WBC; ESV, KJV, NET, NIV, NRSV] is also translated 'let your peace come back to you' [REB], 'let your greeting of peace return to you' [BECNT, BNTC], 'take back your blessing of peace' [CEV, NASB], 'take back the blessing' [NLT], 'take back the peace you wished for them' [NCV], 'take back your greeting' [GW, TEV]. This verb means to return to a point or area where one has been before, with probable emphasis on turning about [LN].

QUESTION—In what sense would the house be 'worthy'?

It means to be receptive to their message [BECNT, BNTC, CC, EBC, ICC, Lns, NICNT, NTC, TH, WBC], to be open to their message and ministry [NAC]. Here of course they are addressing the household, not the dwelling itself [NIGTC, PNTC].

QUESTION—How might someone's 'peace' return to them?

They were to retract or take back their well-wishes [BECNT, NIBC, NAC, TH; CEV, GW, NASB, NCV, NLT, TEV]. The peace of the gospel message would not be experienced by those who were contemptuous of it [CC, PNTC, WBC]. Taking back their peace meant that they were not to stay there [EBC]. The offer of peace is only a blessing if received in faith [NIGTC]. 'Peace to you' was a customary greeting [BNTC, Lns, NIBC, NIGTC, NTC, WBC]; however, if this blessing was not responded to through faith, it bestowed no blessing on the hearers [ICC, NTC]. If such a blessing were not responded to positively, it would be of no effect, similar to a check that is uncashed [NICNT].

10:14 And whoever does- not -receive[a] you nor listen-to[b] your words,[c] going-out[d] outside of-the house or the city shake-off[e] the dust of-your feet.

LEXICON—a. aorist mid. (deponent = act.) subj. of δέχομαι (LN 34.53) (BAGD 1. p. 177): 'to receive' [BAGD, BECNT, CC, LN, NIGTC, NTC, PNTC, WBC; ESV, KJV, NASB, REB], 'to welcome' [BAGD, BNTC, LN, NICNT; CEV, GW, NCV, NET, NIV, NLT, NRSV, TEV], 'to accept, to have as a guest' [LN]. This verb means to accept the presence of a person with friendliness [LN].

b. aorist act. subj. of ἀκούω (LN 31.56) (BAGD 1.b.α. p. 32): 'to listen to' [LN, NICNT, NIGTC, NTC, PNTC, WBC; all versions except KJV, NASB], 'to hear' [BAGD, BNTC, CC; KJV], 'to heed' [BECNT, LN; NASB], 'to listen and respond, to pay attention and respond, to accept' [LN]. This verb means to believe something and to respond to it on the basis of having heard [LN].

c. λόγος (LN 33.98) (BAGD 1.a.δ. p. 477): 'word' [BAGD, BECNT, BNTC, CC, LN, NIGTC, NTC, PNTC, WBC; ESV, KJV, NASB, NIV, NRSV], 'message' [LN, NICNT; CEV, NET, NLT], 'saying, statement' [LN], not explicit [NCV, TEV]. The phrase 'your words' is translated 'what you say' [REB], 'what you have to say' [GW]. This noun denotes that which has been stated or said, with primary focus upon the content of the communication [LN].

d. pres. mid./pass. (deponent = act.) participle of ἐξέρχομαι (LN 15.40) (BAGD 1.a.α. p. 274): 'to go out' [BAGD, LN], 'to depart out of, to leave from within' [LN], 'to come out, to go away' [BAGD]. The participial phrase ἐξερχόμενοι ἔξω 'going out outside' is translated as a temporal circumstance: 'when you leave' [ESV, NIV], 'when ye depart out of' [KJV], 'when you go out of' [PNTC], 'when you are outside' [WBC]; as a coordinate circumstance: 'as you leave' [NIGTC; NET, NLT, NRSV, REB], 'as you go out of' [BECNT, NICNT; NASB], 'as you are going out of' [CC], 'in going out of' [NTC]; as an imperative: 'leave' [CEV, GW, NCV, TEV], 'go out of' [BNTC]. This verb means to move out of an enclosed or well defined two or three-dimensional area [LN].

e. aorist act. impera. of ἐκτινάσσω (LN 16.8) (BAGD 1. p. 246): 'to shake off' [BAGD, LN], 'to shake from, to shake out' [LN]. The phrase 'shake off the dust of your feet' [KJV] is also translated 'shake off the/its dust from your feet' [CC, NICNT, PNTC, WBC; ESV, NRSV], 'shake the/its dust off your feet' [BECNT, NIGTC, NTC; GW, NASB, NCV, NET, NIV, TEV; similarly REB], 'shake its dust from your feet' [NLT], 'shake off the dust that clings to your feet' [BNTC], 'shake the dust from your feet at them' [CEV]. This verb means to shake something out or off of an object in order get rid if it [LN].

QUESTION—What did shaking the dust off one's feet communicate?

It symbolized renunciation and the severing of relationship [BECNT, NAC, NIGTC, PNTC], dissociation [NICNT], or absolute rejection [TH]. It showed they shared nothing in common [NIBC], that they had no fellowship with them [CC], and that God's judgment was to fall on those who did not receive them [BNTC, NIBC]. Since Jews would sometimes remove the dust of a pagan land from their clothing as they were leaving it, this action communicates that people who reject the gospel are being regarded as no better than Gentiles [BECNT, My, PNTC]. Jewish people would brush the dust of pagan lands off themselves so that no contamination of holy things would occur when they returned to their land; doing this after leaving a place that rejected the message of the gospel would symbolize the fact that severe judgment would come on that place [NTC, TRT]. They were showing that they regarded them as no better than Gentiles, whose very dust is defiling [My]. It communicated that they were standing on heathen soil that must not be brought back to the Holy Land [NIBC]. It was a testimony that the feet of those who brought good news of the kingdom were there, and they were leaving their dust as a witness to their having been rejected [Lns]. It would have indicated that they had nothing to do with those people, and that the apostles were not to be blamed for the fate that would befall them [ICC]. It was a prophetic action [WBC].

10:15 Truly[a] I-say to-you, it-will-be more-bearable[b] (for the) land of-Sodom and of-Gomorrah on (the) day of-judgment than (for) that city.

LEXICON—a. ἀμήν (LN 72.6): 'truly' [BECNT, BNTC, CC, LN, NICNT, PNTC, WBC; ESV, NASB, REB], 'amen' [NIGTC], 'solemnly' [NTC], 'verily' [KJV], 'indeed, it is true that' [LN]. This particle is translated as a phrase: 'I promise you' [CEV], 'I assure you' [TEV], 'I tell you the truth' [NCV, NET, NIV, NLT], 'I can guarantee this truth' [GW]. This particle expresses a strong affirmation of what is declared [LN].

b. ἀνεκτός (LN 25.172) (BAGD p. 64) 'bearable, tolerable, endurable' [BAGD, LN]. The comparative form of this adjective is translated 'more bearable' [BECNT, CC, NICNT, NIGTC, PNTC, WBC; ESV, NET, NIV, REB], 'more tolerable' [BNTC, NTC; KJV, NASB], 'easier' [CEV], 'better' [GW, NCV], 'better off' [NLT]. The phrase ἀνεκτότερον ἔσται 'it will be more bearable for' is translated 'God will show more mercy to' [TEV]. This adverb describes what can be borne or endured [LN].

DISCOURSE UNIT—10:16–25 [CEV, ESV, NCV, NET, NRSV, TEV]. The topic is Jesus warns his apostles [NCV], warning about trouble [CEV], coming persecutions [NRSV, TEV], persecutions will come [ESV], persecution of disciples [NET].

DISCOURSE UNIT—10:16–23 [NASB]. The topic is a hard road before them.

10:16 Behold,[a] I send- you -out[b] as[c] sheep[d] in (the) midst[e] of-wolves;[f]

LEXICON—a. ἰδού (LN 91.13) (BAGD 1.c. p. 371): 'behold' [BECNT, BNTC, WBC; ESV, KJV, NASB], 'look' [CC, LN, NICNT, NTC, PNTC; NLT], 'see' [NRSV], 'listen' [LN; NCV, TEV], 'pay attention' [LN], 'remember, consider' [BAGD], not explicit [NIGTC; CEV, GW, NET, NIV, REB]. This particle is a prompter of attention, and serves to emphasize the following statement [LN]. See the discussion about the meaning of this word at 1:20.

b. pres. act. indic. of ἀποστέλλω (LN 15.66) (BAGD 1.b.β. p. 98): 'to send out' [BAGD, BECNT, NICNT, NIGTC, NTC, PNTC; all versions except CEV, KJV], 'to send forth' [BNTC; KJV], 'to send' [LN, WBC; CEV], 'to send away' [BAGD]. This verb means to cause someone to depart for a particular purpose [LN].

c. ὡς (LN 64.12) (BAGD II.2. p. 897): 'as' [BAGD, BECNT, BNTC, CC, LN, NIGTC, NTC, PNTC, WBC; ESV, KJV, NASB, NLT], 'like' [LN, NICNT; CEV, GW, NCV, NET, NIV, NRSV, REB], 'just like' [TEV]. This conjunction is a relatively weak marker of a relationship between events or states [LN].

d. πρόβατον (LN 4.22) (BAGD 1. p. 703): 'sheep' [BAGD, LN; all translations except CEV], 'lamb' [CEV].

e. μέσος (LN 83.9) (BAGD 2. p. 507): 'middle' [BAGD]. The phrase ἐν μέσῳ 'in the midst' [BAGD, NIGTC, NTC, WBC; ESV, KJV, NASB] is also translated 'into the midst' [NRSV], 'in the middle' [PNTC], 'among' [BAGD, CC, LN, NICNT; GW, NCV, NIV, NLT, REB], 'surrounded by' [NET]. The phrase ἐν μέσῳ λύκων 'in the midst of wolves' is translated 'into a pack of wolves' [CEV], 'to a pack of wolves' [TEV]. This adjective describes a position within an area determined by other objects and distributed among such objects [LN].

f. λύκος (LN 4.11) (BAGD 1. p. 481): 'wolf' [BAGD, LN; all translations].

QUESTION—In what way would the disciples be like sheep in the midst of wolves?

This means that Jesus is sending his disciples out among people who will attack them like a wolf will attack harmless and defenseless sheep [TH]. They will be defenseless in themselves and yet they are being sent into a dangerous environment [EBC]. There will be serious trouble ahead [PNTC]. They are vulnerable [NICNT, NIGTC], defenseless [BNTC, Lns, NIBC], and live in a hostile world [NICNT]. Danger threatens them [BECNT, WBC].

so[a] be wise[b] as the serpents[c] and innocent[d] as the doves.[e]

LEXICON—a. οὖν (LN 89.50): 'so' [BECNT, BNTC, LN, NICNT, NIGTC; CEV, ESV, GW, NASB, NCV, NET, NLT, NRSV], 'therefore' [CC, LN, NTC, PNTC, WBC; KJV, NIV], 'consequently, accordingly, then, so then' [LN], not explicit [REB, TEV]. This conjunction indicates result, often implying the conclusion of a process of reasoning [LN].

b. φρόνιμος (LN 32.31) (BAGD p. 866): 'wise' [BAGD, LN, NIGTC; CEV, ESV, KJV, NET, NRSV], 'shrewd' [BECNT, BNTC, CC; NASB, NIV, NLT], 'cunning' [NICNT; GW], 'keen' [NTC], 'crafty' [WBC], 'sensible' [PNTC], 'smart' [NCV], 'wary' [REB], 'cautious' [TEV], 'wisely, with understanding, with insight' [LN]. This adjective describes having understanding resulting from insight and wisdom [LN].

c. ὄφις (LN 4.52) (BAGD 1. p. 600): 'serpent' [BAGD, BECNT, BNTC, CC, NTC, PNTC, WBC; ESV, KJV, NASB, NET, NRSV, REB], 'snake' [BAGD, LN, NICNT, NIGTC; CEV, GW, NCV, NIV, NLT, TEV]. In some ancient eastern cultures, serpents were proverbial for their prudence [EBC].

d. ἀκέραιος (LN 88.32) (BAGD p. 30): 'innocent' [BAGD, BECNT, BNTC, CC, NIGTC, PNTC, WBC; all versions except KJV, NLT, TEV], 'harmless' [NICNT; KJV, NLT], 'guileless' [NTC], 'pure' [BAGD, LN], 'gentle' [TEV], 'untainted' [LN]. This adjective describes being without a mixture of evil and hence to being pure [LN].

e. περιστερά (LN **4.44**) (BAGD p. 652): 'dove' [BAGD, **LN**; all translations], 'pigeon' [BAGD, LN]. Though in English a relatively clear distinction is made between 'doves' (which have pointed tails) and 'pigeons' (which have squared off tails), there seems to be no such distinction in the use of περιστερά and τρυγών in the Greek of the New Testament. In some societies pigeons or doves are not regarded as gentle or peaceful, but rather as wicked and harmful. In fact, in some cultures doves are thought to be symbols of death and of evil. Under such circumstances it is important, therefore, to have some marginal note so as to indicate clearly the symbolic significance of such birds in biblical contexts [LN].

QUESTION—What is the essential element of φρόνιμος 'wise' that he wants them to have?

The term as used here refers to being cautious about danger [EBC, Lns, My, NTC, PNTC, TH, TRT, WBC], or shrewd with respect to self-preservation [ICC, NICNT], not overly naïve [NAC]. He wants them to be able to anticipate and avoid unnecessary danger [NIGTC] and be realistic about and aware of the dangers that surround them [CC]. They need to be sensible about their surroundings and use godly common sense to do the right thing [NTC]. It means being shrewd and tactful [BNTC], but moving on when persecuted [NIBC].

QUESTION—What is the essential element of ἀκέραιος 'innocent' that he wants them to have?

The essential element is harmlessness [NICNT, TH, TRT]. While they are to be shrewd with regard to self-preservation, they are not to harm their opponents [NICNT]. They are to be open to and compassionate toward people [CC]. It is the kind of innocence associated with a consistent and uncompromised integrity [NIGTC]. They must show purity of intention [NAC, NIBC]. They are to be without guile [ICC, Lns, NTC, WBC], and must have a single-minded devotion to duty [ICC]. While showing wisdom, they must also maintain integrity [BECNT] and be free from wrongdoing [BNTC]. They must be upright, refraining from doing anything of a questionable nature [My].

10:17 And[a] beware[b] of people;[c] for they-will-hand- you -over[d] to councils[e] and in their synagogues they-will-flog[f] you;

LEXICON—a. δέ (LN 89.94, 89.124): 'and' [CC, LN (89.94), NTC, PNTC], 'but' [BECNT, BNTC, LN (89.124); KJV, NASB, NLT], not explicit [NICNT, NIGTC, WBC; all versions except KJV, NASB, NLT]. This conjunction may indicate contrast [LN (89.124)], or it may indicate an additive relation, but with the possible implication of some contrast [LN (89.94)].

b. προσέχω (LN 27.59) (BAGD 1.b. p. 714): 'to beware' [BAGD, BECNT, BNTC, CC, NTC, PNTC; ESV, KJV, NASB, NET, NLT, NRSV], 'to be wary' [NIGTC, WBC], 'to be on one's guard against' [BAGD, LN, NICNT; NIV], 'to be on one's guard' [REB], 'to watch out for' [CEV, GW], 'to watch out' [TEV], 'to be careful of' [NCV], 'to keep on the lookout for, to be alert for' [LN], 'to pay attention to' [BAGD, LN]. This verb means to be in a continuous state of readiness to learn of any future danger, need, or error, and to respond appropriately [LN].

c. ἄνθρωπος (LN 9.1) (BAGD 1.b. p. 68). In the plural: 'people' [BECNT, LN, NICNT, NIGTC, WBC; CEV, NCV, NET], 'men' [BAGD, BNTC, CC, NTC, PNTC; ESV, KJV, NASB, NIV, NIV], 'them' [NRSV], 'those who' [TEV], not explicit [NLT, REB]. This noun is conflated with the following clause and translated as specifying the kind of people to avoid: 'people who will take you to court' [CEV], 'people who will hand you over to the Jewish courts' [GW].

d. fut. act. indic. of παραδίδωμι (LN 37.111) (BAGD 1.b. p. 615): 'to hand over' [BAGD, BECNT, BNTC, CC, LN, NICNT, NIGTC, NTC, PNTC, WBC; GW, NASB, NET, NIV, NRSV], 'to be handed over' [NLT, REB], 'to deliver over' [ESV], 'to deliver up' [KJV], 'to turn over to' [BAGD, LN], 'to betray' [LN]. The phrase παραδώσουσιν γὰρ ὑμᾶς εἰς συνέδρια 'they will hand you over to councils' is translated 'they will take you to court' [CEV], 'they will arrest you and take you to court' [NCV; similarly TEV]. This verb means to deliver a person into the control of someone else, involving either the handing over of a presumably guilty person for punishment by authorities or the handing over of an individual to an enemy who will presumably take undue advantage of the victim [LN].

e. συνέδριον (LN **11.79**) (BAGD 3. p. 786): 'council' [NIGTC, NTC; KJV, NET, NRSV], 'local council' [BAGD; NIV], 'city council' [LN], 'council of judges' [LN], 'court' [BECNT, PNTC; CEV, ESV, NASB, NCV, NLT, REB, TEV], 'Jewish court' [GW], 'Sanhedrin' [BNTC, CC, WBC], not explicit [NICNT]. The phrase εἰς συνέδρια 'to councils' is translated 'for trial' [NICNT]. This noun denotes a socio-political group acting as a judicial council [LN].

f. fut. act. indic. of μαστιγόω (LN 19.9) (BAGD 1. p. 495): 'to flog' [BECNT, BNTC, NICNT, NTC, PNTC; ESV, NET, NIV, NRSV, REB], 'to have someone flogged' [NIGTC], 'to be flogged' [NLT], 'to scourge' [BAGD, CC, WBC; KJV, NASB], 'to have someone beaten' [CEV], 'to whip' [LN; GW, NCV, TEV], 'to beat with a whip' [LN], 'to strike with a whip' [BAGD]. This verb means to beat severely with a whip [LN].

QUESTION—What relationship is indicated by δέ 'and'?

It indicates transition to a related idea [CC, EBC, Lns, My, NTC, PNTC]. Presumably those translations that did not translate this conjunction view it as indicating a mild additive relationship and not a significant contrast [NICNT, NIGTC, WBC; CEV, ESV, GW, NCV, NET, NIV, NRSV, REB, TEV]. The dangers in the metaphors of verse 16 are now applied to the situations the disciples will face [EBC, PNTC]. It indicates some level of contrast [BECNT, BNTC; KJV, NASB, NLT].

QUESTION—What is the relationship of the second clause to the first clause?

1. It gives an explanation for the warning to beware of people, which is because they will hand you over, etc. [BECNT, BNTC, CC, NICNT, NIGTC, NTC, PNTC, TRT, WBC; ESV, KJV, NASB, NCV, NET, NIV, NRSV]. It gives an explanation for the warning to beware, which is that they would be handed over, etc, [NLT, REB].

2. It further explains what kind of people to beware of: watch out for people who will hand you over, etc. [CEV, GW, TEV].

QUESTION—Does 'councils' refer to the national Sanhedrin in Jerusalem, or to local councils?

It is referring to smaller, local councils [BNTC, CC, EBC, ICC, Lns, My, NAC, NIBC, NICNT, NIGTC, NTC, PNTC, TH, TRT, WBC]. A local council consisted of twenty-three men, whose task was to keep the peace and also function as a court [Lns, TH]. These are governing councils [NIGTC]. These could be civic councils or synagogue councils [EBC]. Submitting to Roman justice was not optional, whereas submitting to these local councils was required only for those who wanted to take part in Jewish community life [NIGTC].

QUESTION—Do the warnings apply primarily to this mission excursion or to subsequent efforts?

This section seems to focus on future opposition [BNTC, NAC, PNTC]. It refers to the outreach to the Jewish people up to the time of the Roman destruction of Jerusalem in AD 70 [CC]. The earlier part of this discourse is about this limited mission, but some of what Jesus is saying here has a wider perspective that is primarily focused on events up to and including the destruction of Jerusalem, and some of it may even be eschatological [NICNT].

10:18 and you-will-be-led[a] before[b] governors[c] and kings[d] for-the-sake-of[e] me for[f] a-witness[g] to-them and to-(the)-Gentiles.

LEXICON—a. fut. pass. indic. of ἄγω (LN 15.165) (BAGD 2. p. 14): 'to be led' [CC, LN, WBC], 'to be brought' [BECNT, LN, NICNT, NIGTC, PNTC; GW, KJV, NASB, NET, NIV, REB], 'to be brought to trial' [TEV], 'to be dragged' [NTC; CEV, ESV, NRSV], 'to be led away' [BAGD], 'to be led away to trial' [BNTC], 'to be taken to stand' [NCV], 'to be taken into custody, to be arrested' [BAGD]. The phrase ἐπὶ...ἀχθήσεσθε 'you will be led (before)' is translated 'you will stand trial (before)' [NLT]. This verb means to direct or guide the movement of an object, without special regard to point of departure or goal [LN].

b. ἐπί with accusative (LN **83.35**) (BAGD III.1.a.γ. p. 288): 'before' [BAGD, LN; all translations except GW], 'in front of' [GW]. This preposition indicates a position before, with the implication of a relationship of authority [LN].

c. ἡγεμών (LN 37.59) (BAGD 2. p. 343): 'governor' [BAGD, BECNT, BNTC, NICNT, NIGTC, NTC, PNTC, WBC; all versions except CEV, TEV], 'ruler' [CC, LN; CEV, TEV]. This noun denotes one who rules, with the implication of preeminent position [LN].

d. βασιλεύς (LN 37.67) (BAGD 1. p. 136): 'king' [BAGD, LN; all translations]. This noun denotes one who has absolute authority within a particular area and is able to convey this power and authority to a successor [LN].

e. ἕνεκεν (LN 90.43) (BAGD p. 264): 'for the sake of' [BAGD, BECNT, LN, PNTC, WBC; ESV, KJV, NASB, TEV], 'on account of' [BAGD,

BNTC, CC, NIGTC, NTC; NIV, REB], 'because of' [LN, NICNT; CEV, GW, NCV, NET, NRSV]. The phrase ἕνεκεν ἐμοῦ 'for the sake of me' is translated 'because you are my followers' [NLT]. This preposition indicates a participant constituting the reason for an event [LN].
f. εἰς (LN 89.57) (BAGD 4.f. p. 229): 'for' [BNTC, CC, NIGTC, NTC, WBC; KJV], 'as' [BAGD, BECNT, NICNT, PNTC; NASB, NET, NIV, NRSV], 'for the purpose of' [LN], 'in order to' [BAGD, LN], not explicit [CEV, ESV, GW, NCV, NLT, REB, TEV]. This preposition indicates intent, often with the implication of expected result [LN].
g. μαρτύριον (LN 33.262) (BAGD 1.a. p. 493): 'witness' [CC, LN, NICNT, WBC; ESV, NET, NIV], 'testimony' [BAGD, BECNT, BNTC, NIGTC, NTC, PNTC; KJV, NASB, NRSV]. The phrase εἰς μαρτύριον 'for a witness' is translated 'to testify' [GW, REB], 'to tell them...about your faith' [CEV], 'to tell the Good News' [TEV], 'to bear witness' [ESV], 'you will tell them...about me' [NCV], 'this will be your opportunity to tell...about me' [NLT]. This noun denotes the giving of information about a person or an event concerning which the speaker has direct knowledge [LN].

QUESTION—Who are these governors?

The governors spoken of here are rulers of the Gentiles [EBC, Lns, My, NAC], Roman governors [CC, NICNT, TH, WBC]. These rulers were usually Gentiles [BECNT].

QUESTION—Does the dative construction εἰς...αὐτοῖς 'to them' indicate that the witness is *to* them or *against* them?

1. They will be a witness to them [BECNT, BNTC, CC, EBC, ICC, Lns, My, NIBC, NICNT, NIGTC, NTC, PNTC, TRT, WBC; GW, NASB, NET, NIV, NRSV, probably CEV, NCV, NLT, TEV] or a witness before them [ESV, REB].
2. They will be a witness against them [KJV].

QUESTION—To whom does εἰς...αὐτοῖς 'to them' refer?

1. It refers to a witness to the Gentiles, as brought about through trials before governors and kings [NICNT].
2. It refers to a witness to the Jews [Lns, My], who are the principle instigators of the persecutions [Lns].
3. It refers to their witness to governors and kings [BNTC, CC, EBC, ICC, WBC], which probably also includes Jewish authorities [CC]. Their witness will be to Jewish councils and synagogues [NIBC, NIGTC], as well as to Gentile kings and governors and to the Gentiles generally [NIGTC].

10:19 But when they-hand- you -over, do- not -worry-about[a] how or what you-will-say; for it-will-be-given[b] to-you in that hour what to-say. **10:20** For you are not the-ones speaking but the Spirit[c] of- your -Father (will be) the-one speaking in[d] you.

    LEXICON—a. aorist act. subj. of μεριμνάω (LN 25.225) (BAGD 1. p. 505): 'to worry about' [BECNT, LN, NICNT, PNTC; all versions except ESV, KJV], 'to worry' [BNTC, CC], 'to worry as to' [NTC], 'to be worried about' [LN, NIGTC, WBC], 'to take thought' [KJV], 'to be anxious about' [BAGD, LN], 'to be anxious' [ESV], 'to have anxiety, to be unduly concerned' [BAGD]. This verb means to have an anxious concern, based on apprehension about possible danger or misfortune [LN].

    b. fut. pass. indic. of δίδωμι (LN 13.142): 'to be given' [all translations except NLT], 'to be granted' [LN]. This passive verb is translated as active: 'God will give you' [NLT]. The agent of this passive verb is God [Lns, My, PNTC]. This verb means to grant someone the opportunity or occasion to do something [LN].

    c. πνεῦμα (LN 12.18) (BAGD 5.a. p. 676): 'Spirit' [BAGD, LN], 'Spirit of God, Holy Spirit' [LN]. The phrase τὸ πνεῦμα τοῦ πατρός 'the Spirit of your Father' [BECNT, BNTC, CC, NICNT, NIGTC, PNTC, WBC; all versions except CEV] is translated 'the Spirit from your Father' [CEV], 'your Father's Spirit' [NTC]. This noun is a title for the third person of the Trinity [LN].

    d. ἐν (LN 90.6): 'in' [BECNT, BNTC, CC, NICNT, NIGTC, NTC, PNTC; KJV, NASB, REB], 'through' [WBC; ESV, GW, NCV, NET, NIV, NLT, NRSV, TEV], 'by, from' [LN]. The phrase τὸ πνεῦμα τοῦ πατρὸς ὑμῶν τὸ λαλοῦν ἐν ὑμῖν 'the Spirit of your Father will be the one speaking in you' is translated 'The spirit from your Father will tell you what to say' [CEV]. This preposition indicates agent, often with the implication of an agent being used as an instrument, and in some instances relating to general behavior rather than to some specific event [LN].

QUESTION—What relationship is indicated by ἐν 'in'?

    It indicates agency: the Holy Spirit will speak through or by them [BNTC, CC, EBC, ICC, NIBC, TH, WBC; all versions].

10:21 But brother[a] will-betray[b] brother to death and a-father (his) child, and children will-rise-up[c] against parents and put- them -to-death.[d]

    LEXICON—a. ἀδελφός (LN 10.49): 'brother' [LN; all translations except CEV]. The phrase παραδώσει…ἀδελφὸς ἀδελφὸν 'brother will betray brother' is translated 'brothers and sisters will betray one another' [CEV]. This noun denotes a male having the same father and mother as the reference person [LN].

    b. fut. act. indic. of παραδίδωμι (LN 37.111) (BAGD 1.b. p. 615): 'to betray' [BECNT, LN, PNTC; CEV, NASB, NIV, NLT, NRSV], 'to hand over' [BAGD, BNTC, CC, LN, NICNT, NIGTC, WBC; GW, NET, REB,

MATTHEW 10:21

TEV], 'to deliver up' [NTC; KJV], 'to deliver over' [ESV], 'to turn over to' [BAGD, LN], 'to give to be (killed)' [NCV]. This verb means to deliver a person into the control of someone else, involving either the handing over of a presumably guilty person for punishment by authorities or the handing over of an individual to an enemy who will presumably take undue advantage of the victim [LN].

c. fut. mid. indic. of ἐπανίσταμαι (LN 39.34) (BAGD p. 283): 'to rise up against' [BAGD, BECNT, BNTC, CC, NICNT, NIGTC, NTC, PNTC, WBC; KJV, NASB, NET], 'to rise against' [ESV, NRSV], 'to turn against' [CEV, REB, TEV], 'to rebel against' [LN; GW, NIV, NLT], 'to fight against' [NCV], 'to revolt, to engage in insurrection' [LN]. This verb means to rise up in open defiance of authority, with the presumed intention to overthrow it or to act in complete opposition to its demands [LN].

d. fut. act. indic. of θανατόω (LN 20.65) (BAGD 1. p. 351): 'to put to death' [BAGD, BNTC, NICNT], 'to have (someone) put to death' [BECNT, NIGTC, PNTC, WBC; ESV, NCV, NET, NIV, NRSV, TEV], 'to cause to be put to death' [KJV, NASB], 'to kill' [BAGD, CC, LN, NTC; GW], 'to have someone killed' [CEV], 'to cause to be killed' [NLT], 'to send to their death' [REB], 'to execute' [LN]. This verb means to deprive a person of life, with the implication of this being the result of condemnation by legal or quasi-legal procedures [LN].

QUESTION—Does 'put them to death' mean to kill them, or to have them killed?

It means to turn someone over to authorities to have that person put to death [BECNT, ICC, My, NICNT, NIGTC, NTC, PNTC, TH, TRT, WBC; ESV, NCV, NET, NIV, NRSV, TEV]. The guilt is the same, however [NTC].

10:22 And you-will-be hated[a] by all[b] because-of my name;[c] but the-one enduring[d] to (the) end[e] this-one will-be-saved.[f]

LEXICON—a. fut. pass. participle of μισέω (used periphrastically with the verb εἰμί 'to be') (LN 88.198) (BAGD 3. p. 523): 'to be hated' [BAGD, BECNT, BNTC, CC, LN, NICNT, NIGTC, NTC, PNTC, WBC; ESV, KJV, NASB, NET, NRSV], 'to be detested' [LN]. This passive verb is translated as active: 'to hate' [CEV, GW, NCV, NIV, NLT, REB, TEV]. When used periphrastically with the verb it expresses the long duration of the hatred [BAGD]. This verb means to dislike strongly, with the implication of aversion and hostility [LN].

b. πᾶς (LN 59.23) (BAGD 2.a.γ. p. 632): 'all' [BAGD, BNTC, CC, LN, NIGTC, NTC, PNTC; ESV, KJV, NASB, NRSV], 'all people' [NCV], 'all men' [NIV], 'all nations' [NLT], 'everyone' [BAGD, BECNT, WBC; CEV, GW, NET, REB, TEV], 'everybody' [NICNT]. This adjective describes the totality of any object, mass, collective, or extension [LN].

c. ὄνομα (LN 33.126) (BAGD I.4.c.α. p, 572): 'name' [BAGD, LN]. The phrase διὰ τὸ ὄνομά μου 'because of my name' [BECNT, CC, NICNT,

NIGTC, WBC; NASB, NET, NRSV] is also translated 'on account of my name' [PNTC], 'because of me' [CEV, NIV, TEV], 'for my name's sake' [NTC; ESV, KJV], 'because you bear my name' [BAGD, BNTC], 'because you are committed to me' [GW], 'for your allegiance to me' [REB], 'because you are my followers' [NLT], 'because you follow me' [NCV]. This noun denotes the proper name of a person [LN].

d. aorist act. participle of ὑπομένω (LN 25.175) (BAGD 2. p. 845): 'to endure' [BAGD, BECNT, BNTC, CC, LN, NIGTC, NTC, PNTC, WBC; ESV, KJV, NASB, NET, NLT, NRSV, REB], 'to patiently endure' [GW], 'to remain faithful' [NICNT; CEV], 'to keep one's faith' [NCV], 'to stand firm' [NIV], 'to hold out' [TEV], 'to bear up, to demonstrate endurance, to put up with' [LN], 'to remain, to stand one's ground' [BAGD]. This verb means to continue to bear up despite difficulty and suffering [LN].

e. τέλος (LN 67.66) (BAGD 1.d.γ. p. 812): 'end' [BAGD, BECNT, BNTC, LN, NICNT, NIGTC, NTC, PNTC, WBC; all versions]. The phrase 'to the end' is translated 'finally' [CC]. This noun denotes a point of time marking the end of a duration [LN].

f. fut. pass. indic. of σῴζω (LN 21.27) (BAGD 2.b. p. 798): 'to be saved' [BAGD, LN; all translations]. This verb means to cause someone to experience divine salvation [LN].

QUESTION—What does it mean that they will be hated 'by all'?

This is hyperbole [NTC, TRT, WBC], meaning that the hatred will be widespread [EBC, Lns, PNTC, TRT, WBC], that they will be hated by people in general [NTC], hated by all kinds of people [NAC].

QUESTION—Why will Jesus' followers be hated because of Jesus' name?

The world hates Jesus, and because of that it also hates his representatives [NTC]. Jesus' followers will be hated on account of Jesus [EBC, PNTC], that is, because of their connection with him [EBC, ICC, PNTC]. A person's name stands for the person himself and this phrase probably has the same meaning as ἕνεκεν ἐμοῦ 'for the sake of me' in verse 18, both having the idea, 'because you are my followers' [TH]. His followers are committed to Jesus and follow him [GW, NCV, NLT, REB]. They are loyal to him [NAC, NTC].

QUESTION—To what does εἰς τέλος 'to the end' refer?

They must endure to the end of the persecution, which will last until the end of the age, or until the end of their own lives [EBC, NAC, NTC, WBC]. It refers to their enduring until the Parousia, Christ's return [ICC, My]. They must endure to the end of whatever trials they encounter [CC, NIGTC, PNTC, TH]. He wants them to remain undeterred in their loyalty to him during times of persecution [NICNT]. It refers to enduring to the point of death [Lns]. The ambiguity of meaning is probably intentional [EBC].

10:23 But[a] when they-persecute[b] you in this city,[c] flee[d] to the next; for truly I-say to-you, you-will- certainly not[e] -finish[f] the cities of-Israel before[g] the Son of Man comes.

LEXICON—a. δέ (LN 89.94, 89.124): 'but' [BECNT, LN (89.124), NICNT; KJV, NASB], 'and' [CC, LN (89.94), PNTC], 'now' [NTC], 'so' [GW], not explicit [BNTC, NIGTC; CEV, ESV, NCV, NET, NIV, NLT, NRSV, REB, TEV]. This conjunction may indicate contrast [LN (89.124)], or it can indicate an additive relation, but with the possible implication of some contrast [LN (89.94)].

b. pres. act. subj. of διώκω (LN 39.45) (BAGD 2., 3. p. 201): 'to persecute' [BAGD 2, BECNT, BNTC, CC, LN, NICNT, NIGTC, NTC, PNTC; ESV, GW, KJV, NASB, NET, NRSV, TEV], 'to mistreat' [CEV], 'to harass' [LN], 'to drive out, to drive away' [BAGD 3]. This active verb is translated as passive: 'to be persecuted' [NIV, NLT, REB], 'to be treated badly' [NCV]. This verb means to systematically organize a program to oppress and harass people [LN].

c. πόλις (LN 1.88) (BAGD 1. p. 685): 'city' [BAGD, BNTC, CC, LN, NTC; GW, KJV, NASB, NCV], 'town' [BECNT, LN, NICNT, NIGTC, PNTC; CEV, ESV, NLT, NRSV, REB, TEV], 'place' [NET, NIV]. This noun denotes a population center, in contrast with a rural area or countryside and without specific reference to size [LN].

d. pres. act. impera. of φεύγω (LN 15.61) (BAGD 1. p. 855): 'to flee' [BAGD, BECNT, BNTC, CC, LN, NICNT, NIGTC, NTC, PNTC; ESV, GW, KJV, NASB, NET, NIV, NLT, NRSV], 'to take refuge' [REB], 'to hurry' [CEV], 'to run to' [NCV], 'to run away' [LN; TEV]. This verb means to move quickly from a point or area in order to avoid presumed danger or difficulty [LN].

e. οὐ μή. The double negative οὐ μή 'certainly not' [CC, NTC] marks an emphatic negation. It is translated 'not' [BECNT, BNTC, NICNT, NIGTC, PNTC; ESV, KJV, NASB, NCV, NET, NIV, NRSV, TEV], not explicit [CEV, GW, NLT, REB]. This sentence is restructured as a positive statement: the Son of Man will come before you have finished, etc. [CEV, GW, NLT, REB].

f. aorist act. subj. of τελέω (LN 68.22) (BAGD 1. p. 810): 'to finish' [BAGD, LN], 'to finish going through' [BECNT, NTC, PNTC; NASB, NCV, NET, NIV], 'to finish visiting' [BNTC], 'to finish with' [NIGTC], 'to finish your work' [TEV], 'to complete' [BAGD, CC, LN], 'to complete (one's) mission' [WBC], 'to go through' [NICNT; ESV, GW, NRSV, REB], 'to go over' [KJV], 'to go to' [CEV], 'to reach' [NLT], 'to end, to accomplish' [LN]. This verb means to bring an activity to a successful finish [LN].

g. ἕως (LN 67.119) (BAGD I.1.b. p. 334): 'before' [NICNT, NTC, PNTC, WBC; all versions except KJV, NASB], 'until' [BAGD, BECNT, BNTC, CC, LN; NASB], 'till' [KJV]. This conjunction indicates the continuous extent of time up to a point [LN].

QUESTION—What is it that they will not finish before the Son of Man comes?
  Jesus is saying that they would not complete their mission of witness to Israel [CC, Lns, My, NAC, WBC], or to all the towns of Galilee [NICNT]. Jesus is saying they will not finish fleeing from one town to the next, meaning that they will always experience persecution, but there will always be somewhere to go [NIGTC].

QUESTION—What is the 'coming' of the Son of Man to which Jesus here refers?
  The coming of the Son of Man is the same as the coming of the kingdom, which occurs in stages: Jesus was born as a king, he was granted all authority as a result of his passion and resurrection, and there are times of his coming in judgment, whether within history or at the end of history [EBC].
  1. It refers to the end-time Parousia, his second coming [BNTC, ICC, My, NAC, NIGTC, TH].
  2. It refers to Jesus' coming in judgment at the time of the destruction of Jerusalem in AD 70 [CC, EBC, Lns, WBC]. Jesus was saying that they would not complete their ministry to all the towns of Israel prior to that event a few decades later [CC, EBC, WBC]. This refers to Christ's coming in judgment against the Jews when Jerusalem was sacked and the temple was destroyed. It was then the age of the kingdom came into its own [EBC].
  3. It refers to his resurrection and exaltation [NIBC, NICNT, PNTC]. This is his coming in triumph after his resurrection [NIBC]. Here the verb for 'come' is ἔρχομαι, which is unrelated to 'Parousia', the word normally used for Jesus' return in glory; in this passage it refers to his coming before God to be enthroned as the universal king at his resurrection, ascension, and exaltation to glory, in keeping with what was described in Daniel 7 where the one like a son of man came before God to be enthroned as king [NICNT]. Jesus was telling his disciples to carry on with the task he had sent them out to do and they will not have completed it before his work on earth has reached its climax when he comes back from the dead [PNTC].
  4. It refers to his coming to them after his resurrection, as well as to his second coming. This is in keeping with prophetic foreshadowing, in which several events of a similar nature (though separated in time) can be referred to in a single prophetic discourse [NTC].

DISCOURSE UNIT—10:24–39 [NASB]. The topic is the meaning of discipleship.

10:24 **A-disciple[a] is not above[b] the teacher[c] nor a-slave[d] above his master.[e]**
LEXICON—a. μαθητής (LN 36.38) (BAGD 1. p. 485): 'disciple' [BECNT, BNTC, CC, LN, NICNT, NIGTC, PNTC, WBC; CEV, ESV, KJV, NASB, NET, NLT, NRSV], 'follower' [LN], 'pupil' [BAGD, NTC; REB, TEV], 'student' [GW, NCV, NIV], 'apprentice' [BAGD]. This noun denotes a person who is a disciple or follower of someone [LN].

b. ὑπέρ with accusative (LN **87.30**) (BAGD 2. p. 839): 'above' [BECNT, CC, **LN**, NIGTC, PNTC, WBC; ESV, KJV, NASB, NIV, NRSV], 'greater than' [NICNT; NET, NLT, TEV], 'better than' [CEV, GW, NCV], 'superior to' [BAGD, BNTC, LN]. The phrase 'is not above' is translated 'does not outrank' [NTC], 'no (pupil) ranks above' [REB]. This adjective describes a status which is superior to another status [LN].

c. διδάσκαλος (LN **33.243**) (BAGD p. 191): 'teacher' [BAGD, LN; all translations except KJV], 'master' [KJV], 'instructor' [LN]. Note that 'master' may be used in the British sense for 'teacher' [BAGD]. This noun denotes one who provides instruction [LN].

d. δοῦλος (LN 87.76) (BAGD 1.a. p. 205): 'slave' [BAGD, BECNT, CC, LN, NICNT, NIGTC, NTC, PNTC; CEV, GW, NASB, NET, NLT, NRSV, TEV], 'servant' [BNTC, WBC; ESV, KJV, NCV, NIV, REB], 'bondservant' [LN]. This noun denotes one who is a slave in the sense of becoming the property of an owner (though in ancient times it was frequently possible for a slave to earn his freedom) [LN].

e. κύριος (LN 57.12) (BAGD 1.a.β. p. 459): 'master' [LN; all translations except GW, KJV], 'owner' [BAGD, LN; GW], 'lord' [LN; KJV]. This noun denotes one who owns and controls property, especially including servants and slaves, with important supplementary semantic components of high status and respect [LN].

10:25 (It is) enough[a] for- the -disciple that he-be[b] like[c] his teacher or a- slave (to be) like his master. If they-called the master-of-the-house[d] Beelzebul,[e] how-much[f] more his household-members.[g]

LEXICON—a. ἀρκετός (LN **59.45**) (BAGD p. 107): 'enough' [BECNT, BNTC, NICNT, NIGTC, PNTC, WBC; CEV, ESV, GW, KJV, NASB, NET, NIV, NRSV], 'sufficient' [CC, **LN**], 'adequate' [LN]. The phrase ἀρκετὸν τῷ μαθητῇ '(it is) enough for the disciple' is translated 'let the pupil be satisfied' [NTC], 'a pupil should be satisfied' [TEV], 'the pupil should be content' [REB], 'a student should be satisfied' [NCV], 'students are (to be like)' [NLT]. This adjective describes what is sufficient for some purpose and accordingly resulting in satisfaction [LN].

b. aorist mid. (deponent = act.) subj. of γίνομαι (LN 41.1) (BAGD II.1. p. 160): 'to be' [BAGD, BECNT, CC, NIGTC, PNTC, WBC; CEV, ESV, KJV, NIV, NLT, NRSV], 'to become' [BAGD, BNTC, NICNT; GW, NASB, NCV, NET, TEV], 'to conduct oneself, to behave' [LN]. The phrase ἵνα γένηται ὡς ὁ διδάσκαλος αὐτοῦ '(that) he be like his teacher' is translated 'to share his teacher's lot' [NTC; REB]. This verb means to exist and to conduct oneself, with the particular manner specified by the context [LN].

c. ὡς (LN 64.12): 'like' [BECNT, CC, LN, NICNT, NIGTC, WBC; all versions except KJV, REB], 'as' [BNTC, LN, PNTC; KJV], not explicit [NTC; REB]. This conjunction is a relatively weak marker of a relationship between events or states [LN].

d. οἰκοδεσπότης (LN 57.14) (BAGD p. 558): 'master of the house' [BAGD, BECNT, BNTC, NICNT, NIGTC, NTC, WBC; ESV, KJV, NRSV], 'master of the household' [LN; NLT], 'master' [REB], 'head of the house' [PNTC; NASB, NET, NIV], 'owner of the house' [GW], 'head of the family' [CEV, NCV, TEV], 'householder' [CC]. This noun denotes one who owns and manages a household, including family, servants, and slaves [LN].
e. Βεελζεβούλ (LN 93.68) (BAGD p. 139): 'Beelzebul' [BECNT, BNTC, LN, NICNT, NTC, PNTC; ESV, GW, NASB, NCV, NET, NRSV, REB, TEV], 'Beelzeboul' [CC, NIGTC, WBC], 'Beelzebub' [KJV, NIV], 'the prince of demons' [NLT], 'Satan' [CEV]. This proper noun is the name of the Devil as the prince of the demons [LN].
f. πόσος (LN 59.17) (BAGD 1. p. 694): 'how much' [BAGD, BECNT, BNTC, LN, NICNT, NIGTC, NTC, PNTC; NET, NIV, REB], 'much' [CC], 'how extensive' [LN], not explicit [CEV, GW, NCV]. The phrase πόσῳ μᾶλλον 'how much more' is translated 'how much more will they malign/defame' [WBC; ESV, NASB, NET, NRSV], 'how much more shall they call them of his household' [KJV], 'what will they say about' [CEV], 'they will certainly call (the family members) the same name' [GW], '(other members of the family) will be called worse names' [NCV; similarly TEV], '(the members of my household) will be called by even worse names' [NLT]. This interrogative adjective refers to quantity [LN].
g. οἰκιακός (LN 10.11) (BAGD p. 557): 'member of a household' [BAGD, BECNT, BNTC, CC, NICNT, NTC, PNTC, WBC; NASB, NET, NIV, NLT], 'member of a family' [LN; TEV], 'relative' [LN]. This plural noun is translated 'those of his household' [NIGTC; ESV, NRSV], 'them of his household' [KJV], 'his household' [REB], 'family members' [GW], 'other members of the family' [NCV], 'the rest of the family' [CEV]. This noun denotes one who belongs to a particular household or extended family [LN].

QUESTION—Who is the subject of 'they called'?

It is the Jewish leaders who called him that [ICC]. The Pharisees called him that [Lns]. It is a general term, referring to those in society around him [NIGTC].

QUESTION—What does the name 'Beelzebul' mean?

It is being used as another name for Satan [BNTC, CC, EBC, Lns, My, NICNT, NIGTC, NTC, PNTC, TH, WBC; CEV], the prince of the demons [ICC, LN, NIBC, NTC]. The Greek word οἰκοδεσπότης 'master of the house' is a pun on the meaning of 'Beelzebul' [NIBC] since the name of a Canaanite deity was 'Beelzebul,' meaning 'lord of the dwelling or house' [My, NTC], The Jews would pronounce Beelzebul slightly differently so that it meant 'lord of dung' [EBC, NTC, PNTC]. The name 'Beelzebub' means 'lord of the flies' [CC, NAC, PNTC, WBC], and was used as a mocking way of referring to 'Beelzebul' [CC, NAC].

DISCOURSE UNIT—10:26-33 [ESV, NET, NRSV]. The topic is have no fear [ESV], fear God, not man [NET], whom to fear [NRSV].

DISCOURSE UNIT—10:26-31 [ICC; CEV, NCV, TEV]. The topic is fear God, not people [NCV], whom to fear [TEV], the one to fear [CEV], there is no need to fear [ICC].

10:26 Therefore do- not -fear[a] them; for nothing is concealed[b] which will- not -be-uncovered[c] and hidden[d] which will- not -be-made-known.[e]

- LEXICON—a. aorist pass. subj. of φοβέομαι (LN 25.252) (BAGD 1.b.α. p. 863): 'to fear' [BAGD, BNTC, BECNT, CC, LN, NIGTC, WBC; KJV, NASB], 'to have fear' [ESV, NRSV], 'to be afraid' [LN, NICNT, NTC, PNTC; CEV, GW, NCV, NET, NIV, NLT, REB, TEV]. This verb means to be in a state of fearing [LN].
- b. perf. pass. participle of καλύπτω (LN **28.79**) (BAGD 2.b. p. 401): 'to be concealed' [BECNT, CC, LN, NIGTC; NASB, NIV], 'to be hidden' [BAGD, BNTC, **LN**, WBC; CEV, NCV, NET], 'to be covered' [NICNT, NTC, PNTC; ESV, GW, KJV, NLT], 'to be covered up' [NRSV, REB, TEV], 'to be kept secret' [**LN**]. This verb means to cause something not to be known [LN].
- c. fut. pass. indic. of ἀποκαλύπτω (LN 28.38) (BAGD 1. p. 92): 'to be uncovered' [CC, NTC, PNTC; NRSV, REB, TEV], 'to be revealed' [BAGD, BECNT, LN, NICNT, WBC; ESV, KJV, NASB, NET, NLT], 'to be disclosed' [BAGD, BNTC, LN, NIGTC; NIV], 'to be found out' [CEV], 'to be exposed' [GW], 'to be shown' [NCV], 'to be brought to light' [BAGD], 'to be made fully known' [LN]. This verb means to cause something to be fully known [LN].
- d. κρυπτός (LN 28.69) (BAGD 1. p. 454): 'hidden' [BAGD, BECNT, CC, LN, NICNT, NIGTC, NTC, PNTC; ESV, NASB, NIV, REB], 'hid' [KJV], 'secret' [BAGD, BNTC, LN, WBC; GW, NCV, NET, NLT, NRSV], 'not able to be made known' [LN]. This adjective is also translated as a noun: '(every) secret' [CEV, TEV]. This adjective describes not being able to be known, in view of the fact that it has been kept secret [LN].
- e. fut. pass. indic. of γινώσκω (LN 28.1) (BAGD 2.a. p. 161): 'to be made known' [BNTC, NTC, PNTC, WBC; GW, NCV, NET, NIV, REB, TEV], 'to be made known to all' [NLT], 'to become known' [BAGD, BECNT, NIGTC; NRSV], 'to be known' [CC, LN, NICNT; CEV, ESV, KJV, NASB], 'to be known about' [LN], 'to be found out' [BAGD]. This verb means to possess information about [LN].

QUESTION—What relationship is indicated by οὖν 'therefore'?

It indicates a conclusion to be drawn from the statements made in the previous verse [EBC, Lns, NIGTC, PNTC]. Since Jesus will suffer first, before they do, they should not fear it themselves [EBC]. Because Jesus is not dismayed, they should not be dismayed either [Lns, PNTC].

QUESTION—What kinds of things are now hidden, but will be revealed later?
1. It refers to hidden sins [BECNT, BNTC CC, ICC, Lns, NAC, NTC, PNTC], to the sins that people think are hidden [CC, NAC], and believe they have gotten away with [NAC]. It is the sins of the persecutors [BECNT, NTC], including who they are and how they will be punished [NTC]. It is the plots of their opponents [PNTC]. What is now hidden is human wickedness as well as loyalty to Christ [BNTC]. It refers to Christ's enemies and their secrets, but also to the gospel and the disciples themselves [Lns]. All lies will be exposed [ICC]. It also refers to the secret of God's plan in Christ, and the presence of God's rule [CC].
2. It is the gospel, in keeping with the topic of the following verse [EBC, My, NICNT, TH, TRT, WBC]. It is the message about God's kingdom and rule [TRT]. The truth of the gospel will eventually emerge at the end, so they might as well make it known now [EBC].

10:27 What I-say to-you in the darkness[a] speak[b] in the light,[c] and what you-hear in the ear[d] proclaim[e] on the housetops.[f]

LEXICON—a. σκοτία (LN 14.53, **28.71**) (BAGD 1. p. 757): 'darkness' [BAGD, BECNT, BNTC, CC, LN (14.53), NIGTC, PNTC, WBC; KJV, NASB, NLT], 'dark' [BAGD, NICNT, NTC; all versions except KJV, NASB, NLT]. The phrase 'in the darkness' is translated 'secretly' [**LN** (28.71)], 'in secret, in private, privately' [LN (28.71)]. This noun denotes a condition resulting from the partial or complete absence of light [LN (14.53)], and the idiomatic phrase ἐν τῇ σκοτίᾳ 'in the darkness' pertains to not being able to be known by the public but known by some in-group or by those immediately involved [LN (28.71)].

b. aorist act. impera. of λέγω (LN 33.69) (BAGD I.1.a. p. 468): 'to speak' [BECNT, BECNT, BNTC, CC, LN, PNTC, WBC; KJV, NASB, NIV], 'to speak out' [NICNT], 'to say' [BAGD, LN, NIGTC; ESV], 'to tell' [BAGD, LN, NTC; CEV, GW, NCV, NET, NRSV], 'to shout abroad' [NLT], 'to repeat' [REB, TEV]. This verb means to speak or talk, with apparent focus upon the content of what is said [LN].

c. φῶς (LN 14.36, **28.64**) (BAGD 1.a. p. 871): 'light' [BAGD, BECNT, BNTC, CC, LN (14.36), NICNT, NIGTC, PNTC, WBC; CEV, ESV, KJV, NASB, NCV, NET, NRSV], 'daylight' [GW, NIV], 'broad daylight' [NTC; REB, TEV]. This noun denotes light, in contrast with darkness, usually in relation to some source of light such as the sun, moon, fire, lamp, etc. [LN (14.36)]. The idiomatic phrase ἐν τῷ φωτί 'in the light' is translated 'when daybreak comes' [NLT], 'publicly' [**LN**], 'in public' [LN]. It describes being widely known in view of the events in question having taken place in public [LN (28.64)].

d. οὖς (LN 8.24, **24.67**) (BAGD 1. p. 595): 'ear' [BAGD, LN (8.24)]. The phrase εἰς τὸ οὖς 'in the ear' [KJV] is also translated 'into the ear' [CC], 'whispered' [PNTC; CEV, ESV, GW, NRSV, REB], 'whispered into your ear' [NTC], 'whispered in your ear' [BECNT, BNTC, NICNT, WBC;

NASB, NCV, NET, NIV], 'privately in the ear' [NIGTC], 'in secret' [**LN** (24.67)], 'in private' [TEV]. The phrase εἴπατε ἐν τῷ φωτί 'what you hear in your ear' is translated 'what I whisper in your ear' [NLT]. The idiomatic phrase εἰς τὸ οὖς 'in the ear' means to hear something in a secret setting [LN (24.67)].
   e. aorist act. impera. of κηρύσσω (LN 33.206) (BAGD 2.b.β. p. 431): 'to proclaim' [BECNT, LN, NICNT, NTC, PNTC, WBC; ESV, NASB, NET, NIV, NRSV], 'to preach' [BNTC, CC, NICNT; KJV], 'to announce' [LN; CEV, TEV], 'to shout' [GW, NCV, REB], 'to shout for all to hear' [NLT], 'to proclaim aloud, to mention publicly, to spread widely' [BAGD]. This verb means to announce in a formal or official manner by means of a herald or one who functions as a herald [LN].
   f. δῶμα (LN 7.51, **28.64**) (BAGD p. 210): 'housetop' [BAGD, BECNT, BNTC, LN (7.51), NTC, PNTC; all versions except NIV], 'rooftop' [CC, NICNT, NIGTC, WBC], 'roof' [BAGD; NIV]. The phrase 'on the housetops' is translated 'publicly' [**LN** (28.64)], 'in public' [LN (28.64)]. This noun denotes the area on the top of a flat-roof house [LN]. The idiomatic phrase ἐπὶ τῶν δωμάτων 'on the housetops' describes what is widely known in view of the events in question having taken place in public [LN].
QUESTION—What is it that they are supposed to proclaim openly?
   They are to proclaim what Jesus taught them [BECNT, BNTC, Lns, NICNT, PNTC], the message of God's kingdom and rule [TRT], the counsels of the law and gospel of God [CC], the truth [ICC]. They are to proclaim the gospel [NAC, WBC].

10:28 **And do- not -fear those-killing^a the body,^b but not being-able to kill the soul^c; but rather fear the-one being-able to-destroy^d both soul and body in hell.^e**

LEXICON—a. pres. act. participle of ἀποκτείνω (LN 20.61): 'to kill' [BECNT, BNTC, CC, LN, NICNT, NIGTC, NTC, PNTC; all versions], 'to put to death' [WBC]. This verb means to cause someone's death, normally by violent means, with or without intent and with or without legal justification [LN].
   b. σῶμα (LN 8.1) (BAGD 1.b. p. 799): 'body' [BAGD, LN; all translations except CEV]. The clause 'do not fear those killing the body' is translated 'Don't be afraid of people. They can kill you (but)' [CEV]. This noun denotes the physical body of persons, animals, or plants, either dead or alive [LN].
   c. ψυχή (LN 26.4) (BAGD 1.c. p. 893): 'soul' [BAGD, LN; all translations], 'inner self, mind, thoughts, feelings, heart, being' [LN]. This noun denotes the essence of life in terms of thinking, willing, and feeling [LN].
   d. aorist act. infin. of ἀπόλλυμι (LN **20.31**) (BAGD 1.a.α. p. 95): 'to destroy' [BAGD, LN; all translations], 'to ruin' [LN]. This verb means to

374   MATTHEW 10:28

    destroy or to cause the destruction of persons, objects, or institutions [LN].
- e. γέεννα (LN 1.21) (BAGD p. 153): 'hell' [BAGD, BECNT, LN, NICNT, NTC, PNTC; all versions], 'Gehenna' [BAGD, BNTC, CC, LN, NIGTC, WBC]. This noun denotes a place of punishment for the dead [LN].

QUESTION—Who is the one who can destroy body and soul in hell?
    It is God who can destroy body and soul in hell [BECNT, BNTC, CC, EBC, ICC, Lns, My, NAC, NIBC, NICNT, NIGTC, NTC, PNTC, TH, TRT, WBC; CEV, NLT, TEV]. Only God has this authority [PNTC].

QUESTION—Does this statement teach or imply the doctrine of annihilation of the wicked?
1. This verse does not teach annihilation [BECNT, NAC, NTC, PNTC]. The destruction described is an eternal state of punishment for body and soul [BECNT, NTC, PNTC], for the whole person [BECNT, PNTC], not a literal destruction of soul and body [WBC]. This is eternal suffering [NAC], everlasting destruction [My].
2. The destruction is probably an annihilation [NICNT].

QUESTION—What is the soul?
    It is the person's true self [BNTC, NIBC, NICNT, NIGTC, TH], the seat of the spiritual life [Lns]. It transcends earthly life and continues on after death [PNTC]. It is the immaterial element of the human being, and is sometimes called the spirit [NTC]. Here it refers to the inner person as destined either for salvation or damnation [EBC]. In Scripture 'soul' and 'spirit' are more or less used synonymously [Lns, NAC, NTC]. We must be careful though of thinking too much of a division between body and soul [NIGTC].

10:29 Are- not -sold two sparrows[a] for-a-penny[b]? And not one of them falls to the ground apart-from[c] your Father. **10:30** But even the hairs of- your head all are numbered.[d] **10:31** Therefore do- not -fear; you-are- worth-more[e] than-many sparrows.

LEXICON—a. στρουθίον (LN **4.46**) (BAGD p. 771): 'sparrow' [BAGD, BECNT, BNTC, CC, **LN**, NIGTC, NTC, PNTC, WBC; all versions], 'little bird' [NICNT].
- b. ἀσσάριον (LN **6.77**) (BAGD p. 117): 'penny' [BECNT, **LN**, PNTC, WBC; all versions except KJV, NASB, NLT], 'cent' [BAGD, NTC; NASB], 'assarion' [BAGD, BNTC, CC, LN, NIGTC], 'pence' [NICNT], 'farthing' [KJV], 'copper coin' [NLT]. This noun denotes a Roman copper coin worth 1/16 of a denarius [LN].
- c. ἄνευ (LN **89.120**) (BAGD 1. p. 65): 'apart from' [BECNT, LN, PNTC; ESV, NASB, NRSV], 'apart from the will of' [NET, NIV], 'without' [BAGD, CC, **LN**; KJV], 'without the knowledge of' [BNTC, NICNT; REB], 'without the consent of' [NIGTC, WBC; TEV], 'without the knowledge and consent of' [BAGD], 'without the will of' [NTC], 'without the permission of' [GW], 'independent of' [LN]. The phrase ἄνευ τοῦ πατρὸς ὑμῶν 'apart from your Father' is translated 'without

your Father knowing it' [NCV, NLT], 'your Father knows (when)' [CEV]. This preposition indicates negatively linked elements [LN]. In Matthew 10:29 the phrase is elliptical, for it presumes some type of involvement by God in such an event. Some take this to mean 'without your Father's consent', while others interpret it to mean 'without your Father's knowledge.' The particular manner or mode of involvement by God must depend upon the broader context and not upon the meaning of ἄνευ 'apart from' [LN].

d. perf. pass. participle of ἀριθμέω (LN **60.3**) (BAGD p. 106): 'to be numbered' [BECNT, BNTC, CC, **LN**, NICNT, NTC, WBC; ESV, KJV, NASB, NET, NIV, NLT], 'to be counted' [BAGD, LN, NIGTC, PNTC; CEV, GW, NRSV, REB, TEV]. The phrase αἱ τρίχες τῆς κεφαλῆς πᾶσαι ἠριθμημέναι εἰσίν 'even the hairs of your head all are numbered' is translated 'God knows how many hairs are on your head' [NCV]. This verb means to employ numbers in determining a quantity [LN].

e. pres. act. indic. of διαφέρω (LN 65.6) (BAGD 2.b. p. 190): 'to be worth more than' [BAGD, BNTC, CC, NICNT, NTC, PNTC, WBC; GW, NIV, REB], 'to be worth much more than' [CEV, NCV, TEV], 'to be more valuable than' [BECNT; NASB, NET], 'to be more valuable to God than' [NLT], 'to be of more value than' [ESV, KJV, NRSV], 'to be of more importance than' [NIGTC], 'to be valuable, to have worth' [LN], 'to be superior to' [BAGD]. This verb means to be of considerable value, in view of having certain distinctive characteristics [LN].

QUESTION—Does 'apart from your Father' mean simply that God knows about it, or that he is actively involved in that event?

It means 'apart from his will' [EBC, ICC, Lns, NAC, NIGTC, NTC, TH]. He is active in all that happens [BNTC, NIGTC]. Here it speaks of his awareness of what happens [BECNT, CC]. It speaks of both his knowledge as well as his will [TRT, WBC]. Nothing occurs that is outside of God's providential care and knowledge, nor does it frustrate his purposes [NICNT].

QUESTION—Does 'numbered' mean that they are counted, or that every one has been assigned a specific number?

1. It means that they are counted [EBC, ICC, NAC, NICNT, NIGTC, NTC, PNTC, TH, TRT, probably WBC].
2. Not only are all counted, each has its own number [Lns].

DISCOURSE UNIT—10:32-42 [ICC; NCV]. The topic is tell people about your faith [NCV], confession, conflict, compensation [ICC].

DISCOURSE UNIT—10:32-33 [CEV, TEV]. The topic is confessing and rejecting Christ [TEV], telling others about Christ [CEV].

10:32 Therefore everyone[a] who will-acknowledge[b] me before[c] people[d], I-also will-acknowledge before my father in the heavens; **10:33** but whoever would-deny[e] me before people, I-also will-deny him before my father in the heavens.

    LEXICON—a. πᾶς (LN 59.24) (BAGD 1.c.γ. p. 632): 'everyone' [BAGD], 'every, any' [LN]. The phrase πᾶς...ὅστις 'everyone who' [BAGD, BNTC, CC, NICNT, NIGTC, PNTC, WBC; ESV, NASB, NLT, NRSV], is translated 'whoever' [BAGD, NTC; NET, NIV, REB], 'whosoever' [KJV], 'anyone who' [BECNT, LN], 'all those who' [NCV], 'those who' [TEV], 'that person who' [GW]. This third person phrase is also translated as second person in a conditional clause: 'if you' [CEV]. This pronoun denotes any one of a totality [LN].

    b. fut. act. indic. of ὁμολογέω (LN **33.274**) (BAGD 4. p. 568): 'to acknowledge' [BAGD, NICNT, NIGTC, PNTC, WBC; ESV, GW, NET, NIV, NLT, NRSV, REB], 'to confess' [BAGD, BECNT, BNTC, CC, **LN**, NTC; KJV, NASB], 'to declare' [BAGD], 'to profess' [LN]. The phrase 'will acknowledge me' is translated 'tell (others) that you belong to me' [CEV], 'stand...and say they believe in me' [NCV], 'declare they belong to me' [TEV]. This verb means to express openly one's allegiance to a proposition or person [LN].

    c. ἔμπροσθεν (LN 83.33) (BAGD 2.b. p. 257): 'before' [BAGD, BECNT, BNTC, CC, LN, NICNT, NIGTC, NTC, PNTC, WBC; ESV, KJV, NASB, NCV, NET, NIV, NRSV, REB], 'in the presence of' [BAGD], 'in front of' [LN; GW], not explicit [CEV, NLT, TEV]. This preposition indicates a position in front of an object, whether animate or inanimate, which is regarded as having a spatial orientation of front and back [LN].

    d. ἄνθρωπος (LN 9.1) (BAGD 1.a.β. p. 68). 'human being' [BAGD, LN]. In the plural: 'people' [BECNT, LN, NICNT; NET], 'other people' [NIGTC], 'others' [WBC; CEV, GW, NCV, NRSV, REB], 'men' [BAGD, BNTC, CC, NTC, PNTC; ESV, KJV, NASB, NIV], 'mankind' [LN]. The phrase 'before people' is translated 'publicly' [NLT, TEV]. This noun denotes a human being, normally an adult [LN]. In the singular: 'person, human being, individual' [LN].

    e. fut. mid. (deponent = act.) of ἀρνέομαι (LN **33.277**, 34.48) (BAGD 3.2. p. 107, 3.c. p. 108): 'to deny' [BAGD, BECNT, BNTC, CC, LN (**33.277**, 34.48), NICNT, NIGTC, NTC, WBC; ESV, KJV, NASB, NET, NLT, NRSV], 'to disown' [BAGD, PNTC; NIV, REB], 'to repudiate' [BAGD], 'to reject' [CEV, TEV]. The phrase 'would deny me' is translated 'tells others that he doesn't know me' [GW], 'say they do not believe in me' [NCV]. This verb means to say that one does not know about or is in any way related to a person or event [LN 33.277], or it means to deny any relationship of association with someone [LN 34.48].

QUESTION—What relationship is indicated by οὖν 'therefore'?

    It indicates a conclusion to be drawn [BECNT, Lns, NIGTC]. It indicates a conclusion to be drawn from verses 29–30, which is that the disciples' knowledge of their value to God should motivate them not to fear persecution [BECNT]. It indicates a conclusion to be drawn from verses 25–31, that they should not fear persecution [NIGTC]. The conclusion drawn from what has preceded is in the form of a glorious promise [Lns].

QUESTION—What does it mean to acknowledge Jesus?

It means to acknowledge openly that Jesus is Lord of one's life [NTC], to accept his message and follow him in discipleship [WBC]. It is to acknowledge that one belongs to him [Lns, NIBC, NIGTC], follows him [TH, TRT], or believes in him [TRT]. It is to acknowledge him publicly [EBC], to declare allegiance openly to him [NAC, PNTC], and to be faithful in that allegiance to the point of death [NAC]. It is to acknowledge and maintain loyalty to Jesus despite human opposition and hostility [BECNT, NICNT]. It is to preach faithfully and remain loyal [BNTC]. It is to embrace his person, work, and teaching [Lns]. It means to confess that he is the Son of God, the Messiah, and the ransom for sinners [CC].

QUESTION—What does it mean to deny Jesus?

It means to repudiate or disown him [BECNT, EBC, WBC], which is apostasy [CC, WBC], and rejecting God himself [WBC]. It is to fail to maintain loyalty to Jesus because of pressure from public opinion [NICNT]. It is to refuse to be his follower, or to deny that one is his follower [TH], to deny believing in him [TRT]. It is to reject him [BECNT, NAC, PNTC], to disown him [NTC, PNTC], to repudiate him, refusing to acknowledge him [NTC]. It is to side with his opponents [PNTC], to allow fear to cause them to dilute their message or to stop preaching it altogether [BNTC]. It is to fail to confess him because of fear [Lns].

DISCOURSE UNIT—10:34–39 [CEV, ESV, NET, NRSV, TEV]. The topic is not peace, but a sword [ESV, NET, NRSV, TEV], not peace, but trouble [CEV].

10:34 Do- not -think[a] that I-came[b] to bring[c] peace[d] upon the earth; I-came not to bring peace but a-sword.[e]

LEXICON—a. aorist act. subj. of νομίζω (LN 31.29) (BAGD 2. p. 541): 'to think' [BAGD, BECNT, CC, LN, NTC, PNTC; all versions except NIV, NLT], 'to suppose' [BAGD, BNTC, LN, NICNT; NIV], 'to imagine' [LN, WBC; NLT], 'to make (the) judgment' [NIGTC], 'to believe' [BAGD, LN], 'to presume, to assume' [LN]. This verb means to regard something as presumably true, but without particular certainty [LN].

b. aorist act. indic. of ἔρχομαι (LN **15.81**) (BAGD I.1.a. p. 311): 'to come' [BAGD, **LN**; all translations]. This aorist tense verb is translated as perfect tense: 'have come' [BECNT; NET, NIV, NRSV, REB, TEV]. This verb means to move toward or up to the reference point of the viewpoint character or event [LN].

c. aorist. act. infin. of βάλλω (LN **13.14**) (BAGD 2.b. p. 131): 'to bring' [BAGD, BECNT, BNTC, CC, NIGTC, NTC, PNTC, WBC; all versions except KJV], 'to establish' [NICNT], 'to send' [KJV], 'to bring about'

[**LN**], 'to cause' [LN]. This verb means to cause a state or condition, with focus upon the suddenness or force of the action [LN].
  d. εἰρήνη (LN 22.42) (BAGD 1.b. p. 227): 'peace' [BAGD, LN; all translations], 'harmony' [BAGD], 'tranquility' [LN]. This noun denotes a set of favorable circumstances involving peace and tranquility [LN].
  e. μάχαιρα (LN 6.33, **55.6, 39.25**) (BAGD 2. p. 496): 'sword' [BAGD, LN (6.33); all versions except CEV, GW], 'trouble' [CEV], 'conflict' [**LN** (55.6); GW], 'discord' [**LN** (39.25)], 'violence, strife' [LN (39.25)], 'war, fighting' [LN]. This noun denotes a relatively short sword used for cutting and stabbing [LN (6.33)], or by extension a state of discord and strife [LN (39.25)], or of war [LN (55.6)].

QUESTION—What is implied by the statement 'I came'?

It implies his authority [WBC], and expresses a sense of mission [NICNT]. It speaks of Christ's coming into the world [Lns, NTC, PNTC], implying his preexistence [PNTC]. It expresses how he understood his own mission in terms of Christological and eschatological awareness [EBC].

10:35 **For I-came to turn^a a-man against^b his father and a-daughter against her mother and a-daughter-in-law against her mother-in-law, 10:36 and (the) enemies^c of-the man (will be) his household-members.^d**

LEXICON—a. aorist act. infin. of διχάζω (LN **39.41**) (BAGD p. 200): 'to turn' [BAGD, BECNT, BNTC, NIGTC; CEV, GW, NIV], 'to set' [NTC; ESV, NASB, NET, NLT, NRSV, REB, TEV], 'to set at variance' [KJV], 'to divide' [CC, NICNT, PNTC, WBC], 'to separate, to cause a separation' [BAGD], 'to stir up in rebellion against' [**LN**], 'to incite to revolt, to cause to rebel' [LN]. The phrase 'I came to turn a man against' is translated 'I have come so that a son will be against' [NCV]. This verb means to cause people to rebel against, or to reject authority [LN].
  b. κατά with genitive (LN 90.31) (BAGD I.2.b.α. p. 405): 'against' [BAGD, LN; all translations], 'in opposition to, in conflict with' [LN]. This preposition indicates opposition, with the possible implication of antagonism [LN].
  c. ἐχθρός (LN 39.11) (BAGD 2.b.β. p. 331): 'enemy' [BAGD, BECNT, BNTC, CC, NICNT, NIGTC, NTC, PNTC, WBC; ESV, GW, NASB, NCV, NET, NIV, NLT, REB], 'worst enemy' [CEV, TEV], 'foe' [KJV, NRSV], 'being an enemy, in opposition to' [LN]. This pronominal adjective denotes a person who is at enmity with someone [LN].
  d. οἰκιακός (LN **10.11**) (BAGD p. 557): '(one's own) household member' [CC], 'member of (one's own) household' [BAGD, BECNT, BNTC, NTC, PNTC, WBC; NASB, NET, NIV, NRSV], 'those of (one's own) household' [NIGTC; ESV; similarly KJV], 'member of (one's own) family' [LN, NICNT; GW, NCV, TEV], 'those of one's family' [**LN**], 'relative' [LN]. The phrase οἱ οἰκιακοὶ αὐτοῦ 'his own household members' is translated 'right in your own household' [NLT], 'in your own

family' [CEV], 'under his own roof' [REB]. This noun denotes one who belongs to a particular household or extended family [LN].

QUESTION—Does Jesus' statement that he came to turn people against one another indicate purpose, or result?

This statement is hyperbole [BECNT, CC]. The thought that Jesus did not come to bring peace is an example of a kind of hyperbole known as dialectical negation, in which the first part of the statement is an exaggerated negative statement [CC]. Like other aphorisms in the Bible, this statement places emphasis on one aspect of the truth, rather than expressing something that is universally applicable [NTC].

1. It expresses purpose [BECNT, Lns, My, NICNT, NTC, PNTC], in that this result is actually intended [Lns, NICNT, NTC]. This was his purpose, though not the ultimate and primary purpose [My].
2. It expresses result [CC, NIBC, WBC]. It describes the effect of Jesus' coming and preaching [WBC].

10:37 The-one loving[a] father or mother more-than[b] me is not worthy[c] of-me, and the-one loving son or daughter more-than me is not worthy of-me;

LEXICON—a. pres. act. participle of φιλέω (LN **25.33**) (BAGD 1.a. p. 859): 'to love' [BAGD, **LN**; all translations except REB], 'to care for' [REB], 'to have affection for' [BAGD, LN]. This verb means to have love or affection for someone or something based on association [LN].

b. ὑπέρ with accusative (LN 78.29) (BAGD 2. p. 839): 'more than' [BAGD, LN; all translations], 'to a greater degree than' [LN], 'beyond' [BAGD, LN], 'over and above' [BAGD]. This preposition indicates a degree which is beyond that of a compared scale of extent [LN].

c. ἄξιος (LN 65.17) (BAGD 2.a. p. 78): 'worthy' [BAGD, BECNT, BNTC, CC, LN, NICNT, NIGTC, NTC, PNTC, WBC; ESV, KJV, NASB, NET, NIV, NRSV, REB]. The phrase οὐκ ἔστιν μου ἄξιος 'is not worthy of me' is translated 'are not worthy of being mine' [NLT], 'are not worthy to be my followers' [NCV], 'are not fit to be my disciples' [CEV, TEV], 'does not deserve to be my disciple' [GW]. This adjective describes having a relatively high degree of comparable merit or worth [LN].

QUESTION—Is there any significance in the use of the verb φιλέω 'love' as opposed to ἀγαπάω 'love'.

These Greek verbs are often used interchangeably in the NT, and there is no significance in the use of φιλέω here as opposed to ἀγαπάω [CC, NTC, PNTC]. This word indicates the warmest affection [PNTC]. Whereas ἀγαπάω 'love' is a love of purpose and intellect, φιλέω denotes natural affection, such as within a family, and is an affection that is also appropriate in one's love for Jesus [Lns].

QUESTION—What does it mean to be unworthy of Jesus?

It means to be unworthy of being his disciple [Lns, WBC; NLT, NCV, GW], of having a share in his kingdom, and undeserving of what he brings [WBC]. It speaks of being unfit to be his disciple [TH; CEV, TEV]. It means not deserving to be his follower [NAC, TRT], not deserving to belong to him [NTC]. It indicates an unwillingness to see and respond rightly to what God is doing through him [NIGTC].

10:38 and whoever does- not –take-up^a his cross^b and follow^c after^d me, is not worthy of-me.

LEXICON—a. pres. act. indic. of λαμβάνω (LN **24.83**) (BAGD 1.a. p. 465): 'take up' [BNTC, **LN**, NIGTC, NTC, PNTC; CEV, GW, NET, NLT, NRSV, REB, TEV], 'to take' [BECNT, CC, LN, NICNT, WBC; ESV, KJV, NASB, NIV], 'to carry' [LN; NCV], 'to take upon oneself' [BAGD]. The idiom λαμβάνω τὸν σταυρόν 'to take up/take/carry one's cross' means to be prepared to endure severe suffering, even to the point of death [LN].
  b. σταυρός (LN 6.27) (BAGD 2. p. 765): 'cross' [BAGD, LN; all translations]. This noun denotes a pole stuck into the ground in an upright position with a crosspiece attached to its upper part so that it was shaped like a cross. In NT texts about carrying a cross, the reference is probably to the crosspiece of the cross, which normally would have been carried by a man condemned to die [LN].
  c. pres. act. indic. of ἀκολουθέω (LN 15.156) (BAGD 2. p. 31): 'to follow' [BAGD, LN; all translations except CEV], 'to accompany' [BAGD], 'to accompany as a follower' [LN], 'to go along with' [BAGD, LN]. The phrase ἀκολουθεῖ ὀπίσω 'follow after' is translated 'to come with' [CEV]. This verb means to follow or accompany someone who takes the lead in determining direction and route of movement [LN].
  d. ὀπίσω (LN 36.35) (BAGD 2.a.β. p. 575): 'after' [BAGD, BECNT, BNTC, CC, LN, NICNT, NIGTC, NTC, PNTC; NASB], not explicit [WBC; all versions except NASB, TEV]. The phrase ὀπίσω μου 'after me' is translated 'in my steps' [TEV]. This preposition indicates one who is followed as a leader (occurring with a variety of verbs indicating change of state or movement) [LN].

QUESTION—What is meant by taking up a cross?
  This metaphor for self-denial is drawn from the fact that when the Romans crucified a condemned person, he would have to carry the cross-beam to the place of execution [BECNT, My, NIGTC, PNTC, TH]. This form of punishment was usually only for slaves [NICNT, TH], foreigners [TH], or those who stirred up political rebellion [NICNT]. Carrying a cross was always a one-way journey from which one did not return [PNTC]. In addition to the physical torture, crucifixion involved considerable humiliation and shame [CC, NICNT], especially from being paraded through the streets carrying the cross-beam while being mocked by the crowds [NICNT].

10:39 The-one having-found[a] his life will-lose[b] it, and the-one having-lost[c] his life for-the-sake-of me he-will-find it.

LEXICON—a. aorist act. participle of εὑρίσκω (LN 13.17) (BAGD 3. p. 325): 'to find' [BECNT, BNTC, CC, NICNT, NIGTC, NTC, PNTC, WBC; ESV, KJV, NASB, NET, NIV, NRSV], 'to find for oneself' [BAGD], 'to preserve' [GW], 'to cling to' [NLT], 'to gain' [REB], 'to try to gain' [TEV], 'to try to hold on to' [NCV], 'to try to save' [CEV], 'to attain' [BAGD, **LN**], 'to attain to, to discover' [LN]. This verb means to attain a state, with the supplementary implication of discovery [LN]. Nothing has been lost, so 'tries to keep his life ' or 'tries to save his life' is better [TH].
  b. fut. act. indic. of ἀπόλλυμι (LN 57.68) (BAGD 1.b. p. 95): 'to lose' [BAGD, LN; all translations except NCV]. The phrase ἀπολέσει αὐτήν 'will lose it' is translated 'will give up true life' [NCV]. This verb means to lose something which one already possesses [LN].
  c. aorist act. participle of ἀπόλλυμι (LN **23.114**) (BAGD 1.b. p. 95): 'to lose' [BAGD; all translations except CEV, NCV, NLT], 'to give up' [CEV, NCV, NLT]. The idiom ἀπόλλυμι τὴν ψυχήν means 'to suffer the destruction of one's life, to have one's life destroyed, to experience the loss of life' [LN], 'to die' [**LN**]. In Matthew 10:39 some scholars see in the use of ψυχή 'life' a reference not to physical life but to a particular quality of life. This is difficult to justify except in terms of the total context, and it may be that in Matthew 10:39 there is a degree of intentional ambiguity with respect to the meaning of ψυχή [LN].

QUESTION—What is meant by 'having found his life' in the first clause?
  1. It means that someone has evaded martyrdom [BECNT, BNTC, Lns, My, NAC, NIBC, NICNT]. Nothing has been lost, so either 'tries to keep his life' or 'tries to save his life' better expresses the meaning [TH],
  2. Others refer this to one's way of life [EBC, NIGTC, NTC, PNTC, WBC]. It means this person defines life on his own self-centered terms and not any allegiance to Jesus [WBC]. He considers his own interests instead of Christ's interests [NTC]. He has 'made it'' in life by being humanly successful while compromising his loyalty to God and Christ [NIGTC]. He is primarily concerned with what he delights in here and now without regard to eternity [PNTC]. He lives for himself and refuses to do what Christian discipleship requires [EBC].

QUESTION—What is meant by 'the one having lost his life'?
This states the opposite of the first clause [TH]. It involves self-denial that may even lead to martyrdom [BECNT, CC, EBC, ICC, Lns, My, NAC, NIBC, NICNT, NIGTC, NTC, TRT, WBC], or to the loss of cherished relationships [BECNT, CC]. It to die to self [EBC], to face suffering, deprivation, social stigma, and possible execution [NICNT], to sacrifice physical safety in order to remain loyal to Christ's mission [BNTC].

DISCOURSE UNIT—10:40–11:1 [NET, NRSV]. The topic is rewards.

DISCOURSE UNIT—10:40–42 [CEV, ESV, NASB, TEV]. The topic is rewards [CEV, ESV, TEV], the reward of service [NASB].

10:40 **The-one receiving[a] you receives me, and the-one receiving me receives the-one having-sent[b] me.**

LEXICON—a. pres. mid. or pass. (deponent = active) participle of δέχομαι (LN 34.53) (BAGD 1. p. 177): 'to receive' [BAGD, BECNT, BECNT, BNTC, CC, LN, NIGTC, NIGTC, NTC, PNTC, WBC; ESV, KJV, NASB, NET, NIV, NLT, REB], 'to welcome' [BAGD, LN, NICNT; CEV, GW, NRSV, TEV], 'to accept' [LN; NCV]. This verb means to accept the presence of a person with friendliness [LN].
   b. aorist act. participle of ἀποστέλλω (LN 15.66): 'to send' [LN; all translations]. This verb means to cause someone to depart for a particular purpose [LN].

QUESTION—What does it mean to receive Jesus' disciples and how would that be seen as receiving Jesus himself and even God who had sent Jesus?

The person who receives as a guest a disciple whom Jesus has sent on a mission is by that fact receiving Jesus, and receiving Jesus is counted as receiving God who had sent Jesus. That is, any honor paid to the disciple of Jesus would be regarded as something that overflowed to Jesus and to God [PNTC]. It was understood that a man's agent must be received as the man himself [WBC]. It is about accepting and supporting the ministry of any of the disciples [NIGTC], to provide hospitality [BECNT, ICC, NAC, NICNT, NTC, TH], material support and shelter [My, NIBC, NICNT], and to harbor those who are wanted by the authorities for their faith in Jesus [NAC, NIBC]. This could also include accepting their message about Jesus [CC, ICC, Lns, NIGTC, NTC, WBC],

10:41 **The-one having-received a-prophet[a] in (the) name[b] of-a-prophet will-receive (the) reward[c] of-a-prophet, and the one having-received a-righteous[d] (person) in (the) name of-a-righteous (person) will-receive (the) reward of-a-righteous (person).**

LEXICON—a. προφήτης (LN 53.79) (BAGD 4. p. 724): 'prophet' [BAGD, LN; all translations except TEV], 'God's messenger' [TEV], 'inspired preacher' [LN]. This noun denotes one who proclaims inspired utterances on behalf of God [LN].
   b. ὄνομα (LN 58.22) (BAGD II. p. 573): 'category' [BAGD, LN], 'being of the type of' [LN], 'title' [BAGD]. The phrase εἰς ὄνομα προφήτου 'in the name of a prophet' [BECNT, CC, PNTC; KJV, NASB, NET, NRSV] is translated 'as a prophet' [BAGD, NICNT, NIGTC; GW], 'because he is a prophet' [BNTC, NTC; ESV, NIV, REB], 'because that person is a prophet' [WBC], 'just because that person is a prophet' [CEV], 'because he is God's messenger' [TEV], 'as one who speaks for God' [NLT]. The phrase ὁ δεχόμενος προφήτην εἰς ὄνομα προφήτου 'the one having received a prophet in the name of a prophet' is translated 'whoever meets

a prophet and accepts him' [NCV]. This noun denotes the category or kind, based upon an implied designation for a class of entities [LN].
c. μισθός (LN 38.14) (BAGD 2.a. p. 523): 'reward' [BAGD, LN; all translations], 'recompense' [LN]. This noun denotes a recompense based upon what a person has earned and thus deserves, the nature of the recompense being either positive or negative [LN].
d. δίκαιος (LN 88.12) (BAGD 1.b. p. 195): 'righteous' [BAGD, LN], 'just' [BAGD, LN], 'upright' [BAGD]. This adjective is translated pronominally: 'righteous man' [BECNT, BNTC, CC; KJV, NASB, NIV], 'righteous person' [NICNT, NTC, WBC; ESV, GW, NET, NRSV], 'righteous people' [NLT], 'righteous one' [NIGTC], 'good man' [PNTC; REB, TEV], 'good person' [CEV, NCV]. This adjectival noun describes one who lives in accordance with what God requires [LN].

QUESTION—Is there any significant distinction between 'prophet' and 'righteous person'

There seems to be some intended distinction [EBC, Lns, NAC, NTC, PNTC, WBC], the list of the various groups seeming to descend according to prominence, although the different groups are not mutually exclusive [EBC]. A prophet speaks God's message [NAC, NTC, PNTC], and a good man accepts God's sovereignty and walks in God's ways [PNTC], practices true religion [NTC], and obeys God's will by following Jesus [NAC]. 'Prophet' seems to be more specific than 'righteous person' [NICNT]. People are made righteous through heeding the ministry of a prophet [Lns]. Prophets represent God's message and righteous people represent his character [BECNT]. The righteous person witnesses to and stands for God's righteousness [NIGTC]. 'Prophets', 'righteous persons' and 'little ones' are three different ways in which Jesus refers to his disciples [NIBC, NIGTC]. They seem to be used interchangeably here [CC, ICC], the prophet and the just man being essentially the same [ICC]. The terms are used in parallel, and both words describe the apostles [My].

10:42 And whoever gives[a] one of-these little-ones[b] even[c] a-cup[d] of-cold (water) in (the) name of a disciple,[e] truly I-say to-you, he-will- certainly not[f] -lose[g] his reward.

LEXICON—a. aorist act. subj. of ποτίζω (LN 23.35) (BAGD 1. p. 695): 'to give' [BNTC, NICNT, NIGTC, NTC, WBC; all versions except KJV, TEV], 'to give to drink' [BAGD, BECNT, LN, PNTC; KJV], 'to give a drink' [CC; TEV]. This verb means to cause to drink [LN].
b. μικρός (LN 87.58) (BAGD 1.c. p. 521): 'unimportant' [LN], 'most humble' [CEV, GW], 'least' [NLT], 'humble folk' [BAGD], 'low' [LN]. This plural adjective is translated pronominally as 'little ones' [BECNT, BNTC, CC, NICNT, NIGTC, NTC, PNTC, WBC; ESV, KJV, NASB, NCV, NET, NIV, NRSV, REB], 'the least of these my followers' [TEV]. It describes being of low or unimportant status [LN].

c. μόνος (BAGD 2.b. p. 528): 'even' [BECNT, NIGTC; ESV, NASB, NIV, NLT, NRSV, TEV], 'even so much as' [NTC], 'so much as' [REB], 'just' [BNTC], 'just one' [NICNT], 'only' [BAGD, CC, PNTC; KJV, NET], 'merely' [WBC], 'alone' [BAGD], not explicit [CEV, GW, NCV].

d. ποτήριον, (LN 6.121) (BAGD 1. p. 695): 'cup' [BAGD, LN], 'drinking vessel' [BAGD]. The phrase ποτήριον ψυχροῦ 'a cup of cold water' [all translations except CEV, TEV] is also translated 'a cup of cool water' [CEV], 'a drink of cold water' [TEV]. It denotes an object from which one may drink [LN].

e. μαθητής (LN 36.38): 'disciple, follower' [LN]. The phrase 'in the name of a disciple' [BECNT, CC, PNTC; NASB, NET, NRSV] is also translated 'only in the name of a disciple' [KJV], 'because that person/he is a disciple' [BNTC, NTC, WBC; ESV, GW], 'because he is a disciple of mine' [REB], 'because he is my disciple' [NIV; similarly NCV], 'as a disciple' [NICNT, NIGTC], 'because he is my follower' [TEV], 'just because that person is my follower' [CEV], not explicit [NLT]. This noun denotes a person who is a disciple or follower of someone [LN].

f. οὐ μή (LN 69.5) This double negative phrase is translated 'certainly not' [BECNT, CC, LN, NICNT, NTC, PNTC; NIV, REB], 'certainly never' [GW], 'never' [NET], 'not' [BNTC, NIGTC; NASB], 'by no means' [LN, WBC; ESV], 'in no wise' [KJV], 'none (of these)' [NRSV], not explicit [CEV, NCV, NLT, TEV]. This phrase marks an emphatic negation [LN].

g. ἀπόλλυμι (LN 57.68) (BAGD 1.b. p. 95): 'to lose' [BAGD, BECNT, BNTC, CC, LN, NICNT, NIGTC, NTC, PNTC, WBC; ESV, GW, KJV, NASB, NET, NIV, NRSV]. The phrase οὐ μὴ ἀπολέσῃ τὸν μισθὸν αὐτοῦ 'he will certainly not lose his reward' is translated 'will surely be rewarded' [CEV, NLT], 'will truly get their reward' [NCV], 'will certainly not go unrewarded' [REB], 'will certainly receive a reward' [TEV]. This verb means to lose something which one already possesses [LN].

QUESTION—Why does Jesus refer to his disciples as 'little ones'?

It indicates their humility [Lns, WBC], and perhaps their lack of experience [WBC]. They are vulnerable and of little significance, at least in the eyes of the world [CC, NICNT]. It speaks of being an unknown 'nobody' [NTC], of being unimportant [BNTC, TH, TRT], of being insignificant and powerless [PNTC]. It refers here to ordinary believers, who are unobtrusive and even marginalized [NAC]. It refers to those who are least in the kingdom, but who are subject to the opposition of the world [EBC].

QUESTION—What is the sense of μισθός 'reward' here?

It is eschatological reward [CC, ICC], eternal life in heaven [NAC]. It includes present benefits as well as eschatological reward [NIGTC, NTC], that is, peace of mind now, and eternal reward later [NTC]. It is a reward similar to what those in the OT received who welcomed prophets such as Elijah and Elisha [NICNT].

DISCOURSE UNIT—11:1–12:50 [EBC, NAC, PNTC]. The topic is narrative [EBC], opposition experienced in Christ's mission [NAC], responses to Jesus' activity [PNTC].

DISCOURSE UNIT—11:1–30 [ICC]. The topic is this generation: invitation and response.

DISCOURSE UNIT—11:1–19 [CEV, ESV, NCV, NIV, NLT, TEV]. The topic is Jesus and John the Baptist [NCV, NIV, NLT], messengers from John the Baptist [ESV, TEV], John the Baptist [CEV].

DISCOURSE UNIT—11:1–6 [NASB]. The topic is John's questions.

11:1 And it-happened[a] when Jesus finished instructing[b] his twelve disciples, he-departed[c] from-there to-teach[d] and to-preach[e] in their cities.[f]

LEXICON—a. aorist mid. (deponent = act.) of γίνομαι (LN 13.107) (BAGD I.3.f. p. 159): 'to happen' [BAGD, BNTC, LN], 'to take place' [BAGD], 'to come to pass' [PNTC, WBC; KJV], 'to occur, to come to be' [LN], not explicit [BECNT, CC; all versions except KJV]. The phrase καὶ ἐγένετο 'and it happened' is translated 'it so happened' [NIGTC], 'and then' [NICNT], 'now (when)' [NTC]. This verb means to happen, with the implication that what happens is different from a previous state [LN].

b. pres. act. participle of διατάσσω (LN 33.325) (BAGD p. 189): 'to instruct' [BECNT, BNTC, LN, NICNT, NIGTC, NTC, WBC; CEV, ESV, NET, NIV, NRSV], 'to give instructions' [PNTC; GW, NASB, NLT, REB, TEV], 'to order' [BAGD, LN], 'to direct' [BAGD, CC], 'to tell' [LN], 'to tell (these things)' NCV], 'to command' [BAGD, LN; KJV]. This verb means to give detailed instructions as to what must be done [LN].

c. aorist act. indic. of μεταβαίνω (LN 15.2) (BAGD 1.a.α. p. 510): 'to depart' [BNTC, LN; NASB], 'to leave' [CEV, NCV, TEV], 'to go' [BECNT, WBC; REB], 'to go on' [NIGTC, NTC; ESV, NET, NIV, NRSV], 'to go out' [NLT], 'to go away' [PNTC], 'to move on' [NICNT; GW], 'to cross over' [CC], 'to go or pass over' [BAGD], 'to move from one place to another, to change one's location' [LN]. This verb means to effect a change of location in space, with the implication that the two locations are significantly different [LN].

d. pres. act. infin. of διδάσκω (LN 33.224) (BAGD 2.f. p. 192): 'to teach' [BAGD, LN; all translations]. This verb means to provide instruction in a formal or informal setting [LN]. The present infinitive of the verbs 'to teach' and 'to preach' is translated 'to continue teaching and preaching' [CC], 'began teaching and preaching' [CEV].

e. pres. act. infin. of κηρύσσω (LN 33.256) (BAGD 2.b.β. p. 431): 'to preach' [BAGD, BECNT, BNTC, CC, LN, NICNT, NTC, PNTC, WBC; all versions except GW, NRSV], 'to proclaim' [BAGD, NIGTC; NRSV]. The phrase 'teach and preach' is translated 'to teach his message' [GW].

This verb means to publicly announce religious truths and principles while urging acceptance and compliance [LN].

f. πόλις (LN 1.88): 'city' [BECNT, BNTC, CC, LN, NTC, WBC; ESV, GW, KJV, NASB, NRSV], 'town' [LN, NICNT, PNTC; CEV, NET]. The phrase πόλεσιν αὐτῶν 'their towns' is translated 'towns in/of Galilee' [NCV, NIV], 'towns throughout the region' [NLT], 'neighboring towns' [REB], 'towns near there' [TEV]. This noun denotes a population center, in contrast with a rural area or countryside and without specific reference to size [LN].

QUESTION—To whom does αὐτῶν 'their' refer in describing the cities where they were going to preach?

When Matthew uses the term 'their cities' he is referring to Jews in general, and specifically those who opposed Jesus [PNTC]. It refers to preaching in the synagogues of Galilee [EBC, My, NAC, NICNT, NTC, WBC; NIV, NCV]. It refers to the towns of the disciples [NIGTC]. The possessive pronoun 'their' distances Jesus somewhat from the towns in his own home area, indicating a shift in attitude from how his ministry in Galilee had been received before now [NAC].

DISCOURSE UNIT—11:2–16:20 [CC]. The topic is Jesus' ministry is opposed in Israel: the question of Jesus' authority.

DISCOURSE UNIT—11:2–13:53 [EBC]. The topic is teaching and preaching the gospel of the kingdom: rising opposition.

DISCOURSE UNIT—11:2–13:52 [BECNT]. The topic is the growing opposition to the kingdom of heaven.

DISCOURSE UNIT—11:2–12:50 [BECNT, WBC]. The topic is narrative 3: three cycles of unbelief and belief [BECNT], the negative response to Jesus [WBC].

DISCOURSE UNIT—11:2–30 [NIGTC, NICNT; REB]. The topic is varying responses to the Messiah [NICNT], seeing clearly and relating rightly to God's present agenda [NIGTC], recognizing the Messiah [REB].

DISCOURSE UNIT—11:2–19 [NET]. The topic is Jesus and John the Baptist.

DISCOURSE UNIT—11:2–6 [GW, NRSV]. The topic is John sends two disciples [GW], messengers from John the Baptist [NRSV].

11:2 And John having-heard in the prison[a] the works[b] of the Christ (and) having-sent (word) through his disciples **11:3** he-said to-him, "Are-you the-one coming[c] or do-we-wait[d] for another?"

TEXT—Manuscripts reading διὰ τῶν μαθητῶν αὐτοῦ 'through his disciples' are given a B rating by GNT to indicate it was regarded to be almost certain. The variant δύο τῶν μαθητῶν αὐτοῦ 'two of his disciples' is read by KJV only.

MATTHEW 11:2–3

LEXICON—a. δεσμωτήριον (LN 7.24) (BAGD p. 176): 'prison' [BAGD, LN; all translations except NASB], 'jail' [BAGD, LN]. The phrase ἐν τῷ δεσμωτηρίῳ 'in the prison' is translated 'while imprisoned' [NASB]. This noun denotes a place of detention [LN].
- b. ἔργον (LN 42.11) (BAGD 1.c.α. p. 308): 'act' [LN], 'deed' [BAGD, LN, NICNT, NIGTC; ESV], 'accomplishment' [BAGD]. This plural noun is translated 'works' [BECNT, BNTC, CC, PNTC, WBC; KJV, NASB], 'activities' [NTC], 'the things that Christ was doing' [TEV], 'what Christ was doing' [CEV, NCV, NIV, REB], 'what the Messiah was doing' [NRSV], 'all the things the Messiah was doing' [NLT], 'the things Christ had done' [GW], 'the deeds Christ had done' [NET]. This noun denotes that which is done, with possible focus on the energy or effort involved [LN].
- c. pres. mid. or pass. participle (deponent = act.) of ἔρχομαι (LN **15.81**) (BAGD I.1.a.η. p. 311): 'to come' [LN], 'to appear, to come before the public' [BAGD]. This participle is translated 'the Coming One' [BNTC, CC, NIGTC, NTC, PNTC], 'the one who was going to come' [**LN**], 'the one who was to come' [NIV], 'the one John said was going to come' [TEV], 'the one who is to come' [BECNT; ESV, NCV, NET, NRSV, REB], 'the one promised to come' [WBC], 'the one who is coming' [NICNT; GW], 'the one we should be looking for' [CEV], 'he that should come' [KJV], 'the Expected One' [NASB], 'the Messiah we've been expecting' [NLT]. This verb means to move toward or up to the reference point of the viewpoint character or event [LN].
- d. pres. act. indic. of προσδοκάω (LN 30.55) (BAGD 1. p. 712): 'to wait for' [BAGD, BNTC, NIGTC, PNTC, WBC; CEV, NCV, NRSV], 'to look for' [BAGD, BECNT, NTC; ESV, GW, KJV, NASB, NET], 'to keep looking for' [NLT], 'to look forward to' [NICNT], 'to expect' [BAGD, CC, LN; NIV, REB], 'to anticipate' [LN]. This verb means to expect something to happen, whether good or bad [LN].

QUESTION—Should the definite article in the phrase τοῦ Χριστοῦ '(of) the Christ' be understood as indicating a title?

In Greek the definite article is normally used with a name, so the presence of the article here does not indicate whether Χριστός 'Christ' is used here as a title 'the Christ/Messiah' or as a name 'Christ'.
1. It indicates that 'Christ' is used as a title [EBC, BECNT, BNTC, CC, ICC, Lns, NAC, NIBC, NICNT, NIGTC, PNTC, TRT, WBC; ESV, NLT, NRSV]: *the Christ*. The use of the definite article represents the perspective of Matthew, though not necessarily that of John [BECNT, BNTC, EBC, NAC, NIBC, NIGTC]. Matthew may be accenting the importance of whom it was that John doubted [EBC, PNTC].
2. 'Christ' is used here as a name [NTC, TH; CEV, GW, KJV, NASB, NCV, NET, NIV, REB, TEV]: *Christ*.

QUESTION—What does John's question indicate?

John's confidence had been shaken by the delay of God's judgment on sin and by John's own imprisonment [BECNT, CC, Lns, NAC, NTC, NIBC, NICNT, WBC], as well as by the growing opposition to Jesus [BECNT, NICNT, WBC]. The use of ἕτερος 'another' may mean that John is wondering if he should be expecting a different kind of Messiah, so it was really a question about what kind of Messiah Jesus was [BECNT, NIBC]. John was expecting an eschatological judge and deliverer [NIGTC]. John expected Jesus to bring judgment but Jesus didn't do that [Lns, PNTC], and moreover, Jesus abstained from religious practices like fasting [PNTC].

QUESTION—Was the term 'the one coming' understood to be a messianic designation?

1. At that time it was not commonly understood to be a messianic title [BNTC, CC, EBC, NIBC, NICNT, NIGTC, PNTC], but John was using it as a messianic title [BECNT, EBC, ICC, NAC, NICNT, TRT, WBC], and it does reflect OT use [EBC, Lns, NIBC, PNTC, WBC]. It reflected the expectation of a coming deliverer who would usher in the salvation of the last days [CC].
2. It was known and used by the Jews as a messianic title [Lns, My, TH].

11:4 And Jesus answering[a] said to them, "Go[b] report[c] to-John what you(pl)-heard[d] and you(pl)-see;[e]

LEXICON—a. (LN) aorist pass. (deponent = act.) participle of ἀποκρίνομαι (LN 33.184) (BAGD 1. p. 93): 'to answer' [BAGD, BECNT, BNTC, CC, LN, NTC, PNTC, WBC; all versions except NIV, NLT], 'to reply' [BAGD, LN; NIV], 'to respond' [NIGTC], not explicit [NLT]. The phrase ἀποκριθεὶς...εἶπεν 'answering said' is conflated and translated as one verb: 'answered' [PNTC; CEV, ESV, GW, NCV, NET, NRSV, REB, TEV], 'replied' [NIV], 'told (them)' [NLT]. This participle is translated 'in reply' [NICNT]. This verb means to respond to a question asking for information [LN].

b. aorist pass. (deponent = act.) participle of πορεύομαι (used in an imperative sense) (LN 15.34) (BAGD 1. p. 692): 'to go' [BAGD; all translations except GW, NLT, TEV], 'to go back' [GW, NLT, TEV], 'to go away, to leave' [LN], 'to depart' [BAGD]. This verb means to move away from a reference point [LN].

c. aorist act. impera. of ἀπαγγέλλω (LN 33.198) (BAGD 1. p. 79): 'to report' [BAGD, BECNT, NTC; NASB, NIV, REB], 'to tell' [BAGD, BNTC, LN, NICNT, NIGTC, PNTC, WBC; CEV, ESV, GW, NCV, NET, NLT, NRSV, TEV], 'to announce' [BAGD, CC], 'to show' [KJV], 'to inform' [LN]. This verb means to announce or inform, with possible focus upon the source of information [LN].

d. pres. act. indic. of ἀκούω (LN 24.52) (BAGD 1.b.α. p. 32): 'to hear' [BAGD, LN; all translations]. The two present tense verbs 'hear' and 'see' are translated as present progressive: 'you are hearing and seeing'

[BECNT, CC, WBC; TEV]; as past: 'you have heard and seen' [CEV, NLT]. This verb means to see, frequently in the sense of becoming aware of, or taking notice of something [LN].
e. pres. act. indic. of βλέπω (LN 24.7) (BAGD 1.a. p. 143): 'to see' [BAGD, LN; all translations], 'to become aware of, to notice' [LN]. This verb means to see, frequently in the sense of becoming aware of or taking notice of something [LN].

11:5 blind[a] (people) receive- (their) -sight[b] and lame[c] (people) walk, lepers[d] are-cleansed[e] and deaf[f] (people) hear, and dead (people) are-raised[g] and poor[h] (people) are-brought-the-good-news;[i]

LEXICON—a. τυφλός (LN 24.38) (BAGD 1.b. p. 830): 'blind' [BAGD, LN; all translations], 'unable to see' [LN]. This adjective describes being unable to see [LN].
b. pres. act. indic. of ἀναβλέπω (LN 24.42) (BAGD 2.a.α. p. 51): 'to receive sight' [BECNT, BNTC, PNTC, WBC; ESV, KJV, NASB, NRSV, NIV], 'to gain sight' [BAGD, CC, LN, NTC], 'to regain one's sight' [LN], 'to recover sight' [REB], 'to see' [NIGTC; NET, NLT], 'to see again' [NICNT; GW], 'to be able to see' [CEV], 'can see' [NCV, TEV]. This verb means to become able to see, whether for the first time or again [LN].
c. χωλός (LN **23.175**) (BAGD p. 889): 'lame' [BAGD, BNTC, CC, **LN**, NICNT, NIGTC, PNTC, WBC; all versions], 'crippled' [BAGD, NTC], 'one who is lame' [LN]. This adjective describes a disability that involves the imperfect function of the lower limbs [LN].
d. λεπρός (LN 23.162) (BAGD p. 472): 'leper' [BAGD, LN]. See translations of the word at 8:2. This noun denotes a person suffering from a dread skin disease [LN]. This word occurs at 8:2; 10:8; 11:5; 26:6.
e. pres. pass. indic. of καθαρίζω (LN 23.137) (BAGD 1.b.α. p. 387): 'to be healed and made ritually pure/acceptable' [LN], 'to be made clean' [BAGD]. See translations of the word at 8:2. This verb means to heal a person of a disease which has caused ceremonial uncleanness [LN]. This word occurs in this sense at 8:2; 10:8; 11:5.
f. κωφός (LN 24.68) (BAGD 2. p. 462): 'deaf' [BAGD, LN; all translations]. This adjective describes being unable to hear [LN].
g. pres. pass. indic. of ἐγείρω (LN 23.94) (BAGD 2.c. p. 215): 'to be raised' [BAGD, BNTC, CC, NICNT, NIGTC, PNTC, WBC; NET, NIV, NRSV], 'to be raised up' [BECNT, NTC; ESV, KJV, NASB], 'to be raised to life' [LN; CEV, NCV, NLT, REB], 'to be brought back to life' [GW, TEV], 'to be made to live again' [LN]. This verb means to cause someone to live again after having once died [LN].
h. πτωχός (LN 57.53) (BAGD 1.b. p. 728): 'poor' [BAGD, LN; all translations], 'destitute' [LN]. This adjective describes being poor and destitute, implying a continuous state [LN].

i. pass. pres. indic. of εὐαγγελίζω (LN 33.215) (BAGD 2.b.β. p. 317): 'to be brought the good news' [NIGTC; REB], 'to have the good news brought' [NRSV], 'to have the good news preached' [BAGD, BECNT, CC, NTC, PNTC; ESV], 'to have the good news proclaimed' [NET], 'to have the gospel preached' [KJV, NASB], 'to hear the gospel preached' [BNTC], 'to hear the good news' [CEV, GW], 'to hear the good news of salvation' [WBC], 'to be told the good news' [LN, NICNT], 'to have the gospel announced' [LN]. The phrase πτωχοὶ εὐαγγελίζονται 'poor people are brought the good news' is translated 'the Good News is preached to the poor' [NCV, NIV, TEV; similarly NLT]. This verb means to communicate good news concerning something (in the NT a particular reference to the gospel message about Jesus) [LN].

QUESTION—What is meant by πτωχός 'poor'?

They are people who are materially poor [NICNT, TH, WBC], and hence also poor in spirit, as spoken of, in the Beatitudes [NICNT, WBC]. It includes all who are needy as well as those who are afflicted or oppressed [ICC, My, NIGTC, PNTC]. It describes those who recognize their own spiritual poverty [NIBC].

11:6 and blessed[a] is he-who is- not -trapped[b] because-of[c] me."

LEXICON—a. μακάριος (LN 25.119) (BAGD 1.b. p. 486): 'blessed' [BAGD, BECNT, BNTC, CC, NTC, PNTC, WBC; all translations except CEV, NLT, TEV], 'happy' [BAGD, LN, NICNT; TEV], 'fortunate' [BAGD, NIGTC], 'privileged recipient of divine favor' [BAGD]. This adjective is translated as a verb phrase: 'God will bless' [CEV], 'God blesses' [NLT]. It describes being happy, with the implication of enjoying favorable circumstances [LN].

b. aorist mid./pass. subj. of σκανδαλίζομαι (LN 25.180, 88.305, 31.77) (BAGD 1.b. p. 752): 'to be caught, to fall' [BAGD (1.)], 'to fall into a trap' [LN (88.305)]. This verb has only figurative meanings in the NT [LN]: 'to be offended, to take offense' [LN (25.180)], 'to sin, to fall into sin' [LN (88.305)], 'to cease believing, to give up believing' [LN (31.77)], 'to be led into sin, to be repelled by someone, to take offense at someone' [BAGD (1.b.)]. The phrase ὃς ἐὰν μὴ σκανδαλισθῇ ἐν ἐμοί 'he who is not trapped because of me' is translated 'anyone/he who does not take offense at me' [BECNT, BNTC, WBC; NASB], 'anyone who takes no offense at me' [NIGTC; NET, NRSV], 'whosoever shall not be offended in me' [KJV], 'the one who is not offended by me' [ESV], 'the man who does not fall away on account of me' [NIV], 'those who do not turn away because of me' [NLT], 'those who do not find me an obstacle to faith' [REB], 'whoever/the person who is not caused to stumble because of me' [CC, NICNT], 'those who do not stumble in their faith because of me' [NCV], 'anyone who is not tripped up on account of me' [PNTC], 'whoever doesn't lose his faith in me' [GW], 'those who have no doubts about me' [TEV], 'everyone who doesn't reject me because of

what I do' [CEV], 'he who is not repelled by me' [NTC]. This verb means to be offended because of some action [LN 25.180)], or to fall into sin due to certain contributing circumstances [LN (88.30)], or to give up believing what is right and let oneself believe what is false [LN (31.77)].
- c. ἐν (LN 89.26): 'because of' [BECNT, CC, LN, NICNT; NCV, NLT], 'on account of' [LN, PNTC; NIV], 'at' [BNTC, NIGTC, WBC; NASB, NET, NRSV], 'by' [NTC; ESV], 'by reason of' [LN], 'in' [KJV], 'about' [TEV], not explicit [REB]. The phrase ἐν ἐμοί 'because of me' is translated 'because of what I do' [CEV]. This preposition indicates cause or reason, with focus upon instrumentality, either of objects or events [LN].

QUESTION—What does σκανδαλίζομαι 'to be trapped' mean in this verse?

Here Jesus is referring to John's disappointment due to the fact of the Messiah not being in accord with his expectations [CC, WBC]. This assumes that the questioner has begun well and must now avoid stumbling. To do this he must reexamine his presuppositions about the Messiah. John should trust Jesus and not be tripped up by his own preconceived ideas of what the Christ should be and do [PNTC]. It refers to a spiritual defeat, perhaps even a serious loss of faith, [BECNT, My, Lns].

DISCOURSE UNIT—11:7–19 [GW, NASB, NRSV]. The topic is Jesus speaks about John [GW], Jesus praises John the Baptist [NRSV], Jesus' tribute to John [NASB].

11:7 And (as) these were-leaving,ᵃ Jesus began to say to-the crowds about John, "What did-you(pl)-go-out into the wildernessᵇ to see? A-reedᶜ shakenᵈ by (the) wind?

LEXICON—a. pres. mid. or pass. (deponent = act) participle of πορεύομαι [LN 15.34]: 'to leave, to go away' [LN]. The participial phrase 'as these/these-men were leaving' [BECNT, BNTC] is also translated 'as they were leaving' [NICNT; GW], 'as these-men/they went away' [PNTC; ESV, NRSV], 'while they were going away']NET], 'as these men/these-men were going away' [CC, NIGTC; NASB], 'when these messengers were going away' [NTC], 'as they departed' [KJV], 'as these disciples of John were departing' [WBC], 'as/while John's 'disciples/followers were going away/leaving' [CEV, NCV, NIV, NLT, TEV], 'as these disciples of John were departing' [WBC], 'when the messengers were on their way back' [REB]. This verb means to move away from a reference point [LN].
- b. ἔρημος (LN 1.86): 'wilderness' [BNTC, LN, NICNT, NIGTC, NTC, PNTC, WBC; ESV, KJV, NASB, NET, NLT, NRSV, REB], 'desert' [BECNT, CC, LN; CEV, GW, NCV, NIV, TEV], 'lonely place' [LN]. This noun denotes a largely uninhabited region, normally with sparse vegetation [LN].
- c. κάλαμος (LN **3.19**) (BAGD 1. p. 398): 'reed' [BAGD, **LN**; all translations except CEV, GW, TEV], 'tall grass' [CEV, GW], 'blade of grass' [TEV]. This noun denotes a tall-growing grass or sedge [LN].

d. pres. pass. participle of σαλεύω (LN 16.7) (BAGD 1. p. 740): 'to be shaken' [BAGD, BNTC, CC, LN, NICNT, NIGTC, PNTC; ESV, KJV, NASB, NET, NRSV], 'to sway' [BECNT, NTC; GW, REB], 'to be swayed' [NIV], 'to be blown' [WBC; NCV], 'to bend' [TEV], 'to be caused to move to and fro, to be caused to waver or totter' [BAGD]. The question 'A reed shaken by the wind?' is filled out: 'Was he like tall grass blown about by the wind?' [CEV], 'Was he a weak reed, swayed by every breath of wind?' [NLT]. This verb means to cause something to move back and forth rapidly, often violently [LN].

QUESTION—What type of question is the first question?

The first rhetorical question asks, 'What sort of person did you go out to see?' [CEV], or 'What kind of man did you go into the wilderness to see?" [NLT]. Jesus wanted them to think about the type of man John really was [EBC, PNTC, TH]. He starts out by having them eliminate the obviously false answers before arriving at the truth about John in verses 10–12 [EBC].

QUESTION—What type of question is the added question, 'A reed shaken by the wind?'

This is a rhetorical question that anticipates a negative answer [NAC, NIBC]. The reference to a reed describes someone who is weak [BECNT, CC, NAC, NIBC, WBC; NLT], fickle [CC], or wavering and unstable [BECNT, NAC, NIBC, NTC, PNTC, WBC]. It represents someone with no real personal convictions, who sways with popular opinion [Lns]. This was an image used by the rabbis to describe someone who adapts to the prevailing mood in a way similar to how reeds are moved by the wind [NICNT].

11:8 But[a] what did-you(pl)-go-out to-see? A-man dressed in soft[b] (clothing)? Listen, those wearing soft (clothing) are in the houses[c] of kings.

QUESTION—a. ἀλλά (LN 89.125) (BAGD 3. p. 38): 'but' [BAGD, BECNT, BNTC, CC, LN, NICNT, NTC, PNTC, WBC; KJV, NASB], 'instead, on the contrary' [LN], 'or (were you expecting)' [NLT], 'if not' [NIV], 'then' [NIGTC; ESV, NRSV], 'really' [GW], not explicit [CEV, NCV, NET, TEV]. This conjunction indicates an emphatic contrast [LN]. Before independent clauses, ἀλλά 'but' indicates that the preceding is regarded as a settled matter and introduces a transition to something new [BAGD]. This functions as a strong adversative that dismisses the preceding suggestion and leads into something new [PNTC].

b. μαλακός (LN 79.100) (BAGD 1. p. 488): 'soft' [BAGD, BECNT, BNTC, CC, LN, NICNT, NTC, PNTC; ESV, KJV, NASB, NRSV], 'fine' [NIGTC, WBC; CEV, GW, NCV, NIV], 'finery' [REB], 'fancy' [NET, TEV], 'expensive' [NLT], 'luxurious' [LN], 'delicate' [LN]. This adjective describes being soft to the touch [LN]. This type of clothing is mentioned to contrast the luxurious clothing of the rich with the rough garments actually worn by John the Baptist [TH].

c. οἶκος (LN 7.2) (BAGD 1.a.β. p. 560): 'house' [BAGD, BNTC, CC, LN, NIGTC, PNTC, WBC; ESV, KJV], 'home' [NET]. Since this is a house of a king, it is translated 'palace' [BAGD, BECNT, NICNT, NTC; all versions except ESV, KJV, NET]. This noun denotes a building consisting of one or more rooms and normally serving as a dwelling place [LN].

QUESTION—What does this rhetorical question do?

Again this describes someone who is just the opposite of John. It contrasts the luxurious clothing of the rich with the rough garments actually worn by John the Baptist [BECNT, TH]. In 3:4 John is described as wearing the rugged garb of a prophet [EBC], a garment of camel's hair and a leather belt [PNTC, WBC]. Those who are 'yes men' and sycophants to tyrants and have no backbone are rewarded with high office and wear the soft clothing that goes with that position [Lns, NTC]. John was the opposite of the 'yes men' in Herod's court [NICNT]. Not only was he not wearing the soft clothing of those living in king's house, he was languishing in a king's prison [CC, NICNT].

11:9 But what did-you(pl)-go-out to-see? A-prophet[a]? Yes I-say to-you(pl), and more-than[b] a-prophet. **11:10** This is (he) about whom it-is-written, 'Behold I send my messenger[c] before[d] your face,[e] who shall-prepare[f] your(sg) way[g] before you.'

LEXICON—a. προφήτης (LN 53.79) (BAGD 2, 4, p. 723): 'prophet' [BAGD, LN; all translations], 'inspired preacher' [LN]. This noun denotes one who proclaims inspired utterances on behalf of God [LN].
  b. περισσότερος (LN 78.31) (BAGD 2. p. 651): 'more than' [BECNT, BNTC, NICNT, NIGTC, PNTC, WBC; all versions except GW, REB, TEV], 'even more than' [BAGD, NTC], 'much more than' [TEV], 'far more than' [GW, REB], 'greater than' [BAGD, CC], 'surpassing, all the more, much greater' [LN]. This adjective describes a degree which is considerably in excess of some point on an implied or explicit scale of extent [LN].
  c. ἄγγελος (LN 33.195) (BAGD 1.b. p. 7): 'messenger' [BAGD, LN; all translations except REB], 'herald' [REB]. This noun denotes a person who makes an announcement [LN].
  d. πρό (LN 67.17) (BAGD 1. p. 701): 'before' [BAGD, LN], 'in front of' [BAGD]. The phrase πρὸ προσώπου σου 'before your/thy face' [BECNT, CC, NICNT, NTC, PNTC; ESV, KJV], is also translated 'before you' [NIGTC, WBC], 'ahead of you' [BNTC; all versions except ESV, KJV]. This preposition indicates a point of time prior to another point of time [LN].
  e. πρόσωπον (LN 67.19) (BAGD 1.c.ζ. p. 721): 'face' [BAGD, BECNT, CC, NICNT, NTC, PNTC; ESV, KJV]. The phrase προσώπου σου 'your face' is translated 'you' [BNTC, NIGTC, WBC; all versions except ESV, KJV]. The idiom πρὸ προσώπου 'before the face' indicates a point of time, possibly only a short time before another point of time [LN (67.19)].

f. fut. act. indic. of κατασκευάζω (LN 77.6, 77.7) (BAGD 1. p. 418): 'to prepare' [BAGD, LN (77.6); all translations except CEV, TEV], 'to get things ready' [CEV], 'to open' [TEV], 'to make ready' [BAGD, LN]. This verb means to cause to be thoroughly prepared [LN (77.6)]. The idiom κατασκευάζω τὴν ὁδόν 'to prepare the road' means to cause circumstances to be ready or propitious for some event and can also be translated 'to make everything ready for, to prepare for, to prepare the way for, to arrange for' that event [LN (77.7)].

g. ὁδός (LN 1.99) (BAGD 1.a. p. 554): 'way' [BAGD, LN; all translations except CEV], 'road, highway' [BAGD, LN], not explicit [CEV]. The phrase 'who shall prepare your way before you' is translated 'to get things ready for you' [CEV]. This noun is a general term for a thoroughfare, either within a population center or between two such centers [LN].

QUESTION—What is meant by John being more than a prophet'?

John is not just a prophet, he is also the subject of end-time prophecy [BNTC, CC, EBC, ICC, Lns, NIBC, NTC], he is the predicted forerunner of God's Messiah [NTC]. He is more than an ordinary prophet, as he introduces the messianic age [TH]. He is at the dawn of the coming era [BNTC], the last in a series of prophets, bringing the OT era to its culmination [NAC]. Standing on the threshold of the Messiah's coming kingdom, he announces the fulfillment of the OT prophecies [NIBC]. He is the immediate precursor to the coming of the Messiah [NICNT, WBC], and a pivotal figure relative to the coming age of salvation [NICNT], announcing the day of the Lord [EBC]. His ministry shows that the decisive moment in salvation history, and even in world history, has come [CC]. 'More than a prophet' is superlative language [NICNT]. It means that he is abundantly more than a prophet [PNTC], a super-prophet [BECNT]. He is the last and greatest of the OT prophets, and he was sent to proclaim the coming of the Messiah [My].

11:11 Truly I-say to-you(pl) there-has-not-arisen[a] among those-born[b] of-women (one) greater-than[c] John the Baptist; but the least[d] in the kingdom of the heavens is greater than-he.

LEXICON—a. perf. pass. indic. of ἐγείρω (LN **13.83**) (BAGD 2.e. p. 215): 'to arise' [BECNT, CC, **LN**, NICNT, NIGTC, NTC, PNTC, WBC; ESV, NASB, NET, NRSV], 'to rise' [KJV, NIV], 'to appear' [BAGD, BNTC], 'to be caused to exist, to be raised up' [LN], not explicit [CEV, GW, NCV, NLT, REB]. This verb means to cause to come into existence [LN].

b. γεννητός (LN **23.47**) (BAGD p. 156): 'born' [BAGD, BECNT, BNTC, CC, **LN**, NICNT, NIGTC, NTC, PNTC, WBC; ESV, KJV, NASB, NET, NET, NIV, NRSV], 'begotten' [BAGD], 'one born, one who has been born, person' [LN]. This idiom γεννητοῖς γυναικῶν 'born of women' is translated 'born on this earth' [CEV], 'ever born' [GW, NCV], 'ever been born' [REB], 'all who have ever lived' [NLT], 'who have lived' [**LN**; TEV]. This adjective describes having been born [LN].

c. μείζων (comparative form of μέγας) (LN 87.22) (BAGD 2.b.α. p. 498): 'greater than' [BAGD, LN; all translations], 'more important' [LN]. This adjective describes being great in terms of status [LN].

d. μικρότερος (comparative form of μικρός) (LN **87.58**) (BAGD 1.c. p. 521): 'least' [BAGD, BECNT, BNTC, CC, NIGTC, NTC, PNTC, WBC; all versions except GW, NCV, NLT], 'least person' [NLT], 'least important person' [GW, NCV], 'of least importance' [BAGD], 'less important' [NICNT], 'lowest' [LN]. The comparative form is used here with the sense of a superlative [CC, EBC, ICC, NAC]. This adjective describes being of low or unimportant status [LN].

QUESTION—How would someone who is least in the kingdom of heaven be greater than John the Baptist?

The greatness of the least important person in the kingdom is more than the greatness of John solely because that unimportant person belongs to the new era, an era that is so very much superior to the old era of John the Baptist [BNTC, CC, ICC, NAC, NIBC, NIGTC, NTC, PNTC, TH, WBC]. John was the last and greatest prophet in the prophetic era, but he died before the full coming of the greater new covenant era [BECNT, NIBC]. John came at the end of the old era, and was still within that old order, as the kingdom had not yet fully come [BNTC, My]. This is not saying that John is excluded from the messianic salvation, but that he essentially belongs to the old era. He prophesied about the coming time of salvation but did not live long enough to experience it [NAC, NICNT]. The great dividing line between the ages occurred after John's death in the complex of events involved in Jesus' death, resurrection, and the sending of the Spirit [NAC]. John was not able to see the great revelations given by God after John's death or even while he was in prison, so others after him had an advantage over him [Lns]. He is saying that Jesus' disciples are more important than John because they are privileged to participate in God's kingdom [TH].

11:12 And from the days[a] of John the Baptist until now the kingdom of the heavens suffers-violence[b]/advances-forcefully,[b] and violent-ones[c] take- it -by-force.[d]

LEXICON—a. ἡμέρα (LN 67.142) (BAGD 4.b. p. 347): 'day' [BECNT, BNTC, CC, NICNT, NIGTC, NTC, PNTC, WBC; ESV, KJV, NASB, NET, NIV, NRSV], 'time' [BAGD, LN; CEV, GW, NCV, NLT, REB, TEV], 'period' [LN]. This noun denotes an indefinite unit of time (whether grammatically singular or plural), but not particularly long [LN].

b. pres. mid. or pass. indic. of βιάζομαι (LN **20.9**, **20.10**) (BAGD 2.d. p. 140): 'to suffer violence' [BECNT, BNTC, PNTC, WBC; ESV, KJV, NASB, NET, NRSV], 'to be subjected to violence' [NICNT; REB], 'to be violently attacked' [CC], 'to be attacked with violence' [LN], 'to suffer violent attacks' [LN (**20.9**); TEV], 'to use violence' [LN (20.10)], 'to advance forcefully' [GW, NIV, NLT], 'to press forcefully' [NIGTC], 'to go forward in strength' [NCV], 'to press forward vigorously' [NTC], 'to enter forcibly into something' [BAGD], not explicit [CEV]. This verb can mean to experience a violent attack [LN (20.9)], or it can mean to employ violence in doing harm to someone or something [LN (20.10)].

c. βιαστής (LN **20.11**) (BAGD p. 141): 'violent person' [LN], 'violent man' [BAGD, BNTC, CC, **LN**, PNTC; NASB, REB, TEV], 'forceful man' [NIV], 'vigorous man' [NTC], 'impetuous man' [BAGD]. This plural noun is translated 'violent people' [BECNT, NICNT, WBC; CEV, NLT], 'forceful people' [GW, NET], 'those who are violent' [NIGTC], 'the violent' [ESV, KJV, NRSV], 'people' [NCV]. This noun denotes a person who employs violence in order to accomplish his purpose [LN].

d. pres. act. indic. of ἁρπάζω (LN **39.49**) (BAGD 2.b. p. 109): 'to take by force' [ESV, KJV, NASB, NRSV, REB], 'to try to take by force' [NCV], 'to take over by force' [CEV], 'to attack' [NLT], 'to seize' [BAGD, BNTC, LN, PNTC; GW], 'to try to seize' [TEV], 'to snatch (it) away' [CC], 'to plunder' [NICNT, WBC], 'to lay hold of' [NET, NIV], 'to grab at' [NIGTC], 'to take possession' [NTC], 'to claim for oneself' [BAGD], 'to attack' [**LN**]. This verb means to attack, with the implication of seizing [LN].

QUESTION—What does Jesus mean in this statement concerning violence and the kingdom?

1. Jesus is saying that the kingdom is suffering violence [BECNT, BNTC, CC, ICC, NAC, NIBC, NICNT, PNTC, WBC; ESV, KJV, NASB, NET, NRSV, REB, TEV]. This refers to the time when John did his effective preaching in the wilderness and accomplished his life's work. That was the period of time that inaugurated an era in which the kingdom of heaven suffers violence. Violent men are carrying out the violence from which the kingdom suffers [PNTC].

2. Jesus is saying that the kingdom is advancing forcefully [EBC, Lns, My, NIGTC, NTC; GW, NCV, NIV, NLT]. From the days of John the Baptist when Jesus began his ministry the kingdom has been forcefully advancing [EBC].

QUESTION—What did Jesus mean about violent ones taking the kingdom by force?

1. Violent men are forcefully opposing the advancement of the kingdom [BECNT, BNTC, CC, EBC, ICC, NAC, NIBC, NICNT, NIGTC, PNTC, WBC; NLT, NRSV, REB]. Herod was one such example [BECNT, CC, EBC, NAC, NIBC, PNTC]. Opposition was rising, and would get worse, a fact that confused John the Baptist [EBC]. This is a case in which the verb βιάζεται in the first clause is used in the positive sense of advancing forcefully, and its noun cognate βιασταί in the next clause is used in a negative sense, which is that of violence [EBC].

2. Courageous or forceful people are laying hold of it (in a positive sense) [Lns, My, NTC].

3. The statement βιασταὶ ἁρπάζουσιν αὐτήν means that some people are ready to employ violence or military force in order to establish what they regarded as the rule of God on earth [LN].

11:13 **For all the prophets and the law prophesied**[a] **until John;** **11:14** **and if you(pl)-are-willing**[b] **to-accept**[c] **(it), he is Elijah the-one destined**[d] **to-come.** **11:15** **The-one having ears let-him-hear.**[e]

LEXICON—a. aorist act. indic. of προφητεύω (LN 33.459) (BAGD 3. p. 723): 'to prophesy' [BAGD, BECNT, BNTC, CC, LN, NICNT, NTC, PNTC, WBC; ESV, GW, KJV, NASB, NET, NIV, NRSV], 'to prophesy the future' [NIGTC], 'to foretell the future' [BAGD], 'to foretell things to come' [REB], 'to tell what is going to happen' [CEV], 'to tell about what would happen' [NCV], 'to look forward (to this present time)' [NLT], 'to speak about the kingdom' [TEV], 'to make inspired utterances' [LN]. This verb means to speak under the influence of divine inspiration, with or without reference to future events [LN].

b. pres. act. indic. of θέλω (LN 30.58) (BAGD 2. p. 355): 'to be willing' [BECNT, BNTC, CC, NICNT, NIGTC, NTC, PNTC, WBC; ESV, GW, NASB, NET, NIV, NLT, NRSV, TEV], 'to be prepared (to accept), to wish, to want, to be ready' [BAGD], 'to purpose' [LN], not explicit [CEV]. This verb is translated as an auxiliary helping verb: '(if) you will (receive/believe/accept)' [KJV, NCV, REB]. This verb means to purpose, generally based upon a preference and desire [LN].

c. aorist mid. (deponent = act.) infinitive of δέχομαι (LN 31.51) (BAGD 3.b. p. 177): 'to accept' [BAGD, BECNT, BNTC, LN, NICNT, NTC, PNTC, WBC; ESV, GW, NASB, NET, NIV, NLT, NRSV, REB], 'to receive' [CC, NIGTC; KJV], 'to receive readily' [LN], 'to believe' [LN; CEV, NCV, TEV], 'to approve, to tolerate, to put up with' [BAGD]. This verb means to readily receive information and to regard it as true [LN].

d. pres. act. participle of μέλλω (LN 67.62) (BAGD 1.c.β. p. 501): 'to be destined (to come)' [NICNT; REB], 'to be about to' [LN], 'going to' [BAGD]. The phrase ὁ μέλλων ἔρχεσθαι 'the one destined to come' is translated 'who is going to come' [CC], 'who is to come' [BECNT, NIGTC, PNTC; ESV, NET, NRSV], 'who was to come' [BNTC, NTC; GW, NASB, NIV; similarly KJV], 'the one about to come' [WBC], 'whom they said would come' [NCV], 'the prophets said would come' [NLT], 'whose coming was predicted' [TEV], 'you are waiting for' [CEV]. This verb means to occur at a point of time in the future which is subsequent to another event and closely related to it [LN].

e. pres. act. impera. of ἀκούω (LN 31.56) (BAGD 1.a. p. 31): 'to hear' [BAGD, CC, NICNT, NIGTC, NTC, PNTC; ESV, KJV, NASB, NIV, REB], 'to listen' [BECNT, WBC; GW, NET, NRSV], 'to listen and understand' [NLT], 'to accept, to listen to, to listen and respond, to pay attention and respond, to heed' [LN]. This third person imperative is translated as second person imperative: '(then) hear' [REB], 'listen!'

[BECNT; NCV, TEV], 'pay attention!' [CEV]. This verb means to believe something and to respond to it on the basis of having heard [LN].

QUESTION—What relationship is indicate by γάρ 'for'?

It indicates the grounds for what is stated in verse 12 [EBC, ICC]. It gives grounds for the claim that the kingdom has been advancing. The law and prophets prophesied until John, and now there is a new era, and the fulfillment of the prophecy is that the kingdom itself has been forcefully advancing [EBC].

QUESTION—In what sense did the law 'prophesy'?

It pointed forward to a fuller revelation of God's will that was to come [NICNT, PNTC].

QUESTION—To what does εἰ θέλετε δέξασθαι 'if you are willing to accept (it)' refer?

1. It refers to the premise that follows, which is that, though it may be hard to accept, John is the Elijah who was to come [EBC, CC, ICC, Lns, My, NAC, NICNT, NIGTC, NTC, PNTC, TRT, WBC; NLT]. There were other possible interpretations of the Malachi passage that people may have held [NAC].
2. It refers to the law and the prophets, meaning that if you are willing to believe the law and the prophets, John is the Elijah who was to come [CEV, GW].

QUESTION—What is meant by the statement that John is the Elijah who was to come?

It refers to the prophecy of Malachi 4:5–6 [BECNT, CC, ICC, Lns, My, NAC, NIBC, NICNT, NIGTC, NTC, PNTC, TH, WBC]. John is not Elijah returning in the flesh, but he has a ministry that functions in a role prior to the end time that had been ascribed to Elijah [TH, WBC]. John is the forerunner of the day of the Lord, for which Elijah was to prepare the way [CC, NAC, NICNT, NIGTC]. John was to prepare for the coming of the Lord [PNTC]. John was like Elijah in various ways [Lns, NTC, TRT], including his sternness [Lns], the suddenness of his appearance, his call to repentance, his simplicity of lifestyle, and the sharpness of his message [NTC].

11:16 To-what shall-I-compare[a] this generation[b]? It-is like children sitting in the market-places[c] who are-calling to the others **11:17** saying, 'We played-the-flute[d] for-you and you-did- not -dance;[e] we-sang-a-dirge[f] and you-did- not -weep.[g]'

LEXICON—a. fut. act. indic. of ὁμοιόω (LN 64.5) (BAGD 2. p. 567): 'to compare' [BAGD, BECNT, BNTC, CC, LN, NICNT, NIGTC, NTC; ESV, NASB, NET, NIV, NLT, NRSV, TEV], 'to liken' [PNTC, WBC; KJV], 'to describe' [GW, REB]. The phrase 'to what shall I compare this generation? It is like…' is translated 'what can I say about the people of this time? What are they like? They are like…' [NCV], 'you people are

like' [CEV]. This verb means to consider something to be like something else [LN].
b. γενεά (LN 11.4) (BAGD 2. p. 154): 'generation' [BAGD, BECNT, BNTC, CC, NICNT, NIGTC, NTC, PNTC, WBC; ESV, KJV, NASB, NET, NIV, NLT, NRSV, REB], 'you people' [CEV], 'the people who are living now' [GW], 'the people of this time' [NCV], 'the people of this day' [TEV], 'contemporaries' [BAGD], 'those of the same time, those of the same generation' [LN]. This noun denotes people living at the same time and belonging to the same reproductive age-class [LN].
c. ἀγορά (LN 57.207) (BAGD p. 12): 'marketplace' [BAGD, BECNT, BNTC, CC, LN, NICNT, NTC, PNTC, WBC; all versions except CEV, KJV, NLT], 'market' [LN; CEV, KJV], 'public square' [NIGTC; NLT], 'business center' [BAGD, LN]. This noun denotes a commercial center with a number of places for doing business [LN].
d. aorist act. indic. of αὐλέω (LN **6.87**) (BAGD p. 121): 'to play a flute' [BAGD, BECNT, BNTC, CC, LN, NIGTC, NTC, PNTC, WBC; CEV, ESV, NASB, NET, NIV, NRSV], 'to pipe' [NICNT; KJV, REB], 'to play music' [GW, NCV], 'to play wedding music' [TEV], 'to play wedding songs' [NLT].
e. ὀρχέομαι (LN **15.244**) (BAGD p. 583): 'to dance' [BAGD, LN; all translations]. This verb means to engage in patterned rhythmic movements of the whole and/or parts of the body, normally to the accompaniment of music [LN].
f. aorist act. indic. of θρηνέω (LN 33.115) (BAGD 1.b. p. 363): 'to sing a dirge' [BAGD, BECNT, BNTC, NICNT, NTC, WBC; ESV, NASB, NIV], 'to lament' [CC; REB], 'to mourn' [KJV], 'to wail' [NIGTC, PNTC; NRSV], 'to wail in mourning' [NET], 'to sing funeral songs' [LN; CEV, GW, TEV], 'to play funeral songs' [NLT], 'to sing a sad song' [NCV], 'to chant a dirge' [LN]. This verb means to sing or chant expressions of mourning [LN].
g. aorist mid. indic. of κόπτομαι (LN 52.1) (BAGD 2. p. 444): 'to mourn' [BECNT, BNTC, LN, NICNT, NIGTC, WBC; CEV, ESV, NASB, NIV, NLT, NRSV, REB], 'to beat the breast in mourning' [CC], 'to beat the breast' [LN, NTC], 'to show sadness' [GW], 'to lament' [LN, PNTC; KJV], 'to cry' [NCV, TEV], 'to weep' [NET]. This verb means to beat the breast and lament as an expression of sorrow [LN].

QUESTION—What does this comparison describe?

It describes people who cannot be satisfied [BNTC, EBC, Lns, NICNT, NIGTC, NTC, PNTC]. Jesus' contemporaries will have nothing to do with any of the messengers sent to them [WBC]. People would not respond to John's call to repentance, or to Jesus' message of good news and enter into joyful fellowship with others [ICC]. They rejected John's austerity as well as the freedom Jesus offered [NIBC]. In their estimation John was too harsh and Jesus was too liberal; neither matched their expectations [CC, My]. For people to object to John's asceticism and Jesus' supposed indulgence is hypocritical and inconsistent [NAC]. They refused to respond to John's warnings of judgment or Jesus' message of joy [TH].

QUESTION—Who do the children represent, and who do the 'others' represent?

1. The children calling out to the others to suggest games represent Jesus and John, and their companions who are uncooperative with anything that is suggested are like the Jews of Jesus' day [BECNT, BNTC, EBC, NIBC, NICNT, NIGTC, NTC, PNTC, TH]. Jesus and John offered a full spectrum of choice, but the people of their day wanted nothing of what they offered [NIGTC]. The comparison may not be entirely exact, as it is the overall picture that conveys the idea rather than the specific elements [NICNT].

2. The children calling out represent the Jews of Jesus' day and the others to whom they call out represent John and Jesus; at first the Jews call to the ascetic John to dance and be merry, and then they call out to Jesus to live up to their standards of asceticism [CC, ICC, Lns, My]. John and Jesus would not accommodate themselves to the unstable multitudes [Lns].

11:18 For John came neither eating[a] nor drinking,[b] and you(pl)-say, 'He-has a-demon.' **11:19** The Son of Man came eating and drinking, and you(pl)-say, 'Behold a man (who is) a-glutton[c] and a-drunkard,[d] a-friend[e] of-tax-collectors and sinners.'

LEXICON—a. pres. act. participle of ἐσθίω (LN 23.1) (BAGD 1.e.γ. p. 313): 'to eat' [BAGD, LN; all translations except TEV], 'to drink, to consume food, to use food' [LN]. The phrase μήτε ἐσθίων 'neither eating' is translated 'he fasted' [TEV]. This verb means to consume food, usually solids, but also liquids [LN].

b. pres. act. participle of πίνω (LN 23.34) (BAGD 1. p. 658): 'to drink' [BAGD, LN; all translations except TEV]. The phrase μήτε πίνων 'nor drinking' is translated 'he drank no wine' [TEV]. This verb means to consume liquids, particularly water and wine [LN].

c. φάγος (LN **23.19**) (BAGD p. 851): 'glutton' [BAGD, BNTC, LN, NIGTC, NTC, WBC; ESV, GW, NET, NIV, NLT, NRSV, REB, TEV], 'gluttonous man' [BECNT, PNTC; KJV, NASB], 'a greedy fellow' [NICNT]. The phrase ἄνθρωπος φάγος 'man who is a glutton' is translated 'the man is a glutton' [CC], 'that man/he eats too much!' [CEV, NCV]. This noun denotes a person who habitually eats excessively [LN].

d. οἰνοπότης (LN 88.288) (BAGD p. 562): 'drunkard' [BAGD, BNTC, BECNT, CC, LN, NIGTC, WBC; ESV, NASB, NIV, NLT, NRSV], '(a) drunk' [GW, NET], 'drinker' [NTC; REB], 'wine drinker' [BAGD, PNTC; TEV], 'wine bibber' [KJV], 'heavy drinker' [LN], 'who likes his drink' [NICNT], '(that man) drinks too much!' [CEV], '(he) drinks too much wine' [NCV]. This noun denotes a person who habitually drinks too much and thus becomes a drunkard [LN].

e. φίλος (LN 34.11) (BAGD 2.a.α. p. 861): 'friend' [BAGD, LN; all translations]. This noun denotes a male person with whom one associates and for whom there is affection or personal regard [LN].

QUESTION—What does it mean that John came neither eating nor drinking?

It refers to John's asceticism [ICC, NAC, NIBC, NICNT, NIGTC, PNTC, TH, WBC]. He wasn't known for eating and drinking [CEV]. He didn't use alcohol or go to dinner parties [EBC]. He didn't eat or drink like other people do [NCV], or spend his time eating and drinking [NLT]. He fasted and drank no wine [TH; TEV]. He is contrasted with Jesus who feasts and drinks [NICNT, NIGTC; NLT].

And-yet[a] wisdom[b] is-proved-right[c] by her deeds.[d]"

TEXT—Manuscripts reading ἀπὸ τῶν ἔργων αὐτῆς 'by her deeds' are given a B rating by GNT to indicate it was regarded to be almost certain. Some manuscripts have ἀπὸ τῶν τέκνων αὐτῆς 'by her children'. Only KJV follows this reading.

LEXICON—a. καί (LN 89.92): 'and yet' [BNTC, NIGTC, PNTC], 'yet' [NTC; CEV, ESV, GW, NASB, NRSV, REB], 'and' [LN, NICNT, WBC], 'and so' [CC], 'but' [BECNT; KJV, NCV, NET, NIV, NLT], 'however' [TEV]. This conjunction marks coordinate relations [LN].

b. σοφία (LN 32.32) (BAGD 4. p. 760): 'wisdom' [BAGD, LN; all translations except REB, TEV], 'God's wisdom' [REB, TEV], 'to be prudent' [LN]. This noun denotes the capacity to understand and, as a result, to act wisely [LN].

c. aorist pass. indic. of δικαιόω (LN 88.16) (BAGD 2. p. 197): 'to be proved right' [PNTC; GW, NIV, REB], 'to be proven to be right' [LN; NCV], 'to be vindicated' [BAGD, BECNT, NIGTC, NTC; KJV, NASB, NET, NRSV], 'to be justified' [BAGD, BNTC, NICNT, WBC; ESV], 'to be declared innocent' [CC], 'to be shown to be right' [LN; CEV, NLT], 'to be shown to be true' [TEV]. This verb means to demonstrate that something is morally right [LN].

d. ἔργον (LN 42.11): 'deed' [LN], 'act' [LN]. This plural noun is translated 'deeds' [BECNT, NICNT, NIGTC, WBC; ESV, NASB, NET, NRSV], 'works' [BNTC, CC, NTC], 'actions' [PNTC; GW, NIV], 'what it does' [CEV, NCV], 'results' [NLT, REB, TEV]. This noun denotes that which is done, with possible focus on the energy or effort involved [LN].

QUESTION—What is the point of this statement about wisdom?

How Jesus lived, that is, his actions will eventually vindicate him as being right [WBC]. God's wisdom is proved right by the lifestyles lived by Jesus and John, both of whom are living righteously, though differently from one another [EBC]. John and Jesus both exemplify living the good life that comes as the fruit of practical wisdom [NICNT]. John and Jesus are envoys of Wisdom personified [NIGTC]. The wisdom Jesus taught is lived out and proved right in how his followers live [PNTC]. God's wisdom, which Jesus and John taught, is proved to be right by the results in the lives of people who live by it [TRT]. Jesus' works make his identity plain [ICC]. The message of repentance that John preached, and the message of salvation that Jesus preached, have been vindicated by the fruit shown in the lives of those who responded to them [NTC]. Regardless of how people may have responded, what Jesus did gave clear evidence that the kingdom had arrived [NIBC]. What Jesus and John did were works of divine Wisdom, so when people contradict themselves by slandering first Jesus and then John, they are actually proving Wisdom to be innocent by their own contradictory accusations [Lns].

DISCOURSE UNIT—11:20–24 [CEV, ESV, GW, NASB, NCV, NET, NIV, NLT, TEV]. The topic is Jesus warns Chorazin, Bethsaida, and Capernaum [GW], Jesus warns unbelievers [NCV], judgment for the unbelievers [NLT], the unbelieving towns [CEV, TEV], woe to unrepentant cities [ESV, NRSV], woes on unrepentant cities [NET], woe on unrepentant cities [NIV], the unrepenting cities [NASB].

11:20 Then he-began to-denounce^a the cities in which most^b of-his miracles happened,^{c} because they-did- not -repent;^{d}

LEXICON—a. pres. act. infin. of ὀνειδίζω (LN 33. 422) (BAGD 2. p. 570): 'to denounce' [BECNT; ESV, GW, NASB, NIV, REB], 'to reprimand' [**LN**], 'to reproach' [BAGD, BNTC, CC, LN, NICNT, NIGTC, NTC, PNTC; NRSV, TEV], 'to criticize' [NCV], 'to criticize openly' [NET], 'to upbraid' [KJV]. This verb is translated as a phrase: 'Jesus was upset with them and said' [CEV]. This verb means to reproach someone, with the implication of that individual being evidently to blame [LN].

b. πολύς (LN 59.1) (BAGD III.1.a. p. 689): 'most of' [BAGD], 'many, a great deal of, a great number of' [LN]. The phrase αἱ πλεῖσται δυνάμεις αὐτοῦ 'most of his miracles' [BECNT; CEV, GW, NASB, NCV, NIV, REB, TEV] is also translated 'most of his mighty works' [BNTC, NIGTC, NTC, PNTC; ESV, KJV], 'most of his deeds of power' [NRSV], 'the majority of his miracles' [WBC], 'his many miracles' [NICNT], 'many of his miracles' [CC; NET], 'so many of his miracles' [NLT]. This adjective describes a relatively large quantity of objects or events [LN].

c. aorist mid. (deponent = active) indic. of γίνομαι (LN 13.107) (BAGD I.2.a. p. 158): 'to happen' [CC, LN, NIGTC], 'to be done' [BAGD, BECNT, BNTC, PNTC; ESV, KJV, NASB, NRSV], 'to be performed' [NTC; NIV, REB], 'to take place' [BAGD, NICNT], 'to occur, to come to be' [LN]. The verb ἐγένοντο 'happened' is translated 'he had done…(miracles)' [WBC; NET, REB], 'he had worked…(miracles)' [CEV, GW], 'he had performed…(miracles)' [TEV], 'he did' [NCV]. This verb means to happen, with the implication that what happens is different from a previous state [LN].

d. aorist act. indic. of μετανοέω (LN 41.52) (BAGD p. 512): 'to repent' [BAGD, BECNT, BNTC, CC, LN, NICNT, NIGTC, NTC, PNTC, WBC; ESV, KJV, NASB, NET, NIV, NRSV], 'to repent of one's sins and turn to

God' [NLT], 'to turn from one's sins' [TEV], 'to turn to God' [CEV], 'to change the way one thinks and acts' [GW], 'to change one's life and stop sinning' [NCV], 'to change one's way' [LN], 'to change one's mind, to be converted' [BAGD]. The phrase ὅτι οὐ μετενόησαν 'because they did not repent' is translated 'for their impenitence' [REB]. This verb means to change one's way of life as the result of a complete change of thought and attitude with regard to sin and righteousness [LN].

11:21 "Woe[a] to-you(sg), Chorazin, woe to-you(sg) Bethsaida; for if the miracles which occurred among you(pl) happened in Tyre and Sidon they-would-have-repented long-ago[b] in sackcloth[c] and ashes.[d]

LEXICON—a. οὐαί (LN 22.9) (BAGD 1.a. p. 591): 'woe' [BAGD, BECNT, BNTC, CC, NICNT, NIGTC, NTC, PNTC; ESV, KJV, NASB, NET, NIV, NRSV], 'alas' [BAGD; REB], 'how horrible' [GW], 'how terrible' [NCV, TEV], 'disaster, horror' [LN]. The phrase Οὐαί σοι, Χοραζίν 'woe to you Chorazin' is translated 'You people of Chorazin are in for trouble!' [CEV], 'What sorrow awaits you, Korazin' [NLT]. This noun denotes a state of intense hardship or distress [LN].

b. πάλαι (LN 67.24) (BAGD 1. p. 605): 'long ago' [BAGD, LN; all translations except NCV], 'a long time ago' [NCV]. This adverb describes a point of time preceding another point of time, with an interval of considerable length [LN].

c. σάκκος (LN 6.164) (BAGD p. 740): 'sackcloth' [BAGD, **LN**; all translations except NCV, NLT, TEV]. The phrase 'in sackcloth' is translated 'clothing themselves in burlap' [NLT], 'they would have worn rough cloth (to show…)' [NCV], 'would have put on sackcloth (to show)' [TEV]. This noun denotes a heavy material normally used for making sacks, but worn by persons in mourning and as a sign of repentance [LN].

d. σποδός (LN 14.73) (BAGD p. 763): 'ashes' [BAGD, BECNT, BNTC, CC, LN, NICNT, NIGTC, NTC, PNTC, WBC; ESV, GW, KJV, NASB, NET, NIV, NRSV, REB]. The phrase 'in…ashes' is translated 'they would have…put ashes on their heads/on themselves' [CEV, NCV], 'would have sprinkled ashes on themselves' [TEV], 'throwing ashes on their heads' [NLT]. This noun denotes the residue from a burned substance [LN].

QUESTION—What is communicated by οὐαί σοι 'woe to you'?

It expresses regret, not vengeance [NIBC, PNTC], and combines both compassion and warning [PNTC]. It is almost the same as a curse [NTC]. It mixes an announcement of doom with pity [EBC, NAC]. It expresses threat or warning [ICC, TRT]. It is a prophetic formula conveying blame [CC, NICNT], or impending judgment [CC], but not sympathy [NICNT]. It is a prophetic lament [NIGTC]. It is a lament that expresses painful displeasure [WBC]. It is the opposite of 'blessed' in 5:3 [TH].

QUESTION—What relationship is indicated by εἰ 'if'?

It indicates a contrary to fact conditional construction, something that did not in fact occur [BECNT, CC, TRT].

11:22 But[a] I-say to-you(sg), it-will-be more-tolerable[b] (for) Tyre and Sidon in (the) day of-judgment than for-you(pl).

LEXICON—a. πλήν (LN 89.130) (BAGD 1.b. p. 669): 'but' [BAGD, BNTC, CC, LN, NTC; ESV, KJV, NCV, NET, NIV, NRSV, REB], 'nevertheless' [BAGD, BECNT, LN, PNTC, WBC; NASB], 'indeed' [NICNT], 'in fact' [NIGTC], 'however' [BAGD], not explicit [CEV, GW, NLT, TEV]. This conjunction indicates contrast, implying the validity of something irrespective of other considerations [LN].

b. ἀνεκτότερον (comparative of ἀνεκτός) (LN **25.172**) (BAGD p. 64): 'more tolerable' [BAGD, BECNT, BNTC, **LN**, NIGTC, NTC, WBC; KJV, NASB, NRSV], 'more bearable' [BAGD, CC, LN, NICNT, PNTC; ESV, NET, NIV, REB], 'more endurable' [BAGD, LN], 'better (for)' [GW, NCV]. The phrase Τύρῳ καὶ Σιδῶνι ἀνεκτότερον ἔσται 'it will be more tolerable for Tyre and Sidon' is translated 'Tyre and Sidon will be better off' [NLT], 'the people of Tyre and Sidon will get off easier than you' [CEV], 'God will show more mercy to the people of Tyre and Sidon than to you' [TEV]. This adjective describes what can be borne or endured [LN].

QUESTION—What is shown about those who will be punished on the day of judgment?

There will be degrees of torment in hell [EBC]. Those who had greater opportunities will be judged more severely than those who have had less [PNTC].

11:23 And you(sg), Capernaum, will-you-be-lifted-up[a] to[b] heaven[c]? No,[d] to Hades[e] you-will-go-down;[f] for if the miracles happened in Sodom which happened in you(sg), it-would-have-remained[g] until today. **11:24** Yet I-say to-you(pl) that it-will-be more-tolerable for Sodom in (the) day-of-judgment than for-you(sg)."

TEXT—Manuscripts reading μὴ ἕως οὐρανοῦ ὑψωθήσῃ 'will you be lifted up to heaven? No!' are given a B rating by GNT to indicate that it was regarded to be almost certain. Manuscripts that have ἢ ἕως οὐρανοῦ ὑψωθεῖσα 'who are lifted up to heaven' are followed by KJV only.

TEXT—Manuscripts reading καταβήσῃ 'you will go down' are given a C rating by GNT to indicate that choosing it over a variant text was difficult. This reading is followed by BECNT, BNTC, CC, NICNT, NTC, WBC; CEV, GW, NASB, NIV, NLT. Manuscripts that have καταβιβασθήσῃ 'you will be brought down' are followed by NIGTC, PNTC; ESV, KJV, NCV, NET, NRSV, REB, TEV.

LEXICON—a. fut. pass. indic. of ὑψόω (LN 87.20) (BAGD 1. p. 851): 'to be lifted up' [BAGD, CC; NCV, NIV], 'to be lifted' [GW], 'to lift oneself' [TEV], 'to be exalted' [BECNT, BNTC, LN, NICNT, NIGTC, NTC,

MATTHEW 11:23–24

PNTC, WBC; ESV, KJV, NASB, NET, NRSV, REB], 'to be raised high' [BAGD], 'to be honored' [CEV, NLT], 'to be given high position' [LN]. This verb means to cause someone to have high status [LN].

b. ἕως (LN 84.19) (BAGD II.2.a. p. 335): 'to' [LN; all translations except CEV, NLT], 'as far as' [BAGD, LN], 'in' [CEV, NLT], 'up to' [LN]. This preposition indicates extension up to or as far as a goal [LN].

c. οὐρανός (LN 1.11, 1.5) (BAGD 1.b. p. 594): 'heaven' [LN (1.11), all translations except NIV], 'the skies' [NIV], 'sky' [BAGD, LN (1.5)]. This noun denotes the supernatural dwelling place of God and other heavenly beings. Although this noun has a component denoting that which is 'above' or 'in the sky,' the element of abode' is evidently more significant than a location above the earth [LN]. The Heaven–Hades contrast could be metaphorical for exaltation–humiliation, but in view of the surrounding references to the day of judgment, Hades has more sinister overtones [EBC].

d. μή. This negating particle (which was in the previous sentence) indicates that the question asked expects a negative answer [Lns, NTC]. It is translated as 'you will…will you?' [BECNT], 'will you…?' [BNTC, NTC, WBC; ESV, GW, NCV, NET, NIV, NLT, NRSV, REB], 'you will…?' [PNTC], 'you will not…will you?' [CC; NASB], 'will you really…?' [NICNT], 'do you think you will…?' [NIGTC; CEV], 'do you want to…' [TEV].

e. ᾅδης (LN 1.19) (BAGD 1. p. 17): 'Hades' [BECNT, BNTC, CC, LN, NICNT, NIGTC, NTC, PNTC, WBC; ESV, NASB, NET, NRSV, REB], 'hell' [CEV, GW, KJV, TEV], 'the depths' [NCV, NIV], 'the place of the dead' [NLT], 'the world of the dead' [LN]. This noun denotes a place or abode of the dead, including both the righteous and the unrighteous (in most contexts ᾅδης is equivalent to the Hebrew term Sheol) [LN].

f. fut. mid. (deponent = act.) indic. of καταβαίνω (LN 15.107) (BAGD 2. p. 408): 'to go down' [CC, LN, NICNT, WBC; CEV, GW, NIV, NLT], 'to descend' [BECNT, BNTC, LN, NTC; NASB], 'to move down, to come down' [LN]. The variant textual reading (in the passive voice) is translated 'to be brought down' [BAGD, NIGTC, PNTC; ESV, KJV, NRSV, REB], 'to be thrown down' [NCV, NET, TEV]. This verb means to move down, irrespective of the gradient [LN].

g. aorist act. indic. of μένω (LN **13.89**) (BAGD 1.c.β. p. 504): 'to remain' [BECNT, CC, LN, NIGTC, PNTC, WBC; ESV, KJV, NASB, NIV, NRSV], 'to continue' [LN; NET], 'to continue to exist' [LN], 'to survive' [BNTC, NICNT], 'to be standing' [NTC], 'to be still standing' [CEV, REB], 'to still be there/here' [GW, NLT], 'to still be a city' [NCV], 'to still be in existence' [**LN**; TEV]. This verb means to continue to exist [LN].

QUESTION—What does being lifted up to heaven mean?

The people of Capernaum believed that they were going to heaven [PNTC, TRT]. There they expected to receive great eschatological blessings [WBC].

It refers to the fact that they had the great distinction of Jesus having lived and worked there [My]. The people of Capernaum had optimistic expectations that were not realistic in view of the disaster coming upon them [NIGTC]. They had great pride [TH]. Heaven refers to God's saving presence [CC].

QUESTION—What does going down to Hades mean here?

Jesus is saying that they will go to the place of torment for the dead [BECNT, Lns, NTC, PNTC]. It means going to hell [CC, Lns, My, NTC, TRT]. It refers to eternal judgment [EBC, NAC]. Hades represents the place of the dead [NIBC, NICNT, WBC], which is not the same as hell, though it does symbolize destruction [NICNT]. Here it is only a figure of speech representing abasement [ICC]. This is an allusion to Isaiah 14:15 [BECNT, BNTC, CC, EBC, ICC, NAC, NIBC, NICNT, NIGTC, NTC, PNTC, WBC].

QUESTION—Who is Jesus addressing in verse 24?

1. He was continuing to address Capernaum [My, PNTC]. The plural 'you' is addressed to the inhabitants of Capernaum, and the singular 'you' is addressed to the city [My]. All translations seem to imply that Jesus was continuing to address Capernaum.
2. Jesus had been addressing the cities in the preceding verse with the singular pronoun 'you', so probably this change to the plural 'you' is directed to the people in the crowd of verse 7 who were listening to Jesus [EBC]. The plural 'you' is addressed to anyone who hears his statement about Capernaum's fate [NICNT].

DISCOURSE UNIT—11:25–30 [CEV, ESV, GW, NASB, NCV, NET, NIV, NLT, NRSV, TEV]. The topic is Jesus praises the Father and invites disciples to come to him [GW], Jesus offers rest to people [NCV], come to me and rest [CEV, TEV], come to me and I will give you rest [ESV], come to me [NASB], Jesus' invitation [NET], rest for the weary [NIV], Jesus thanks his father [NRSV], Jesus' prayer of thanksgiving [NLT].

11:25 At that time answering Jesus said, "I-praise[a] you(sg), Father, Lord of-the heaven and the earth, that you-hid[b] these (things) from (the) wise[c] and (the) intelligent[d] and revealed[e] them to-little-children;[f]

LEXICON—a. pres. mid. (deponent = act.) indic. of ἐξομολογέομαι (LN **33.351**) (BAGD 2.c. p. 277): 'to praise' [BAGD, BECNT, BNTC, CC, NICNT, NTC, PNTC, WBC; GW, NASB, NCV, NIV], 'to thank' [**LN**, NIGTC; ESV, KJV, NET, NLT, NRSV, REB, TEV], 'to give thanks to' [LN], 'to be grateful to' [CEV]. This verb means to acknowledge one's thankfulness, and its NT use is restricted to contexts in which God is the one being thanked [LN].

b. aorist act. indic. of κρύπτω (LN **28.79**) (BAGD 2.a. p. 454): 'to hide' [BAGD, **LN**; all translations], 'to keep secret, to conceal' [BAGD, LN].

c. σοφός (LN 32.35) (BAGD 2. p. 760): 'wise' [BAGD; all translations except NLT, REB], 'learned' [BAGD; REB], 'one who is wise, a wise man' [LN]. The phrase σοφῶν καὶ συνετῶν 'the wise and the intelligent' is translated 'those who think themselves wise and clever' [NLT]. This pronominal adjective denotes a person of professional or semi-professional status who is regarded to be particularly capable in understanding the philosophical aspects of knowledge and experience [LN].

d. συνετός (LN 32.27) (BAGD p. 788): 'intelligent' [BAGD, BECNT, BNTC, LN, NICNT, WBC; GW, NASB, NET, NRSV], 'wise' [BAGD, BECNT; REB], 'smart' [NCV], 'learned' [NTC; NIV, TEV], 'educated' [CEV], 'clever' [PNTC], 'insightful' [LN], 'understanding' [CC, LN, NIGTC; ESV], 'prudent' [KJV]. This pronominal adjective describes a person who is able to understand and evaluate [LN].

e. aorist act. indic. of ἀποκαλύπτω (LN 28.38) (BAGD 2. p. 92): 'to reveal' [LN; all translations except CEV, NCV, TEV], 'to show' [CEV, NCV, TEV], 'to reveal something to someone' [BAGD], 'to disclose, to make fully known' [LN]. This verb means to cause something to be fully known [LN].

f. νήπιος (LN 9.43) (BAGD 1.b.β. p. 537): 'little child' [NICNT; ESV, GW, NET, NIV], 'those who are like little children' [NCV], 'small child' [LN], 'childlike' [BAGD, WBC; NLT], 'child' [BNTC], 'babe' [NTC; KJV], 'baby' [PNTC], 'infant' [BECNT, CC, NIGTC; NASB, NRSV], 'ordinary people' [CEV], 'simple' [REB], 'unlearned' [TEV], 'innocent' [BAGD]. This noun denotes a small child above the age of a helpless infant but probably not more than three or four years of age [LN]. In this verse the noun is used in the figurative sense of people who view spiritual things from the standpoint of a child, people who are child-like, innocent, and unspoiled by learning [BAGD].

QUESTION—What does ἐν ἐκείνῳ τῷ καιρῷ 'at that time' indicate?

It is not precise [EBC, NAC, PNTC, TH], but connects the passage to what has immediately preceded [BNTC, NIGTC, TH, WBC]. It links generally to the thought of opposition expressed in the previous passage [EBC, NAC]. It is linked to what has been expressed in verses 16–24, which describe how Jesus' ministry seems to be failing [CC]. It occurred in the same general period as what has just been narrated [PNTC]. It occurred after the apostles returned from the mission trip for which they were commissioned earlier in chapter 10 [Lns, My, NTC].

QUESTION—Why is this dialogue introduced with the statement 'answering Jesus said'?

'Answered and said' is a Semitic idiom that does not necessarily respond to a specific statement made previously [BNTC, EBC, ICC, NICNT, PNTC]. The phrase ἀποκριθεὶς Ἰησοῦς εἶπεν 'answering Jesus said' is translated 'Jesus answered and said' [BNTC, CC, NTC], 'Jesus said' [BECNT; CEV, GW, NASB, NET, NIV, NCV, NRSV, TEV], 'Jesus answered' [PNTC], 'Jesus said in response' [NIGTC], 'Jesus, responding to this unbelief, said' [WBC], 'Jesus declared' [NICNT; ESV], 'Jesus spoke these words' [REB], 'Jesus prayed this prayer' [NLT]. When not preceded by specific statements, this idiom is used in Matthew's to introduce a significant new statement as in 15:15 and 17:4 [NICNT]. It is the response to a situation, and not necessarily to a specific statement made by someone, and in this case, it was a response to the report of the disciples on returning from their mission trip [Lns, My, NTC]. It is a response to the unbelief of those whom he has been criticizing [WBC].

QUESTION—In what sense does Jesus call God 'Father'?

God is uniquely Jesus' father [BNTC, NTC, PNTC]. Jesus has existed eternally as the Son [CC]. He is son in his essence, the eternal Son of the eternal Father [Lns]. Jesus had an exclusive sense of sonship that is further explicated in verse 27 [EBC]. God is his Father in a messianic sense [NTC], but also in the Trinitarian sense [BECNT, NTC]. This statement is a decisive step toward the formulation of the doctrine of the Trinity [NICNT]. Although it was not unknown in Judaism for God to be considered as a Father, it was unprecedented for someone to call God 'my Father' [NICNT].

QUESTION—What are 'these things' that are hidden?

It refers to what God was doing and communicating through the ministries of John the Baptist and Jesus [CC, NIGTC], particularly their eschatological significance [CC]. It refers to the presence of the kingdom, which could not be known through human excellence or wisdom, but only by revelation and simple trust [PNTC]. It refers to the things concerning God's kingdom [NTC]. It refers to divine wisdom [NICNT]. It refers to the eschatological significance of Jesus' mighty works [BECNT, ICC, WBC], the significance of his mission [NAC], the meaning of his message and healings [BNTC, ICC], the truth he has taught and the truth about who he really is [NICNT], that the kingdom is present in Jesus himself [ICC]. It refers to the content of Jesus' teaching, the mostly unnoticed unfolding of the messianic age, and the significance of the miracles Jesus did [EBC]. It refers to all the substance of Christ's teaching, namely the gospel of salvation by grace through faith [Lns]. It refers to things related to Christ's messianic kingdom [My]. It has to do with the things of the kingdom, which some people were unable to comprehend [TRT].

QUESTION—What is meant by 'little children'?

It refers to the most humble of people, who gain knowledge of spiritual truth through simple faith [PNTC]. They are those who are conscious of their dependence [CC, EBC, Lns, NAC, NTC, WBC], who are willing to be taught [EBC, NICNT], and who are not wise in their own estimation [CC, EBC, NTC]. They are meek and humble [ICC], they are trusting and innocent, and don't allow preconceived ideas about what God's way should be like to prevent them from responding rightly to Jesus' message and miracles [BNTC]. They don't know much [TH]. They have a childlike dependence on their Father in heaven [BECNT]. The 'children' are Jesus' disciples [My, NIBC, NICNT], who are willing to receive revelation, and whose response in simple faith stands in contrast to the scribes and Pharisees [My, NIBC]. They are not important in the world's eyes [NICNT]. The poor and oppressed are included here [WBC]. It speaks of ordinary people with ordinary limits [NIGTC], the humble [TRT].

11:26 **Yes, Father, for thus it-was (your) good-pleasure[a] before[b] you(sg).**

LEXICON—a. εὐδοκία (LN 25.88) (BAGD 2. p. 319): 'good pleasure' [BAGD], 'desire, what is wished for' [LN 25.8)], 'what pleases' [LN (25.88)]. The clause ὅτι οὕτως εὐδοκία ἐγένετο ἔμπροσθέν σου 'for thus it was your good pleasure before you' is translated 'for this way was well-pleasing in your sight' [NASB], 'for this was your good pleasure' [WBC; NIV; similarly NIC, NTC], 'that is what pleased you.' [CEV], 'for such/this was your gracious will' [ESV, NET, NRSV], 'such was your choice' [REB], 'this was how you were pleased to have it happen' [TEV], 'for so it seemed good in thy sight' [KJV], 'this is what pleased you' [GW], 'this/that was pleasing to you' [BECNT, BNTC], 'so it was well pleasing before you' [PNTC], 'in this way good pleasure happened before you' [CC], 'something which was your good pleasure happened in front of you' [NIGTC], 'this is what you wanted' [NCV], 'it pleased you to do it this way' [NLT]. This noun denotes that which pleases someone [LN (25.88)], or the noun is a derivative of the verb εὐδοκέω 'to prefer' and refers to that which is desired on the basis of its appearing to be beneficial [LN 25.8].

b. ἔμπροσθεν (LN **90.20**) (BAGD 2.d. p. 257): 'before' [BAGD, CC, PNTC], 'in the sight of' [BAGD, LN], 'in the opinion of, in the judgment of' [LN]. See translation of this word in the preceding lexical item. This preposition indicates a participant whose viewpoint is relevant to an event [LN].

QUESTION—What is the significance of beginning this sentence with ναί 'yes'?

Although the particle 'yes' is usually an affirmative response to another's question or statement, here it used as the emphatic affirmation 'yes indeed' of one's own previous statement [BAGD (3.), BECNT, LN (69.1), Lns, NIGTC, PNTC]. Here it affirms the conclusion stated in this sentence concerning what was just said [WBC].

QUESTION—In what sense was οὕτως 'thus' the Father's εὐδοκία 'good pleasure'?

God takes pleasure in revealing things pertaining to salvation to humble people [Lns, NTC, PNTC]. It expresses God's sovereignty in election, which in no way diminishes human responsibility [EBC]. This term indicates God's deliberate choice and intent [NICNT]. The note of predestination should be held in tension with the affirmation of human culpability in verses 20–24 [WBC].

11:27 Everything[a] was-handed-over[b] to-me by my Father, and no-one knows[c] the Son except[d] the Father, nor does- anyone -know the Father except the Son and (anyone) to-whom the Son chooses[e] to reveal[f] (him).

LEXICON—a. πᾶς (LN 63.2) (BAGD 2.a.δ. p. 632): 'entire, whole, total' [LN]. This plural adjective is translated substantively: 'everything' [BAGD, NICNT, NIGTC, WBC; CEV, GW, NLT, REB], 'all things' [BAGD, BECNT, BNTC, CC, NTC, PNTC; ESV, KJV, NASB, NCV, NET, NIV, NRSV, TEV]. This adjective describes being entire or whole, with focus on the totality [LN].

b. aorist pass. indic. of παραδίδωμι (LN 57.77) (BAGD 3. p. 615): 'to be handed over' [BECNT, LN, NTC, PNTC; ESV, NASB, NET, NRSV], 'to be given' [WBC], 'to be given over' [LN], 'to be committed' [BNTC; NIV], 'to be entrusted' [CC, NICNT; REB], 'to be passed on' [BAGD, NIGTC], 'to be delivered' [KJV]. This passive verb is translated as active: 'to give' [CEV, NCV, TEV], 'to turn over' [GW], 'to entrust' [NLT]. This verb means to hand over to or to convey something to someone, particularly a right or an authority [LN].

c. pres. act. indic. of ἐπιγινώσκω (LN **28.2**) (BAGD 2.a. p. 291): 'to know' [BAGD, BECNT, BNTC, **LN**, NIGTC, NTC, PNTC, WBC; all versions except NLT], 'to truly know' [CC; NLT], 'to fully know' [WBC], 'to recognize' [NICNT], 'to know about, to know definitely about, knowledge about' [LN]. This verb means to possess more or less definite information about, possibly with a degree of thoroughness or competence [LN].

d. εἰ μή (LN 89.131) (BAGD VI.8.a p. 220): 'except' [BAGD, BECNT, BNTC, CC, NICNT, NIGTC, PNTC, WBC; all versions except CEV, KJV, REB], 'but' [NTC; KJV, REB], 'except that, however, instead, but only' [LN], not explicit [CEV]. The exclusion expressed by the phrase οὐδεὶς...εἰ μή 'no one...except' is stated positively: 'is the only one who' [CEV]. This phrase indicates contrast by designating an exception [LN].

e. pres. mid. or pass. (deponent = act.) subjunctive of βούλομαι (LN 30.56) (BAGD 2.b. p. 146): 'to choose' [BECNT, BNTC, NIGTC, WBC; ESV, NCV, NIV, NLT, NRSV, REB, TEV], 'to be willing' [BAGD, NICNT, NTC; GW], 'to will' [PNTC; NASB], 'to wish' [BAGD, CC], 'to decide' [NET], 'to want' [CEV], 'to purpose, to plan, to intend' [LN]. The phrase βούληται... ἀποκαλύψαι 'chooses to reveal' is translated 'will reveal' [KJV]. This verb means to think, with the purpose of planning or deciding on a course of action [LN].

f. aorist act. infin. of ἀποκαλύπτω (LN 28.38) (BAGD 2. p. 92): 'to reveal' [BAGD, LN; all translations except CEV, NCV], 'to tell' [CEV, NCV], 'to disclose, to make fully known' [LN]. This verb means to cause something to be fully known [LN].

MATTHEW 11:27

QUESTION—What does πάντα 'everything' refer to?

Here it refers to all knowledge [EBC, PNTC], or knowledge about God [TH, TRT], or revelation of the truth [NICNT, WBC]. It refers to all God's revelation [CC, ICC, NIGTC], which is eschatological in its focus [ICC]. It refers to all authority [EBC, My, NAC, NIGTC], all power [TRT]. It refers to all created things and beings everywhere, plus salvation, grace, judgment, truth, righteousness and everything else [Lns]. It refers not only to understanding the Son's authority and power to do miracles, but to everything involved in revealing and executing God's purposes [BNTC]. It refers to everything necessary for granting salvation and blessing, which would include authority over evil, over nature, over all people and spirits, as well as having the Spirit of God and all spiritual qualities such as wisdom, love, peace, and much more [NTC]. Jesus is unique in his role of revealing God [WBC]. Jesus has a privileged status as God's Son and heir of all that is God's [NIGTC].

QUESTION—What is meant by the verb 'know' here?

It means to know who he really is in his essential being [PNTC]. It speaks of a very intimate and full acquaintance [NAC], a full, mutual knowledge [CC, EBC, Lns, TRT], a knowledge drawn from an intimate and unique Father and Son relationship that is open to others only by invitation and revelation [EBC, Lns]. It is a complete, intimate, and mutual knowledge [WBC]. It speaks of a unique and intimate relationship [TH]. It means fully recognizing the Son as the one chosen to reveal God and his purpose fully, which even the disciples understood only poorly; likewise, only the Son really knows the Father and his purposes, power, grace, and nature [BNTC]. It speaks of the eternal Father-Son relationship within the Trinity, and that only the Father and Son understand the depth of knowledge, wisdom, and love that exists in the heart of the other, which are resources that are the inexhaustible reservoir from which the weary and burdened may have their needs met [NTC]. The Father knows the Son in his whole nature, and in all he thinks and does [My]. The Father and the Son acknowledge, take account of, and concern themselves with each other [ICC]. It speaks of a deep personal relationship in which they each know the other for who he truly is [NICNT].

QUESTION—What is implied by the phrase 'and to whomever the Son chooses to reveal him'?

It means that salvation is dependent not upon anything in man, but upon revelation, which in turn is dependent on the will and pleasure of the Father and the Son [NICNT, NTC]. It speaks of those who are willing to receive the revelation, as indicated by the open invitation expressed in the next verse to anyone who hungers for the peace and rest that only God can give [PNTC]. This speaks of an electing revelation [BECNT, NAC], but which is also balanced by the language of free will in verses 20–24 and 28–29 [CC, NAC]. It means that the Son wants to tell others about the Father [CEV]. It indicates an enormous emphasis on the person and authority of Jesus, including the fact that Jesus' sonship precedes and is the basis for his being the Messiah

[EBC]. It is saying that people only come to know the Father through the gracious and freely chosen act of the Son who reveals him [BNTC]. In the matter of revelation, the will of the Son is on a par with the will of the Father; the universal invitation given in the following verse is a counterbalance to the restriction implied in verse 27 [NICNT]. He is God's unique agent and his sole mediator [WBC].

11:28 Come[a] to me all the-ones being-weary[b] and being-burdened,[c] and-I will-give-rest[d] to-you(pl).

LEXICON—a. aorist act. impera. of δεῦρο, used with plural subject (LN 84.24) (BAGD 2. p. 176): 'to come (to)' [BAGD; all translations], 'come here' [LN]. This verb means to move toward a goal at or near the speaker [LN].
- b. pres. act. participle of κοπιάω (LN **23.78**, 42.47) (BAGD 1. p. 443): 'to be weary' [BECNT, BNTC, LN (23.78), NIGTC, NTC, PNTC; NASB, NET, NIV, NLT, NRSV, REB], 'to become weary' [BAGD], 'to be tired' [BAGD, **LN** (23.78); CEV, GW, NCV, TEV], 'to labor' [CC, WBC; ESV, KJV], 'to toil' [NICNT], 'to work hard' [LN (42.47)]. This verb means to be tired or weary, as the result of hard or difficult endeavor [LN (23.78)], or to work hard LN (42.47)].
- c. perf. pass. participle of φορτίζω (LN 15.207) (BAGD p. 865): 'to be burdened' [BAGD, BNTC, NIGTC, NTC; NET, NIV], 'to be heavily burdened' [CC, PNTC], 'to carry heavy burdens' [CEV, NLT, NRSV], 'to bear burdens' [WBC], 'to be heavy laden' [ESV, KJV, NASB], 'to carry heavy loads' [GW, TEV], 'to have heavy loads' [NCV], 'to be loaded' [BAGD], 'to be heavily loaded' [NICNT], 'to be loaded down' [BECNT], 'to be caused to bear a load' [LN], 'to be caused to carry something' [BAGD, LN]. This participle is translated as a phrase: 'whose load is heavy' [REB]. This verb means to cause to carry or bear a load [LN].
- d. fut. act. indic. of ἀναπαύω (LN **23.84**) (BAGD 1. p. 59): 'to give rest' [BAGD, **LN**; all translations except PNTC], 'to refresh' [PNTC], 'to cause to rest' [BAGD, LN].

QUESTION—In what way are such people weary and burdened?
It is the heavy religious burden of rules and regulations from religious leaders [CC, EBC, NIBC, NICNT, NTC, TH, TRT, WBC]. There is also the heavy burden brought by sin and guilt, as well as the uncertainties of life [CC]. The focus is not on the fact of work, but of need [PNTC]. It is an invitation to those who are hurting and recognize their spiritual need [NAC]. He is speaking generally of the burdens of life [PNTC], the neediness of God's people [NIGTC]. He is speaking of those laboring to earn salvation [Lns]. This invitation is given to those who are not yet disciples [WBC].

QUESTION—What is the nature of the 'rest' of which he speaks?
It includes peace of mind and heart, and relief from uncertainty and anxiety [NTC]. It is a deep refreshment that enables a person to go back to his or her tasks with renewed strength and energy [PNTC]. It is relief from sin and guilt, and from striving after salvation [Lns]. It is an eschatological rest, and

reflects the language of Jeremiah 6:16 [EBC, NICNT, NIGTC, WBC], but it is also a present reality [EBC, WBC]. This 'rest' is a proper fellowship with God [TH]. It is not idleness or inaction [BNTC, ICC], but the contentment and full life that come from knowing and living by the truth which God's Son reveals [ICC]. It is eternal, eschatological salvation by faith [CC]. It speaks of a refreshing and fulfillment that looks forward to the eschatological Sabbath [WBC].

11:29 Take my yoke[a] upon you(pl) and learn[b] from me, for I-am gentle[c] and humble[d] in-heart,[e] and you(pl)-will-find rest[f] for your(pl) souls;[g]

LEXICON—a. ζυγός (LN 6.8) (BAGD 1. p. 339): 'yoke' [BAGD, LN; all translations except NCV]. The phrase ἄρατε τὸν ζυγόν μου ἐφ' ὑμᾶς 'take my yoke upon you' is translated 'accept my teachings' [NCV]. This noun denotes a bar or frame of wood by which two draft animals are joined at the head or neck in order to work together effectively in pulling a plow, harrow, or wagon [LN].

b. aorist act. impera. of μανθάνω (LN 27.12) (BAGD 1. p. 490): 'to learn' [BAGD, LN; all translations except NLT], 'to be instructed, to be taught' [LN]. The phrase μάθετε ἀπ' ἐμοῦ 'learn from me' is translated 'let me teach you' [NLT]. This verb means to acquire information as the result of instruction, whether in an informal or formal context [LN].

c. πραΰς (LN **88.60**) (BAGD p. 699): 'gentle' [BAGD, BECNT, CC, **LN**, NIGTC, PNTC; all versions except KJV, NLT], 'mild' [LN], 'meek' [BAGD, BNTC, LN, NICNT, NTC, WBC; KJV], 'humble' [BAGD; NLT], 'considerate' [BAGD]. This adjective describes being gentle and mild [LN].

d. ταπεινός (LN **88.52**) (BAGD 2.b. p. 804): 'humble' [BAGD, BECNT, BNTC, CC, **LN**, NIGTC, PNTC, WBC; CEV, GW, NASB, NCV, NET, NIV, NRSV, TEV], 'lowly' [BAGD, NICNT, NTC; ESV, KJV], 'gentle' [NLT]. The phrase ταπεινὸς τῇ καρδίᾳ 'humble in heart' is translated 'humble-hearted' [REB]. This adjective describes being unpretentious in one's behavior [LN].

e. καρδία (LN 26.3) (BAGD 1.b.η. p. 404): 'heart' [BAGD, BECNT, BNTC, CC, LN, NICNT, NIGTC, NTC, PNTC, WBC; ESV, KJV, NASB, NET, NIV, NLT, NRSV], 'spirit' [NCV, TEV], 'inner self, mind' [LN], not explicit [CEV, GW]. This noun denotes the causative source of a person's psychological life in its various aspects, but with special emphasis upon thoughts [LN].

f. ἀνάπαυσις (LN **22.37**) (BAGD 2. p. 58): 'rest' [BAGD; all translations], 'relief' [LN]. This noun denotes relief from trouble and related anxiety [LN].

g. ψυχή (LN 26.4) (BAGD 1.c. p. 893; 1.f. p. 894): 'soul' [BAGD 1.c. p. 893, BECNT, BNTC, CC, NICNT, NIGTC, NTC, PNTC; ESV, KJV, NASB, NET, NIV, NLT, NRSV, REB], 'life' [CC; NCV], 'self' [BAGD 1.f. p. 894, NIGTC, WBC; GW], 'inner self, mind, thoughts, feelings, heart, being' [LN], not explicit [CEV, TEV]. This noun denotes the essence of life in terms of thinking, willing, and feeling [LN].

QUESTION—Is Jesus referring to a yoke for draft animals, or a yoke that people put upon their own shoulders for carrying loads?

It is a yoke used for draft animals when plowing [EBC, Lns, NAC, NIGTC, TH, TRT]. It focuses not on the fact of yoking animals together as a pair, but of putting them into service [NIGTC]. Some take it to refer to a yoke that a person would wear to carry loads [CC, NICNT]. It could be either [PNTC].

QUESTION—What is meant by the metaphor 'take my yoke upon you'?

It means to accept and submit to Jesus' teaching [BNTC, EBC, ICC, NICNT, NTC, PNTC, TH, TRT, WBC; NCV], to follow his teaching and example of humility [BECNT], to yield to the gospel and the doctrine of faith [Lns]. It is a metaphor for discipleship [CC, EBC], of being subject to his guidance and discipline [My]. Jewish rabbis described the obligation to fulfill the law in terms of a yoke that must be taken upon oneself [BECNT, BNTC, ICC, NAC, NICNT, NTC, PNTC, TRT, WBC], but often interpreted that law in terms that many people felt were a difficult burden [NTC, PNTC]. Jesus now identifies himself as the new Torah, or new revelation of God, that they were to take upon themselves [ICC]. What Jesus requires is challenging, but it is accomplished through the strength the Holy Spirit provides [NAC]. It speaks of service, obedience, and subordination [NIGTC].

QUESTION—Does the phrase μάθετε ἀπ' ἐμοῦ mean 'learn *from* me' or 'learn *about* me'?

1. It means to learn from him [BECNT, BNTC, CC, EBC, Lns, NICNT, NIGTC, NTC, PNTC, TH, TRT, WBC; all versions except KJV which uses the ambiguous phrase 'learn of me'].

2. It means to learn about him; as other Jews learned Torah, they are to 'learn' about Jesus, who is the functional equivalent of the Torah [ICC].

QUESTION—What relationship is indicated by ὅτι 'for'?

1. It indicates the grounds for the exhortation [BECNT, BNTC, My, NICNT, NIGTC, NTC, PNTC, TH, TRT, WBC; all versions except CEV]: *because*.

2. It indicates the content of what they are to learn [CC, Lns, NIBC]: *that*.

QUESTION—What does πραΰς...καὶ ταπεινός 'gentle and humble' mean in this context?

Jesus is claiming to be peaceful and peace-loving [NTC]. He is considerate [PNTC, TRT], patient, and kind [TRT]. It contrasts with religious teachers who were proud and ostentatious [BECNT]. He has the gentleness of a servant [EBC]. He is humble, not overbearing [Lns]. 'Meek' and 'humble in heart' are essentially synonymous terms [WBC]. Here it describes Jesus' moderation and concern for others [NIGTC].

QUESTION—Does the phrase τῇ καρδίᾳ 'in heart' refer only to 'humble' or to 'gentle and humble'?

1. It refers to the second quality: he is humble-hearted [CC, Lns, NIGTC, TRT, WBC; REB].

2. It refers to both qualities [My, PNTC].

11:30 **for my yoke is easy[a] and my burden[b] light.[c]"**

LEXICON—a. χρηστός (LN **22.40**) (BAGD 1.a.α. p. 886): 'easy' [BAGD, BECNT, BNTC, **LN**, NIGTC, PNTC; ESV, GW, KJV, NASB, NCV, NIV, NRSV, TEV], 'easy to bear' [CEV, NET, NLT], 'easy to wear' [REB], 'pleasant' [BAGD, CC, LN], 'kind' [NICNT, WBC], 'kindly' [NTC]. This adjective describes that which is pleasant or easy, with the implication of suitability [LN].
  b. φορτίον (LN 15.208) (BAGD 2. p. 865): 'burden' [BAGD, BECNT, CC, LN, NICNT, NIGTC, NTC, PNTC, WBC; CEV, ESV, GW, KJV, NASB, NIV, NRSV], 'burden I give you' [NLT], 'load' [BAGD, LN; NET, REB], 'load I impose' [BNTC], 'load I will put on you' [TEV], 'load I give you to carry' [NCV]. This noun denotes a relatively heavy object which is carried [LN].
  c. ἐλαφρός (LN **22.38**) (BAGD 1. p. 248): 'light' [BAGD, LN; all translations except NET], 'not hard to carry' [NET], 'easy' [LN], 'easy to bear' [BAGD, **LN**]. This adjective describes that which is easy to bear or to endure [LN].

QUESTION—What is meant by his yoke being easy and his burden light?

Although he is calling people to service and not careless ease, the service to which he calls them is not burdensome or drudgery [PNTC]. Whereas trying to earn salvation by scrupulously obeying the rules imposed by the religious leaders produces slavery, Jesus grants salvation to those who simply believe, which then enables them to serve him gratefully, with peace and joy and enthusiasm [NTC]. What makes it light is that it is a response of loyalty to a person as opposed to obedience to external commandments [NIBC]. He is saying that the 'yoke' of discipleship that he gives is good and comfortable [EBC]. The load he gives them to carry comes with his companionship and help [BNTC]. He gives power and consolation to help people bear his yoke [Lns]. The discipline and duty that he imposes is that of love [My]. Jesus requires his disciples to go beyond the concern for detailed regulation and instead live according to God's deeper underlying purposes [NICNT]. The Pharisees made following the law heavy and burdensome, but Jesus' teaching went directly to the heart of the Law [WBC]. Following and serving Jesus is pleasant, and all that he requires brings benefits to his follower [TRT]. Jesus' way will be easy to follow, causing the disciple no harm [TH].

DISCOURSE UNIT—12:1–50 [NIGTC; REB]. The topic is conflict with the Pharisees [NIGTC; REB].

DISCOURSE UNIT—12:1–45 [NICNT]. The topic is Jesus' authority is challenged.

DISCOURSE UNIT—12:1–21 [ICC]. The topic is two Sabbath controversies and the servant of Deutero-Isaiah.

DISCOURSE UNIT—12:1–14 [NET, NIV]. The topic is Lord of the Sabbath.

DISCOURSE UNIT—12:1–8 [CEV, ESV, GW, NCV, NLT, NRSV, TEV]. The topic is Jesus has authority over the day of worship [GW], Jesus is lord of the Sabbath [ESV, NCV], the question about the Sabbath [CEV, TEV], plucking grain on the Sabbath [NRSV], a discussion about the Sabbath [NLT].

DISCOURSE UNIT—12:1–7 [NASB]. The topic is Sabbath questions.

12:1 At that time[a] Jesus went through the grainfields[b] on-the Sabbath; and his disciples were-hungry[c] and began to-pick[d] (the) heads-of-grain[e] and to-eat.

LEXICON—a. καιρός (LN 67.78) (BAGD 1. p. 394): 'time' [BAGD, LN], 'period of time' [LN]. The phrase ἐν ἐκείνῳ τῷ καιρῷ 'at that time' [BECNT, BNTC, CC, NICNT, NIGTC, NTC, PNTC; ESV, KJV, NASB, NCV, NET, NIV NRSV] is also translated 'at about that time' [NLT], 'about that time' [WBC; REB], 'not long afterward' [TEV]. Some indicate in other ways that it is an expression referring to the general period of the preceding events: 'One Sabbath...' [CEV], 'Then on a day of worship...' [GW]. This noun denotes an indefinite unit of time, the actual extent of time being determined by the context [LN]. It can mean either a point of time or a period of time [BAGD]. There are two temporal markers in this verse that may result in nonsense in a literal translation: 'At that time Jesus took a walk one Sabbath day through the cornfields'. An option quite close to 'At that time' is 'About that time' [TH].

b. σπόριμα (LN 43.7) (BAGD p. 763): This plural noun is translated 'grainfields' [BAGD, BECNT, LN, NICNT, PNTC; ESV, GW, NASB, NIV, NLT, NRSV], 'grain fields' [BNTC, CC, LN, WBC; NET], 'wheat fields' [CEV, TEV], 'fields of grain' [NCV], 'field of standing grain' [NTC], 'standing grain' [BAGD, LN], 'cornfields' [REB], 'corn' [KJV]. (Note that in British usage 'corn' can simply mean 'grain', as opposed to what Americans call 'corn', but others call 'maize'.) This noun denotes grain growing in a field [LN].

c. aorist act. indic. of πεινάω (LN 23.29) (BAGD 1. p. 640): 'to be hungry' [BAGD, CC, LN, NICNT, NIGTC, NTC, PNTC, WBC; all versions except NASB, KJV, REB], 'to become hungry' [BECNT, BNTC; NASB], 'to hunger' [BAGD], 'to be an hungred' [KJV], 'to have hunger' [LN], 'to feel hungry' [REB]. This verb means to be in a state of hunger, without any implications of particular contributing circumstances [LN].

d. pres. act. infin. of τίλλω (LN 18.9) (BAGD p. 817): 'to pick' [BAGD, BECNT, BNTC, LN, NICNT, NTC; CEV, GW, NASB, NCV, NET, NIV, TEV], 'to pluck' [BAGD, CC, LN, NIGTC, PNTC, WBC; ESV, KJV, NRSV, REB], 'to break off' [NLT]. This verb means to pluck or pick by pulling off or out of [LN].

e. στάχυς (LN 3.40) (BAGD 1. p 765): 'head of grain' [BAGD, BECNT, BNTC, NIGTC, NTC, PNTC; ESV, GW, NASB, NIV, NLT, NRSV], 'ear of grain' [BAGD, CC, NICNT], 'grain' [NCV], 'ear' [WBC], 'ear of corn' [KJV, REB], 'ear of wheat' [LN], 'head of wheat' [LN; NET, TEV], 'grains of wheat' [CEV]. This noun denotes the dense spiky cluster in which the seeds of grain such as wheat and barley grow (in NT contexts it always refers to wheat) [LN].

QUESTION—What specific time is referred to by the phrase 'at that time'?

It was generally about the same period of time as what was just narrated [EBC, NAC, NTC, PNTC, TH, WBC], though not necessarily on the same day [EBC]. It was during the period of opposition described in chapter 11 [BECNT, Lns, PNTC]. It expresses a conceptual link with the issue of rest in 11:25ff [CC, ICC, NICNT, NIGTC]. Matthew organized his material topically, not chronologically [NAC]. The link with chapter 11 is conceptual, involving the yoke of discipleship versus the yoke of the law, and also the idea of rest [NAC]. The events described in chapter 12 may have even taken place shortly before the Sermon on the Mount [NTC].

12:2 But the Pharisees having-seen (this) said to-him, "Behold,ᵃ your disciples are-doing what is- not -lawfulᵇ on (the) Sabbath."

LEXICON—a ἰδού (LN 91.13) (BAGD 1.b. p. 370): 'behold' [BAGD, BNTC; KJV], 'look' [BAGD, BECNT, CC, LN, NICNT, NIGTC, PNTC, WBC; all versions except KJV, CEV], 'see' [BAGD], 'see here' [NTC], 'listen, pay attention' [LN], not explicit [CEV]. See translations of this word at 1:20. This particle is a prompter of attention, and serves to emphasize the following statement [LN].

b. pres. act. indic. of ἔξεστι (LN **71.32**) (BAGD 1. p. 275): 'to be lawful' [BECNT, BNTC, CC, PNTC, WBC; ESV, KJV, NASB, NCV, NIV, NRSV], 'to be permitted' [BAGD, NIGTC, NTC], 'to be possible' [BAGD], 'to be proper' [BAGD], 'must' [LN], 'ought to' [**LN**]. The phrase ὃ οὐκ ἔξεστιν 'what is not lawful' is translated 'what is forbidden' [REB], 'what is against the law' [NET], 'it is against our Law' [TEV], 'something which ought not to be done' [NICNT], 'that is not right to do' [GW], '(they are) not supposed to do that' [CEV], '(your disciples) are breaking the law' [NLT]. This verb means to be obligatory [LN]. The finite form of this verb occurs only in the third person singular [BAGD].

QUESTION—What was wrong with doing this on the Sabbath?

These Pharisees considered the disciples to be breaking the rabbinical laws against working on the Sabbath since they considered the action of picking the heads of wheat to be the work of reaping [BNTC, EBC, ICC, Lns, NAC, NIBC, NICNT, NTC, PNTC, TH, TRT, WBC]. The Pharisees who were present also viewed rubbing the heads of grain together as threshing [NIBC, NICNT, NTC, PNTC], blowing away the chaff as winnowing [NIBC, PNTC], and eating the grain as preparing a meal [NIBC].

12:3 But he-said to them, "Have-you- not -read what David did when he- was-hungry and those with him, **12:4** how he entered into the houseᵃ of

God and they-ate the consecrated[b] bread, which was not lawful for-him to eat nor for-those with him but-only[c] for-the priests[d]?

TEXT—Manuscripts reading ἔφαγον 'they ate' are given a C rating by GNT to indicate that choosing it over a variant text was difficult. This reading is followed by NIGTC, PNTC, WBC; CEV, NASB, NCV, NET, NIV, NLT, TEV. The reading ἔφαγεν 'he ate' is followed by BECNT, BNTC, CC, NICNT, NTC; ESV, GW, KJV, NRSV, REB.

LEXICON—a. οἶκος (LN 7.2) (BAGD 1.a.β. p. 560): 'house' [BAGD, LN; all translations], 'temple, sanctuary' [LN]. This noun denotes a building consisting of one or more rooms and normally serving as a dwelling place, and it may also include certain public buildings, for example, a temple [LN].

b. πρόθεσις (LN **53.26**) (BAGD 1. p. 706): 'presentation, setting forth, putting out' [BAGD]. The idiom ἄρτοι τῆς προθέσεως (literally 'bread of the placing forth') is translated 'consecrated bread' [BECNT, LN, NTC; NASB, NIV], 'bread of the Presence/presence' [ESV, GW, NRSV], 'bread of the Presentation' [CC], 'loaves of the presence' [WBC], 'loaves of presentation' [BAGD, BNTC], 'presentation loaves' [NIGTC], 'ceremonial loaves' [NICNT], 'loaves of offering' [PNTC], 'sacred loaves of bread' [CEV], 'sacred loaves' [NLT], 'sacred bread' [NET, REB], 'holy bread' [NCV], 'showbread' [KJV], 'bread offered to God' [**LN**; TEV]. This idiom denotes bread which was set out as an offering in the presence of God in the Tabernacle and later in the Temple [LN].

c. εἰ μή (LN 89.131) (BAGD VI.8.b. p. 220): 'but only' [BECNT, BNTC, LN, NICNT, NTC; ESV, KJV, NET, NIV, NRSV, REB], 'only' [CEV, GW, NCV, NLT, TEV], 'except only '[CC], 'alone' [NIGTC], 'but alone' [PNTC, WBC; NASB], 'but' [BAGD, LN], 'except that' [LN]. This phrase marks contrast by designating an exception [LN].

d. ἱερεύς (LN 53.87) (BAGD 1.b.α. p. 372): 'priest' [BAGD, LN; all translations]. This noun denotes one who performs religious rites and duties on behalf of others [LN].

QUESTION—What answer is anticipated by the question Jesus asks?

The form of the question assumes an affirmative answer [BECNT, CC, TH]. He knows they have read the passage, but his point is that they did not understand what they read [BECNT, CC]. The question is rhetorical, for they had certainly read it [TH, TRT, WBC].

QUESTION—What was the 'consecrated bread'?

It was 'the bread of the presence', twelve loaves representing the twelve tribes of Israel, placed in two rows in the sanctuary, that is, in the presence of the Lord. It symbolized the fellowship that people enjoy with God and their consecration to him, and also symbolized the fact that he provided their bread [NTC]. They were placed on a table of gold [Lns, My, NIBC]. This bread was replaced every Sabbath [My, NIBC]. Each loaf was made with six pounds of flour [Lns]. This bread was supposed to be eaten by the priests in a holy place [TH].

MATTHEW 12:5–6   419

12:5 Or have-you(pl)- not -read in the law that on-the Sabbath the priests in the temple profane^a the Sabbath and are guiltless^b? **12:6** But I-say to you(pl) (something) greater-than^c the temple is here.

TEXT—Some manuscripts have μείζων, a masculine form for the adjectival phrase 'greater than', which would be understood as modifying an implied masculine subject, 'someone'. Most manuscripts read μεῖζον, which is a neuter form, and would be understood as modifying an implied neuter subject, 'something'. GNT does not mention this variant. KJV, NIV, and NLT translate the implied subject as 'one', where all others translate it as 'something'.

LEXICON—a pres. act. indic. of βεβηλόω (LN 53.33) (BAGD p. 138): 'to profane, to desecrate' [BAGD], 'to make unclean, to defile' [LN]. The phrase τὸ σάββατον βεβηλοῦσιν 'profane the Sabbath' [CC, NIGTC, PNTC; ESV, KJV] is also translated 'desecrate the Sabbath' [BECNT, BNTC, WBC; NET], 'on the Sabbath…desecrate the day' [NIV], 'violate the Sabbath' [NICNT], 'break the Sabbath' [NTC; NASB, NRSV, REB], 'break the Sabbath law' [TEV], 'break the law about the Sabbath' [NCV], 'do things they shouldn't on the day of worship' [GW], 'may work of the Sabbath' [NLT], 'are allowed to work on the Sabbath' [CEV]. This verb means to cause something to become unclean, profane, or ritually unacceptable [LN].

b. ἀναίτιος (LN 88.316) (BAGD p. 55): 'guiltless' [BNTC, LN, NIGTC, NTC, PNTC; ESV, NRSV], 'innocent' [BAGD, BECNT, CC, LN, WBC; NASB, NIV], 'not guilty' [**LN**], 'blameless' [KJV]. The phrase καὶ ἀναίτιοί εἰσιν 'and are not guilty' is translated 'and yet they are not guilty' [NET, TEV], 'yet remain innocent' [GW], 'they are not held guilty' [REB], 'without incurring guilt' [NICNT], 'but the priests are not wrong for doing that' [NCV], 'no one says that they are guilty of breaking the law of the Sabbath' [CEV]. This adjective describes not being guilty of wrongdoing [LN].

c. μεῖζον, comparative of μέγας (LN 87.22) (BAGD 2.b.α. p. 498): 'greater than' [BECNT, BNTC, CC, NICNT, NIGTC, NTC, PNTC; all versions except NLT], 'even greater than' [WBC; NLT], 'greater' [BAGD, LN], 'more important' [LN]. This adjective describes being great in terms of status [LN].

QUESTION—Why does Jesus say that some*thing* greater than the temple is here, as opposed to some*one*?

The neuter pronoun can be used to refer to a person if a quality of the person is what is being emphasized, as opposed to the person himself [EBC, ICC]. The use of the neuter focuses on his quality of greatness as opposed to his personal identity [ICC]. The neuter pronoun is used because Jesus is being compared to two impersonal things, the temple and the tabernacle [Lns]. The use of the neuter pronoun, which refers to Jesus' own person and character, shows more emphasis than the use of the masculine pronoun would [My]. The neuter pronoun is used because the focus is on Jesus' role in ministry as the mediator between God and his people [NICNT]. The neuter pronoun refers to Jesus' ministry and the reality of the kingdom of God that is beginning to dawn [WBC]. It refers to a new claim or new truth [TH]. What is greater is Jesus himself and his ministry of manifesting God's kingdom [CC]. Jesus' claim to be greater than the temple was radical [NAC], and would have been astonishing or even shocking to those who heard [CC, Lns, NIGTC, TRT, WBC], and the position of 'temple' at the beginning of this clause gives emphasis to this statement [TH, WBC]. The grammatical distinctions between masculine and neuter were often blurred in NT Greek [NAC].

12:7 If you(pl)-had-known what (this) is,[a] 'I-desire[b] mercy[c] and not sacrifice',[d] you(pl)-would- not -have-condemned[e] the innocent.[f]

LEXICON—a pres. act. indic. of εἰμί (LN 13.4) (BAGD II.3. p. 224): 'to be' [CC, LN, NIGTC], 'to mean' [BAGD, BECNT, BNTC, NICNT, NTC, PNTC, WBC; ESV, GW, KJV, NASB, NCV, NET, NRSV, TEV]. The phrase τί ἐστιν 'what (this) is' is translated 'what this text means' [REB], 'what these words mean' [NIV], 'the meaning of this Scripture' [NLT], 'what the Scriptures mean when they say' [CEV]. This verb means to be identical with [LN].

b. pres. act. indic. of θέλω (LN 25.1, 25.102) (BAGD 4.b. p. 355): 'to desire' [BECNT, BNTC, CC, LN, NIGTC, NTC, PNTC, WBC; ESV, NASB, NIV, NRSV], 'to want' [LN (25.1), NICNT; CEV, GW, NCV, NET, NLT, TEV], 'to require' [REB], 'to wish' [LN (25.1)], 'to take pleasure in' [BAGD], 'to like' [LN (25.102)]. This verb is translated 'I would have' [KJV]. This verb means to desire to have or experience something [LN (25.1)], or to take pleasure in something in view of its being desirable [LN (25.102)].

c. ἔλεος (LN 88.76) (BAGD 1. p. 250): 'mercy' [BAGD, BNTC, CC, LN, NICNT, NIGTC, NTC, PNTC, WBC; ESV, GW, KJV, NET, NIV, NRSV, REB], 'compassion' [BECNT; NASB], 'kindness' [NCV, TEV]. This noun is translated as a verb phrase: 'to show mercy' [NLT], 'to be merciful to others' [CEV]. This noun denotes the act of showing kindness or concern for someone in serious need [LN].

d. θυσία (LN 53.20) (BAGD 2.a. p. 366): 'sacrifice' [BAGD, LN; all translations except CEV, NCV, NLT], 'animal sacrifices' [NCV], 'offering' [BAGD]. This noun is translated as a phrase: 'to offer sacrifices' [NLT], 'offering sacrifices to me' [CEV]. This noun denotes that which is offered as a sacrifice [LN].

e. aorist act. indic. of καταδικάζω (LN **56.31**) (BAGD p. 410): 'to condemn' [BAGD, **LN**; BECNT, BNTC, CC, NIGTC, NTC, PNTC, WBC; all versions except NCV], 'to pass judgment' [NICNT], 'to judge' [NCV], 'to find or pronounce guilty' [BAGD], 'to render a verdict of guilt' [LN]. This verb means to judge someone as definitely guilty and thus subject to punishment [LN].

f. ἀναίτιος (LN 88.316) (BAGD p. 55): 'innocent' [BAGD, BECNT, CC, LN, WBC; NASB, NET, NIV, REB], 'innocent people' [GW], 'guiltless' [BNTC, LN, NICNT, NIGTC, NTC, PNTC; ESV, KJV, NRSV], 'people who are not guilty' [TEV], 'these innocent disciples of mine' [CEV], 'my innocent disciples' [NLT], 'those who have done nothing wrong' [NCV]. This adjective describes not being guilty of wrongdoing [LN].

QUESTION—How are we to understand the statement that God did not desire sacrifice?

The contrast is the important element; that is, he desires mercy *more than* sacrifice [CC, ICC, NICNT, PNTC, TRT].

DISCOURSE UNIT—12:8–21 [NASB]. The topic is Lord of the Sabbath.

12:8 For[a] the Son of Man is Lord[b] of[c]-the Sabbath."

LEXICON—a γάρ (LN 89.23): 'for' [LN; all translations except CEV, GW, NCV], 'so' [CEV, NCV], 'because' [LN], not explicit [GW]. This conjunction indicates cause or reason between events, though in some contexts the relationship is often remote or tenuous [LN].

b. κύριος (LN 37.51) (BAGD 1.a.α. p. 459): 'Lord' [BAGD, BECNT, BNTC, CC, LN, NICNT, NIGTC, NTC, WBC; CEV, KJV, ESV, NCV, NIV, NLT, TEV], 'lord' [PNTC; ESV, NET, NRSV, REB], 'ruler' [LN], 'master' [BAGD, LN]. The phrase κύριος...ἐστιν 'is Lord' is translated 'has authority (over)' [GW]. This noun denotes one who rules or exercises authority over others [LN].

c. There is no lexical entry for 'of', but it is used in translation to express the relationship indicated by the genitive case of τοῦ σαββάτου 'the Sabbath'. It is translated 'of' [all translations except CEV, GW, NLT], 'over' [CEV, GW, NLT].

QUESTION—What relationship is indicated by γάρ 'for'?

It gives the grounds for what he has just said [NTC, PNTC, WBC]. Jesus was the one who had the authority to decide what loyalty to the Sabbath day really means [WBC]. The disciples were innocent because he was Lord of the Sabbath and he had allowed, and even wanted them to do what they were doing [NTC]. It gives the grounds for his authority to make the statements in verse 3–7, and especially for what is said in verse 7, which is that he, who is greater than David and the temple, is Lord of the Sabbath, which means that he has the authority to condemn these religious leaders [CC]. It gives grounds for all that has been said since verse 1, which is that Jesus is the Lord who instituted the Sabbath, so he knows what the Sabbath is about and how it should be observed [Lns].

QUESTION—What is the basis of Jesus' defense of his disciples' actions?

Note that Jesus' arguments center around three main ideas: an approach to law itself; focus on compassion for human need; and a lesser-to-greater argument based on Jesus' superiority to the religious institutions that gives him authority over them. These three elements are not mutually exclusive.

1. The scripture does not condemn David for doing what was unlawful, so Jesus is challenging the Pharisees' very approach to using the law [EBC]. His opponents were wrong to treat man-made rules as binding without allowing any exceptions to it [NTC]. The fact that priests can work on the Sabbath shows that ceremonial requirements are not absolute [Lns, NIGTC, TH]. Even scripture allows some exception to the rule about the Sabbath [ICC].
2. Jesus puts human need as being above the oral legal tradition [BECNT, BNTC, TH] or ceremonial regulations [ICC, Lns, NIBC, NIGTC]. Compassion has a higher priority than ritual [My, NAC, NIBC, NICNT]. It is always right to show mercy [NTC].
3. Jesus says that the priests are guiltless of Sabbath breaking because the work of the temple takes precedence over Sabbath rest. So because he is greater than the temple and the sacrificial system he takes precedence over them [BECNT, CC, ICC, My, NIBC, PNTC]. Jesus is more important than the temple, and by implication, greater than David, so he has the authority to determine how the Sabbath is to be observed in this new age of the kingdom [NAC]. If priests can violate Sabbath laws because their work in the temple takes precedence over Sabbath regulations, how much more are Jesus and his disciples innocent, because Jesus is greater than the temple [EBC, NICNT, NIGTC] and because he and his disciples are busy with the work of God [WBC]. David was permitted to do what was not lawful because of who he was as the anointed successor to Saul, and also because he was on a holy mission; Jesus is implying that he is greater than David, and as such is innocent just as David was [NICNT]. Jesus had authority to interpret what was acceptable on the Sabbath because he was Lord over it [BECNT, BNTC, CC, EBC, Lns, NIBC, NTC, PNTC, TH, TRT, WBC].

QUESTION—What does it mean to be Lord of the Sabbath?

Because of who Jesus is, he can determine what the rules for Sabbath observance should be [BECNT, BNTC, EBC, Lns, NIBC, NTC, PNTC, TH, TRT], and can override them when necessary [NIBC]. The authority of the Messiah is greater than the law about the Sabbath, and that law is subject to him [My]. He is one of the persons of the triune God who instituted the Sabbath, and he knows the correct meaning of the Sabbath [CC]. Jesus, who is greater than the temple, is also greater than the Sabbath [WBC].

DISCOURSE UNIT—12:9–15 [GW]. The topic is Jesus heals on the day of worship.

DISCOURSE UNIT—12:9–14 [CEV, ESV, NCV, NLT, NRSV, TEV]. The topic is Jesus heals a man's hand [NCV], a man with a crippled hand [CEV], the man with a paralyzed hand [TEV] a man with a withered hand [ESV], the man with a withered hand [NRSV], Jesus heals on the Sabbath [NLT].

12:9 And having-left from-there he-went into their synagogue; **12:10** and behold, (there was) a man having a-withered[a] hand[b]. And they-asked him saying, "Is-it-lawful on-the Sabbath to heal[c]?" so-that they-might-accuse[d] him.

LEXICON—a. ξηρός (LN **23.173**) (BAGD 2. p. 548): 'withered' [BAGD, BECNT, BNTC, CC, LN, NIGTC, PNTC, WBC; ESV, KJV, NASB, NET, NRSV, REB], 'paralyzed' [BAGD, LN, NICNT; GW, TEV], 'shriveled' [NTC; NIV], 'crippled' [CEV, NCV], 'deformed' [NLT], 'shrunken and paralyzed' [**LN**]. This adjective describes a shrunken, withered, and hence immobile part of the body [LN].

b. χεῖρα (LN 8.30) (BAGD 1. p. 880): 'hand' [BAGD, BECNT, BNTC, CC, LN, NIGTC, NTC, PNTC, WBC; all versions except REB], 'arm' [NICNT; REB]. This noun denotes a hand or any relevant portion of the hand, including, for example, the fingers [LN].

c. aorist act. infin. of θεραπεύω (LN 23.139) (BAGD 2. p. 359): 'to heal' [BAGD, LN; all translations except NLT, NRSV], 'to work by healing' [NLT], 'to restore' [BAGD], 'to cure' [LN; NRSV], 'to take care of' [LN]. This verb means to cause someone to recover health, often with the implication of having taken care of such a person [LN].

d. aorist act. subj. of κατηγορέω (LN 33.427) (BAGD 1.a. p. 423): 'to accuse' [BAGD, BECNT, BNTC, CC, LN, NIGTC, PNTC, WBC; ESV, KJV, NASB, NCV, NET, NIV, NRSV], 'to accuse of doing wrong/something wrong' [CEV, GW, TEV], 'to bring a charge' [NICNT, NTC; REB], 'to bring charges' [BAGD, LN; NLT]. This verb means to bring serious charges or accusations against someone, with the possible connotation of a legal or court context [LN].

QUESTION—To whom does 'their' refer in the phrase 'their synagogue'?

It refers to the Pharisees just mentioned [BNTC, EBC, Lns, My, NIBC, NICNT, WBC]. It was the synagogue of the Jews in that town [TH], so 'their' refers to the local people [PNTC].

QUESTION—What part of the body is described by the word 'hand'?

It usually refers only to the hand itself [BECNT, BNTC, CC, LN, NIGTC, NTC, PNTC, TH, WBC], though it could have included the forearm as well [NICNT, TH, TRT; REB].

QUESTION—What was the specific problem with his hand?

The muscles were atrophied [PNTC, TRT], such that he could not move it [TRT]. It was paralyzed [BECNT, NICNT, TH; GW, TEV].

QUESTION—Who questioned Jesus?

'They' are the Pharisees mentioned in the previous section [BECNT, CC, ICC, My, NAC, NICNT, WBC].

QUESTION—Was it considered unlawful to heal on the Sabbath?

Although there was a difference of opinion on this issue, many rabbis considered it permissible to heal on the Sabbath only if the patient's life was endangered [BECNT, CC, EBC, ICC, My, NIBC, NICNT, NIGTC, NTC, PNTC, WBC]. This ruling referred to using medical help, not miraculous healing [EBC]. It is hard to see how a miraculous healing like this would be considered work [BECNT, Lns], but in any case, this healing did not violate anything in the Torah [BECNT, ICC]. In Jerusalem a more strict interpretation was generally held, whereas in Galilee a more lenient view was more commonly held [NTC].

QUESTION—What sort of accusation is in view here?

They wanted to bring a legal charge against him [BECNT, ICC, Lns, My, NAC, TH]. It could be a legal charge, but might simply refer to a slanderous accusation [PNTC].

12:11 And[a] he-said to-them, "What man is-there among you who will-have one sheep[b] and if this-one falls[c] into a-pit[d] on the Sabbath, will-he- not - take-hold-of[e] it and lift-(it)-up[f]?

LEXICON—a. δέ (LN 89.94, 89.87, 89.124): 'and' [LN (89.87, 89.94); KJV, NASB, NLT], 'but' [CC, LN (89.124), PNTC, WBC; REB], 'so' [BECNT], 'and then' [LN (89.87)], not explicit [BNTC, NICNT, NIGTC, NTC; CEV, ESV, GW, NCV, NET, NIV, NRSV, TEV]. This conjunction indicates a sequence of closely related events [LN (89.87)], or may indicate an additive relation, but with the possible implication of some contrast [LN (89.94)], or, it may simply mark contrast [LN (89.124)].

b. πρόβατον (LN 4.22) (BAGD 1. p. 703): 'sheep' [BAGD, LN; all translations]. The phrase πρόβατον ἕν 'one sheep' [BNTC, NICNT, PNTC, WBC; KJV, NET, REB] is also translated 'only one sheep' [NRSV], 'a sheep' [BECNT, CC, NIGTC, NTC; CEV, ESV, GW, NASB, NCV, NIV, NLT, TEV].

c. aorist act. subj. of ἐμπίπτω (LN **15.121**) (BAGD 1. p. 256): 'to fall into' [BAGD, **LN**; all translations]. This verb means to fall into a particular location [LN].

d. βόθυνος (LN **1.55**) (BAGD p. 144): 'pit' [BAGD, BECNT, BNTC, LN, NTC, WBC; ESV, GW, KJV, NASB, NET, NIV, NRSV], 'ditch' [**LN**, NIGTC, PNTC; CEV, NCV, REB], 'hole' [LN, NICNT], 'deep hole' [TEV], 'well' [NLT]. This noun denotes a hole, trench, or pit, either natural or dug [LN].

e. fut. indic. act. of κρατέω (LN 18.6) (BAGD 1.b. p. 448): 'to take hold of' [BAGD, BECNT, BNTC, NIGTC, PNTC; ESV, GW, NASB, NET, NIV, TEV], 'to grab hold of' [NTC, WBC], 'to get hold of' [NICNT], 'to lay hold of' [NRSV], 'to lay hold on' [KJV], 'to catch hold of' [REB], 'to grab' [CC], 'to grasp' [BAGD], 'to seize' [BAGD, LN], 'to hold on to, to retain in the hand [LN], not explicit [CEV, NCV, NLT]. This verb means to hold on to an object [LN].

f. fut. act. indic. of ἐγείρω (LN **17.10**) (BAGD 1.a.β. p. 214): 'to lift up' [NIGTC], 'to lift out' [BECNT, BNTC, NTC, PNTC; CEV, ESV, GW, KJV, NASB, NET, NIV, NRSV, REB, TEV], 'to raise up' [BAGD], 'to raise' [BAGD, CC], 'to pull out' [NICNT, WBC], 'to help to rise' [BAGD], 'to help (it) out (of the ditch)' [NCV], 'to cause to stand up'

[LN], 'to get (it) on its feet' [**LN**]. The phrase κρατήσει αὐτὸ καὶ ἐγερεῖ 'take hold of it and lift it up' is translated 'work to pull it out' [NLT]. This verb means to cause to stand up, with a possible implication of some previous incapacity [LN].

QUESTION—Does the 'you' in 'among you' refer exclusively to the Pharisees in the discussion or more generally to all present in the synagogue?

This is addressed to the Pharisees [EBC, NICNT], but it also refers generally to everyone present in the synagogue [NICNT, TH].

QUESTION—Does the use of ἕν 'one' mean that the man would have had only one sheep?

1. The numeral ἕν is used here as an indefinite article: 'a sheep' [EBC, CC, TRT]. It is translated as indefinite by BECNT, CC, NIGTC, NTC; CEV, ESV, GW, NASB, NCV, NIV, NLT, TEV. The use of ἕν does not imply that there are no other sheep, but gives emphasis to the one that is lost [NICNT].
2. It is definite, and speaks of only one sheep [Lns, My, PNTC, TH; NRSV]. It may be that the focus is not so much on it being the only sheep the man had, but on the fact that someone would do the work required to rescue even one animal on the Sabbath [Lns]. It is the more dear to him for being the only one he owns [My, PNTC].

12:12 So[a] by-how-much-more[b] is- a-man[c] -valuable[d] (than) a-sheep. So-then[e] it-is-lawful to-do good[f] (on) the Sabbath.

LEXICON—a. οὖν (LN 89.50, 91.7) (BAGD 1.c.γ. p. 593): 'so' [BAGD, LN (89.50), NICNT], 'therefore' [BAGD, CC, LN (89.50), WBC], 'so then, consequently, accordingly' [LN (89.50)], 'then' [BAGD, BECNT, LN (89.50, 91.7); KJV, NASB], 'now' [BNTC], 'surely, indeed' [LN (91.7)], not explicit [NIGTC, NTC, PNTC; all versions except KJV, NASB]. This conjunction may indicate emphasis [LN (91.7)], or may indicate result, often implying the conclusion of a process of reasoning [LN (89.50)].

b. πόσος (LN 59.17) (BAGD 1. p. 694): 'how much more…than' [BAGD, BECNT, NICNT, NIGTC, NTC, PNTC; ESV, NASB, NET, NIV, NLT, NRSV], 'much more than' [WBC; CEV, TEV], 'far more…than' [BNTC], 'certainly…more than' [GW], 'surely…more than' [NCV], 'surely…far more than' [REB], 'by how much' [CC], 'how much' [BAGD, LN; KJV]. This interrogative adjective describes quantity [LN].

c. ἄνθρωπος (LN 9.1) (BAGD 1.a.β. p. 68): 'man' [BAGD, BNTC, CC, NTC, PNTC; ESV, KJV, NASB, NIV, REB], 'person' [BECNT, LN, NIGTC; NET, NLT], 'human being' [BAGD, LN, NICNT, WBC; NCV, NRSV, TEV], 'human' [GW], 'people' [CEV]. This noun denotes a human being (normally an adult) [LN].

d. pres. act. indic. of διαφέρω (LN 65.6) (BAGD 2.b. p. 190): 'to be valuable' [BECNT, LN; GW, NASB, NET, NIV, NLT, NRSV], 'to be of value' [NIGTC, NTC; ESV], 'to have worth' [LN], 'to be worth' [BNTC, NICNT, PNTC, WBC; CEV, REB, TEV], 'to be worth more than'

[BAGD], 'to be better than' [KJV], 'to matter' [CC], 'to be important' [NCV]. This verb means to be of considerable value, in view of having certain distinctive characteristics [LN].

e. ὥστε (LN **89.52**) (BAGD 1.a. p. 899): 'so then' [BECNT, CC, LN, PNTC, WBC; NASB, TEV], 'so' [BAGD, BNTC, **LN**, NIGTC; ESV, GW, NCV, NET, NRSV], 'and so' [CEV], 'well then' [NICNT], 'therefore' [BAGD, LN, NTC; NIV, REB], 'wherefore' [KJV], 'yes' [NLT], '(so) accordingly, as a result, so that, and so' [LN]. This conjunction indicates result, often in contexts implying an intended or indirect purpose [LN].

f. καλῶς (LN 65.23) (BAGD 3. p. 401): 'good' [BAGD, LN; all translations except KJV, NCV, TEV], 'good things' [NCV], 'well' [LN; KJV], 'fine, excellent, well done' [LN]. The phrase καλῶς ποιεῖν 'to do good' is translated 'to help someone' [TEV]. This adverb describes events which measure up to their intended purpose [LN].

12:13 Then he-says to-the man, "Stretch-out^a your hand." And he-stretched-(it)-out and it-was-restored^b (as) healthy^c as the other. **12:14** And having-gone-out the Pharisees took counsel-together^d against him so-that/how^e they-might-destroy^f him.

LEXICON—a. aorist act. impera. of ἐκτείνω (LN 16.19) (BAGD 1. p. 245): 'to stretch out' [BAGD, BECNT, BNTC, CC, LN, NICNT, NIGTC, PNTC, WBC; ESV, NASB, NET, NIV, NRSV, REB, TEV], 'to stretch forth' [KJV], 'to hold out' [NTC; CEV, GW, NCV, NLT], 'to extend, to reach out' [LN]. This verb means to cause an object to extend in space (for example, by becoming straight, unfolded, or uncoiled) [LN].

b. aorist pass. indic. of ἀποκαθίστημι (LN 13.65) (BAGD 1. p. 92): 'to be restored' [BAGD, BECNT, BNTC, CC, LN, NICNT, NIGTC, NTC, PNTC, WBC; ESV, KJV, NASB, NET, NLT, NRSV], 'to be completely restored' [NIV], 'to become normal again' [GW], 'to become well again' [NCV, TEV], 'to be made sound again' [REB], 'to be caused again to be' [LN], 'to become (as healthy as...)' [CEV]. This verb means to change to a previous good state [LN].

c. ὑγιής (LN 23.129) (BAGD 1.a. p. 832): 'healthy' [BAGD, CC, LN; ESV, GW, NET], '(to) health' [NICNT, WBC], '(to a) healthy condition' [BNTC], '(to) normal' [NASB], 'whole' [NIGTC, PNTC; KJV], 'well' [LN], 'sound' [BAGD, NTC; NIV, NRSV], 'good' [BECNT]. The phrase ὑγιὴς ὡς ἡ ἄλλη 'as healthy as the other one' [CEV], is translated 'just like the other one' [NLT], 'like the other' [REB], 'like the other hand' [NCV]. This adjective describes the state of being healthy or well (in contrast with sickness) [LN].

d. συμβούλιον (LN 30.74) (BAGD 1. p. 778): 'counsel' [CC, NIGTC, NTC, PNTC, WBC], 'plans' [NCV, TEV], 'plans (against)' [LN], 'plot' [BAGD, LN]. The verb phrase συμβούλιον ἔλαβον 'took counsel together' is translated 'consulted together' [NICNT], 'conspired'

[BECNT, ESV, NASB, NRSV], 'plotted' [BNTC; GW, NET, NIV, REB], 'held a counsel' [KJV], 'called a meeting to plot' [NLT], 'started making plans' [CEV]. This noun denotes joint planning so as to devise a course of common action, often one with a harmful or evil purpose [LN].

e. ὅπως (LN 89.59; 89.86) (BAGD 2.b. p. 577): 'so that' [BECNT, LN (89.59), NIGTC, PNTC], 'to' [BAGD, BNTC; CEV, GW, NCV, NLT], 'in order to' [LN (89.59)], 'in order that' [CC], 'with a view to' [NICNT], 'for the purpose of' [LN (89.59)], 'how' [LN (89.86), NTC, WBC; ESV, KJV, NIV, NRSV, REB, TEV], 'as to how' [NASB, NET], 'in what manner' [LN (89.86)], 'that' [BAGD]. This conjunction may indicate purpose for events and states (sometimes occurring in highly elliptical contexts) [LN (89.59)], or it may indicate how an event would take place [LN (89.86)]. It may also indicate the content of a question or decision [BAGD].

f. aorist act. subj. of ἀπόλλυμι (LN 20.31) (BAGD 1.a.α. p. 95): 'to destroy' [BAGD, BECNT, CC, LN, NIGTC, NTC, WBC; ESV, KJV, NASB, NRSV], 'to kill' [PNTC; CEV, GW, NCV, NIV, NLT, TEV], 'to assassinate' [NET], 'to bring about (Jesus') death' [REB], 'to get rid of' [NICNT], 'to ruin' [BAGD, LN]. This verb means to destroy or to cause the destruction of persons, objects, or institutions [LN].

QUESTION—Why does the author use the present tense verb λέγει 'he says'?
It gives special emphasis [NIGTC], making it more vivid [PNTC].

QUESTION—When was the man's hand healed?
It was healed as he extended it [BECNT, My, NIGTC]. It was healed as soon as he extended it [TRT]. It was healed before he extended it, because he was unable to extend it before it was healed [PNTC]. Jesus told him to extend it to prove that it was healed [NAC]. It was healed because he extended his hand, demonstrating his faith by his obedience, but we are not told when it was healed [NICNT].

QUESTION—What relationship is indicated by ὅπως 'so that'?
1. It indicates the content of the counsel, either *to* kill Jesus (as indicated by the use of an infinitive) [BAGD, BNTC; CEV, GW, NASB, NCV, NET, NLT], or more specifically *how to* kill Jesus [NTC, WBC; ESV, KJV, NIV, NRSV, REB, TEV].
2. It indicates purpose [BECNT, CC, NICNT, NIGTC, PNTC].

QUESTION—What was their motivation for wanting to destroy Jesus?
The real concern of the Pharisees was that their authority was being challenged and their influence and control threatened [BECNT, NIBC, NICNT, PNTC]. They were concerned about their prestige as well as what they conceived to be God's truth [BNTC]. The issue at stake here is Jesus' authority [EBC, NIBC] and his messianic claims, not disputes about Sabbath observance [EBC]. The Sabbath question never entered into the formal accusations for which Jesus was crucified [ICC].

DISCOURSE UNIT—12:15–21 [CEV, ESV, NCV, NET, NIV, NLT, NRSV, TEV]. The topic is Jesus is God's chosen servant [ESV, NCV], God's chosen servant [CEV, NIV, NLT, NRSV, TEV], God's special servant [NET].

12:15 **But Jesus knowing[a] (this) departed from-there. And many crowds[b] followed him, and he-healed[c] them all**

TEXT—The word ὄχλοι 'crowds' is not in some Greek manuscripts. It is included in brackets by GNT and given a C rating to indicate that choosing it over a variant text was difficult. It is included in brackets by WBC.

LEXICON—a. aorist act. participle of γινώσκω (LN 28.1): 'to know' [CC, LN, NICNT, PNTC, WBC; GW, KJV, NCV, NLT], 'to learn' [BNTC; NET], 'to find out' [CEV], 'to become aware' [NRSV], 'to be aware' [REB], 'to hear about' [TEV], 'to know about, to have knowledge of' [LN]. This verb is translated adjectivally: 'aware (of this)' [BECNT, NIGTC, NTC; ESV, NASB, NIV]. This verb means to possess information about something [LN].

b. ὄχλος (LN 11.1): 'crowd, multitude' [LN]. The phrase ὄχλοι πολλοι 'many crowds' [CC, WBC; NRSV] is also translated 'great crowds' [NIGTC; NET], 'large crowds' [CEV, TEV], 'great multitudes' [KJV], 'many people' [NICNT; GW, NCV, NLT], 'many' [BAGD, BECNT, BNTC, NTC, PNTC; ESV, NASB, NIV, REB]. This noun denotes a casual non-membership group of people, fairly large in size and assembled for whatever purpose [LN].

c. aorist act. indic. of θεραπεύω (LN 23.139): 'to heal' [LN; all translations except GW, NRSV], 'to cure' [LN; GW, NRSV]. This verb means to cause someone to recover health, often with the implication of having taken care of such a person [LN].

QUESTION—Was Jesus' knowledge of their intent to kill him a supernatural knowledge?

He knew the thoughts of the Pharisees without anyone having to tell him [WBC]. It may have been a supernatural knowledge [ICC]. He probably received a report [NIBC]. It is not known how he knew that [BECNT, BNTC, PNTC].

QUESTION—What is meant by πάντας 'all'?

It means that all who needed healing were healed [Lns, My, NIBC, NIGTC, NICNT, PNTC, TH, TRT, WBC], not that everybody in the crowd needed healing [NIBC, NIGTC]. The 'many' who followed him were sick people wanting healing [BNTC].

DISCOURSE UNIT—12:16–21 [GW]. The topic is Jesus is God's servant.

12:16 **and he-warned[a] them that-they- not -make him known,[b]** **12:17** **so-that might-be-fulfilled[c] what was-spoken through Isaiah the prophet saying,**

LEXICON—a. aorist act. indic. of ἐπιτιμάω (LN 33.331) (BAGD 1. p. 303): 'to warn' [BAGD, BECNT, NICNT, NTC, WBC; CEV, NASB, NCV,

MATTHEW 12:16–17

NIV, NLT], 'to warn sternly' [NET], 'to charge' [KJV], 'to charge sternly' [BNTC], 'to order' [ESV, GW, NRSV], 'to order sternly' [NIGTC], 'to give orders' [TEV], 'to give strict instructions' [PNTC; REB], 'to rebuke' [CC], 'to command' [LN]. This verb means to command, with the implication of a threat [LN].
b. φανερός (LN 28.28) (BAGD 1. p. 852): 'known, evident, seen, open' [BAGD], 'well known, widely known' [LN]. The verb phrase φανερὸν αὐτὸν ποιήσωσιν 'make him known' [BECNT, BNTC, NIGTC, NTC, PNTC, WBC; ESV, KJV, NRSV, REB] is also translated 'to tell others about him' [NICNT; TEV], 'to tell anyone about him' [CEV], 'tell/tell-people who he was' [GW, NASB, NCV, NIV], 'to reveal who he was' [NLT]. This adjective describes being widely and well known [LN].
c. aorist pass. subj. of πληρόω (LN 13.106) (BAGD 4.a. p. 671): 'to be fulfilled' [BAGD, BNTC, CC, LN, NIGTC, NTC, PNTC, WBC; KJV], 'to come true' [CEV, GW], 'to be caused to happen, to be made to happen' [LN]. This passive subjunctive verb is translated as an active infinitive: 'to fulfill' [BECNT; ESV, NASB, NET, NIV, NRSV, REB], 'to bring about' [NCV], 'to make come true' [TEV]; as an active finite verb: '(this) fulfilled' [NLT]. This verb means to cause to happen, with the implication of fulfilling some purpose [LN].

QUESTION—Why did Jesus not want them to make him known?
He did not want his messianic ministry to be interpreted according to their royal or militaristic notions of what the Messiah was to be [EBC, WBC]. He did not want popular misunderstandings about what the Messiah was supposed to be to interfere with the ministry God had given him [TRT]. He wanted to avoid premature arrest and execution [NAC], and avoided premature confrontation [NICNT]. He did not want to excite more opposition [Lns, My]. People who were interested in the spectacular would only cause those opposed to Jesus to intensify their effort [BECNT]. Jesus was not seeking publicity [BNTC, ICC, NIGTC, PNTC] or fame [NTC]. He wanted the central focus to be on the message of the kingdom, not on himself [BNTC].

QUESTION—Does ἵνα 'so that' represent Jesus' purpose, or simply the conclusion that Matthew draws from Jesus' warning?
The wording reflects how Matthew interprets the situation [BNTC, EBC, ICC, Lns, NAC, NIBC, NICNT, NIGTC, NTC, PNTC, TH, WBC; CEV, GW, NET, NIV, NLT].

12:18 "Behold my servant[a] whom I-chose,[b] my beloved[c] in whom my soul was-well-pleased[d]; I-will-put my Spirit upon him, and he-will-proclaim[e] justice[f] to-the nations/Gentiles[g]

LEXICON—a. παῖς (LN 87.77) (BAGD 1.b.γ. p. 604): 'servant' [BAGD, LN; all translations], 'slave' [LN]. This noun denotes a slave, possibly serving as a personal servant, which would imply that he was kindly regarded by his master [LN].

b. aorist act. indic. of αἱρετίζω (LN **30.91**) (BAGD p. 24): 'to choose' [BAGD, **LN**; all translations except CEV], 'to select' [LN]. This verb is also translated as a participle used adjectivally: 'my chosen servant' [CEV]. It means to choose or select for the purpose of showing special favor to or concern for [LN].

c. ἀγαπητός (LN **25.45**) (BAGD 2. p. 6): 'beloved' [BAGD, BECNT, BNTC, CC, LN, NICNT, NIGTC, NTC, PNTC, WBC; ESV, KJV, NASB, NLT, NRSV, REB], 'dear' [BAGD, LN], 'one who is loved' [**LN**], 'object of one's affection' [LN]. This adjective is translated as a verb phrase: 'I love him' [CEV, NCV], 'whom I love' [GW], 'the one I love' [NET, NIV, TEV]. This pronominal adjective describes one who is loved. It is also possible to understand ἀγαπητός in Matthew 12:18 as 'the only beloved one' (LN 58.53) and then the meaning may be simply 'only' or 'unique' [LN].

d. aorist act. indic. of εὐδοκέω (LN 25.87) (BAGD 2.a. p. 319): 'to be well pleased' [BECNT, BNTC, CC, NTC, PNTC, WBC; ESV, KJV, NASB, NRSV], 'to be pleased' [BAGD, LN; NCV, TEV], 'to take delight' [BAGD; NET, REB], 'to delight in' [NIGTC; GW, NIV], 'to be delighted with' [NICNT], 'to take pleasure in' [LN]. The phrase εἰς ὃν εὐδόκησεν ἡ ψυχή μου 'in whom my soul was well pleased' is translated 'he pleases me' [CEV], 'who pleases me' [NLT]. This verb means to be pleased with something or someone, with the implication of resulting pleasure [LN].

e. fut. act. indic. of ἀπαγγέλλω (LN 33.198) (BAGD 2. p. 79): 'to proclaim' [BAGD, BECNT, BNTC, NTC, PNTC, WBC; ESV, NASB, NET, NIV, NLT, NRSV, REB], 'to announce' [CC, NIGTC; GW, TEV], 'to tell openly' [BAGD], 'to be a messenger (of)' [NICNT], 'to bring' [CEV], 'to show' [KJV], 'to tell' [LN; NCV], 'to inform' [LN]. This verb means to announce or inform, with possible focus upon the source of information [LN].

f. κρίσις (LN 56.25) (BAGD 3. p. 453): 'justice' [BAGD, LN; all translations except KJV, NCV, TEV], 'my justice' [NCV], 'judgment' [KJV, TEV], 'righteousness' [BAGD], 'fairness' [LN]. This noun denotes the administration of justice [LN].

g. ἔθνη, the plural form of ἔθνος 'nation' (LN 11.37, 11.55): The singular form ἔθνος means 'nation, people' [LN (1.55)]. The plural form ἔθνεσιν is translated 'nations' [CC, NICNT, NIGTC, NTC, PNTC, WBC; CEV, GW, NET, NIV, NLT, REB, TEV], 'all people' [NCV], or it may have the extended meaning 'Gentiles' [BECNT, BNTC; ESV, KJV, NASB, NRSV], 'heathen, pagans' [LN]. The singular noun denotes the largest unit into which the people of the world are divided on the basis of their constituting a socio-political community [LN (11.55)], and the plural form 'nations' may have the extended meaning of people who do not belong to the Jewish or Christian faith [LN (11.37)].

MATTHEW 12:18 431

QUESTION—What did God mean when he said 'I will put my Spirit on him'?
Most translate this literally. Others translate this as 'I will give him my Spirit' [CEV], 'I will send my Spirit upon him' [TEV]. God poured his spirit on his servant to empower him for a specific mission [EBC, NIGTC, PNTC, WBC], which is to proclaim justice to the nations [BECNT, PNTC, WBC], to declare prophetically what God's will is and to call sinners to repent [NTC]. Endowment with God's spirit marks him as the Messiah [NICNT].

QUESTION—What is the nature of the κρίσις 'justice' spoken of here?
It is the righteousness seen in the broad view of God's character being revealed for the benefit and blessing of all nations [EBC]. This means that ultimately justice will be done for people of all nations, just as salvation was made available to people of all nations [PNTC]. Justice is what is right, that is, what is the will of God, namely that people repent, believe, be saved, and live for the glory of God [NTC]. It is redemption, the bringing of forensic righteousness [Lns], the saving work of God [TH]. It is the divine judgment to be brought about at the last day [My]. It is the establishment of a just order that will remove and replace all the injustice that currently exists [NIGTC]. It is God working out his own good purposes for his people [NICNT].

12:19 He-will- not -quarrel[a] nor shout,[b] nor will- anyone -hear his voice in the streets.

LEXICON—a. fut. act. indic. of ἐρίζω (LN 33.447) (BAGD p. 309): 'to quarrel' [BAGD, BECNT, BNTC, CC, LN, NICNT, NIGTC, NTC, PNTC, WBC; ESV, GW, NASB, NET, NIV], 'to shout' [CEV], 'to argue' [**LN**; NCV, TEV], 'to strive' [KJV, REB], 'to fight' [NLT], 'to wrangle' [BAGD; NRSV], 'to dispute' [LN]. This verb means to express differences of opinion, with at least some measure of antagonism or hostility [LN].

b. fut. act. indic. of κραυγάζω (LN 33.83) (BAGD 2.a. p. 449): 'to shout' [LN, NTC, PNTC; GW, NLT, REB, TEV], 'to shout out' [NIGTC], 'to shout aloud' [NICNT], 'to cry out' [BAGD, BECNT, BNTC, CC, WBC; NASB, NCV, NET, NIV], 'to cry aloud' [ESV, NRSV], 'to cry' [KJV], 'to yell' [CEV], 'to scream' [BAGD, LN]. This verb means to shout or cry out, with the possible implication of the unpleasant nature of the sound [LN].

QUESTION—What does it mean that no one will hear his voice in the streets?
1. He does not raise his voice or shout to attract attention publicly [PNTC]. He avoids public wrangling [Lns, My, NIBC, NICNT, NIGTC, NTC]. He will avoid publicity and quarrelling [ICC, TH, WBC]. He ministers in gentleness and humility, not in brashness or arrogance [EBC]. He does not try to incite the crowds with rhetoric [BECNT, NIGTC].
2. It means that few will truly listen to his voice in the sense of responding adequately [NAC], or by choosing to believe [CC].

12:20 A-reed[a] having-been-crushed[b] he-will- not -break[c] and a- smoldering[d] -wick[e] he-will- not -extinguish,[f] until he-leads[g] justice[h] to victory.[i]

LEXICON—a. κάλαμος (LN 3.55) (BAGD 1. p. 398): 'reed' [BAGD, LN; all translations except GW, NCV], 'cattail' [GW], 'blade of grass' [NCV]. This noun denotes the stalk of a reed plant [LN].
- b. perf. pass. participle of συντρίβω (LN **19.46**) (BAGD 1.a. p. 793): 'to be crushed' [**LN**], 'to be bruised' [LN]. This participle is translated adjectivally: 'bent' [BECNT, BNTC; CEV, TEV], 'bruised' [NTC, WBC; ESV, KJV, NET, NIV, NRSV], 'crushed' [CC, NIGTC; NCV], 'broken' [REB], 'shattered' [PNTC], 'battered' [NASB], 'damaged' [NICNT; GW], 'weakest' [NLT]. This verb means to cause damage to an object by crushing [LN].
- c. fut. act. indic. of κατάγνυμι (LN **19.35**) (BAGD p. 409): 'to break' [BAGD, BECNT, BNTC, CC, LN, NICNT, NIGTC, NTC, PNTC; CEV, ESV, KJV, NCV, NET, NIV, NRSV], 'to break off' [GW, NASB, TEV], 'to snap off' [REB], 'to crush' [NLT]. This verb means to break or to shatter a rigid object [LN].
- d. pres. pass. participle of τύφομαι (LN **14.64**) (BAGD p. 831): 'to smolder' [BAGD, **LN**], 'to flicker' [LN], 'to smoke, to give off smoke' [BAGD]. This participle is translated 'smoldering' [BNTC, NIGTC, NTC, WBC; ESV, NASB, NET, NIV, NRSV, REB], 'smoking' [BECNT, CC, NICNT, PNTC; GW, KJV], 'flickering' [NLT, TEV], 'dying' [CEV], 'weak' [NCV]. This verb describes the process of burning slowly, with accompanying smoke and relatively little glow [LN].
- e. λίνον (LN **6.158**) (BAGD 1. p. 475): 'wick' [BECNT, BNTC, CC, **LN**, NICNT, NIGTC, NTC, PNTC, WBC; ESV, GW, NASB, NET, NIV, NRSV, REB], 'lamp' [TEV], 'lamp-wick' [BAGD], 'flame' [CEV, NCV], 'candle' [NLT], 'flax' [KJV]. This noun denotes a linen cord in a lamp that draws up the oil [LN].
- f. σβέννυμι (LN 14.70) (BAGD 1. p. 745): 'to extinguish' [BAGD, BNTC, LN, NIGTC; NET], 'to put out' [BAGD, BECNT, LN, NICNT, WBC; CEV, GW, NASB, NCV, NLT, TEV], 'to quench' [CC, NTC; ESV, KJV, NRSV], 'to snuff out' [PNTC; NIV, REB]. This verb means to cause a fire to be extinguished [LN].
- g. aorist act. subj. of ἐκβάλλω (LN **13.68**) (BAGD 3. p. 237): 'to lead' [BAGD, BECNT, BNTC; NASB, NIV], 'to lead on' [NTC; REB], 'to bring' [WBC; ESV, NET, NRSV], 'to bring forth' [NIGTC], 'to bring out' [PNTC], 'to bring right through' [NICNT], 'to make' [GW], 'to make to win' [NCV], 'to make (to do something)' [**LN**], 'to cause (to do something)' [**LN**; TEV], 'to cause to be' [NLT, LN], 'to cast forth' [CC], 'to send forth' [KJV], 'to make become' [LN]. The phrase ἐκβάλῃ εἰς νῖκος τὴν κρίσιν 'he leads justice to victory' is translated 'he will make sure that justice is done' [CEV]. This verb means to cause a significant change of state by decisive action [LN].

h. κρίσις (LN **56.25**) (BAGD 3. p. 453): 'justice' [BAGD, BECNT, CC, **LN**, NICNT, NIGTC, NTC, PNTC, WBC; all versions except KJV], 'judgment' [KJV], 'the right' [BNTC], 'righteousness' [BAGD], 'fairness' [LN]. This noun denotes the administration of justice [LN]. It may be difficult to speak of 'justice triumphing', so in some languages it may be necessary to translate this 'so that all accusations are judged justly,' or 'so that everyone receives what he should' or 'until all judgments are just' [LN].

i. νῖκος (LN 39.57) (BAGD 1. p. 540): 'victory' [BAGD, BECNT, BNTC, LN, NICNT, NTC, PNTC; ESV, KJV, NASB, NCV, NET, NIV, NRSV, REB], 'triumph' [WBC], not explicit [CEV]. The phrase εἰς νῖκος 'to victory' is translated 'victorious' [GW], 'finally victorious' [NLT], 'successfully' [NIGTC], '(cause) to triumph' [TEV], 'forever' [CC]. This noun denotes a victory over someone [LN].

QUESTION—What do the metaphors of the reed and the wick refer to?

The imagery expresses the fact that Jesus is gentle [BECNT, BNTC, EBC, Lns, My, NAC, NIBC, PNTC, TH, TRT], merciful to those who are weak [BECNT, EBC, TH], kind to the weak and helpless [NTC], gentle with broken and damaged lives [BNTC]. He is loving, caring, and patient with people who are wounded or broken, and with whom others would not concern themselves [PNTC]. The broken reed and the smoldering wick represent those who have been worn down by life's hardships [NIBC], who are about to perish because of sin [Lns]. His character stands in contrast to the Pharisees' indifference to the suffering of the handicapped man and their cruelty in planning to murder Jesus [NTC]. He revives and strengthens the moral life of those who are spiritually helpless and miserable [My]. He offers hope to the harassed outcasts at the margins of society, however wretched or unimportant they may appear to be [ICC]. God is patient with people who are downtrodden, needy, rejected, and sinful [WBC]. Jesus reaches out to people who are marginalized or considered to be of little value [NIGTC]. He will be sympathetic and gentle with people whose faith is weak [TRT].

QUESTION—In what sense would he lead justice 'to victory'?

'To victory' means to do it 'successfully' [ICC, Lns, NIGTC, WBC]. He will cause justice to prevail [BECNT, Lns, My, NTC, PNTC, TRT; GW, NCV, NLT, TEV]. 'He will make sure that justice is done' [CEV], and he will right the wrongs of the world [NAC], overcoming all evil opposition [My]. This will happen when sin and the consequences of sin are banished forever from God's redeemed universe [NTC]. He will fully bring divine judgment on evil, and salvation for the poor [BNTC]. This is a paraphrase of Isaiah 42:3 and 42:4 [EBC, ICC, WBC]. He will encourage damaged and vulnerable people rather than discard them [NICNT].

12:21 And in- his -name[a] (the) nations/Gentiles[b] will-hope.[c]"

LEXICON—a. ὄνομα (LN 33.126) (BAGD I.4.b. p. 571): 'name' [BAGD, LN]. The phrase 'in his name' [BECNT, BNTC, CC, NICNT, NIGTC, NTC, PNTC, WBC; ESV, KJV, NASB, NET, NIV, NLT, NRSV] is also translated 'in him' [CEV, NCV, REB], 'on him' [TEV], 'because of him' [GW]. This noun denotes the proper name of a person or object [LN].

b. ἔθνη, the plural form of ἔθνος 'nation' (LN 11.55, 11.37): 'nations' [LN (11.55), NICNT, NIGTC, PNTC, WBC; GW, NIV, REB], 'all the world' [NLT], 'all peoples' [TEV]. Others think an extended meaning of this noun is intended: 'Gentiles' [BECNT, BNTC, NTC; CEV, ESV, KJV, NASB, NET, NRSV], 'non-Jewish people' [NCV], 'peoples' [LN (11.55)]. The singular noun denotes the largest unit into which the people of the world are divided on the basis of their constituting a socio-political community [LN (11.55)], and the plural form 'nations' may have the extended meaning of people who do not belong to the Jewish or Christian faith [LN (11.37)].

c. fut. act. indic. of ἐλπίζω (LN 25.59) (BAGD 3. p. 252): 'to hope in' [BECNT, CC, NIGTC, NTC, WBC; ESV, NASB, NET, NRSV], 'to hope' [LN], 'to place one's hope in' [NICNT; CEV], 'to put one's hope in' [BAGD, BNTC; NIV, REB], 'to put one's hope on' [TEV], 'to find one's hope in' [NCV], 'to have hope (because of)' [GW], 'to set one's hope in' [PNTC], 'to trust in' [KJV], 'to hope for' [LN]. This verse is translated 'And his name will be the hope of all the world' [NLT]. This verb means to look forward with confidence to that which is good and beneficial [LN].

QUESTION—Is there any significant difference between how the noun ἔθνη 'nations/Gentiles' is translated in this verse as opposed to how it is translated in verse 18??

In this passage ἔθνη is translated as having the same meaning in both verses by BECNT, BNTC, CC, ICC, NICNT, NIGTC, PNTC, NTC, WBC; CEV, ESV, GW, KJV, NASB, NIV, NRSV, REB. However, four translations have changed the wording they used in verse 18. In verse 18 ἔθνη is translated 'nations' [NET, NLT, TEV], and in verse 21 it is translated 'the world' [NLT], 'all peoples' [TEV]. 'Gentiles' [NET]. In verse 18 it is translated 'all people', but in verse 21 it is translated 'non-Jewish people' [NCV].

1. The focus is on all the nations of the world [NAC, NIBC, NICNT, NIGTC, PNTC, TH, TRT, WBC; GW, NIV, REB] and Israel is included in this term [NIGTC, TRT]. The Greek word for 'nations' is often translated 'Gentiles', but here the focus is on what the servant will do for all the nations of the world as a whole [PNTC].
2. The focus is on the Gentiles being distinct from the Jews [BECNT, BNTC, Lns, My, NTC, WBC; CEV, ESV, KJV, NASB, NET, NRSV].

QUESTION—What does it mean that they will hope 'in his name'?

'Name' stands for the person [PNTC, TH], so this means either they will trust on him or in him [TH]. All that the name 'Messiah' implies will be the

MATTHEW 12:21 435

basis for their hope [My]. 'In his name' means according to how he is revealed; that is, they will trust in Christ as he has been revealed to the world [NTC]. They will come to trust in God as he is in his essential character, that is, all that he truly is [PNTC]. They will rest their hopes in him [NIBC]. This refers to their allegiance to Jesus [NIGTC]. They will trust him to save them [TRT]. The Hebrew text of the passage from Isaiah that Jesus is quoting has 'law', whereas the LXX has 'name', but this is not strange in view of the fact that in Matthew's gospel the law is seen as pointing to Jesus [BECNT].

DISCOURSE UNIT—12:22–50 [ICC]. The topic is an objection story, a testing story, a correction story.

DISCOURSE UNIT—12:22–37 [GW, NIV, NLT]. The topic is Jesus and Beelzebub [NIV], Jesus and the prince of demons [NLT], Jesus is accused of working with Beelzebul [GW].

DISCOURSE UNIT—12:22–32 [CEV, ESV, NCV, NET, NRSV, TEV]. The topic is Jesus' power is from God [NCV], blasphemy against the Holy Spirit [ESV], Jesus and Beelzebul [NET, NRSV, TEV], Jesus and the ruler of the demons [CEV].

DISCOURSE UNIT—12:22–29 [NASB]. The topic is the Pharisees rebuked.

12:22 Then was-brought to-him a-demonized (man) (who was) blind and mute,[a] and he healed him, so-that the mute (man) (was able) to speak and to see. **12:23** And all the crowds were-amazed[b] and were saying, "This (man) is not[c] the Son of-David (is he)?"

LEXICON—a. κωφός (LN 33.106, 24.68) (BAGD 1. p. 462): 'mute' [BAGD, BECNT, CC, LN (33.106), WBC; NASB, NET, NIV, NRSV], 'dumb' [BAGD, NICNT, LN, PNTC; KJV, REB], 'unable to speak' [BNTC], 'unable to talk' [GW], 'could not speak' [NTC], 'couldn't speak' [NLT], 'could not talk' [CEV, NCV, TEV], 'unable to speak, incapable of talking' [LN (33.106)], 'deaf' [LN (24.68)], 'deaf and mute' [NIGTC]. This adjective describes someone as being unable to speak or talk [LN (33.106)], or it describes someone as being unable to hear [LN (24.68)].

b. imperf. mid. indic. of ἐξίστημι (LN 25.220) (BAGD 2.b. p. 276): 'to be amazed' [BAGD, BECNT, NTC; all versions except NIV], 'to be astonished' [BAGD, BNTC, CC, NICNT, NIGTC, PNTC, WBC; NIV], 'to be astonished greatly, to be greatly astounded, to be astounded completely' [LN]. This verb means to cause someone to be so astounded as to be practically overwhelmed [LN].

c. μήτι (LN 69.16) (BAGD p. 520). The question is introduced by this negative interrogative particle and it is translated 'could this man/one be?' [BECNT, WBC; GW, NET], 'could this be?' [NIV], 'could he be?' [TEV], 'could Jesus be?' [CEV], 'could it be that Jesus is?' [NLT], 'can this be?' [NIGTC, PNTC; ESV, NRSV, REB], 'is this perhaps?' [BNTC], 'is not this?' [KJV]. Translation choices expressing some element of disbelief are: 'can this man really be?' [NICNT], 'this one isn't...is he?' [CC], 'this man cannot be...can he?' [NASB], 'surely this cannot be?' [NTC]. This sentence is also translated as expressing a statement, not a question: 'perhaps this man is the Son of David' [NCV]. This interrogative marker indicates a somewhat emphatic negative response [LN], and it is often left untranslated [BAGD].

QUESTION—What relationship is indicated by τότε 'then'?

It indicates a loose connection with what was related in the previous section [EBC, PNTC], only that it occurred sometime later [PNTC], and in fact probably took place much later [EBC]. It is indefinite [NTC]. It indicates that this event occurred after what was narrated in verse 15, where Jesus withdrew from the place where a confrontation with the Pharisees had occurred [TH].

QUESTION—What relationship is indicated by μήτι '(is) not'?

1. It expresses uncertainty, but at least sees the proposition as a possibility that he could be the Son of David [BECNT, BNTC, ICC, Lns, My, NIBC, NICNT, NIGTC, NTC, PNTC, TH, TRT, WBC; CEV, NCV, NET, NIV, NLT, TEV]. The question is framed as though expecting a negative answer [NTC]. Although they were perplexed, they still thought that it might be possible that Jesus was in fact the Messiah [NTC, PNTC]. The miracles indicated that he might be the Messiah, but since he didn't fulfill the political aspect of what they expected, they were puzzled [EBC, NICNT].

2. It expects a negative answer to the question [BAGD, CC, EBC, NAC; NASB]: This man isn't the Son of David, is he?

3. It expects a positive answer to the question [KJV]: Isn't this the Son of David?

12:24 But the Pharisees having-heard said, "This (man) does- not -cast-out demons except[a] by[b] Beelzebul (the) ruler[c] of-the demons."

LEXICON—a. εἰ μή (LN 89.131) (BAGD VI.8.a. p. 220): 'except' [BAGD, CC, NICNT, PNTC; NET], 'only' [BECNT, BNTC, NIGTC, WBC; ESV, GW, NASB, NIV, NRSV, REB, TEV], 'if not' [BAGD], 'but' [LN, NTC; KJV], 'except that, however, instead, but only' [LN], not explicit [CEV, NCV, NLT]. This phrase indicates contrast by designating an exception [LN].

b. ἐν (LN 90.6): 'by' [BECNT, BNTC, LN, NIGTC, NTC, PNTC; ESV, KJV, NASB, NIV, NRSV, REB], 'by the power of' [NICNT; CEV, NET], 'through' [WBC], 'in connection with' [CC], 'with the help of' [GW]. This preposition is also translated by a verb phrase: '(Jesus) uses the power of' [NCV], 'he gets his power from' [NLT], '(Beelzebul) gives him power' [TEV]. This preposition indicates agency, often with the implication of an agent being used as an instrument, and in some instances relating to general behavior rather than to some specific event [LN].

c. ἄρχων (LN 37.56) (BAGD 3. p. 114): 'ruler' [BAGD, BECNT, BNTC, CC, LN, NICNT, NIGTC, PNTC, WBC; CEV, GW, NASB, NCV, NET, NRSV, TEV], 'prince' [BAGD, NTC; ESV, KJV, NIV, NLT, REB], 'governor' [LN]. This noun denotes one who rules or governs [LN].

QUESTION—What was it that the Pharisees heard and responded to?

They heard that the crowds were wondering if Jesus was the Messiah [BECNT, ICC, Lns, My, NIBC, NICNT, NIGTC, NTC, PNTC, WBC]. They could have heard and reacted to the fact that the people were wondering if Jesus was the Messiah, or to the news about the healing [TH, TRT], or to both [TRT].

QUESTION—What is implied by the Pharisees' use of the pronoun οὗτος 'this (man)'?

The pronoun οὗτος 'this (man)' is used in a somewhat pejorative or dismissive sense [CC, NIGTC, PNTC], implying contempt [ICC]. It is used in a highly derogatory sense [Lns]. It is emphatic [My].

12:25 But knowing[a] their thoughts[b] he-said to them, "Every kingdom having-been-divided[c] against itself is-destroyed[d] and every city or house having-been-divided against itself will- not -stand.[e]

LEXICON—a. perf. act. participle of οἶδα (LN 32.4) (BAGD 4. p. 556): 'to know' [BECNT, BNTC, CC, NICNT, NTC, PNTC, WBC; all versions except NET], 'to understand' [LN], 'to see' [NIGTC], 'to realize' [NET], 'to comprehend' [LN]. This verb means to comprehend the meaning of something, with focus upon the resulting knowledge [LN].

b. ἐνθύμησις (LN 30.15) (BAGD p. 266): 'thought' [BECNT, BNTC, CC, LN, NIGTC, NTC, PNTC, WBC; ESV, KJV, NASB, NIV, NLT], 'what is thought, opinion' [LN]. This noun is translated as a phrase: 'what they were thinking' [NICNT; CEV, GW, NCV, NET, NRSV, TEV], 'what was in their minds' [REB]. This noun denotes the content of thinking and reasoning [LN].

c. aorist pass. participle of μερίζω (LN **63.23**) (BAGD 1.a. p. 504): 'to be divided' [BAGD, **LN**; all translations except CEV, NLT, TEV], 'to be disunited' [LN]. The clause 'Every kingdom having been divided against itself is destroyed' is translated 'Any kingdom where people fight against each other will end up ruined' [CEV], 'Any country that divides itself into groups which fight each other will not last very long' [TEV], 'Any kingdom divided by civil war is doomed' [NLT]. This verb means to divide into separate parts [LN].

d. pres. pass. indic. of ἐρημόομαι (LN 20.41) (BAGD p. 309): 'to be destroyed' [LN; NCV, NET], 'to be laid waste' [BAGD, BECNT, CC, NICNT, NIGTC; ESV, NASB, NRSV, REB], 'to be devastated' [BNTC], 'to be ruined' [PNTC; GW, NIV], 'to end up ruined' [CEV], 'to be on its way to ruin' [NTC], 'to suffer ruin' [WBC], 'to be brought to desolation' [KJV], 'to be doomed' [NLT], 'to suffer destruction, to suffer desolation'

[LN], 'to not last long' [TEV]. This verb means to suffer destruction, with the implication of being deserted and abandoned [LN].
e. future pass. indic. of ἵσταμαι (LN **13.90**) (BAGD II.1.d. p. 382): 'to stand' [BECNT, BNTC, CC, NIGTC, NTC, PNTC, WBC; ESV, KJV, NASB, NET, NIV, NRSV, REB], 'to stand firm' [BAGD], 'to survive' [NICNT], 'to last' [GW], 'to continue to exist' [**LN**], 'to continue' [LN; NCV], 'to continue to be, to keep on existing' [LN]. The clause 'and every city or house having been divided against itself will not stand' is translated 'and a town or family that fights will soon destroy itself' [CEV], 'a town or family splintered by feuding will fall apart' [NLT], 'any town or family that divides itself into groups which fight each other will fall apart' [TEV]. This passive verb means to continue to exist, with the probable implication of some resistance involved [LN].

12:26 And if Satan casts-out[a] Satan, he-has-been-divided against[b] himself; how then will his kingdom stand?

LEXICON—a. pres. act. indic. of ἐκβάλλω (LN 53.102) (BAGD 1. p. 237): 'to cast out' [BAGD, LN], 'to make go out, to exorcise' [LN], 'to drive out, to expel' [BAGD]. The clause 'if Satan casts out Satan' [BECNT, NIGTC, PNTC, WBC; ESV, KJV, NASB, NET, NRSV; similarly NLT] is also translated 'if Satan is casting out Satan' [CC], 'if Satan is engaged in casting out Satan' [NTC], 'if Satan expels Satan' [BNTC], 'if Satan forces Satan out' [GW], 'if Satan drives out Satan' [NIV], 'if Satan throws out Satan' [NICNT], 'if it is Satan who drives out Satan' [REB], 'if Satan forces out himself' [NCV], 'if Satan fights against himself' [CEV], 'if one group is fighting another in Satan's kingdom' [TEV]. This verb means to cause a demon to no longer possess or control a person [LN].

b. ἐπί (LN 90.34) (BAGD III. 1.a.ε. p. 288): 'against' [LN]. The phrase 'he has been divided against himself' [CC] is translated 'he is divided against himself' [BECNT, BNTC, NICNT, NIGTC, NTC, PNTC, WBC; ESV, GW, KJV, NASB, NET, NIV, NRSV, REB; similarly NCV], 'he is divided and fighting against himself' [NLT], '(...Satan's kingdom), this means that it is already divided into groups' [TEV], not explicit [CEV]. This preposition indicates opposition in a judicial or quasi-judicial context [LN].

QUESTION—What relationship is indicated by εἰ 'if' in verses 26–27?
It indicates a condition which is assumed true only for the sake of argument [BECNT, EBC, Lns, NAC, PNTC, TH]. The condition is obviously false [PNTC, TRT].

QUESTION—How could Satan cast out Satan?
The Pharisees had accused Jesus of casting out demons by Beelzebul (Satan) and this would mean that Satan was in effect casting himself out when he enabled Jesus to deliver people from his own power [PNTC]. Since the demons do Satan's work, for Satan to cast them out would mean casting

MATTHEW 12:26 439

himself out [EBC, Lns]. The name of the leader of the group of demons is Satan and his name is used to represent one of Satan's demons or a group of Satan's demons [TH].

QUESTION—What kind of question is 'how then will his kingdom stand'?
This is a rhetorical question that makes the statement that his kingdom could not stand [TH]. The question shows the inherent contradiction [NIGTC] and reveals the absurdity [Lns, NTC, WBC], and even the impossibility of the idea [WBC]. Through the question, Jesus is stating the obvious [CC, EBC, NICNT]. Some translate this as a definite statement: 'His kingdom will not continue' [NCV], 'His own kingdom will not survive' [NLT], 'and will soon fall apart!' [TEV].

12:27 And if I cast-out the demons by[a] Beelzebul, by whom do- your sons[b] -cast-(them)-out? Therefore[c] they will-be your judges.[d]

LEXICON—a. ἐν (LN 90.6): 'by' [BECNT, BNTC, LN, NIGTC, NTC, PNTC; ESV, KJV, NASB, NET, NIV, NRSV, REB], 'by the power of' [NICNT], 'with the help of' [GW], 'through' [WBC], 'in connection with' [CC]. The phrase 'by Beelzebul' is translated 'I use the power of Beelzebul (to cast/force out)' [CEV, NCV], '(I am) empowered by Satan' [NLT], 'because Beelzebul gives me the power to do so' [TEV]. This preposition indicates agent, often with the implication of an agent being used as an instrument [LN].

b. υἱός (LN **36.39**, 9.4) (BAGD 1.c.α. p. 833): 'son' [BAGD, BECNT, BNTC, CC, NICNT, NIGTC, NTC, PNTC; ESV, NASB, NET], 'disciple' [LN (36.39)], 'follower' [BAGD, **LN** (36.39); CEV, GW, TEV], 'person of ..., one who is ...' [LN (9.4)]. The phrase οἱ υἱοὶ ὑμῶν 'your sons' is translated 'your children' [KJV], 'your people' [NCV, NIV], 'your own people' [REB], 'those associated with you' [WBC], 'your own exorcists' [NLT, NRSV]. This noun may denote one who is a disciple or follower of someone, with the implication of being like the one whom he follows [LN (36.39)], or may denote a person of a class or kind, specified by the following genitive construction [LN (9.4)].

c. διὰ τοῦτο (LN 90.44): 'therefore' [BECNT, BNTC, NICNT, NIGTC, NTC, PNTC; ESV, KJV, NRSV], 'for this reason' [LN; NASB, NET], 'because of this' [CC, LN], 'so then' [NIV], 'so' [NCV, NLT], 'that's why' [GW], 'because of this charge' [WBC], 'if this is your argument' [REB], not explicit [CEV, TEV].

d. κριτής (LN 56.28) (BAGD 1.b. p. 453): 'judge' [BAGD, BECNT, BNTC, CC, LN, NICNT, NIGTC, NTC, PNTC, WBC; ESV, GW, KJV, NASB, NCV, NET, NIV, NRSV]. This noun is translated as a phrase: 'the ones who will judge' [CEV], 'they will condemn you' [NLT], 'they themselves will refute you' [REB], 'will prove you are wrong' [TEV]. It denotes one who presides over a court session and pronounces judgment [LN].

QUESTION—What is meant by the term 'your sons'?

It refers to the Pharisees' disciples or followers [BNTC, ICC, NIBC, NTC, PNTC, TH, TRT], those who have been trained by the Pharisees [My], the Pharisees' own exorcists [BECNT, ICC, Lns]. It refers to Jewish exorcists [CC, NICNT, NIGTC, WBC]. It could refer either to disciples of the Pharisees or to Jewish people more generally [EBC].

QUESTION—Is there any significance to the use of the personal pronouns ἐγώ 'I' and αὐτοί 'they'?

They are not needed grammatically, so their presence indicates emphasis [CC]. There is also emphasis in the contrast between 'I' and 'your sons' [Lns, My, NIGTC].

QUESTION—What relationship is indicated by διὰ τοῦτο 'therefore'?

It indicates a conclusion to be drawn from the implied answer to the rhetorical question in the first part of this verse [Lns, WBC].

QUESTION—In what way would their 'sons' be their judges?

Apparently there were Jews who claimed to cast out demons and some of them could be referred to as the 'sons' of the Pharisees. Those exorcists would testify to the fact casting out demons was not a work of Satan [PNTC]. The implication is that the miraculous deeds performed by those followers of the Pharisees were sufficient evidence to prove that the Pharisees' argument was faulty. The idea is 'Their actions demonstrate how wrong your argument is' or 'What they are doing proves that your accusations cannot be right' [TH]. If those among the Pharisees' disciples who performed exorcisms were to affirm that it was done by the power of Satan, it would condemn their own practice; but if they were to acknowledge that it was done by God's power, it would vindicate Jesus [NTC]. The simple fact that those exorcists did what they did and were appreciated shows that the Pharisees' explanation of Jesus' powers was an evasion of the truth [NIGTC].

12:28 But if by (the) Spirit of-God I cast-out the demons, then the kingdom of-God has-come[a] upon you.

LEXICON—a. aorist act. indic. of φθάνω (LN **13.123**) (BAGD 2. p. 856): 'to come upon' [BAGD, BECNT, CC, **LN**, NIGTC, NTC, PNTC, WBC; ESV, NASB, NIV], 'to catch up with' [NICNT], 'to come, to arrive' [BAGD]. The phrase 'has come upon you' [BECNT, CC, NIGTC, NTC, PNTC; ESV, NASB, NIV] is translated 'has indeed come upon you' [WBC], 'has already come upon you' [REB, TEV], 'has come to you' [GW, NCV, NRSV], 'is come unto you' [KJV], 'has just come to you' [BNTC], 'has caught up with you' [NICNT], 'has already come to you' [CEV], 'has already overtaken you' [NET], 'has arrived among you' [NLT]. This verb means to happen to someone prior to a particular point in time [LN].

QUESTION—What relationship is indicated by εἰ 'if'?
   It assumes the stated condition to be true [CC, BECNT, NTC, PNTC; CEV, TEV]. However, in this statement translating εἰ as 'if' instead of 'since' heightens the rhetorical force by inviting the reader to think about the logical connection involved [CC].
QUESTION—What is the relationship between 'the kingdom of God' and 'the kingdom of the heavens' which Matthew has used earlier in this gospel?
   There is no distinction between the terms [BECNT, EBC, Lns, NIGTC, NTC, PNTC, WBC]. This variation is probably stylistic, used for the sake of parallelism with 'Spirit of God' [BECNT, EBC, ICC, Lns, NICNT, NIGTC] and in opposition to the idea of Satan's kingdom mentioned two verses earlier [ICC, NICNT, WBC]. Here the use of 'of God' instead of 'of heaven' provides a more personal reference to God, which balances 'Spirit of God' in the previous clause [NICNT].
QUESTION—What is the connotation of the phrase ἔφθασεν ἐφ' ὑμᾶς 'has come upon you'?
   It carries a negative sense [CC, PNTC], and possibly even means 'has come *against* you' [CC]. It implies an unwelcome surprise [NICNT], a challenge that they must come to terms with [NIGTC]. It has actually become present, not just near [Lns, WBC]. The kingdom is present in the person of the Christ [ICC]. It means that God has now established his rule among you [TH]. The age of the kingdom has dawned [EBC]. It has begun to appear [BNTC]. The kingdom of God was already present in the form of Jesus' miracles, which were encroaching on Satan's territory [BECNT]. It was already a present reality [NAC, NTC, TRT], at least in some sense [NAC]. It had arrived, but not in its fullness [My, NIBC].

12:29 Or how is- anyone -able[a] to-enter[b] into the house of the strong-man[c] and seize[d] his goods,[e] unless first he-would-bind[f] the strong-man? And then he-will-plunder[g] his house.

LEXICON—a. pres. mid. or pass. (deponent = act.) indic. of δύναμαι (LN 74.5): 'to be able to' [CC, LN], 'can' [BECNT, BNTC, LN, NICNT, NIGTC, NTC, PNTC; all versions except NCV, NLT], 'to be powerful enough' [NLT], 'to be possible for' [WBC], not explicit [NCV]. This verb means to be able to do or to experience something [LN].
   b. aorist act. infin. of εἰσέρχομαι (LN 15.93) (BAGD 1.a.β. p. 232): 'to enter' [BECNT, BNTC, CC, LN, NIGTC, NTC, PNTC, WBC; ESV, KJV, NASB, NCV, NET, NIV, NLT, NRSV], 'to get into' [NICNT], 'to break into' [CEV, REB, TEV], 'to move into' [LN], 'to come into' [BAGD, LN], 'to go into' [BAGD, LN; GW]. This verb means to move into a space, either two-dimensional or three-dimensional [LN].
   c. ἰσχυρός (LN 79.63) (BAGD 1.a. p. 383): 'strong' [BAGD, LN], 'mighty, powerful' [BAGD], 'vigorous' [LN]. This adjective is translated as a substantive: 'strong man' [BECNT, BNTC, CC, NICNT, NTC, PNTC, WBC; all versions except NCV, NLT], 'strong man like Satan' [NLT],

'strong person' [NIGTC; NCV]. It describes being physically strong and vigorous [LN].
   d. aorist act. infin. of ἁρπάζω (LN **57.235**) (BAGD 1. p. 109): 'to seize' [BNTC, PNTC], 'to forcefully seize' [LN], 'to steal' [BAGD, NICNT, WBC; CEV, GW, NCV, NET], 'to take away' [TEV], 'to drag away' [BAGD], 'to carry off' [BAGD, BECNT, **LN**, NTC; NASB, NIV], 'to snatch away' [CC], 'to plunder' [LN, NIGTC; ESV, NLT, NRSV], 'to make off with' [REB], 'to spoil' [KJV], 'to rob' [LN]. This verb means to forcefully take something away from someone else, often with the implication of a sudden attack [LN].
   e. σκεῦος (LN 57.20) (BAGD 1.a. p. 754): 'goods' [LN, NIGTC, NTC, PNTC, WBC; ESV, KJV, NLT, REB], 'possessions' [BECNT, NICNT; NIV], 'belongings' [LN; TEV], 'property' [BAGD, BNTC; GW, NASB, NET, NRSV], 'vessels' [CC], 'things' [CEV, NCV], 'household furnishings' [LN]. This noun, which occurs only in the plural, denotes objects which are possessed [LN].
   f. aorist act. subj. of δέω (LN 18.13) (BAGD 1.b. p. 177): 'to bind' [BAGD, CC, NTC, PNTC, WBC; ESV, KJV, NASB], 'to tie up' [BECNT, BNTC, LN, NICNT, NIGTC; all versions except ESV, KJV, NASB], 'to tie' [BAGD, LN], 'to tie together' [LN]. This verb means to tie objects together [LN].
   g. fut. act. indic. of διαρπάζω (LN 57.238) (BAGD p. 188): 'to plunder' [BECNT, BNTC, CC, LN, NICNT, NIGTC, PNTC; ESV, NASB, NLT, NRSV, TEV], 'to plunder thoroughly' [WBC; NET], 'to ransack' [NTC; REB], 'to take everything' [CEV], 'to steal property' [GW], 'to steal things' [NCV], 'to spoil' [KJV], 'to plunder thoroughly' [BAGD], 'to rob' [LN; NIV]. This verb means to plunder something thoroughly or completely [LN].

QUESTION—What relationship is indicated by ἤ 'or'?
   It indicates another argument to be considered [EBC, Lns, My, NIGTC, TH, TRT], an alternative way of looking at the situation [BECNT]. It introduces a variation on the argument just given [ICC]. This function of indicating another aspect of the argument is expressed in translation: 'or again' [NIV, REB], 'furthermore' [WBC], 'how else (can)' [NET].

QUESTION—Who is the strong man?
   Jesus is referring to Satan [BECNT, CC, EBC, ICC, Lns, My, NAC, NIBC, NICNT, NIGTC, NTC, PNTC, TH, TRT, WBC], or to the demons [BNTC].

DISCOURSE UNIT—12:30–32 [NASB]. The topic is the unpardonable sin.

12:30 The-one not being with[a] me is against[b] me, and the-one not gathering[c] with me scatters.[d]

LEXICON—a. μετά (with the genitive) (LN **90.42**) (BAGD A.II.1.c.δ. p. 509): 'with' [BAGD, **LN**; all translations except CEV, TEV], 'for' [TEV], 'on the same side as' [LN], 'on someone's side' [BAGD]. The phrase μετ' ἐμοῦ 'with me' is translated 'on my side' [CEV]. This preposition

indicates association in which one party acts or exists for the benefit of another [LN].
  b. κατά (with the genitive) (LN 90.31) (BAGD I.2.b.γ. p. 406): 'against' [BAGD, LN; all translations except NLT], 'in opposition to, in conflict with' [LN]. The phrase κατ' ἐμοῦ ἐστιν 'is against me' is translated 'opposes me' [NLT]. This preposition indicates opposition, with the possible implication of antagonism [LN].
  c. pres. act. participle of συνάγω (LN 15.125) (BAGD 1. p. 782): 'to gather' [BAGD, BECNT, BNTC, CC, NICNT, NIGTC, NTC, PNTC, WBC; ESV, GW, KJV, NASB, NET, NIV, NRSV, REB], 'to gather in the harvest' [CEV], 'to help (me) gather' [TEV], 'to gather together, to call together' [LN]. The phrase συνάγων μετ' ἐμοῦ 'gathering with me' is translated 'work with me' [NCV], 'working with me' [NLT]. This verb means to cause to come together, whether of animate or inanimate objects [LN].
  d. pres. act. indic. of σκορπίζω (LN 15.135) (BAGD 1. p. 757): 'to scatter' [BAGD, LN; all translations except KJV, NCV, NLT], 'to scatter abroad' [KJV], 'to disperse' [BAGD], 'to cause to disperse' [LN]. The verb is translated 'working against me' [NCV, NLT]. This verb means to cause a group or a gathering to disperse or scatter [LN].

QUESTION—What does it mean to be 'with' Jesus?
He is saying that no one can be neutral about Jesus [EBC, BECNT, BNTC, CC, ICC, Lns, NICNT, NIGTC, NTC, PNTC, TH]. To be 'with' Jesus means to be his ally, to be on his side [Lns, PNTC, TH, TRT], to actively support him and his kingdom [BECNT], to be in intimate association with him [NTC]. It means to help him gather in the lost ones of Israel [NIBC].

QUESTION—What life situation is the metaphorical reference to gathering or scattering drawn from?
  1. It is drawn from shepherding [BECNT, ICC, Lns, NIBC, NIGTC, NTC, PNTC]. The sheep in a flock tend to scatter and if a person takes no part in gathering the scattered members of the flock, he in effect scatters them, since by doing nothing he casts his vote in favor of scattering them [PNTC].
  2. It is drawn from the harvest [EBC, TH, TRT, WBC; CEV]. The idea is of gathering people to God, much as one gathers in crops at harvest time. But the one who doesn't help gather people is scattering them, or driving them away from God [TH].

12:31 **Therefore I-say to you(pl), every sin[a] and blasphemy[b] will-be-forgiven[c] people, but the blasphemy (against[d]) the Spirit will- not -be-forgiven.**

  LEXICON—a. ἁμαρτία (LN 88.289): 'sin' [LN; all translations except CEV], 'sinful thing you do' [CEV]. This noun denotes acting contrary to the will and law of God.

b. βλασφημία (LN 33.401) (BAGD 1., 2.b. p. 143): 'blasphemy' [BAGD, BECNT, BNTC, CC, LN, NICNT, NIGTC, NTC, PNTC, WBC; ESV, KJV, NASB, NET, NIV, NLT, NRSV], 'slander' [BAGD; REB], 'sinful thing you say' [CEV], 'evil thing they say' [TEV], '(everything) they say against God' [NCV], 'cursing' [GW], 'defamation' [BAGD], 'serious insult' [LN]. This noun denotes the content of a defamation [LN].

c. fut. pass. indic. of ἀφίημι (LN 40.8) (BAGD 2. p. 126): 'to be forgiven' [BAGD, BECNT, BNTC, CC, LN, NIGTC, NTC, PNTC, WBC; all versions], 'to be pardoned' [BAGD, LN]. The future tense of this verb is translated as indicating a possibility: 'can be forgiven' [CEV, NCV, NLT, REB, TEV], 'may be forgiven' [NICNT]. This verb means to remove the guilt resulting from wrongdoing [LN].

d. There is no lexical entry for the English word 'against'. It is used to represent the relationship indicated by the genitive case of τοῦ πνεύματος 'the Spirit'. This relationship is translated 'against' [BECNT, BNTC, NICNT, NIGTC, NTC; all versions except GW], 'of' [CC, PNTC, WBC]. The phrase 'blasphemy against the Spirit' is translated 'cursing the Spirit' [GW].

QUESTION—What relationship is indicated by the genitive case of τοῦ πνεύματος 'the Spirit'?

It indicates that the Spirit is the one being blasphemed [BECNT, BNTC, CC, Lns, NAC, NIBC, NICNT, NIGTC, NTC, PNTC, TH, TRT, WBC; all versions].

QUESTION—What does it mean that 'every' sin and blasphemy will be forgiven except that one?

It means only that it is possible for such sins to be forgiven, not that they will automatically be forgiven [CC, ICC, NICNT, NIGTC, PNTC, TRT; CEV, NCV, NLT, REB, TEV]. In order to receive forgiveness for such sins, forgiveness must be sought [NTC, PNTC, TRT].

QUESTION—What is the blasphemy against the Spirit that cannot be forgiven?

It is a self-conscious, thoughtful, and even willful rejection of the work of the Spirit of God and willfully turning away from what one knows to be true. This would be the case with anyone who perceives that Jesus' ministry is empowered by the Holy Spirit but then ascribes it to Satan [EBC]. Those who deny that the Spirit of God is working through Jesus are in effect saying that the Spirit-empowered ministry of Jesus is actually demonic [CC]. It is to attribute the working of the Spirit of God to Satan, in the outright rejection of God's saving power that is being shown in actions of overthrowing Satan's kingdom [WBC]. In their case it was willfully ascribing an obvious work of God to Satan [NTC, TH]. Since the power of the Spirit is behind Jesus' miracles, to attribute those works to Satan is to slander the Spirit, an eternal sin that goes far beyond mere unbelief [BECNT]. Such people come to the point where they can no longer repent or seek forgiveness [NTC, PNTC]. It is to so refuse the clear conviction of the Holy Spirit that the person comes to a state wherein the Spirit is no longer able to produce

MATTHEW 12:31					445

conviction and repentance [Lns]. It is rejecting the clear revelation of the Holy Spirit and willfully shutting out the light of revelation, such that one's opposition to God is expressed in speech; this leaves the person in a state of heart that is unable to seek forgiveness or receive any influence from the Holy Spirit [My]. It is to call the evident working of God a work of Satan [NICNT, NIGTC], which excludes a person from what God is doing in Jesus; however, even this may be repented of, and is unforgiveable only if it is ongoing and sustained [NIGTC]. It is on-going rejection of Jesus [CC].

12:32 And whoever[a] would-speak[b] a-word against the Son of Man, it-shall-be-forgiven him; but whoever would-speak (a-word) against the Holy Spirit, it-will- not -be-forgiven him neither in this age[c] nor in the coming[d] (one).

LEXICON—a. ὅς (LN 92.27): The phrase ὅς ἐάν 'whoever' [BNTC, CC, NIGTC, NTC, PNTC, WBC; ESV, GW, NASB, NET, NRSV], is also translated 'whosoever' [KJV], 'who' [LN], '(if) anyone' [BECNT, NICNT], 'anyone who' [NCV, NIV, NLT, REB, TEV], 'you' [CEV], 'the one who' [LN]. The relative pronoun ὅς denotes any entity, event, or state, either occurring overtly in the immediate context or clearly implied in the discourse or setting [LN].

b. aorist act. subj. of λέγω (aorist form εἶπον) (LN 33.69): 'to speak, to say' [LN]. The phrase λόγον λέγω κατά 'to speak a word against' [BECNT, CC, NICNT, NIGTC, NTC, PNTC; ESV, GW, KJV, NASB, NIV, NRSV, REB] is also translated 'to speak against' [CEV, NCV, NET, NLT], 'to say a word against' [BNTC, WBC], 'to say anything against' [TEV]. This verb means to speak or talk, with apparent focus upon the content of what is said [LN].

c. αἰών (LN **67.143**) (BAGD 2.a. p. 27): 'age' [BAGD, BECNT, BNTC, CC, **LN**, NICNT, NIGTC, NTC, PNTC, WBC; ESV, NASB, NET, NIV, NRSV, REB], 'life' [CEV], 'world' [GW, KJV, NLT], 'era' [LN]. The phrase τούτῳ τῷ αἰῶνι 'this age' is translated 'now' [NCV, TEV]. This noun denotes a unit of time as a particular stage or period of history [LN].

d. μέλλω (LN 67.135) (BAGD 2. p. 501): 'to come' [BAGD, LNC]. The phrase ἐν τῷ μέλλοντι 'in the coming one' [BNTC, WBC] is also translated 'in the one that is coming' [CC], 'in the age to come' [BECNT, NICNT, NIGTC, NTC; ESV, NASB, NET, NIV, NRSV, REB], 'in that to come' [PNTC], 'in the world to come' [KJV, NLT], 'in the life to come' [CEV], '(in this world) or the next' [GW], 'in the future' [NCV], '(now) or ever' [TEV]. The phrase τὸ μέλλον 'the future' refers to an unlimited extent of time beginning with the time of the discourse [LN].

QUESTION—Does this mean that the Holy Spirit is more important than Jesus? The Holy Spirit is not more important than Jesus [EBC]. Anyone who blasphemes the Holy Spirit is also rejecting Jesus' own claims about himself [EBC]. Someone could make a mistake about who Jesus was [NICNT, PNTC, WBC]. It was not obvious that he was the Son of God, but to call obvious works of the power of the Holy Spirit a work of Satan was inexcusable [PNTC] and shows one's own moral bankruptcy [BNTC]. The contrast seems to be one of rejecting Jesus when the evidence is unclear versus rejecting him when he is clearly operating in the power of the Holy Spirit [My, NAC, NIGTC].

DISCOURSE UNIT—12:33–37 [CEV, ESV, NASB, NCV, NET, NRSV, TEV]. The topic is people know you by your words [NCV], a tree and its fruit [CEV, NRSV, TEV], trees and their fruit [NET], a tree is known by its fruit [ESV], words reveal character [NASB].

12:33 Either make^a the tree good^b and the fruit^c of-it good, or make the tree bad^d and the fruit bad; for from the fruit the tree is-known.^e

LEXICON—a. aorist act. impera. of ποιέω (LN 42.29) (BAGD I.1.e.β. p. 682): 'to make' [BECNT, BNTC, CC, NICNT, NIGTC, PNTC, TH, WBC; ESV, GW, KJV, NASB, NCV, NET, NIV, NRSV], 'to get' [REB], 'to consider' [NTC], 'to assume, to suppose, to take as an example' [BAGD]. The phrase 'make the tree good' is translated 'a good tree produces' [CEV], 'if a tree is good' [NLT], 'you must have a healthy tree' [TEV], 'get a good tree' [REB]. This verb means to produce something new [LN].

b. καλός (LN 65.22) (BAGD 2.a. p. 400): 'good' [BAGD, LN; all translations except TEV], 'healthy' [TEV], 'fine' [BAGD, LN]. This adjective describes the condition of having acceptable characteristics or functioning in an agreeable manner, often with the focus on outward form or appearance [LN].

c. καρπός (LN 3.33) (BAGD 1.a. p. 404): 'fruit' [BAGD, LN; all translations]. This noun denotes any fruit part of plants, including grain as well as pulpy fruit [LN].

d. σαπρός (LN 65.28) (BAGD 1. p. 742): 'bad' [BAGD, BNTC, LN, NIGTC, WBC; all versions except GW, KJV, TEV], 'worthless' [BECNT], 'rotten' [CC, NICNT, PNTC; GW], 'sickly' [NTC], 'corrupt' [KJV], 'poor' [TEV], 'unusable, unfit' [BAGD], 'diseased' [LN]. This adjective describes the condition of being poor or bad in quality and hence of little or no value (particularly in reference to plants, either in the sense of seriously diseased or of seedling stock, that is, not budded or grafted) [LN].

e. pres. pass. indic. of γινώσκω (LN 28.1) (BAGD 1.a. p. 160): 'to be known' [BAGD, BECNT, BNTC, LN, NICNT, NIGTC, NTC, PNTC; ESV, KJV, NASB, NCV, NET, NRSV, TEV], 'to be being known' [CC], 'to be recognized' [NIV], 'to be identified' [NLT], 'to be proven' [WBC], 'to known about' [LN]. The phrase ἐκ γὰρ τοῦ καρποῦ τὸ δένδρον γινώσκεται 'from the fruit the tree is known' is translated 'you can tell a tree by its fruit' [REB], 'you can tell what a tree is like by the fruit it produces' [CEV], 'a person can recognize a tree by its fruit' [GW]. This verb means to possess information about [LN].

MATTHEW 12:33

QUESTION—In what sense is the verb 'make' used here?

It is used to introduce a supposition [BECNT, Lns, NIBC, NICNT, NTC, TRT]. To get good fruit, one must make the tree good by proper cultivation [NIGTC]. It means to judge the tree to be good or bad [My]. They must be consistent in their thinking: that is, if the fruit is good, the tree must also be good [BECNT, My, NIBC, NTC, TH, TRT]. This appears to be a popular proverb [NICNT]. It appears to introduce a supposition, though it may be an appeal to action [PNTC].

QUESTION—Do 'good' and 'bad' refer to the relative health of the tree, or to the kind of tree it is?

Note that while the choice seems to be between either the wrong kind of tree producing the wrong kind of fruit, as opposed to a diseased or rotten tree producing diseased or rotten fruit, it may be that the metaphor is not that clear and specific. Some commentators appear not to distinguish between those choices [PNTC, possibly EBC, NIBC].

1. It refers more generally to the nature of the tree, the kind if tree it is [BAGD, BNTC, Lns, probably NICNT]. Since rotten trees don't bear fruit at all, it denotes a more general meaning [BAGD].
2. It refers to the health of the tree [NTC, TH, TRT].
3. It refers to the cultivation of the tree, which may involve both of the above positions [ICC, NIGTC].

QUESTION—What is the point Jesus is making?

It is an appeal to action, to make what the tree in the metaphor represents to be good [CC, EBC, ICC, NIGTC]. This is a challenge and call to repentance [CC]. Jesus is saying that if his works are good, then the Pharisees should conclude that he is good [BECNT, Lns, My, NTC, TH, TRT]. The bad 'fruit' of the Pharisees' accusations demonstrates that they themselves are bad [BECNT, BNTC, EBC, ICC, NAC, NIBC, NICNT, NIGTC, NTC, PNTC, WBC].

12:34 Offspring[a] of-vipers,[b] how can-you speak good-things[c] being evil[d]? For from the abundance[e] of-the heart[f] the mouth speaks.

LEXICON—a. γέννημα (LN 23.53, 58.26) (BAGD p. 156): 'offspring' [BAGD, CC, LN (23.53, 58.26), NIGTC, NTC, PNTC, WBC; NET], 'brood' [BAGD, BECNT, BNTC, LN, NICNT; ESV, NASB, NIV, NLT, NRSV, REB], 'bunch' [CEV], 'generation' [KJV], 'child' [BAGD, LN (23.53)], 'son of, child of, kind of, one who has the characteristics of, person of' [LN (58.26)], not explicit [GW, NCV, TEV]. This noun can denote that which has been produced or born of a living creature [LN (23.53)], or a kind or class of persons, with the implication of possessing certain derived characteristics [LN (58.26)].

b. ἔχιδνα (LN **88.123**) (BAGD p. 331): 'viper' [BAGD, BECN\T, BNTC, CC, **LN**, NICNT, NIGTC, NTC, WBC; ESV, KJV, NASB, NET, NIV, NRSV, REB], 'snake' [LN, PNTC; CEV, NCV, NLT, TEV], 'poisonous

snake' [GW], 'evil person' [LN]. This noun denotes a dangerous and despised person [LN].
   c. ἀγαθός (LN 88.1): 'good things' [BNTC, CC, PNTC, WBC; KJV, NRSV, TEV], 'good' [LN, NIGTC; ESV, REB], 'what is good' [BECNT, NTC; NASB], 'what is good and right' [NLT], 'anything good' [NICNT; CEV, GW, NCV, NET, NIV], 'goodness, good act' [LN]. The adjective describes positive moral qualities of the most general nature [LN].
   d. πονηρός (LN 88.110) (BAGD 1.b.α. p. 691): 'evil' [BAGD, BECNT, BNTC, CC, LN, NIGTC, NTC, PNTC, WBC; all versions], 'bad' [BAGD, NICNT], 'immoral' [LN], 'wicked' [BAGD, LN], 'base, worthless' [BAGD]. This adjective describes what is morally corrupt and evil [LN].
   e. περίσσευμα (LN 59.53) (BAGD 1. p. 650): 'abundance' [BAGD, BNTC, CC, LN, NIGTC, NTC, PNTC, WBC; ESV, KJV, NRSV], 'fullness' [BAGD; REB], 'overflow' [NIV], 'what overflows from' [BECNT, NICNT], 'what fills' [NET], 'that which fills' [NASB], 'a great deal of' [LN]. The phrase τοῦ περισσεύματος τῆς καρδίας 'the abundance of the heart' is translated 'what/whatever is in your hearts' [CEV, NLT], 'the things that are in the heart' [NCV], 'what the heart is full of' [TEV], 'what comes from inside you' [GW]. This noun denotes that which exists in abundance [LN].
   f. καρδία (LN 26.3) (BAGD 1.b.ε. p. 404): 'heart' [BAGD, LN; all translations except GW], 'inside you' [GW], 'inner self, mind' [LN]. This noun denotes the causative source of a person's psychological life in its various aspects, but with special emphasis upon thoughts [LN].
QUESTION—What is the imagery behind the phrase 'the abundance of the heart'?
   The picture is of a substance overflowing from a container [EBC, Lns, My, NTC, NIV]. The heart is pictured as a container, and whatever fills it—either good or evil—overflows through the mouth in the form of the words a person speaks [TH]. Whatever fills a person's heart determines what that person says [PNTC].
QUESTION—What does 'heart' signify?
   It is the center of personality [EBC, TH, WBC], the inner person [NIBC], the seat of the whole inner life [PNTC], of thinking, feeling and willing [NTC, PNTC]. It is the inner faith and character [BNTC].

12:35 The good[a] man from the treasure[b] of good[c] draws-out[d] good-things, and the evil[e] man from the treasure of evil[f] draws out evil-things.
LEXICON—a. ἀγαθός (LN 88.1) (BAGD 1.b.α. p. 3). 'good' [BAGD, LN; all translations].
   b. θησαυρός (LN 65.10) (BAGD 1.b. p. 361): 'treasure' [BECNT, BNTC, CC, LN, NIGTC, PNTC; ESV, KJV, NASB, NRSV, TEV], 'store' [NICNT; REB], 'inner storehouse' [NTC], 'treasury' [BAGD, WBC; NET, NLT], 'wealth, riches' [LN]. The phrase τοῦ ἀγαθοῦ θησαυροῦ

'treasure of good' is translated 'the good things that are in them' [GW], 'the good stored up in him' [NIV], 'good things in their hearts' [NCV], '(bring) good things out of their hearts' [CEV]. This noun denotes that which is of exceptional value and kept safe [LN].
- c. ἀγαθός (LN 88.1) (BAGD 1.b.β. p. 3): 'good' [BAGD, BECNT, BNTC, CC, LN, NICNT, NIGTC, NTC, PNTC, WBC; CEV, ESV, KJV, NASB, NET, NIV, NRSV, REB], 'good things' [NCV, TEV], 'good heart' [NLT], not explicit [GW].
- d. pres. act. indic. of ἐκβάλλω (LN 15.68) (BAGD 3. p. 237): 'to bring out' [BAGD, BECNT, CC, NIGTC, NTC, PNTC; CEV, NASB, NET, NIV, NRSV, TEV], 'to bring forth' [BNTC, WBC; ESV, KJV], 'to produce' [NICNT; NLT, REB], 'to take out, to remove' [BAGD], 'to send, to send out, to send forth' [LN]. The phrase 'draws out good things' is translated 'do the good things' [GW], 'say good things' [NCV]. This verb means to send out or away from, presumably for some purpose [LN].
- e. πονηρός (LN 88.110) (BAGD 1.b.α. p. 690): 'evil' [BECNT, BNTC, CC, NIGTC, NTC, PNTC, WBC; all versions except TEV], 'bad' [NICNT; TEV],
- f. πονηρός (LN 88.110) (BAGD 1.b.α. p. 690): 'evil' [BECNT, BNTC, CC, NIGTC, NTC, PNTC, WBC; all versions except TEV], 'bad things' [NICNT; TEV].

QUESTION—Does the word θησαυρός 'treasure' signify the treasure or the treasury from which it is drawn?

The word 'treasure' can signify both something that is valuable and also the place were valuable things are kept [TH, PNTC]. Although either meaning is possible in this verse, in the end there is not a great deal of difference [PNTC].
1. It signifies the treasure that has been drawn out [BNTC, CC, ICC, NIGTC, TRT].
2. It signifies the treasury from which it is drawn [My, NTC, TH, WBC; NET, NLT]. It is clear from the context of verse 34 that this is speaking of the place where the treasure is stored [TH].
3. It signifies both the treasure and the treasury [Lns].

12:36 And I-say to-you(pl) that every careless[a] word which men will-speak they-will-give account[b] for it in (the) day of-judgment[c]; **12:37** for by[d] your(sg) words you(sg)-will-be-justified,[e] and by your(sg) words you(sg)-will-be-condemned.[f]

LEXICON—a. ἀργός (LN **30.44**, 72.21) (BAGD 3. p. 104): 'careless' [BAGD, BECNT, BNTC, **LN** (30.44, 72.21), NTC, PNTC, WBC; CEV, ESV, GW, NASB, NCV, NIV, NRSV], 'worthless' [CC; NET], 'empty' [NICNT], 'idle' [NIGTC; KJV, NLT], 'thoughtless' [REB], 'without thought' [LN (30.44)], 'indifferent' [LN (72.21)], 'useless' [BAGD; TEV], 'unproductive' [BAGD]. This adjective describes not giving careful consideration to something [LN (30.44)], or it describes showing indifference as to whether something is as it should be [LN (72.21)].

b. λόγος (LN 57.228) (BAGD 2.a. p. 478): 'account' [BAGD, LN; all translations except NASB, NCV], 'accounting' [NASB], 'reckoning' [BAGD], 'credit, debit' [LN]. The phrase ἀποδώσουσιν…λόγον 'they will give account' is translated '(people) will be responsible' [NCV]. This noun denotes a record of assets and liabilities [LN].

c. κρίσις (LN 30.110) (BAGD 1.a.α. p. 452): 'judgment' [BAGD, LN; all translations], 'judging' [BAGD], 'decision, evaluation' [LN]. This noun denotes the content of the process of judging [LN].

d. ἐκ (LN 89.77) (BAGD 3.i. p. 235): 'by' [BECNT, BNTC, CC, NICNT, NIGTC, NTC, PNTC; ESV, GW, KJV, NASB, NET, NIV, NRSV], 'by means of' [LN], 'from' [LN, WBC], 'because of' [CEV], 'out of' [REB], 'according to, in accordance with' [BAGD], not explicit [NCV, NLT, TEV]. This preposition indicates means as constituting a source [LN].

e. fut. pass. indic. of δικαιόω (LN 56.34) (BAGD 3.a. p. 197): 'to be justified' [NIGTC, NTC, PNTC, WBC; ESV, KJV, NASB, NET, NRSV], 'to be acquitted' [BAGD, BNTC, CC, LN, NICNT; NIV, REB], 'to be vindicated' [BECNT], 'to be told (they are) innocent' [CEV], 'to be declared innocent' [GW], 'to be pronounced righteous' [BAGD], 'to be set free, to have guilt removed' [LN]. The phrase ἐκ…τῶν λόγων σου δικαιωθήσῃ 'by your words you will be justified' is translated 'some of your words will prove you right' [NCV], 'the word you say will acquit you' [NLT], 'your words will be used to judge you–to declare you…innocent' [TEV]. This verb means clearing someone of transgression [LN].

f. fut. pass. indic. of καταδικάζω (LN 56.31) (BAGD p. 410): 'to be condemned' [BAGD, BECNT, BNTC, CC, LN, NICNT, NIGTC, NTC, PNTC, WBC; ESV, KJV, NASB, NET, NIV, NRSV, REB], 'to be told (they are) guilty' [CEV], 'to be declared guilty' [GW], 'to be found guilty, to be pronounced guilty' [BAGD], 'to have a verdict of guilt rendered' [LN]. The phrase ἐκ τῶν λόγων σου καταδικασθήσῃ 'by your words you will be condemned' is translated 'the words you say will condemn you' [NLT], 'the words you have said will be used to judge you…some of your words will prove you guilty' [NCV], 'your words will be used to judge you–to declare you…guilty' [TEV]. This verb means to judge someone as definitely guilty and thus subject to punishment [LN].

QUESTION—What is meant here by ἀργός 'careless'?

It describes what is apparently insignificant, and even the apparently insignificant things a person says reveal what is in his heart [EBC]. It is irresponsible speech [BNTC]. Their words are morally useless [My], useless because they don't help anyone, but actually do harm [TH]. It is worthless speech [BECNT, CC, WBC], useless for accomplishing anything good [NTC], something best left unspoken [NIBC, WBC], something that emanates from the 'rotten' inner life [CC]. It describes what is carelessly said, without concern for the effect on other people, but which actually shows what is really in the heart [PNTC]. Careless or casual remarks sometimes indicate what is in the heart more than carefully chosen words [BNTC, NAC, NIBC]. They are words without substance, such as empty promises or unpaid vows, and in this case they are words that are spoken as though defending God's truth, but which actually impede his work of salvation [NICNT].

QUESTION—What relationship is indicated by γάρ 'for'?

It indicates grounds for the statement in the previous verse: they will have to give account, because judgment will be on the basis of what one says [PNTC, TH].

QUESTION—In what sense will people be 'justified' by their words?

They will be declared innocent or guilty based on what they have said [BECNT, EBC, TH]. Judgment is based on what we are, and what we say reveals what we are [PNTC]. Words reflect what is in the heart [ICC, My, NICNT, NIGTC, NTC, WBC]. In 10:32–33 Jesus says that people will be rejected or accepted on the basis of their denial or confession of a relationship with Jesus [NAC]. Those who are friendly, reverent, responsible, and kind in speech will be acquitted, but those who are hostile, irresponsible, and profane in their speech will be condemned [BNTC]. Words of faith will enable a person to be acquitted, and words of unbelief will cause them to be condemned [CC].

QUESTION—Why does Jesus shift from the plural 'you' to the singular 'you' in this passage?

This saying may have come from an independent source, such as a proverb [EBC, ICC, NICNT, NIGTC, WBC]. It gives emphasis in applying what he is saying to each individual hearing it [NTC, TH], which in this case is specifically being applied to the Pharisees [TH].

DISCOURSE UNIT—12:38–45 [GW, NASB, NIV, NLT]. The topic is the sign of Jonah [GW, NIV, NLT], the desire for signs [NASB].

DISCOURSE UNIT—12:38–42 [CEV, ESV, NCV, NET, NRSV, TEV]. The topic is the people ask for a miracle [NCV], the demand for a miracle [TEV], the sign of Jonah [ESV, NET, NRSV], a sign from heaven [CEV].

12:38 **Then some of the scribes and Pharisees answered him saying, "Teacher, we-want to-see a sign^a from you."**

LEXICON—a. σημεῖον (LN 33.477) (BAGD 2.a. p. 748): 'sign' [BECNT, BNTC, CC, LN, NICNT, NIGTC, NTC, PNTC, WBC; ESV, KJV, NASB, NET, NRSV, REB], 'sign from heaven' [CEV], 'miraculous sign' [GW, NIV], 'miraculous sign to prove your authority' [NLT], 'miracle' [BAGD; TEV], 'a miracle as a sign' [NCV], 'wonder' [BAGD]. This noun denotes an event which is regarded as having some special meaning [LN].

QUESTION—What is implied by 'answered' in verse 38?
1. These men were responding to what Jesus had been saying in the preceding passage [BECNT, NIBC, NIGTC, PNTC, TH, WBC]. It indicates a response to Jesus' strong warning about sin that will not be forgiven [BECNT]. They were responding to the healing of the demoniac described in verse 24 [Lns].
2. It does not necessarily indicate a specific answer to a particular statement [EBC; CEV, GW, NASB, NIV, NLT, NRSV, REB, TEV]. It does not necessarily indicate a response to the specific controversy just narrated, but serves generally to introduce the next conversation in the narrative [EBC].

QUESTION—What is indicated by the use of the term 'teacher'?
It was a respectful title [EBC, PNTC, TH]. The title appears respectful, but in this case it was insincere [BECNT, CC, Lns, NTC]. This term of respect may actually indicate a certain amount of resistance to Jesus [WBC]. They address him with a title indicating that he is on a level equal to themselves [NIGTC]. In Matthew's gospel only those who are not Jesus' followers call him 'teacher' [BECNT, CC, NIBC, NICNT, WBC].

QUESTION—What kind of a sign were they looking for?
They were looking for a sign from heaven that would clearly show that God was at work in Jesus' miracles [NAC, PNTC, TH]. They wanted an especially significant miracle [BECNT], compelling proof [BNTC], some miraculous token to be performed on command [EBC, NAC, PNTC]. They wanted something sensational [ICC, NTC], something that appealed to the senses [My], something that would amaze or impress [WBC]. They wanted signs such as those that Moses performed [ICC, NIBC]. They wanted him to predict some clear sign to occur in the near future, such as occasionally happened in the OT [CC].

12:39 But Jesus answering said to-them, "An-evil[a] and adulterous[b] generation[c] seeks[d] a-sign, and a-sign will- not -be-given to-it except the sign of-Jonah the prophet.

LEXICON—a. πονηρός (LN 88.110) (BAGD 1.b.α. p. 691): 'evil' [BAGD, BECNT, BNTC, CC, LN, NIGTC, NTC, PNTC, WBC; all versions except NIV, REB], 'wicked' [BAGD, LN, NICNT; NIV, REB], 'immoral' [LN], 'bad, worthless, degenerate' [BAGD]. This adjective describes being morally corrupt and evil [LN].

b. μοιχαλίς (LN **31.101**) (BAGD 2.a. p. 526): 'adulterous' [BAGD, BECNT, BNTC, CC, LN, NICNT, NIGTC, NTC, PNTC, WBC; ESV, KJV, NASB, NET, NIV, NLT, NRSV], 'unfaithful' [**LN**; GW], 'sinful' [NCV], 'godless' [REB, TEV], '(you) won't believe' [CEV]. This adjective describes being unfaithful to one's earlier and true beliefs [LN].

c. γενεά (LN 11.4) (BAGD 2. p. 154): 'generation' [BAGD, BECNT, BNTC, CC, NICNT, NIGTC, NTC, PNTC, WBC; ESV, KJV, NASB, NET, NIV, NLT, NRSV, REB], 'people of an era' [GW], 'people of this

day' [TEV], 'people' [NCV], 'contemporaries' [BAGD], 'those of the same time, those of the same generation' [LN], not explicit [CEV]. This noun denotes people living at the same time and belonging to the same reproductive age-class [LN].
   d. pres. act. indic. of ἐπιζητέω (LN 25.9) (BAGD 2.b. p. 292): 'to seek' [BECNT, CC, NIGTC, PNTC; ESV, KJV], 'to seek for' [BECNT], 'to seek after' [WBC], 'to look for' [NTC; GW], 'to demand' [BAGD, NICNT; NLT], 'to desire' [BAGD, BNTC, LN], 'to crave' [NASB], 'to want' [CEV], 'to want to see' [NCV], 'to want to' [LN], 'to ask for' [NET, NIV, NRSV, REB, TEV]. This verb means to desire to have or experience something, with the probable implication of making an attempt to realize one's desire [LN].

QUESTION—In what way could the people of Jesus' day have been described as adulterous?

Here it describes being unfaithful to God [BNTC, CC, ICC, Lns, My, NIBC, NTC, PNTC, TH, TRT, WBC], being disobedient [TH], being idolatrous [NAC], or being guilty of religious apostasy [EBC, NIBC]. Their unfaithfulness is shown in their lack of repentance and faith [CC]. This is a biblical metaphor for sin [BECNT]. It describes a break in their covenant relationship with God [Lns].

QUESTION—What is the connotation of ἐπιζητέω 'seek'?

It indicates a demand [Lns, My, NIBC, NICNT, PNTC; NLT]. It means to seek or request [BECNT, NTC; NET, NIV, NRSV, REB, TEV].

QUESTION—Who is the agent of the passive verb 'will be given'?

God is the one who would give the sign [ICC, PNTC, TH, WBC].

QUESTION—What is the relationship between the nouns in the genitive construction τὸ σημεῖον Ἰωνᾶ 'the sign of Jonah'?

The experience of Jonah is primarily in mind [NICNT, PNTC]. It doesn't mean that Jonah performed a miracle. The meaning is 'the only visible action God will do for you is the same one he did for the prophet Jonah' [TH] and what God did is explained in the next verse [TH, WBC].

QUESTION—What was that sign?

The sign is Jesus' resurrection [BNTC, CC, ICC, My, NTC], or death and resurrection [Lns, NAC, NICNT], or the death, burial and resurrection [TRT]. Both Jesus and Jonah were delivered from death as a sign attesting the validity of their message [BECNT, EBC]. For Jesus' disciples, his authority is grounded in his death and resurrection [EBC]. It was Jesus' interment for three days, just as Jonah was in the fish for three days [NIGTC].

12:40 For just-as Jonah was in the belly[a] of-the big-fish[b] three days and three nights, so the Son of Man will-be in the heart of-the earth three days and three nights.

LEXICON—a. κοιλία (LN 8.67) (BAGD 1. p. 437): 'belly' [BAGD, LN; all translations except CEV, NCV, TEV], 'stomach' [BAGD; CEV, NCV],

'internal organs' [LN], not explicit [TEV]. This noun denotes the entire digestive apparatus, including stomach and intestines [LN].
- b. κῆτος (LN **4.61**) (BAGD p. 431): 'big fish' [**LN**; CEV, NCV, TEV], 'great fish' [ESV, NLT], 'huge fish' [LN; GW, NET, NIV], 'whale' [WBC; KJV], 'sea monster' [BAGD, BECNT, BNTC, CC, NICNT, NIGTC, NTC, PNTC; NASB, NRSV, REB]. This noun denotes any large sea monster [LN].

QUESTION—How are we to reconcile the 'three days and three nights' in the heart of the earth with the fact that Jesus' resurrection occurred on the morning of the second day after he died?

In Jewish reckoning, any portion of the day counted as the whole [BECNT, CC, EBC, ICC, Lns, My, NAC, NICNT, NTC, PNTC]. The phrase 'three days and three nights' is a quote from the Septuagint Greek translation of Jonah 1:17 [ICC, NICNT, TH, WBC]. Matthew also records Jesus saying he will rise *on* the third day [PNTC]. What is described as three days and nights in Esther 4:16 is also described in Esther 5:1 as ending on the third day, not after the third day [CC, Lns, NTC].

QUESTION—To what does 'the heart of the earth' refer here?
1. It refers to the grave [BECNT, EBC, Lns, NIGTC, NTC, PNTC, TH], not to Hades as the realm of the dead [EBC, Lns, TH]. This refers to the grave rather than the world of the dead and could be translated 'deep in the earth (or ground)' or 'buried in the ground' [TH].
2. It refers to the realm of the dead [NIBC, WBC], which is not the same as the grave [NIBC].

12:41 (The)[a] **men of-Nineveh will-rise-up**[b] **in the (day of) judgment**[c] **with**[d] **this generation and condemn**[e] **it,**

LEXICON—a. There is no definite article in the text. It is translated as having the definite article [BECNT, CC, NICNT, PNTC; all versions]. The phrase ἄνδρες Νινευῖται 'men of Nineveh' is translated 'Ninevites' [WBC], 'Ninevite men' [NIGTC].
- b. fut. mid. indic. of ἀνίσταμαι (LN 17.6) (BAGD 2.c. p. 70): 'to rise up' [BAGD, BNTC, CC, NICNT, NIGTC, PNTC, WBC; ESV, NRSV], 'to stand up' [BECNT, LN, NTC; GW, NASB, NCV, NET, NIV, NLT, TEV], 'to stand there' [CEV], 'to rise' [KJV], 'to arise' [BAGD]. The phrase 'will rise up in the day of judgment with this generation' is translated 'will appear in court when this generation is on trial' [REB]. This verb means to assume a standing position [LN].
- c. κρίσις (LN 30.110) (BAGD 1.a.α. p. 452): 'judgment' [BAGD, LN; all translations except REB], 'decision, evaluation' [LN], not explicit [REB]. This noun denotes the content of the process of judging [LN].
- d. μετά with genitive (LN 89.108): 'with' [LN; all translations except NLT, REB, TEV], 'in the company of, together with' [LN], 'against' [NLT], not explicit [TEV]. The phrase 'with this generation' is translated 'when this

generation is on trial' [REB]. This preposition indicates an associative relation, usually with the implication of being in the company of [LN].
  e. fut. act. indic. of κατακρίνω (LN 56.31) (BAGD p. 412): 'to condemn' [BAGD, LN; all translations except NCV, REB, TEV], 'to show that you are guilty' [NCV], 'to ensure one's condemnation' [REB], 'to accuse (you)' [TEV], 'to render a verdict of guilt' [LN]. This verb means to judge someone as definitely guilty and thus subject to punishment [LN].

QUESTION—Is there any significance in the absence of the definite article in the phrase ἄνδρες Νινευῖται '(The) men of Nineveh'?

It emphasizes the nature or character of the people so described, that is, men of Nineveh as contrasted with Jews [Lns, NTC].

QUESTION—Is there any significance in the use of ἄνδρες 'men', which normally connotes adult males?

Here the term is used generically to mean 'people' [ICC, PNTC, TH, WBC; CEV, NCV, NET, NLT, NRSV, TEV]. It reflects the dominance of men in ancient society [NIGTC]. This word is customary with adjectives describing race or locality [Lns].

QUESTION—What is the connotation of 'rise up'?

It means to rise up against someone, and here it refers to the people of Nineveh rising to bear witness against them in court [CC, EBC, NTC, PNTC]. They will stand up to accuse [NIBC, TH]. They will appear as witnesses [My]. It refers to their rising from the dead at the time of eschatological judgment [ICC, NICNT, NIGTC, WBC].

because they-repented[a] at the preaching[b] of-Jonah, and behold, (something/someone) greater-than[c] Jonah (is) here.

LEXICON—a. aorist act. indic. of μετανοέω (LN 41.52) (BAGD p. 512): 'to repent' [BAGD, BECNT, BNTC, CC, LN, NICNT, NIGTC, NTC, PNTC, WBC; ESV, KJV, NASB, NET, NIV, NRSV, REB], 'to repent of one's sins' [NLT], 'to turn from one's sins' [TEV], 'to turn to God' [CEV], 'to turn to God and change the way one thinks and acts' [GW], 'to be sorry and change one's life' [NCV], 'to be converted, to change one's mind' [BAGD], 'to change one's way' [LN]. This verb means to change one's way of life as the result of a complete change of thought and attitude with regard to sin and righteousness [LN].
  b. κήρυγμα (LN 33.258) (BAGD 2. p. 431): 'preaching' [BAGD, BECNT, CC, LN, NIGTC, NTC, PNTC, WBC; ESV, KJV, NASB, NIV, NLT, REB], 'message' [BNTC], 'proclamation' [BAGD, NICNT; NRSV], 'what is preached' [LN]. The phrase εἰς τὸ κήρυγμα Ἰωνᾶ 'at the preaching of Jonah' is translated 'when Jonah preached' [CEV], 'when Jonah preached to them' [NCV, NET], 'when they heard Jonah preach' [TEV], 'when Jonah spoke his message' [GW]. This noun denotes the content of what is preached [LN].
  c. πλεῖον (LN 78.28) (BAGD II.2.c. p. 689): 'greater than' [BAGD], 'more than' [LN], 'more, to a greater degree, even more' [LN]. This pronominal

adjective is neuter in the phrase πλεῖον Ἰωνᾶ 'greater than Jonah' and the phase is translated 'something greater than Jonah' [BECNT, BNTC, NTC, PNTC; ESV, NASB, NET, NRSV, TEV; similarly CEV], 'something more than Jonah' [CC, NICNT, NIGTC, WBC], 'what is here is greater than Jonah' [REB], 'someone greater than Jonah' [GW, NCV, NLT], 'one greater than Jonah' [NIV], 'a greater than Jonah' [KJV]. This adjective describes a degree which surpasses in some manner a point on an explicit or implicit scale of extent [LN].

QUESTION—To what does the neuter adjective πλεῖον 'something greater' refer?

It refers to Jesus [BECNT, EBC, NAC]. It is neuter because it represents everything the Jews had in Christ [Lns]. The use of the neuter pronoun shows more emphasis than the use of the masculine pronoun would show [My]. Distinctions of grammatical gender were not always sharply observed in NT Greek [NAC]. It emphasizes the quality of greatness, as opposed to personal identity [CC, NIBC]. It speaks of Jesus, his message, and his inauguration of the kingdom of God [WBC]. Πλεῖον is neuter because it points to God's work overall in Jesus, including providing his son for the salvation of sinners, and the inauguration of the kingdom [PNTC]. It refers to the coming of God's kingdom and its herald, Jesus [ICC]. It refers to the eschatological judgment [ICC].

12:42 (The) queen[a] of-(the) South[b] will-rise-up[c] in the judgment with this generation and condemn it, because she-came from the ends[d] of the earth to-hear the wisdom[e] of-Solomon, and behold, (one) greater-than Solomon (is) here.

LEXICON—a. βασίλισσα (LN 37.68) (BAGD p. 137): 'queen' [BAGD, LN; all translations]. This noun denotes a female ruler who has absolute authority within a particular area and who is able to pass on the power to rule to a successor [LN].
  b. νότος (LN 82.4) (BAGD 3. p. 544): 'south' [BAGD, LN], 'a country in the south' [BAGD], 'Sheba' [NLT, TEV]. This noun in the genitive case, and which lacks the definite article, is translated using the definite article: 'the South/south' [all translations except NLT, TEV].
  c. fut. pass. indic. of ἐγείρω (LN 17.10) (BAGD 2.e. p. 215): 'to be caused to stand up' [LN], 'to get up' [LN], 'to appear' [BAGD]. This passive verb is translated as a true passive: 'to be raised up' [CC, NICNT, NIGTC]. It is also translated as having an active meaning: 'to rise up' [BECNT, BNTC, PNTC, WBC; ESV, KJV, NASB NET, NRSV], 'to rise' [NIV], 'to arise' [NTC], 'to stand up' [GW, NCV, NLT, TEV], 'to stand (there)' [CEV],'to appear' [BAGD; REB]. This verb means to cause to stand up, with a possible implication of some previous incapacity [LN].
  d. πέρας (LN 80.6) (BAGD 1. p. 644): 'end' [BAGD, BECNT, BNTC, CC, LN, NICNT, NIGTC, NTC, PNTC, WBC; ESV, GW, NASB NET, NIV, NRSV, REB], 'uttermost part' [KJV], 'limit' [BAGD, LN]. The phrase ἐκ

τῶν περάτων τῆς γῆς 'from the ends of the earth' is translated 'from far away' [NCV], 'from a distant land' [NLT], 'all the way from her country' [TEV], 'a long way' [CEV]. This noun denotes limit as the distant end of a space [LN]. The phrase 'from the ends of the earth' is a Semitic idiom meaning 'a very long distance' [TH].

e. σοφία (LN 32.37) (BAGD 2. p. 759): 'wisdom' [BAGD, LN; all translations except NCV, TEV], 'wise teaching' [NCV, TEV], 'insight, understanding' [LN]. This noun denotes the content of what is known by those regarded as wise [LN].

DISCOURSE UNIT—12:43–45 [CEV, ESV, NCV, NET, NRSV, TEV]. The topic is people today are full of evil [NCV], return of an evil spirit [CEV], the return of the evil spirit [TEV], the return of the unclean spirit [NET, NRSV], return of an unclean spirit [ESV].

12:43 And whenever the[a] unclean spirit goes-out[b] from a[c] man, it-goes[d] through waterless[e] places seeking[f] a-resting-place[g] and[h] does- not -find[i] it.

LEXICON—a. The neuter definite article τό is translated as definite: 'the' [BECNT, BNTC, NICNT, NTC, WBC; ESV, KJV, NASB, NRSV]. It is translated as indefinite: 'an' [CC, NIGTC, PNTC; CEV, GW, NCV, NET, NIV, NLT, REB, TEV].

b. aorist act. subj. of ἐξέρχομαι (LN 15.40) (BAGD 1.a.δ. p. 274): 'to go out' [BAGD, BECNT, BNTC, CC, LN, NTC, PNTC; ESV, KJV, NASB, NET, NRSV, TEV], 'to come out' [BAGD, WBC; GW, NCV, NIV, REB], 'to be expelled' [NICNT], 'to depart' [NIGTC], 'to leave' [CEV, NLT], 'to depart out of, to leave from within' [LN]. This verb means to move out of an enclosed or well-defined two or three-dimensional area [LN].

c. The masculine definite article τοῦ is translated as definite: 'the' [BNTC]. It is translated as indefinite: 'a' [BECNT, CC, NICNT, NIGTC, NTC, PNTC, WBC; all versions except REB], not explicit [REB].

d. pres. mid. or pass. (deponent = indic.) of διέρχομαι (LN 15.21) (BAGD 1.b.α. p. 194): 'to go through' [BAGD], 'to travel around through, to journey all through' [LN]. The phrase διέρχομαι διά 'to go-through through' is translated 'to go through' [PNTC; GW, NIV], 'to pass through' [BECNT, CC, NIGTC; ESV, NASB, NET], 'to wander through' [BNTC, NICNT, NTC, WBC; NRSV], 'to travel through' [CEV, NCV], 'to walk through' [KJV], 'to go into' [NLT], 'to wander over' [REB], 'to travel over' [TEV], 'to travel around through, to journey all through' [LN]. This verb means to travel around through an area, and implies both an extensive and thorough movement throughout an area [LN].

e. ἄνυδρος (LN 2.8) (BAGD p. 76): 'waterless' [BAGD, BECNT, BNTC, CC, LN, NIGTC, NTC, PNTC, WBC; ESV, NASB, NET, NRSV], 'arid' [NICNT; NIV], 'dry' [LN; GW, KJV, NCV, TEV]. The phrase ἀνύδρων τόπων 'waterless places' is translated 'the desert' [CEV, NLT], 'the

desert sands' [REB]. This adjective describes the absence of water or moisture [LN].
- f. pres. act. participle of ζητέω (LN 27.41) (BAGD 1.a.β. p. 338): 'to seek' [BECNT, BNTC, CC, LN, NIGTC, NTC, WBC; ESV, KJV, NASB, NIV, NLT, REB], 'to look for' [LN, NICNT, PNTC; CEV, GW, NCV, NET, NRSV, TEV], 'to try to learn where something is, to look for, to try to find' [LN]. This verb means to try to learn the location of something, often by movement from place to place in the process of searching [LN].
- g. ἀνάπαυσις (LN **23.87**) (BAGD 3. p. 58): 'resting-place' [BAGD, NIGTC, WBC; NRSV, REB], 'place to rest' [**LN**; CEV, GW, NCV], 'rest' [BECNT, BNTC, CC, NTC, PNTC; ESV, KJV, NASB, NET, NIV, NLT], 'somewhere to settle' [NICNT]. This noun denotes a location for resting.
- h. καί (LN 89.92) (BAGD I.2.g. p. 392): 'but' [BAGD, BNTC, CC, NTC; CEV, ESV, GW, NCV, NET, NLT, NRSV], 'yet' [BECNT], 'and' [LN, NICNT, NIGTC, PNTC, WBC; KJV, NASB, NIV, REB], not explicit [TEV]. This conjunction indicates coordinate relations [LN].
- i. pres. act. indic. of εὑρίσκω (LN 27.27) (BAGD 1.a. p. 324): 'to find' [BAGD, LN; all translations], 'to discover' [BAGD, LN], 'to come upon' [BAGD], 'to learn the whereabouts of something, to happen to find' [LN]. This verb means to learn the location of something, either by intentional searching or by unexpected discovery [LN].

QUESTION—Should the evil spirit be referred to as 'he' or 'it'?

In referring to the evil spirit all commentary translations and all versions except KJV use the neuter form 'it' as the implied subject of the third person singular verbs, and 'itself' to translate ἑαυτοῦ, which grammatically could be masculine or neuter. KJV uses 'he' and 'himself'.

QUESTION—Why is a demon called an 'unclean' spirit?

It is called 'unclean' because it defiles the person [BNTC, NIBC]. It seeks to stir up what is unclean and morally vile, and to make a person to be inwardly unclean and disordered [Lns].

QUESTION—Why are definite articles used with 'spirit' and 'man'?

1. It is not referring to any specific instance, so indefinite articles should be used with 'spirit' and 'man' [EBC, NICNT, NIGTC, PNTC, TRT, TH]. This passage is a parable [BECNT].
2. He is describing a specific case, not a general principle [Lns]. It is drawing on the exorcism in verses 22–30 to illustrate a principle [NAC, WBC], which in this case is a potential problem with the Jewish people [WBC].

QUESTION—What does the metaphor of dry places signify, and what does it tell us about unclean spirits?

In Jesus' day people associated demons with wilderness areas [EBC, ICC, Lns, NIBC, NIGTC, PNTC, WBC], or waterless places [BNTC, TH], places where conditions for human well-being are not good [NIGTC]. The parable was not intended to give details about demon possession, so care must be

MATTHEW 12.43

taken not to generalize about demons from this brief passage [CC, NIGTC, NTC, WBC]. The demon is only truly at home in a human host [NICNT].

QUESTION—What is the connotation of 'rest'?

It refers to a place of shelter, a place to stay, and has no connotation of being tired [TH]. The demon has no 'rest' in isolation because it is the nature of demons to torment others [EBC, ICC], so it returns to where it can harm or destroy someone [NIBC]. Demons want to reside in human hearts so they can carry out their evil purposes, and when they cannot do that, it is painful to them [NTC]. The evil spirit is looking for some abode wherein he may fulfill his vile desires [Lns].

12:44 Then it-says, "I-will-return^a into my house^b from-where I-went-out; and having-come it-finds (it) standing-empty^c having-been-swept^d and having-been-put-in-order.^e

LEXICON—a. fut. act. indic. of ἐπιστρέφω (LN 15.90) (BAGD 1.b.α. p. 301): 'to return to' [BECNT, BNTC, CC, LN, NICNT, NIGTC, WBC; ESV, KJV, NASB, NET, NIV, NLT, NRSV], 'to go back to' [LN, NTC, PNTC; CEV, GW, NCV, REB, TEV], 'to turn around, to turn back' [BAGD]. This verb means to return to a point or area where one has been before, with probable emphasis on turning about [LN].

b. οἶκος (LN 7.2) (BAGD 1.b.β. p. 560): 'house' [BECNT, BNTC, CC, LN, NIGTC, NTC, PNTC, WBC; ESV, KJV, NASB, NCV, NIV, NRSV, TEV], 'home' [NICNT; CEV, GW, NET, REB], 'person' [NLT], 'dwelling, habitation' [BAGD], 'temple, sanctuary' [LN]. This noun denotes a building consisting of one or more rooms and normally serving as a dwelling place [LN].

c. pres. act. participle of σχολάζω (LN **59.43**) (BAGD 2. p. 798): 'to stand empty' [BAGD, CC], 'to be empty' [**LN**], 'to be unoccupied' [BAGD], 'to be vacant' [LN]. This participial form is translated adjectivally: 'empty' [BNTC, NIGTC, PNTC; CEV, ESV, KJV, NCV, NET, NLT, NRSV, TEV], 'unoccupied' [BECNT, NICNT, NTC, WBC; GW, NASB, NIV, REB]. This verb means to be empty, with special reference to a dwelling [LN].

d. perf. pass. participle of σαρόω (LN 46.19) (BAGD p. 744): 'to be swept' [BAGD, CC, LN; ESV]. This participial form is translated adjectivally: 'swept' [BECNT, BNTC, NIGTC, PNTC; KJV, NASB, NLT, NRSV], 'clean' [CEV, TEV], 'swept clean' [NICNT, NTC, WBC; GW, NCV, NET, NIV, REB]. This verb means to sweep by using a broom [LN].

e. perf. pass. participle of κοσμέω (LN 79.12) (BAGD 1. p. 445; 2.a.β. p. 445): 'to be put in order' [BAGD 1, CC], 'to be fixed up' [CEV], 'to be all fixed up' [TEV], 'to be tidied up' [NICNT], 'to be tidied' [PNTC], 'to be beautified' [LN], 'to be adorned' [BAGD 2, LN], 'to be decorated' [BAGD 2, LN, NIGTC]. This participial form is translated adjectivally: 'put in order' [BECNT, BNTC, NTC, WBC; ESV, NASB, NET, NIV, NRSV], 'in order' [GW, NLT], 'made neat' [NCV], 'tidy' [REB], 'garnished' [KJV]. This verb means to cause something to be beautiful by decorating [LN].

QUESTION—What does the metaphor of an empty and ordered house describe? The empty house represents people who rejected the proclamation of Jesus [CC, ICC], and consequently are not occupied by the Spirit of God [CC]. The vacancy must be filled by the Spirit of God and discipleship [NICNT]. The core elements of Jesus' ministry had not really found a place in the hearts of the people [NIGTC]. The person was essentially unchanged since nothing good or positive had come to fill the void [BECNT, BNTC, ICC, WBC]. The empty house symbolizes people who have a temporary amendment of habits but without radical commitment and change brought about by the new birth and expressed in true fellowship with Christ [My]. The man's life was outwardly reformed, but he did not become a child of God and did not have the Holy Spirit living within [Lns]. He lacked power and spiritual resources to make his change permanent [PNTC].

QUESTION—What is the relationship of the last clause in this verse to the first? Although it is not written as a conditional sentence, it should be understood as presenting a conditional proposition: *if* he finds it empty when he returns, etc. [EBC, ICC, PNTC].

12:45 Then it-goes and takes-along[a] with it seven other spirits more-evil[b] than-itself and having-entered (they)-dwell[c] there; and the last[d] (condition)[e] of that man becomes worse[f] than-the first[g]. Thus it-will-be also to-this evil[h] generation.

LEXICON—a. pres. act. indic. of παραλαμβάνω (LN 15.168) (BAGD 1. p. 619): 'to take along' [BAGD, CC, LN, NIGTC, PNTC; NASB], 'to take with' [BAGD, BNTC; KJV, NIV], 'to bring along' [BAGD, BECNT, LN; GW, NRSV, TEV], 'to bring with' [WBC; ESV, NET], 'to bring back' [NTC], 'to go out and bring' [NCV], 'to recruit' [NICNT], 'to collect' [REB], 'to find' [CEV, NLT]. This verb means to take or bring someone along with [LN].

b. πονηρότερος (comparative form of πονηρός, for which see verse 39). This comparative form is translated 'more evil' [BNTC, CC, NIGTC, PNTC, WBC; ESV, GW, NET, NLT, NRSV], 'more wicked' [BECNT, NTC; KJV, NASB, NIV, REB], 'worse' [NICNT], 'even worse' [CEV, TEV].

c. pres. act. indic. of κατοικέω (LN 85.69) (BAGD 1.b. p. 424): 'to dwell' [BAGD, BNTC, CC, LN; ESV, KJV], 'to make (their) dwelling' [WBC], 'to make (their) home' [CEV], 'to live' [BAGD, BECNT, LN, NICNT, NTC; NASB, NCV, NET, NIV, NLT, NRSV, TEV], 'to take up residence' [NIGTC], 'to take up permanent residence' [GW], 'to reside' [BAGD, LN], 'to settle down' [BAGD, PNTC], 'to settle' [REB]. This verb means to live or dwell in a place in an established or settled manner [LN]. In Greek a neuter plural subject frequently takes a singular verb, so in all translations except BNTC the implied subject of this singular verb is assumed to be plural, that is, all of the spirits, but in BNTC the implied subject is assumed to be the first unclean spirit.

d. ἔσχατος (LN **61.13**) (BAGD 3.a. p. 314): 'last' [BAGD, BECNT, BNTC, CC, **LN**, NIGTC, PNTC, WBC; ESV, KJV, NASB, NET, NRSV], 'final' [LN, NICNT, NTC; NIV], 'in the end' [GW, REB], not explicit [CEV, NCV, NLT, TEV]. The phrase γίνεται τὰ ἔσχατα τοῦ ἀνθρώπου ἐκείνου χείρονα τῶν πρώτων 'the last condition of that man becomes worse than the first' is translated 'the person ends up in worse shape than before' [CEV], 'the person has even more trouble than before' [NCV], 'that person is worse off than before' [NLT], 'when it is all over, the person is in worse shape than at the beginning' [TEV]. This adjective describes being the last in a series of objects or events [LN].

e. There is no lexical entry for this word in the Greek text. It is supplied in translation as being the implied noun modified by the adjective ἔσχατος 'last'. It is translated 'condition' [NTC, WBC; GW, NIV], 'state' [BECNT, BNTC, NICNT, NIGTC, PNTC; ESV, KJV, NASB, NET, NRSV], 'shape' [CEV, TEV], 'things' [CC], 'plight' [REB], not explicit [NCV, NLT].

f. χείρων (LN 65.29) (BAGD p. 881): 'worse' [BAGD, LN; all translations except CEV, NCV, NLT], 'worse off' [NLT], 'more severe' [BAGD], not explicit [CEV, NCV]. This adjective describes being less satisfactory than something else [LN].

g. πρῶτος (LN 60.46) (BAGD 1.a. p. 725): 'first' [BAGD, BECNT, BNTC, CC, LN, NIGTC, PNTC; ESV, KJV, NASB, NET, NIV, NRSV], 'former' [NTC, WBC], 'earlier' [BAGD]. This adjective is translated adverbially: 'before' [CEV, GW, NCV, NLT, REB], 'at first' [NICNT], 'at the beginning' [TEV]. This adjective describes what is first in a series involving time, space, or set [LN].

h. πονηρός. See entry 'b' above.

QUESTION—What is the point of this parable?

Satan's kingdom was in retreat and God's kingdom had begun to come, but unless the people of Jesus' day would repent, commit to Jesus, accept his message and enter the dawning kingdom, they would be overtaken by evil [BNTC]. Jesus was describing the incorrigibility of the people of his day, who were only content with minor amendment of their ways, but were not interested in major change or repentance [My]. People who would refuse Jesus and his message leave a vacancy in their lives that would leave them more evil than ever before [TH]. Jesus' miracles of healing and demon exorcism are signs of the kingdom and also are a benefit to people; but if those people who have experienced these signs don't repent and turn to him in faith and commitment, they will wind up worse off than before [NICNT, NIGTC, WBC]. Jesus' point is that, despite all his work in casting out demons, healing the sick, and stilling the storm, the spiritual condition of those people in the end would be worse than before if they don't follow him in faith [CC]. The rejection of Jesus and his ministry would eventually result in their being beset by unprecedented evil [ICC]. The people of Jesus' day had been helped temporarily by John the Baptist and then by Jesus, but it was not a permanent change, and they were already in a worse spiritual condition than before, as evidenced by their accusing Jesus of being connected with Satan [Lns]. Jesus had brought messianic deliverance and the message of the kingdom to the people of his day, but their repentance was shallow and the Holy Spirit had not been invited into their lives [NIBC]. Responding to John's ministry in confessing sins and being baptized was not enough; Jesus must have the full devotion of their hearts [NTC]. If the people of that generation continued as they were doing, empty and without the Holy Spirit, they would only come to ruin [PNTC]. Apart from repentance, their future would be bleak [BECNT].

DISCOURSE UNIT—12:46–50 [NICNT; CEV, ESV, GW, NASB, NCV, NET, NIV, NLT, NRSV, TEV]. The topic is the true family of Jesus [GW, NLT], Jesus' true family [NICNT; NCV, NET], Jesus' mother and brothers [CEV, ESV, NIV, TEV], changed relationships [NASB].

12:46 **While-he-(was)- still -speaking to-the crowds, behold, his mother and brothers were-standing outside seeking to-speak with-him.** **12:47** **And someone said to-him, "Behold, your mother and brothers are-standing outside seeking to speak to-you(sg)."** **12:48** **And answering Jesus said to-the one-speaking to-him, "Who is my mother and who are my brothers?"** **12:49** **And having-stretched-out**[a] **his hand to his disciples he-said, "Behold, my mother and my brothers.** **12:50** **For whoever does the will**[b] **of my Father in (the) heavens this-one is my brother and sister and mother."**

TEXT—Manuscripts that include verse 47 are given a C rating by GNT to indicate that choosing it over a variant text was difficult. GNT, BECNT, WBC include it in brackets. It is not included by ESV.

LEXICON—a. aorist act. participle of ἐκτείνω (LN 16.19) (BAGD): 'to stretch out' [BECNT, BNTC, CC, LN, NICNT, NIGTC, NTC, PNTC, WBC; ESV, NASB], 'to stretch forth' [KJV], 'to extend, to reach out' [LN]. The phrase ἐκτείνας τὴν χεῖρα αὐτοῦ 'having stretched out his hand to' is translated 'he pointed to' [CEV, NCV, NLT, TEV], 'pointing to' [NIV, NRSV, REB], 'pointing toward' [NET], 'pointing with his hand' [GW]. This verb means to cause an object to extend in space (for example, by becoming straight, unfolded, or uncoiled) [LN].

b. θέλημα (LN 25.2) (BAGD 1.c.γ. p. 354): 'will' [BAGD, BNTC, BECNT, CC, NICNT, NIGTC, NTC, PNTC, WBC; ESV, KJV, NASB, NET, NIV, NLT, NRSV, REB], 'wish, desire' [LN]. The phrase τὸ θέλημα τοῦ πατρός μου 'the will of my Father' is translated 'what my Father wants' [GW, NCV, TEV], 'obeys my Father' [CEV]. This noun denotes that which is desired or wished for [LN].

QUESTION—How reliable is the inclusion of verse 47 in the text, as opposed to its omission in some important manuscripts?

It was probably part of the original text, but most likely was omitted accidentally in some manuscripts due to the fact that both verse 46 and verse 47 end with λαλῆσαι; after transcribing verse 46 the copyist probably went to λαλῆσαι at the end of verse 47, thinking he was picking up where he left off previously [BECNT, BNTC, EBC, ICC, NAC, NIBC, NICNT, NIGTC, NTC, PNTC, WBC].

QUESTION—Who are the 'disciples' he is referring to here?

This was the inner circle of his disciples [NTC]. It is primarily the twelve, though it may also include a wider group [NICNT]. It includes other followers besides the twelve closest ones [My, TRT, WBC], which would also include women [WBC].

QUESTION—What point was Jesus making about relationships within the family with respect to doing the will of God?

Loyalty to God's kingship is more important that family ties [NICNT]. The kingdom of God takes precedence over human relationships, including that of family [BECNT, ICC, NAC, WBC]. Jesus is not dissolving family bonds, but rather is putting them in perspective relative to the higher priority of the kingdom of God [BECNT, ICC]. He is not showing disrespect for his mother, but giving priority to doing the will of God his Father [EBC]. Putting the importance of the kingdom above his family would have been shocking in Jesus' day [CC]. Doing the will of God means believing and following Jesus [CC, NAC]. It means accepting the fact that Jesus' mighty deeds are an indication that the messianic kingdom has come [NIBC]. Doing the will of his Father is the evidence that they are Jesus' kin, though it is not what makes them such [EBC]. The will of God is that people repent and believe in Jesus, receive forgiveness by faith [Lns, NTC], and live for the glory of God [NTC]; such people have the most intimate spiritual relationship with Jesus [Lns]. Those who were close to him in the service of God were most like family to Jesus [PNTC].

DISCOURSE UNIT—13:1–16:20 [NAC]. The topic is a progressive polarization of response to Jesus.

DISCOURSE UNIT—13:1–58 [WBC; REB]. The topic is the third discourse: teaching in parables [WBC], parables [REB].

DISCOURSE UNIT—13:1–53 [EBC, NICNT, NIGTC]. The topic is the kingdom of heaven–proclamation and response: the parable discourse [NICNT], parables of the kingdom [NIGTC], third discourse: the parables of the kingdom [EBC].

DISCOURSE UNIT—13:1–52 [BECNT, NAC, PNTC]. The topic is discourse 3: parables of the kingdom of heaven [BECNT], the polarization explained: kingdom parables [NAC], teaching in parables [PNTC].

464   MATTHEW 13:1

DISCOURSE UNIT—13:1–23 [ICC; GW, NET, NIV, NLT]. The topic is a story about a farmer [GW], the parable of the sower [NET, NIV], the parable of the sower and its interpretation [ICC], the parable of the farmer scattering seed [NLT].

DISCOURSE UNIT—13:1–9 [CEV, ESV, NASB, NCV, NRSV, TEV]. The topic is a story about planting seed [NCV], the parable of the sower [ESV, NRSV, TEV], Jesus teaches in parables [NASB], a story about a farmer [CEV].

13:1 On that[a] day having-gone-out[b] of-the house Jesus was-sitting[c] beside[d] the lake;[e]

LEXICON—a. ἐκεῖνος (LN 92.30) (BAGD 2.b.γ. p. 239): 'that' [BAGD, LN, all translations]. The phrase ἐν τῇ ἡμέρᾳ ἐκείνῃ 'on that day' [BNTC, CC, NIGTC, PNTC, WBC; NET], is also translated 'that day' [BECNT, NTC; NASB], 'that same day' [NICNT; all versions except NASB, NET]. This pronoun refers to an entity regarded as relatively absent in terms of the discourse setting [LN].

b. aorist act. participle of ἐξέρχομαι (LN 15.40) (BAGD 1.a.α. p. 274): 'to go out' [BAGD, BECNT, BNTC, CC, LN, NICNT, NIGTC, PNTC, WBC; ESV, KJV, NASB, NCV, NET, NIV, NRSV, REB], 'to leave' [NTC; CEV, GW, NLT, TEV], 'to come out, to go away' [BAGD], 'to depart out of, to leave from within' [LN]. This verb means to move out of an enclosed or well defined two or three-dimensional area [LN].

c. imperf. mid. or pass. (deponent = act.) of κάθημαι (LN 17.12) (BAGD 2. p. 389): 'to sit' [LN], 'to sit down' [BAGD, LN], 'to be seated' [LN]. This verb means to be in a seated position or to take such a position [LN]. This verb in the imperfect is translated as imperfect: 'was sitting' [BECNT, CC, NTC; NASB]; as past tense: 'sat' [BNTC, NICNT, PNTC; ESV, KJV, NCV, NET, NIV, NLT, NRSV, REB], 'sat down' [NIGTC, WBC; CEV, GW, TEV].

d. παρά with the accusative (LN 83.25) (BAGD III.1.b.α. p. 611): 'beside' [BECNT, BNTC, NIGTC, WBC; CEV, ESV, NLT, NRSV], 'by' [BAGD, CC, LN, NICNT, PNTC; GW, KJV, NASB, NCV, NCV, NET, NIV, REB], 'on' [NTC], 'to' [TEV], 'at' [BAGD, LN], 'alongside' [LN]. This preposition describes a position near another location or object, usually with the implication of being alongside or close to [LN].

e. θάλασσα (LN 1.70) (BAGD 2. p. 350): 'lake' [BAGD, LN, NICNT, WBC; NCV, NET, NIV, NLT], 'Lake Galilee' [CEV], 'sea' [BAGD, BECNT, BNTC, CC, LN, NIGTC, PNTC; ESV, NASB, NRSV], 'Sea of Galilee' [GW]. The phrase παρὰ τὴν θάλασσαν 'beside the lake' is translated 'on the seashore' [NTC], 'by the seaside' [KJV], 'by the lakeside' [REB], 'to the lakeside' [TEV]. This noun denotes a particular body of water, normally rather large [LN].

QUESTION—To what particular day does 'that day' refer?

It is the same day as the events reported at the end of chapter 12 [BECNT, CC, EBC, Lns, NAC, NICNT, NIGTC, PNTC, TH, WBC].

MATTHEW 13:1

QUESTION—What house is being referred to here?

It is the house mentioned in 12:46ff [BECNT, BNTC, EBC, My, NICNT, NIGTC, PNTC, TH, WBC], which is probably Peter's house in Capernaum [ICC, WBC]. It was the home of Jesus' extended family, into which Jesus had gone with his mother and brothers for a while and then walked to the seashore [Lns].

13:2 and great[a] crowds were-gathered to him, so that he got-into[b] a-boat[c] to-sit-down, and all the crowd stood[d] on the shore.[e]

LEXICON—a. πολύς (LN 59.1) (BAGD I.1.a.β. p. 687): 'great, large, many' [BAGD], 'many, a great number of' [LN]. The phrase 'great crowds were gathered to him' [NIGTC], is translated 'great crowds were gathered around him' [PNTC], 'large crowds gathered to him' [BECNT; NASB], 'large crowds gathered and came to him' [BNTC], 'many crowds gathered to him' [CC], 'large crowds gathered beside him' [WBC], 'great/large crowds gathered around him' [NICNT; ESV, NCV], 'great multitudes were gathered together unto him' [KJV], 'such great/large crowds gathered around him (that)' [CEV, NIV, NRSV], 'the crowds that gathered about him were so large' [NTC]. This same group of people is referred to with a singular noun in the following clause, 'all the crowd stood on the shore' and some translations use the singular form here also: 'a large crowd soon gathered around him' [NLT], 'such a large crowd gathered around him' [NET], 'the crowd that gathered around him was so large (that)' [GW, TEV], 'so many people gathered round him (that)' [REB]. This adjective indicates a relatively large quantity of objects [LN]. In this verse the phrase 'great crowds' is probably better translated 'the great crowd' [TH] or 'many people' [BAGD, TH].

b. aorist act. participle of ἐμβαίνω (LN 15.225) (BAGD p. 254): 'to get into' [BAGD, BECNT, CC, NICNT, NIGTC, PNTC, WBC; all versions except CEV, KJV], 'to go into' [LN; KJV], 'to enter' [BNTC], 'to step into' [LN, NTC]. The phrase εἰς πλοῖον ἐμβάντα καθῆσθαι 'he got into a boat to sit down' is translated 'he had to sit in a boat' [CEV]. This verb means to step into some area [LN].

c. πλοῖον (LN 6.41) (BAGD 2. p. 673): 'boat' [BAGD, LN, all translations except KJV], 'ship' [LN; KJV]. This noun denotes any kind of boat, from small fishing boats, as on Lake Galilee, to large seagoing vessels [LN].

d. pluperfect act. indic. of ἵσταμαι (LN 17.1) (BAGD II.2.b.β. p. 382): 'to stand' [BAGD, BECNT, LN, all translations]. This verb means to be in a standing position [LN].

e. αἰγιαλός (LN 1.63) (BAGD p. 21): 'shore' [BAGD, BECNT, BNTC, CC, LN, NICNT, NIGTC, NTC, WBC; all versions except ESV, NASB, NRSV], 'beach' [BAGD, LN, PNTC; ESV, NASB, NRSV]. This noun denotes a strip of land immediately bordering the edge of a body of water and gradually sloping down into the water [LN].

QUESTION—What part of this discourse was given to the crowds, and what part was spoken privately to the disciples?
1. The parables of the sower, the weeds, the mustard seed, and the yeast were spoken publicly, but the explanations as well as the parables of the hidden treasure, the pearl and the dragnet were spoken privately to the disciples [BECNT, CC, EBC, My, NIGTC, NTC, PNTC, TRT, WBC].
2. All the parables in the chapter are spoken for the crowds, but the explanations are given only to the disciples [NICNT].

QUESTION—Why did Jesus get into the boat to teach?
He got into the boat to get some distance between him and the crowd [NIGTC], to avoid the press of the crowd [BNTC, NAC, NIBC, NICNT, NTC, PNTC, TRT, WBC], or perhaps to see them better [BNTC, CC], and for the acoustical advantage provided by the water [WBC].

QUESTION—Why did Jesus sit down?
He sat to teach the people [EBC, ICC, NICNT, NIGTC, NTC, PNTC, TH, WBC; CEV, TEV], since sitting was the normal posture for teaching [Lns, NTC, PNTC, WBC].

13:3 And he-spoke[a] to-them many-things[b] in parables[c] saying, "Behold[d] the sower[e] went-out to sow.[f]

LEXICON—a. aorist act. indic. of λαλέω (LN **33.70**) (BAGD 2.b. p. 463): 'to speak' [BAGD, BECNT, BNTC, CC, LN; KJV, NASB], 'to speak about' [**LN**], 'to tell' [**LN**, NIGTC, NTC, PNTC, WBC; ESV, NET, NIV, NLT, NRSV, REB, TEV], 'to say' [NICNT], 'to talk' [LN]. The phrase ἐλάλσεν...ἐν παραβολαῖς 'he spoke...in parables' is translated 'taught...by using stories' [CEV], 'used stories as illustrations' [GW], 'used stories to teach' [NCV]. This verb means to speak or talk [LN].

b. πολύς (LN 59.1) (BAGD I.2.b.α. p. 688): 'many things' [BAGD, BECNT, CC, NICNT, NIGTC, NTC, PNTC, WBC; all versions except NLT], 'much' [BAGD, BNTC], 'many stories' [NLT], 'many, a great deal of, a great number of' [LN]. This adjective describes a relatively large quantity of objects or events [LN].

c. παραβολή (LN **33.15**) (BAGD 2. p. 612): 'parable' [BAGD, BECNT, BNTC, CC, **LN**, NICNT, NIGTC, NTC, PNTC, WBC; ESV, KJV, NASB, NET, NIV, NRSV, REB, TEV], 'stories in the form of parables' [NLT], 'stories' [CEV, NCV], 'stories as illustrations' [GW], 'illustration' [BAGD], 'figure, allegory, figure of speech' [LN]. This noun denotes a relatively short narrative with symbolic meaning [LN].

d. ἰδού (LN 91.13) (BAGD 1.b.γ. p. 371): 'behold' [BAGD, BECNT, BNTC; KJV, NASB], 'see' [BAGD], 'look' [BAGD, CC, LN, NIGTC, WBC], 'listen' [LN; GW, NET, NLT, NRSV], 'pay attention' [LN], 'once' [NICNT; TEV], 'once upon a time' [NTC], not explicit [PNTC; CEV, ESV, NCV, NIV, REB]. This particle is a prompter of attention, and serves to emphasize the following statement [LN].

MATTHEW 13:3

e. pres. act. participle of σπείρω (LN 43.6) (BAGD 1.a.α. p. 761): 'sower' [BAGD, BECNT, BNTC, NICNT, NTC, PNTC, WBC; ESV, KJV, NASB, NET, NRSV, REB], 'one who sows' [CC, LN, NIGTC], 'farmer' [CEV, GW, NCV, NIV, NLT], 'man (who went out to sow grain)' [TEV]. This participle denotes someone who scatters seed over tilled ground [LN].

f. pres. act. infin. of σπείρω (LN 43.6) (BAGD 1.a.α. p. 761): 'to sow' [BAGD, BECNT, BNTC, CC, LN, NICNT, NIGTC, NTC, PNTC, WBC; ESV, KJV, NASB, NET, NRSV, REB], 'to sow seed' [NIV], 'to sow grain' [TEV], 'to plant seed/s' [GW, NCV, NLT], 'to scatter seed in a field' [CEV]. This verb means to scatter seed over tilled ground [LN].

QUESTION—What were parables?

Parables were illustrations [BNTC], analogies that illustrated a point, though the meaning might also be unclear [NAC]. This is the NT equivalent of the OT Hebrew term *mashal*, which could refer broadly to a variety of speech forms, including proverbs, riddles, taunts, allegorical stories or even similes [BECNT, CC, EBC, ICC, NAC, NIBC, NICNT, TH]. In Hebrew culture generally a *mashal* or parable could be a short, one-line statement or something more extensive, and often referred to any figure of speech that is to some degree enigmatic; these would convey truth vividly and in a way that would prompt the listener to think, though a certain level of commitment was necessary on the part of the hearer before it could be understood [PNTC]. The parables were brief stories that Jesus told that would communicate indirectly or allegorically in order to convey a deeper meaning, and could be seen as metaphors extended to the level of narrative [CC]. The parables were stories taken from everyday life [NIBC, PNTC], events that actually could have occurred [My]. Parables communicated deep truths by using analogies drawn from ordinary things [WBC]. Most parables were extended metaphors or similes [EBC]. Parables were limited allegories containing symbolic elements, with interpretations that would have come readily to mind to the first century Jewish audience that Jesus addressed. What is common to all the parables is the use of analogy for the sake of illustration, though that could also be perplexing [NAC]. This passage marks a turning point in the narrative of this gospel, in which Jesus began to use parables much more than before due to growing opposition and the rejection of his message; however, he still continued to speak very directly and forcefully on some occasions [BECNT, NAC]. Parables were used both to reveal truth as well as to conceal it [EBC ICC, NAC, NIBC, NTC, PNTC, WBC]. Jesus used parables to reveal truth to those who accepted by faith what is mysterious, and to conceal it from those who rejected the obvious [NTC]. Jesus used parables to illustrate and explain a point, but also to capture the imagination and penetrate the dullness of those who heard, and lead them to respond in obedience [BNTC]. In the synoptic gospels the word always refers to something that is not to be taken literally [NIGTC].

468   MATTHEW 13:3

QUESTION—What crop was being sown in this story?
It would have been either wheat or barley [Lns, NICNT, NTC, TH].

13:4 And as^a he sowed some^b (seeds) fell beside^c the path,^{d} and having-come the birds ate- them -up.^{e}

LEXICON—a. ἐν (LN **67.136**) (BAGD II.3. p. 260): 'as' [BECNT, BNTC, **LN**, NICNT, NIGTC, PNTC, WBC; ESV, NASB, NET, NIV, NLT, NRSV, REB, TEV], 'while' [BAGD, CC, NTC; CEV, NCV], 'when' [BAGD; KJV], 'during' [BAGD, LN], 'in the course of' [LN], not explicit [GW].
  b. ὅς. This relative pronoun is translated as 'some seeds' [BECNT, BNTC, NTC, PNTC, WBC; ESV, GW, KJV, NASB, NET, NLT, NRSV], 'some seed' [NCV], 'some of the seed' [NICNT; REB], 'some lots of seed' [NIGTC], 'some of it' [CEV, TEV], 'some' [NIV], 'there were seeds that' [CC]. Note that the neuter relative pronoun ἅ is plural, but the verb ἔπεσεν 'fell' is singular, and likewise in the following passage the verb forms are sometimes plural, and sometimes singular, since in Greek plural neuter nouns and pronouns can take a singular or plural verb. In verses 19ff the relative pronoun is masculine singular and apparently represents a shift from the seed to the person the seed represents. Also, the implied collective noun 'seed' can be thought of either as collective singular 'seed' or as plural 'seeds', and this variation is seen in the translations.
  c. παρά with the accusative (LN 83.25) (BAGD III.1.d. p. 611): 'beside' [BECNT, BNTC, LN, NICNT, NTC; NASB], 'by' [CC, LN; KJV, NCV], 'along' [NIGTC, NTC; CEV, ESV, GW, NET, NIV, REB, TEV], 'along the edge of' [WBC], 'alongside' [LN], 'on' [BAGD; NLT, NRSV]. This preposition describes a position near another location or object, usually with the implication of being alongside or close to [LN].
  d. ὁδός (LN 1.99) (BAGD 1.a. p. 554): 'path' [BECNT, CC, NICNT, NIGTC, NTC, PNTC, WBC; ESV, NET, NIV, NRSV, TEV], 'footpath' [NLT, REB], 'road' [BAGD, BNTC, LN; CEV, GW, NASB, NCV], 'way, highway' [BAGD, LN], 'wayside' [KJV]. This noun is a general term for a thoroughfare, either within a population center or between two such centers [LN].
  e. aorist act. indic. of κατεσθίω (LN **23.11**) (BAGD 1. p. 422): 'to eat up' [BAGD, BECNT, **LN**, NICNT; NASB, NCV, NIV, NRSV, REB, TEV], 'to eat' [BNTC, WBC; CEV, NLT], 'to gobble up' [NTC], 'to devour' [BAGD, CC, NIGTC, PNTC; ESV, GW, NET], 'to devour up' [KJV]. This verb means to devour something completely [LN].

13:5 And other (seed) fell on the rocky-ground^a where it-did- not -have much soil,^{b} and immediately^c it-sprouted^d because-of not having depth^e of-soil.

LEXICON—a. πετρῶδες (LN **2.22**) (BAGD p. 655): 'rocky ground' [BAGD, CC, **LN**, NTC; CEV, ESV, GW, NCV, NET, NRSV, REB, TEV], 'rocky place' [BECNT, BNTC, PNTC; NASB, NIV], 'rocky area' [NICNT, NIGTC], 'stony place' [KJV], 'stony ground' [WBC], '(soil) with under-

lying rock' [NLT]. This noun denotes a rocky substance or bedrock covered by a thin layer of earth [LN].
b. γῆ (LN **2.14**) (BAGD 1. p. 157): 'soil' [BAGD, **LN**; all versions except KJV, NCV, CEV], 'earth' [BAGD; KJV], 'dirt' [NCV], 'ground' [LN]. The phrase 'did not have much soil' is translated as an adjective describing rocky ground: 'thin' [CEV].
c. εὐθέως (LN 67.53) (BAGD p. 320): 'immediately' [BAGD, BECNT, CC, LN, NTC, PNTC, WBC; ESV; NASB], 'at once' [BAGD, BNTC, NIGTC], 'quickly' [NICNT; CEV, GW, NET, NIV, NLT, NRSV, REB], 'very fast' [NCV], 'forthwith' [KJV], 'soon' [TEV], 'right away' [LN]. This adverb describes a point of time immediately subsequent to a previous point of time (the actual interval of time differs appreciably, depending upon the nature of the events and the manner in which the sequence is interpreted by the writer) [LN].
d. aorist act. indic. of ἐξανατέλλω (LN 23.195) (BAGD p. 272): 'to sprout' [LN, NIGTC, PNTC; GW, NLT, REB], 'to spring up' [BAGD, BECNT, BNTC, NTC, WBC; ESV, KJV; NASB, NET, NIV, NRSV, TEV], 'to come up' [CC], 'to grow up' [NICNT], 'to start growing' [CEV], 'to grow' [NCV], 'to sprout leaves' [LN]. This verb means to begin vegetative growth, with special emphasis upon the sprouting of leaves [LN].
e. βάθος (LN **81.8**) (BAGD 1. p. 130): 'depth' [BAGD, BECNT, BNTC, CC, LN, NICNT, NIGTC, NTC, PNTC; ESV; NASB, NRSV, REB], 'deepness' [KJV]. The phrase τὸ μὴ ἔχειν βάθος γῆς 'not having depth of soil' is translated 'there was not much soil' [WBC], 'the soil wasn't/was not deep' [GW, NET, TEV], 'the soil wasn't very deep' [CEV], 'the ground was not so deep' [NCV], 'the soil was shallow' [NIV, NLT]. This noun denotes the distance beneath a surface [LN].

QUESTION—What is the nature of the 'rocky ground'?

This is soil over a layer of bedrock that lies close to the surface, and it does not mean soil that was mixed with rocks [BECNT, BNTC, EBC, Lns, NIBC, NICNT, NIGTC, NTC, PNTC, TH, TRT]. The sun bakes the moisture out of shallow soil [BNTC, EBC, NICNT], and would also heat the rock just below the surface, such that the warmth would cause the seed to sprout more quickly than the other seed [Lns, NIGTC, TH]. The sprouts break through the surface too soon and are not yet ready for exposure to sunlight [NIGTC]. They can't send roots down very far, so they grow in an upward direction, with too little root to sustain growth [My, NTC].

13:6 But[a] (the) sun having-risen[b] it-was-scorched[c] and because-of not having root[d] it-withered.[e]

LEXICON—a. δέ (LN 89.124, 89.94): 'but' [BECNT, BNTC, CC, LN (89.124), NICNT, NTC, PNTC, WBC; all versions except KJV], 'and' [LN (89.94); KJV], not explicit [NIGTC]. This conjunction indicates contrast [LN

(89.124)], or may indicate an additive relationship with possible implication of some contrast [LN (89.94)].
b. aorist act. participle of ἀνατέλλω (LN 15.104) (BAGD 2. p. 262): 'to rise' [BAGD, BNTC, CC, LN, PNTC; NASB, NCV, NRSV, REB], 'to come up' [BECNT, LN, NICNT, NIGTC, NTC; CEV, GW, NET, NIV, TEV], 'to be up' [KJV]. This verb means to move up, especially of the upward movement of the sun, stars, or clouds [LN].
c. aorist pass. indic. of καυματίζω (LN **14.68**) (BAGD p. 425): 'to be scorched' [BAGD, **LN**; all translations except NCV, NLT, TEV], 'to be burned' [BAGD], 'to be harmed by heat' [LN], not explicit [NCV]. This passive verb is translated as active: 'to burn' [TEV], 'to wilt' [NLT]. This verb means to cause to suffer because of intense heat [LN].
d. ῥίζα (LN 3.47) (BAGD 1.a. p. 736): 'root' [BAGD, LN; all translations]. This noun denotes the underground part of a plant [LN].
e. aorist pass. indic. of ξηραίνω (LN 79.82) (BAGD 2.a. p. 548): 'to wither' [BECNT, BNTC, CC, LN, WBC; GW, NET, NIV], 'to wither up' [NIGTC], 'to wither away' [NTC, PNTC; KJV, NASB, NRSV, REB], 'to shrivel up' [NICNT], 'to dry up' [LN; CEV, NCV, TEV], 'to dry out' [LN]. This passive verb is translated as passive: 'to be withered' [CC]; all others translate it as active. This verb means to cause something to become dry [LN].

13:7 And other (seed) fell among[a] the thorns,[b] and the thorns grew-up[c] and choked[d] them.
LEXICON—a. ἐπί with accusative (LN 83.9) (BAGD III.1.a.γ. p. 288): 'among' [BAGD, BECNT, BNTC, LN, NIGTC, NTC, PNTC, WBC; all versions except CEV], 'on' [CC, NICNT]. The phrase 'among the thorns' is translated 'where thornbushes grew up' [CEV]. This preposition describes a position within an area determined by other objects and distributed among such objects [LN].
b. ἄκανθα (LN 3.17) (BAGD p. 29): 'thorn' [BECNT, BNTC, CC, NTC; ESV, KJV, NASB, NET, NIV, NLT, NRSV], 'thorny patch' [NICNT], 'thornbushes' [NIGTC, PNTC, WBC; CEV, GW, TEV], 'thorny weed' [NCV], 'thorn plant' [BAGD, LN], 'brier' [LN], 'thistle' [LN; REB]. This noun denotes any kind of thorny plant [LN].
c. aorist act. indic. of ἀναβαίνω (LN 23.196) (BAGD 1.b. p. 50): 'to grow up' [BECNT, BNTC, NICNT, NIGTC, PNTC, WBC; all versions except KJV, NASB, NCV], 'to grow' [NCV], 'to come up' [BAGD, CC; NASB], 'to shoot up' [NTC], 'to spring up' [KJV], 'to sprout and grow' [LN]. This verb means to grow, as of plants, from the time of sprouting to mature size [LN].
d. aorist act. indic. of πνίγω (LN **23.120**) (BAGD 1.c. p. 679): 'to choke' [BAGD; all translations], 'to cause plants to die' [**LN**]. This verb means to cause the death of plants by other plants crowding them out and/or overshadowing them [LN].

13:8 And other (seed) fell on the good[a] soil and it-produced[b] fruit,[c] some one-hundred,[d] some sixty, and some thirty.

LEXICON—a. καλός (LN 65.22) (BAGD 2.a. p. 400): 'good' [BAGD, LN; all translations except NLT], 'fertile' [NLT], 'fine' [BAGD, LN]. This adjective describes having acceptable characteristics or functioning in an agreeable manner, often with the focus on outward form or appearance [LN].

  b. imperf. act. indic. of δίδωμι (LN 23.199) (BAGD 4. p. 193): 'to produce' [LN, NICNT, NIGTC, PNTC, WBC; CEV, ESV, GW, NCV, NET, NIV, NLT, REB], 'to yield' [BAGD, BECNT, BNTC, LN, NTC; NASB], 'to bring forth' [KJV, NRSV], 'to bear' [LN; TEV], 'to give' [CC]. The verb phrase καρπὸν δίδωμι means to produce fruit or seed (of plants) [LN].

  c. καρπός (LN 3.33) (BAGD 1.a. p. 404): 'fruit' [BAGD, BNTC, CC, LN, NIGTC, WBC; KJV], 'crop' [BECNT, NICNT, NTC, PNTC; NASB, NCV, NIV, NLT, REB], 'grain' [ESV, GW, NET, NRSV, TEV], not explicit [CEV]. This noun denotes any fruit part of plants, including grain as well as pulpy fruit [LN].

  d. ἑκατόν (LN 60.33) (BAGD p. 236): 'one hundred' [BAGD, LN], 'a hundred' [CC], 'a hundredfold' [BNTC, LN, NICNT, NIGTC, NTC, PNTC, WBC; ESV, KJV, NASB, NRSV, REB]. The phrase ὃ μὲν ἑκατόν 'some one-hundred' is translated 'a hundred times more' [NCV], 'a hundred times as much' [NET], 'a hundred times as much as was scattered' [CEV], 'one hundred times as much as was/had been planted' [GW, NLT], 'a hundred times what was sown' [NIV], 'some had a hundred grains' [TEV].

QUESTION—Is it unusual to have a yield of sixty to one hundred kernels from a single seed?

Plants that have thirty grains would be somewhat less than normal [NICNT]; a one hundred-fold yield would be quite good, but not miraculous [NICNT, WBC]. The yield described here is not out of the ordinary [BECNT, EBC]. A normal head of grain would have about thirty kernels, and sometimes plants could have multiple heads of grain; overall yield, which is affected by other factors than just kernels per plant, would be more in the range of five to fifteen times what was sown, but in good conditions the yield that Jesus describes here is not impossible, particularly if the quality of the seed is exceptional, which may be a significant point of his parable here concerning the power of Jesus' own teaching [NIGTC]. The yield Jesus describes would be extraordinary [NAC, PNTC, TRT, WBC], as a tenfold to twentyfold increase would be a normal yield [NAC, TRT]. An increase of thirtyfold would be a very good crop [PNTC]. A sevenfold to tenfold increase would be average, but a one hundredfold increase would not be impossible [NIBC, TRT].

13:9 The-one having[a] ears let-(him)-hear.[b]"

LEXICON—a. pres. act. participle of ἔχω (LN 57.1, 24.59): 'to have' [LN (57.1)].The phrase ὁ ἔχων οὖς 'the one having ears' is translated 'the one who has ears' [CC, NIGTC; NET], 'whoever has ears' [NICNT], 'who hath ears' [KJV], 'he who has ears' [BNTC, NTC, PNTC; ESV, NASB, NIV], 'anyone with ears' [BECNT; NRSV], 'anyone with ears to hear' [NLT], 'the person who has ears' [WBC; GW], 'if you have ears' [CEV, REB, TEV], 'you people who can hear me' [NCV]. This verb means to have or possess objects or property [LN (57.1)]. The idiom ἔχω οὖς 'to have ear' means to be able to hear, with the implication of being expected to hear or having the obligation to hear with a further implication of related mental activity [LN (24.59)].
  b. pres. act. (third person) impera. of ἀκούω (LN 31.56) (BAGD 1.a. p. 31): 'to hear' [BAGD, BNTC, CC, NICNT, NIGTC, NTC, PNTC, WBC; ESV, KJV, NASB, NIV, REB], 'to listen' [BECNT, LN; GW, NCV, NET, NRSV, TEV], 'to listen and understand' [NLT], 'to pay attention' [CEV], 'to accept, to listen and respond, to pay attention and respond, to heed' [LN]. This verb means to believe something and to respond to it on the basis of having heard [LN].

QUESTION—What does this admonition mean?
  It is an invitation to grasp the meaning of the parable [BECNT, Lns, TRT, WBC], to think about what has been said [PNTC]. It is an invitation to people, including even those who normally are undiscerning, to open themselves up to new insights [NIGTC]. He is inviting anyone who has the spiritual capacity to ponder this parable and apply it to his or her own life to do so [NTC]. The statement implies that there is a hidden meaning to be discovered for those who will apply themselves to understand it [Lns].

DISCOURSE UNIT—13:10–17 [CEV, ESV, NASB, NCV, NRSV, TEV]. The topic is why Jesus used stories to teach [NCV], why Jesus used stories [CEV], the purpose of the parables [ESV, NRSV, TEV], an explanation [NASB].

13:10 And having-approached[a] (him) the disciples said to him. "Why do-you(sg)-speak to-them in parables?" **13:11** And answering he-said to-them, "Because[b] to-you(pl) it-has-been-given[c] to-know[d] the mysteries[e] of the kingdom of-the heavens, but to-them it-has-not-been-given.

LEXICON—a. aorist act. participle of προσέρχομαι (LN 15.77) (BAGD 1. p. 713): 'to approach' [BAGD, BNTC, CC, LN, NTC], 'to come to' [BAGD, BECNT, NICNT, NIGTC, PNTC; CEV, NCV, NET, NIV, REB, TEV], 'to come' [WBC; ESV, KJV, NASB, NLT, NRSV], 'to go to' [BAGD], 'to come near to' [LN], not explicit [GW]. This verb means to move toward a reference point, with a possible implication in certain contexts of a reciprocal relationship between the person approaching and the one who is approached [LN].
  b. ὅτι (LN 89.33): 'because' [BECNT, CC, LN, NICNT, NIGTC, PNTC, WBC; KJV], 'since, for' [LN], not explicit [BNTC, NTC; all versions

except KJV]. This conjunction indicates cause or reason, based on an evident fact [LN].
  c. perf. pass. indic. of δίδωμι (LN 13.142) (BAGD 1.b.β. p. 193): 'to be given' [BAGD, BECNT, CC, NICNT, NIGTC, NTC, PNTC, WBC; ESV, GW, KJV, NASB, NIV, NRSV, TEV], 'to be permitted' [NLT], 'to be granted' [BAGD, LN; REB], 'to be allowed' [LN]. The phrase ὑμῖν δέδοται γνῶναι 'to you it has been given to know' is translated 'you have been given the opportunity to know' [NET], 'you have been chosen to know' [NCV], 'I have explained...to you' [CEV]. This verb means to grant someone the opportunity or occasion to do something [LN].
  d. aorist act. infin. of γινώσκω (LN **32.16**, 28.1) (BAGD 1.a. p. 160): 'to know' [BECNT, CC, LN (28.1), NICNT, NIGTC, NTC, PNTC, WBC; ESV, KJV, NASB, NCV, NET, NRSV, REB], 'to understand' [BNTC, **LN** (32.16); NLT], 'to know about, to have knowledge of' [LN (28.1)], 'knowledge' [GW, NIV, TEV], not explicit [CEV]. This verb means to come to an understanding as the result of ability to experience and learn [LN (32.16)], or to possess information about [LN (28.1)].
  e. μυστήριον (LN **28.77**) (BAGD 1. p. 530): 'mystery' [BECNT, BNTC, CC, LN, NIGTC, NTC, PNTC, WBC; GW, KJV, NASB], 'secret' [**LN**, NICNT; all versions except GW, KJV, NASB]. This noun denotes the content of that which has not been known before but which has been revealed to an in-group or restricted constituency [LN].

QUESTION—When did this conversation occur?
  1. It occurred while Jesus was still in the fishing boat [BECNT, My, NICNT, NIGTC, TH, TRT]. This conversation occurred in the middle of the discourse, while Jesus was still engaged in speaking to the crowds, after which he resumed speaking to the crowds, relating the parables in verses 24–35 [BECNT, My, NICNT].
  2. It was probably at the end of the larger discourse [EBC, Lns, NAC, NTC]. It was when they were away from the crowds [CC]. They were probably back in the house [Lns, NTC], at which time he told the disciples the other four parables narrated in this chapter [NTC].

QUESTION—What relationship is indicated by ὅτι 'because'?
  1. It indicates his reason for telling parables [BECNT, CC, EBC, ICC, LN, My, NICNT, NIGTC, PNTC, TRT, WBC; KJV]: 'because'.
  2. It indicates the content of speech, which in English would be marked by quotation marks: 'He answered and said to them, "To you...."' [Lns]. It is translated as indicating the content of speech by BNTC, NTC; CEV, ESV, GW, NASB, NCV, NET, NIV, NLT, NRSV, REB, TEV, though possibly only for reasons of English style.

QUESTION—Who is the agent of the passive verb 'it has been given'?
God is the one who has given them the knowledge [BECNT, BNTC, CC, My, Lns, PNTC, TH, TRT].

QUESTION—In what sense is the term μυστήρια 'mysteries' used?
The term 'mystery' refers to that which can only be known by divine revelation [BECNT, CC, EBC, Lns, My, NAC, NICNT, NIGTC, NTC, PNTC, TH, WBC], and it often refers to eschatological realities and events [EBC, WBC]. People cannot understand God's divine purpose and work unless God enables them [BNTC]. They must first become disciples before they will understand these things [NICNT]. The secret or mystery in question here is about how God establishes his kingdom on earth [TH]. It is the mystery about how God's kingdom has already entered into the world and is at work secretly [EBC, CC, NAC, NTC, WBC], about the present growth of God's kingdom [BECNT], about God's purposes and how he works [BNTC], about the mixed character of the kingdom in its present form, as opposed to its future purity and perfection [NTC], about the fact that it is present in Jesus [NIBC], or about the fact that it is not yet present with irresistible power [NAC]. The use of 'mystery' or 'secret' here has no correlation to its use in the pagan mystery religions [EBC, PNTC].

13:12 For whoever has,[a] to-him (more) will-be-given[b] and he-will-have-in-abundance;[c] but to-whoever does- not -have, even what he-has will-be-taken-away[d] from him.

LEXICON—a. pres. act. indic. of ἔχω (LN 57.1) (BAGD I.2.a. p. 332): 'to have' [BAGD, BECNT, BNTC, CC, LN, NICNT, NIGTC, NTC, PNTC, WBC; ESV, KJV, NASB, NET, NIV, NRSV, REB], 'to have something' [CEV, TEV], 'to own' [LN], 'to possess' [BAGD, LN]. The phrase ὅστις...ἔχει 'whoever has' is translated 'those who have understanding' [NCV], 'those who understand these mysteries' [GW], 'those who listen to my teaching' [NLT]. This verb means to have or possess objects or property [LN].

b. fut. pass. indic. of δίδωμι (LN 57.71): 'to be given' [BECNT, BNTC, CC, LN, NICNT, NIGTC, NTC, PNTC; all versions]. The implied element that is given is translated 'more' [BECNT, BNTC, NICNT, NIGTC, WBC; all versions except GW, KJV, NLT], 'more knowledge' [GW], 'more understanding' [NLT], 'it' [CC, PNTC], not explicit [NTC; KJV]. This verb means to give an object, usually implying value [LN].

c. fut. pass. indic. of περισσεύω (LN 59.54) (BAGD 2.a. p. 651): 'to have in abundance' [BAGD, NIGTC, PNTC], 'to have abundance' [BNTC], 'to have an abundance' [ESV, NASB, NET, NIV, NRSV], 'to have more abundance' [KJV], 'to have a great abundance' [BECNT], 'to have abundantly' [NTC], 'to have more than enough' [NICNT; TEV], 'to have enough and to spare' [REB], 'to have all they need' [NCV], 'to be provided in abundance' [LN], 'to be caused to abound' [BAGD, CC], 'to be provided a great deal of, to be caused to be abundant' [LN], not explicit [CEV]. The phrase καὶ περισσευθήσεται 'he will have in abundance' is translated 'they will have an abundance of knowledge' [NLT], 'they will excel in understanding them' [GW].

MATTHEW 13:12

d. fut. pass. indic. of αἴρω (LN 90.96): 'to be taken away' [BECNT, BNTC, NICNT, NIGTC, NTC, PNTC; all versions except CEV, REB, TEV], 'to be taken' [CC], 'to take away from, to remove from' [LN]. The phrase ὃ ἔχει ἀρθήσεται 'what he has will be taken away' is translated 'the person…will have taken away from him' [TEV], 'people…will lose what little they have' [CEV], 'those…will forfeit even what they have' [REB]. This verb means to cause someone to no longer experience something [LN].

QUESTION—What did Jesus mean by this statement?

He is referring to their ability to understand [BECNT, BNTC, CC, Lns, My, NAC, NIBC, NICNT, NIGTC, NTC, PNTC, TH, WBC]. What the person has or does not have is receptivity to Jesus' message of the kingdom [WBC]. This statement is probably proverbial, based on the observation that the rich tend to get richer and the poor to get poorer [My]. It is referring to people having (or lacking) understanding of how God is establishing his kingdom in this world; those who have understanding will gain more [BECNT, TH]. Those who understand what is being revealed will receive more revelation, but those who do not accept the revelation of the message of the kingdom will lose everything [NAC, NICNT]. Those who use the spiritual truth they are given will gain more, but those who do not make use of it will lose it [PNTC]. It describes the growing polarization that was happening in Jesus' ministry: those with insight that led them to embrace Jesus and his kingdom would be given more, whereas those with limited insight and who have not accepted the gospel would lose what they had, or what they thought they had [NAC]. What could be taken away, if they are not appreciative of their spiritual blessings, is their standing as members in God's kingdom [EBC]. It is not possible to stand still spiritually, as people will either progress or decline [Lns, NTC]. Apart from God's revelation about how his reign is being expressed through Jesus a person's spiritual condition can only go from bad to worse [CC]. If, through neglect, people fail to grow in spiritual graces they will eventually lose what progress they have made, and especially in regard to knowledge of spiritual things, and so much the more so if they actively reject what Christ teaches [NTC]. If someone lacks basic understanding and loyalty to Christ, both of which presuppose repentance, faith, and obedience to him, they will not be given clearer insight [BNTC].

13:13 For-this-reason[a] I-speak to-them in parables, because[b] while-seeing[c] they-do- not -see and while-hearing[d] they-do- not -hear or understand,[e]

LEXICON—a. διὰ τοῦτο (LN 90.44) (BAGD B.II.2. p. 181): 'for this reason' [BAGD, BNTC, LN, PNTC, WBC; NET], 'it is for this reason that' [NTC], 'the reason…is' [NIGTC; NRSV, TEV], 'therefore' [BAGD, BECNT; KJV, NASB], 'this is why' [ESV, GW, NCV, NIV], 'that is why' [NICNT; NLT, REB], 'because of all this' [CC], 'on account of, because of' [BAGD], not explicit [CEV]. The preposition διά indicates a participant constituting the cause or reason for an event or state [LN].

b. ὅτι (LN 89.33): 'because' [BECNT, BNTC, CC, LN, NICNT, NTC, PNTC, WBC; CEV, ESV, KJV, NASB], 'that' [NIGTC; NRSV, TEV], 'for' [LN; NLT, REB], 'since, in view of the fact that' [LN], not explicit [GW, NCV, NET, NIV]. This conjunction indicates cause or reason, based on an evident fact [LN].

c. pres. act. participle of βλέπω (LN 24.7) (BAGD 1.d. p. 143): 'to see' [BAGD, LN; ESV, GW, KJV, NASB, NCV, NET, NIV, NRSV], 'look' [BAGD; CEV, NLT, REB, TEV]. The phrase βλέποντες οὐ βλέπουσιν 'while seeing they do not see' [NASB] is translated 'seeing they do not see' [NIGTC, NTC, PNTC; ESV], 'seeing they see not' [KJV], 'although seeing they do not see' [WBC], 'though seeing, they do not see' [NIV], 'although they see they do not see' [CC; NET], 'they see, but they don't really see' [NCV], 'although they see, they do not perceive' [BECNT], 'seeing they do not perceive' [NRSV], 'though they see they do not really see' [BNTC], 'when they see they do not see' [NICNT], 'they see, but they're blind' [GW], 'they look, but do not see' [TEV], 'they look but they don't really see' [NLT], 'they look without seeing' [REB], 'when they look they cannot see' [CEV]. This verb means to see, frequently in the sense of becoming aware of or taking notice of something [LN].

d. pres. act. participle of ἀκούω (LN 24.52) (BAGD 1.a. p. 31): 'to hear' [BAGD, LN; WBC; all translations except CEV, REB, TEV], 'to listen' [CEV, REB, TEV]. The phrase ἀκούοντες οὐκ ἀκούουσιν 'while hearing they do not hear' [NASB] is also translated 'hearing they do not hear' [NIGTC, NTC, PNTC; ESV], 'hearing they hear not' [KJV], 'hearing they do not listen' [NRSV], 'although they hear, they do not hear' [CC; NET], 'although hearing they do not hear' [WBC], 'though hearing they do not hear' [NIV], 'when they hear they do not hear' [NICNT], 'although they hear, they do not listen' [BECNT], 'they hear, but they don't really hear' [NCV], 'they hear, but they don't listen' [GW], 'they hear, but they don't really listen' [NLT], 'though they hear they do not really hear' [BNTC], 'when they listen they cannot hear' [CEV], 'they...listen without hearing' [REB], 'they listen, but do not hear' [TEV].

e. pres. act. indic. of συνίημι (LN 32.5) (BAGD p. 790): 'to understand' [BAGD, LN; all translations except GW], 'to try to understand' [GW], 'to comprehend' [BAGD, LN], 'to perceive, to have insight into' [LN]. This verb means to employ one's capacity for understanding and thus to arrive at insight [LN].

QUESTION—What relationship is indicated by διὰ τοῦτο 'for this reason'?

1. It refers to what follows: because although seeing, they don't see, etc. [CC, EBC, Lns, NAC, NIGTC, TH, WBC; CEV, NCV, NET, NIV, NRSV, TEV]. The phrase διὰ τοῦτο 'for this reason' and ὅτι 'because' are a double causal construction, both indicating the reason that Jesus speaks in parables [CC, NIGTC].

2. It refers to what had just been said [BECNT, BNTC, My, NTC, PNTC, TRT; ESV, GW, KJV, NASB]. Jesus speaks in parables to the crowds because the privilege of knowing the mysteries of the kingdom has been given to the disciples, but not to them [BNTC, PNTC]. He speaks in parables because the growing resistance against him shows hardness of heart, which cannot go unpunished [NTC]. He speaks in parables because those with understanding tend to gain more, and those with little tend to lose what they have [My].

QUESTION—What is indicated in the use of the word ὅτι 'because'?

It indicates the reason he speaks to them in parables [BNTC, CC, EBC, Lns, My, NAC, NIBC, NICNT, NTC, PNTC, TH, WBC]. He does this to accommodate people whose thinking is shallow or who reject Christ, allowing them to remain uncomprehending, since that is what they prefer [PNTC]. The divine reason for their lack of comprehension involves the mystery of election [EBC, NAC, PNTC, WBC], but the human reason is their own spiritual dullness and resistance [EBC, NAC, WBC], or their rejection of Christ [PNTC]. He withholds spiritual truth from those who don't want it in order to avoid increasing their liability to judgment for having rejected that truth [NIBC]. The biblical authors see much more compatibility between divine sovereignty and human responsibility than modern readers do [EBC]. Jesus uses parables to penetrate the denseness of the people [BNTC].

13:14 **and the prophecy^a of-Isaiah is-fulfilled^b in-them that says, 'Hearing you-will-hear and by-no-means^c understand, and seeing you-will-see and will- by-no-means -perceive.^d**

LEXICON—a. προφητεία (LN 33.460) (BAGD 3.a. p. 722): 'prophecy' [BAGD, **LN**; all translations except CEV, NCV], 'promise' [CEV], 'the things (Isaiah) said' [NCV], 'inspired utterance' [LN]. This noun denotes an utterance inspired by God [LN].

b. pres. pass. indic. of ἀναπληρόω (LN **13.106**) (BAGD 2. p. 59): 'to be fulfilled' [BAGD, BECNT, BNTC, CC, LN, NICNT, NIGTC, NTC, PNTC, WBC; ESV, KJV, NASB, NET, NIV, NRSV, REB], 'to fulfill' [NLT], 'to come true' [CEV, GW], 'to be true' [NCV], 'to apply to' [**LN**; TEV], 'to be caused to happen, to be made to happen' [LN]. This verb means to cause to happen, with the implication of fulfilling some purpose [LN].

c. οὐ μή 'by no means': This emphatic double negative is translated 'never' [BECNT, NICNT, NTC; CEV, ESV, GW, NET, NIV, NRSV, REB], 'surely not' [CC], 'certainly not' [NIGTC], 'not at all' [WBC], 'not' [BNTC, PNTC; KJV, NASB, NCV, NLT, TEV].

d. aorist act. subj. of ὁράω (LN 32.11): 'to perceive' [BECNT, BNTC, CC, LN, NICNT, NIGTC, NTC; ESV, KJV, NASB, NIV, NRSV], 'to comprehend' [GW, NET, NLT], 'to understand' [LN], 'to see' [LN; CEV,

REB, TEV], 'to learn' [NCV]. This verb means to come to understand as the result of perception [LN].

QUESTION—In what sense is the prophecy of Isaiah fulfilled?

The people of Jesus' day fulfill Isaiah's prophecy in that they repeat the same pattern of behavior as the people whom Isaiah described in his own day [BECNT, CC, EBC, NAC, NICNT, NTC]. It is a typological fulfillment in that what the people had done in Isaiah's day was being repeated by Jesus' Jewish contemporaries [WBC]. Isaiah predicted that most Jewish people would not accept or understand what Jesus taught [BNTC].

QUESTION—What is being expressed by the phrases 'hearing you will hear' and 'seeing you will see'?

It describes a continual hearing and seeing [EBC, NICNT, NTC, TRT; NIV]. They continue to have sensory perception, though without real understanding [NAC]. This use of the noun ἀκοῇ 'in hearing' in the dative case along with its cognate verb ἀκούσετε 'you will hear' reflects how the Greek Septuagint translated the Hebrew infinitive absolute construction [EBC, Lns].

13:15 For the heart[a] of-this people has-been-made-dull,[b] and they-have-barely[c] -heard[d] with-the ears and they-closed[e] their eyes, lest[f] they-see with-the eyes, and hear with-the ears and understand with-the heart and turn[g] and I-would-heal[h] them'.

LEXICON—a. καρδία (LN 26.3): 'heart' [BECNT, BNTC, CC, LN, NICNT, NIGTC, NTC, PNTC, WBC; ESV, KJV, NASB, NET, NIV, NLT, NRSV], 'mind' [LN; CEV, NCV, REB, TEV], 'inner self' [LN], not explicit [GW]. This noun denotes the causative source of a person's psychological life in its various aspects, but with special emphasis upon thoughts [LN].

b. aorist pass. indic. of παχύνω (LN **32.45**) (BAGD 2. p. 638): 'to become dull' [BAGD, BECNT, BNTC, NTC, PNTC; NASB, NET, REB], 'to be dull' [TEV], 'to grow dull' [ESV, NRSV], 'to grow hard' [WBC], 'to be hardened' [NLT], 'to become calloused' [NIV], 'to become fat' [CC, NICNT], 'to grow fat' [NIGTC], 'to wax gross' [KJV], 'to become stubborn' [NCV], 'to be unable to understand' [**LN**], 'incapable of understanding' [**LN**], 'to be mentally dull' [**LN**]. The phrase 'for the heart of this people has been made dull' is translated 'all of them have stubborn minds' [CEV], 'these people have become close-minded' [GW]. This verb means to become unable to understand or comprehend as the result of being mentally dull or spiritually insensitive [LN].

c. βαρέως (LN 32.46) (BAGD p. 133): 'barely' [ESV], 'with difficulty' [BAGD, BNTC, CC], 'scarcely' [BECNT, NASB], 'heavily' [LN, NICNT], 'poorly' [WBC], 'hardly' [NIV]. The phrase τοῖς ὠσὶν βαρέως ἤκουσαν 'they have barely heard with the ears', is translated 'they are hard of hearing' [BAGD, NTC; NET], 'they have become hard of hearing' [NTC; GW], 'their ears are hard of hearing' [NRSV], 'their ears are dull of hearing' [KJV], 'their ears are stopped up' [CEV], 'they have stopped/stopped-up their ears' [REB, TEV], 'their ears cannot hear' [NLT], 'they do not hear' [NCV], 'they heard with heavy ears' [NIGTC]. The idiom τοῖς ὠσὶν βαρέως ἀκούω 'to hear heavily with the ears' means to be mentally slow or dull in comprehending [LN].

d. aorist act. indic. of ἀκούω (LN 24.52) (BAGD 1.a. p. 31): 'to hear' [BAGD, BECNT, BNTC, CC, LN, NICNT, PNTC, WBC; ESV, NASB, NIV, NLT], not explicit [NTC; CEV, GW, KJV, NET, NLT, NRSV, REB, TEV]. This aorist tense of this verb is translated by a verb or verb phrase in the past tense [NIGTC]; in the perfect tense [CC, NICNT, NTC; REB, TEV]; in the present tense [BECNT, BNTC, PNTC, WBC; CEV, ESV, GW, KJV, NASB, NCV, NET, NIV, NLT, NRSV]. The verb phrase 'they have barely heard with the ears' is translated 'their ears have become hard of hearing' [NTC], 'these people have become hard of hearing' [GW], 'their ears are dull of hearing' [KJV], 'their ears are hard of hearing' [NRSV], 'they are hard of hearing' [NET], 'their ears are stopped up' [CEV], 'they have stopped/stopped up their ears' [REB, TEV], 'their ears cannot hear' [NLT],

e. aorist act. indic. of καμμύω (LN 27.50) (BAGD p. 402): 'to close (the eyes)' [BAGD, BECNT, BNTC, CC, NTC; ESV, KJV, NASB, NCV, NIV, NLT, TEV], 'to shut (the eyes)' [NICNT, PNTC, WBC; GW, NET, NRSV, REB]. The phrase τοὺς ὀφθαλμοὺς αὐτῶν ἐκάμμυσαν 'they closed their eyes' is translated 'their eyes are covered' [CEV]. The idiom καμμύω τοὺς ὀφθαλμούς 'to close the eyes' means to be unwilling to learn and to evaluate something fairly, to refuse to learn, to refuse to recognize [LN].

f. μήποτε (LN 89.62) (BAGD 2.b.α. 519): 'lest' [BNTC, CC, LN, NTC, PNTC, WBC; ESV, KJV], 'so that...not' [BECNT, LN, NICNT, NIGTC; NET, NRSV; similarly NLT], 'in order that...not' [BAGD, LN], 'so that...never' [GW], 'otherwise' [NASB, NCV, NIV, REB, TEV], 'if they could, they would...' [CEV]. This conjunction indicates negative purpose, often with the implication of apprehension [LN].

g. aorist act. subj. of ἐπιστρέφω (LN 41.51) (BAGD 1.b.β. p. 301): 'to turn' [BAGD, BECNT, CC, NIGTC, PNTC; ESV, NET, NIV, NRSV], 'to turn back' [BAGD, BNTC], 'to turn around' [NICNT], 'to turn again' [NTC], 'to turn to me' [LN; CEV, NLT, REB, TEV], 'to return' [GW, NASB], 'to come back (to me)' [NCV], 'to repent' [WBC], 'to be converted' [KJV], 'to change one's ways' [LN]. This verb means to change one's manner of life in a particular direction, with the implication of turning back to God [LN].

h. fut. mid. (deponent = act.) indic. of ἰάομαι (LN **13.66**) (BAGD 2. p. 368): 'to heal' [BAGD, **LN**; all translations except GW, NCV], 'to be healed' [NCV], 'to renew' [LN]. The phrase ἐπιστρέψωσιν καὶ ἰάσομαι αὐτούς 'turn and I would heal them' is translated 'return to me for healing' [GW]. This verb means to cause something to change to an earlier, correct, or appropriate state [LN].

QUESTION—What relationship is indicated by μήποτε 'lest'?
1. It indicates the purpose for which people have closed their eyes, ears, and hearts, which is to avoid seeing, hearing, or understanding [BNTC, Lns, My, NTC, PNTC, TH; ESV, NET, NRSV]. It also reflects God's purpose, which is a judicial hardening in which he is judging them for their failure to understand by making them even less able to understand [BECNT, EBC, Lns, NTC].
2. It indicates the result of closing their eyes, ears, and hearts, which is that they can no longer see, hear, or understand [BECNT, EBC, NICNT; CEV; probably GW, NLT]. This has occurred as a result of divine judgment on them for their refusal to listen and respond properly [BECNT, EBC].

QUESTION—What is indicated by the future tense of the statement ἰάσομαι αὐτούς 'I would heal them'?
It speaks of the consequences that would occur *if* the people were to turn to God [BECNT, CC, Lns, My, NIBC, NICNT, NIGTC, NTC, PNTC, WBC; CEV, ESV, KJV, NASB, NET, NIV, NRSV, REB, TEV]. The future indicative is functioning as a subjunctive [WBC]. Since this quotation is introduced as a prophecy of Isaiah, the reader must be able to understand that Isaiah was quoting a message from God, and that the pronoun 'I' refers to God and not Isaiah. The TEV indicates that God is speaking in the last line of the quotation, 'and they would turn to me, says God, and I would heal them.' This last line could be more direct 'If they did, God says, "They would turn to me and I would heal them."' Or 'God' could be kept in the third person, 'then they would turn to God for him to heal them'. Some translators prefer to indicate at the beginning of the quotation in verse 14 that Isaiah was speaking for God, 'what Isaiah predicted when he spoke God's word' [TH].

13:16 But your(pl) eyes (are) blessed[a] because they-see and your(pl) ears because they hear.

LEXICON—a. μακάριος (LN 25.119) (BAGD 3.a. p. 487): 'blessed' [BAGD, BECNT, BNTC, CC, NTC, PNTC, WBC; ESV, GW, KJV, NASB, NET, NIV, NLT, NRSV], 'fortunate' [BAGD, NIGTC], 'happy' [BAGD, LN, NICNT; REB]. The phrase ὑμῶν δὲ μακάριοι οἱ ὀφθαλμοὶ ὅτι βλέπουσιν 'blessed are your eyes because they see' is translated 'but God has blessed you, because your eyes can see' [CEV], 'but you are blessed, because you see with your eyes' [NCV], 'As for you, how fortunate you are! Your eyes see' [TEV]. This adjective describes being happy, with the implication of enjoying favorable circumstances [LN].

QUESTION—What is meant by μακάριος 'blessed'?
It carries the same sense as in the beatitudes of chapter 5 [EBC, Lns, NICNT, NIGTC, NTC, PNTC]. It describes the favor of God resting upon them [NTC, PNTC]. It means that God has been very good to them and has blessed them [TH]. It describes their fortunate and happy state [NICNT, NIGTC, PNTC]. They have been greatly privileged [BECNT, EBC], blessed

with perception of wonderful things that previous generations of godly people longed to see [BECNT].

QUESTION—Where is the emphasis in verse 16?

'Your' is emphatic by virtue of being first in the sentence [BNTC, CC, Lns, My, WBC]: *your* eyes however are blessed, unlike theirs. 'Blessed' is emphatic by virtue of being placed before the noun 'eyes', which it modifies [CC].

13:17 **For truly I-say to-you(pl) that many prophets and righteous-people[a] eagerly-desired[b] to-see what you(pl)-see and they-did- not -see (it), and to-hear what you(pl)-hear and they-did- not -hear (it).**

LEXICON—a. δίκαιος (LN 88.12) (BAGD 1.b. p. 195): 'righteous' [BAGD, LN], 'just' [BAGD, LN], 'upright' [BAGD]. This plural adjective is translated pronominally as 'righteous people' [BECNT, NICNT, NIGTC; ESV, NET, NLT, NRSV], 'righteous men' [BNTC, CC, PNTC; KJV, NASB, NIV], 'righteous persons' [NTC, WBC], 'saints' [REB], 'good people' [CEV, NCV], 'God's people' [GW, TEV]. This adjective describes being in accordance with what God requires [LN].

b. aorist act. indic. of ἐπιθυμέω (LN 25.12) (BAGD p. 293): 'to desire' [BAGD, BNTC, BNTC, WBC; KJV, NASB], 'to long' [BAGD, BECNT, LN, NIGTC, NTC; ESV, GW, NET, NIV, NLT, NRSV, REB], 'to be eager' [NICNT; CEV], 'to want' [PNTC; NCV], 'to want very much' [TEV], 'to desire very much' [LN]. This verb means to greatly desire to do or have something [LN].

QUESTION—What is the function of the introductory clause ἀμὴν γὰρ λέγω ὑμῖν 'For truly I say to you'?

It emphasizes the importance of the following assertion [Lns, NTC, PNTC, TH]. The disciples have an incomparable privilege of seeing and hearing the messianic fulfillment that is now occurring [WBC].

DISCOURSE UNIT—13:18–23 [CEV, ESV, NASB, NCV, NRSV, TEV]. The topic is Jesus explains the seed story [NCV], Jesus explains the parable of the sower [TEV], the parable of the sower explained [ESV, NRSV], the sower explained [NASB], Jesus explains the story about the farmer [CEV].

13:18 **You, therefore,[a] hear[b] the parable of-the sower.**

LEXICON—a. οὖν (LN 89.50): 'therefore' [BNTC, CC, LN, PNTC, WBC; KJV], 'then' [BECNT, NIGTC, NTC; ESV, NASB, NIV, NRSV, REB, TEV], 'so' [LN, NICNT; NCV, NET], 'now' [CEV, NLT], 'consequently, accordingly, so then' [LN], not explicit [GW]. This conjunction indicates result, often implying the conclusion of a process of reasoning [LN].

b. aorist act. impera. of ἀκούω (LN 24.52, 32.1) (BAGD 1.b.α. p. 32): 'to hear' [BAGD, LN (24.52)], 'to understand, to comprehend' [LN (32.1)]. The phrase ἀκούσατε τὴν παραβολὴν 'hear the parable' [BECNT, BNTC, CC, NIGTC; ESV, KJV, NASB, NRSV, REB] is also translated 'listen to the parable' [NTC, PNTC, WBC; NET], 'listen to what the parable...means' [NIV], 'listen to the meaning of the parable/that-story' [NICNT; NCV], 'listen to the explanation of the parable' [NLT], 'listen and learn what the parable...means' [TEV], 'listen to what the story...means' [GW], 'listen to the meaning of the story' [CEV]. This verb means to hear something [LN (24.52)], or to hear and understand something [LN (32.1)]. Jesus is not telling the disciples to hear the parable again, but to understand its meaning [TH].

QUESTION—What is given emphasis in this sentence?

'You' is emphatic by its being placed first in the sentence [CC, EBC, ICC, Lns, My, NIBC, NICNT, NIGTC, PNTC, TH, WBC]. 'You' stands in contrast to the crowds [CC, EBC, NICNT, PNTC, TH], who were not privileged to have the insight given to the disciples [NICNT, NIGTC], or in contrast to people such as the scribes who lacked genuine religious seriousness [PNTC]. It also stands in contrast to the prophets and righteous men who never saw what the disciples were being allowed to see [EBC].

13:19 **Anyone**[a] **hearing the message of-the kingdom and not understanding,**[b] **the evil-one comes and snatches-away**[c] **the-thing having-been-sown in his heart, this is**[d] **what**[e] **was-sown beside the road.**

LEXICON—a. πᾶς (LN 59.23) (BAGD 1.a.α. p. 631): 'any' [BAGD], 'every, each' [BAGD, LN], 'all, whole' [LN]. The singular personal pronoun παντός 'anyone' and the singular possessive pronoun αὐτοῦ 'his' in the second clause are translated 'Anyone...his' [CC, NTC, PNTC; ESV, KJV, NASB, NET, NIV, REB], 'Anyone...the (heart)' [NRSV], 'Anyone... their' [NICNT], 'Anyone...that person's' [BECNT], 'everyone...his' [BNTC], 'everyone...their' [NIGTC], 'every person...that person's' [WBC], 'the person...that person's' [NCV], 'people...their' [CEV], 'someone...in him' [GW], 'those who...their' [NLT], 'those who...in them' [TEV]. The pronoun πᾶς denotes the totality of any object, mass, collective, or extension [LN].

b. pres. act. participle of συνίημι (LN 32.5) (BAGD p. 790): 'to understand' [BAGD, BECNT, BECNT, BNTC, CC, LN, NICNT, NIGTC, PNTC, WBC; all versions], 'to grasp' [NTC], 'to comprehend' [BAGD, LN], 'to gain an insight into' [BAGD], 'to perceive, to have insight into' [LN]. This verb means to employ one's capacity for understanding and thus to arrive at insight [LN].

c. pres. act. indic. of ἁρπάζω (LN **18.4**) (BAGD 2.a. p. 109): 'to snatch away' [BAGD, BECNT, BNTC, CC, **LN**, NIGTC, NTC, PNTC; ESV, GW, NASB, NIV, NLT, NRSV, TEV], 'to snatch' [NICNT; NET], 'to catch away' [KJV], 'to take away' [BAGD, LN; NCV], 'to carry away' [REB], 'to seize' [LN, WBC; CEV]. This verb means to grab or seize by force with the purpose of removing and/or controlling [LN]. In Matthew 13:19 the context as a whole is figurative, but a more or less literal rendering of 'snatches' or 'seizes' is probably satisfactory [LN].

d. The verb ἐστιν 'is' [BECNT, BNTC, CC, NICNT, NIGTC, NTC, PNTC, WBC; CEV, ESV, KJV, NASB, NET, NIV, NRSV, REB] is also translated 'represents' [NLT], 'illustrates' [GW], 'is like' [NCV], 'are like' [TEV].
e. ὁ (LN 92.11): The masculine participle phrase ὁ σπαρείς 'what was sown' [BECNT, NIGTC, WBC; ESV, NRSV] is translated in reference to the seed: 'what had/has been sown' [NIGTC], 'the seed sown' [BNTC; NET, NIV, REB], 'the seed planted' [GW], 'the seed/s that fell' [CEV, NLT, TEV]. It is translated in reference to a person: 'the one who/that was sown' [CC, NTC], 'the person sown' [NICNT], 'he who was sown' [PNTC], 'he which received the seed' [KJV], 'the one on whom seed was sown' [NASB], 'that seed is like the person' [NCV].

QUESTION—How is 'Anyone hearing the message of the kingdom and not understanding' connected with the rest of the verse?

This initial clause identifies the person who is represented by the first example given in the parable and it is variously connected with the rest of the verse.

1. Some translate the clause as a temporal participial phrase: 'When anyone hears the word…' [BECNT, CC, NICNT, NTC, PNTC; ESV, NASB, NET, NIV, NRSV, REB; similarly KJV].
2. One makes it a separate sentence to give the setting: 'Someone hears the word about the kingdom but doesn't understand it.' [GW].
3. Some make it a prepositional phrase completing the thought of the main verb: 'From every one who hears the word about the kingdom…the Evil One snatches away' [BNTC], 'In the case of everyone who hears the word…the evil one comes and snatches away' [NIGTC; similarly WBC].
4. Some connect it with the last clause of the verse: 'What is the seed that fell by the road? That seed is like the person who hears…'[NCV], 'The seed that fell on the footpath represents those who hear the message…' [NLT], 'The seeds that fell along the road are the people who hear the message…' [CEV], 'Those who hear the message about the kingdom but do not understand it are like the seeds that fell along the path' [TEV].

QUESTION—What is the message of the kingdom?

This is another way of saying 'the gospel of the kingdom' [EBC, NIGTC, TH, WBC], which is Jesus' claim that the kingdom of God is coming in and through his ministry [WBC]. It is the message about the messianic kingdom [My]. It is the Son of Man's message [NTC], the whole message that tells of the kingdom [PNTC].

QUESTION—How is the word 'heart' used here?

The heart is the seat of thinking and willing, which some would render 'mind' [TH]. It is the seat of decision making, the center of personality [EBC], the innermost being [PNTC].

QUESTION—What is the connection between the seed and the response of the person to the message?

This is a very abbreviated expression [My, NICNT, NTC]. Not all the details of the interpretation of the parable are completely consistent with each other [ICC]. The seed that was sown represents what happens with people as they respond to Jesus' message [BECNT, ICC, Lns, My, NTC, PNTC, TH, TRT, WBC]. While this seems to equate the person with the seed as a slight mixing of images, it is a compressed way of representing the story, the person representing the instance of seed being sown in the particular kind of soil [WBC]. The masculine participles, pronouns, articles and adjectives in verses 19–23 show that the seeds he is describing really stand for people, since 'soil' would require feminine forms and 'seed' would require neuter forms [CC]. The masculine gender of the pronoun οὗτος 'this' and the participle σπαρείς 'sown' indicate that this ultimately refers to the persons being described, even though 'sown' obvious refers to seed; the reason for this is that Matthew has a very compressed way of moving from the story itself to the application [NICNT].

13:20 And what was-sown on the rocky-ground, this is the-(one) hearing the message and immediately[a] receiving[b] it with joy,[c]

LEXICON—a. εὐθύς (LN 67.53): 'immediately' [BECNT, CC, LN, NTC, PNTC, WBC; ESV, NASB, NET, NLT, NRSV], 'at once' [BNTC, NIGTC; GW, NIV, REB], 'quickly' [NICNT; NCV], 'right away' [CEV], 'anon' [KJV], 'as soon as they hear it' [TEV]. This adverb indicates a point of time immediately subsequent to a previous point of time (the actual interval of time differs appreciably, depending upon the nature of the events and the manner in which the sequence is interpreted by the writer) [LN].

b. pres. act. participle of λαμβάνω (LN 31.50) (BAGD 1.e.β. p. 464): 'to receive' [BAGD, BECNT, BNTC, CC, LN, NIGTC, PNTC, WBC; ESV, KJV, NASB, NET, NIV, NLT, NRSV, TEV], 'to accept' [LN, NICNT, NTC; CEV, GW, NCV, REB], 'to come to believe' [LN]. This verb means to come to believe something and to act in accordance with such a belief [LN].

c. χαρά (LN 25.123) (BAGD 1. p. 875): 'joy' [BAGD, BECNT, BNTC, CC, LN, NIGTC, NTC, PNTC, WBC; all versions except CEV, TEV], 'enthusiasm' [NICNT], 'gladness, great happiness' [LN]. The phrase μετὰ χαρᾶς 'with joy' is translated 'gladly' [CEV, TEV]. This noun denotes a state of joy and gladness [LN].

13:21 but does- not -have root[a] in himself but-rather is temporary,[b] but when- affliction[c] or persecution[d] -happens[e] because-of[f] the message immediately he- falls-away/is-caused-to-fall-away.[g]

LEXICON—a. ῥίζα (LN 3.47) (BAGD 1.b. p. 736): 'root' [BAGD, BNTC, CC, LN, NICNT, NIGTC, NTC, PNTC, WBC; ESV, GW, KJV, NET, NIV, NRSV, REB], 'deep root' [CEV, NLT], 'firm root' [BECNT; NASB].

The phrase οὐκ ἔχει...ῥίζαν 'does not have root in himself' is translated 'does not let the teaching go deep into his life' [NCV], 'it does not sink deep into them' [TEV]. This noun denotes the underground part of a plant [LN].

b. πρόσκαιρος (LN **67.109**) (BAGD p. 715): 'temporary' [BAGD, BECNT, CC, LN, NIGTC, PNTC; NASB], 'short-lived' [NICNT], 'transitory' [BAGD], 'lasting only for a time' [BAGD], 'not long' [**LN**], 'for a little while, for a while' [LN]. The phrase πρόσκαιρός ἐστιν '(he) is temporary' is translated 'lasts only a little while' [BNTC; GW], 'lasts but a short while' [NTC], 'lasts only for a time' [WBC], 'lasts only a short time' [NIV], 'don't last long' [NLT, TEV], 'don't last very long' [CEV], 'endures for a while' [ESV, KJV; similarly NRSV], 'keeps it only a short while' [NCV], 'does not endure' [NET], 'has no staying power' [REB]. This adjective describes a relatively short period of time, with emphasis upon the temporary nature of the event or state [LN].

c. θλῖψις (LN 22.2) (BAGD 1. p. 362): 'affliction' [BECNT, BNTC, NTC; NASB], 'tribulation' [BAGD, CC, WBC; ESV, KJV], 'trouble' [PNTC; NCV, NET, NIV, NRSV, REB], 'suffering' [LN, NICNT; GW], 'oppression' [BAGD, NIGTC], 'life gets hard' [CEV], 'to have problems' [NLT], 'trouble and suffering, persecution' [LN]. This noun denotes trouble involving direct suffering [LN].

d. διωγμός (LN 39.45) (BAGD p. 201): 'persecution' [BAGD, LN; all translations except NLT, CEV], 'be persecuted' [NLT], 'in trouble' [CEV]. This noun denotes a systematically organized program to oppress and harass people [LN].

e. γίνομαι (LN 13.107) (BAGD I.1.b.β. p. 158): 'to happen' [BECNT, LN], 'to occur' [LN, WBC], 'to come' [BNTC, CC; NCV, NET, NIV], 'to be' [NIGTC, PNTC; REB], 'to come to be' [LN], 'to come along' [GW], 'to come about' [BAGD], 'to arise' [BAGD, NICNT, NTC; ESV, KJV, NASB, NRSV], not explicit [CEV, NLT]. This verb means to happen, with the implication that what happens is different from a previous state [LN].

f. διά with accusative (LN 90.44) (BAGD B.II.1. p. 181): 'because of' [BAGD, BECNT, CC, LN, NIGTC; GW, KJV, NASB, NCV, NET, NIV, TEV], 'for the sake of' [BAGD], 'on account of' [BNTC, LN, NICNT, NTC, PNTC, WBC; ESV, NRSV, REB], not explicit [CEV]. The phrase διὰ τὸν λόγον 'because of the message' is translated 'for believing God's word' [NLT]. This preposition indicates a participant constituting the cause or reason for an event or state [LN].

g. pres. pass. indic. of σκανδαλίζομαι (LN **31.77**) (BAGD 1. a. p. 752): 'to fall away' [BAGD, BECNT, BNTC, NTC, WBC; ESV, NASB, NET, NIV, NLT, NRSV], 'to fall from faith' [GW], 'to lose faith' [REB], 'to stumble' [NICNT], 'to be caused to stumble' [CC, NIGTC], 'to take offense' [PNTC], 'to be offended' [KJV], 'to give up' [TEV], 'to be caused to sin' [BAGD]. This passive verb may have an active meaning:

'to cease believing, to give up believing' [LN], 'to fall into sin' [LN]. The verb σκανδαλίζεται 'he falls away/is caused to fall away' is translated 'he gives up' [CEV, NCV]. This verb means to give up believing what is right and let oneself believe what is false [LN].

QUESTION—What is the nature of the θλῖψις 'affliction' mentioned here?

It is persecution [NICNT, NIGTC, NTC, WBC]. It is personal difficulty or opposition that comes from following Jesus [CC]. It is external pressure from the non-Christian world [NTC].

QUESTION—What does the phrase διὰ τὸν λόγον 'because of the message' modify?

1. It modifies both 'affliction' and 'persecution' [BECNT, BNTC, CC, NICNT, NIGTC, NTC, PNTC, WBC; all translations except CEV, NLT]: when, because of the message, affliction or persecution happen, they fall away.
2. It modifies 'persecution' [CEV, NLT]: when problems happen, or when there is persecution because of the message, they fall away.

13:22 **And what was-sown in the thorns, this is the-one hearing the word, and the worries[a] of-the world[b] and the deceitfulness[c] of-wealth[d] choke the message and it-becomes unfruitful.[e]**

LEXICON—a. μέριμνα (LN 25.224) (BAGD p. 504): 'worry' [BAGD, BNTC, CC, LN, NICNT, NIGTC, PNTC; GW, NASB, NCV, NIV, NLT, TEV], 'care' [NTC; ESV, KJV, NET, NRSV, REB], 'anxiety' [BAGD, LN, WBC], 'concern (for)' [BECNT], 'anxious concern' [LN]. The phrase ἡ μέριμνα τοῦ αἰῶνος 'the worries of the world' is translated 'they start worrying about the needs of this life' [CEV]. This noun denotes a feeling of apprehension or distress in view of possible danger or misfortune [LN].

b. αἰών (LN 67.143) (BAGD 2.a. p. 27): 'world' [BECNT, NICNT, NIGTC, PNTC, WBC; ESV, KJV, NASB, NRSV], 'present world' [NTC], 'present age' [BAGD], 'age' [BAGD, CC, LN], 'life' [CEV, GW, NCV, NIV, NLT, TEV], 'era' [LN]. The phrase τοῦ αἰῶνος 'of the world' is translated 'worldly' [NET, REB], '(the worry) the world excites' [BNTC]. This noun denotes a unit of time as a particular stage or period of history [LN].

c. ἀπάτη (LN 31.12) (BAGD 1. p. 82): 'deceitfulness' [BAGD, PNTC; ESV, KJV, NASB, NIV], 'deceit' [CC], 'deception' [BAGD, BECNT, BNTC, LN], 'deceitful glamour' [NTC], 'deceitful pleasure' [GW], 'false glamour' [REB], 'lure' [NLT, NRSV], 'false lure' [NICNT], 'allure' [NIGTC], 'seduction' [BAGD, WBC], 'seductiveness' [NET], 'love for' [TEV], 'temptation' [NCV]. The phrase 'the deceitfulness of wealth' is translated 'they are fooled by the desire to get rich' [CEV]. This noun denotes the act of causing someone to have misleading or erroneous views concerning the truth [LN].

d. πλοῦτος (LN 57.30) (BAGD 1. p. 674): 'wealth' [BAGD, BECNT, BNTC, CC, LN, NICNT, NIGTC, PNTC; CEV, NASB, NCV, NET, NIV,

NLT, NRSV, REB], 'riches' [BAGD, LN, NTC, WBC; ESV, GW, KJV, TEV]. This noun denotes an abundance of possessions exceeding the norm of a particular society and often with a negative connotation [LN].

e. ἄκαρπος (LN 23.202) (BAGD 2. p. 29): 'unfruitful' [BAGD, BNTC, CC, NIGTC, NTC, PNTC, WBC; ESV, KJV, NASB, NIV], 'useless, unproductive' [BAGD], 'without fruit, bearing no fruit, producing no harvest' [LN]. The phrase ἄκαρπος γίνεται 'it becomes unfruitful' is translated 'it yields nothing' [NRSV], 'it does not yield a crop' [BECNT], 'it cannot produce a crop' [NICNT], 'it can't produce anything' [GW], 'they never produce anything' [CEV], 'it produces nothing' [NET], 'it proves barren' [REB], 'no fruit is produced' [NLT], 'they don't bear fruit' [TEV], 'stop that teaching from growing' [NCV]. This adjective describes not producing seed, fruit, or harvest [LN].

QUESTION—What is the relationship between the nouns in the genitive construction μέριμνα τοῦ αἰῶνος 'worries of the world'?

The worry or concern is for the world, that is, for the things of the world [BECNT]. The world stimulates or excites the worry [BNTC]. It is concern for the ordinary matters of everyday living [NIBC, NTC, TH], and although such concern is not evil, it may become evil if allowed to dominate life [TH]. Every age has its own kinds of worry [Lns]. Note that αἰών can be conceived of temporally, meaning this age as opposed to the age to come [EBC, NICNT, PNTC], or spatially, meaning this world as opposed to heaven [NIGTC], or even in terms of this world as opposed to Messiah's kingdom [My].

QUESTION—In what sense might wealth be considered 'deceitful'?

It means that such people are misled by their desire for wealth [BECNT; CEV]. Wealth cannot actually provide the security that it would seem to offer [NICNT]. A person may be deceived into depending on wealth instead of God [TRT], or into thinking that riches would bring contentment or satisfaction [Lns, NTC, PNTC], or may be deceived about the worth and importance of wealth [BNTC].

13:23 And what was-sown on the good soil, this is the-one hearing and understanding the message, who indeed[a] bears-fruit[b] and produces[c] one-hundred, or sixty, or thirty."

LEXICON—a. δή (LN 91.6) (BAGD 1. p. 178): 'indeed' [BAGD, BECNT, CC, LN, NICNT, PNTC, WBC; ESV, NASB, NRSV], 'then' [LN], 'also' [KJV], not explicit [BNTC, NIGTC, NTC; ESV, GW, NCV, NET, NIV, NLT, TEV]. The phrase ὃς δὴ καρποφορεῖ 'who indeed bears fruit' is translated 'he does bear fruit' [REB]. This particle indicates relatively weak emphasis, and it is frequently not translated but may be reflected in the word order [LN]. It denotes that a statement is definitely established [BAGD, PNTC].

b. pres. act. indic. of καρποφορέω (LN **23.199**) (BAGD 2. p. 405): 'to bear fruit' [BAGD, BECNT, BNTC, CC, **LN**, NIGTC, NTC, PNTC, WBC;

ESV, KJV, NASB, NET, NRSV, REB, TEV], 'to produce a crop/crops' [NICNT; GW, NIV], 'to produce a harvest' [NLT], 'to produce fruit, to yield' [LN], 'to grow' [NCV], not explicit [CEV]. This verb means to produce fruit or seed (of plants) [LN].

c. pres. act. indic. of ποιέω (LN 13.9): 'to produce' [BNTC, CC, NIGTC, PNTC, WBC; CEV, GW], 'to produce fruit' [NCV], 'to yield' [BECNT, NICNT, NTC; ESV, NET, NIV, NRSV, REB], 'to bring forth' [KJV, NASB], 'to bring about, to cause to be' [LN], not explicit [NLT, TEV]. This verb means to cause a state to be [LN].

QUESTION—What is the fruit that is produced?

It is probably conduct such as Jesus described in the Sermon on the Mount [WBC]. It is how a disciple works out a commitment to serving God [NICNT]. It is discipleship expressed in obedience to God's law [BECNT]. It is general, including any outcome befitting the Christian life [NIGTC]. It is genuine conversion, resulting in faith, love, joy, peace, and also bringing others to Christ [NTC]. It is consistent obedience to God's will [NAC]. The fruit is worship and obedience [BNTC].

DISCOURSE UNIT—13:24–43 [ICC]. The topic is three more parables.

DISCOURSE UNIT—13:24–30 [CEV, GW, NASB, NCV, NET, NIV, NLT, NRSV, TEV]. The topic is a story about weeds in the wheat [GW], a story about wheat and weeds [NCV], the parable of the wheat and weeds [NLT], the parable of the weeds [ESV, NET, NIV, TEV], the parable of the weeds among the wheat [NRSV], weeds among the wheat [CEV], tares among wheat [NASB].

13:24 He put-before[a] them another parable saying, "The kingdom of-the heavens is-like/has-become-likened-to[b] to-(a)-man having-sown[c] good seed in his field.

LEXICON—a. aorist act. indic. of παρατίθημι (LN 33.16) (BAGD 1.b. p. 623): 'to put before' [BAGD, BECNT, BNTC, NICNT, NIGTC, PNTC; ESV, NRSV], 'to put forth' [KJV], 'to place before' [CC], 'to set before' [WBC], 'to present to' [NTC; NASB], 'to present (someone) with' [NET], 'to tell' [CEV, NCV, NIV, NLT, TEV], 'to give' [REB]. The phrase 'He put before them another parable' is translated 'Jesus used another illustration' [GW]. The idiom παρατίθημι τὴν παραβολήν (literally 'to place a parable alongside') means to tell a parable [LN].

b. aorist pass. indic. of ὁμοιόω (LN 64.5) (BAGD 1. p. 567): 'to be like, to become like' [BAGD], 'to compare' [LN]. Here this aorist passive verb is translated 'is likened to/unto' [PNTC; KJV], 'is like' [BAGD, NIGTC, NTC; CEV, GW, NCV, NET, NIV, NLT, REB], 'has become like' [CC], 'is like this' [TEV], 'may/can be compared to' [BAGD, BECNT, BNTC, NICNT; ESV, NASB, NRSV], 'is similar to' [WBC]. This verb means to consider something to be like something else [LN].

c. aorist act. participle of σπείρω (LN 43.6) (BAGD 1.a.γ. p. 761): 'to sow' [BAGD, BECNT, BNTC, CC, LN, NICNT, NIGTC, NTC, PNTC, WBC;

ESV, KJV, NASB, NET, NIV, NRSV, REB, TEV], 'to plant' [GW, NCV, NLT], 'to scatter seed' [CEV]. This verb means to scatter seed over tilled ground [LN].

QUESTION—To whom does 'them' refer?

It refers to the crowds [BECNT, CC, EBC, My, NICNT, NIGTC, NTC, PNTC, TH, TRT, WBC].

QUESTION—What is the significance of the use of the aorist passive indicative Ὡμοιώθη 'is likened to' for introducing a comparison as opposed to the more commonly used present indicative form of that verb?

All references translate this verb as if it were in the present tense. Some think there is no significant difference in meaning for the aorist form as opposed to the present tense form when it just introduces a comparison [BNTC, NTC, PNTC]. A future passive would focus on the kingdom in its final coming, whereas the aorist passive tense is used to describe the kingdom in the degree to which it has already been inaugurated [EBC]. It indicates that the situation has happened or developed [NIGTC]. It means that the kingdom has already been inaugurated [EBC, ICC, Lns]. It indicates that God's reign has already come in Jesus' ministry, and was present at the time Jesus told the parable [CC, My]. It is used to introduce a more extended story with multiple characters [NICNT].

QUESTION—What is the actual comparison being made here?

The kingdom is being compared to what happened in the *situation* or *case* or *story* of a man who planted good seed [EBC, ICC, NICNT, NIGTC, NTC, TH, TRT, WBC; CEV], not to the man himself [EBC].

13:25 But while- the people[a] were-sleeping his enemy[b] came and sowed-in-addition[c] weeds[d] among[e] the wheat and went-away.[f]

LEXICON—a. ἄνθρωπος (LN 9.1): (in the plural) 'people, persons, mankind' [LN]. This plural noun with the definite article is translated as though not having the definite article: 'people' [BECNT, CC, NICNT, NIGTC; GW], 'men' [BNTC, NTC, PNTC; KJV], 'everyone' [CEV, NCV, NET, NIV, REB, TEV], 'everybody' [NRSV]. It is translated with the definite article, and as though referring to the servants mentioned in verse 27: 'his men' [ESV, NASB], 'his servants' [WBC], 'the workers' [NLT].

b. ἐχθρός (LN 39.11) (BAGD 2.b.β. p. 331): 'enemy' [BAGD; all translations], 'being an enemy' [LN]. This pronominal adjective describes a person who is at enmity with someone [LN].

c. aorist act. indic. of ἐπισπείρω (LN 43.8) (BAGD p. 300): 'to sow in addition' [LN], 'to add a sowing' [BNTC], 'to make a further sowing' [NICNT], 'to scatter seeds' [CEV], 'to sow afterward' [BAGD], 'to sow on top' [CC], 'to sow on top of' [LN], 'to sow where something else is sown' [**LN**], 'to sow' [BECNT, NIGTC, NTC, PNTC, WBC; ESV, KJV, NASB, NET, NIV, NRSV, REB, TEV], 'to plant' [GW, NCV, NLT]. This verb means to sow in addition to a previous sowing [LN].

d. ζιζάνιον (LN 3.30) (BAGD p. 339): 'weed' [BECNT, CC, NICNT, PNTC, WBC; ESV, GW, NCV, NET, NIV, NLT, NRSV, TEV], 'darnel' [BAGD, BNTC, **LN**; REB], 'tares' [NTC; KJV, NASB], 'zizania' [NIGTC], 'cheat' [BAGD]. The phrase ἐπέσπειρεν ζιζάνια 'sowed in addition weeds' is translated 'scattered weed seeds' [CEV]. This noun denotes a particularly undesirable weed resembling wheat and possessing a seed that is poisonous. In this one passage in which ζιζάνιον occurs in the NT it is possible to use an expression such as 'poisonous weed' or 'bad weed' [LN].

e. μέσος (LN **83.9**) (BAGD 2. p. 507): 'among' [BAGD, BECNT, BNTC, CC, **LN**, NICNT, NIGTC, NTC, WBC; all versions except CEV, GW], 'in the middle of' [PNTC], 'with' [LN]. The phrase ἀνὰ μέσον τοῦ σίτου 'among the wheat' is translated 'in the field' [CEV], 'in the wheat field' [GW]. This adjective describes a position within an area determined by other objects and distributed among such objects [LN].

f. aorist act. indic. of ἀπέρχομαι (LN 15.37) (BAGD 1.a. p. 84): 'to go away' [BAGD, BECNT, BNTC, CC, LN, NICNT, NTC, PNTC; ESV, GW, NASB, NET, NIV, NRSV, TEV], 'to go his way' [KJV], 'to go off' [NIGTC], 'to leave' [LN; CEV, NCV], 'to depart' [LN, WBC], 'to slip away' [NLT], 'to make off' [REB]. This verb describes the action of motion away from a reference point with emphasis upon the departure, but without implications as to any resulting state of separation or rupture [LN].

QUESTION—To whom does τοὺς ἀνθρώπους 'the people' refer?
1. It refers generally to people [BECNT, BNTC, CC, ICC, Lns, My, NICNT, NIGTC, NTC, PNTC, TH; CEV, GW, KJV, NCV, NET, NIV, NRSV, REB, TEV].
2. It refers specifically to the men described in verse 26, the land-owner's servants [NIBC, WBC; ESV, NASB, NLT].

QUESTION—What is the nature of the ζιζάνιον 'weed' in this story?
It is a kind of darnel [BNTC, EBC, Lns, My, NAC, NICNT, NIGTC, PNTC, TH, WBC]. It is the bearded darnel [EBC, NIGTC, NTC], which is difficult to distinguish from wheat when the plants are young, and the roots of which entangle around the roots of the wheat plants [EBC]. The bearded darnel is host to a fungus that is poisonous to people or animals when eaten [NIGTC, NTC]. It is a poisonous weed [LN]. The grains are poisonous [NICNT].

13:26 And when the shoots sprouted and produced fruit, then the weeds appeared[a] also. **13:27** And the servants[b] of-the landowner having-approached-him said to-him, 'Sir,[c] did-you- not -sow good seed in your field? From-where[d] then does-it-have weeds?'

LEXICON—a. aorist pass. indic. of φαίνομαι (LN 24.18) (BAGD 2.b. p. 851): 'to appear' [BAGD, BECNT, BNTC, CC, LN, PNTC, WBC; ESV, GW, KJV, NET, NIV, NRSV], 'to become visible' [BAGD, LN, NICNT], 'to become evident' [NIGTC; NASB], 'to be seen' [NTC; REB], 'to show

up' [TEV], 'to be revealed' [BAGD], not explicit [CEV]. The phrase ἐφάνη καὶ τὰ ζιζάνια 'the weeds appeared also' is translated 'the weeds also grew' [NCV, NLT], 'the farmer's servants could see the weeds' [CEV]. This verb means to become visible to someone [LN].
- b. δοῦλος (LN 87.76): 'servant' [BNTC, CC, NTC, WBC; CEV, ESV, KJV, NCV, NIV, TEV], 'slave' [BECNT, LN, NICNT, NIGTC, PNTC; NASB, NET, NRSV], 'worker' [GW, NLT], 'the farmer's men' [REB], 'bondservant' [LN]. This noun denotes one who is a slave in the sense of becoming the property of an owner (though in ancient times it was frequently possible for a slave to earn his freedom) [LN].
- c. κύριος (LN **87.53**) (BAGD 1.a.β. p. 459): 'sir' [CC, **LN**, NIGTC, NTC, PNTC, WBC; all versions except ESV, NCV, NRSV], 'master' [BECNT, NICNT; ESV, NRSV], 'lord' [BNTC], not explicit [NCV]. This noun is title of respect used in addressing or speaking of a man [LN].
- d. πόθεν (LN 84.6) (BAGD 2. p. 680): 'from where?' [LN, NICNT, NTC, WBC; all versions except ESV, KJV, NASB], 'from what source?' [BAGD, BNTC], 'whence?' [CC, LN, PNTC], 'from whence' [KJV], 'how?' [BECNT, NIGTC; ESV, NASB], 'where?' [LN]. The interrogative πόθεν 'from where' can also be used to indicate a person as opposed to a location as a source [EBC]. This adverb describes extension from a source, with an incorporated interrogative point of reference [LN].

13:28 And he-said to-them, '(An) enemy did this.' And the servants say to him, 'Then do-you-wish that going-out we-gather^a them?' **13:29** But he said, 'No, lest^b while-gathering the weeds you-uproot^c the grain with^d them.
  LEXICON—a. aorist act. subj. of συλλέγω (LN 18.10) (BAGD p. 777): 'to gather in, to collect' [BAGD], 'to pick' [BAGD, LN], 'to pluck' [LN]. The phrase 'gather them' [BNTC, NTC; ESV, NET, NRSV] is also translated 'gather them up' [PNTC; KJV, NASB], 'gather the darnel' [REB], 'gather the weeds' [WBC], 'pull them up' [BECNT; NIV], 'pull up the weeds' [CEV, NCV, TEV], 'pull out the weeds' [NICNT; CEV, NLT], 'collect them' [CC, NIGTC]. This verb means to pluck or pick by pulling off or out of, with the intent of gathering together [LN].
- b. μήποτε (LN 89.62) (BAGD 2.b.α. p. 519): 'lest' [BNTC, CC, LN, NTC, PNTC, WBC; ESV, KJV], 'in case you might' [NICNT], 'otherwise you might' [NIGTC], 'no, you might' [CEV, NCV, REB, TEV], 'no, you may' [BECNT; GW, NASB, NET, NIV], 'no, you would' [NRSV], 'no, you will' [NLT], 'in order that ... not' [BAGD, LN], 'so that ... not' [LN]. This conjunction indicates negative purpose, often with the implication of apprehension [LN].
- c. aorist act. subj. of ἐκριζόω (LN 43.11) (BAGD 1. p. 244): 'to uproot' [BAGD, BECNT, BNTC, CC, LN, NICNT, NIGTC, NTC; NASB, NET, NLT, NRSV], 'to root up' [PNTC; ESV, KJV, NIV], 'to root out' [WBC], 'to pull up' [CEV, NCV, REB, TEV], 'to pull out' [GW], 'to pull out by

the roots' [BAGD, LN]. This verb means to remove a plant, including its roots [LN].

d. ἅμα (LN **89.114**, 67.34) (BAGD 2. p. 42): 'with' [BECNT, BNTC, PNTC; GW, NASB, NET, NIV], 'together with' [BAGD, CC, **LN** (89.114)], 'along with' [NICNT, NTC, WBC; ESV, NRSV, TEV], 'also with' [KJV], 'also' [CEV, NCV], 'in addition' [LN (89.114)], 'at the same time' [LN (67.34), NIGTC; REB], not explicit [NLT]. This preposition indicates association, involving additional items affected by some event [LN (89.114)]. It may also indicate a point of time which is emphatically simultaneous with another point of time [LN (67.34)].

QUESTION—Why is λέγουσιν 'say' in the present tense?

It gives emphasis [CC] and vividness to the account [PNTC].

QUESTION—Why would removing the weeds uproot the grain?

The roots of the weeds would be intertwined with the roots of the wheat, making it impossible to remove them without uprooting the wheat [BNTC, CC, ICC, My, NAC, NICNT, NTC]. The roots of darnel are deeper and stronger than wheat roots, and in pulling them up much of the wheat would also be affected [WBC].

13:30 Allow[a] both to-grow-together[b] until the harvest, and in (the) time of-the harvest I-will-say to-the reapers,[c] "Gather first the weeds and tie[d] them into bundles[e] in-order-to burn them, but the wheat gather-together into my barn.[f]" "

LEXICON—a. aorist act. impera. of ἀφίημι (LN 13.140) (BAGD 4. p. 126): 'to allow' [BAGD, CC, LN; NASB], 'to let' [BAGD, BECNT, BNTC, LN, NIGTC, NTC, PNTC, WBC; all versions except CEV, NASB], 'to leave' [NICNT], 'to leave alone' [CEV], 'to leave it to' [LN], 'to permit' [BAGD]. This verb means to leave it to someone to do something, with the implication of distancing oneself from the event [LN].

b. pres. pass. infin. of συναυξάνομαι (LN **23.192**) (BAGD p. 785): 'to grow together' [BAGD, **LN**; all translations except CEV], 'to grow side by side' [BAGD], 'to grow with' [LN], not explicit [CEV]. This verb means to become larger together with, in the sense of growing in essentially the same area and at the same time [LN].

c. θεριστής (LN **43.16**) (BAGD p. 359): 'reaper' [BAGD, BECNT, BNTC, **LN**, NICNT, NTC; ESV, KJV, NASB, NET, NRSV, REB], 'harvester' [BAGD, CC, LN, NIGTC, PNTC, WBC; NIV, NLT], 'worker' [CEV, GW, NCV], 'harvest worker' [TEV]. This noun denotes a person who gathers in a crop [LN].

d. aorist act. impera. of δέω (LN **18.13**) (BAGD 1.a. p. 177): 'to tie' [BAGD, BECNT, BNTC, **LN**, NICNT, NTC; GW, NET, NIV, NLT, REB, TEV], 'to bind' [BAGD, CC, NIGTC, PNTC, WBC; ESV, KJV, NASB, NRSV], 'to tie together' [LN; NCV], 'to tie up' [LN; CEV]. This verb means to tie objects together [LN].

e. δέσμη (LN **18.16**) (BAGD p. 176): 'bundle' [BAGD, BECNT, BNTC, CC, **LN**, NICNT, NIGTC, NTC, PNTC; all versions except CEV, NCV, 'bunch' [WBC], not explicit [CEV, NCV]. This noun denotes that which has been tied up or tied together [LN].

f. ἀποθήκη (LN 7.25) (BAGD p. 91): 'barn' [BAGD, BECNT, LN, NICNT, NTC, PNTC, WBC; all versions], 'storehouse' [BAGD, BNTC, LN], 'granary' [CC, NIGTC]. This noun denotes a building for storage [LN].

DISCOURSE UNIT—13:31–35 [GW, NCV, NIV]. The topic is stories about a mustard seed and yeast [GW], stories of mustard seed and yeast [NCV], the parables of the mustard seed and the yeast [NIV].

DISCOURSE UNIT—13:31–33 [CEV, ESV]. The topic is the mustard seed and the leaven [ESV], stories about a mustard seed and yeast [CEV].

DISCOURSE UNIT—13:31–32 [NASB, NET, NRSV, TEV]. The topic is the parable of the mustard seed [NET, NRSV, TEV], the mustard seed [NASB].

13:31 **He put-before them another parable saying, "The kingdom of-the heavens is like a-seed[a] of-mustard,[b] which a-man having-taken sowed in his field; 13:32 which is smaller[c] than-all the seeds, but whenever it-grows it-is greater-than[d] the garden-plants[e] and becomes a-tree, so-that the birds of-the air come and nest[f] in its branches."**

LEXICON—a. κόκκος (LN 3.35) (BAGD 1. p. 440): 'seed' [BAGD, LN; all translations except ESV, KJV], 'grain of (mustard) seed' [ESV, KJV], 'grain' [BAGD]. This noun denotes the kernel part of fruit [LN].

b. σίναπι (LN **3.20**) (BAGD p. 751): 'mustard' [BAGD, **LN**; all translations], 'mustard plant' [LN]. This noun denotes a large herb noted for its very small seeds and in some instances growing to a height of three meters (about ten feet) [LN].

c. μικρός (LN **79.125**) (BAGD 2.a. p. 521): 'small' [BAGD, LN], 'little' [LN]. This comparative form is translated 'smallest' [**LN**, NTC, PNTC, WBC; all versions except KJV, NASB, REB], 'smaller than' [BECNT, BNTC, CC, NICNT, NIGTC; NASB, REB], 'least of' [KJV].

d. μέγας (LN 79.123) (BAGD 2.b.β. p. 498): 'large, big' [LN], 'great' [BAGD, LN]. This comparative form is translated 'greatest' [WBC; KJV, NET, NRSV], 'biggest' [NTC; TEV], 'largest' [NIV, NLT], 'one of the largest' [NCV], 'larger than' [BECNT, BNTC, NIGTC, PNTC; CEV, ESV, NASB], 'taller than' [GW, REB], 'bigger than' [NICNT], 'greater than' [CC]. This adjective describes what is large in size, relative to the norm for the class of objects in question [LN].

e. λάχανον (LN **3.29**) (BAGD p. 467): 'garden plant' [BECNT, **LN**, PNTC; CEV, ESV, GW, NASB, NCV, NET, NIV, NLT], 'garden herb' [CC, NTC], 'garden vegetable plants' [BNTC], 'plants that belong to the vegetable garden' [NIGTC], 'plant' [WBC; REB, TEV], 'vegetable' [BAGD, NICNT], 'herb' [KJV], 'shrub' [NRSV], 'edible garden herb'

[BAGD]. This noun denotes any one of the smaller plants cultivated in a garden such as herbs and vegetables [LN].
f. pres. act. infin. of κατασκηνόω (LN **6.147**) (BAGD 2. p. 418): 'to nest' [BAGD, BECNT, BNTC, CC, **LN**; CEV, GW, NASB, NET], 'to make a nest' [NIGTC; ESV, NLT, NRSV, TEV], 'to build a nest' [NCV], 'to roost' [NICNT, PNTC; REB], 'to lodge' [NTC; KJV], 'to dwell' [WBC], 'to perch' [NIV]. This verb means to make a nest (or possibly to find shelter) [LN].

QUESTION—What is the point of Jesus' comparison?

He is describing the growth and expansion of the kingdom, which despite small and seemingly insignificant beginnings, brings great growth and results [BECNT, BNTC, CC, EBC, ICC, Lns, My, NAC, NIBC, NIGTC, NTC, PNTC, TRT, WBC]. A beginning that is unimpressive or almost imperceptible can result in a dramatic transformation [NICNT]. What looks insignificant to the world will fulfill God's promises and will eventually triumph [NAC]. There is an organic unity between the kingdom's small beginning and its final, mature state [EBC, ICC]. It also describes the fact that Christ's rule comes into human hearts by something being implanted from outside the heart [NTC].

QUESTION—How large does a mustard plant grow to be?

It can grow to a height of eight feet or more [PNTC, TH, WBC], or even up to ten or fifteen feet [CC, LN, NICNT, NTC]. This may be an example of hyperbole or exaggeration for effect [CC, NICNT, WBC], which does occur in some of the other parables [CC, NICNT].

QUESTION—Do birds actually build nests in the branches of the mustard plant?

The idea of birds taking shelter in the branches reflects imagery from Daniel 4 and Ezekiel 17 and 31 [EBC, NICNT, TH, WBC].

1. This verb refers to finding shelter [NICNT, NTC], perching [EBC, My], or roosting [NAC, NICNT, PNTC; REB], not to nest building or raising young, because the mustard plant does not reach sufficient size by early spring when nesting takes place [NICNT]. Birds could find shelter from a storm or shade from the sun in it [NTC].
2. It is translated as though referring to nesting or nest building [BECNT, BNTC, CC, ICC, NIBC, NIGTC, TRT, WBC; CEV, ESV, GW, NASB, NCV, NET, NLT, NRSV, TEV]. Though nest building in mustard plants in modern Palestine has occasionally been observed, normally the mustard plant is unlikely to attract nesting [NIGTC]. Like other parables, this one is not necessarily intended to be accurate to the details of real life [ICC].

DISCOURSE UNIT—13:33–35 [NASB, NLT]. The topic is the leaven [NASB], parable of the yeast [NLT].

DISCOURSE UNIT—13:33 [NET, NRSV, TEV]. The topic is the parable of the yeast.

13:33 He told them another parable; "The kingdom of-the heavens is like leaven,[a] which a-woman having-taking (it) hid[b] in three measures[c] of fine-flour until (the)-whole was-leavened.[d]"

LEXICON—a. ζύμη (LN 5.11) (BAGD 1. p. 340): 'leaven' [BAGD, BECNT, BNTC, CC, NICNT, NIGTC, PNTC, WBC; ESV, KJV, NASB], 'yeast' [BAGD, LN, NTC; all translations except ESV, KJV, NASB]. This noun denotes leaven employed in making bread rise [LN].
  b. aorist act. indic. of ἐγκρύπτω (LN **85.50**) (BAGD p. 216): 'to hide in' [BECNT, BNTC, CC, LN, NICNT, NIGTC; ESV, KJV, NASB, NCV], 'to hide' [BAGD], 'to put into' [BAGD, **LN**, NTC, PNTC], 'to put in' [NLT], 'to mix into' [WBC; CEV, GW, NIV], 'to mix in' [NRSV], 'to mix with' [NET, REB, TEV]. This verb means to put into, with the implication of the substance no longer being visible [LN]. Here the verb ἐγκρύπτω means 'to put something into something' and in this context the translation 'mixed' is good. The usage of the verb κρύπτω 'to hide' in verse 35 and 44 are best interpreted in different ways [NRSV].
  c. σάτον (LN **81.23**) (BAGD p. 745): 'measure' [BNTC, LN, NTC, PNTC, WBC; ESV, KJV, NET, NLT, NRSV, REB], 'large measure' [NICNT], 'peck' [BECNT; NASB], 'saton' [LN, NIGTC], 'big batch' [CEV], 'batch' [**LN**]. The phrase σάτα τρία 'three measures' is translated 'ten gallons [forty liters]' [CC], 'a bushel' [TEV], 'a large amount' [GW, NIV], 'a large tub' [NCV]. This noun denotes the Hebrew measure for grain, about a peck and a half or somewhat less than one-half bushel (a bushel consists of four pecks) or approximately twelve liters in the metric system. In Matthew 13:33 the precise amount of flour is not important. What is important is to provide some type of measurement which will indicate a considerable quantity [LN].
  d. aorist pass. indic. of ζυμόω (LN **5.12**) (BAGD p. 340): 'to be leavened' [BAGD, BECNT, BNTC, CC, NIGTC, PNTC, WBC; ESV, KJV, NASB, NRSV, REB], 'to use yeast' [LN], 'to ferment' [BAGD]. The phrase ἕως οὗ ἐζυμώθη ὅλον 'until the whole was leavened' is translated 'until the whole batch of dough rises' [TEV], 'until the whole lump/batch had risen' [**LN**, NTC], 'until the dough had all risen' [NICNT; similarly NET], 'until it made all the dough rise' [NCV], 'finally all the dough rises' [CEV], 'until the yeast/it had worked its way all through the dough' [GW, NIV], 'it permeated every part of the dough' [NLT]. This verb means to employ yeast in the process of making bread rise [LN].

QUESTION—Is there any difference between yeast and leaven?
  They are not the same thing; leaven could be a portion of fermented dough from a previous baking [BECNT, NICNT, PNTC, TRT].
QUESTION—How much flour is this?
  It is about 40 liters [BECNT, NIGTC, TH, WBC] or 50 pounds [NIGTC, TH], which is about ten gallons [CC], and will bake enough bread to feed 100 people [TH] or even 150 [BECNT, WBC].

QUESTION—What is the point of this parable?
Something very small can affect something very large [BECNT, BNTC, NIGTC, TRT]. The kingdom will show significant growth from small beginnings [BNTC, ICC, NIBC], and produces results all out of proportion to its small beginnings [EBC]. The kingdom of God will have widespread, pervasive influence [NAC, NIBC]. In addition to the principle of growth as described in the last parable, this one also describes the work of the Holy Spirit bringing about change, beginning from within and permeating everything [EBC, NTC]. The influence of the Messiah's kingdom penetrates its future subjects so thoroughly that they are brought completely into the spiritual condition required for entrance into the kingdom [My]. What appears insignificant at first will become large and all-encompassing, so the disciples should not despair, but have confidence in what Jesus is doing [CC]. It points out the contrast between the small beginnings of the kingdom and the great consummation of it, as well as the fact that the cause of the change came from the outside [PNTC]. The kingdom works secretly and invisibly, works from within, and penetrates all nations and lands [Lns]. Like leaven, the kingdom has a pervasive and permeating effect in its growth [BECNT, CC, NICNT, NTC, WBC], and a dramatic effect on human society [NICNT].

DISCOURSE UNIT—13:34–35 [CEV, ESV, NET, NRSV, TEV]. The topic is Jesus' use of parables [TEV], prophecy and parables [ESV], the purpose of parables [NET], the use of parables [NRSV], the reason for teaching with stories [CEV].

13:34 All these (things) Jesus spoke in parables to-the crowds and he-said nothing to them apart-from[a] parables, **13:35** so-that[b] it-might-be-fulfilled what was-spoken through the prophet saying, "I-will-open my mouth in parables, I-will-utter[c] things-having-been-hidden[d] from (the) foundation[e] of-(the) world."

TEXT—Manuscripts reading ἀπὸ καταβολῆς κόσμου 'from the foundation of the world' are given a C rating by GNT to indicate that choosing it over those texts that read only ἀπὸ καταβολῆς 'from the foundation' was difficult. It is included by NICNT, PNTC; CEV, ESV, GW, KJV, NASB, NCV, NET, NIV, NLT, NRSV, REB, TEV. It is included in brackets by BECNT, GNT, NIGTC, WBC. It is omitted by BNTC, CC, NTC.

LEXICON—a. χωρίς (LN 89.120) (BAGD 2.b.β. p. 890): 'apart from' [BAGD, CC], 'apart from using' [WBC], 'without' [BAGD, BECNT, BNTC, LN, NICNT, NIGTC, NTC, PNTC; ESV, KJV, NASB, NET, NRSV], 'without using' [BNTC, NTC; CEV, NIV, NLT, TEV], 'without illustrating it with' [GW], 'except in' [REB], not explicit [NCV]. This preposition indicates negatively linked elements [LN].
  b. ὅπως (LN 89.59) (BAGD 2.a.α. p. 577): 'so that' [LN, NIGTC, PNTC, WBC], 'in order that' [BAGD, BECNT, CC], 'that' [BNTC, NTC; KJV], 'so' [CEV, NIV], 'in order to, for the purpose of' [LN]. The phrase ὅπως

MATTHEW 13:34–35

πληρωθῇ 'so that it might be fulfilled' is translated 'this was to fulfill' [NICNT; ESV, NASB, NRSV, REB], 'this fulfilled' [NET, NLT], 'so…came true' [CEV, GW], 'he did this to make come true' [TEV], 'this is as (the prophet said)' [NCV]. This conjunction indicates purpose for events and states (sometimes occurring in highly elliptical contexts) [LN].

c. ἐρεύγομαι (LN 33.192) (BAGD p. 308): 'to utter' [BAGD, BECNT, CC, NICNT, NTC, PNTC, WBC; ESV, KJV, NASB, NIV, REB], 'to proclaim' [BAGD, BNTC, LN; NRSV], 'to announce' [**LN**; NET], 'to pour forth' [NIGTC], 'to explain' [CEV, NLT], 'to tell' [GW, TEV]. This verb means to announce in a sudden and emphatic manner (with an implication of 'blurting out') [LN].

d. perf. pass. participle of κρύπτω (LN 28.79) (BAGD 2.a. p. 454): 'to be hidden' [BAGD, LN], 'to be kept secret, to be concealed' [BAGD, LN]. This participle is translated 'things hidden' [BECNT, BNTC, CC, NICNT, WBC; NASB, NIV, NLT], 'things that have been hidden' [CEV], 'what has been hidden' [NIGTC; ESV, GW, NET, NRSV], 'things secret' [PNTC], 'things kept secret' [REB], 'things which have been secret' [NCV], 'things which have been kept secret' [KJV], 'things unknown' [TEV], 'mysteries' [NTC]. This verb means to cause something not to be known [LN].

e. καταβολή (LN 42.37) (BAGD 1. p. 409): 'foundation' [CC, NICNT, NIGTC, PNTC, WBC; ESV, KJV, NASB, NET, NRSV], 'creation' [LN; CEV, NIV, NLT, TEV], 'beginning' [BECNT, BNTC]. The phrase 'from the foundation of the world' is translated 'from ancient times' [NTC], 'since the world was made' [GW, NCV, REB]. This noun denotes creation, particularly of the world, with focus upon the beginning phase [LN].

QUESTION—What relationship is indicated by ὅπως 'so that'?
1. It indicates Jesus' own purpose for teaching with parables [CC, PNTC, TH].
2. It indicates the result, in that Jesus' teaching had the effect of fulfilling prophecy [EBC, TRT]. Jesus fulfilled OT typology and patterns that ultimately looked forward to Jesus' fulfillment of them [WBC].

QUESTION—What hidden things is Jesus explaining?
He is explaining God's righteous acts in redemption, as shown in the teaching and miracles of Jesus, and ultimately in his death and resurrection [EBC]. He is explaining the mysteries of the kingdom [My]. In Psalm 78 Asaph was teaching profound truths about God's redemptive work in history, which might or might not have been obvious to later generations [BECNT, NAC], and Jesus typologically fulfills the patterns of that same OT redemptive history [BECNT, ICC, NAC]. Just as Asaph teaches about God's work in the salvation history of Israel, so also God's salvation is being described in Jesus' parables [NTC, PNTC]. Jesus' message and mission were the outworking of God's plan for salvation and for the redemption of his people that have been in place from the beginning [WBC]. Jesus uses

parables, which may or may not be clearly understood [NIBC, NIGTC], and he is revealing spiritual truths that cannot be known apart from revelation [NIBC, NICNT, NIGTC, PNTC], which in this case are truths about God's sovereign rule [NIBC]. The psalmist explained God's saving work in Israel's history, and Jesus now manifests and explains God's new work in salvation history, fulfilling the Law and Prophets and the history of Israel [CC]. There may be a bit of hyperbole in the statement about the things being hidden [BECNT].

DISCOURSE UNIT—13:36–43 [CEV, GW, NASB, NCV, NET, NIV, NLT, NRSV, TEV]. The topic is the meaning of the weeds in the wheat [GW], Jesus explains the story about the weeds [CEV], Jesus explains about the weeds [NCV], Jesus explains the parable of the weeds [NRSV, TEV], the parable of the weeds explained [NIV], the parable of the wheat and weeds explained [NLT], explanation for the disciples [NET], the tares explained [NASB].

13:36 Then having-left/having-dismissed[a] the crowds he-went into the house. And his disciples approached him saying, "Explain[b] for-us the parable of-the weeds of-the field." **13:37** And answering he-said, "The-one-sowing the good seed is the Son of Man, **13:38** and the field is the world, and the good seed, these are the sons[c] of-the kingdom; and the weeds are the sons of-the evil-(one),[d]

LEXICON—a. aorist act. participle of ἀφίημι (LN 15.43, 15.48) (BAGD 1.a.α. p. 125): 'to leave' [BECNT, BNTC, CC, LN (15.48), NICNT, NIGTC, PNTC; all versions except GW, KJV, REB], 'to depart from' [LN (15.48)], 'to dismiss' [LN (15.43), NTC, WBC], 'to let go, to send away' [BAGD; GW, KJV, REB], 'to let go away' [LN (15.43)]. This verb means to cause (or permit) a person or persons to leave a particular location [LN (15.43)], or to move away from [LN (15.48)].

b. aorist act. impera. of διασαφέω (LN 33.143) (BAGD 1. p. 188): 'to explain' [BAGD, **LN**; all translations except KJV, TEV], 'to declare' [KJV], 'to tell what it means' [TEV], 'to make clear, to make evident' [LN]. This verb means to make an obscurity clear by a thorough explanation [LN].

c. υἱός (LN 11.13) (BAGD 1.c.δ. p. 834): 'son' [BNTC, CC, NIGTC, NTC, PNTC; ESV, NASB, NIV]. The idiomatic phrase οἱ υἱοὶ τῆς βασιλείας 'sons of the kingdom' is also translated 'children of the kingdom' [BECNT, NICNT, WBC; KJV, NRSV, REB], 'people of the kingdom' [NET, NLT], 'people/those who belong to the kingdom' [CEV, GW, TEV], 'all of God's children who belong to the kingdom' [NCV]. This phrase refers to people who should properly be or were traditionally regarded as a part of the kingdom of God [LN].

d. ὁ πονηρός (LN 12.35) (BAGD 2.b. p. 691): 'the evil one' [BAGD, BECNT, BNTC, CC, NTC, PNTC, WBC; all versions except NCV, KJV, TEV], 'the Evil One' [LN, NICNT; NCV, TEV], 'he who is evil' [LN], 'the wicked one' [KJV], 'evil' [NIGTC]. The phrase ὁ πονηρός 'the evil one' is a title for the Devil, the one who is essentially evil or in a sense personifies evil [LN].

QUESTION—Does ἀφεὶς τοὺς ὄχλους 'having left/having dismissed the crowds' mean that he dismissed the people or that he left them?
1. He left them [BECNT, BNTC, CC, NIBC, NICNT, NIGTC, PNTC, TRT; CEV, ESV, NASB, NCV, NET, NIV, NLT, NRSV, TEV].
2. He dismissed them [Lns, NTC, WBC; GW, KJV, REB].

QUESTION—What house did he go into?
It is the same house as in 12:46 and 13:1 [EBC, My, NAC, PNTC, TRT]. It may have belonged to Peter or Matthew [TRT]. It is the house in Capernaum referred to in 8:14 and 9:10 [TH]. It is a house in Capernaum that may well have belonged to some friend or follower, as mentioned in 9:28 and 12:14 [NTC]. It was the home of his extended family [Lns].

QUESTION—What does the phrase 'the sons of the evil one' mean?
It refers to people who belong to Satan [ICC, NICNT, NTC, PNTC, TH, TRT] or who are associated with him [WBC]. They are those whose ethical nature is derived from Satan [My]. They are characterized by wickedness [Lns].

13:39 and the enemy having-sown them is the devil,[a] and the harvest is (the) end[b] of-(the) age,[c] and the harvesters are (the) angels.

LEXICON—a. διάβολος (LN 12.34) (BAGD 2. p. 182): 'the devil' [BECNT, BNTC, CC, NIGTC, NTC, PNTC; all versions except TEV], 'the Devil' [BAGD, LN, WBC; TEV]. This noun is a title for the Devil, literally 'slanderer' and denotes the principal supernatural evil being [LN].

b. συντέλεια (LN 67.66) (BAGD p. 792): 'end' [BAGD, BECNT, BNTC, LN, NICNT, NTC, PNTC, WBC; all versions except ESV], 'consummation' [CC], 'completion' [BAGD, NIGTC], 'close' [BAGD; ESV]. This noun denotes a point of time marking the end of a duration [LN].

c. αἰών (LN 67.143) (BAGD 2.a. p. 27): 'age' [BAGD, BECNT, BNTC, CC, LN, NICNT, NIGTC, NTC, PNTC, WBC; ESV, NASB, NET, NIV, NRSV, TEV], 'time' [CEV, REB], 'era' [LN], 'world' [GW, KJV, NCV, NLT]. This noun denotes a unit of time as a particular stage or period of history [LN].

QUESTION—What is the end of the age?
It is the end of the world [Lns, TH, TRT], the end of the present world order [NICNT]. It is the great consummation [Lns, NTC, PNTC], the time of final judgment [My, NAC, NIBC, TRT, WBC].

13:40 So-then[a] just-as[b] the weeds are-gathered and burned by-fire, so[c] it-will-be at the end of the age; **13:41** the Son of Man will-send-out his angels, and he-will-gather from his kingdom all causes-of-sin[d] and the-ones practicing[e] lawlessness.[f]

LEXICON—a. οὖν (LN 89.50): 'so then' [LN], 'then' [BECNT, BNTC, LN, NIGTC, NTC], 'therefore' [BAGD, CC, PNTC, WBC; KJV], 'so' [LN, NICNT; NASB], 'consequently, accordingly' [LN], not explicit [all versions except KJV, NASB]. This conjunction indicates result, often implying the conclusion of a process of reasoning [LN].

b. ὥσπερ (LN 64.13) (BAGD 1. p. 899): 'just as' [BAGD, BECNT, CC, LN, NICNT, NIGTC, WBC; ESV, GW, NASB, NCV, NLT, NRSV, TEV], 'as' [BNTC, LN, NTC, PNTC; KJV, NET, NIV, REB], not explicit [CEV]. This conjunction indicates similarity between events and states [LN].

c. οὕτως (LN 61.9) (BAGD 1.a. p. 597): 'so' [BAGD, BECNT, BNTC, CC, LN, NIGTC, NTC, PNTC; all versions except CEV], 'thus' [BAGD, LN, WBC], 'in this way' [LN], 'in this manner' [BAGD], 'that's how' [CEV]. This adverb indicates a reference to that which precedes [LN].

d. σκάνδαλον (LN **88.306**) (BAGD 3. p. 753): 'that which causes someone to sin, one who causes someone to sin' [LN], 'that which gives offense' [BAGD]. The phrase πάντα τὰ σκάνδαλα 'all causes of sin' [ESV, NRSV] is translated as referring to things: 'all things that offend' [KJV], 'all things that give offense' [BNTC], 'everything that is offensive' [BAGD, NTC], 'all stumbling blocks' [NICNT; NASB], 'all causes of stumbling' [CC, NIGTC], 'everything that causes stumbling' [WBC], 'everything that causes sin' [NET, NIV, NLT], 'every cause of sin' [REB], 'everything that causes people to sin' [GW], 'all the things that cause sin' [PNTC]. Others take this phrase to specifically refer to people: 'all those who cause people to sin' [TEV], 'all who cause people to sin' [**LN**], 'everyone who causes others to sin' [CEV], 'all who cause sin' [BECNT; NCV]. This is a figurative extension of the meaning of the noun σκάνδαλον 'trap' and it denotes *that which*, or *the one who*, causes someone to sin [LN]. The neuter words πάντα τὰ σκάνδαλα 'all causes of sin' are followed by the phrase 'and the ones practicing lawlessness,' so this might indicate that we should take the neuter word 'all' to refer to persons instead of things [BAGD]. Although the form is neuter, in the present context of judgment, the phrase makes no sense unless people are the cause of stumbling (sinning) [TH].

e. pres. act. participle of ποιέω (LN 90.45) (BAGD I.1.c.γ. p. 682): 'to practice' [LN], 'to do' [BAGD, BNTC, CC, LN; CEV, GW, KJV, NCV, NIV, NLT, TEV], 'to commit' [BAGD, BECNT, PNTC; NASB], 'to produce' [NIGTC], 'to perpetrate' [NTC], 'to be guilty of' [BAGD, WBC], not explicit [NICNT; ESV, NET, NRSV]. This verb indicates an agent relationship with a numerable event [LN].

f. ἀνομία (LN **88.139**) (BAGD 2. p. 72): 'lawlessness' [BAGD, BECNT, CC, LN, NIGTC, NTC, PNTC, WBC; NASB], 'lawless deed' [BAGD, BNTC], 'lawless living' [LN], 'wrong' [CEV], 'evil' [GW, NCV, NIV, NLT], 'evil things' [TEV], 'iniquity' [KJV]. The phrase 'the ones practicing lawlessness' is translated 'those who live lawlessly' [NICNT], 'lawbreakers' [ESV, NET], 'evildoers' [NRSV], 'whose deeds are evil' [REB]. This noun denotes acting with complete disregard for the laws or regulations of a society [LN].

QUESTION—Is the kingdom of the Son of Man the same as the kingdom of God?
1. The two terms represent the same kingdom [EBC, Lns, NICNT, TH]. The kingdom of the Son of Man and the kingdom of God are best taken as synonyms since in 16:28 and 20:21 the kingdom of the Son of Man definitely refers to the kingdom in its final consummation [TH].
2. The kingdom of the Son of Man is the sovereignty given to the Son following his being raised from the dead, whereas the kingdom of God refers to God's eternal rule following the final judgment [NIBC].

13:42 And they-will-throw[a] them into the furnace[b] of-the fire;[c] there-will-be weeping[d] and the gnashing[e] of-teeth there. **13:43** Then the righteous will-shine[f] as the sun in the kingdom of-their father. The-one having ears let-(him)-hear.

LEXICON—a. fut. act. indic. of βάλλω (LN 15.215) (BAGD 1.b. p. 131): 'to throw' [BAGD, BECNT, CC, LN, NICNT, NIGTC, NTC; all versions except KJV, REB], 'to cast' [PNTC, WBC; KJV]. This active verb is also translated as passive: 'they will be thrown' [REB].

b. κάμινος (LN 7.73) (BAGD p. 402): 'furnace' [BAGD, LN; all translations], 'oven' [BAGD], 'kiln' [LN]. This noun denotes a construction used for the smelting of ore and burning of ceramic ware, but in this verse it is used figuratively of hell [LN].

c. πῦρ (LN 2.3) (BAGD 1.b. p. 730): 'fire' [BAGD, LN]. This noun in the genitive case is translated 'of fire' [BECNT; KJV, NASB, NRSV]. It is translated as an adjective modifying 'furnace': 'fiery' [BNTC, CC, NIGTC, NIGTC, NTC; ESV, NET, NIV, NLT, TEV], 'burning' [NICNT], 'blazing' [PNTC; GW, NCV, REB], 'flaming' [CEV].

d. κλαυθμός (LN 25.138) (BAGD p. 433): 'weeping' [BAGD, BECNT, BNTC, CC, LN, NICNT, NIGTC, NTC, PNTC, WBC; ESV, NASB, NET, NIV, NLT, NRSV], 'wailing' [KJV, REB], 'crying' [BAGD, LN]. The phrase 'there will be weeping' is translated 'people will cry' [CEV, GW, NCV], 'they will cry' [TEV]. This noun denotes weeping or wailing, with emphasis upon the noise accompanying the weeping [LN].

e. βρυγμός (LN 23.41) (BAGD p. 148): 'gnashing (of teeth)' [BAGD, BECNT, BNTC, CC, LN, NICNT, NIGTC; ESV, KJV, NASB, NET, NIV, NLT, NRSV], 'grinding' [NTC, PNTC, WBC; REB]. The phrase 'the gnashing of teeth' is translated 'they will gnash their teeth' [TEV], 'people will…grit their teeth in pain' [CEV], 'people will grind their teeth with pain' [NCV], 'people will…be in extreme pain' [GW]. This noun denotes the grinding or the gnashing of the teeth, whether involuntary as in the case of certain illnesses, or as an expression of an emotion such as anger or of pain and suffering [LN].

f. fut. act. indic. of ἐκλάμπω (LN **14.38**) (BAGD p. 242): 'to shine' [BECNT, BNTC, NICNT, NTC, PNTC; all versions except CEV, KJV, NASB], 'to shine forth' [CC, **LN**, NIGTC; CEV, KJV, NASB], 'to shine out' [BAGD], 'to glimmer' [WBC]. This verb means to shine forth from a source, and occurs only in this verse where it is used in a figurative context [LN].

QUESTION—What is the furnace of fire?

It is hell [Lns, My, NAC, NICNT, TH, WBC], the final destination of the wicked [PNTC]. When readers are not familiar with furnaces, possible translations are 'the fires of hell' or 'into hell, which is like a great fire' [TH].

QUESTION—What is the main point of the parable?

Although the judgment, represented by the harvest, is coming, that time has not yet arrived [NTC, WBC]. At the time of the judgment the kingdom will be cleansed of those who don't belong in it, but it will not happen before then, so patience is needed [NTC]. It explains why the coming of the kingdom in Jesus' present ministry seems not to be overwhelming and conclusive [CC]. This parable is about the kingdom, not just the church [EBC, NAC, NTC, PNTC], though it can be applied to the church [EBC, NTC, PNTC]. The kingdom is mysterious and hidden at the present time, but it will triumph in the end [ICC].

QUESTION—Is this parable intended to account for the fact that both believers and unbelievers are mixed together in the church?

The focus is not on the mixing of believers and unbelievers in the church [Lns, NIBC, NICNT, PNTC]. In verse 38 Jesus explained that the field in which the seeds were sown is the world, so the focus is on the presence of both kinds of people in the world generally [BECNT, EBC, NAC, NICNT, PNTC]. This parable was not given for the purpose of limiting or moderating discipline within the church [EBC, ICC, Lns, NAC]. Here 'the world' would not have been understood by Matthew or his readers as referring to the church [WBC]. While the mixing is described with reference to the world, it is also a reality in the church, which the scope of this parable also includes [CC, NTC].

DISCOURSE UNIT—13:44–53 [GW]. The topic is stories about a treasure, a merchant, and a net.

DISCOURSE UNIT—13:44–52 [ICC; NET]. The topic is parables on the kingdom of heaven [NET], three more parables and the conclusion of the discourse [ICC].

DISCOURSE UNIT—13:44–50 [NRSV]. The topic is three parables.

DISCOURSE UNIT—13:44–46 [NCV, NIV]. The topic is stories of a treasure and a pearl [NCV], the parables of the hidden treasure and the pearl [NIV].

DISCOURSE UNIT—13:44–45 [NLT]. The topic is parables of the hidden treasure and the pearl.

DISCOURSE UNIT—13:44 [CEV, ESV, NASB, TEV]. The topic is the parable of the hidden treasure [ESV, TEV], the hidden treasure [NASB], a hidden treasure [CEV].

13:44 The kingdom of-the heavens is like a-treasure hidden in the field, which a-man having-found (it), hid,[a] and because-of his joy[b] he-goes-away and he-sells everything[c] as-much-as he-has and he-buys that field.

LEXICON—a. aorist act. indic. of κρύπτω (LN 24.30) (BAGD 1.a. p. 454): 'to hide' [BAGD, BNTC, CC, LN, NICNT, NIGTC, PNTC; KJV, NET, NRSV], 'to hide again' [BECNT, WBC; NASB, NCV, NIV, NLT], 'to cover up' [NTC; ESV], 'to cover up again' [TEV], 'to bury again' [CEV, GW, REB], 'to cover, to conceal' [BAGD], 'to make hidden and safe' [LN]. This verb means to cause something to be invisible (in the sense of being hidden), but for the purpose of safekeeping and protection [LN].
  b. χαρά (LN 25.123) (BAGD 1. p. 875): 'joy' [BAGD, LN], 'gladness, great happiness' [LN]. The phrase ἀπὸ τῆς χαρᾶς αὐτοῦ 'because of his joy' [BNTC; NET], is translated 'because of his joy over it' [BECNT], 'because of their joy' [NIGTC], 'in his joy' [ESV, NIV, NRSV; REB], 'in his joy over it' [NTC], 'from his joy' [CC], 'from joy over it' [PNTC; NASB], 'for joy thereof' [KJV], 'out of joy' [WBC], 'in his delight' [NICNT], 'in his excitement' [NLT], 'a person like that is happy' [CEV], 'he was/is so happy that' [NCV, TEV], 'he was so delighted with it' [GW]. This noun denotes a state of joy and gladness [LN].
  b. πᾶς (LN 59.23): 'everything' [WBC; CEV, GW, NCV, NLT, TEV], 'all' [BECNT, LN, NICNT, NICNT, NTC, PNTC; ESV, KJV, NASB, NET, NIV, NRSV, REB], 'every, each' [LN]. The phrase πάντα ὅσα ἔχει 'everything as much as he has' is translated 'all–whatever he did have' [CC], 'what he owns' [BNTC]. This adjective describes the totality of any object, mass, collective, or extension [LN].

QUESTION—How had the treasure been hidden in the field?
  It had been buried [BECNT, BNTC, ICC, Lns, NIBC, NICNT, NIGTC, NTC, PNTC, TH, WBC; GW, REB].
QUESTION—How did the man hide the treasure he found?
  He buried it again [TH; CEV, GW, REB].
QUESTION—What does this parable imply about the ethics of the man's actions?
  The question about the ethics of the man's actions is not relevant to the point that Jesus was making with this story [BECNT, CC, ICC, NAC, NIBC, NICNT, PNTC, TH, WBC]. Sometimes people buried their wealth, which could subsequently become lost or forgotten, or sometimes the person who buried it died without anyone else knowing where it was, and it would then belong to whomever found it [Lns, NIBC, NIGTC, PNTC, TRT]. Buying the field would insure that the man's claim to the treasure would not be contested by the previous owner of the field [PNTC, NIGTC].

MATTHEW 13:45-46

DISCOURSE UNIT—13:45–46 [CEV, ESV, GW, NASB, TEV]. The topic is the parable of the pearl [GW, TEV], the parable of the pearl of great value [ESV], a costly pearl [NASB], a valuable pearl [CEV].

13:45 Again[a] the kingdom of-the heavens is like a-man (who is) a-merchant[b] seeking fine[c] pearls;[d] **13:46** And having-found one valuable[e] pearl having-gone-away he-sold everything that he-had and he-bought it.

LEXICON—a. πάλιν (LN 89.97) (BAGD 3. p. 607): 'again' [BECNT, BNTC, CC, LN, NICNT, NIGTC, NTC, PNTC, WBC; ESV, KJV, NASB, NET, NIV, NLT, NRSV, REB], 'furthermore' [BAGD], 'also' [LN; GW, NCV, TEV], 'and' [LN], not explicit [CEV]. This adverb indicates an additive relationship involving repetition [LN].

b. ἔμπορος (LN 57.203) (BAGD p. 257): ἔμπορος (LN 57.203) (BAGD p. 257): 'merchant' [BAGD, LN], 'trader' [LN]. The phrase ἀνθρώπῳ ἐμπόρῳ 'a man who is a merchant' is translated 'a merchant man' [CC; KJV], 'a merchant' [BECNT, BNTC, NTC, PNTC, WBC; ESV, GW, NASB, NET, NIV, NLT, NRSV, REB], 'a person who was a merchant' [NIGTC], 'a trader' [NICNT], 'a shop owner' [CEV], 'a man' [NCV, TEV]. This noun denotes one who is engaged in commerce and trade [LN].

c. καλός (LN 65.22) (BAGD 2.a. p. 400): 'fine' [BAGD, BECNT, LN, NICNT, NIGTC, NTC, PNTC; all versions except KJV, NLT], 'beautiful' [BNTC, CC, WBC], 'choice' [NLT], 'goodly' [KJV], 'good' [BAGD, LN]. This adjective describes having acceptable characteristics or functioning in an agreeable manner, often with the focus on outward form or appearance [LN].

d. μαργαρίτης (LN 2.43) (BAGD 1. p. 491): 'pearl' [BAGD, LN; all translations]. This noun denotes a smooth, rounded concretion formed within the shells of certain mollusks and that is valued as a gem because of its lustrous color [LN].

e. πολύτιμος (LN 65.3) (BAGD p. 690): 'valuable' [BAGD, LN; GW], 'very valuable' [BECNT, BNTC, CC, NIGTC; CEV, NCV], 'immensely valuable' [NICNT], 'of great value' [NTC; ESV, NASB, NET, NIV, NLT, NRSV], 'of very special value' [REB], 'of great price' [PNTC; KJV], 'very precious' [BAGD], 'precious' [WBC], 'unusually fine' [TEV], 'expensive' [LN]. This adjective describes being of great value or worth, implying in some contexts a monetary scale [LN].

QUESTION—What is the function of πάλιν 'again'?
It connects this parable closely with the preceding one [EBC, NIGTC, TH]. It introduces a formula that he has used previously [PNTC]. It introduces a second, similar comparison [Lns, My]. It means 'Here is another parable about God's rule' or 'The rule of God can also be said to be like this' [TH].

MATTHEW 13:45-46 505

QUESTION—What does the pearl represent and what is the main point?
1. The pearl represents the kingdom of God that a person should want to give up anything to be a part of [BNTC, EBC, Lns, My, NICNT, NIGTC, NTC, PNTC, TH, WBC]
2. The pearl in this parable, as well as the field and the treasure in the previous parable, represent people whom Jesus wants to redeem [CC].

DISCOURSE UNIT—13:47–52 [NASB, NCV, NIV, NLT]. The topic is a story of a fishing net [NCV], the parable of the net [NIV], the parable of the fishing net [NLT], a dragnet [NASB].

DISCOURSE UNIT—13:47–50 [CEV, ESV, TEV]. The topic is the parable of the net [ESV, TEV], a fish net [CEV].

13:47 Again the kingdom of-the heavens is like a-net[a] having-been-cast into the sea and it-gathered (fish) from all kinds;[b] **13:48** which when it-was-filled[c] having-pulled-(it)-up[d] on the shore and having-sat-down they-gathered the good-(ones)[e] into a-container,[f] but the bad-(ones)[g] they-threw out.

LEXICON—a. σαγήνη (LN **6.13**) (BAGD p. 739): 'net' [BECNT, **LN**, NICNT; all versions except NASB, NLT], 'dragnet' [BAGD, BNTC, CC, NTC, PNTC, WBC; NASB], 'fishing net' [NIGTC; NLT], 'seine net' [LN]. This noun denotes a long seine net used in fishing [LN].

b. γένος (LN **58.23**) (BAGD 4. p. 156): 'kind' [BAGD, BECNT, BNTC, CC, **LN**, NICNT, NIGTC, PNTC, WBC; all versions], 'variety' [NTC], 'type' [LN], 'class' [BAGD]. This noun denotes a category or class based upon an implied derivation and/or lineage [LN].

c. aorist pass. indic. of πληρόω (LN **59.37**) (BAGD 1.a. p. 670): 'to be filled' [BAGD, CC, LN, PNTC; NASB]. This passive verb is translated as a descriptive phrase: 'was full' [BECNT, BNTC, **LN**, NICNT, NIGTC, NTC, WBC; all versions except CEV, NASB, TEV], 'is full' [CEV, TEV]. This verb means to cause something to become full [LN].

d. aorist act. participle of ἀναβιβάζω (LN 15.213) (BAGD p. 50): 'to pull up' [BAGD, BECNT, BNTC, **LN**, NICNT; NIV], 'to pull' [GW, NCV, NET, TEV], 'to drag up' [CC; NLT], 'to drag' [NTC], 'to draw up' [LN, NIGTC; NASB], 'to draw' [ESV, KJV, NRSV], 'to bring up' [BAGD, WBC], 'to haul' [REB], 'to be dragged' [CEV]. This verb means to pull or draw something in an upward direction [LN].

e. καλός (LN 65.22) (BAGD 2.a. p. 400): 'good' [BAGD, LN; all translations], 'fine' [LN], 'useful' [BAGD]. This adjective describes having acceptable characteristics or functioning in an agreeable manner, often with the focus on outward form or appearance [LN].

f. ἄγγος (LN **6.120**) (BAGD p. 8): 'container' [BAGD, BNTC, LN, NICNT, NTC, WBC; ESV, GW, NASB, NET], 'vessel' [BAGD, CC, **LN**; KJV], 'basket' [BECNT, NIGTC, PNTC; NCV, NIV, NRSV, REB], 'crate' [NLT], 'bucket' [TEV], not explicit [CEV]. This noun denotes a container, primarily for liquids or wet objects, containing perhaps some sixteen to twenty liters (or about four to five gallons) [LN].

g. σαπρός (LN 65.28) (BAGD 1. p. 742): 'bad' [BAGD, BECNT, BNTC, LN, NIGTC, NTC, PNTC, WBC; all versions except REB, TEV], 'worthless' [NICNT; REB, TEV], 'rotten' [CC], 'unwholesome, unfit, unusable' [BAGD]. This adjective describes being of poor or bad quality and hence of little or no value [LN].

QUESTION—What kind of net was this, and how did it function?

It was a large net with floats on the top and weights on the bottom, and it was dragged through the water [BECNT, NIGTC, PNTC, TH], potentially catching a great number of fish [BECNT, PNTC], plus a wide variety of other things, including junk and weeds [NIGTC]. It was either drawn between two boats or pulled by one boat while tied to something on shore on the other end [EBC, PNTC].

QUESTION—What do the fish of 'all kinds' represent?

The phrase 'of all kinds' simply represents good and bad fish; that is, those that are useful and those that are not [EBC, Lns, NICNT, TH]. The variety of fish is not significant to the point of the parable, which focuses primarily on the decisive judgment that is coming upon people [NIBC, NTC]. It recalls the mission mandate to be fishers of men, calling all kinds of people into the visible community of the church [CC]. It emphasizes the universality of God's judgment of people [NAC], all of whom will be separated for judgment at the end of the age [NIBC]. It seems to signify the universality of the kingdom, that it is preached to peoples of all nations [BECNT, My, WBC].

13:49 So[a] it-will-be in the end of-the age; the angels will-go-out and they-will-separate[b] the wicked[c] from among[d] the righteous **13:50** and they-will-throw them into the furnace of-the fire; there-will-be wailing and the gnashing of-teeth there.

LEXICON—a. οὕτως (LN 61.9) (BAGD 1.b. p. 597): 'so' [BAGD, BECNT, BNTC, CC, LN, NIGTC, NTC, PNTC; ESV, KJV, NASB, NRSV], 'thus' [BAGD, LN, WBC], 'that is how' [NICNT; CEV, REB], 'this is how' [NIV], 'this way' [NCV, NET], 'in this way' [LN], 'that is the way' [NLT], 'in this manner' [BAGD], 'like this' [TEV]. The phrase οὕτως ἔσται 'so it will be' is translated 'the same thing will happen' [GW]. This adverb indicates a reference to that which precedes [LN].

b. fut. act. indic. of ἀφορίζω (LN 63.28) (BAGD 1. p. 127): 'to separate' [BAGD, BNTC, CC, LN, NICNT, NIGTC, NTC, PNTC, WBC; all versions except KJV, NASB, TEV], 'to set one apart from another' [LN], 'to remove' [BECNT], 'to sever' [KJV], 'to take out' [NASB], 'to gather up' [TEV], 'to take away' [BAGD]. This verb means to separate into two or more parts or groups, often by some intervening space [LN].

c. πονηρός (LN 88.110) (BAGD 2.a. p. 691): 'wicked' [BAGD, BECNT, BNTC, LN, NICNT, NTC, PNTC; KJV, NASB, NIV, REB], 'wicked

MATTHEW 13:49-50 507

people' [NLT], 'evil' [CC, LN, NIGTC, WBC; ESV, NET, NRSV], 'evil people' [CEV, GW, NCV, TEV], 'evildoer' [BAGD]. This adjective describes what is morally corrupt and evil [LN].

d. μέσος (LN **83.9**) (BAGD 2. p. 507): 'among' [BAGD, BECNT, BNTC, LN, NICNT; KJV, NASB, TEV], 'the midst of' [CC, NIGTC, WBC], 'with' [LN], not explicit [NTC, PNTC; all versions except KJV, NASB, TEV]. This adjective describes a position within an area determined by other objects and distributed among such objects [LN].

QUESTION—What is the point of this parable?

It describes the absolute certainty of the coming judgment [BNTC, Lns, NAC, NTC, PNTC], and the finality of the sentence when it is pronounced [NTC, PNTC]. It describes the state of the kingdom of God at the time of the judgment. There will be both righteous and wicked people [EBC, NICNT, PNTC, WBC], and a great sorting will occur [EBC, ICC, NIBC, NICNT, NIGTC, PNTC, WBC]. At the judgment the wicked will be separated from the righteous and suffer punishment [ICC]. The disciples should not discriminate as they preach the gospel, since it is for all nations [BECNT, CC].

DISCOURSE UNIT—13:51-53 [NRSV]. The topic is treasures new and old.

DISCOURSE UNIT—13:51-52 [CEV, ESV, TEV]. The topic is new truths and old [TEV], new and old treasures [CEV, ESV].

13:51 Did-you(pl)-understand[a] all these-(things)?" They-said to him, "Yes." **13:52** And he-said to-them, "Therefore every scribe having-become-a-disciple[b] for-the kingdom of-the heavens is like a-man (who is) master-of-a-household,[c] who brings-out of-his storeroom[d] new-(things)[e] and old-(things).[f]"

TEXT—Manuscripts beginning this verse with Συνήκατε 'Did you understand...?' are followed by GNT, which does not mention any variant reading. A variant reading is Λέγει αὐτοῖς ὁ Ἰησοῦς εἶπεν αὐτοῖς, Συνήκατε 'Jesus says to them, "Did you understand..."' and it is followed by KJV.

TEXT—Manuscripts reading Ναί. 'Yes.' are followed by GNT, which does not mention any variant reading. A variant reading is Ναί, κύριε. 'Yes, Lord.' and it is followed by KJV.

LEXICON—a. aorist act. indic. of συνίημι (LN 32.5) (BAGD p. 790): 'to understand' [BAGD, LN; all translations], 'to comprehend' [BAGD, LN], 'to perceive, to have insight into' [LN], 'to gain an insight into' [BAGD]. This aorist verb is translated using a perfect tense verb form: 'have you understood' [BECNT, BNTC, NICNT, NTC, PNTC, WBC; ESV, GW, KJV, NASB, NET, NIV, NRSV, REB]; using a past tense verb form: 'did you understand' [CC, NIGTC], 'if they understood' [CEV]; using a present tense verb form: 'do you understand' [NCV, NLT, TEV]. This verb means to employ one's capacity for understanding and thus to arrive at insight [LN].

b. aorist pass. participle of μαθητεύω (LN 36.31, 36.37) (BAGD 2. p. 485): 'to become a disciple' [BAGD], 'to be a disciple of' [LN 36.31)], 'to be made a disciple or follower of' [LN (36.37)]. The phrase 'every scribe having become a disciple for the kingdom of the heavens' is translated 'every scribe who has become a disciple of the kingdom of heaven' [BNTC; GW, NASB], 'every scribe who has become a disciple in the kingdom of heaven' PNTC], 'every scribe who has become a disciple of the reign of heaven' [CC], 'everyone discipled to be a scribe for the kingdom of heaven' [NIGTC], 'every scribe who has been made a disciple for the kingdom of heaven' [NICNT], 'every scribe who has been instructed in the kingdom of heaven' [WBC], 'every scribe who has been trained for the kingdom of heaven' [NTC; ESV, NRSV], 'every scribe which is instructed unto the kingdom of heaven' [KJV], 'every student of the Scriptures who becomes a disciple in the kingdom of heaven' [CEV], 'every expert in the law who has been trained for the kingdom of heaven' [NET], 'every legal expert who has become a disciple of the kingdom of heaven' [BECNT], 'every teacher of the law who becomes a disciple in the Kingdom of heaven' [TEV], 'every teacher of the law who has been taught/instructed about the kingdom of heaven' [NCV, NIV], 'every teacher of the law who becomes a disciple in the Kingdom of Heaven' [NLT], 'when a teacher of the law has become a learner in the kingdom of heaven' [REB]. This verb means to be a follower or a disciple of someone in the sense of adhering to the teachings or instructions of a leader and in promoting the cause of such a leader [LN (36.31)], or to cause someone to become a disciple or follower of someone [LN (36. 37)].

c. οἰκοδεσπότης (LN 57.14) (BAGD p. 558): 'master of a household' [LN, WBC; NRSV], 'master of a house' [BAGD, BNTC, NICNT; ESV], 'head of a household' [BECNT, NTC; NASB], 'householder' [CC, PNTC; KJV, REB], 'homeowner' [GW, NLT, TEV], 'owner of a house' [NCV, NET, NIV]. The phrase ἀνθρώπῳ οἰκοδεσπότῃ 'a man who is master of a household' is simple referred to as 'someone' [CEV]. This noun denotes one who owns and manages a household, including family, servants, and slaves [LN].

d. θησαυρός (LN **7.32**) (BAGD 1.a.β. p. 361): 'storeroom' [BAGD, BECNT, **LN**, NICNT; CEV, NIV, NLT], 'storehouse' [BAGD, NTC, WBC], 'storage room' [TEV], 'store' [REB], 'treasure-store' [CC], 'treasure chest' [GW], 'treasure room' [LN], 'treasure' [BNTC, PNTC; ESV, KJV, NASB, NET, NRSV]. The phrase 'out of his storeroom' is translated as a phrase describing the new and old items: 'he has saved' [NCV]. This noun denotes a room for the storage of valuables [LN].

e. καινός (LN 67.115) (BAGD 1. p. 394): 'new' [BAGD, LN; all translations], 'unused' [BAGD], 'recent' [LN]. This adjective describes something as having been in existence for only a short time [LN]. The

MATTHEW 13:51–52

implied noun or noun phrase being modified by 'new' and 'old' is translated 'things' [BECNT, BNTC, CC, NICNT, NIGTC, NTC, PNTC, WBC; GW, KJV, NASB, NCV, REB, TEV], 'treasures' [CEV, NIV], 'what (is)' [ESV, NET, NRSV], 'gems of truth' [NLT].

f. παλαιός (LN 67.97) (BAGD 1. p. 605): 'old' [BAGD, LN; all translations]. This adjective describes something as having existed continuously for a relatively long time [LN].

QUESTION—What are 'all these things' that they said they understood?

Jesus was asking if they understood what he was communicating in parables [EBC, NIBC, TRT], which included both the parables that he explained as well as the ones he didn't explain [EBC]. It refers to all the parables in this chapter [BNTC, NIGTC, WBC], which are about the kingdom [WBC]. The phrase refers to what he was telling them about the growth of the kingdom despite opposition [BECNT]. This refers to information about the kingdom that he had been giving to them [NTC]. It also refers to the secrets of the kingdom mentioned in verse 11 [EBC]. It is what he had told them since verse 36 [My]. It relates to what he said in verses 44–50 in the three parables about the kingdom, but especially in verses 49–50 where he explained them to the disciples [NICNT].

QUESTION—What relationship is indicated by διὰ τοῦτο 'therefore'?

Because they understood, or thought they understood, certain things must follow [BECNT, Lns, PNTC, TH]. Because they understood, they are like a householder, etc. [My]. Because they understood the nature of the kingdom, they, as Christian 'scribes', could be described in the statement that follows [WBC]. Because things in the kingdom of heaven are the way Jesus had been describing, certain things must follow about discipleship [NIGTC].

QUESTION—Who are the 'scribes' who have been 'discipled for the kingdom'?

This refers to Jesus' disciples who, having been instructed, will then instruct others [BECNT, BNTC, CC, EBC, ICC, Lns, NAC, NICNT, NIGTC, NTC, PNTC, WBC]. The term γραμματεύς 'scribe' refers to one who teaches, and having been discipled by Jesus for the kingdom is what makes his disciples 'scribes'. They, as well as all Christians to come, are responsible for teaching and discipling others in a similar way [BECNT, EBC]. The term 'scribe' refers to any kingdom worker, as the one who has been trained has the responsibility to train others [NTC]. It refers to any well-instructed disciple [BNTC, PNTC]. It refers to Christian teachers [ICC, My]. It is the disciple who is able to proclaim both the old as well as the new deeds of Israel's God [CC]. In addition to becoming teachers, the disciples would also administer justice in the church [NIGTC].

QUESTION—What relationship is indicated by the dative case construction τῇ βασιλείᾳ 'for the kingdom'?

It describes having been made or having become a disciple *of* the kingdom, meaning that there is a transformation of the person's entire allegiance [EBC]. They are disciples of the kingdom in that they will teach the kingdom message [BECNT]. It means to have committed oneself to all the kingdom stands for [PNTC], to be dedicated to the kingdom [BNTC], to be instructed in the truths about the kingdom [ICC], or to be trained concerning the nature of the kingdom as Jesus taught about it in these parables [WBC]. Being a disciple of the kingdom means being a disciple of Jesus, who represents the kingdom [My].

QUESTION—What are the 'things new and old'?

Jesus' disciples were to draw from what Jesus taught them to teach new truths that are tied to the older truths [BECNT], though the new things are primary [BECNT, EBC]. Jesus' disciples were to draw out the meaning of the OT scriptures, which were being fulfilled in the new age, and they would also show how they were to be applied [NAC, NICNT]. There was one revelation, the focus of which was the new gospel of the kingdom, which was fulfilling the old in that it completed and took precedence over the revelation of the OT prophets [EBC]. Jesus had come to fulfill the law and the prophets [BECNT], and the faith his disciples were to hold and teach must encompass both testaments [BECNT, WBC]. A well-trained disciple would have to draw from his Jewish heritage together with the new perspective Jesus had given in his teaching about the kingdom [BNTC]. The new, fresh insights did not do away with the old, which have stood the test of time, but because a new age has dawned, the old could only be understood in terms of how it prepared the way for the new [PNTC]. New truths built on the old ones [Lns, NIBC]. The prophecies of the OT prophets, the teaching of the law, and the use of parables and similes belong to what was taught in the OT era, but now the predictions were fulfilled, the teachings of the law were being developed and perfected by Christ, and the way Christ used parables for messianic teaching were all new [My].

DISCOURSE UNIT—13:53–19:2 [BECNT]. The topic is opposition to the kingdom continues.

DISCOURSE UNIT—13:53–18:35 [PNTC]. The topic is the end of Jesus' ministry in Galilee.

DISCOURSE UNIT—13:53–17:27 [BECNT]. The topic is narrative 4: various responses to the Son of God.

DISCOURSE UNIT—13:53–16:20 [NAC]. The topic is the polarization enacted: from Jew to Gentile.

DISCOURSE UNIT—13:53–58 [ICC, PNTC; CEV, ESV, NASB, NCV, NET, NIV, NLT, TEV]. The topic is a prophet without honor [PNTC; NIV], Jesus goes to his hometown [NCV], Jesus is rejected at Nazareth [NLT, TEV], Jesus rejected at Nazareth [ESV], the rejection at Nazareth [ICC], rejection at Nazareth [NET], Jesus revisits Nazareth [NASB], the people of Nazareth turn against Jesus [CEV].

13:53 And it-happened when Jesus finished[a] these parables, he went-away from-there.

LEXICON—a. aorist act. indic. of τελέω (LN 68.22) (BAGD 1. p. 810): 'to finish' [BAGD, BECNT, BNTC, LN, NIGTC, NTC, PNTC, WBC; all versions], 'to complete' [BAGD, CC, LN], 'to come to an end' [NICNT], 'to bring to an end' [BAGD], 'to end' [LN]. This verb means to bring an activity to a successful finish [LN].

DISCOURSE UNIT—13:54–19:2 [EBC]. The topic is the glory and the shadow: progressive polarization.

DISCOURSE UNIT—13:54–17:27 [EBC]. The topic is narrative.

DISCOURSE UNIT—13:54–16:20 [NIGTC]. The topic is Jesus interpreted, but also rejected.

DISCOURSE UNIT—13:54–14:12 [NICNT]. The topic is further hostile response.

DISCOURSE UNIT—13:54–58 [GW, NRSV]. The topic is Nazareth rejects Jesus [GW], the rejection of Jesus at Nazareth [NRSV].

13:54 And having-gone to his hometown[a] he-was-teaching them in the synagogue, so-that they-were-amazed[b] and were-saying, "Where[c] did- this- (man) -get this wisdom[d] and the miracles?[e]

LEXICON—a. πατρίς (LN 1.81) (BAGD 2. p. 637): 'hometown' [BECNT, LN, CC, NIGTC, NTC, PNTC; all versions except KJV, REB], 'home town' [BAGD, BNTC, WBC; REB], 'home village' [NICNT], 'own country' [KJV], 'homeland' [LN]. This noun denotes the region or population center from which a person comes, that is to say, the place of one's birth or childhood or the place from which one's family has come [LN].

b. pres. pass. infin. of ἐκπλήσσομαι (LN 25.219) (BAGD 2. p. 244): 'to be amazed' [BAGD; CEV, GW, NCV, NIV, NLT, TEV], 'to be astonished' [BECNT, CC, NICNT, NIGTC, NTC, PNTC, WBC; ESV, KJV, NASB, NET], 'to be astounded' [BNTC; NRSV], 'to be greatly astounded' [LN], 'to be overwhelmed' [BAGD]. This verb is translated as a phrase: 'in amazement' [REB]. This verb means to be so amazed as to be practically overwhelmed [LN].

c. πόθεν (LN 84.6) (BAGD 2. p. 680): 'where?' [BECNT, LN, NICNT, NIGTC, NTC, PNTC; all versions except KJV], 'from where' [LN], 'whence' [CC, LN; KJV], 'from what source' [BAGD, BNTC], 'brought about or given by whom?' [BAGD]. The phrase 'where did this man get…?' is translated 'how did this…come to this man?' [WBC]. This adverb describes extension from a source, with an incorporated interrogative point of reference [LN].

d. σοφία (LN 32.32) (BAGD 3.a. p. 760): 'wisdom' [BAGD, LN; all translations]. This noun denotes the capacity to understand and, as a result, to act wisely [LN].

e. δύναμις (LN 76.7) (BAGD 4. p. 208): 'miracle' [BAGD, BNTC, CC, LN, NICNT; TEV], 'mighty work' [NIGTC; ESV, KJV], 'mighty deed' [LN], 'wonder' [BAGD], 'powerful deed' [BECNT], 'deed of power' [BAGD; NRSV], 'miraculous power' [PNTC; NASB, NET, NIV, REB], 'the power to do/work miracles' [NTC; CEV, GW, NCV, NLT]. This noun denotes a deed manifesting great power, with the implication of some supernatural force [LN].

QUESTION—Is this rejection at home the same incident as reported in Luke 4:16–31?

1. It is the same incident [BECNT, BNTC, ICC, Lns, NAC, NIBC, NICNT, NTC, PNTC, TH]. It may be the same incident, but that is not certain [EBC].
2. It is not the same incident; what is reported in Luke 4:16–36 is referred to in Matthew 4:12–13 [My].

QUESTION—What was the nature of their amazement?

They were astonished and perplexed, but also skeptical [BECNT]; their amazement gave way to skepticism [NICNT], and even produced skepticism [WBC]. They were amazed in part because they knew that his upbringing did not include training as a rabbi [My, NAC]. They were amazed and astounded at his teaching and the miracles they knew about, but also at the fact that he was just a local person from their own town [BNTC].

QUESTION—What may be implied by the use of τούτῳ 'this man'?

It is used to express contempt [Lns, My, NIBC, PNTC]. Its use here shows their skepticism [WBC].

13:55 Is not this the son of-the carpenter[a]? Is not his mother called Mary and his brothers James and Joseph and Simon and Judas? **13:56** And are-not- all his sisters –here with us? So where (does he get)[b] all these things?"

LEXICON—a. τέκτων (LN 45.9) (BAGD p. 809): 'carpenter' [BAGD, BNTC, CC, **LN**, NICNT, NIGTC, NTC, PNTC, WBC; all versions], 'builder' [BAGD, BECNT, LN], 'woodworker' [BAGD]. This noun denotes one who uses various materials (wood, stone, and metal) in building. There is every reason to believe that in biblical times one who was regarded as a τέκτων would be skilled in the use of wood and stone and possibly even metal [LN].

b. There is no lexical entry for this implied phrase. It is represented in translation as 'did he get?' [BECNT, NTC; NET, TEV], 'did this fellow get?' [NIGTC], 'does this man get' [BNTC; ESV, NASB, NCV], 'does he get' [REB], 'did this man get?' [PNTC; GW, NIV, NRSV], 'does this man have?' [CC], 'hath this man?' [KJV], 'has this man gotten?' [NICNT], 'did (these things) come?' [WBC], 'did he learn?' [NLT], 'can he do?' [CEV].

MATTHEW 13:55-56 513

QUESTION—What skill or trade is described by the term ὁ τέκτων 'the carpenter'?

It could be used of any craftsman [ICC, NIGTC, PNTC], but usually denotes someone who works in wood, a carpenter [Lns, My, PNTC]. Here we should understand it to mean 'carpenter' [ICC, Lns, NIGTC, PNTC]. It can mean 'carpenter' [EBC, ICC], or 'builder' [BECNT, EBC, ICC, NICNT, WBC], which would mean someone who constructed homes of mud brick [EBC]. He worked in wood, making things such as furniture, doors, or roofing beams [NIGTC]. The noun that most translate as 'carpenter' could refer to a mason who builds with stone [BECNT, NAC, NIBC, NIGTC, TH].

QUESTION—What does 'all' imply about the number of sisters Jesus had?

It implies that there were at least three sisters [BNTC, Lns, My].

QUESTION—What is meant by the question, 'Where does he get all these things'?

This asks about the source of his authority or power [BECNT, EBC, NIBC, PNTC, TH, WBC], possibly in view of the fact that he was not trained as a rabbi [BECNT, NAC]. In their eyes he was no better than anyone else from that village [PNTC]. They did not see that his wisdom and power came from God [BNTC, Lns]. His origins were not from a sufficiently high level of society to warrant such fame and prestige [NIGTC].

13:57 And they-were-taking-offense[a] in him. But Jesus said to-them, "A-prophet is not without-honor[b] except in (his) hometown and in his household.[c]" **13:58** And he-did- not -do many miracles there because-of their unbelief.[d]

  LEXICON—a. imperf. pass. indic. of σκανδαλίζομαι (LN 31.77) (BAGD 1.b. p. 752): 'to take offense at, to be repelled by' [BAGD], 'to cease believing, to give up believing' [LN]. The phrase 'they were taking offence in him' is translated 'they took offense at him' [BECNT, BNTC, NICNT, NIGTC, NTC, PNTC; ESV, GW, NASB, NET, NIV, NRSV], 'they were offended in him' [KJV], 'they turned against him' [REB], 'they rejected him' [TEV], 'the people were upset with Jesus' [NCV], 'the people were very unhappy because of what he was doing' [CEV], 'they were deeply offended and refused to believe in him' [NLT], 'they were scandalized by him' [WBC], 'they began to be caused to stumble because of him' [CC]. This is a figurative extension of the verb 'to fall into a trap,' and means to give up believing what is right and let oneself believe what is false [LN].
  b. ἄτιμος (LN 87.72) (BAGD 1. p. 120): 'without honor' [BECNT, NICNT, NIGTC, NTC, PNTC, WBC; ESV, KJV, NASB, NET, NIV, NRSV], 'isn't honored' [GW], 'lacking in honor' [LN], 'lack honor' [BNTC; REB], 'dishonored' [BAGD, CC, LN]. The litotes οὐκ ἔστιν...ἄτιμος εἰ μή 'is not without honor except' is translated 'is honored everywhere except' [BAGD; NCV, NLT], 'is honored by everyone, except' [CEV], 'is

respected everywhere except' [TEV]. This adjective describes being of low status on the basis of not having honor or respect [LN].

c. οἰκία (LN 10.8) (BAGD 2. p. 557): 'household' [BAGD, BECNT, LN, NICNT, PNTC; ESV, NASB], 'house' [CC, NIGTC, WBC; GW, KJV, NET, NIV, NRSV], 'home' [BNTC; NCV], 'family' [BAGD, LN, NTC; CEV, NLT, REB, TEV]. This noun denotes the family consisting of those related by blood and marriage, as well as slaves and servants, living in the same house or homestead [LN].

d. ἀπιστία (LN 31.105) (BAGD 2.a. p. 85): 'unbelief' [BAGD, BECNT, BNTC, CC, NICNT, NIGTC, NTC, WBC; ESV, KJV, NASB, NET, NLT, NRSV], 'lack of faith' [PNTC; GW, NIV], 'want of faith' [REB], 'lack of belief' [BAGD], 'not believing' [LN]. This noun is translated as a phrase: 'the people did not have any faith' [CEV], 'they had no faith' [NCV], 'they did not have faith' [TEV]. This noun and the cognate verb describe not believing in the good news about Jesus Christ and hence not becoming a follower [LN].

QUESTION—Why did Jesus not do many miracles?

He did few miracles because few people would come to him for healing [NTC]. Jesus chose not to do miracles just to please skeptics or impress people [BECNT, NAC]. Although Jesus sometimes actually did do miracles where faith was lacking, in this instance if he had done miracles in the face of such rejection he would be turning his mission into a sideshow [EBC]. Their unbelief shut the door to blessings they might otherwise have been granted [BNTC]. He was unwilling to perform miracles to counteract unbelief on their part [CC, ICC, My, NIGTC, WBC].

DISCOURSE UNIT—14:1–12 [ICC, PNTC; CEV, ESV, GW, NASB, NCV, NET, NIV, NLT, NRSV, REB, TEV]. The topic is recalling John's death [GW], how John the Baptist was killed [NCV], the death of John the Baptist [ICC, PNTC; CEV, ESV, NET, NLT, NRSV, REB, TEV], John the Baptist beheaded [NASB, NIV].

14:1 At that time Herod the tetrarch[a] heard the report[b] (about) Jesus, **14:2** and said to his servants,[c] "This is John the Baptist; he rose from those-dead and because of-this (these) miraculous-powers[d] are-at-work in him.

LEXICON—a. τετραάρχης (LN **37.78**) (BAGD p. 814): 'tetrarch' [BAGD, BECNT, BNTC, CC, **LN**, NICNT, NIGTC, NTC, PNTC, WBC; ESV, KJV, NASB, NET, NIV, REB], 'ruler' [CEV, NRSV], 'ruler of Galilee' [GW, NCV, NLT, TEV], 'governor of a region' [LN]. This noun denotes a ruler with rank and authority lower than that of a king and one who ruled only with the approval of Roman authorities [LN].

b. ἀκοή (LN 33.213) (BAGD 2.a. p. 31): 'report' [BAGD, CC, LN, PNTC; NCV, NET, NIV, NRSV, REB], 'news' [BECNT, LN, NTC; CEV, GW, NASB], 'fame' [BAGD, BNTC, NIGTC, WBC; ESV, KJV], 'what people

were saying' [NICNT], 'information' [LN], 'about' [NLT, TEV]. This noun denotes the content of the news which is heard [LN].
c. παῖς (LN 87.77) (BAGD 1.a.γ. p. 64): 'servant' [BAGD, CC, NICNT, NIGTC, NTC, PNTC, WBC; ESV, KJV, NASB, NCV, NET, NRSV], 'attendant' [BAGD, BECNT, BNTC; NIV, REB], 'official' [CEV, GW, TEV], 'adviser' [NLT], 'courtier' [BAGD], 'slave' [BAGD, LN]. This noun denotes a slave, possibly serving as a personal servant and thus with the implication of kindly regard [LN].
d. δύναμις (LN 76.7, 12.44) (BAGD 1. p. 207): 'miracle, mighty deed' [LN (76.7)], 'power' [BAGD, LN (12.44)]. The phrase 'these miraculous powers are at work in him' [NTC; ESV, NASB, NET, REB; similarly BECNT, PNTC; NIV] is also translated 'these powers are at work in him' [BNTC, NICNT, NIGTC; NRSV; similarly CC, WBC], 'mighty works do show forth themselves in him' [KJV], 'he has the power to work/perform these miracles' [CEV; GW; similarly TEV], 'he can work these miracles' [NCV], 'he can do such miracles' [NLT]. This noun denotes a deed manifesting great power, with the implication of some supernatural force [LN (76.7)], or it can denote a supernatural power having some particular role in controlling the destiny and activities of human beings [LN (12.44)].

QUESTION—To what particular point in time does 'at that time' refer?
It is used for transition and does not reference any particular point in time [WBC]. It should not be tied to the section immediately preceding this [EBC, NAC]. It refers generally to the period of opposition in Jesus' ministry described in the two previous chapters [Lns]. It connects this passage loosely with the topic of the wrong understanding the people of Nazareth had about Jesus by adding the wrong understanding Herod had [NAC]. It gives a thematic link to the question asked previously by the people of Nazareth concerning where he got these powers [NIGTC]. It connects the account of John's death with the account of Jesus' rejection at Nazareth, though it does not indicate an exact time [TH].

QUESTION—Who is the Herod in this passage?
This is Herod Antipas who ruled in Galilee and Perea. He was a son of Herod the Great (of the birth narrative) [CC, EBC, ICC, NAC, NICNT, NIGTC, PNTC, TRT, WBC]. He ruled from about 4 BC to about AD 39 [CC, ICC, NAC, NICNT, PNTC, TH].

QUESTION—What is the difference between a tetrarch and a king?
The term 'tetrarch' was originally used to denote the ruler of one fourth of a kingdom [BECNT, ICC, NIBC, NIGTC, NTC, PNTC, TH, WBC], though the term could be used for other petty rulers as well [ICC, NIGTC, NTC, PNTC]. A tetrarch was below an ethnarch, which in turn was below a king [NTC, PNTC]. Herod Antipas had been appointed to rule one fourth of the kingdom of Herod the Great [BECNT]. Although Herod Antipas was not actually a king, that term was used popularly [EBC], and people sometimes may have used the term 'king' more generally to refer to their rulers, as is

done in verse 9 [PNTC, WBC]. The term 'king' was used as a courtesy to Herod Antipas [ICC, Lns], but also by some for the sake of flattery [NICNT, PNTC].

14:3 **For Herod having-arrested John bound him and put- (him) -away^a in prison because-of^b Herodias the wife of-Philip his brother; 14:4 For John was-saying to-him, "It-is- not -lawful for-you to-have^c her."**

LEXICON—a. aorist mid. indic. of ἀποτίθημι (LN 85.44) (BAGD 2. p. 101): 'to put away' [CC, LN, NICNT, NTC], 'to put' [BECNT, BNTC, **LN**, NIGTC, PNTC, WBC; all versions except NLT, REB], 'to throw (into)' [REB], 'to put out of the way, to remove' [LN]. The phrase ἐν φυλακῇ ἀπέθετο 'put him away in prison' is translated 'imprisoned' [NLT]. This verb means to put or take something away from its normal location; the semantic element of 'out of the way' is implied in the activity of 'putting in prison' [LN].

    b. διά with the accusative (LN 90.44): 'because of' [BECNT, BNTC, LN, NIGTC, PNTC, WBC; NASB, NCV, NIV, TEV], 'on account of' [CC, LN, NICNT, NTC; NET, NRSV], 'for the sake of' [ESV, KJV], 'for' [GW], 'as a favor to' [NLT], not explicit [CEV]. This preposition indicates a participant constituting the cause or reason for an event or state [LN].

    c. pres. act. infin. of ἔχω (LN 57.1) (BAGD I.2.b.α. p. 332): 'to have' [BECNT, BNTC, CC, LN, NIGTC, NTC, PNTC, WBC; ESV, KJV, NASB, NET, NIV, NRSV], 'to take' [CEV], 'to marry' [NLT], 'to be married to' [GW, NCV, TEV], 'to have as one's own' [BAGD], 'to possess' [BAGD, LN]. The phrase 'it is not lawful for you to have her' is translated 'you have no right to her' [REB]. This verb means to have or possess objects or property [LN].

QUESTION—Who was Herodias?

Herodias had been the wife of Herod Philip, the half-brother of Herod Antipas, and she was the daughter of Aristobulus, the half-brother of Philip and Antipas, which means that Philip and Antipas were her uncles [EBC, NTC, PNTC]. Aristobulus, Philip, and Antipas were sons of Herod the Great, and Herodias was his granddaughter [PNTC].

QUESTION—What is implied by the use of the imperfect tense of the verb 'saying'?

It indicates that John said it more than once [BECNT, EBC, Lns, NIBC, NICNT, PNTC, TH]. He was repeatedly saying this [CC, NICNT, NTC, TH, WBC]. John's criticism of Herod would have been public [NICNT].

QUESTION—What was unlawful about this relationship?

In Jewish law it was forbidden to marry a brother's wife while the brother was still living [BECNT, CC, EBC, ICC, NIBC, NICNT, NIGTC, NTC, PNTC, TH, TRT, WBC]. It may not have even come to the point of marriage yet and John was warning that such a marriage, if it were to occur, would be forbidden [NIBC]. The relationship was adulterous [BNTC, Lns, NTC]. Two marriages were being violated, that of Herod Antipas to his own wife and that of Herodias to Antipas' brother Philip [BNTC, NICNT]. In addition to being a forbidden union, the new union was not actually a marriage, it was no more than adultery [Lns]. As a woman, Herodias was not permitted under Jewish law to divorce her husband, so she may have appealed to Roman law to do that, which would not have been acceptable to many Jews [NICNT].

14:5 And wanting[a] to-kill him he-feared the people,[b] because they-regarded[c] him as a-prophet.

LEXICON—a. pres. act. participle of θέλω (LN 25.1): 'to want, to desire, to wish' [LN] The participial phrase 'wanting to kill him' is translated 'Herod/he wanted to kill him/John, but' [NICNT, NIGTC, PNTC; CEV, NCV, NIV, NLT, TEV], 'Herod would have liked to put him to death, but...' [REB], 'So Herod wanted to kill John. However...' [GW], 'although Herod wanted to kill John' [NET], 'although he/Herod wanted to put him to death' [ESV, NASB, NRSV], 'although Herod wanted to execute him' [BECNT], 'although he wanted to kill him' [BNTC, NTC], 'although he wanted to have him killed' [WBC], 'although he was wanting to kill him' [CC], 'when he would have put him to death' [KJV]. This verb means to desire to have or experience something [LN].

b. ὄχλος (LN 87.64) (BAGD 2. p. 601): '(the) people' [BAGD, BNTC, NTC, PNTC; CEV, ESV, GW, NCV, NIV, REB], '(the) Jewish people' [TEV], 'crowd' [BECNT, CC, NICNT, NIGTC, WBC; NASB, NET, NRSV], 'multitude' [KJV], 'common people, rabble' [BAGD, LN]. The phrase 'he feared the people' is translated 'he was afraid of a riot, because all the people believed...' [REB]. This noun denotes the common people, in contrast with those who are rich, leaders, and/or authorities in the society, often with the implication of disdain and low esteem [LN].

c. imperf. act. indic. of ἔχω (LN 31.1) (BAGD I.5. p. 333): 'to regard' [BECNT, BNTC, LN, NICNT, WBC; NASB, NRSV], 'to consider' [BAGD, **LN**, NIGTC; NIV, TEV], 'to hold (someone) as/to-be' [CC, NTC, PNTC; ESV], 'to hold a view' [LN], 'to think' [CEV, GW], 'to believe (to be)' [NCV, NLT], 'to count as' [KJV], 'to accept as' [NET], 'to look upon' [BAGD]. The phrase 'they regarded him as a prophet' is translated 'in whose eyes John was a prophet' [REB]. This verb means to hold a view or have an opinion with regard to something [LN].

14:6 Now at-(the)-birthday-celebration[a] of-Herod it-happened-that the daughter of Herodias danced[b] in (their) midst[c] and it-pleased[d] Herod, **14:7** so he-promised with an-oath[e] to-give to-her whatever she-would-ask-for.

LEXICON—a. γενέσια (LN **51.12**) (BAGD p. 154): 'birthday celebration' [BAGD, BNTC, **LN**, NICNT; REB], 'birthday' [BECNT, CC, NIGTC, NTC, PNTC, WBC; all versions except NLT, REB], 'birthday party' [NLT], 'birthday festival' [LN]. This noun denotes a celebration or a festivity marking the anniversary of someone's birth [LN].

b. aorist mid. (deponent = act.) indic. of ὀρχέομαι (LN 15.244) (BAGD p. 583): 'to dance' [BAGD, LN; all translations]. This verb describes a patterned rhythmic movements of the whole and/or parts of the body, normally to the accompaniment of music [LN].

c. μέσος (LN **83.10**) (BAGD 2. p. 507): 'in the midst' [LN], 'among' [BAGD], 'before' [BAGD], 'in the middle' [**LN**]. The phrase ἐν τῷ μέσῳ 'in the midst' [BNTC, CC] is translated 'in their midst' [NIGTC], 'before them' [BECNT, NTC, PNTC; KJV, NASB, NET], 'before the company' [ESV, NRSV], 'before the guests' [REB], 'among the guests' [NICNT, WBC], 'for them' [NIV], 'for the guests' [CEV, GW], 'for Herod and his guests' [NCV], 'in front of the whole group' [TEV]. This pronominal adjective denotes a position in the middle of an area [LN].

d. aorist act. indic. of ἀρέσκω (LN 25.90) (BAGD 2.a. p. 105): 'to please' [BAGD, LN], 'to be pleasing to' [BAGD]. This verb is translated with the dancer as the stated or implied subject: '(she) pleased Herod/him' [BECNT, BNTC, CC, NICNT, NIGTC, PNTC, WBC; CEV, ESV, KJV, NASB, NCV, NET, NIV, NRSV], 'she fascinated Herod' [NTC]. It is translated with the dance itself as the subject: 'a dance that greatly pleased Herod' [NLT]. It is translated passively with Herod as the subject: 'Herod was so pleased' [TEV], 'Herod was delighted' [GW, REB]. This verb means to cause someone to be pleased with someone or something [LN].

e. ὅρκος (LN **33.463**) (BAGD p. 581): 'oath' [BAGD, BECNT, BNTC, CC, LN, NICNT, NIGTC, PNTC, WBC; ESV, KJV, NASB, NCV, NET, NIV, NRSV, REB], 'vow' [NLT]. The phrase 'promised with an oath' is translated 'promised by swearing' [**LN**], 'promised her, "I swear"' [TEV], 'he swore' [CEV, GW]. This noun denotes the action of affirming the truth of a statement by calling on a divine being to execute sanctions against a person if the statement in question is not true [LN].

QUESTION—Who was this girl who danced?

This was Salome, daughter of Herodias and Herod Philip [EBC, ICC, Lns, NAC, NTC, TH, WBC]. Salome would later marry her own half-uncle, Philip the tetrarch, thus becoming her mother's sister-in-law and aunt [NTC].

QUESTION—What kind of dance was this?

Although nothing sensuous is implied in the use of the word ὀρχέομαι, judging from the reputation for immorality among the Herods the dance could well have been sensual [EBC, NAC]. It was probably immodest and provocative [BNTC, CC, My, NIBC, NTC, PNTC]. The dance was thoroughly pagan, probably learned while the girl was living in Rome [Lns]. The entire atmosphere of the party was one of debauchery [NICNT]. Such dancing at a party like this would normally have been done by a prostitute [TRT]. The dancing may or may not have been erotic [NIGTC].

14:8 And she having-been-prompted[a] by her mother said, "Give to-me here on a-platter[b] the head of John the Baptist."

LEXICON—a. aorist pass. participle of προβιβάζω (LN **33.299**) (BAGD p. 703): 'to be prompted' [BECNT, PNTC; ESV, NASB, NIV, NRSV, REB], 'to be urged' [**LN**; GW], 'to be urged on' [BNTC, NTC], 'to be put forward' [BAGD, CC, **LN**, WBC], 'to be put up to (something)' [NICNT], 'to be directed' [NIGTC], 'to be instructed' [NET], 'to be instructed before' [KJV]. The phrase προβιβασθεῖσα ὑπὸ τῆς μητρὸς αὐτῆς 'having been prompted by her mother' is translated 'at her mother's urging' [NLT], 'at her mother's suggestion' [TEV], 'the girls' mother told her to say' [CEV], 'Herodias told her daughter what to ask for' [NCV]. This verb means to speak in such a way as to encourage a particular type of behavior or action [LN].

b. πίναξ (LN **6.134**) (BAGD p. 658): 'platter' [BAGD, BECNT, BNTC, CC, LN, NIGTC, NTC, WBC; CEV, ESV, GW, NASB, NCV, NET, NIV, NRSV], 'plate' [**LN**, PNTC; TEV], 'dish' [BAGD, NICNT; REB], 'tray' [NLT], 'charger' [KJV]. This noun denotes a relatively flat, large dish [LN].

QUESTION—What kind of dish was a πίναξ 'platter'?

It would have been a flat, wooden platter [NIBC]. It would have been something flat like a pine board, and thus a flat plate of some kind [Lns, NTC, PNTC, TH].

14:9 And the king being-distressed[a] because of the oaths and the dinner-guests[b] ordered (that) it-be-given, **14:10** and having-sent[c] beheaded John in the prison. **14:11** And his head was-brought on a-platter and was-given to-the girl,[d] and she-took (it) to- her -mother.

LEXICON—a. aorist pass. participle λυπέομαι (LN 25.274) (BAGD 2.a. p. 481): 'to be distressed' [BAGD, BNTC, LN, NIGTC, NTC, WBC; NIV, REB], 'to be grieved' [BECNT, CC, NTC; NASB, NET, NRSV], 'to be sad' [BAGD, LN; TEV], 'to be very sad' [NCV], 'to regret' [GW], 'to be sorry' [CEV, ESV, KJV], 'to become sorrowful' [BAGD]. It is translated as an adverb: 'reluctantly' [NICNT]. This passive verb is translated as active: 'the king regretted (what he had said)' [NLT]. It means to be sad as the result of what has happened or what one has done [LN].

b. pres. mid. or pass. (deponent = act.) participle of συνανάκειμαι (LN 34.10) (BAGD p. 784): 'to recline at table with, to eat with' [BAGD], 'to eat together, to associate in a meal' [LN]. The phrase τοὺς συνανακειμένους (literally 'the (ones) reclining at table with') is translated 'the dinner guests' [BAGD, BECNT, BNTC, NTC; NASB, NCV, NET, NIV], 'the guests' [PNTC; CEV, ESV, GW, NLT, NRSV, REB, TEV], 'those who were reclining with him' [CC], 'those reclining at dinner with him' [NIGTC], 'those reclining at the meal with him' [WBC],

'those who were feasting with him' [NICNT], 'them which sat with him at meat' [KJV]. This verb means to be associated with others in eating [LN].
  c. aorist act. participle of πέμπω (LN 15.66) (BAGD 1. p. 642): 'to send' [BAGD, LN]. The phrase πέμψας ἀπεκεφάλισεν τὸν Ἰωάννην 'having sent he beheaded John' is translated 'he sent, and beheaded John' [BNTC, CC, WBC; KJV], 'he sent and had John beheaded' [BECNT, NICNT, NIGTC, PNTC; ESV, NASB, NRSV; similarly NET], 'he had John's head cut off in prison' [GW], 'had John beheaded' [NIV, REB], 'so he had John beheaded' [NTC; TEV], 'so John was beheaded' [NLT], 'he sent soldiers to the prison to cut off John's head' [NCV], '(he ordered a guard) to go to the prison and cut off John's head' [CEV]. This verb means to cause someone to depart for a particular purpose [LN].
  d. κοράσιον (LN **9.40**) (BAGD p. 444): 'girl' [BAGD, BECNT, BNTC, **LN**, NICNT, NIGTC, NTC, PNTC, WBC; all versions except KJV], 'young girl' [CC], 'damsel' [KJV]. This noun denotes a girl about the age of puberty. It is impossible to determine the age of Herodias' daughter, but in view of her role as an attractive dancer, she was probably of the age of puberty [LN].
QUESTION—Why is the word 'oaths' plural here, but singular in verse 7?
  It is plural because Herod probably repeated what he said for emphasis [Lns, My, PNTC]. It refers to the one oath Herod had made [BECNT, EBC, WBC; GW, KJV, NCV, NET, NLT, REB, TEV].
QUESTION—Does the phrase 'because of his oaths and his dinner guests' indicate why the king gave the order for John's execution or why the king was distressed?
  1. He gave the order because of his oaths and guests [BECNT, BNTC, CC, ICC, Lns, My, NIBC, NICNT, NIGTC, NTC, PNTC, TRT; all versions]: the king was distressed, but because of his oaths and the dinner guests he gave the order.
  2. He was distressed because of his oaths before his dinner guests [EBC, WBC]: the king, distressed because of his oaths and the dinner guests, gave the order.
QUESTION—What does the term κοράσιον 'girl' indicate about the age of this girl?
  It indicates that she was about the age of puberty [LN], about twelve years old [NAC, PNTC, WBC], or older than twelve [Lns], between twelve and fourteen years [ICC, NICNT]. Salome would have been eighteen to twenty years old at this time [TH].

14:12 And having-gone his disciples took[a] the body[b] and buried it and having-come they-told[c] Jesus.
LEXICON—a. aorist act. indic. of αἴρω (LN 15.203) (BAGD 3. p. 24): 'to take' [CC, NICNT, NIGTC, PNTC, WBC; CEV, ESV, NET, NIV, NRSV], 'to take away' [BECNT, LN, NTC; NASB, REB], 'to take up' [KJV], 'to carry away' [BAGD, BNTC, LN; TEV], 'to get' [NCV], 'to remove'

[BAGD, LN], 'to carry off' [LN], not explicit [GW, NLT]. This verb means to lift up and carry (away) [LN].
   b. πτῶμα (LN 8.7) (BAGD p. 728): 'body' [BECNT, BNTC, NICNT, NTC, PNTC, WBC; all versions], 'dead body' [BAGD, LN], 'corpse' [BAGD, CC, LN, NIGTC]. This noun denotes a dead body, whether of an animal or a human being [LN].
   c. aorist. act. indic. of ἀπαγγέλλω (LN 33.198) (BAGD 1. p. 79): 'to tell' [BAGD, BNTC, LN, NICNT, NIGTC, PNTC; all versions except NASB], 'to bring a report' [BECNT], 'to report' [BAGD, NTC, WBC; NASB], 'to inform' [LN], 'to announce' [BAGD, CC]. This verb means to announce or inform, with possible focus upon the source of information [LN].

DISCOURSE UNIT—14:13–16:12 [REB]. The topic is more miracles and teaching.

DISCOURSE UNIT—14:13–36 [NICNT, PNTC]. The topic is miracles around the lake [NICNT], some miracles of Jesus [PNTC].

DISCOURSE UNIT—14:13–21 [ICC; CEV, ESV, GW, NASB, NCV, NET, NIV, NLT, NRSV, TEV]. The topic is Jesus feeds more than five thousand [GW], more than five thousand fed [NCV], Jesus feeds five thousand men [TEV], Jesus feeds the five thousand [ESV, NIV], Jesus feeds five thousand [CEV, NLT], the feeding of the five thousand [ICC; NET], feeding the five thousand [NRSV], five thousand fed [NASB].

14:13 And having-heard^a Jesus withdrew^b from-there in a-boat to a-desolate^c place privately;^d and the crowd having-heard followed him on-foot^e from the cities.

LEXICON—a. aorist act. participle of ἀκούω (LN 33.212) (BAGD 3.a. p. 32): 'to hear' [LN; all translations], 'to receive news' [LN], 'to learn' [BAGD], 'to be informed about' [BAGD]. The temporal relationship indicated by the aorist participle is translated 'when Jesus/he heard' [BECNT, BNTC, CC, NICNT, NIGTC, PNTC, WBC; all versions except CEV, NLT], 'upon hearing' [NTC], 'as soon as Jesus heard' [NLT], 'after he heard' [CEV]. This verb means to receive information about something, normally by word of mouth [LN].
   b. aorist act. indic. of ἀναχωρέω (LN **15.53**) (BAGD 2.b. p. 63): 'to withdraw' [BAGD, BECNT, CC, LN, NICNT, NIGTC, NTC; ESV, NASB, NIV, NRSV, REB], 'to leave' [NCV, NLT, TEV], 'to depart' [KJV], 'to depart privately' [BNTC], 'to go off' [LN], 'to go away' [LN, NTC, WBC; NET], 'to take refuge' [BAGD]. This verb is translated by a phrase: 'he crossed Lake Galilee to go to some place' [CEV], 'he left and went to a place' [GW]. This verb means to move away from a location, implying a considerable distance [LN].
   c. ἔρημος (LN **1.86**) (BAGD 1.a. p. 309): 'desolate' [BAGD; ESV], 'isolated' [BECNT; NET], 'solitary' [NIV], 'remote' [NLT, REB], 'secluded' [NASB], 'lonely' [**LN**, NTC; NCV, TEV], 'deserted' [CC,

PNTC, WBC; NRSV], 'uninhabited' [NICNT], 'desert' [LN; KJV], 'wilderness' [LN, NIGTC], 'abandoned, empty' [BAGD], not explicit [CEV, GW]. This adjective describes a largely uninhabited region, normally with sparse vegetation (in contrast with πόλις 'a population center') [LN].
d. κατ' ἰδίαν (LN 28.67) (BAGD 4. p. 370): 'privately' [BAGD, BNTC, CC, LN, NTC, PNTC, WBC; NET, NIV, REB], 'by himself' [BAGD, BECNT; ESV, NASB, NCV, NRSV, TEV], 'alone' [NIGTC], 'to be alone' [NICNT; NLT], 'where he could be alone' [CEV, GW], 'apart' [KJV]. The idiom κατ' ἰδίαν (literally 'according to that which is private') describes what occurs in a private context or setting, in the sense of not being made known publicly [LN].
e. πεζῇ (LN **8.50**) (BAGD p. 638): 'on foot' [BECNT, BNTC, **LN**, NICNT, NIGTC, NTC, PNTC, WBC; all versions except TEV], 'by land' [BAGD, CC, **LN**; TEV]. This adverb describes travel by foot overland [LN].

QUESTION—What did Jesus hear that prompted him to withdraw?
1. He heard of what had happened to John [BNTC, ICC, Lns, My, NICNT, TH, TRT, WBC; CEV, NASB, NCV, NIV, NLT, REB, TEV; probably KJV, NRSV]. Jesus retreated in order to pray, with the death of John possibly prompting him to think more about his own upcoming passion, but he was not fleeing from Herod [WBC].
2. Jesus retreated when he learned of Herod's response to his preaching and miracles referred to in verses 1–2 (verses 3–12 constitute an excursus or flashback to explain what happened to John) [CC, EBC, NAC, NIBC, PNTC]. The γάρ 'for' in verse 3 introduces an excursus from the topic in verses 1–2, and the δέ 'and' here in verse 13 brings the excursus to a close; that is, when Jesus learned what Herod was thinking about Jesus' ministry, which is described in verses 1–2, he withdrew [EBC]. Jesus heard about Herod's fear that Jesus was actually John the Baptist returned from the dead [CC, NIBC].

QUESTION—Does κατ' ἰδίαν 'privately' imply that Jesus was alone, or were his disciples also with him?
His disciples were with him [BECNT, CC, EBC, Lns, NICNT, NTC, PNTC, TH, TRT]. He was trying to get away from the crowds to be alone with his disciples [NTC]. A boat would have required a crew, so Jesus could not have traveled by boat alone [NICNT]. Another view is that only Jesus went there by boat while his disciples traveled by land to join him there [WBC].

14:14 And having-gone-out[a] he-saw a- great -crowd and he-had-compassion[b] on them and healed[c] their sick.[d]
LEXICON—a. aorist act. participle of ἐξέρχομαι (LN 15.40) (BAGD 1.a.β. p. 274): 'to go out' [LN, NICNT], 'to get out of (a boat)' [BAGD, NIGTC; CEV, GW, NET, TEV], 'to step from a boat' [NLT], 'to disembark' [BAGD, BNTC, WBC], 'to come ashore' [PNTC; REB], 'to go ashore' [BECNT; ESV, NASB, NRSV], 'to land' [NIV], 'to arrive'

[NCV], 'to come out' [CC, NTC], 'to go forth' [KJV], 'to depart out of, to leave from within' [LN]. This verb means to move out of an enclosed or well defined two or three-dimensional area [LN].
   b. aorist pass. σπλαγχνίζομαι (deponent = act.) of (LN 25.49) (BAGD p. 762): 'to have compassion' [CC, NIGTC, PNTC; ESV, NET, NIV, NLT, NRSV], 'to feel compassion' [BECNT, LN; NASB], 'to be moved with compassion' [NTC, WBC; KJV], 'to have pity' [BAGD], 'to feel sorry for' [CEV, GW, NCV], 'to feel sympathy' [BAGD, BNTC], 'to have great affection for' [LN]. The phrase ἐσπλαγχνίσθη ἐπ' αὐτοῖς 'he had compassion on them' is translated 'his heart went out to them' [NICNT; REB], 'his heart was filled with pity' [TEV]. This verb means to experience great affection and compassion for someone [LN].
   c. aorist act. indic. of θεραπεύω (LN 23.139): 'to heal' [LN; all translations except GW, NRSV], 'to cure' [LN; GW, NRSV]. This verb means to cause someone to recover health, often with the implication of having taken care of such a person [LN].
   d. ἄρρωστος (LN **23.147**) (BAGD p. 109): 'sick' [BAGD, BECNT, BNTC, CC, **LN**, NIGTC, NTC, PNTC, WBC; all versions], 'ill' [BAGD, LN, NICNT]. This adjective describes being sick or ill, as a state of powerlessness [LN].

QUESTION—Does the participle ἐξελθών 'having gone out' refer to Jesus getting out of the boat, or leaving the privacy of the place to which he had retreated?
   1. The participle refers to his getting out of the boat; the crowds had arrived first [BECNT, BNTC, EBC, ICC, NIBC, NIGTC, PNTC, TH, TRT, WBC; CEV, ESV, GW, NASB, NCV, NET, NIV NLT, NRSV, REB, TEV].
   2. The participle refers to his leaving the place of retreat and seeing the crowds, who arrived after he did [Lns, My, NTC].

14:15 And evening[a] having-come the disciples came to him saying, "The place is deserted and the hour[b] has- already -passed; dismiss the crowds, so-that having-gone-out into the villages they-may-buy food for-themselves."

LEXICON—a. ὀψίας (LN 67.197) (BAGD 2. p. 601): 'evening' [BAGD, BECNT, BNTC, LN, NICNT, NTC, PNTC; all versions]. The phrase ὀψίας δὲ γενομένη 'evening having come' is translated 'when it had become/became late' [CC, NIGTC]. This noun denotes the period after sunset and before darkness [LN].
   b. ὥρα (LN 67.199) (BAGD 1. p. 896): 'hour' [LN], 'time of day' [BAGD]. The phrase ἡ ὥρα ἤδη παρῆλθεν 'the hour has already passed' [BNTC], is translated 'the hour has already passed away' [CC], 'the time for the evening meal has already passed' [NIGTC], 'the time is now past' [KJV], 'the time is already late' [BECNT, PNTC], 'the hour is now late' [NRSV], 'the hour is already late' [NASB, NET], 'it's already getting late' [NIV, NLT], 'it's getting late' [NICNT], 'it's already late' [CEV, GW, NCV], 'it

is already very late' [TEV], 'it is already late in the day' [NTC], 'the day is already gone' [WBC], 'the day has gone' [REB], 'the day is now over' [ESV]. This noun denotes the twelfth part of a day, measured from sunrise to sunset [LN].

QUESTION—What time of day was it at this point?

It was between three and six o'clock in the evening [My]. It was late afternoon [PNTC, TRT], sometime before sunset [NTC]. It was the end of the day [WBC], just before sunset [CC, Lns, TH]. It was already after time for the evening meal [Lns, NIBC]. The noun ὀψίας 'evening' could refer to any time from mid-afternoon until just after dark, but here it refers to the earlier period [EBC].

14:16 But Jesus said to-them, "They-have no need to-go-away, you give to-them (something) to-eat." **14:17** But they-said to-him, "We-do- not -have (anything) here except five loaves[a] and two fish.[b]" **14:18** But he-said, "Bring them here to me."

LEXICON—a. ἄρτος (LN **5.8**) (BAGD 1.a. p. 110): 'loaf' [BECNT, BNTC, CC, NICNT, PNTC, WBC; ESV, KJV, NASB, NET, NRSV, REB, TEV], 'loaf of bread' [BAGD, **LN**, NIGTC; CEV, GW, NCV, NIV, NLT], 'bread' [BAGD], 'bread-cake' [NTC]. This noun denotes a relatively small and generally round loaf of bread that is considerably smaller than present-day typical loaves of bread and thus more like 'rolls' or 'buns' [LN].

b. ἰχθύς (LN 4.59) (BAGD p. 384): 'fish' [BAGD, LN; all translations].

QUESTION—What may be inferred from the use of the pronoun ὑμεῖς 'you' in verse 16?

Since the pronoun is unnecessary, its presence indicates emphasis: *you* give them something [CC, EBC, ICC, NAC, NTC, PNTC, TH, WBC].

QUESTION—How large would these loaves have been?

1. Such a loaf would be about the size of a bun, and five of them would suffice for a meal for one person [PNTC].
2. Three loaves would have been enough for a meal for one person [TH], so five loaves might suffice for two people [TH, TRT].
3. One loaf would have been enough for a meal for one person [NICNT].
4. A normal sized loaf would have fed about three people [NAC]. It was about a half inch thick and the size of a plate in diameter [My].

14:19 And having-commanded the crowds to-recline[a] on the grass,[b] (and) having-taken the five loaves and the two fish, having-looked-up[c] to the heaven he-blessed[d] and having-broken[e] (them) he-gave the bread to the disciples, and the disciples (gave them) to-the crowds.

LEXICON—a. aorist pass. infin. of ἀνακλίνω (LN **17.24**) (BAGD 2. p. 56): 'to recline' [BAGD, BECNT, BNTC, CC, PNTC, WBC], 'to lie down' [BAGD], 'to sit' [NICNT], 'to sit down' [NTC; all versions], 'to be seated' [NIGTC], 'to cause to recline to eat' [LN], 'to have someone sit down to eat' [**LN**]. This verb means to cause someone to assume a

MATTHEW 14:19

reclining (or possibly sitting) position as part of the process of eating [LN].
- b. χόρτος (LN 3.15) (BAGD p. 884): 'grass' [BAGD, LN; all translations]. This noun denotes small green plants, and in NT contexts it refers primarily to green grass in a field or meadow [LN].
- c. aorist act. participle of ἀναβλέπω (LN 24.10) (BAGD 1. p. 50): 'to look up' [BAGD, LN; all translations except NCV], 'to look' [NCV]. This verb means to direct one's vision upward [LN].
- d. aorist act. indic. of εὐλογέω (LN 33.470, 33.356) (BAGD 1. p. 322): 'to bless' [BNTC, CC, LN (33.470), WBC; CEV, GW, KJV, NASB, NLT, NRSV], 'to pronounce the blessing' [BECNT], 'to say a/the blessing' [NICNT, NIGTC; ESV, REB], 'to give thanks' [NTC, PNTC; NET, NIV], 'to thank God' [NCV], 'to give thanks to God' [TEV], 'to give thanks and praise' [BAGD], 'to praise' [LN (33.356)]. This verb means to ask God to bestow divine favor on, with the implication that the verbal act itself constitutes a significant benefit [LN (33.470)]. It may also refer to the act of speaking of something in favorable terms [LN (33.356)].
- e. aorist act. participle of κλάω (LN **19.34**) (BAGD p. 433): 'to break' [BAGD, BECNT, BNTC, CC, **LN**, NICNT, NIGTC, NTC, PNTC; all versions except GW, NCV, NLT], 'to break into pieces' [WBC; NLT], 'to break apart' [GW], 'to divide' [NCV], 'to break bread' [LN]. This verb means to break an object into two or more parts, and in the NT it is used exclusively for breaking bread [LN].

QUESTION—What is suggested by the verb ἀνακλίνω 'recline'?

It suggests that they are at a banquet or feast [BNTC, NICNT, PNTC, WBC], one that perhaps anticipates the messianic banquet [NICNT, PNTC]. It is possible that this is to be seen as a celebratory meal or banquet [NIGTC]. Reclining would have been the normal position for a regular meal [TH, TRT].

QUESTION—What does the action of looking up signify?

It was the normal posture of prayer at meals for a head of household [EBC, ICC, Lns, My, NAC, NICNT, PNTC, WBC]. The actions of looking up, taking, blessing, breaking, and giving are normal actions at a Jewish meal, but these same verbs are repeated in the account of the Last Supper, suggesting a correlation [ICC, NICNT, NIGTC].

QUESTION—What is the implied object of εὐλόγησεν 'blessed' here?

1. God is the implied object; Jesus is blessing, thanking, or praising God for providing the food [BECNT, BNTC, CC, EBC, ICC, My, NAC, NIBC, NICNT, NIGTC, NTC, PNTC, TH, TRT, WBC; NCV, NET, NIV, TEV]. The traditional Jewish blessing for meals was 'Blessed are you O Lord our God, king of the universe, who brings forth food from the earth' [EBC, ICC, NAC, PNTC, WBC].
2. The food is the implied object; Jesus is blessing the food or asking a blessing on the food [CEV, GW, NASB, NLT, NRSV].

14:20 And all ate and were-satisfied,[a] and they-carried-away what-was-leftover[b] of-the fragments twelve baskets full.[c] **14:21** And those-eating were about five-thousand men apart-from[d] women and children.

LEXICON—a. aorist pass. indic. of χορτάζω (LN 23.16) (BAGD 2.a. p. 884): 'to be satisfied' [BECNT, CC, LN, NIGTC, PNTC; ESV, NASB, NCV, NET, NIV, REB], 'to be satisfied with food' [LN], 'to be filled' [BAGD, BNTC, NTC; KJV, NRSV], 'to be full' [WBC], 'to have enough' [TEV], 'to eat as much as one wants' [CEV, GW, NLT], 'to have as much as one wants' [NICNT], 'to be caused to eat one's fill' [BAGD, LN]. This verb means to cause to eat so as to become satisfied [LN].

b. pres. act. participle of περισσεύω (LN 57.24) (BAGD 1.a.α. p. 650): 'to be left over' [BAGD], 'to be more than enough' [BAGD], 'to have (much) more than enough, to have an overabundance' [LN]. This participle is translated as a verb phrase: 'that were left over' [BECNT; NIV], 'what was left over' [BNTC, NIGTC, NTC; NASB, NRSV, REB, TEV], 'that remained' [KJV], 'what remained over' [PNTC], 'left over' [ESV, NET]. It is also translated as a noun: 'leftovers' [NICNT; CEV, NLT], 'abundance' [WBC]; as an adjective: 'leftover (fragments/pieces)' [WBC; GW, NCV]. This verb means to have such an abundance as to be more than sufficient [LN].

c. πλήρης (LN 59.35) (BAGD 1.a.β. p. 669): 'full' [BAGD, BECNT, BNTC, CC, LN, NICNT, NIGTC, NTC, PNTC, WBC; ESV, KJV, NASB, NET, NRSV, TEV], 'filled' [BAGD], not explicit [CEV, NLT]. The phrase 'twelve baskets full' is translated '(they) filled twelve baskets' [GW, NCV], 'twelve baskets were filled' [REB], 'twelve basketfuls' [NIV]. This adjective describes a quantity of space as being completely occupied by something [LN].

d. χωρίς (LN 89.120) (BAGD 2.a.γ. p. 890): 'apart from' [BAGD, CC, LN, NICNT, PNTC], 'besides' [BECNT, BNTC, NIGTC; ESV, NASB, NIV, NRSV], 'beside' [KJV], 'not counting' [NTC, WBC; CEV, NCV, NET, REB, TEV], 'in addition to' [NLT], 'without' [BAGD, LN], 'not with, no relationship to, independent of' [LN]. This preposition is translated as a phrase: 'This number does not include' [GW]. This preposition indicates negatively linked elements [LN].

QUESTION—Is there any significance in Matthew's mention of the fact that there were twelve baskets of leftovers?

He may be intending an association with the twelve tribes of Israel [CC, EBC, NAC, WBC]. Jesus is in the process of forming a new Israel, and the twelve baskets may foreshadow the messianic banquet to come [NAC]. It is a sign of messianic provision and fulfillment, an indication that the Messiah is among them [WBC]. It may be intended to communicate the fact that the Messiah supplies enough to provide abundantly for Israel, as represented by the twelve disciples [CC, EBC]. The twelve baskets symbolize food for all Israel [NIGTC].

QUESTION—How many people were fed in all?
Counting women and children there could have been as many as fifteen to twenty thousand people [EBC, NAC]. It was well over five thousand [NICNT]. Since difficulty of travel and the terrain itself would have made it less likely that women and children could go to where Jesus was, probably the five thousand men made up the majority of the crowd [NIGTC, NTC].

DISCOURSE UNIT—14:22-36 [GW, NASB, NCV, NET, NIV, NLT]. The topic is Jesus walks on the sea [GW], Jesus walks on water [NASB, NCV, NLT], Jesus walks on the water [NIV], walking on water [NET].

DISCOURSE UNIT—14:22-33 [ICC; CEV, ESV, NRSV, TEV]. The topic is Jesus walks on the water [TEV], Jesus walks on water [CEV, ESV, NRSV], the Lord of the sea walks on the waves [ICC].

14:22 **And immediately^a he-compelled^b the disciples to-get-into^c the boat and to-go-ahead-of him to-the other-side, while^d he-would-dismiss^e the crowds.**

LEXICON—a. εὐθέως (LN 67.53): 'immediately' [BECNT, CC, LN, NICNT, NIGTC, NTC, PNTC, WBC; ESV, NASB, NCV, NET, NIV, NLT, NRSV], 'at once' [BNTC], 'right away' [LN; CEV], 'quickly' [GW], 'straightway' [KJV], 'as soon as they had finished' [REB], 'then' [LN; TEV]. This adverb indicates a point of time immediately subsequent to a previous point of time, the actual interval of time differing appreciably, depending upon the nature of the events and the manner in which the sequence is interpreted by the writer [LN].

b. aorist act. indic. of ἀναγκάζω (LN 37.33) (BAGD 2. p. 52): 'to compel' [BNTC, CC, LN], 'to urge' [BAGD, BECNT], 'to make (someone)' [NICNT, NIGTC, NTC, PNTC; all versions except KJV, NCV, NLT], 'to instruct' [WBC], 'to constrain' [KJV], 'to tell' [NCV], 'to insist' [NLT], 'to force' [LN]. This verb means to compel someone to act in a particular manner [LN].

c. aorist act. infin. of ἐμβαίνω (LN 15.95) (BAGD p. 254): 'to get into (a ship/boat)' [BAGD, BECNT, CC, LN, NICNT, NIGTC, NTC, WBC; all versions except REB], 'to embark' [BAGD, BNTC, LN, PNTC; REB]. This verb means to go into or onto, as in the case of a boat [LN].

d. ἕως (LN **67.139**) (BAGD II.1.b.g. p. 335): 'while' [BAGD, BECNT, BNTC, CC, **LN**, NICNT, NIGTC, WBC; all versions except CEV, NCV], 'until' [PNTC], 'till' [NTC], 'as long as' [LN]. The phrase 'while he would dismiss the crowds' is translated 'But he stayed until he had sent the crowds away' [CEV], 'He stayed there to send the people home' [NCV]. This preposition refers to an extent of time of the same length as another extent or unit of time [LN].

e. aorist act. subj. of ἀπολύω (LN **15.43**) (BAGD 2.b. p. 96): 'to dismiss' [BAGD, BNTC, CC, **LN**, NIGTC, WBC; ESV, NIV, NRSV, REB], 'to send away' [BAGD, BECNT, NICNT, NTC, PNTC; CEV, GW, KJV,

NASB, TEV], 'to send home' [NCV, NLT], 'to disperse' [NET], 'to let (people) leave' [**LN**], 'to let go away' [LN]. This verb means to cause (or permit) a person or persons to leave a particular location [LN].

QUESTION—What is implied by the use of the verb ἀναγκάζω 'compel'?

It suggests that the disciples did not want to leave [BNTC]. They wanted to stay with Jesus [My]. Jesus' reason for sending them away so urgently may have been related to what was reported in John 6:15 about people wanting to make him king by force [NAC]. Jesus may have sensed that the disciples would have liked to stay and share in the excitement present among the crowd [NIBC], including perhaps the political interests of those who wanted to make him king [NTC]. Jesus did not want his disciples to become involved in any messianic insurgency [EBC, Lns, PNTC, WBC] or to be infected with the unhealthy enthusiasm of some of the people [NICNT].

14:23 And having-dismissed the crowds he-went-up on the mountain by himself to pray. Evening having- (already) -come, he-was alone there. **14:24** And by-this-time the boat was-away-from the land many stadia,[a] being-buffeted[b] by the waves,[c] for the wind was contrary.[d]

TEXT—Manuscripts reading σταδίους πολλοὺς ἀπὸ τῆς γῆς ἀπεῖχεν 'was away from the land many stadia' are given a C rating by GNT to indicate that choosing it over a variant text that omit 'from the land' was difficult. However, all translations but KJV follow GNT. A variant reading is μέσον τῆς θαλάσσης ἦν 'was in the midst of the sea' is this is followed by only KJV.

LEXICON—a. στάδιος (LN **81.27**) (BAGD 1. p. 764): 'stade' [BAGD, BNTC, CC, LN]. The phrase σταδίους πολλούς 'many stadia' [NIGTC, NTC, PNTC] is translated 'a long way' [BECNT; CEV, ESV], 'a long distance' [WBC; NASB], 'quite a distance' [**LN**], 'a considerable distance' [NIV], 'some distance' [REB], 'hundreds of yards' [GW], 'miles' [NICNT], 'far from' [NCV, NET, NRSV], 'far away from' [NLT], 'far out' [TEV]. This noun denotes a measure of distance of about 600 feet or 185 meters [LN].

b. fut. pass. participle of βασανίζω (LN 38.13) (BAGD 3. p. 134): 'to be buffeted' [NICNT; NIV], 'to be battered' [BECNT, NIGTC, NTC; NASB, NRSV], 'to be beaten' [ESV], 'to be hit' [NCV], 'to be harassed' [BAGD, BNTC], 'to be tossed' [PNTC; KJV], 'to be tossed about/around' [WBC; CEV, TEV], 'to be thrown around' [GW], 'to take a beating' [NET], 'to be tormented' [CC, LN]. The phrase 'being buffeted by the waves' is translated 'they were fighting heavy waves' [NLT], 'battling...a rough sea' [REB]. This verb normally means to punish by physical torture or torment [LN].

c. κῦμα (LN 14.25) (BAGD p. 457): 'wave' [BAGD, LN; all translations except REB], 'rough sea' [REB], 'billow, surge' [LN]. This noun denotes a moving ridge or succession of swells on the surface of a body of water [LN].

d. ἐναντίος (LN 82.11) (BAGD 1. p. 262): 'contrary' [BAGD, CC, NIGTC, WBC; KJV, NASB], 'against (them/it)' [BECNT, BNTC, LN, NICNT; ESV, NET, NIV, NRSV], 'blowing against (it)' [NCV, TEV], 'from the opposite direction' [NTC], 'opposed, hostile' [BAGD]. The phrase 'the wind was contrary' is translated 'there was a headwind' [PNTC], 'battling with a headwind' [REB], 'it was going against the wind' [CEV, GW], 'a strong wind had risen' [NLT]. This adjective describes something that is oriented in the direction opposite to a movement [LN].

QUESTION—What time of day is described here?

In verse 15 ὀψίας 'evening' referred to the end of the day, and here it refers to a time somewhat later on after that [WBC]. It was about six o'clock or after [My]. It was after dark [EBC, TH], possibly a long time after dark [NICNT, TRT].

QUESTION—How far had they gotten in their journey across the lake?

The boat was somewhere around the middle of the lake [EBC, Lns, PNTC] possibly farther [PNTC]. They were far from land [NICNT, TH]. They had probably rowed about three or four miles in a section of the lake that was about no more than five miles wide [NAC, NTC]. They were a mile or two from the shore from which they had embarked [WBC].

14:25 In- (the) -fourth watch[a] of-the night he-came to them walking on the lake. **14:26** And the disciples having-seen him walking on the lake were-terrified[b] saying "It-is a-ghost,[c]" and they-cried-out[d] from fear[e].

LEXICON—a. φυλακή (LN 67.196) (BAGD 4. p. 868): 'watch' [BAGD, BECNT, BNTC, CC, LN, NICNT, NIGTC, NTC, PNTC, WBC; ESV, KJV, NASB, NIV], 'a watch of the night' [BAGD], 'a fourth of the night' [LN]. The phrase τετάρτῃ δὲ φυλακῇ τῆς νυκτὸς 'in the fourth watch of the night' is translated 'a little while before morning' [CEV], 'early in the morning' [NRSV], 'as night was ending' [NET], 'between three and six o'clock in the morning' [GW, NCV, TEV; similarly REB], 'about three o'clock in the morning' [NLT]. This noun denotes one of four periods of time into which the night was divided and during which time certain assigned persons would be on the lookout [LN].

b. aorist pass. indic. of ταράσσω (LN 25.244) (BAGD 2. p. 805): 'to be terrified' [BAGD, BECNT, BNTC, NICNT, NIGTC, WBC; all versions except KJV, NCV, REB], 'to be disturbed' [BAGD], 'to be troubled' [BAGD, CC; KJV], 'to be frightened' [BAGD, NTC, PNTC], 'to be afraid' [NCV], 'to be shaken' [REB], 'to be caused great mental distress' [LN]. This verb means to cause acute emotional distress or turbulence [LN].

c. φάντασμα (LN **12.42**) (BAGD p. 853): 'ghost' [BAGD, **LN**; all translations except KJV], 'spirit' [KJV], 'apparition' [BAGD]. This noun denotes an apparition [LN].

d. aorist act. indic. of κράζω (LN 33.83) (BAGD 1. p. 447): 'to cry out' [BAGD, BECNT, BNTC CC, NICNT, NIGTC, PNTC, WBC; all versions

except CEV, GW, TEV], 'to shout' [LN], 'to scream' [BAGD, LN, NTC; CEV, GW, TEV]; 'to shriek' [BAGD]. This verb means to shout or cry out, with the possible implication of the unpleasant nature of the sound [LN].
  e. φόβος (LN 25.251) (BAGD 2.a.α. p. 863): 'fear' [BAGD, BECNT, BNTC, CC, LN, NICNT, NIGTC, NTC, PNTC, WBC; ESV, KJV, NASB, NET, NIV, NLT, NRSV, TEV], 'terror' [REB], 'alarm, fright' [BAGD], not explicit [CEV]. The phrase 'in fear' is translated 'they were afraid' [GW, NCV]. In this context this word means 'terror' [Lns, NAC, NIGTC; REB]. This noun denotes a state of severe distress, aroused by intense concern for impending pain, danger, evil, etc., or possibly by the illusion of such circumstances [LN].
QUESTION—What does the term φάντασμα 'ghost' refer to?
  It means a disembodied spirit or apparition from the realm of the dead [NAC, NICNT], or the spirit of a dead person [TRT]. They thought they were seeing a haunting specter from the world of evil [NTC]. It was popularly believed that the sea was the home of evil spirits [NICNT, WBC], so they probably believed that it was a ghost that meant to harm them [WBC]. They thought it was a spirit floating on the waves, in something of a parody of Jesus [NIGTC].

14:27 **But immediately Jesus spoke to-them saying, "Have-courage,ᵃ it-is I; do- not -be-afraid.ᵇ" 14:28 And having-answered him Peter said, "Lord, if it-is you, command me to-come to you on the water." 14:29 And he said, "Come.ᶜ" And getting-out from the boat Peter walked on the water and came to Jesus.**

TEXT—Manuscripts reading καὶ ἦλθεν 'and came' are given a B rating by GNT to indicate it was regarded to be almost certain. Other manuscripts read ἐλθεῖν 'to come'. Only KJV reads 'to come'.
LEXICON—a. pres. act. impera. of θαρσέω (LN 25.156) (BAGD p. 352): 'to have courage' [BAGD, LN; NCV, NET], 'to take courage' [BECNT, NTC, PNTC; NASB, NIV, NLT], 'to be courageous' [BAGD, CC, LN], 'to be of good courage' [WBC], 'to be of good cheer' [KJV], 'to take heart' [NIGTC; ESV, NRSV, REB], 'to calm down' [GW], 'to be bold' [LN]. This imperative is translated 'Courage!' [BNTC; TEV], 'Don't worry' [NICNT; CEV] This verb means to have confidence and firmness of purpose in the face of danger or testing [LN].
  b. pres. pass. impera. of φοβέομαι (LN 25.252) (BAGD 1.a. p. 862): 'to be afraid' [BAGD, LN; all translations], 'to fear' [LN]. This present imperative is translated as indicating that an ongoing action should cease: 'stop being afraid' [CC]. This verb means to be in a state of fearing [LN].
  c. aorist act. impera. of ἔρχομαι (LN 15.81) (BAGD I.1.a.β. p. 310): 'to come' [BAGD, BECNT, BNTC, CC, LN, NIGTC, NTC, PNTC, WBC; all versions except CEV, NLT]. This imperative is translated 'Come on' [CEV], 'Come on then' [NICNT], 'Yes, come' [NLT]. This verb means to

move toward or up to the reference point of the viewpoint character or event [LN].

QUESTION—Is there any particular significance in Jesus' statement ἐγώ εἰμι 'it is I'?

1. This is an intentional echo of God's self-revelation in Ex 3:14 [EBC, ICC, NAC, WBC], and is the clearest claim to deity by Jesus up to this point in the gospel of Matthew [NAC]. It indicates the presence of the living God [NIBC]. Any Christian reading this after the resurrection would recognize the ἐγώ εἰμι (literally 'I am') as echoing the self-disclosure of God in the Septuagint of Exodus 3:14, Isaiah 43:10 and 51:12 [EBC, WBC]. It is suggestive of God's power and authority [BNTC, PNTC]. He is identifying himself as the one who chose them, who has guided them, and who has given them numerous proofs of his love and power [NTC]. It does not reflect the 'I am' of Exodus 3:14, but does echo some of the statements of divine self-disclosure from Isaiah [CC].

2 ἐγώ εἰμι 'it is I' would be the most natural way for Jesus to identify himself, so we do not need to conclude that this is an echo of the divine name [NICNT].

QUESTION—Does the question εἰ σὺ εἶ 'if it is you' presuppose the actual reality of the condition?

This is a first class conditional sentence which does assume that the condition is actually true, which in this case is that it really is Jesus: 'since it is you' [EBC, Lns, NAC, NTC, PNTC, WBC]. It could mean 'if' or 'since' in this context [ICC].

14:30 But seeing[a] the strong[b] wind he-was-afraid, and having-begun to-sink[c] he-cried-out saying, "Lord, save[d] me."

TEXT—Manuscripts reading ἰσχυρόν 'strong' are given a C rating by GNT to indicate that choosing it over those texts that omit it was difficult. It is omitted by BNTC, NIGTC, NTC; ESV, NASB, NCV, NIV.

LEXICON—a. pres. act. participle of βλέπω (LN 24.7) (BAGD 7.a. p. 143): 'to see' [LN; all translations except GW, NRSV], 'to notice' [GW, NRSV], 'to perceive, to feel' [BAGD], 'to become aware of, to notice, to glance at' [LN]. This verb means to see, frequently in the sense of becoming aware of or taking notice of something [LN].

b. ἰσχυρός (LN 79.63) (BAGD 2. p. 383): 'strong' [BECNT, CC, LN, NICNT, WBC; CEV, GW, NET, NLT, NRSV, TEV], 'violent' [BAGD], 'boisterous' [PNTC; KJV], 'vigorous' [LN]. The phrase ἄνεμον ἰσχυρόν 'strong wind' is translated 'the strength of the gale' [REB]. This adjective describes being physically strong and vigorous [LN].

c. pres. pass. infin. of καταποντίζω (LN 15.117) (BAGD p. 417): 'to sink' [BAGD, LN; all translations except TEV], 'to sink down' [TEV], 'to drown' [BAGD, LN]. This verb means to cause something or someone to sink into deep water [LN].

d. aorist act. impera. of σῴζω (LN **21.18**) (BAGD 1.a. p. 798): 'to save' [BAGD; all translations], 'to rescue' [BAGD, **LN**], 'to deliver, to make safe' [LN]. This verb means to rescue from danger and to restore to a former state of safety and well being [LN].

QUESTION—What did Peter actually see?

He perceived the strength of the wind [CC, NIBC, NIGTC, NTC, PNTC]. He saw its effect on the waves and the boat [PNTC]. He was distracted by the fierceness of the wind [WBC]. Here the word 'wind' is a synecdoche for 'storm', which means that Peter became more aware of the storm [EBC].

14:31 And immediately Jesus having-stretched-out his hand took-hold[a] of-him and he-says to-him, "You-(of)-little-faith,[b] why did-you-doubt?[c]"

LEXICON—a. aorist mid. (deponent = act.) indic. of ἐπιλαμβάνομαι (LN **18.2**) (BAGD 1. p. 295): 'to take hold of' [BAGD, BECNT, BNTC, CC, **LN**, NICNT, NIGTC, PNTC, WBC; ESV, NASB], 'to catch hold of' [GW, REB], 'to catch' [BAGD; KJV, NCV, NET, NIV, NRSV], 'to grab' [NTC; NLT], 'to grab hold of' [TEV], 'to help (him) up' [CEV], 'to grasp' [BAGD, LN]. This verb means to take hold of or grasp, with focus upon the goal of the motion' [LN].

b. ὀλιγόπιστος (LN 31.96) (BAGD p. 563): 'of little faith' [BAGD, LN], 'of insufficient faith' [LN]. This pronominal adjective (in the vocative case) is translated 'You of little faith' [BECNT, NIGTC, WBC; NASB, NET, NIV, NRSV], 'O you of little faith' [ESV; similarly KJV], 'Little-faith' [CC], 'You feeble believer' [BNTC], 'You faithless man' [NICNT], 'Man of little faith' [PNTC], 'O man of little faith' [NTC], 'You have so little faith' [GW, NLT], 'How little faith you have' [REB; similarly TEV], 'You surely don't have much faith' [CEV], 'Your faith is small' [NCV]. This adjective describes having relatively little faith [LN].

c. aorist act. indic. of διστάζω (LN **31.37**) (BAGD 1. p. 200): 'to doubt' [BAGD, BECNT, BNTC, CC, **LN**, NICNT, NIGTC, PNTC, WBC; all versions except NLT, REB], 'to waver' [NTC], 'to hesitate' [REB], 'to be uncertain about' [LN]. The question 'Why did you doubt?' is translated 'Why did you doubt me?' [NLT]. This verb means to think that something may not be true or certain [LN].

QUESTION—What is Jesus specifically asking in his question to Peter?

Jesus is asking him what purpose such doubt could serve [EBC, Lns, My], and the answer to that is 'none' [Lns]. The normal expression for a 'why?' question would be διὰ τί, for which the obvious answer would be 'the storm', but here Jesus says εἰς τί, which seems to be asking what would be the purpose for this doubt, now that Peter has already come this far [EBC]. He is making the statement that Peter did not need to yield to dismay and doubt [BNTC].

14:32 And as- they -were-going-up into the boat, the wind ceased.ᵃ **14:33** And those in the boat worshippedᵇ him saying, "Truly you-are (the) Son of-God."

LEXICON—a. aorist act. indic. of κοπάζω (LN **68.42**) (BAGD p. 443): 'to cease' [BAGD, BNTC, LN, NIGTC, NTC; ESV, KJV, NET, NRSV], 'to stop' [BAGD, BECNT, LN, WBC; NASB, NLT], 'to stop blowing' [GW], 'to abate' [BAGD, CC], 'to die down' [CEV, NIV, TEV], 'to die away' [NICNT], 'to drop' [PNTC; REB], 'to become calm' [NCV]. The phrase ἐκόπασεν ὁ ἄνεμος 'the wind ceased' is translated 'the wind stopped blowing' [**LN**]. This verb means to cease, in reference to some type of movement [LN].

  b. aorist act. indic. of προσκυνέω (LN 53.56) (BAGD 5. p. 717): 'to worship' [BAGD, BECNT, BNTC, CC, LN, NIGTC, NTC, PNTC, WBC; all versions except GW, REB], 'to bow down before' [NICNT], 'to bow down in front of' [GW], 'to fall at (his) feet' [REB], 'to prostrate oneself in worship, to bow down and worship' [LN], 'to do obeisance to, to do reverence to' [BAGD]. This verb means to express by attitude and possibly by position one's allegiance to and regard for deity [LN].

QUESTION—What did the disciples mean by their worship and confession that Jesus was the Son of God?

At this point 'Son of God' would have had mostly a messianic meaning to them, though after the resurrection they would have understood it in its fullest ontological sense; Matthew's testimony seems to focus on the significance that is beyond what the disciples would have understood at that moment [EBC]. Matthew is presenting an answer to the question of who Jesus really is, which is that he is exercising prerogatives that were reserved only for Yahweh in the OT, though the disciples' confession probably lacks adequate understanding of who he really is [NAC]. The worship they give assigns to Jesus the highest possible place and acknowledges him as one who is uniquely related to the one God; however, they may not have understood this term as precisely as they would later [PNTC]. Their humble adoration was genuine worship, and convinced of the limitlessness of Jesus' power and love, they now acknowledge the truth of what the Father had said from heaven at Jesus' baptism and what the demons had confessed in 8:29 concerning Jesus being God's Son [NTC]. It is a worshipful response [BNTC, NIBC], and anticipates Peter's subsequent confession at Caesarea Philippi (in Matthew 16:16) that Jesus is God's Son [NIBC]. At this point they recognize him as God's unique messenger and Messiah, but as Matthew's narrative progresses their recognition of all that that means grows, reaching a climax in 16:16, which is a turning point in this gospel [WBC]. The overwhelming miracle causes the disciples to recognize that he is more than human; they also remember that he has called God 'Father' in 7:21, 10:32–33, 11:25–27, and 12:50, and that he has been called 'Son of God' by God at his baptism and by demons, so it is not surprising for them to acknowledge here that he is Son of God [NICNT]. It is not sufficient to use a simile here for the sake of cultures that reject the notion that God would have a son, saying that Jesus is *like* a son to God, because that does not give a sufficiently strong statement of his divine origin [TH].

DISCOURSE UNIT—14:34-36 [ICC; CEV, ESV, NRSV, TEV]. The topic is Jesus heals the sick in Gennesaret [ESV, NRSV, TEV], Jesus heals sick people in Gennesaret [CEV], the Lord heals the sick at evening [ICC].

14:34 **And having-crossed-over they-came to the land at Gennesaret. 14:35 And having-recognized[a] him the men of that place sent into all that region and they-brought to-him all those-having-illness 14:36 and they-were-begging[b] him that they-might- only -touch the fringe[c] of his garment;[d] and as-many-as touched (it) were-healed.[e]**

LEXICON—a. aorist act. participle of ἐπιγινώσκω (LN 27.61): 'to recognize' [BECNT, LN; all translations except CEV, KJV], 'to have knowledge of' [KJV]. The phrase ἐπιγνόντες αὐτὸν οἱ ἄνδρες τοῦ τόπου ἐκείνου 'having recognized him the men of that place…' is translated 'The people found out he was there' [CEV]. This verb means to identify newly acquired information with what had been previously learned or known [LN].

b. imperf. act. indic. of παρακαλέω (LN 33.168) (BAGD 3. p. 617): 'to beg' [NICNT, NTC; all versions except ESV, KJV, NASB], 'to implore' [BECNT, BNTC; ESV, NASB], 'to appeal to' [BAGD, LN, NIGTC], 'to beseech' [CC, PNTC; KJV], 'to plead with' [WBC], 'to ask, plead for' [LN], 'to entreat' [BAGD], 'to request' [BAGD, LN]. This verb means to ask for something earnestly and with propriety [LN].

c. κράσπεδον (LN 6.180) (BAGD 1. p. 448): 'fringe' [BECNT, LN, NICNT; ESV, NASB, NLT, NRSV], 'hem' [BAGD, CC, WBC; KJV], 'tassel' [BNTC, NIGTC, NTC, PNTC], 'edge' [BAGD; GW, NCV, NET, NIV, REB, TEV], 'border' [BAGD], not explicit [CEV]. This noun denotes the border of a garment [LN].

d. ἱμάτιον (LN 6.172): 'cloak' [BECNT, LN, PNTC; NASB, NET, NIV, NRSV, REB, TEV], 'garment' [BNTC, NTC, WBC; ESV, KJV], 'coat' [LN, NIGTC; NCV], 'clothes' [CEV, GW], 'robe' [LN; NLT]. This noun denotes any type of outer garment [LN].

e. aorist pass. indic. of διασῴζω (LN 23.136) (BAGD p. 189): 'to be healed' [CC, LN, PNTC; CEV, NCV, NET, NIV, NLT, NRSV], 'to be cured' [BAGD, BECNT, BNTC, LN, NTC; NASB], 'to be completely cured' [REB], 'to be restored to health' [NICNT], 'to be made whole' [WBC], 'to be made perfectly whole' [KJV], 'to be made well' [LN; ESV, GW, TEV], 'to be made completely well' [NIGTC]. This particular word may carry additional emphasis, meaning *complete* healing [ICC, My, NAC, NIBC, NIGTC, PNTC; KJV, REB]. This verb means to cause someone to become well again after having been sick [LN].

MATTHEW 15:1–2

DISCOURSE UNIT—15:1–16:12 [PNTC]. The topic is opposition and loyalty.

DISCOURSE UNIT—15:1–28 [NIV]. The topic is clean and unclean.

DISCOURSE UNIT—15:1–20 [ICC, NICNT; GW, NCV, NLT]. The topic is a further challenge: the question of purity [NICNT], Jesus challenges the Pharisees' traditions [GW], the Pharisaic tradition; clean and unclean [ICC], obey God's law [NCV], Jesus teaches about inner purity [NLT].

DISCOURSE UNIT—15:1–14 [NASB]. The topic is tradition and commandment.

DISCOURSE UNIT—15:1–9 [CEV, ESV, NET, NRSV, TEV]. The topic is the teaching of the ancestors [CEV, TEV], traditions and commandments [ESV], breaking human traditions [NET], the tradition of the elders [NRSV].

15:1 Then Pharisees and scribes come to Jesus from Jerusalem saying, **15:2** "Why do- your disciples -transgress[a] the tradition[b] of-the elders[c]? For they-do- not -wash[d] their hands when they-eat bread.[e]"

LEXICON—a. pres. act. indic. of παραβαίνω (LN **36.28**) (BAGD 2.a. p. 611): 'to transgress' [BAGD, BNTC, CC, LN, NTC, WBC; KJV], 'to break' [BAGD, BECNT, NIGTC, PNTC; ESV, GW, NASB, NIV, NRSV, REB], 'to go against' [NICNT], 'to disobey' [**LN**; CEV, NET, NLT, TEV], 'to not follow' [NCV], 'to break the law' [LN]. This verb means to act contrary to established custom or law, with the implication of intent [LN].

b. παράδοσις (LN **33.239**) (BAGD 2. p. 615): 'tradition' [BAGD, **LN**; all translations except NCV, TEV], 'unwritten laws' [NCV], 'teaching' [LN; TEV]. The phrase 'tradition of the elders' is translated 'what our ancestors taught us to do' [CEV]. This noun denotes the content of traditional instruction [LN].

c. πρεσβύτερος (LN **53.77**) (BAGD 1.b. p. 699): 'elder' [BECNT, BNTC, CC, LN, NICNT, NIGTC, NTC, PNTC, WBC; ESV, KJV, NASB, NET, NIV, NRSV], 'ancestor' [CEV, GW]. The phrase τῶν πρεσβυτέρων 'of the elders' is translated 'that have been handed down to us' [NCV], 'handed-down by our ancestors' [TEV], 'age-old (tradition)' [NLT], 'ancient (tradition)' [REB], 'of the ancients' [BAGD]. This noun denotes a person of responsibility and authority in matters of socio-religious concerns, both in Jewish and Christian societies [LN].

d. pres. mid. indic. of νίπτω (LN **47.9**) (BAGD 2.b. p. 540): 'to wash' [BAGD, BECNT, BNTC, CC, LN, NICNT, NIGTC, PNTC, WBC; all versions except NLT], 'to rinse' [NTC]. The phrase 'wash their hands' is translated 'ceremonial hand-washing' [NLT]. This verb means to wash a part of a body, usually the hands or feet [LN].

e. ἄρτος (LN **5.1**): 'bread' [BECNT, BNTC, CC, NICNT, NTC, PNTC, WBC; KJV, NASB], 'food' [LN, NIGTC]. The phrase 'they eat bread' is translated simply 'they eat' [all translations except KJV, NASB, REB], 'eating' [REB]. This noun denotes any kind of food or nourishment [LN].

QUESTION—What is the function of τότε 'then' in this passage?

It introduces something that happens after what has already been narrated but does not reference any specific moment in time [PNTC]. It is frequently used in Matthew as a loose connective between narrated events [EBC]. It is not precise and just means that this occurred at about that time [Lns, NTC]. It indicates that the narrative is continuing [TH]. It indicates that these events occurred while he was still at Gennesaret [My].

QUESTION—What was the relationship between Pharisees and scribes?

Most scribes were Pharisees [BNTC, NIBC, PNTC], but many Pharisees were not scribes [NIBC, PNTC]. The scribes were OT scholars and were considered experts in interpreting the law, whereas the Pharisees were a religious order, consisting for the most part of laymen, and who devoted themselves to a strict observance of the law [NIBC]. The scribes were professional expounders and teachers of OT law [NTC]. Both the scribes and prominent Pharisees were allowed to teach in the synagogues [BNTC].

QUESTION—What was the significance of the visit by this delegation from Jerusalem?

They would have been seen as a semi-official delegation [EBC, NICNT, WBC], and would have been held in high esteem by the locals [EBC]. They were an official delegation from Jerusalem [TH], which had been sent to investigate Jesus [TRT]. This may even be an official inquiry [BECNT]. That they were from Jerusalem suggests that they would have represented a greater authority and even a great threat than others from Galilee [NAC]. It was out of the ordinary for them to visit this rural area in Galilee, and they would have been treated with respect. This shows the degree of hostility that Pharisees in Jerusalem felt toward Jesus, since they apparently came to provoke an argument [PNTC]. They had more prestige than local members of their sect [Lns]. This visit foreshadows the intense conflicts that will arise in Jerusalem later on in the gospel account [CC, ICC, NICNT, NIGTC].

QUESTION—What was the παράδοσις 'tradition' of the elders?

It was the oral tradition of interpreting OT law to which the Pharisees adhered, and it was intended to be a hedge around the Torah to prevent people from violating it [WBC]. It was drawn primarily from OT laws given for the Levitical priests, but the Pharisees had added more to it and applied it to all the Jewish people [BECNT, CC, ICC, NICNT, WBC]. It was the teaching that had been handed down for generations and had developed into a vast body of doctrine that was difficult to know completely, and some of it was very burdensome [PNTC]. The scribes and Pharisees considered the oral tradition to be as binding as the law itself [NIBC, NTC, TH]. This was a fairly large body of oral teaching commenting on rules of conduct derived from OT law, though in many cases it reflected conflicting opinions [EBC, NTC]. The Pharisees believed that the oral law, which explained and applied the written law, was given to Moses at the same time as the written law. The oral tradition that had grown up around the law was eventually put into writing about AD 200 in what came to be called the Mishnah [BECNT]. The

Pharisees considered the oral tradition to be equally valid as the law of Moses, though the Sadducees did not acknowledge it as such [BNTC, CC]. In practice the tradition was considered to be above the scripture itself [Lns]. The Pharisees held to traditions that went beyond what the OT scriptures required, and viewed them as being obligatory for all Jewish people [NIGTC]. Their ritual concerning hand washing may actually have been relatively recent [NICNT].

QUESTION—What was the nature of the washing to which the Pharisees referred?

It was not so much a washing to get the hands clean as a ritual cleansing done by pouring water over the hands in a certain way [NTC, TH]. The point was not cleanliness or hygiene, but ceremonial purification [EBC, ICC, NAC, NIBC, NTC, PNTC, TRT, WBC]. A specific amount of water had to be poured over the hands up to the wrist in a particular manner [EBC, PNTC, TRT], first with the fingers pointing up, then with the fingers pointing down, and then by rubbing the washed hand with the other fist [NIBC].

15:3 But^a answering he-said to-them, "And you, why do-you-transgress the commandment^b of God because-of your tradition? **15:4** For God said, 'Honor^c (your) father and (your) mother', and 'The-one-reviling^d father or mother let-him-be-put-to-death.'^{e}"

TEXT—Manuscripts reading θεὸς εἶπεν 'God said' are given a B rating by GNT to indicate it was regarded to be almost certain. Some manuscripts read θεὸς ἐνετείλατο λέγων 'God commanded saying' but only KJV follows this reading. CEV and ESV read 'commanded' in place of 'said', though that may be for stylistic reasons only.

LEXICON—a. δέ (LN 89.87, 89.124): 'but' [BECNT, CC, LN (89.124), PNTC; KJV], 'and' [LN (89.87), WBC; NASB], not explicit [BNTC, NICNT, NIGTC, NTC; all versions except KJV, NASB]. This conjunction can mark contrast [LN (89.124)], or it can indicate a sequence of closely related events [LN (89.87)].

b. ἐντολή (LN 33.330): 'commandment' [BECNT, BNTC, LN, NICNT, NIGTC, NTC, WBC; ESV, GW, KJV, NASB, NET, NRSV, REB], 'command' [CC; NCV, NIV, TEV], 'direct commandment' [NLT], 'order' [LN], not explicit [CEV]. This noun denotes that which is authoritatively commanded [LN].

c. pres. act. impera. of τιμάω (LN **87.8**) (BAGD 2. p. 817): 'to honor' [BAGD, **LN**; all translations except CEV, TEV], 'to respect' [LN; CEV, TEV], 'to revere' [BAGD]. This verb means to attribute high status to someone by honoring him [LN].

d. pres. act. participle of κακολογέω (LN **33.399**) (BAGD p. 397): 'to revile' [BAGD, CC, **LN**; ESV], 'to insult' [BAGD; NET], 'to speak evil of' [BAGD, BECNT, BNTC, NICNT, NIGTC, WBC; NASB, NRSV], 'to speak disrespectfully of' [NLT], 'to curse' [NTC; CEV, GW, KJV, NIV,

REB, TEV], 'to say cruel things to' [NCV], 'to denounce' [LN]. This verb means to insult in a particularly strong and unjustified manner LN].
e. pres. act. impera. of τελευτάω (LN 23.102) (BAGD p. 810): 'to die' [BAGD, LN]. The phrase θανάτῳ τελευτάτω 'let him be put to death' [PNTC], is derived from a Hebrew idiom meaning 'let him surely die' [BAGD]. It is translated 'is to be put to death' [BECNT, NICNT; NASB], 'must be put to death' [GW, NCV, NET, NIV, NLT], 'must certainly be put to death' [NTC], 'you are to be put to death' [TEV], 'shall be put to death' [REB], 'let (him) most certainly be put to death' [WBC], 'let him die the death' [KJV], 'let him die without fail' [BNTC], 'let him surely die' [CC], 'must surely die' [NIGTC; ESV, NRSV], 'put to death (all who)' [CEV]. This verb means to come to the end of one's life, as a euphemistic expression for death [LN].

QUESTION—Why does Jesus describe the tradition of the elders only as 'your' tradition?

He did not even allow it the dignity of being called the tradition 'of the elders' [CC, NIGTC]. He was contrasting their tradition with the commandment of God to emphasize that they are not on a par [BECNT, CC, NICNT, NIGTC, NTC, PNTC]. He calls it 'your tradition' to emphasize that they themselves had embraced it and were not compelled by some higher authority to follow it [PNTC]. He was emphasizing their personal responsibility for accepting and promoting it [Lns], and that they had wrongly attached paramount importance to it, putting it above God's law [NTC].

QUESTION—What does 'reviling' parents consist of?

It means to speak evil of them [PNTC, WBC], or to insult them [EBC]. It may also include other forms of abuse or neglect as well [TH].

15:5 You, however, say, 'Whoever would-say to-(his)-father or to-(his)-mother, "Whatever you(sg)-might-have-been-benefited[a] from me (is) a-gift,[b]"

LEXICON—a. aorist pass. subj. of ὠφελέω (LN 35.2) (BAGD 1.a. p. 900): 'to be benefited' [BAGD], 'to benefit' [NTC, PNTC, WBC], 'to be used for (your) benefit' [REB], 'to gain (from)' [NIGTC; ESV], 'to be profited' [KJV], 'to profit (you)' [BECNT], 'to give (to you)' [NLT], 'to help' [NASB, NCV, TEV], 'to be helped' [BAGD, CC, LN], 'to receive help' [BNTC; NET, NIV], 'to expect help' [NICNT], 'to receive support' [GW], 'to have support' [NRSV], 'to be aided' [BAGD]. The phrase ἐξ ἐμοῦ ὠφεληθῇς 'you might have been benefited from me' is translated 'whatever I have that would help you' [NASB], 'helping (their) parents as they should' [CEV]. This verb means to provide assistance, with emphasis upon the resulting benefit [LN].
b. δῶρον (LN 57.84) (BAGD 2. p. 211): 'gift' [BAGD, BNTC, CC, LN, NTC, WBC; KJV], 'gift to God' [PNTC], 'gift devoted to God' [NIV], 'given to God' [BECNT; GW, NASB, NCV, NET, NRSV], 'set apart for God' [NICNT; GW], 'vowed to give to God' [NLT], 'belongs to God'

[TEV], 'offered to God' [CEV], 'offering to God' [NIGTC], 'offering' [BAGD]. This noun denotes that which is given or granted [LN].

QUESTION—What did it mean to say that it is a gift?

It meant that it was devoted or offered to God as a gift to God [BECNT, EBC, NICNT, NIGTC, PNTC; CEV, ESV, GW, NASB, NCV, NET, NIV, NLT, NRSV, REB, TEV]. Food, money or property could be dedicated to the temple treasury in this manner [NICNT]. It was a vow to support the temple [WBC]. Declaring something to be a gift in this manner appears to be a deliberate attempt to avoid the possibility of anyone else having a claim on it [NICNT]. This practice could be used as a legal fiction in which there was never any actual giving of the item or money, but which avoided giving it to the parents [ICC]. Such funds or goods could continue to be used by the one who pledged them, but could not be transferred to someone else [BECNT, BNTC, NIBC, NICNT, TH]. The gift was payable at the time of the death of the person who had dedicated it, but was available for use until that time [NAC]. In many cases it was simply a legal device that would allow a person to avoid having to provide for their parents, but without actually having to give anything to the temple [NIGTC].

15:6 he-will- certainly-not^a -honor his father;' and you-invalidate^b the word of God because-of^c your tradition.

TEXT—Manuscripts reading τὸν πατέρα αὐτοῦ 'his father' are given a C rating by GNT to indicate that choosing it over a variant text was difficult. Some texts read τὸν πατέρα αὐτοῦ ἢ τὴν μητέρα αὐτοῦ 'his father or his mother.' BNTC, KJV, NASB, NCV, REB follow this reading. Manuscripts reading τὸν πατέρα ἢ τὴν μητέρα 'father or mother' are followed by BECNT, WBC; CEV, NLT (translated 'parents' by WBC; CEV, NLT).

TEXT—Manuscripts reading τὸν λόγον 'the word' are given a B rating by GNT to indicate it was regarded to be almost certain. Other manuscripts read τὴν ἐντολήν 'the commandment', and this reading is followed by KJV, TEV. Some manuscripts read τὸν νόμον 'the law', and this reading is followed by REB. CEV translates 'commands', though this may be for stylistic reasons only.

LEXICON—a. οὐ μή (LN 69.3) (BAGD D.2. p. 517): 'not' [BAGD, LN; KJV]. The clause 'he will certainly not honor his father' is translated as a continuation of what the scribes and Pharisees say to, or about, whoever says to his father, "Whatever you might have been benefited from me is a gift': 'then that person need not honor the father' [NRSV], 'need not honor their father' [NIGTC], 'he does not need to honor his father' [NET; similarly ESV], 'surely does not have to honor his father' [NTC], 'he does not have to honor his father' [GW, NASB], 'they do not need to honor their father' [TEV], 'must not honor his father' [REB], 'this person must not honor father or mother' [BECNT], 'shall not honor his father or his mother' [BNTC], 'shall surely not honor his father' [CC], 'is not to honor his father' [PNTC], 'he is not to honor his father with it' [NIV], 'they are not

to honor their parent' [NICNT], 'And honor not his father, he shall be free' [KJV], 'one need not at all support one's parents' [WBC]. The clause is translated as Jesus' comment to the scribes and Pharisees: 'You teach that person not to honor his father' [NCV], 'In this way, you say they don't need to honor their parents' [NLT], 'Is this any way to show respect to your parents?' [CEV]. Both of these particles indicate negative propositions [LN], and when used together the negation is strengthened [BAGD].
- b. ἀκυρόω (LN 76.25) (BAGD p. 34): 'to invalidate' [BECNT; NASB], 'to invalidate the authority of' [LN], 'to make void' [BNTC, NICNT, NIGTC; ESV, NRSV], 'to make null and void' [NTC; REB], 'to nullify' [CC, PNTC; NET, NIV], 'to cancel' [NLT], 'to cancel out' [WBC], 'to make of none effect' [KJV], 'to ignore' [CEV], 'to reject' [LN; NCV], 'to destroy the authority of' [GW], 'to disregard' [LN; TEV]. This verb means to refuse to recognize the force or power of something [LN].
- c. διά with accusative (LN 89.26): 'because of' [LN, PNTC, WBC; GW], 'on account of' [CC, LN; NET], 'for the sake of' [BECNT, BNTC, NIGTC, NTC; ESV, NASB, NCV, NIV, NLT, NRSV], 'on the basis of' [NICNT], 'in order to follow' [CEV, TEV], 'by' [KJV], 'out of regard for' [REB], 'by reason of' [LN]. This preposition indicates cause or reason, with focus upon instrumentality, either of objects or events [LN].

QUESTION—What is the force of the phrase οὐ μή 'certainly not'?

It has the force of an imperative: the man *shall not* honor the parents [BECNT, BNTC, CC, Lns, My, NAC, NICNT, PNTC; NASB, NIV, REB]. Since it has been vowed to God, there is nothing left to give to the parents [PNTC]. It indicates that the person is definitely freed from the *obligation* to honor the parents [ICC, NIGTC, NTC, WBC; ESV, GW, NET, NLT, NRSV, TEV].

QUESTION—What relationship is indicated by the conjunction καί 'and'?

It indicates the consequence of the teaching Jesus is criticizing [CC, My, TH]. It is translated 'and so' [CC; NLT], 'so' [NICNT; ESV, NRSV], 'thus' [KJV, NIV].

15:7 Hypocrites,[a] Isaiah prophesied accurately[b] concerning you saying, **15:8** 'This people[c] honors me with-the lips,[d] but their heart is-removed far-away[e] from me;

TEXT—Some manuscripts add ἐγγίζει μοι…τῷ στόματι αὐτῶν 'draws near to me with their mouth'. GNT makes no mention of this variant, and only KJV follows it.

LEXICON—a. ὑποκριτής (LN 88.228) (BAGD p. 845): 'hypocrite' [BAGD, LN; all translations except CEV], 'pretender' [BAGD, LN], 'show off' [CEV], 'one who acts hypocritically' [LN]. This noun denotes one who pretends to be other than he really is [LN].
- b. καλῶς (LN **72.12**) (BAGD 4.b. p. 401): 'rightly' [BAGD, **LN**, WBC; NASB, NRSV], 'accurate' [LN] 'correctly' [BAGD, BECNT, LN; NET],

'well' [BNTC, CC, NIGTC, PNTC; ESV, KJV], 'right' [LN]. The phrase καλῶς ἐπροφήτευσεν 'prophesied accurately' is translated 'made an excellent prophecy' [NICNT], 'was right when he prophesied/said' [NTC; GW, NCV, NIV, NLT], 'how right was (Isaiah) when he prophesied' [REB, TEV], 'was right when he wrote' [CEV]. This adjective describes what is accurate and right, with a possible implication of being commendable [LN].

c. λαός (LN 11.55) (BAGD 3.a. p. 466): 'people' [BAGD, LN (11.55); all translations except CEV], 'nation' [LN (11.55)], 'people of God' [BAGD, LN (11.12)]. The phrase Ὁ λαὸς οὗτος 'this people' is translated 'all of you' [CEV]. This noun denotes the largest unit into which the people of the world are divided on the basis of their constituting a socio-political community [LN (11.55)]. It is also used as a collective noun describing a group of people who belong to God (whether Jews or Christians) [LN (11.12)].

d. χεῖλος (LN 33.74) (BAGD 1. p. 879): 'lip' [BAGD, BECNT, BNTC, CC, NICNT, NIGTC, NTC, PNTC, WBC; ESV, GW, KJV, NASB, NET, NIV, NLT, NRSV], 'speech' [LN], 'lip service' [REB], 'words' [CEV, NCV, TEV]. This noun is used figuratively to denote the action of communicating orally [LN].

e. πόρρω (LN 83.31) (BAGD 1. p. 693): 'far away' [BAGD, LN], 'far' [BAGD], 'at a distance, a long way off' [LN]. This adverb describes being in a position at a relatively great distance, with the possible implication of comparison [LN]. The phrase πόρρω ἀπέχει ἀπ' ἐμοῦ 'is removed far away from me' is translated 'is/are far from me' [BECNT, NIGTC, NTC; all versions except CEV, NASB, TEV], 'is far away from me' [NICNT, PNTC; NASB], 'is really far away from me' [TEV], 'is distant from me' [WBC], 'is far distant from me' [BNTC, CC]. The phrase ἡ δὲ καρδία αὐτῶν πόρρω ἀπέχει ἀπ' ἐμοῦ 'their heart is removed far away from me' is translated 'you never really think about me' [CEV].

QUESTION—In what sense was Isaiah speaking about the people of Jesus' day?

What Isaiah said in his day also fit the situation in Jesus' time [BECNT, NAC, NTC]. Jesus was saying that, whatever Isaiah may have intended concerning the people of his own time, what he had prophesied fit the situation in Jesus' day [NICNT, PNTC]. Isaiah's words addressed to his own generation had typological correspondence to the people of Jesus' day [WBC]. Like the Jews in Jerusalem that Isaiah criticized, these Jews, who were also from Jerusalem, had religious practices that often focused on eternals at the expense of principle [EBC]. The Pharisees and scribes were repeating the error of the people of Isaiah's day [Lns]. The fact that Isaiah's words were recorded in scripture suggests that it can be related to other situations as well [NIGTC]. Jesus sees Isaiah's words as a prediction [My].

QUESTION—What does it mean to honor God with the lips but not the heart? It means that they say the right things, but don't really mean it [PNTC, TH, TRT]; they had good words, but lacked good works [PNTC]. There was a difference between what they said and what was really in their hearts [WBC]. They praised God with their words, but their hearts were corrupt [NTC].

15:9 and in-vain[a] they-worship[b] me teaching (as) doctrines[c] (the) commandments[d] of men.[e]' "

LEXICON—a. μάτην (LN 89.54) (BAGD p. 495): 'in vain' [BAGD, BECNT, BNTC, CC, **LN**, NICNT, NIGTC, NTC, PNTC; ESV, KJV, NASB, NET, NIV, NRSV, REB], 'vainly' [WBC], 'useless' [CEV], 'pointless' [GW], 'worthless' [NCV], 'a farce' [NLT], 'to no avail, with no result' [LN]. This adjective is translated 'it is no use' [**LN**; TEV]. This adjective describes a condition of being without any result [LN].

b. pres. mid. indic. of σέβομαι (LN 53.53) (BAGD 2.a. p. 746): 'to worship' [BAGD, LN; all translations except GW, NCV, NLT], 'to venerate' [LN]. This verb is translated as a noun: '(their) worship' [GW, NCV, NLT]. This verb means to express in attitude and ritual one's allegiance to and regard for deity [LN].

c. διδασκαλία (LN 33.236 (BAGD 2. p. 191): 'doctrine' [BAGD, BECNT, LN, NTC, PNTC, WBC; ESV, KJV, NASB, NET, NRSV, REB], 'what is taught' [LN], 'teaching' [CC, LN, NIGTC], 'ideas' [NLT], '(my) laws' [TEV], not explicit [BNTC; CEV]. The phrase διδάσκοντες διδασκαλίας 'teaching as doctrines' is translated 'teaching people to obey' [NICNT], 'the things they teach' [NCV], 'their teachings' [GW, NIV]. This noun denotes the content of what is taught [LN].

d. ἔνταλμα (LN 33.330) (BAGD p. 268): 'commandment' [BAGD, BNTC, CC, LN, PNTC, WBC; ESV, KJV, NET, REB], 'command' [NIGTC; NLT], 'rule' [NICNT; CEV, GW, NCV, NIV, TEV], 'precept' [BECNT, NTC; NASB, NRSV], 'order' [LN]. This noun denotes that which is authoritatively commanded [LN].

e. ἄνθρωπος (LN 9.1) (BAGD 1.a.β. p. 68): 'person, individual, human being' [LN], The plural form of this noun refers to 'men' [BAGD], 'human beings' [BAGD], 'people, mankind' [LN]. The genitive noun ἀνθρώπων 'of men' [CC, NTC; ESV, KJV, NASB, NET, REB] is translated 'taught by men' [NIV], 'men's' [PNTC], 'human' [BECNT, WBC; NCV, NRSV, TEV], 'merely human' [BNTC, NICNT], 'but human' [NIGTC], 'man-made' [NLT], 'made up/made by humans' [CEV, GW]. This noun denotes a human being, normally an adult [LN].

DISCOURSE UNIT—15:10–20 [CEV, ESV, NET, NRSV, TEV]. The topic is the things that make a person unclean [TEV], what really makes people unclean [CEV], what defiles a person [ESV], true defilement [NET], things that defile [NRSV].

15:10 And calling- the crowd -to-himself he-said to-them, "Listen[a] and understand;[b] **15:11** not what enters into the mouth defiles[c] the man, but what comes-out-of[d] the mouth this defiles the man."

LEXICON—a. pres. act. impera. of ἀκούω (LN 24.52) (BAGD 1.c. p. 32): 'to listen' [BAGD, NICNT, PNTC; GW, NCV, NET, NIV, NLT, NRSV, REB, TEV], 'to hear' [BAGD, BECNT, BNTC, LN, NIGTC, NTC, WBC; ESV, KJV, NASB], 'to pay attention' [CEV]. This present imperative is translated 'to begin to hear' [CC].

b. pres. act. impera. of συνίημι (LN 32.5) (BAGD p. 790): 'to understand' [BAGD, BECNT, BNTC, LN, NICNT, NIGTC, NTC, PNTC, WBC; all versions except CEV, GW, NLT], 'to try to understand' [CEV, GW, NLT], 'to comprehend' [BAGD, LN], 'to perceive, to have insight into' [LN]. This present imperative is translated 'to begin to understand' [CC]. This verb means to employ one's capacity for understanding and thus to arrive at insight [LN].

c. pres. act. indic. of κοινόω (LN 53.33) (BAGD 1.a. p. 438): 'to defile' [BAGD, BNTC, CC, LN, NIGTC, NTC, PNTC, WBC; ESV, KJV, NASB, NET, NLT, NRSV, REB], 'to make unclean' [LN, NICNT; GW, NCV, NIV], 'to make ritually unclean' [TEV], 'to make (you) unclean and unfit to worship God' [CEV], 'to make impure' [BAGD, BECNT], 'to profane' [LN]. This verb means to cause something to become unclean, profane, or ritually unacceptable [LN].

d. pres. mid. or pass. (deponent = act.) participle of ἐκπορεύομαι (LN 15.40) (BAGD 2. p. 244): 'to come out of' [BECNT, WBC; all versions except CEV, NASB, NLT], 'to exit out of' [CC], 'to go out of' [BNTC, LN, NICNT, NIGTC, NTC, PNTC], 'to proceed out of' [NASB], 'to come from' [LN], 'to depart out of, to leave from within' [LN]. The phrase 'what goes out of the mouth' is translated 'the words that come out of your mouth' [CEV, NLT]. This verb means to move out of an enclosed or well defined two or three-dimensional area [LN].

15:12 Then having-approached, the disciples say to-him, "Do-you-know[a] that the Pharisees having-heard (this) statement[b] were-offended[c]?"

LEXICON—a. perf. act. indic. of οἶδα (LN 28.1) (BAGD 1.e. p. 556): 'to know' [BAGD, BECNT, BNTC, CC, LN, NIGTC, NTC, PNTC, WBC; all versions except GW, NLT], 'to realize' [NICNT; GW, NLT], 'to know about, to have knowledge of' [LN]. This verb has a perfect tense form but a present tense meaning. It means to possess information about something [LN].

b. λόγος (LN 33.98) (BAGD 1.a.γ. p. 477): 'statement' [BAGD, BECNT, LN, WBC; GW, NASB], 'saying' [LN, PNTC; KJV, ESV, NET], 'what you said' [BNTC, NICNT, NTC; CEV, NCV, NRSV, TEV], 'what you have been saying' [REB], 'what you just said' [NLT], 'word' [CC, LN], 'words' [NIGTC], not explicit [NIV]. This noun denotes that which has

been stated or said, with primary focus upon the content of the communication [LN].
   c. aorist pass. indic. of σκανδαλίζομαι (LN **25.180**) (BAGD 2. p. 753): 'to be offended' [BNTC, **LN**, NTC; ESV, GW, KJV, NASB, NET, NIV], 'to take offense' [BECNT, LN, NICNT, PNTC; KJV, REB], 'to be scandalized' [NICNT, WBC], 'to be angry' [NCV], 'to be caused to stumble' [CC], 'to have one's feelings hurt' [TEV], 'to be given offense' [BAGD], 'to be shocked, to be angered' [BAGD]. This passive verb is translated by an active voice construction with Jesus as the acting subject: 'you insulted (the Pharisees)' [CEV], 'you offended (the Pharisees)' [NLT]. This verb means to be offended because of some action [LN].

QUESTION—What statement was it that offended them?
   1. It was Jesus' statement to the crowds in verse 11 about what did and did not constitute defilement EBC, ICC, Lns, My, NICNT, PNTC, WBC]. This would have been seen as usurping the teaching role of the Pharisees and scribes [Lns]. It could possibly also include all that was said previously in this confrontation [ICC].
   2. It was Jesus' sharp criticism in verse 3–9 of their regard for tradition over the law of God [BECNT, BNTC, NIBC, NTC, probably NAC].

QUESTION—Why did the disciples say this to Jesus?
They apparently held the Pharisees and scribes in high regard, and were surprised at Jesus' stern rejection of them [EBC, WBC]. They may have feared that Jesus' rebuke would stimulate further opposition [BECNT, CC]. They also were aware that the Pharisees and scribes were popular as interpreters of God's law [BECNT, CC]. They recognized that the point Jesus was making was quite radical and they want to be sure they understood what he intended [NAC]. The disciples were reluctant to offend the religious leaders [NIBC]. They perceived bitter resentment on the part of the Pharisees and scribes over what Jesus had said to them [NTC].

15:13 But answering he-said, "Every plant^a that my heavenly Father did-not -plant^b will-be-uprooted.^c

LEXICON—a. φυτεία (LN **3.1**) (BAGD p. 870): 'plant' [BAGD, BECNT, BNTC, LN, NICNT, NIGTC, PNTC, WBC; all versions], 'planted thing' [CC], 'growth' [NTC], 'that which is planted' [BAGD]. This noun denotes any kind of plant, whether tree, bush, or herb [LN].
   b. aorist act. indic. of φυτεύω (LN **43.5**) (BAGD p. 870): 'to plant' [BAGD, LN; all translations except NLT, REB]. This active verb is also translated as passive: 'to be planted' [NLT]. The phrase ἣν οὐκ ἐφύτευσεν ὁ πατήρ μου ὁ οὐράνιος 'that my heavenly Father did not plant' is translated 'not of my heavenly Father's planting' [REB]. This verb means to plant, used primarily in relation to vines, bushes, and trees [LN].
   c. fut. pass. indic. of ἐκριζόω (LN **43.11**) (BAGD 1. p. 244): 'to be uprooted' [BAGD, BECNT, CC, LN, NIGTC, NTC; GW, NASB, NET, NLT, NRSV], 'to be rooted up' [KJV, REB], 'to be pulled up' [**LN**;

TEV], 'to be rooted out/up' [NICNT, PNTC; ESV], 'to be pulled out/up by the roots' [BAGD, BNTC, LN; CEV, NCV, NIV]. This verb means to remove a plant, including its roots [LN].

QUESTION—What does the metaphor of uprooting signify?

It speaks of impending judgment [BECNT, ICC, Lns, NAC, NICNT, NTC]. It represents total destruction [WBC]. It refers only to the teaching of the Pharisees, a teaching that will not continue to stand [My, PNTC]. Or instead of referring to every false doctrine, this refers to the Pharisees, the leaders of the Jewish people, who were not reliable as spiritual guides because they were not truly part of God's planting [ESVSB]. It means, 'Those Pharisees are like plants which my Father in heaven did not plant and he will pull up every one of them' [TH]. What has bee made known by God is what counts. What he has not made known, but which the Pharisees teach so authoritatively has no future [PNTC].

15:14 Leave- them -alone[a]; they-are blind guides[b] of-blind-people; and if a-blind (person) guides[c] a-blind (person), both will-fall[d] into a-pit."[e]

TEXT—Manuscripts reading τυφλοί εἰσιν ὁδηγοί τυφλῶν 'they are blind guides of blind people' are given a C rating by GNT to indicate that choosing it over a variant text that omits 'of blind people' was difficult. Manuscripts that include 'of blind people' are followed by BECNT, BNTC, CC, NTC, PNTC, WBC; CEV, KJV, NASB, NLT, NRSV, TEV. Manuscripts that omit that variant are followed by NICNT, NIGTC, NTC; ESV, GW, NCV, NET, NIV, REB.

LEXICON—a. aorist act. impera. of ἀφίημι (LN 13.140) (BAGD 4. p. 126): 'to leave alone' [BNTC, NICNT, PNTC; GW, REB], 'to leave' [NET, NIV], 'to let alone' [BECNT; ESV, KJV, NASB, NRSV], 'to let be' [NIGTC, WBC], 'to let go' [NTC], 'to leave behind' [CC], 'to let, to allow' [BAGD, LN], 'to let go' [BAGD]. The phrase ἄφετε αὐτούς 'leave them alone' is translated 'Stay away from those/the Pharisees' [CEV, NCV], 'ignore them' [NLT], 'don't worry about them' [TEV]. This verb means to leave it to someone to do something, with the implication of distancing oneself from the event [LN].

b. ὁδηγός (LN 36.4) (BAGD 2. p. 553): 'guide' [BAGD, BECNT, BNTC, CC, LN, NICNT, NIGTC, PNTC, WBC; ESV, NASB, NET, NIV, NRSV, REB], 'leader' [BAGD, LN, NTC; GW, KJV, NCV, TEV], not explicit [CEV]. The phrase 'blind guides of blind people' is translated 'blind guides leading blind people' [NLT]. This noun denotes one who guides or leads [LN].

c. pres. act. subj. of ὁδηγέω (LN **15.182**) (BAGD 1. p. 553): 'to guide' [BAGD, BECNT, BNTC, **LN**, NIGTC, PNTC; NASB, NLT, NRSV, REB], 'to lead' [BAGD, CC, LN, NICNT, NTC, WBC; CEV, ESV, GW, KJV, NCV, NET, NIV, TEV]. This verb means to guide or to direct, with the implication of making certain that people reach an appropriate destination [LN].

d. fut. mid. (deponent = act.) indic. of πίπτω (LN 15.118) (BAGD 1.a. p. 659): 'to fall' [BAGD, LN; all translations]. This verb means to fall from one level to another [LN].

e. βόθυνος (LN 1.55) (BAGD p. 144): 'pit' [BECNT, BNTC, CC, LN, NTC, WBC; ESV, GW, NASB, NET, NIV, NRSV], 'ditch' [LN, NICNT, NIGTC, PNTC; CEV, KJV, NCV, NLT, REB, TEV], 'hole' [LN]. This noun denotes a hole, trench, or pit, natural or dug [LN].

DISCOURSE UNIT—15:15–20 [NASB]. The topic is the heart of man.

15:15 And having-answered Peter said to-him, "Explain[a] to-us this parable.[b]" **15:16** But he said, "Are-you(pl) also still[c] without-understanding[d]?

TEXT—Manuscripts reading τὴν παραβολὴν ταύτην 'this parable' are given a C rating by GNT to indicate that choosing it over a variant text that omits 'this' was difficult. Manuscripts that include 'this' are followed by BECNT, CC, NICNT, PNTC, WBC; GW, KJV, NET, NRSV, TEV. Manuscripts that omit 'this' are followed by BNTC, NIGTC, NTC; ESV, NASB, NCV, NIV, NLT,

LEXICON—a. aorist act. impera. of φράζω (LN **33.141**) (BAGD p. 865): 'to explain' [BAGD, **LN**; all translations except CEV, KJV, REB], 'to declare' [KJV], 'to tell' [REB], 'to interpret' [BAGD]. The phrase Φράσον ἡμῖν 'explain to us' is translated 'what did you mean?' [CEV]. This verb means to explain the meaning of something, with the implication that the text in question is difficult or complex [LN].

b. παραβολή (LN 33.15) (BAGD 2. p. 612): 'parable' [BAGD, BECNT, BNTC, CC, LN, NIGTC, NTC, PNTC; ESV, KJV, NASB, NET, NIV, NLT, NRSV, REB], 'analogy' [WBC], 'illustration' [BAGD; GW], 'example' [NCV], 'saying' [TEV], 'figure, allegory, figure of speech' [LN], not explicit [CEV]. This noun denotes a relatively short narrative with symbolic meaning [LN].

c. ἀκμήν (LN **67.128**) (BAGD p. 30): 'still' [BAGD, **LN**], 'even yet' [BAGD], 'yet' [LN]. The phrase Ἀκμὴν καί 'also still' [BECNT, BNTC; ESV, NRSV] is translated 'still also' [NIGTC; NASB], 'still' [NCV, NIV, REB, TEV], 'by now' [CEV], 'even now' [PNTC], 'even now still' [NICNT], 'also even now' [CC], 'also even yet' [NTC], 'also yet' [KJV], 'even yet also' [WBC], 'yet' [GW, NLT], 'even after all this' [NET]. This adverb describes extension of time up to and beyond an expected point [LN].

d. ἀσύνετος (LN 32.49) (BAGD 1. p. 118): 'without understanding' [BNTC, CC, **LN**, NIGTC, NTC, PNTC, WBC; ESV, KJV, NRSV], 'lacking in understanding' [BECNT; NASB], 'not able to understand' [NICNT], 'senseless, foolish' [BAGD, LN]. The phrase ὑμεῖς ἀσύνετοί ἐστε; 'are you without understanding?' is translated 'don't you understand?' [GW, NLT], 'do you not understand?' [NCV], 'don't any of you know what I am talking about?' [CEV], 'are you so foolish?' [NET], 'are you so dull?' [NIV], 'are you as dull as the rest?' [REB], 'you are no more intelligent than the others' [TEV]. This adjective describes a lack of proper use of mental capacity for insight and understanding [LN].

QUESTION—What was the 'parable' that the disciples were asking about?

It was what Jesus said in verse 11 about the thing that defiles a man [BECNT, BNTC, CC, EBC, ICC, Lns, My, NIBC, NICNT, NTC, PNTC, TH, TRT, WBC].

QUESTION—In what sense was what Jesus said a parable?

A parable is something that is not to be taken literally, but applied in another way [NIGTC]. A parable does not have to be a story, [PNTC], it may simply be a proverb [WBC], a wise saying [NTC, PNTC, WBC], or even an enigmatic saying or riddle [BNTC, NIBC, WBC]. A parable was a pithy statement of a general nature, which would need to be understood and applied in specific cases [NICNT]. What Jesus said in verse 11 is framed as an antithetical proverb or wisdom saying, the application of which was not clear to the disciples [ICC]. In this case, the statement was puzzling because it was so radical, challenging their basic understanding of what religion is [NIBC]. It was enigmatic for the idea that something coming from *within* could defile a person [BNTC]. What Jesus said is a parable in the sense that he was *indirectly* comparing the Pharisees' teaching on what constitutes purity with his own teaching [CC].

15:17 Do-you(pl)- not -understand[a] (that) everything[b] entering into the mouth goes into the stomach[c] and is-expelled[d] into the latrine[e]? **15:18** But the-things going-out of the mouth come-out from the heart, and-those-things defile the man.

LEXICON—a. pres. act. indic. of νοέω (LN 32.2) (BAGD 1.b. p. 540): 'to understand' [BAGD, BECNT, BNTC, LN; KJV, NASB, NET, TEV], 'to know' [NTC; CEV, GW, NCV], 'to perceive' [BAGD, PNTC], 'to see' [ESV, NIV, NRSV, REB], 'to be aware' [WBC], 'to comprehend' [CC, LN], 'to realize' [NICNT, NIGTC], 'to gain insight into, to apprehend' [BAGD], not explicit [NLT]. This verb means to comprehend something on the basis of careful thought and consideration [LN].

b. πᾶν (LN 59.23) (BAGD 1.c.γ. p. 632): 'everything' [BAGD, BECNT, BNTC, CC, NICNT, NIGTC, PNTC, WBC; NASB], 'whatever' [NTC; ESV, GW, NET, NIV, NRSV, REB], 'anything' [NLT, TEV], 'whatsoever' [KJV], 'the food' [CEV], 'all the food' [NCV], 'all, every' [LN]. This adjective describes the totality of any object, mass, collective, or extension [LN].

c. κοιλία (LN 8.67) (BAGD 1. p. 437): 'stomach' [BAGD, BECNT, NIGTC, NTC, PNTC, WBC; all versions except KJV], 'digestive system' [BNTC], 'belly' [BAGD, CC, LN, NICNT; KJV], 'internal organs' [LN]. This noun denotes the entire digestive apparatus, including stomach and intestines [LN].

d. pres. pass. indic. of ἐκβάλλω (LN 15.44) (BAGD 3. p. 237): 'to be expelled' [CC, LN, NIGTC; ESV], 'to be passed out' [NICNT], 'to be evacuated' [BNTC], 'to be eliminated' [NASB], 'to be discharged' [REB], 'to be cast out' [KJV], 'to be sent away, to be driven out' [LN], 'to be taken out, to be removed' [BAGD]. This passive verb is also translated as an active verb: 'to pass' [BECNT, NTC, WBC], 'to pass out' [NET], 'to go out' [PNTC; CEV, NCV, NIV, NRSV, TEV], 'to go' [GW, NLT]. This verb means to cause to go out or leave, often, but not always, involving force [LN].

e. ἀφεδρῶν (LN **7.72**) (BAGD p. 124): 'latrine' [BAGD, BNTC, CC, **LN**, NIGTC, NTC, PNTC, WBC], 'toilet' [BECNT, LN, NICNT; GW], 'sewer' [NET, NLT, NRSV], 'drain' [REB], 'draught' [KJV], not explicit [ESV, NASB]. The phrase 'into the latrine' is translated 'out of the/your body' [CEV, NCV, NIV, TEV].

QUESTION—What is the ἀφεδρῶν 'latrine'?

It is not a drain, but a privy, a place to which someone retires and sits down [Lns, PNTC]. It is probably a disposal bucket [NAC].

15:19 For from the heart come evil thoughts,ª murders,ᵇ adulteries,ᶜ fornications,ᵈ thefts,ᵉ false-testimonies,ᶠ blasphemies.ᵍ **15:20** These are what defile the person, but eating with-unwashed hands does- not -defile the person."

LEXICON—a. διαλογισμός (LN 30.10) (BAGD 1. p. 186): 'thought' [BAGD, BECNT, BNTC, NICNT, PNTC; all versions except NET, NRSV, TEV], 'argument' [CC], 'inclination' [NIGTC], 'scheme' [NTC], 'deliberation' [WBC], 'idea' [NET, TEV], 'intention' [NRSV], 'reasoning' [BAGD, LN]. This noun denotes the act of thinking or reasoning with thoroughness and completeness [LN].

b. φόνος (LN 20.82) (BAGD p. 864): 'murder' [BAGD, LN; all translations except TEV], 'to kill' [TEV], 'killing' [BAGD]. This noun denotes the action of depriving a person of life by illegal, intentional killing [LN].

c. μοιχεία (LN 88.276) (BAGD p. 526): 'adultery' [BAGD, LN; all translations except CEV], 'unfaithfulness in marriage' [CEV]. This noun denotes sexual intercourse of a man with a married woman other than his own spouse [LN].

d. πορνεία (LN 88.271) (BAGD 1. p. 693): 'fornication' [BAGD, BECNT, BNTC, CC, LN, NIGTC, PNTC, WBC; KJV, NASB, NRSV, REB], 'sexual immorality' [ESV, NET, NIV, NLT], 'sexual offense' [NICNT], 'sexual sin' [NTC; GW, NCV], 'vulgar deed' [CEV], '(do other) immoral things' [TEV], 'prostitution' [BAGD, LN]. This noun denotes the act of engaging in sexual immorality of any kind, often with the implication of prostitution [LN].

e. κλοπή (LN 57.232) (BAGD p. 436): 'theft' [BAGD, BECNT, BNTC, LN, NICNT, NIGTC, NTC, PNTC; ESV, KJV, NASB, NET, NIV, NLT, NRSV, REB], 'thievery' [CC], 'robbery' [WBC], 'stealing' [BAGD;

CEV, GW, NCV], 'to rob' [TEV]. This noun denotes the act of taking secretly and without permission the property of someone else [LN].
   f. ψευδομαρτυρία (LN 33.272) (BAGD p. 892): 'false testimony' [BAGD, LN, NICNT, NTC; NET, NIV], 'false witness' [BAGD, BECNT, BNTC, NIGTC; ESV, KJV, NASB, NRSV], 'false witnessing' [CC], 'perjury' [PNTC; REB], 'telling lies' [CEV], 'lying' [GW, NCV, NLT], 'lie' [WBC], 'to lie' [TEV]. This noun denotes the content of what is testified falsely [LN].
   g. βλασφημία (LN **33.400**) (BAGD 1. p. 143): 'blasphemy' [BAGD, CC, PNTC, WBC; KJV], 'slander' [BAGD, BECNT, BNTC, NICNT, NIGTC; ESV, NASB, NET, NIV, NLT, NRSV, REB], 'reviling' [**LN**], 'abusive speech' [BAGD, NTC], 'defamation' [BAGD], 'insulting others' [CEV], 'to slander others' [TEV], 'speaking evil of others' [NCV], 'cursing' [GW]. This noun denotes the act of speaking against someone in such a way as to harm or injure his or her reputation [LN].

QUESTION—What is the relationship of 'evil thoughts' to the rest of this list of vices?

The rest of the vices listed flow from the evil thoughts [ICC, My, NIGTC; TEV]. Evil thoughts can lead to all sorts of evil actions [NICNT, NTC, PNTC]. All the other sins originate in the heart, where the evil thoughts occur [NICNT]. Jesus began with internal thoughts and moved to external actions [BECNT, NTC]. The six vices that follow 'wicked considerations' are in apposition to it, listing what some of those considerations consist of [Lns]. (Note that the other commentaries consulted made no mention of any relationship between the evil thoughts and the sins listed subsequently, so presumably they saw no causal connection.)

QUESTION—Is there any significance in the particular sins that are listed?

They are sins prohibited in the second table of the Ten Commandments [BECNT]. They follow the order of commandments six through nine in the Ten Commandments [EBC, ICC, NAC, NIBC, NIGTC, PNTC, TH, WBC]. This list follows Jesus' discussion of the violation of the fifth commandment concerning honoring one's parents [NIBC].

QUESTION—What is the range of behaviors covered by πορνεία 'fornication'?

It is a general term for sexual sin or immorality [NIGTC, NTC; ESV, GW, NCV, NET, NIV, NLT], for sexual sin of any kind [NICNT, PNTC, TH, TRT; NLT].

QUESTION—Is βλασφημία 'blasphemy' critical speech directed toward God or toward other people?

Here it refers to slander of other people [BNTC, My, NICNT, TH]. It includes slanders against both God and other people [PNTC, TRT]. It is verbal sin against God [ICC]. Jesus may have been referring to the Pharisees' attempts to defame him [BECNT].

DISCOURSE UNIT—15:21-39 [NICNT]. The topic is the Messiah's mission extended beyond Israel.

DISCOURSE UNIT—15:21-31 [GW]. The topic is the faith of a Canaanite woman.

DISCOURSE UNIT—15:21-28 [ICC; CEV, ESV, NASB, NCV, NET, NLT, NRSV, TEV]. The topic is Jesus helps a non-Jewish woman [NCV], a woman's faith [CEV, TEV], a Canaanite woman's faith [NET], the Canaanite woman's faith [NRSV], the faith of a Canaanite woman [ESV], the faith of a Gentile woman [NLT], the Syrophoenician woman [NASB], the Canaanite woman [ICC].

15:21 **And having-gone-out from-there Jesus withdrew**[a] **into the region**[b] **of-Tyre and Sidon.**

LEXICON—a. aorist act. indic. of ἀναχωρέω (LN 15.53) (BAGD 2.b. p. 63): 'to withdraw' [BAGD, BECNT, CC, LN, NICNT, NIGTC; ESV, NASB, NIV, REB], 'to depart' [BNTC; KJV], 'to retire' [BAGD, LN, NTC], 'to go' [WBC; CEV, GW, NCV, NET, NLT], 'to go away' [LN, PNTC; NRSV], 'to go off' [LN; TEV], 'to take refuge' [BAGD]. This verb means to move away from a location, implying a considerable distance [LN].

b. μέρος (LN 1.79) (BAGD 1.b.g. p. 506): 'region' [BAGD, BECNT, BNTC, **LN**, NICNT, PNTC; GW, NET, NIV, NLT, REB], 'territory' [LN; CEV, TEV], 'district' [BAGD, NIGTC, NTC; ESV, NASB, NRSV], 'area' [NCV], 'land' [LN]. This plural noun, which is normally translated as singular, is translated using a plural form: 'regions' [WBC], 'parts' [CC], 'coasts' [KJV]. This noun, which is always in the plural, denotes a region or regions of the earth, normally in relation to some ethnic group or geographical center, but not necessarily constituting a unit of governmental administration [LN].

QUESTION—What does the phrase ὁ Ἰησοῦς ἀνεχώρησεν 'Jesus withdrew' imply about Jesus' motives for this journey?

He is withdrawing from conflict and confrontation [BECNT, CC, Lns, My, NICNT, PNTC], from potential danger [ICC, NIGTC]. He is going into an area where he would be less well-known [WBC]. He is withdrawing from ministry responsibilities [BNTC]. He wants to avoid a further escalation of opposition, at least for the present [CC]. He is avoiding Jewish opposition and Jewish crowds [NICNT].

QUESTION—How long a journey would this have been?

It was a distance of about fifty miles [BECNT, NIBC]. Tyre was about twenty-five miles northwest of Lake Galilee and Sidon was about twenty-five miles north of Tyre [EBC, PNTC, TH]. The round trip could have taken months [PNTC]. He may have been gone for as much as six months [NTC].

QUESTION—Did Jesus actually leave Jewish territory?
1. He entered non-Jewish territory [BECNT, CC, EBC, Lns, NAC, NIBC, NICNT, NTC, PNTC, TH, WBC, probably BNTC, NIGTC], as is made more clear by Mark 7:31 [EBC].
2. He remained in Jewish territory [My].

15:22 And behold,[a] a-Canaanite woman from that region[b] having-come-out was-crying-out saying, "Have-mercy[c] on-me, Lord, Son-of David; my daughter is- severely[d] -demonized.[e]"

LEXICON—a. ἰδού (LN 91.13): 'behold' [BNTC; ESV, KJV], 'lo and behold' [NTC], 'look' [CC, LN, PNTC, WBC], 'suddenly' [BECNT; CEV], 'just then' [NRSV], 'listen, pay attention' [LN], not explicit [NICNT, NIGTC; GW, NASB, NCV, NET, NIV, NLT, REB, TEV]. This particle is a prompter of attention, and serves to emphasize the following statement [LN].

b. ὅριον (LN 1.79) (BAGD p. 581): 'region' [BAGD, CC, LN, NIGTC, NTC; ESV, NASB, NRSV, TEV], 'regions' [WBC], 'territory' [LN; GW], 'land' [LN], 'district' [BAGD, BNTC, LN], 'vicinity' [BECNT; NIV], 'area' [NICNT; NCV, NET], 'parts' [PNTC; REB], 'coasts' [KJV]. The phrase ἀπὸ τῶν ὁρίων 'from that region' is translated 'from there' [CEV], 'who lived there' [NLT]. This noun, which is always in the plural, denotes a region or regions of the earth, normally in relation to some ethnic group or geographical center, but not necessarily constituting a unit of governmental administration [LN].

c. aorist act. impera. of ἐλεάω (LN **88.76**) (BAGD p. 249): 'to have mercy on' [BAGD, BECNT, BNTC, CC, **LN**, NIGTC, PNTC, WBC; all versions except CEV, REB], 'to show mercy' [BAGD, NICNT], 'to be merciful to/toward' [BAGD, LN], 'to take pity on' [NTC], 'to have pity on' [BAGD; CEV, REB]. This verb means to show kindness or concern for someone in serious need [LN].

d. κακῶς (LN **78.17**) (BAGD 1. p. 398): 'severely' [BAGD, BECNT, LN, NICNT, NTC, WBC; ESV], 'grievously' [**LN**; KJV], 'completely' [BNTC], 'terribly' [CC, NIV], 'horribly' [NET], 'badly' [BAGD, NIGTC], 'wickedly' [PNTC], 'cruelly' [NASB], 'seriously, dangerously' [LN], not explicit [CEV, GW, NRSV, REB]. This adverb is translated 'she is suffering very much' [NCV], 'that torments her severely' [NLT], 'she is in a terrible condition' [TEV]. This adverb describes a high point on a scale of extent and implying harm and seriousness of the state [LN].

e. pres. mid. or pass. (deponent = act.) indic. of δαιμονίζομαι (LN 12.41) (BAGD p. 169): 'to be demon possessed' [BECNT, CC, LN, PNTC; NASB, NET], 'to be possessed by a demon' [BAGD, BNTC, NIGTC; NLT], 'to be oppressed by a demon' [ESV], 'to suffer from being possessed by a demon' [WBC], 'to suffer from demon-possession' [NIV], 'to be tormented by a demon' [BAGD, NICNT, NTC; GW, NRSV], 'to be tormented by a devil' [REB], 'to have a demon' [NCV, TEV], 'to be vexed with a devil' [KJV]. The phrase κακῶς δαιμονίζεται 'is severely demonized' is translated 'is full of demons' [CEV]. This verb means to be possessed by a demon [LN].

QUESTION—What is the function of ἰδού 'behold' in this verse?

It is used to introduce the woman as an important character for the story [NIGTC, PNTC]. It draws attention to something unexpected [BECNT, CC, EBC, ICC, TRT, WBC], or remarkable [Lns], a new development [NICNT], which in this case is a Gentile woman approaching Jesus to ask something of him [CC, WBC]. It is an attention getter [TH].

QUESTION—What is implied by the use of the term 'Canaanite' as opposed to the more commonly used 'Phoenician' or 'Greek'?

It has OT associations with those pagans displaced by the people of Israel, and who stand in contrast to the people of God [WBC]. The term recalls OT accounts of Israel's ancient enemies [EBC, ICC, Lns, NICNT, NIGTC, TRT]. As a Canaanite, this woman would have had no covenantal basis for a claim on Israel's God [EBC]. This name had associations with evil in previous eras [NAC]. She is distinctly different ethnically, and her ancestors were traditional enemies of Israel [NIBC]. The Canaanites were among Israel's most persistent and dangerous enemies, yet in Matthew's genealogy of Jesus two of the women, Rahab and Tamar, are Canaanites [NICNT].

QUESTION—In what sense did she 'come out'?

1. It means that she went out of her home [PNTC, TH] or her village [NICNT, TH]. It reflects either the fact that her ancestry was there, or that she came out of her home [EBC]. She left her district and met him on the eastern border of the Phoenician area [BNTC, Lns].
2. She came out of the Gentile region and crossed into the area of the Jews, where Jesus had remained [My].

QUESTION—What did the woman intend by using the term κύριος 'Lord'?

It expresses reverence and respect [BNTC, NTC], worshipful reverence [NIGTC]. It comes from faith, and is the same way Jesus' disciples would address him [CC]. Here it has its fullest meaning, expressing Jesus' Lordship [PNTC]. She understands it as a messianic title [Lns, NICNT]. It is unclear what she may have meant, though Matthew's readers would certainly have seen its full meaning [EBC].

QUESTION—Why did this foreign woman call him 'Son of David'?

She was acknowledging Jesus as the Jewish Messiah [EBC, CC, Lns, My, NAC, NIBC, NICNT, NIGTC, NTC, PNTC, TH, TRT, WBC]. She understood something important about Jesus and his mission [BECNT]. She knew of his Davidic descent [BNTC].

MATTHEW 15:23–24

15:23 But he did- not -answer[a] her a-word. And his disciples having-approached were-asking[b] him saying, "Send- her -away, for she-cries-out after us." **15:24** But he having-answered said, "I-was-sent only[c] to the lost[d] sheep of-(the) house[e] of-Israel."

LEXICON—a. aorist pass. (deponent = act.) indic. of ἀποκρίνομαι (LN 33.28) (BAGD 1. p. 93): 'to answer' [BAGD, BECNT, BNTC, CC, NIGTC, NTC, PNTC, WBC; ESV, GW, KJV, NASB, NCV, NET, NIV, NRSV], 'to reply' [BAGD, NICNT], 'to say' [LN; CEV, TEV], 'to say...in reply' [REB], 'to give reply' [NLT], 'to speak, to declare' [LN]. This verb means to introduce or continue a somewhat formal discourse [LN].

b. imperf. act. indic. of ἐρωτάω (LN 33.161) (BAGD 2. p. 312): 'to ask' [BAGD, BECNT, CC, WBC; CEV], 'to beg' [NICNT; ESV, NCV, NET, TEV], 'to press' [NIGTC], 'to urge' [NTC; GW, NIV, NLT, NRSV, REB], 'to request' [BAGD, BNTC, LN, PNTC], 'to implore' [NASB], 'to beseech' [KJV], 'to ask for' [LN]. This verb means to ask for, usually with the implication of an underlying question [LN].

c. εἰ μή (LN 89.131): 'only' [BECNT, NIGTC, NTC; all versions except KJV], 'not...except' [BNTC, CC], 'not anyone except' [NICNT], 'no one except' [WBC], 'not...but' [PNTC; KJV], 'except that, but, however, instead, but only' [LN]. This phrase indicates contrast by designating an exception [LN].

d. perf. act. participle of ἀπόλλυμι (LN 27.29) (BAGD 2.b. p. 95): 'to be lost' [BAGD], 'to lose, to no longer know where something is' [LN]. This participle is translated as an adjective: 'lost' [all translations]. This verb means to become unaware of the location of something [LN].

e. οἶκος (LN 11.58) (BAGD 3. p. 561): 'house' [BAGD, BECNT, BNTC, CC, NICNT, NIGTC, NTC, PNTC, WBC; ESV, KJV, NASB, NET, NRSV, REB], 'people' [CEV, NCV, NLT, TEV], 'descendants' [BAGD], 'nation' [BAGD; GW], not explicit [NIV].

QUESTION—Were the disciples asking Jesus to grant her request and then send her away, or simply to send her away?

1. They expected him to grant her request and then dismiss her [BNTC, CC, EBC, Lns, My, NAC, NICNT, PNTC, WBC]. They had never seen Jesus turn anyone away and did not expect him to do so now [PNTC]. In the next verse Jesus will give a reason for not helping her rather than for not sending her away [EBC].
2. They just wanted him to send her away, without granting her request [BECNT, NIBC, NIGTC, NTC, TH].

QUESTION—To whom was Jesus' speaking?

Jesus responds to the disciples' having asked that he grant her request, but it is left unstated whether he was responding to the disciples, or to the woman, or to both [BNTC, NAC]. The answer to this question depends in part on how the previous question was answered If the disciples were asking him to send her away *without* helping her, his reply would more naturally be seen as

addressing the woman, whereas if they are asking him to grant her request, his reply could more reasonably be seen as being addressed to them.
1. He was addressing the disciples [CC, EBC, My, NICNT, PNTC, WBC].
2. He was addressing the woman [BECNT, NIGTC, NTC, TH; NLT].

QUESTION—Does 'the lost sheep of the house of Israel' refer to the whole nation as being lost sheep, or only to certain ones who were lost?
1. It refers to all the people of Israel, all of whom are like lost sheep [BECNT, CC, EBC, ICC, Lns, NAC, NICNT, WBC; CEV, NCV, NLT].
2. It refers to those of Israel who are lost, not to all of Israel as being lost [BNTC, NIBC, NIGTC].

15:25 But she having-come was-bowing-down[a] to-him saying, "Lord,[b] help[c] me." **15:26** But he having-answered said, "It-is not good[d] to take the bread[e] of-the children and throw (it) to the dogs.[f]"

LEXICON—a. imperf. act. indic. of προσκυνέω (LN 17.21) (BAGD 5. p. 717): 'to bow down' [BECNT; GW], 'to bow down before' [NICNT; NASB, NET], 'to bow before' [NCV], 'to worship' [WBC; KJV, NLT], 'to fall reverently before' [BNTC], 'to do obeisance to' [NIGTC], 'to pay homage' [CC], 'to kneel down' [CEV], 'to kneel before' [PNTC; ESV, NIV, NRSV], 'to fall at (someone's) feet' [NTC; REB, TEV], 'to prostrate oneself before' [LN], 'to fall down and worship, to prostrate oneself before, to do reverence to' [BAGD]. This verb means to prostrate oneself before someone as an act of reverence, fear, or supplication [LN].

b. κύριος (LN 12.9, 87.53) (BAGD 2.c.β. p. 459): 'Lord' [BAGD, LN (12.9); all translations except REB, TEV], 'sir' [LN (87.53); REB, TEV], 'mister' [LN (87.53)]. As a title for God and for Christ this noun denotes one who exercises supernatural authority over mankind [LN (12.9)]. It may also be used as a title of respect used in addressing or speaking of a man [LN (87.53)].

c. pres. act. impera. of βοηθέω (LN 35.1) (BAGD 2. p. 144): 'to help' [BAGD, LN; all translations]. This verb means to assist in supplying what may be needed [LN].

d. καλός (LN 88.4) (BAGD 3.b.,c. p. 400): 'good' [BECNT, BNTC, CC, LN, NIGTC, PNTC; NASB], 'right' [NICNT, WBC; all versions except KJV, NASB, NRSV], 'proper' [NTC], 'fair' [NRSV], 'meet' [KJV], 'praiseworthy' [BAGD 3.b., LN], 'morally good, pleasing to God' [BAGD 3.b], 'better' [BAGD 3.c.]. This adjective describes a positive moral quality, with the implication of being favorably valued [LN].

e. ἄρτος (LN 5.1) (BAGD 1.a. p. 110): 'bread' [BAGD, BECNT, BNTC, CC, NICNT, NIGTC, NTC, PNTC, WBC; ESV, KJV, NASB, NCV, NET, NIV, REB], 'food' [LN; CEV, GW, NLT, NRSV, TEV]. This noun denotes any kind of food or nourishment [LN].

f. κυνάριον (LN 4.35) (BAGD p. 457): 'dog' [BAGD, BECNT, CC, NICNT, NIGTC, PNTC, WBC; all versions], 'puppy' [BNTC], 'house dog' [LN, NTC], 'little dog' [BAGD, LN].

QUESTION—What is being expressed by the term προσκυνέω 'bowing down'?

She was kneeling to plead for help [EBC, PNTC, TH; CEV, ESV, NIV, NRSV]. Her bowing down was also intended as an act of worship [BECNT, NTC, PNTC, WBC], as was her use of the title 'Lord' [BECNT]. Whatever she may have intended, Matthew sees it as an act of worship [NAC]. It was obeisance that was not far from the full sense of 'worship' [NIGTC].

QUESTION—What is the connotation of the term 'dog' as Jesus uses it here?

This noun denotes a house dog [BAGD, Lns, NIBC, NTC, PNTC, TRT, WBC], or pet [BAGD, ICC, Lns, NAC, NTC, TH], as opposed to dogs of the farm or in the street [BAGD]. It clearly has a negative implication [CC, EBC, NICNT, NIGTC], implying Israel's superior privilege over Gentiles in spiritual things [CC, NIGTC, WBC]. It is very blunt [CC]. Although the expression is rather harsh, Jesus' use of it was without insult or bitterness [BECNT, BNTC, NIBC, PNTC, TRT]. Jesus was not speaking in a derogatory manner here [TH, TRT], but is indicating the priority of one group over another, that the people of Israel would be ministered to first [TH]. Jesus is testing her faith [TRT]. Jesus' statement primarily reflects an attitude of pastoral concern for Israel as the covenant people of God, and the recognition that the Gentiles were not part of that covenant [BECNT]. Jewish people described Gentiles this way because Gentiles did not make distinctions between clean and unclean foods [NIBC]. This diminutive form is not as harsh as the normal word for 'dog' [My]. In the NT the diminutive force of this noun may have become lost, though a component of emotive attachment or affection is no doubt retained and thus the reference is presumably to a house dog [LN].

15:27 But she-said, "Yes, Lord, for[a] even the dogs eat from the crumbs[b] falling from the table of their masters."

LEXICON—a. γάρ (BAGD 1.e. p. 152): 'for' [BAGD]. The phrase ναί, καὶ γάρ 'yes, for even' [BNTC, CC, PNTC], is translated 'yes, it is, for even' [NICNT], 'yes, yet even' [ESV, KJV, NRSV], 'yes, but even' [BECNT; NASB, NCV, NET, NIV], 'right, but even' [NTC; similarly GW], 'that's true, but even' [CEV, NLT, TEV; similarly WBC], 'true, and yet' [REB], 'yes, to be sure, and' [NIGTC].

b. ψιχίον (LN 5.5) (BAGD p. 893): 'crumb' [BAGD, BECNT, BNTC, CC, **LN**, NICNT, WBC; CEV, ESV, KJV, NASB, NCV, NET, NIV, NRSV], 'scrap' [LN, NIGTC, NTC, PNTC; GW, NLT, REB], 'leftovers' [TEV], 'very little bit' [BAGD]. This noun denotes a small piece of food (normally bread) [LN].

QUESTION—What is communicated by the phrase Ναί κύριε καὶ γάρ 'Yes, Lord, for even'?

The woman agrees with Jesus about the priority of the Jews over Gentiles in his mission [CC, ICC, Lns, My, NAC, NIGTC, PNTC, TRT, WBC], that the Jews have a claim on the Messiah that Gentiles do not have [EBC], and then she extends the application of his illustration about the dogs to show that even the dogs have a place in the household, getting crumbs that fall from the table [BECNT, CC, EBC, ICC, Lns, My, NAC, NIGTC, NTC, PNTC, TRT]. She is asking only that she be treated like the little house dogs that are allowed to pick up the scraps that fall to the floor [NIBC]. Her reply is a feisty refusal to accept what Jesus is implying; even while acknowledging that Jesus' first priority is with the Jews, she presses the point that it does not have to stop there [NICNT].

15:28 Then Jesus having-answered said to-her, "O woman,[a] great[b] (is) your faith. Be-it-done for-you as you-wish.[c]" And her daughter was-healed[d] from that hour.[e]

LEXICON—a. γυνή (LN 9.34) (BAGD 1. p. 168): 'woman' [BAGD, LN]. The vocative ῏Ω γύναι 'O woman' [BECNT, BNTC, CC, NTC, PNTC, WBC; ESV, KJV, NASB], is translated 'Woman' [NIGTC; GW, NCV, NET, NIV, NRSV], 'Dear woman' [CEV, NLT], 'My dear woman' [NICNT], 'Lady' [LN], not explicit [REB]. The phrase 'O woman, great is your faith' is translated 'You are a woman of great faith' [TEV]. This noun denotes an adult female person of marriageable age [LN]. As a form of address, γυνή 'woman' was used in Koine Greek in speaking politely to a female person [LN].

b. μέγας (LN 78.2) (BAGD 2.a.γ. p. 498): 'great' [BAGD, BECNT, BNTC, CC, LN, NICNT, NIGTC, NTC, PNTC, WBC; ESV, KJV, NASB, NCV, NET, NIV, NLT, NRSV], 'strong' [GW], 'firm' [BAGD], 'to a great degree, intense' [LN]. The phrase μεγάλη σου ἡ πίστις 'great is your faith' is translated 'you really do have a lot of faith' [CEV], 'you are a woman of great faith' [TEV], 'what faith you have' [REB]. This adjective describes the upper range of a scale of extent, with the possible implication of importance in relevant contexts [LN].

c. pres. act. indic. of θέλω (LN 25.1): 'to wish' [BECNT, BNTC, CC, LN, NIGTC, PNTC; NAS, NRSV, REB], 'to desire' [LN, NTC; ESV], 'to want' [LN, WBC; CEV, GW, NET, TEV], 'to will' [KJV], 'to ask' [NCV]. The phrase γενηθήτω σοι ὡς θέλεις 'be it done for you as you wish' is translated 'your wish is granted' [NICNT], 'your request is granted' [NIV, NLT]. This verb means to desire to have or experience something [LN].

d. aorist pass. indic. of ἰάομαι (LN 23.136) (BAGD 1. p. 368): 'to be healed' [BAGD, BECNT, BNTC, CC, LN, NIGTC, NTC, PNTC, WBC; all versions except GW, KJV, REB], 'to be cured' [BAGD, LN, NICNT; GW], 'to be made whole' [KJV], 'to be restored to health' [REB], 'to be made well' [LN]. This verb means to cause someone to become well again after having been sick [LN].

e. καιρός (LN 67.1): 'time, occasion' [LN]. The phrase ἀπὸ τῆς ὥρας ἐκείνης 'from that hour' [BNTC, CC, PNTC; NET] is translated 'from that very hour' [NIGTC, WBC; KJV, NIV], 'from then on' [BECNT, 'from that moment' [NICNT; REB], 'from that very moment' [NTC], 'at that moment' [CEV, GW, NCV], 'at that very moment' [TEV], 'instantly' [ESV, NLT, NRSV], 'at once' [NASB]. This noun denotes points of time consisting of occasions for particular events [LN].

QUESTION—What is signified by the use of ᾦ 'O' with the vocative γύναι 'woman'?

It is emphatic [BECNT, NICNT], expressing admiration [NICNT] and emotion [EBC, ICC, PNTC], and shows how Jesus was moved by her faith [BECNT, WBC]. It indicates special solemnity, since it is relatively uncommon [Lns]. It adds intensity [NIGTC].

DISCOURSE UNIT—15:29–39 [ICC; NIV]. The topic is Jesus feeds the four thousand [NIV], the feeding of the four thousand [ICC].

DISCOURSE UNIT—15:29–31 [CEV, ESV, NASB, NCV, NET, NLT, NRSV, TEV]. The topic is Jesus heals many people [CEV, NCV, NLT, TEV], Jesus cures many people [NRSV], Jesus heals many [ESV], healing many others [NET], healing crowds [NASB].

15:29 And having-departed from-there Jesus went[a] along[b] Lake Galilee, and having-gone-up on the mountain[c] he-sat there.

LEXICON—a. aorist act. indic. of ἔρχομαι (LN 15.81) (BAGD I.1.a.β. p. 310): 'to go' [CC, NICNT, NTC, PNTC; CEV, GW, NASB, NCV, NET, NIV, TEV], 'to come' [BAGD, BNTC, LN, NIGTC, WBC; KJV], 'to pass' [BECNT; NRSV], 'to walk' [ESV], 'to return' [NLT], 'to take the road' [REB]. This verb means to move toward or up to the reference point of the viewpoint character or event [LN].

b. παρά with accusative (LN 83.25) (BAGD III.1.b.β. p. 611): 'along' [BECNT, NTC, PNTC; CEV, GW, NET, NIV, NRSV], 'along by' [NICNT; NASB, TEV], 'alongside' [LN], 'by' [CC, LN; REB], 'beside' [NIGTC, WBC; ESV], 'near' [KJV], 'to' [NLT]. The phrase ἦλθεν παρά 'went along' is translated 'went along the shore of' [NCV], 'came to the shore of' [BNTC]. This preposition describes a position near another location or object, usually with the implication of being alongside or close to [LN].

c. ὄρος (LN 1.46) (BAGD p. 582): 'mountain' [BAGD, BECNT, CC, LN, NIGTC, PNTC, WBC; ESV, GW, KJV, NASB, NET, NRSV], 'mountainside' [NIV], 'hill' [BAGD, NTC; CEV, NCV, NLT, REB, TEV], 'hill country' [BNTC], 'hills' [NICNT]. This noun, which has a definite article is translated without it by CC, NIGTC, NTC; CEV, GW, KJV, NCV, NET, NIV, NLT, REB, TEV. It is translated with the definite article by BECNT, BNTC, NICNT, PNTC, WBC; ESV, NASB, NRSV. This noun denotes a relatively high elevation of land, in contrast with βουνός 'hill', which is by comparison somewhat lower [LN].

d. imperf. mid. or pass. (deponent = act.) of κάθημαι (LN 17.12) (BAGD 2. p. 389): 'to sit down' [BAGD, LN], 'to sit' [LN], 'to be seated, to be sitting' [LN]. This verb in the imperfect tense is translated as indicating a single action of taking a seat: 'he sat' [BNTC, NICNT, PNTC; GW, NCV], 'he sat down' [NIGTC, WBC; CEV, ESV, KJV, NET, NIV, NLT, NRSV, REB, TEV]; as indicating an ongoing action of being in a sitting position: 'he was sitting' [BECNT, CC, NTC; NASB]. This verb means to be in a seated position or to take such a position [LN].

QUESTION—Where did this event take place?
  1. It was on the eastern side of Lake Galilee, in Gentile territory [EBC, Lns, NAC, NIBC, NICNT, NTC, PNTC], in the Decapolis [EBC, Lns, PNTC]. Jesus is doing for Gentiles what he previously did for Jews [NAC]. It may be in or near the Decapolis, but the Decapolis had a sizeable majority of Jews [CC], and so the crowd was probably composed of both Jews and Gentiles [CC, NTC].
  2. It was probably in a Jewish area near Lake Galilee [BECNT, ICC, WBC].

QUESTION—Is there any significance to the presence of the definite article in the phrase τὸ ὄρος 'the mountain'?

Even though the article is present, it is not necessarily definite in the sense of referring to a known hill [CC, Lns, NICNT, NTC, PNTC]. It may mean no more than that he went into the hilly region [NICNT, PNTC]. The article has no significance here, as the presence or absence of the article in prepositional phrases in Greek does not appear to follow a predictable pattern [CC]. It refers to a particular mountain nearby [My].

15:30 **And great crowds came to-him having with them (the) lame,[a] blind, crippled,[b] mute,[c] and many others and put[d] them at his feet, and he-healed[e] them;**

LEXICON—a. χωλός (LN 23.175) (BAGD p. 889): 'lame' [BAGD, LN; all translations except CEV], 'crippled' [BAGD; CEV], 'one who is lame' [LN]. This adjective describes a disability that involves the imperfect function of the lower limbs [LN].
  b. κυλλός (LN 23.176) (BAGD p. 457): 'crippled' [BAGD, BECNT, BNTC, **LN**, NICNT, NTC, PNTC; ESV, NASB, NCV, NET, NIV, NLT, REB, TEV], 'deformed' [BAGD, CC, WBC], 'disabled' [GW], 'maimed' [NIGTC; KJV, NRSV], 'lame' [CEV]. This adjective describes a disability in one or more limbs, especially the leg or foot, often as the result of some deformity [LN].
  c. κωφός (LN 33.106) (BAGD 1. p. 462): 'mute' [BAGD, BECNT, CC, LN, NIGTC, WBC; ESV, NASB, NET, NIV, NRSV], 'dumb' [BAGD, BNTC, LN, NICNT, PNTC; KJV, REB, TEV], '(who) could not speak' [NCV, NLT], 'lacking the power of speech' [NTC], 'unable to talk' [CEV, GW], 'unable to speak, incapable of talking' [LN]. This adjective describes not being able to speak or talk [LN].
  d. aorist act. indic. of ῥίπτω (LN 85.37) (BAGD 2. p. 736): 'to put' [ESV, NCV, NRSV, REB], 'to put down' [BAGD, LN, NICNT, PNTC], 'to place' [BNTC, **LN**; CEV, TEV], 'to place down' [LN], 'to lay' [CC,

WBC; GW, NET, NIV, NLT], 'to lay down' [BAGD, BECNT, NTC; NASB], 'to cast' [NIGTC], 'to cast down' [KJV]. This verb means to put or place something down, with the possible implication of rapidity of action [LN].
- e. aorist act. indic. of θεραπεύω (LN 23.139): 'to heal' [LN; all translations except GW, NRSV], 'to cure' [LN; GW, NRSV]. This verb means to cause someone to recover health, often with the implication of having taken care of such a person [LN].

15:31 so-that[a] the crowd marveled[b] seeing (the) mute speaking, (the) crippled healthy and (the) lame walking-about[c] and (the) blind seeing; and they-glorified[d] the God of-Israel.

LEXICON—a. ὥστε (LN 89.52) (BAGD 2.a.β. p. 900): 'so that' [BAGD, BECNT, BNTC, LN, NICNT, NTC, PNTC; ESV, NRSV], 'the result was that' [NIGTC], 'with the result that' [CC, WBC], 'as a result' [LN; NET], 'insomuch that' [KJV], 'so' [NASB], 'therefore, (so) accordingly, so then, and so' [LN], not explicit [CEV, GW, NCV, NIV, NLT, REB, TEV]. This conjunction indicates result, often in contexts implying an intended or indirect purpose [LN].
- b. aorist act. infin. of θαυμάζω (LN 25.213) (BAGD 1.a.α. p. 352): 'to marvel' [BNTC, CC, LN, WBC; NASB], 'to be amazed' [BECNT, LN, NICNT, NIGTC; CEV, GW, NCV, NET, NIV, NLT, NRSV, TEV], 'to be astonished' [NTC, PNTC], 'to wonder' [LN; ESV, KJV]. The phrase τὸν ὄχλον θαυμάσαι 'the crowd marveled' is translated 'great was the amazement of the people' [REB]. This verb means to wonder or marvel at some event or object, though whether the reaction is favorable or unfavorable depends on the context [LN].
- c. pres. act. participle of περιπατέω (LN 15.227) (BAGD 1.c. p. 649): 'to walk' [BECNT, CC, LN, NICNT, NIGTC, NTC, PNTC, WBC; all versions except CEV, NCV], 'to go about' [BAGD], 'to go' [LN]. The phrase χωλοὺς περιπατοῦντας 'the lame walking about' is translated 'the crippled/lame could walk' [CEV, NCV]. This verb means to walk along or around [LN].
- d. aorist act. indic. of δοξάζω (LN 33.357) (BAGD 1. p. 204): 'to glorify' [CC, LN, NIGTC, NTC, PNTC, WBC; ESV, KJV, NASB], 'to praise' [BAGD, BECNT, LN; CEV, GW, NCV, NET, NIV, NLT, NRSV, TEV], 'to give glory' [NICNT], 'to give praise' [REB], 'to honor, to magnify' [BAGD]. This verb means to speak of something as being unusually fine and deserving honor [LN].

QUESTION—What does the statement 'they glorified the God of Israel' imply about the audience?
1. This expression demonstrates that this event occurred in Gentile territory and that the people saying 'the God *of Israel*' are Gentiles [EBC, Lns, NAC, NIBC, NICNT, NTC, PNTC]. The crowd was probably composed of both Jews and Gentiles, though predominantly of Gentiles [Lns].

2. It shows that the speakers are Jewish [CC, ICC, NIGTC, WBC]. This could have been spoken by Jewish people [BECNT]. The crowd was probably composed of both Jews and Gentiles, but praising 'the God of Israel' is essentially Jewish [CC].

DISCOURSE UNIT—15:32–39 [CEV, ESV, GW, NASB, NCV, NET, NLT, NRSV, TEV]. The topic is Jesus feeds more than four thousand [GW], more than four thousand fed [NCV], Jesus feeds four thousand men [TEV], Jesus feeds four thousand [CEV, NLT], Jesus feeds the four thousand [ESV], the feeding of the four thousand [NET], feeding the four thousand [NRSV], four thousand fed [NASB].

15:32 And having-called-to-himself his disciples Jesus said, "I-feel-compassion for the crowd, for already they-are-remaining with-me three days and they-do not -have anything to-eat; and I-do- not -want[a] to dismiss[b] them hungry,[c] lest they-faint[d] on the way (home).

LEXICON—a. pres. act. indic. of θέλω (LN 30.58) (BAGD 2. p. 355): 'to want' [BAGD, BECNT, NICNT, NIGTC, NTC, PNTC, WBC; all versions except CEV, KJV], 'to purpose' [LN]. The phrase οὐ θέλω 'I do not want' is translated 'I am unwilling' [BNTC; ESV], 'I am not willing' [CC], 'I will not' [KJV]. This verb means to purpose, generally based upon a preference and desire [LN]. It refers to one's purpose and resolve [BAGD].

b. aorist act. infin. of ἀπολύω (LN 15.43) (BAGD 2.b. p. 96): 'to dismiss' [BAGD, BNTC, LN, NIGTC, WBC], 'to send away' [BAGD, BECNT, CC, NICNT, NTC, PNTC; all versions], 'to let go away' [LN]. This verb means to cause (or permit) a person or persons to leave a particular location [LN].

c. νῆστις (LN **23.31**) (BAGD p. 538): 'hungry' [BAGD, BNTC, BECNT, CC, NICNT, NIGTC, NTC, WBC; all versions except KJV, TEV], 'really hungry' [**LN**], 'fasting' [PNTC; KJV], 'without feeding them' [TEV], 'quite hungry' [LN], 'not eating' [BAGD]. This adjective describes the state of being very hungry, presumably for a considerable period of time and as the result of necessity rather than choice [LN].

d. aorist pass. subj. of ἐκλύομαι (LN **23.79**) (BAGD p. 243): 'to faint' [**LN**, PNTC; all versions except GW, NIV], 'to give out' [BAGD, CC, LN, NIGTC, WBC], 'to become exhausted' [BECNT; GW], 'to collapse' [BNTC, NICNT, NTC; NIV], 'to become weary' [BAGD], 'to become extremely weary, to faint from exhaustion' [LN]. This verb means to become so tired and weary as to give out (possibly even to faint from exhaustion) [LN].

15:33 And the disciples say to-him, "Where in (this)-desolate-place[a] (could come) to-us enough loaves[b] so-as to-satisfy[c] such a-crowd?" **15:34** And Jesus-says to-them, "How many loaves do-you-have?" And they-say, "Seven and a-few small-fish."

LEXICON—a. ἐρημία (LN 1.86) (BAGD p. 309): 'desolate place' [ESV, NASB, NET], 'desert' [BAGD, CC, LN; CEV, NRSV, TEV], 'remote place' [BECNT; NIV, REB], 'uninhabited place' [BNTC], 'uninhabited area' [NICNT], 'uninhabited region' [BAGD, NTC], 'wilderness' [LN, NIGTC, PNTC, WBC; KJV, NLT], 'place where no one lives' [GW], 'lonely place' [LN]. The phrase ἐν ἐρημίᾳ 'this deserted place' is translated 'we are far away from any town' [NCV]. This noun denotes a largely uninhabited region, normally with sparse vegetation (in contrast with πόλις 'a population center') [LN].

b. ἄρτος (LN 5.8) (BAGD 1.a. p. 110): 'loaf' [BAGD, BECNT, BNTC, CC, NICNT, PNTC, WBC; NASB], 'loaf of bread' [BAGD, LN], 'bread' [BAGD, NIGTC, NTC; ESV, GW, KJV, NCV, NET, NIV, NRSV, REB], 'food' [CEV, NLT, TEV]. This noun denotes a relatively small and generally round loaf of bread (considerably smaller than present-day typical loaves of bread and thus more like 'rolls' or 'buns') [LN].

c. aorist act. infin. of χορτάζω (LN **23.16**) (BAGD 2.a. p. 884): 'to satisfy' [BAGD, CC, **LN**, NIGTC, PNTC; NASB, NET], 'to feed' [BAGD, BECNT, BNTC, NTC; CEV, ESV, GW, NCV, NIV, NRSV, REB, TEV], 'to fill' [BAGD; KJV], 'to be filled' [WBC], 'to cause to eat one's fill, to satisfy with food, to cause (someone) to have as much as they want' [LN]. The phrase ὥστε χορτάσαι ὄχλον τοσοῦτον 'so as to satisfy such a crowd' is translated 'that we can give such a large crowd all they want to eat' [NICNT], 'for such a huge crowd' [NLT]. This verb means to cause to eat so as to become satisfied [LN].

d. ἰχθύδιον (LN 4.60) (BAGD p. 384): 'small fish' [BECNT, BNTC, NTC, WBC; all versions except CEV, KJV], 'little fish' [BAGD, LN, NICNT, NIGTC, PNTC; CEV, KJV], 'fish' [CC]. This noun denotes any kind of relatively small fish [LN].

15:35 And having-directed[a] the crowd to-recline[b] on the ground **15:36** he-took the seven loaves and the fishes and having-given-thanks he-broke-(them) and gave (them) to-the disciples, and the disciples (gave them) to-the crowds.

LEXICON—a. aorist act. participle of παραγγέλλω (LN 33.327) (BAGD p. 613): 'to direct' [BNTC; ESV, NASB], 'to instruct' [BAGD, CC; NET], 'to give orders' [BAGD], 'to order' [BECNT, LN, NTC, WBC; GW, NRSV, REB, TEV], 'to tell' [NICNT, PNTC; CEV, NCV, NIV, NLT], 'to command' [BAGD, LN, NIGTC; KJV]. This verb means to announce what must be done [LN].

b. aorist act. infin. of ἀναπίπτω (LN 17.23) (BAGD 1. p. 59): 'to recline' [BAGD, BECNT, BNTC, CC, LN, PNTC, WBC], 'to sit down' [NIGTC;

all versions except NCV], 'to sit' [NICNT; NCV], 'to take (one's) place' [NTC], 'to sit down to eat' [LN], 'to lie down' [BAGD]. This verb means to be in a reclining position as one eats (with the focus either upon the position or the act of eating) [LN].

15:37 And all ate and were-satisfied. And the left-over of-the fragments[a] were seven baskets[b] full. 15:38 And those eating were four-thousand men apart-from women and children. 15:39 And having-dismissed the crowds he-got-into the boat and went to the region[c] of Magadan.

TEXT—Manuscripts reading Μαγαδάν 'Magadan' are given a C rating by GNT to indicate that choosing it over a variant text that reads Μαγδαλά 'Magdala' was difficult. Only KJV reads 'Magdala'.

LEXICON—a. κλάσμα (LN 19.40) (BAGD p. 433): 'fragment' [BAGD, BNTC, CC, LN, WBC], 'broken piece' [BECNT, NIGTC, PNTC; ESV, NASB, NIV, NRSV], 'broken loaf' [NICNT], 'piece' [BAGD, LN, NTC; GW, NCV, NET, TEV], 'food' [NLT], 'broken meat' [KJV], not explicit [CEV, REB]. This noun denotes a fragment or piece resulting from the action of breaking [LN].

b. σπυρίς (LN **6.149**) (BAGD p. 764): 'basket' [BAGD, BECNT, BNTC, LN, NICNT, NIGTC, PNTC, WBC; ESV, KJV, NCV, NET, NRSV, REB, TEV], 'large basket' [LN; CEV, GW, NASB, NLT], 'hamper' [BAGD, CC, NTC]. The phrase ἑπτὰ σπυρίδας πλήρεις 'seven baskets full' is translated 'seven basketfuls' [NIV]. This noun denotes a basket which is presumably somewhat larger than a κόφινος (the basket used in 14:20) [LN].

c. ὅριον (LN 1.79) (BAGD p. 581): 'region' [BAGD, BECNT, LN, NIGTC, NTC, WBC; ESV, NASB, NET, NLT, NRSV], 'area' [NICNT; NCV], 'territory' [LN; GW, TEV], 'district' [BAGD], 'vicinity' [NIV], 'neighborhood' [REB], 'town' [CEV], 'land' [LN]. This plural noun, which is normally translated as singular, is translated using a plural form: 'regions' [CC], 'districts' [PNTC], 'coasts' [KJV]. This noun, which is always in the plural, denotes a region or regions of the earth, normally in relation to some ethnic group or geographical center, but not necessarily constituting a unit of governmental administration [LN].

QUESTION—What difference would there have been between the baskets used to gather leftovers in 14:20 and the baskets used in this account?

The σπυρίς baskets referred to in this verse were large baskets [Lns, NICNT, NTC, TH, TRT; CEV, GW, NASB, NLT], probably somewhat larger than the large baskets used in 14:20 [LN, NAC, NIBC]. The σπυρίς basket was made of marsh grass and was the kind of basket in which Paul was lowered from the city wall in Acts 9:25 [TH]. There is little distinguishable difference between the κόφινος basket of 14:20 and the σπυρίς basket in this verse [CC]. The κόφινος basket of 14:20 was made of more rigid material (probably wicker) than the σπυρίς basket in this verse [EBC, PNTC, WBC]. The word for basket in this verse, σπυρίς, is a more

Hellenistic term than κόφινος [NAC, NICNT]. Both words are general words used for 'basket' though κόφινος used in 14:20 might be smaller [ICC, NIGTC].

QUESTION—Where is Magadan?
The location of this town is unknown, as is the location of Dalmanutha in Mark's account of the same event [BECNT, BNTC, CC, EBC, ICC, Lns, NAC, NIBC, NICNT, NIGTC, PNTC, TH, TRT, WBC]. Perhaps Magadan is the same as Magdala, which is on the west side of Lake Galilee [BECNT, NAC]. Magadan is somewhere in Jewish territory, on the west side of Lake Galilee [EBC, NAC, NIBC, NICNT].

DISCOURSE UNIT—16:1–17:20 [NIGTC]. The topic is anticipating a future through suffering and beyond.

DISCOURSE UNIT—16:1–12 [NICNT; NASB]. The topic is the end of the Galilean mission [NICNT], Pharisees test Jesus [NASB].

DISCOURSE UNIT—16:1–4 [ICC; CEV, ESV, GW, NCV, NET, NIV, NLT, NRSV, TEV]. The topic is the Pharisees ask for a sign from heaven [GW], the leaders ask for a miracle [NCV], the leaders demand a miraculous sign [NLT], the demand for a sign [NET, NIV, NRSV], a demand for a sign from heaven [CEV], the demand for a miracle [TEV], the Pharisees and Sadducees demand signs [ESV], the request for a sign from heaven [ICC].

16:1 **And having-approached, the Pharisees and Sadducees testing[a] (him) asked[b] him to-show them a-sign[c] from the heaven.[d]**

LEXICON—a. pres. act. participle of πειράζω (LN **27.31**) (BAGD 2.c. p. 640): 'to test' [BECNT, NICNT, NIGTC, PNTC, WBC; all versions except KJV, NCV, TEV], 'to put to the test' [BAGD], 'to want to trap' [TEV], 'to try to trap' [**LN**], 'to tempt' [BNTC, CC, NTC; KJV], 'to make trial of' [BAGD], 'to attempt to catch in a mistake' [LN], 'to trick' [NCV]. This verb means to obtain information to be used against a person by trying to cause that person to make a mistake [LN].

b. aorist act. indic. of ἐπερωτάω (LN **33.161**) (BAGD 2. p. 285): 'to ask (to)' [**LN**; all translations except CEV, KJV, NLT], 'to ask for' [BAGD, LN; CEV], 'to desire (that)' [KJV], 'to demand' [NLT], 'to request' [LN]. This verb means to ask for, usually with the implication of an underlying question [LN].

c. σημεῖον (LN 33.477) (BAGD 2.a. p. 748): 'sign' [BAGD, BECNT, BNTC, CC, LN, NICNT, NIGTC, NTC, PNTC, WBC; CEV, ESV, KJV, NASB, NET, NIV, NRSV, REB], 'miraculous sign' [GW, NLT], 'miracle' [BAGD; NCV, TEV]. The phrase σημεῖον ἐκ τοῦ οὐρανοῦ ἐπιδεῖξαι αὐτοῖ 'to show them a sign from heaven' is translated 'to show them a miraculous sign from heaven to prove his authority' [NLT], 'to perform a miracle for them to show that God approved of him' [TEV]. This noun denotes an event which is regarded as having some special meaning. 'Sign' as an event with special meaning was inevitably an unusual or even miraculous type of occurrence, and in a number of contexts it may be rendered as 'miracle' [LN].

d. οὐρανός (LN **12.16**) (BAGD 2.a. p. 594): 'heaven' [BAGD; all translations except NCV, TEV], 'God' [BAGD, LN; NCV, TEV]. This noun, which is a figurative extension of meaning of οὐρανός 'heaven,' is a reference to God based on the Jewish tendency to avoid using a name or direct term for God [LN].

QUESTION—What relationship is indicated by the use of the participial form of the verb πειράζω 'testing'?

It expresses purpose: they wanted to test, temp, or trap him [BECNT, CC, EBC, LN, NICNT, NIGTC, NTC, TH, TRT, WBC; ESV, GW, NCV, NET, NRSV, REB, TEV].

QUESTION—For what specifically are Jesus' critics asking in requesting a 'sign from the heaven'?

1. They are asking for a sign from God, 'heaven' being used as a circumlocution for 'God' [NICNT, TH, WBC]. They wanted a spectacular miracle with divine significance to prove that God was with him [PNTC; NLT, TEV], something only possible to divine power [BNTC].
2. They are asking for a sign in the heavens, that is in the sky itself [ICC, Lns, My, NTC, probably NIGTC]. They wanted something clearly apocalyptic [NAC].

16:2 **But answering he-said to-them, "(When) evening having-come you say, 'Fair-weather,ᵃ for the skyᵇ is-red.ᶜ'**

TEXT—Some manuscripts omit the quoted material beginning with 'When evening having come' all the way to the end of verse 3, so that the quotation does not begin until verse 4. GNT includes this portion in brackets with a C rating to indicate that choosing it over a variant text was difficult. Only REB omits this variant reading. BNTC includes it, but comments that it is probably not original.

LEXICON—a. εὐδία (LN **14.1**) (BAGD 1. p. 319): 'fair weather' [BAGD, BECNT, BNTC, CC, **LN**, NIGTC, NTC, WBC; ESV, KJV, NASB, NET, NIV, NLT, NRSV], 'fine weather' [NICNT, PNTC; GW, TEV], 'good weather' [CEV, NCV]. This noun denotes sunny, mild weather without strong winds [LN].

b. οὐρανός (LN **1.5**) (BAGD 1.d. p. 594): 'sky' [LN; all translations except CC (REB omits this)], 'heaven' [BAGD, CC]. This noun denotes space above the earth, including the vault arching high over the earth from one horizon to another, as well as the sun, moon, and stars [LN].

c. pres. act. indic. of πυρράζω (LN **79.32**) (BAGD p. 731): 'to be red' [BECNT, CC, NICNT, NIGTC, NTC, PNTC, WBC; all versions except NLT (REB omits this)], 'to be fiery red' [BAGD, **LN**], 'to glow red' [BNTC]. The phrase 'Fair weather for the sky is red' is translated 'Red sky at night means fair weather tomorrow' [NLT].

QUESTION—Why would a red sky in the evening indicate good weather for the following day?

Clouds that bring rain come from the Mediterranean in the west, but winds from the east blow those clouds out to sea, allowing a red glow from the setting sun, thus indicating that rain clouds were gone and clear weather was ahead [Lns, NAC].

16:3 **And (in the) morning, 'Bad-weather[a] today, for the sky is-red (and) overcast.[b]' You know how to interpret[c] the appearance[d] of the sky, but the signs of the times[e] you are- not –able (to-discern).**

LEXICON—a. χειμών (LN 14.2) (BAGD 1. p. 879): 'bad weather' [BAGD, LN, NTC], 'storm' [BECNT, NICNT; GW, NASB], 'stormy' [BNTC, CC, NIGTC, PNTC, WBC; ESV, NIV, NET, NRSV], 'rainy and stormy weather' [BAGD], 'rainy day' [NCV], 'foul weather' [KJV, NLT], 'stormy weather' [LN]. The phrase σήμερον χειμών 'bad weather today' is translated 'it is going to rain' [CEV, TEV]. This noun denotes stormy weather involving strong wind, overcast sky, and often cold temperature; thunder and lightning may also be present [LN].

b. pres. act. participle of στυγνάζω (LN **14.56**) (BAGD 2.b. p. 771): 'to be overcast' [GW, NIV], 'to be gloomy' [BAGD, BECNT, **LN**; CEV], 'to become dark and gloomy' [LN], 'to be dark' [BAGD, NIGTC, PNTC, WBC; NCV, TEV], 'to get darker' [CC], 'to be darkening' [NET], 'to be lowering' [NTC; KJV], 'to be threatening' [ESV, NASB, NRSV], 'to be angry' [NICNT], 'to become dark' [BAGD], not explicit [NLT]. The phrase πυρράζει γὰρ στυγνάζων ὁ οὐρανός 'the sky is red and is overcast' is translated 'the sky glows with an ominous red' [BNTC]. This verb means to become both dark and gloomy, with the implication of threatening [LN].

c. pres. act. infin. of διακρίνω (LN 30.109) (BAGD 1.c.β. p. 185): 'to interpret' [BECNT, BNTC, NICNT, PNTC; ESV, NIV, NLT, NRSV], 'to discern' [CC, WBC; KJV, NASB], 'to judge' [BAGD, NIGTC], 'to judge correctly' [BAGD; NET], 'to judge carefully, to evaluate carefully' [LN]. The phrase τὸ μὲν πρόσωπον τοῦ οὐρανοῦ…διακρίνειν 'to interpret the appearance of the sky' is translated 'forecast the weather by judging the appearance of the sky' [GW], 'tell what the weather will be like by looking at the sky' [CEV], 'predict the weather by looking at the sky' [TEV], 'you see these signs in the sky and know what they mean' [NCV]. This verb means to make a judgment on the basis of careful and detailed information [LN].

d. πρόσωπον (LN **24.24**) (BAGD 1.d. p. 721): 'appearance' [BAGD, BECNT, BNTC, CC, **LN**, NICNT, NIGTC, PNTC; ESV, GW, NASB, NET, NIV, NRSV], 'face' [WBC; KJV], 'weather signs' [NLT], not explicit [CEV, TEV]. The phrase 'the appearance of the sky' is translated 'what the sky looks like' [**LN**], 'these signs in the sky' [NCV]. This noun denotes the form or characteristics of something as seen [LN].

e. καιρός (LN 67.145) (BAGD 4. p. 395): 'age, era' [LN]. The phrase τὰ δὲ σημεῖα τῶν καιρῶν 'the signs of the times' [BECNT, BNTC, CC, NICNT, NIGTC, PNTC, WBC; ESV, GW, KJV, NASB, NET, NIV, NLT, NRSV] is translated 'the signs concerning these times' [TEV], 'what is happening now' [CEV], 'the things I am doing now' [NCV]. This noun denotes an indefinite period of time, but probably with the implication of the relationship of a period to a particular state of affairs [LN].

QUESTION—What were 'the signs of the times' that they should have understood?

The 'times' were the eschatological times set by God, in which personal decisions had to be made [ICC]. The response of the people, the miracles of Jesus, and the fulfillment of OT prophecy were among the signs of the times [Lns, My]. People should have understood the significance of Jesus' present ministry [CC, NAC, NIBC, NICNT, NIGTC, TH, WBC; CEV, NCV]. The events taking place among them showed that God was visiting his people [PNTC]. They should have been able to perceive that there was a crisis at hand and that judgment was impending [BNTC]. The times here were eschatological times set by God, in which personal decisions had to be made [ICC]. He was teaching about the kingdom of God [TRT]. They should especially have realized the significance of the miracles performed by Jesus [BECNT, CC, EBC, Lns, My, NTC, TH, TRT].

QUESTION—Is the second sentence in this verse a question or a statement?
1. It is a statement [BECNT, BNTC, CC, Lns, NICNT, NIGTC, NTC, PNTC, TH, TRT; all versions except KJV, NASB].
2. It is translated as a question [WBC; KJV, NASB]: 'can ye not discern?' [KJV], 'how…are you not able to discern?' [WBC], 'you cannot discern?' [NASB]. It is punctuated as a question by GNT.

16:4 An-evil[a] and adulterous[b] generation[c] seeks[d] a-sign, and a-sign will-not -be-given to-it except the sign of-Jonah." And having-left them he-went-away.

LEXICON—a. πονηρός (LN 88.110) (BAGD 1.b.α. p. 691): 'evil' [BAGD, BECNT, BNTC, CC, LN, NIGTC, NTC, PNTC, WBC; CEV, ESV, GW, NASB, NCV, NLT, NRSV, TEV], 'wicked' [BAGD, LN, NICNT; KJV, NET, NIV, REB], 'immoral' [LN], 'worthless, degenerate' [BAGD]. This adjective describes being morally corrupt and evil [LN].

b. μοιχαλίς (LN 31.101) (BAGD 2.a. p. 526): 'adulterous' [BAGD, BECNT, BNTC, CC, LN, NICNT, NIGTC, NTC, PNTC, WBC; ESV, KJV, NASB, NET, NIV, NLT, NRSV], 'unfaithful' [LN; GW], 'sinful' [NCV], 'godless' [REB, TEV]. The phrase 'an evil and adulterous generation' is translated 'you are evil and won't believe' [CEV]. This adjective describes being unfaithful to one's earlier and true beliefs [LN].

c. γενεά (LN 11.4) (BAGD 2. p. 154): 'generation' [BECNT, BNTC, CC, NICNT, NIGTC, NT, PNTC, WBC; ESV, KJV, NASB, NET, NIV, NLT,

NRSV, REB], 'people' [GW, NCV], 'people of this day' [TEV], 'those of the same time, those of the same generation' [LN], not explicit [CEV]. This noun denotes people living at the same time and belonging to the same reproductive age-class [LN].
   d. pres. act. indic. of ἐπιζητέω (LN 25.9) (BAGD 2.b. p. 292): 'to seek' [CC, NIGTC, WBC], 'to seek for' [ESV], 'to seek after' [KJV, NASB], 'to look for' [NTC, PNTC; GW, NIV], 'to ask for' [NCV, NET, NRSV, REB, TEV], 'to demand' [BAGD, NICNT; NLT], 'to want' [BECNT, LN; CEV], 'to desire' [BAGD, BNTC, LN]. This verb means to desire to have or experience something, with the probable implication of making an attempt to realize one's desire [LN].
QUESTION—What is the sign of Jonah?
   It will be Jesus' resurrection [BNTC, CC, ICC, Lns, NIBC, NTC, PNTC, WBC]. Jesus and Jonah were both delivered from death as a sign attesting the validity of their message [BECNT, EBC]. See discussion of this question also at 12:39.
QUESTION—What was the significance of Jesus' going away?
   It symbolized the incompatibility of Jesus and those religious leaders [BECNT]. Jesus abandoned them to the hardness of heart that they had chosen [NTC]. Jesus left them to think about what the sign of Jonah meant [PNTC]. Jesus showed that he is making a decisive break with the Jewish leaders [NICNT]. He once again withdrew from hostility [NAC]. He refused to waste any more words on them [Lns] and left them to judgment [Lns, My]. He left those who refused to be persuaded to their own devices [ICC].

DISCOURSE UNIT—16:5–12 [ICC; CEV, GW, NCV, NET, NIV, NLT, NRSV, TEV]. The topic is the yeast of the Pharisees [GW], guard against wrong teachings [NCV], the yeast of the Pharisees and Sadducees [CEV, NET, NIV, NLT, NRSV, TEV], the leaven of the Pharisees and Sadducees [ICC].

16:5 And the disciples having-come to the other-side forgot[a] to-take bread.
16:6 But Jesus said to-them, "Watch-out[b] and beware[c] of the yeast[d] of-the Pharisees and Sadducees.
LEXICON—a. aorist. mid. (deponent = act.) indic. of ἐπιλανθάνομαι (LN 29.17) (BAGD 1. p. 295): 'to forget (to do)' [BAGD, LN; all translations], 'to neglect, to overlook' [LN]. The aorist tense of this verb is translated as perfect tense: 'had forgotten' [BECNT, BNTC, CC, NICNT, NIGTC, PNTC, WBC; all translations except NET, NIV, TEV]. This verb means to not recall and thus to fail to do something [LN].
   b. pres. act. impera. of ὁράω (LN 30.45) (BAGD 2.b. p. 578): 'to watch out' [NIGTC; CEV, NASB, NET, NLT, NRSV], 'to look out' [NICNT, NTC, PNTC], 'to watch' [CC; ESV], 'to be on one's watch' [WBC], 'to pay attention to' [BECNT, LN], 'to take care' [BAGD, BNTC; REB, TEV], 'to be careful' [GW, NCV, NIV], 'to take heed' [KJV], 'to see to' [BAGD], 'to take notice of, to consider to concern oneself with' [LN].

This verb means to take special notice of something, with the implication of concerning oneself [LN].

c. pres. act. impera. of προσέχω (LN 27.59) (BAGD 1.b. p. 714): 'to beware' [BECNT, CC, NICNT, NIGTC, PNTC, WBC; ESV, KJV, NASB, NCV, NET, NLT, NRSV], 'to be on one's guard against' [BNTC, LN, NTC; CEV, NIV, REB, TEV], 'to watch out for' [GW], 'to pay attention to' [BAGD, LN], 'to keep on the lookout for, to be alert for' [LN]. This verb means to be in a continuous state of readiness to learn of any future danger, need, or error, and to respond appropriately [LN].

d. ζύμη (LN 88.237) (BAGD 2. p. 340): 'yeast' [BAGD, NTC; CEV, GW, NCV, NET, NIV, NLT, NRSV, TEV], 'leaven' [BAGD, BECNT, BNTC, CC, NICNT, NIGTC, PNTC, WBC; ESV, KJV, NASB, REB], 'hypocrisy, pretense' [LN]. This noun is a figurative extension of meaning of ζύμη 'yeast', and denotes hypocritical behavior, probably implying hidden attitudes and motivations. In this passage the ζύμη 'yeast' of the Pharisees and the Sadducees is equated with their teaching, but the context would indicate clearly that this was a type of hypocritical teaching, since the religious leaders said one thing but did something quite different [LN].

QUESTION—Where had Jesus and the disciples gone?

They left the western shore of Lake Galilee [EBC, BNTC, Lns, My, NAC, NTC, WBC], and went to the east side [Lns, My, NAC, NTC, WBC], or possibly to the northeast side [BNTC, Lns, NTC, TRT].

16:7 But they-were-discussing[a] among themselves saying "(It is) because we-did- not -bring bread." **16:8** And having-known-(this)[b] Jesus said, "You-of-little-faith, why do-you-discuss among yourselves that you-do- not -have bread?

LEXICON—a. imperf. mid. or pass. (deponent = act.) indic. of διαλογίζομαι (LN 33.158) (BAGD 1. p. 186): 'to discuss' [BECNT, BNTC, CC, LN, NICNT, NIGTC; ESV, GW, NASB, NCV, NET, NIV, TEV], 'to reason' [BAGD, NTC, PNTC; KJV], 'to talk something over' [CEV], 'to argue' [NLT], 'to say' [NRSV, REB], 'to converse' [LN], 'to consider' [BAGD, WBC]. This verb means to engage in some relatively detailed discussion of a matter [LN].

b. aorist act. participle of γινώσκω (LN 27.2) (BAGD 4.b. p. 161): 'to perceive, to notice, to realize' [BAGD], 'to learn, to find out' [LN]. The phrase γνοὺς δὲ ὁ Ἰησοῦς 'and having known this, Jesus' is translated 'when Jesus became aware of this' [BECNT], 'Jesus, aware of this' [ESV, NASB], 'aware of their discussion, Jesus' [NIV], 'becoming aware of it, Jesus' [NRSV], 'Jesus realized this' [BNTC], 'but because Jesus knew' [CC], 'Jesus knew what they were saying' [NICNT; TEV, NLT], 'knowing what they were talking about' [NIGTC; NCV], 'Jesus knew about their conversation' [GW], 'knowing what they were talking about' [NCV], 'knowing what they were discussing' [REB], 'when Jesus noticed this' [NTC], 'but when Jesus knew this' [PNTC], 'when Jesus learned of this' [NET], 'when Jesus perceived' [KJV], 'Jesus knew their thoughts' [WBC], 'Jesus knew what they were thinking' [CEV]. This verb means to acquire information by whatever means, but often with the implication of personal involvement or experience [LN].

QUESTION—What relationship is indicated by the conjunction ὅτι 'because'?
1. It indicates a causal relation: *because* we didn't bring bread [BECNT, EBC, My, NICNT, NTC, PNTC; CEV, KJV, NASB, NCV, NET, NIV, NLT, NRSV, TEV].
2. It indicates the content of speech: saying, 'We didn't bring bread' [BNTC, CC, Lns, NIGTC, WBC; ESV, GW, REB].

QUESTION—How did Jesus know what they were discussing?
1. He heard what they were talking about [NAC, NTC, PNTC].
2. He knew what they were thinking [Lns, My, NIBC, WBC; CEV].

16:9 Do-you- not-yet -understand,ᵃ and-do-you not -remember the five loaves of-the five-thousand and how-many baskets you-took-(up)ᵇ? **16:10** Or the seven loaves of-the four-thousand and how-many baskets you-took-(up)?

LEXICON—a. pres. act. indic. of νοέω (LN 32.2) (BAGD 1.e. p. 540): 'to understand' [BAGD, BECNT, BNTC, LN, NIGTC, PNTC; all versions except ESV, NRSV], 'to comprehend' [CC, LN, WBC], 'to realize' [NICNT], 'to perceive' [BAGD, LN; ESV, NRSV], 'to gain insight into' [LN]. The phrase οὔπω νοεῖτε 'do you not yet understand?' is translated 'do you still lack understanding?' [NTC]. This verb means to comprehend something on the basis of careful thought and consideration [LN].

b. aorist act. indic. of λαμβάνω (LN 57.55): 'to take up' [BNTC, LN, NIGTC, PNTC, WBC; KJV, NET], 'to gather' [BECNT; ESV, NIV, NRSV], 'to pick up' [CC, NTC; NASB, NLT, REB], 'to collect' [NICNT], 'to fill' [GW, NCV, TEV], 'to take' [LN], not explicit [CEV]. This verb means to acquire possession of something [LN].

16:11 Howᵃ do-you- not -understand that I-did- not -speak to-you about bread? But beware of the yeast of-the Pharisees and Sadducees." **16:12** Then they-understoodᵇ that he-did- not -say to-beware of the yeast of bread but of-the teachingᶜ of-the Pharisees and Sadducees.

TEXT—Manuscripts reading τῶν ἄρτων 'about bread' are given a C rating by GNT to indicate that choosing it over a variant text that omits this was difficult. These words are omitted only by NICNT.

LEXICON—a. πῶς (LN 92.16) (BAGD 1.b. p. 732): 'how?' [BAGD, LN], 'by what means?' [LN]. This interrogative adverb is translated 'how could you?' [BECNT; NET, NRSV], 'how do you?' [CC], 'how is it that?' [BNTC, NIGTC, NTC, PNTC, WBC; ESV, KJV, NASB, TEV], 'how can you?' [NICNT; REB], 'how is it possible?' [BAGD], 'how is it' [NIV], 'why (don't you)?' [GW, NCV], 'why (can't you)?' [NLT], not explicit [CEV]. This adverb is an interrogative reference to means [LN].

570   MATTHEW 16:11–12

b. aorist act. indic. of συνίημι (LN 32.5) (BAGD p. 790): 'to understand' [BAGD, BECNT, BNTC, CC, LN, NICNT, NIGTC, NTC, WBC; all versions except CEV], 'to comprehend' [BAGD, LN], 'to perceive' [LN, PNTC], 'to know' [CEV], 'to have insight into' [LN]. This verb means to employ one's capacity for understanding and thus to arrive at insight [LN].

c. διδαχή (LN 33.236) (BAGD 2. p. 192): 'teaching' [BAGD, LN; all versions except GW, KJV, NLT], 'teachings' [GW], 'deceptive teaching' [NLT], 'doctrine' [LN; KJV], 'what is taught' [LN]. This noun denotes the content of what is taught [LN].

QUESTION—What was the teaching that Jesus considered to be like yeast?

Jesus' critics held expectations about what the Messiah was supposed to be like that didn't fit Jesus, and they taught accordingly [TRT]. It refers to their teaching that righteousness could be attained by one's own efforts through outward conformity to certain behavioral standards [NTC]. Their teachings expressed their opposition to Jesus [BECNT, CC, NICNT, NIGTC, PNTC, WBC], and it was their influence with the people that eventually led to Jesus' execution [NIGTC]. What the Pharisees taught did not always agree with what the Sadducees taught, but both groups shared the same attitude toward divine revelation that kept them from believing that Jesus could be the Messiah. That attitude is what the disciples must avoid [EBC]. It was the influence of those two groups that could destroy a disciple's loyalty to Jesus [BNTC]. Since both groups opposed Jesus, whatever they said about him would have tended to block others from putting their faith in Jesus [ICC].

DISCOURSE UNIT—16:13–17:27 [REB]. The topic is Jesus the Son of God.

DISCOURSE UNIT—16:13–17:13 [PNTC]. The topic is the Christ made known.

DISCOURSE UNIT—16:13–20 [ICC, NICNT; CEV, ESV, GW, NASB, NCV, NET, NIV, NLT, NRSV, TEV]. The topic is the Messiah recognized by his disciples [NICNT], Peter declares his belief about Jesus [GW], Peter says Jesus is the Christ [NCV], Peter's declaration about Jesus [NLT, NRSV, TEV], Peter confesses Jesus as the Christ [ESV], Peter's confession of Christ [NASB, NIV], Peter's confession [NET], who is Jesus? [CEV], Jesus, the Messiah and Son of God founds his church [ICC].

16:13 **And having-come into the regions of Caesarea Philippi Jesus was-questioning his disciples saying, "Who do- people -say (that) the Son of Man is?" 16:14 And they said, "Some (say) John the Baptist, and others Elijah, and others Jeremiah or one of-the prophets."**

TEXT—Manuscripts reading Τίνα λέγουσιν οἱ ἄνθρωποι εἶναι τὸν υἱὸν τοῦ ἀνθρώπου; 'Who do people say that the Son of Man is?' are given a B rating by GNT to indicate it was regarded to be almost certain. Some manuscripts add με somewhere in the sentence, giving the translation 'Who do people say that I, the Son of man, am?' Only KJV follows this variant reading.

QUESTION—Where was Caesarea Philippi?

It was a town at the base of Mt. Hermon [CC, EBC, ICC, NIBC, NTC, PNTC, WBC], about twenty-five miles north of Lake Galilee [BECNT, CC, EBC, NAC, NIBC, NICNT, NTC, PNTC, WBC] and near the source of the Jordan River [BECNT, NTC, PNTC]. This may be the most northerly point that Jesus traveled to in his ministry, unless his journey to the regions of Sidon actually took him all the way to that city [CC, NICNT].

QUESTION—What was the point of Jesus' question "Who do people say that the Son of Man is?"

'Son of Man' was Jesus' favorite designation for himself, so he was asking who people understood Jesus himself to be [EBC, NIBC, PNTC]. He wanted to know how the people outside his circle understood the term in Dan 7:14 as it applied to him, and whether they really thought it did apply to him in its messianic sense [My].

QUESTION—What is meant by 'one of the prophets'?

Some people were expecting a series of prophetic forerunners in the last days [EBC]. Some expected that the greatest prophets of the OT era would return before the last days to usher in that age [WBC]. They supposed that Jesus was one of the OT prophets that had returned from the dead [My, NTC]. Some Jewish people expected the Messiah to be the prophet mentioned in Deut 18:15–18 [BECNT, NAC, NICNT]. Some thought he was a new prophet, and others thought he was a re-incarnation of one of the prophets of old [PNTC]. The idea of his being a prophet was what was common in all of the answers [ICC, PNTC].

16:15 He-says to-them, "But you(pl),[a] who do- you -say I am?" **16:16** And answering Simon Peter said, "You are the Christ, the son of-the living God." **16:17** And answering Jesus said to him, "Blessed[b] are-you, Simon son-of Jonah,[c] for flesh and blood[d] did- not -reveal[e] (this) to-you but my Father in the heavens.

LEXICON—a ὑμεῖς 'you(p)' This personal plural pronoun is emphatic, both from its forefronted position in the sentence as well as from the fact that its presence is normally not necessary, being included in the second person plural verb λέγετε 'you say'. The phrase Ὑμεῖς δὲ τίνα λέγετε 'But you...who do you say' [BNTC, CC, NTC, PNTC], is also translated 'But you yourselves, who do you say' [WBC], 'And you—who do you say' [NIGTC; REB], 'But what about you? Who do you say' [NICNT; NIV, TEV]. It is also translated with no emphasis indicated: 'But who do you say' [BECNT; CEV, ESV, GW, NASB, NET, NLT, NRSV], 'And who do you say' [NCV], 'But whom say ye' [KJV].

b. μακάριος (LN 25.119) (BAGD 1.b. p. 486): 'blessed' [BAGD, BECNT, BNTC, CC, NTC, PNTC, WBC; all versions except REB, TEV], 'happy' [BAGD, LN, NICNT], 'fortunate' [BAGD, NIGTC], 'favored' [REB],

572 MATTHEW 16:15–17

'good for you!' [TEV]. This adjective describes being happy, with the implication of enjoying favorable circumstances [LN].

c. Βαριωνᾶ or Βαριωνᾶς (LN **93.64**) (BAGD p. 133): 'son of Jonah' [BECNT, CC; CEV, GW, NCV, NET, NIV, NRSV, REB], 'son of John' [NLT, TEV], 'Bar-Jona' [BAGD, LN, NICNT, PNTC; KJV, NASB], 'Bar Jonah' [BNTC, NIGTC, NTC, WBC; ESV], 'Bar-Jonas' [LN]. This is the family name of the apostle Simon Peter [LN].

d. σὰρξ καὶ αἷμα (LN 9.14) (BAGD 1.a. p. 22, 3. p. 743). This idiomatic phrase is translated 'flesh and blood' [BECNT, BNTC, CC, NICNT, NIGTC, NTC, PNTC, WBC; ESV, KJV, NASB, NET, NRSV], 'person' [**LN**; NCV], 'human' [GW], 'man' [NIV], 'human being' [BAGD, **LN**; NLT, REB, TEV], not explicit [CEV]. It denotes a human being in contrast with a divine being [LN].

e. aorist act. indic. of ἀποκαλύπτω (LN 28.38) (BAGD 2. p. 92): 'to reveal' [BAGD, BECNT, BNTC, CC, LN, NICNT, NIGTC, NTC, PNTC; ESV, GW, KJV, NASB, NET, NIV, NRSV], 'to teach' [NCV], 'to disclose, to make fully known' [LN]. The phrase 'flesh and blood did not reveal this' is translated 'flesh and blood are not the source of this revelation' [WBC], 'you didn't discover this on your own' [CEV], 'you did not learn this/that from any human being' [NLT, REB], 'this truth did not come to you from any human being' [TEV]. This verb means to cause something to be fully known [LN].

QUESTION—What was the point of Jesus' question, "But you, who do you say I am?"

This question was intended to contrast the opinion of persons who were outside the circle of the disciples with the opinion that the disciples themselves held of Jesus [TH]. Jesus turns away from the opinions of the general pubic which had only casual contacts with him to ask his disciples the same question. They had left all to follow Jesus and had been with him for quite some time. They had seen all he did and had heard what he taught. In the light of this, how did they themselves view him? [ESV]. He wanted to elicit from his disciples a clear confession that he was the Christ (Messiah) [My, WBC]. He also wanted to correct any misconceptions they might have about his role as the Christ [NAC, NIBC].

QUESTION—When Peter answered Jesus, was he speaking for himself or as a spokesman for the group?

Peter spoke as a spokesman for the disciples [BECNT, BNTC, EBC, My, NAC, NICNT, NIGTC, NTC, PNTC, WBC], at least in part [EBC, NIGTC]. Although Peter was the spokesman for the group, he appeared to be ahead of the rest in comprehending who Jesus is [NICNT]. Jesus wanted to elicit from the disciples a clear confession that he was the Christ [My, WBC], but particularly to correct misconceptions they might have about his role as Messiah [NAC, NIBC].

MATTHEW 16:15–17

QUESTION—What is the significance of the designations 'Christ' and 'Son of the living God'?

Although 'Son of God' may have had purely messianic significance to Peter, it later came to indicate divinity [EBC]. This confession is the Christological high point of this gospel, just as the high priest's demand in 26:63 that Jesus identify himself is its low point [BECNT]. As the 'Christ' he is the long-awaited anointed one, ordained by the Father to be prophet, priest and king for his people; on the other hand he is 'Son of the living God' in a unique and eternal sense that does not apply to any mortal, and his reference to God as his Father speaks of the warm love within the Trinity as well as of the eternal-essence relationship between him and the Father [NTC]. 'Christ' is the central figure of OT expectation and of Jewish hopes and dreams, but 'Son of God' speaks of Jesus' own consciousness of a unique and intimate relationship with his heavenly Father [NIBC]. Taken together the two descriptions form the most comprehensive expression of Jesus' essential being found in the gospels [PNTC]. 'Christ' designates him as Israel's leader, sent from God, and 'Son of God' describes his unique nature and his filial relationship to God, his Father [BNTC]. In calling him 'Son of God' Peter recognized Jesus' unique relationship with God his Father [NAC]. It is unclear how much Peter may have understood and differentiated the two terms, but at least for Matthew's readers, 'Messiah' was a functional title describing Jesus' saving activity, and 'Son of God' went beyond that to describe who Jesus really is [NICNT]. As the Christ, the Messiah, Jesus was the one climatic figure in whom God's purposes would ultimately be accomplished [CC, NICNT]. As Messiah, he was *the* coming one who would usher in the messianic age that would transform the present order, but as 'Son of God' he was more than just a human; he was a manifestation of God, God's agent who participates in God's own being [WBC]. That Jesus is the 'Son of God' is probably the central and most important affirmation about him in this gospel, though since it has already been said about him before in this gospel it is not new; in this passage it is Peter's acknowledgement that Jesus is the 'Christ' that is the startling new revelation, for in him all the hopes of Israel would be realized [CC]. Together these two designations constitute the sum of the Christian confession [My]. As the Christ he was the royal descendant of David whom the people expected would restore the fortunes of God's people, but as the Son of God he was one to be worshiped and one in whom God is directly encountered [NIGTC]. Whereas 'Christ' refers to his role as the promised savior, 'Son of God' describes him in terms of his deity and divine origin [TH].

QUESTION—What does it mean for God to be called 'the living God'?

It distinguishes him as Israel's true God as opposed to pagan false gods [BECNT]. He is the living God in contrast with the false gods of the pagans, which are dead, but he also is the source of all life [NTC, WBC]. God alone has life in himself and is able to impart life to others [ICC, NAC, TH]. This title distinguishes him from lifeless idols [My, NAC]. He is the true God who is alive and active in his world and in Israel's history [NICNT]. He is one to be reckoned with and who works with divine power in earthly situations [NIGTC]. He is the only God who is alive, and he lives forever [TRT].

QUESTION—Why is Peter sometimes also called the son of John, as in John 1:42?

Peter was probably known as *Bar Johanan*, 'Son of John,' and *Bar Jonah* in this verse is just a shortened form of that name [BECNT, CC, EBC, NAC, NICNT, NIGTC, TH], so then it also means 'Son of John' [NLT, TEV]. But it is possible that Peter's father had two names. Then it could have the meaning 'someone like Jonah' [PNTC], in which case Jesus was describing Peter as a spiritual son of the prophet Jonah [NIBC].

QUESTION—What is meant by the statement 'flesh and blood did not reveal this'?

'Flesh and blood' is a Jewish way of referring to man as a mortal human being [BNTC, EBC, My, NAC, NICNT, TH]. It refers to human agency [ICC, WBC], particularly in contrast to God [ICC, NICNT, NIGTC]. Here it describes the difference between receiving information by revelation of God as opposed to receiving it from human sources [BNTC, CC, NIBC], or from merely human reasoning [NTC, WBC] or effort [WBC], or from tradition [NTC], or from deep human insight or cleverness [PNTC], or from human deduction [NAC].

16:18 And I say to-you(sg) that you are Peter,[a] and on this rock[b] I-will-build[c] my church[d] and (the) gates of-Hades[e] will- not -prevail-against[f] it.

LEXICON—a. Πέτρος (LN 93.296) (BAGD p. 654): 'Peter' [BAGD, BECNT, BNTC, CC, LN, NICNT, NIGTC, NTC, PNTC, WBC; ESV, GW, KJV, NASB, NCV, NET, NIV, NRSV], 'Peter, the rock' [REB], 'Peter, which means 'a rock'' [CEV], 'Peter (which means a rock)' [NLT], 'Peter: you are a rock' [TEV]. This is the Greek name of the leader of the twelve apostles, who was also called Cephas and whose name was originally Simon [LN].

b. πέτρα (LN 2.21) (BAGD 1.b. p. 654): 'rock' [BAGD, LN; all translations except TEV], 'rock foundation' [TEV], 'bedrock' [LN]. This noun denotes bedrock (possibly covered with a thin layer of soil), rocky crags, or mountain ledges, in contrast with separate pieces of rock normally referred to as λίθος (see 2.23) [LN].

c. fut. act. indic. of οἰκοδομέω (LN 45.1) (BAGD 2. p. 558): 'to build' [BAGD, LN; all translations], 'to construct' [LN]. This verb means to make or erect any kind of construction [LN].

d. ἐκκλησία (LN **11.33**) (BAGD 4.d. p. 241): 'church' [BAGD, **LN**; all translations]. This noun denotes the totality of congregations of Christians [LN]. This refers to the church universal, to which all believers belong [BAGD].

e. ᾅδης (LN **12.50**) (BAGD 1. p. 17): 'Hades' [BAGD], 'death' [**LN**], 'the underworld' [BAGD]. The idiom πύλαι ᾅδου 'gates of Hades' [BECNT, BNTC, NICNT, NIGTC, NTC, PNTC, WBC; NASB, NET, NIV, NRSV] is also translated 'Hades' gates' [CC], 'the gates of hell' [ESV, GW, KJV], 'the power of hell' [NLT], 'death' [TEV], 'death itself' [CEV], 'the power/powers of death' [NCV, REB]. The idiom 'gates of Hades' describes death as an impersonal supernatural power. Some scholars, however, understand πύλαι ᾅδου to mean Satanic powers of evil [LN].

f. fut. act. indic. of κατισχύω (LN 39.56) (BAGD 2. p. 424): 'to prevail against' [ESV, KJV, NRSV], 'to overpower' [BECNT, NICNT, NTC, PNTC, WBC; GW, NASB, NET], 'to have power over' [CEV], 'to prevail over' [LN], 'to defeat' [**LN**; NCV], 'to conquer' [NLT, REB], 'to overcome' [NIV, TEV], 'to prove stronger than' [NIGTC], 'to prove victor over' [BNTC], 'to win a victory over' [BAGD, CC]. This verb means to prevail over something or some person so as to be able to defeat, with the implication that the successful participant has greater strength [LN].

QUESTION—What relationship is indicated by κἀγὼ δέ 'and I'?

This is an emphatic transitional formula [TH] The word κἀγώ emphasizes the first person pronoun ἐγώ 'I' [NIGTC, PNTC], and the phrase κἀγὼ δέ means 'But I, for my part' [BAGD 3.b. p. 386]. It indicates that Jesus' response about who Peter is, corresponds with Peter's declaration of who Jesus is [Lns, My, NAC, NICNT, NIGTC, PNTC, WBC].

QUESTION—Is there any clear distinction in Greek between πέτρα 'rock' and Πέτρος 'Peter'?

Matthew's Greek readers would not have perceived any distinction between the two forms [NICNT], and there is no difference in Aramaic between the word *kepha* 'rock' and *Kepha* used as a name [EBC, NAC, NICNT, NTC, TH, WBC]. Grammatical precision is not relevant in the use of metaphors [BECNT, WBC]. The reason for the difference between πέτρα 'rock' and Πέτρος 'Peter' is that, in order to be used as a man's name, the feminine noun πέτρα 'rock' must be given a masculine form, which would be Πέτρος [EBC, ICC, NAC, NICNT, NTC, WBC].

QUESTION—Was 'Rock' a name newly coined just for Peter?

Some think this name was virtually unknown prior to Jesus applying it to Peter [CC, NIBC, NICNT]. Others think Kepha 'rock' was an accepted name in Jesus' day [EBC, ICC, NIGTC]. Peter was already known by this name [BNTC, NAC, My, PNTC, WBC], as is indicated by John 1:42 [My, NAC, TRT]. It was used as a nickname [NIBC, PNTC]. Here Jesus gave that name a new significance [My, WBC].

QUESTION—What is the rock upon which Jesus will build his church?

The rock is Peter himself [BNTC, EBC, ICC, My, NAC, NICNT, NTC, TH]. It is principally Peter, as the confessing apostle, but the other apostles are also included [BECNT, CC]. It is Peter as the first believer in Christ, and who exercised basic leadership in the early days of the church, as we see in

Acts 1–5 [BNTC, NICNT]. Peter was preeminent in evangelism in the early days of the church, and had a prominence that none of the others had [ICC]. Peter is prominent in the work of the early church as first among equals [BECNT, CC, EBC, NICNT, NTC], but he was not dominant over the other apostles and elders [EBC]. 'Rock' refers to Peter's office and function as the leader of the apostolic group [WBC]. The rock is Peter as well as his confession of faith in Jesus, which cannot be separated from Peter [NIBC]. The rock is Peter himself, but Jesus' statement is made in view of the faith that Peter has professed [My]. It is to be built on Peter *as the man who has received this revelation,* and we should not separate the man from the confession. Peter is the foundation of the church in the sense that it began with him and his confession, but ultimately the church is built on Christ and depends on Christ, not on Peter [PNTC]. Jesus expected Peter to exercise prominent leadership in the church [BNTC], but this passage implies nothing about infallibility [EBC], exclusive authority [EBC, NTC], succession [EBC, ICC, My], of any elaborate ecclesiology [NAC]. Peter is at the forefront of the leadership in the early church, though this is more in the sense of his being chronologically the first disciple and the first to confess him as Messiah, as opposed to being superior in any hierarchy [NAC]. Not all of the early church was built on or by Peter, as there were segments of the church that did not have a connection to him [PNTC]. That Peter is clearly the one referred to here is confirmed by his being called a stumbling stone immediately thereafter [NICNT].

QUESTION—What does the term ἐκκλησία 'church' connote?

In the NT ἐκκλησία 'church' is always a community of people, never a building [NICNT]. Here the term refers to all believers [NTC, TRT], the community of believers [My, TH]. The basic meaning of ἐκκλησία 'church' is an assembled community [BECNT, NAC, NICNT]. In Acts and the epistles the term usually refers to Christian congregations or to all God's people redeemed by Christ, and in the Greek translation of the OT it can refer to various kinds of assemblies such as a synagogue or even a crowd [EBC]. Jesus' assertion that he will build his church is a claim to be the Messiah [EBC], with the church being the messianic community [EBC, WBC], a fellowship established in direct continuity with OT Israel [EBC, NIGTC]. The Messiah would be expected to have such a community linked to him and following his teachings [PNTC]. Christ's church is the new Israel and is the NT counterpart to the OT congregation of the elect [NIBC].

QUESTION—How does the concept of the church relate to the concept of the kingdom?

The kingdom and the church are closely related but are not identical; 'kingdom' is the rule of God, and 'church' is the people of God [PNTC]. Jesus' kingdom or rule is not to be equated with his church, which is his people of the new covenant; however, kingdom and church are not opposed to one another, as the Messiah's reign (or kingdom) calls out the Messiah's people, the church, and in the establishment of the church God's kingdom is being manifested [EBC]. It is the church that extends God's kingdom on the earth [BECNT]. Although 'kingdom' is a broader concept than 'church', in this passage they are used almost interchangeably [NTC]. Christ's church is composed of all those who submit to God's kingly rule [NAC]. The kingdom will be given to the church, as Jesus will teach in 21:43 [ICC]. The church will be transformed into the kingdom at the second coming of Christ [My].

QUESTION—What does the term 'gates of Hades' refer to?
1. It refers to the power of death [BNTC, EBC, My, NIBC, NICNT, NIGTC, TH, WBC]. The church that Messiah is building cannot die [EBC, WBC]. It is a metaphor for death, and stands in clear contrast to the phrase 'the living God' in verse 16 [NICNT]. It refers to the power of death to draw people now living into eternal doom, and from which the church will rescue them [NIGTC]. 'Gates' represent death's power to imprison [BNTC, My, NIBC, NICNT, TH], but the church of the living God will not be held back or imprisoned, nor will it be swallowed up [NICNT]. Death does not have the power to keep Jesus from rising and leading the church to victory [BNTC]. Believers will certainly experience the resurrection [NIBC].
2. It refers to evil spiritual powers that oppose the church [BECNT, CC, ICC, NAC, NTC]. The church will never be extinguished no matter how badly it is attacked [NAC].

16:19 I-will-give to-you(sg) the keys[a] of-the kingdom of-the heavens, and whatever you-bind[b] on the earth will-be bound[c] in the heavens, and whatever you-loose[d] on the earth will-be loosed in the heavens.

LEXICON—a. κλείς (LN 6.220) (BAGD 1. p. 434): 'key' [BAGD, LN; all translations]. This noun denotes an instrument used for locking and unlocking doors and gates [LN].
b. aorist act. subj. of δέω (LN **37.46**) (BAGD 4. p. 178): 'to bind' [BAGD, BECNT, BNTC, CC, NIGTC, NTC, PNTC, WBC; ESV, KJV, NASB, NET, NIV, NRSV], 'to tie up' [NICNT], 'to imprison' [GW], 'to prohibit' [**LN**; TEV], 'to not allow' [LN; CEV, NCV], 'to forbid' [NLT, REB], 'to not permit' [LN]. This verb means to exercise authority over something on the basis that it is not legitimate [LN].
c. The phrase ἔσται δεδεμένον 'will be bound' is formed from the future form of the verb εἰμί 'to be' and the perfect passive participle of δέω 'to bind', which is equivalent to a future perfect passive verb form: 'will have been (bound, etc.)'. It is translated as future perfect passive by CC, NICNT, PNTC, WBC; NASB, NET. It is translated as future passive: 'will be (bound, etc.)' by BECNT, BNTC, NIGTC, NTC; ESV, KJV, NIV, NLT, NRSV, REB, TEV. It is translated as future active 'God will (allow, etc)' by CEV, GW, NCV.
d. aorist act. subj. of λύω (LN **37.47**) (BAGD 5. p.484): 'to loose' [BAGD, BECNT, BNTC, CC, NIGTC, NTC, PNTC; ESV, KJV, NASB, NIV, NRSV], 'to set loose' [WBC], 'to release' [NET], 'to set free' [GW], 'to

untie' [NICNT], 'to permit' [**LN**; NLT, TEV], 'to allow' [LN; CEV, NCV, REB]. This verb means to exercise authority over something on the basis of its being legitimate [LN].

QUESTION—What do the keys of the kingdom represent, and how does that relate to the church?

The keys represent the power to grant people permission to enter the kingdom or to exclude people from it [BECNT, CC, EBC, My, NTC, WBC], based on the gospel message as Jesus established it [BECNT, EBC]. The proclamation of the truth about Jesus opens God's reign to all who believe it, but shuts it from those who reject it; it also relates especially to forgiving the sins of the penitent and retaining the sins of the impenitent, a function that is now exercised by pastors [CC]. Peter is able to admit people into the kingdom through pointing to Jesus as the Christ and as the Son of God, and through communicating to them what Jesus taught [NIGTC]. It also represents authority over acceptable behavioral standards within the Christian community [BECNT, NTC]. In this passage Peter and the apostles are also charged with the ongoing proclamation of the gospel message [BECNT]. The authority Jesus grants here is exercised through the preaching of the gospel and the exercise of discipline in the Church [NTC]. Peter and the apostles have the power to determine what conduct is appropriate to those who live under God's rule, and what is not [NIBC]. It refers to evangelism, by which others are admitted to the church, but also to teaching authority, which is connected with authority over how life should be lived within the community [ICC]. It is on the basis of his confession of faith that Peter is granted the 'keys', and we see him exercise this gift in Acts 2 and 3 where he brings many into the kingdom by the message he preaches [PNTC]. The keys represent access to the storehouse, which in the case of the church means making appropriate provision for the household, which is not the same as controlling admission to the kingdom [NICNT].

QUESTION—What is involved in the binding and loosing that Jesus is describing here?

1. It refers to admittance into God's kingdom [BECNT, EBC, NAC]. Peter and the apostles control entrance into the kingdom based on people echoing the apostolic confession of Jesus as the Messiah and Son of God [BECNT]. Entrance into the kingdom is made available or prohibited through the apostles' witness and preaching [NAC]. By the proclamation of the gospel Peter will open the kingdom of heaven to some, as in Acts 2:14–39 and 3:11–26, and shut it against others, as in Acts 4:11–12 and 8:20–23 [EBC]. Peter will determine what prohibited things will disqualify someone from entering the future kingdom [My].

2. It refers to regulating conduct in the church [BNTC, NIBC, NICNT, NIGTC, PNTC]. It concerns teaching what is forbidden or allowed [BNTC, NICNT]. Inspired by the Holy Spirit, the church has the ability to determine what things are permitted and what things are forbidden, so the keys refer to admission and exclusion from membership, whereas binding

and loosing mainly refer to regulating conduct [PNTC]. The basis of the binding and loosing, that is, the regulation of behavior, is the teaching of Jesus [NIGTC, WBC]. Peter is responsible to see that what Jesus taught is applied to how people live [NIGTC].
3. It is the exercise of the office of the keys, in which pastors forgive the sins of the penitent and retain the sins of the impenitent [CC].
4. It refers to admittance as well as conduct [ICC, NTC, WBC]. Peter and the apostles have authority over faith and morals when exercised in harmony with the teachings of Jesus and the word of God, meaning that they admit into the kingdom those whose faith is genuine and in accord with the gospel, but they also discipline those whose behavior falls below biblical standards [NTC].

QUESTION—Does this statement apply only or primarily to Peter, or does it apply also to the rest of the apostles?
1. Jesus' commission applies to all of the apostles [BECNT, BNTC, CC, EBC, NAC, NIBC, NICNT, PNTC, WBC], though especially to Peter [NICNT]. It applies to Peter as representing the other apostles, but ultimately the whole church [NTC]. That it refers to Peter and the other apostles can be seen in 18:18, though Peter does have a special place and role [EBC]. This implies nothing about successors to Peter [BNTC, EBC, NICNT].
2. It refers primarily to Peter [ICC, NIGTC].

QUESTION—What is the significance of the future perfect periphrastic construction of the verbs 'bind' and 'loose'?
Whatever Peter binds and looses will have already been bound or loosed in heaven by God, and the action by the human agent brings the binding and loosing power of God to bear in the lives of the people they deal with [CC]. Since Peter binds and looses by proclaiming a gospel that has already been given, and by making application on the basis of the gospel as already given, then whatever he binds or looses will already have been bound or loosed in heaven, provided that he adheres to the gospel as it has been divinely revealed [EBC]. The future perfect tense probably indicates that their decisions about life and belief in the new community should and will be based on divine inspiration and guidance given to the leaders; the future aspect of the future perfect tense probably points to a fulfillment sometime after the resurrection [PNTC]. Peter's decisions will have God's approval when they are made in faith and loyalty [BNTC]. In this passage Jesus is saying that those who enter the kingdom will do so in accordance with the sovereign purposes of God, but without specifying whether God or the apostles caused the specific responses [NAC]. It means that Peter will be given divine guidance to make decisions according to what God has already ordained [NICNT]. Peter speaks on behalf of heaven, and his judgments, as well as the judgments of the church, reflect what is settled in heaven as God's will; the future tense of the verb combined with the perfect participle indicates the final authority of the binding and loosing [WBC]. What Peter

determines about things that prohibit a person's entrance into the future kingdom will be ratified by God [My]. The perfect participles indicate coordinated action, in that what is bound or loosed on earth is likewise bound or loosed in heaven at the same time [NIGTC].

16:20 Then he-warned^a the disciples that they-tell no-one that he is the Christ.^b

TEXT—Some manuscripts include the name 'Jesus' before 'the Christ'. Manuscripts that omit it are given a B rating by GNT to indicate that the shorter reading was regarded to be almost certain. Only KJV includes the name 'Jesus'.

LEXICON—a. aorist mid. indic. of διαστέλλομαι (LN 33.323) (BAGD p. 188): 'to warn' [NASB, NCV, NIV, NLT], 'to sternly warn' [BNTC], 'to charge' [KJV], 'to strictly charge' [ESV], 'to strictly order' [GW], 'to sternly order' [NRSV], 'to order' [BAGD, BECNT, CC, LN, NIGTC, WBC; TEV], 'to give orders' [BAGD], 'to give strict orders' [NTC; REB], 'to command' [LN], 'to impress on' [NICNT], 'to admonish' [PNTC], 'to instruct' [NET], 'to tell' [CEV]. This verb means to state with force and/or authority what others must do [LN]. It is a strong term for giving orders [NICNT].

b. Χριστός (LN 53.82) (BAGD 1. P. 887): 'the Christ' [BAGD, BECNT, BNTC, CC, LN, NIGTC, NTC, WBC; ESV, KJV, NASB, NCV, NET, NIV], 'the Messiah' [BAGD, LN, NICNT, PNTC; CEV, GW, NLT, NRSV, REB, TEV], 'the Anointed One' [BAGD]. This noun denotes a title for Jesus as the Messiah in the NT. In a number of languages Χριστός (or Μεσσίας) as a reference to the Messiah occurs in a transliterated form based either on Χριστός in Greek or on Messiah in Hebrew. However, in some languages an attempt is made to represent the significance of the terms Χριστός and Μεσσίας by translating 'God's appointed one' or 'God's specially chosen one' or 'the expected one,' in the sense of one to whom everyone was looking for help and deliverance [LN].

QUESTION—Why didn't Jesus want them to tell others that he was the Christ?
Jesus wanted to reveal his messianic identity through symbol-charged actions and words that would prompt people to answer the question of who he really was. He wanted people to come to penitent faith based on obedience and submission to him, not on the basis of nationalistic fervor that might short-circuit the events leading to the cross [EBC]. Jesus was concerned about the sentiment of the crowds, who viewed the role of Messiah primarily in political terms [BECNT, NTC, PNTC]. He did not want to stir up nationalistic hopes in the people [BNTC, My, NICNT]. He was also concerned about the increasing opposition of Jewish leaders [BECNT]. He knew that many Jewish people held nationalistic expectations about the Messiah, and since even his own disciples poorly understood what his messiahship really meant, including what he must suffer, he knew that

other Jews would have understood it even less [NIBC]. The conventional understanding of what Messiah was supposed to be and do was very different from Jesus' own understanding [CC, NICNT]. Although Jesus is the Messiah, he was not the national-political Messiah the masses expect [WBC].

DISCOURSE UNIT—16:21–28:20 [CC; NAC]. The topic is the climax of Jesus' ministry [NAC], part **3:** the road to the cross, the empty tomb, and all the nations [CC].

DISCOURSE UNIT—16:21–20:32 [CC]. The topic is passion predictions and disciples' incomprehension.

DISCOURSE UNIT—16:21–18:35 [NAC]. The topic is focus on coming death and resurrection.

DISCOURSE UNIT—16:21–17:27 [NAC, WBC]. The topic is implications for discipleship: correcting misunderstandings [NAC], the turning point: the announcement of the cross [WBC].

DISCOURSE UNIT—16:21–17:13 [NICNT]. The topic is a glimpse into the future: messianic suffering and glory.

DISCOURSE UNIT—16:21–28 [CEV, NCV, NET, NIV, NLT, TEV]. The topic is Jesus says that he must die [NCV], Jesus speaks about his suffering and death [CEV, TEV], first prediction of Jesus' death and resurrection [NET], Jesus predicts his death [NIV, NLT].

DISCOURSE UNIT—16:21–24 [GW]. The topic is Jesus foretells that he will die and come back to life.

DISCOURSE UNIT—16:21–23 [ICC; ESV, NASB, NRSV]. The topic is Jesus foretells his death and resurrection [ESV, NRSV], Jesus foretells his death [NASB], the passion and resurrection predicted [ICC].

16:21 **From that-time**[a] **Jesus began to-explain**[b] **to-his disciples that it-was-necessary**[c] **for-him to-go to Jerusalem and to-suffer many-things from the elders and high-priests and scribes and to-be-killed and to-be-raised**[d] **on-the third day.**

TEXT—Some manuscripts include the title Χριστός 'Christ' after the name Jesus. GNT does not mention this variant reading. Only BNTC has 'Jesus Christ'.

LEXICON—a. τότε (LN 67.47) (BAGD 1.a. p. 823): 'at that time' [BAGD], 'then' [BAGD, LN]. The phrase ἀπὸ τότε 'from that time' [BECNT, BNTC, NICNT, NIGTC, NTC, WBC; ESV, NASB, REB] is also translated 'from that time on' [GW, NCV, NET, NIV, NRSV, TEV], 'from that time forth' [KJV], 'from then' [BECNT, CC, PNTC], 'from then on' [CEV, NLT]. This adverb describes a point of time subsequent to another point of time [LN].

b. pres. act. infin. of δείκνυμι (LN 33.150) (BAGD 2. p. 172): 'to explain' [BAGD, BNTC, LN; NIV], 'to make known' [BECNT], 'to show' [CC, LN, NICNT, NIGTC, PNTC, WBC; ESV, KJV, NASB, NET, NRSV], 'to say plainly' [NTC; TEV], 'to make clear' [LN; REB], 'to inform' [GW], 'to tell plainly' [NLT], 'to tell' [CEV, NCV]. This verb means to explain the meaning or significance of something by demonstration [LN].

c. pres. act. indic. of δεῖ (LN 71.34): 'to be necessary' [CC, LN, NICNT, NIGTC, PNTC, WBC; NLT], 'must' [BECNT, BNTC, LN, NTC; all versions except GW, REB], 'to have to' [GW, REB]. This verb means to be that which must necessarily take place, often with the implication of inevitability [LN].

d. aorist pass. infin. of ἐγείρω (LN 23.94) (BAGD 2.c. p. 215): 'to be raised' [BAGD, CC, NICNT, NIGTC, PNTC; ESV, NET, NRSV], 'to be raised up' [BECNT, NTC; NASB] 'to be raised to life' [LN, WBC; NIV, TEV], 'to be raised again' [KJV, REB], 'to be raised from the dead' [NCV, NLT], 'to be brought back to life' [GW], 'to made to live again' [LN]. This passive verb is translated as active: 'to rise to life' [CEV]. This verb means to cause someone to live again after having once died [LN].

QUESTION—What is the function of the phrase Ἀπὸ τότε 'from that time'?

Just as in 4:17, this phrase marks a turning point in the account [BECNT, BNTC, CC, EBC, Lns, My, NAC, NICNT, NIGTC, WBC]. It introduces a second main portion of Jesus' teaching [BNTC]. It marks a new stage in Jesus unveiling who he is to his disciples [NIBC]. Now that they understand that he is the Messiah, they need to understand what that actually means, which is something very different from what they expect [PNTC]. The occurrence of the phrase merely links what follows with what precedes [EBC].

QUESTION—What is implied by the use of ἤρξατο 'he began' to explain?

Jesus explained this to them multiple times [EBC]. Getting them to understand would be a slow process [CC, PNTC].

QUESTION—What is implied by the use of δεῖ 'it was necessary'?

It indicates that what must happen to him was a divine necessity [BECNT, My, NIGTC, PNTC, TH, WBC]. It was the will of God [BNTC, CC, ICC, Lns, NIGTC, NIBC, WBC], and Jesus would submit to the Father's will [EBC, NTC]. It was necessary to fulfill the demands of the law and pay the penalty for sin [NTC].

QUESTION—Who are the πρεσβυτέρων 'elders'?

They are respected leaders of the community [BECNT, NIBC], leaders of the tribal or sub-tribal divisions [NTC]. Their leadership standing was based on their age, experience, and piety [WBC]. They had been judges in local courts [Lns]. They were from influential families, and often were aligned with the priests [NICNT]. They are members of the ruling Sanhedrin who are not part of some other specific party or profession [NAC]. Together, with the chief priests and scribes they make up the Sanhedrin [BNTC, EBC, ICC, Lns, NICNT, PNTC].

MATTHEW 16:21

QUESTION—Who is the agent of the passive verb 'to be raised'?
The agent of the action is God [ICC, Lns, NICNT, PNTC, TH, TRT, WBC].
QUESTION—How are the days being counted such that the resurrection is said to have happened on the third day?
This is inclusive reckoning, the crucifixion being counted as being on the first day [BNTC, EBC, NAC, NTC, PNTC, TRT, WBC].

16:22 And having-taken- him -aside,ᵃ Peter began to-rebukeᵇ him saying, "**Mercy to-you,ᶜ Lord; this shall- certainly-not -happenᵈ to you.**"

LEXICON—a. aorist mid. participle of προσλαμβάνομαι (LN 15.180) (BAGD 2.a. p. 717): 'to take (someone) aside' [BAGD, LN; all translations except KJV, REB], 'to take (someone)' [KJV], 'to take hold of (someone)' [REB], 'to lead aside' [LN]. This verb means to take or lead off to oneself [LN].

b. pres. act. infin. of ἐπιτιμάω (LN 33.419) (BAGD 1. p. 303): 'to rebuke' [BAGD, BECNT, CC, **LN**, NICNT, NIGTC, NTC; ESV, KJV, NASB, NET, NIV, NRSV, REB, TEV], 'to denounce' [LN], 'to reprove' [BAGD, BNTC, WBC], 'to remonstrate' [PNTC], 'to reprimand' [NLT], 'to object (to this)' [GW]. The phrase ἤρξατο ἐπιτιμᾶν αὐτῷ 'began to rebuke him' is translated 'told him to stop talking like that' [CEV; similarly NCV]. This verb means to express strong disapproval of someone [LN].

c. ἵλεως (LN 88.77, **88.78**) (BAGD p. 376): 'merciful' [BAGD, LN (88.77)], 'gracious' [BAGD]. The phrase ἵλεώς σοι 'mercy to you' is translated 'mercy on you' [BNTC, NTC], 'God be merciful on/to you' [CC, NIGTC], 'God forbid' [BAGD, BECNT, NICNT, PNTC; NASB, NET, NRSV, TEV], 'God save you from those things' [NCV], 'heaven forbid' [GW, NLT, REB], 'God forbid it, may it not happen' [**LN** (88.78)], 'far be this/it from you' [WBC; ESV, KJV], 'never!' [NIV]. The phrase Ἵλεώς σοι, κύριε 'mercy to you, Lord' is conflated with οὐ μὴ ἔσται σοι τοῦτο 'this shall certainly not happen to you' and translated 'God would never let this happen to you, Lord!' [CEV]. This adjective describes the act of showing mercy [LN (88.77)]. The idiom Ἵλεώς σοι 'mercy to you' is a highly elliptical expression equivalent in meaning to the statement 'may God be merciful to you in sparing you from having to undergo some experience' [LN (88.78)].

d. fut. mid. (deponent = act.) indic. of εἰμί (LN 13.104) (BAGD I.4. p. 223): 'to happen' [BAGD, LN; all translations except CC; KJV], 'to take place, to occur' [BAGD], 'to be' [CC, LN; KJV]. The use of the double negative οὐ μή 'certainly not' with a future indicative instead of a subjunctive makes the statement very emphatic [EBC, NIGTC, PNTC]. This verb means to occur, of an event [LN].

16:23 But having-turned he-said to Peter, "Get-away[a] behind[b] me, Satan; you-are a-stumbling-block[c] to me, for you- are-not –thinking-on[d] the-(things)[e] of God but the-(things) of-man."

LEXICON—a. pres. act. impera. of ὑπάγω (LN 15.52) (BAGD 1. p. 836): 'to go away' [BAGD, LN], 'to be gone' [BAGD], 'to depart, to leave' [LN]. See next entry for renderings. This verb means to depart from someone's presence, with the implication of a changed relation [LN].

b. ὀπίσω (LN 83.40) (BAGD 2.a.α. p. 575): 'behind' [BAGD, LN], 'in back of' [LN]. The phrase Ὕπαγε ὀπίσω μου 'get away behind me' is translated 'get behind me' [BECNT, BNTC, WBC; ESV, KJV, NASB, NET, NIV, NRSV], 'go away behind me' [PNTC], 'go away from me' [NCV], 'get away from me' [NIGTC; CEV, NLT, TEV], 'leave behind me' [CC], 'away with you; get behind me' [NICNT], 'get out of my way' [GW], 'get out of my sight' [NTC], 'out of my sight' [REB]. This preposition describes a position behind an object or other position [LN].

c. σκάνδαλον (LN 25.181) (BAGD 2. p. 753): 'stumbling block' [BECNT, CC, NICNT; NASB, NET, NIV, NRSV, REB], 'temptation' [BNTC], 'cause of stumbling' [NIGTC, WBC], 'trap' [NTC, PNTC], 'a dangerous trap' [NLT], 'obstacle' [TEV], 'hindrance' [ESV], 'offense' [LN; KJV], 'what causes offense' [LN], 'temptation to sin, enticement' [BAGD]. The phrase σκάνδαλον εἶ ἐμοῦ 'you are a stumbling block to me' is translated 'you are in my way' [CEV], 'you are tempting me to sin' [BAGD; GW], 'you are not helping me' [NCV]. This noun denotes that which causes offense and thus arouses opposition [LN].

d. pres. act. indic. of φρονέω (LN 30.20) (BAGD 2. p. 866): 'to think' [PNTC; GW, REB], 'to set one's mind on' [BAGD, BECNT, CC, WBC; ESV, NASB, NET, NRSV], 'to have in mind' [NIV], 'to be concerned about' [NIGTC], 'to care about' [NCV], 'to be intent on' [BAGD], 'to savour' [KJV], 'to ponder, to let one's mind dwell on, to keep thinking about, to fix one's attention on' [LN]. The phrase οὐ φρονεῖς τὰ τοῦ θεοῦ 'you are not thinking on the things of God' is translated 'your thoughts are not those of God' [NICNT], 'these thoughts of yours don't come from God' [TEV], 'your thinking reflects the thoughts not of God' [BNTC], 'you are looking at things not from God's point of view' [NTC], 'you are seeing things (from a human point of view) not from God's' [NLT], 'you think (like everyone else and) not like God' [CEV]. This verb means to keep on giving serious consideration to something [LN].

e. This neuter plural definite article is translated 'things' [CC, NIGTC, WBC; ESV, KJV, NCV, NIV, NRSV], 'interests' [BECNT; NASB, NET], 'thoughts' [BNTC, NICNT, PNTC], 'the way God thinks' [GW], 'as God thinks' [REB], not explicit [CEV, TEV].

QUESTION—Did Jesus turn toward Peter or away from him?

1. Jesus turned toward Peter [BNTC, EBC, Lns, NICNT, NTC, PNTC, TH; CEV, NLT].
2. Jesus turned his back on Peter [My, NIBC].

MATTHEW 16:23

QUESTION—Does Ὕπαγε ὀπίσω μου 'Get away behind me' express something about discipleship, as with ὀπίσω μου 'after me' in 4:19, 10:38, and 16:24, or about repudiation, as with Ὕπαγε 'Get away' in 4:10?
1. It expresses repudiation [BNTC, CC, My, Lns, NAC, NIBC, NICNT, NIGTC, NTC, PNTC, TH; CEV, NCV, NLT, TEV], that he should get out of Jesus' way [EBC, WBC; CEV, GW], that he should get behind Jesus so he can be ignored [PNTC], that he should get out of Jesus' sight [BNTC, Lns, NAC, NTC, TH; REB].
2. It probably means that Peter needed to return to a position of following behind Jesus as a disciple [BECNT].

QUESTION—Why does Jesus address Peter as 'Satan'?
Instead of operating by divine revelation as in the previous passage, here Peter was aligning himself with Satan's view of things [EBC]. Peter has taken a position that is the same as that of Satan, who earlier tried to deter Jesus from doing his Father's will, so it is as though Peter's response was inspired by Satan [NICNT, WBC]. Peter's suggestion comes from Satan himself, and is essentially the same as what Satan proposed in the temptation account [PNTC]. Just as Satan tried to divert Jesus from doing the will of God in the temptation, Peter has become Jesus' adversary by his opposition to the cross [BECNT]. Satan is using Peter to tempt Jesus to seek the crown apart from the cross, so Jesus addresses Satan directly, or at least whatever in Peter is being influenced by Satan [NTC]. Anyone who opposes God's plan and will is acting as an emissary of Satan [NIBC]. Thwarting God's plan is Satan's role [My, NAC, TH], not a disciple's role [NAC]. Peter is playing the role of Satan, though he is not being possessed by him [ICC]. He unwittingly became an agent of Satan [Lns], the mouthpiece of the great adversary [CC].

DISCOURSE UNIT—16:24–28 [ICC; ESV, GW, NASB, NRSV]. The topic is what it means to follow Jesus [GW], take up your cross and follow Jesus [ESV], the cross and self-denial [NRSV], discipleship is costly [NASB], the cost of discipleship [ICC].

16:24 Then Jesus said to-his disciples, "If anyone wants[a] to-come[b] after me, let-him-deny[c] himself and let-him-take-up[d] his cross and let-him-follow[e] me.

LEXICON—a. pres. act. indic. of θέλω (LN 25.1): 'to want' [CC, LN, NICNT, NIGTC; CEV, GW, NCV, NET, NLT, NRSV, TEV], 'to wish' [BECNT, BNTC, LN, NTC; NASB, REB], 'to desire' [LN, WBC], 'to set one's will on' [PNTC]. The phrase θέλει...ἐλθεῖν 'wants to come' is translated 'would come' [ESV, NIV], 'will come' [KJV]. This verb means to desire to have or experience something [LN].
  b. aorist act. infin. of ἔρχομαι (LN 15.81) (BAGD II. p. 311): 'to come' [LN], 'to go' [BAGD]. The phrase ὀπίσω μου ἐλθεῖν 'to come after me' [BECNT, BNTC, CC, NIGTC, WBC; ESV, KJV, NASB, NIV] is also translated 'on coming after me' [PNTC], 'to come behind me' [NTC], 'to

come with me' [GW, TEV], 'to follow me' [NCV], 'to become/be my follower/s' [CEV, NET, NLT, NRSV], 'to be a follower of mine' [REB], 'to be my disciple' [NICNT]. This verb means to move toward or up to the reference point of the viewpoint character or event [LN].

c. aorist mid. (deponent = act.) impera. of ἀπαρνέομαι (LN 30.52) (BAGD p. 81): 'to deny' [BAGD, BNTC, CC, NICNT, NIGTC, NTC, PNTC; ESV, KJV, NASB, NET, NIV, NRSV], 'to renounce' [REB], 'to forget' [TEV], 'to disregard, to pay no attention to, to say No to' [LN]. The phrase ἀπαρνησάσθω ἑαυτόν 'deny himself' is translated 'practice self-denial' [BECNT, WBC], 'forget about yourself' [CEV], 'say no to the things they want' [GW], 'give up the things they want' [NCV], 'turn from your selfish ways' [NLT]. This verb means to refuse to give thought to or express concern for [LN].

d. aorist act. impera. of αἴρω (LN 15.203, **24.83**) (BAGD 2. p. 24): 'to take up' [BECNT, BNTC, CC, **LN** (24.83), NICNT, NIGTC, NTC, PNTC; all versions except GW NCV, TEV], 'to take' [WBC], 'to pick up' [GW], 'to carry' [TEV], 'to carry away' [LN (15.203)], not explicit [NCV]. This verb means to lift up and carry (away) [LN]. The phrase αἴρω τὸν σταυρόν 'to take up (one's) cross' [**LN** (24.83)] is also translated 'to be prepared to suffer even unto death' [**LN** (24.83)], 'to be willing even to give up (their) lives' [NCV]. This verb means to be prepared to endure severe suffering, even to the point of death [LN].

e. pres. act. impera. of ἀκολουθέω (LN 36.31): 'to follow' [LN; all translations], 'to be a disciple of' [LN]. This present tense imperative form is translated 'to continue to follow' [CC], 'to keep following' [WBC]. This verb means to be a follower or a disciple of someone, in the sense of adhering to the teachings or instructions of a leader and in promoting the cause of such a leader [LN].

QUESTION—What did the phrase 'take up his cross' mean to those who heard Jesus say this?

Someone condemned to die by crucifixion had to carry part of the cross to the place of execution [BECNT, EBC, NICNT, NIGTC, PNTC, TH] where the vertical post was already erected [BECNT], so carrying one's own cross was a symbol of death [EBC, TH]. Crucifixion was for slaves and political rebels, and was viewed with horror by the Jewish population [NICNT]. The condemned criminal carrying his cross through the streets had to endure insults from people along the way [NIBC, NICNT]. It means to decisively accept shame, persecution, and pain for Jesus' sake [NTC].

QUESTION—What is meant by 'follow me'?

It meant to deliberately die to oneself or deny oneself [WBC]. It is to live in self-denying service even to the point of following Jesus in crucifixion [BECNT]. It meant to trust, to obey, and even to be willing to suffer for Christ's cause [NTC]. Jesus meant that they should follow him to Jerusalem, and more generally follow him in self-sacrificial discipleship without concern for themselves [BNTC]. It meant to be his disciple, but here it also had the sense of following him willingly to his crucifixion and resurrection, accepting whatever suffering comes because of faith in Christ [Lns]. It means to join Jesus as he begins to risk his own life by what he is doing [NIGTC].

QUESTION—What does the use of the present imperative of 'to follow' indicate?

The two other imperatives are in the aorist, but 'follow' is in the present imperative because the action of following is to be ongoing [CC, ICC, NIBC, NTC, PNTC, WBC]. Following him is a way of life [PNTC]. A disciple must follow and keep on following [NTC]. The first two verbs represent momentary actions that are preparatory to the ongoing, continuous course of action [Lns].

16:25 For whoever wishes to-save[a] his life will-lose[b] it; whoever would-lose his life for- my -sake[c] will find[d] it.

LEXICON—a. aorist act. infin. of σῴζω (LN 21.18) (BAGD 1.a. p. 798): 'to save' [BAGD, BECNT, BNTC, CC, NICNT, NIGTC, NTC, PNTC; all versions except NLT], 'to preserve' [BAGD, WBC], 'to hang on to' [NLT], 'to rescue' [BAGD, LN], 'to deliver, to make safe' [LN]. This verb means to rescue from danger and to restore to a former state of safety and well being [LN].

b. fut. act. indic. of ἀπόλλυμι (LN 57.68) (BAGD 1.b. p. 95): 'to lose' [BAGD, LN; all translations except CEV, NCV], 'to destroy' [CEV]. The phrase ἀπολέσει αὐτήν 'will lose it' is translated 'will give up true life' [NCV]. This verb means to lose something which one already possesses [LN].

c. ἕνεκεν with the genitive (LN 90.43 (BAGD p. 264): 'for (my) sake' [BECNT, BNTC, CC, NIGTC, NTC, PNTC; ESV, KJV, NASB, NET, NLT, NRSV, REB, TEV], 'for the sake of' [BAGD, LN], 'on (my) account' [WBC], 'on account of' [BAGD], 'because of' [BAGD, LN, NICNT], 'for' [CEV, GW, NCV, NIV]. This preposition indicates a participant constituting the reason for an event [LN].

d. fut. act. indic. of εὑρίσκω (LN 13.17) (BAGD 3. p. 325): 'to find' [BAGD; all translations except NCV, NLT], 'to save' [NLT], 'to obtain' [BAGD], 'to attain to, to discover' [LN]. The phrase εὑρήσει αὐτήν 'will find it' is translated 'will have true life' [NCV]. This verb means to attain a state, with the supplementary implication of discovery [LN].

QUESTION—What relationship is indicated by the conjunction γάρ 'for'?

It indicates a reason for what Jesus has just stated [ICC, Lns, NIGTC, PNTC]. It introduces the first of three reasons Jesus gives for his statement about full discipleship requiring death to oneself [BECNT, CC, WBC]. What he said in verse 24 is the core of his teaching, and verses 25–28 support verse 24 [CC].

QUESTION—What does ψυχή 'life' mean in this verse?
It refers to life in the deepest sense of one's true being [PNTC, WBC], which transcends death [WBC]. It does not mean 'soul' as opposed to the body, but refers to the whole person [CC, TH], including body and soul [CC]. It speaks both of the physical life as well as ones' true or essential life or existence [BNTC, NIBC, TH]. Here it is more a reference to the physical life, as contrasted with the true self or eternal life in the next verse [NICNT, TRT]. In the first clause saving one's physical life will result in the loss of true life, and in the second clause losing physical life will result in true life [NCV].

16:26 For what will- a-man -be-benefited[a] if he-would-gain[b] the whole world[c] but would-forfeit[d] his life/soul[e]? Or what will- a-man -give in-exchange-for[f] his life/soul?

LEXICON—a. fut. pass. indic. of ὠφελέω (LN 35.2) (BAGD 1.a. p. 900): 'to be helped' [BAGD, CC, LN], 'to be profited' [PNTC; KJV]. The phrase τί ὠφεληθήσεται ἄνθρωπος 'what will a man be benefited' is translated 'what will it profit a-man/them' [BECNT; ESV, NASB, NRSV], 'what does it benefit a person' [NET], 'what do you benefit' [NLT], 'what benefit will a man get' [BNTC], 'what good will it be/do for a-man/people' [BAGD, NICNT; GW, NIV], 'what will anyone profit' [WBC], 'what will you/anyone gain' [CEV, REB], 'will you gain anything' [TEV], 'it is worth nothing for them' [NCV]. This verb means to provide assistance, with emphasis upon the resulting benefit [LN].
   b. aorist act. subj. of κερδαίνω (LN 57.189) (BAGD 1.a. p. 429): 'to gain' [BAGD, BECNT, BNTC, CC, LN, NICNT, PNTC, WBC; ESV, KJV, NASB, NET, NIV, NLT, NRSV], 'to win' [GW, REB, TEV], 'to own' [CEV], 'to have' [NCV]. This verb means to gain by means of one's activity or investment [LN].
   c. κόσμος (BAGD 6. p. 446): 'world' [BAGD; all translations].
   d. aorist pass. subj. of ζημιόομαι (LN **57.69**) (BAGD 1. p. 338): 'to forfeit' [BAGD, BECNT, BNTC, NICNT, NTC; ESV, NASB, NET, NIV, NRSV], 'to lose' [CC, **LN**, PNTC, WBC; GW, KJV, NCV, NLT, TEV], 'to suffer loss' [BAGD], 'to destroy' [CEV]. The phrase δὲ ψυχὴν αὐτοῦ ζημιωθῇ 'but would forfeit his soul/life' is translated 'at the cost of his life' [REB]. This verb means to suffer the loss of something which one has previously possessed, with the implication that the loss involves considerable hardship or suffering [LN].
   e. ψυχή (LN 23.88) (BAGD 1.c. p. 893): 'life' [BNTC, CC, LN, NICNT, NTC, PNTC, WBC; ESV, GW, KJV, NCV, NET, NRSV, REB, TEV], 'soul' [BAGD, BECNT; NASB, NIV, NLT]. CEV translates this noun as '(your) life' in verse 25, as '(your)self' in the first occurrence in this verse, and as '(your) soul' in the second occurrence in this verse.
   f. ἀντάλλαγμα (LN 57.143) (BAGD p. 72): 'in exchange for' [BECNT, NICNT, NIGTC, NTC, WBC; GW, KJV, NASB, NET, NIV], 'as an exchange for' [CC, PNTC], 'in return for' [ESV, NRSV], 'something

given in exchange' [BAGD, LN]. The phrase 'in exchange for his life/soul' is translated 'to get back your soul' [CEV], 'to buy back their souls' [NCV], 'to buy his life back' [REB], 'to regain your life' [TEV]. This entire sentence is translated 'Is anything worth more than your soul'? [NLT]. This noun denotes that which is exchanged or given in exchange [LN].

QUESTION—What relationship is indicated by γάρ 'for'?

It gives a reason for Jesus' statement in 16:25 concerning why the person who wants to save his life will lose it [CC]. It indicates a second reason for doing what he tells them about full discipleship [CC, Lns, WBC], which builds upon the first reason given in verse 24 [WBC]. It indicates an explanation supporting what he has expressed in verse 24 [BECNT, NIGTC].

QUESTION—What is meant by ψυχή 'life/soul' in this verse?

It can be difficult to draw distinctions between one meaning and another of this word [BAGD]. Here it could be seen as meaning 'one's very self' [EBC, Lns, NTC], one's essential being [PNTC, WBC], that which transcends or survives death [ICC, TH, WBC], eternal life [TRT], the true self [NICNT], the higher life, life in the ultimate sense [NIBC], life in the world to come [ICC]. It is the soul, which inherits or experiences eternal life [My]. It is the whole person [CC].

16:27 For the Son of Man is-going[a] to-come in the glory of his Father with his angels and then he-will-reward[b] each-(person) according-to[c] his action.[d]

TEXT—Manuscripts reading τὴν πρᾶξιν αὐτοῦ 'his action' are given a B rating by GNT to indicate it was regarded to be almost certain. Some manuscripts read τὰ ἔργα αὐτοῦ 'his works'. This reading is followed by KJV only. This phrase is translated 'his/their deeds' by NTC; NASB, NLT, TEV, though this may be for stylistic reasons only.

LEXICON—a. pres. act. indic. of μέλλω (LN 67.62) (BAGD 1.c.δ. p. 501): 'to be going to' [BECNT; ESV, NASB, NIV], 'to be about to' [BNTC, CC, LN, WBC; TEV], 'to be destined' [BAGD, NICNT], 'must' [BAGD]. The phrase μέλλει...ἔρχεσθαι 'is going to come' is translated 'is to come' [NIGTC; NRSV, REB], 'shall/will come' [NTC, PNTC; GW, KJV, NET, NLT], 'will soon come' [CEV], 'will come again' [NCV]. This verb means to occur at a point of time in the future which is subsequent to another event and closely related to it [LN].

b. fut. act. indic. of ἀποδίδωμι (LN 38.16) (BAGD 3. p. 90): 'to reward' [BAGD, LN, NIGTC; CEV, KJV, NCV, NET, NIV, TEV], 'to give (due) reward' [REB], 'to repay' [BECNT, CC, NICNT; ESV, NASB, NRSV], 'to recompense' [BAGD, BNTC, LN, PNTC], 'to render' [BAGD, NTC, WBC], 'to pay back' [GW], 'to judge' [NLT]. This verb means to recompense someone, whether positively or negatively, depending upon what the individual deserves [LN].

c. κατά with accusative (LN 89.8) (BAGD II.5.a.β. p. 407): 'according to' [BAGD, BECNT, BNTC, CC, NICNT, NIGTC, NTC, PNTC, WBC; ESV, KJV, NASB, NET, NIV, NLT, TEV], 'in accordance with' [BAGD, LN], 'in conformity with, corresponding to' [BAGD], 'in relation to' [LN], 'based on' [GW], 'due' [REB], 'for' [CEV, NCV, NRSV]. This preposition indicates a relation involving similarity of process [LN].
d. πρᾶξις (LN **42.8**) (BAGD 1. p. 697): 'deed' [LN], 'work' [CC], 'activity' [BAGD, NIGTC], 'behavior' [PNTC], not explicit [REB]. This singular noun is translated as a plural noun: 'deeds' [NTC; NASB, NLT, TEV]; as a phrase: 'what that person/he has done' [BECNT, BNTC, **LN**; ESV, GW, NET, NIV], 'what they have done' [NICNT, WBC; CEV, NCV], 'what has been done' [NRSV], 'what he did' [BAGD]. This noun denotes carrying out some activity (with possible focus upon the procedures involved) [LN].

QUESTION—What relationship is indicated by the conjunction γάρ 'for'?

It indicates a third reason for the call to commitment given in verse 25 [CC, WBC], and gives a reason why all that he has said in verses 24–26 is true [CC]. It links verse 27 with everything he has said since verse 24 [TH]. It indicates another explanation supporting what he has expressed in verse 24 [BECNT]. It indicates a justification and confirmation of what he has said in verse 26 about the loss of the soul [My], the true self [NICNT].

QUESTION—What is the 'glory of his Father'?

It is the same glory that God his Father enjoys [EBC, My], the splendor now surrounding the Father in heaven [BNTC]. It describes the glory, splendor, and brilliance of the second coming, but also the oneness of the Father and the Son [PNTC]. Jesus will fully exhibit all the divine attributes, which he possesses equally with the Father [Lns]. The Father imparts his own glory to him [NTC]. Christ's glory reflects the radiance of God the Father [NAC]. The coming of the Son of Man will manifest the glory of God [NIGTC]. It is the power or authority that God will give him [TH].

QUESTION—What is the 'coming' referred to in this verse?

It is Jesus' coming in final judgment [BECNT, BNTC, CC, Lns, NICNT, NIGTC, NTC, WBC], the second coming of Christ [My, PNTC]. It is related to the coming of the Son of Man before the Ancient of Days in the courtroom scene depicted in Dan 7, which is a picture of the great final judgment [NICNT].

QUESTION—To whom does the possessive adjective αὐτοῦ 'his' refer in the phrase 'his angels'?

They are the angels of the Son of Man [BECNT, CC, EBC, Lns, NICNT, NIGTC, NTC, PNTC, WBC; ESV, NET, NLT, NRSV]. In 25:31 the angels come with the Son of Man, and in 13:41 and 24:31 the angels are the angels of the Son of Man. Thus, 'his angels' likely refers to the Son of Man's angels in this verse also [CC].

MATTHEW 16:28 591

16:28 Truly I-say to-you there-are some of-those-standing[a] here who will-certainly-not -taste[b] death until[c] they-see the Son of Man coming in his kingdom.[d]"

LEXICON—a. perf. act. participle of ἵσταμαι (or ἵστημι) (LN **85.8**) (BAGD II.2.b.α. p. 382): 'to be (in a location)' [BAGD, LN]. The phrase 'some of those standing here' [BECNT, BNTC, NICNT, NIGTC, PNTC; CEV, REB] is translated 'some of those who/that are standing here' [CC, NTC; NASB; similarly NIV], 'some standing here' [WBC; ESV, NET, NRSV], 'some standing here right now' [NLT], 'some people standing here' [NCV; similarly GW], 'there be some standing here' [KJV], 'some here' [**LN**; TEV]. This verb means to be in a location, with the possible implication of standing but with the focus upon location [LN]. With this verb the emphasis is less on standing than on being or existing [BAGD].

b. aorist mid. (deponent = act.) subj. of γεύομαι (LN **90.78**) (BAGD 2. p. 157): 'to taste' [BECNT, BNTC, CC, NICNT, NIGTC, NTC, PNTC; ESV, KJV, NASB, NIV, NRSV, REB], 'to experience' [BAGD, **LN**; NET], 'to come to know something' [BAGD]. The idiom 'taste death' is translated 'die' [WBC; CEV, GW, NCV, NLT, TEV]. This verb means to experience, probably focusing on personal involvement [LN].

c. ἕως (LN 67.119): 'until' [BECNT, BNTC, CC, LN, NTC, PNTC, WBC; ESV, GW, KJV, NASB, TEV] 'before' [NICNT, NIGTC; CEV, NCV, NET, NIV, NLT, NRSV, REB]. This conjunction describes the continuous extent of time up to a point [LN].

d. βασιλεία (LN 37.64): 'kingdom' [BECNT, BNTC, NICNT, NIGTC, PNTC, WBC; all versions except TEV], 'reign' [CC, LN], 'royal dignity' [NTC]. The phrase 'coming in his kingdom' is translated 'come as King' [TEV]. This noun denotes the rule of a king, with the implication of complete authority and the possibility of being able to pass on the right to rule to one's son or near kin [LN].

QUESTION—What is the function of the word ἀμήν 'truly'?
It indicates that what follows is solemn [NICNT, NTC, PNTC], or gravely important [WBC]. It expresses emphasis [BNTC]. It introduces an emphatic promise that reinforces what he had just been saying [CC].

QUESTION—What does it mean to 'taste death'?
It means to die [CC, EBC, My, NICNT, NTC, PNTC, TH, WBC; CEV, GW, NCV, NLT, TEV]. 'Taste' is a metaphorical way to describe death's bitterness, which even the disciples must experience, as all sinners will do [Lns].

QUESTION—In what sense is the conjunction ἕως 'until' used here?
The intent is to say that they will still be living when that event happens, but it does not predict when their death will come [NICNT]. It does not mean that they won't die, just that they won't die before that event occurs [EBC].

QUESTION—What is meant by the Son of man 'coming in his kingdom'?
1. It refers inclusively to his resurrection, the outpouring of the Holy Spirit, and the subsequent spread of the gospel and growth of the church [EBC,

NTC, PNTC], including the mission to the Gentiles [EBC, NTC], all of which demonstrate his rule at the Father's right hand [NTC]. The chiastic structure of verses 24–28 indicates a parallelism between taking up one's cross in the immediate future and the fact of seeing the Son of Man coming in his kingdom, which would presumably be in the near future also [EBC]. It speaks of his resurrection and consequent open declaration of his divine sonship (as in Rom 1:3–4), and of his reign in and through his church [NIBC]. After the resurrection all of the disciples except Judas heard Jesus announce that all authority in heaven and earth had been given to him, after which time that newly established authority became more and more apparent in various ways, at least for those with eyes to see it; the first aspect of fulfillment however is related in what immediately follows in the account of the transfiguration [NICNT]. The fulfillment of this statement probably comes in stages, beginning with the transfiguration and possibly including various other subsequent events [NIGTC].
2. It refers to the transfiguration [BECNT, NAC]. The transfiguration narrated in the next passage is at least a foretaste of what he would have been referring [CC, NIGTC, NICNT], a foreshadowing or preview of his eventual glorious return [BECNT, NAC]..
3. It refers to the resurrection, which is a foretaste of his final coming in glory [ICC].
4. It refers to the destruction of Jerusalem [Lns, WBC], which is a foretaste of the final eschatological judgment [WBC].
5. This promise is partially fulfilled in the transfiguration, but it is primarily fulfilled, though in a paradoxical way, in Jesus' agony in Gethsemane, where he demonstrated full obedience to the will of his Father [CC].

www.ingramcontent.com/pod-product-compliance
Lightning Source LLC
Chambersburg PA
CBHW052013040526
R18239600001BA/R182396PG44108CBX00011BA/21